Interaction of the Rocky Mountain Foreland and the Cordilleran Thrust Belt

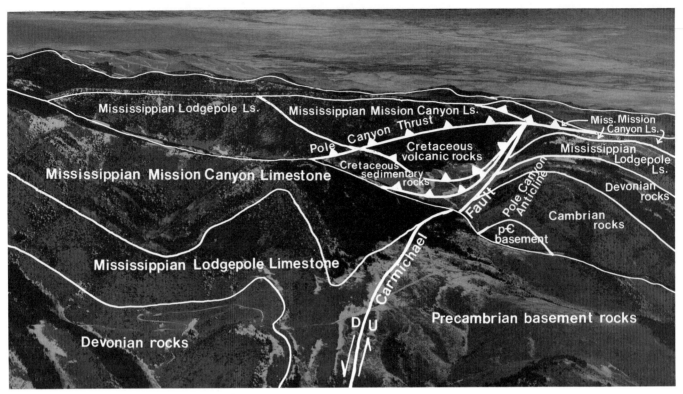

Oblique aerial photograph of the north-central Tobacco Root Mountains, looking northwest, with a down-plunge view of the Pole Canyon anticline. The Pole Canyon anticline is a basement-cored Rocky Mountain foreland structure on the hanging wall of the Carmichael fault. Thin skinned thrusts of the frontal Cordilleran thrust belt in Montana are warped over the hinge of the anticline (see Schmidt and others, this volume, Figure 10). The Jefferson River Valley is in the background. Photo by Hugh Dresser, Montana College of Mineral Science and Technology.

The Geological Society of America
Memoir 171

Interaction of the Rocky Mountain Foreland and the Cordilleran Thrust Belt

Edited by

Christopher J. Schmidt
Department of Geology
Western Michigan University
Kalamazoo, Michigan 49008

William J. Perry, Jr.
U.S. Geological Survey
MS 940, Box 25046
Denver Federal Center
Denver, Colorado 80225

1988

MR

Published by The Geological Society of America, Inc.
3300 Penrose Place, P.O. Box 9140, Boulder, Colorado 80301

GSA Books Science Editor Campbell Craddock

Printed in U.S.A.

Library of Congress Cataloging-in-Publication Data

Interaction of the Rocky Mountain Foreland and the Cordilleran Thrust
    Belt / edited by Christopher J. Schmidt, William J. Perry, Jr.
        p.   cm.
    Many of the papers were presented at the GSA Rocky Mountain
Section Meeting in Flagstaff, Arizona, May 1–2, 1986.
    Includes bibliographies and index.
    ISBN 0-8137-1171-1
    1. Geology, Structural—Congresses.   2. Geology—Rocky Mountains
Region—Congresses.   3. Thrust faults (Geology)—West (U.S.)-
-Congresses.   I. Schmidt, Christopher J.   II. Perry, William J.
III. Geological Society of America.   IV. Geological Society of
America.   Rocky Mountain Section.   Meeting (39th : 1986 : Flagstaff,
Ariz.)
QE606.5.U6I54   1988
551.8'0978—dc19   88-13899
                                                CIP

10 9 8 7 6 5 4 3 2

iv

7-27-89

Contents

Styles of Deformation in the Foreland

General or Comparative Structural Studies
of Interaction and Overlap

Regional Structural and Geophysical Studies
of Interaction and Overlap

Contents   vii

Contents

Plates (in pocket inside back cover)

Complete Bouger Gravity Map of the Dubois, Idaho; Montana 1° × 2°
sheet; scale 1:250,000.
   Dolores Kulik and William J. Perry

Geologic Map of the Southern and Central Beaverhead Mountains, Idaho and
Montana —Plate I.
Tectonic Map of the Beaverhead Mountains showing distribution
of thrust plates — Plate II.
   Betty Skipp

Geologic Map of the Hoback area, Teton and Sublette Counties Wyoming;
Figure 3.
   Robert B. Hunter

Microfiche (in pocket inside back cover)

Appendices for Cordilleran Foreland Basin evolution in response to interactive Cretaceous
thrusting and foreland partitioning, southwestern Montana
   1. Framework grain abundance for Kootenai, Blackleaf, and Frontier Formations
   2. Blackleaf Formation; Sedimentology and Basin Configuration
   3. Frontier Formation; Sedimentation and Interpretations Relative to Basin
     Configuration
       Robert K. Schwartz and Peter G. DeCelles

Preface

We conceived the idea for this volume during the GSA National Convention in Reno, Nevada, in November 1984, and issues a preliminary call for papers in the February 1985 *Structure and Tectonics Division Newsletter*. Many of the papers were presented orally at the GSA Rocky Mountain Section Meeting in Flagstaff, Arizona, May 1–2, 1986. This collection of papers grew out of our realization that a substantial number of earth scientists (from academia, industry, and the U.S. Geological Survey) were actively working on problems related to interaction of the Rocky Mountain foreland and Cordilleran thrust belt.

Although recognition of low-angle thrusting in the western United States goes back to the early years of the twentieth century, with Bailey Willis' (1902) discovery of the Lewis thrust in northwestern Montana, the concept of an originally continuous thrust belt from Alaska to Mexico is still questioned (for example, Love, 1983). Deformation of the Rocky Mountain foreland was observed by the early territorial surveys, more than 100 years ago, but a consensus about the style of deformation and the timing is still elusive.

Compressive deformation and crustal shortening of the Colorado Rockies were perhaps first recognized by Chamberlin (1919, 1923). However, many workers (for example, Prucha and others, 1965; Tweto, 1975; and Matthews, 1978) have considered Laramide (Late Cretaceous and early Tertiary) deformation of the Rocky Mountain foreland to be primarily due to vertical tectonics. During the 1960s and 1970s, Robert R. Berg and Donald L. Blackstone were among the few who remained strong proponents of horizontal compression and low-angle basement-involved thrusting (for example, Berg, 1962; and Blackstone, 1963). Brown (this volume) summarizes the evidence for compressive deformation in the Rocky Mountain foreland. A separate school of thought (for example, Sales, 1968; Stone, 1969; and Chapin, 1983) has emphasized the role of wrench faulting. A few workers (for example, Gries, 1983) have inferred a sequence of deformation in the Rocky Mountain foreland involving early east-west compression and later north-south compression. Others have argued for a more or less consistent southwest-northeast or east-west direction of compression and have related the diversity of structural trends to the reactivation of previous fault zones (for example, Schmidt and Garihan, 1983; Brown, this volume).

Armstrong (1968) suggested restricting the term Laramide orogeny to the Late Cretaceous and early Tertiary basement-involved deformation of the Rocky Mountain foreland. He introduced the term Sevier orogenic belt for the thin-skinned thrust belt of Nevada and Utah, which he believed to be entirely Cretaceous in age; he also believed there was little temporal overlap between the Laramide and Sevier events. Beutner (1977) extended the term Sevier northward to include the thrust belt in Idaho, Wyoming, and southwestern Montana. Most workers now use the term Cordilleran thrust belt (for example, Powers, 1983) to include the belt of thin-skinned deformation between Alaska and Mexico. The term Laramide is restricted to the Rocky Mountain foreland; we follow this usage and recognize, as do many volume authors, a considerable temporal overlap between deformation of the foreland and thrust belt. Laramide is now often used alternatively as a style term (Laramide-type or Laramide style) for the basement-involved deformation of the Rocky Mountain foreland, but it still has the original time connotation of Late Cretaceous through early Eocene. Because of this ambiguity, we have cautioned all contributors to this volume to define what they mean by Laramide, if they use the term.

Interaction of "thick-skinned" and thin-skinned" deformation was first described as occurring in the Swiss Alps by Heim (1919), who noted that the folds of the northeastern Jura Mountains were crowded against the Black Forest massif. Interaction of these two deformational styles has recently been recognized as occurring in the Precordillera and Sierras Pampeanas region of west-central South America (Fielding and Jordan, this volume), an area which has been cited as a modern analog of the Central Rocky Mountains (Dickinson and Snyder, 1978; Jordan and Allmendinger, 1986). Interaction of foreland uplifts and the Cordilleran thrust belt in North America was first described in detail by Horberg and others (1949). It now appears that a wide spatial overlap of the two structural styles can be demonstrated for the region (for example, Hamilton, 1978, Scholten, 1983; Kulik and Schmidt, this volume; Kulik and Perry, this volume; Kraig and others, this volume; Perry and others, this volume; Schmidt and

and others, this volume; and Skipp, this volume). Structural interaction has strongly influenced basin evolution and sedimentation in the region of overlap (for example, Schuster and Steidtman, this volume; Schwartz and DeCelles, this volume).

This volume emphasizes the interaction of the Cordilleran thrust belt and Rocky Mountain foreland in studies of regional structural geology, geophysics, and sedimentology from west-central Montana to Arizona. The nature of the Rocky Mountain foreland and its deformation are shown to affect the geometry of the Cordilleran thrust belt in two primary ways: (1) buttressing and related effects on the eastward-propagating frontal zone of the thrust belt by pre-existing uplifts, fault-bounded blocks or other pre-existing basement irregularities of the adjacent Rocky Mountain foreland; and (2) deformation of the frontal zone of the Cordilleran thrust belt by subsequent basement-involved deformation of the foreland. Major promontories and reentrants of the craton margin provide a dominant control on the position of later salients and recesses in the Cordilleran thrust belt (Beutner, 1977), similar to that suggested by Thomas (1977) for the Appalachian and Ouachita thrust belts. Secondary effects include lateral ramps and related features controlled by stratigraphic variations in the thrust belt, which in turn, may be controlled by older foreland events (Woodward, this volume). Most of the structural and geophysical studies reported in this volume address the question of which structures—foreland or thrust belt—developed first in a specific region and discuss how early-formed structures influenced later ones. Because of the continuing debate concerning Rocky Mountain foreland deformation, we have included several chapters that address the nature and style of foreland deformation. Although this subject is perhaps not as controversial as it was several years ago, we believe it worthwhile to present some of the current views of the geometry and mechanics of the foreland before proceeding with chapters dealing with its interaction with the thrust belt.

The sedimentological studies in this volume address the development of the first-order foreland basin, including structural control by thrust-belt and foreland elements on sedimentation. Such studies provide insight into stages of Rocky Mountain foreland and Cordilleran thrust belt development, which cannot be inferred from preserved structural features. They indicate that the thrust belt and attendant first-order foreland basin migrated eastward into regions where Rocky Mountain foreland structures were episodically reactivated to form second-order basins and intervening highs within the first-order basin (Schwartz and DeCelles, this volume).

When we began working on this volume we assumed that the nature and degree of interaction of the thrust belt and foreland would be fairly well defined, although we were aware of some disagreements. We soon found, from reviewer comments and from authors who describe the same areas but arrive at completely different conclusions, that the style and degree of interaction in some areas, as in the Teton–Gros Ventre region, are much disputed (compare Craddock and others, this volume, with Woodward, this volume). Degree and sequence of temporal overlap is likewise debated (compare Johnson and Sears, this volume, with Coryell and Spang, this volume). These controversies should focus attention on the many problems yet to be resolved in the region where the Cordilleran thrust belt and Rocky Mountain foreland merge or overlap.

A summary of the ideas related to the causal link between shortening in the Cordilleran thrust belt and the Rocky Mountain foreland and relative plate motions has recently been presented by Engebretson and others (1985). Several chapters in this volume indicate that there is currently a controversy about the nature of that linkage. Some authors see the compressive shortening of the Cordilleran thrust belt as having the same causative link to plate convergence as the Rocky Mountain foreland (for example, Brown this volume; Kulik and Schmidt, this volume). Others suggest that the thrust belt and foreland may each be linked to somewhat different plate interactions which overlapped in time (Hamilton, 1981, this volume).

It is fitting that this volume be dedicated to two geologists who have had divergent ideas concerning interaction in the area in which the Idaho-Wyoming salient of the thrust belt meets the Gros Ventre foreland uplift. Jack Dorr carefully mapped the Hoback Canyon region in Wyoming and worked to recognize and date the synorogenic deposits derived from both the foreland and the thrust belt. Steve Oriel meticulously mapped large areas of the adjacent thrust belt in this region of interaction and was a pioneer in recognizing the importance of the age and source of synorogenic conglomerates. Several chapters in this volume rely heavily on the pioneering work of these two geologists.

William J. Perry, Jr.
U.S. Geological Survey

Christopher J. Schmidt
Western Michigan University

REFERENCES CITED

Armstrong, R. L., 1968, Sevier orogenic belt in Nevada and Utah: Geological Society of America Bulletin, v. 79, p. 429–458.

Beutner, E. C., 1977, Causes and consequences of curvature in the Sevier orogenic belt, Utah to Montana, *in* Heisey, E. L., and others, eds., Rocky Mountain thrust belt geology and resources: Wyoming Geological Association 29th Annual Field Conference Guidebook, p. 353–365.

Berg, R. R., 1962, Mountain flank thrusting in Rocky Mountain foreland, Wyoming and Colorado: American Association of Petroleum Geologists Bulletin, v. 46, p. 2019–2032.

Blackstone, D. L., 1963, Development of geologic structure in the Central Rocky Mountains: American Association of Petroleum Geologists Memoir 2, p. 160–179.

Chamberlin, R. T., 1919, The building of the Colorado Rockies: Journal of Geology, v. 27, p. 145–164.

—— , 1923, On the crustal shortening of the Colorado Rockies: American Journal of Science, 5th series, v. 6, p. 215–221.

Chapin, C. E., 1983, An overview of the Laramide wrench faulting in the southern Rocky Mountains, with emphasis on petroleum exploration, *in* Lowell, J. D., and Gries, R., eds., Rocky Mountain foreland basins and uplifts: Rocky Mountain Association of Geologists, p. 169–179.

Dickinson, W. R., and Snyder, W. S., 1978, Plate tectonics of the Laramide orogeny, *in* Matthews, V., III, Laramide folding associated with basement block faulting in the western United States: Geological Society of America Memoir 151, p. 355–366.

Engebretson, D. C., Cox, A., and Gordon, R. G., 1985, Relative motions between oceanic and continental plates in the Pacific basin: Geological Society of America Special Paper 206, 59 p.

Gries, R., 1983, An overview of Laramide wrench faulting in the southern Rocky Mountains with emphasis on petroleum exploration, *in* Lowell, J. D., and Gries, R., eds., Rocky Mountain foreland basins and uplifts: Rocky Mountain Association of Geologists, p. 169–179.

Hamilton, W., 1978, Mesozoic tectonics of the western United States, *in* Howell, D. G., and McDougall, K. A., eds., Mesozoic paleogeography of the western United States: Society of Economic Paleontologists and Mineralogists Pacific Section, Pacific Coast Paleogeography Symposium 2, p. 33–70.

——, 1981, Plate-tectonic mechanism of Laramide deformation, *in* Boyd, D. W., and Lillegraven, J. A., eds., Rocky Mountain foreland basement tectonics: University of Wyoming Contributions to Geology, v. 19, p. 87–92.

Heim, A., 1919, Geologie der Schweiz, v. 1: Leipzig, 704 p.

Horberg, L., Nelson, V., and Church, V., 1949, Structural trends in central western Wyoming: Geological Society of America Bulletin, v. 60, p. 183–216.

Jordan, T. E., and Allmendinger, R. W., 1986, The Sierras Pampeanas of Argentina; A modern analogue of Laramide deformation: American Journal of Science, v. 286, p. 737–764.

Love, J. D., 1983, A possible gap in the western thrust belt in Idaho and Wyoming, *in* Powers, R. B., ed., Geologic studies of the Cordilleran thrust belt—1982: Rocky Mountain Association of Geologists, v. 1, p. 247–259.

Matthews, V., III, ed., Laramide folding associated with basement block faulting in the western United States: Geological Society of America Memoir 151, 370 p.

Powers, R. B., ed., 1983, Geologic studies of the Cordilleran thrust belt—1982: Rocky Mountain Association of Geologists, 3 volumes, 976 p.

Prucha, J. J., Graham, J. A., and Nickelsen, R. P., 1965, Basement controlled deformation in Wyoming province of Rocky Mountain foreland: American Association of Petroleum Geologists Bulletin, v. 49, p. 966–992.

Schmidt, C. J., and Garihan, J. M., 1983, Laramide tectonic development of the Rocky Mountain foreland of southwestern Montana, *in* Lowell, J. D., and Gries, R., eds., Rocky Mountain foreland basins and uplifts: Rocky Mountain Association of Geologists, p. 271–294.

Scholten, R., 1983, Continental subduction in the northern U.S. Rockies; A model for back-arc thrusting in the western Cordillera, *in* Powers, R. B., ed., Geologic studies of the Cordilleran thrust belt—1982: Rocky Mountain Association of Geologists, v. 1, p. 123–136.

Stone, D. S., 1969, Wrench faulting and Rocky Mountain tectonics: The Mountain Geologist, v. 6, no. 2, p. 67–79.

Thomas, W. A., 1977, Evolution of Appalachian–Ouachita salients and recesses from reentrants and promontories in the continental margin: American Journal of Science, v. 227, p. 1233–1278.

Tweto, O., 1975, Laramide (Late Cretaceous–early Tertiary) orogeny in the southern Rocky Mountains: Geological Society of America Memoir 155, p. 1–43.

Willis, B., 1902, Stratigraphy and structure, Lewis and Livingstone Ranges, Montana: Geological Society of America Bulletin, v. 13, p. 305–352.

Acknowledgments

Much of our initial interest in this project was spawned by a Penrose Conference on Laramide tectonics of the Rocky Mountain foreland that was convened by Gary Couples and David Lageson in 1982. Many of the authors of papers in this volume were participants.

Many individuals and groups helped us along the way from inception to completion of this volume. In particular, we thank the Center for Tectonophysics at Texas A & M University for helping Schmidt in some of his early organization of authors, titles, and reviewers. He thanks John Spang, David Wiltschko, John Logan, and James Evans (now at Utah State University) for their initial encouragement and logistical support.

Our colleagues at the U.S. Geological Survey and Western Michigan University offered many helpful suggestions and also provided logistical support. In particular, we thank Mitchell Reynolds for some of his early suggestions, Beverly Britt and Carol Harkness for typing correspondence with authors and reviewers, and Robert Versical and Barry McBride for help with the final editing of the manuscripts.

Of course, we thank all of the authors for their contributions, and we especially thank Donald Cook for his willingness to withdraw his manuscript from acceptance in another publication to include it here. Dr. Cook is one of several people who have developed methods for balancing cross sections of basement-cored folds, and we are pleased that he chose this volume to publish his method.

We were fortunate to have a large number of very competent and dedicated reviewers, some of whom reviewed two or more papers. A list of reviewers is provided below.

We gratefully acknowledge the helpful encouragement of Cam Craddock during all phases of this project.

Finally we thank our wives, Carolyn Rutland and Diane Perry, for helping us keep our sanity and friendship during the frustrating times encountered with coordinating the efforts of so many authors and reviewers.

REVIEWERS

M. J. Bartholomew
William Bilodeau
Myrl E. Beck
Robert Berg
Donald L. Blackstone
William E. Bonini
Steven E. Boyer
Ronald R. Bruhn
David Brumbaugh
Bruce Bryant
David L. Campbell
Charles E. Chapin
Ronald B. Chase
James W. Collinson
Donald G. Cook
Earle R. Cressman
Hugh Dresser
Thaddeus Dyman
Eric Erslev
James P. Evans
Thomas D. Fouch
David Fountain
John J. Garihan
Robbie Gries
L. Trowbridge Grose
Richard Groshong
Warren Hamilton
Paul L. Heller
Lehi F. Hintze
Paul Hoffman
Richard Hoppin
Raymond Ingersoll
W. Calvin James
Roy M. Kligfield
Charles F. Kluth

Bart J. Kowallis
Timothy F. Lawton
David A. Lindsey
J. David Love
James E. Lowell
Greg Mack
David Moore
William R. Muehlberger
Neil D. Opdyke
Steven S. Oriel
Robert Pearson
Rex Pilger
Lucian Platt
Raymond A. Price
Victor A. Ramos
Stephen Reynolds
Frank Royse
E. T. Ruppel
John Sales
William Seager
Jay R. Scheevel
James G. Schmitt
Sandro Serra
John Spang
Deborah A. Spratt
Edward J. Sterne
Lee J. Suttner
David T. A. Symons
William A. Thomas
Carl R. Vondra
David Wiltschko
Donald U. Wise
Lee A. Woodward
Nicholas B. Woodward

DEDICATION TO
JOHN A. DORR, JR.

Jack Dorr's curiosity about the complex relations between thin-skinned thrusting and basement-involved deformation in western Wyoming began while he was conducting his Ph.D. research in the Hoback Basin in the late 1940s. Later, as a professor in Michigan's Department of Geology and Mineralogy, his interest in thrust belt–foreland interactions was rekindled, and he began to steer his research and graduate students toward the problem of spatial and temporal relations between these two structural provinces. His yeas of observing sedimentary responses to faulting in the ranges adjacent to the Hoback Basin, and his previous association with A. J. Eardley, had convinced Jack that there were important problems to be solved. Thus, in 1962 he began a research program that was to continue for more than 20 years, providing research training for both undergraduate and graduate students, and culminating with numerous publications. Perhaps most important among his papers are GSA Special Paper 177 (*Deformation and deposition between a foreland uplift and an impinging thrust belt: Hoback Basin, Wyoming*) and the 1983 AAPG paper entitled *Timing of deformation in the overthrust belt and foreland of Idaho, Wyoming and Utah,* both of which Jack co-wrote.

During the 1960s, Jack spent much of each summer field season running Michigan's field station at Camp Davis near Jackson, Wyoming, where he taught and was director. Few students who had the experience will forget the instructions in plane tabling from Jack, or the many hours he spent with them in the field teaching the stratigraphic section, mapping complex local structures on air photographs, or even going through the Paleozoic section in an avalanche scar near Teton Pass. In spite of his teaching and administrative duties, however, Jack found a few days each week to continue his own research in the area near camp and to oversee the work of graduate students.

With vertebrate paleontology as his own specialty and first love, Jack's work centered on dating tectogenic sediments by identifying vertebrate remains and thus dating the uplift that had shed the sediment. This was frustrating work at best, especially with conglomerates. As Jack pointed out, "Horses didn't like running through boulders in the Eocene any more than they do now." However, despite the many difficulties inherent in this approach, his work provided some of the first chronologies for thrusting and for uplift in the adjacent foreland.

In addition to his propensity for hard work (he never seemed to tire of searching for vertebrates, no matter what the conditions), much of Jack's success was due to the fact that he brought a wide variety of skills to bear on a problem. Few vertebrate paleontologists, for example, can claim his ability as a mapper or his knowledge of regional Paleozoic and Mesozoic stratigraphy. When the bridge to Camp Davis washed out and the local rancher wouldn't let students cross his land, Jack used skills acquired in the Army Corps of Engineers during World War II to build a ferry which transported everyone back and forth across the Hoback River for most of the field season.

Jack passed away suddenly on April 6, 1986 at his home in Ann Arbor. For those of us who knew him he leaves a legacy of excitement and fun in learning about the world around us. It is fitting that this book be dedicated to Jack Dorr, for much of his excitement in learning took place in that wonderfully confusing area in western Wyoming where thrusts and foreland uplifts meet. His work there has helped us all to learn.

James R. Steidtmann
Laramie, Wyoming
July, 1986

DEDICATION TO
STEVEN S. ORIEL

Steve Oriel (1923–1986) mapped in the Idaho-Wyoming thrust belt every field season from 1954 to 1985. His contributions to our knowledge of the stratigraphy and tectonics of that area include detailed tracing of facies changes in Tertiary rocks in the Fort Hill quadrangle, Wyoming, separating the geometries and ages of several sets of flat and steep faults in Proterozoic rocks southeast of Malad City, Idaho, and mapping practically every hill in between. No one was as intimately familiar as Steve was with this region, which spans three degrees across strike and encompasses more than 50,000 km^2.

Drawing geologic contacts and faults was what Steve did, and he did it with accuracy and pace. Because he covered so much ground, a few remarks on his *modus operandi* might be instructive. Every summer started with a three-day course in field methods for new assistants, teaching them how to set up a plane table and how to keep located on a map or aerial photo with an accuracy equal to the point of a sharp pencil. He spent time training his assistants to see the geology in the landscape and especially in the ever-present aerial photos, and showing them how to depict what they saw on topographic maps. He stressed how the current work would contribute to the solution of regional problems. On the fourth day the assistant was encouraged to begin mapping. Another field season was off and running, with all hands enthusiastically working over the hills and then sharing a gin and tonic after a good day in the field. Steven's informal course should be a model for teaching students how to draw useful lines and to make pertinent annotations that will produce a meaningful geologic map.

Through the decades in Wyoming and Idaho, he mapped on foot, on horseback, by Jeep, by helicopter, and from a small fixed-wing airplane. Many a stranger, lulled by Steve's quiet demeanor, was surprised at the way he drove a Jeep—and the places he drove one. As Steve charged through the bush, he urged his passengers to keep their hands on the ceiling of the Jeep if they wished to stay in their seats; between bounces he described the stratigraphic and structural details visible in any direction. One technique missing from his field-methods course was how to keep the Jeep from getting stuck, but many summers provided practical lessons on how to get it "unstuck."

Steve grew up in New York City and enrolled at Columbia, intending to major in journalism. Following service in World War II, he completed an undergraduate degree in geology and went to Penn State for a semester, during which he was co-author of a paper on ostracodes, the first publication in what became a long list. He then went to Yale and received his Ph.D. in 1949. After a few years with Stanolind (Amoco), he moved to the U.S. Geological Survey in Denver, where he worked the rest of his life.

Steve made major contributions to the development and preparation of the Geological Survey's paleotectonic map series, e.g., Professional Paper 515. He chaired the American Commission on Stratigraphic Nomenclature, and edited that commission's new *Stratigraphic Code* published in the AAPG *Bulletin* in 1983. He played a role in revitalizing GSA publications, and served on various committees in and outside the Survey. His dedication to field mapping led to an administrative post as program manager of the Survey's mapping program. For these and other accomplishments he received the Meritorious Service Award of the Department of the Interior in 1979, and the Department's Distinguished Service Award in 1985, though I never heard him mention either one.

Steven contributed something else year after year. He gave much of his precious field time to visit almost every geologist working in southeastern Idaho and the surrounding area. He helped solve technical difficulties for some and explained stratigraphic subtleties to many. But especially he encouraged these geologists and moved their mapping forward. He spent more field time with some graduate students than their thesis advisors did. We had hoped these contributions would continue.

It is appropriate that this book be dedicated to Steven S. Oriel as an indication of our fondness for him and our respect for his contributions to the geology and the geologists of the Cordilleran thrust belt.

Lucian B. Platt
August 1, 1986

Geological Society of America
Memoir 171
1988

Deformational style of Laramide uplifts in the Wyoming foreland

William G. Brown
Department of Geology, Baylor University, Waco, Texas 76798

ABSTRACT

The evidence presented in this chapter supports the conclusion that there is no one, single structural style in the Wyoming foreland, and that the orientation of various structures is extremely important when deciding which structural model should apply. For instance, foreland features displaying the basic characteristics of compressional uplifts are those that trend northwest, whereas those features displaying the characteristics of vertical uplifts are those that trend northeast, or east-west.

The development of drape folds and upthrust structures in a compressional system requires a local concentration of the vertical uplift component, satisfying the theoretical and experimental models of Hafner and Sanford. Concentration of these vertical stresses (σ_1) takes place along east- or northeast-trending faults that segment or compartmentalize the northwest-trending thrust, or fold-thrust structures. These compartmental faults may have inherited their location and trend from Precambrian zones of weakness reactivated during the Laramide orogeny. Experimental studies have shown that small amounts of lateral movement may occur along these faults without exposure of a strike-slip fault at the surface.

Folding of the sedimentary section is commonly a response to the tectonic loading by the Precambrian basement forcing block. If the forcing block moves along a reverse fault, the resulting fold in the sedimentary section is a compressional fold, which displays the volumetric problems and bed-length adjustments typical of flexural folding. If the forcing block is uplifted along a more nearly vertical fault, the resulting structure is a drape fold in the overlying sedimentary section, which requires certain bed-lengthening mechanisms to develop. Continued uplift will result in the development of an upthrust structure.

INTRODUCTION

To maximize the benefits to be derived from this volume, it is necessary to understand fully the structural styles of the foreland and thrust belt provinces individually. This chapter describes the geometry and kinematics of foreland structures, developed during the Laramide orogeny, which are well depicted in outcrops and the subsurface of Wyoming.

Although the areal extent of Laramide structural basins is as great as that of the Laramide uplifts, most structural studies have concentrated on the positive structural features. The role that Laramide basins have played in the interaction of the Wyoming foreland and Cordilleran thrust belt is recorded primarily in the syn- and post-tectonic sediments deposited and preserved in the basins. It is the structural uplifts that provide the most dramatic evidence of interaction with the foreland and thrust belt; therefore, the Laramide uplifts are emphasized in this chapter.

The term "Wyoming foreland," as used here, refers to the area of basement-involved structures formed during the Laramide orogeny, which lie east of the Wyoming overthrust belt (Fig. 1). The Wyoming foreland is also a major part of the tectonic province referred to as the Rocky Mountain foreland (Woodward, 1976), and is nearly coincident with the Wyoming Province of Prucha and others (1965). The larger Rocky Mountain foreland includes the Precambrian-involved mountain ranges of Colorado, Montana, New Mexico, and Utah. Although most examples presented in this discussion are from the Wyoming foreland, a few are from the larger Rocky Mountain foreland area. The Laramide orogeny was first mentioned by Dana in 1896, wherein he related the orogeny to the time of deposition of the Laramie Formation of Upper Cretaceous age. Armstrong (1968) has shown that there was an overlap in timing of what he called the "Sevier orogeny" and the classic Laramide orogeny. As there is overlap of thin-skin and basement-involved deformation in time (late Sevier–early Laramide) and space—the theme of this volume—I herein limit the term "Laramide" to those basement-involved features that developed in Late Cretaceous through Eocene time, and the subsidiary features related to them.

HISTORICAL REVIEW

It is useful both to review briefly the significant studies that have influenced the present structural interpretations of the Wyoming foreland and also to understand the chronological development of various concepts. The early years of geologic study of the Wyoming foreland were concerned with initial mapping of the major structural features. This was followed closely by studies of the water and mineral resources of the region. Maps of major foreland areas began to be published around the beginning of the twentieth century. The early interpretations of the structural style of the Wyoming foreland concentrated on the major uplifts and the mode of deformation in the Precambrian basement rocks.

Until the 1950s, structural interpretations generally supported the concept of horizontal compression as the cause of the major structural uplifts, and most mountain-bounding reverse faults were depicted as dipping at angles of less than 30° (Wilson, 1934; Beckwith, 1938; Blackstone, 1940); however, an early vertical uplift interpretation of Rattlesnake Mountain anticline was published by Johnson (1934).

Two significant research papers were published during the 1950s. The first (Hafner, 1951) presented the results of theoretical mathematical models of structural development—one of horizontal compression, and another one of vertical uplift. The second paper (Sanford, 1959) presented the results of theoretical and experimental models of vertical uplift. I consider the term "vertical uplift" to be synonymous with "vertically driven" and "vertical σ_1."

A significant modification of the low-angle thrust concept was introduced by Berg (1961, 1962b), who predicted that major foreland structures such as the Wind River Mountains are bounded by an overturned limb and rotated between two low-angle reverse faults, as evidenced by subsurface well control in other areas. He called his model the fold-thrust, because he recognized that a major component of folding must have preceded the thrusting that developed the large basement overhangs on several mountain fronts.

Osterwald (1961) published one of the first interpretations of foreland structures using the vertical uplift models postulated by Hafner (1951) and Sanford (1959). The terms "upthrust" and

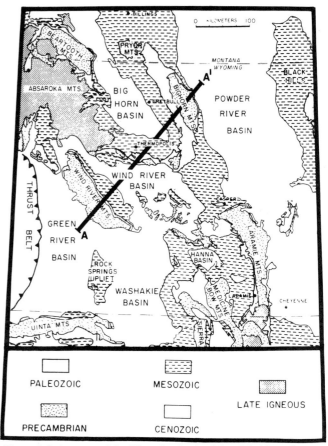

Figure 1. Index map of the Wyoming foreland (modified from Stearns, 1978). Precambrian basement crops out in cores of major mountain uplifts between thrust belt and Black Hills uplift. Line A-A′ is a regional structural cross shown in Figure 19.

"drape folding," which are applied to most interpretations utilizing the vertical uplift concept today, were formalized by Prucha and others (1965). The publication of these works marked a departure in the interpretation of the mode of uplift of foreland structural features from the prevailing compressional model. The concept of horizontal compression as the deforming force was gradually replaced by the concept of σ_1 oriented vertically.

Sales (1968) created experimental models using a "barite mud" medium and deforming the rectangular confining-box frame into a parallelogram, simulating a rotational torque stress field. The results of these experiments reproduced the map patterns of many Wyoming foreland structures, and cross sections through the hardened barite models displayed the structural geometry often encountered in subsurface well control.

The concept of wrench fault tectonics was applied to the Wyoming foreland by Stone (1969, 1970, 1975). This concept added a new dimension to the concept of horizontal compression, that of possible large lateral offsets.

The concept of vertical uplift received widespread attention when Stearns (1971) published his work on Rattlesnake Mountain anticline, near Cody, Wyoming. The literature on the structural style of the Wyoming foreland was dominated by the concept of vertically driven uplifts for the next decade. A significant aspect of this work has been the study of experimentally created drape folds, which were deformed under confining pressures simulating depth of burial during the Laramide orogeny (Friedman and others, 1976; Stearns and Weinberg, 1975). These experimental models display an amazing similarity to features observed in outcrop, and were created by compression parallel to the long axis of the models (which is actually vertical, due to the configuration of the deformational rig).

During the period from 1971 to the present, differences among the present foreland structural concepts have been brought into sharp focus as a result of new well control and better seismic data. Since the early 1980s, a number of articles have been published documenting the model of horizontal compression during the Laramide orogeny (Blackstone, 1981, 1984; Brown, 1981; Gries, 1981). The fold-thrust geometry encountered in wells drilled since Berg (1962b) formulated the model was documented by Gries (1983a). Brown (1983) documented the sequential development of Berg's fold-thrust model, and also presented a reverse fault interpretation (Brown, 1984a) of Rattlesnake Mountain anticline (near Cody, Wyoming) as an alternative to the drape fold interpretation of Stearns (1971).

Modern seismic data have been published that demonstrate that significant basement overhangs exist on the flanks of several major uplifts (Gries, 1983a,b; Lowell, 1983; Skeen and Ray, 1983; Sprague, 1983). The Consortium On Continental Reflection Profiling (COCORP) shot reflection seismic lines across the Wind River Mountains (Smithson and others, 1978) and the Laramie Range (Johnson and Smithson, 1985) in an attempt to obtain deep crustal data. The COCORP data establish the low-angle nature of the bounding reverse faults for both mountain uplifts.

I consider a return to the earlier held concept of horizontal compression as the active agent in Laramide deformation to be more compatible with the large-scale horizontal movements involved in the modern understanding of plate tectonics, than is the vertical uplift concept.

FORELAND STRUCTURAL STYLE

Basic models of foreland deformation

There are five basic models applied to the foreland (Fig. 2): (1) uplift on near-vertical faults, with draping of the sedimentary section (Stearns, 1971); (2) the upthrust structure (Prucha and others, 1965); (3) the thrust uplift (Berg, 1962b), or the "thrust-fold" uplift (Stone, 1983; 1984a,b); (4) the fold-thrust structure (Berg, 1962b); and (5) uplifts created by wrench faulting (Stone, 1969, 1970, 1975). The first two are models of uplifts driven by predominantly vertical forces; the following two are models of uplifts driven predominantly by horizontal compression. The last model is also related to horizontal compression, but is considered to involve predominantly strike-slip movements and internal rotation.

Uplift on vertical faults, with drape folding. The vertical uplift model was derived from the interpretation that the sedimentary section drapes passively over the edge of a vertically rising basement block. One of the major consequences of this model is that there is no requirement for crustal (basement) shortening.

In the draping mechanism of Prucha and others (1965), the length of the sedimentary section (Fig. 2a) before deformation (line *ab*) has obviously been extended during deformation (line *a'b*). The bed thickness, however, has remained the same, which introduces the problem of how structural balance (constant bed volume) is maintained during deformation.

One obvious way to accommodate an increase in bed length is to "thin" the sedimentary section on the steep limb of the fold over the edge of the basement block (Fig. 3a). A second method of accommodation is to extend the length of the sedimentary section through normal faulting (Fig. 3b).

A third mechanism is the development of a detachment above the basement surface in the sedimentary section (Fig. 3c). The detachment would be activated during the vertical movement of the basement block so that the sediments could deform independently. The original thickness of the sedimentary section would be maintained by allowing the section to slide toward the area of the drape fold from outside the immediate area (Hoppin, 1970). This would result in the development of a void (Fig. 3c), from which all of the sedimentary section above the detachment would have been removed by horizontal motion on the plane of detachment.

It should be made clear that drape folds do exist, but one or more of the bed-length accommodations noted above must be present with sufficient magnitude to account for the vertical relief on the basement. If these accommodations are not present on the fold, perhaps a different deformational model should be applied to the structure.

Upthrust structures. In the upthrust model of differential vertical uplift, the uplifted block is bounded by a concave downward fault; a shallow, gently dipping thrust fault is portrayed as steepening to near-vertical downward in the basement (Prucha and others, 1965; Fig. 2b). This fault shape was predicted by the theoretical vertical uplift models of Hafner (1951) and Sanford (1959), as well as by Sanford's sandbox experiments.

The shape of the upthrust brings forth the same problem of shortening in the sedimentary section vs. the lack of shortening of the basement, as in the drape fold. Theoretical studies (Hafner, 1951) show that the upthrust geometry necessitates having normal faults (extensional mechanism) on the hanging wall. The upthrust model has been applied to many foreland structures without recognizing the need for extensional features in the interpretation.

The upthrust structure is a viable model for uplift created by vertical forces, but as with the drape fold, it requires bed-length changes to maintain structural balance. This compensation is most likely to be achieved through extension by normal faulting.

Thrust uplift structures. Many early interpretations of

FORELAND STRUCTURAL MODELS

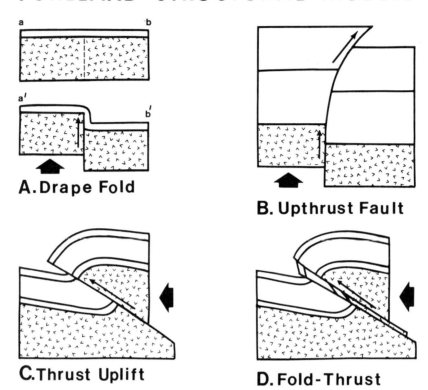

A. Drape Fold

B. Upthrust Fault

C. Thrust Uplift

D. Fold-Thrust

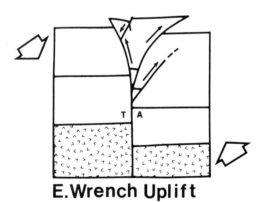

E. Wrench Uplift

Figure 2. Five basic models of foreland deformation are the drape fold
(a), upthrust fault (b), thrust uplift (c), fold-thrust uplift (d), and wrench-
related uplifts (e). Models a and b after Prucha and others (1965); models
c and d after Berg (1962b).

foreland structures display the boundaries of the uplifts as low-angle thrust faults that carry the basement and sedimentary rocks over the adjacent basins. It is unclear which worker first proposed this style, but Berg (1962b) used the term "thrust uplift" for those structures that attained their great vertical relief along low-angle thrust faults (Fig. 2c). Early interpretations employing this model include the Five Springs area in the Bighorn Mountains (Wilson, 1934), the east flank of the Medicine Bow Range (Beckwith, 1938), the Wind River Canyon area of the Owl Creek Mountains (Fanshawe, 1939), the Elk Mountain area at the north end of the Sierra Madre Range (Beckwith, 1941), and the Pryor Mountains of southern Montana–northern Wyoming (Blackstone, 1940).

The thrust uplift model implies horizontal compression as the mode of deformation. This model maintains structural balance more readily than vertical uplift models by moving basement and sedimentary section over the same near-planar fault geometry. The anticipated low angle of dip of the thrust (Hafner, 1951) results in the development of mountain-front overhangs. Areas where low-angle, apparently planar, reverse faults have resulted in the development of major overhangs are the north side of the Laramie Range, south of Glenrock, Wyoming (Gries, 1983b), which was drilled by True Oil Company; the southwest side of the Sweetwater-Granite Mountain uplift, north of Sheep Ridge anticline (Berg, 1962b), which was drilled by Amoco Production Company, and the Piney Creek fault on the east side of the Bighorn Mountains (Blackstone, 1981), which is now drilled by Gulf Oil Corporation.

Fold-thrust structures. The fold-thrust model of foreland deformation (Fig. 2d), as postulated by Berg (1962b), was based on evidence from fewer than a half-dozen wells that penetrated areas of basement overhang in the foreland at that time. Berg applied the model to the Wind River Mountains and postulated that this major foreland structure was bounded by a fold-thrust feature. In the fold-thrust model, a dual fault zone (Brown, 1982) commonly develops, which ultimately places Precambrian basement over an inverted sedimentary section of Paleozoic or Mesozoic rocks. In thrust contact, this inverted section overlies right-side-up Mesozoic or Cenozoic rocks. The overturned flank between the dual system of faults is usually thinned, often with less competent shales missing. The dual fault zone dips at shallow angles of between 20° and 40°. Subthrust synclinal rocks usually

continue to dip under the uplift, placing the bottom of the adjacent syncline, or basin, under the fold-thrust uplift.

Berg (1962b) described the sequential development of the fold-thrust, with the first stage of development characterized by an asymmetric anticline. The second stage in the sequence is characterized by the overturning of the steep limb and the development of a second reverse fault near the synclinal hinge. The third stage in the sequence is the formation of the basement overhang. The development and preservation of the overturned limb, rotated between two reverse faults, convinced Berg that the process of development was one of folding and thrusting, not vertical block uplift nor simple thrust uplift.

More recently, some workers (Stone, 1983, 1984a,b; Scheevel, 1984) have suggested that this feature should be called the "thrust-fold" model, in that the folding in the sedimentary section is a consequence of thrusting of the basement. Because of the priority of usage established by Berg (1962b), this writer has adopted the "fold-thrust" terminology.

In the absence of clear surface exposures, distinguishing a "fold-thrust" uplift from a "thrust" uplift is almost totally dependent on the presence of properly placed, and sufficiently deep, well control. Only then can the presence or absence of the dual fault zone and overturned flank ("fault sliver" of Skeen and Ray, 1983) be determined.

Uplifts related to wrench faulting. Stone (1969, 1970, 1975) has proposed a wrench fault pattern encompassing the entire Wyoming foreland area. Application of this concept to the foreland requires variable magnitudes of lateral movements on many Laramide faults. Numerous Laramide faults display lateral "separation" in two dimensions on outcrop. Difficulty arises when trying to quantify actual amounts of lateral "slip." An absence of sufficient linear geologic elements, which would produce "piercing points" when intersected by fault planes, frequently precludes actual determination of lateral slip.

There are a few areas where such determinations can be made with some accuracy. In the Five Springs area (Hoppin, 1970), at its southeastern end, the Five Springs thrust turns to strike northeast, and steepens to vertical. Hoppin reported slickensides, which he interpreted as indicating oblique-slip along the northeast-trending portion of the fault. The panel of vertical dip, which strikes northwest-southeast along the mountain front,

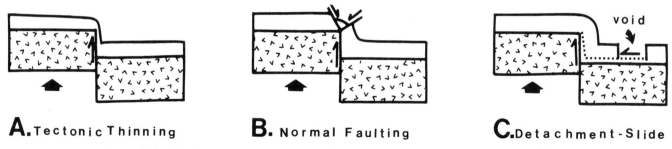

A. Tectonic Thinning   **B.** Normal Faulting   **C.** Detachment-Slide

Figure 3. Bed-length accommodations needed to maintain structural balance of drape folds: tectonic thinning of the beds (a), extension by normal faulting (b), development of a bedding plane detachment to allow the sedimentary section to slide into the fold with normal stratigraphic thickness (c). Model c will result in the creation of an area devoid of the same volume of rock that slides to the drape fold.

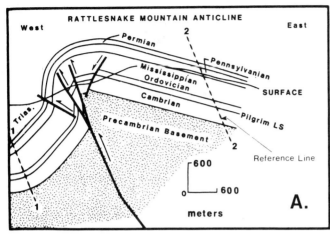

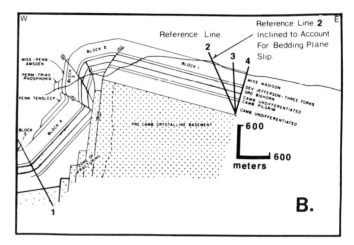

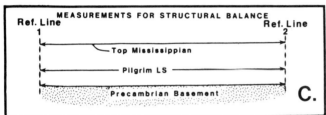

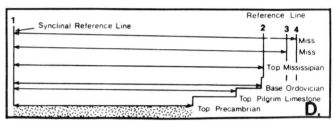

Figure 4. Comparison of structural models in the interpretation of Rattlesnake Mountain anticline. a, Reverse fault interpretation (after Brown, 1984a) shows an upward fault-to-fold interchange and an upward rotated footwall basement block. b, Drape fold interpretation (after Stearns, 1971) shows an upward change from normal (extension) faulting to reverse (contraction) faulting; configuration of basement surface on the downthrown blocks added by this author. c, Bed-length measurements (Brown, 1984a) of the Mississippian, Cambrian Pilgrim Limestone, and Precambrian basement surface between reference lines (1) and (2) demonstrates structural balance of cross section. d, Bed-length measurements (Brown, 1987) of Mississippian, Cambrian Pilgrim Limestone and Precambrian basement surface between reference lines (1) and (2) indicate that, compared to the length of the Mississippian, the Precambrian basement surface is approximately 1,524 m (5,000 ft) too short, and the Pilgrim Limestone is approximately 609 m (2,000 ft) too short, or out of balance. Measurements of these same surfaces between reference line (1) and (3) or (4) will show even greater imbalance.

is offset along this tear fault, with left-lateral slip of approximately 1 km.

Another area where determination of lateral slip can be made is the Piney Creek tear fault, at the northwest end of the Piney Creek thrust (Blackstone, 1981). Blackstone's depiction of approximately 4.8 km of right-lateral offset is confirmed by the Gulf well, which established approximately 5 km of heave on the Piney Creek thrust. This area is discussed more fully below in the section on the corner problem.

Few areas in the foreland display the classic en echelon arrangement of folds and acute angle between folds and postulated wrench faults. Rather, the common pattern is that of block-like outlines, with folds intersected by faults at high angles. This pattern is discussed below, in the section on compartmental deformation.

Comparison of vertically and horizontally driven models

Interpretations of the same foreland structures by the proponents of both vertically driven (vertical σ_1) and horizontally

driven (horizontal σ_1) blocks allow direct comparison of the two models, as applied to that area. The following section reviews two such areas.

Rattlesnake Mountain anticline, Wyoming. Brown (1984a) has published a comparison of his reverse fault interpretation (Fig. 4a) of Rattlesnake Mountain anticline, with the drape fold interpretation of Stearns (1978; Fig. 4b). Both of these interpretations were drawn along the same surface profile. The drape fold interpretation requires the presence of bed-lengthening mechanisms. The normal faults at the surface are not of sufficient magnitude in extending the section to account for the vertical relief. The Paleozoic carbonates are continuous over the fold, and thinning of the section is insignificant (Stearns, 1971).

Brown (1984a) has shown that, in the reverse fault interpretation, the bed lengths of the basement and sedimentary section are in structural balance. However, in the drape fold interpretation, the Mississippian and Ordovician are 1,524 m (5,000 ft) longer than the basement, and 610 m (2,000 ft) longer than the Cambrian Pilgrim Limestone (Brown, 1987).

Stearns (1971) proposed that the structural imbalance between the sedimentary section and the basement surface could be explained by the development of a bedding plane detachment at the Heart Mountain detachment surface. Movement along this detachment, concurrent with development of the fold, allowed the overlying sedimentary section to slide into the steep limb of the anticline, thus maintaining stratigraphic thickness without significant extension (normal faults) or thinning.

Application of this method requires the development of an area that is devoid of sedimentary section (Fig. 3c) equivalent to the amount needed to balance the bed-length problems described above. In the case of Rattlesnake Mountain anticline, such a void could possibly exist west of the structure, in the area covered with late Eocene volcanic rocks. However, application of this model elsewhere in the Bighorn basin would result in voids that seismic and well data prove do not exist.

Soda Lakes area, Colorado. Both Osterwald (1961) and Berg (1962a) have published interpretations of the Soda Lakes area, along the Colorado Front Range. These two interpretations (Fig. 5) contrast the upthrust (Fig. 5a) and fold-thrust (Fig. 5b) models. The major differences between these two interpretations are the attitudes of the reverse faults and the geometry at the top of the crystalline basement in the vicinity of the faults. The difference in crustal shortening between the two interpretations is readily apparent, but the difference would be even greater if Berg had allowed the upturned sedimentary section and basement surface to continue for a greater distance under the uplift.

Application of the concept of structural balance to these two interpretations (Fig. 5, c and d) demonstrates the same problem in applying the upthrust model where the necessary extension is absent or insufficient, as in the drape fold. The difference in lengths of the Cretaceous Dakota (Kd) and Precambrian basement surface represents the amount by which each interpretation is out of volumetric (structural) balance. On Osterwald's section, the basement is approximately 15 to 20 percent shorter (Fig. 5c) than the sedimentary section (Kd); on Berg's section, the basement is less than 5 percent shorter (Fig. 5d) than the Dakota. Berg's section could be brought into complete balance by keeping the two faults dipping at a low angle, and allowing the basement to project farther to the west. The absence of the second well in Osterwald's interpretation does not affect the interpreted length of the basement surface. Large differences in bed lengths may indicate that the wrong model has been applied in the interpretation.

In summary, the best evidence for the occurrence of the drape fold and upthrust structures in the foreland (i.e., extension to the depth of the Precambrian basement surface via normal faulting and documented thinning of the sedimentary section) is generally localized on those structures that strike east-west, or northeast-southwest (Brown, 1982, 1987; e.g., the north-northeast–striking Deep Creek normal fault in the southern Bighorn Mountains; Paleozoic section across the west-striking high-angle reverse fault bounding the north flank of the Owl

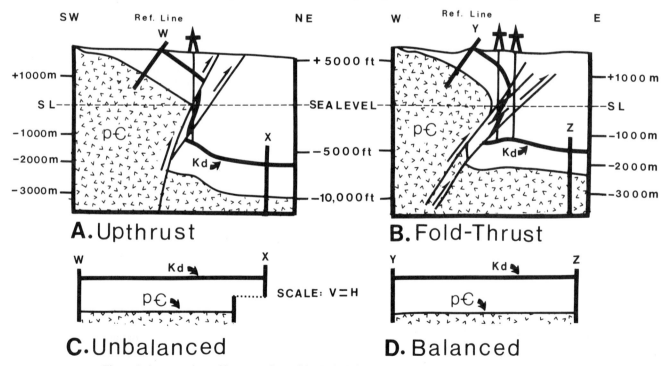

Figure 5. A comparison of interpretations of the Soda Lakes area, Colorado, utilizing the upthrust model (a) modified from Osterwald (1961), and the fold-thrust model (b) modified from Berg (1962a). Comparison of bed-length measurements of the Dakota Sandstone (Kd) and the top of the Precambrian basement between reference lines (W-X), and (Y-Z), indicates the upthrust model (c) is out of structural balance by approximately 20 percent, whereas the fold-thrust model (d) is balanced to less than 5 percent error (after Brown, 1987).

Creek uplift; Figs. 14, 15). It was along these trends that maximum "differential vertical uplift" was concentrated as the structures developed.

It is apparent that thrust uplift structures also occur in the foreland, but what is not clear is whether these structures develop the major overhang of basement rocks, as seen with the fold-thrust structures. The penetration of a single reverse fault by a well bore does not resolve the problem of whether the feature drilled a thrust uplift or a fold-thrust structure. This was borne out by the drilling on the west flank of the Casper arch, where the dual fault system (fault sliver) was not encountered by the wells drilled near the leading edge of the uplift, but it was documented by wells that drilled through the overhang of the Precambrian basement.

It has not been clearly documented whether the presence or absence of the dual fault zone (fault sliver) is significant enough to separate the fold-thrust from a thrust uplift. The presence of such a fault sliver (fold-thrust) may merely represent the more ductile yielding of the basement, whereas the absence of the fault sliver (thrust uplift) may be due to a more brittle yielding of the basement. However, Brown (1987) has shown initial evidence that there are slight differences in the trends of those features that are interpreted as fold-thrust uplifts (northwest) and those interpreted as thrust uplifts (north-northwest). Such a slight change in trend of some foreland faults may have resulted in oblique slip, with displacement occurring on a single fault plane.

The documented examples of fold-thrust structures from Wyoming are northwest-trending structures (Berg, 1962b; Gries, 1981; Brown, 1987). Sequential stages of development of the fold-thrust, postulated by Berg (1962b), have been documented in outcrop and subsurface (Brown, 1983).

In a later section (Plate tectonic setting: Direction of Laramide compression), it is shown that the direction of regional compression determined for the Laramide orogeny was along a N40° to 50°E line. The fold-thrust structures are oriented at right angles to this direction of compression, display overhangs that face either northeast or southwest, and are here interpreted to represent conjugate sets of low-angle reverse faults in the basement (Hafner, 1951) during the Laramide orogeny. These reverse faults developed as a response to the northeast-directed regional compressive forces.

Concept of compartmental deformation

The northwest-trending primary Laramide thrust and fold-thrust structures are often interrupted by less prominent east- or northeast-striking cross faults. These cross faults segment, or compartmentalize, mountain uplifts and/or terminate individual anticlines along plunge. The resulting pattern outlines a series of linear structural blocks.

Characteristics. I have applied the term "compartmental faults" (Brown, 1975, 1982) to those high-angle faults that strike obliquely to, and segment, the primary basement-involved Laramide foreland structures. Compartmentalized deformation has

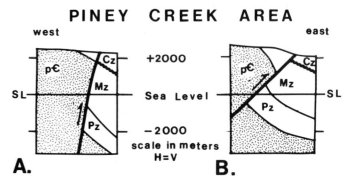

PINEY CREEK AREA

Figure 6. Contrasting interpretations of the Piney Creek thrust, east flank of the Bighorn Mountains. a, Upthrust (vertically driven) interpretation (Palmquist, 1978) of Piney Creek thrust shows minor overhang of mountain front. Area above hachured line is from north of the Piney Creek block. b, Thrust uplift (horizontally driven) interpretation of the Piney Creek thrust (Blackstone, 1981) requires sedimentary section beneath the Precambrian overhang of the mountain front.

the following characteristics: (1) compartmental faults trend east, or northeast, and their lengths are short relative to the scale of the structures that they segment; (2) abrupt changes in anticlinal asymmetry may occur across these faults; (3) northwest-trending structures may terminate at, or against, the compartmental fault; and (4) structural balance across a fold trend is maintained from one compartment to another.

The corner problem. Objections to a horizontal compressional origin for the Laramide orogeny have focused on the apparent absence of demonstrable strike-slip movement on the east- or northeast-trending faults that terminate structures such as the Horn (Palmquist, 1978) and the Rattlesnake Mountain anticline (Stearns, 1971; Brown, 1987). The intersection of northwest-trending anticlines with oblique or transverse faults sets up a geometry referred to by Stearns (1978, Fig. 7) as the "corner problem."

In the vertical uplift concept, the intersection of these trends would result in a vertically rising "block corner"; thus drape folds would be formed on both sets of faults. In the horizontal compressional model, however, the northwest-trending fault should be a thrust or fold-thrust feature, and the east- or northeast-trending compartmental fault should be a high-angle normal or reverse fault, with possible oblique slip. Stearns (1978) has argued that lateral offset along these transverse trends is not observed in the foreland.

Contrasting views of the "corner problem" are presented by Palmquist (1978) and Blackstone (1981) in their interpretations of the Piney Creek "block" (Fig. 6) on the east flank of the Bighorn Mountains. Palmquist interpreted the Piney Creek thrust (Fig. 6a) as having the typical upthrust shape, and concluded that the structure was the result of "... dominant early vertical uplift and minor late lateral expansion, or thrusting" (p. 131, 1978). Blackstone (1981) interpreted the Piney Creek thrust (Fig. 6b) to dip 45° westward, and showed reverse dip-slip offset of as much as 4 km (2.5 mi). He also projected the Upper Cretaceous rocks

PINEY CREEK AREA

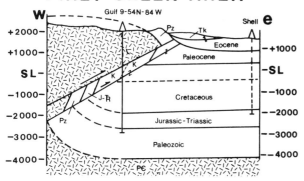

Scale in Meters : H=V

Figure 7. True-scale cross section, from southwest to northeast, across the Piney Creek thrust (Brown, 1987). Gulf Oil Corporation 1-9-2D Granite Ridge well penetrated approximately 1,765 m (5,790 ft) of Precambrian basement, approximately 465 m (1,510 ft) of Cretaceous(?), interpreted as overturned and steeply dipping, and a normal stratigraphic section from Upper Cretaceous to Mississippian. Total depth of well is 4,790 m (15,710 ft). If Tertiary/Paleozoic contact on surface is the trace of the Piney Creek thrust, then the thrust plane dips a maximum of 35°; as interpreted here, the surface contact is unconformable and the thrust dips approximately 25°.

on the footwall *under* the interpreted overhang of the Precambrian basement, and stated, "These Cretaceous formations *must* exist in the footwall and only the position of the cutoff by faulting is in question" (p. 118, 1981).

Gulf Oil Corporation drilled the Piney Creek "block" in 1983–1984, plugging the Granite Ridge 1-9-2D well at a total depth of 4,790 m (15,710 ft). The well (Fig. 7) drilled through approximately 1,768 m (5,790 ft) of Precambrian basement, and encountered Cretaceous(?) rocks, which are interpreted here to be overturned, and stretched due to dip, to a depth of approximately 2,225 m (7,300 ft). Below this, to total depth, a normal stratigraphic section from Upper Cretaceous Parkman Formation to Mississippian Madison Limestone was encountered. The *maximum* dip that can be drawn for the Piney Creek thrust is 35°, but is interpreted here to be as shallow as 25°, resulting in a horizontal displacement of approximately 5.36 km (3.3 mi).

Rock deformation models have been used to study the "corner problem" in the laboratory (Logan and others, 1978). In Figure 8a, the forcing block has been precut, to simulate fault planes observed in nature. The no. 1 precut is vertical and parallel to the direction of loading (simulating the northeast-trending compartmental faults), while the no. 2 precut dips 65° and strikes perpendicular to the direction of loading (representing the main northwest-trending reverse faults). The forcing block is made to move up the 65° precut, and obliquely across the vertical cut.

Repetition of this experiment (with increasing displacement) produced a series representing the sequence of development. The last experiment in the series (Fig. 8b) displays all of the features that developed progressively throughout the experiments. The initial movement along the no. 1 precut (compartmental trend)

does not reach the surface of the model (fault a); however, a drape fold does develop over the edge of the forcing block.

Progressively greater displacement results in a fault (b) that first surfaces at the *lower* hinge of the drape fold, and then moves progressively up the flank of the drape fold (c), until the faulting approaches the *upper* hinge of the drape fold (d). The conclusion to be drawn from such experiments is that some as yet unquantified amounts of lateral slip may occur at block corners *without the fault reaching the surface*! Increasing amounts of offset are needed before the fault that bounds the block corner will propagate vertically to the surface as a strike-slip fault, located over the edge of the basement block. Between these two extremes, intermediate amounts of offset would be expressed as a fault on the flank of the drape fold, having the concave downward shape of an upthrust. Brown (1987) has applied this model to the termination of the south end of Rattlesnake Mountain anticline by an east-west–striking upthrust.

Structures developed in the sedimentary section

The profile of Laramide structures is controlled by three factors that interact during the time of deformation: (1) the upward movement of basement forcing block; (2) the deformational mechanisms active in the sedimentary section, which are controlled by lithology, depth of burial, and pore pressure; and (3) the thickness and arrangement of the various lithologies into "packages" that are of the same lithology (same deformational mechanism) or of different lithologies. These combine into a composite package such that the resulting deformational mechanism is determined by the dominant lithology.

The structural configuration of a basin-flank anticline will thus display a variety of geometries (Fig. 9). The Precambrian basement is typically faulted up into the overlying Cambrian rocks, forming a large, relatively simple anticline in the overlying Paleozoic section. The form of the fold is controlled by the dominant member of the Paleozoic package, which is composed of the Ordovician through Mississippian carbonates. Adjustments in fold shape are accomplished by detachments in the Devonian shaly limestone and the Pennsylvanian Amsden Shale, which develop by flexural slip, out of the adjacent synclines as a consequence of volume problems.

The overlying Mesozoic rocks are more broadly folded upward through the section, and display numerous subsidiary folds on the flanks of the structures, which are the result of volumetric crowding in the adjacent synclines. Multiple detachments (Dahlstrom, 1969) allow the broadly folded anticline to tighten downward, detach, and continue downward as a broad fold, often changing directions of asymmetry as it does so.

Laramide basins do play a significant role in the creation of local structural features as a consequence of volumetric problems that develop in upward tightening synclines. Based on my work in the foreland (Brown, 1981, 1983, 1987), I have recognized the presence of three styles of structures that result from flexural slip on bedding planes, activated by volumetric adjustments required

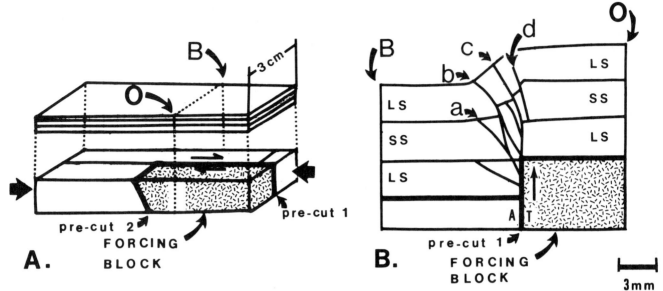

Figure 8. Deformational model of block corner (a), which makes use of a forcing block that is compressed parallel to its long dimension. The forcing block moves up the no. 2 precut as a reverse fault block, and obliquely up the no. 1 precut as an oblique slip-fault having a component of right-lateral strike-slip. The forcing block deforms the overlying sedimentary rocks into a geometry observed at foreland block corners. b, A cross section along line O-B crosses the no. 1 precut and shows that the precut has both vertical and horizontal components of movement (T = toward, A = away). Repetitions of the experiment with increasing offset of the forcing block establishes the sequence of fault formation from a through d (after Logan and others, 1978).

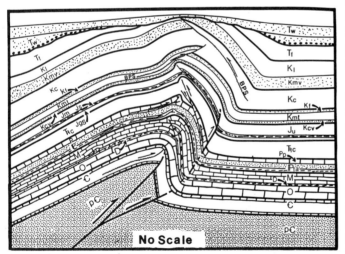

Figure 9. The composite foreland basin-flank anticline (Brown, 1987) is derived from observations from a number of structures in the Wyoming foreland. The basement acts as the forcing block, causing the sedimentary section to conform to the block in overall size and shape. Stratigraphic variations control the deformation mechanisms in the sedimentary section, one of which is the development of detachment zones that are activated as bedding-plane slip horizons (BPS) as a consequence of volumetric adjustments in adjacent synclines. Multiple detachments allow the concentric-like parallel fold to propagate to depth, with changes in asymmetry associated with major zones of detachment.

by parallel folding. Typical "S"- and "Z"-drag folds have formed on many foreland structures at almost every stratigraphic level of the sedimentary section, and at all scales. I have named these features (Fig. 10), based on their mode of formation and/or their pattern in cross section and map view: back-limb folds, cross-crestal structures, and rabbit-ear structures.

Back-limb folds (Fig. 10a) are essentially large-scale S- or Z-drag folds that develop by simple shear along bedding planes, as a response to the volumetric problems created in upward-tightening parallel synclines (Brown, 1982). Cross-crestal structures (Fig. 10b) are created by the same volume problem and fold mechanism as back-limb folds; however, the appearance in cross section is somewhat different. The cross-crestal structure originates where bedding-plane slip develops on the gentle flank, then overrides an anticlinal hinge and offsets the crest of the fold. The rabbit-ear structure (Fig. 10c; Tomlinson, 1952) is so-named for the appearance, both in map and cross section view, as that of a "long-eared" subsidiary fold on the steep flank of an anticline.

Back-limb folds. When stratigraphic layers are flexed during parallel folding of a syncline, bedding-plane slip occurs, which is directed away from the synclinal hinge and up the flanks of the structure. An out-of-the-syncline crowd structure may develop on the gentle limb of the adjacent anticline (as an S or Z drag fold), but more importantly, such a fold may also form on the flank of a basin, and seemingly have no relationship to an underlying anticline. The initial movement is usually along a bedding-plane fault, which may subsequently remain confined in the bedding (in the manner of a "blind" thrust fault), or may cut up-section in one or more ramps (or steps), giving rise to anticlines, as shown (Fig. 10a).

Such features are developed at Spring Creek anticline in the Bighorn basin (Petersen, 1983). Well and seismic data substantiate the interpretation that the faulting dies out at the synclinal hinge.

Cross-crestal structures. The primary difference between cross-crestal (Fig. 10b) and back-limb folds is that, in the cross-crestal feature, the bedding-plane slip has shifted the crest of a shallow anticlinal structure, with respect to the deeper crest. While the trajectory of the bedding-plane slip is shown to remain confined to a single bed until the crest of the anticline is encountered, this is not a rigid requirement for the development of the model.

Petersen (1983) recognized the cross-crestal nature of subsurface faults in the Pitchfork anticline in the Bighorn basin. The detachment originated in a syncline and moved as bedding-plane slip along a horizontal distance of 4,877 m (4.8 km, more than 3 mi) before it cut up-section as a reverse fault. The stratigraphic duplication of the fault increased from 0 to 76 m (250 ft) as the fault crossed the crest of the deeper structure, and shifted the shallow crest approximately 305 m (1,000 ft) to the west.

An aerial down-plunge view of Horse Center anticline (Fig. 11; Bighorn basin) shows the crest of the structure at the Cretaceous level to have been offset from the crest at the Triassic level by a cross-crestal detachment that soles-out in Jurassic shales. This geometry has been confirmed in the field.

Rabbit-ear structures. The primary difference between the rabbit-ear structure (Fig. 11c) and cross-crestal and back-limb fold is the localization of the drag fold on the steep flank of the adjacent anticline to form the rabbit-ear. Bedding-plane slip originates at the hinge of the adjacent syncline, with movement taking place all along the steep limb of the fold. Physical rock models of "rabbit-ear"–like folds on the steep limbs of asymmetric folds have been created in laboratory experiments (Chester, 1985; Chester and others, this volume). The bedding-plane slip remains confined to bedding as long as the bedding remains constant dip, as determined by the orientation of the lower portion of the anticlinal flank. As the bedding planes curve around the hinge of the anticline, they cross the original trajectory of the bedding-plane slip, and the movement becomes that of a reverse fault, cutting up-section in the direction of tectonic transport. Eventually, the slip trajectory is at a high angle to the bedding, and the reverse faulting dies out upward into a fold (the rabbit-ear).

Spring Creek anticline (Bighorn basin; Petersen, 1983) also demonstrates that back-limb folds and rabbit-ear structures, both originating from volume problems, can exist on adjacent flanks of the same syncline.

FORELAND BASEMENT COMPLEX

The principal distinction between thrust belt structures and the foreland structures with which they interact is the nature and degree of the involvement of the basement complex in deforma-

tion. In the "thin-skinned" structures of the thrust belt, particularly the part nearest the foreland, the basement rocks are only incidentally involved in the thrusting. In the Wyoming foreland "thick-skinned" structures, the basement complex is fundamentally involved in deep-rooted thrust faults. It is appropriate to briefly examine the nature of these basement rocks for a more complete understanding of the Wyoming foreland.

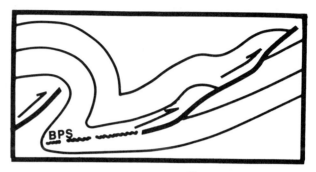

A.Back–Limb Fold

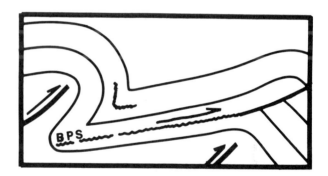

B.Cross–Crestal Fold

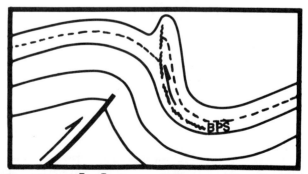

C.Rabbit–Ear Fold

Figure 10. Synclinal parallel folding of the sedimentary layers results in volumetric problems that are resolved by bedding-plane slip (BPS) away from synclinal axes. The BPS results in formation of reverse-faulted structures of three styles: back-limb folds (a), cross-crestal structures (b), and rabbit-ear structures (c) (modified from Brown, 1982).

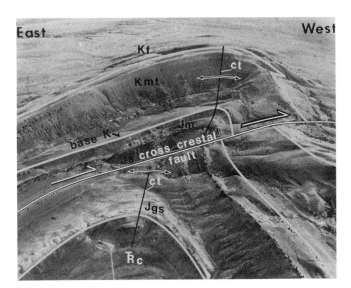

Figure 11. A south-looking, aerial, down-plunge view of Horse Center anticline (T.51N.,R.101W.) shows a cross-crestal structure that has developed as a consequence of bedding plane slip in Jurassic shales. The crest of the anticline in the Cretaceous rocks is offset to the west of the crest in the Triassic rocks.

Age of basement rocks

The Precambrian basement complex of the Wyoming foreland comprises a series of igneous and metamorphic rocks that have been dated as older than 1,400 Ma. The area of exposure of the oldest Precambrian rocks (older than 1,750 Ma) makes up the Wyoming Province (Houston, 1971). The central core of older Precambrian rocks represents the southwestern extension of the Superior Province of the Canadian shield. The oldest rocks exposed in the foreland (older than 2,900 Ma) crop out in the Beartooth, Bighorn, and Wind River uplifts, and are surrounded by rocks that date between 2,600 and 2,900 Ma. The 2,600-Ma and older complex (Archean) is in tectonic contact with rocks 1,750 Ma and younger (Early Proterozoic) along the Mullen Creek–Nash Fork "shear zone" in southeastern Wyoming (Houston and others, 1968).

Precambrian granitic and mafic dikes have been mapped throughout the Wyoming foreland (Johnson and Hills, 1976; Heimlich and others, 1973, 1974; Armbrustmacher, 1972). Granite and pegmatite dikes in the northern Laramie Range have been dated at approximately 2,500 Ma (Johnson and Hills, 1976). Manzer and Heimlich (1974) have age-dated metadolerite dikes in the northern Bighorn Mountains at approximately 2,750 Ma, and dolerite dikes at younger than 2,750 Ma. The *Geologic Map of Wyoming* (Love and Christiansen, 1985) indicates the presence of late Archean/Proterozoic mafic dikes in several of the Wyoming mountain ranges. Also, Middle Proterozoic (1,400 Ma) rhyolite and diabase porphyry dikes are indicated in the Laramie Range, and Early to Middle Proterozoic dikes are shown in the Teton Range. There are clearly two, perhaps three, ages of dikes

present in the Precambrian basement of the Wyoming foreland, most of which trend east and northeast.

Basement rock types

The following discussion clarifies a commonly held misconception that the foreland basement is predominantly *granite*; it is not a detailed review of the Archean and Early Proterozoic basement of Wyoming. The many exposures of Precambrian rocks within the Wyoming foreland are best described as an "igneous and metamorphic complex." The petrology of the basement complex includes plutonic, metaigneous, metasedimentary, and metavolcanic rocks of various types. The metasedimentary suite includes marble, quartzite, iron formations, metaconglomerates, and a variety of granitic and felsic gneisses, and pelitic and graphitic schists. Houston (1971) presented a brief synthesis of regional relationships of Precambrian outcrops in Wyoming. Of significance to later discussions of the structural characteristics of foreland basement rocks is the observation that large areas of the foreland basement are not igneous rocks, but are composed of metasedimentary and metavolcanic rocks.

Many foreland workers place major importance on the role that Precambrian basement has played in the development of the foreland structural style. Basement outcrops of the foreland display a complex structural fabric that includes foliation, folds, shear zones, mafic igneous dikes and pegmatites, and lithologic boundaries of Precambrian age.

The Precambrian structural fabric trends from north to east, with a northeast trend being dominant (Hoppin, 1961; Jennings, 1967; Heimlich, 1969; Brown, 1975; Mitra and Frost, 1981). However, Palmquist (1967) noted that the foliation in the Horn area of the Bighorn Mountains strikes primarily north-south, parallel to the Horn fault. Contrasting the dominance of northeast-trending Precambrian features with the observation of the predominant northwest trend of major Laramide structures had led some workers to conclude that Laramide structures have no relationship to Precambrian trends (Houston, 1971). Perhaps the major understanding gained from a study of these Precambrian trends is that the less obvious Laramide structures, which trend east, northeast, and north-northeast, are controlled by faults that were apparently localized by Precambrian structural fabric (see section below on primary vs. inherited trends; Hoppin and Palmquist, 1965). For example, the Laramide Tensleep fault (east-west trend) apparently represents reactivation of a major Precambrian shear zone (Hoppin and others, 1965). The Laramide Tongue River "lineament" (northeast trend), in the northern Bighorn Mountains, comprises a number of Precambrian shear zones and igneous dikes (Jennings, 1967). The north-northeast–trending Deep Creek fault, of the southern Bighorn Mountains, is adjacent to a Precambrian dolerite dike (Nichols, 1965). The Boysen normal fault strikes east-west, and dips 60° south, parallel to the Precambrian foliation. Although Schmidt and Garihan (1983, 1986) cited evidence that northwest-trending Laramide faults in Montana have Precambrian ancestry, no such relationship has been demonstrated in Wyoming. To the contrary, Mitra and Frost (1981) have shown that Laramide faults in the core of the Wind River Mountains cut undeformed basement and overlying Paleozoic sedimentary rocks, as well as Late Precambrian "deformation zones." Some basement discontinuities may have been so thoroughly recrystallized as to have no longer been mechanical discontinuities during the Laramide orogeny (R. A. Hoppin, personal communication); however, it can also be concluded that there are numerous zones of anisotropy present within the foreland basement complex that do appear to have controlled the location and trend of the east-, northeast-, and north-northeast–striking Laramide structures.

Mechanical basement

Stearns (1971, 1975, 1978) has applied the term "mechanical basement" to the Wyoming foreland by stating that the basement is statistically homogeneous and isotropic, and has behaved brittlely to depths of at least 15,240 m (50,000 ft). He specifically excluded all bedded and foliated rocks, envisioning that Precambrian crystalline granitic rocks make up most of the "basement." I find the occurrence of Precambrian rocks containing numerous shear zones, fractures, foliations, and dikes difficult to equate with a statistically isotropic basement.

Laramide deformation was concentrated along primary northwest trends, with generally brittle yielding of the crust due to horizontal compressive stresses. Deformation also occurred along secondary structural trends that strike to the east and northeast (see the section on Regional structural trends: Primary vs. inherited). These secondary trends may have resulted from the reactivation of Precambrian zones of weakness, which were oriented obliquely with respect to the primary Laramide trends, and subparallel to the direction of regional compressive stress. Deformation within the various blocks may have been controlled by small-scale inhomogeneities within the basement.

To illustrate this development, consider the crust in the foreland as a slab of homogeneous and isotropic material with numerous vertical "cuts" of various depths and lengths, all of which are oriented northwest-southeast and scattered randomly over the slab (Brown, 1987). If a stress were applied from the southwest (as during the Laramide orogeny), the cuts would close under the compression and the slab would deform as if the cuts were not present (i.e., as a homogeneous, isotropic material). The result would be some kind of folding at the upper surface of the slab (if the material were ductile), or conjugate sets of reverse faults (if the material were brittle), all of which would trend northwest-southeast, perpendicular to the applied compressive stress.

Now consider the same slab, but this time with some of the cuts oriented northeast-southwest (Brown, 1987). As before, the compressive stress would be applied from the southwest. Again, the result would be a series of northwest-trending folds or conjugate reverse faults, but this time some of the folds and reverse faults would be cut off against northeast-trending "compartmental" faults. In this case, the material *between* the northeast-

trending cuts is homogeneous and isotropic, but the "cuts" control the lengths of the folds and reverse faults along strike. These cuts represent anisotropies, or zones of weakness that were properly oriented to the applied stress, and were therefore reactivated during the deformation (Laramide orogeny).

From the previous discussion, the following conclusions can be made: (1) the assumption of homogeneous and isotropic conditions is acceptable in theoretical modeling; (2) the conjugate reverse faults observed in the Wyoming foreland may be related to a mechanically homogeneous basement, which was deformed by a horizontal compressive stress; (3) this homogeneous basement was segmented (compartmentalized) into discrete individual blocks by structural discontinuities inherited from the Precambrian history of the foreland; and (4) small-scale Precambrian structural fabric exerted variable control on local Laramide structures.

It is reasonable to exclude rocks of the Belt Series and Uinta Group, but all the rest of the Precambrian exposed in the Wyoming foreland should be considered basement. It appears that the only homogeneous, isotropic bodies are the truly igneous, granitic intrusions that have unknown areal extent. Although many of the basement rocks are igneous, it is erroneous to restrict the Wyoming foreland basement to only homogeneous and isotropic conditions. The presence of many planes of weakness in these rocks must be considered in the overall development of the structural style of the foreland. Therefore, I conclude that the basement of the Wyoming foreland will behave in several different ways, depending on rock type and orientation of various anisotropic discontinuities.

Geometry of upper basement surface

Observations made on several foreland structures demonstrate that there is no unique geometry associated with the basement surface, and that various geometries can be observed on both upthrown and downthrown blocks. The observed geometric shapes are: (1) a flat, planar basement surface; (2) a rotated planar basement surface; (3) an anticlinal curvature (usually on the hanging wall of reverse faults); and (4) a synclinal curvature (on the footwall block). Several of these geometries are controlled by the basic shapes of the fault surfaces in the basement; others depend on the action of multiple faults to achieve rotation. The angle between the basement surface and the fault plane at the time of fault development (cut-off angle) may be used to interpret the curvature and geometry of the fault plane deeper within the basement (Brown, 1984a).

The presence of a dipping planar (rotated) basement surface on the upthrown blocks is the most frequently portrayed geometry in published vertical uplift interpretations (Prucha and others, 1965; Hoppin, 1970; Stearns, 1971, 1975). This geometry is observed on outcrop in several areas throughout the foreland, including Rattlesnake Mountain anticline, west of Cody, Wyoming. There are no exposures of Precambrian rocks on the downthrown side of the exposed fault, but the interpretation by

Stearns (1971; 1975, Fig. 11; 1978) shows the basement surface on the downthrown side of the fault zone to be flat and planar.

Downthrown fault blocks are seldom purposely drilled in oil exploration, and recording of seismic reflection data originating from the basement, or from lower Paleozoic sediments from the footwall position under a basement overhang, is difficult for reasons related to the seismic ray paths (Sacrison, 1978). It is critical to the interpretation of foreland structural styles to study those areas that are eroded deeply enough to expose the geometry of the basement surface on the downthrown block such as the Five Springs (Hoppin, 1970) and Porcupine Creek areas (Brown, 1984b) of the Bighorn Mountains, and Clarks Fork Canyon (Wise, 1983) of the Beartooth uplift.

The reverse fault that controls the Porcupine Creek anticline is exposed at basement level (Brown, 1987, 1984b). The basement surface on the upthrown block is flat and planar; however, on the downthrown block the basement surface dips approximately 45° westward in conformity with the overlying sedimentary section, and is interpreted to flatten westward into a shallow syncline on the footwall of the Porcupine fault, but still on the uplifted mountain block. This geometry suggests that the basement and the sedimentary section folded or rotated together.

The geometry of the folded basement surface is significant in that it provides a measure of the minimum crustal shortening in the structure. The seldom-seen geometry of the basement surface on the downthrown block is therefore critical to understanding the total geometry of Laramide structures.

Many areas in the Wyoming foreland display the geometry of an anticlinal fold at the basement surface. Examples of this geometry include: (1) Sunshine "nose" (T.19N.,R.70W.), (2) Richeau dome (T.21N.,R.69W.), (3) southeastern plunge of the Wind River Mountains, (4) southern Bighorn Mountains (T.39 to 40N.,R.86 to 88W.), and (5) Sheep Ridge anticline (T.30N.,R.96 to 97W.). This geometry may be derived by several methods, including cataclastic deformation, macrofracturing, rigid-body rotation, flexural slip mechanisms, and fault-bend folding. All of these mechanisms may have operated during Laramide deformation.

An example of cataclastic deformation (microfracturing) in the core of a small anticline west of Manitou Springs, Colorado, was presented by Hudson (1955) and discussed by Stearns (1971). Microfracturing has been the most commonly reported basement deformation mechanism. Examples of this mechanism include Coad Mountain (Houston and Barnes, 1969), Sheephead anticline (Banks, 1970), and the Five Springs area (Wilson, 1934; Wise, 1964; Hoppin, 1970). Rigid rotation of the upper surface of the Precambrian basement has been applied to the Clarks Fork area by Stearns and Weinberg (1975), and to Rattlesnake Mountain anticline by Brown (1984a). Flexural slip of basement rocks is anathema to many workers; however, Schmidt and Garihan (1983) have described flexural slip on Precambrian foliation in Montana. Brown (1987) has suggested that flexural slip in basement rocks could occur on subhorizontal fractures created under horizontal compression.

Figure 12. Photo of curved Precambrian basement surface on the south canyon wall of Clarks Fork River (T.56N.,R.103W.). Dip angle on the basement surface increases toward the east (left) before possible termination by reverse fault.

In the Five Springs area (Bighorn Mountains), Wilson (1934) demonstrated the rotation and bending of horizontal sheeting joints (his A-2 set) in conformity with the Cambrian/Precambrian contact, and stated " . . . practically every joint surface of any block of granite one may pick up has been slickensided. . . ." The presence of slickensides on originally horizontal sheeting joints that are not bent into an antiformal shape suggests that slippage on those joints may have aided in the "bending" of the granite and its upper surface.

Observations from several areas show instances where the basement surface dips into a major reverse fault, resulting in a basement anticline on the upthrown block. Examples of this geometry include Clarks Fork Canyon (T.56N.,R.103 to 104W.), Bald Mountain anticline (T.25N.,R.81W.; Blackstone, 1983), Ferris Mountains (T.30N.,R.88W.), La Prelle anticline (T.31N., R.72 to 74W.), and Hunt Mountain anticline (T.54 to 55N.,R.91W.). Exposure of the Precambrian basement surface on the south side of Clarks Fork Canyon in the Beartooth Range also displays this geometry (Fig. 12).

Wise (1964) and D. W. Stearns (personal communication) have pointed out that many of the erosional ravines in the face of the basement exposure show cataclastic deformation, as if along faults. The question then becomes whether the basement curvature is the result of small-scale faulting and offset along the zones of cataclasis, or whether the cataclastic deformation is the brittle response of the basement to attempted buckling under compressive stresses. The large fault cutoff angle (Brown, 1982, 1984a) suggests that the fault was at a steeper angle as it broke the basement surface and has flattened somewhat as the basement was uplifted. It is possible that the anticlinal shape represents a fault-bend fold (Suppe, 1985), the shape of which was induced by the geometry of the fault plane. If so, the Beartooth thrust may also flatten at depth, and have a ramp-like geometry in the subsurface.

Orientations of basement faults

The questions of what the structural style of the Wyoming foreland is, and what model should be applied to subsurface interpretations, are directly related to a knowledge of the orientation and geometry of the bounding fault(s). Field observations must be combined with subsurface well and geophysical data in order to determine the answers to the above questions. Also, variation in trends and geometries should be expected, based on the structural patterns inherited from the Precambrian. A major concept of this chapter is that there is a strong relationship between the strike orientation and the dip of foreland mountain-bounding fault systems, and that the geometric model applied may therefore vary from one range to another.

Structural observations. The reported dips of fault planes in the Precambrian basement throughout the Wyoming foreland generally range from 60° to vertical for normal faults, and 20° to 70° for reverse faults (Brown, 1987). Prucha and others (1965) discussed the significance of plunge associated with the adjacent uplift to the exposure of the entire geometry of a fault along trend. For this very reason, the method of "down-plunge viewing" (Mackin, 1959) of geologic maps and outcrops is critical to the full understanding of the structural geometry exposed along foreland mountain fronts.

The geometry and dip of many of the major Laramide uplifts of the Wyoming foreland are now documented by surface, well, and geophysical data (Gries, 1983a; Skeen and Ray, 1983). Documented examples of uplifts bounded by low-angle (20° to 45°) reverse faults include: (1) the southwest flank of the Wind River Mountains (Smithson and others, 1978; Gries, 1981, 1983a); (2) the southwest flank of the Casper arch (Keefer, 1965, 1970; Brown, 1982; Gries, 1981, 1983a; Skeen and Ray, 1983; Sprague, 1983); (3) the southwest flank of Immigrant Trail anticline (Berg, 1962b; Gries, 1983a); (4) the EA thrust, on the southwest flank of the western Owl Creek Mountains (Berg, 1962b; Hamilton, 1978; Gries, 1983a); (5) the northeast flank of the Beartooth Range (Bonini and Kinnard, 1983; now drilled through by Amoco Production Company); (6) the east flank of the Piney Creek block (Brown, 1987; this volume); and (7) the east flank of the Laramie Range (Johnson and Smithson, 1985). Note that all of these structures trend northwest-southeast; of the above-listed faults, one through four dip to the northeast, and faults five through seven dip to the southwest. These dip orientations may represent conjugate reverse faults, an interpretation compatible with Hafner's (1951) mathematical model of horizontal compression (see Fig. 16b).

Although the Wyoming foreland is considered to have remarkable outcrops, few mountain-bounding fault zones are exposed to the extent that the question as to the dip and geometry of the faults involved can be unequivocally answered. One of the first areas in which there was sufficient well control to calculate the dip of a major subsurface fault was the Waltman field, on the west flank of the Casper arch. The arch has been thrust from northeast to southwest, along a thrust that subcrops under the Eocene Wind River Formation. Three-point structural calculations on the thrust plane yield a 20° dip to the east-northeast at the Upper Cretaceous stratigraphic level, and a 43° northeast dip at the Precambrian basement level (Brown, 1987). The downward increase from 20° to 43° is suggestive of the upthrust geometry (Prucha and others, 1965); however, Skeen and Ray (1983) and Sprague (1983) have interpreted seismic data as indicating that the Casper arch thrust flattens again and dips very gently to the northeast in the basement for some distance under the Casper arch. Skeen and Ray have also suggested that the process of steepening and flattening could be repeated again (Fig. 13). Such repeated steepening and flattening of the fault plane gives it a stair-step appearance, and defines the geometry of a "ramp," similar to that displayed by thin-skinned overthrust faults (Rich, 1934).

There are a number of faults in the Wyoming foreland that have documented dip angles greater than 45°. Those faults that trend east-west generally dip between 60° and 80° (Brown, 1987); examples include Casper Mountain fault (Brown, 1975), Tensleep fault (Palmquist, 1967; Hoppin and others, 1965), Boysen normal fault (Fanshawe, 1939; Wise, 1963), and the north end of Laramie Range (Gries, 1983a).

Those faults that strike essentially northeast, parallel to the regional direction of shortening, exhibit near-vertical dips. Examples of these include the tear faults of the Clear Creek thrust (Hoppin, 1961); the East Medicine Butte tear fault of the Five Springs thrust (Hoppin, 1970); the Corral Creek fault, northwest end of the Laramie Range (Brown, 1975); and the tear faults in the Shirley Mountains (Brown, 1987).

The relationship between northwest-striking and east-west–striking faults can be demonstrated with the North Owl Creek area (Brown, 1987). The North Owl Creek fault bounds the northeast side of the western Owl Creek uplift (Fig. 14), and changes strike in T.8N.,R.1E.(W.R.M.), from a northwest to an east-west trend. The northwest-trending portion of the North Owl Creek fault is a low-angle reverse fault that dips 20° to the southwest (Fig. 15a), and becomes a high-angle reverse fault that dips to the south (Fig. 15b) when the strike changes to the west. A number of northwest-trending, reverse-faulted structures are terminated at their north ends against this west-trending fault (Figs. 14, 15b). The absence of equivalent folds north of the east-west fault indicates that the northwest-trending folds and low-angle reverse faults developed *concurrently* with the east-west high-angle reverse fault. Additional evidence (Brown, 1987) such as this suggests that other east-west–trending faults also developed concurrently with primary northwest-trending structures. It is not necessary to call on a later compressive pulse, reoriented north-south, to account for the east-west trends such as this, as postulated by Gries (1983b).

Primary vs. inherited trends. In this discussion, "primary" trends refer to those that apparently owe their existence entirely to Laramide stresses, whereas "inherited" trends refer to those that were probably generated during the Precambrian and were reactivated during the Laramide orogeny. Geologists have long speculated on the role that various Precambrian "zones of weakness" may have played in controlling the development of Laramide structures (Hoppin, 1961; Hoppin and Palmquist, 1965; Houston, 1971).

The northwest trends are considered the primary Laramide trends in the Wyoming foreland. Schmidt and Garihan (1983, 1986) documented a Precambrian ancestry for northwest-trending Laramide-age faults in southern Montana; however, no data have been published that establish a Precambrian ancestry for the northwest-trending Laramide-age faults of the Wyoming foreland. Mitra and Frost (1981) demonstrated the presence of a number of Precambrian and Laramide "deformation zones" in the Precambrian basement of the Wind River Mountains. The Precambrian zones do not cut overlying Cambrian sedimentary rocks, but are cut by a series of northwest-striking, northeast-dipping Laramide deformation zones that transect both the Precambrian rocks and the overlying sedimentary rocks. Examples of Precambrian-age basement shear zones that have been mapped in the foreland include the northeast-trending Mullen Creek–Nash Fork shear zone (Houston and others, 1968), the east-trending Tensleep fault zone (Hoppin and others, 1965), the northeast-trending Tongue River zone (Jennings, 1967; Hoppin and Jennings, 1971), the northeast-trending Florence Pass fault

(Hodgson, 1965), and the north-south–trending shear zones in the Beartooth uplift (Foose and others, 1961).

Several workers (Brown, 1975; Hoppin, 1961, 1970; Nichols, 1965) have recognized a relationship between the orientation of Laramide faults and Precambrian igneous dikes in the foreland. A few Precambrian dikes trend northwest (Love and Christiansen, 1985), but most trend east, northeast, and north-northeast. All of the above trends have been recognized during systematic studies of fractures in the basement cores of the major uplifts (Hodgson, 1965; Hoppin, 1965; Jennings, 1967; Wilson, 1934; Wise, 1963, 1964).

Trends of Precambrian foliation are highly variable throughout the foreland. In the Bighorn Mountains, the foliation strikes primarily east-west and northeast-southwest (Heimlich, 1969), but changes to north-south strike in the Horn area (Palmquist, 1967). Precambrian foliation exposed in the Wind River Canyon of the Owl Creek Mountains strikes primarily east-west, and dips approximately 60° south. Foliation in the basement at Casper Mountain trends generally east-west and northeast in the northern Laramie Range (Sears and Sims, 1954).

Examples of Precambrian "zones of weakness," which have also been documented as having been reactivated during the Laramide orogeny, include (1) the Tensleep fault, which transects the Bighorn Mountains along an east-west trend (Hoppin and others, 1965); (2) the northeast-trending Florence Pass fault (Hodgson, 1965); (3) the north-northeast–trending Deep Creek

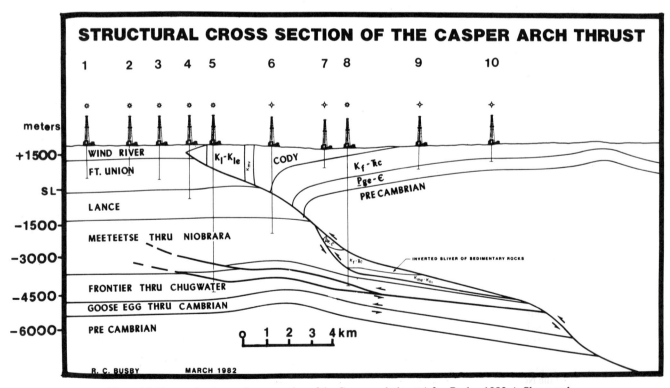

Figure 13. True-scale structural cross section of the Casper arch thrust (after Busby, 1982: *in* Skeen and Ray, 1983), based on well and seismic data. Geometry suggests a stair-step arrangement of the fault plane in the basement, typical of faults of the thin-skinned thrust belt.

fault (Nichols, 1965); (4) the northeast-trending Tongue River lineament (Jennings, 1967); (5) the east-west–trending Casper Mountain fault (Brown, 1975); (6) the northeast-trending Corral Creek fault (Brown, 1975); (7) the east-west trending Boysen normal fault (Wise, 1964); (8) the tear faults in the Clear Creek thrust (Hoppin, 1961); (9) the tear faults in the Five Springs thrust (Hoppin, 1970); (10) the northeast-trending south-bounding fault of Quealy Dome, along the projection of Mullen Creek–Nash Fork shear zone (Stone, 1985); (11) the tear faults in the Shirley Mountains (Brown, 1987); and (12) the Horn fault in the Bighorn Mountains (Palmquist, 1967).

Theoretical and experimental models. Theoretical and experimental models have exerted great influence on the interpretation of foreland structural styles. The results have been widely applied, but often with certain basic data omitted. It is important, therefore, to understand fully the assumptions and limitations of these models.

The two most widely quoted works on theoretical deformation models are those of Hafner (1951) and Sanford (1959). If the assumption of these two workers concerning the homogeneous and isotropic nature of the deformed material is correct, their models should be applied only to "mechanical" basement and not to the layered sedimentary section.

Hafner calculated stress trajectories for mathematical models of both vertical uplift and horizontal compression. From the stress trajectories he derived the geometry of various fault planes

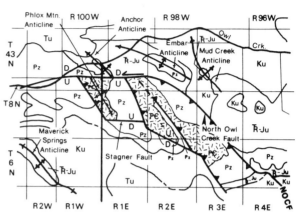

Figure 14. Map of Owl Creek Mountains, central Wyoming (modified from Love and Christiansen, 1985). Northwest-trending North Owl Creek fault has been thrust to the northeast, but changes strike in T.8N.,R1E.. Southeast-plunging basement structures are terminated at their north ends by the NOCF. The angle between Anchor anticline and the NOCF suggests a component of left-lateral slip along the west-trending segment of the North Owl Creek fault.

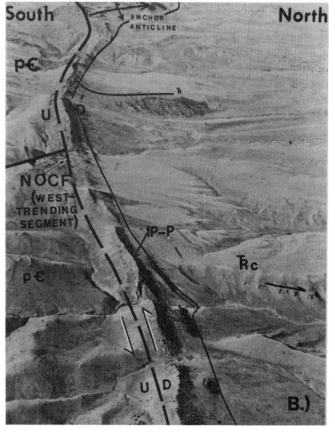

Figure 15. Paleozoic rocks thrust northeast over overturned Triassic rocks (curved arrow) along the 20° southwest-dipping North Owl Creek fault (a), where it strikes northwest. Southeast-plunging structures are abruptly terminated along the high-angle, west-trending segment of the North Owl Creek fault (b), resulting in localization of vertically directed forces along this portion of the fault. Steeply dipping Upper Paleozoic and Triassic rocks flatten rapidly northward, away from the fault. There are no structures north of the North Owl Creek fault equivalent to those basement structures on the south side of the fault (i.e., Phlox Mountain), which are truncated by the west-trending segment of the North Owl Creek fault.

(Fig. 16), which would develop under those specific conditions. His solutions for differential vertical uplift (vertical sigma 1) have been widely quoted as the models of upthrust fault profiles (Prucha and others, 1965). If Figure 16a is examined closely, it can be seen that the left-hand portion of the model displays a pattern of normal faults on the uplifted block of the upthrust. The normal faults are necessary in order for the concave downward fault geometry to develop. The change from no structural shortening along the lower, vertical portion of the fault, to structural repetition (shortening) across the low-dipping, upper portion of the fault, necessitates a progressive increase upward in extension somewhere on the upthrown block in order to maintain structural balance.

Sanford's (1959) experimental physical models (Fig. 17) show the development of the characteristic concave downward shape of the upthrust fault bounding the uplifted blocks. Also shown in these examples is the development of the normal faults, antithetic to the upthrusts on the upthrown blocks, which satisfy the requirement for extension mentioned above.

Most published examples of upthrust faults (Bald Mountain: Prucha and others, 1965; Piney Creek: Palmquist, 1978) do not display normal faults on the hanging wall. If the normal faults are not indicated by the geological data, it would appear that the upthrust model was applied in error.

In the case of Hafner's (1951) model of horizontal compression (Fig. 16b), the reverse faults leave the basement at low angles. One of the conjugate sets of faults would even tend to steepen upward into the overlying sediments, giving it a "sled runner" geometry. Many published interpretations of structures created by horizontal compression show low-angle reverse faults that also display a concave-upward geometry (Blackstone, 1983, 1984; Skeen and Ray, 1983; Brown, 1984a; Stone, 1984a,b).

TIMING AND SEQUENCE OF UPLIFTS

It is well established by dating synorogenic conglomerates that the overall deformation in the Cordilleran thrust belt of western Wyoming, Utah, and Idaho progressed from west to east through time (Armstrong and Oriel, 1965; Royse and others, 1975). The oldest of the basement-involved foreland structures in western Wyoming are the combined Targhee-Teton uplift (Love, 1977, 1983) and the Moxa arch (Gries, 1983b; Kraig and others, this volume; Wach, 1977). The time of formation of these early features is coincidental with the emplacement of the Absaroka thrust sheet (Campanian; Lamerson, 1983) to the west. The Hogsback thrust—the youngest and easternmost in the thrust belt (Paleocene to early Eocene; Lamerson, 1983)—actually overrode features such as the Moxa arch (Murray, 1960; Kraig and others, this volume).

Deformation of the basement-involved features also began in the west, in the vicinity of the Moxa arch, in the Campanian (Gries, 1983b; Wach, 1977) and migrated northeastward in time (Fig. 18). Evidence of uplift of the Wind River Mountains, in Maastrichtian time (Late Cretaceous; Gries, 1983b), is recorded

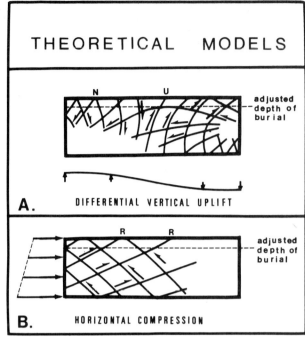

Figure 16. Orientation of potential fault planes determined from theoretical mathematical stress analyses (after Hafner, 1951) for differential vertical uplift (a) and horizontal compression (b). N = normal fault; R = reverse fault; U = upthrust fault. Dashed line represents adjusted level of basement surface for depth of burial at onset of Laramide orogeny (Stearns, 1975).

by the presence of feldspar fragments in Paleocene Fort Union rocks in the Green River basin west of the present Wind River uplift (W. G. Brown, unpublished data). Paleocene rocks dip gently to the northeast into the Wind River basin, and overlap uppermost Cretaceous Maastrichtian (Lance Formation) and Campanian rocks (Mesaverde Formation) with angular unconformity on the northeast flank of the Wind River Mountains near Hudson, Wyoming. Farther east, the northern margin of the Wind River basin was downwarped approximately 1,676 m (5,500 ft) during Maastrichtian time, and the adjacent Owl Creek Range (to the north) was first uplifted during Paleocene time (Keefer, 1965, 1970).

Laramide deformation culminated in the Bighorn basin in late Paleocene to early Eocene, as documented by the deep infolding of Paleocene rocks in synclines around the flanks of the basin and the angular relationship with the gently dipping overlying Eocene rocks. Local areas such as the northeast flank of the basin were subjected to early pulses of uplift (Maastrichtian), as evidenced by the slight angularity between the Lance and Fort Union Formations just west of Greybull, Wyoming. The latest stage of Laramide uplift is documented on the east flank of the Bighorn Mountains just west of Buffalo, Wyoming, where Eocene rocks are deformed along the mountain front.

Interpretation of eastward progression of the onset of deformation does not necessarily imply a cessation of all tectonic activity to the west as deformation began farther east. Instead, it should be visualized as the eastward movement of a "tectonic front," which probably had subtle, early deformation in front of it, and continued, active deformation behind it. The timing of individual structural features must be considered very carefully.

In summary, primary Laramide structures generally trend northwest, with secondary, less conspicuous structures that trend toward the east, northeast, and north. Thus, four different fault orientations developed in response to Late Cretaceous to Eocene (Laramide orogeny) horizontal compression. Movements along these different trends may include reverse and normal dip-slip, reverse and normal oblique-slip, and left- and right-lateral strike-slip. Many of the secondary trends appear to be controlled by Precambrian zones of weakness in the basement.

CRUSTAL SHORTENING ACROSS FORELAND TRENDS

Shortening of the sedimentary section is observable in many different areas within the foreland. An integrated interpretation of the foreland structural style should recognize the variation in crustal (basement) shortening dictated by the different models of

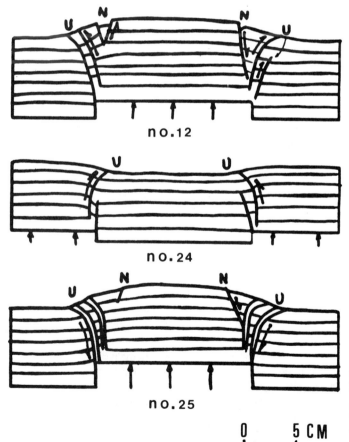

Figure 17. Development of upthrust fault geometry in sandbox experiments (after Sanford, 1959) via vertically driven piston. Numbers 12, 24, and 25 refer to different runs of experiment with different materials. N = normal fault; U = upthrust fault.

foreland deformation already presented. For the entire foreland province to be in structural balance, the amount of crustal shortening interpreted on the upper surface of the Precambrian basement should be equal to that demonstrated for the sedimentary section.

A regional, true-scale cross section (Fig. 19) has been drawn along line A-A' (Fig. 1) oriented N.40°E., parallel to the direction of maximum shortening (and assumed maximum compression). The cross section is controlled by outcrops, well control, and seismic data. A measurement of the original length of basement and sedimentary bedding surfaces indicates that the cross section is in structural balance. Comparing the original and present-day map separation of the ends of the cross section yields the figure of

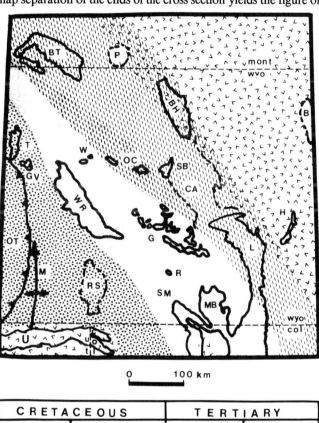

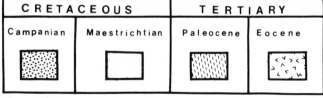

Figure 18. Onset of the Laramide orogeny began in the west and migrated eastward through time as a wave of deformation, with some slight deformation preceding the wavefront, and continued deformation behind it. Therefore some areas show possible multiple periods of deformation (modified from Gries, 1983b, Fig. 7). B = Black Hills; BH = Bighorn Mountains; BT = Beartooth uplift; CA = Casper arch; G = Granite Mountains; GV = Gros Ventre uplift; H = Hartville uplift; L = Laramie Range; M = Moxa arch; MB = Medicine Bow Range; OC = Owl Creek Range; OT = Overthrust Belt; P = Pryor Mountains; R = Rawlins uplift; RS = Rock Springs uplift; SB = Southern Bighorn Mountains; SM = Sierra Madre Range; T = Teton-Targhee uplift; U = Uinta Mountains; W = Washakie Range; WR = Wind River Mountains.

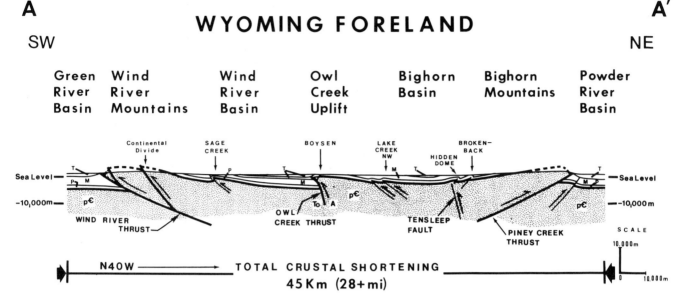

Figure 19. Regional true-scale structural cross section (line A-A′, Fig. 1) drawn parallel to direction of shortening and assumed direction of maximum compression (N.40°E.), demonstrates the conjugate nature of major foreland crustal faults. Different strike orientations of foreland structures result in differing amounts of crustal shortening, as shown by crossing the east-west–trending Owl Creek thrust and Tensleep fault, as compared to the northwest-trending Wind River thrust and the Piney Creek thrust in the Bighorn Mountains. Total crustal shortening along this line of section is 45 km (about 28 mi). T = Tertiary; M = Mesozoic; P = Paleozoic; p€ = Precambrian basement complex; To = toward; A = away.

45 km (about 28 mi) of total crustal shortening across this segment of the foreland (based on the concept of minimum displacement; Brown, 1982). This figure represents a 13 to 15 percent shortening of the foreland crust.

The bimodal sense of vergence of these reverse faults in the crust is shown in the oppositely directed asymmetry and thrusting of the Wind River and Bighorn uplifts, and represents a conjugate system of reverse faults. The east-west–trending Tensleep fault is depicted as a high-angle fault having reverse oblique-slip because of the angle that it makes with the northeast-southwest direction of compression; thus, it may be intermediate between a drape fold and an upthrust fault. The upthrust geometry has been applied to the thrust bounding the south flank of the Owl Creek Mountains (Wind River Canyon area) because of its east-west trend, plus extension on the hanging wall accomplished by the Boysen normal fault and other smaller faults. The trends of both the upthrust and Boysen normal fault are parallel to exposed Precambrian foliation on the hanging wall, suggesting Precambrian control of these faults.

Measurement of crustal shortening in the foreland yields a maximum value when measured in a northeast-southwest direction (e.g., perpendicular to the Wind River Mountains). The east-west, northeast, and north-south–trending faulted structures are here interpreted (in the absence of piercing points) to have undergone oblique-slip. Therefore, maximum crustal shortening is not perpendicular to these secondary trends, but oblique to them, parallel to the regional northeast-southwest direction of compression.

PLATE TECTONIC SETTING

Direction of Sevier orogeny plate collision

Coney (1978) described plate interactions along the west coast of North America from the breakup of Pangea (Late Triassic) to the present. In general, the North American plate has moved in a westerly direction since Jurassic time. Subduction has occurred along the western margin of the continent throughout this period, until initiation of transform movements along the San Andreas fault system in Oligocene time, approximately 30 Ma (Atwater, 1970). Specifically, Coney described the plate tectonic setting of western North America during the time period of 155 to 89 Ma, which closely approximates the duration of the Sevier orogeny (Fig. 20a) as defined by Armstrong (1968).

During this period, North America was moving northwestward at approximately 6.5 cm/yr, and the Farallon plate was moving northeastward at 7 cm/yr. The directions and rates of plate movement resulted in collision between the two plates along a line trending N.72°E., at a rate of 8 cm/yr. The structures that developed in Utah, Idaho, and western Wyoming during this plate interaction were a series of east-verging thrust sheets that are interpreted as being older in the west (Armstrong and Oriel, 1965; Royse and others, 1975).

Direction of Laramide orogeny plate collision

Armstrong (1968) stated that the Laramide orogeny began in Campanian time and ended in Eocene time. Coney's (1978)

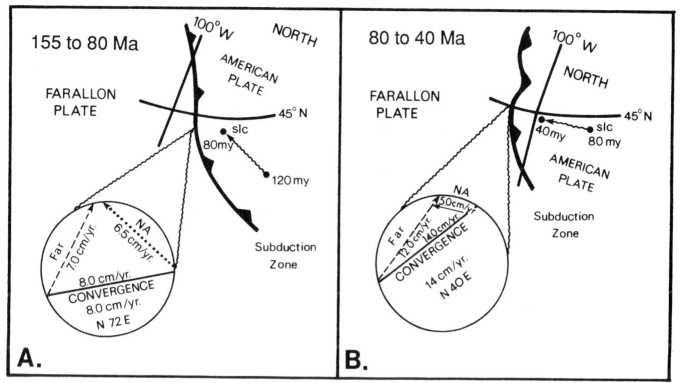

Figure 20. Plate tectonic setting during the Sevier (a) and Laramide (b) orogenies (after Coney, 1978). Far = Farallon plate; NA = North American plate; SZ = subduction zone; SLC = Salt Lake City, for reference. Convergence between the Farallon and North American plates changed from 8 cm/yr (N.72°E.) during the Sevier orogeny to 14 cm/yr (N.40°E.) during the Laramide orogeny.

plate tectonic reconstruction for the period 80 to 40 Ma (Fig. 20b) effectively brackets this time range.

During this period, the North American plate moved almost due west at a rate of 5 cm/yr, while the Farallon plate moved northeastward at 12 cm/yr. These plate movements resulted in plate convergence (collision) during the Laramide orogeny along a line trending N.40°E., at a rate of 14 cm/yr. This represents a rotation of the North American plate movement (Engebretson and others, 1984) from northwest to west, and a speeding-up of the rate of collision from 8 to 14 cm/yr (approximately 1.7 times as fast as during the Sevier orogeny). This period of rapid collision resulted in the formation of the primary, northwest-trending, basement-involved foreland structures.

The plate tectonic setting of western North America during the Laramide orogeny can be compared to the present-day subduction zone along the Chile-Peru trench and the Andean mountain belt (Dickinson and Snyder, 1978; Jordan and others, 1983; Fielding and Jordan, this volume). Stauder (1975) has shown that compressive stresses in the crust exist 700 km inland (east) of the present-day subduction zone.

Comparison of the present-day Andean model with the Late Cretaceous western North America must take into account the several hundred kilometers of crustal extension created by the post–Laramide Basin and Range taphrogeny. Palinspastic restoration of extension of the Basin and Range province (Hamilton and Meyer, 1966) demonstrates that the Wyoming foreland was a

similar distance from the subduction zone during the Laramide orogeny, as the Andes are from the Chile-Peru subduction zone today. It is reasonable to conclude that the crustal compressive stresses generated during the Laramide orogeny would have reached inland to the Wyoming foreland.

The greatly increased rate of Laramide convergence (Coney, 1978; Jurdy, 1984) resulted in a flattening of the subduction zone (Dickinson and Snyder, 1978; Engebretson and others, 1984), which shifted the areas of high heat flow hundreds of kilometers eastward into the Wyoming foreland during the Laramide orogeny (Bird, 1984). Displacement of the high heat flow under the foreland resulted in a thermally weakened crust, which yielded along low-angle reverse faults when subjected to compressive forces. Schmidt and others (1985) calculated the spacing of crustal structures based on heat flow considerations and concluded that there were two levels of crustal detachment: one at the base of the crust, and a second, more shallow one in the upper crust.

Direction of Laramide compression

It is important to separate the direction of plate movement from the direction of plate collision when discussing the direction of regional compression. The direction in which collision occurs can be taken to represent the direction of maximum compressive deformation, and thus the average direction in which the maximum principal stress, σ_1, acts.

The analogy of western North America during the Laramide orogeny to the present-day Andean model shows that compressive stress is developed parallel to the direction of plate convergence (Jordan and others, 1983; Burchfiel and Davis, 1975; Stauder, 1975).

The N.72°E. direction of convergence during the Sevier orogeny can be taken as the direction of σ_1, which created the generally north-south trend of the Idaho-Utah-Wyoming thrust belt. The N.40°E. direction of convergence during the time period 80 to 40 Ma can be taken as the direction of maximum compressive stress during the Laramide orogeny. This stress field resulted in the development of major northwest-trending foreland uplifts at right angles to the maximum compression.

This concept of a constant direction of regional compression during the Laramide orogeny (80 to 40 Ma) differs from other workers. For instance, Gries (1983b) called for a change from northeast-southwest compression to north-south compression to explain the multiple trends of mountain fronts in Wyoming that appear to have basement overhangs. A unidirectional compression (N.40°E.) also differs from the concept of compression generated by rotation of the Colorado Plateau in two stages, as put forth by Hamilton (1981; this volume).

Chapin and Cather (1983) concluded that the direction of compression changed from east-northeast to N.45°E. during the Paleocene. However, they stated that the Colorado Plateau was then transported to the north-northeast. This N.45°E. direction of compression would have resulted in convergent right wrenching on the more north-south–oriented structures of the southern Rocky Mountains. The same model may apply to the Colorado Front Range and the Laramie Range of southeastern Wyoming. East-west–trending features (such as the Owl Creek and Uinta Mountains) would also be oblique to the N.40° to 50°E. direction of compression. All of these structures display varying amounts of basement overhang, which may have resulted from reverse left-oblique slip on the east-west–striking fault zones.

In addition to these large-scale inferences of the direction of compression for the foreland, there are features observable in the field that also indicate a northeast-southwest orientation for σ_1. Allison (1983) mapped numerous small-scale structural features along the east flank of the Bighorn basin (T.47N.,R.88 to 89W.) that individually and collectively confirm a northeasterly compression direction (σ_1). Tectonic stylolites are oriented such that the shortening direction (implied σ_1) is parallel to the long axis of the "teeth," as seen in cross section, and perpendicular to the strike of the stylolite zone. Bedding-normal stylolites mapped by Allison indicate a N.61°E. direction of compression. Joint orientations also indicated a σ_1 direction of N.52°E.; plumose structures on fracture faces indicates a σ_1 direction of N.50°E. Finally, slickensides on fault surfaces indicated a N.48°E. direction for σ_1 orientation.

Features such as the Wind River thrust (Berg, 1962b; Gries, 1981; Smithson and others, 1978), the Casper Arch thrust (Gries, 1981; Skeen and Ray, 1983), and the Beartooth thrust display major heave components of displacement (overhang) which have been verified by drilling and seismic data. These major reverse faults, which dip northeast and southwest, represent primary brittle yielding of the upper crust along conjugate sets of reverse faults, as postulated by Hafner (1951). The northwest trend of these oppositely dipping fault zones suggests that the assumption that the N.40°E. direction of plate convergence also represents the regional direction of maximum compression (σ_1) is valid.

CONCLUSIONS

There is no one, single structural style in the Wyoming foreland. The evidence presented in this section clearly leads to the conclusion that the orientation of the structural feature is extremely important when deciding which structural model to apply. Features displaying the basic characteristics of fold-thrust uplifts are the major northwest-trending structures of the foreland. Thrust uplifts also trend generally northwest but may be at slight angles to the trends of the fold-thrusts.

Those features that display the basic characteristics of the drape fold and upthrust structures are the east- and northeast-trending foreland structures. These latter structures are generally perpendicular or oblique to the fold-thrust trends, and are therefore parallel or subparallel to the regional direction of compression.

Northwest-trending structures that have been interpreted as drape folds, such as Rattlesnake Mountain anticline (Stearns, 1971), are structurally out of balance. The imbalance between the sediments and the basement surface results from a general lack of extensional mechanisms in the upthrown block. These features can be balanced by flattening of the fault(s) into low-angle reverse faults, and/or by interpreting curvature on the basement/sediment contact of the hanging wall, footwall, or both. Such modifications ultimately result in a fold-thrust interpretation.

Development of drape folds and upthrust structures result from localization of vertical uplift components along east- or northeast-trending faults that segment, or compartmentalize, the northwest-trending structures. These east- or northeast-trending faults may have inherited their location and orientation from Precambrian shear zones, igneous dikes, or other "zones of weakness." Localization of vertical movements resulted from reactivation of these zones during the Laramide orogeny. A northeast-southwest, horizontal stress field should have resulted in a high degree of oblique slip with lateral offset along these trends. However, a lack of piercing points makes this difficult to prove.

Experimental studies have shown that small amounts of lateral movement may occur without surface exposure of the fault. The fault will develop the shape of an upthrust, and reach the surface first low on the flank of the associated drape fold, and then develop progressively higher onto the drape fold, with increasing amounts of lateral and vertical displacement.

The folding in the sedimentary section responds to tectonic loading by the Precambrian basement forcing block. If the forcing block moves along a reverse fault, the resulting fold in the sedimentary section will be a compressional fold displaying the volumetric problems and bed-length adjustments (out-of-the-syncline crowd structures, i.e., back-limb folds, and cross-crestal and rabbit-ear structures) typical of such compression. If the forcing block is uplifted along a more vertical fault (as in compartmental deformation), the resulting structure will be a drape fold in the overlying sedimentary section. As such, certain bed-lengthening mechanisms (thinning of the steep limb, and extensional normal faults) should become the predominant style (i.e., North Owl Creek area, Wind River Canyon).

It is therefore critical to the interpretation of foreland structural styles that particular attention be paid to the orientation of structures, both within the regional stress system and also with one another, for comparisons to be meaningful.

ACKNOWLEDGMENTS

I thank Robert Berg, Richard Hoppin, and Christopher Schmidt for reviewing this paper; their comments have greatly improved the text. I also gratefully acknowledge my 23-year association with Chevron USA, Inc., and the benefits derived from this association through the exchange of ideas and concepts with numerous Chevron geologists and geophysicists. The concepts presented in this chapter are the outgrowth of this association, but I am solely responsible for interpretations made herein.

REFERENCES CITED

Allison, M. L., 1983, Deformation styles along the Tensleep fault, Bighorn basin, Wyoming: Wyoming Geological Association 34th Annual Field Conference Guidebook, p. 63–75.

Armbrustmacher, T. J., 1972, Mafic dikes of the Clear Creek drainage area, eastern Bighorn Mountains, Wyoming: Contributions to Geology, v. 11, p. 31–40.

Armstrong, F. C., and Oriel, S. S., 1965, Tectonic development of Idaho-Wyoming thrust belt: American Association of Petroleum Geologists Bulletin, v. 49, no. 11, p. 1847–1866.

Armstrong, R. L., 1968, Sevier orogenic belt in Nevada and Utah: Geological Society of America Bulletin, v. 79, no. 4, p. 429–458.

Atwater, T., 1970, Implication of plate tectonics for the Cenozoic tectonic evolution of Western North America: Geological Society of America Bulletin, v. 81, no. 12, p. 3513–3536.

Banks, C. E., 1970, Precambrian gneiss at Sheephead Mountain, Carbon County, Wyoming, and its relationship to Laramide structure [M.S. thesis]: Laramie, University of Wyoming, 36 p.

Beckwith, R. H., 1938, Structure of the southwest margin of the Laramie basin, Wyoming: Geological Society of America Bulletin, v. 49, p. 1515–1544.

——, 1941, Structure of the Elk Mountain district, Carbon County, Wyoming: Geological Society of America Bulletin, v. 52, p. 1445–1486.

Berg, R. R., 1961, Laramide tectonics of the Wind River Mountains, *in* Symposium on Late Cretaceous rocks: Wyoming Geological Association 16th Annual Field Conference Guidebook, p. 70–80.

——, 1962a, Subsurface interpretation of Golden fault at Soda Lakes, Jefferson County, Colorado: American Association of Petroleum Geologists Bulletin, v. 46, no. 5, p. 704–707.

——, 1962b, Mountain flank thrusting in Rocky Mountain foreland, Wyoming and Colorado: American Association of Petroleum Geologists Bulletin, v. 46, no. 11, p. 2019–2032.

Bird, P., 1984, Laramide crustal thickening event in the Rocky Mountain foreland and Great Plains: Tectonics, v. 3, no. 7, p. 741–758.

Blackstone, D. L., Jr., 1940, Structure of the Pryor Mountains, Montana: Journal of Geology, v. 48, p. 590–618.

——, 1981, Compression as an agent in deformation of the east-central flank of the Bighorn Mountains, Sheridan and Johnson Counties, Wyoming: Contributions to Geology, v. 19, no. 2, p. 105–122.

——, 1983, Laramide compressional tectonics, southeastern Wyoming: Contributions to Geology, v. 22, no. 1, p. 1–38.

——, 1984, Quealy dome, Albany County, Wyoming; A Rocky Mountain foreland structural trap oil field: Mountain Geologist, v. 21, no. 3, p. 85–90.

Bonini, W. E., and Kinard, R. E., 1983, Gravity anomalies along the Beartooth front, Montana, *in* Geology of the Bighorn Basin: Wyoming Geological Association 34th Annual Field Conference Guidebook, p. 89–95.

Brown, W. G., 1975, Casper Mountain area, Wyoming; A model of Laramide deformation [abs.]: American Association of Petroleum Geologists Bulletin, v. 59, no. 5, p. 906.

——, 1981, Surface and subsurface examples of the Wyoming foreland as evidence of a regional compressional origin for the Laramide orogeny [abs.]: Contributions to Geology, v. 19, no. 2, p. 175–177.

——, 1982, New tricks for old dogs; A shortcourse in structural geology: American Association of Petroleum Geologists Southwest Sectional Meeting, 79 p.

——, 1983, Sequential development of the fold-thrust model of foreland deformation *in* Lowell, J. D., ed., Rocky Mountain foreland basins and uplifts: Rocky Mountain Association of Geologists, p. 57–64.

——, 1984a, Rattlesnake Mountain Anticline; A reverse fault interpretation: Mountain Geologist, v. 21, no. 2, p. 32–35.

——, 1984b, Basement involved tectonics; Foreland areas: American Association of Petroleum Geologists Continuing Education Course Note Series 26, 92 p.

——, 1987, Structural style of the Laramide orogeny, Wyoming foreland [Ph.D. thesis]: Geophysical Institute, University of Alaska–Fairbanks, 343 p.

Burchfiel, B. C., and Davis, G. A., 1975, Nature and controls of Cordilleran orogenesis, western United States; Extensions of an earlier synthesis: American Journal of Science Bulletin, v. 275-A, p. 363–396.

Chapin, C. E., and Cather, S. M., 1983, Eocene tectonics and sedimentation in the Colorado Plateau; Rocky Mountain area, *in* Lowell, J. D., ed., Rocky Mountain foreland basins and uplifts: Rocky Mountain Association of Geologists, p. 33–56.

Chester, J. S., 1985, Deformation of layered rocks in the ramp regions of thrust faults; A study with rock models [M.S. thesis]: College Station, Texas A&M University, 137 p.

Coney, P. J., 1978, Mesozoic-Cenozoic Cordilleran plate tectonics, *in* Smith, R. B. and Eaton, G. P., eds., Cenozoic tectonics and regional geophysics of the western Cordilleran: Geological Society of America Memoir 152, p. 33–50.

Dahlstrom, C.D.A., 1969, The upper detachment in concentric folding: Canadian Petroleum Geology Bulletin, v. 17, no. 3, p. 326–346.

Dana, J. D., 1896, Manual of geology, 4th ed.: New York, American Book Company, 1987 p. (1895).

Dickinson, W. R., and Snyder, W. S., 1978, Plate tectonics of the Laramide orogeny, *in* Matthews, V., III, ed., Laramide folding associated with basement block faulting in the western United States; Geological Society of America Memoir 151, p. 355–366.

Engebretson, D. C., Cox, A., and Thompson, G. A., 1984, Correlation of plate motions with continental tectonics; Laramide to Basin-Range: Tectonics, v. 3, no. 2, p. 115–119.

Fanshawe, J. R., 1939, Structural geology of the Wind River Canyon area, Wyoming: American Association of Petroleum Geologists Bulletin, v. 23, p. 1439–1492.

Foose, R. M., Wise, D. U., and Garbarini, G., 1961, Structural geology of the Beartooth Mountain block, Montana and Wyoming: Geological Society of America Bulletin, v. 72, p. 1147–1172.

Friedman, M., Handin, J., Logan, J. M., Min, K. D., and Stearns, D. W., 1976, Experimental folding of rocks under confining pressure; Part III, Faulted drape folds in multilithologic layered specimens; Geological Society of

America Bulletin, v. 87, p. 2049–2066.

Gries, R., 1981, Oil and gas prospecting beneath the Precambrian of foreland thrust plates in the Rocky Mountains: Mountain Geologist, v. 18, p. 1–18.

——, 1983a, Oil and gas prospecting beneath Precambrian of foreland thrust plates in the Rocky Mountains: American Association of Petroleum Geologists Bulletin, v. 67, no. 1, p. 1–26.

——, 1983b, North-south compression of Rocky Mountain foreland structures, *in* Lowell, J. D., ed., Rocky Mountain foreland basins and uplifts: Rocky Mountain Association of Geologists, p. 9–32.

Hafner, W., 1951, Stress distribution and faulting: Geological Society of America Bulletin, v. 62, no. 4, p. 373–398.

Hamilton, W., 1978, Mesozoic tectonics of the western United States: Pacific Section, Society of Economic Paleontologists and Mineralogists Pacific Coast Paleogeography Symposium 2, p. 33–70.

——, 1981, Plate tectonic mechanism of Laramide deformation: Contributions to Geology, v. 19, p. 87–92.

Hamilton, W., and Meyer, W. B., 1966, Cenozoic tectonics of the western United States: Review of Geophysics, v. 4, p. 509–549.

Heimlich, R. A., 1969, Reconnaissance petrology of Precambrian rocks in the Bighorn Mountains, Wyoming: Contributions to Geology, v. 8, no. 1, p. 47–61.

Heimlich, R. A., Nelson, G. C., and Gallagher, G. L., 1973, Metamorphosed mafic dikes from the southern Bighorn Mountains, Wyoming: Geological Society of America Bulletin, v. 84, p. 1439–1449.

Heimlich, R. A., Gallagher, G. L., and Shotwell, L. B., 1974, Quantitative petrography of mafic dikes from the central Bighorn Mountains, Wyoming: Geology Magazine, v. 111, p. 97–106.

Hodgson, R. A., 1965, Genetic and geometric relations between structures in basement and overlying sedimentary rocks with examples from Colorado plateau and Wyoming: American Association of Petroleum Geologists Bulletin, v. 49, no. 7, p. 935–939.

Hoppin, R. A., 1961, Precambrian rocks and their relationship to Laramide structure along the east flank of the Bighorn Mountains near Buffalo, Wyoming: Geological Society of America Bulletin, v. 72, no. 3, p. 351–367.

——, 1970, Structural development of Five Springs Creek area, Bighorn Mountains, Wyoming: Geological Society of America Bulletin, v. 81, p. 2403–2416.

Hoppin, R. A., and Jennings, T. V., 1971, Cenozoic tectonic elements, Bighorn Mountain region Wyoming-Montana: Wyoming Geological Association 23rd Field Conference Guidebook, p. 39–74.

Hoppin, R. A., and Palmquist, J. C., 1965, Basement influence on later deformation; The problem, techniques of investigation, and examples from Bighorn Mountains, Wyoming: American Association of Petroleum Geologists Bulletin, v. 49, no. 7, p. 993–1003.

Hoppin, R. A., Palmquist, J. C., and Williams, L. O., 1965, Control by Precambrian basement structure on the location of the Tensleep–Beaver Creek faults, Bighorn Mountains, Wyoming: Journal of Geology, v. 73, p. 189–195.

Houston, R. S., 1971, Regional tectonics of the Precambrian rocks of the Wyoming Province and its relationship to Laramide structure: Wyoming Geological Association 23rd Annual Field Conference Guidebook, p. 19–28.

Houston, R. S., and Barnes, C. W., 1969, Basement response to the Laramide orogeny at Coad Mountain, Wyoming: Contributions to Geology, v. 8, p. 37–43.

Houston, R. S., and others, 1968, A regional study of rocks of Precambrian age in that part of the Medicine Bow Mountains lying in southeastern Wyoming; With a chapter on the relationships between Precambrian and Laramide structures: Geological Survey of Wyoming Memoir 1, 167 p.

Hudson, F. S., 1955, Folding of unmetamorphosed strata super-jacent to massive basement rocks: American Association of Petroleum Geologists Bulletin, v. 39, p. 2038–2052.

Jennings, T. V., 1967, Structural analysis of the northern Bighorn Mountains, Wyoming [Ph.D. thesis]: Iowa City, University of Iowa, 224 p.

Johnson, G. D., 1934, Geology of the mountain uplift transected by the Shoshone Canyon, Wyoming: Journal of Geology, v. 42, n. 8, p. 809–835.

Johnson, R. A., and Smithson, S. B., 1985, Thrust faulting in the Laramie Mountains, Wyoming from reanalysis of COCORP data: Geology, v. 13, no. 8, p. 534–537.

Johnson, R. C., and Hills, F. A., 1976, Precambrian geochronology and geology of the Boxelder Canyon area, northern Laramie Range, Wyoming: Geological Society of America Bulletin, v. 87, p. 809–817.

Jordan, T. E., Isacks, B. L., Allmendinger, R. W., Brewer, J. A., Ramos, V. A., and Ando, C. J., 1983, Andean tectonics; Lateral segmentation in Central Andes, related to geometry of subducted plate: Geological Society of America Bulletin, v. 94, no. 3, p. 341–361.

Jurdy, D. M., 1984, The subduction of the Farallon plate beneath North America as derived from relative plate motions: Tectonics, v. 3, no. 2, p. 107–114.

Keefer, W. R., 1965, Stratigraphy and geologic history of the uppermost Cretaceous, Paleocene, and lower Eocene rocks in the Wind River basin, Wyoming: U.S. Geological Survey Professional Paper 495-A, p. A1–A77.

——, 1970, Structural geology of the Wind River basin, Wyoming: U.S. Geological Survey Professional Paper 495-D, 35 p.

Lamerson, P. R., 1983, The Fossil basin area, and its relationship to the Absaroka thrust fault system, *in* Powers, R. B., ed., Geologic studies of the Cordilleran thrust belt, 1982: Rocky Mountain Association of Geologists, p. 279–340.

Logan, J. M., Friedman, M., and Stearns, M. T., 1978, Experimental folding of rocks under confining pressure, Part VI, Further studies of faulted drape folds, *in* Matthews, V., III, ed., Laramide folding associated with basement block faulting in the western United States: Geological Society of America Memoir 151, p. 79–99.

Love, J. D., 1977, Summary of Upper Cretaceous and Cenozoic stratigraphy, and of tectonic and glacial events in Jackson Hole, northwestern Wyoming: Wyoming Geological Association 29th Annual Field Conference [in conjunction with Montana Geological Society and Utah Geological Society] Guidebook, p. 585–593.

——, 1983, A possible gap in the western thrust belt in Idaho and Wyoming, *in* Powers, R. B., ed., Geologic studies of the Cordilleran thrust belt, 1982: Rocky Mountain Association of Geologists, p. 247–260.

Love, J. D., and Christiansen, A. C., 1985, Geologic map of Wyoming: U.S. Geological Survey, scale 1:500,000.

Lowell, J. D., 1983, Foreland deformation, *in* Lowell, J. D., ed., Rocky Mountain foreland basins and uplifts: Rocky Mountain Association of Geologists, p. 1–8.

Mackin, J. H., 1959, The down-structure method of viewing geologic maps: Journal of Geology, v. 58, no. 1, p. 55–72.

Manzer, G. K., and Heimlich, R. A., 1974, Petrology and geochemistry of mafic and ultramafic rocks from the northern Bighorn Mountains, Wyoming: Geological Society of America Bulletin, v. 85, no. 5, p. 703–708.

Mitra, G., and Frost, B. R., 1981, Mechanisms of the deformation within Laramide and Precambrian deformation zones in basement rocks of the Wind River Mountains: Contributions to Geology, v. 19, no. 2, p. 161–173.

Murray, F. E., 1960, An interpretation of the Hilliard thrust fault, Lincoln and Sublette Counties, Wyoming, *in* McGooky, D. P., and Miller, D. N., Jr., eds., Overthrust belt of southwest Wyoming and adjacent areas: Wyoming Geological Association 15th Annual Field Conference Guidebook, p. 161–186.

Nichols, C. E., 1965, Geology of a segment of Deep Creek fault zones, southern Bighorn Mountains, Wyoming [Ph.D. thesis]: Iowa City, University of Iowa.

Osterwald, F. C., 1961, Critical review of some tectonic problems in Cordilleran foreland: American Association of Petroleum Geologists Bulletin, v. 45, no. 2, p. 219–237.

Palmquist, J. C., 1967, Structural analysis of the Horn area; Bighorn Mountains, Wyoming: Geological Society of America Bulletin, v. 78, p. 282–298.

——, 1978, Laramide structure and basement block faulting; Two examples from the Bighorn Mountains, Wyoming, *in* Matthews, V., III, ed., Laramide folding associated with basement block faulting in the western United States: Geological Society of America Memoir 151, p. 125–128.

Petersen, F. A., 1983, Foreland detachment structures, *in* Lowell, J. D., ed., Rocky Mountain foreland basins and uplifts: Rocky Mountain Association of Geologists, p. 65–77.

Prucha, J. J., Graham, J. A., and Nickelsen, R. P., 1965, Basement-controlled deformation in Wyoming province of Rocky Mountain foreland: American Association of Petroleum Geologists Bulletin, v. 49, no. 7, p. 966–992.

Rich, J. W., 1934, Mechanics of low-angle overthrust faulting as illustrated by Cumberland thrust block, Virginia, Kentucky, and Tennessee: American Association of Petroleum Geologists Bulletin, v. 18, no. 12, p. 1584–1596.

Royse, F., Jr., Warner, M. A., and Reese, D. L., 1975, Thrust belt structural geometry and related stratigraphic problems, Wyoming, Idaho, northern Utah, *in* Bolyard, D. W., ed., Symposium on Deep drilling frontiers in the central Rocky Mountains: Rocky Mountain Association of Geologists, p. 41–45.

Sacrison, W. R., 1978, Seismic interpretation of basement block faults and associated deformation, *in* Matthews, V., III, ed., Laramide folding associated with basement block faulting in the western United States: Geological Society of America Memoir 151, p. 39–49.

Sales, J. K., 1968, Cordilleran foreland deformation: American Association of Petroleum Geologists Bulletin, v. 52, p. 2000–2015.

Sanford, A. R., 1959, Analytical and experimental study of simple geologic structures: Geological Society of America Bulletin, v. 79, p. 19–51.

Scheevel, J. R., 1984, Fold-thrust versus thrust-folds, *in* Forum: Mountain Geologist, v. 21, n. 3, p. 73–74.

Schmidt, C. J., and Garihan, J. M., 1983, Laramide tectonic development of the Rocky Mountain foreland of southwestern Montana, *in* Lowell, J. D., ed., Rocky Mountain foreland basins and uplifts: Rocky Mountain Association of Geologists, p. 271–294.

——, 1986, Role of recurrent movement on northwest-trending basement faults in the tectonic evolution of southwestern Montana, *in* Aldrich, J., ed., Proceedings of 6th International Conference on Basement Tectonics: Salt Lake City, International Basement Tectonics Association.

Schmidt, C. J., Evans, J. P., Fletcher, R. C., and Spang, J. H., 1985, Spacing of Rocky Mountain foreland arches and Laramide magmatic activity: Geological Society of America Abstracts with Programs, v. 17, p. 710.

Sears, W. A., Jr., and Sims, F. C., 1954, Structural geology of the Casper Mountain area: Wyoming Geological Association 9th Annual Field Conference Guidebook, p. 27–31.

Skeen, R. C., and Ray, R. R., 1983, Seismic models and interpretation of the Casper arch thrust; Application to Rocky Mountain foreland structure, *in* Lowell, J. D., ed., Rocky Mountain foreland basins and uplifts: Rocky Mountain Association of Geologists, p. 99–124.

Smithson, S. B., Brewer, J., Kaufman, S., Oliver, J., and Hurich, C., 1978, Question of the Wind River thrust, Wyoming, resolved by COCORP deep reflection data and by gravity, *in* Boyd, R. G., ed., Resources of the Wind River Basin: Wyoming Geological Association 30th Annual Field Conference Guidebook, p. 227–234.

Sprague, E. L., 1983, Geology of the Tepee Flats–Buffington Fields, Natrona County, Wyoming, *in* Lowell, J. D., ed., Rocky Mountain foreland basins and uplifts: Rocky Mountain Association of Geologists, p. 339–343.

Stauder, W. J., 1975, Subduction of the Nazca Plate under Peru as evidenced by focal mechanisms and by seismicity: Journal of Geophysical Research, v. 80, p. 1053–1064.

Stearns, D. W., 1971, Mechanisms of drape folding in the Wyoming province: Wyoming Geological Association 23rd Annual Field Conference Guidebook, p. 125–144.

——, 1975, Laramide basement deformation in the Bighorn basin; The controlling factor for structure in the layered rocks: Wyoming Geological Association 27th Annual Field Conference Guidebook, p. 149–158.

——, 1978, Faulting and forced folding in the Rocky Mountains foreland, *in* Matthews, V., III, ed., Laramide folding associated with basement block faulting in the western United States: Geological Society of America Memoir 151, p. 1–37.

Stearns, D. W., and Weinberg, D. M., 1975, A comparison of experimentally created and naturally formed drape folds: Wyoming Geological Association 27th Annual Field Conference Guidebook, p. 159–166.

Stone, D. S., 1969, Wrench faulting and the Rocky Mountain tectonics: Mountain Geologist, v. 6, no. 2, p. 67–79.

——, 1970, Principal horizontal stress in the central Rocky Mountains versus California: Mountain Geologist, v. 7, no. 2, p. 69–82.

——, 1975, A dynamic analysis of subsurface structure in northwestern Colorado, *in* Bolyard, D. W., ed., Symposium on deep drilling frontiers in the central Rocky Mountains: Rocky Mountain Association of Geologists, p. 33–40.

——, 1983, The Greybull Sandstone pool (Lower Cretaceous) on the Elk Basin thrust-fold complex, Wyoming and Montana, *in* Lowell, J. D., ed., Conference on Rocky Mountain foreland basins and uplifts: Rocky Mountain Association of Geologists, p. 345–356.

——, 1984a, Seismic profile; South Elk Basin area, Bighorn basin, Wyoming, *in* Bally, W. W., ed., Seismic expression of structural styles, v. 3: American Association of Petroleum Geologists, p. 3.2.2-20–3.2.2.-24.

——, 1984b, The Rattlesnake Mountain, Wyoming, debate; A review and critique of models: Mountain Geologist, v. 21, no. 2, p. 37–46.

——, 1985, Quealy Dome; A Rocky Mountain foreland structural trap oil field, *in* Forum: Mountain Geologist, v. 22, no. 1, p. 1–3.

Suppe, J., 1985, Principles of structural geology: Englewood Cliffs, N.J., Prentice-Hall, 537 p.

Tomlinson, C. W., 1952, Odd geologic structures of southern Oklahoma: American Association of Petroleum Geologists Bulletin, v. 36, no. 9, p. 1820–1840.

Wach, P. H., 1977, The Moxa Arch, an overthrust model?: Wyoming Geological Association 29th Annual Field Conference Guidebook (in conjunction with Montana Geological Society and Utah Geological Society), p. 651–664.

Wilson, C. W., Jr., 1934, A study of the jointing in the Five Springs Creek area, east of Kane, Wyoming: Journal of Geology, v. 42, p. 498–522.

Wise, D. U., 1963, Keystone faulting and gravity sliding driven by basement uplift of Owl Creek Mountains, Wyoming: American Association of Petroleum Geologists Bulletin, v. 47, n. 4, p. 586–598.

——, 1964, Microjointing in basement, middle Rocky Mountains of Montana and Wyoming: Geological Society of America Bulletin, v. 75, p. 287–306.

——, 1983, Overprinting of Laramide structural grains in the Clark's Fork Canyon area and eastern Beartooth Mountains of Wyoming: Wyoming Geological Association 34th Annual Field Conference Guidebook, p. 77–88.

Woodward, L. A., 1976, Laramide deformation of Rocky Mountain foreland; Geometry and mechanics: New Mexico Geological Society Special Publication 6, p. 11–17.

MANUSCRIPT ACCEPTED BY THE SOCIETY FEBRUARY 9, 1988

Printed in U.S.A.

Geological Society of America
Memoir 171
1988

Laramide crustal shortening

Warren B. Hamilton
U.S. Geological Survey, Box 25046, Denver Federal Center, Denver, Colorado 80225

ABSTRACT

North America rapidly overrode buoyant oceanic lithosphere during late Late Cretaceous and early Paleogene time. The southwestern United States was retarded by drag against the overridden slab and advanced slightly more slowly than did the continental interior. This resulted in crustal shortening, in a broad zone between the continental subplates, that produced the variably overthrust Laramide basement uplifts of the Rocky Mountain region. The thrust faults flatten downward into the middle crust and are reflective in seismic profiles, likely because diverse crystalline rocks have been transposed along them by ductile shear and flattening.

The increase northward and northwestward, from New Mexico to Wyoming, of crustal shortening across the Laramide belt, and the fanning pattern of northwest-broadening arcs defined by the compressive structures throughout the Rocky Mountain region, indicate that the Colorado Plateau region rotated clockwise, as though about an Euler pole in or near central New Mexico, by perhaps 4° relative to the continental interior. This rotation, combined with the subsequent clockwise relative rotation of the plateau by about 3° about an Euler pole in central Colorado as the Rio Grande rift opened in middle Tertiary time, can be seen in paleomagnetic data.

INTRODUCTION

The North American craton was deformed compressively during latest Cretaceous and early Tertiary time, 75 to 40 m.y. ago, to form the Laramide belt of structures extending the length of the U.S. Rocky Mountains. This deformation occurred as the continental North American plate was rapidly overriding, and probably dragging on, gently inclined, subducting oceanic lithosphere (Bird, 1984, 1988; Chapin and Cather, 1981; Cross, 1986; Dickinson, 1981; Dickinson and Snyder, 1978; Hamilton, 1981; Liviccari and others, 1981; Molnar and Atwater, 1978). In pre-Laramide Cretaceous time, when convergence was relatively slow and the subducting plate dipped steeply, an accretionary wedge of mélange, a fore-arc basin, a magmatic arc, and a foreland thrust belt were produced (Hamilton, 1978). Toward the end of Cretaceous time, convergence accelerated, the lithosphere being subducted was younger and sank more slowly, arc magmatism spread far inland, and Laramide deformation began. The Laramide crustal shortening represented a relative slowing of the southwest part of the continent and can be viewed as the product of slight clockwise rotation of the Colorado Plateau relative to the continental interior as though about an Euler pole in or near northwest Texas (Hamilton, 1978, 1981) or central New Mexico (this report).

LARAMIDE DEFORMATION OF THE CRATON

The Rocky Mountain region of the North American craton, from central New Mexico to northern Montana, was distorted by shortening during the Laramide episode in late Late Cretaceous, Paleocene, and Eocene time. The typical products of this deformation are large, asymmetric anticlines of Precambrian basement rocks, bounded on one or both sides by thrust faults or steep monoclines against deep basins that subsided and received sediments concurrent with rise of uplifts (Fig. 1). The major uplifts and basins have lengths of hundreds of kilometers, and the structural relief between some paired uplifts and basins exceeds 10 km. Some basin axes are beneath the fronts of overriding basement uplifts. The main structures define a belt trending northward and widening through northern New Mexico into Colorado, where they splay out in successive arcs to the west, west-northwest, northwest, and north, through northern Utah, Wyoming, Montana, and, in part in the subsurface, western South and North Dakota. The amount of total shortening across the belt increases northward and northwestward along it as both the width of the belt and the number of major structures within it increase. Much less shortening, expressed as monoclines, affected the Colorado Plateau.

Geologic structures requiring major shortening have long

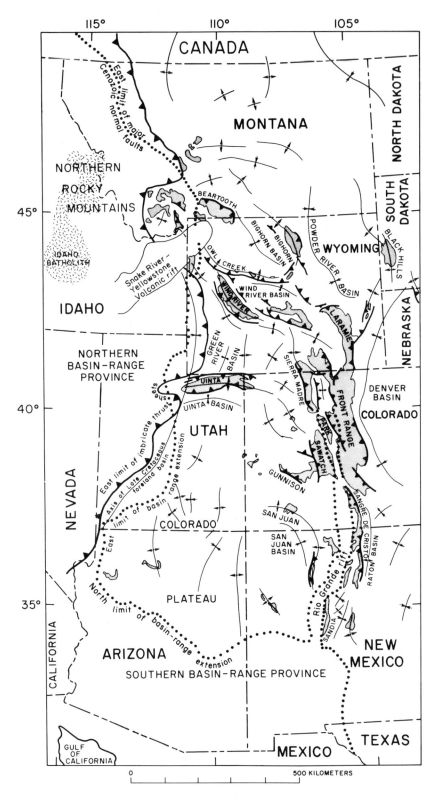

Figure 1. Selected structural elements of the Rocky Mountain region. Most of the uplifts and basins indicated are of Laramide age—very late Cretaceous and early Paleogene. Outcrops of Precambrian rocks east of the foreland fold-and-thrust belt and north of the southern Basin and Range province are shaded.

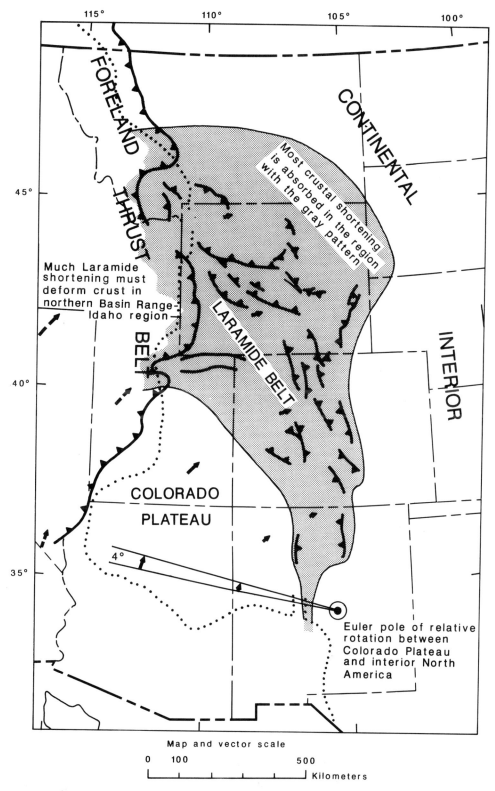

Figure 2. Map illustrating rotation of the Colorado Plateau relative to interior North America, as the cause of the Laramide deformation of the Rocky Mountain region. The vectors depict, to scale, the relative rotation of the plateau by 4° as though about the inferred Euler pole in New Mexico. The motion was absorbed by crustal shortening in the Laramide belt.

been known from field observations. Modern detailed geologic maps of complex basement-involved thrust-and-fold structures include those by Baltz and O'Neill (1984), Snyder (1980), and Tysdal (1976). Although many Rocky Mountain geologists assume that Laramide overthrust deformation represents surficial overflow of blocks bounded by vertical faults, their "verticalist" speculation is disproved by deep drilling, reflection profiling, and mapped structural geometry.

The widths of individual Laramide uplifts and basins are less than the wavelength of isostatic compensation so they are represented by conspicuous, paired highs and lows in the informative isostatic-residual-gravity field (Jachens and others, 1985; Simpson and others, 1986). The increase in crustal shortening from central New Mexico to Wyoming and the decrease beyond in Montana can be seen graphically in the isostatic-residual gravity highs of the uplifts, which reach maximum values near +70 milligals in Wyoming. The gravity highs require excess crustal loads—shortening—and cannot be explained by vertical uplift of crustal prisms (Simpson and others, 1986).

Deep-crustal deformation

Reflection profiling and oil-exploration drilling have demonstrated the compressive character of Laramide structures in many places (Blackstone, 1983, 1986; Brewer and others, 1982; Smithson and others, 1979; and papers by many authors in the volumes edited by Gries and Dyer, 1985, and by Lowell and Gries, 1983). Thrust faults flatten downward into the middle crust where constrained and probably owe their reflectivity at depth to contrasting crystalling lithologies transposed into parallel layers by ductile shear. Ambiguous deep-reflection records can be interpreted to indicate that faults splay in the middle crust into anastomosing zones of ductile faulting that separate relatively unsheared lenses (Sharry and others, 1985). The deep crust may have been uncoupled from the upper crust to a considerable extent, and an increase with increasing temperature downward of pervasiveness of deformation is to be expected on rock-mechanic grounds.

Analogy is suggested with exposed lower-crust structures of the Proterozoic Grenville province of Ontario, where northwest-verging imbrication of great lenses of deep-crustal granulites between thick zones of mylonite of granulite and amphibolite facies has been demonstrated by Davidson (1984, 1985, 1986; also Lindia and others, 1983; Mawer, 1983; and White and Mawer, 1988; Fig. 3). The aggregate thickness of the shear zones over which shortening is distributed increases in a general way downward in the Grenville crust, for the zones affect deep, granulite-facies rocks more than they do shallower, amphibolite-facies rocks. Similar deep-crustal lenses separated by zones of ductile shear may be imaged by COCORP deep-reflection profiles (Klemperer and others, 1985; they did not make this interpretation) in the Adirondack Mountains region of the Grenville province.

Other analogs for Laramide structures include the great

midcrustal basement thrusts formed about 2,500 m.y. ago, and also marked by thick cataclasites, exposed in northern Ontario (Percival and McGrath, 1986); the modern Sierras Pampeanas of Argentina (Jordan and Allmendinger, 1986); and many more (Rodgers, 1987).

Uplift of the Western Interior

The Colorado Plateau, the basins of the early-Laramide Rocky Mountains, the foreland basin in front of the advancing thrust wedge of the Sevier belt, and the Great Plains were all near sea level—marine strata are widespread—very late in Cretaceous time. Local relief was much increased by Laramide shortening, but the rise of the entire region to its present general altitudes of 1 to 2.5 km above sea level occurred during Neogene time. Crustal thickness (Allenby and Schnetzler, 1983) is mostly near 40 km, a standard stable-continent value. Locally, it exceeds 50 km, presumably as a result of Laramide shortening, although at the present state of fragmentary knowledge the overthick regions correlate only in part with those of shortening and of current altitude. Uppermost mantle velocities are near normal—8.0 to 8.2 km/sec (Allenby and Schnetzler, 1983)—so the regional uplift must be largely compensated deeper in the mantle. The broad correlation between the region of uplift and the region beneath which Pacific lithosphere was earlier subducted at shallow depth (Bird, 1984, 1988) permits inference that the Neogene uplift was due to some delayed effect of that plate interaction, perhaps in slow heating of the subducted slab, or in peeling away and sinking of the lower part of the tectonically overthickened mantle lithosphere (Bird, 1988).

Age of deformation

Laramide deformation took place during very late Cretaceous and early Paleogene time. Regional syntheses of evidence for dating the structures were made recently by Cross (1986), using primarily structural evidence, and Dickinson and others (1988), using higher resolution stratigraphic data. More limited analyses include those by Chapin and Cather (1981), Dickinson and others (1986), Gries (1983), and Tweto (1975). Near the tight arcs of Sevier belt thrusts in the complex foreland knot of southwesternmost Montana, minor deformation may have occurred as early as Aptian time, late Early Cretaceous (DeCelles, 1986; Nichols and others, 1985), and major deformation occurred during late Campanian or earliest Maastrichtian time, about 75 Ma (Cross, 1986). Throughout the rest of the province, deformation began within Maastrichtian or early Paleocene time, 75 to 60 Ma, climaxed in the Paleocene and early and middle Eocene, and was over by earliest Oligocene time, about 35 Ma (Cross, 1986; Dickinson and others, 1988). There are no consistent relationships between orientations and geographic positions of structures and the ages of their inception, climax, and termination, except that deformation in the south continued after that in the north had ended (Cross, 1986; Dickinson and others, 1988), contrary inferences by Chapin and Cather (1981) and Gries (1983) notwithstanding. Structures in east and west, and structures trending variously north, northwest, and west, all include early and late members. As Dickinson and others (1988, quoted from a prepublication draft of their report) emphasized, "the intricate geometry of Laramide uplifts and basins with diverse structural trends probably developed jointly within a complex but generally synchronous strain field imposed across a region of varied crustal architecture."

Shortening on a regional scale was continuous in space, and probably in time (Cross, 1986, noted evidence for a lull at about 60 Ma), but individual structures waxed and waned. The sequential development of individual structures can perhaps be viewed as a large-scale analog of kink folding: a structure grew until it reached a semistable configuration, at which it was easier mechanically to break a new structure through elsewhere than to continue shortening on the initial structure. Specific sites of failure within the stressed domain were controlled by local factors either within or at the base of the lithosphere. Geographic and temporal variations in shortening likely reflect complex variations in the degree and location of coupling between the overriding continental plate and the subducting materials beneath, much complicated by beam-strength effects.

"Reactivation"

Tweto (e.g., 1975), among others, long argued that reactivation of Precambrian and late Paleozoic structures dominated the geometry and location of Laramide uplifts and basins. This concept is unsupported by field evidence; no major structures have been demonstrated to have the predicted multistage histories. It was for Tweto, however, an expression of his conviction, shown graphically (Tweto, 1983) and shared by many Rocky Mountain geologists, that all fundamental crustal motion is vertical, and hence, that strike-slip, extensional, and shortening deformations are but minor surficial products of jostling between vertically moving prisms and that any appropriately oriented deep vertical fault will be used repeatedly.

By contrast, I see a nearly random correlation on a regional scale between the structures of diverse ages. Precambrian structural grains commonly were cut at high angles by Laramide structures, although minor structures were indeed reactivated where orientations were favorable (Schmidt and Garihan, 1983). Laramide structures share general trends with Paleozoic basins and ranges in part of western Colorado, but almost no correspondence exists even there between the locations of basins and ranges of the two episodes, and no major structure has yet been proved to have been active during both events.

ROTATION OF THE COLORADO PLATEAU

It is a theorem of spherical geometry that the net result of any motion between two plates, each internally rigid, on the surface of a sphere can be expressed in terms of a finite rotation of one plate relative to the other about a pole of rotation. This pole is commonly referred to as an Euler pole, after Leonhard Euler, the 18th-century Swiss mathematician who demonstrated the validity of this theorem. The Colorado Plateau and the continental interior behaved as quasi-rigid plates during compressive Laramide deformation, so the net motion of the plateau relative to the interior can be expressed in terms of a rotation about such a pole. The approximate location of the pole and amount of relative rotation can be inferred from geologic data.

The total amount of crustal shortening—the relative convergence of Colorado Plateau and continental interior—increased markedly northwestward and northward along the Laramide belt, and the trends of structures swing in broadening arcs in those directions (Fig. 1). North-trending structures in northwest New Mexico display a strong right-slip component (Baltz, 1967; Chapin and Cather, 1981), whereas structures trending west and west-northwest in the Wyoming region display a left-slip component (Sales, 1968), as northwest-trending structures in southwest Montana (Schmidt and Garihan, 1983) also may do. There is little Laramide deformation of any sort at the south end of the belt in central New Mexico (Kelley, 1972). These regional variations require that the rotation of the plateau relative to the continental interior was clockwise about an Euler pole nearby to the east or southeast of the southern part of the Colorado Plateau.

Figure 2 illustrates a relative rotation of the Colorado Plateau that accounts for the systematic regional changes in amount and directions of relative offsets. The illustrated rotation of 4° is fit to the assumption that about half the width of each of the basement ranges represents crustal shortening. This amount accords with shortening inferred in regional cross sections well constrained by structural-geologic and geophysical data (e.g., Brown, this volume); I doubt that a rotation of as little as 2° or as much as 8° could be fit to such constraints.

Reasonably good fits to the constraints could be obtained with an Euler pole moved as much as a few hundred kilometers to the east or southeast from the location illustrated; likely limits are smaller in other directions. A pole 400 km to the east of that used here was illustrated by Hamilton (1981, Fig. 2), but I now regard the pole location of the present paper as better fit to the structural data.

As individual structures are not continuous, shortening does not increase smoothly along them away from the Euler pole, but rather waxes and wanes; local slip vectors will only approximately follow the smooth rotational vectors illustrated in Figure 2.

Colorado Plateau

The Laramide monoclines of the Colorado Plateau record only minor shortening (Davis, 1978). The structures are approximately perpendicular to the predicted rotation vectors in Figure 2 only in the northern part of the plateau; elsewhere, monoclinal trends are irregular but mostly northward. I infer that the plateau plate was slightly shortened in an east-west direction as it rotated clockwise relative to the continental interior.

Figure 3 (this and facing page). Deep-crustal mylonites about 1,100 m.y. old in the Grenville province, in Ontario east of Lake Huron. Davidson (1984, 1985) found thick zones of these rocks to separate northwest-imbricated lenses of less-deformed deep-crustal rocks. Layering is inherited from compositional contrasts in older rocks but represents primarily transposition and flattening accompanying mylonitization. The deep-crustal structure of the Laramide belt may be analogous to that exposed here, and shear-transposed rocks such as these may produce the reflections seen on deep seismic-reflection profiles. (a) Granulite-facies mylonite. Dark lens at lower left is of relatively little-sheared garnet-hypersthene tonalite. Rest of cut is of fine-grained mylonite consisting of light-colored layers of magnetite metagranite, quartzite, and subordinate metapegmatite, finely lined by thin, dark layers of garnet-plagioclase rock. Roadcut is about 15 m high; location is 18 km east-southeast of Huntsville. (b) Mylonitized anorthositic gabbro, showing variably transposed layers of differing compositions. The rolled feldspars, from shredded pegmatites, show sense of shearing was top to the north (left). Coin is 2 cm in diameter; location is 2 km northeast of Parry Sound. (c) Variably mylonitized and transposed gabbroic anorthosite, 2 km northeast of Parry Sound.

Composite motions

The regional variations in Laramide deformation are so systematic—the relationship of trends and aggregate widths of structures to rotational vectors is so tidy (Fig. 2)—that I assume that the pole of relative rotation remained approximately fixed relative to both plateau and interior plates throughout the period of rotation. Some other Rocky Mountain geologists who seek mobilistic explanations—many are still verticalists—view Laramide shortening as produced by relative motions of the Colorado Plateau by fixed amounts in constant directions. (Such proposals imply sequential rotations about distant Euler poles but are not commonly expressed in such terms.) Gries (1983) inferred straight motions in complex sequential directions to explain di-versely oriented structures singly, but her rationale is disproved by the ages of the structures in question. Gries further argued that shifts in sites of deformation required major changes of directions of convergence between Colorado Plateau and continental interior because, she reasoned, shortening on structures close to the Colorado Plateau would necessarily precede that on more distant structures during any one episode of motion of the plateau relative to the continental interior; this rationale is mechanically invalid.

"Wrench faults"

Some Rocky Mountain geologists (e.g., Stone, 1969) appeal to reactivation of neatly geometric sets of intersecting "wrench

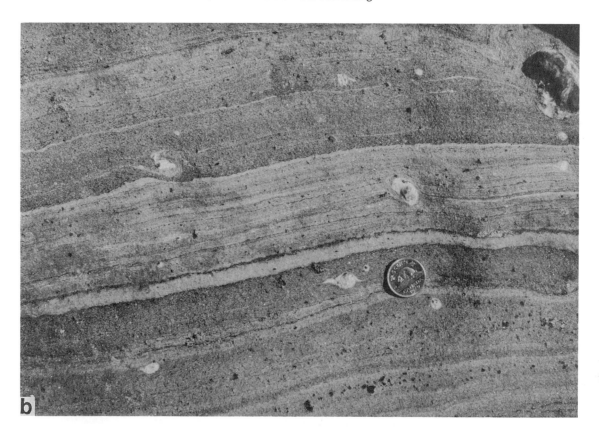

faults," hidden deep in the crust and only uncommonly shown directly by the surface geology, as the cause of Laramide deformation. Chapin and Cather (1981) deduced, incorrectly, that early and late Laramide regional compression were differently oriented, and proposed that the different stress fields activated different sets of such deep-crustal "wrench faults" that complexly controlled the observed very different structures of the upper crust. I view such "wrench faults" as both unnecessary and mechanically improbable. Although patterns of strike-slip faulting may indeed change downward in the crust (Sibson, 1983), I know of no deeply eroded terrains in which detailed mapping has demonstrated fault patterns like those required by "wrench faulting" hypotheses.

OTHER BOUNDARIES

The Colorado Plateau plate must continue westward and southward to other zones of relative motion between plates, but the character of those boundaries is little understood.

Southern structures

The plateau must have moved relative to Mexico, for much deformation affected southern Arizona and New Mexico during very late Cretaceous and early Paleogene time, but overall kinematics are not yet obvious. Upper-crust basement uplifts bounded by thrust faults of Laramide age and type and general northwest trends are present in southern New Mexico and southeast Arizona (Davis, 1979; Hayes and Raup, 1968; Seager and Mack, 1986). In mid-crust terrains deformed synmetamorphically during latest Cretaceous time, exposed farther west in southern Arizona and southeastern California, a number of geologists (e.g., Reynolds and others, 1980, 1986) have inferred major thrust faults to be present. In most exposures of such inferred structures that I have examined, including some of those cited by Reynolds and his associates, I see by contrast pervasive synmetamorphic recumbent folding and ductile flattening affecting almost unbroken basement-and-cover and granite-and-wallrock sequences (Hamilton, 1987), not discrete major faults. Whether such synmetamorphic deformation affected the middle crust on a regional scale or was limited to areas heated by magmatism (or by voluminous hot water expelled from oceanic sediments subducted beneath the truncated base of the continental crust: Hoisch, 1987), and in any case what sort of deformation simultaneously affected the upper crust, is not yet known. Rehrig and Heidrick (1976) showed that the numerous upper-crustal dikes of Laramide age in southern Arizona trend generally east-northeastward, so the direction of least principal stress was oriented approximately north-northwestward.

Inferences by Drewes (1981) that stratified and basement rocks of southern Arizona were deformed during Laramide time into a foreland thrust belt that records about 200 km of northeast-directed overthrusting are, in my view, invalid. Paleozoic and lower Mesozoic strata compose a thin cratonic section only 2 km or so thick in most of the region (although basin fills of upper Mesozoic strata are present in parts of it) and Drewes' own maps indicate to me that the imbricate faults he postulates to be present in Paleozoic strata do not exist. For example, Drewes and Thorman (1980) mapped in detail a complete, continuous section of the cratonic Paleozoic section, and yet depicted in cross section great thrust faults, with 10 km or more of slip each, whose unlikely effect is to precisely reassemble the complete section of thin, distinctive Paleozoic units just as the faults reach the irregular ground surface. I follow Dickinson (1987) and most other geologists active in the region in regarding most of the structures assumed by Drewes to be Cretaceous basement-involving megathrusts to be in fact low-angle normal faults (detachment faults) of middle Tertiary age, for the faults in question widely place steep-dipping middle Tertiary rocks upon mid-crust crystalline rocks of which many are themselves of middle Tertiary age. Foreland thrusting affected upper Mesozoic strata in trans-Pecos Texas and northeastern Mexico, but no belt of similar structures through Arizona and southeastern California connects this terrain with the Sevier belt.

Great Basin

Laramide crustal shortening must have continued westward or northwestward through the Great Basin and Idaho regions, although no details can yet be specified. The great structural complexity of the foreland fold-and-thrust belt in Idaho, northern Utah and Nevada, and southern and central Montana contrasts markedly with the simplicity of the belt in British Columbia and Alberta, and may record in part Laramide basement shortening oblique to the general direction of advance of the growing wedge of generally supracrustal thrusts, although major contributions to the complexity certainly were made also by late Mesozoic and Cenozoic magmatism and by middle and late Cenozoic crustal extension. The poorly known Cretaceous and Eocene clastic strata of northern Nevada might relate to compressive structures yet to be defined.

About 125 km of crustal shortening is predicted by my model along the small circle that passes through southwest Montana, but less than half that amount is accounted for by shortening on exposed Montana structures. The excess must, in my terms, have been absorbed by structures in northwest Utah and southeast Idaho that have gone unrecognized because of the severity of superimposed deformations there.

Interference with thrust belt

Eastward imbrication of the stratal wedge of the Sevier belt—the foreland fold-and-thrust belt west of the Colorado Plateau and of the Laramide Rocky Mountains of northern Utah, Wyoming, and Montana (Fig. 1)—occurred during late Early Cretaceous, Late Cretaceous, and early Paleogene time (Cross, 1986; Heller and others, 1986), so late Sevier thrusting overlapped in time with early and middle Laramide deformation. The thrust wedge was driven gravitationally by crustal thickening, arguably itself the product either of arc magmatism or of crustal shortening, farther west. Eastward-advancing frontal thrusts broke like waves against rising Laramide uplifts, sheared off basement slices, and were raised with the uplifts. The contrasted structures formed nearly at right angles in Utah but at decreasing angles northward from there.

The zone of interaction in Wyoming and Montana between late thrust sheets of the foreland-thrust belt and the rising uplifts of the Laramide belt is described in this volume by Kulik and Schmidt, who infer both the basement uplifts and the thrust belt to be products of east-west shortening of the continental plate. I see the deformation documented by these authors as representing instead interference between a growing wedge of thrust sheets advancing relatively eastward and basement structures that were rising in response to crustal shortening that in this area was oriented north-northeastward in the south and east-northeastward in the north (Fig. 2).

My inferred New Mexico Euler pole contains the prediction that the general direction of Laramide shortening in southwest Montana was about 065°. Laramide compressional structures there appropriately trend mostly northwestward or northward (e.g., Tysdal, 1976, 1986), and fold axes in Paleozoic and Mesozoic rocks mostly plunge gently. Schmidt and Garihan (1983), however, concluded from small-scale indicators of fault-slip directions that northwest-trending structures record oblique left-slip transpression and that shortening was oriented east-west, in a zone of moderately plunging structures within 30 km or so east of the foreland thrust belt. They argued that this east-west shortening disproves my thesis, whereas I see this shortening, if indeed of Laramide age, as indicative of local complications in the zone of interference between Laramide and Sevier structures. Schmidt (written communication, 1986) now puts the average direction of shortening in this area at about 080°, closer to my 065°. The oblique-slip structures shown by Schmidt and Garihan (1983, Fig. 2) lie mostly in Precambrian rocks so that their Laramide history is in doubt. Further, middle and late Cenozoic crustal extension in this region may have had much greater effects than have been incorporated in the analysis by Schmidt and Garihan.

Idaho batholith

Laramide uplifts of Wyoming and southwest Montana are trending generally northwestward toward the Idaho batholith where last clearly defined. The Cretaceous granites and gneisses of the batholith are shown by their petrology (e.g., primary muscovite in granites, and aluminum-silicate triple-point assemblages in gneisses) to have crystallized at depths on the order of 15 km, whereas Eocene volcanic rocks and epizonal granites are widespread in the eastern part of the batholith. I earlier suggested (Hamilton, 1978, 1981) that latest Cretaceous and early Paleogene uplift and erosion might have been due to unrecognized Laramide shortening. Recent zircon dating (Bickford and others, 1981; Chase and others, 1983) has, however, shown that deep-

seated Eocene gneisses also are exposed in the northeast part of the batholith. I now believe that much of the present juxtaposition of rocks of deep and shallow origins is likely due to tectonic denudation by Eocene extensional (detachment) faulting, allied to that of northern Washington and south-central British Columbia, whether or not uplift and erosion also reflect Laramide shortening. Skipp (1987) proposed that major northeast-directed basement-involving overthrusts are present in east-central Idaho.

RELATION TO MEGAPLATE MOTIONS

The timing and geometry of Laramide deformation correspond to changes in motions of North American and eastern Pacific megaplates, and a causal relationship is presumed (Coney, 1976; Cross, 1986; Engebretson and others, 1984, 1985; Jurdy, 1984; Rea and Duncan, 1986). Global reorganizations of plate motions resulted in convergence between Farallon and North American plates that was much more rapid during latest Cretaceous and early Paleogene time—the span of the Laramide orogeny—than it was either before or after. Details of timing and rates are disputed; indeed, it is not yet clear whether the eastern Pacific lithosphere subducted beneath the western United States during Cretaceous time belonged to the Farallon or the Kula plate.

Mechanism of subduction

An understanding of the mechanism of subduction is critical to tectonic analysis of western North America. Much published paleotectonic analysis incorporates the misconception that plate shortening necessarily accompanies plate convergence. Too often subduction is visualized as the sliding of oceanic lithosphere down a slot fixed in the mantle beneath an overriding plate; this would indeed require extreme shortening of an advancing upper plate if it occurred. The common case, however, is that the hinge rolls back, away from the overriding plate, with a horizontal velocity equal to or greater than the velocity of advance of the overriding plate. Among those who have documented wide-ranging evidence for this are Carlson and Melia (1984), Chase (1978), Dewey (1980), Garfunkel and others (1986), Hamilton (1979), Malinverno and Ryan (1986), Molnar and Atwater (1978), and Uyeda and Kanamori (1979). Subduction commonly occurs at an angle steeper than the inclination of the seismic Benioff zone, which marks a position, not a trajectory, of the subducting plate, and which varies with rates of convergence, hinge rollback, and slab sinking.

The common regime in overriding plates above sinking slabs is in consequence one of extension or neutrality, not shortening. Laramide intraplate shortening is exceptional. Even during that episode of shortening, the subduction hinge was retreating at almost the velocity of plate convergence, and only a small proportion of the total convergence was absorbed in Laramide compressive structures. The shortening represents a slight slowing of the rate of advance of the Colorado Plateau subplate of North America.

PLATE INTERACTIONS IN THE WESTERN UNITED STATES

Subduction was steep during slow-convergence Cretaceous time, and the magmatic arc then lay within 300 km of the west margin of the North American plate and formed the Sierra Nevada, Peninsular, and Idaho batholiths. During rapid-convergence latest Cretaceous time, subduction flattened, particularly beneath the southwestern United States where young, buoyant oceanic lithosphere was involved. Perhaps the crust of that lithosphere was uncommonly thick (Cross, 1986; Livaccari and others, 1981). The continental lithosphere was eroded tectonically from beneath, against the buoyant subducting slab, during the rapid-convergence period. Older Cretaceous arc-magmatic rocks that had formed 100 km or so above the steeply subducting slab of the slow-convergence period were truncated from beneath, and meatmorphosed oceanic sediments were plated directly against rocks formed only 30 km or so deep in that older arc. The oceanic rocks are now exposed tectonically beneath the truncated arc rocks in southern California uplifts, where they are termed variously the Pelona, Orocopia, and Rand Schists, and the structure separating them from the truncated continental crust above is termed variously the Vincent, Orocopia, Chocolate Mountains, and Rand thrusts. The leading edge of the continent also may have been eroded tectonically far back in the central Coast Ranges of California, where Cretaceous arc-magmatic granites equivalent to those of the medial Sierra Nevada lie upon coeval Franciscan accretionary wedge materials along the Sur-Nacimiento megathrust (Page, 1982). This great fault cuts out about 150 km of rocks that lay between magmatic arc and accretionary wedge when they formed. The continental crustal materials removed by the frontal and basal tectonic erosion must have been moved back under the continent and likely contributed to the buoyancy of subducted materials and hence to the drag against the overriding continental plate. Crustal drag during the same episode is probably recorded by the kilometer-thick zones of mid-crust Santa Rosa mylonites that bound lenses of relatively undeformed plutonic rocks, imbricated with westward vergence (that is, eastward underdrag) in the eastern Peninsular Ranges of southern California.

The magmatic arc swung far inland as convergence accelerated and subduction flattened (Coney and Reynolds, 1977). When covergence slowed in middle Paleogene time and subduction again became steep (what became of the prior gently inclined slab is not yet clear), severe extension began in the Basin and Range province and the Rio Grande rift.

The Laramide rotation of the Colorado Plateau is a consequence of the retardation of the southwestern United States by drag on the subducted slab. Laramide crustal shortening absorbed only a small fraction of the correlative convergence of at least 3,000 km (Engebretson and others, 1984; Jurdy, 1984) of the Pacific and Farallon plates. The previously cratonic region affected by Laramide shortening corresponds to that part of the continent beneath which particularly low-angle subduction is indicated by convergence rates and by age (hence, buoyancy) patterns of Farallon lithosphere; the rotation of the Colorado Plateau is in agreement with torques predicted from these patterns (Bird, 1984, 1988).

OTHER ROTATIONS OF THE COLORADO PLATEAU REGION

In addition to the Laramide rotation, the Colorado Plateau region moved relative to the continental interior in late Paleozoic time and again in middle and late Cenozoic time.

Late Paleozoic event

A series of broad basins and basement uplifts was formed during Pennsylvanian and Permian time in a wide zone trending east-southeastward across what had previously been the cratonic interior of southwestern North America, from the Pacific continental paleomargin in the Nevada-Utah sector to the Ouachita paleomargin in the Texas-Oklahoma sector. Oquirrh uplifts and basins in the west, the Uncompahgre uplift and other "Ancestral Rocky Mountains" of southern Wyoming, Colorado, and New Mexico in the middle, and west Texas and Wichita-Anadarko-Arbuckle structures in the east are components of this system. Published seismic reflection surveys prove crustal shortening of Laramide type in Oklahoma, where the Wichita Mountains basement uplift is thrust north-northeastward over the syntectonic Anadarko Basin (Brewer and others, 1983; Kluth, 1986). Thrusting of the basement Uncompahgre uplift of Colorado relatively southwestward over its paired basin is proved by industry drilling and reflection profiling (references in Kluth, 1986). The dimensions of the other large basins and basement uplifts, and the marked positive isostatic-residual gravity anomalies of the uplifts (Jachens and others, 1985; Simpson and others, 1986), make it likely that they too are due to crustal shortening of Laramide type (Goldstein, 1984; Hamilton, 1978, 1981; Kluth, 1986). The region to the southwest of this belt of late Paleozoic structures must have moved relatively toward the continental interior. As the structures fall within a belt trending west-northwestward from Oklahoma through Utah, I infer that the Euler pole to which this motion can be related is distant.

Middle and late Cenozoic event

The Rio Grande rift system of extensional basins and ranges trends northward across New Mexico into Colorado, and at least in the south opened mostly in late Oligocene and early Miocene time, to a lesser extent in the late Miocene, and still less in middle Miocene, Pliocene, and Quaternary time (Morgan and others, 1986). The extension accompanied the slowing of North America and the steepening of subduction beneath it. The Rio Grande extensional terrain narrows, and hence the amount of separation of Colorado Plateau from continental interior decreases, irregularly northward to a poorly defined terminus in central Colorado.

A rotation of the plateau region of 3° clockwise, relative to an Euler pole in central Colorado, would provide about 30 km of extension at the south end of the rift system. Such a motion requires shortening between plateau and continental interior along a zone or zones radiating in other directions from that pole. Despite the common assumption that post-Laramide compressive structures do not exist in the region, some are in fact present. The major belt of requisite shortening involving middle Tertiary strata appears to me to be present primarily in a zone trending westward through the Uinta region of northwestern Colorado and northeastern Utah (see, for example, Rowley and others, 1985). Farther south in Utah, west-trending thrust faults cut strata as young as middle Oligocene (Davis and Krantz, 1986).

PALEOMAGNETIC DATA

Adding the rotations inferred for the middle and late Cenozoic opening of the Rio Grande rift (3° clockwise about a pole in central Colorado) and for the Laramide shortening (4° clockwise about a pole in central New Mexico) yields a net clockwise rotation of the Colorado Plateau relative to the continental interior of about 6° during very late Cretaceous and Cenozoic time. Paleomagnetic pole positions determined from plateau rocks should diverge by some such amount from those of correlative rocks in the continental interior. The rotations at issue are near the limit of detection by present paleomagnetic methods and data sets.

Steiner (1986) analyzed the most reliable paleomagnetic data from correlative upper Paleozoic and Triassic strata of plateau and craton and concluded that a clockwise rotation of about 11° of plateau relative to craton had occurred. Bryan and Gordon (1986) derived and compared separate polar-wander curves for plateau and craton from paleomagnetic data for Middle Permian

through Lower Cretaceous strata. They also saw a clockwise rotation, but one of only about 4°; as their curves are poorly constrained for one or the other plate during most time increments, their 4° estimate is less soundly based than is Steiner's 11°. Steiner (written communication, 1986) perceived a slight additional northward shift of Pennsylvanian and Lower Permian rocks of the southern Colorado Plateau relative to correlative rocks of the craton; this shift, if real, could record crustal shortening across the late Paleozoic Wichita-Uncompahgre belt. Irving and Strong (1985) also saw a relative clockwise rotation of the plateau, which Irving (oral communication, 1986) estimated as about 10°.

Published North American polar-wander paths commonly contain poles based on, or biased by, plateau data, and accordingly are likely displaced from proper cratonic paths. Conversely, Frei (1986) mistakenly sought to constrain relative rotations between Sierra Nevada and Colorado Plateau by comparing Cretaceous paleomagnetic orientations of the Sierra Nevada with those (which themselves make up a data set of dubious validity) of the continental interior.

ACKNOWLEDGMENTS

I am particularly indebted to Christopher Schmidt, who disagrees with many of my conclusions but nevertheless provided penetrating and helpful comments on successive drafts of this essay. The manuscript was further improved as a result of criticism by Charles Chapin and Robbie Gries, both of whom also disagree with many of my conclusions, and by John Sales and Peter Ward. Anthony Davidson gave me a field tour of exposed deep-crustal shear zones in Ontario, which may be analogs for deep Laramide structures seen on reflection profiles.

REFERENCES CITED

Allenby, R. J., and Schnetzler, C. C., 1983, United States crustal thickness: Tectonophysics, v. 93, p. 13–31.

Baltz, E. H., 1967, Stratigraphy and regional tectonic implications of part of Upper Cretaceous and Tertiary rocks, east-central San Juan basin, New Mexico: U.S. Geological Survey Professional Paper 552, 101 p.

Baltz, E. H., and O'Neill, J. M., 1984, Geologic map and cross sections of the Mora River area, Sangre de Cristo Mountains, Mora County, New Mexico: U.S. Geological Survey Map I–1456, scale 1:24,000.

Bickford, M. E., Chase, R. B., Nelson, K. K., Shuster, R. D., and Arruda, E. C., 1981, U-Pb studies of zircon cores and overgrowths, and monazite; Implications for age and petrogenesis of the northeastern Idaho batholith: Journal of Geology, v. 89, p. 433–457.

Bird, P., 1984, Laramide crustal thickening event in the Rocky Mountain foreland and Great Plains: Tectonics, v. 3, p. 741–758.

—— , 1988, Formation of the Rocky Mountains, western United States—A continuum computer model: Science, v. 239, p. 1501–1507.

Blackstone, D. L., Jr., 1983, Laramide compressional tectonics, southeastern Wyoming: University of Wyoming Contributions to Geology, v. 22, p. 1–38.

—— , 1986, Foreland compressional tectonics; Southern Bighorn Basin and adjacent areas, Wyoming: Geological Survey of Wyoming Report of Investigations 34, 32 p.

Brewer, J. A., Allmendinger, R. W., Brown, L. D., Oliver, J. E., and Kaufman, S., 1982, COCORP profiling across the Rocky Mountain Front in southern Wyoming; Part 1, Laramide structure: Geological Society of America Bulletin, v. 93, p. 1242–1252.

Brewer, J. A., Good, R., Oliver, J. E., Brown, L. D., and Kaufman, S., 1983, COCORP profiling across the southern Oklahoma aulacogen; Overthrusting of the Wichita Mountains and compression within the Anadarko Basin: Geology, v. 11, p. 109–114.

Bryan, P., and Gordon, R. G., 1986, Rotation of the Colorado Plateau; An analysis of paleomagnetic data: Tectonics, v 5, p. 661–667.

Carlson, R. L., and Melia, P. J., 1984, Subduction hinge migration: Tectonophysics, v. 102, p. 399–411.

Chapin, C. E., and Cather, S. M., 1981, Eocene tectonics and sedimentation in the Colorado Plateau–Rocky Mountain area: Arizona Geological Society Digest, v. 14, p. 173–198.

Chase, C. G., 1978, Extension behind island arcs and motions relative to hot spots: Journal of Geophysical Research, v. 83, p. 5385–5387.

Chase, R. B., Bickford, M. E., and Arruda, E. C., 1983, Tectonic implications of Tertiary intrusion and shearing within the Bitterroot dome, northeastern Idaho batholith: Journal of Geology, v. 91, p. 462–470.

Coney, P. J., 1976, Plate tectonics and the Laramide orogeny: New Mexico

Geological Society Special Publication 6, p. 5–10.

Coney, P. J., and Reynolds, S. J., 1977, Cordilleran Benioff zones: Nature, v. 270, p. 403–406.

Cross, T. A., 1986, Tectonic controls of foreland basin subsidence and Laramide style deformation, western United States: International Association of Sedimentology Special Publication 8, p. 15–39.

Davidson, A., 1984, Identification of ductile shear zones in the southwestern Grenville Province of the Canadian Shield, *in* Kroner, A., and Greiling, R., eds., Precambrian tectonics illustrated: Stuttgart, Schweizerbart'sche Verlagsbuchhandlung, p. 263–279.

—— , 1985, Tectonic framework of the Grenville Province in Ontario and western Quebec, Canada, *in* Tobi, A. C., and Touret, J.L.R., eds., The deep Proterozoic crust in the North Atlantic provinces: Dordrecht, D. Reidel, p. 133–149.

—— , 1986, New interpretations in the southwestern Grenville Province: Geological Association of Canada Special Paper 31, p. 61–73.

Davis, G. H., 1978, Monocline fold pattern of the Colorado Plateau: Geological Society of America Memoir 151, p. 215–233.

—— , 1979, Laramide folding and faulting in southeastern Arizona: American Journal of Science, v. 279, p. 543–569.

Davis, G. H., and Krantz, R. W., 1986, Post-"Laramide" thrust faults in the Claron Formation, Bryce Canyon National Park, Utah: Geological Society of America Abstracts with Programs, v. 18, p. 98.

DeCelles, P. G., 1986, Sedimentation in a tectonically partitioned, nonmarine foreland basin; The Lower Cretaceous Kootenai Formation, southwestern Montana: Geological Society of America Bulletin, v. 97, p. 911–931.

Dewey, J. F., 1980, Periodicity, sequence, and style at convergent plate boundaries: Geological Association of Canada Special Paper 20, p. 553–573.

Dickinson, W. R., 1981, Plate tectonic evolution of the southern Cordillera: Arizona Geological Society Digest, v. 14, p. 113–135.

—— , 1987, General geologic map of Catalina core complex and San Pedro trough: Arizona Bureau of Geology and Mineral Technology, Miscellaneous Map Series 87-A, 18 p. + 15 maps.

—— , 1984, Reinterpretation of Lime Peak thrust as a low-angle normal fault; Implications for the tectonics of southeastern Arizona: Geology, v. 12, no. 10, p. 610–613.

Dickinson, W. R., and Snyder, W. S., 1978, Plate tectonics of the Laramide orogeny: Geological Society of America Memoir 151, p. 355–366.

Dickinson, W. R., Lawton, T. F., and Inman, K. F., 1986, Sandstone detrital modes, central Utah foreland region—stratigraphic record of Cretaceous-Paleogene tectonic evolution: Journal of Sedimentary Petrology, v. 56, p. 276–293.

Dickinson, W. R., Klute, M. A., Hayes, M. J., Janecke, S. V., Lundin, E. R., McKittrick, M. A., and Olivares, M. D., 1988, Paleogeographic and paleotectonic setting of Laramide sedimentary basins in the central Rocky Mountain region: Geological Society of America Bulletin, v. 100, p. 1023–1039.

Drewes, H., 1981, Tectonics of southeastern Arizona: U.S. Geological Survey Professional Paper 1144, 96 p.

Drewes, H., and Thorman, C. H., 1980, Geologic map of the Cotton City Quadrangle and the adjacent part of the Vanar Quadrangle, Hidalgo County, New Mexico: U.S. Geological Survey Map I-1221, scale 1:24,000.

Engebretson, D. C., Cox, A., and Thompson, G. A., 1984, Correlation of plate motions with continental tectonics; Laramide to Basin-Range: Tectonics, v. 3, p. 115–119.

Engebretson, D. C., Cox, A., and Gordon, R. G., 1985, Relative motions between oceanic and continental plates in the Pacific Basin: Geological Society of America Special Paper 206, 59 p.

Frei, L. S., 1986, Additional paleomagnetic results from the Sierra Nevada; further constraints on Basin and Range extension and northward displacement of the western United States: Geological Society of America Bulletin, v. 97, p. 840–849.

Garfunkel, Z., Anderson, C. A., and Schubert, G., 1986, Mantle circulation and the lateral migration of subducted slabs: Journal of Geophysical Research, v. 91, p. 7205–7223.

Goldstein, A., 1984, Tectonic controls of late Paleozoic subsidence in the south-central United States: Journal of Geology, v. 92, p. 217–222.

Gries, R. R., 1983, North-south compression of Rocky Mountain foreland structures, *in* Lowell, J. D., and Gries, R. R., eds., Rocky Mountain foreland basins and uplifts: Rocky Mountain Association of Geologists, p. 9–32.

Gries, R. R., and Dyer, R. C., eds., 1985, Seismic exploration of the Rocky Mountain region: Rocky Mountain Association of Geologists Folio, 300 p.

Hamilton, W. B., 1978, Mesozoic tectonics of the western United States: Pacific Section, Society of Economic Paleontologists and Mineralogists, Pacific Coast Paleogeography Symposium 2, p. 33–70.

—— , 1979, Tectonics of the Indonesian region: U.S. Geological Survey Professional Paper 1078, 345 p.

—— , 1981, Plate-tectonic mechanism of Laramide deformation: University of Wyoming Contributions to Geology, v. 19, p. 87–92.

—— , 1987, Mesozoic geology and tectonics of the Big Maria Mountains region, southeastern California: Arizona Geological Society Digest, v. 18, p. 33–47.

Hayes, P. T., and Raup, R. B., 1968, Geologic map of the Huachuca and Mustang Mountains, southeastern Arizona: U.S. Geological Survey Map I-509, scale 1:48,000.

Heller, P. L., Bowdler, S. S., Chambers, H. P., Coogan, J. C., Hagen, E. S., Shuster, M. W., Winslow, N. S., and Lawton, T. F., 1986, Time of initial thrusting in the Sevier orogenic belt, Idaho-Wyoming and Utah: Geology, v. 14, p. 388–391.

Hoisch, T. D., 1987, Heat transport by fluids during Late Cretaceous regional metamorphism in the Big Maria Mountains, southeastern California: Geological Society of America Bulletin, v. 98, p. 549–553.

Irving, E., and Strong, D. F., 1985, Paleomagnetism of rocks from Burin Peninsula, Newefoundland; Hypothesis of late Paleozoic displacement of Acadia criticized: Journal of Geophysical Research, v. 90, p. 1949–1962.

Jachens, R. C., Simpson, R. W., Blakely, R. J., and Saltus, R. W., 1985, Isostatic residual gravity map of the United States: U.S. Geological Survey, scale 1:2,500,000.

Jordan, T. E., and Allmendinger, R. W., 1986, The Sierras Pampeanas of Argentina—A modern analogue of Rocky Mountain foreland deformation: American Journal of Science, v. 286, p. 737–764.

Jurdy, D. M., 1984, The subduction of the Farallon plate beneath North America as derived from relative plate motions: Tectonics, v. 3, p. 107–113.

Kelley, V. C., 1972, New Mexico lineament of the Colorado Rockies front: Geological Society of America Bulletin, v. 83, p. 1849–1852.

Klemperer, S. L., Brown, L. D., Oliver, J. E., Ando, C. J., Czuchra, B. L., and Kaufman, S., 1985, Some results of COCORP seismic reflection profiling in the Grenville-age Adirondack Mountains, New York State: Canadian Journal of Earth Sciences, v. 22, p. 141–153.

Kluth, C. F., 1986, Plate tectonics of the Ancestral Rocky Mountains: American Association of Petroleum Geologists Memoir 41, p. 353–369.

Lindia, F. M., Thomas, M. D., and Davidson, A., 1983, Geological significance of Bouguer gravity anomalies in the region of Parry Sound Domain, Grenville Province, Ontario: Geological Survey of Canada Paper 83-1B, p. 261–266.

Livaccari, R. F., Burke, K., and Sengor, A.M.C., 1981, Was the Laramide orogeny related to subduction of an oceanic plateau?: Nature, v. 289, p. 276–278.

Lowell, J. D., and Gries, R. R., eds., 1983, Rocky Mountain foreland basins and uplifts: Rocky Mountain Association of Geologists, 392 p.

Malinverno, A., and Ryan, W.B.F., 1986, Extension in the Tyrrhenian Sea and shortening in the Apennines as result of arc migration driven by sinking of the lithosphere: Tectonics, v. 5, p. 227–245.

Mawer, C. K., 1987, Shear criteria in the Grenville Province, Ontario, Canada: Journal of Structural Geology, v. 9, p. 531–539.

Molnar, P., and Atwater, T., 1978, Interarc spreading and Cordilleran tectonics as alternates related to the age of subducted oceanic lithosphere: Earth and Planetary Science Letters, v. 41, p. 330–340.

Morgan, P., Seager, W. R., and Golombek, M. P., 1986, Cenozoic thermal, mechanical, and tectonic evolution of the Rio Grande Rift: Journal of Geophysical Research, v. 91, p. 6263–6276.

Nichols, D. J., Perry, W. J., Jr., and Haley, J. C., 1985, Reinterpretation of the palynology and age of Laramide syntectonic deposits, southwestern Montana, and revision of the Beaverhead Group: Geology, v. 13, p. 149–153.

Page, B. M., 1982, Migration of Salinian composite block, California, and disappearance of fragments: American Journal of Science, v. 282, p. 1694–1734.

Percival, J. A., and McGrath, P. H., 1986, Deep crustal structure and tectonic history of the northern Kapuskasing uplift of Ontario; An integrated petrological-geophysical study: Tectonics, v. 5, p. 553–572.

Rea, D. K., and Duncan, R. A., 1986, North America plate convergence; A quantitative record of the past 140 m.y.: Geology, v. 14, p. 373–376.

Rehrig, W. A., and Heidrick, T. L., 1976, Regional tectonic stress during the Laramide and early Tertiary intrusive periods, Basin and Range province, Arizona: Arizona Geological Society Digest, v. 10, p. 205–229.

Reynolds, S. J., Keith, S. B., and Coney, P. J., 1980, Stacked overthrusts of Precambrian basement and inverted Paleozoic sections emplaced over Mesozoic strata, west-central Arizona: Arizona Geological Society Digest, v. 12, p. 45–51.

Reynolds, S. J., Spencer, J. E., Richard, S. M., and Laubach, S. E., 1986, Mesozoic structures in west-central Arizona: Arizona Geological Society Digest, v. 16, p. 35–51.

Rodgers, J., 1987, Chains of basement uplifts within cratons marginal to orogenic belts: American Journal of Science, v. 287, p. 661–692.

Rowley, P. D., Hansen, W. R., Tweto, O., and Carrara, P. E., 1985, Geologic map of the Vernal 1° by 2° Quadrangle, Colorado, Utah, and Wyoming: U.S. Geological Survey Map I-1526, scale 1:250,000.

Sales, J. K., 1968, Crustal mechanics of Cordilleran foreland deformation; A regional and scale-model approach: American Association of Petroleum Geologists Bulletin, v. 52, p. 2016–2044.

Schmidt, C. J., and Garihan, J. M., 1983, Laramide tectonic development of the Rocky Mountain foreland of southwestern Montana: Rocky Mountain Association of Geologists 1983 Symposium, p. 271–294.

Seager, W. R., and Mack, G. H., 1986, Laramide paleotectonics of southern New Mexico: American Association of Petroleum Geologists Memoir 41, p. 667–685.

Sharry, J., Langan, R. T., Jovanovich, D. B., Jones, G. M., Hills, N. R., and Guidish, T. M., 1985, Enhanced imaging of the COCORP seismic line, Wind River Mountains: American Geophysical Union Geodynamics Series v. 13, p. 223–236.

Sibson, R. H., 1983, Continental fault structure and the shallow earthquake source: Geological Society of London Journal, v. 140, p. 741–767.

Simpson, R. W., Jachens, R. C., Blakely, R. J., and Saltus, R. W., 1986, A new isostatic residual gravity map of the conterminous United States with a discussion on the significance of isostatic residual anomalies: Journal of Geophysical Research, v. 91, p. 8348–8372.

Skipp, B., 1987, Basement thrust sheets in the Clearwater orogenic zone, central Idaho and western Montana: Geology, v. 15, p. 220–224.

Smithson, S. B., Brewer, J. A., Kaufman, S., Oliver, J. E., and Hurich, C. A., 1979, Structure of the Laramide Wind River uplift, Wyoming, from COCORP deep reflection data and from gravity data: Journal of Geophysical Research, v. 84, p. 5955–5972.

Snyder, G. L., 1980, Geologic map of the northernmost Park Range and southernmost Sierra Madre, Jackson and Routt Counties, Colorado: U.S. Geological Survey Map I-1113, scale 1:48,000.

Steiner, M. B., 1986, Rotation of the Colorado Plateau: Tectonics, v. 5, p. 649–660.

Stone, D. S., 1969, Wrench faulting and central Rocky Mountain tectonics: Mountain Geologist, v. 6, p. 67–79.

Tweto, O., 1975, Laramide (Late Cretaceous–early Tertiary) orogeny in the southern Rocky Mountains: Geological Society of America Memoir 144, p. 1–44.

——, 1983, Geologic sections across Colorado: U.S. Geological Survey Map I-1416, scale 1:500,000.

Tysdal, R. G., 1976, Geologic map of northern part of Ruby Range, Madison County, Montana: U.S. Geological Survey Map I-951, scale 1:24,000.

——, 1986, Thrust faults and back thrusts in Madison Range of southwestern Montana foreland: American Association of Petroleum Geologists Bulletin, v. 70, p. 360–376.

Uyeda, S., and Kanamori, H., 1979, Back-arc opening and the mode of subduction: Journal of Geophysical Research, v. 84, p. 1049–1061.

White, J. C., and Mawer, C. K., 1988, Dynamic recrystallization and associated exsolution in perthites—Evidence of deep crustal thrusting: Journal of Geophysical Research, v. 93, p. 325–337.

MANUSCRIPT ACCEPTED BY THE SOCIETY FEBRUARY 9, 1988

Printed in U.S.A.

Geological Society of America
Memoir 171
1988

Geometrical and mechanical constraints on basement-involved thrusts in the Rocky Mountain foreland province

John H. Spang and James P. Evans*
Center for Tectonophysics and Department of Geology, Texas A&M University, College Station, Texas 77843-3115

ABSTRACT

A review of the kinematics, mechanics, and mechanisms of deformation in Precambrian basement rocks and in the Paleozoic and younger sedimentary rocks is combined with recent data on foreland structures for the purpose of developing models of basement-involved structures. This chapter concentrates on the deformation of isotropic, crystalline basement rocks since other foreland basement rock types (i.e., foliated metamorphic rocks and low-grade metasedimentary rocks) can fold on shorter wavelengths. Precambrian crystalline rocks of the foreland and overlap provinces deformed at low to moderate temperatures and confining pressures; the deformation mechanisms consisted of brittle and semi-brittle fracture and cataclasis. Sedimentary rocks were highly anisotropic during the Laramide deformation, and the mechanical properties of the sedimentary rocks may have changed as the loading conditions and the dip of the rocks changed over time. The kinematic models of foreland structures presented here consist of monoclinal flexures that formed ahead of a wide zone of faults, ramp anticlines in the Precambrian rocks that develop above a dip change in the underlying fault, wedge-shaped shear zones in the Precambrian rocks, and structures above curved faults.

INTRODUCTION

Structures in the thrust belt and foreland provinces are complicated to varying degrees by the timing of the basement-involved structures with respect to the thin-skinned structures, the different rock types, and the difference in deformation mechanisms in the basement rocks and the sedimentary rocks. "Foreland style" and "thin-skinned style" structures are often intimately related in the thrust belt, overlap, and the foreland provinces. Many foreland structures provide exposures of basement-involved structures that have been inferred to exist in the subsurface in the overlap zone as defined by Kulik and Schmidt (this volume). In this chapter we review the deformation mechanisms and geometry of structures in the crystalline basement rocks and in the sedimentary rocks of foreland structures. We then develop kinematic models for the interaction of basement and sedimentary rocks that agree with the mechanics and mechanisms of deformation in the Precambrian and sedimentary rocks. These models examine how basement-cover rock relationships may develop through time. This review is necessary in order to show the potential interaction of thin-skinned thrust sheets and underlying basement-involved structures with time.

MECHANICAL BEHAVIOR OF PRECAMBRIAN ROCKS

The mechanical behavior of rocks is a function of lithology, pressure, temperature, fluids, strain rate, and loading conditions during deformation (Griggs and Handin, 1960). We briefly review the deformation mechanisms in crystalline (i.e., nonfoliated) basement rocks, which have been deformed under relatively low confining pressure and temperature. Field observations and down-plunge projections (e.g., Schmidt and Garihan, 1983) show that foliated metamorphic rocks involved in foreland or overlap deformation have folded relatively easily. Foliated metamorphic rocks of the Gallatin Range deformed by flexural slip that was accomplished by cracking and faulting of quartz and feldspar grains (Miller and Lageson, 1986); this resulted in thin zones of cataclasis. Experimental data (Borg and Handin, 1966; Handin, 1966; Donath, 1961; Paterson, 1978) support these observations

*Present address: Department of Geology, Utah State University, Logan, Utah 84322-0705.

by showing that slip along foliation planes is the dominant deformation mechanism in foliated crystalline rocks. Foliated rocks thus behave as a layered, anisotropic material, and few mechanical differences appear to exist between the cover and basement rocks in these cases. Some degree of mechanical anisotropy clearly exists in many of the Precambrian rocks throughout the foreland province. However, in only a limited number of places does the anisotropy of the Precambrian rocks appear to play an important role in the deformation of the foreland structure (for example, the Uinta Mountain Group; Matthews, 1986). We limit our discussion to regions in which the Precambrian rocks likely behaved as an isotropic material at the shallow depths and thus at the low temperatures (<300°C) and low mean pressures (<200 Mpa). We do not treat the behavior of the deeper crust (C. J. Schmidt and others, in preparation) nor the anisotropic behavior of the basement rocks.

Osterwald (1961), Hodgson (1965), Prucha and others (1965), and Stearns (1978) have suggested that the Precambrian rocks of the foreland province deformed by motion along steeply dipping, narrow faults that are concave downward. Brittle deformation was proposed to extend to depths of 10,000 to 15,000 m. The faults were observed or interpreted to be narrow (Hodgson, 1965; Osterwald, 1961), which led these workers to suggest that the large-scale motion of the Precambrian rocks was that of translation and rigid rotation of large blocks of rock.

More recent studies of Laramide structures have shed new light on the deformation mechanisms within and on the form of faults in several Foreland structures. Precambrian rocks in the hanging wall of the Wind River thrust sheet (Fig. 1) sustained significant amounts of internal shortening by motion along zones of faults distributed throughout the range (Mitra and Frost, 1981; see also Mitra and others, this volume). Deformation mechanisms in these faults consist of fracture and subsequent cataclasis. The White Rock thrust, an imbricate to the Wind River thrust (see Smithson and others, 1979), may have developed first by fracture and faulting, causing the fault zone to strain harden and thus widen with time (Mitra, 1984). Continued grain-size reduction may have then led to diffusion-controlled mechanisms and strain localization along a narrow part of the fault zone (Mitra, 1984).

Precambrian rocks of the Washakie Range (Fig. 1) deformed by motion along wide zones of faults near the front of the range and by small-scale faulting within the range (Evans, 1985, 1986). Brittle deformation early in the fault history promoted alteration of feldspars to phyllosilicates, which weakened the faults over time. Continued cataclasis and slip resulted in fault zones 100 to 250 m wide with a foliated-cataclasite texture. Net slip on the 30° dipping basement faults ranges from 4 to 9 km, and structural relief varies from 1 to 3 km. Young and others (1983) show that Precambrian rocks in the Madison Range (Montana) deformed by motion along closely spaced faults, which lie in a zone 1 km wide and are responsible for at least 1.5 km of structural relief on the upper basement surface. Deformation of the Precambrian rocks consists of slip along narrow, discrete faults, fault-gouge zones, and/or wide zones of faults with

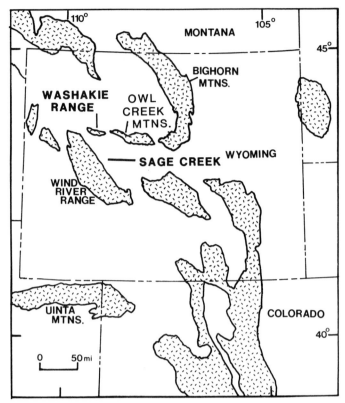

Figure 1. Location map showing outlines of major basement-cored structures in the Foreland Province.

highly sheared rocks separated by undeformed protolith. A smoothly folded upper basement surface can then form by motion along faults and closely spaced fractures. It must be emphasized that the dominant deformation mechanisms in the crystallline basement rocks considered herein are brittle fracture and subsequent faulting. However, folding by slip along foliation planes or folding by minute adjustments along closely spaced fractures may also result in folded Precambrian rocks.

Deformation within the thrust sheets is recorded by several types of faults in Laramide Precambrian-cored thrust sheets. Gilliland (1959) and Granger and others (1971) documented steeply dipping faults, some 300 to 400 m wide, on the northeast side of the Wind River Range. In several localities these faults cut the Paleozoic rocks and form east-facing monoclines with structural relief (measured on the top of the Precambrian rocks) of at least 400 m, and possibly more. Yonkee and others (1984) have proposed that these faults, along with shallowly dipping thrusts, serve to deform the internal part of the Wind River thrust sheet. Deformation of the Washakie thrust sheet occurred by slip along steeply dipping reverse faults and small displacement thrusts (Evans, 1986).

Erslev (1986) has suggested that faults which bound foreland structures are narrow and curved, and that the faults flatten with depth. Rigid blocks are rotated and translated along the main faults, and curved secondary faults form within the blocks to accommodate deformation within the blocks. Sharry and others (1985) suggested that the Wind River thrust consists of a wide zone of anastomosing faults. The interpretations of these authors, along with the data and observations referenced above, suggest that single, narrow fault models are not representative in all cases.

Early models for the mechanical behavior of the crystalline Precambrian rocks of the foreland province and adjacent areas used the results of experimental studies (e.g., Borg and Handin, 1966) as support for the proposed strong behavior of the rocks. This strong behavior was extrapolated to the field to support the hypothesis that the Precambrian rocks deformed by motion along narrow faults. Folds with Precambrian rocks in them were often attributed to artifacts or errors in seismic processing or incorrect interpretation of field or subsurface data (see Matthews, 1986). However, some authors (e.g., Blackstone, 1980) have interpreted basement rocks to have been folded on short wavelengths. It is important to distinguish between strength and ductility of the rocks. Experiments on granitic rocks conducted over a wide range of conditions (Tullis and Yund, 1977, 1985; see also Tullis, 1983) show that granitic rocks may sustain significant amounts of strain by brittle fracture, faulting, and cataclasis at temperatures of less than 350°C. Extrapolation of the experimentally derived strengths of granitic rocks (Tullis and Yund, 1985) to natural pressure and temperature conditions and the data of Mitra and Frost (1981), Mitra (1984), and Evans (1985) all suggest that naturally deformed granitic rocks may not be as strong as previously thought. Moreover, experimental deformation of limestones and dolomites over a wide range of pressures and temperatures (Handin, 1966) indicates these sedimentary rocks can be as strong as gneisses and granites. Also note that crystalline rocks may be as much as five times weaker in extension than they are in compression (N. L. Carter, personal communication, 1986). Thus, in some instances the Precambrian crystalline rocks may be weaker than we previously thought, and the differences in strength between some of the units in the sedimentary rocks and the Precambrian rocks may be quite small.

From our field work and a survey of relevant literature, there appear to be several different fault configurations common in the Foreland province. Narrow, discrete faults are common and well documented in the Precambrian rocks; they probably form by localized fracture and faulting. Wide faults or zones of faults may also result. These two types of faults can result in very different geometries in the Precambrian rocks. Narrow faults yield sharp, angular structures in the basement, which would provide areas of high-stress concentration for the nucleation of structures in the sedimentary rocks (Wiltschko and Eastman, 1983, this volume) or provide corners of basement rocks which get clipped off as thin-skinned thrusts impinge on the preexisting basement structure (Coryell and Spang, this volume; Schmidt and others, this volume). Wide zones of deformation result in broad "folded" shapes in the Precambrian rocks, forming ramp folds or frontal monoclines. These broad folds are less effective as stress concentrators and produce gradual deflections in thin-skinned structures above (Kraig and others, this volume).

MECHANICAL BEHAVIOR OF THE SEDIMENTARY ROCKS

The influence of the mechanical behavior of the sedimentary rocks on the geometry and history of foreland structures has often been ignored. The presumed strong, rigid behavior of the Precambrian rocks was thought to control the geometry, location, and style of deformation in the sedimentary (cover) rocks (Stearns, 1978; Cook, this volume). Although the stratigraphy of the sedimentary rocks varies across the foreland and overlap provinces, several points regarding the mechanical behavior of the sedimentary rocks can be used to better interpret and constrain the kinematics of the basement-involved structures. Sedimentary rocks have been used as line-length markers for cross-section constructions (e.g., Spang and others, 1985), but their mechanical influence on the evolution of foreland structures has not been discussed.

Two of the factors controlling the behavior of the sedimentary rocks are the strengths of the individual units and the anisotropy of the entire sequence. Some units in the Paleozoic section are strong and relatively isotropic (as, for example, the Ordovician Bighorn Dolomite and the Mississippian Madison Limestone), but others are highly anisotropic and have very low shear strengths (e.g., Cambrian Gros Ventre Formation). The Bighorn Dolomite does contain a distinct detachment horizon near its base, which may influence some of the foreland structures (Stearns, 1971). Common deformation mechanisms in the sedimentary rocks in the foreland and overlap provinces are folding accomplished by bedding plane slip, folding by flexural or cataclastic flow, and faulting.

The mechanical anisotropy of the sedimentary section may have significant influence on the development of the Precambrian-involved structures. The data of Donath (1961) suggest sedimentary rocks are weakest in shear when loaded at 30° to the bedding. Layered rocks deformed at confining pressures comparable to those at the base of the Paleozoic section during the beginning of the Laramide deformation are two to three times as strong when loaded parallel to bedding as when they are loaded at 30° to bedding. Rotation of an anisotropic material through an angle of 45° reverses the shear modulus and bulk modulus of a material (Biot, 1965). If a material initially has a low shear strength and a high compressive strength, rotation through an angle of 45° reverses the modulii so that the material becomes strong in shear and weak in compression. Thus, the experimental data and the model for anisotropic materials suggest that bedded rocks can be both weak and strong, depending on their orientation relative to the applied compressive stresses. The layered rocks will slip along bedding when loaded at shallow angles to bedding, whereas in other cases, bedding-parallel slip, and thus folding, will be difficult when the rocks are loaded either parallel to or at high angles to bedding (see also Chester and others, this volume). Thus, the mechanical behavior of the sedimentary rocks may be expected to change as the structures develop.

The experimental data and theoretical models for anisotropic materials discussed above suggest that the sedimentary rocks—in particular, the competent carbonate units—may be strong when loaded parallel to bedding, weak when dipping at 20° to 40° relative to the local compression direction, and then strong when dipping more than 40° relative to the local compression direction. The above arguments apply to the entire sedimentary section as well. Little shortening due to folding of the sedimentary rocks could occur early in the development of the structure, as the entire sequence, including the strong carbonates, would be loaded parallel to bedding. Evidence for early layer-parallel shortening of the sedimentary rocks has been documented by Hennings and Spang (1986). Increased shortening of the Precambrian rocks by faulting would cause the overlying beds to rotate, making bedding parallel slip and folding easy. As the beds steepen, presumably with more displacement along the basement faults, the sedimentary rocks would again be stronger, as they would be loaded at increasingly higher angles to bedding. This could cause the fold above and ahead of the basement fault(s) to "lock up." Further shortening would occur by increased displacement along the basement fault(s), resulting in a faulted fold (Berg, 1962; Spang and others, 1985). This model predicts that faults at low angles to bedding would form relatively early in the history of the basement-cored structure, and might not always be the result of the crowding out of the syncline later in the history of the fold (Brown, 1983, this volume).

Thinly bedded shales and limestones near the base of the sedimentary rocks may serve as a décollement horizon along which the sedimentary rocks can decouple from the Precambrian rocks. Décollement behavior of the Cambrian shales has been documented in the Rattlesnake Mountain structure (see Stone, 1984). This decoupling may not always occur, however. Hennings and Spang (1986) have shown that the Ordovician and Mississippian carbonates were thinned above the steeply dipping Dry Fork Ridge fault, and Berg (1976) showed that the Triassic shales thinned above the Hamilton Dome fault. Mechanical models (Evans, 1987) predict that this thinning occurs only if the sedimentary rocks are mechanically coupled to the Precambrian rocks.

EFFECTS OF STRESS FIELD ON FAULT GEOMETRIES

Orientation of tectonic stresses

Theoretical models of stress distributions and displacements have often been used to support arguments about the geometry of faults at depth and about the actual orientation of the tectonic stresses in the Foreland province during the Laramide event. Figure 2 has been modified from Hafner (1951). The fault trajectories are derived by choosing an Airy stress function, which represents a geologically reasonable stress distribution. Principal stress magnitudes and orientations can be calculated for any point within the area (cross section) under consideration. It is possible to calculate the trajectories of conjugate faults by using a Mohr-Coulomb failure criterion. The calculations consider the body to be a homogeneous, isotropic, elastic medium, and the model breaks down when the first fault forms. It is important to note that at any single point, either of the two conjugate faults might form. In natural settings, the local geology (layering, rock type, preexisting structures) may well play a role in determining which of the two faults actually forms. Theoretical models by necessity make simplifying assumptions about rock behavior. However, they are useful in anticipating how structures form and provide mechanical constraints on kinematic models.

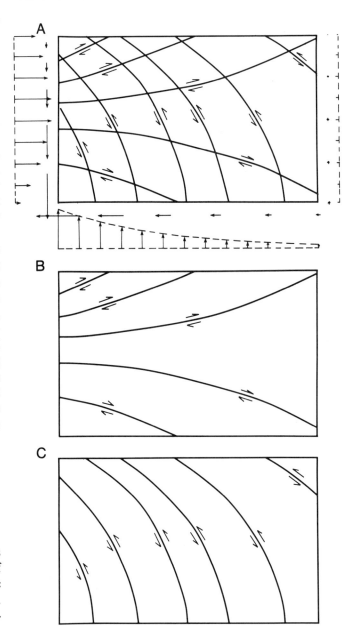

Figure 2. Fault trajectories for an isotropic, homogeneous, elastic block (after Hafner, 1951). A, Both sets of faults, which result from loads shown along the sides of the block. B, Shallowly dipping faults only. C. Steeply dipping faults.

Figure 2a shows the stresses on the outside of a block that are necessary to satisfy static equilibrium. Various authors have taken the normal stresses acting on the base and inferred that upthrusts, or curved high-angle reverse faults, would result (Fig. 2b). Conversely, some authors have taken the normal stresses acting on the sides and inferred that thrusts or fold-thrusts would result (Fig. 2c). These are meaningless arguments since whatever stress system (normal or shear stress applied at the base or sides) represents the "true" tectonic stress, *all* of the other stresses are required to satisfy the conditions of the model. When the results of the theoretical models are applied to a natural setting, it may be concluded, based on the observations, that one system of faults would be dominant while the other system of faults would develop only locally. The theoretical models do not predict which of the fault sets will be dominant—only that they may form.

Fault propagation from basement to cover rocks

Deformation associated with a discrete fault may be modeled with crack solutions (see, for example, Rodgers and Rizer, 1981). Secondary faults may occur near the fault tips and propagate away from the tip. Secondary faults associated with a thrust that dips 30° and 60° relative to compression (Fig. 3) show that secondary synthetic faults above and ahead of the fault tip curve downward and antithetic faults dip steeply. Secondary faults may propagate from a substrate through an overlying layer with approximately the same dip, curving gently away from the tip when both the substrate and layer have the same elastic properties.

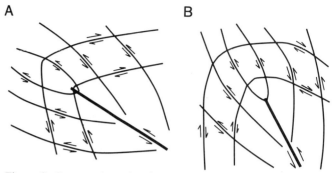

Figure 3. Cross sections showing secondary faults associated with a dipping thrust. A, Fault dips 30° relative to the compression. B, Fault dip 60° relative to compression. Fault projectures determined from Mohr-Coulomb failure criterion with the plane of failure oriented 30° to the maximum principal stress. Stresses near the thrust calculated from an elastic crack solution for a shear crack (Evans, 1987).

When the layer is weaker than the substrate, both synthetic and antithetic secondary fault trajectories flatten away from the fault tip (Rodgers and Rizer, 1981).

BASEMENT-COVER ROCK GEOMETRIES

Single discrete fault in basement

Figure 4a diagrammatically depicts a single discrete fault in basement with no displacement on the basement fault. The cover

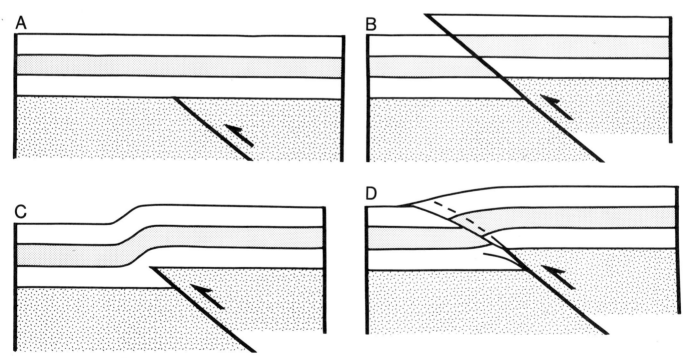

Figure 4. A number of possible basement fault geometries for the case of a single, relatively discrete fault in basement. Specific examples are discussed in detail in the text. A, Restored planar fault. B, Planar fault with displacement. C, Fold in the sedimentary rocks above a basement fault. D, Fault that becomes shallower in the sedimentary rocks, forming a ramp anticline in the sedimentary rocks.

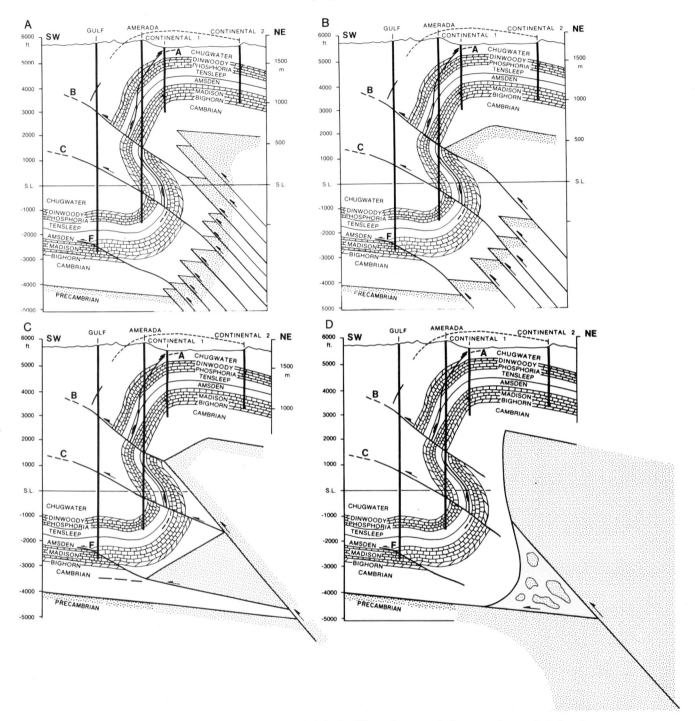

Figure 5. Illustration of how a number of distinctly different basement fault geometries may be inferred for the Sage Creek Anticline, Wyoming (using data from Berg, 1962, are modified by Spang and others, 1985) in order to satisfy the same geometry for the sedimentary cover rocks; see text for details. The faults in the sedimentary cover rocks have been labeled alphabetically to correspond to the terminology of Berg (1962). A, Fold in the sedimentary rocks above a wide zone of faults in the Precambrian rocks. B, Modified wide zone with a small fold in the hanging wall. C, Ramp anticline that has been faulted through along a fault parallel to the main basement fault. D, Interpretation of Erslev (1986). E, Shear zone geometry for a basement uplift. F, Fault zone that becomes narrow at depth, after Cook, 1983.

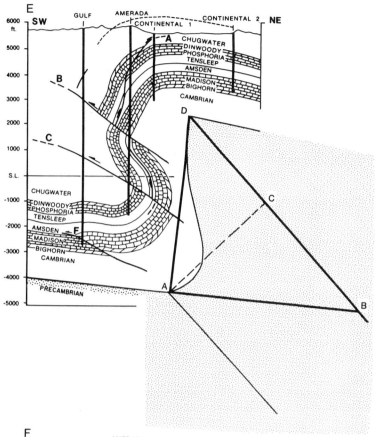

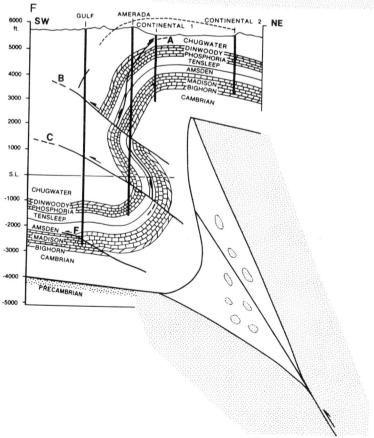

rocks have been arbitrarily depicted as three layers of equal thickness that can have identical or different mechanical properties, but the cover rocks would in any case be more ductile than the underlying basement. A perfectly planar fault can propagate parallel to itself, requiring no internal deformation of either basement or cover rocks (Fig. 4), resulting in a plateau uplift. Structural relief, as measured on the top of basement, must return to zero at some point out of the cross section. There must be either another fault or the basement must be gently folded with a very large radius of curvature (so as not to exceed its ductility), which would allow the structural relief to be zero.

Structurally higher secondary faults would cut the folded cover rocks at progressively larger cutoff angles, and folds may form in the hanging wall when the main or secondary faults flatten in the cover rocks (Fig. 4c). The fold(s) that forms above the fault develops in response to the change in underlying fault shape, and thus is a ramp anticline, albeit a somewhat different ramp fold than what most geologists are used to. This hanging-wall imbrication allows development of a footwall syncline, which has an overturned, attenuated limb even though basement in the hanging wall may be only slightly deformed (see also Fig. 5). For the case of a relatively steep reverse fault (dip >60°), the secondary faults also flatten as they cut up-section through the cover rocks. Deformation in the hanging wall will result in either a ramp anticline or in beds that are extended above the fault.

Figure 4d depicts a situation in which the lowest unit of the cover rocks is extremely ductile and may correspond to the Cambrian shales, where present, in the foreland. This diagram depicts the transfer of displacement from all faulting in basement to all folding in the upper two layers of the cover rocks. The ductile unit thickens in the footwall of the basement fault and thins in the hanging wall of the fault. This geometry has been observed in nonscaled rock models for the case of a 60° dip (Logan and others, 1978) and a 30° dip (J. H. Spang, unpublished data) on the basement fault. Similar results can be inferred from theoretical models for 60° and 30° dip (Rodgers and Rizer, 1981). Secondary faults have been interpreted in natural analogs for the case of steeply dipping faults (e.g., Stearns, 1978) or more shallowly dipping faults (e.g., Spang and others, 1985). The secondary faults are generally interpreted to occur when the folds in the cover rocks have locked up due to room problems in their cores. However, as noted earlier, the local stress field may have been reoriented so that bedding plane slip is no longer relatively easy. The upward younging of the secondary faults enables the folded cover rocks to increase in structural relief even after the folds have locked up.

Examples of possible basement configurations for given cover rock geometry

Cross-section balancing of foreland structures is complicated by the involvement of the Precambrian rocks, which generally lack uniform layering or reference horizons. However, if the configuration of the sedimentary rocks at some level above the Pre-cambrian rocks is known or can be determined in the hanging wall, and is at least partially constrained in the footwall, the lengths of these beds must equal the lengths of units lower in the section and/or the original line length of the contact between the sedimentary rocks and the Precambrian rocks. These line-length calculations can be used to iteratively determine the geometry of the faults in the Precambrian rocks at depth (Spang and others, 1985). The measurements are commonly made between pinning points or lines, which are chosen so that they are at some distance from the fault and are perpendicular to bedding in regions where little or no deformation, shear, or translation has occurred. This provides an area within which bed length and bed area must be conserved. If cross sections do not balance or do not agree with the data, then the section is incorrect or the assumptions about rock behavior are invalid. This method usually provides a range of values of fault dips at depth, since bed length between the footwall cutoff and the footwall pin line is not known exactly for most foreland structures. These line-length/fault-dip calculations do provide an estimate of fault form, based on the assumption that bed area is conserved.

In order to illustrate some of the points discussed above regarding the relationships between the mechanical behavior of the rocks and the resulting geometries of the structures, Spang and others (1985) redrew the original cross section of Berg (1962) to provide a balanced cross section for the cover rocks above the Sage Creek Anticline, a basement-cored structure on the northeastern slope of the Wind River Mountains, Wyoming. At least seven significantly different geometries for deformed basement can be inferred for this structure (Fig. 5). All but one of the basement configurations can be constructed as locally balanced cross sections (i.e., those cross sections that balance within the limits of the cross section).

Figure 5a is a locally balanced cross section in which the line length of the Ordovician Big Horn Dolomite is equal to the line length of the upper basement surface. The shape of the cover rocks depicts a box-shaped, overturned anticline and adjacent syncline. Fault A has a geometry similar to an out-of-syncline crowding fault (Brown, 1983). This type of fault has been interpreted as solving room problems that develop in the core of the adjacent syncline. However, fault A occurs in the outer portion of the syncline rather than in the more tightly folded core of the syncline. Faults B and C are interpreted to offset fault A and therefore are younger than fault A. Out-of-syncline faults may have formed very early as antithetic secondary faults, when bedding plane slip was relatively difficult due to the orientation of the beds relative to the regional stress field. We interpret faults B and C as relatively late secondary faults. These are termed mountain flank thrusts (Berg, 1962) or curved high-angle reverse faults (upthrusts) (Stearns, 1978). Fault F could be either an early synthetic secondary fault or a late antithetic secondary fault. Spang and others (1985) interpreted the basement geometry as a zone of parallel faults with stair-step–like offset, and this zone of faults becomes narrower as the cross section is sequentially restored.

Figure 5b (from Spang and others, 1985) depicts an uppermost fault that has a ramp anticline in the Precambrian rocks above it. This requires that the basement rocks must have deformed internally to allow the hanging wall to conform to the footwall geometry of the fault; in general, such behavior is not expected in crystalline rocks unless they are highly faulted (see Fig. 6).

A single large ramp anticline in the basement rocks (Fig. 5c) may form above a fault that came out of basement and flattened somewhere in the Cambrian rocks, and later faulted through the ramp anticline along a fault parallel to the master fault in the basement. A single large ramp anticline also requires substantial deformation of the basement rocks. Figure 5c may not be a locally balanced cross section, since the line length of the upper basement surface is approximately 3,400 ft longer than the line length of the Ordovician Big Horn Dolomite, but given the internal deformation of basement inferred in this model, the present line length of the upper basement surface may not reflect the true (i.e., original) line length. For this cross section to balance on a regional scale there would have to be an equivalent amount of shortening of the cover rocks and/or elongation of the basement rocks beyond the limits of the cross section in Figure 5. A ramp anticline model may not be appropriate for the Sage Creek structure, but other structures, such as the Washakie thrust system, may be best interpreted as ramp anticlines (see Fig. 6).

Figure 5d depicts a geometry originally proposed by Erslev (1986). This interpretation requires that the leading edge of the hanging wall is broken off and left behind in the footwall as a wedge-shaped mass. This geometry is possible only if the broken-off wedge is highly deformed, although some large, relatively undeformed masses may be present within the highly deformed wedge (Fig. 5d). If the top of the basement block were exposed, the steep face on the hanging-wall block would lead some workers to interpret a much steeper fault within the basement at depth. The apparently steep leading edge of the hanging-wall block is an artifact, and the true leading edge of the hanging wall has been broken off and left behind during subsequent slip on the fault.

Figure 5e shows an apparently folded upper basement surface developed ahead of a zone of distributed simple shear within the basement. The depth, width, and amount of angular shear strain within the fault zone, represented by the zone of distributed simple shear, is constrained by the local geology. In the simplest case, AB represents the original line length of the upper basement surface that would continuously change from AB to AC to AD in the final configuration. The cover rocks must initially shorten by an amount equivalent to the difference in line length between AB and AC. As the deformation continues, the cover rocks must lengthen by an amount equal to the difference in line length between AC and AD. Shortening in the cover rocks could be accommodated early by thickening or displacement along faults A and F. Similarly, the elongation of the cover rocks could be accomplished by later faults B and C. Although we think of faults

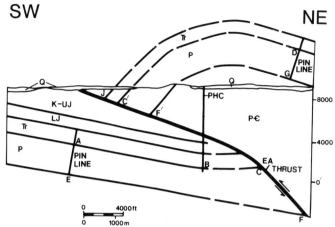

Figure 6. Northeast-southwest cross section through the front of the Washakie thrust system, northwestern Wyoming (see Fig. 1 for location). The frontal fold probably formed as a ramp fold above a change of dip in the underlying EA thrust. Hanging-wall fold shape determined by downplunge projection of outcrop data. The form of the EA thrust is determined by balancing the cross section between pin lines. Line lengths AB + BC + C′D = EF + F′G. The line lengths AB, C′D and F′G are well constrained. Dip of the footwall rocks is inferred to be shallow along the line length BC. Thus, EF is the only unknown and can be found with the relationship given above. EA thrust steepens to a dip of 40° to 50° at depth. Symbols: Q = Quaternary sediments; K-UJ = Cretaceous and Upper Jurassic rocks; LJ = Lower Jurassic rocks; Tr = Triassic rocks; P = Paleozoic rocks; PC = Precambrian rocks; PHC = Phillips Horse Creek drill hole. Simplified from J. P. Evans (1987, in preparation).

B and C as thrusts, they cut bedding at high angles and extend the layering (Spang and others, 1985). Thus, if the amount of layer-parallel shortening and elongation is known, we can adjust the dip of the shear zone to account for the relative lengths of lines AB, AC, and AD, and generate a locally balanced cross section for this model (Fig. 5e).

Figure 5f depicts a wedge-shape shear zone, which narrows with depth and has been drawn after a configuration originally used by Cook (1983) for the Rattlesnake Mountain structure (see also Cook, this volume). Although the shear zone would be a region of relatively high strain, it may contain blocks of relatively undeformed country rock, several of which have been shown diagrammatically in Figure 5f.

All of the examples shown in Figure 5 have the same amount of structural relief on basement and accommodate the same geometry in the folded cover rocks. With the exception of Figure 5C, all of the cross sections are locally balanced, and the basement has been shortened by the same amount as the cover rocks in the plane of the section. In a geometrical sense, all of these cross sections are possible, but all of them require a different style of deformation within the basement rocks. Depending on the actual nature of the basement rocks for any given natural basement structure, one or more of these geometries or those outlined in Figure 5 may be much more likely to form than the others.

SUMMARY

At low temperatures and confining pressures, crystalline basement rocks deform by a variety of mechanisms. The most common are fracture and subsequent cataclasis, along with minor amounts of plastic deformation, kinking, and sliding along phyllosilicates. Faults that result range from discrete, narrow faults to complex zones of faulting. The strength of the sedimentary cover rocks may vary substantially, since the relative ease of bedding-plane slip is a function of the orientation of bedding relative to local or regional stress fields. Theoretical and model studies should be applied with caution, since at any point they cannot uniquely predict which faults would form. However, one general result of these studies is that over a wide range of possible fault dips, faults tend to flatten as they propagate from a strong to a weak medium.

For any basement-cored structure, a number of distinctly different basement geometries may be inferred, each requiring a different mechanical response of the basement rocks. The cover rocks initially respond to shortening in the basement by folding and faulting (either synthetic or antithetic secondary faults). The initial response of the sedimentary rocks, coupled with the variable strength of the cover rocks due to their anisotropy, may affect the response of the basement during later stages of shortening.

REFERENCES CITED

Berg, R. R., 1962, Mountain flank thrusting in Rocky Mountain foreland, Wyoming and Colorado: American Association of Petroleum Geologists Bulletin, v. 46, p. 2019–2032.
—— , 1976, Deformation of Mesozoic shales at Hamilton Dome, Bighorn Basin, Wyoming: American Association of Petroleum Geologists Bulletin, v. 60, p. 1425–1433.
Biot, M. A., 1965, Mechanics of incremental deformation: New York, John Wiley and Sons, 563 p.
Blackstone, D. L., 1980, Foreland deformation; Compression as a cause: Contributions to Geology, v. 18, p. 83–101.
Borg, I., and Handin, J. W., 1966, Experimental deformation in crystalline rock: Tectonophysics, v. 3, p. 251–323.
Brown, W. G., 1983, Sequential development of the fold-thrust model of foreland deformation, *in* Lowell, J. D., and Gries, R. R., eds., Rocky Mountain foreland basins and uplifts: Rocky Mountain Association of Geologists, p. 57–64.
Cook, D. G., 1983, The northern Franklin Mountains, Northwest Territories, Canada; A scale model of the Wyoming Province, *in* Lowell, J. D., and Gries, R. R., eds., Rocky Mountain foreland basins and uplifts: Rocky Mountain Association of Geologists, p. 315–338.
Donath, F. A., 1961, Experimental study of shear failure in anisotropic rocks: Geological Society of America Bulletin, v. 72, p. 985–989.
Erslev, E. A., 1986, Basement balancing of Rocky Mountain foreland uplifts: Geology, v. 14, p. 259–262.
Evans, J. P., 1985, Deformation mechanisms and textures in feldspar-rich rocks; Examples from Laramide fault zones, Wyoming: EOS Transactions of the American Geophysical Union, v. 66, p. 1068.
—— , 1986, Development of a monocline due to compression and its relationship to Laramide basement thrusts: Geological Society of America Abstracts with Programs, v. 18, p. 354.
—— , 1987, Geometry, mechanisms, and mechanics of a Precambrian-cored Laramide thrust sheet, Wyoming [Ph.D. thesis]: College Station, Texas A&M University, 217 p.
Gilliland, J. D., 1959, Geology of the Whisky mountain area, Fremont County, Wyoming [M.S. thesis]: Laramie, University of Wyoming, 89 p.
Granger, H. C., McKay, E. J., Mattick, R. E., Patten, L. L., and McIlroy, P., 1971, Mineral resources of the Glacier Primitive area, Wyoming: U.S. Geological Survey Bulletin 1319-F, 113 p.
Griggs, D., and Handin, J. W., 1960, Observations on fracture and a hypothesis of earthquakes, *in* Griggs, D., and Handin, J., eds., Rock deformation: Geological Society of America Memoir 79, p. 347–364.
Hafner, W., 1951, Stress distribution and faulting: Geological Society of America Bulletin, v. 62, p. 373–398.
Handin, J. W., 1966, Strength and ductility, *in* Clark, S. P., Jr., ed., Handbook of physical constants: Geological Society of America Memoir 97, p. 223–290.
Hennings, P. H., and Spang, J. S., 1986, Petrofabric implications for cover rock adjustment in a basement cored anticline, Dry Fork Ridge, Bighorn Mountains, Wyoming: Geological Society of America Abstracts with Programs, v. 18, p. 635.
Hodgson, R. A., 1965, Genetic and geometric relations between structures in basement and overlying sedimentary rocks, with examples from Colorado Plateau and Wyoming: American Association of Petroleum Geologists Bulletin, v. 49, p. 935–949.
Logan, J. M., Friedman, M., and Stearns, D. W., 1978, Experimental folding of rocks under confining pressure; Part VI, Further studies of faulted drape folds, *in* Matthews, V., III, ed., Laramide folding associated with basement block faulting in the western United States: Geological Society of America Memoir 151, p. 79–100.
Matthews, V., III, 1986, A case for brittle deformation of the basement rocks during the Laramide revolution in the Rocky Mountain foreland province: Mountain Geologist, v. 23, p. 1–5.
Miller, E. W., and Lageson, D. R., 1986, Laramide basement deformation in the southern Bridger Range and northern Gallatin Range, Montana: Geological Society of America Abstracts with Programs, v. 18, p. 396.
Mitra, G., 1984, Brittle to ductile transition due to large strains along the White Rock thrust, Wind River Mountains, Wyoming: Journal of Structural Geology, v. 6, p. 51–61.
Mitra, G., and Frost, B. R., 1981, Mechanisms of deformation within Laramide and Precambrian deformation zones in basement rocks in the Wind River Mountains: Contributions to Geology, v. 19, p. 161–173.
Osterwald, F. W., 1961, Critical review of some tectonic problems in Cordilleran foreland: American Association of Petroleum Geologists Bulletin, v. 45, p. 219–237.
Paterson, M. S., 1978, Experimental rock deformation; The brittle field: New York, Spinger-Verlag, 254 p.
Prucha, J. J., Graham, J. A., and Nickelsen, R. P., 1965, Basement controlled deformation in Wyoming province of Rocky Mountain foreland: American Association of Petroleum Geologists v. 49, p. 966–992.
Rodgers, D. A., and Rizer, W. D., 1981, Deformation and secondary faulting near the leading edge of a thrust, *in* McClay, K., and Price, N. J., eds., Thrust and nappe tectonics: Geological Society of London, p. 65–77.
Schmidt, C. J., and Garihan, J. M., 1983, Laramide tectonic development of the Rocky Mountain foreland of southwestern Montana, *in* Lowell, J. D., and Gries, R. R., eds., Rocky Mountain foreland basins and uplifts: Rocky Mountain Association of Geologists, p. 271–294.
Sharry, J., Langan, R. T., Jovanovich, D. B., Jones, G. M., Hill, N. R., and Guidish, T. M., 1985, Enhanced imaging of the COCORP seismic line, Wind River Mountains, *in* Deep structure of the continental crust: American Geophysical Union Geodynamics Series, v. 13, p. 223–236.
Smithson, S. B., Brewer, J. A., Kaufman, S., Oliver, J. E., and Hurich, C. A.,

1979, Structure of the Laramide Wind River uplift, Wyoming, from CO-CORP deep reflection data and from gravity data: Journal of Geophysical Research, v. 84, p. 5955–5971.

Spang, J. H., Evans, J. P., and Berg, R. R., 1985, Balanced cross sections of small fold-thrust structures: The Mountain Geologist, v. 22, p. 41–46.

Stearns, D. W., 1971, Mechanisms of drape folding in the Wyoming province: Wyoming Geological Association 23rd annual guidebook, Wyoming tectonics symposium, p. 125–144.

—— , 1978, Faulting and forced folding in the Rocky Mountain foreland, *in* Matthews, V., III, ed., Laramide folding associated with basement block faulting in the western United States: Geological Society of America Memoir 151, p. 1–37.

Stone, D. S., 1984, The Rattlesnake Mountain, Wyoming, debate; A review and critique of models: Mountain Geologist, v. 21, p. 137–148.

Tullis, J., 1983, Deformation of feldspar: Mineralogical Society of America Reviews in Mineralogy, v. 2, p. 247–323.

Tullis, J., and Yund, R. A., 1977, Experimental deformation of dry Westerly Granite: Journal of Geophysical Research, v. 82, no. 36, p. 5705–5718.

—— , 1985, Cataclastic flow of feldspars; An experimental study: Geological Society of America Abstracts with Programs, v. 17, p. 737.

Wiltschko, D. V., and Eastman, D., 1983, Role of basement warps and faults in localizing thrust fault ramps, *in* Hatcher, R. D., Jr., Williams, H., and Zietz, I., eds., Contributions to the tectonics and geophysics of mountain chains: Geological Society of America Memoir 158, p. 177–190.

Yonkee, A., Mitra, G., and Hull, J., 1984, Basement-cover relationship in Laramide foreland thrust sheets of the Wyoming province: Geological Society of America Abstracts with Programs, v. 16, p. 702.

Young, S., Werkema, M. A., and Sheedlo, M. A., 1983, Mechanisms of rock deformation in basement-involved thrusts of southwest Montana: Geological Society of America Abstracts with Programs, v. 15, p. 725.

MANUSCRIPT ACCEPTED BY THE SOCIETY FEBRUARY 9, 1988

Geological Society of America
Memoir 171
1988

Balancing basement-cored folds of the Rocky Mountain foreland

Donald G. Cook
Geological Survey of Canada, 3303 33rd St. N.W., Calgary, Alberta T2L 2A7, Canada

ABSTRACT

In structures involving faulted crystalline basement and folded sedimentary cover rocks, an understanding of the geometry of the folded and faulted sedimentary cover rocks enables a unique interpretation of the basement fault, provided that three critical assumptions are valid: (1) Basement deformation was primarily by rigid-body rotation and translation on a single master fault, which in many cases is completely masked near the basement-cover contact by the development of a zone of subsidiary splays, brecciation, and cataclastic flow. If this assumption is valid, the initial hanging-wall and footwall cut-off points probably will not be observable, but must, for reconstruction purposes, lie in the projected hanging-wall and footwall planar basement surfaces. (2) The structure balances locally; shortening of the cover was in direct response to and exactly equal to shortening of the basement. If so, then any accurate determination of predeformation bedding length is also an accurate determination of predeformation basement length in a given cross section. It follows that any cut-off point selected in the hanging wall has a corresponding cut-off point fixed in the footwall. (3) Volume changes accompanying deformation are negligible or can be estimated.

Assumptions 1 and 2 permit the establishment of a family of potential faults, each of which satisfies the requirement that basement length was equal to the measured bedding length. Only one of those potential faults satisfies the further requirement that the postdeformational cross-sectional area of each unit must either be equal to the predeformational area or must reflect any established or assumed volume change. Restoration of the hanging wall establishes three points that define the trace of the fault in the cross section. In the case of a rotated block, the three points are nonrectilinear and define the curvature of the fault plane. In summary, the three assumptions constrain the interpretation to a unique solution of the master fault with respect to dip, position in the cross section, and curvature (if any).

INTRODUCTION

In basement-cored structures in the Rocky Mountain foreland, the geometry of the deformed sedimentary cover is commonly better known than that of the deformed basement. As a consequence, published interpretations of basement faults include a full range of normal faults, vertical faults, reverse faults (both concave upward and concave downward), or combinations thereof. Stone (1984) republished examples of all of the above in a review of interpretations of Rattlesnake Mountain near Cody, Wyoming. Basement has been considered by some authors to have deformed by brittle deformation and rigid-body block rotation (e.g., Matthews, 1986) and by others by folding (e.g., Blackstone, 1983, p. 33) or some combination of faulting and folding. Such structures have been called fold-thrusts (Berg, 1962), thrust

folds (Stone, 1983), drape folds (Stearns, 1971), and forced folds (Stearns, 1978). An excellent review and critique of models was provided by Stone (1984).

The continuing debate and controversy are focused on the geometry and mechanisms of deformation of the basement; the cover rocks are commonly better known and not the subject of controversy. This chapter shows that, if the fold geometry in the cover is known, the dip, location, and curvature of the underlying basement fault can be unequivocally determined, provided that three critical assumptions are valid: (1) that the structure is in fact due to displacements related to a master fault in the basement; (2) that the structure balances locally; and (3) that volume changes during deformation are negligible, or can be determined. In this chapter, cross sections are considered to represent plane strain, and consequently, volumes or volume changes are considered to be proportionately represented by cross-sectional areas.

If these assumptions are valid, then the dip, position, and curvature of the master fault can be uniquely determined, even though this fault may be completely obscured at upper basement levels by the generation of subsidiary splay faults and zones of brecciation and cataclasis. Cataclastic flow may be extensive enough to generate apparent folding of the basement surface.

ASSUMPTION 1. THE SINGLE MASTER FAULT

Published cross sections commonly show single major basement faults underlying Rocky Mountain foreland structures. There are abundant examples in the work of many authors, including Mathews and Work (1978), Schmidt and Garihan (1983), Blackstone (1983), Brown (1984, this volume), and Erslev (1985). Many of the cross sections portray basement as folded adjacent to the master fault (e.g., Schmidt and Garihan, 1983; Blackstone, 1983; Brown, 1984, this volume). Other sections (e.g., Blackstone, 1983, p. 27) show unfaulted Precambrian in the cores of folds. A continuing controversy among Rocky Mountain foreland geologists relates to whether crystalline basement was capable of folding during Laramide deformation. For example, Stearns (1978, p. 9) argued, on the basis of rock mechanics experiments, that basement had to behave as a brittle material under the burial conditions prevalent in the foreland during Laramide deformation. Conversely, Blackstone (1983, p. 1) observed that highly fractured basement rocks can be flexed into folds, and cited numerous cases (p. 10) in which basement is deformed with the overlying sedimentary cover. Most structurally oriented papers dealing with the foreland illustrate cross sections that display rigidly planar hanging-wall and footwall blocks, and any interpreted folding of basement is confined to the area of the steep forelimb of the folded sedimentary cover and immediately adjacent to the master basement fault (for example, see Brown, 1984, p. 33). The folding–vs.–brittle failure controversy is resolved if subsidiary splays, brecciation, and cataclasis related to the master fault are severe enough to permit cataclastic flow and the generation of a pseudo-folded basement surface.

An experimental test specimen (Friedman and others, 1976, p. 1058; Stearns, 1978, p. 29), although not a dynamically scaled model of foreland structures, nonetheless provides an analogue for a pseudo-fold generated by brittle failure and cataclastic flow. Friedman has kindly loaned the original photograph for reproduction here (Fig. 1). Sandstone (brittle material), overlain by limestone (ductile material), was shortened under confining pressures appropriate to the Rocky Mountain foreland. Initial failure was localized by pre-cutting in the sandstone a fault surface dipping at 60° (Stearns, 1973, p. 29). If the resulting deformational geometry provides an analogue for basement failure in the foreland, then a number of very important observations can be made as follows:

1. The original fault, dipping at 60°, is identifiable only at lower levels. At upper levels it is masked by brecciation, cataclasis, and subsidiary splays, some shallower, and some steeper, than the original fault.

2. Rotation of coherent blocks of "basement" has been permitted by cataclastic flow in adjacent brecciated zones.

3. The "basement" surface in gross form appears folded, but in fact it is a composite of fault segments and rotated stratigraphic segments. The "basement/sediment" contact is thus in part stratigraphic and in part structural, and the length of that contact is meaningless for calculating shortening or extension across the structure.

4. The "basement" surface, a tectonic contact over much of its length in the deformed zone, includes segments dipping to the right and others dipping to the left, so that at some points the contact appears to be a normal fault, and at others, a reverse fault. Consequently, at any given point in the deformed zone, the dip of the "basement" surface has no reliable significance as a stress or kinematic indicator.

The suggestion that faults may expand upward into a zone of subsidiary splays and cataclasis is supported by a number of published cross-sections (e.g., Gries, 1983, p. 19, 22; Skeen and Ray, 1983, p. 102; Prucha and others, 1965, p. 978; Blackstone, 1983, p. 14).

In summary, as an analogue, Friedman's test specimen suggests that cataclstic flow can generate a deformed basement surface that appears to have been folded, and that the master fault can be obscured by the development of subsidiary splays, brecciation, and cataclasis. The master fault, if it exists, may nonetheless be identified precisely if the geometry of overlying strata is accurately known and if two further assumptions are valid.

ASSUMPTION 2.
THE STRUCTURE BALANCES LOCALLY

If the structure balances locally, then at unspecified distances from the structure the sedimentary cover can be considered attached or "spiked" to the basement with no relative movement between them (symbolic spikes are shown on most figures here). It follows that any accurate determination of the original bedding length is also an accurate determination of predeformation basement length (Fig. 2). In structures where the cover rocks are significantly deformed by ductile or cataclastic flow, the original bedding length must be calculated from a knowledge of the undeformed stratigraphic thickness and the deformed cross-sectional area. In examples used here, it is assumed or known that the penetrative strain of competent beds is negligible; consequently, initial bedding lengths can be measured directly from the deformed sections. The method applies only if the *initial* bedding length can be measured or reasonably calculated. If so, the dip of the basement fault can be determined by first selecting any potential cut-off point in the hanging wall. A corresponding cut-off point in the footwall (Fig. 3) is determined by the consideration that total length of basement in hanging wall and footwall must be equal to the measured bedding length in the folded sedimen-

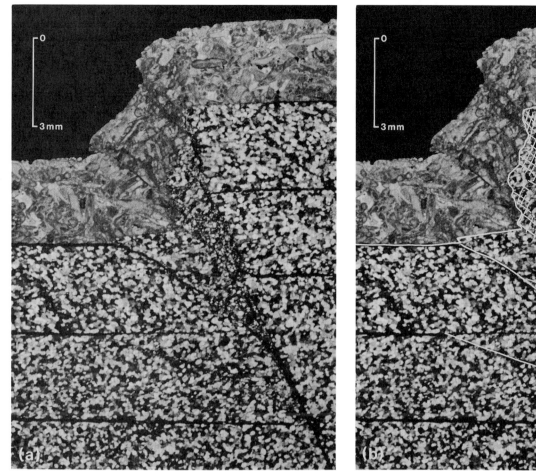

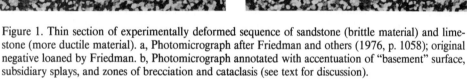

Figure 1. Thin section of experimentally deformed sequence of sandstone (brittle material) and limestone (more ductile material). a, Photomicrograph after Friedman and others (1976, p. 1058); original negative loaned by Friedman. b, Photomicrograph annotated with accentuation of "basement" surface, subsidiary splays, and zones of brecciation and cataclasis (see text for discussion).

tary rocks. A family of potential solutions, all with identical dips, exists (Fig. 3b); each satisfies the requirement that the interpreted total basement length is equal to the measured bedding length. Thus, even though the precise location is yet to be found, at this point in the analysis the dip of the fault is determined.

ASSUMPTION 3. VOLUME CHANGE ACCOMPANYING DEFORMATION IS NEGLIGIBLE OR CAN BE DETERMINED

The countless possible determinations, all of which will yield the correct dip, are represented by three possibilities shown in Figure 3b. All three will balance bedding length with basement length, but only Figure 4b balances before-and-after volumes (cross-sectional areas). Figure 4a implies a volume expansion, Figure 4c implies contraction, and Figure 4b implies no volume change accompanying deformation.

It follows that, if a volume change were known or could be assumed, a fault could be interpreted that would accommodate

that change. It is suggested in this chapter that, in many structures, basement has been deformed in large part by brecciation and cataclastic flow. Although a volume increase in that case would undoubtedly result, it is assumed in all examples analyzed here that such increase is negligible, and volume changes are considered to be zero. Any reinterpretation accommodating a volume expansion will result in shifting the position of the interpreted fault toward the hanging wall (Fig. 4a); the dip will not be affected.

BASEMENT CONFIGURATION

If a basement corner has been displaced from the hanging wall to the footwall, the hanging-wall and footwall cut-off points will be lost or obscured. The master fault can still be determined because the initial cut-off points had to fall in the hanging-wall and footwall planes of the basement surface (Fig. 5), and the selected fault must balance the volume of rock transferred from the hanging wall with the volume of rock transferred to the footwall (Fig. 5a).

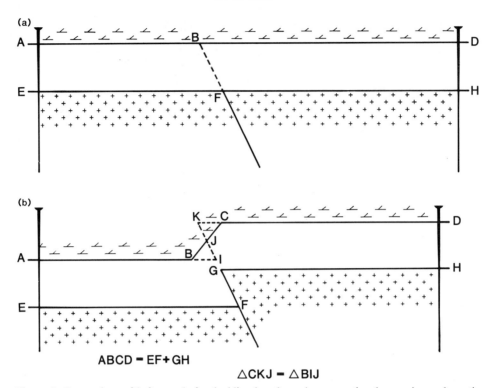

Figure 2. Comparison of before-and-after bedding lengths and cross-sectional areas in a schematic basement-cored fold with no volume change and no penetrative strain of competent strata. Spikes at either end symbolize no motion of cover relative to basement at those points. Line lengths and cross-sectional areas between the spikes after deformation must be equal to those between the spikes before deformation. a, Before deformation. Bedding length AD is equal to basement length EH. b, Schematic balanced basement-cored fold. Bedding lengths and cross-sectional areas are equal to those in a. Triangles KCJ and JBI are made to be congruent isosceles triangles so that before-and-after bedding lengths and before-and-after cross-sectional areas can be easily compared. Thus, ABCD is equal to the original bedding length AI+KD, which is also equal to the original basement length EF+GH. During deformation a volume (CKJ) of the ductile unit has been displaced from the hanging wall and an equal volume (BIJ) has been added to the footwall.

Any interpretation of the basement configuration must balance before-and-after basement volumes, as represented by cross-sectional areas (Fig. 5b). With no other controls on basement geometry, a variety of such interpretations is possible. Thus, to interpret the shape of the cataclastically deformed or "folded" basement, some specific control points are needed. The problem is nicely illustrated by two real folds interpreted below. One, Rattlesnake Mountains, is limited in the range of interpretations because part of the basement surface is observed in outcrop; the other, Sage Creek anticline, is open to a broad range of interpretations because there are no outcrop or borehole basement control points in the critical area of the structure.

The development of forced folds is greatly facilitated by the presence of a ductile unit (Cambrian shales in Wyoming), which serves as a transfer zone from the faulted and block rotation style of basement deformation to the fold style of the sedimentary cover. Before-and-after volumes of the ductile unit must also balance (Fig. 5c). In fact, if the bulk balancing to locate the fault (Fig. 5a) and the basement balancing to interpret basement geometry (Fig. 5b) have both been done accurately, the before-

and-after volumes of the ductile unit will automatically balance, but they can be compared as an independent check (Fig. 5c) on the accuracy of the other construction.

APPLICATION TO REAL STRUCTURES

The method is here applied to three real structures as published. It is applied to the test specimen of Friedman and others (1976), essentially as a test of the method, and it is used to reinterpret Rattlesnake Mountain and Sage Creek anticlines. For Rattlesnake Mountain, the data for fold geometry, and hence bedding-lengths, are taken from Stearns (1971). For Sage Creek anticline, the fold geometry is taken from Spang and others (1985), but basement dip in the hanging-wall block is drawn parallel to the base of the Bighorn Dolomite, as shown by Berg (1981).

TEST SPECIMEN OF FRIEDMAN AND OTHERS

The test specimen shown in Figure 1 is used to test the area-balancing part of this method (Fig. 6). The dip of the origi-

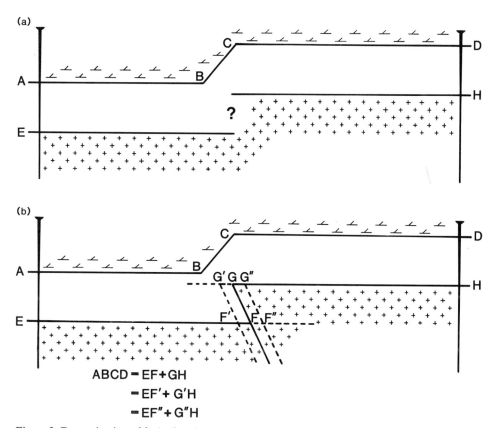

Figure 3. Determination of fault dip where only the fold geometry is known. a, Schematic basement-cored fold with known fold geometry but unknown basement geometry. Accurate measurement of the bedding length ABCD permits identification of the basement fault (see Figs. 3b, 4). b, Fault dip is determined by the consideration that an accurate measurement of bedding length is also an accurate measurement of original basement length. Thus, for any cut-off point G interpreted in the hanging wall, a corresponding point F is fixed in the footwall, because EF plus GH must be equal to the measured bedding length ABCD. A great number of interpretations are possible, but all have the same dip. Only one interpretation will also balance cross-sectional areas (see Fig. 4).

nal fault does not have to be determined because it is known to be 60° (Stearns, 1978, p. 29). Line-length balancing cannot be tested because the limestone is deformed and bedding lengths cannot be determined. During deformation, a corner of the "basement" sandstone has been redistributed so that there has been a net transfer of "basement" across the plane of the original 60° dipping fault. The fault is obscured in upper levels, but its original position relative to hanging wall and footwall can be determined by selecting the 60° dipping line that balances the area of "basement" missing from the hanging wall with the area of "basement" added to the footwall (Fig. 6). That fault, projected to lower levels, virtually coincides with the preserved section of the original fault. This known situation provides on the one hand a neat analogue of deformation and redistribution of a basement corner, and, on the other hand, a confirmation of the area-balancing method to locate the master fault once the dip is known.

Balancing of before-and-after areas of this structure indicates that there has been no significant volume change in the sandstone "basement." This differs from the findings of Logan and others (1978, p. 89–94), who calculated substantial volume increases for

similar test specimens. At present I have no convincing explanation for the difference.

RATTLESNAKE MOUNTAIN REINTERPRETED

Rattlesnake Mountain has been a popular subject for structural interpretation. Stone (1984) traced the history of successive interpretations from Johnson (1934) to Brown (1984); a recent addition is Erslev (1986). On Rattlesnake Mountain an exposed west-dipping fault forms the contact between Paleozoic rocks and Precambrian crystalline basement in the critical forelimb area. Early workers showed it to be a west-dipping normal fault; apparently they were not concerned with the contradiction implied by a structure that simultaneously portrayed compressional deformation (the folded strata) with extensional deformation (the basement normal fault). Stearns (1971) rationalized the apparent contradiction by concluding that the structure could not be balanced locally. Accordingly, he implemented a regional detachment, postulated to exist in the Ordovician Bighorn Dolomite. Stearns' interpretation (Fig. 7) required that the sedimentary

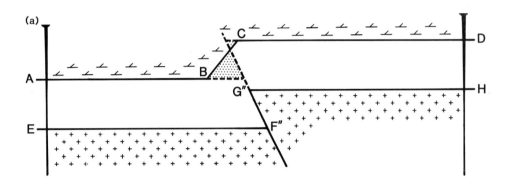

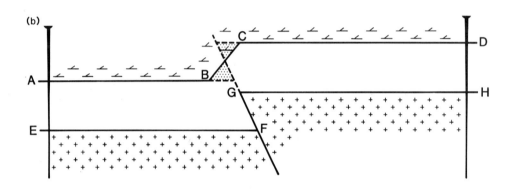

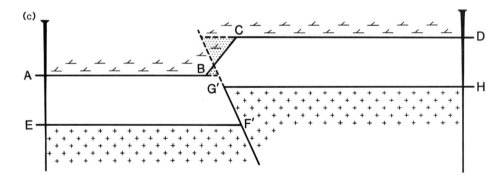

Figure 4. Position of the fault is determined by the consideration that volumes (i.e., cross-sectional areas) before and after deformation are equal (assuming negligible volume changes accompanying deformation). Of three potential solutions presented, G″ F″ (Fig. 4a) implies a volume expansion, G′F′ (Fig. 4c) implies a volume contraction, and GF (Fig. 4b) implies no volume change and is thus the unique fault that balances this structure. No other fault interpretation will balance before-and-after bedding lengths and before-and-after volumes.

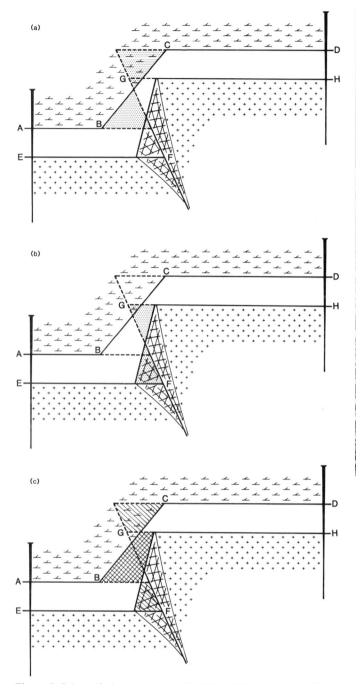

Figure 6. Area balancing applied to test specimen (see Fig. 1) to determine the master fault. Dip is given (Stearns, 1978) as 60°. The fault with 60° dip that balances "basement" missing from the hanging wall with "basement" added to the footwall is the one shown. Projected to depth, that fault coincides with the preserved section of the original fault.

Figure 5. Schematic basement-cored fold in which a "corner" of basement has been redistributed through brecciation and cataclastic flow (cf., Fig. 1) and a ductile shale unit accommodates changes in geometry from cataclastically deformed basement to folded competent cover rocks. Although the original master fault is obscured, its location can nonetheless be identified. The initial hanging-wall and footwall cut-off points, G and F, must fall in the hanging-wall and footwall planes of the basement surface, and satisfy the requirement that bedding length ABCD must be equal to the original basement-length EF+GH; a great number of solutions is possible, all with the same dip (see Fig. 3b). The position of the fault and the configuration of the basement are determined and interpreted respectively by balancing the various shaded areas in figure 5a through c. a, Position of the main fault is determined as per Figure 3. Of the family of potential faults that will balance line lengths, only the one shown will balance before-and-after areas. The shaded areas outside the folded surface ABCD was originally in the hanging wall, and must be equal to the shaded area under ABCD, which has been added to the footwall. b, Configuration of the basement surface is open to interpretation but is subject to the restriction that volumes (cross-sectional areas) of crystalline basement before-and-after deformation must balance. The shaded area missing from the hanging wall must be equal to the shaded area added to the footwall. c, If the gross balancing (Fig. 5a) and the basement balancing (Fig. 5b) have been done accurately, before-and-after volumes of ductile shale must also balance but can be compared as a check. Single-ruled areas represent volumes of shale that existed before deformation but have been displaced during deformation. Double-ruled area represents space into which shale has been displaced (i.e., single-ruled area must be equal to double-ruled area in a balanced section).

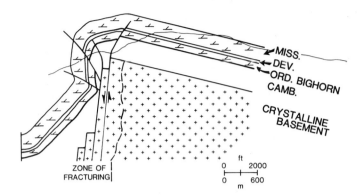

Figure 7. Cross-section of Rattlesnake Mountain anticline after Stearns (1971). Critical data from this figure, incorporated in a reinterpretation (Fig. 8), are the fold geometry, the attenuation of Cambrian shales virtually to zero thickness at the west face of the structure, and the steep westward dip of the basement-shale contact.

cover was completely decoupled from its basement and was more or less free to conform to whatever geometry was imposed by deformation of the underlying basement.

Others (e.g., Cook, 1983; Brown, 1984, this volume; Erslev, 1986) believed that the structure probably balanced locally; that is to say, that shortening of the folded strata was equal to, and in direct response to, shortening in the basement. Cook (1983, p. 323) presented a cross section, balanced by the method presented here, as an ancillary item to a comparison of Canadian Franklin Mountains with Wyoming province. Brown (1984, this volume) concentrated on balancing bedding lengths and treated the present basement/sediment contact as a stratigraphic surface, which he portrayed as having been folded in the footwall. His analysis required that the present basement surface has been neither lengthened nor shortened as a consequence of the basement "folding" process. As noted by Erslev (1986, p. 260) and Mathews (1986, p. 4), Brown's cross section displays an excess of basement relative to what existed prior to deformation. Brown's fault would have to be moved to the west in order to balance before-and-after basement volumes.

Erslev's (1986) mathematical analysis of Rattlesnake Mountain is very similar in overall approach to the graphical method used here. He calculated both dip and curvature from a knowledge of bedding lengths and fold geometry, and he recognized the need for some transfer of rock from the hanging wall to the footwall in order to balance cross-sectional areas of basement. One principal difference between the two methods is that Erslev concentrated on determining fault dips and fault curvatures required by tilted hanging-wall blocks. He recognized the need, but did not provide the method, for precisely balancing before-and-after cross-sectional areas. One major philosophical difference distinguishes Erslev's concept of basement deformation from my own. He achieved transfer from the hanging wall to the footwall by interpreting a rigid hanging-wall corner or basement wedge

being faulted off and transferred en bloc to the foot wall, whereas I have achieved that transfer by brecciation and cataclastic flow across a broad zone that includes rotation and displacement of coherent basement blocks. It is important to note that the area-balancing method presented in this chapter is applicable in either case.

Rattlesnake Mountain is used as the primary example here, not because of its obvious popularity, but because the available data make it ideally suited for analysis by the method described herein. Stearns (1971) established that Paleozoic carbonates maintain an essentially constant thickness around the fold, clearly demonstrating negligible internal strain and, therefore, negligible bedding-length deformation. The interpretation (Fig. 8) accommodates what I consider to be the critical facts established by Stearns' field studies: (1) folding of the Paleozoic carbonates with no significant internal shortening or extension, (2) attenuation of the ductile Cambrian shales to zero thickness, and (3) a west dip of the Precambrian surface at the west face of the structure. In Figure 8a, the approximate dip of the master fault is determined by balancing the original basement length with the length of the base of the Bighorn Dolomite, and the approximate position is determined by balancing the total volume (basement and Cambrian strata) missing from the hanging wall with the total volume added to the footwall. Dip and position are approximate because curvature has not yet been determined.

In Figure 8b, a basement configuration is interpreted. Several geometries are possible, but any viable interpretation must incorporate the west-dipping basement surface observed in outcrop and the observed attenuation of Cambrian shales. It must also balance basement rocks missing from the hanging wall with those interpreted as having been added to the footwall. Before-and-after volumes of Cambrian shale must also balance (Fig. 8c).

Finally, as indicated by Erslev (1986), the fault must be curved in order to accomplish rotation of the hanging wall relative to the footwall. That curvature can be simply determined by restoring the hanging wall to its original horizontal position (Fig. 8d). The resultant three points (AA'C') all lie in the plane of the fault., are nonrectilinear, and define the curvature for the distance joining the three points. The curved fault, so defined, no longer precisely balances the various before-and-after cross-sectional areas and has to be shifted slightly to the right in order to do so.

The final interpretation (Fig. 8e) shows a curved master fault with radius of curvature equal to 11,600 m, and forming an angle of 57° with the reconstructed basement surface in both hanging wall and footwall. The fault cannot be observed in outcrop and, indeed, probably does not exist as an identifiable entity at upper levels. Nonetheless, if the three key assumptions are valid, and if Stearns' data set is accurate, this is the *only* fault (within limits of construction accuracy) to which the Rattlesnake Mountain structure can be attributed. Note that Erslev (1986) has shown a much shallower dipping fault than that determined here. He appears to have modified Stearns' fold geometry, which may account for the difference.

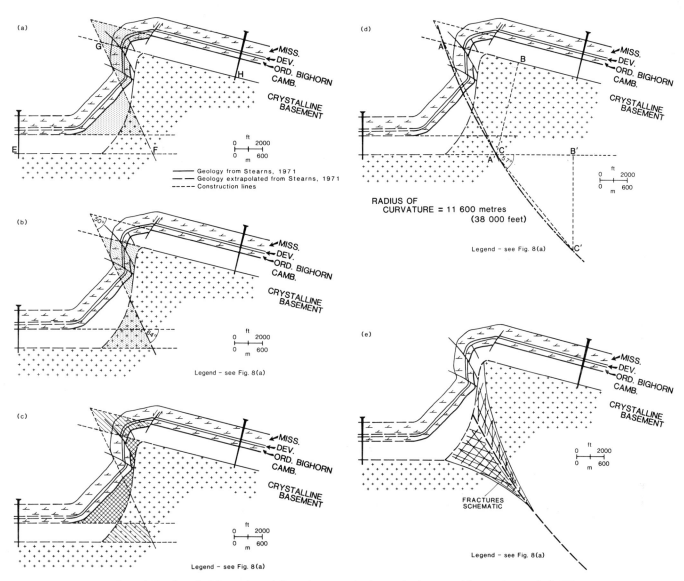

Figure 8. Rattlesnake Mountain anticline reinterpreted using method presented here. a, Master fault GF is interpreted such that the original basement length EF+GH is equal to the length of the base of the Bighorn Dolomite, and such that the gross area (volume) missing from the hanging wall is equal to the new area (volume) created in the footwall (shaded areas). Fault is approximate because curvature required by the rotation of hanging wall relative to footwall, has yet to be determined (see Fig. 8d). b, Interpretation of basement configuration as per Figure 5b. Interpretation is restricted by observation in outcrop of west-dipping basement surface, and virtual juxtaposition of Bighorn Dolomite and basement. c, Balancing of ductile Cambrian shale area (volume) as a check (see Fig. 5c). d, Establishment of curvature on the fault. When hanging wall is restored to horizontal position, the triangle ABC restores to A′B′C′. The three points AA′C′ are nonrectilinear and define the curvature of the fault. The various cross-sectional areas will no longer balance, and the curved fault must be shifted slightly eastward in order that they do so. e, Final interpretation. If the three key assumptions are valid, then the heavy curved dashed line represents the only fault that will balance the cross-section.

SAGE CREEK ANTICLINE REINTERPRETED

Sage Creek anticline was interpreted by Berg (1981). In a reinterpretation, Spang and others (1985) used the line-balancing procedure outlined here to determine the fault dip, but they interpreted the deformation as having been distributed across a series of parallel faults rather than attributed to a single master fault (Fig. 9a). Erslev (1985) challenged the existence of distributed parallel faults in deeper exposures and presented an alternate interpretation involving a single basement fault. Sage Creek anticline is reinterpreted here on the assumption that the structure is due to displacements related to a master basement fault. That fault has been determined (Fig. 9,b and d) with respect to dip and position following the procedure outlined in Figures 5 and 8. During deformation, the hanging wall was rotated approximately 4° relative to the footwall. The fault curvature required to accomplish that rotation has not been established.

Although the master fault has been uniquely determined, the configuration of the deformed basement surface is open to a variety of interpretations because there are no basement control data in the critical area of the structure. The range of interpretations possible is illustrated by Figure 9,b and d (also see Erslev, 1985; Spang and Evans, this volume). Figure 9b is a modification of the interpretation (Fig. 9a) of Spang and others (1985), whereas Figure 9d is a modification of the interpretation (Fig. 9c) of Berg (1981). Each of these interpretations (Fig. 9,b and d) is viable because each is balanced with respect to before-and-after line lengths and before-and-after cross-sectional areas of both basement and ductile Cambrian shale. The overturned forelimb of the fold suggests that there may be significant dislocation of basement, and I am therefore biased toward some interpretation similar to Figure 9d. Note that the master fault has the same dip and position in both cases and is not open to an alternate interpretation for this data set. Erslev's (1985) interpretation of the master fault is virtually identical in dip to my interpretations, but his fault is placed farther to the southwest than mine. It would appear from casual inspection that his placement of the fault has resulted in a basement wedge in the footwall that is too small to balance the basement corner missing from the hanging wall.

SOME ADDITIONAL COMMENTS

The method presented here depends on having an accurate determination of predeformational bedding length. If the strata have been penetratively deformed, the initial bedding length must be calculated on volumetric considerations. If, however, penetrative strain is negligible in the competent strata, then no matter how badly faulted the strata may be, the length of a stratigraphic unit, accurately determined, also represents the initial length of the basement surface in the line of section, and the dip and position of the master fault can be determined. Realistically, most structures contain small unrecognized faults that will introduce unknown errors into bedding-length measurement. If such faults shorten bedding, the measured length will be too short, and the

fault as determined will be steeper than actual. In many foreland folds, however—for example, Sage Creek anticline—beds are probably attenuated in the overturned or steeply dipping forelimb, and thus the measured bedding length is probably too long. The fault dip determined in such cases will be less than actual.

SUMMARY

If basement-cored folds can be attributed to a controlling master basement fault, that fault can be identified, provided that the structure balances locally, that volume changes during deformation are negligible or are known, and that the geometry of the enveloping fold is accurately known.

Many folds probably have attenuated beds in the steep forelimb, and the bedding-length measurement is probably too long. In such cases the calculated fault dip will be lower than actual.

The basement/sediment contact is here assumed to have been faulted and pseudo-folded by the development of splays from the master fault and the generation of zones of brecciation and cataclastic flow. If so, the basement surface in the fold core comprises some combination of stratigraphic segments, fault segments, and cataclastically deformed segments, and its measured length cannot be used in bedding-length comparisons for balancing considerations. Moreover, the basement surface, even where it is known to be a fault contact, is unreliable as an indicator of the geometry and genesis of the master fault. Whether basement corners have been relocated by brecciation and cataclasis as preferred here, or by displacement and rotation of rigid hanging-wall corners or wedges as suggested by Erslev (1986), the volume added to the footwall must exactly balance the volume missing from the hanging wall. This chapter has presented a method for establishing these volumes.

If the geometry of the folded sedimentary cover is known, the dip, position, and curvature of the master fault can be uniquely determined. However, without control points on the deformed basement surface, a great variety of basement configurations is possible. The viability of any one interpretation can nonetheless be tested by comparing before-and-after cross-sectional areas.

Figure 9. Interpretations of Sage Creek Anticline. a, Sage Creek anticline from Spang and others (1985). Fold geometry is controlled by data from wells (vertical heavy lines), whereas basement interpretation is uncontrolled. They considered displacement of basement to have been distributed across a shear zone. Their fold geometry is here taken as data and used to reinterpret Sage Creek anticline as due to displacements related to a single master fault (Fig. 9,b and d). b, Sage Creek anticline reinterpreted using method presented here. Fault, determined as in Figure 5 and 8, is approximate because curvature required by the 4° rotation of hanging wall relative to footwall has not been determined. Basement geometry cannot be uniquely identified with available data, but any interpretation is subject to the restriction that the shaded area (volume) missing from the hanging wall must be equal to the shaded area (volume) added to the footwall. The interpretation presented here approximates the surface in Figure 9a. c, As interpreted by Berg (1981). d, Balanced interpretation approximating Berg's (1981) configuration for basement.

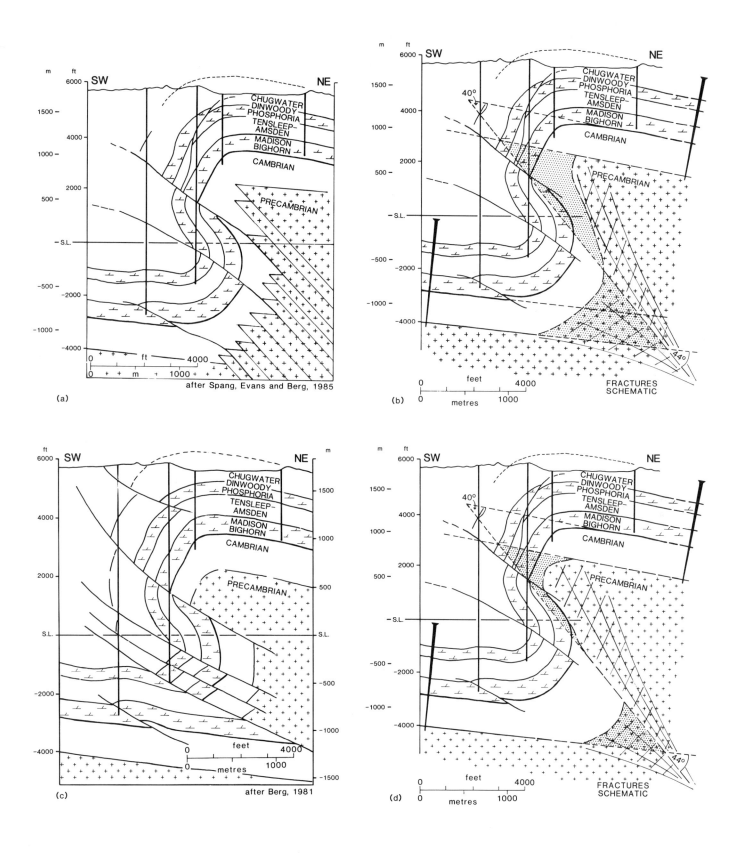

(a) after Spang, Evans and Berg, 1985

(b) FRACTURES SCHEMATIC

(c) after Berg, 1981

(d) FRACTURES SCHEMATIC

ACKNOWLEDGMENTS

I thank David Stearns, who introduced me to the Wyoming province and who piqued my interest in its fascinating complexities. I also thank Elspeth Snow for her efficient assistance in preparing this work, particularly in the construction and drafting of the figures.

REFERENCES CITED

Berg, R. R., 1962, Mountain flanks thrusting in Rocky Mountain foreland, Wyoming and Colorado: American Association of Petroleum Geologists Bulletin, v. 46, p. 2019–2032.
——, 1981, Review of thrusting in the Wyoming foreland: University of Wyoming Contributions to Geology, v. 19, p. 93–104.
Blackstone, D. L., Jr., 1983, Laramide compressional tectonics, southeastern Wyoming: Univerity of Wyoming Contributions to Geology, v. 22, p. 1–38.
Brown, W. G., 1984, A reverse fault interpretation of Rattlesnake Mountain anticline, Big Horn Basin, Wyoming: Mountain Geologist, v. 21, p. 31–36.
Cook, D. G., 1983, The northern Franklin Mountains, Northwest Territories, Canada; A scale model of the Wyoming province, *in* Lowell, J. D., and Gries, R. eds., Rocky Mountain foreland basins and uplifts: Denver, Colorado, Rocky Mountain Association of Geologists, p. 314–338.
Erslev, E. A., 1985, Balanced cross sections of small fold-thrust structures; Comment: Mountain Geologist, v. 22, p. 91–93.
——, 1986, Basement balancing of Rocky Mountain foreland uplifts: Geology, v. 14, p. 259–262.
Friedman, M., Handin, J., Logan, J. M., Min, K. D., and Stearns, D. W., 1976, Experimental folding of rocks under confining pressure; Part III, Faulted drape folds in multilithologic layered specimens: Geological Society of America Bulletin, v. 87, p. 1049–1066.
Gries, R., 1983, North-south compression of Rocky Mountain foreland structures, *in* Lowell, J. D. and Gries, R., eds., Rocky Mountain foreland basins and uplifts: Denver, Colorado, Rocky Mountain Association of Geologists, p. 9–32.
Johnson, G. D., 1934, Geology of the mountain uplift transected by the Shoshone Canyon, Wyoming: Journal of Geology, v. 42, p. 809–838.
Logan, J. M., Friedman, M., and Stearns, M. T., 1978, Experimental folding of rocks under confining pressure; Part VI, Further studies of faulted drape folds, *in* Matthews, V., III., ed., Laramide folding associated with basement block faulting in the western United States: Geological Society of America Memoir 151, p. 79–100.
Matthews, V., III, 1986, A case for brittle deformation of the basement during the Laramide revolution in the Rocky Mountain foreland province: Mountain Geologist, v. 23, p. 1–5.
Matthews, V., III, and Work, D. F., 1978, Laramide folding associated with basement block faulting along the northeastern flank of the Front Range, Colorado, *in* Matthews, V., III, ed., Laramide folding associated with basement block faulting in the western United States: Geological Society of America Memoir 151, p. 101–124.
Prucha, J. J., Graham, J. A., and Nickelsen, R. P., 1985, Basement-controlled deformation in Wyoming Province of Rocky Mountain foreland: American Association of Petroleum Geologists Bulletin, v. 49, p. 966–1003.
Schmidt, C. J., and Garihan, J. M., 1983, Laramide tectonic development of the Rocky Mountain foreland of southwestern Montana, *in* Lowell, J. D., and Gries, R., eds., Rocky Mountain foreland basins and uplifts: Denver, Colorado, Rocky Mountain Association of Geologists, p. 271–294.
Skeen, R. C., and Ray, R. R., 1983, Seismic models and interpretation of the Casper Arch Thrust; Application to Rocky Mountain foreland structure, *in* Lowell, J. D. and Gries, R., eds., Rocky Mountain foreland basins and uplifts: Denver, Colorado, Rocky Mountain Association of Geologists, p. 99–124.
Spang, J. H., Evans, J. P., and Berg, R. R., 1985, Rocky Mountain structures; Balanced cross sections of small fold-thrust structures: Mountain Geologist, v. 22, p. 41–46.
Stearns, D. W., 1971, Mechanisms of drape folding in the Wyoming Province: Wyoming Geological Association, 23rd Annual Field Conference, Wyoming Tectonics Symposium, Guidebook, p. 125–143.
——, 1978, Faulting and forced folding in the Rocky Mountains foreland, *in* Matthews, V., III., ed., Laramide folding associated with basement block faulting in the western United States: Geological Society of America Memoir 151, p. 1–38.
Stone, D. S., 1983, The Greybull Sandstone pool (lower Cretaceous) on the Elk Basin thrust fold complex, Wyoming and Montana, *in* Lowell, J. D., and Gries, R., eds., Rocky Mountain foreland basins and uplifts: Denver, Colorado, Rocky Mountain Association of Geologists, p. 345–356.
——, 1984, The Rattlesnake Mountain, Wyoming debate; A review and critique of models: Mountain Geologist, v. 21, p. 37–46.

MANUSCRIPT ACCEPTED BY THE SOCIETY FEBRUARY 9, 1988
GEOLOGICAL SURVEY OF CANADA CONTRIBUTION 31786

Geological Society of America
Memoir 171
1988

Comparison of thrust fault rock models to basement-cored folds in the Rocky Mountain foreland

Judith Savaso Chester, John H. Spang, and John M. Logan
Center for Tectonophysics and Department of Geology, Texas A&M University, College Station, Texas 77843

ABSTRACT

Nonscaled rock models of the ramp regions of thrust faults develop structures at a late stage of shortening that are similar in geometry, relative mechanical properties, and deformation mechanisms to some basement-cored folds in the Rocky Mountain foreland. Based on these similarities, the models suggest that a ramp anticline in crystalline basement could evolve into a foreland-style fold. The configuration consists of a 20° dip-ramp in a single, thick layer of sandstone overlain by a layered veneer of limestone and mica. The models are deformed at a confining pressure of 50 MPa and displacement rate of $8(10)^{-3}$ cm s^{-1}. Although designed to simulate thin-skinned tectonics, the configuration allows comparison with any layered sequence overlying a low-angle reverse fault.

The late-stage structure produced in the model is a flat-topped, asymmetric fold with a near-vertical forelimb overlying an uplifted, faulted sandstone layer. Critical to the development of this structure is the change in mechanisms of shortening from translation of the hanging wall along a décollement to deformation within the hanging wall. The latter enhances the vertical displacement field. The change in mechanisms appears to be caused by deformation-induced changes in rheology and geometry of the layers that weaken the hanging wall and promote locking of the décollement.

The comparison presented here may be particularly applicable to structures in the interaction zone between the foreland and thrust belt. Ramp anticlines and basement uplifts are end members in a continuum of potential structures that may be present in this zone, and evolution from one style to the other may be possible.

INTRODUCTION

The origin of basement-cored uplifts and the mechanics of the associated folding of the sedimentary cover in the Rocky Mountain foreland have long been subjects of study and debate (e.g., Thom, 1923; Bucher and others, 1934; Chamberlin, 1945; Osterwald, 1961; Berg, 1962; Blackstone, 1963; Prucha and others, 1965; Stearns, 1975, 1978; Gries, 1983; Couples, 1986). The relationship of the basement deformation to that of the sedimentary cover rock, the nature of the basement deformation other than offset of rigid blocks along large, discrete faults, the geometry of the major basement faults at depth, and the tectonic significance of relatively small-scale layer-parallel compressive features in the sedimentary cover are some of the subjects that have been addressed.

Observational data suggest that several characteristic structural features of the Rocky Mountain foreland must be incorpo-rated in any model of its origin (e.g., Bucher and others, 1934; Chamberlin, 1945; Foose and others, 1961; Blackstone, 1963; Prucha and others, 1965; Stearns, 1978; Brown, this volume). These include a variety of basement-fault geometries, large absolute vertical motions of basement blocks (both up and down) often associated with tilting or rotation, and asymmetric folds in the sedimentary cover rock that do not show a single direction of vergence.

Rock models of low-angle reverse faults deformed under confining pressure (Chester, 1985) generate structures that bear geometric similarity to basement-cored folds characteristic of this region. In light of the similarity, this chapter describes the geometry and kinematics of the model suite, and discusses the implications suggested by these models. Inasmuch as the style of interaction between the thrust belt and foreland structures de-

HIGH–ANGLE REVERSE FAULT

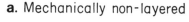

a. Mechanically non-layered   **b.** Mechanically layered

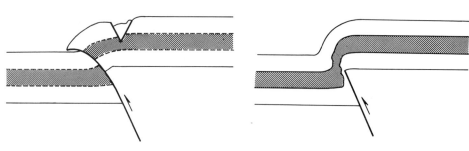

LOW–ANGLE REVERSE FAULT

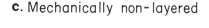 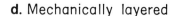

c. Mechanically non-layered   **d.** Mechanically layered

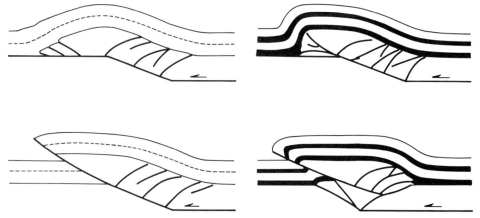

Figure 1. Schematic representations of the geometries produced in drape fold models (a, b: 100 MPa confining pressure) and thrust fault models (c, d: 50 MPa confining pressure). Cases without mechanical layering in the veneer (a, c) and cases with mechanical layering (b, d). Layering in (a) and (b) is the same except in (b) where interfaces are lubricated with MoS_2 to produce mechanical layering. Diagrams are based on models of (a) Friedman and others (1976, specimen 298), (b) Friedman and others (1980, specimen 729), (c) Morse (1978, specimen 385 and 382), and (d) Chester (1985, specimen 1815 and 1812).

pends partly on the style of the foreland structures themselves, the observed model geometries may also have direct application to observed or inferred styles of interaction (e.g., Kulik and Schmidt, this volume; Kraig and others, this volume).

The use of rock models to gain insight into the geometry and kinematics of basement-cored folds in the foreland is not new (e.g., Friedman and others, 1976, 1980; Logan and others, 1978; Stearns and Weinberg, 1975; Weinberg, 1979; Couples, 1983). Previous rock models were designed to have some similarity to an initial geometry and loading condition hypothesized for foreland folds. Generally, they consist of a precut forcing member, representing faulted basement, overlain by a layered rock veneer, representing sedimentary cover. The models best known to

workers have precut faults oriented at angles of approximately 65° to 90° to the layered veneer and are called drape fold models (Fig. 1a, b). Such models are represented by two end members: those in which the sedimentary veneer is welded to the basement and mechanical layering is not significant (Fig. 1a), and those in which the veneer is mechanically layered and slip within the veneer is promoted during deformation (Fig. 1b).

Other rock models relevant to the investigation of basement uplifts and their interaction with the thrust belt are models of the ramp regions of thrust faults (Morse, 1977, 1978; Chester, 1985). Although these models were constructed to investigate the deformation of sedimentary rocks in thin-skinned fold and thrust belts, the configuration also is similar to sedimentary rock overlying basement containing a low-angle reverse fault. Rock models of thrust faults by Morse (1977, 1978) studied the case of a veneer in which mechanical layering is not significant (Fig. 1c). The model suite described here is part of a study in which the mechanical layering is pronounced and the mechanisms of interlayer-slip and intralayer-flow are enhanced (Chester and others, 1986).

The method for applying the results of rock model studies to help understand natural processes has been discussed extensively (Stearns and Weinberg, 1975; Friedman and others, 1976; Morse, 1977; Logan and others, 1978, 1983). Use of rock precludes the models from being mechanically scaled (Hubbert, 1937), which in some ways restricts their utility. However, all techniques used to study geologic systems are limited to some extent (Currie, 1962). The use of rock materials and a high-pressure apparatus produces deformation in the models by some of the same mechanisms that operate in nature. The models provide a way to study the interaction of these mechanisms within a relatively complex deformation scheme. By using a material that promotes a particular mechanism (such as mica, which promotes interlayer-slip), the role of that mechanism in the total deformation may be investigated.

As with all model studies, the application of rock model data to natural deformation involves an intermediate step of comparison and interpretation (Morse, 1977). It appears that the best framework for interpreting and applying the models to nature is in terms of the degree of similarity outlined by Hubbert (1937). For example, if a resultant model structure is geometrically similar to a natural structure, then the kinematics of the model might also be similar (Logan and others, 1983). In this way, the models can provide valuable insight and act as guides for further analysis of the natural structure.

MODEL DESIGN

The specimen configuration consists of a forcing block of Coconino Sandstone containing a precut fault inclined 20° to the overlying, unfaulted, thinly interlayered sequence of limestone and mica (Fig. 2). For the purposes of this chapter, the sandstone represents faulted basement, and the veneer represents the unfaulted sedimentary cover rock. A rigid block of Tennessee sandstone or granite is placed beneath the forcing blocks, which constrains displacements of the forcing blocks during the experiment and remains undeformed. The veneer and rigid block are separated from the loading pistons by two clay spacers. Prior to deformation, the models are rectangular, 11 by 3.2 by 2.9 cm in size. Ink grids were drawn on the sides of the assembled specimens to allow identification of macroscopic slip surfaces and determination of the magnitude and sense of slip between layers.

The models are jacketed with lead and heat-shrink polyolefin tubing and placed under a confining pressure of 50 MPa in the large specimen triaxial apparatus described by Handin and others (1972). They are then loaded in compression parallel to their longest dimension and shortened at an average displacement

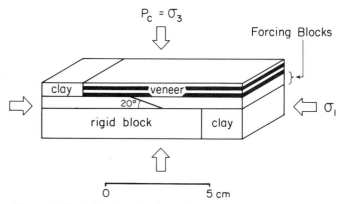

Figure 2. Block diagram showing initial configuration of models. The Coconino Sandstone forcing block contains a precut fault oriented at 20° to the initial layering; the rigid block is composed of Tennessee sandstone or granite, and the veneer of Indiana limestone (white) and mica (black). Locations of the clay spacers are shown. Arrows indicate loading scheme.

rate of $8(10)^{-3}$ cm s^{-1} under room-dry and room-temperature conditions. Under the experimental conditions, the clay deforms easily and supports practically no differential stress; thus only the forcing blocks are end-loaded directly (Fig. 3). The presence of the lower clay spacer ensures that the rigid block will not influence the deformation in any way other than to constrain the forcing block displacements. The models were shortened to three different amounts to allow investigation of the sequential development of structures (S/Lr = 0.20, 0.55, 1.20). The dimensionless term S/Lr normalizes the shortening by the horizontal length of the precut fault (Fig. 3b).

The model materials and experimental conditions were chosen to promote interlayer-slip and to obtain contrasting layer thickness, strength, and ductility, and a pronounced mechanical anisotropy. The Coconino Sandstone is mechanically homogeneous, isotropic, and brittle under the experimental conditions. It deforms by faulting and localized cataclastic flow. The Indiana limestone also is homogeneous and isotropic, and under the imposed experimental conditions, is weaker than the sandstone and mechanically ductile. It deforms by microscopic fracturing and mechanical twinning. Prior to model assembly, the mica is separated along the (001) cleavage planes and stacked to produce two units composed of thin, continuous sheets. Under the experimental conditions, it deforms primarily by fracture and frictional slip along cleavage planes, and by kink folding. The mica is mechanically anisotropic; the shear strength under compression normal to the cleaved surfaces is approximately 10 times greater than for shear along the cleaved surfaces (Chester, 1985). The shear strength normal to the cleavage is approximately 1.5 times greater than that for Coconino Sandstone.

Deformation in the models is characterized, in part, by measurements of the vertical (D_v) and horizontal (D_h) components of displacement of the upper forcing block, dips on the fold limbs, and magnitude and sense of slip between the layers (Fig. 3b). The

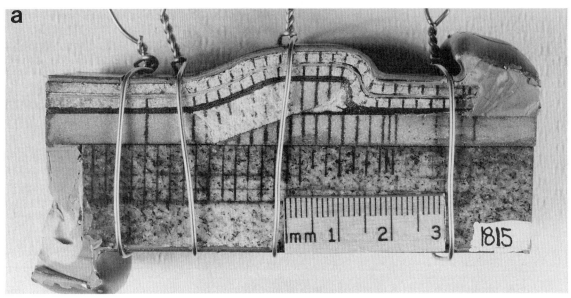

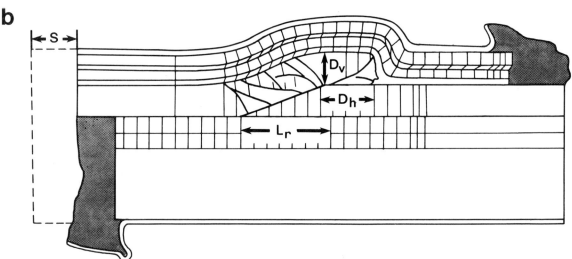

Figure 3. Photograph (a) and tracing (b) of specimen 1815 which represents maximum shortening tested (S/Lr = 1.20). Both (a) and (b) show the deformation of the clay (shaded) and grid used for slip measurements; (b) also shows location of measurements made on deformed specimens, horizontal displacement (D_h), vertical displacement (D_v), shortening (S), and horizontal component of ramp length (Lr).

deformed rock models were further characterized by mapping the deformational features on photographs of petrographic sections.

MODEL RESULTS

The resultant macroscopic geometry and deformational features depend on the degree of shortening (Fig. 4). At the initiation of deformation, the low-angle basement fault terminates at the unfaulted layers of the veneer. By the first stage of shortening (S/Lr = 0.2), the fault has cut up-section to a décollement horizon that is established within the lowest mica unit (Fig. 4a). The layered veneer and upper basement forcing block respond to the shortening by translating along the décollement (left-lateral shear for a right-dipping basement fault) into the clay spacer, and by folding concave downward. Up to an S/Lr of 0.55, approximately 90 percent of the shortening is transferred by slip along the décollement to the clay spacer. The thrusted wedge of the upper basement block remains relatively undeformed, with fracturing and minor cataclasis accommodating the folding through the upper ramp hinge (Fig. 4b). Folding of the upper basement block through the lower ramp hinge is achieved by the formation of curved reverse faults, referred to as backthrusts (Figs. 3, 4). These form in response to the stress concentration at the lower ramp hinge and are carried up the ramp as shortening continues (Morse, 1977, 1978). The translation and folding of the upper basement block produce a symmetric ramp anticline at an S/Lr of 0.55 (Fig. 4b).

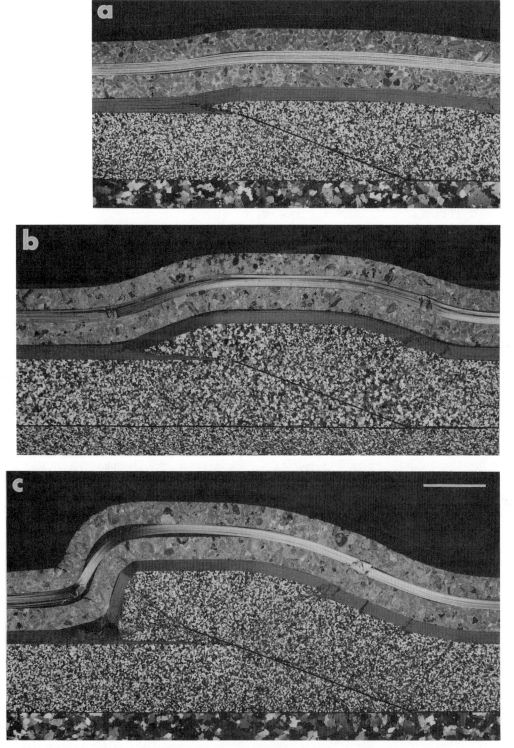

Figure 4. Photomicrographs of thin sections of the deformed models showing stages of fold development. Views are under crossed polarizers; scale bar = 0.5 cm. Specimens shown in (a), (b), and (c) are models with an S/Lr of 0.20, 0.55, and 1.20, respectively (specimens 1814, 1559, and 1815).

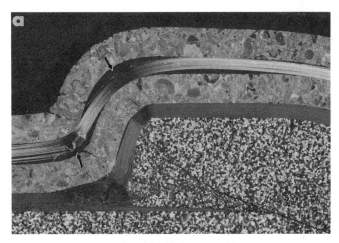 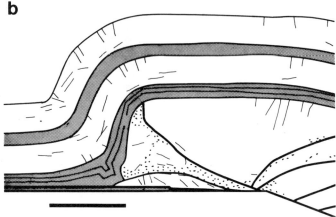

Figure 5. Photomicrograph (a) and line drawing (b) of the thrusted basement block and asymmetrically folded veneer at an S/Lr of 1.20. Scale bar = 0.5 cm. In line drawing, thin lines represent microfractures, thick lines are faults, and stippled pattern indicates cataclastic zones. Arrows point to gaps formed on release of the confining pressure; gaps are closed on line drawing.

By an S/Lr of 1.20, horizontal translation of the hanging wall along the décollement (D_h) is reduced to approximately 57 percent of the shortening. The reduction reflects nominal slip along the décollement after an S/Lr of approximately 0.55. Subsequent shortening is achieved by formation of, and movement along, two imbricate faults in the upper basement block, and further folding of the layered veneer (Figs. 4c, 5). One imbricate fault is concave downward, oriented approximately parallel to the décollement horizon below. The other is concave upward, oriented parallel to the sawcut fault at the base, but steepening to approximately a 40° dip midway through the upper basement block, and to near vertical at the upper surface of the block. Extensive cataclasis and rotation of large, relatively undeformed blocks between the two imbricate faults are associated with movement along these faults (Figs. 5, 6). The portion of the basement that lies above both the upper imbricate fault and the uppermost backthrust fault remains relatively undeformed; it is translated as a single, rigid block without significant rotation. These mechanisms produce an uplifted, faulted block. The surface of this block displays both continuous and abrupt changes in dip such that it appears to be folded. Overlying this block is a continuous, flat-topped, asymmetric kink fold in the veneer having one near-vertical limb.

The ratio of maximum vertical uplift to horizontal displacement of the upper basement block at an S/Lr of 0.20 and 0.55 is similar to that expected for translation along the 20°-dipping precut fault (Fig. 7). At an S/Lr of 1.20, however, the ratio is equal to that expected for translation along a fault having a dip of approximately 33° (Fig. 7). The increased ratio reflects shortening that is achieved by internal deformation between an S/Lr of 0.55 and 1.20; this enhances the vertical displacement field.

Dips on the upper limestone layer in the frontal and trailing fold limbs are 68° and 22°, respectively. The separation of the

layers that occurred upon release of the confining pressure at the end of the experiment suggests that the frontal limb dips were even greater under confining pressure (Fig. 5). Dips on the upper surface of the basement in the frontal-fold limb range from 52°, to vertical, to 68° overturned; the average dip is 85°. The sequential development in this model suite to produce the final asymmetric fold at an S/Lr of 1.20 is reproducible (Chester, 1985).

Folding of the veneer is by microscopic fracturing and mechanical twinning in the limestone, and interlayer-slip and kink folding in the mica. Nominal layer–parallel displacements occur in the mica units where they are in contact with the apparatus piston (right side in Fig. 2) and at the apex of the anticline. Significant interlayer slip occurs on the limbs of the fold and is evenly distributed between the cleaved planes throughout the layer (Fig. 3). Interlayer slip on the limbs increases approximately linearly with limb dip and has the sense of shear expected for flexural-slip folding (Chester, 1985).

DISCUSSION

The generation of a continuous, asymmetric fold with a near-vertical limb overlying a forcing member cut by a low-angle reverse fault has been formed only in rock models of thrust sheets layered with mica. Critical to the development of this fault-cored fold is the change in mechanisms of deformation in the upper basement block from horizontal translation to imbricate faulting and internal deformation at a moderate S/Lr. The early response of the model to shortening by establishing a décollement within the mica and translating the hanging wall into the clay spacer is consistent with both the shear properties of the mica and the clay spacer boundary condition. Experiments testing the frictional properties of cleaved mica show that it has an extremely low coefficient of sliding friction under experimental conditions similar to those used here (Savaso, 1983). This low coefficient of friction promotes the formation of a décollement within the lower mica unit. In addition, the clay spacer located in front of the veneer produces a condition of relatively low resistance to horizontal translation of the hanging wall along the décollement.

Locking of the décollement, steepening of the frontal fold limb, and formation of imbricate thrust faults in the sandstone layer indicate that the resistance to translation of the hanging wall along the décollement increases relative to the resistance to folding and faulting within the hanging wall. Such an increase could result from (1) a change in the clay-spacer boundary condition if all of the clay were squeezed out, (2) an increase in the coefficient of friction along the décollement, (3) changes in the mechanical response of the layers, and (4) changes in the orientation of the layering with respect to the local stresses.

The fact that clay is still present at the end of the veneer at the final stage of shortening indicates that the clay-spacer condition remains constant and cannot be responsible for the change in structural style. The resistance to slip along the mica décollement probably increases, as friction tests on cleaved mica show work hardening during frictional slip. However, based on the response of other rock models from the same study, the increase expected would not be sufficient to cause the change in style (Chester, 1985). Possibly more important are (1) the fracturing that occurs in the thrusted sandstone wedge during the early stages of shortening that weakens it to further deformation, (2) the development of distinct fold hinges within the veneer, and (3) the rotation of the mica cleavage with respect to the local principal stresses that occurs during folding of the veneer. The latter would increase the shear stress across the cleavage and enhance interlayer-slip, weakening the hanging wall to further folding about the weakened hinges. Thus, after an S/Lr of 0.55, there is apparently a sufficient decrease in the resistance of the hanging wall to folding and shearing, relative to the resistance to slip along the décollement, that these mechanisms take over. This interpretation is supported by other model data (Chester, 1985).

Thrust fault models with the same initial configuration and boundary conditions, but with nonlayered veneers (Morse, 1977, 1978) or with different types of mechanical layering in the veneers (Chester, 1985), do not produce the same structural style. Thus, the presence of the mechanically anisotropic mica, and the extremely thin layering and anisotropy it imparts to the veneer, are critical to the development of the final model geometry. As such, the models illustrate that the mechanical properties of the veneer can affect not only the deformational style of the veneer unit, but also the sandstone forcing block below.

The similarities of the resultant model structure at a S/Lr of 1.20 to basement-cored folds in the Rocky Mountain foreland include (1) the flat-topped, asymmetric fold in the cover rock with one near-vertical and locally overturned limb; (2) a basement surface that is curved or displays abrupt changes in dip such that it appears to be folded; (3) the presence of faults at or near the basement surface that have both relatively steep and shallow dips and which may be curved; (4) the presence of rotated, relatively undeformed, fault-bounded basement blocks adjacent to the steep limb, and a relatively large, undeformed basement block

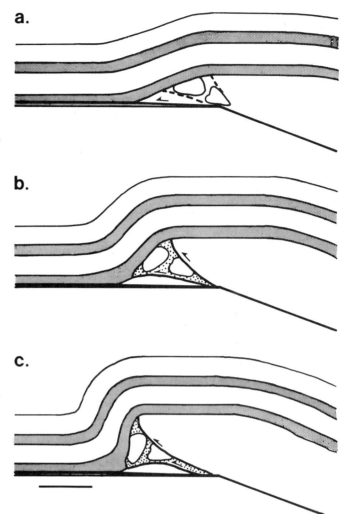

Figure 6. Line drawings showing the development of the curved basement surface through fracture, imbricate faulting, and rotation of basement blocks between zones of cataclasis. (a) S/Lr = 0.55; (b) hypothesized stage between an S/Lr of 0.55 and 1.20; (c) S/Lr = 1.20. Scale bar = 0.5 cm.

making up the rest of the fold-core; and (5) large relative motion upward. These similarities suggest that the structural development in the model suite might be used as an analogue to the development of some basement-cored folds by equating the sandstone to basement and veneer to sedimentary cover. However, because the deformation path leading to the development of a final structure may be nonunique, the validity of such an application must be examined.

If the specific model suite described is an accurate analogue to some basement-cored folds in the foreland or in the interaction zone, then structures representing all stages of development in the model suite should be present in these regions. This means that natural structures representing the early stages of shortening should resemble a thrusted basement wedge that is folded to produce a ramp anticline. In light of field, experimental, and

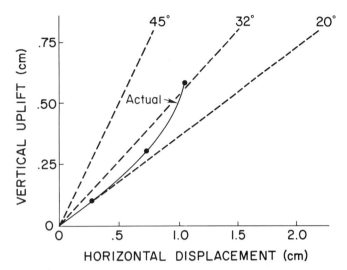

Figure 7. Plot of vertical uplift (D_v) versus horizontal displacement (D_h) of the upper basement block. Black dots represent the three stages of shortening tested. Dashed lines indicate the ratio expected for displacement along faults with dips of 20°, 32° and 45°.

theoretical data, several workers have argued against folding of the basement such as that suggested in cross sections by Berg (1962) (e.g., Stearns, 1971, 1978; Stearns and Weinberg, 1975; Matthews, 1986). Berg (1962) did not specify the mechanisms for folding in his earlier paper; however, his cross-section implied that folding of the basement surface preceded faulting. Later he proposed two possible models of the fold-thrust hypothesis that could produce an apparently folded basement surface (Spang and others, 1985). One model incorporates a ramp anticline somewhat similar to that in the rock model. In the rock model, folding occurs only after formation and movement along a basement fault, and primarily reflects the local stress state of the uplifted basement wedge. Therefore it does not imply buckling of the crust.

Ramp anticlines in basement are not typically described in literature concerning the foreland. The present work offers the hypothesis that the formation of such a structure in basement-type rocks could give rise to foreland-style folds. This hypothesis may be particularly applicable to structures between the foreland and thrust belt. Ramp anticlines and basement uplifts are end members to a sequence of potential structures that may be present in such a region, and the evolution from one style to the other may be possible.

In the model, folding of the thrusted wedge occurs by fracturing and minor cataclasis. If folding of basement wedges does occur in nature, it may involve more distributed cataclastic flow, as well as discrete faulting and rotation of blocks. Such mechanisms are activated in the model at the advanced stage of shortening and are responsible for producing the curved basement surface. The generation of curved basement surfaces below continuously folded sedimentary sections in the foreland has been attributed to the operation of one or more of these mechanisms,

as suggested by several cross sections (e.g., Wise, 1963; Cook, 1983; Schmidt and Garihan, 1983; Brown, 1983; Spang and others, 1985; Erslev, 1986; Evans, 1987). The mechanisms have been noted in crystalline basement-cored folds in both the foreland (e.g., Hudson, 1955) and other structural provinces (e.g., Hill, 1930). Similarly, Stearns (1971, 1978) and Stearns and Weinberg (1975) have noted that cataclastic flow at the corners of fault blocks of crystalline basement can produce small, highly broken, curved contacts that appear to be folded. Although the latter two authors considered these structures to be minor, their data are consistent with others', and document that the deformation mechanisms in the sandstone are similar to those described for crystalline basement.

Because the models are not scaled, the similarity between the mechanical response of the model components and their natural counterparts also should be evaluated (e.g., Logan and others, 1978, 1983; Morse, 1977; Stearns and Weinberg, 1975; Weinberg, 1979). Several questions relevant to such an evaluation include the correlation between the sandstone unit and crystalline basement. Is mica a good analogue for layered sedimentary rocks? Can basement be weaker than the cover rock at some time during deformation? And finally, what is the natural counterpart to the upper clay spacer?

The sandstone is mechanically homogeneous, isotropic, brittle, and strong relative to the limestone and mica (for shear parallel to the cleavage). The mechanical description is based on triaxial compression tests on solid cylinders of sandstone deformed under similar experimental conditions used in the thrust fault models. In comparing the sandstone to basement, if one uses the mechanical definition of basement suggested by Stearns (p. 9, 1978), i.e., a "mass of rock which is statistically homogeneous, isotropic, and continuous," and notes that the upper basement in the foreland deforms by brittle mechanisms (e.g., Hudson, 1955; Stearns, 1971), then it would appear that the sandstone in the models may be considered mechanically similar to basement.

Whether the mechanical anisotropy of the veneer, due to the presence of mica, models layered sedimentary rock cannot be answered because the effective anisotropy of natural sedimentary sections is not accurately known. However, many theoretical treatments of deformation of layered sedimentary rock assume or infer relative strength or viscosity ratios between layers on the order of 5 to 30 (e.g., Sherwin and Chapple, 1968; Stein and Wickman, 1980). The strength anisotropy of the mica-layered veneer is within this range.

In reference to the relative strength between the basement and cover rock, if the basement is locally weakened from previous deformation, i.e., pre-Laramide, then it could in fact be weaker than portions of the sedimentary section at some time during deformation. Strengths determined for perfectly intact, undeformed samples of rock representative of basement (e.g., granite) deformed in experiments that simulate shallow crustal conditions exceed the strengths of sedimentary rocks (Handin and Hager, 1957; Borg and Handin, 1966). However, the bulk strength of representative basement rock containing fractures and faults may be much lower, possibly equivalent to the frictional strength of rock (e.g., Brace and Kohlstedt, 1980), which is essentially the same for crystalline and most sedimentary rocks (Byerlee, 1978). When Laramide deformation was initiated, the basement may have consisted of a weakened, fractured and faulted rock unit (e.g., Hudson, 1955; Spencer, 1959; Blackstone, 1981, 1983), whereas the sedimentary section was probably intact. In this sense the bulk strength of some massive dolomites and sandstones in the sedimentary section may have been close to or even greater than that of basement at the time of Laramide folding. Thus, the relative strength of the sandstone and the mica do not appear to restrict the application of the models to these basement-cored folds.

The clay spacers are used to simulate different loading conditions that might be imposed on a propagating thrust by a neighboring rock mass. In the model suite here, they produce a condition of relatively low resistance to horizontal translation of the hanging wall in the transport direction. This might arise in nature when structures that can accommodate the displaced hanging-wall section are forming nearby. An example would be a fold forming in the cover rock above a high-angle basement fault having the opposite sense of vergence as the low-angle thrust. The thrust-cored fold would require translation of rock out of the folded region, whereas the steeper fault-cored fold would require the opposite (e.g., Spang and others, 1985). In order for the thrust-cored fold to balance, the neighboring fold must be taken into account. Critical to the transfer of displacement between the two folds is the existence of a décollement. The models suggest that if mechanical layering is present, a décollement may form within the sedimentary rock section, and the basement/sedimentary rock contact may remain welded.

CONCLUSIONS

The fault-cored fold produced at a late stage in the rock model suite is similar in geometry, relative mechanical properties of components, and deformation mechanisms operative during

shortening to some basement-cored folds described in the foreland. Based on these similarities, the models suggest that the formation of a ramp anticline in crystalline basement could give rise to a foreland-style fold. Critical to the development of the final model structure is the presence of a veneer having a high degree of mechanical anisotropy that enhances interlayer-slip and the development of kink folds. The model suggests that sedimentary cover rocks of this type may influence the deformational style of the upper basement significantly. In the models the effect of the cover rocks appears to become more important with increased shortening as a result of deformation-induced changes in geometry and mechanical properties of the components. Changes in these parameters appear to cause the change from horizontal translation along a décollement to internal deformation within the hanging wall. Thus, the effects of deformation on both basement and sedimentary rock rheology and geometry, as well as the mechanical role of the cover rocks should be considered when interpreting the genesis of such structures.

The application of the rock model data to basement-cored folds can only be evaluated in light of field data. The model may be particularly applicable to structures in the interaction zone between the foreland and thrust belt. Ramp anticlines and basement uplifts are end members in a continuum of potential structures that may be present in this zone, and the evolution from one style to the other may be possible.

ACKNOWLEDGMENTS

This work was generously supported by grants to J.S.C. from Amoco Production Company, ARCO Oil and Gas Company, the American Association of Petroleum Geologists, and the Houston Geological Society. We thank F. M. Chester, M. Friedmen, C. J. Schmidt, S. Serra, and R. H. Groshong for their critical reviews of this manuscript. J.S.C. acknowledges F. M. Chester, M. Friedman, R. C. Fletcher, and W. G. Brown for stimulating discussions during the course of the model study.

REFERENCES CITED

Berg, R. R., 1962, Mountain flank thrusting in Rocky Mountain foreland, Wyoming and Colorado: American Association of Petroleum Geologists Bulletin, v. 48, p. 2019–2032.

Blackstone, D. L., Jr., 1963, Development of geologic structure in central Rocky Mountains, *in* Backbone of the Americas: American Association of Petroleum Geologists Memoir 2, p. 160–179.

——, 1981, Compression as an agent in deformation of the east-central flank of the Bighorn Mountains, Sheridan and Johnson Counties, Wyoming: University of Wyoming Contributions to Geology, v. 19, no. 2, p. 105–122.

——, 1983, Laramide compressional tectonics southeastern Wyoming: University of Wyoming Contributions to Geology, v. 22, no. 1, p. 1–38.

Borg, I., and Handin, J. W., 1966, Experimental deformation of crystalline rocks: Tectonophysics, v. 3, p. 249–368.

Brace, W. F., and Kohlstedt, D. L., 1980, Limits on lithospheric stress imposed by laboratory experiments: Journal of Geophysical Research, v. 85, p. 6248–6252.

Brown, W. G., 1983, Sequential development of the fold-thrust model of foreland

deformation, *in* Lowell, J. D., and Gries, R., eds., Rocky Mountain foreland basins and uplifts: Denver, Colorado, Rocky Mountain Association of Geologists, p. 57–64.

Bucher, W. H., Thom, W. T., Jr., and Chamberlin, R. T., 1934, Geologic problems of the Beartooth-Bighorn region: Geological Society of America Bulletin, v. 45, p. 167–188.

Byerlee, J. D., 1978, Friction in rocks: Pure and Applied Geophysics, v. 116, p. 6248–6252.

Chamberlin, R. T., 1945, Basement control in Rocky Mountain deformation: American Journal of Science, Daly Volume, p. 98–116.

Chester, J. S., 1985, Deformation of layered rocks in the ramp regions of thrust faults; A study with rock models [M.S. thesis]: College Station, Texas A&M University, 138 p.

——, Logan, J. M., and Spang, J. H., 1986, Role of layering in the deformation of thrust sheets: Geological Society of America Abstracts with Programs, v. 18, p. 346.

Cook, D. G., 1983, The northern Franklin Mountains, Northwest Territories,

Canada,—A scale model of the Wyoming province, *in* Lowell, J. D., and Gries, R., eds., Rocky Mountain foreland basins and uplifts: Denver, Colorado, Rocky Mountain Association Geologists, p. 315–338.

Couples, G. D., 1983, Effects of interlayer slip in multilayer folds: Geological Society of America Abstracts with Programs, v. 15, p. 10.

—— , 1986, Kinematic and dynamic considerations in the forced folding process as studied in the laboratory (experimental models) and in the field (Rattlesnake Mountain, Wyoming) [Ph.D. thesis]: College Station, Texas A&M University, 193 p.

Currie, J. B., Patnode, H. W., and Trump, R. P., 1962, Development of folds in sedimentary strata. Geological Society of America Bulletin, v. 73, p. 655–674.

Erslev, E. A., 1986, Basement balancing of Rocky Mountain foreland uplifts: Geology, v. 14, p. 259–262.

Evans, J. P., 1987, Geometry, mechanisms, and mechanics of deformation in a Laramide thrust sheet [Ph.D. thesis]: College Station, Texas A&M University, 217 p.

Foose, R. M., Wise, D. U., and Garbarini, G. S., 1961, Structural geology of the Beartooth Mountains, Montana and Wyoming: Geological Society of America Bulletin, v. 72, p. 1143–1172.

Friedman, M., Handin, J. W., Logan, J. M., Min, K. D., and Stearns, D. W., 1976, Experimental folding of rocks under confining pressure; Part III, Faulted drape folds in multilithologic layered specimens: Geological Society of America Bulletin, v. 87, p. 1049–1066.

—— , Hugman, R.H.H., III, and Handin, J., 1980, Experimental folding of rocks under confining pressure, Part VIII—Forced folding of unconsolidated sand and lubricated layers of limestone and sandstone: Geological Society of America Bulletin, v. 91, p. 307–312.

Griess, R., 1983, North-south compression of Rocky Mountain foreland structures, *in* Lowell, J. D., and Gries, R., eds., Rocky Mountain foreland basins and uplifts: Denver, Colorado, Rocky Mountain Association Geologists, p. 9–32.

Handin, J. W., and Hager, R. V., 1957, Experimental deformation of rocks under confining pressure; Tests at room temperature on dry samples: American Association of Petroleum Geologists Bulletin, v. 41, p. 1–50.

Hill, M. L., 1930, Structure of the San Gabriel Mountains, north of Los Angeles: University of California Publications in Geologic Science, v. 19, no. 6, p. 136–169.

Hubbert, M. K., 1937, Theory of scale models as applied to the study of geologic structures: Geological Society of America Bulletin, v. 48, p. 1459–1520.

Hudson, F. S., 1955, Folding of unmetamorphosed strata superjacent to massive basement rocks: American Association of Petroleum Geologists Bulletin, v. 39, p. 2038–2052.

Logan, J. M., Friedman, M., and Stearns, M. T., 1978, Experimental folding of rocks under confining pressure; Part VI, Further studies of faulted drape folds, in Matthews, V., III, ed., Laramide folding associated with basement block faulting in the western United States: Geological Society of America Memoir 151, p. 79–99.

—— , Savaso, J. A., Patton, T. L., 1983, Rock models; A major tool for investigating mechanical processes [abs.]: EOS American Geophysical Union Transactions, v. 64, p. 317–318.

Matthews, V., III, 1986, A case for brittle deformation of the basement during the Laramide revolution in the Rocky Mountain foreland province: Mountain Geologist, v. 23, no. 1, p. 1–5.

Morse, J. D., 1977, Deformation in ramp regions of overthrust faults—experiments with small-scale rock models: Wyoming Geological Association, 29th Annual Field Conference, Guidebook, p. 457–470.

—— , 1978, Deformation in the ramp regions of thrust faults; Experiments with rock models [M.S. thesis]: College Station, Texas A&M University, 138 p.

Osterwald, F. W., 1961, Critical review of some tectonic problems in the Cordilleran foreland: American Association of Petroleum Geologists Bulletin, v. 45, p. 219–237.

Prucha, J. J., Graham, J. A., and Nickelsen, R. P., 1965, Basement-controlled deformation in the Wyoming Province of Rocky Mountain foreland: American Association of Petroleum Geologists Bulletin, v. 49, p. 966–992.

Savaso, J. A., 1983, Experiments investigating the effect of interlayer slip in non-scaled rock models of thrust faults: Geological Society of America Abstracts with Programs, v. 15, p. 10.

Schmidt, C. G., and Garihan, J. M., 1983, Laramide tectonic development of the Rocky Mountain Foreland of southwestern Montana, *in* Lowell, J. D., and Gries, R., eds., Rocky Mountain foreland basins and uplifts: Denver, Colorado, Rocky Mountain Association of Geologists, p. 271–294.

Sherwin, J., and Chapple, W. M., 1968, Wavelength of single layer folds; A comparison between theory and observation: American Journal of Science, v. 266, p. 167–179.

Spang, J. H., Evans, J. P., and Berg, R. R., 1985, Balanced cross sections of small fold-thrust structures: Mountain Geologist, v. 22, p. 41–46.

Spencer, E. W., 1959, Geologic evolution of the Beartooth Mountains, Montana and Wyoming; Part 2, Fracture patterns: Geological Society of America Bulletin, v. 70, p. 467–508.

Stearns, D. W., 1971, Mechanisms of drape folding in the Wyoming Province: Wyoming Geological Association 23rd Annual Field Conference, Guidebook, p. 125–144.

—— , 1975, Laramide basement deformation in the Bighorn Basin—the controlling factor for structures in the layered rocks: Wyoming Geological Association 27th Annual Field Conference, Guidebook, p. 149–158.

—— , 1978, Faulting and forced folding in the Rocky Mountains foreland: in Matthews, V., III, ed., Laramide folding associated with basement block faulting in the western United States: Geological Society of America Memoir 151, p. 1–37.

—— , and Weinberg, D. M., 1975, A comparison of experimentally created and naturally deformed drape folds: Wyoming Geological Association 27th Annual Field Conference, Guidebook, p. 159–166.

Stein, R., and Wickman, J., 1980, Viscosity-based numerical model for fault-zone development in drape folding: Tectonophysics, v. 66, p. 225–251.

Thom, W. T., Jr., 1923, The relation of deep-seated faults to the surface structural features of central Montana: American Association of Petroleum Geologists, v. 7, p. 1–13.

Weinberg, D. M., 1979, Experimental folding of rocks under confining pressure; Part VII, Partially scaled models of drape folds: Tectonophysics, v. 54, p. 1–24.

Wise, D. W., 1963, Keystone faulting and gravity sliding driven by basement uplift of Owl Creek Mountains, Wyoming: American Association of Petroleum Geologists Bulletin, v. 47, p. 586–599.

MANUSCRIPT ACCEPTED BY THE SOCIETY FEBRUARY 9, 1988

Geological Society of America
Memoir 171
1988

Region of overlap and styles of interaction of Cordilleran thrust belt and Rocky Mountain foreland

Dolores M. Kulik
U.S. Geological Survey, Box 25046, Denver Federal Center, Denver, Colorado 80225
Christopher J. Schmidt
Department of Geology, Western Michigan University, Kalamazoo, Michigan 49008

ABSTRACT

The Cordilleran thrust belt and Rocky Mountain foreland overlap in a zone 120 to 160 km wide, extending at least from the central Montana salient to the northern edge of the Colorado Plateau, along the area of transition from the North American craton to the Cordilleran miogeocline. Current literature describes the Cordilleran thrust belt and Rocky Mountain foreland structural provinces as a paired belt with two distinct styles of deformation. Eastward-directed, décollement-soled thrusts are described as typical of the thrust belt, whereas fault-bounded, basement-cored uplifts with various trends and intervening deep basins have been identified with the Rocky Mountain foreland.

The overlap zone is characterized by the overlap in space and in time of structures of the thrust belt and foreland provinces, by the interaction between thrust belt and foreland structures, and by superposed deformation at two crustal levels.

Timing of thrust sheet movement and foreland uplift employs chiefly paleontologic, and especially palynologic, dating of associated synorogenic deposits, stratigraphic bracketing based on paleontology, and radiometric dating of syntectonic igneous rocks. The results of numerous studies of this kind in the overlap province define an overlap between late Campanian (Late Cretaceous) and early Eocene time, a span of approximately 25 m.y.

Interaction of structures of the Rocky Mountain foreland and those of the Cordilleran thrust belt has been described from many local areas within the overlap province. The styles of interaction include ramping of thrust faults over fault-bounded foreland uplifts and folding of thrust sheets by postthrust foreland uplift.

The position of the overlap zone is controlled in part by the presence of the transitional margin between the Proterozoic cratonic shelf and the Cordilleran miogeocline. Thrusting in the miogeoclinal wedge is assumed to have been initiated at a zone of brittle-ductile transition and to have been controlled principally by the layering in the sedimentary section. We believe detachment in the region from the hingeline eastward occurred at two crustal levels: the upper one controlled by mechanical decoupling in the sedimentary overburden, and the lower one controlled by the zone of transition from brittle to ductile behavior in the basement. Deformation in the foreland also may have been controlled by compressional reactivation of zones of crustal weakness inherited from earlier orogenic events, particularly Middle and Late Proterozoic normal faults along the cratonic margin.

INTRODUCTION

From Montana to New Mexico, uplift of basement-cored ranges in the region termed the Rocky Mountain foreland is characteristic of a distinct style of deformation. The terms "Laramide" or "thick-skinned" have often been applied to this deformational style. However, because of disagreement about how the term Laramide should be applied (age and/or style and/or orogenic event), we have herein adopted the usage "foreland style" for the uplifts of the Rocky Mountain foreland. The foreland style has also recently been referred to as the "Wind River type" by Hatcher and Williams (1986). In the foreland style, cratonic sedimentary sequences and basement rocks consisting of Archean and Proterozoic igneous and metamorphic complexes were shortened by deeply rooted thrust faults having a variety of orientations (Fig. 1). In this type of uplift, basement rocks of the craton are *fundamentally* involved in deformation along major faults or fault systems. Basement rocks are present in thrust plates in the hinterland of the Cordilleran fold and thrust belt. However, in the frontal part of the belt, which overlaps the Rocky Mountain foreland to the east, sedimentary rocks of the continental margin wedge, from Middle Proterozoic to early Tertiary, were transported eastward on décollement-soled thrusts that involved basement rocks only *incidentally* as "chips" removed from structural highs in the paths of advancing thrusts (type 1 basement involvement of Hatcher and Williams, 1986; see Skipp, this volume).

These two basic styles of deformation—a thrust belt style and a foreland style—are well described in the geological literature, but despite local studies that have described buttressing, impingement, and interaction, most authors have treated them as separate and distinct entities. Although the temporal overlap (Late Cretaceous–early Eocene) of thrust belt and foreland deformation has been recognized for at least 40 years (Horberg and others, 1949) and probably longer, recent studies have increasingly focused on the wide spatial overlap of 100 to 150 km, the variety of types of interaction, and geometric similarities between the two styles (Burchfiel and Davis, 1975; Hamilton, 1978; Gries, 1983a; Kulik, 1984). Many of the studies during the past 10 to 15 years that have provided this information and insight are reviewed or contained within this volume. The paleontological dating of thrusts and associated uplifts in both the thrust belt and foreland has been outlined by Wiltschko and Dorr (1983) for the Wyoming salient and adjacent foreland. Palynostratigraphic techniques have been employed by Nichols and others (1985) in dating foreland uplifts and thrust sheet emplacement in southwestern Montana. Radiometric age determinations, only marginally useful in the Wyoming region, have been employed extensively in the thrust belt and adjacent foreland in Montana where syntectonic igneous rocks are common (Schmidt and O'Neill, 1983; Ruppel and Lopez, 1984; Tysdal and others, 1986).

Seismic reflection studies have been valuable in defining the subsurface geometry of both thrust belt and foreland structures

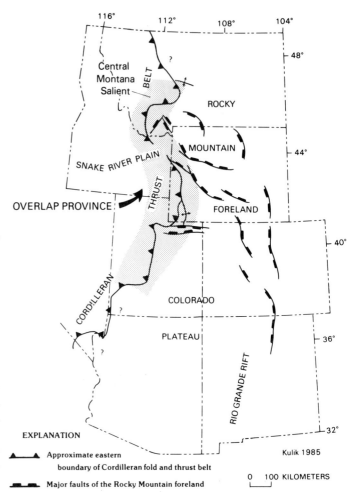

Figure 1. Location of the overlap province between the Cordilleran thrust belt and the Rocky Mountain foreland.

and in defining subsurface overlap (e.g., Royse and others, 1975; Smithson and others, 1978; Dixon, 1982; Gries, 1983a; Skeen and Ray, 1983; Stone, 1984a, 1985a,b; Livesey, 1985; Ray and Berg, 1985; Lopez and Schmidt, 1985). Drilling has further aided subsurface interpretation (Gries, 1981). For example, the understanding that most of the mountain flank thrusts of the foreland dip moderately at mountain flanks and flatten at depth has been derived principally from seismic information augmented with drilling data. The general lack of basement involvement in the eastern part of the thrust belt has been known since the 1950's (for example, Misch, 1960), but most of the proof of this fact has been obtained from seismic information. Gravity and aeromagnetic data commonly show large anomalies over the crystalline cores of foreland uplifts which are identifiable even where the anomalies are overlapped by patterns produced by thrust belt terranes. Modeling of these anomalies has been shown to be effective in constraining subsurface geometries of the foreland structures (Hurich and Smithson, 1982; Kulik and Perry, 1982, this volume). Paleomagnetic studies have identified areas where thrust sheets were rotated when they encountered uplifted fore-land blocks, thereby providing good evidence of thrust belt/fore-land interaction (Grubbs and Van der Voo, 1976; Schwartz and Van der Voo, 1984; Eldredge and Van der Voo, 1985, this volume).

Model studies of various kinds have been particularly effective in elucidating the nature of thrust belt–foreland interaction and the similarities of thrust belt and foreland deformational styles. Nonscaled layered rock models, with a variety of loading conditions and layer types, have been investigated to determine the influence of layering on the deformational style in thrusts (Chester and others, 1986, this volume). Physical models using such materials as clay or corn starch and "Play-doh" have been used to show various aspects of the true geometries of foreland and thrust-belt structures (e.g., Rodgers and Rizer, 1981; Stone, 1984b, 1985b). Photoelastic-model studies have shown the relative effectiveness of various types of basement structures in localizing stress concentrations and thrust ramps (Wiltschko and Eastman, 1983, 1986, this volume) and the nature of secondary fault splay patterns in a layered half space applicable to both thrust belt and foreland styles (Rodgers and Rizer, 1981). Analytical models for shortening of two layers with different rheologic properties have been applied to determine at what depths foreland detachment faults might occur (Fletcher, 1984; Schmidt and others,1985) and what the sequence of thrust imbrication might be for a thrust sheet pushed from the rear and subjected to frontal buttressing (Mandl and Shippam, 1981). Balancing of cross sections is basically a modeling procedure. Balancing of sections in thrust belt terranes is a procedure that has been used for nearly 20 years (Dahlstrom, 1969), whereas balancing of sections in the foreland is relatively new (e.g., Cook, 1983, this volume; Brown, 1984; Spang and others, 1985; Erslev, 1985). Such sections (models) provide realistic constraints on subsurface geometry and are particularly important and revealing when applied to the region where thrust belt structures and foreland structures overlap (e.g., Kraig and others, 1986, this volume).

The many recent studies, only a few of which we have cited here, provide justification for recognizing a separate structural terrane—the overlap province (Fig. 1)—where the Rocky Mountain foreland spatially and temporally overlaps with the Cordilleran thrust belt. The purposes of this chapter are to: (1) review and compare the deformational styles of the Cordilleran thrust belt and the Rocky Mountain foreland; (2) review the temporal overlap between the two deformational styles; (3) examine some of the various types of interaction between the styles; and (4) suggest possibilities for the causes of overlap.

SIMILARITY IN DEFORMATIONAL STYLE

The structural style in the Cordilleran thrust belt has been described by numerous authors. An excellent history of this literature was presented by Perry and others (1984) and is only briefly reviewed here. Major features characteristic of thrust belt structures are: (1) low-angle, thin-skinned, décollement-soled, craton-ward-directed faults (Price, 1981) (Fig. 2); (2) concentric folds over ramps in competent strata (Rich, 1934; Royse and others, 1975); (3) transfer zones and lateral ramps that shift major displacement from one plate to another (Dahlstrom, 1970; Royse and others, 1975); and (4) imbricate faults and duplex zones (Dahlstrom, 1970).

The characterization of the major faults in the Rocky Mountain foreland has been subject to a wider range of interpretations (Fig. 3). Despite a long-lived controversy over horizontal vs. vertical components (Berg, 1962; Keefer and Love, 1963; Stearns, 1971; Brown, 1983, this volume; Stone, 1984a), deformation in the foreland has been generally considered to be accomplished on variously oriented, deep-crustal faults that produce uplifts cored by crystalline basement rocks of the craton.

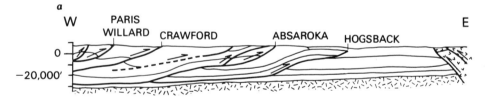

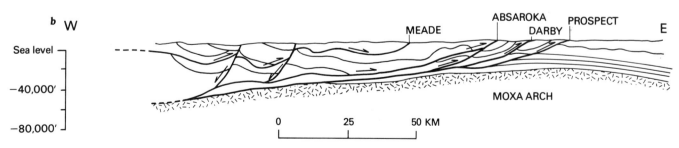

Figure 2. Style of deformation in the Cordilleran thrust belt. a, After Dixon (1982). b, After Royse and others (1975).

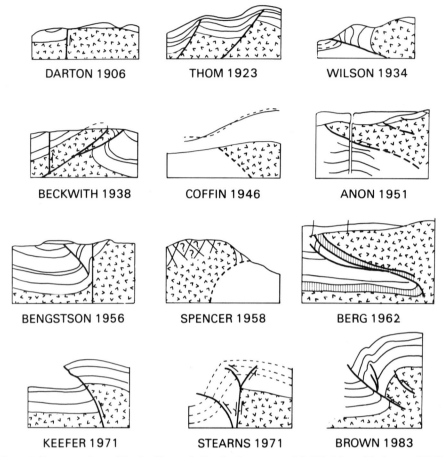

Figure 3. Interpretations of Rocky Mountain Foreland structures. Modified from Blackstone (1963).

The foreland style of deformation was seen as sufficiently unique that Prucha and others (1965, p. 966) recommended that it be "considered apart from other terranes of the North American cordillera." Cross sections that span the Rocky Mountain foreland and Cordilleran thrust belt are scarce in the literature; most of those that do appear (such as those in Fig. 4) have perpetuated the view of separate, different, and distinct structural provinces.

The fault geometry, orientation, and thrust sheet thickness, in addition to the degree of involvement of Precambrian crystalline rocks, are the major characteristics that have been used to differentiate between thrust belt and foreland structures. We believe, however, that the thrust belt and foreland share many structural similarities. Geophysical and drilling data have consistently supported interpretations of low-angle major faults in the Rocky Mountain foreland (Berg, 1962). Interpretations of the Wyoming COCORP line across the Wind River Range strongly suggest that a low-angle major fault underlies the range and overrides the adjacent basin (Smithson and others, 1978). Cross sections by Gries (1981, 1983a), Love (1970), and Lowell (1983), based on seismic and drill-hole data, show low-angle major faults beneath foreland uplifts. Gravity modeling (Kulik, 1982; Kulik and Perry, 1982) also requires low-angle faults beneath foreland uplifts in the Gros Ventre Mountains and the Snowcrest Range.

Simple comparisons of dips and other geometric aspects of several of these faults with those in the thrust belt indicate some noteworthy similarities (Fig. 5). Superimposing the dip angles interpreted from gravity and seismic data of the EA, Uinta, and Snowcrest foreland thrusts (dashed black lines of Fig. 5d,e,f) on cross sections of the Absaroka, Meade, and Crawford thrusts of the thrust belt shows the similarity between several of the important faults of the Rocky Mountain foreland and those of the Cordilleran thrust belt in terms of dip, fault trajectory, and footwall cutoff angles.

The basement surface dips gently westward beneath the frontal edge of the thrust belt. With few exceptions, the faults in the hinterland of the thrust belt involve only sedimentary rocks. However, according to Royse and others (1975), these faults originate at depths greater than 20 km, and the deformation here extends through the entire brittle crust as it does in the foreland. However, the upper crust in the thrust belt comprises primarily rocks of the miogeoclinal sedimentary wedge, and the detachment horizons where the faults are initiated are within the sedimentary sequence.

Cross sections such as those shown in Figure 4 suggest that the faults in the sedimentary rocks of the shelf sequence represent the only crustal deformation in the shelf area. However, we be-

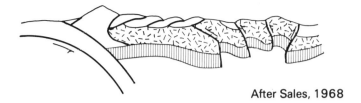

After Sales, 1968

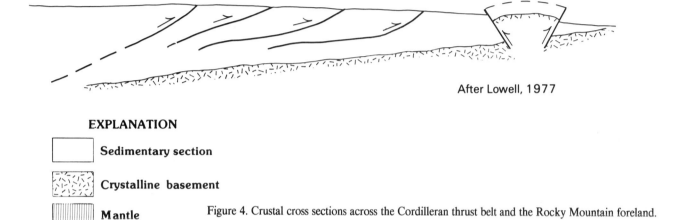

After Lowell, 1977

EXPLANATION

☐ **Sedimentary section**

▨ **Crystalline basement**

▥ **Mantle**

Figure 4. Crustal cross sections across the Cordilleran thrust belt and the Rocky Mountain foreland.

lieve that the region from the leading edge of the thrust belt westward for 100 to 160 km is deformed at two crustal levels: one within the sedimentary sequence, the other within the basement rocks. We define this region as the overlap province (Fig. 1). It extends at least from west-central Montana to the northern edge of the Colorado Plateau and is inferred to follow the broad area of transition between the Cordilleran miogeocline and the craton.

OVERLAP IN TIME

A general view exists from much of the older literature that thrust belt deformation preceded Rocky Mountain foreland deformation and that the thrust belt deformaion had ceased before foreland deformation began (Armstrong, 1968). However, deformation in those areas traditionally described as thrust belt and foreland overlapped in time (Armstrong and Oriel, 1965; Dorr and others, 1977; Wiltschko and Dorr, 1983; Kulik, 1984). In the Montana part of the overlap province, minor uplift began in mid-Cretaceous (Cenomanian) time (Schwartz, 1983; Dyman, 1986), and active foreland uplift began as early as Coniacian time in the Blacktail-Snowcrest uplift (Nichols and others, 1985) and extended into late Paleocene or early Eocene time (Schmidt and O'Neill, 1983; Schmidt and Garihan, 1983; Lageson and others, 1984) in other areas (Fig. 6). Thrust-belt deformation in the southwestern Montana part of the overlap province was in progress during late Campanian and early Maastrichtian time (Brumbaugh and Hendrix, 1981; Schmidt and O'Neill, 1983; Ruppel and Lopez, 1984; Perry and others, 1986) and advanced

into the eastern margin of the central Montana (Helena) salient in late Paleocene to early Eocene time (Skipp and others, 1968; Schmidt and O'Neill, 1983) (Fig. 7). Therefore, although foreland uplift in the overlap zone in Montana was slightly earlier than the arrival of the frontal thrust belt sheets in the southwestern Montana recess, both styles of deformation overlapped from late Campanian to early Eocene time (Fig. 6).

In Wyoming, foreland uplift also may have begun as early as Coniacian time in the north (Targhee uplift of Love, 1973); progressed southeastward to the ancestral Teton–Gros Ventre, Wind River, and Moxa uplifts; and continued through early Eocene time at least in the northern Wind River uplift and Washakie Mountains north of the Wind River uplift (Dorr and others, 1977; Love, 1973; Wiltschko and Dorr, 1983; Beck and others, this volume) (Fig. 7). Movement on the more easterly thrust-belt sheets (Absaroka, Darby, Prospect) within the overlap zone in Wyoming progressed from Santonian time on the Absaroka thrust to the Paleocene-Eocene boundary on the Prospect thrust (Wiltschko and Dorr, 1983). These more closely constrained dates, therefore, agree very well with the time of overlap in the Montana part of the overlap zone (Figs. 6, 7).

Timing of overlap in the Uinta region of northern Utah was documented and summarized by Crittenden (1976) and Bradley (1986). The overlap in time in this region covers about the same period as that in Montana and Wyoming. Strong folding along the Uinta axis began in latest Cretaceous (Campanian to Maastrichtian) time and continued through early Eocene time. Thrust belt movement on the Absaroka thrust system in the region dates

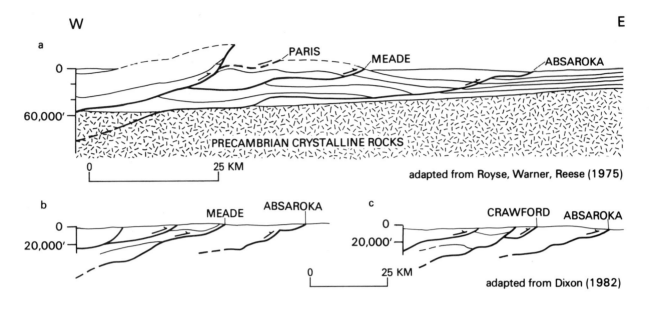

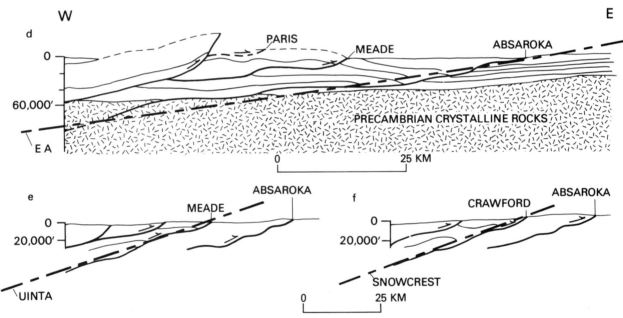

Figure 5. A. Cross sections of the Absaroka (a), Meade (b), and Crawford (c) faults of the Cordilleran thrust belt. Heavy lines superimposed on the cross sections represent the angle of the faults derived from gravity and seismic data for the EA (d), Uinta (e), and Snowcrest (f) faults of the Rocky Mountain foreland.

from about mid-Santonian time (Bradley, 1986) and continues into Paleocene time (Fig. 6). The existence of any pre-Cretaceous thrusting has been recently questioned by Heller and others (1986) as a result of reevaluation of the timing of events in the thrust belt.

In summary, it appears that deformation of the Cordilleran thrust belt, the Rocky Mountain foreland—and the overlap province between them—took place not during consecutive, mutually exclusive orogenies with different causes, but during the same period of protracted compression.

STYLE OF INTERACTION BETWEEN FORELAND AND THRUST BELT

Several types of interaction between foreland structures and thrust belt structures have been described or hypothesized for the overlap province. Our approach here is to first describe the

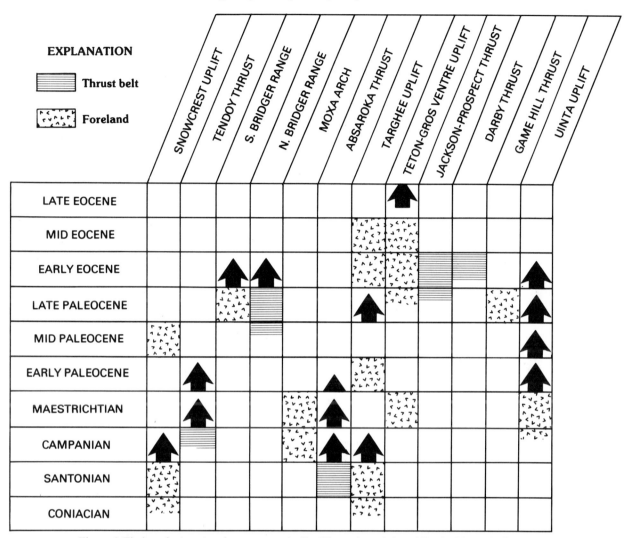

Figure 6. Timing of selected major structures in Cordilleran thrust belt and Rocky Mountain foreland. Partially adapted from Gries (1983b) and other sources mentioned in text. Arrows indicate deformation continued intermittently.

general types of interaction either hypothesized as possible or identified in the field, and then to examine specific examples and possible variations of the general types. The general types of interaction may be assigned to one of two groups depending on the relative timing of the two structural styles at the interaction location. In the first group, we describe structures in the foreland that formed at some time prior to the emplacement of thrust-belt plates. This group includes any earlier structure that produced an irregularity in the basement surface, regardless of whether it is strictly a Late Cretaceous or early Tertiary Rocky Mountain foreland structure or a structure formed in the overlap province during an earlier deformation event. The second group includes examples in which foreland structures formed after the emplacement of a thrust plate.

Thrust ramps

The most distinct structures produced when décollement thrusts encounter various types of foreland structures are thrust ramps or upward deflections in the thrust surface, usually across younger and stronger rocks. The role of basement surface irregularities in localizing thrust ramps has recently been investigated by Wiltschko and Eastman (1983, this volume). They have suggested that three types of irregularities of the basement surface control the position of ramps: normal faults, basement warps or arches, and reverse faults.

For the foreland/thrust belt interaction in the overlap province, we propose three general models of foreland structures that may control the position of ramps in the leading edge of the thrust belt (Fig. 8); these are very similar to the models proposed in the photoelastic studies of Wiltschko and Eastman (1983; this volume). They are: (1) a normal fault in which the relatively high footwall block faces an impinging thrust sheet (Fig. 8a); (2) a reverse fault and associated foreland fold in which the uplifted hanging-wall block and steep anticlinal limb faces a thrust sheet (Fig. 8b); and (3) a reverse fault and associated foreland fold in which the fault dips toward the thrust sheet and the hanging-wall

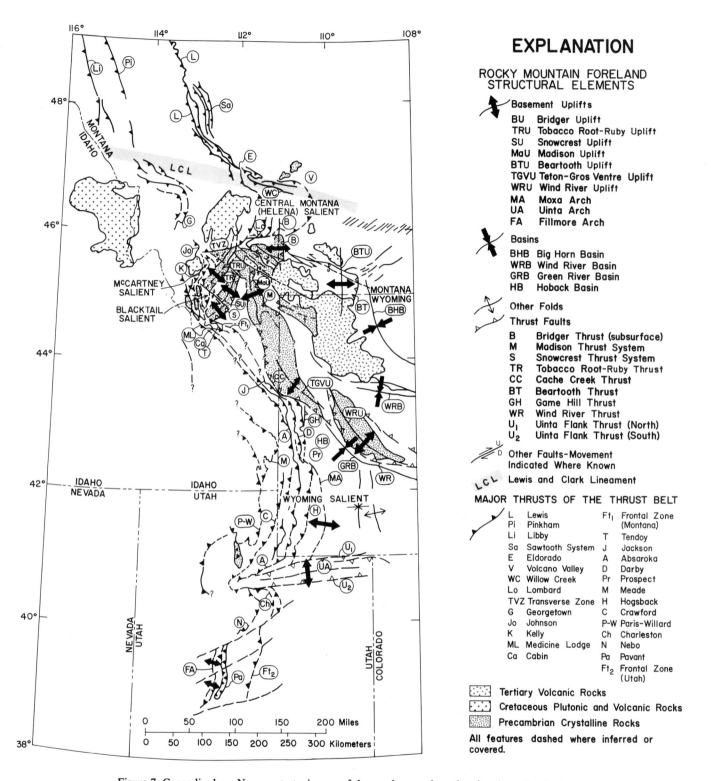

EXPLANATION

ROCKY MOUNTAIN FORELAND STRUCTURAL ELEMENTS

Basement Uplifts

BU	Bridger Uplift
TRU	Tobacco Root-Ruby Uplift
SU	Snowcrest Uplift
MaU	Madison Uplift
BTU	Beartooth Uplift
TGVU	Teton-Gros Ventre Uplift
WRU	Wind River Uplift
MA	Moxa Arch
UA	Uinta Arch
FA	Fillmore Arch

Basins

BHB	Big Horn Basin
WRB	Wind River Basin
GRB	Green River Basin
HB	Hoback Basin

Other Folds

Thrust Faults

B	Bridger Thrust (subsurface)
M	Madison Thrust System
S	Snowcrest Thrust System
TR	Tobacco Root-Ruby Thrust
CC	Cache Creek Thrust
BT	Beartooth Thrust
GH	Game Hill Thrust
WR	Wind River Thrust
U_1	Uinta Flank Thrust (North)
U_2	Uinta Flank Thrust (South)

Other Faults-Movement Indicated Where Known

LCL Lewis and Clark Lineament

MAJOR THRUSTS OF THE THRUST BELT

L	Lewis	Ft_1	Frontal Zone (Montana)
Pi	Pinkham		
Li	Libby	T	Tendoy
Sa	Sawtooth System	J	Jackson
E	Eldorado	A	Absaroka
V	Volcano Valley	D	Darby
WC	Willow Creek	Pr	Prospect
Lo	Lombard	M	Meade
TVZ	Transverse Zone	H	Hogsback
G	Georgetown	C	Crawford
Jo	Johnson	P-W	Paris-Willard
K	Kelly	Ch	Charleston
ML	Medicine Lodge	N	Nebo
Ca	Cabin	Pa	Pavant
		Ft_2	Frontal Zone (Utah)

Tertiary Volcanic Rocks

Cretaceous Plutonic and Volcanic Rocks

Precambrian Crystalline Rocks

All features dashed where inferred or covered.

Figure 7. Generalized pre-Neogene tectonic map of the overlap province showing the major foreland and thrust belt structures and structural relationships described in text. Principal sources are: Armstrong (1968), Blackstone (1977), Lamerson (1983), Love (1983), Perry and Sando (1982), Ruppel and Lopez (1984), Schmidt and Garihan (1983), Schmidt and O'Neill (1983), Scholten (1983), and Winston (1986).

block is tilted such that the basement/cover contact also dips toward the thrust sheet (Fig. 8c). Several field examples of these general models are described below and in other papers in this volume.

The three generalized models (Fig. 8) can have many variations because foreland structures and thrust-belt structures are commonly observed to have divergent strikes, particularly where the foreland structures and/or the thrust-belt structures follow earlier fault trends (Schmidt and O'Neill, 1983; Schmidt and Garihan, 1983). Ramps may therefore be frontal, lateral, or oblique, depending on the relative orientations of the thrust belt and foreland structures. Anomalous and unexplained relationships within the thrust belt (such as younger-over-older thrusts and thrusts that cut down section in the direction of transport) may be caused by interaction with foreland structures.

It seems useful to speculate on the possible nature of some interactions. In the case of a preexisting normal fault (Fig. 8a), for example, if the strata were identical in the hanging wall and footwall block, a thrust ramp might produce a younger-over-older thrust relationship (Fig. 9a). If the uplifted block were originally eroded, filling the downthrown block with sediment, subsequent ramping might place the detrital rock over its original source rock (Fig. 9b). A thrust ramp over a particularly steep normal fault with a sharp footwall corner may cut across basement rocks that would subsequently be translated over the ramp (Fig. 9c). Where a preexisting reverse fault and foreland fold faces the impinging thrust sheet (Fig. 8b), the stratigraphic throw in the thrust sheet would be expected to change abruptly as the thrust crosses the foreland structure, in some cases producing younger-over-older thrust relationships (Fig. 10a,b,c). If the displacement on the reverse fault were large, the thrust sheet likely would cut crystalline basement rocks on the hanging wall of the reverse fault (Fig. 10b). In this way, pieces of basement would be translated on otherwise thin-skinned thrust sheets. Movement on the foreland reverse fault might produce wedging of the foreland structure along a weak horizon and initiate thrusting in the opposite direction (Fig. 10d). Where a foreland reverse fault dips toward the thrust belt (Fig. 8c), if the resulting warp were gentle, décollement surfaces may climb in elevation without climbing stratigraphically for long distances and may stack up in imbricate fashion because of the buttressing effect of the warp (Wiltschko and Eastman, 1983) (Fig. 11a). If the warp were steep, thrusts might not follow bedding up the steep limb, and instead might cut across bedding on a gently dipping fault surface. They would therefore cut down-section locally in the direction of transport (Fig. 11b).

The general examples and several of the variations are represented by structures in the overlap province of the frontal Cordilleran thrust belt and Rocky Mountain foreland. Several of these are described in detail in this volume. Normal faults that control the position of ramps may have formed along both southern and northern boundaries of the Helena embayment of the Belt basin in Middle Proterozoic time (Fig. 12) (Thom, 1957; Harris, 1957; McMannis, 1963; Robinson, 1963; Harrison and others,

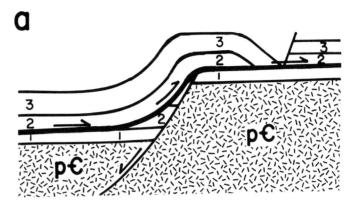

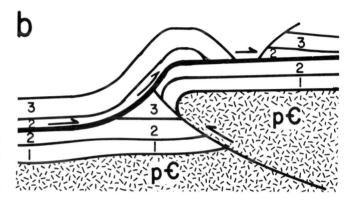

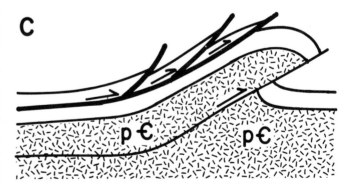

Figure 8. Schematic cross sections of the types of ramps produced by foreland structures. Precambrian crystalline basement rocks are represented by hachured pattern. In sequence of hypothetical layers, 1 is oldest. Modified in part from Wilschko and Eastman (1983).

1974; Zieg, 1981; Godlewski and Zieg, 1984; Schmidt and Garihan, 1986). These boundaries now compose the leading edge of thrusted terranes in the southern and northern parts of the central Montana (Helena) salient of the Montana thrust belt. The thrusts on both these boundaries (Lewis and Clark lineament and

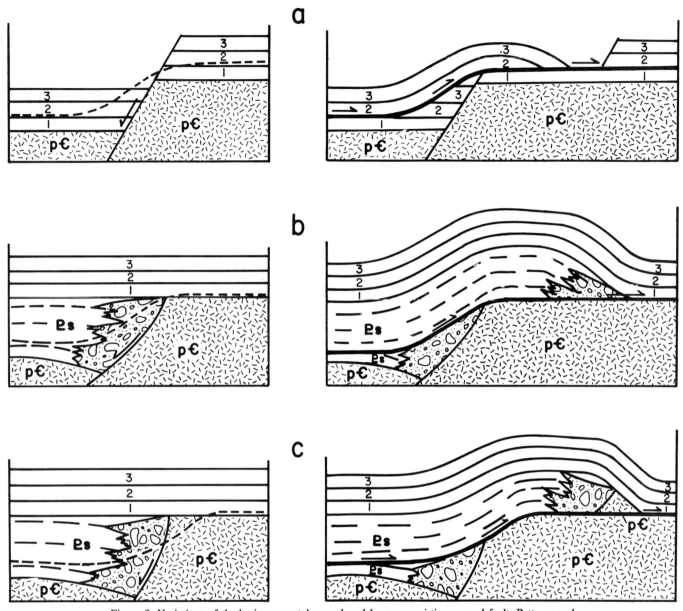

Figure 9. Variations of the basic ramp styles produced by a pre-existing normal fault. Patterns and numbering are the same as in Figure 7. P̲ s refers to Proterozoic sedimentary rocks, which are locally coarse conglomerates on the downthrown sides of the normal faults. The cases are discussed in text.

southwest Montana transverse zone) show evidence of having had significant strike-slip motion (Smedes and Schmidt, 1979; Woodward, 1981; Schmidt and Hendrix, 1981) and have been interpreted to be major oblique and lateral ramps, respectively, in which thin-skinned thrusts have been deflected by normal faults (Schmidt and others, 1984; Sears, 1983, 1984) (cf. Figs. 7, 12). Pieces of Archean basement, exposed in the hanging wall of the major thrust in the southwest Montana transverse zone, have been interpreted as having been removed by thrusting from the footwall of the Proterozoic normal fault that initiated the thrust ramp (Schmidt and Garihan, 1986).

The Cordilleran hingeline, an elongate boundary between the late Precambrian Cordilleran geosyncline and the cratonic shelf (Hill, 1976), has been interpreted as a rifted passive margin that was formed during continental separation in late Precambrian time (Stewart, 1972). The general coincidence between the hingeline and the Cordilleran thrust belt, particularly in Utah and Nevada, has been recognized for a long time (e.g., Harris, 1959; Stokes, 1976). Thrust ramps may have been localized by normal faults associated with the Cordilleran hingeline. Thrusts localized by normal faults of a previous passive margin have been described from several places in the Appalachian thrust belt (Jacobsen and Kanes, 1974, 1975; Thomas, 1977, 1983, 1986, and personal communication, 1985). There are, however, no

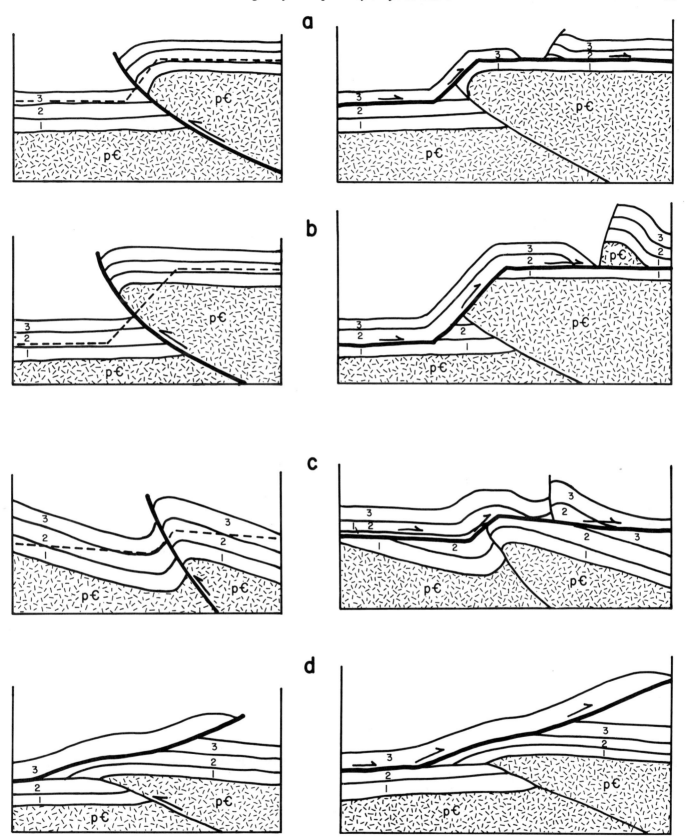

Figure 10. Variations of ramps produced by foreland anticline/reverse fault verging opposite to transport direction of thrusts. All variations are discussed in text except example C, which is that of homoclinal gentle limbs of a foreland fold transected by a flat thrust.

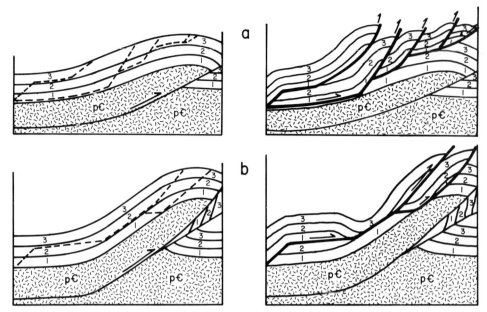

Figure 11. Two examples of overlapping thrust belt and foreland structures that verge in the same direction. The examples discussed in text and the imbrication/ramp style are related primarily to steepness of dip on the gentle limb of the foreland structure.

certain examples of this style of interaction in the Cordilleran thrust belt. Picha and Gibson (1985) and Picha (1986) have described several late Precambrian features (a horst called the Fillmore arch and the ancient Ephram fault) in central Utah, which they believe localized the Pavant-Canyon thrust system and the frontal Sevier thrust system (Fig. 12). Several cross-strike structural discontinuities in the thrust belt here appear to be largely lateral ramps controlled by lineaments of probable Precambrian ancestry normal to the hingeline. The pattern of salients and recesses in central and southern Utah may therefore be related to promontories and embayments of the late Precambrian continental margin in a way similar to that hypothesized by Thomas (1977, 1983, 1985) for the Appalachian-Ouachita Paleozoic thrust belt.

Foreland anticlines and associated reverse faults that verge generally toward the thrust belt have been described in the southwestern Montana part of the overlap zone (Schmidt and O'Neill, 1983; Schmidt and Garihan, 1983; Brandon, 1984; Schmidt and Geiger, 1985). In this region, northwest-trending Laramide reverse faults of Proterozoic ancestry are an important component of the structural style of the foreland. Where thrust faults of the southwest Montana transverse zone impinge on anticlines associated with these reverse faults, the thrusts ramp over the anticlinal hinges and change in both orientation and transport direction (Schmidt and others, this volume) (Fig. 7). The foreland anticline above the reverse fault with the greatest displacement (Brooks Creek anticline–Bismarck fault of Garihan and others, 1983) has produced a younger-over-older thrust relationship (Mississippian over Cambrian) where the thrust ramps over the anticlinal hinge.

Ruppel and Lopez (1984) have described oblique tearing of frontal thrust sheets on the northwest-trending Blacktail and McCartney reverse faults (Fig. 7). The situation they described might also be interpreted as oblique ramping of the frontal thrusts over the foreland anticlines associated with the reverse faults (Schmidt and Geiger, 1985).

Precambrian (Archean?) crystalline basement rocks are present in several thrust plates in the Tendoy and Beaverhead Ranges and the Armstead Hills in extreme southwestern Montana (Fig. 7) (Scholten, 1983; Dubois, 1983; Coryell and Spang, this volume; Johnson and Sears, this volume; Skipp, this volume). Scholten (1983) suggested that these thrusts are "rooted" in basement rocks. Coryell and Spang (this volume) have offered the alternative hypothesis that some thrusts may have encountered basement blocks uplifted along earlier reverse faults. This hypothesis appears to be an attractive alternative, inasmuch as northeast-trending reverse faults of the foreland are known from geophysical data (Kulik and Perry, this volume) to have extended well into the region of the thrust belt, and the foreland deformation began prior to thrusting (Schmidt and O'Neill, 1983). Furthermore, Wiltschko and Eastman (this volume) demonstrated that reverse fault corners are efficient stress concentrators; therefore, it should not be surprising to find these basement corners cut by thrusts at locations where the thrusts ramp across the anticlinal hinges on the hanging walls of the reverse faults (Fig. 10b). Kulik and others (1983) and Kulik and Perry (this volume) have suggested that the thrust sheets may have encountered the northeast-trending Blacktail-Snowcrest uplift.

The Moxa arch in southwestern Wyoming has been described as being a broad arch in basement rocks near the leading

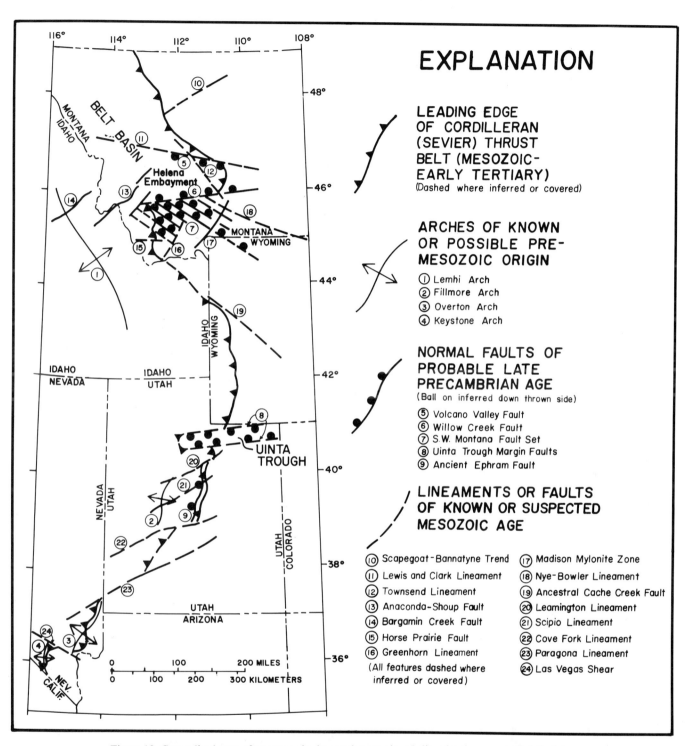

Figure 12. Generalized map of structures in the overlap province believed to have controlled the later position of thrust ramps or Laramide foreland structures. Principal sources are: Blackstone (1963), Harrison and others (1974), O'Neill and Lopez (1985), Picha and Gibson (1985), Ruppel (1978), Schmidt and Garihan (1986), Sears and others (1982), and Stewart (1972).

edge of the thrust belt (Royse and others, 1975; Blackstone, 1979; Dixon, 1982) (Fig. 7). Wiltschko and Eastman (1983) suggested that ramps in the Prospect and Darby thrusts may have been localized by the arch because it acted as a fault deflector. This suggestion was further refined by Kraig and others (1985, this volume) on the basis of seismic profiles and sequential cross-section reconstructions. They indicated that the arch is subtended by an east-dipping thrust in basement rocks; the thrust shallows upward and is parallel to bedding at the base of the Triassic section. These authors suggested that the initial westward movement on this foreland thrust, and arching of the Phanerozoic section above it, produced initial eastward movement on the Prospect thrust (including ramping of the thrust over the west-dipping flank of the arch). The way in which the westward movement on the foreland thrust produces initial eastward movement on the Prospect thrust is similar to the development of intercutaneous wedges or triangle zones described for the frontal thrust belt in the Canadian Rockies (Jones, 1983; Charlesworth and Gagnon, 1985) (Fig. 10d). Later movement on the Prospect thrust and ramping of the more westerly Darby thrust was also controlled by this west-dipping flank of the arch (Fig. 10d).

Broad arching of the basement produced by foreland thrusts that dip westward below the thrust belt in southwestern Montana has been described by Brandon (1984), Schmidt and others (1984), and Lopez and Schmidt (1985). Uplift along the Snowcrest foreland thrust system or on the Tobacco Root–Ruby thrust system immediately to the northwest (Fig. 7) produced a west-dipping contact between basement and cover rocks, which is considerably steeper in parts of southwestern Montana than in adjacent areas of west-central Montana or western Wyoming. This more steeply dipping basement-cover contact may have been partly responsible for the closely spaced stacking of thrust sheets in areas like the eastern McCartney salient (Brandon, 1984; Lopez and Schmidt, 1985). Where the trends of the basement uplifts are oblique or transverse to the thrust belt trends, as in extreme southwestern Montana near the Idaho border, abrupt changes in strike and stratigraphic throw occur in several of the frontal thrust sheets (Perry and Sando, 1983; Perry and Hossack, 1984; Kulik, 1984).

Buttressing

The concept of buttressing of thin-skinned thrusts and folds was recognized by Heim (1919), who noted that folds of the northeastern Jura Mountains were crowded against the Black Forest massif. Buttressing of thrust sheets by foreland uplifts along the front of the Cordilleran thrust belt was first described by Horberg and others (1949) for the area along the northern edge of the Wyoming salient; it has since been frequently mentioned as an important mechanical interaction between the two styles of deformation. Buttressing commonly involves shortening of advancing thrust sheets against already uplifted foreland blocks and may precede or accompany actual deflection (ramping) of thrust sheets. Among the various effects ascribed to buttressing are: (1)

crowding and/or convergence of fold hinges in front of foreland uplifts (Horberg and others, 1949; Blackstone, 1977; Schmidt and O'Neill, 1983); (2) deflection of the trend of fold hinges to parallelism or near parallelism with the strike of foreland buttresses (Beutner, 1977; Corbett, 1983); (3) intensification of thrusting, increased stacking, or increased imbrication (Horberg and others, 1949; Bregman, 1976; Blackstone, 1977; Beutner, 1977; Corbett, 1983; Schmidt and others, this volume); (4) production of out-of-sequence (break-back) thrust imbrication (Beutner, 1977; Kopania, 1983; Dimitre-Dunn, 1983; Schmidt and others, this volume; Craddock and others, this volume; Hunter, this volume); (5) formation of layer-parallel shortening fabrics (especially solution cleavage) and minor folds in thrust sheets ahead of foreland buttresses (Pecora, 1981; Schmidt and Geiger, 1985; Craddock and others, this volume; Schmidt and others, this volume); and (6) rotation or change in trend of thrust sheets against buttresses aligned oblique to initial transport direction (Horberg and others, 1949; Rubey, 1955; Grubbs and Van der Voo, 1976; Love, 1977, 1983; Beutner, 1977; Wiltschko and Eastman, 1983; Wiltschko and Dorr, 1983; Kopania, 1983; Davis, 1983; Eldredge and Van der Voo, 1985, this volume; Craddock and others, this volume).

One or more of these effects has been described for nearly every part of the overlap province from the northern portion of the central Montana (Helena) salient (Bregman, 1976) to southwestern Utah (Davis, 1983). Beutner (1977) ascribed the major salient and recess pattern of the thrust belt from central Montana to central Utah to the effect of buttressing, and Davis (1983) suggested that curvature of the thrust belt in southwestern Utah (Pavant Mountains) was also the result of buttressing against uplifts to the north and south of the salient (Fig. 7).

Several examples of presumed buttressing have been reevaluated or challenged. The interaction of the Bridger Range foreland structure and the thrust belt at the southern margin of the central Montana (Helena) salient (Fig. 7), described as a buttressing phenomenon by Schmidt and O'Neill (1983), has been reinterpreted by Lageson and others (1984) as postthrust foreland uplift. Deflection of thrusts and folds around the western margin of the transverse Uinta arch (Fig. 7) was also interpreted to be a result of buttressing by relatively rigid quartzites that had filled the late Precambrian Uinta trough (Beutner, 1977). However, the same pattern of thrust deflection has also been ascribed to postthrust uplift of the Uinta arch (Crittenden, 1976; Bruhn and others, 1983; Bradley, 1986; Bradley and Bruhn, this volume).

The best documented evidence for buttressing occurs in the northern Wyoming salient where the ancestral Teton–Gros Ventre uplift developed prior to the young thrust movements (Fig. 7) (Horberg and others, 1949; Dorr and others, 1977; Love, 1977; Wiltschko and Dorr, 1983; Craddock and others, this volume). Even here, however, some of the supposed effects of buttressing have been questioned by Moore and others (1984), Oriel and Moore (1985), and Woodward (this volume). These authors have found no evidence that the abundance of thrust imbricates in the Absaroka thrust system in front of the hypothetical Targhee or ancestral Teton–Gros Ventre uplifts indicates a mechanical interaction between the thrust belt and foreland. Woodward has also questioned the existence of the out-of-sequence thrusts in this region, which have been cited as evidence of buttressing (Hunter, this volume). Counterclockwise rotations of the frontal Darby and Jackson-Prospect thrust systems, as a result of interaction with the ancestral Teton–Gros Ventre foreland uplift, are well documented from paleomagnetic data and seem unassailable (Grubbs and Van der Voo, 1976; Wiltschko and Eastman, 1983; Wiltschko and Dorr, 1983; Kopania, 1983). However, the actual mechanism for thrust-sheet rotation is not so clear.

Although buttressing of thrust sheets by foreland uplifts may have occurred in the eastern overlap province, the extent of this phenomenon and the nature of its effects are not at all clear.

Effects of postthrust foreland uplift

Geometries of interaction that result from uplift of a foreland structure below or adjacent to an already existing thrust sheet are not easily distinguished from thrust ramp geometries or from buttressing effects (Couples and Lewis, this volume). Furthermore, because of the temporal and spatial overlap of the two styles, many structures likely are a product of continued uplift of foreland blocks during emplacement of thrust sheets; thus they are not distinctly either ramp/buttress structures or thrust modification structures.

Examples of actual truncation of a thrust sheet by a foreland thrust are rare. The best known examples are the truncation of the Hogsback thrust by the Uinta north flank thrust (Crittenden, 1976; Blackstone, 1977; Bruhn and others, 1983) and the truncation of the Jackson (Prospect) thrust by the Cache Creek foreland thrust that borders the ancestral Teton–Gros Ventre uplift (Love, 1983; Dimitre-Dunn, 1983) (Fig. 7). Other occurrences of truncation are equivocal. For example, the Game Hill fault, a west-verging reverse fault bordering a partially uplifted segment of the Hoback basin, has been interpreted to cut the Cliff Creek (Prospect) thrust (Schroeder, 1973; Corbett, 1983). Others (e.g., Dorr and others, 1977; Wiltschko and Dorr, 1983; Hunter, this volume) have indicated that the Cliff Creek (Prospect) thrust overrides the Game Hill fault.

Folding of thrust sheets by foreland uplifts is the most commonly recognized thrust modification. A variety of geometries is possible, depending on the trend and plunge and sense of vergence of the foreland uplift relative to the orientation and transport direction of the thrusts. Three different models are illustrated (Fig. 13). In two of these (Fig. 13, a and b), the foreland fault and the thrust belt fault are assumed to trend in the same direction, but the sense of vergence is the same in (a) and opposite in (b). The third model (c) shows a foreland uplift transverse to and plunging toward the thrust belt. In the first model (Fig. 13a), the resulting geometry is not significantly different from folded thrusts or antiformal thrust stacks produced by the forward progression of thrust duplex development (Boyer and Elliott, 1982) or by thrust ramping from below (Dahlstrom, 1970). Map patterns of such geometries would be similar or identical to thrust

culminations. The only significant difference is that basement rocks would ultimately be involved in the underlying uplift and there would be no branch line between the foreland fault and the thrust belt fault. In asymmetrical foreland arches verging in the opposite direction from the thrust belt (Fig. 13b), the geometry would be somewhat more easily distinguished from ordinary thrust belt geometries, particularly if thrusts were overturned opposite to their transport direction. The map patterns of thrusts and associated folds for a transverse foreland uplift would be that of a sharp recess into the thrust belt (Fig. 13d).

Examples of either of the first two models (specifically, those illustrated in Fig. 13, a and b) have not been described in the overlap province. Corbett (1983), Dimitre-Dunn (1983), and Woodward (this volume) have described local steepening of thrusts in the Absaroka thrust system and Jackson (Prospect) thrust system south of the present Teton Range; this steepening may be the result of late-stage foreland uplift of the hypothetical Targhee and ancestral Teton–Gros Ventre uplifts along the Cache Creek thrust. Rubey (1973) showed southwest-verging folds on the Jackson thrust sheet. These folds, also described by Blackstone (1977), Corbett (1983), and Dimitre-Dunn (1983), may have been formed during earlier emplacement of the Jackson thrust sheet and rotated to a southwest-verging position by a foreland uplift on the east similar to that illustrated in Figure 13b. Because the thrusts are exposed only on one side of the foreland uplift, it is not easy to distinguish the observed geometries from the effects of thrust ramping or buttressing. In the vicinity of the Georgetown thrust in the Montana thrust belt (Fig. 7), anomalous west-verging folds and thrusts have been described (Mutch, 1961; Gwinn, 1961; McGill, 1959; Baken, 1981) and attributed to a variety of mechanisms including westward forceful intrusion of the Boulder batholith (Gwinn, 1961). We suggest that these anomalous west-verging structures might be explained by the folding of the thrusts over a foreland anticline developed above an east to northeast-dipping basement thrust (as shown in Fig. 13b).

Several field examples of thrust modification by transverse foreland uplifts have been documented. The best known of these is the interaction of the Uinta uplift and the thrusts of north-central Utah. North of the Uinta axis, the easternmost thrust (Hogsback thrust) is probably truncated by the foreland thrust that bounds the north flank of the arch (Bradley and Bruhn, this volume). The thrust traces of the more westerly Absaroka thrust system bend to the west near the arch (Fig. 7) and are locally cut by the North Flank thrust (Bryant and Nichols, this volume). The Charleston thrust is deflected south of the Uinta axis in a similar way. These deflections have been interpreted as folding of the thrust sheets resulting from the uplift of the Uintas similar to that depicted in Figure 13c (Crittenden, 1969, 1974, 1976; Bruhn and others, 1983; Bradley, 1986; Bryant and Nichols, this volume). However, the observation that the development of the Hogsback thrust and the Uinta uplift were coeval has resulted in a considerably more complex interpretation than that in Figure 13c (Bradley and Bruhn, this volume).

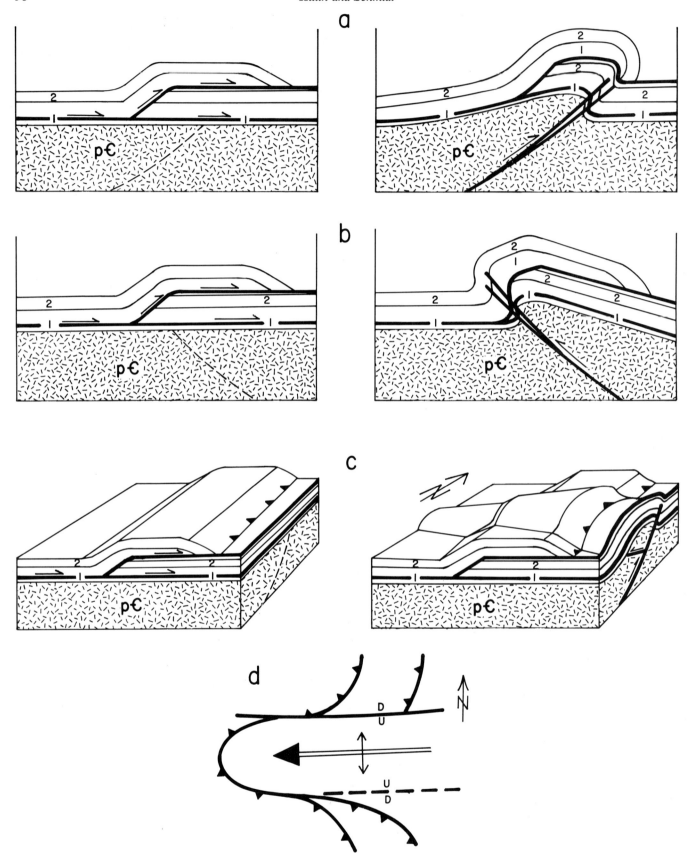

Figure 13. Three examples of modification of thrust sheet geometry by postthrust folding and faulting (cases are described in text).

In southwestern Montana, the foreland Blacktail-Snowcrest uplift strikes transverse to the leading edge of the thrust belt (Tendoy thrust) and is overridden by it (Fig. 7). However, post-thrust reactivation on the Snowcrest thrust system that bounds the foreland uplift is a possible cause for later folding of the Tendoy thrust along an east-northeast trend (Perry and others, this volume). The Bridger Range at the southern margin of the central Montana (Helena) salient (Fig. 7) is a north-plunging foreland structure that is transverse to the southwest Montana transverse zone (lateral ramp) (Schmidt and O'Neill, 1983). Several enigmatic northwest-trending faults in the northern part of the range have been interpreted by Lageson and others (1984) to be the eastern sides of lateral ramps folded by uplift of the Bridger Range along a west-dipping foreland-style thrust. This example is similar to that in Figure 13b, except that the thrust belt structures have significant right-lateral movement. In two other locations along the transverse zone, early formed thrusts with evidence of ramping over northwest-trending foreland anticlines are themselves folded by later uplift of those anticlines, giving reasonably good evidence of coeval thrust belt and foreland activity (Schmidt and Geiger, 1985; Schmidt and others, this volume). Tysdal (this volume) has interpreted the thrusts that define the northern Blacktail Mountains salient in southwestern Montana as being turned up and reoriented by uplift along a northwest-trending foreland block.

CAUSES OF OVERLAP

Major zones of faulting in the basement rocks along the Cordilleran hingeline and adjacent craton that existed prior to Mesozoic and early Cenozoic deformation (Fig. 12) (Picha, 1986) contributed to the development of the overlap province. The northwest-trending reverse faults of the Montana foreland, for example, have been shown to have a Precambrian ancestry (Reid, 1957; Schmidt and Garihan, 1983, 1986). The east- and northeast-trending structures are also probably inherited from Proterozoic time (Harrison and others, 1974; Ruppel and Lopez, 1984; O'Neill and Lopez, 1985). Elsewhere, the Uinta flank thrusts are almost certainly inherited from Precambrian features (Sears and others, 1982; Bruhn and others, 1983; Bryant and Nichols, this volume), and the ancestral Teton–Gros Ventre uplift is likewise suspected to have had an earlier history (Blackstone, 1963). It is reasonably certain, therefore, that reactivation of favorably oriented preexisting fault zones in the basement occurred at about the same time as deformation in the Cordilleran thrust belt.

The development of the overlap province may also be related to a major zone of regional delamination in the crystalline basement. Field studies, drilling data, seismic profiles, and gravity studies that have been made in the last decade consistently support interpretations of low-angle major thrust faults in the Rocky Mountain foreland. Although subsurface geometries may be explained by several models (Fig. 14), we believe the most plausible model closely resembles a low-angle thrust geometry in which a zone of decoupling exists at some level in the crystalline basement (Fig. 14d). As pointed out by Bally (1981) and Sibson (1983), low-angle thrust faulting that involves basement rocks indicates the existence of horizons of decoupling or delamination in the continental lithosphere: "It is concluded that decoupling within the lower crust and perhaps the upper mantle is essential to explain thrust faulting of continental basement slabs" (Bally, 1981, p. 25).

By analogy to décollement thrusting in layered rocks, the most commonly cited cause for decoupling at the base of crystalline thrust sheets is mechanical layering. This mechanical layering in the otherwise isotropic crystalline rocks is thought to be thermally controlled; that is, rocks below a certain depth behave in a sufficiently ductile manner because of elevated temperatures, and the cooler and more brittle rocks above them detach along the brittle-ductile transition zone. This is not a new suggestion for either the Rocky Mountain foreland or for other regions of the Cordillera. Armstrong and Dick (1974) and Lowell (1977) suggested that involvement of crystalline basement in thrust sheets in the hinterland of the thrust belt was the result of detachment along the boundary between the brittle lithosphere and its ductile infrastructure as a result of an elevated thermal gradient in retro-arc settings. Burchfiel and Davis (1975) speculated that basement shortening in the Rocky Mountain foreland in Late Cretaceous and early Tertiary time was related to a thermally controlled increase in crustal ductility beneath the region of basement uplifts. Bruhn and others (1983) proposed that the Uinta North Flank thrust was a major foreland fault ramp that soled into a detachment zone along the brittle-ductile transition zone at a depth of 15 to 20 km.

We propose that, if decoupling along the brittle-ductile transition is a valid concept, the boundaries of the overlap province can be defined on the basis of the superposition of decoupling at two crustal levels: a relatively shallow level, controlled by the anisotropy and ductility contrasts in the sedimentary section, and a deeper level controlled by the thermally dependent rheological contrast in otherwise mechanically isotropic basement. The extent of the overlap province therefore depends heavily on what the depth and dip of the brittle-ductile transition was at the onset of deformation. Although relatively little is known about the position of this zone in the crust, estimates have been made on the basis of (1) laboratory data on the frictional and rheological properties of various crustal rocks over a wide range of experimental conditions, and (2) mechanical analyses of rheological models broadly consistent with experimental data.

The passage from brittle behavior to ductile behavior (frictional to quasiplastic in the usage of Sibson, 1983, 1984) in quartzofeldspathic crustal rocks is determined principally by the mechanical response of quartz to shear stress as temperature increases (Sibson, 1983). Experimentally, quartz-rich rocks weaken and flow plastically at temperatures between 250° and 350°C (e.g., Brace, 1965; Brace and Kohlstedt, 1980; Tullis and Yund, 1977, 1980; Tullis and others, 1982; Turcotte and Schubert, 1982). Shear-resistance profiles based on experimental data gen-

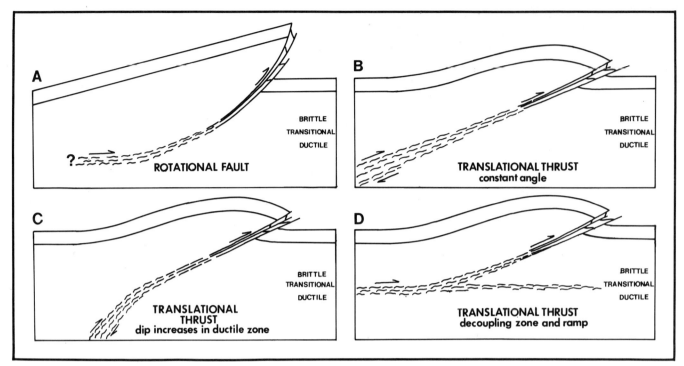

Figure 14. Possible subsurface geometries of thrusts in basement rocks of the foreland and overlap province.

erally show a relatively sharp transition from purely frictional behavior in the brittle field to quasiplastic behavior in the ductile field (Fig. 15; Sibson, 1983). Estimates of the depth of this transition in the crust depend on geothermal gradient and, for strain rates on the order of 10^{-14}/sec, range from 5 km for 40°C/km to 20 km for 10°C/km (Sibson, 1983). N. H. Carter and M. C. Tsenn (unpublished manuscript, 1986) have suggested that two mechanically weak zones of potential decoupling exist within the crust: the shallower between 8 and 18 km where a quartz rheology dominates, and the other at 25 to 35 km where a feldspar/pyroxene rheology dominates. Although the geothermal gradient in the overlap province during the time of thrust belt/foreland deformation is not known, it is assumed that gradients were somewhat higher than in the Rocky Mountain foreland, in part because of proximity to large Cretaceous plutons such as the Idaho and Boulder batholiths (Fig. 7). If this is true, the brittle-ductile transition would have dipped eastward toward the foreland and shallowed westerly under the thrust belt, where it eventually emerged from the basement and transected the sedimentary section in the miogeoclinal prism. Ductile behavior of rocks in the miogeoclinal prism is common in its western region. However, because of the anisotropic layered sequence here, it is inappropriate to assume a single simple surface as the brittle-ductile transition.

A different approach to determination of the depth of the brittle-ductile transition in the Rocky Mountain foreland was taken by Fletcher (1984). He reasoned that regional first-order uplifts in the basement rocks of the foreland could be treated as folds or arches of long wavelength for which the wavelength was governed by the thickness of the brittle layer. Following an earlier analysis of a two-layer case under extension (Fletcher and Hallet, 1983), the brittle layer (above the brittle-ductile transition) was modeled as a power-law fluid with a very large exponent, and the underlying ductile layer was modeled as a power-law fluid with a small exponent. Results obtained from an analysis of shortening of the model crust suggested that the ratio of spacing (dominant

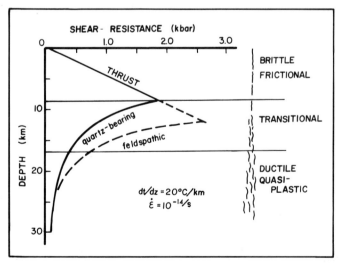

Figure 15. Shear resistance profile for a quartz-bearing rock (Westerly Granite) flow law, a strain rate of 10^{-14}/sec, and a linear geotherm of 25°C/km, modified from Sibson (1983, 1984).

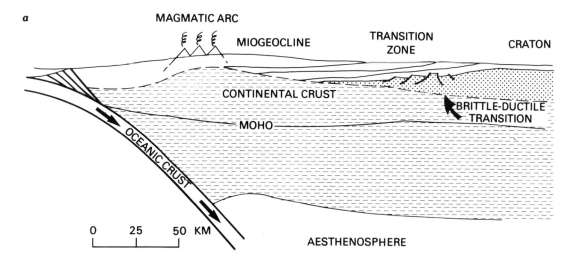

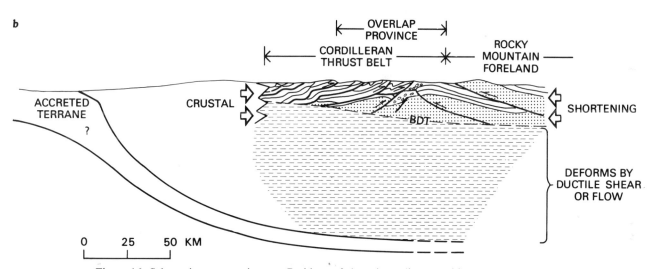

Figure 16. Schematic cross sections. *a*, Positions of the miogeocline, transition zone, craton, and brittle-ductile transition zone prior to compressional deformation. *b*, Relationships of deformational structures in the Cordilleran thrust belt, Rocky Mountain foreland, and the overlap province. Arrows indicate crustal shortening. Crust below brittle-ductile transition deforms by ductile shear and flow.

wave length) to thickness of the brittle layer was in the range of 4 to 6. By this analysis, the range of depths to the brittle-ductile transition, which permits folding of the brittle layer, may be determined by measuring the spacing of the dominant foreland uplifts. Application of this approach to the foreland arches in Montana and Wyoming indicates that the depth to the brittle-ductile transition rises westward toward the overlap province because the spacing of uplifts is progressively shorter in that direction (Schmidt and others, 1985). The mean spacing of foreland uplifts in the Montana portion of the overlap province is 45 km, corresponding to a shallow depth (7 to 11 km) of the brittle-ductile transition. This shallow depth may be related to an elevated heat flow resulting from syntectonic igneous activity in this part of the overlap province. In Wyoming, the spacing of foreland uplifts also decreases westward toward the overlap province, but

the shortest spacing (between the Wind River and Moxa structures) is 100 km, which corresponds to a depth of 17 to 25 km to the brittle-ductile transition. Although no uplifts are known west of the Moxa arch, the brittle-ductile transition possibly continued to shallow and, farther west, intersected the miogeoclinal prism.

The line of intersection of the presumed eastward-dipping brittle-ductile transition and the westward-dipping upper basement surface largely controlled the preshortening western boundary of the overlap zone. West of that boundary, faulting initiated at the brittle-ductile transition was within the miogeoclinal sedimentary wedge. In Montana, seismic profiles show that basement-involved, foreland-style reverse faults exist at least 20 km west of the leading edge of the thrust belt (Lopez and Schmidt, 1985), where the depth to basement is presently about 5 km. Basement blocks in thrust sheets with several tens of kilometers of eastward translation are found at least 40 km west of the leading edge of the thrust belt (Scholten, 1983). Presumably, the line of intersection of the brittle-ductile transition and the basement-cover contact was somewhat west of the original palinspastic position of these blocks.

Craddock (1986) estimated that for the Wyoming salient, the temperature along the basal detachment for the western thrust sheets (Paris, Meade, Crawford, and Absaroka) was in excess of 300°C, and therefore the basement below these sheets probably underwent ductile flow (Craddock, 1986). This may explain why no foreland structures like the Moxa arch have been found beneath the Absaroka and the more westerly thrust sheets in the Wyoming salient, as predicted by Hamilton (1978). It also suggests a very narrow overlap province in the region and a particularly steep eastward dip of the brittle-ductile transition (7° to 10°). Minimum depth to the brittle-ductile transition below the Moxa arch was estimated by Schmidt and others (1985) to be about 17 km, based on arch spacing and the analytic model of Fletcher (1984). This is compatible with a geothermal gradient of about 18°C/km, which is somewhat lower than the value of 25°C/km assumed by Craddock (1986).

We suggest that Mesozoic and early Cenozoic compression caused decoupling at a brittle-ductile transition zone that initiated deformation in both the thrust belt and the foreland. In the hinterland of the thrust belt, in rocks of the miogeoclinal wedge, the faults were initiated by brittle-ductile decoupling, and as they propagated eastward to northeastward and upward, deformation was taken up by decoupling between competent and incompetent sedimentary units in the upper and frontal parts of the thrust belt. Brittle-ductile decoupling remained an active deformation mechanism at depth across the boundary between the miogeocline and the crystalline craton beneath the frontal part of the thrust belt resulting in reactivation of basement structures in the foreland and in superposed structures in the overlap province (Fig. 16). Thus, the overlap province is defined by deformation at two crustal levels with interaction of structures within the brittle crust.

CONCLUSIONS

A unique structural province—the overlap province—occurs across the area of transition from the North American craton to the Cordilleran miogeocline, from the central Montana (Helena) salient into southwestern Montana, and along the Idaho-Wyoming-Utah segment of the thrust belt and adjacent foreland. In the overlap province, structures of the Cordilleran thrust belt and those of the Rocky Mountain foreland overlap in space and time, are similar in deformational style, and interact in identifiable and predictable ways.

The Cordilleran thrust belt and Rocky Mountain foreland, along with the overlap province, should be considered as an entity and united by several elements: (1) deformation exists through the entire brittle crust, whether that crust was formed predominantly of sedimentary rocks of the miogeoclinal wedge in the thrust belt, predominantly of crystalline rocks of the craton in the foreland, or of a combination of both types across the miogeocline-shelf-craton transition in the overlap province where deformation took place at two crustal levels; (2) deformation took place on low-angle major thrust faults, which are initiated in a brittle-ductile transition zone that spans the miogeocline-craton boundary, and propagated through the brittle crust along lithologic mechanical boundaries between units of varying ductility; (3) deformation occurred intermittently from the Cretaceous to the Eocene within a dominantly compressive stress regime; and (4) many individual structures were reactivated, and those of the thrust belt and those of the foreland in some places alternated in the overlap province.

The interpretation of a stress regime that can accommodate concurrent, episodic, and alternating deformation in the Cordilleran thrust belt, the Rocky Mountain foreland, and the interactive overlap province between them suggests a model of orogenesis in which fundamental compressional stresses responsible for early thrust-belt deformation continued during the breakup of the foreland.

Resolution of the structural interrelationships of the Cordilleran thrust belt and Rocky Mountain foreland, recognition and characterization of the overlap province between them, and interpretation of the factors that controlled the location of the overlap may have application in other orogenic belts; for example, the Precordillera/Sierras Pampeanas belt of Argentina (Fielding and Jordan, this volume).

ACKNOWLEDGMENTS

We acknowledge particularly Jim Evans, Ray Fletcher, Bill Perry, Betty Skipp, Dave Wiltschko, and Nick Woodward for stimulating discussions of the ideas presented in this chapter. We also thank Warren Hamilton, Tom Hildenbrand, Dave Love, Bill Perry, William A. Thomas, and Lee A. Woodward for critical and constructive reviews of the manuscript. Freddy Thorsten and Nancy Arnold typed numerous drafts for which we are grateful.

REFERENCES CITED

Armstrong, F. C., and Oriel, S. S., 1965, Tectonic development of Idaho-Wyoming thrust belt: American Association of Petroleum Geologists Bulletin, v. 49, no. 11, p. 1847–1866.

Armstrong, R. L., 1968, Sevier orogenic belt in Nevada and Utah: Geological Society of America Bulletin, v. 79, p. 429–458.

Armstrong, R. L., and Dick, H.J.B., 1974, A model for the development of thin overthrust sheets of crystalline rock: Geology, v. 2, p. 35–40.

Baken, J. F., 1981, Structural geology and tectonic history of the northern Flint Creek Range, west-central Montana, *in* Tucker, T. E., ed., Southwest Montana: Montana Geological Society 1981 Field Conference Guidebook, p. 161–166.

Bally, A. W., 1981, Thoughts on the tectonics of folded belts, *in* McClay, K. R., and Price, N. J., eds., Thrust and nappe tectonics: Oxford, Blackwell Scientific Publications, p. 13–32.

Berg, R. R., 1962, Mountain flank thrusting in Rocky Mountain foreland, Wyoming and Colorado: American Association of Petroleum Geologists Bulletin, v. 46, p. 2019–2032.

Beutner, E. C., 1977, Causes and consequences of curvature in the Sevier orogenic belt, Utah to Montana: Wyoming Geological Association 29th Annual Field Conference Guidebook, p. 353–365.

Blackstone, D. L., Jr., 1963, Development of geologic structure in central Rocky Mountains: American Association of Petroleum Geologists Memoir 2, p. 160–179.

——, 1977, The overthrust belt salient of the Cordilleran fold belt western Wyoming–southeastern Idaho–northeastern Utah, *in* Rocky Mountain thrust belt geology and resources: Wyoming Geological Association 29th Annual Field Conference Guidebook, p. 367–384.

——, 1979, Geometry of the Prospect-Darby and La Barge faults at their junction with the La Barge Platform, Lincoln and Sublette Counties, Wyoming: Geological Survey of Wyoming Report of Investigations, p. 18–34.

Boyer, S. E., and Elliott, D., 1982, Thrust systems: American Association of Petroleum Geologists Bulletin, v. 66, p. 1196–1230.

Brace, W. F., 1965, Some new measurements of linear compressibility of rocks: Journal of Geophysical Research, v. 70, p. 391–398.

Brace, W. F., and Kohlstedt, D. L., 1980, Limits of lithospheric stress imposed by experiments: Journal of Geophysical Research, v. 85, p. 6248–6252.

Bradley, M. D., 1986, Thrust splay correlation in the Absaroka thrust system of north central Utah: Geological Society of America Abstracts with Programs, v. 18, p. 343.

Brandon, W. C., 1984, An origin for the McCartney's Mountain salient of the southwestern Montana fold and thrust belt [M.S. thesis]: Missoula, University of Montana, 128 p.

Bregman, M. L., 1976, Change in tectonic style along the Montana thrust belt: Geology, v. 4, p. 775–778.

Brown, W. G., 1983, Sequential development of the fold-thrust model of foreland deformation, *in* Lowell, D., and Gries, R., eds., Rocky Mountain foreland basins and uplifts: Denver, Colorado, Rocky Mountain Association of Geologists, p. 57–64.

——, 1984, A reverse fault interpretation of Rattlesnake Mountain anticline, Big Horn Basin, Wyoming: Mountain Geologist, v. 21, p. 31–36.

Bruhn, R. L., Picard, M. D., and Beck, S. L., 1983, Mesozoic and early Tertiary structure and sedimentology of the central Wasatch Mountains, Uinta Mountains, and Uinta Basin: Utah Geological and Mineral Survey Special Studies 59, p. 63–105.

Brumbaugh, D. S., and Hendrix, T. E., 1981, The McCarthy Mountain structural salient, southwestern Montana, *in* Tucker, T. E., ed., Southwest Montana: Montana Geological Society 1981 Field Conference Guidebook, p. 201–209.

Burchfiel, B. C., and Davis, G. A., 1975, Nature and controls of Cordilleran orogenesis, western United States; Extensions of an earlier synthesis: American Journal of Science, v. 275-A, p. 363–396.

Charlesworth, H.A.K., and Gagnon, L. G., 1985, Intercutaneous wedges, the triangle zone, and structural thickening of the Mynheer coal seam at Coal Valley in the Rocky Mountain foothills of central Alberta: Bulletin of Canadian Petroleum Geology, v. 33, p. 22–30.

Chester, J. S., Spang, J. H., and Logan, J. M., 1986, Comparison of thrust fault rock models to Wyoming foreland structure: Geological Society of America Abstracts with Programs, v. 18, p. 346.

Coney, P. J., 1978, Mesozoic-Cenozoic Cordilleran plate tectonics, *in* Smith, R. B., and Eaton, G. P., eds., Cenozoic tectonics and regional geophysics of the western Cordillera: Geological Society of America Memoir 152, p. 33–50.

Cook, D. G., 1983, The northern Franklin Mountains, Northwest Territories, Canada; A scale model of the Wyoming province, *in* Lowell, J. D., and Gries, R., eds., Rocky Mountain foreland basins and uplifts: Denver, Colorado, Rocky Mountain Association of Geologists, p. 315–338.

Corbett, M. K., 1983, Superposed tectonism northern Idaho-Wyoming thrust belt, *in* Powers, R. B., ed., Geologic studies of the Cordilleran thrust belt-1982: Denver, Colorado, Rocky Mountain Association of Geologists, v. 1, p. 341–356.

Coryell, J. J., 1983, Structural geology of the Heeneberry Ridge area, Beaverhead County, Montana [M.S. thesis]: College Station, Texas A&M University, 108 p.

Craddock, J. P., 1986, Possible thermal controls on thin and thick-skinned faulting, overthrust region, Idaho and Wyoming: Geological Society of America Abstracts with Programs, v. 18, p. 349.

Crittenden, M. D., Jr., 1969, Interaction between Sevier orogenic belt and Uinta structures near Salt Lake City Utah: Geological Society of America Abstracts with Programs, v. 1, p. 18.

——, 1976, Stratigraphic and structural setting of the Cottonwood area, Utah, *in* Hill, J. G., ed., Symposium on geology of the Cordilleran hingeline: Denver, Colorado, Rocky Mountain Association of Geologists, p. 363–379.

——, 1974, Regional extent and age of thrusts near Rockport Reservoir and relation to possible exploration targets in northern Utah: American Association of Petroleum Geologists Bulletin, v. 58, no. 12, p. 435–442.

Dahlstrom, C.D.A., 1969, Balanced cross sections: Canadian Journal of Earth Sciences, v. 6, p. 743–757.

——, 1970, Structural geology in the eastern margin of the Canadian Rocky Mountains: Bulletin of Canadian Petroleum Geology, v. 18, p. 332–406.

Davis, L., 1983, Geology of the Dog Valley–Red Ridge area, southern Pavant Mountains, Millard County, Utah: Geological Society of America Abstracts with Programs, v. 15, p. 379.

Dickinson, W. R., and Snyder, W. S., 1978, Plate tectonics of the Laramide folding associated with basement block faulting in the western United States: Geological Society of America Memoir 151, p. 355–366.

Dimitre-Dunn, S. L., 1983, Timing of foreland and thrust-belt deformation in an overlap area, Teton Pass, Idaho and Wyoming, *in* Lowell, J. D., and Gries, R., eds., Rocky Mountain foreland basins and uplifts: Denver, Colorado, Rocky Mountain Association of Geologists, p. 263–269.

Dixon, J. S., 1982, Regional structural synthesis, Wyoming structural salient of western overthrust belt: American Association of Petroleum Geologists Bulletin, v. 66, p. 1560–1580.

Dorr, J. A., Jr., Spearing, D. R., and Steidtmann, J. R., 1977, Deformation and deposition between a foreland uplift and an impinging thrust belt, Hoback Basin, Wyoming: Geological Society of America Special Paper 177, 82 p.

Dubois, D. P., 1983, Tectonic framework of basement thrust terrane, northern Tendoy Range, southwest Montana, *in* Powers, R. B., ed., Geologic studies of the Cordilleran thrust belt, 1982; Denver, Colorado, Rocky Mountain Association of Geologists, v. 1, p. 145–158.

Dyman, T. S., 1986, Mid-Cretaceous sedimentation and tectonism in the southwest Montana foreland basin: Geological society of America Abstracts with Programs, v. 18, p. 353.

Eldridge, S., and Van der Voo, R., 1985, Paleomagnetic study of thrust-sheet rotations in the Helena salient southwest Montana: Geological Society of America Abstracts with Programs, v. 17, p. 573.

Erslev, E. A., 1985, Balanced cross sections of small fold-thrust structures; Comment: Mountain Geologist, v. 22, p. 91–93.

Fletcher, R. C., 1984, Instability of lithosphere undergoing shortening; A model for Laramide foreland structures: Geological Society of America Abstracts with Programs, v. 16, p. 83.

Fletcher, R. C., and Hallet, B., 1983, Unstable extension of the lithosphere; A mechanical model for Basin-and-Range structure: Journal of Geophysical Research, v. 88, p. 7457–7466.

Garihan, J. M., Schmidt, C. J., Young, S. W., and Williams, M. A., 1983, Recurrent movement history of the Bismark–Spanish Peaks–Gardiner fault system, southwest Montana, in Lowell, J. D., and Gries, R., eds., Rocky Mountain foreland basins and uplifts: Denver, Colorado, Rocky Mountain Association of Geologists, p. 295–314.

Godlewski, D. W., and Zieg, G. A., 1984, Stratigraphy and depositinal setting of the Precambrian Newland Limestone, in Hobbs, S. W., ed., The Belt: Montana Bureau of Mines and Geology Special Publication 90, p. 2–4.

Gries, R. R., 1981, Oil and gas prospecting beneath the Precambrian of foreland thrust plates in the Rocky Mountains: Mountain Geologist, v. 18, no. 1, p. 1–18.

——, 1983a, Oil and gas prospecting beneath the Precambrian of foreland thrust plates in the Rocky Mountains: American Association of Petroleum Geologists Bulletin, v. 67, p. 1–26.

——, 1983b, North-south compression of Rocky Mountain foreland structures, in Lowell, J. D., and Gries, R., eds., Rocky Mountain foreland basins and uplifts: Denver, Colorado, Rocky Mountain Association of Geologists, p. 9–32.

Grubbs, K. L., and Van der Voo, R., 1976, Structural deformation of the Idaho-Wyoming overthrust belt (U.S.A.), as determined by Triassic paleomagnetism: Tectonophysics, v. 33, p. 321–336.

Gwinn, V. E., 1961, Geology of the Drummond area central-western Montana: Montana Bureau of Mines and Geology Map GM4, 1 section with descriptive text, Special Publication 21, p. 17.

Hamilton, W., 1978, Mesozoic tectonics of the western United States, in Howell, D. G., and McDougall, K. A., eds., Mesozoic paleogeography of the western United States: Pacific Section, Society of Economic Paleontologists and Mineralogists, Pacific Coast Paleogeography Symposium 2, p. 33–70.

——, 1981, Plate-tectonics mechanisms of Laramide deformating, in Boyd, D. W., and Lillegraven, J. A., eds., Rocky Mountain foreland basement tectonics: University of Wyoming Contributions to Geology, v. 19, p. 87–92.

Harris, H. D., 1959, A late Mesozoic positive area in western Utah-Nevada: American Association of Petroleum Geologists Bulletin, v. 43, p. 2636–2652.

Harris, S. A., 1957, The tectonics of Montana as related to the Belt Series: Billings Geological Society 8th Annual Field Conference Guidebook, p. 22–23.

Harrison, J. E., Griggs, A. B., and Wells, J. D., 1974, Tectonic features of the Precambrian Belt basin and their influence on post-Belt structures: U.S. Geological Survey Professional Paper 866, 15 p.

Hatcher, R. D., and Williams, R. T., 1986, Mechanical models for single thrust sheets and their relationships to the mechanical behavior of orogenic belts: Geological Society of America Bulletin, v. 97, p. 975–985.

Heim, A., 1919, Geologie der Schweiz, v. 1: Leipzig, 704 p.

Heller, P. L., Bowdler, S. S., Chambers, H. P., Coogan, J. C., Hagen, E. S., Shuster, M. W., Winslow, N. S., and Lawton, T. F., 1986, Time of initial thrusting in the Sevier orogenic belt, Idaho-Wyoming and Utah: Geology, v. 14, p. 388–391.

Hill, J. G., 1976, Editors introduction, in Hill, J. G., ed., Geology of the Cordilleran hingeline: Denver, Colorado, Rocky Mountain Association of Geologists, p. 6.

Horberg, L., Nelson, V., and Church, V., 1949, Structural trends in central western Wyoming: Geological Society of America Bulletin, v. 60, p. 183–216.

Hunter, R. B., 1986, Structural and timing relations between the Prospect thrust system, the antithetic Game Hill thrust, and the Gros Ventre foreland uplift: Geological Society of America Abstracts with Programs, v. 18, p. 363.

Hurich, C. A., and Smithson, S. B., 1982, Gravity interpretation of the southern

Wind River Mountains, Wyoming: Geophysics, v. 47, no. 11, p. 1550–1561.

Jacobsen, F., Jr., and Kanes, W. H., 1974, Structure of the Broadtop synclinorium and its implications for Appalachian structural style: American Association of Petroleum Geologist Bulletin, v. 58, p. 362–375.

——, 1975, Structure of the Broadtop synclinorium, Wills Mountain anticlinorium, and Allegheny frontal zone: American Association of Petroleum Geologists Bulletin, v. 59, p. 1136–1150.

Jones, P. B., 1983, Oil and gas beneath east dipping underthrust faults, Alberta Foothills, in Powers, R. B., ed., Geological studies of the Cordilleran thrust belt, 1982: Denver, Colorado, Rocky Mountain Association of Geologists, p. 61–74.

Keefer, W. R., and Love, J. D., 1963, Laramide vertical movements in central Wyoming: University of Wyoming Contributions to Geology, v. 2, no. 1, p. 47–54.

Kopania, A. A., 1983, Deformation consequences of the impingement of the foreland and northern thrust belt, eastern Idaho and western Wyoming: Geological Society of America Abstracts with Programs, v. 15, p. 296.

Kraig, D. H., Wiltschko, D. V., and Spang, J. H., 1986, Interaction of the northern segment of the Moxa arch with the western overthrust belt, southwestern Wyoming: Geological Society of America Abstracts with Programs, v. 18, p. 368.

Kulik, D. M., 1982, Illustrations of gravity models of the southeast limb of the Blacktail-Snowcrest uplift, southwest Montana: U.S. Geological Survey Open-File Report 82-823, 7 p.

——, 1984, A structural model for the overlap zone between the Rocky Mountain foreland and the Cordilleran thrust belt in southwestern Montana: Geological Society of America Abstracts with Programs, v. 16, p. 227.

Kulik, D. M., and Perry, W. J., Jr., 1982, Gravity modeling of the steep southeast limb of the Blacktail-Snowcrest uplift: Geological Society of America Abstracts with Programs, v. 14, p. 318.

Kulik, D. M., Perry, W. J., Jr., and Skipp, B., 1983, A model for Rocky Mountain foreland and overthrust belt development; Geophysical and geological evidence for spacial overlap: Geological Society of America Abstracts with Programs, v. 15, p. 318.

Lageson, D. R., Zim, J. C., and Kelly, M. C., 1984, Superimposed styles of deformation in the Bridger Range, southwestern Montana: Geological Society of America Abstracts with Programs, v. 16, p. 567.

Lamerson, P. R., 1983, The fossil basin and its relationship to the Absaroka thrust system, Wyoming and Utah, in Powers, R. B., ed., Geologic studies of the Cordilleran thrust belt, 1982; Denver, Colorado, Rocky Mountain Association of Geologists, p. 279–340.

Livesey, G. B., 1985, Laramide structures of the southeastern Sand Wash basin, in Gries, R. R., and Dyer, R. C., eds., Seismic exploration of the Rocky Mountain region: Denver, Colorado, Rocky Mountain Association of Geologists and Denver Geophysical Society, p. 87–94.

Lopez, D. A., and Schmidt, C. J., 1985, Seismic profile across the leading edge of the fold and thrust belt of southwest Montana, in Gries, R.R., and Dyer, R. C., eds., Seismic exploration of the Rocky Mountain region: Denver, Colorado, Rocky Mountain Association of Geologists and Denver Geophysical Society, p. 45–50.

Love, J. C., 1970, Cenozoic geology of the Granite Mountain area, central Wyoming: U.S. Geological Survey Professional Paper 495C, p. C1–C154.

——, 1973, Harebell Formation (Upper Cretaceous) and Pinyon Conglomerate (uppermost Cretaceous and Paleocene), northwestern Wyoming: U.S. Geological Survey Professional Paper 734-A, p. A1–A54.

——, 1977, Summary of Upper Cretaceous and Cenozoic stratigraphy and of tectonic and glacial events in Jackson Hole, northwestern Wyoming, in Rocky Mountain thrust belt geology and resources: Wyoming Geological Association Guidebook 29th Annual Field Conference, p. 585–593.

——, 1983, A possible gap in the western thrust belt in Idaho and Wyoming, in Powers, R. B., ed., Geological studies of the Cordilleran thrust belt, 1982: Denver, Colorado, Rocky Mountain Association of Geologists, v. 1, p. 247–259.

Lowell, J. D., 1977, Underthrusting origin for thrust-fold belts with applications to the Idaho-Wyoming belt: Wyoming Geological Association 19th Annual Field Conference Guidebook, p. 449–455.

—— , 1984, Plate tectonics and foreland basement deformation: Geology, v. 2, p. 275–278.

—— , 1983, Foreland deformation, *in* Lowell, J. D., ed., Rocky Mountain foreland basins and uplifts: Denver, Colorado, Rocky Mountain Association of Geologists, p. 1–18.

Mandl, G., and Shippam, G. K., 1981, Mechanical model of thrust sheet gliding and imbrication, *in* McClay, K. R., and Price, N. J., eds., Thrust and nappe tectonics: Oxford, Blackwell Scientific Publications, p. 79–98.

McGill, G. E., 1959, Geologic map of the northwestern flank of the Flint Creek Range, western Montana: Montana Bureau of Mines and Geology Map GM3, 1 section with descriptive text, Special Publication 18.

McMannis, W. J., 1963, LaHood Formation; A coarse facies of the Belt Series in southwest Montana: Geological Society of America Bulletin, v. 74, p. 407–436.

Misch, P., 1960, Regional structural reconnaissance in central northeast Nevada and some adjacent areas; Observations and interpretations, *in* Geology of east-central Nevada: Intermountain Association of Petroleum Geologists and Eastern Nevada Geological Society 11th Annual Field Conference Guidebook, p. 17–42.

Moore, D., Woodward, N. B., and Oriel, S. S., 1984, Geologic map of the Mt. Baird Quadrangle: U.S. Geological Survey Open-File Report 84-776, 12 p., scale 1:24,000.

Mutch, T. A., 1961, Geologic map of the northeast flank of the Flint Creek Range, western Montana: Montana Bureau of Mines and Geology Special Publication 22 (Geologic Map 5).

Nichols, D. J., Perry, W. J., Jr., and Haley, J. C., 1985, Reinterpretation of the palynology and age of Laramide syntectonic deposits, southwestern Montana, and revision of the Beaverhead Group: Geology, v. 13, p. 149–153.

O'Neill, J. M., and Lopez, D. A., 1985, Character and regional significance of Great Falls tectonic zone, east-central Idaho and west-central Montana: American Association of Petroleum Geologists Bulletin, v. 69, p. 437–447.

Oriel, S. S., and Moore, D.W., 1985, Geologic map of the West and East Palisades Roadless areas, Idaho and Wyoming: U.S. Geological Survey Miscellaneous Field Studies Map MF-1619B, scale 1:50,000.

Pecora, W. C., 1981, Bedrock geology of the Blacktail Mountains, southwestern Montana [M.A. thesis]: Middletown, Connecticut, Wesleyan University (also U.S. Geological Survey Open-File Report 81-999), 203 p.

Perry, W. J., Jr., and Hossack, J. R., 1984, Structure of the frontal zone, southwest Montana section of the Cordileran thrust belt: Geological Society of America Abstracts with Programs, v. 14, p. 318.

Perry, W. J., Jr., and Sando, W. J., 1983, Sequence of deformation of Cordilleran thrust belt in Lima, Montana, region, *in* Powers, R. B., ed., Geologic studies of the Cordilleran thrust belt, 1982: Denver, Colorado, Rocky Mountain Association of Geologists, v. 1, p. 137–144.

Perry, W. J., Jr., Ryder, R. T., and Moughan, E. K., 1981, The southern part of the southwest Montana thrust belt, *in* Tucker, T. E., ed., Southwest Montana: Montana Geological Society 1981 Field Conference Guidebook, p. 261–273.

Perry, W. J., Jr., Roeder, D. H., and Lageson, D. R., eds., 1984, North American thrust-faulted terranes: American Association of Petroleum Geologists Reprint Series 27.

Perry, W. J., Jr., Haley, J. C., and Nichols, D. J., 1986, Interactions of Rocky Mountain foreland and Cordilleran thrust belt in the Lima region, southwest Montana: Geological Society of America Abstracts with Programs, v. 18, p. 402.

Picha, F., 1986, The influence of preexisting tectonic trends on geometrics of the Sevier orogenic belt and its foreland in Utah, *in* Peterson, J. A., ed., Paleotectonics and sedimentation of the Rocky Mountain region: American Association of Petroleum Geologists Memoir 41, p. 309–320.

Picha, F., and Gibson, R. I., 1985, Cordilleran hingelines; Late Precambrian rifted margin of the North American craton and its impact on the depositional and structural history, Utah and Nevada: Geology, v. 13, p. 465–468.

Price, R. A., 1981, The Cordilleran foreland thrust and fold belt in the southern Canadian Rocky Mountains, *in* Thrust and nappe tectonics: Geological Society of London, p. 427–448.

Prucha, J. J., Graham, J. A., and Nickelsen, R. P., 1965, Basement controlled deformation in Wyoming province of Rocky Mountain foreland: American Association of Petroleum Geologists Bulletin, v. 49, p. 966–992.

Ray, R. R., and Berg, C. R., 1985, Seismic interpretation of the Casper arch thrust, Tepee Flats field, Wyoming, *in* Gries, R. R., and Dyer, R. C., eds., Seismic exploration of the Rocky Mountain region: Denver, Colorado, Rocky Mountain Association of Geologists and Denver Geophysical Society, p. 51–58.

Reid, R., 1957, Bedrock geology of the north end of the Tobacco Root Mountains, Madison County, Montana, Montana Bureau of Mines and Geology Memoir 36, 25 p.

Rich, J. L., 1934, Mechanics of low-angle overthrust faulting as illustrated by Cumberland thrust block, Virginia, Kentucky, and Tennessee: American Association of Petroleum Geologists Bulletin, v. 18, p. 1584–1596.

Robinson, G. D., 1963, Geology of the Three Forks Quadrangle, Montana: U.S. Geological Survey Professional Paepr 370, 143 p.

Rodgers, D. A., and Rizer, W. D., 1981, Deformation and secondary faulting near the leading edge of a thrust fault, *in* McClay, K. R., and Price, N. J., eds., Thrust and nappe tectonics: Oxford, Blackwell Scientific Publications, p. 65–77.

Royse, F., Jr., Warner, M. A., and Reese, D. L., 1975, Thrust belt structural geometry and related stratigraphic problems, Wyoming–Idaho–northern Utah, *in* Bolyard, D. W., ed., Symposium on deep drilling in the central Rocky Mountains: Denver, Colorado, Rocky Mountain Association of Geologists, p. 41–54.

Rubey, W. W., 1955, Early structural history of the overthrust belt of western Wyoming and adjacent states: Wyoming Geological Association Guidebook 10th Annual Field Conference, p. 125–126.

—— , 1973, Geologic map and structure sections of the Afton Quadrangle and part of the Big Piney Quadrangle, Lincoln and Sublette Counties, Wyoming: U.S. Geological Survey Miscellaneous Field Investigation Map I-686, 2 sheets, scale 1:62,500.

Rubey, W. W., and Hubbert, M. K., 1959, Role of fluid pressure in mechanics of overthrust faulting; II, Overthrust belt in geosynclinal area of western Wyoming in light of fluid-pressure hypothesis: Geological Society of America Bulletin, v. 70, p. 167–206.

Ruppel, E. T., 1978, Medicine Lodge thrust system, east-central Idaho and southwest Montana: U.S. Geological Survey Professional Paper 1031, 23 p.

Ruppel, E. T., and Lopez, D. A., 1984, The thrust belt in southwest Montana and east-central Idaho: U.S. Geological Survey Professional Paper 1278, 41 p.

Sales, J. K., 1968, Crustal mechanics of Cordilleran foreland deformation; A regional and scale-model approach: American Association of Petroleum Geologists Bulletin, v. 52, p. 2016–2044.

Schmidt, C. J., and Garihan, J. M., 1983, Laramide tectonic development of the Rocky Mountain foreland of southwestern Montana, *in* Lowell, J., and Greise, R., eds., Rocky Mountain foreland basins and uplifts: Denver, Colorado, Rocky Mountain Association of Geologists, p. 271–294.

—— , 1986, Middle Proterozoic and Laramide tectonic activity along the southern margin of the Belt Basin, *in* Roberts, S. M., ed., Belt supergroup; A guide to Proterozoic rocks of western Montana and adjacent areas: Montana Bureau of Mines and Geology Special Publication 94, p. 217–235.

Schmidt, C. J., and Geiger, B., 1985, Nature of deformation in foreland anticlines and impinging thrust belt; Tobacco Root and southern Highland Mountains, Montana: Tobacco Root Geological Society Guidebook of the 10th Annual Field Conference, p. 41–65.

Schmidt, C. J., and Hendrix, T. E., 1981, Tectonic controls for thrust belt and Rocky Mountain foreland structures in the northern Tobacco Root Mountains, Jefferson Canyon area, southwestern Montana, *in* Tucker, T. E., ed., Southwest Montana: Montana Geological Society 1981 Field Conference Guidebook, p. 167–180.

Schmidt, C. J., and O'Neill, J. M., 1983, Structural evolution of the southwest

Montana transverse zone, *in* Powers, R. B., ed., Geologic studies of the Cordilleran thrust belt—1982: Denver, Colorado, Rocky Mountain Association of Geologists, p. 193–218.

Schmidt, C. J., O'Neill, J. M., and Branden, W. C., 1984, Influence of foreland structures on the geometry and kinematics of the frontal fold and thrust belt, southwestern Montana: Geological Society of America Abstracts with Programs, v. 16, p. 647.

Schmidt, C. J., Evans, J. P., Fletcher, R. C., and Spang, J. H., 1985, Spacing the Rocky Mountain foreland arches and Laramide magmatic activity: Geological Society of America Abstracts with Programs, v. 17, p. 710.

Scholten, R., 1983, Continental subduction in the northern U.S. Rockies; A model for back-arc thrusting in the western Cordillera, *in* Powers, R. B., ed., Geologic studies of the Cordilleran thrust belt, 1982: Denver, Colorado, Rocky Mountain Association of Geologists, v. 1, p. 123–136.

Schroeder, M. L., 1973, Geologic map of the Clause Peak Quadrangle, Lincoln, Sublette, and Teton Counties, Wyoming: U.S. Geological Survey Map GQ-1092, scale 1:24,000.

Schwartz, R. K., 1983, Broken Early Cretaceous foreland basin in southwestern Montana: Sedimentation related to tectonism, *in* Powers, R. B., ed., Geologic studies of the Cordilleran thrust belt, 1982: Denver, Colorado, Rocky Mountain Association of Geologists, p. 159–183.

Schwartz, S. Y., and Van der Voo, R., 1984, Paleomagnetic study of thrust sheet rotation during foreland impingement in the Wyoming-Idaho overthrust belt: Journal of Geophysical Research, v. 89, p. 10077–10086.

Sears, J., 1983, A continental margin ramp in the Cordilleran thrust belt along the Montana lineament: Geological Society of America Abstracts with Programs, v. 15, p. 682.

——, 1984, The Uinta and Belt basins; Proterozoic rifts, Phanerozoic ramps: Geological Society of America Abstracts with Programs, v. 16, p. 254.

Sears, J. W., Graff, P. J., and Holden, G. S., 1982, Tectonic evolution of lower Proterozoic rocks, Uinta Mountains, Utah and Colorado: Geological Society of America Bulletin, v. 93, p. 990–997.

Sibson, R. H., 1983, Continental fault structure and the shallow earthquake source: Journal of the Geological Society of London, v. 140, p. 747–767.

——, 1984, Roughness at the base of the seismogenic zone; Contributing factors: Journal of Geophysical Research, v. 89, p. 5791–5799.

Skeen, R. C., and Ray, R. R., 1983, Seismic models and interpretations of the Casper arch thrust; Application to Rocky Mountain foreland structure, *in* Lowell, J. D., and Gries, R., eds., Rocky Mountain foreland basins and uplifts: Denver, Colorado, Rocky Mountain Association of Geologists, p. 99–124.

Skipp, B., 1986, Cordilleran thrust belt and faulted foreland in the Beaverhead Mountains, Idaho and Montana: Geological Society of America Abstracts with Programs, v. 18, p. 414.

Skipp, B., Hepp, M. M., and McGrew, L. W., 1968, Late Paleocene thin-skinned deformation of the western edge of the Crazy Mountains Basin, Montana: Geological Society of America Special Paper 115, Abstracts for 1967, p. 446–447.

Smedes, H. W., and Schmidt, C. J., 1979, Regional geologic setting of the Boulder batholith, Montana, *in* Suttner, L. J., ed., Guidebook for Penrose Conference—Granite II: p. 1–36.

Smithson, S. B., Brewer, J., Kaufman, S., Oliver, J., and Hurich, C. A., 1978, Nature of the Wind River thrust, Wyoming, from COCORP deep-reflection data and from gravity data: Geology, v. 6, p. 648–652.

——, 1979, Structure of Laramide Wind River uplift, Wyoming, from COCORP deep-reflection data and gravity data: Journal of Geophysical Research, v. 84, p. 5955–5972.

Spang, J. H., Evans, J. P., and Berg, R. R., 1985, Balanced cross sections of small fold-thrust structures: Mountain Geologist, v. 22, p. 41–46.

Stearns, D. W., 1971, Mechanisms of drape folding in the Wyoming Province, *in* Symposium on Wyoming tectonics and their economic significance: Wyoming Geological Association 23rd Annual Field Conference Guidebook, p. 125–143.

Stewart, J. H., 1972, Initial deposits in the Cordilleran geosyncline; Evidence of a Late Precambrian (<850 m.y.) continental separation: Geological Society of America Bulletin, v. 83, p. 1345–1360.

Stokes, W. L., 1976, What is the Wasatch Line?, *in* Hill, J. G., ed., Geology of the Cordilleran hingeline: Denver, Colorado, Rocky Mountain Association of Geologists, p. 11–25.

Stone, D. S., 1984a, The Rattlesnake Mountain, Wyoming, debate; A review and critique of models: Mountain Geologist, v. 21, p. 37–46.

——, 1984b, Structure along the Arlington fault zone, Pass Creek area, southern Hanna basin, Wyoming: Mountain Geologist, v. 21, p. 77–84.

——, 1985a, Geologic interpretation of seismic profiles, Big Horn basin, Wyoming; Part I, East flank, *in* Gries, R. R., and Dyer, R. C., eds., Seismic exploration of the Rocky Mountain region: Denver, Colorado, Rocky Mountain Association of Geologists and Denver Geophysical Society, p. 165–174.

——, 1985b, Geologic interpretation of seismic profiles, Big Horn basin, Wyoming; Part II, West flank, *in* Gries, R. R., and Dyer, R. C., eds., Seismic exploration of the Rocky Mountain region: Denver, Colorado, Rocky Mountain Association of Geologists and Denver Geophysical Society, p. 175–186.

Thom, W. T., Jr., 1957, Tectonic relationships, evolutionary history, and mechanics of origin of the Crazy Mountain basin, Montana: Billings Geological Society 8th Annual Field Conference Guidebook, p. 9–21.

Thomas, W. A., 1977, Evolution of Appalachian-Ouachita salients and recesses from reentrants and promontories in the continental margin: American Journal of Science, v. 277, p. 1233–1278.

——, 1983, Continental margins, orogenic belts, and intracratonic structures: Geology, v. 11, p. 270–272.

——, 1986, A Paleozoic synsedimentary structure in the Appalachian fold-thrust belt in Alabama, *in* McDowell, R. C., and Glover, L., eds., The Lowry Volume; Studies in Appalachian geology: Virginia Polytechnic Institute and State University Department of Geological Sciences Memoir 3, p. 1–12.

Tullis, J., and Yund, R. A., 1977, Experimental deformation of dry Westerly Granite: Journal of Geophysical Research, v. 82, p. 5705–5718.

——, 1980, Hydrolytic weakening of experimentally deformed Westerly Granite and Hale Albite rock: Journal of Structural Geology, v. 2, p. 439–451.

Tullis, J., Snoke, A. W., and Todd, V. R., 1982, Significance and petrogenesis of mylonitic rock (Penrose Conference Report): Geology, v. 10, p. 227–230.

Turcotte, D. L., and Schubert, G., 1982, Geodynamics; Applications of continuum physics to geological problems: New York, John Wiley & Sons, 450 p.

Tysdal, R. G., Marvin, R. F., and DeWitt, E., 1986, Late Cretaceous stratigraphy, deformation, and intrusion in the Madison Range of southwestern Montana: Geological Society of America Bulletin, v. 97, p. 859–868.

Wiltschko, D. V., and Dorr, J. A., Jr., 1983, Timing of deformation in overthrust belt and foreland of Idaho, Wyoming, and Utah: American Association of Petroleum Geologists Bulletin, v. 67, p. 1304–1322.

Wiltschko, D. V., and Eastman, D., 1983, Role of basement warps and faults in localizing thrust fault ramps, *in* Hatcher, R. D., Jr., Williams, H., and Zietz, I., Contributions to the tectonics and geophysics of mountain chains: Geological Society of America Memoir 158, p. 177–190.

——, 1986, Comparison of the mechanical role of basement normal and reverse faults in localizing deformation in the overlying cover rocks: Geological Society of America Abstracts with Programs, v. 18, p. 423.

Winston, D., 1986, Sedimentation and tectonics of the Middle Proterozoic Belt basin and their influence on Phanerozoic compression and extension in western Montana and northern Idaho, *in* Peterson, J. A., ed., Paleotectonics and sedimentation in the Rocky Mountain region: American Association of Petroleum Geologists Memoir 41, p. 87–118.

Woodward, L. A., 1981, Tectonic framework of Disturbed Belt of west-central Montana: American Association of Petroleum Geologists Bulletin, v. 65, no. 2, p. 291–302.

Woodward, N. B., 1986, Thrust geometry of the Snake River Range, Idaho and Wyoming: Geological Society of America Bulletin, v. 97, p. 178–193.

Zieg, G. A., 1981, Stratigraphy, sedimentology, and diagenesis of the Precambrian upper Newland Limestone, central Montana [M.S. thesis]: Missoula, University of Montana, 182 p.

Manuscript Accepted by the Society February 9, 1988

Geological Society of America
Memoir 171
1988

"Thrust belt" structures with "foreland" influence; The interaction of tectonic styles

Gary D. Couples*
Amoco Production Co., P.O. Box 800, Denver, Colorado 80201
Helen Lewis
Consulting Geologist, 7456 Empire Road, Boulder, Colorado 80303

ABSTRACT

The Rocky Mountain foreland and adjacent thrust belt have long been considered as separate tectonic entities, with primary consideration of interaction limited to a narrow frontal zone. Basement in the thrust belt has usually been interpreted as a passive floor, but we question that view. Models are presented in which cover folds, caused by basement faulting, initiate thrust ramp development, and where basement faulting causes folding of preexisting thrust sheets. The structures so created would generally be interpreted as purely thrust features, given the usual exposure or subsurface penetration. Typically, the transported hanging-wall geometry is identical in the two modes of formation. The models illustrate how basement faulting can participate in the development of geometries typical of thrust belts, and that a number of classical thrust-belt geometries could have a foreland element in their genesis. The models are geometric, but they incorporate the concept of mechanical stratigraphy and are illustrated by means of schematic cross sections and maps.

INTRODUCTION

The Rocky Mountain foreland and the thrust belt of western Wyoming have been investigated separately for decades, with each area generally being treated as a distinct tectonic province having a definite style (e.g., thrust belt: Royse and others, 1975; foreland: Prucha and others, 1965). Consideration of interaction, or overlap, of the provinces is relatively recent. In southwestern Montana, Schmidt and co-workers have discussed spatial and temporal overlap of these two provinces (i.e., the thrust belt sensu largo) for several years (Schmidt and Hendrix, 1981; Schmidt and O'Neill, 1982). Others have discussed impingement of the Wyoming thrust belt against the Teton-Targhee and Uinta promontories (Dimitre-Dunn, 1983; Beutner, 1977). Still more recently, the frontal portions of the Wyoming thrust belt have been interpreted to show the effect of the subjacent Moxa-LaBarge Uplift (Kraig and others, this volume), and that of other structures (Fahy, 1987).

These interpretations refer to interaction occurring in a rather narrow thrust-belt leading edge. We have derived from these and other published works the concept that thrust belt/foreland interaction consists primarily of a buttress effect, or at least an impediment to the continued motion of advancing thrust sheets. The mechanical analyses of interaction of which we are aware (e.g., Wiltschko and Eastman, 1983; this volume) are closely aligned with the buttress concept, although they were designed to evaluate stress concentrations that might localize ramps.

Most interpretations of structural development *within* the thrust belt have excluded foreland-type structures (i.e., those with basement involvement), and have considered basement rocks within the thrust belt to be allochthonous slices. In a broader sense, a primary premise in thrust-belt geology in western North America has been that the basement constitutes a gently dipping, undeformed planar floor beneath the allochthonous sheets (e.g., Dixon, 1982). Consequently, thrust-belt structures are perceived as initiating and developing in a realm of planar strata.

We question the paradigm that holds that basement is not involved in thrust-belt structures. Specifically, we address possibilities for structural development if "foreland" structures were

---

*Present address: Consulting Geologist, 7456 Empire Road, Boulder, Colorado 80303.

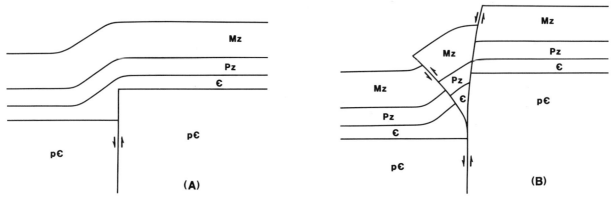

Figure 1. (A), Simple schematic basement uplift with forced fold modeled on the Rocky Mountain Foreland. pЄ = Precambrian basement (statistically isotropic, homogeneous, and continuous; see Stearns, 1971); Є = Cambrian sequence (mostly shales); Pz = Paleozoic carbonates; Mz = Mesozoic sequence (dominantly clastics, with significant shale intervals). (B), Faulting breaks through previously continuous folded layers at high magnitude of uplift. Note that there are no rotational motions. Such rotations are the normal case in the foreland, and they lead to discrete anticlines as opposed to monoclines. We eliminate rotation of blocks in the remaining illustrations for comparison purposes. Symbols same in remaining figures. Scale is general; Pz is ±1,000 m thick.

also present in a thrust belt, and challenge the view that the two structural styles are spatially distinct (see also Kulik and Schmidt, this volume). We approach the prediction of geometries by incorporating a consideration of the mechanical stratigraphy; both provinces have a similar stratigraphic succession, and so are expected to exhibit a similar response to deformation (with comparable slip surfaces defining mechanical units having similar strengths and stiffnesses). By setting up scenarios for the sequences of structural growth, we predict several results of the interaction.

This chapter does not advocate that all thrust-belt features have a foreland genesis. Rather it suggests that it is geometrically and mechanically possible for foreland deformation to cause *some* thrust-belt features. The Rocky Mountain foreland and the western Wyoming thrust belt serve as settings for our models; however, the principles and concepts are thought to be applicable to other thrust belts. Because models, and not field examples, are the subject matter of the chapter, no attempt is made to quantify the frequency of either mode of genesis.

BACKGROUND MATERIAL

Foreland model

Deformation within the Rocky Mountain foreland is characterized by a major vertical component (with some horizontal translation), where uplifted crystalline basement underlies uplifted and folded sediments. The degree of horizontal translation involved is a subject of debate (as summarized by Couples and Lageson, 1985; also Brown, this volume). In this chapter we emphasize the interplay of vertical and horizontal motions. Partly for that reason, but primarily because we feel it is most applica-

ble, we use a simple foreland geometry, as described by Stearns (1971), in which magnitude of uplift is significantly greater than the horizontal shortening of the basement (Fig. 1A). (The other end-member interpretation, where horizontal shortening exceeds vertical uplift, is outlined by Brown, this volume; it is also discussed by numerous other authors referenced therein.) Although the final geometry certainly differs depending on the basement fault angle, there is a noticeable commonality to structural configuration of both high-angle and low-angle models. Thus, much of our work is equally applicable in cases with low-angle basement faults.

In the Rocky Mountain region, we consider the crystalline Precambrian basement to be translated and rotated by faulting but internally almost unstrained. Above the basement, weak (flowable) Cambrian shales are overlain by a package of strong (stiff) strata, the Paleozoic carbonates. Above, the interlayered Mesozoic clastics are of intermediate strength and stiffness (Stearns, 1978; Stearns and Weinberg, 1975). This three-layer division of the layered rocks is the first-order mechanical stratigraphy (Couples, 1986), discussed more fully below.

One interpretation of foreland geometries is that uplift and rotation of faulted Precambrian basement blocks leads to forced folding of the overlying layered rocks (Stearns, 1978). For many of the foreland structures, the carbonate package is interpreted to have detached from the basement during folding and displaced (laterally translated) into the fold as a component of the necessary balancing (Stearns, 1971, 1978). For this stratigraphic package, fewer than 1,700 m of basement-fault displacement generally produces a continuous (unfaulted) fold in the Paleozoic carbonates (Couples, 1986; Fig. 1A). If uplift exceeds 1,700 m, faults tend to propagate up through the sedimentary section from the basement fault, disrupting the previous continuity of the fold (Fig. 1B).

Mechanical stratigraphy

For our purpose here, we use "mechanical stratigraphy" to represent both the vertical variation of rock properties (e.g., strength and ductility) and the prediction of bedding-parallel slip/shear. The prediction of slip surfaces is based on both field and experimental observations, as well as on theoretical considerations (Couples, 1986).

Because the Rocky Mountain foreland stratigraphic sequence is very similar to that of the western Wyoming thrust belt, their mechanical stratigraphies are likely to be similar (Fig. 2). For example, the major detachment below the Paleozoic carbonates was active in both the foreland (as discussed in the previous paragraph), and as a basal décollement in the adjacent thrust belt (see for example, Lamerson, 1983; Dixon, 1982).

The referenced décollement at the base of the Paleozoic carbonates is defined as a first-order mechanical boundary. It, and the Paleozoic/Mesozoic interface, bound the three-layer, first-order mechanical stratigraphy used throughout this chapter. Second- and higher order units can be distinguished, but these complicate the predictions and are generally only applicable at the scale of a local structure. It is the specific consideration of mechanical stratigraphy that distinguishes the models of this chapter from those described previously for basement/thrust interaction (e.g., Wiltschko and Eastman, 1983), where the sedimentary-layer responses have been treated less specifically, or not at all.

The slip surfaces predicted for the stratigraphic section, together with expected strengths (resistance to shape-change) of the packages bounded by the slip surfaces, are used to develop the models. Basement faulting and lateral displacements are defined, and the sequential geometries are then predicted using the expected mechanical stratigraphy and rock responses.

The models we describe are necessarily conceptual, since numerical models with such properties and displacements are presently not achievable, and experimental models with the appropriate sequences of loading would be exceedingly difficult to create.

Thrust belt terminology

Thrust faults have been discussed for more than a century (cf. Perry and others, 1984). The terminology that has developed is somewhat variable, so it is important to briefly describe our usage. The terms "ramp" and "flat," when unmodified, denote portions of a thrust fault surface (Fig. 3A). We find it useful to have terms to describe the angular relationship of bedding to the fault surface (see also Butler, 1982). Thus, a hanging-wall ramp (HWR) can be located on a flat, which in the case shown (Fig. 3B), is also a footwall flat (FWF). The truncations that constitute the HWR are an essential part of the dip changes that lead to closed and, hence, prospective anticlines (see, for example, Jamison, 1987; Couples and others, 1987).

Note that, in the example shown, an HWF is adjacent to the ramp (also here an FWR). A reason for not equating the terms ramp and FWR is that faults might not develop in planar beds, or faults might be subjected to subsequent folding (Fig. 3C). Finally, transverse ramps (Fig. 3D) are also common structures (and equally HWTRs and FWTRs), generally linking longitudinal ramps (implied by the unmodified ramp) and HWRs and FWRs.

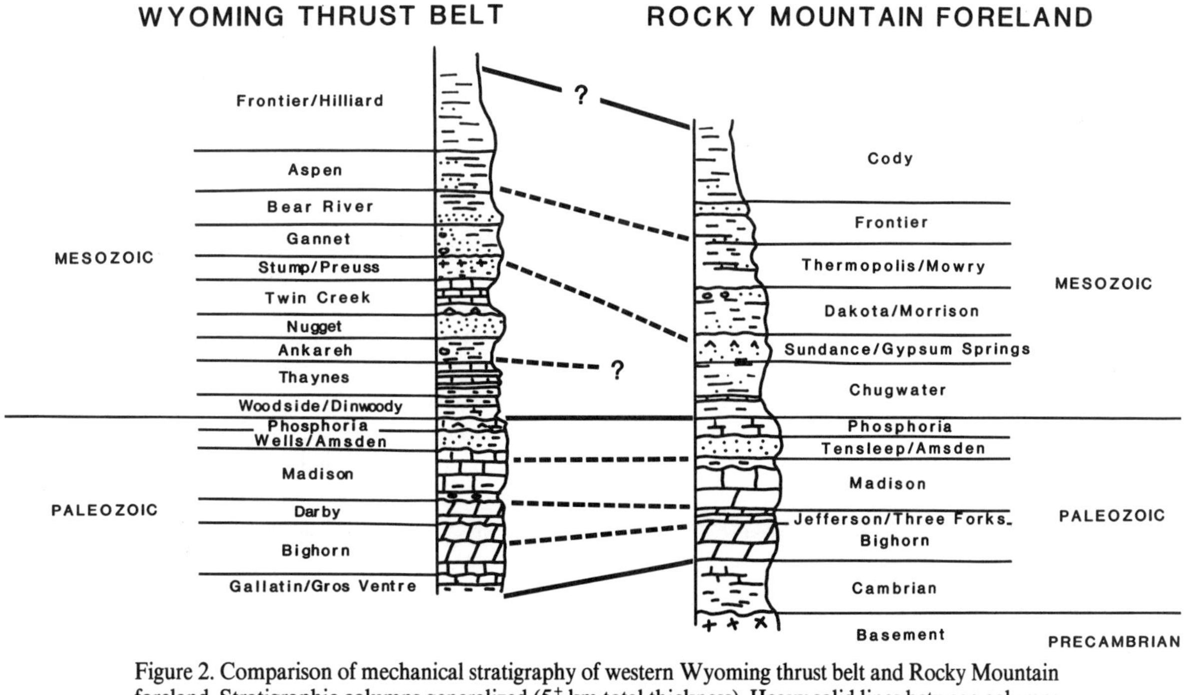

Figure 2. Comparison of mechanical stratigraphy of western Wyoming thrust belt and Rocky Mountain foreland. Stratigraphic columns generalized (5⁺ km total thickness). Heavy solid lines between columns are first-order mechanical boundaries; dashed lines represent second-order surfaces.

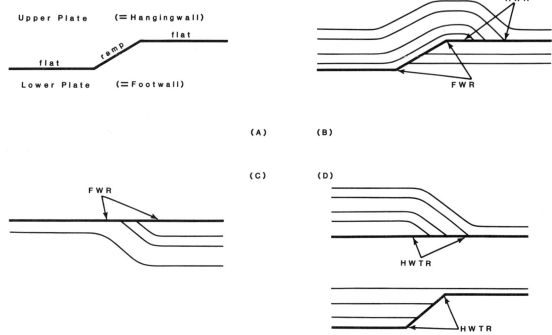

Figure 3. Terminology for thrust-belt structures. (A), Idealized ramp/flat geometry for a thrust surface. (B), Simple fault-bend fold (Suppe, 1983). Note that regional west dip would lead to a localized, discrete anticline rather than the broad, flat-topped structure illustrated. Also referred to as a truncation anticline (see Couples and others, 1987). (C), One situation in which FWR does not equate with "ramp" [see (A)]. (D), Strike-parallel cross sections defining hanging-wall transverse ramp. Note also the possibility of having an HWTR if beds are planar, but thrust surface experiences a step.

Interaction possibilities

The term "interaction" carries an implication of relative timing. In our models, we treat block uplift and thrusting as distinct events, with first block uplift, and then thrusting, occurring first. We do this to more clearly illustrate the portions of the structural development attributable to each, but we believe that a simultaneous growth of uplifts and thrusts (as addressed by Kulik and Schmidt, this volume) is equally likely. Thus, the slip surfaces activated during deformation, which are characteristic of a given style, may assist the structural growth continued by the other.

We first treat two-dimensional situations, considering only cross-sectional views, and then extend the analysis to some cases in which map patterns indicate three-dimensional shape changes. Because this volume is primarily concerned with the western U.S. Cordillera, we use the conventions accepted for this region, with thrusting occurring from west to east, and all cross sections having west on the left side.

TWO-DIMENSIONAL CASES (CROSS SECTIONS)

Thrust ramp formation due to previous forced fold

If foreland structures predate thrusting, they may cause or localize thrust ramps. When an earlier forced fold's steep flank faces west, the detachment surface(s) operating during forced

folding can be utilized again during the thrusting event. In this case, the bedding plane thrust can follow the inclined bedding up the forelimb and across the anticlinal crest (Fig. 4), cutting upsection when the gently dipping limb is reached. The resulting hanging-wall geometry is, after translation away from the causative site, indistinguishable from ramp anticlines resulting from a fault-bend fold (Suppe, 1983; Jamison, 1987). Rarely, the two causative mechanisms might be distinguishable by a detailed structural analysis of the area surrounding the transported fold (this is discussed under three-dimensional cases), but they are geometrically identical in cross section.

If the forced-fold steep limb faces east, and the thrust fault cuts across bedding in the forelimb (Fig. 5), the end result is again a hanging-wall ramp indistinguishable in a local cross section (when away from the causative site) from the case of a thrust ramp developed in planar beds.

Returning to a west-facing steep limb, a thrust may continue its previous trajectory, and cut downsection across the folded rocks (Fig. 6). Although such down-cutting is considered anomalous in thrust belts, it is known to occur.

Figures 4 and 6 illustrate two different responses of a thrust to an apparently similar preexisting uplift. A third response, buttressing, is treated separately below. These responses seem to be controlled by factors such as type of hinge deformation during folding, as well as normal and shear stresses that develop along (potential) slip surfaces.

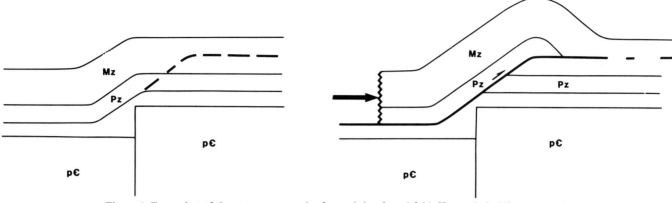

Figure 4. Formation of thrust ramp as result of preexisting forced fold. Heavy dashed line represents future thrust surface; heavy solid line is active thrust fault. Heavy arrow represents translation of thrust sheet. Note development of truncation anticline in hanging wall of thrust. Again, note that regional west dip would lead to local anticline after thrust translation. Scale is general; see caption to Figure 1.

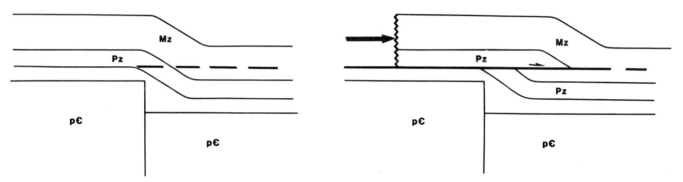

Figure 5. Alternate formation of thrust ramp. See caption to Figure 4.

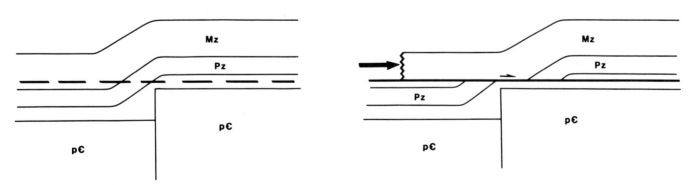

Figure 6. Illustration of thrust fault cutting across preexisting structure and "down section." Note planarity of thrust fault. See caption to Figure 4.

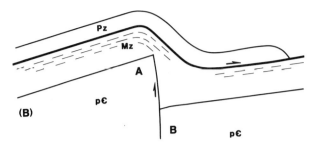

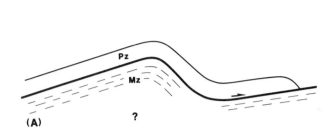

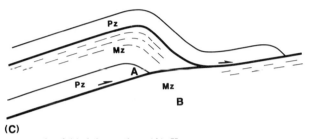

Figure 7. Illustration showing two ways of interpreting an east-verging folded thrust plate. (A), Known geometry; short dashes imply bedding dips in Mesozoic strata. (B), Forced-fold interpretation. (C), Effect of interpreting a blind thrust. Points A and B referenced in text. Scale as in Figure 1.

Thrusts deformed by block uplift

Thrust plates could be folded and faulted by later block uplift. If a thrust surface and adjacent rocks are folded by an east-facing uplift, the fold is likely to be interpreted as resulting from a deeper thrust, rather than as the response to uplifted basement (Fig. 7). Both situations are geometrically possible, and without deep exposure or subsurface penetration of areas A or B, they are indistinguishable in cross section.

If a west-facing block uplift folded a thrust, the thrust-sheet fold would probably be interpreted as the result of a backthrust arising from a deeper thrust, rather than as a faulted forced fold associated with a west-facing block fault (Fig. 8). Again, both cases are geometrically possible; only outcrop or subsurface penetration of area ABC would differentiate the two cases in cross section.

Previously, we suggested that preexisting basement faults could act as sites for thrust ramp development. If such a thrust ramp (associated with a block-fault below) were subjected to additional block uplift, a near-surface geometry would develop, which is normally interpreted as resulting from a listric normal fault (Fig. 9). However, in the model illustrated, the normal fault is not listric into an earlier thrust surface, but is, instead, an upward continuation of the underlying block-bounding fault (refer to Fig. 1B). Basement-block rotations, along with syntectonic sedimentation, could create an apparent "half-graben," as is seen in many thrust-belt interpretations, but the listric normal

fault—which is the generally presumed cause of the half-graben—is not present. Again, in the absence of appropriate outcrop, the differentiation of the possibilities requires subsurface penetration at positions A or B.

One further example warrants attention. If, after thrusting, a new basement block is greatly elevated in the thrust-belt hinterland (i.e., to the west), erosion could result in outcropping basement rocks. One interpretation of the resulting map pattern would be that the basement rocks were thrusted. This interpretation contrasts with the case of an autochthonous basement, where the uplifted thrust plate(s) have been eroded from the uplifted block, leaving a thrust-plate klippe to the east (Fig. 10).

Foreland buttress

Thus far, the models describe cases in which thrust motions are not restrained by foreland uplifts, only altered. An early, large-displacement basement uplift could effectively buttress against the forward motion of thrust sheets (Fig. 11), the situation most commonly cited as evidence for interaction. Where only the forward part of a sheet stops, the continued motion must be taken up by processes such as imbrication, close buckle folding, and possibly, pressure solution (see Kulik and Schmidt, this volume; Mitra and others, this volume).

In the case illustrated, the foreland uplift has faulted through the sedimentary sequence, rather than causing a fold, although a limited amount of folding could be incorporated in this explana-

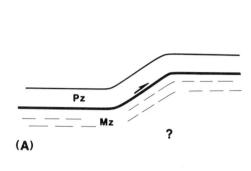

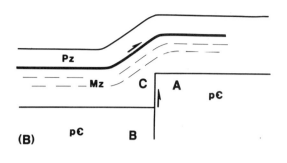

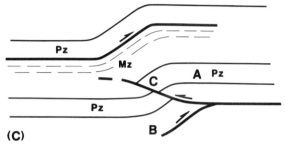

Figure 8. Illustration showing two ways of interpreting a west-verging folded thrust. (A), Known geometry; short dashes imply bedding dips in Mesozoic strata. (B), Forced-fold interpretation. (C), Backthrust in subjacent thrust sheet causing fold. Points A, B, C referenced in text. Scale as in Figure 1.

tion. Such a situation might arise from very low confining pressures (to weaken the strata) or from very high pressures (bed-normal stress inhibits slip, thus reducing the layered response of the sediments; both of these situations are anomalies). In these cases, what has essentially occurred is a disruption of the layering, and hence the mechanical stratigraphy. The convenient slip surface was no longer available, and thus the fold did not develop as the block rose. Consequently, there was no path to continue the thrust motion over the uplift.

A similar disruption of the mechanical stratigraphy can result from situations somewhat more subtle than that illustrated in Figure 11. If the basement fault is a low-angle reverse fault, then crowding and west-verging folding might develop in the layered sequence. Imbricate faults arising from the basement might also interrupt the continuity of the layering. These and other situations can lead to a buttress effect in that a well-defined trajectory does not exist for the thrust plane to continue over the uplifted block.

THREE-DIMENSIONAL CASES (MAP VIEWS)

Basement block corners are quite common in the Rocky Mountain foreland (Stearns and Stearns, 1978), leading to uplift boundaries that are irregular and angular in map view. If such angularity also characterizes basement blocks under a thrust belt, then consideration must be given to its effect on thrust-sheet structures.

Commonly, a thrust belt exhibits transverse features. We

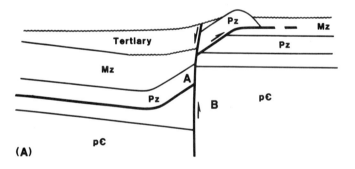

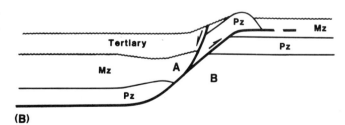

Figure 9. Alternate interpretations of valley-fill adjacent to high-angle surface fault. (A), Thrust ramp offset by faults associated with basement uplift. (B), Listric normal fault sliding down previous thrust surface ("relaxation"). Points A and B referenced in text. Scale as above; no exaggeration.

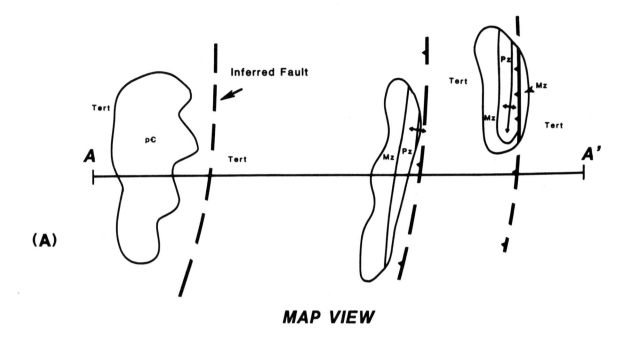

MAP VIEW

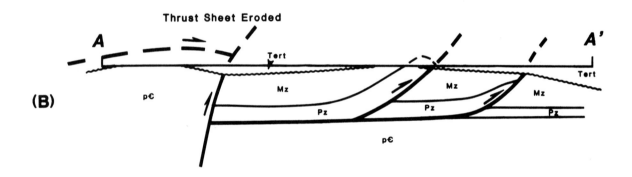

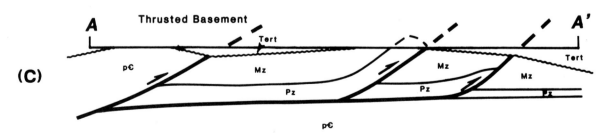

Figure 10. Autochthonous vs. allochthonous basement. (A), Known map relations. Tert = "postorogenic" clastic fill and overlap sequence. Length of section in tens of kilometers. (B), Cross section
(vertically exaggerated) showing autochthonous basement; thrust belt is isolated klippe. (C), Alternate
cross section showing allochthonous basement as part of thrusted mass.

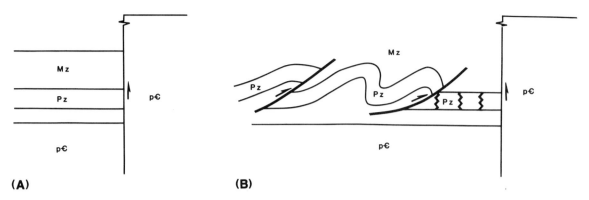

Figure 11. Effect of buttressing due to previously uplifted block. (A), One possible initial configuration (see text for other options that might disrupt bedding and/or continuity of slip surfaces). (B), Postthrusting geometry, with imbrication, buckle folding, and pressure solution (wavy lines) demonstrating contractional strains. Scales as in Figure 1.

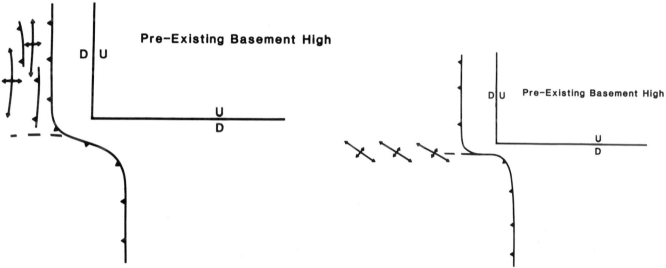

Figure 12. Map view of thrust sheet where internal shortening results from stoppage against preexisting uplift. Dashed line represents trace of tear fault in the sheet. Tear fault extent may be small if pile-up shortening equals advance of unrestrained part of thrust sheet. Scale similar to that in Figure 10.

Figure 13. Map view of thrust sheet stopped by preexisting uplift without any pile-up deformation. Forward motion of unrestrained portion occurs across tear or wrench, perhaps with local wrench-associated oblique folds. Scale as in Figure 10.

propose that some of these are the response to basement block corners, caused by uplift before, during, or after thrusting. This section addresses the geometries that can develop when thrust sheets encounter block corners, and therefore addresses the geologic map patterns associated with transverse features. Because there are a large number of geometric possibilities, we discuss only those few that seem especially relevant to our experiences in thrust-belt interpretation.

If a single, isolated block uplift was present in a thrust belt, and it was surrounded by a uniformly dipping and otherwise continuous panel of strata, the anomalously high elevation of the block, as well as singular structural features in the affected thrust sheets, would betray the mode of origin. In a case more like that observed for the Rocky Mountain foreland, and which we infer to be representative of the western Wyoming thrust belt, uplifted

and downdropped basement blocks are distributed throughout an area, and "regional" dip and elevation are difficult to identify (e.g., Fahy, 1987).

There are several types of interaction that might occur as the leading edge of a thrust sheet approaches a basement block with a corner. Part of the thrust sheet might ramp over the uplift (as described earlier under two-dimensional cases) while the remainder would proceed unaffected. The thrust surface would exhibit a change in elevation, and there would probably be differences in the pattern of deformation. Another possibility is that the uplift acts as a buttress, leading to a local pile-up of deformation (Fig. 12). Still another possibility is that the buttressed sheet comes to a halt, with the development of a tear between that portion and the unrestrained, still advancing thrust (Fig. 13). The results of the scenarios are expressed as differences in cross section and in map view related to position with respect to the block corner. Because these sequences have common elements, they can be difficult to differentiate, particularly in the subsurface.

The interaction scenarios described here for block corners all result in the development of a jog or apparent offset in either a fault trace or some other structural "reference" line, such as truncation anticlines. However, with the exception of tearing caused by buttressing, most of these do not have any real component of relative transverse offset within the thrust sheet, and the jogs are only apparent.

One such possibility of an apparent change in the thrust trace is the case of a postthrusting uplift, which was followed by erosion of the elevated portion of a previous thrust sheet. Perhaps this latter case could be identified by knowing the distribution of a reference line, such as a straight-line facies transition (Fig. 14). As a complication, a prethrust uplift could be rejuvenated, leading to the appearance of offset, which includes a real component of offset.

A change in map position of a thrust-sheet truncation-anticline does not require a tear within the sheet. Transverse ramps can link hanging-wall anticlines, making their apparent offset unsuitable for determining tear faults in the thrust sheet. The explanation normally used for hanging-wall transverse anticlines, and their associated truncations, is that the original thrust fault had a "dog-leg" in its ramp (Fig. 15). After translation of the hanging wall to a regional flat, the two longitudinal truncation anticlines would be linked by a transverse fold caused by the HWTR. This sequence of events does not involve a foreland component.

Transverse ramps (and their associated transverse folds) can also develop by severing and translating existing basement-cored folds. If block uplift previously created a fold pattern with corners or "dog-legs," and this was cut off and transported as part of the hanging wall (Fig. 16), an HWTR would result, linking two

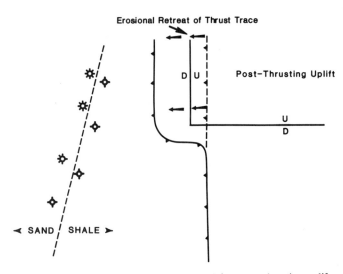

Figure 14. Map view of thrust sheet eroded from postthrusting uplift. Dashed line is constrained facies change, which disproves tearing in the thrust sheet. Scale as in Figure 10.

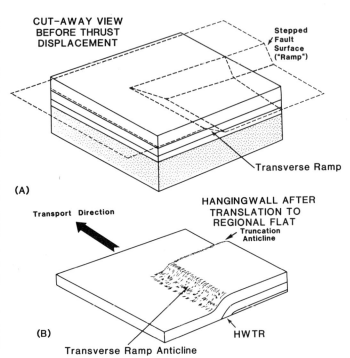

Figure 15. (A), Block diagram of thrust ramp geometry where dog-leg (i.e., transverse ramp) cuts planar beds. Dashed lines outline thrust surfaces. (B), Postthrusting geometry. Note transverse anticline in hanging wall at termination of (longitudinal) truncation anticline. As shown, "anticlines" are really monoclines, but refer to caption of Figures 1 and 4 for explanation of effects of regional dip and treatment of scale.

apparently normal truncation anticlines. As in the two-dimensional cases, the blocks could face into or away from the direction of thrusting; this example illustrates the case that faces away. If thrust motions are large enough so that the FWR area is not observed, the two cases (Figs. 15, 16) yield hanging-wall fold patterns that are the same, and unless microstructural information (for example, that visible in thin sections) could resolve the mode of fold formation, there would be no local technique for distinguishing between the two modes of formation.

CONCLUSIONS

In this chapter we have shown some alternate interpretations of thrust-belt structures, specifically the effect of foreland tectonics on a "pure" thrust-belt style. Our interpretations were developed from field and subsurface interpretation problems we have encountered primarily, but not solely, in the western Wyoming thrust belt. The models, represented first as cross sections and then with map considerations, were developed to test the plausibility of a foreland component influencing the thrust-belt style. They were constructed from our understanding of the mechanical stratigraphy, especially to examine the question of whether foreland influence results in diagnostic features.

We find that typically it is not possible to find features that

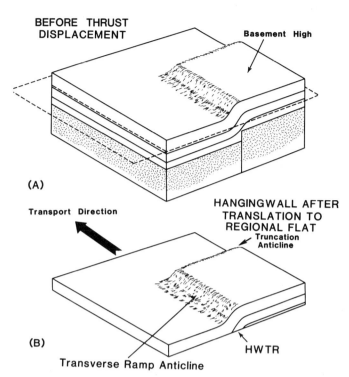

BEFORE THRUST
DISPLACEMENT

Basement High

(A)

Transport Direction

HANGINGWALL AFTER
TRANSLATION TO
REGIONAL FLAT

Truncation
Anticline

(B)

HWTR

Transverse Ramp Anticline

Figure 16. (A), Block diagram of planar thrust plane cutting folds above preexisting basement block uplift. Dashed lines outline future thrust surface. (B) Hanging-wall geometry after thrusting. Compare with geometry of hanging wall in Figure 15. See also caption to Figure 15 for explanation of use of "anticline."

are unequivocally diagnostic of interaction. The overlying thrust plate is geometrically very similar or identical in many common cases. Exposures and data density nearly always leave unresolved ambituities. For most of the scenarios we describe, the primary difference between the various modes of formation resides only in the site of formation, which in the thrust belt is usually some distance west and in the deep subsurface.

We believe that the models we have described are valid interpretation possibilities, and in actual cases they may represent the more likely interpretation. We suggest that these models, or other derivatives of the concept, should be considered when making interpretations in thrust belts.

ACKNOWLEDGMENTS

We thank Rick Davis, Chuck Kluth, Chris Schmidt, and especially John Sales for careful and helpful reviews of this manuscript. We also extend thanks to an anonymous reviewer from whom we discovered some topics we were miscommunicating in our writing. Finally, we express great appreciation to Chris Schmidt and Bill Perry for their patience, help, and most importantly, their encouragement toward the preparation and revision of this manuscript.

REFERENCES CITED

Beutner, E. C., 1977, Causes and consequences of curvature in the Sevier orogenic belt, Utah to Montana: Wyoming Geological Association, 29th Annual Field Conference Guidebook, p. 353–365.

Butler, R.W.H., 1982, The terminology of structures in thrust belts: Journal of Structural Geology, v. 4, p. 239–245.

Couples, G. D., 1986, Kinematic and dynamic considerations in the forced folding process as studied in the laboratory (experimental models) and in the field (Rattlesnake Mountain, Wyoming) [Ph.D. thesis]: College Station, Texas A&M University, 193 p.

Couples, G. D., and Lageson, D. R., 1985, Penrose Conference report; Laramide tectonics of the Rocky Mountain foreland: Geology, v. 13, p. 311.

Couples, G. D., Weir, G. M., and Jamison, W. R., 1987, Structural development and hydrocarbon entrapment at Whitney Canyon and Yellow Creek fields, Wyoming overthrust belt: Wyoming Geological Association, 38th Annual Field Conference Guidebook, p. 275–285.

Dimitre-Dunn, S. L., 1983, Timing of foreland and thrust-belt deformation in an overlap area, Teton Pass, Idaho, and Wyoming, *in* Lowell, J. D., and Gries, R., eds., Rocky Mountain foreland basins and uplifts: Denver, Colorado, Rocky Mountain Association of Geologists, p. 263–269.

Dixon, J. S., 1982, Regional structural synthesis, Wyoming salient of western overthrust belt: American Association of Petroleum Geologists Bulletin, v. 66, p. 1560–1580.

Fahy, M., 1987, Pre-thrusting basin morphology; Influence on geochemical "fairways" and subsequent thrust deformations in the Wyoming-Idaho thrustbelt: Wyoming Geological Association, 38th Annual Field Conference Guidebook, p. 267–274.

Jamison, W. R., 1987, Geometric analysis of fold development in overthrust terranes: Journal of Structural Geology, v. 9, p. 207–219.

Lamerson, P. R., 1983, The Fossil Basin and its relationship to the Absaroka thrust system Wyoming and Utah, *in* Powers, R. B., ed., Geologic studies of the Cordilleran thrust belt, 1982: Denver, Colorado, Rocky Mountain Association of Geologists, p. 279–340.

Perry, W. J., Jr., Roeder, D. H., and Lageson, D. R., 1984, Introduction, *in* North American thrust-faulted terranes: American Association of Petroleum Geologists Reprint Series no. 27, p. v–xi.

Prucha, J. J., Graham, J. A., and Nickelsen, R. P., 1965, Basement-controlled deformation in Wyoming Province of Rocky Mountain foreland: American Association of Petroleum Geologists Bulletin, v. 49, p. 966–992.

Royse, F., Jr., Warner, M. A., and Reese, D. L., 1975, Thrust belt structural geometry and related stratigraphic problems, Wyoming–Idaho–northern Utah, *in* Bolyard, D. W., ed., Deep drilling frontiers in the central Rocky Mountains: Denver, Colorado, Rocky Mountain Association of Geologists, Guidebook, p. 41–54.

Schmidt, C. J., and Hendrix, T. E., 1981, Tectonic controls for thrust belt and Rocky Mountain foreland structures in the Northern Tobacco Root Mountains, Jefferson Canyon area, southwestern Montana, *in* Tucker, T., ed., Field Conference and Symposium to southwest Montana: Montana Geological Society, p. 167–180.

Schmidt, C. J., and O'Neill, J. M., 1983, Structural evolution of the southwest Montana transverse zone, *in* Powers, R. B., ed., Geologic studies of the Cordilleran thrust belt, 1982: Denver, Colorado, Rocky Mountain Association of Geologists, p. 193–218.

Stearns, D. W., 1971, Mechanisms of drape folding in the Wyoming Province: Wyoming Geological Association, 23rd Annual Field Conference Guidebook, p. 125–144.

——— , 1978, Faulting and forced folding in the Rocky Mountains foreland, *in* Matthews, V., ed., Laramide folding associated with basement block faulting in the western United States: Geological Society of America Memoir 151, p. 1–37.

Stearns, D. W., and Weinberg, D. M., 1975, A comparison of experimentally created and naturally formed drape folds: Wyoming Geological Association, 27th Annual Field Conference Guidebook, p. 159–166.

Stearns, M. T., and Stearns, D. W., 1978, Geometric analysis of multiple drape folds along the northwest Big Horn Mountains front, Wyoming, *in* Matthews, V., ed., Laramide folding associated with basement block faulting in the western United States: Geological Society of America Memoir 151, p. 139–156.

Suppe, J., 1983, Geometry and kinematics of fault-bend folding: American Journal of Science, v. 283, p. 684–721.

Wiltschko, D. V., and Eastman, D., 1983, Role of basement warps and faults in localizing thrust fault ramps, *in* Hatcher, R. D., Jr., Williams, H., and Zietz, I., eds., Contributions to the tectonics and geophysics of mountain chains: Geological Society of America Memoir 158, p. 177–190.

MANUSCRIPT ACCEPTED BY THE SOCIETY FEBRUARY 9, 1988

Geological Society of America
Memoir 171
1988

A photoelastic study of the effects of preexisting reverse faults in basement on the subsequent deformation of the cover

David V. Wiltschko
Center for Tectonophysics and Department of Geology, Texas A&M University, College Station, Texas 77843-3115
Daniel B. Eastman
Exxon USA, P.O. Box 4697, Houston, Texas 77210-4697

ABSTRACT

Published deep reflection seismic data show that the top of the basement surface beneath fold-thrust belts, although largely flat, does contain some topography. Basement highs are often caused by motion on normal and/or reverse faults whose formation in many cases predated deformation of the sedimentary cover. Two-layer, two-dimensional, geometrically similar plane strain photoelastic models designed to elucidate the mechanical role of these basement structures in localizing thrust fault ramps and other zones of disturbance show that (1) any basement topography will produce a stress concentration (local stress divided by regional stress); (2) the highest stress concentration will be produced above those structures with the sharp corners, i.e., gentle warps are not as effective as fault-block corners; (3) reverse faults are generally more efficient stress concentrators than high-angle normal faults; and (4) basement faults may have little effect on the stresses in the cover if there is a sufficiently thick layer of weak rock blanketing the basement topography. Quantitatively, basement reverse faults produce stress concentrations as much as 4.6 in our models, nearly a factor of 2 larger than basement warps or normal faults.

INTRODUCTION

A useful generalization in fold-thrust belts is that basement is both flat and not involved in the deformation of the sedimentary cover. However, as more information has become available on the shape of the basement-sediment contact, it has become clear that basement faults do occur and in some instances may have affected the subsequent deformation of the cover. In this chapter we review and further investigate the nature of the interaction between abrupt basement uplifts and the overlying sedimentary rocks, focusing on the mechanisms by which preexisting basement uplifts may localize future deformation in the cover.

BACKGROUND

Preexisting basement structures occur in several foreland fold-thrust belts. They have been observed in the southern and central Appalachians (Thomas, 1982; Jacobeen and Kanes, 1974, 1975), the Overthrust Belt of Wyoming (Wach, 1977; Blackstone, 1979; Royse and others, 1975; Kraig and others, 1985, 1986a, 1987, this volume), the Montana segment of the western Cordillera (Schmidt and O'Neill, 1983; Schmidt and others, this volume; Skipp, this volume), the Salt Range in Pakistan (Lillie and others, 1985; Lillie and Yousuf, 1986; Baker and others, 1988), and are suspected in other areas. Many of these faults are interpreted as normal faults that formed during production of the passive margin on which the sedimentary cover was built. Others are reverse faults that are interpreted to have been produced or reactivated at the same time that thrusting took place in the cover.

Wiltschko and Eastman (1983) reviewed three kinds of structures that could localize thrust fault ramps: preexisting folds, sedimentary facies and thickness changes, and basement topography. Considering the latter, they showed that, at the corners of the fault blocks of preexisting normal faults of various angles of dip, the deviatoric stress is locally raised as much as 2½ times the regional stress value. These areas of locally high stress serve as

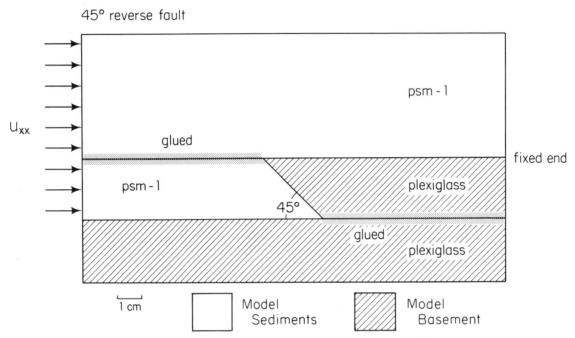

Figure 1. Model configuration for 45° reverse fault showing materials, types of joints, and the loading configuration. Basement and the sedimentary cover are modeled using stiff Plexiglass and Photoelastic Corporation's PSM-1 plastic, respectively. The 30° reverse fault model was constructed and loaded in the same manner, the only difference being the dip of the model basement fault.

loci for the initiation of faulting in the sedimentary cover; the faults form at the basement corner and propagate both up toward the surface and down toward the basal detachment. Finite element models of the same geometries by Schedl and Wiltschko (1987) substantiate these results; they further show that the stress concentrations may be even larger, depending on the strength of the contact between the model basement and cover, as well as the acute angle between the basement top and the fault. Advani and others (1978) examined the specific case of the Rome Trough in eastern Kentucky. They showed that anomalous joint orientations overlying the Rome Trough may be due to the reorientation of the stress field over one of the trough's buried faults.

STATEMENT OF THE PROBLEM

Not all basement faults observed to date are of the normal fault variety; in parts of the western Cordillera, preexisting normal faults in basement may be the exception and not the rule (see Kraig and others, 1985, this volume; Skipp, this volume; Schmidt and others, this volume). Therefore it is important to investigate the role of reverse faults in localizing thrust fault ramps, especially since a close association has been observed by a few workers (Schmidt and others, this volume; Schmidt and O'Neill, 1983; Skipp, this volume; Fielding and Jordan, this volume).

THE MODELS

We have produced two new models for a reverse fault in basement using photoelastic techniques. The models differ only in

the dip of the basement fault. Both models were constructed using 0.64-cm- (¼ in) thick high-polymer plastic sheets: the basement was represented by stiff Plexiglass, and the sedimentary cover was represented by Photoelastic Corporation's PSM-1 (Fig. 1). The Young's Modulus (E) of PSM-1 is 23,440 bars (340,000 psi), and the ratio $E_{Plexiglass}/E_{PSM-1}$ is approximately 2.0. The models were produced by machining rectilinear pieces of both materials and then gluing them with glues appropriate for the elastic moduli of each material. The interface between the two different materials was not glued. The models were analyzed in a 20.3- × 30.5-cm (8 × 12 in.) biaxial deformation apparatus described in Wiltschko and Eastman (1983, p. 189), using standard photoelastic techniques (e.g., Dally and Riley, 1978). The results are shown in Figures 2 through 6.

The results of the two models differ in degree but not in the essential features of the stress distributions and magnitudes. For the 45° reverse fault model, there is a stress concentration of about 4.6 in the vicinity of the upper sharp basement (near point X in Fig. 2) corner. There is also another region of elevated stress beneath the overhang of the fault (Z on Fig. 2). Faults would normally start in one of these two regions of higher stress and propagate toward the other. For significant motion to occur on these faults, however, they must link the basal detachment and the surface. The stress trajectories converge on the region of high stress (Fig. 3). The resulting faults that one would predict using a Mohr-Coulomb criteria involving an angle of internal friction of 30° are shown in Figure 3.

For the 30° reverse fault model, the stress concentration in

45° Reverse fault: magnitudes

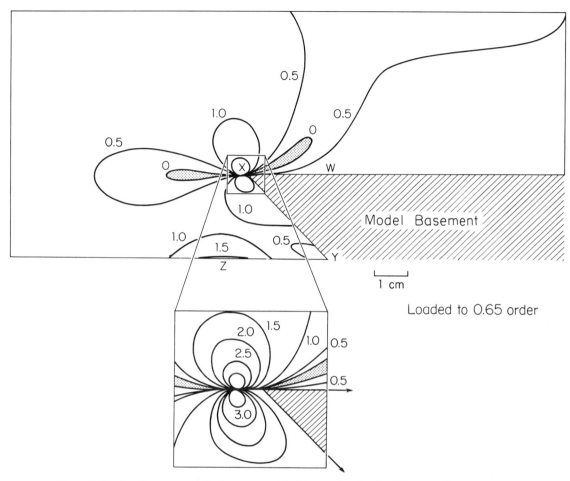

Figure 2. Deviatoric stress magnitudes, expressed in fringe orders for the 45° reverse fault model. The maximum stress concentration (local stress divided by stress applied at boundary) is 4.6 for this model.

the vicinity of the point X (Fig. 5) is 3.9. In addition, there is a stress concentration in the vicinity of point Z. As in the 45° model, the stress trajectories converge in the vicinity of point X (Fig. 6) and therefore predict fault trajectories essentially the same as those of the 45° fault model.

Motion on some of these potential faults would be difficult due to their topography. There is a region beneath the underhang of the basement fault (largely included in a triangle with points X, Y, and Z as apices) that would not be caught up in faults of appreciable displacement, even though the deviatoric stress there is higher than the regional level (Figs. 2, 5). One would expect in the real situation that the rocks there would be fractured, perhaps severely, but would remain largely stratigraphically intact. If a region of basement in the hanging wall subtended by the fault and basement top (the fault "corner," or region WXY, in Figs. 2, 5) were sufficiently narrow at some level, pieces of the upper basement corner could be broken off and transported along some of these faults toward the surface. The result of this process would be to remove the region of high stress, but at the same time

perhaps remove the evidence for it ever having existed. Portions of basement rock caught up in thrust faults are relatively common in the thrust terrane of southwest Montana where thrust faults have impinged upon uplifted basement blocks (see Coryell and Spang, this volume; Skipp, this volume).

APPLICATION OF RESULTS TO LAYERED ROCKS

The model presented above may be unrealistic as applied to rocks for three major reasons. First, because the model is a few tens of centimeters in length, the role of gravity in the model deformation is inconsequential; this may not be true for larger structures. Second, because the plastic sheets used are isotropic and homogeneous, the effects of layering cannot be incorporated into the model. Third, it is unclear whether a basement corner as sharp as that which we have employed will survive the process of forming the basement fault; it may be blunted by deformation.

If the rocks in the modeled structures follow a (linear) Mohr-Coulomb criterion, then the effect of gravity would be to

45° Reverse fault: principal stress directions

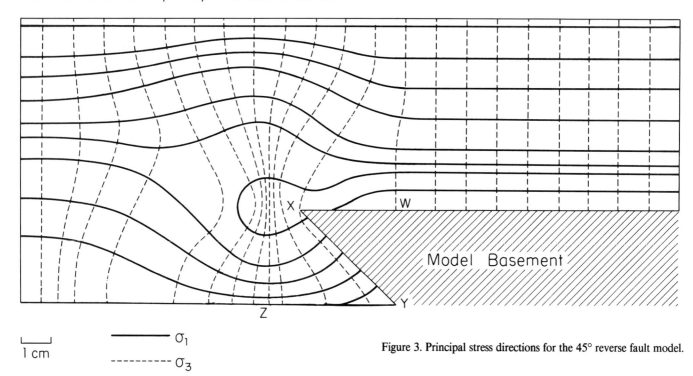

1 cm

——————— σ_1

---------- σ_3

Figure 3. Principal stress directions for the 45° reverse fault model.

45° Reverse fault: potential fault trajectories

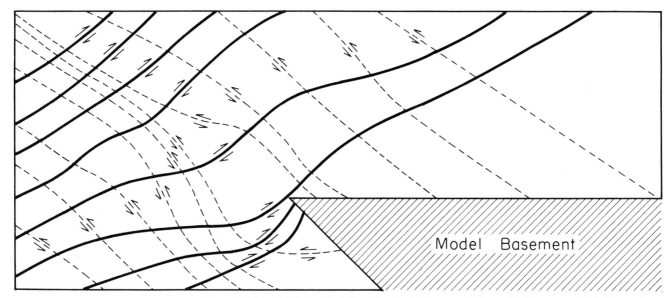

Figure 4. Potential fault orientations for the 45° reverse fault model. The potential faults are drawn assuming a Mohr-Coulomb criterion with an angle of internal friction of 30°. Displacement on the lower two right-verging faults (solid lines) is impossible unless the basement rocks fail.

1 cm

30° Reverse fault: magnitudes

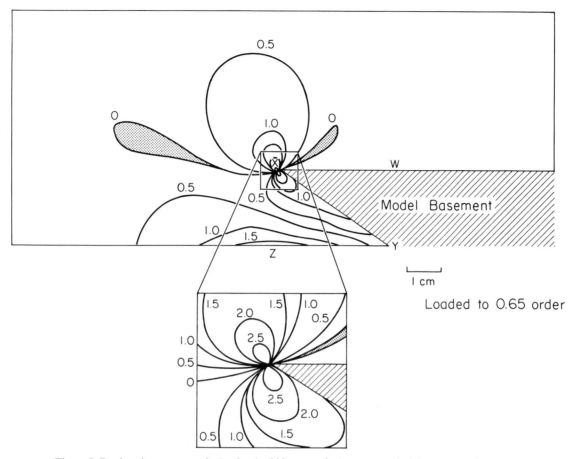

Figure 5. Deviatoric stress magnitudes for the 30° reverse fault, expressed in fringe orders. The maximum stress concentration (local divided by stress applied at boundary) is 3.9 for this model.

alter the positions, but not the shapes, of the potential faults. All other factors being the same, stress concentrations at sharp basement corners that occur higher in the section would more likely cause failure than those that occur deeper due to the normal stress dependence on failure. Therefore, smaller, deeply buried, basement faults have less effect than larger ones simply due to the position of the induced stress concentrations in the stratigraphic section.

The role of layering is potentially more complex and involves, in part, a knowledge of both the way the sedimentary section is stressed as well as the lateral distributions and positions in the sedimentary stack of strong and weak layers. To illustrate possible effects, consider two possible scenarios for the timing of basement faulting, and therefore the configuration of the cover over the basement structure.

Postdepositional faulting in basement

Consider a stiff basement overlain by a thick basal phyllosilicate-rich shaley clastic sequence that passes upward into a thickly bedded carbonate (largely dolomite) unit, which is in turn overlain by more thick clastics. As a result of regional compression, a fault in the basement develops, extending into the overlying sedimentary cover. If displacement on the basement fault is small, the hanging wall basement corner will not extend out of the basal shale. Because the stress level in a particular layer and at a specific applied load is a function of the stiffness of the material, a large stress concentration will not develop within the relatively less stiff phyllosilicate-rich shale. Moreover, the small throw of the basement fault does not present a large barrier to motion on faults confined to the sedimentary cover; i.e., the cover rocks will slide over the small basement corner. Therefore, the anisotropy introduced by the extension of the basement fault into the sedimentary cover may have more control on the localization of thrust faults than the stress concentration due to the basement cover itself.

If displacement on the fault in basement is larger, however, the displacement constraints are larger; rocks below the upper corner of the basement fault will not move unless the intervening basement segment is broken. The failure of the basement corner is

30° Reverse fault: principal stress directions

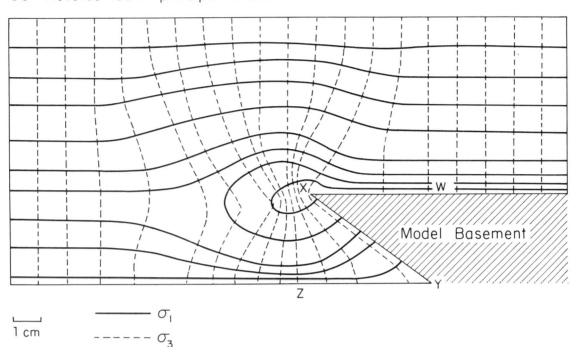

1 cm

——— σ_1

- - - - - σ_3

Figure 6. Principal stress trajectories for 30° reverse fault model. These predict potential fault orientations essentially similar to those shown for the 45° reverse fault model (Fig. 4).

in turn a function of the strength of the basement rocks. As a result, the precise effect of a basement fault will depend on both its displacement and strength relative to that of the sedimentary cover, as well as on the nature of the layering of the cover.

Predepositional faulting in basement

Consider instead the case of a basement fault formed early in the depositional history of a particular area. As is presumed to be the case in several instances, an unequal thickness of sediments would be deposited on the hanging wall and footwall of the basement fault (see Thomas, 1982). In addition, if the fault moved several times within the depositional history of the area, then some bending of preexisting layers over the fault would take place. As a result, the sedimentary layers are not flat-lying and therefore contain other potential areas for concentration of stress. Preexisting bends in sediments can be potent stress concentrators in addition to any that may exist around the basement corner (Dieterich and Carter, 1969; see the discussion in Wiltschko and Eastman, 1983).

We have machined the model basement to a sharp corner in both models with a flat model sediment–model basement contact in both the hanging wall and footwall. How appropriate is this configuration as a model for actual field examples of reverse faults in basement? First, broad generalizations are difficult to make because of a meager data set; there are few documented cases of these kinds of faults. However, those cases that have been

well documented show that there is some dip reversal on the basement-sediment contact near the fault. That is, the basement smoothly curves, even up to the point of cutoff by the basement reverse fault (Schmidt and others, this volume). However, the degree of curvature varies a great deal among basement faults in the Rocky Mountain foreland in general. Examples of interpreted sharp basement corners include Gries (1983a, b), Erslev (Forellen fault: 1986), Brown (this volume), Blackstone (1986), and Kraig and others (this volume). The model we present is an extreme situation, and as such illustrates the possible stress effects of sharp basement corners. Until careful subsurface studies are conducted that document in more detail the geometries of basement reverse faults, as well as the fabrics around particular basement steps, it will not be possible to justify further refinements in the geometry of such models.

COMPARISON OF THE EFFECTS OF REVERSE AND NORMAL BASEMENT FAULTS

As shown by Advani and others (1978), Wiltschko and Eastman (1983), and Schedl and Wiltschko (1987), normal faults produce stress concentrations. In general, however, these are lower than those we have found in the present models. Schedl and Wiltschko (1987) show that photoelastic methods tend to underestimate the stress concentrations for a particular geometry because, as a result of the way in which the load is applied, the exact loading condition (constant stress or constant displacement) is rarely attained exactly. The stress concentrations attained by them for normal faults using the finite element method were larger by as much as a factor of 1.5 than those found by Wiltschko and Eastman (1983). Nevertheless, it is clear that reverse faults produce larger stress concentrations than normal faults, although the actual stress concentration we have predicted may be low. The contrast is especially high between a vertical fault and a 45° reverse fault where the stress concentrations are 1.5 and 4.6, respectively.

CONCLUSIONS

1. Basement faults, where present, can have a significant effect on the local stress in the sedimentary cover.

2. In the ideal case, the stress concentration at the sharp corner of a 45° reverse fault may be as high as 4.6, whereas that for a 30° reverse fault is 3.9. Deformation of the corner and enveloping sedimentary rocks will reduce this concentration, perhaps significantly.

3. Sufficiently thin basement corners may produce stress concentrations that in turn concentrate deformation in their vicinity. Subsequent faulting will tend to fault these corners off, which may be an explanation for the inclusion of small basement blocks in some thrust sheets.

4. Both 45° and 30° reverse faults are more efficient stress concentrators than are basement normal faults.

ACKNOWLEDGMENTS

This work was supported through National Science Foundation Grants EAR-7815477 and EAR-8212714 (to D.V.W.). Additional funding for the photoelastic laboratory at the University of Michigan, where the analyses were performed, came from the F. Scott Turner Bequest, a Rackham Faculty Research grant, and a grant from the Division of Research Development and Administration, University of Michigan. The comments of Richard Groshong, Jr., Sandro Serra, and an anonymous reviewer measurably improved the manuscript. We also thank Chris Schmidt for his thorough and diligent editing, and for many helpful comments, criticisms, and insights.

REFERENCES CITED

Advani, S. H., Gango Rao, H.U.S., Chang, H. Y., Dean, C. S., and Oversby, W. K., 1978, Stress trajectory simulations across the Appalachian Plateau Province in West Virginia, *in* Shott, G., and others, eds., Proceedings of the first eastern gas shales symposium: Morgantown Energy Research Center, MERC/SP-77/5, p. 442–448.

Baker, D. M., Lillie, R. S., Yeats, R. S., Johnson, G. D., Yousuf, M., and Zamin, A.S.H., 1988, Development of the Himalayan frontal thrust zone: Salt Range, Pakistan: Geology, v. 16, p. 3–7.

Blackstone, D. L., Jr., 1979, Geometry of the Prospect-Darby and La Barge faults at their junction with the La Barge Platform, Lincoln and Sublette Counties, Wyoming: Geological Survey of Wyoming Report of Investigations 18, 34 p.

——, 1986, Foreland compressional tectonics; Southern Bighorn Basin and adjacent areas, Wyoming: Geological Survey of Wyoming Report of Investigations 34, 32 p.

Dally, J. W., and Riley, W. F., 1978, Experimental stress analysis: New York, McGraw-Hill, 571 p.

Dieterich, J. H., and Carter, N. L., 1969, Stress history of folding: American Journal of Science, v. 267, p. 129–154.

Erslev, E. A., 1986, Basement balancing of Rocky Mountain foreland uplifts: Geology, v. 14, p. 259–262.

Gries, R., 1983a, North-south compression of Rocky Mountain foreland structure, *in* Lowell, J. D., and Gries, R., eds., Rocky Mountain foreland basins and uplifts: Denver, Colorado, Rocky Mountain Association of Geologists, p. 9–32.

——, 1983b, Oil and gas prospecting beneath the Precambrian of foreland thrust plates in the Rocky Mountains: American Association of Petroleum Geologists Bulletin, v. 67, p. 1–26.

Jacobeen, F., Jr., and Kanes, W. H., 1974, Structure of the Broadtop synclinorium and its implications for Appalachian structural style: American Association of Petroleum Geologists Bulletin, v. 58, p. 362–375.

——, 1975, Structure of the Broadtop synclinorium, Wills Mountain anticlinorium, and Allegheny frontal zone: American Association of Petroleum Geol-

ogists Bulletin, v. 59, p. 1136–1150.

Kraig, D. H., Wiltschko, D. V. and Spang, J. H., 1985, Emplacement of the Moxa Arch and related initiation of the ancestral Prospect thrust, southwestern Wyoming: Geological Society of America Abstracts with Programs, v. 17, p. 634.

——, 1986a, Interaction of the northern segment of the Moxa Arch with the western overthrust belt, southwestern Wyoming: Geological Society of America Abstracts with Programs, v. 18, p. 368.

——, 1986b, Interaction of the La Barge Platform with the western overthrust belt, southwestern Wyoming: Geological Society of America, Abstracts with Programs, v. 18, p. 367–368.

——, 1987, Interaction of basement uplift and thin-skinned thrusting: Moxa Arch and the western overthrust belt, Wyoming: Geological Society of America Bulletin, v. 99, p. 654–662.

Lillie, R. J., and Yousuf, M., 1986, Modern analogs for some midcrustal reflections observed beneath collisional mountain belts, *in* Barazangi, M., and Brown, L., eds., Reflection seismology: The continental crust: American Geophysical Union Geodynamics Series, v. 4, p. 55–65.

Lillie, R. J., Yeats, R. S., Leathers, M., Baker, D., and Yousuf, M., 1985, Interpretation of seismic reflection data across the Himalayan foreland thrust belt in Pakistan: Geological Society of America Abstracts with Programs, v. 17, p. 644.

Royse, F., Jr., Warner, M. A., and Reese, D. L., 1975, Thrust belt structural geometry and related stratigraphic problems, Wyoming, Idaho, northern Utah: Denver, Colorado, Rocky Mountain Association Geologists, 1975, Symposium on Deep Drilling Frontiers in Central Rocky Mountains, p. 41–54.

Schedl, A., and Wiltschko, D. V., 1987, The role of basement in thrust fault ramping: Journal of Structural Geology, v. 9, p. 1029–1037.

Schmidt, C. J., and O'Neill, J. M., 1983, Structural evolution of the southwest Montana transverse zone, *in* Powers, R. B., ed., Geologic studies of the Cordilleran thrust belt, 1982; Denver, Colorado, Rocky Mountain Association of Geologists, p. 193–218.

Thomas, W. A., 1982, Stratigraphy and structure of the Appalachian fold and thrust belt in Alabama: *in* Thomas, W. A., and Neathery, T. L., eds., Appalachian thrust belt in Alabama; Tectonics and sedimentation: 95th Annual Meeting of the Geological Society of America Guidebook for field trip no. 13, p. 55–78.

Wach, P. H., 1977, The Moxa Arch; An overthrust model?: Wyoming Geological Association 29th Annual Field Conference Guidebook, p. 651–664.

Wiltschko, D. V., and Eastman, D., 1983, Role of basement warps and faults in localizing thrust fault ramps: Geological Society of America Memoir 158, p. 177–190.

Manuscript Accepted by the Society February 9, 1988

Printed in U.S.A.

Geological Society of America
Memoir 171
1988

Comparison of mesoscopic and microscopic deformational styles in the Idaho-Wyoming thrust belt and the Rocky Mountain foreland

Gautam Mitra
Department of Geological Sciences, University of Rochester, Rochester, New York 14627
Joseph M. Hull
Department of Geological Sciences, Rutgers University–Newark College of Arts and Sciences, Newark, New Jersey 07102
W. Adolph Yonkee
Department of Geology and Geophysics, University of Utah, Salt Lake City, Utah 84112
Gretchen M. Protzman*
Department of Geological Sciences, University of Rochester, Rochester, New York 14627

ABSTRACT

A comparison of mesoscopic and microscopic structures in the Idaho-Utah-Wyoming thrust belt and the Rocky Mountain deformed foreland in Wyoming reveals regional variations in structural style and a decrease in regional shortening from the thrust belt (~60 percent shortening) to the foreland (~30 percent shortening). Deformation in the thrust belt is thin-skinned and is achieved by regional-scale simple shear in the sedimentary cover, which is separated from the basement by a regional décollement. Detailed studies on the Crawford thrust sheet show that large-scale shortening in the cover was produced by thrust faults and associated folds, while internal shortening was achieved by pressure solution (recorded by spaced cleavage), plastic deformation (recorded by deformed fossils), and cataclasis (recorded by contraction faults).

In the foreland, both basement and cover are deformed by regional-scale pure shear, although this may be the secondary effect of even larger, lithospheric-scale thrusting. Detailed studies in the Wind River Mountains (of the Wyoming foreland) show that large folds in the cover are directly related to major deformation zones in the basement. Localized strain softening along these zones allowed large displacements by cataclastic and diffusional processes, while basement blocks between zones underwent only minor deformation by fracturing and faulting. Minor internal shortening in the cover was produced by contraction faults, buckle folds, and rare tectonic stylolites. The regional change in structural style from the thrust belt to the foreland may reflect a change in the physical conditions of deformation, caused (at least partly) by significant differences in the thickness of the sedimentary cover in the two areas.

INTRODUCTION

The eastern margin of the North American Cordillera in Idaho, Utah, and Wyoming consists of two adjoining but distinct structural provinces. These are a fold-and-thrust belt characterized by the "foothills family" of structures (Dahlstrom, 1970; Boyer and Elliott, 1982), and a deformed foreland that lies farther to the east and is characterized by large-scale basement uplift along major faults (Fig. 1).

The Idaho-Utah-Wyoming thrust belt forms a broad salient that is convex to the east (Fig. 1). This belt is typified by major thrusts that transported a thick sequence of Paleozoic and Mesozoic beds eastward. The geometry of major structures is well documented (Royse and others, 1975; Dixon, 1982; Lamerson, 1983). The thrusts are listric in shape and cut up-section in the direction of transport in a stair-step fashion. Large-scale folds with concentric to kink geometries are associated with the thrust faults. A regional décollement separates the folded and faulted sedimentary rocks of the cover from the underlying Precambrian crystal-

---

*Present address: Geology Department, University of California at Davis, Davis, California 95616.

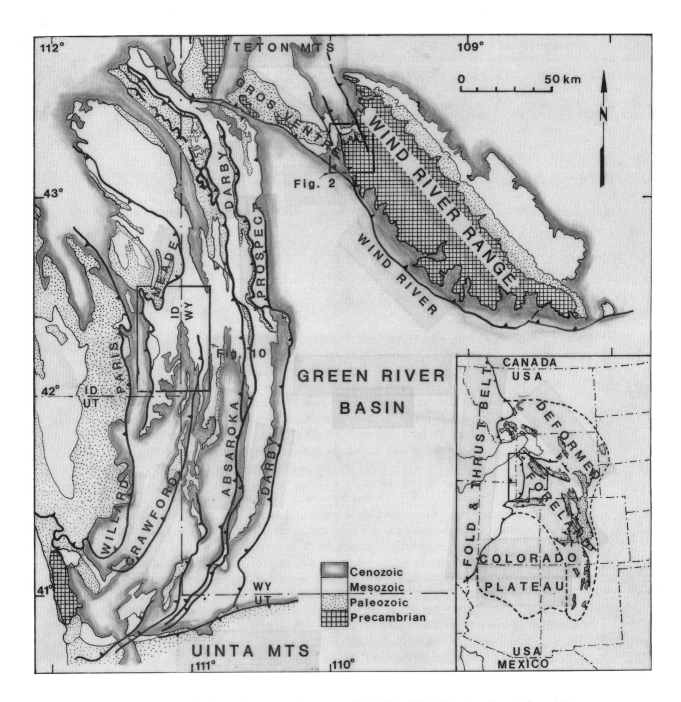

Figure 1. Map showing major structural patterns of the Idaho-Utah-Wyoming thrust belt and the deformed foreland. Major thrusts are labeled, and the areas of detailed study are indicated. Inset index map shows location of the tristates area with respect to major tectonic subdivisions of the Cordillera.

line basement. Thus, the overall deformation is "thin-skinned," although the basement does become involved farther to the west where metamorphism reaches greenschist facies (Bruhn and Beck, 1981).

East of the Idaho-Utah-Wyoming thrust belt, the deformed foreland forms another salient convex to the east that extends from central Montana to New Mexico (Fig. 1). This region is characterized by blocks of Precambrian basement that were uplifted along major reverse faults (Berg, 1962; Blackstone, 1981; Brown, 1984). The reverse faults generally strike north to northwest, and the sense of motion and symmetry is variable for different faults (Gries, 1983a,b). The uplifted blocks are separated by deep basins, and there is as much as 15 km of structural relief on the basement-cover unconformity from the basins to the uplifts. Unlike the thrust belt, the deformation in the sedimentary rocks of the cover is closely related to the basement deformation. Thus, the overall deformation is "thick-skinned," being strongly controlled by the large-scale deformation of basement.

In the tri-state area of Idaho, Utah, and Wyoming, the timing of deformation in both the thrust belt and the deformed foreland is recorded by synorogenic deposits. Synorogenic conglomerates preserved in the Idaho-Utah-Wyoming thrust belt record the motion on major thrust faults. This gives perhaps the most refined and complete timing of thrusting of any thrust belt in the world (Royse and others, 1975; Wiltschko and Dorr, 1983; Heller and others, 1986). The thrust sheets were emplaced sequentially from west to east during the early Cretaceous to middle Eocene. Motion along some reverse faults in the foreland is also recorded by other synorogenic conglomerates (Dorr and others, 1977; Gries, 1983a,b), which indicate that these faults were active from latest Cretaceous to the Eocene during the Laramide orogeny. Thus, the development of these two structural provinces overlapped in time.

The close spatial and temporal association of the provinces provides an excellent opportunity to study and compare the two different structural styles of the deformed foreland and the fold and thrust belt. Why is there an overall change in the structural style between these two adjoining provinces? Although we may not yet be able to answer this question completely, it is useful to compare and contrast detailed structural patterns in these two areas. In particular, what are the detailed differences and similarities in structural geometry at both the megascopic and mesoscopic scales? What differnces are there in the relative importance of different deformation mechanisms at the microscopic scale? In this chapter, we address these fundamental questions based on a comparison of detailed structures from two areas: the northern part of the Wind River mountains in the deformed foreland, and parts of the Crawford and Meade thrust sheets in the Idaho-Utah-Wyoming thrust belt (Fig. 1).

WIND RIVER MOUNTAINS

Large-scale structure

The Wind River mountain range of western Wyoming consists of a northwest-trending, doubly plunging anticline that is cored by Precambrian crystalline basement (Fig. 1). The basement is composed mainly of Archean granitoids and gneisses, with minor metamorphosed supracrustal rocks, and is overlain by a thin sequence of Paleozoic and Mesozoic sedimentary beds. The first-order antiform is asymmetric with a long, gently dipping northeast limb and a steeper, shorter southwest limb. Along the western flank of the range, the Archean basement is thrust over Phanerozoic sediments in the Green River basin along the Wind River thrust (Fig. 1). This major fault can be traced to a depth of 20 km on seismic sections at the southern end of the range

(Zawislak and Smithson, 1981), with an average dip of 35° and a displacement of about 20 km. The northern end of the range (Richmond, 1945) is perhaps the best exposure of a thick-skinned Laramide foreland thrust sheet and shows deformation features developed in both the basement and the overlying sedimentary cover (Fig. 2). Initial uplift in the Wind River Range began in Campanian time about 72 Ma and continued at least until early Eocene (52 Ma) when the Precambrian crystalline rocks were first breached (Dorr and others, 1977).

The basement rocks in the core of the anticline are cut by deformation zones of different ages formed at various metamorphic grades (Mitra and Frost, 1981). Laramide deformation is represented by an anastomosing series of small brittle deformation zones or BDZs (Mitra, 1980), which produce internal shortening of the basement, and occasionally reach up into the adjoining Phanerozoic cover (Fig. 2). The BDZs bound blocks that are internally less deformed. There are three main sets of BDZs: (1) a set of prominent zones that dip moderately to the east, with reverse sense of slip; (2) a set of zones that dip steeply to the west, and have a reverse sense of slip; and (3) a less well developed set of oblique slip zones that are steeply dipping and strike west-northwest. Figure 2 also shows a series of second-order anticlines that are cored by basement and are associated with the BDZs. These folds plunge to the north (approximately 30° toward N10W) and thus a range of structural levels is exposed in the northern Wind River mountains.

A down-plunge projection of this area (Fig. 3) shows the two sets of deformation zones that strike parallel to regional structural trends, and cut both the basement and the sedimentary cover. One set of BDZs dips 40° to the east and includes the White Rock and Wind River thrusts. The basement-cover unconformity is displaced by about 5 km on each thrust. The thrusts are marked by anastomosing footwall imbricates that bound complexly deformed sedimentary rocks. Beds in the footwalls of the thrusts are rotated into synforms with overturned limbs adjacent to the faults. Bedding is thinned by movement along numerous high-angle and low-angle extension faults that formed during simple shear near the thrusts (Fig. 4A).

Figure 3 also shows a second set of reverse slip zones that dip steeply to the west, and include the New Fork, Osborn, Battleship, and Saltlick BDZs (Richmond, 1945). These zones rapidly lose displacement upward into tip antiforms in the sedimentary cover. The antiforms are asymmetric, with gently dipping western limbs and steep to overturned eastern limbs where bedding is locally thinned (Fig. 4B). These folds have amplitudes of as much as 3 km and kink geometries, with approximately planar limbs and relatively narrow hinges. Many of the kink band boundaries defining these folds intersect the BDZs near the basement-cover unconformity, an intersection geometry that does not require folding of the basement. The basement blocks are locally rotated due to movement along the BDZs. The two sets of BDZs probably formed synchronously, as indicated by the partially rotated tip antiform beneath the White Rock thrust. Folding in the sedimentary rocks is locally disharmonic, as shown by an

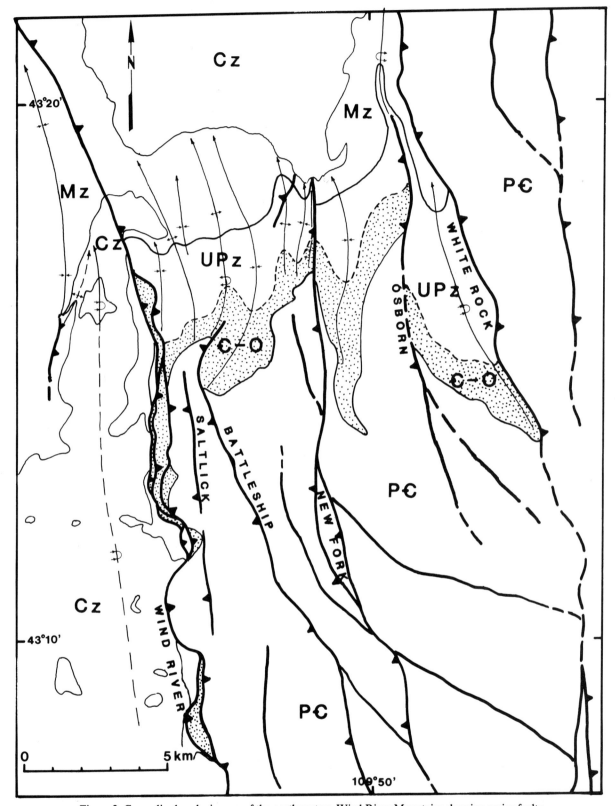

Figure 2. Generalized geologic map of the northwestern Wind River Mountains showing major faults and anastomosing deformation zones within the Precambrian basement, and north-plunging folds in the sedimentary cover. Symbols: PЄ = Precambrian, Є-O = Cambrian-Ordovician, UPz = Upper Paleozoic, Mz = Mesozoic, Cz = Cenozoic.

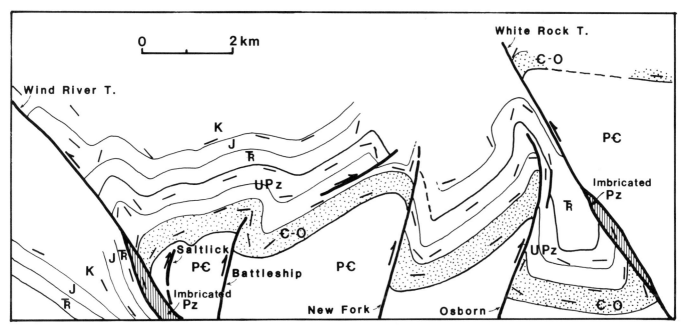

Figure 3. Down-plunge projection (looking north) of northwestern part of the Wind River Mountains. East-dipping reverse faults juxtapose basement against footwall synclines in the sedimentary cover. Steeply west-dipping faults end in the cores of tip-anticlines. Stratigraphic units: PC = Precambrian, C-O-Cambrian-Ordovician, Pz = Paleozoic, UPz = Upper Paleozoic, Tr = Triassic, J = Jurassic, K = Cretaceous.

antiform that was formed above a local detachment in Devonian limestones (Fig. 3). This fold has an amplitude of about 0.5 km and probably formed as shortening was tranferred out of the syncline that lies to the west.

The overall structural style is characterized by deformation of both the basement and the overlying sedimentary cover. Shortening in the basement results dominantly from slip on a conjugate set of reverse slip BDZs that produce significant components of both horizontal and vertical displacement. Most large-scale structures in the sedimentary covers are directly related to the BDZs that cut the basement. There is an overall transfer of shortening from movement on BDZs in the basement to folding in the sedimentary cover. There is no major regional décollement, although there is some localized disharmonic folding in the cover.

Mesoscopic and microscopic structures in basement

The deformation in the basement is concentrated along the BDZs that bound less deformed blocks. The BDZs are characterized by intense fracturing and widespread chlorite alteration, and are typically strongly weathered. The zone of fracturing and weathering may reach 0.5 km in width, although the most intense cataclasis typically occurs in zones 1 to 10 m wide (Mitra, 1984). Within these zones there are numerous thinner anastomosing zones of ultracataclasite, microbreccia, and fine-grained gouge (Fig. 5A) surrounding less-deformed lithons. There are also thin (less than 1 m) BDZs with small displacements (less than 10 m) within the lithons, as well as numerous shear and tension frac-

tures. Much of this fracturing extends into the cover at the basement-cover unconformity and is likely to have formed during Laramide deformation. The fracture spacing is variable, but shortening values from fracturing are generally less than 5 percent (engineer's strain).

There is a general correlation between the overall width and displacement of BDZs (Robertson, 1983), suggesting that the BDZs probably grew in thickness with time and with increasing displacement (Mitra, 1980). Thus, the progression of structures from the edge to the middle of a BDZ provides a time sequence for the development of the BDZ. Studies across the New Fork and White Rock BDZs illustrate the changes in deformation mechanisms that are responsible for concentration of strain in the BDZs during progressive deformation.

Deformation in the granitic basement begins with the development of unstable (transgranular) fractures (Lawn and Wilshaw, 1975) (Fig. 5B) and associated minor plastic deformation. A series of closely spaced fractures with small shear displacements develop with increasing deformation. These unstable fractures can result from two main micromechanisms, cleavage 1 and cleavage 2 (following Ashby and others, 1979; Gandhi and Ashby, 1979; Atkinson, 1982; Mitra, 1984), which are microscopically indistinguishable. In cleavage 1, fracturing is controlled by preexisting cracks with no plastic deformation except locally at crack tips. In cleavage 2, fracturing is controlled by cracks nucleated at stress concentrations due to dislocation pile-ups after small amounts of plastic strain (less than 1 percent) within grains.

The fractures locally anastomose with one another, forming

lenticular fragments and producing wear fragments by frictional sliding; this results in an overall decrease in grain size (Fig. 5C). Grain-size reduction results in strain hardening, with higher stresses required to propagate new fractures according to the Hall-Petch relationship (Lawn and Wilshaw, 1975; Mitra, 1978). With continued deformation, the very fine-grained material forms a ductile matrix that controls the mechanical behavior of the rock when it makes up as little as 10 percent of the rock by volume (Mitra, 1978). Large grains of quartz and feldspar continue to deform by fracturing, but the fractures are blunted (stabilized) at grain boundaries by the ductile matrix. This stable fracturing continues to reduce the average grain size until the larger grains are "floating" in the fine-grained matrix.

The matrix consists of fine-grained quartz with minor amounts of feldspars, micas, and iron oxides. The grain size of the matrix generally varies from less than 2 μm to 15 μm, with a mean grain size of about 6 μm in the most deformed samples (Fig. 5D). Mitra (1984) has suggested that the grain-size reduction results in a change in deformation mechanism to diffusional mass transfer processes accommodated by some form of grain boundary sliding. Evidence for diffusional creep includes pressure solution along quartz grains that are indented into one another and pressure shadows filled with syntectonic chlorite. The very low temperatures of this fluid-assisted deformation suggest that its accommodating mechanism was a low-temperature, viscous

grain boundary sliding or particulate flow (Borradaile, 1981) that is different from both the frictional grain boundary sliding usually invoked for fault gouge and the high temperature grain boundary sliding associated with superplastic mylonites. This change from dominantly brittle deformation to a strain-softening ductile deformation localizes strain along narrow zones within the major BDZs and allows large strains to accumulate along these zones.

Discrete gouge zones and unstable brittle fractures locally cut across the matrix and record periodic strain hardening later in the deformation history (Fig. 5A). Cycles of strain hardening and softening are also suggested by breccia-in-breccia structures,

Figure 4. A, Photograph of complex deformation in overturned limb of footwall syncline of the White Rock thrust. Steep normal faults (at high angles to bedding) and reactivated wedge faults (at low angles to bedding) extend bedding that is rotated into the stretching direction. Highly fractured Precambrian basement is seen in the hanging wall of the thrust. B, Photograph looking down the plunge of the tip anticline of the Battleship BDZ. Bedding is locally thinned in the eastern limb of the anticline, which has long planar limbs and a sharp hinge. Highly fractured and altered basement along the BDZ is exposed in the foreground.

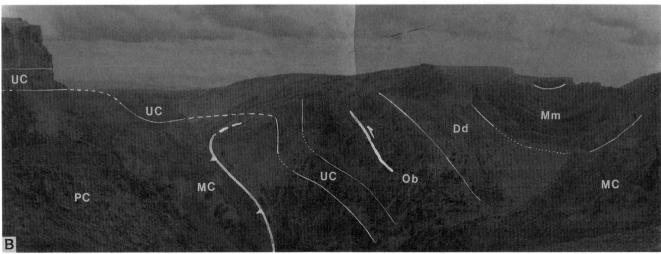

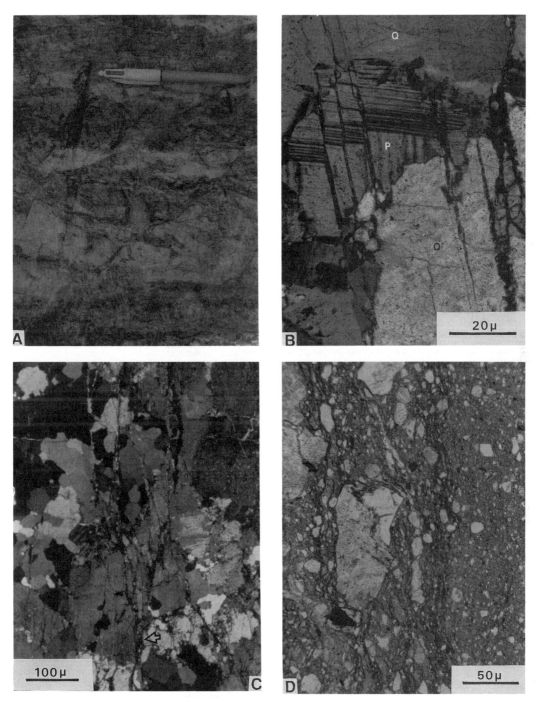

Figure 5. A, Anastomosing zones of ultracataclasite and microbreccia in the central part of the New Fork BDZ. Note ductile flowage of fine-grained matrix around fractured lenses of granite. B, Photomicrograph showing microstructures developed at the edge of a BDZ in P€ granitic basement. Unstable fractures cut across plagioclase (P) and quartz (Q) grains, with small offsets of albite twin planes across each fracture. Crossed polarizers. C, Photomicrograph showing anastomosing unstable fractures produce lenticular fragments in P€ granitic basement. Early fractures develop thin gouge zones (arrow) as wear fragments are produced from frictional sliding. Crossed polarizers. D, Photomicrograph of fine-grained cataclasite (grain size <5 μm) in P€ granitic basement shows ductile deformation textures, with matrix flowing around coarse, brittle fragments. Concentration of opaque minerals into bands by pressure solution, and growth of pressure shadow tails produce a crude foliation. Plane polarized light.

where clasts of breccia are surrounded by almost identical matrix material (Fig. 5D). The presence of late-stage fluids is recorded by local veins of less-deformed calcite within the BDZs, but fluid pressures may have fluctuated during the deformation history. One mechanism of strain hardening involving changing fluid pressure is dilatancy hardening (Frank, 1965; Orowan, 1966; Rudnicki, 1984), where fluid flow cannot keep pace with dilatancy, resulting in a drop in pore pressure and an increase in the strength of the rock.

Basement strain estimates

In rocks undergoing brittle deformation, a population of faults can be used to estimate principal strain or stress directions (Arthaud, 1969; Angelier, 1979, 1984; Aleksandrowski, 1985). The orientation of net slip lineations and M-lines (perpendicular to the net slip on the fault) define the symmetry of deformation. The minimum strain energy requirement predicts that faults will form in certain orientations, depending on the strain state and the angle of friction (Reches, 1978, 1983). In plane-strain pure shear, M-lines cluster about the intermediate principal strain direction (Y), while the net slip lineations define a great circle that contains the principal stretching (X) and shortening (Z) directions. The acute bisector of an Anderson-type conjugate set of brittle faults (Anderson, 1942) corresponds to the Z direction. Thus, for isotropic materials undergoing irrotational strain, principal strain directions can be easily estimated. For rotational plane strain, rotation about the Y direction does not change the orientation of most M-lines, and net-slip lineations remain in the XZ plane. Thus, principal directions can also be estimated for other simple strain states such as simple shear.

Slickenlines (Fleuty, 1975) on discrete gouge and fracture surfaces within the New Fork BDZ define an east-west girdle with a broad point maximum that plunges gently to the west (Fig. 6A,i). This girdle reflects essentially east-west displacements and approximately plane strain. The M lines define a north-south girdle with a strong point maximum (Y) that plunges very gently to the south (Fig. 6A,ii). Fold axes (generally parallel to Y) are also very gently plunging in this area. Poles to gouge and slickenside surfaces define two diffuse maxima that are steeply plunging and separated by about 50° (Fig. 6A,iii). These maxima probably correspond to a conjugate fault set with an acute bisector (Z) that plunges gently to the west and coincides with the broad maximum in the slickenline girdle.

A smaller data set from the White Rock thrust shows similar patterns. Slickenlines define a broad east-west girdle with a gently plunging maximum (Fig. 6B,i). The broad great circle is consistent with approximately plane strain, although the greater variability suggests a more complicated strain history. M-lines define a diffuse north-south girdle with a point maximum (Y) that plunges gently to the north (Fig. 6B,ii). The X direction is steeply plunging, defined by the intersection of the M line and slickenline girdles. Poles to the slickenside surfaces define a very broad maxi-

mum that plunges steeply to moderately to the southwest (Fig. 6B,iii); a conjugate fault set is not apparent.

The BDZs offset a set of Late Archean, unmetamorphosed, internally undeformed, planar diabase dikes. The net slip direction for a BDZ is defined by the intersection of the BDZ boundary and the XZ plane, and the amount of net slip can be estimated using the separation of the dikes along the BDZ. For example, a net slip of about 3,500 m, with a slip vector plunging 80° to the west, can be calculated from a steeply dipping diabase dike that has a left-lateral separation of 1,500 m across the New Fork BDZ. This slip is considerably greater than the 2,000 m of displacement of the basement-cover unconformity shown in the down-plunge projection. The difference may reflect an upward decrease in slip along a propagating BDZ. Because the intersection of the dike and the BDZ is at a low angle to the slip direction, the estimated slip is very sensitive to small changes in the geometry. The Battleship BDZ has a similar orientation and a calculated net slip of about 1,500 m. There are several smaller BDZs in this area that have net slips on the order of 100 to 200 m.

The diabase dikes are buried beneath the sedimentary cover in the footwalls of the White Rock and Wind River thrusts. Hence, the net slips on these faults must be calculated by other means. The down-plunge projection (Fig. 9) is drawn parallel to the XZ plane for these faults, and the net slip can be estimated from the separation of the basement-cover unconformity. Both thrusts show about 5 km of displacement of the unconformity. A set of conjugate faults with oppositely directed net slips will approximate bulk pure shear (Bell, 1981), with the principal directions parallel to the bisectors of the set. The major BDZs just described form a conjugate set with a 60° dihedral angle, and have opposite shear senses and similar net slips on subparallel movement planes; these features are all consistent with bulk deformation of the basement by plane strain pure shear.

The BDZs exposed in the study area are approximately planar to anastomosing, and the basement-cover unconformity shows only small amounts of rotation. As most of the strain in the basement is concentrated along major BDZs, the bulk strain in the rocks can be estimated by summing individual displacements on the BDZs. The elongation and orientation of two markers is sufficient to estimate the average bulk deformation gradient for such sets of faults (W. A. Yonkee and others, unpublished data). Using this method, the principal shortening axis is determined to have a rake of 3° east on the XZ plane in the Green River Lakes area (see Fig. 9). The rotation of the principal directions during deformation is less than 5°, indicating approximately pure shear deformation. The principal quadratic elongations are $\lambda_3 = 0.53$ and $\lambda_1 = 1.44$, corresponding to about 30 percent shortening (engineer's strain) parallel to λ_3. The east-west subhorizontal bulk shortening direction is subparallel to the shortening directions estimated from the slickensides. Although the calculated bulk deformation matrix is only a crude approximation of the total displacement field, the matrix provides qualitative insights into the overall deformation and supports the slickenside analysis.

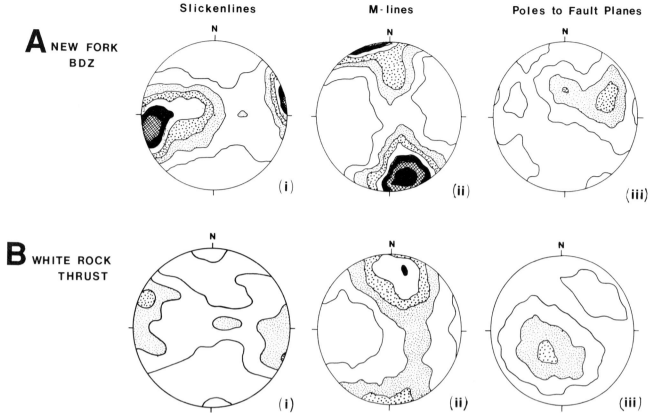

Figure 6. A, Equal-area projection of data from 135 slickenside surfaces in the New Fork BDZ. Contours drawn by the Kamb method at 1σ intervals. (i) Slickenlines define an east-west girdle that records approximately plane strain. (ii) M-lines define a north-south girdle with a south-plunging point maximum. (iii) Poles to slickenside surfaces define broad, steeply plunging, double maxima. B, Data from 38 slickenside surfaces in the White Rock thrust zone. (i) Slickenlines define an east-west girdle that records approximately plane strain. (ii) M-lines define a north-south girdle with a north-plunging point maximum. (iii) Poles to slickenside surfaces define a broad point maximum representing faults dipping moderately to the northeast.

Sedimentary cover structures

Internal shortening in the sedimentary cover is produced by a variety of mesoscopic and microscopic structures. Most of the shortening is accomplished by movement along small-scale faults or BDZs. Several sets of BDZs are developed, the most common being contraction faults (Fig. 7A) that account for approximately 5 percent shortening (engineer's strain) at the outcrop scale. Many contraction faults are at a low angle to bedding around large-scale folds, and thus probably formed prior to large-scale folding. Other contraction faults locally cut bedding at high angles in steeply dipping fold limbs and thus formed later in the deformation. Small-scale extension faults are also widespread, especially in overturned fold limbs where faults extend and thin beds that have been rotated into the stretching direction. Additionally, early formed contraction faults may be rotated and reactivated as extension faults, producing further stretching of bedding. Cross-fractures are locally developed and produce minor extension parallel to the major fold axis.

The BDZs are marked by thin zones of gouge and breccia that form by cataclasis. Fractures in the zones generally propagate across grain boundaries and fossil fragments. Fine-grained zones containing opaque residue and fibrous calcite parallel to the fault boundaries suggest local pressure solution within fault zones (Fig. 7B). The calcite fibers trend approximately east-west on most faults, parallel to the overall translation. Local calcite-filled veins that crosscut all other structures indicate that fracturing was important through the late stages of deformation.

Small-scale disharmonic buckle folds in thinly bedded limestones also record early layer-parallel shortening (Fig. 7C). Most of these folds have axes that plunge gently to the north, subparallel to the major fold axes (Fig. 8A). Axial surfaces of the buckle folds strike north-south and partially fan about the large-scale folds. Shortening from these buckle folds is less than 5 percent at the outcrop scale. Cross-folds, with axes at a high angle to the major fold axes, are less well developed, and produce only minor local shortening parallel to the major fold axes.

Petrographic examination of the sedimentary rocks, particularly limestones, reveals evidence for a variety of deformation mechanisms. Wide-spaced tectonic stylolites in some bioclastic

Figure 7. A, Wedge (contraction) faults in Paleozoic limestone at Green River Lake. Bedding is vertical and the faults are at low angle (<30°) to bedding. Both bedding and the faults have been rotated to steep dips during large-scale folding. View looking north. B, Photomicrograph of thin BDZ (upper right) in Paleozoic dolomite. Note local concentration of insoluble residue in the BDZ gouge giving rise to a crude foliation. The rock also shows well-developed veins (V) cut by stylolites (S) (lower left). C, Small-scale buckle folds in Paleozoic medium-bedded limestone at Green River Lake. The folds are disharmonic, and shorten bedding by as much as 5 percent. View looking north. D, Stylolites and associated calcite-filled sigmoidal veins in a small shear zone in Paleozoic limestone on Sheep Mountain. Note undeformed coral within zone, indicating absence of penetrative plastic deformation. View looking down on subhorizontal bedding surface, north toward top of photograph.

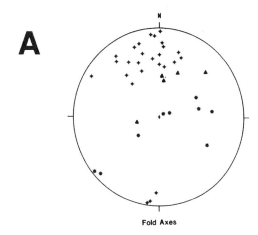

Fold Axes

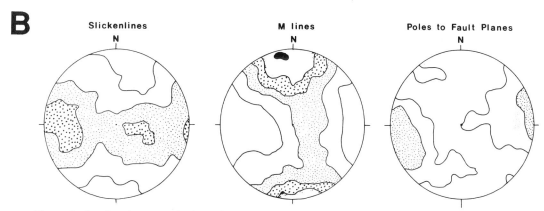

Figure 8. A, Equal-area projection of fold axes for small-scale buckle folds. Most axes (+) are subparallel to the gently north plunging, large-scale fold axis. Axes of small conical folds are shown by triangles. Axes of cross-folds (*) define an east-west girdle at a large angle to the regional fold axis. B, Equal-area projection of data from 37 slickenside surfaces in the sedimentary cover. The data are contoured by the Kamb method using a contour interval of 1σ. (i) Slickenline and calcite fiber lineations define an east-west girdle that records approximately plane strain. (ii) M-lines define a north-south girdle with a point maximum that plunges gently northward, subparallel to the regional fold axis. (iii) Poles to slickenside surfaces define a broad maximum plunging gently westward.

limestones (Fig. 7D) truncate otherwise undeformed fossil fragments, and are marked by insoluble residue (Fig. 7B and D). The stylolites dissolve calcite veins and in turn are cut by other veins (Fig. 7D), indicating concurrent development of veins and stylolites. The stylolites, which generally strike north-south and are oriented at moderate to high angles to bedding, account for less than 5 percent shortening by pressure solution. A very minor amount of plastic shortening is recorded by mechanical twinning of calcite, but fossils are not significantly changed in shape. These microstructures are similar to those in the adjacent Idaho-Wyoming thrust belt, but are less well developed; cataclasis appears to be the dominant deformation mechanism in most cover lithologies in the Wind River Mountains.

Strain estimates in sedimentary rocks

The principal strain directions in the sedimentary cover can be estimated from populations of slickensides and corresponding calcite-fiber slickenlines. Most slickenlines in the sedimentary rocks define a broad east-west girdle recording slip subperpendicular to the major fold axes (Fig. 8B,i). M-lines define a north-south great circle with a point maximum (Y) that plunges gently to the north (Fig. 8B,ii) parallel to the fold axes. This geometry is consistent with approximately plane strain parallel to the plane of the down-plunge projection (Fig. 9). Poles to the slickenside surfaces define a diffuse pattern with a very weak maximum that plunges gently westward (Fig. 8B,iii). The bulk principal extension (X) is probably parallel to the intersection of the M-line and slickenline girdles. Rotation of slickenside surfaces and the anisotropic nature of the cover complicates the interpretation of the pattern, but there is a close correspondence between the strain directions estimated for both the sedimentary cover and the basement.

The magnitude of shortening of the sedimentary cover can be estimated by measuring deformed bed lengths in the down-plunge projection (Fig. 3). Shortening from small-scale structures

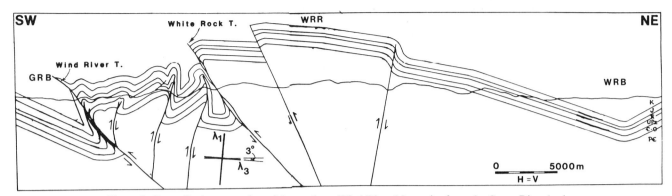

Figure 9. Generalized cross section of the northern Wind River Mountains from the Green River basin (GRB) to the Wind River basin (WRB). Two sets of faults shorten the basement and are associated with folds in the sedimentary cover. Total basement shortening is approximately 30 percent. In the sedimentary cover, fold shortening ranges from 21 percent in Cambrian strata to 23 percent in Jurassic strata; additional shortening of 7 to 9 percent is achieved by internal shortening of beds. Orientation of maximum (λ_1) and minimum (λ_3) principal axes of strain are shown.

is generally less than 5 percent, and bed thicknesses remain approximately constant (except locally in overturned fold limbs). Taking this internal shortening of the beds into account, the total shortening in the sedimentary cover is approximately 30 percent, similar to the shortening estimates for the basement. Large-scale folds show both east and west vergence, reflecting the conjugate set of BDZs in the basement. The deformation in the cover probably approximates bulk pure shear as in the basement, although there are more complex local rotations.

Summary

Regional shortening of the sedimentary cover is best calculated by drawing a line-length balanced section for the northern Wind River Mountains, between basins where the bedding returns to horizontal (Fig. 9). Overall, there is general agreement in both the geometry and magnitude of deformation in the cover and basement. The strain approximates plane strain bulk pure shear in both, and both show approximately equal amounts of subhorizontal shortening (30 percent, engineer's strain). In the basement, slip on conjugate BDZs produces significant components of horizontal and vertical displacement resulting in more than 10 km of structural relief on the basement-cover unconformity. There is an overall transfer of shortening from slip on basement BDZs to folding in the sedimentary cover.

CRAWFORD THRUST SHEET

Large-scale structure

Large-scale structure style of the Idaho-Utah-Wyoming thrust belt is characterized by translation and shortening along major thrust faults. The thrust faults have a stair-step geometry, with each having as much as 20 km of displacement. The thrusts generally dip to the west at less than 30°; thus, there is a dominant

component of horizontal translation. Major folds formed in the hanging walls of the thrusts, as strata were translated over the stair-step geometry and tip anticlines formed locally during propagation of the thrusts. The folds have concentric to kink geometries, and a regional décollement separates the folded and faulted sedimentary cover from crystalline basement. There are also major décollement horizons in the cover that separate sedimentary packages that shorten by different amounts and with different styles (Coogan and Boyer, 1985). There is significant and complex internal shortening within the thrust sheets associated with small-scale imbricate thrusts and folding.

The Crawford and Meade thrust sheets are located in the central part of the Idaho-Utah-Wyoming thrust belt (Fig. 1). Major movement on the Crawford thrust is recorded by the Middle Coniacian (88 Ma) Echo Canyon conglomerate (Wiltschko and Dorr, 1983). The eastern boundary of the Crawford sheet is marked by the Crawford thrust, which places Paleozoic to Lower Mesozoic strata over Upper Mesozoic strata (Fig. 10A); northward, the thrust cores a major tip anticline that marks the eastern boundary of the sheet. The western boundary is marked by the trace of the Meade thrust, which parallels the Crawford thrust for a considerable strike distance. The structures described here are those developed between the Meade and Crawford thrusts in this broad transfer zone, where structural relationships have been documented by previous work (Mansfield, 1927; Cressman, 1964; Rubey and others, 1975, 1980; Oriel and Platt, 1980; Evans and Spang, 1984; Mitra and Yonkee, 1985; Coogan and Yonkee, 1985).

The subsurface geometry of the Crawford thrust is shown in Figure 10B, which is derived from a series of cross sections presented by Dixon (1982). The Crawford thrust ramps up from the basal décollement in Lower Paleozoic strata to a glide horizon in the Jurassic Preuss Formation. The thrust then glides subparallel to Preuss salt beds for as much as 20 km before ramping to the surface (Coogan and Yonkee, 1985). A cross section across the northern part of the sheet illustrates the typical ramp-flat geometry of the major thrust faults (Fig. 11). The Sublette anticline (Evans and Spang, 1984)—the dominant feature in the eastern part of the thrust sheet—is a major ramp anticline formed where the hanging-wall ramp cutoffs were rotated during translation onto a footwall flat in the Preuss Formation. West of the anticline is the broad Red Mountain syncline, which folds the Jurassic and Cretaceous strata. West of the syncline, a fold train is developed above a décollement at the base of the Jurassic Twin Creek Formation (Coogan and Boyer, 1985; Protzman and Mitra, 1985). This décollement represents the frontal portion of the Sheep Creek thrust that produced further internal shortening within the Crawford sheet. A hanging-wall ramp anticline, the Western anticline, developed above this thrust. The dominant feature in the westernmost part of the Crawford sheet is the Home Canyon anticline (Cressman, 1964), which folds the Pa-

leozoic and Mesozoic sections and overlying Meade thrust sheet (Fig. 11). Although the Meade thrust is folded, its original ramp-flat geometry is still apparent. The thrust ramps upward from Mississippian limestones to glide horizons in the Twin Creek and Preuss Formations, following these horizons for about 20 km before ramping to the surface.

Mesoscopic and microscopic structures

Further internal shortening within the thrust sheet is associated with mesoscopic and microscopic structures. Detailed structural relationships between these minor structures and the large-scale features provide insights into the structural history of the Crawford sheet. Strain markers, including cleavage, vein arrays, and deformed fossils, are particularly useful for understanding the deformation history of the sheet. All of these features are

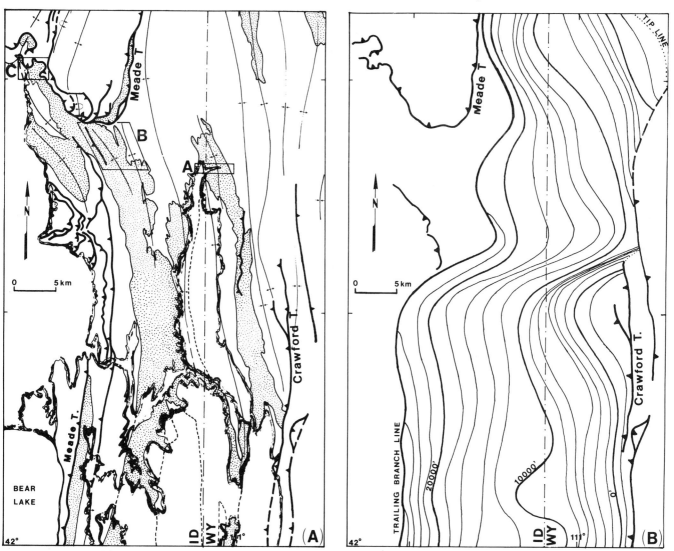

Figure 10. A, Generalized geologic map of the northern part of the Crawford thrust sheet. Jurassic Twin Creek Formation is stippled. Areas of detailed study are outlined: A = Salt Canyon, B = Whiskey Flat, C = Georgetown Canyon. B, Structure contour map of northern part of Crawford thrust plane superposed on map showing thrust traces.

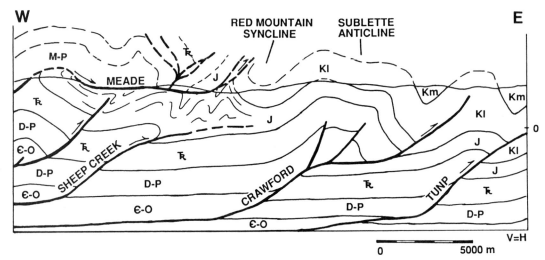

Figure 11. Generalized cross section across the northern part of the Crawford thrust sheet. Note the stair-step geometry of the thrusts and the folds associated with that geometry. Also note the folding of the overlying Meade sheet, and the significant shortening in the Crawford sheet due to imbricate faults and associated folds.

present in the micrites of the Jurassic Twin Creek Formation, which is well exposed over most of the sheet. Three representative areas have been studied in detail (Fig. 10A): the Salt Canyon area, which covers part of the Sublette anticline; the Whiskey Flat area, which includes the fold train above the Sheep Creek décollement; and the Georgetown Canyon area, which illustrates folding in the footwall of the Meade thrust.

Salt Canyon area

The Salt Canyon area covers part of a hanging-wall ramp anticline that approximates a double kink (Fig. 12). The cleavage is strongly fanned about this fold and remains subperpendicular to bedding in both the crest and the limbs (Fig. 13A). Cleavage intensity (spacing) is nearly constant around the fold, and cleavage does not refract between micrite and sparry limestone layers. Thus, cleavage formed during layer-parallel shortening early in

the deformation history, and accounts for most of the early strain. Cleavage was later passively rotated during large-scale folding concurrent with major movement on the Crawford thrust.

Small-scale buckle folding within thin-bedded interlayered siltstones and micrites produced minor shortening. Cleavage in these buckle folds is almost axial planar, with small amounts of refraction between the siltstone and micrite layers (Fig. 13B). Thus, the cleavage and the small-scale buckle folds formed concurrently during early shortening. Small-scale contraction faults also produced minor internal shortening. Cleavage is better developed near these contraction faults and becomes asymptotic to the faults, suggesting concurrent development with simple shear along the faults. The amount and sense of shear along the faults does not vary systematically across the large-scale anticline, again suggesting that the cleavage and contraction faults formed prior to large-scale folding.

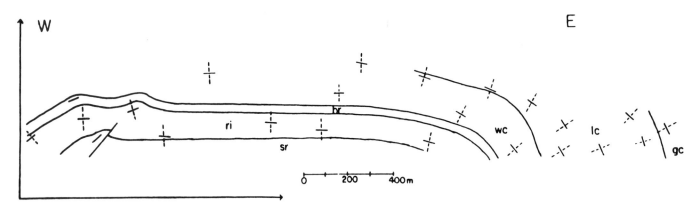

Figure 12. Down-plunge projection showing double kink anticline in the Salt Canyon area. Cleavage (short dashed lines) is strongly fanned, remaining subperpendicular to bedding around the fold. Members of the Twin Creek Formation: gc = Giraffe Creek, lc = Leeds Creek, wc = Watton Canyon, br = Boundary Ridge, ri = Rich, sl = Sliderock.

Figure 13. A, Cleavage in micrites of the Twin Creek Formation is defined by closely spaced partings in outcrop along Montpelier Canyon. Cleavage (steeply dipping) is approximately perpendicular to bedding. Meter stick for scale. View looking north. B, Photomicrograph of small-scale buckle fold with cleavage parallel to the axial plane. Note small amounts of refraction of cleavage between micrite and siltstone layers. C, Photomicrograph showing cleavage defined by spaced anastomosing seams of dark insoluble residue that bound less deformed micrite lithons. Calcite-filled veins are at high angle to the cleavage seams. Veins offset cleavage seams and are offset by cleavage seams, indicating that both features formed at the same time. Plane polarized light. D, Breccia zone (BR, lower right) along first-order kink band boundary (of Salt Canyon kink fold) illustrating the importance of cataclasis late in the deformation history. Cleavage (S_1) is folded adjacent to the zone and a weak, fanned second cleavage (S_2) has formed. Bedding (S_0) is steeply dipping.

Microscopically, the cleavage is defined by spaced seams of insoluble residue that bound relatively less deformed micrite lithons (Fig. 13C). The seams truncate undeformed fossil fragments and ooids, and cut across some calcite-filled veins and are offset by others (Fig. 13C). Thus, the veins and the cleavage formed concurrently, with material dissolved from the cleavage seams being precipitated in the veins. These features are all characteristic of pressure-solution cleavage (Durney, 1972), indicating that early in the deformation history the dominant deformation mechanism within the micrites was pressure solution. The wide variety of vein arrays gives some indication of the complicated deformation history. A set of bed-parallel planar fractures produced extension perpendicular to bedding, concurrent with the shortening perpendicular to the cleavage seams. Straight to sigmoidal fractures in en echelon arrays occur in two conjugate sets of shear zones. One set strikes north-south and produced minor shortening perpendicular to the direction of transport of the thrust sheet. Another set strikes east-west and accommodated differential translation and minor variations in strain parallel to the transport direction of the sheet. The overall deformation in the shear zones was probably produced by a combination of low-temperature grain boundary sliding, pressure solution, and unstable fracturing. Some fractures contain fibrous calcite that shows evidence of formation by the crack-seal mechanism (Ramsay, 1981).

There is a significant amount of early layer-parallel shortening produced by the development of the pressure solution cleavage. The cleavage seams are subparallel to calcite fibers in veins and pressure shadows, indicating that the seams formed subperpendicular to the principal shortening direction. The widths of the cleavage seams are proportional to the amount of calcite dissolved along the seams and to the amount of insoluble residue originally in the micrite. Thus, shortening associated with cleavage development can be estimated from the width of the seams, and shortening values (engineer's strain) range from 5 to 25 percent (with an average value of about 15 percent) in the Salt Canyon area (Yonkee, 1983).

Flexural slip during later large-scale folding occurred along discrete gouge horizons that are subparallel to bedding. Breccia zones also occur along the kink band boundaries of the anticline (Fig. 13D). Thus, the dominant deformation mechanism changed from pressure solution early in the deformation history to cataclasis by the time of major movement on the Crawford thrust. The cleavage is locally folded next to the breccia zones, and a very weak second cleavage parallel to the axial surfaces of the folds records some minor pressure solution continuing late in the deformation.

Whiskey Flat Area

A second-order fold train is developed in the Jurassic rocks in the hanging wall of the Sheep Creek thrust where it glides in the gypsum beds at the base of the Twin Creek Formation (Fig. 14). The folds are upright to overturned eastward and concentric to chevron in shape, accounting for a significant amount

of internal shortening of the Jurassic section within the Crawford sheet. Anticlinal fold hinges are truncated by the last imbricates of the Meade thrust (Protzman, 1985), indicating that the folding occurred concurrently with the final phases of movement on the overlying Meade thrust. The folded Twin Creek beds also show evidence for significant amounts of internal shortening by pressure solution and plastic deformation.

Cleavage is very well developed in the clay-rich micrites, which show gradations from spaced cleavage seams to an almost penetrative fabric. Cleavage is typically oriented at a high angle to bedding and is strongly fanned around folds (Fig. 14). The cleaner limestones show well-developed stylolites that are parallel to cleavage seams in the adjacent micrites (Fig. 15A). Shortening strains have been estimated from the stylolites by assuming that the average height of the stylolite teeth represents the amount of material removed by solution from the stylolitic surface (Stockdale, 1926). Engineer's strain values range from 3 to 18 percent, similar to the pressure solution strains in the Salt Canyon area.

Plastic strains within the Twin Creek limestones can be determined from deformed *Pentacrinus* ossicles that occur in several fossil hash layers (Fig. 15B). Strains can be determined from bed-parallel and bed-normal fossils using angular changes (Fig. 15C) from the original pentameral symmetry of *Pentacrinus* (Protzman, 1985). Strain ellipse axial ratios range from 1.2 to 4.2, corresponding to engineer's strain shortening values of 2 to 47 percent. The higher strain values are associated with observed discrete deformation zones (containing strongly deformed *Pentacrinus*), which bound less-deformed rock. The overall plastic strain has a large component of flattening oriented at high angles to bedding with the stretching direction fanned around later folds. The long axis of the plastic strain ellipse in the XZ principal plane closely tracks the orientation of the cleavage traces, as seen in down-plunge projections (Fig. 14). This strain geometry suggests that the plastic deformation took place during early layer-parallel shortening, and accompanied pressure solution deformation.

In thin section, deformed fossils are truncated along solution seams and are crosscut by undeformed calcite-filled veins (Fig. 15C). Such relationships indicate that the plastic deformation occurred at the same time or slightly earlier than the pressure solution strain. Thus, both the cleavage planes and the plastic strain stretching direction began at high angles to bedding during early layer-parallel shortening; both underwent passive rotation during later folding in the Meade footwall.

Some of these deformed rocks are incorporated into the Meade hanging wall during late-stage footwall imbrication of the Meade thrust. The Twin Creek strata in these frontal slices of the Meade sheet do not exhibit multiple cleavages as is seen in the Montpelier Canyon and Salt Canyon sections (Mitra and Yonkee, 1985). Apparently the conditions that favor cleavage development no longer existed in these rocks, as they were plucked from the footwall and rapidly brought up to shallower levels by imbricate faults. Mesoscopic structures such as folds and faults continued to evolve within the hanging-wall slices, and the earlier formed cleavage was rotated to low angles to the thrust faults.

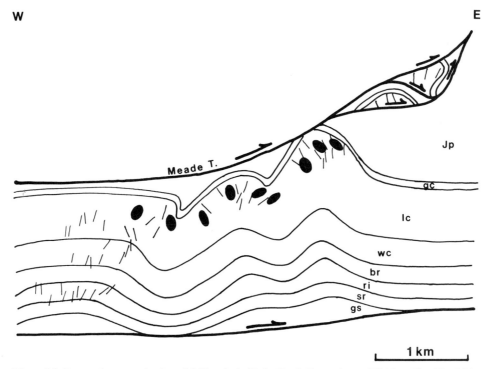

Figure 14. Down-plunge projection of fold train in Twin Creek Formation at Whiskey Flat. The folds form above a detachment in the Gypsum Spring Member. Both cleavage (short dashes) and the long axes of plastic strain (ellipses) are strongly fanned around the folds, and are at high angles to bedding. Penetrative strain took place early in the deformation history (during layer-parallel shortening); the strain markers were passively rotated during later folding. Stratigraphic units: Jp = Jurassic Preuss Formation, gc = Giraffe Creek, lc = Leeds Creek, wc = Watton Canyon, br = Boundary Ridge, ri = Rich, Sr = Sliderock, gs = Gypsum Spring members of the Jurassic Twin Creek Formation.

This late stage cleavage rotation must take place by some form of low-temperature grain boundary sliding or grain-scale particulate flow (Borradaile, 1981).

Georgetown Canyon area

The overturned limb of a complex footwall syncline that developed during movement on the main Meade thrust is exposed along Georgetown Canyon (Fig. 16). Cleavage forms a slightly convergent fan in the syncline with cleavage-bedding angles decreasing from 90° in the hinge to about 20° in the overturned limb near the thrust. Cleavage is also oriented at a low angle to the thrust and the cleavage intensity increases toward the thrust, indicating that cleavage was developing during simple shear associated with emplacement of the overlying Meade sheet. Silt layers in the micrites locally show normal offsets of several centimeters across cleavage seams and rotate into subparallelism with the seams. Some cleavage seams also show normal offsets across silt layers, resulting in an overall decrease in the average cleavage-bedding angle. The pressure solution cleavage did not track the rotating strain directions during simple shear close to the thrust fault. Some form of grain boundary sliding or particulate flow (Borradaile, 1981) is interpreted to have accommodated slip along the seams and silt layers.

Cleavage that had been rotated into shallow dips during early shear was later shortened by small-scale buckle folds and conjugate kinks (Fig. 15D). A weak second cleavage is developed subparallel to the axial surfaces of the buckle folds and cuts across the preexisting structures. Contraction faults at a low angle to the cleavage account for a significant component of this later shortening, and record an increase in the relative importance of cataclasis. Both the thrust and its footwall syncline were later rotated into an antiformal kink during the formation of the Home Canyon ramp anticline. This late antiformal kink passively rotated the cleavage so that cleavage-bedding relationships are similar on both limbs of the kink.

Strain estimates

The Twin Creek Formation was shortened at various scales within the Crawford sheet. The bedding datum has been shortened by about 50 percent in the cross section shown in Figure 11. Early layer parallel shortening produced approximately an additional 15 percent shortening within the micrites. The internal shortening is somewhat variable, and different structures (cleavage in micrites, folds in interlayered siltstones, and contraction faults) produced the shortening in different lithologies. This gives a combined shortening of about 60 percent, significantly greater

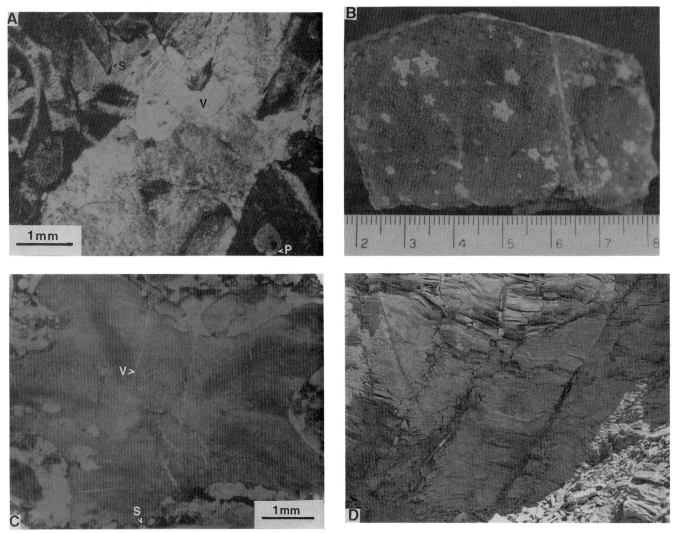

Figure 15. A, Photomicrograph of "clean" limestones of the Twin Creek Formation at Whiskey Flat showing well-developed stylolites (S) where material is dissolved, and veins (V) and pressure shadows (P) where calcite is reprecipitated. The height of the stylolite teeth can be used to determine the minimum amount of shortening by pressure solution. Plane polarized light. B, Deformed *Pentacrinus* ossicles (Twin Creek Formation at Whiskey Flat) lose their original pentameral symmetry. Their change in shape can be used to determine the plastic strain. Scale is in centimeters and millimeters. C. Photomicrograph of deformed *Pentacrinus* (Twin Creek Formation at Whiskey Flat) truncated by a solution seam (S) and crosscut by undeformed calcite-filled veins (V). Plastic deformation preceded or was contemporaneous with pressure solution. Plane polarizd light. D, Cleavage deformed by late stage cross-kinks in the Georgetown Canyon area.

than the estimated 30 percent shortening in the Wind River Mountains.

Conditions of deformation

The temperatures of deformation have been estimated by the crystallinities of illite in the cleavage seams (Mitra and Yonkee, 1985). Mineralogy, fluid characteristics, and time also influence illite crystallinities. Average illite-breadth values (Kisch, 1980) range from about 0.6 to 0.7 in the Crawford sheet and record deformation temperatures between about 150° and 200°C. Thermal models of the Crawford sheet indicate that these temperatures probably resulted from emplacement of the overriding Meade sheet. Intracrystalline plasticity and pressure solution could have been facilitated by the increased temperatures and pressures that accompany the emplacement of a relatively hotter thrust sheet over shallower cooler rocks (Yonkee, 1983). Maximum temperatures and pressures would have been reached soon after emplacement of the overlying Meade sheet, consistent with presure solution and plastic deformation during early layer-parallel shortening of the Crawford sheet.

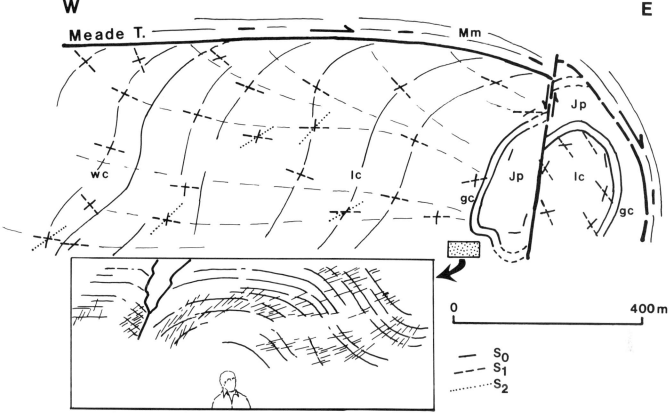

Figure 16. Down-plunge projection of Georgetown Canyon area, showing the complex footwall syncline of the Meade thrust. Both the Meade thrust and its footwall structures are folded into a first-order fold during motion on the later, lower Crawford thrust. Orientations of bedding (S_0), cleavage (S_1) and second cleavage (S_2) are shown. Stratigraphic units: Mm = Mississippian Madison Formation, wc = Watton Canyon, lc = Leeds Creek, gc = Giraffe Creek members of the Jurassic Twin Creek Formation, and the Jurassic Preuss Formation (Jp).

Summary

Structural features developed within the Crawford thrust sheet are typical of other thrust sheets within the Idaho-Wyoming thrust belt. Detailed structural studies can be used to give the overall deformation history of the Crawford sheet. Early layer-parallel shortening of beds that are to form the future thrust sheet are accomplished by pressure solution (giving rise to cleavage), plastic deformation (as indicated by deformed fossils), cataclasis (producing small-scale contraction faults), and small-scale buckle folding. Some of these features in the trailing edge of the future thrust sheet formed concurrently with late-stage footwall imbrication of the overlying Meade thrust. The pressure-temperature conditions for deformation within the Crawford sheet may have been partly imposed by the emplacement of the earlier overriding Meade sheet (Mitra and Yonkee, 1985).

Thrust sheets closer to the foreland in the Idaho-Wyoming thrust belt show similar features, although penetrative structures, such as cleavage, are not as well developed as in the Crawford sheet (Mitra and others, 1984; Mitra and Yonkee, 1985; Bradley and Bruhn, this volume). The Absaroka, Prospect, and Darby thrusts carry progressively thinner sedimentary sections in their hanging walls, and show more inhomogeneous cataclastic deformation. The Meade and the Williard thrusts, closer to the hinterland, carry thicker sections and show more complex internal deformation within the lower parts of the sheets (Cashman and others, 1986). All of these thrust faults have a stair-step geometry and generally dip shallowly to the west. The constant slip sense on the thrusts is interpreted to reflect plane-strain simple shear in the sedimentary cover.

DISCUSSION

A comparison of structures in the Wind River Mountains of the deformed foreland and the Crawford thrust sheet of the Idaho-Wyoming thrust belt reveals two distinct structural styles. The lithologic package in both areas consists of massive Precambrian crystalline basement overlain by a layered sedimentary cover. The mechanical response of this package to deforming forces and the geometry of shortening are quite different in these two areas.

The structural style of the northern part of the Wind River Mountains is characterized by shortening of the basement along an anastomosing set of BDZs that produce dominantly bulk pure shear in the basement. The deformation was concentrated in the BDZs due to strain softening along narrow zones where diffusion processes became dominant as grain size decreased during progressive cataclasis. Shortening in the sedimentary cover is achieved primarily by large-scale folds that are kinematically related to the BDZs in the basement. There is about 30 percent horizontal shortening of both the basement and the sedimentary cover, and also a large component of vertical displacement. Internal shortening in the sedimentary cover is less than 5 percent and is produced by contraction faults, buckle folds, and rare tectonic stylolites. Basement blocks between major BDZs also generally have less than 5 percent internal shortening along discrete shear fractures. Cataclasis was the dominant deformation mechanism for internal shortening in both the sedimentary cover and the basement.

On a more regional scale, basement was thrust westward in the northern Wind River Mountains, to the southwest in the central and south-central parts of the range, and to the south at the very southeastern tip. This variation in transport direction is also seen throughout the deformed foreland, but maximum shortening occurs in a northeast-southwest direction (Kanter and others, 1981). One possible explanation for the variable structural trends in the foreland is that preexisting mechanical anisotropy within the basement (e.g., layering or older faults) controls the orientation of Laramide faults (Stearns, 1975; Schmidt and Garihan, 1983). Detailed mapping in the northern Wind River Mountains, however, shows that Archean fabrics are quite variable over small distances and are frequently crosscut by uniform Laramide structures (Worl, 1967; Mitra and Frost, 1981). Similarly, in the southern Wind River Mountains, metamorphosed supracrustal rocks are crosscut by several sets of Laramide deformation zones, despite their strong mechanical anisotropy (Hull and others, 1986).

In the Crawford thrust sheet, shortening of the sedimentary cover takes place by displacement on thrust faults with stair-step geometry and by associated folding. A regional décollement separates the shortened sedimentary cover from apparently undeformed basement (Royse and others, 1975). There is approximately 50 percent shortening of the sedimentary cover by large-scale structures, and horizontal displacements are dominant. All the thrusts have the same west-to-east direction of motion, reflecting the consistent transport direction throughout the thrust belt. All these observations indicate that overall deformation was produced by bulk simple shear. There is also significant internal shortening of the sedimentary cover, achieved by penetrative plastic deformation, the development of pressure solution cleavage, contraction faults, and small-scale buckle folds during early layer-parallel shortening. Internal shortening strains reach values as high as 20 percent, with the western (trailing edge) part of the sheet showing higher strains and a more complex deformation history. Horizontal shortening of the sedimentary cover is important in both the deformed foreland and in the thrust belt. However, the shortening associated with large-scale structures is greater in the thrust belt. The sedimentary rocks in both structural

provinces also show internal deformation in the form of early layer-parallel shortening, although the shortening values are significantly greater in the thrust belt and locally exceed 20 percent.

Horizontal shortening of basement rocks in the deformed foreland is equivalent to the shortening in the cover. This equivalence may reflect the control of structures in the sedimentary rocks by structures developed in the basement. The sedimentary cover, which forms a thin veneer, is perhaps accommodating relatively small-scale structural features formed at the basement-cover interface as a result of much larger scale structures formed at deeper levels within the basement. The major reverse faults do not flatten into bedding-parallel thrusts in the cover, and there is little or no slip on the basement-cover unconformity.

In the thrust belt, on the other hand, the sedimentary rocks are stripped from the basement along a basal décollement and are shortened independently of the basement. The apparent lack of shortening of the basement underneath the frontal thrust can be partially accounted for by shortening of basement in the hinterland, but not all of the basement can be accounted for in this way (Elliott, 1973; Price, 1981). The basement underneath the frontal thrust sheets may be homogeneously shortened by a network of small ductile deformation zones (Mitra, 1979) or by folding of anisotropic and incompetent units. Both of these types of minor structures are present in the Archean gneisses of the Farmington Canyon complex (Bruhn and Beck, 1981; Bryant, 1984; Yonkee and Bruhn, 1986), and may extend farther toward the foreland under the frontal thrust sheets.

On a larger scale, the basement may be duplexed; this could produce a tremendous amount of shortening in a relatively small volume (Boyer and Elliott, 1982). The duplex geometry in the basement is almost *required* (Boyer and Elliott, 1982; Elliott and Johnson, 1980; Elliott and others, 1982; Butler, 1985), given the large amount of "rootless" shortening in the cover. A similar large-scale mechanism would be partial subduction of basement or underthrusting (Price, 1981), which would probably produce a large-scale duplex geometry as well.

Whereas most of the structures observed at the surface in the deformed foreland formed by cataclasis, structures resulting from plasticity and diffusive mass-transfer processes are more widespread in the thrust belt. Cleavage is a pervasive fabric element in deformed micrites of the thrust belt, but is essentially absent in the adjacent foreland cover. These differences in structural style might be related to differences in the physical conditions of deformation. Higher pressures and temperatures would favor more homogeneous, ductile deformation and thermally activated micromechanisms (such as diffusion and plasticity). Lower pressures and temperatures would promote heterogeneous deformation by brittle failure, at least in the early stages of deformation.

The illite crystallinity of cleavage seams suggests temperatures near 200°C in the thrust belt; similar studies have not been completed in the foreland. However, rough estimates of deformation conditions in each area can be made based on the thickness of the cover. The sedimentary cover in the northern Wind River Mountains is uniformly thin, measuring about 2 km from the base of the Cambrian to the top of the Jurassic (4.5 km including the Cretaceous) (Richmond, 1945; Keefer, 1957, 1970). The same section in the fold and thrust belt varies from about 2 km in the frontal sheets to 6 km in the Crawford (8.5 km including the Cretaceous), to as much as 10 km(?) in the Willard sheet (Royse and others, 1975). Thus, the initial physical conditions in the Crawford sheet and the Wind River Mountains differed by at least a few kilobars and 100°C, assuming a normal geotherm. Significant differences in pressure and temperature were also produced in the thrust belt by emplacement of relatively hot thrust sheets (Mitra and Yonkee, 1985). Rapid overthrusting produced relatively high pressure-temperature conditions initially, followed by slow heating in the footwall as the isotherms rose and equilibrated. These differnces in deformation conditions may be responsible for the variations in small-scale structures, although lithology, strain rate, and fluid characteristics are also important. However, the variation in large-scale structural style from the thrust belt to the foreland is difficult to explain solely from P-T differences.

The ultimate driving force for the deformation in the thrust belt is probably farther toward the hinterland where the sedimentary section is thicker and metamorphic grades are higher. It is tempting to suggest that higher initial pressures and temperatures in the hinterland of the fold and thrust belt produced far-traveled, basement-involved thrust sheets, which in turn raised the pressures and temperatures in the footwall, promoting deformation in frontal sheets. The higher grade deformation in the hinterland also helped emplace the frontal thrusts either by pushing them from behind (Chapple, 1978; Davis and others, 1983), or by creating a surface slope that allowed them to be emplaced by gravitational spreading (Elliott, 1976). For the pressure-temperature conditions at the base of the frontal sedimentary wedge, the yield stress for the sedimentary cover is significantly lower than that for the basement, causing the cover to detach from the basement along this major mechanical discontinuity.

In the foreland, ductile shortening occurred first in deep to middle crustal levels. The crust may have been thermally softened during flat plate subduction during the Late Mesozoic, as suggested by calc-alkaline volcanics scattered throughout the eastern Cordillera (Lowell, 1974). The ductile shortening below the brittle-plastic transition was transferred up into the brittle crust along discrete fault zones. These zones are probably listric in shape overall, as suggested for the Wind River thrust (Hurich, 1981; Erslev, 1986), and root into shallow-dipping ductile deformation zones or zones of homogeneous strain at deep levels (greater than 20 km) of the crust.

CONCLUSIONS

At the largest scale of observations considered in this chapter, we have shown that deformation in the thrust belt takes place dominantly by simple shear, with the mechanically anisotropic sedimentary cover being stripped from the basement and transported unidirectionally along major low angle thrusts. At the same scale, deformational fabric in the foreland is characterized by an anastomozing set of BDZs, motion on which is consistent with a regional pure shear deformation. At a larger scale, gross mechanical behavior of the foreland may be related to mirustal delamination (Bengston, 1983), in which case we could consider foreland strain to be a result of regional simple shear above this detachment. Thus, interpretations of regional bulk strain are scale dependent, and comparisons between structural provinces are meaningful only if they consider structures of comparable scales.

ACKNOWLEDGMENTS

We thank our colleagues at the University of Rochester and University of Wyoming for useful discussions during the course of this work. The constructive criticisms by Peter Geiser, Lee Woodward, two anonymous reviewers, and Chris Schmidt were very helpful. Thanks to Margrit Gardner for typing various versions of the paper. Part of the work was supported by National Science Foundation Grants EAR-8207395 and EAR-8507039 (to G.M.).

REFERENCES CITED

Aleksandrowski, P., 1985, Graphical determination of principal directions of slickenside lineation populations; An attempt to modify Arthaud's method: Journal of Structural Geology, v. 7, p. 73–82.

Anderson, E. M., 1942, The dynamics of faulting and dyke formation, with applications to Britain: Edinburgh, Oliver & Boyd, 191 p.

Angelier, J., 1979, Determination of the mean principal directions of stress for a given fault population: Tectonophysics, v. 56, p. T17–T26.

—— , 1984, Tectonic analysis of fault slip data sets: Journal of Geophysical Research, v. 89, p. 5835–5848.

Arthaud, F., 1969, Methode de determination graphique des directions de raccourcissement, d'allongement et intermediaire d'une population de failles: Bulletin of the Geological Society of France, Series 7, v. 11, p. 729–737.

Ashby, M. F., Gandhi, C., and Taplin, D.M.R., 1979, Fracture mechanism maps and their construction for F.C.C. metals and alloys: Acta Metallurgica, v. 27, p. 699–729.

Atkinson, B. K., 1982, Subcritical crack propagation in rocks; Theory, experimental results, and applications: Journal of Structural Geology, v. 4, p. 41–56.

Bell, T. H., 1981, Foliation development; The contribution, geometry, and significance of progressive, bulk, inhomogeneous shortening: Tectonophysics, v. 75, p. 273–296.

Bengston, C. A., 1983, Relation of foreland tectonics to the von Mises yield condition for ductile crustal failure: Geological Society of America Abstracts with Programs, v. 15, p. 1.

Berg, R. R., 1962, Mountain flank thrusting in the Rocky Mountain foreland from Wyoming and Colorado: American Association of Petroleum Geologists Bulletin, v. 46, p. 2019–2032.

Blackstone, D. L., Jr., 1981, Compression as an agent in deformation of the east-central flank of the Bighorn Mountains, Sheridan and Johnson Counties, Wyoming: University of Wyoming Contributions to Geology, v. 19, p. 105–122.

Borradaile, G. J., 1981, Particulate flow of rock and the formation of cleavage: Tectonophysics, v. 72, p. 305–321.

Boyer, S. E., and Elliott, D., 1982, Thrust systems: American Association of Petroleum Geologists Bulletin, v. 66, p. 1196–1230.

Brown, W. G., 1984, A reverse fault interpretation of Rattlesnake Mountain anticline, Bighorn Basin, Wyoming: Mountain Geologist, v. 21, p. 31–35.

Bruhn, R. L., and Beck, S. L., 1981, Mechanics of thrust faulting in crystalline basement, Sevier orogenic belt, Utah: Geology, v. 9, p. 200–204.

Bryant, B., 1984, Reconnaissance geologic map of the Precambrian Farmington Canyon complex and surrounding rocks in the Wasatch Mountains between Ogden and Bountiful, Utah: U.S. Geological Survey Miscellaneous Investigations Map I-1447, scale 1:50,000.

Butler, R.W.H., 1985, The restoration of thrust systems and displacement continuity around the Mont Blanc massif, N.W. external Alpine thrust belt: Journal of Structural Geology, v. 7, p. 569–582.

Cashman, P. H., Bruhn, R. L., Parry, W. T., and Yonkee, W. A., 1986, Regional variations in crustal rheology and structure, Sevier orogenic belt, Utah: Geological Society of America Abstracts with Programs, v. 18, p. 559.

Chapple, W. M., 1978, Mechanics of thin-skinned fold-and-thrust belts: Geological Society of America Bulletin, v. 89, p. 1189–1198.

Coogan, J. C., and Boyer, S. E., 1985, Variable shortening mechanisms in fold-thrust belts and implications for cross section balancing; An example from the Idaho-Wyoming thrust belt: Geological Society of America Abstracts with Programs, v. 17, p. 552.

Coogan, J. C., and Yonkee, W. A., 1985, Salt detachment in the Jurassic Preuss Redbeds within the Meade and Crawford thrust systems, Idaho and Wyoming, in Kerns, G. J., and Kerns, R. L., eds., Orogenic patterns and stratigraphy of north-central Utah and southeastern Idaho: Utah Geological Association Publication 14, p. 75–82.

Cressman, E. R., 1964, Geology of the Georgetown Canyon–Snowdrift Mountain area, southeastern Idaho: U.S. Geological Survey Bulletin 1153, 150 p.

Dahlstrom, C.D.A., 1970, Structural geology in the eastern margin of the Canadian Rocky Mountains: Bulletin of Canadian Petroleum Geology, v. 18, p. 332–406.

Davis, D., Suppe, J., and Dahlen, F. A., 1983, Mechanics of fold-and-thrust belts and accretionary wedges: Journal of Geophysical Research, v. 88, p. 1153–1172.

Dixon, J. S., 1982, Regional structural synthesis, Wyoming salient of western overthrust belt: American Association of Petroleum Geologists Bulletin, v. 66, p. 1560–1580.

Dorr, J. A., Jr., Spearing, D. R., and Steidtmann, J. R., 1977, Deformation and deposition between a foreland uplift and an impinging thrust belt, Hoback basin, Wyoming: Geological Society of America Special Paper 177, 82 p.

Durney, D. W., 1972, Solution transfer, an important geological deformation mechanism: Nature, v. 235, p. 315–317.

Elliott, D., 1973, Plate tectonics and the problem of too much granitic basement: Geology, v. 1, p. 111.

——— , 1976, The motion of thrust sheets: Journal of Geophysical Research, v. 81, p. 949–963.

Elliott, D., and Johnson, M.R.W., 1980, Structural evolution in the northern part of the Moine thrust belt, N.W. Scotland: Transactions of the Royal Society of Edinburgh, Earth Sciences, v. 71, p. 69–96.

Elliott, D., Fisher, G. W., and Snelson, S., 1982, A restorable cross section through the central Appalachians: Geological Society of America Abstracts with Programs, v. 14, p. 482.

Erslev, E. A., 1986, Basement balancing of Rocky Mountain foreland uplifts: Geology, v. 14, p. 259–262.

Evans, J. P., and Spang, J. H., 1984, The northern termination of the Crawford thrust, western Wyoming: University of Wyoming Contributions to Geology, v. 23, p. 15–31.

Fleuty, M. J., 1975, Slickensides and slickenlines: Geology Magazine, v. 112, p. 319–322.

Frank, F. C., 1965, On dilatancy in relation to seismic sources: Reviews in Geophysics, v. 3, p. 485–503.

Gandhi, C., and Ashby, M. F., 1979, Fracture mechanism maps for materials which cleave; F.C.C., B.C.C., and H.C.P. metals and ceramincs: Acta Metal-lurgica, v. 27, p. 1956–1602.

Gries, R., 1983a, North-south compression of Rocky Mountain foreland structure, in Lowell, J. D., and Gries, R., eds., Rocky Mountain foreland basins and uplifts: Denver, Colorado, Rocky Mountain Association of Geologists, p. 9–32.

——— , 1983b, Oil and gas prospecting beneath the Precambrian of foreland thrust plates in the Rocky Mountains: American Association of Petroleum Geologists Bulletin, v. 67, p. 1–26.

Hurich, C. A., 1981, Gravity interpretation and deep crustal structure of the Wind River range, Wyoming: University of Wyoming Contributions to Geology, v. 19, p. 177.

Heller, P. L., Bowdler, S. S., Chambers, H. P., Coogan, J. C., Hagen, E. S., Shuster, M. W., Winslow, N. S., and Lawton, T. F., 1986, Time of initial thrusting in the Sevier orogenic belt, Idaho-Wyoming and Utah: Geology, v. 14, p. 388–391.

Hull, J., Koto, R., and Bizub, R., 1986, Deformation zones in the Highlands of New Jersey: Geological Association of New Jersey Guidebook, v. 3, p. 19–66.

Kanter, L. R., Dyer, R., and Dohman, T. E., 1981, Laramide crustal shortening in the northern Wyoming Province: University of Wyoming Contributions to Geology, v. 19, p. 135–142.

Keefer, W. R., 1957, Geology of the Du Noir area, Fremont County, Wyoming: U.S. Geological Survey Professional Paper 294-E, p. 155–221.

——— , 1970, Structural geology of the Wind River Basin, Wyoming: U.S. Geological Survey Professional Paper 695-D, 35 p.

Kisch, H. J., 1980, Incipient metamorphism of Cambro-Silurian clastic rocks from the Jamatland Supergroup, central Scandinavian Caledonides, western Sweden; Illite crystallinity and vitrinite reflectance: Journal of the Geological Society of London, v. 137, p. 271–286.

Lamerson, P. R., 1983, The Fossil Basin and its relationship to the Absaroka thrust system, Wyoming and Utah, in Powers, R. B., ed., Geologic studies of the Cordilleran thrust belt, 1982: Denver, Colorado, Rocky Mountain Association of Geologists, p. 279–340.

Lawn, B. R., and Wilshaw, T. R., 1975, Fracture of brittle solids: Cambridge, Cambridge University Press, 204 p.

Lowell, J. D., 1974, Plate tectonics and foreland basement deformation: Geology, v. 2, p. 275–278.

Mansfield, G. R., 1927, Geography, geology, and mineral resources of part of southeastern Idaho: U.S. Geological Survey Professional Paper 152, 453 p.

Mitra, G., 1978, Ductile deformation zones and mylonites; The mechanical processes involved in the deformation of crystalline basement rocks: American Journal of Science, v. 278, p. 1057–1084.

——— , 1979, Ductile deformation zones in Blue Ridge basement rocks and estimation of finite strains: Geological Society of America Bulletin, v. 90, p. 935–951.

——— , 1980, Brittle and ductile deformation zones in granitic basement rocks of the Wind River Mountains, Wyoming; A look at the brittle-ductile transition: Geological Society of America Abstracts with Programs, v. 12, p. 485.

——— , 1984, Brittle to ductile transition due to large strains along the White Rock thrust, Wind River Mountains, Wyoming: Journal of Structural Geology, v. 6, p. 51–61.

Mitra, G., and Frost, B. R., 1981, Mechanisms of deformation within Laramide and Precambrian deformation zones in basement rocks of the Wind River Mountains: University of Wyoming Contributions to Geology, v. 19, p. 161–173.

Mitra, G., and Yonkee, W. A., 1985, Relationship of spaced cleavage to folds and thrusts in the Idaho-Utah-Wyoming thrust belt: Journal of Structural Geology, v. 7, p. 361–373.

Mitra, G., Yonkee, W. A., and Gentry, D. J., 1984, Solution cleavage and its relationship to major structures in the Idaho-Utah-Wyoming thrust belt: Geology, v. 12, p. 354–358.

Oriel, S. S., and Platt, L. B., 1980, Geologic map of the Preston 1°×2° Quadrangle, southeastern Idaho and western Wyoming: U.S. Geological Survey Miscellaneous Investigation Map I-1127, scale 1:250,000.

Orowan, E., 1966, Dilatancy and the seismic focal mechanism: Reviews of Geophysics, v. 4, p. 395–404.

Price, R. A., 1981, The Cordilleran foreland thrust and fold belt in the southern Canadian Rocky Mountains, *in* McClay, K. R., and Price, N. J., eds., Thrust and nappe tectonics: Geological Society of London Special Publication 9, p. 427–448.

Protzman, G. M., 1985, The emplacement and deformation history of the Meade thrust sheet, southeastern Idaho [M.S. thesis]: Rochester, New York, University of Rochester, 117 p.

Protzman, G. M., and Mitra, G., 1985, Emplacement history of a thrust sheet based on analysis of pressure solution cleavage and deformed fossils: Geological Society of America Abstracts with Programs, 17, p. 694.

Ramsay, J. G., 1981, Tectonics of the Helvetic Alps, *in* McClay, K. R., and Price, N. J., eds., Thrust and nappe tectonics: Geological Society of London Special Publication 9, p. 293–309.

Reches, Z., 1978, Analysis of faulting in three-dimensional strain field: Tectonophysics, v. 47, p. 109–129.

—— , 1983, Faulting of rocks in three-dimensional strain field; Part II, Theoretical analysis: Tectonophysics, v. 95, p. 133–156.

Richmond, G. M., 1945, Geology of the northwest end of the Wind River Mountains, Sublette County, Wyoming: U.S. Geological Survey Oil and Gas Investigations Preliminary Map no. 31, scale ~1 inch to 1 mile.

Robertson, E. C., 1983, Relationship of fault displacement to gouge and breccia thickness: Transactions of the Society of Petroleum Engineers of the American Institute of Mining, Metallurgical, and Petroleum Engineers, p. 1426–1432.

Royse, F., Warner, M. A., and Reese, D. L., 1975, Thrust belt structural geometry and related stratigraphic problems, Wyoming-Idaho-northern Utah: Rocky Mountain Association of Geologists Symposium Proceedings, p. 41–54.

Rubey, W. W., Oriel, S. S., and Tracey, J. I., Jr., 1975, Geology of the Sage and Kemmerer 15-minute Quadrangles, Lincoln County, Wyoming: U.S. Geological Survey Professional Paper 855, 18 p.

—— , 1980, Geologic map and structure sections of the Cokeville 30-minute Quadrangle, Lincoln and Sublette Counties, Wyoming; U.S. Geological Survey Miscellaneous Investigations Map I-1129, scale 1:62,500.

Rudnicki, J. W., 1984, Effects of dilatant hardening on the development of concentrated shear deformation in fissured rock masses: Journal of Geophysical Research, v. 89, p. 9259–9270.

Schmidt, C. J., and Garihan, J. M., 1983, Laramide tectonic development of the Rocky Mountain foreland of southwestern Montana, *in* Lowell, J., and Gries, R., eds., Rocky Mountain foreland basins and uplifts: Denver, Colorado, Rocky Mountain Association of Geologists, p. 271–294.

Stearns, D. W., 1975, Laramide basement deformation in the Bighorn Basin; The controlling factor for structures in the layered rocks: Wyoming Geological Association 27th Annual Field Conference Guidebook, p. 149–158.

Stockdale, P. B., 1926, The stratigraphic significance of solution in rocks: Journal of Geology, v. 34, p. 399–414.

Wiltschko, D. V., and Dorr, J. A., 1983, Timing of deformation in overthrust belt and foreland of Idaho, Wyoming, and Utah: American Association of Petroleum Geologists Bulletin, v. 67, p. 1304–1322.

Worl, R. G., 1967, Taconite and migmatite in the northern Wind River Mountains, Fremont, Sublette, and Teton Counties, Wyoming [Ph.D. thesis]: Laramie, University of Wyoming, 130 p.

Yonkee, W. A., 1983, Mineralogy and structural relationships of cleavage in the Twin Creek Formation within part of the Crawford thrust sheet in Wyoming and Idaho [M.S. thesis]: Laramie, University of Wyoming, 125 p.

Yonkee, W. A., and Bruhn, R. L., 1986, Geometry and mechanics of basement deformation, Sevier orogenic belt, northern Utah: Geological Society of America Abstracts with Programs, v. 18, p. 798.

Zawislak, R. A., and Smithson, S. B., 1981, Problems and interpretation of COCORP deep seismic reflection data, Wind River range, Wyoming: Geophysics, v. 46, p. 1684–1701.

MANUSCRIPT ACCEPTED BY THE SOCIETY FEBRUARY 9, 1988

Geological Society of America
Memoir 171
1988

Active deformation at the boundary between the Precordillera and Sierras Pampeanas, Argentina, and comparison with ancient Rocky Mountain deformation

Eric J. Fielding and Teresa E. Jordan
Institute for the Study of the Continents and the Department of Geological Sciences, Cornell University, Ithaca, New York 14853

ABSTRACT

The Precordillera and Sierras Pampeanas of western Argentina are active thin-skinned and thick-skinned deformational provinces in the foreland of the Andean orogenic system and occur above a subhorizontal segment of the subducting plate. The two morphostructural provinces are analogous to the Idaho-Wyoming thrust belt and Rocky Mountain foreland provinces, respectively, that were formed in the western United States in Late Cretaceous to early Cenozoic time. Comparisons of the younger structures at the boundary between the Precordillera and Sierras Pampeanas with analogous, more eroded, structures in North America aid in the interpretation of the subsurface structural geometry of both orogenic belts and shed some light on the factors that control the style of deformation at the contact between thin- and thick-skinned deformational provinces.

The Eastern Precordillera subprovince is bordered on the east by the Sierras Pampeanas basement block-uplift province. It has been deformed in late Cenozoic to Recent time into a set of folds and thrusts that verge westward, as opposed to the eastward vergence of the structures in the adjoining Central Precordillera subprovince. While few subsurface data are available, we have interpreted this subprovince to have been deformed by a combination of basement-involved and thin-skinned structures, in a manner analogous to that of the Moxa Arch in the zone of overlap between the thin-skinned and thick-skinned thrust belts in North America. We suggest that the change in structural style between the Precordillera and the Sierras Pampeanas provinces is most likely related to paleogeographic contrasts, and that the change in vergence between the Eastern and Central Precordillera subprovinces may be due to the presence of a reactivated Paleozoic fault zone.

INTRODUCTION

The American Cordillera is a nearly continuous chain of mountains that extends along the Pacific margins of both North and South America. In this chapter we examine the geology of the cratonic side of two segments of the Cordilleran orogenic belt, comparing the Late Cretaceous–early Cenozoic Rocky Mountains and the late Cenozoic Andes Mountains. The Andean Cordillera of central Chile and Argentina (Fig. 1) is an active orogenic belt, over a flat subduction zone, with many similarities to the Late Cretaceous–Early Tertiary Rocky Mountains of the western United States (e.g., Sales, 1968; Coney, 1976; Jordan and others, 1983a). In both areas, a thin-skinned thrust belt is located on the hinterland side of a region of uplifted and rotated blocks of crystalline basement. The thin-skinned thrust belts are the Idaho-Wyoming segment of the Sevier thrust belt and the Precordillera thrust belt of Argentina. The ancient Wyoming and Colorado Rocky Mountain (or "Laramide") foreland province of North America and the modern Sierras Pampeanas of Argentina are the basement-uplift provinces (Fig. 2).

The thin-skinned and basement-uplift deformation overlapped in time for both the North and South American orogenic belts that are discussed here. There is an extensive literature concerning the mechanisms for the deformation of the crust within

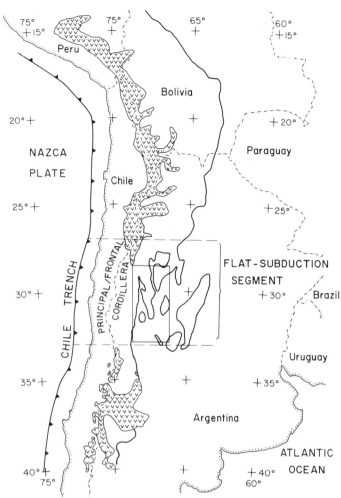

Figure 1. Location map of flat-slab subduction segment in the central Andes of Chile and Argentina. Modern volcanic arc, marked by "V" pattern, is not active over flat slab. Box shows area in Figure 2. Solid line outlines major mountain ranges and eastern edge of Andean Cordillera and Precordillera.

stresses, applied by the coupling of the continental lithosphere with the subhorizontal subducting plate (e.g., Bird, 1984); and the material properties of the lithosphere that are determined by its thermal state (e.g., Sibson, 1983) and its paleogeographic distribution of earlier structures and depositional basins. Kulik and Schmidt (this volume) define and describe an "overlap zone" that is a broad expression of the zone of contact between thin- and thick-skinned deformational provinces in the North American Cordillera. In parallel with their work, we describe and discuss a similar zone of contact between the Precordillera thrust belt and the Sierras Pampeanas deformational provinces. We also compare specific geometries and timing relations of the active Argentine contact zone to the more thoroughly explored but eroded overlap zone of the Rocky Mountains. We describe the spatial relations between the subducted plate geometry and the contact zone, and attempt to show that paleogeography is a key factor in the evolution of this contact region. The role of the thermal regime in controlling the location of the contact zone is poorly constrained by existing data, but crustal earthquake data appear to be inconsistent with some of the models of the brittle-ductile transition (BDT) that have been put forth for the western U.S., as discussed below.

Much more subsurface information is available on the North American Rocky Mountain Foreland and Sevier thrust belt, the result of active petroleum exploration in the United States (e.g., Royse and others, 1975; Dixon, 1982; Gries, 1983), than is available for the Argentine Precordillera and Sierras Pampeanas, which have no producing petroleum fields and less intense exploration. Conversely, the age of deformation of the Precordillera is much younger (Miocene through possibly Recent time) and the duration of deformation much shorter (15 m.y.) than the age and duration of analogous deformation in North America (Cretaceous through Eocene, a period of 40 to 50 m.y.). Thus, the structures still visible at the surface of the Precordillera and Sierras Pampeanas may provide a view of the more eroded Rocky Mountains province at an early stage of development.

Most of the structural geology presented here has been mapped and published by a number of Argentine geologists. We have compiled the available regional geologic data with Landsat Thematic Mapper (TM) images and Space Shuttle photography. We present a more detailed discussion of the structures of the Sierra de Huaco, a well-exposed part of the contact zone, based on the results of our own mapping. Our intent is to present these data and some of our interpretations from a point of view that will be helpful to workers who are addressing questions about the structural evolution of the thin-skinned and basement-involved deformational provinces in either North or South America.

PRECORDILLERA AND SIERRAS PAMPEANAS

Regional tectonic setting

The Precordillera thrust belt and the Sierras Pampeanas basement-uplift provinces are located on the eastern flank of the

the two types of foreland shortening provinces. A separate question is the nature of, and controls on, the regions of contact between thin-skinned and basement-involved foreland provinces. Across the contact zone, deformation that appears to be limited mostly to the sedimentary section of the thin-skinned belt changes to deformation that fundamentally involves the cratonic basement. These contact zones occur both parallel and normal to the direction of maximum shortening. The change *along* strike (normal to the shortening) is exemplified in North America by the Rocky Mountain system of southern Montana, and in South America by the northern margin of the Sierras Pampeanas, north of the area in Figure 2 (Allmendinger and others, 1983b).

In this chapter we discuss the zone of contact *across* strike, in the direction of the shortening, and concentrate on the Andean Cordillera. The controls on the deformational style (i.e., thin- or thick-skinned) are likely to be a combination of two factors: the

Andean orogenic belt in west-central Argentina. They occur in the approximately 500-km-long Andean segment between 28°S and 33°S where the subducted Nazca plate is subhorizontal beneath the South American plate (Fig. 1; Barazangi and Isacks, 1976; Jordan and others, 1983a). The subducting Nazca plate descends with a moderate eastward dip (~30°) from the Chile trench to a depth of 100 km, before flattening to a dip of less than 5° east farther eastward (Barazangi and Isacks, 1976; Bevis and Isacks, 1984). Numerous intermediate-depth earthquakes in the region clearly define the subducted plate geometry (Bevis and Isacks, 1984; Cahill and Isacks, 1985; Smalley and Isacks, 1987). Kadinsky-Cade and others (1985) illustrated that the flattening of the subducted plate occurs beneath the crest of the Andean Cor-

dillera, about 80 km to the west of the foreland deformational belts discussed here. In this flat-slab segment, the Andean Cordillera consists of the narrow and high Principal and Frontal Cordilleras (Fig. 1), which are composed in part of a Miocene volcanic arc complex and deformed by local thrust and reverse faulting during the Miocene. The extinct volcanic arc of this segment was active before about 10 Ma (Jordan and Gardeweg, 1988; Kay and others, 1988), implying that the change of the subducted plate from a moderately east-dipping to a subhorizontal configuration was completed before 10 Ma (Jordan and others, 1983b; Kay and others, 1988).

The Precordillera thrust belt forms the foothills of the Andean Cordillera, while the Sierras Pampeanas are a distinct mor-

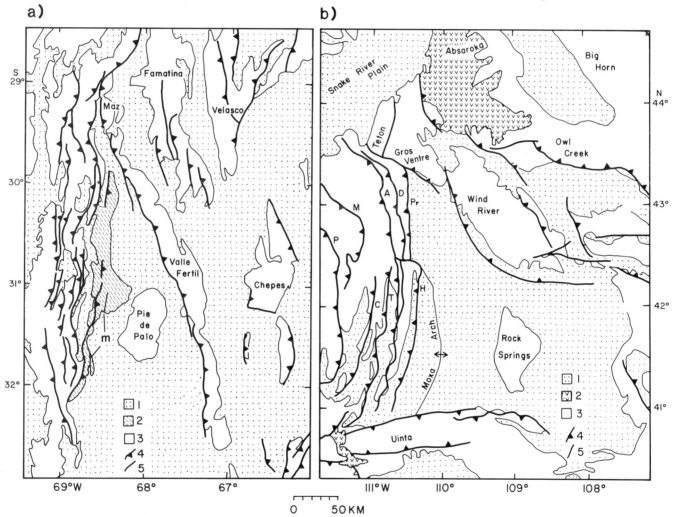

Figure 2. Comparison map. Precordillera fold-thrust belt and western Sierras Pampeanas basement-uplift province of Argentina. b, Analogous Sevier fold-thrust belt and Laramide basement-uplift province at the same scale (after King and Beikman, 1974). Names of major mountain ranges of the Sierras Pampeanas and Laramide provinces are noted. Symbols in 2a are: (1) Quaternary alluvium, (2) Eastern Precordillera subprovince, (3) Precambrian through Neogene rocks of Sierras Pampeanas and Central and Western Precordilleras, (4) thrust and reverse faults, (5) other faults; m indicates melange zones discussed in text. Symbols in 2b are: (1) postorogenic upper Eocene rocks through Quaternary alluvium, (2) Eocene volcanic rocks, (3) Eocene and older rocks, (4) thrust and reverse faults, (5) other faults. Letters for Sevier thrusts are: A, Absaroka; D, Darby; Pr, Prospect; H, Hogsback; T, Tump, C, Crawford, P, Paris, M, Meade.

phostructural province of mountain blocks and broad valleys. The Precordillera and Sierras Pampeanas have a high level of crustal seismicity (Jordan and others, 1983a; Smalley, 1988). These crustal earthquakes provide constraints on the subsurface rheology and deformation (e.g., Chinn and Isacks, 1983; Kadinsky-Cade, 1985; Kadinsky-Cade and others, 1985). Large earthquakes and their associated aftershock zones, studied using teleseismic and local data (e.g., Kadinsky-Cade and others, 1985), and small earthquakes located by local network data (Smalley, 1988) show that the crust of the western Sierras Pampeanas and Eastern Precordillera is being deformed in a brittle (seismogenic) manner to a depth of 25 to 40 km. Large crustal earthquakes have not been recorded from most of the Precordillera, although this could be an artifact of the short duration of the instrumental earthquake data base (Chinn and Isacks, 1983). Throughout the Precordillera and Sierras Pampanas, there is ample evidence of late Cenozoic deformation: earthquakes, fault scarps in alluvium, and youthful morphology all indicate that the present topography is a dynamic feature that is a result of recent and ongoing deformation.

Regional structural geology

Ortiz and Zambrano (1981) divided the Precordillera fold-thrust belt into three parallel morphostructural subprovinces: the Western, Central, and Eastern Precordilleras. Each subprovince persists along strike for more than 300 km. In this study, we concentrate on the Central and Eastern Precordillera subprovinces and do not discuss the Western Precordillera. The Central Precordillera is an eastward-verging, thin-skinned thrust belt, developed in a Paleozoic miogeoclinal shelf sequence (Figs. 2, 3, 4; Baldis and Chebli, 1969). The Eastern Precordillera was defined by Ortiz and Zambrano (1981) as the west-verging portion of the Precordillera on the eastern side of the fold-thrust province (Fig. 2). The boundary between the Central and Eastern subprovinces lies within a series of longitudinal valleys, the largest of which is the Matagusanos Valley (Figure 3; Rolleri, 1969; Ortiz and Zambrano, 1981). The Eastern Precordillera, the main focus of this chapter, is discussed following the description of the bordering morphostructural provinces.

Central Precordillera thrust belt. The structural geology of the Central Precordillera is known from regional surface mapping (Furque, 1963, 1972, 1979, 1983), and is illustrated in regional cross sections published by Heim (1952), Baldis and Chebli (1969), Ortiz and Zambrano (1981), and Vasquez and Gorroño (1982). To date there have been no seismic profiles nor other subsurface data collected in the relatively inaccessible Central Precordillera, but roughly 3,000 m of topographic relief and excellent exposure permit adequate definition of the gross structural geometry.

A major zone of décollement has been inferred to exist in the lowest unit of the known Paleozoic sedimentary section, the Ordovician San Juan Limestone, which is exposed in a series of imbricate thrust faults (Figs. 3, 4, 5; e.g., Baldis and Chebli, 1969). The faults are accompanied by east-verging folds, primarily anticlines preserved at the leading edges of the thrust plates. Neither crystalline basement nor sedimentary units below the San Juan Limestone are exposed in the Central Precordillera (e.g., Baldis and others, 1982). The remainder of the Phanerozoic section consists of clastic sedimentary rocks and minor volcanic units (Fig. 5), so that the repeated slivers of the lithologically distinctive and resistant San Juan Limestone clearly identify the major thrust faults (Figs. 3, 4). In general, four or five major thrust faults splay off of the basal décollement and reach the surface in the Central Precordillera.

Baldis and Chebli (1969) estimated, from the thickness of the stratigraphic sections and structural geometries, that the basal décollement deepens from 3 to 4 km below the surface in the eastern Central Precordillera to 5 to 8 km beneath the western Central Precordillera (Fig. 4), following a pre-Cenozoic westward dip of the San Juan Limestone. The major thrust faults are parallel to bedding in the limestone but cut overlying units as steeper faults in hanging-wall and footwall cutoffs (Baldis and Chebli, 1969). The horizontal component of net slip on any one fault is not well known, but existing cross sections suggest a minimum of about 20 km (30 percent) (Baldis and Chebli, 1969) to 50 km (50 percent) (R. Allmendinger, unpublished data) of shortening across the Central Precordillera thrust system.

The structural style and stratigraphic position of the thrusts are similar throughout the southern two-thirds of the map area, south of 30°S (Fig. 3), which makes the definition of thin-skinned thrust sheets fairly simple. To the north, there are variations in the Paleozoic units, particularly in the Ordovician units (e.g., Baldis and others, 1982). Consequently, without the resistant San Juan Limestone to mark the leading edges of the thrust plates, the thrust sheets of the northwestern Central Precordillera are less well defined, and more folds are apparent. At about 29°S, the northerly trending Precordillera structures are overprinted by northwest-trending structures related to interaction with the Sierra de Maz, a basement uplift in the Sierras Pampeanas (Fig. 2a, Fig. 3).

Matagusanos Valley system. The boundary between east-verging and west-verging structural subprovinces of the Precordillera fold-thrust belt lies in the Matagusanos Valley and its northern extension, the Huaco Valley (Fig. 3). The valley system widens to about 25 km near 31.5°S, but it pinches to about 1 km width to the north (Figs. 2a, 3) and farther to the south. Unconsolidated deposits mantle much of the Cenozoic synorogenic strata in the valley. The depth to basement beneath the Matagusanos Valley system is constrained by data from one test well and by the downward projection of stratigraphy. There are at least 5 to 6 km of Cenozoic strata (Fig. 6) underlain by an uncertain thickness of Mesozoic and Paleozoic units (Fig. 5), giving a total of about 8 to 10 km of strata above the crystalline basement. Structural thickening of this section would increase the estimate of the depth to basement. The well drilled through the Cenozoic strata in the Matagusanos Valley (YPF well S.J.M.es-1) penetrated Ordovician limestone at a depth of 5930 m, without passing through the upper Paleozoic units expected in this part of the

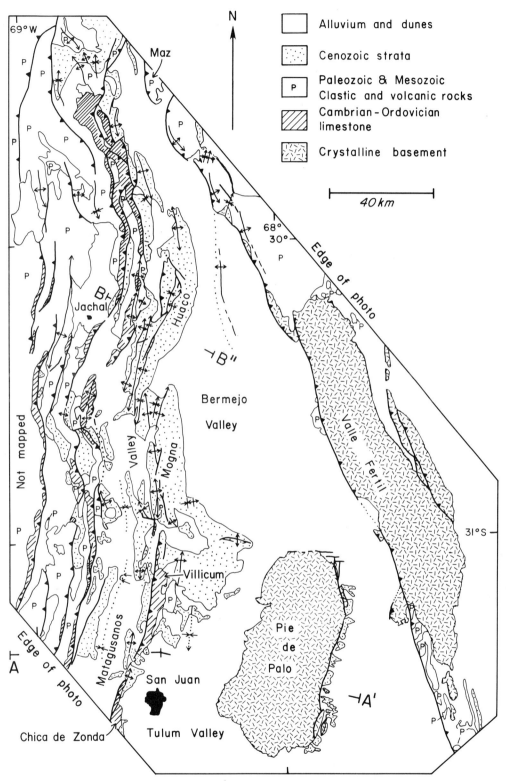

Figure 3. Structural map of Central Precordillera, Eastern Precordillera, and western Sierras Pampeanas, based on stereo Large Format Camera photographs taken by Space Shuttle *Challenger,* Landsat Thematic Mapper images, and published geologic maps. A-A′ indicates cross section of Figure 4; B-B′ is cross section of Figure 8.

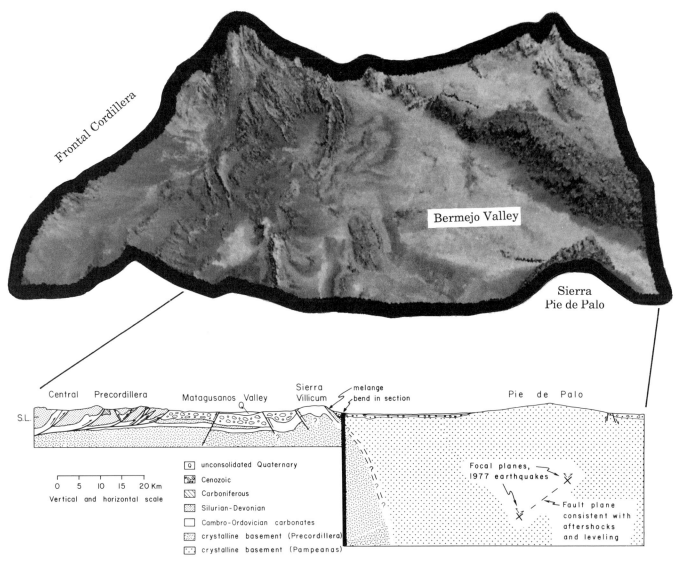

Figure 4. Perspective 3-D view of Landsat Thematic Mapper scene covering Precordillera north of about 31°S, with generalized cross section of the Central Precordillera, Matagusanos Valley, Eastern Precordillera, and Sierra Pie de Palo of the Sierras Pampeanas. Cross section modified slightly from Baldis and Chebli (1969) for the western portion; eastern portion modified from Kadinsky-Cade (1985, and others, 1985). Heavy line marks bend in section and join between western and eastern sections. Double dashed line marks inferred continuation of Devonian melange as terrane boundary between major basement blocks. Location of section A-A′ shown in Fig. 3, near 30°20′S. Topographic data used to compute the vertically exaggerated perspective view from B. L. Isacks.

Precordillera. About 2.5 km of stratigraphic section would be expected below the top of the Ordovician, giving a depth to basement of about 8.5 km at the well location.

Within the Matagusanos Valley, structures consist of north-trending folds and apparently minor, parallel faults in the Cenozoic rocks exposed along the west and east sides. In the southern part, the alluvium-filled valley appears to be synclinal (Fig. 3), but without detailed surface data, the vergence of structures in the Matagusanos Valley is not well defined. Our interpretation of satellite imagery suggests that the folds are east-verging and locally overturned to the east (Fig. 3), although Baldis and others

(1979) noted west-verging folds in the southern part of the valley. Thus the reversal between east and west vergences apparently occurs within the valley or at the faults on its eastern margin. Rolleri (1969) suggested that the southward continuation of the Matagusanos Valley structures crosses over to the eastern side of Sierra Chica de Zonda (Fig. 3). Other studies of Sierra Chica de Zonda, however, have shown that it is a west-verging structure similar to the rest of the Eastern Precordillera (Ortiz and Zambrano, 1981; Baldis and Bordonaro, 1984), so it is more reasonable to infer that the Matagusanos Valley structures continue southward on the west side of Sierra Chica de Zonda.

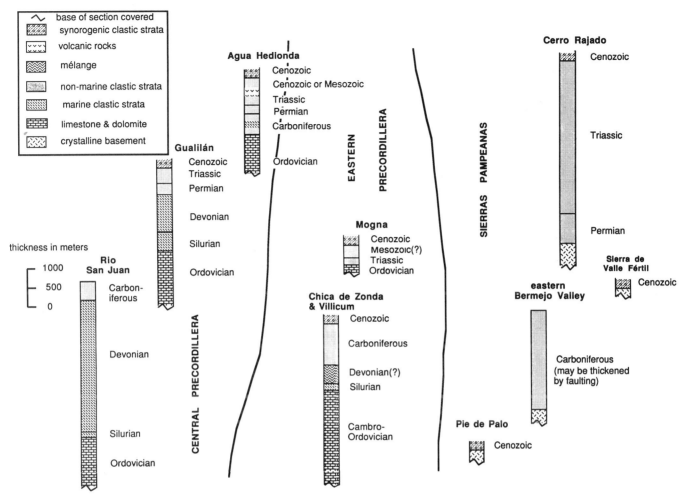

Figure 5. Stratigraphic summary of bedrock predating the late Cenozoic deformation, comparing sections in the Central Precordilla, Eastern Precordillera, and Sierras Pampeanas. Based on Ortiz (1968), Baldis and Chebli (1969), Polanski (1970), Gentili (1972), Mirre (1976), Furque (1979 and 1983), Cingolani and others (1981), Cuerda and others (1981, 1984), Baldis and others (1982), and Baldis and Bordonaro (1984).

The Matagusanos Valley has the highest level of crustal seismicity in the Precordillera. Many small earthquakes, well located by a local network, occur at depths of 10 to 35 km (Smalley and Isacks, 1986; Smalley, 1988). Most of these crustal earthquakes are probably located in the basement, below the deformed sedimentary section that may be decoupled from the basement (Smalley and Isacks, 1986; Smalley, 1988).

Sierras Pampeanas. The Precordillera is flanked on the east by the broad basins and mountains of the Sierras Pampeanas. The crystalline basement block uplifts of the Sierras Pampeanas are bounded by reverse and thrust faults that trend primarily to the north and verge variably to the west or east (Fig. 2a). The ranges expose basement rocks that were metamorphosed during the late Precambrian (600 to 900 Ma) (Caminos and others, 1982; Spinelli, 1983) with numerous intrusions of Paleozoic plutons in the central and eastern Sierras Pampeanas (Rapela and others, 1982). The two ranges closest to the Precordillera (the

Sierra de Valle Fértil and Pie de Palo) and the Bermejo Valley are described here, along with the nature of their contact with the Eastern Precordillera.

Pie de Palo. Pie de Palo, the westernmost range of the Sierras Pampeanas province, is located about 30 km east of the Paleozoic exposures that are uplifted in the southern part of the Eastern Cordillera (Figs. 2a, 3, 4). The range is an elliptical dome with a north-trending summit crest line and topographic relief of about 2,500 m. It is composed of medium-grade, strongly layered, metamorphic rocks that are overlain, around the margins of the range, by only Cenozoic clastic strata.

The crust beneath Pie de Palo is seismically active. A major ($M_S = 7.4$) earthquake and its aftershock sequence in 1977 have been interpreted to have occurred as a blind thrust extending between about 17 and 35 km depth, on a 35° west-dipping fault plane beneath the range, based on seismic and leveling data (Fig. 4; Kadinsky-Cade, 1985; Kadinsky-Cade and others, 1985).

Such a blind thrust is thought to be the principal structure controlling uplift of the range (Jordan and Allmendinger, 1986). North-trending reverse faults and some antithetic normal faults are mapped locally along both the east and west margins of the range (Baldis and others, 1979; Uliarte and Lendaro de Gianni, 1982; Whitney and Bastias, 1984), and are probably minor expressions of the deep reverse fault. The northern flank of the range is also faulted, with east-striking faults. Oblique slip on the east-striking fault system is suggested by the en-echelon pattern of the fault strands and the inferred eastward thrusting of the Pie de Palo block (Fig. 3). The southern margin of the range is not faulted; the gentle southward slope of the basement surface is onlapped by Quaternary deposits.

The contact between the crystalline basement to the east and the Paleozoic units of the Eastern Precordillera to the west is concealed in a valley north of the city of San Juan that is largely covered by alluvial and eolian deposits (Fig. 3). Discontinuous exposures of the Cenozoic strata in the valley appear to define an undulatory series of broad folds, and their distribution implies that the valley is a synclinorium (Fig. 4). At the north end of the valley, north-striking Tertiary strata of the Sierra de Mogna in the Eastern Precordillera connect eastward with east-striking strata, projecting toward the northern boundary of Pie de Palo. These strata are affected by east-striking folds with steeply plunging axes in the valley near Pie de Palo that are probably associated with the inferred oblique-slip fault system at the north end of Pie de Palo (Fig. 3).

To the south of the city of San Juan, in the Tulum Valley, Quaternary deposits and other Cenozoic strata overlie crystalline basement at a shallow depth (e.g., Gray de Cerdan, 1969). The lateral contact between Sierras Pampeanas basement and the thick Paleozoic sequence of the Eastern Precordillera can be more precisely located here. A series of small, isolated hills (too small to map at the scale of Fig. 2) expose crystalline basement, similar to that of Pie de Palo, in a trend southwest along the strike of the western margin of Pie de Palo. These basement exposures come within 10 km of Paleozoic strata of the Eastern Precordillera that crop out in the Sierra Chica de Zonda. Between the basement exposures and the Paleozoic exposures are Quaternary scarps along a regional set of east-dipping thrust faults that cut the Cenozoic strata (Rolleri, 1969; Uliarte and Lendaro de Gianni, 1982; Bastias and others, 1984). These faults closely parallel the trend of the Eastern Precordillera rather than the trend of the isolated basement exposures to their east.

Sierra de Valle Fértil and Bermejo Valley. To the north of Pie de Palo, the Sierra de Valle Fértil system is the westernmost series of ranges of the Sierras Pampeanas. It trends N30°W, oblique to the Eastern Precordillera, and intersects the Eastern Precordillera at the Sierra de Maz (Figs. 2a, 3). The western border of Sierra de Valle Fértil is a reverse fault system with a minimum vertical throw at the center of the range of about 10 km in the late Cenozoic. Its subsurface geometry is not well known, but it is interpreted as a fault dipping 30 to 35° east (Jordan and Allmendinger, 1986). In the segment to the east of Pie de Palo,

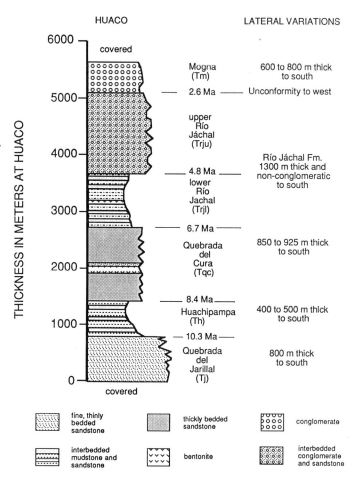

Figure 6. Stratigraphy of Cenozoic units exposed in Sierra de Huaco, as described and dated by Johnsson and others (1984) and Johnson and others (1986). The variations in thickness that are noted occur over about a 100-km distance, along strike of Eastern Precordillera (from Cuerda and others, 1981, 1984).

the Sierra de Valle Fértil thrust-fault system cuts Quaternary sediments (Whitney and Bastias, 1984), and seismic reflection data show that the fault dips about 30° east (Snyder and others, 1986). Young deformation may also be indicated at the north end of the Sierra de Valle Fértil, where an earthquake at a depth of 30 km occurred east of the range (Chinn and Isacks, 1983), possibly generated by the fault system that has uplifted the range (Jordan and others, 1983a; Jordan and Allmendinger, 1986).

Sierra de Valle Fértil is separated from the Eastern Precordillera by the triangular, alluvium-covered Bermejo Valley, which is 65 km wide at its south end and narrows northward. Cenozoic strata in the basin are 6 km thick on the western side and are thought to thicken eastward (see the section on Cenozoic stratigraphy below; Ortiz and Zambrano, 1981; Jordan and Allmendinger, 1986). This asymmetrical shape is consistent with gravity data from the basin (D. Snyder, personal communication, 1986). The Tertiary synorogenic strata exposed in the northern half of the Eastern Precordillera were apparently deposited in a continuation of the Bermejo basin to the west that was subsequently deformed and uplifted. Continued subsidence of the present basin is indicated by thick Quaternary deposits.

The northwestern end of the Sierra de Valle Fértil system (the Sierra de Maz) contacts the northern Precordillera (Figs. 2a, 3). Although that zone has been mapped at regional scale (e.g., de Alba, 1954), we are not aware of any studies focused on the geometry or relative timing of structures in that zone. Sierra de Maz is a crystalline basement block uplifted along its west side by a northwest-trending fault that is a continuation of the Sierra de Valle Fértil system. The strike line of the Sierra de Valle Fértil/ Sierra de Maz intersects the nearly north-south structures of the Precordillera in a little-studied zone of complex folding that apparently includes folds of both trends. The Sierra de Valle Fértil fault system has been interpreted as a major crustal feature with fault activity at various times through the Phanerozoic (e.g., Baldis and others, 1982), so it may continue beneath the northern Precordillera. This juxtaposition of the Sierras Pampeanas deformation with the thin-skinned structures of the Precordillera has some similarities with the Gros Ventre/Sevier belt interaction of the North American Cordillera, although the difference in strike between the thin- and thick-skinned structures in the South American example is less than in the North American case (Fig. 2).

EASTERN PRECORDILLERA

Parts of the Eastern Precordillera have been mapped at both regional and local scales, and the structural geometry has been illustrated in regional and local cross sections (Baldis and Chebli, 1969; Rolleri, 1969; Baldis and others, 1979; Furque, 1979; Contreras, 1981; Cuerda and others, 1981; Ortiz and Zambrano, 1981; Vasquez and Gorroño, 1982; Baldis and others, 1982; Baldis and Bordonaro, 1984; Cuerda and others, 1984). These data have been combined with Landsat TM imagery, stereo pairs of Large Format Camera photographs taken by the space shuttle, and reconnaissance field mapping to make a new map (scale originally about 1:780,000) of the northern part of the Eastern Precordillera (Fig. 3).

The Eastern Precordillera consists of four principal mountain ranges in a roughly north-south chain (Fig. 3). The structural level exposed in the ranges generally decreases northward, so that Paleozoic strata exposed in the cores of the southern structures are not exposed in the north. The Paleozoic and Mesozoic stratigraphy is reviewed briefly in the section on paleogeography below; here we summarize only the synorogenic upper Cenozoic units.

Cenozoic stratigraphy

Cenozoic clastic strata are the most widespread rock units exposed in the Eastern Precordillera and have recently been studied at several locations (e.g., Contreras, 1981; Cuerda and others, 1981; Johnsson and others, 1984; Johnson and others, 1986; Bercowski and others, 1986). Where they have been dated in the northern part of the Eastern Precordillera, the lower 5,400

m of the approximately 6,000-m-thick section were deposited between about 14 Ma and 2.3 Ma, a period that includes the inferred time of deformation in the Central Precordillera thrust belt to the west (Fig. 6; Johnson and others, 1986; Jordan and others, 1988). The fluvial sequence coarsens upward, representing a progression from a low-relief depositional environment to a proximal alluvial fan setting, probably indicating the progressive eastward development of Central Precordillera thrusting from the west (Cuerda and others, 1981; Johnson and others, 1986; Beer and others, 1986).

The base and top of the Cenozoic section are not exposed at Huaco (see Fig. 6), and the thicknesses of some of the formations vary, but the entire section appears conformable in the Sierra de Huaco and the Sierra de Mogna to the south (Cuerda and others, 1981; Johnson and others, 1986). The stratigraphy and lithologies of the strata are summarized in Figure 6; here, we describe only a few interesting stratigraphic features. The Huachipampa Formation (Th) tends to flow in the tighter anticlinal hinges, causing thickness changes from 600 m on the limbs of folds to only 20 m in the nose of an anticline at Mogna (Furque, 1979; Cuerda and others, 1981; Furque, 1983; Johnson and others, 1986). Because several of the structures of the Sierra de Huaco are expressed at the surface only within the Rio Jáchal Formation, we have mapped this thick formation as two members (upper, Trju, and lower, Trjl; Figs. 6, 7) and locally have shown marker beds that further trace structures.

Structural geology

The structures of the Eastern Precordillera are presumed to be basically similar along strike, but due to differences in erosional levels, are expressed differently at the surface. In the southern part of the subprovince, surface exposures reveal imbricate, east-dipping thrust faults in the Paleozoic strata. In the northern part of the subprovince, surface exposures show large-amplitude folds and associated faults in the Cenozoic strata. We first summarize the structural geology of the Sierra Chica de Zonda, which is the best-described part of the southern area. The Sierra de Villicum is presumed to be similar in structural style to Chica de Zonda, but only generated cross sections across it have been published (e.g., Fig. 4). We next describe the surficial geology of Sierra de Huaco and surrounding areas, in the northern part of the Eastern Precordillera, based on our own data. The structures of the Eastern Precordillera have similarities to regions in the Northern Cordillera, and are compared in the following section.

Evidence of basement faulting in the southern region.
The Sierra Chica de Zonda is uplifted and tilted to the east along a principal east-dipping reverse fault along its western flank (Fig. 3) and several parallel imbricate thrusts within the range (Baldis and Bordonaro, 1984; not shown in Fig. 3). Baldis and Bordonaro (1984) proposed that the southern part of the Eastern Precordillera is a Sierras Pampeanas–type structure, controlled by a fault that penetrates crystalline basement, with secondary detachment of the carbonate-based sedimentary section along thrust

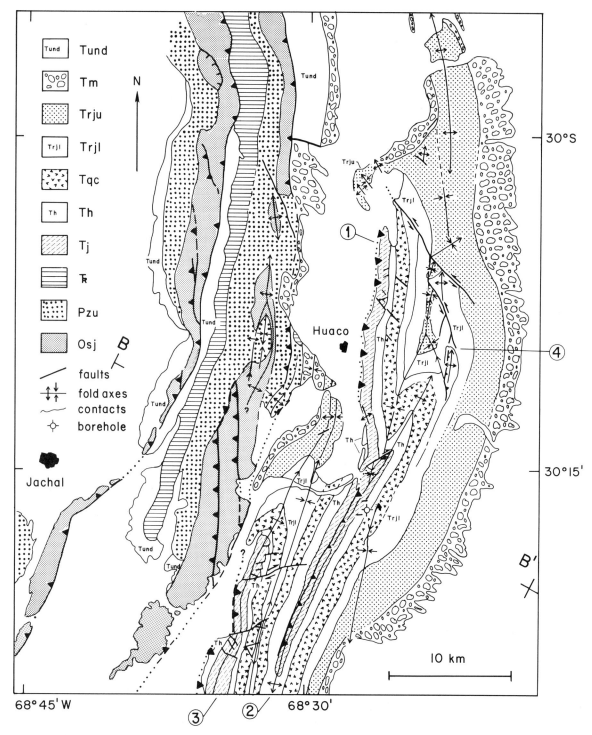

Figure 7. Geologic map of Precordillera near town of Huaco, illustrating deformation of upper Tertiary and older strata. Sources of data are described in text. Western portion is the Agua Hedionda Ranges, part of the east-verging Central Precordillera; eastern portion is the Sierra de Huaco, part of west-verging Eastern Precordillera. Symbols for stratigraphic units that are not defined in Figure 6 include: "Tund" (undifferentiated Tertiary clastic rocks), "T$_R$" (Triassic rocks), "Pzu" (clastic Paleozoic strata), and "Osj" (Ordovician San Juan Limestone). Faults, fold axes, and contacts are dashed where inferred and dotted where projected. Triangles are on upper plates of thrust faults. Cross section B-B′ extends beyond the edge of this figure to the east (see Fig. 3) and is shown in Figure 8.

faults. These authors based their interpretation on three observations: that the Lower Cambrian limestone exposed along the western fault of Chica de Zonda is the deepest stratigraphic level exposed anywhere in the Central or Eastern Precordillera, that isolated exposures of crystalline basement occur within 10 km east of Paleozoic strata, and that facies relations indicate that the Eastern Precordillera was a faulted and uplifted structural feature during the deposition of part of the middle Paleozoic section (Baldis and Chebli, 1969; Baldis and others, 1982).

Support for the interpretation of basement-faulting beneath the Eastern Precordillera is also indicated by crustal earthquake activity. A 1972 earthquake ($M_S = 6.0$) was located to the east of the southeast side of the Sierra de Mogna at a depth of 20 km, with a thrust-type focal mechanism (Chinn and Isacks, 1983). The strike of the nodal planes parallels the surface structures of Sierra de Mogna (Chinn and Isacks, 1983), and an upward extrapolation of one of the nodal planes as a 34° east-dipping fault from the hypocenter intersects the surface near the principal surface thrust fault on the west side of the Sierra de Mogna. A large ($M_S = 7.5$) earthquake that destroyed the city of San Juan in 1944 was also probably located within the Eastern Precordillera to the west of Sierra Pie de Palo (Castellanos, 1945; Kadinsky-Cade, 1985) but without adequate seismic records the depth of this earthquake is unknown. No primary faulting was observed at the surface (Castellanos, 1945), so the earthquake may have occurred on a basement fault decoupled from at least the shallowest surface sediments. Two other large earthquakes caused extensive damage in the Eastern Precordillera in the last 100 years, but there are not enough data to locate them accurately. As described above, numerous small earthquakes have been recorded beneath the southern part of the Matagusanos Valley and the Eastern Precordillera at depths of 10 to 35 km, which is primarily within the crystalline basement (Smalley, 1988).

Surficial structure of the northern region. We have examined in some detail the well-exposed portion of the Precordillera shown in Figure 7 to better understand the nature of the boundary between the Central and Eastern Precordillera subprovinces. The western half of Figure 7, west of the town of Huaco, contains ranges here called the Agua Hedionda Ranges that are part of the east-verging Central Precordillera. East of the town of Huaco is the Sierra de Huaco, part of the west-verging Eastern Precordillera. We have mapped the structures by photo interpretation of enhanced Landsat TM digital imagery, Large Format Camera (LFC) stereo photographs collected by the space shuttle, and stereo low-altitude air photos. The structural and stratigraphic interpretations were checked, and the strikes, dips, and plunges of most of the major structures were measured during reconnaissance field work. The LFC color infra-red photograph set, collected by the Space Shuttle *Challenger* flight 41-G in October 1984, provided a cartographically accurate base for the map and a synoptic view of the structures not available from the air photos. The TM data, from scene ID 50787-13514, acquired on 27 April 1986, provided additional spectral ("color") information on the lithologic units that complements the LFC photos. An enlargement of LFC frame 1684, covering the northern part of the Eastern Precordillera, was interpreted at a scale of approximately 1:170,000 for Figure 7.

Agua Hedionda Ranges. We here refer to the set of mountains between the town of Huaco and the city of Jáchal (Figs. 3, 7) as the Agua Hedionda Ranges. The structures exposed here are typical of the Central Precordillera, consisting of imbricated east-verging thrust sheets containing primarily Paleozoic rocks (Fig. 5). The resistant Ordovician San Juan Limestone crops out in two subparallel cuestas along the leading edges of two west-dipping thrust sheets (Heim, 1952; Rolleri, 1969; Furque, 1979). The strike of the strata is close to north, as in the Sierra de Huaco, with some eastward convexity. One sharp kink in the strike of the limestone occurs about 5 km south of the city of Jáchal (Fig. 7), suggesting the presence of a transverse structure or lateral ramp in the subsurface.

The two major thrust faults are generally not exposed at the surface in the Agua Hedionda Ranges, but their traces are generally well constrained. The western thrust has stratigraphic throw from the San Juan Limestone to at least the upper part of the Triassic, approximately 2.5 km of vertical throw. The eastern cuesta is formed by a tight anticlinal fold along its central part and by a set of imbricate thrust plates and a buried range-bounding thrust to the south. The anticline has a near-vertical to overturned east limb and an approximately 45° west-dipping west limb. Smaller, nearly isoclinal folds are present in the upper Paleozoic section of the east limb.

Sierra de Huaco. The Sierra de Huaco is a series of north-south–trending, west-verging folds and faults that expose Upper Tertiary synorogenic strata in the northern part of the Eastern Precordillera, with more folds than faults exposed at the surface (Fig. 7). The folds generally have axial surfaces that are upright or east-dipping, and the thrust faults appear to dip to the east.

A Cities Service test well (Las Salinas Ax-1) drilled near the core of the Las Salinas Anticline (anticline II of Fig. 7) passed through the lower part of the Tertiary section and some of the Paleozoic and Mesozoic section, before penetrating the San Juan Limestone near the total depth of 3631 m (A. Ortiz, 1984, personal communication). The line-length balanced cross sections of Figure 8 pass through the well location and show two possible interpretations of the subsurface geometry that agree with the well data.

The higher elevations of the Sierra de Huaco are three long, narrow ridges that are formed by the resistant, and apparently more competent, Jarillal Formation (Tj) in the cores of anticlines. These three anticlines (1, 2, and 3 in Fig. 7) are each more than 20 km long and nearly linear. The hinge lines of the major anticlines are horizontal for most of the length of the folds, plunging gently only near their ends. The large folds have wavelengths of about 5 km and varying amplitudes of about 1 to 6 km. Most of the folds of all sizes have sharp angular hinges and straight limbs.

Anticlines 1 and 3 (Fig. 7) are the westernmost structures in this part of the Eastern Precordillera. The change in vergence

a)

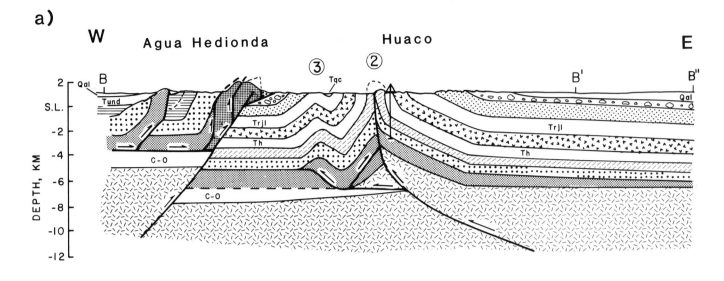

b)

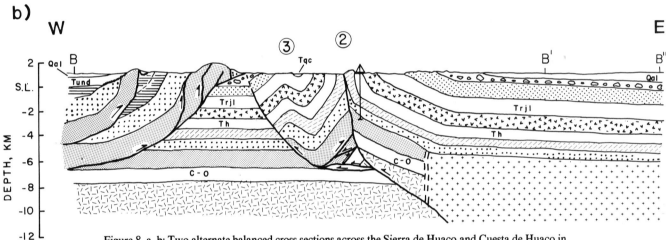

Figure 8. a, b: Two alternate balanced cross sections across the Sierra de Huaco and Cuesta de Huaco in the northern part of the Eastern Precordillera, based on data described in text (location shown in Figs. 3, 7). Cities Service test well "Las Salinas Ax-1" is shown. Vertical and horizontal scales are equal. Stratigraphic units same as those of Figure 7, except a, with the addition of crystalline basement (random tick pattern), and b, with Precordilleran basement in random tick pattern and Pampean basement in small plus pattern with Paleozoic suture (double dashed line) between them; basement ages unknown. Differences between cross sections described in text.

between the Central and Eastern Precordilleras occurs within the narrow valley between these anticlines of the Sierra de Huaco and the Agua Hedionda Ranges (Figs. 7, 8). The west limb and hinge of the northern anticline (1) are not exposed along most of its length. Its east limb dips 80° east, in the section east of the town of Huaco, and presumably has been uplifted relative to the buried west limb by an east-dipping thrust. The southwestern anticline (3) apparently has a more open fold hinge than anticline 2 to its east (Fig. 8). The syncline between the two southern anticlines (2 and 3) has a west-verging asymmetry, with dips of 60° west on the east limb and only 30° east on the west limb. The partially exposed west limb of anticline 3 is less than 1 km from the easternmost east-verging thrust plate, carrying Ordovician

San Juan Limestone (Fig. 7), closely constraining the surface trace of the boundary between the east- and west-verging structural subprovinces.

Anticline 2 and anticline 4, the eastern series of folds in the Sierra de Huaco, are examples of folds that we have interpreted as being formed over basement faults (Figs. 7, 8). Anticline 2 is the site of the Cities Service test well and is the eastern anticline on the cross section of Figure 8. It has a tight, somewhat rounded, hinge at its north end, but farther south, a west-verging thrust fault in the core of the anticline repeats the Jarillal Formation on the west side (Figs. 7, 8). Folds and faults, too small to map at this scale, are common along the fold hinge and are probably related to space problems in the very tight core of the anticline (Fig. 8).

Modeling the steep dips (near vertical) of the limbs and the tightness of the hinge of anticline 2 is difficult with Suppe's (1983) fault-bend fold theory or his fault-propagation fold theory (Suppe and Medwedeff, 1984; Woodward and others, 1985), primarily because the dip of the faults closest to the limbs in both theories must be at least as steep as the dip of the limbs. Farther north, on strike of anticlines 2 and 4, a series of more open, west-verging folds are expressed at the service in the Rio Jáchal Formation.

The detailed kinematics of the faults of the Huaco area are not well known, but it appears that most of the faults exposed at the surface are consistent with nearly east-west shortening. A thrust fault duplicates the Jarillal Formation in the hinge of anticline 2, and a buried thrust is inferred to have uplifted the east limb of anticline 1 and the southern part of anticline 3; these thrusts are apparently parallel to bedding in the steeply dipping limbs of anticlines 1, 2, and 3. Several minor thrust faults, also parallel to bedding, that pass along strike into tight syncline-anticline pairs are visible on the air photos, but are too small to map on Figure 7. There are also traverse faults that have possible strike-slip displacement. One of the larger transverse faults, northeast of the town of Huaco, cuts the north end of anticline 1, truncates the syncline located between anticlines 1 and 4, and terminates in the core of anticline 4. The displacement direction and dip of this fault are difficult to interpret on the air photos, but it appears to be a near-vertical, left-lateral, strike-slip fault (similar to some parallel smaller scale strike-slip faults investigated in the field farther south). The axes of the syncline and anticline 4 are displaced across the southern major splay of the fault and do not continue north of the northern branch (Fig. 7), indicating a complex fault displacement history probably synchronous with the folding. All of these large-scale faults at the surface are consistent with the estimated east-west shortening across the Eastern Precordillera, and they may be related to underlying basement faults (Fig. 8). It is unclear whether or not the steeply dipping thrusts, which are parallel to bedding, were originally low-angle and have been rotated to their present dips after thrusting.

There are also two conjugate sets of smaller scale faults that trend east-northeast and southeast across the folds and are probably high-angle strike-slip faults. Many minor faults are visible on the air photos, and many small faults are visible in the field. Only the larger faults of the two conjugate sets are shown in the map (Fig. 7); they are especially common where they cut the apparently more brittle Jarillal Formation exposed in the anticlinal cores. Field checks of a few of the faults confirmed that at least some are near-vertical, and revealed mutual cross-cutting relationships between the two sets, showing that faults of both strikes were contemporaneous. The two conjugate sets are present in scales of offset ranging from a kilometer to a few millimeters, and are consistent with east-southeast–directed shortening and minor north-northeast–directed extension. Some of the minor faults visible on the air photos have steep dips and apparent normal displacement, another indication of some nearly north-south extension.

COMPARISONS TO STRUCTURAL PROVINCES OF THE ROCKY MOUNTAINS

Comparisons of the Eastern Precordillera with areas in North America that may have analogous structural geometries aid in the interpretation of the subsurface geometries of the structures of the Eastern Precordillera, where there is little subsurface control.

General comparisons

The Idaho-Wyoming salient of the Sevier thrust belt consists of a set of five major north-trending thrust plates that have translated the Phanerozoic strata to the east, resulting in about 100 km (50 percent) shortening above the crystalline basement (Fig. 2b). The thrusts were active between the Late Jurassic and Eocene; in general, successively younger thrust faults ramped to the surface at successively more eastward (cratonward) positions (Armstrong and Oriel, 1965; Royse and others, 1975). The Central Precordillera is similar in structural style to the Idaho-Wyoming thrust belt (Fig. 2; e.g., Baldis and Chebli, 1969), and preliminary dating suggests that Precordillera thrusts also progressed from west to east (Jordan and others, 1985).

The basement uplifts and intervening basins of the Rocky Mountain Foreland area formed during the Late Cretaceous through middle Eocene by shortening across thrust and reverse faults (e.g., Chapin and Cather, 1981; Gries, 1981; Lowell, 1985; Brown, this volume; Hamilton, this volume). The basement faulting produced a structural relief that locally exceeds 10 km and horizontal overlap of as much as 30 km (Berg, 1962; Gries, 1981, 1983; Brown, this volume). The trends of the uplift-bounding faults are much more variable than the thrusts of the adjacent Idaho-Wyoming thrust belt, perhaps due to a rotation through time of the maximum shortening direction (Chapin and Cather, 1981; Gries, 1983) or to reactivation of variably trending basement lineations (Blackstone, 1963). The subsurface geometry of the range-bounding faults at mid- or lower crustal depths is not yet well known, although they are commonly interpreted to flatten to décollement-style thrusts at a mid-crustal detachment (e.g., Bally, 1981; Schmidt and others, 1985). Locally, this geometry has been confirmed by deep seismic reflection profiling, such as the COCORP profiles across the Wind River Mountains (e.g., Sharry and others, 1986). The Sierras Pampeanas ranges and basins of Argentina are similar in scale and structural style to those of the Rocky Mountain basement uplift province (Jordan and Allmendinger, 1986).

The deformation of the Rocky Mountain basement uplifts and the Idaho-Wyoming thrust belt was coeval during the Late Cretaceous to early Eocene (e.g., Wiltchko and Dorr, 1983). Similarly, incomplete age constraints indicate that the basement faults in the Sierras Pampeanas have been active during the last 10 m.y. (Jordan and Allmendinger, 1986), and thrust faults of the Central Precordillera spanned the last 15 m.y. (Jordan and others, 1985; Johnson and others, 1986; Reynolds and others, 1987).

Kulik and Schmidt (this volume) recognize an "overlap zone" in which structures typical of the Sevier thrust belt and the Rocky Mountain basement uplift zone overlap in time and space. We interpret the Eastern Precordillera, and the Sierra de Maz to its north, to be an analogous "overlap zone" in the Andean Cordillera. The North American and South American overlap zones are not exactly equivalent, however, in either dimension or duration. Specifically, the overlap zone of the western United States exceeds 100 km in width over much of its length, and activity characteristic of the structural overlap spanned about 25 m.y. (Kulik and Schmidt, this volume), although the overlap zone structures in any one transect of the zone were typically active for a much shorter time period (e.g., Moxa Arch discussion below). In contrast, the overlap zone in Argentina is only about 30 to 50 km in width (Figs. 2a, 3), and deformation within the zone has been active for a maximum of 10 to 15 m.y. Along some transects of the Eastern Precordillera, such as that shown in Figure 8, deformation has only been active for 2 to 3 m.y. (Jordan and others, 1985; Johnson and others, 1986). The difference in duration of deformation appears to be consistent with the different amounts of shortening in the two foreland provinces: an estimated 2 percent in the Sierras Pampeanas during 10 m.y. (Jordan and Allmendinger, 1986) versus an estimated 13 to 15 percent in the Rocky Mountain Foreland during 40 m.y. (Brown, this volume). Thus, the present stage of development of the Eastern Precordillera and Sierra de Maz zone may be similar to that of the overlap zone of the western United States at an early point in its history. Perhaps the width of the overlap zone in Argentina will increase with continued deformation.

Specific structural comparisons

The existing data for the Eastern Precordillera suggest several possible subsurface geometries and alternative explanations of its structural history. Some of the possible models can be illuminated by comparison to analogous structures in the Rocky Mountains whose three-dimensional form is better known.

Potential explanations of the Eastern Precordillera include: (1) It is a triangle or delta zone (not involving basement) and accommodates crowding problems at the eastern boundary of the thin-skinned Precordillera. (2) It is the surface expression of buried basement-involved thrusts or reverse faults typical of the Sierras Pampeanas; the thick sedimentary cover is locally detached along secondary décollements. (3) It is an "out-of-the-basin" thrusted anticline related to broad folding of the basement beneath the Bermejo basin. (4) It is a combination or superposition of one or more of the above.

Triangle zones or delta zones are exemplified by the Alberta foothills of the Canadian Cordilleran thrust belt, which are north of the region of interference with the Rocky Mountain basement uplifts (e.g., Jones, 1983). Locally, triangle zones are also described along the eastern margin of the Idaho-Wyoming thrust belt (e.g., Game Hill thrust: Royse, 1985). Since triangle zones result in a series of folds and faults that verge opposite to the principal structures of the fold-thrust belt, they could be analo-

gous to the Eastern Precordillera structures. Backthrusts (opposed in vergence to the main part of the thrust belt) are common on the cratonic flanks of thin-skinned thrust belts (Lowell, 1985). By analogy to the Alberta foothills or the frontal Idaho-Wyoming thrust belt, a triangle zone would be localized at the position of the Eastern Precordillera by the decrease in thickness of the Paleozoic sedimentary wedge (Fig. 5).

The two sets of faults that constitute the Alberta triangle zone are described by Price (1981) and Jones (1983, see Fig. 9b). The first is a set of eastward-directed blind thrusts, climbing up-section eastward from the regional décollement level of the thrust belt. Simultaneously, a second set of westward-directed thrust faults formed, with a décollement at the same or higher structural level than the regional thrust-belt décollement. Where the east-directed thrusts join the west-directed faults in the upper décollement, offset diminishes to zero; this occurs beneath the Alberta syncline. The development of successive splays in the blind thrust package results in folding of both the east-directed and west-directed thrusts, and in some cases results in steep or overturned folds (Jones, 1983, Fig. 19). As discussed below, we interpret this as a possible, but not the most likely, explanation of the Eastern Precordillera structures.

The second model, with significant basement faulting, is perhaps the most likely explanation for the Eastern Precordillera, as first suggested by Baldis and Chebli (1969) and supported by the data presented in this paper and by local earthquake data (Smalley and Isacks, 1987; Smalley, 1988). There are several examples in the North American Cordillera of basement fault systems that spatially overlap the thin-skinned thrust system. These include instances where the thin-skinned and basement faults intersect with significantly different strikes (e.g., Gros Ventre and Uinta Mountains) and where the two systems are subparallel to one another (e.g., Moxa Arch-La Barge Platform). We discuss the Moxa Arch-La Barge system in some detail because it is similar to the Eastern Precordillera in scale, in map geometry, and in probable involvement of crystalline basement.

For about 200 km, the north-striking Moxa Arch-La Barge platform is subparallel to and east of the easternmost thrusts of the southern half of the Idaho-Wyoming thrust belt (Fig. 2b). To the north, it intersects the thrust belt, apparently causing an inflection in strike of the Darby/Hogsback/Prospect thrust systems, and has been hypothesized to continue northward underneath the thin-skinned thrusts (Blackstone, 1979). The history of shortening and uplift on the Moxa Arch is complex. During the Early and Middle Cretaceous, it may have formed as a flexural bulge due to the crustal loading of thrust faults to the west of the arch (Jordan, 1981). Arching in the Late Cretaceous that is indicated by an erosional unconformity beneath the Tertiary strata (Garing and Tainter, 1985; Stockton and Hawkings, 1985) may have had the same cause and geometry as contemporaneous basement uplifts to the east. The eastern margin of the thrust belt, north of the intersection of the Moxa Arch and thrust belt, was folded above a basement fold or fault during the early Eocene (Royse, 1985), but this did not occur to the south along the trend of the Cretaceous

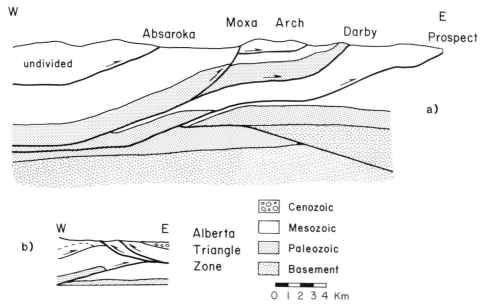

Figure 9. Cross sections of North American Cordillera structures that are possibly analogous to the Eastern Precordillera. a, Moxa Arch system, showing interrelations between east-dipping basement fault and west-dipping thin-skinned thrusts of Idaho-Wyoming thrust belt (from Kraig and others, this volume). b, The Alberta foothills triangle zone, from Jones (1982). The sections in a and b are drawn at same scale, with no vertical exaggeration.

Moxa Arch (Royse, 1985; Stockton and Hawkins, 1985; Garing and Tainter, 1985). In the area of intersection with the thrust belt, the sum of the basement motions caused an asymmetrical arch, with a steeper flank on the west (Blackstone, 1979; Royse, 1985). To the south, the arch is asymmetrical to the east (Stockton and Hawkins, 1985).

Blackstone (1979) and Kraig and others (this volume) illustrated the geometry of structures near the intersection of the Moxa Arch and thrust belt. South of the intersection, the Calpet fault is an east-dipping thrust fault (Blackstone, 1979) that is an expression of the regional Moxa Arch; however, Blackstone's cross sections do not clarify whether the Calpet fault cuts basement. The Calpet fault is truncated by the Eocene La Barge thrust, which is the easternmost major west-dipping thrust fault (Blackstone, 1979). To the north of the intersection, Kraig and others (this volume) inferred that an east-dipping basement thrust controls the structure of the eastern margin of the thrust belt (Fig. 9a). The inferred basement fault is blind, flattening upward until it parallels bedding in the Triassic section (Fig. 9a). Motion on the east-verging Prospect thrust may be a consequence of motion on the basement thrust. Evidence for similar basement faulting beneath the Eastern Precordillera is discussed below.

The third possible explanation of the Eastern Precordillera, an "out-of-the-basin" thrusted anticline, can be illustrated by comparison to folds within the Rocky Mountain basement uplift province. This type of structure is analogous to "out-of-the-syncline crowd" or "rabbit-ear" structures, discussed by Brown (this volume), that are caused by crowding in a synclinal axis during flexural-slip folding. The space problems in the hinge zone

become more severe at stratigraphically higher levels and can produce bedding-parallel thrust faults (Brown, 1984, this volume; Lowell, 1985 [who refers to these as one type of "foreland detachment structure"]).

Whether these can operate at a scale adequate to generate the Eastern Precordillera depends on the degree to which the crystalline basement can fold. The Sheep Mountain anticline in the eastern Big Horn Basin may be a large-scale example of basement involvement in folding (Brown, 1984), while somewhat smaller structures in the northwestern Wind River basin, Elk Mountain area, and other locations contain this type of structure in the absence of basement folding (Lowell, 1985). The fact that the thrusts of the Eastern Precordillera are not parallel to the axis of the Bermejo Valley basin and Sierra de Valle Fértil block uplift, and that they persist south of the area where Pie de Palo intersects the Bermejo Valley (Fig. 3), implies that the Eastern Precordillera is not a simple expression of an out-of-the-basin structure.

The final possible model for the Eastern Precordillera is that it has formed by the spatial superposition of one or more of the structural models described above. There are numerous analogues of the superposition of thin-skinned and thick-skinned structures in the overlap zone of the western United States. Kulik and Schmidt (this volume) discuss a variety of geometries of structures that can result from this superposition, depending on the relative vergence directions and age relations of the interfering structures. However, lack of known constraints on the subsurface geometries of the Eastern Precordillera make interpretations of complex overlapping structures difficult to evaluate.

PROJECTING THE STRUCTURAL INTERPRETATIONS OF THE EASTERN PRECORDILLERA TO DEPTH

There are two challenges in determining the subsurface structural geometry and genesis from the surface structures in the Eastern Precordillera: how to project the surface structures downward to evaluate whether there is basement faulting, and how to connect the Eastern Precordillera structures with the Central Precordillera structures to the west. The surface geometries, stratigraphy, earthquake data, and structural analogies constrain the interpretations.

A previous interpretation of the subsurface structure beneath the south-central part of the Eastern Precordillera and the adjacent Central Precordillera by Baldis and Chebli (1969) is shown in Figure 4. These authors interpreted a sharp change in the structural style between the Central Precordillera, a classic thin-skinned fold-thrust belt, and the Eastern Precordillera, formed above high-angle basement faults. Little new geologic information is available to refine the interpretation of the subsurface structure of this southern part of the Eastern Precordillera.

We have constructed two cross sections through the northern part of the Eastern Precordillera and part of the adjacent Central Precordillera, illustrating alternative interpretations of the subsurface structure (Fig. 8). There are few constraints on the deeper levels of the structure in this section. The sections were constructed from surface dips measured in the field, formation depths from the Cities Service test well, and the geometric constraints of line-length section-balancing.

A major component of the first structural model (Fig. 8a) is the interpretation of two zones of basement faulting: a west-dipping fault under the eastern side of the Agua Hedionda Ranges, which is part of the Central Precordillera subprovince, and an east-dipping fault under the Sierra de Huaco, which is in the Eastern Precordillera. The crystalline basement of the Bermejo basin just to the east of the Sierra de Huaco is at least 6 km deep (beneath the exposed Tertiary strata; see Fig. 6) and probably 7 to 9 km deep (e.g., Fig. 5 and section below on paleogeography). Baldis and Chebli's (1969) structural reconstructions indicate that the depth to the décollement at the base of the San Juan Limestone is 3 to 4 km beneath the easternmost Central Precordillera, with little or no thickness of Tertiary strata. The Cambro-Ordovician carbonate sequence that underlies the San Juan Limestone in the southern part of the Eastern Precordillera (Sierras Villicum and Chica de Zonda: Baldis and Bordonaro, 1984) is inferred to lie between the décollement and basement in the Central Precordillera.

The basement fault under the eastern edge of the Central Precordillera (Fig. 8a) is inferred from the difference in the estimated depths to basement between the Eastern and Central Precordilleras. The steep dips of the limbs of the anticline formed along this fault (Fig. 8a) imply a steeply dipping ramp, which may be more simply explained by high-angle basement faulting than by an anticlinal stack of many fault-bend folds (e.g., Suppe,

1983). Baldis and Chebli (1969) also showed basement faults on the east side of the Central Precordillera, accommodating a similar inferred discontinuity in the projected depth to basement (Fig. 4). Uplift of the Central Precordillera along this fault during the Cenozoic could explain the apparent lack of thick Upper Tertiary synorogenic strata west of the Eastern Precordillera at this latitude, and pre-Cenozoic movement on this fault could also explain differences in the thicknesses of the upper Paleozoic and Mesozoic units (Fig. 5). The dip of this fault is not constrained, but was chosen to be similar to the 45° dip typical of Sierras Pampeanas faults (Jordan and Allmendinger, 1986). The abundance of crustal earthquakes in the basement at depths greater than 10 km in the southern Matagusanos Valley (Smalley and Isacks, 1987; Smalley, 1988) is consistent with this interpretation but does not require it.

An alternative explanation of the subsurface structure of the eastern edge of the Central Precordillera is shown in Figure 8b. In this interpretation, a local triplication of the thick section of Ordovician limestone beneath the Agua Hedionda Ranges fills much of the space above a basement surface at the 8-km depth that is inferred for the basement beneath the Sierra de Huaco. This structural geometry implies a much greater amount of shortening in the eastern part of the Central Precordillera than the first alternative (more than 100 percent of the present width) and a much greater paleogeographic width of the Cambro-Ordovician shelf. We believe this interpretation is less likely, but existing data are not sufficient to rule it out.

The basement fault under the Sierra de Huaco (on the east side of Figs. 8a, b) is inferred from the shortening of the overlying Tertiary strata, the very steep dip of the limbs of anticline 2, and from the along-strike persistence of the west-verging structures that define the Eastern Precordillera (Fig. 4). A ~20° dip of the fault at depth (Fig. 8a) was estimated using the method suggested by Spang and others (1985) from the amount of shortening in the Cenozoic strata. The measured 6.3 km, or 16 percent, shortening is a minimum, as the closure of anticline 2 has been eroded away (Fig. 4b); greater shortening would require a shallower dip on the underlying basement fault. The basement fault is inferred to underlie anticlines 2 and 4, and to have decreasing throw northward. The steep dips of both of the limbs and tightness of the hinge on anticline 2 would appear to preclude the explanation of this fold as a fault-bend or fault-propagation fold (Suppe, 1983; Suppe and Medwedeff, 1984; Woodward, and others, 1985). Active basement faulting at depths of 10 to 35 km within the Eastern Precordillera is also indicated by the medium-sized 1972 earthquake and numerous small earthquakes described above (Chinn and Isacks, 1983; Smalley, 1988).

The cross section in Figure 8b shows an additional west-verging thrust on the west limb of anticline 3 that has been inferred near the surface south of the section (Fig. 7), but probably decreases in throw northward and may or may not extend near to the surface at the latitude of the section. Other than this minor difference, both of the alternative cross sections in Figure 8 share a similar fault geometry between the Sierra de Huaco, but illustrate different rock units at depth. Figure 8b shows a major terrane boundary (as described by Ramos and others, 1986) that separates a block with no Cambro-Ordovician carbonates to the east from the Precordillera basement overlain by those units. The Cenozoic deformation may have reactivated that preexisting crystalline basement fault at depth (Fig. 8b, and see section below on paleogeography), although the presence of the Ordovician limestone in anticline 2 indicates that a new fault plane was developed in the upper crust.

A second possible explanation, as described above in the comparison section, for the observed west-verging shortening in the Sierra de Huaco is that it has been shortened over a décollement that connects with the décollement under the Central Precordillera to the west, in a geometry similar to the "triangle zone" structure of the Alberta Foothills (Fig. 9b). This possibility seems unlikely if the depth to the basement in the Eastern Precordillera is considerably greater than that in the adjacent part of the Central Precordillera (Fig. 8a). This interpretation of basement depths is dependent on estimates of the thicknesses of overlying strata that are not exposed. However, it seems most reasonable that the structures in the northern portion of the Eastern Precordillera developed for similar reasons as those in the southern part of the Eastern Precordillera. As described above and illustrated in Figure 4, the stratigraphic level of the décollement in the southern part of the Eastern Precordillera, at Sierra Chica de Zonda, is quite clearly deeper than that of the Central Precordillera (Baldis and Chebli, 1969), which is inconsistent with its development as a triangle zone.

CONTROLS ON LOCATION OF THIN- TO THICK-SKINNED TRANSITION

The active orogenic system in South America is an informative place to study the controls on the location of the transition between thin- and thick-skinned deformational provinces. Kulik and Schmidt (this volume) suggest that the location of the "overlap zone" in the North American Cordillera is controlled by the presence of a Paleozoic–early Mesozoic hingeline, by reactivation of preexisting zones of crustal weakness, and by changes in depth to the brittle-ductile transition (BDT) of deformational mode within the crust. Similarly, location of the Eastern Precordillera is coincident with a Paleozoic basin margin and with a possible ancient fault zone.

Paleogeography

Paleogeography is the most outstanding difference between the Precordillera and the Sierras Pampeanas. The existence of a thick Phanerozoic sedimentary section in the Precordillera permitted the development of a thin-skinned thrust belt, while there are only discontinuous depocenters of thinner strata overlying the crystalline basement of the Sierras Pampeanas (Allmendinger and others, 1983a). The paleogeography of the Precordillera and Sierras Pampeanas can be inferred from the stratigraphy of the rocks

deposited before the development of the present structural provinces. The stratigraphy of the Eastern Precordillera subprovince, where the transition between thin- and thick-skinned deformation occurs, shares elements with the Central Precordillera subprovince to the west and with the Sierras Pampeanas province to the east (Fig. 5; Ortiz and Zambrano, 1981), but it is a zone of important change of thickness and mechanical properties of the units. The crystalline basement (generally of Precambrian age) that is exposed at the surface in most of the Sierras Pampeanas is not exposed in the Precordillera nor in the main Cordillera of the Andes to the west, so the nature of the basement is unknown west of the Sierras Pampeanas province.

The lowest units exposed in the Eastern Precordillera are a group of carbonates of Early Cambrian to Middle Ordovician age (Fig. 5), exposed from the southern end of the Sierra de Mogna southward. The Ordovician San Juan Limestone, the upper unit in that carbonate section, is the lowest unit exposed in the thrust plates of the Central Precordillera (e.g., Baldis and Chebli, 1969).

In the eastern Precordillera, the San Juan limestone is overlain by a series of Ordovician and Silurian conglomerates and shales (Fig. 5; Baldis and others, 1982). The overlying Devonian(?) unit is a layer of deformed shales and sandstones that enclose blocks of San Juan Limestone and blocks of conglomerate and is exposed in a broad belt along the eastern flanks of Sierras Chica de Zonda and Villicum (Figs. 2a, 3). Its origin has been debated and it has been variably interpreted as a depositional mixture of the lithologies (e.g., Baldis, and others, 1982) or as a tectonic melange (e.g., Ramos and others, 1984, 1986). The deformed sequence is overlain with angular unconformity by local Carboniferous clastic strata (e.g., Polanski, 1970) and Triassic redbeds (e.g., Cuerda and others, 1984) (Fig. 5). Units that unconformably overlie the Triassic redbeds at the Sierra de Mogna are of uncertain age (Fig. 5); little is known about the regional geologic history during the Mesozoic and early Cenozoic.

The Paleozoic sequence of the Eastern Precordillera thus differs in important ways from that to the east and west (Fig. 5). The Central Precordillera is characterized by pseudoconcordant contacts between units spanning the Ordovician through Carboniferous; therefore, it has been interpreted as a region of tectonic stability throughout the Paleozoic (Baldis and Chebli, 1969; Baldis and others, 1982). The Sierras Pampeanas lack any clear record of sediment accumulation from the late Precambrian until the Carboniferous. Instead, early and middle Paleozoic plutonism and dynamic metamorphism were widespread (as summarized in Ramos and others, 1984, 1986). Carboniferous to Triassic nonmarine strata overlie the crystalline basement, with a major depocenter located to the east of and overlapping the basement of the northern part of the Sierra de Valle Fértil system (Ortiz, 1968; Gentili, 1972; Andreis and others, 1975; Figs. 3, 5).

The paleogeographic contact between the Central and Eastern Precordillera is covered by the Matagusanos valley system. The point of closest approach between the two subprovinces is at the Huaco Valley (Fig. 7). There, the Central Precordillera section lacks typical Silurian and Devonian units (Agua Hedionda Ranges in Fig. 5). The lack of surface exposure of the Paleozoic strata in the Sierra de Huaco makes it difficult to interpret the nature of the contact. Our alternative interpretations in the cross sections of Figure 8 show either a gradual eastward thinning of the Paleozoic units, or no change in thickness; both interpretations are compatible with the thicknesses penetrated by the Cities test well.

The important stratigraphic changes across the Eastern Precordillera indicate the possible existence of a major crustal boundary. Ramos and others (1984, 1986) suggested that the Devonian(?) melange on the eastern side of the Eastern Precordillera may have been a terrane boundary, with Paleozoic faulting and uplift of the Eastern Precordillera (e.g., Baldis and others, 1982) related to the terrane margin. Their inference that it was primarily a zone of strike-slip fault motion implies that it might project as a steeply dipping feature in the subsurface. Such a fault zone would be a major mechanical break in the continental crust. The melange crops out along the eastern flank of Chica de Zonda and Villicum (Figs. 2a, 4), and because the facies and structural trends of the Paleozoic strata parallel the Cenozoic structural trends (Baldis and others, 1982), a similar pre-Cenozoic feature probably continues in the subsurface farther to the north in the Eastern Precordillera and may be located beneath the Sierra de Huaco (Fig. 8b).

The boundary in the Eastern Precordillera of the Paleozoic basin sequence may explain the difference in the structural style between the Central Precordillera terrane and the Sierras Pampeanas terrane. As mentioned by Kulik and Schmidt (this volume), the presence of a thick section of sedimentary rocks, such as that of the Central Precordillera, may favor the formation of a thin-skinned fold-thrust belt that deforms only above the basement (with basement shortening occurring farther west under the Frontal Cordillera), while the absence of thick sedimentary rocks forces the shortening to involve the basement.

Brittle-ductile transition constraints

The depth of the BDT in the Precordillera and Sierras Pampeanas is constrained only by the occurrence of crustal earthquakes at depths of up to 35 to 40 km beneath the Eastern Precordillera and westernmost Sierras Pampeanas (Stauder, 1973; Chinn and Isacks, 1983; Kadinsky-Cade and others, 1985; Smalley, 1988); there is, of course, no way to know the depth of paleoseismicity of the Laramide province during the time of deformation. Farther west, under the Central Precordillera, there are few crustal earthquakes, so the depth of the BDT is not directly constrained there. The lack of earthquakes under the Central Precordillera, if not due to the sampling method, could be due to a lack of basement deformation there (i.e., basement shortening is taken up farther west) or to a shallower BDT allowing aseismic deformation within the crystalline basement and overlying sedimentary rocks. There are no published heat-flow data from the Precordillera or Sierras Pampeanas, so the geothermal gradient and thermal state of the lithosphere are unknown, but the seismicity indicates elastic deformation in the middle to lower crust.

The wavelength of deformation in the North American foreland has been related to the thickness of the brittle layer by Fletcher (1984). The wavelength of the deformation in the Sierras Pampeanas is about 60 km in the western part of the province, and nearly 120 km as an overall average (Jordan and Allmendinger, 1986), compared to the minimum 100-km wavelength of the foreland arches in Wyoming (Kulik and Schmidt, this volume). This reasoning would suggest that the BDT of the western Sierras Pampeanas is shallower than its estimated depth of 17 to 25 km in the Wyoming foreland (Kulik and Schmidt, this volume), which contradicts the earthquake data. Perhaps there are other controls, such as preexisting fault zones, on the wavelength of the Sierras Pampeanas blocks. Therefore, west to east deepening of the BDT, as hypothesized by Kulik and Schmidt (this volume) for the North American Cordillera, is not adequately tested by presently available data from the South American Cordillera, but preliminary data do not support a shallowing within the Sierras Pampeanas province. Farther west, under the Central Precordillera, the BDT may be at a shallower level within the crystalline basement or the thick Paleozoic sedimentary section. This would be consistent with the occurrence of Miocene volcanic centers from the Principal Cordillera to the Central Precordillera and the lack of crustal seismicity there today. The Miocene volcanism may have heated and somewhat softened the crust of what shortly thereafter became the Precordillera fold-thrust belt.

CONCLUSIONS

Study of the continuing active deformation of the South American orogenic system can provide insights into aspects of the extinct North American Cordillera deformational belt that are no longer observable. The geometry of the subducting oceanic Nazca plate is well defined by earthquakes that occur within the downgoing plate. Both the Precordillera and Sierras Pampeanas deformational provinces occur to the east of the zone of flattening of the subducted plate, above a subhorizontal subducted plate. It has been suggested that the Sevier thrust belt and Rocky Mountain foreland were formed above a similar "flat slab" (Dickinson and Snyder, 1978).

The Eastern Precordillera is a structural subprovince between the basement-involved deformation in the Sierras Pampeanas to the east and the thin-skinned deformation of the Central Precordillera to the west. The subsurface structure of the Eastern Precordillera is not well constrained, but the existing data suggest that basement-involved faulting underlies the series of west-verging folds and faults that deform the near-surface synorogenic deposits. Furthermore, there may also be west-dipping faults that cut into the basement beneath the easternmost Central Precordillera. The mid-crustal earthquake activity under the Matagusanos Valley and central Eastern Precordillera is consistent with the presence of the basement-involved faulting under the

Eastern Precordillera. The increasingly deeper structural level along strike from north to south can be explained by a southward increase in throw on the underlying basement fault, or the dip of the fault may change along strike, resulting in different amounts of vertical uplift for the same amount of horizontal shortening.

Although the surface structural geometry of the northern portion of the Eastern Precordillera is similar to that of the Alberta foothills triangle zone, it is more nearly analogous to the Moxa Arch because of the likelihood of basement control on the deformation. Like the Moxa Arch, a west-verging basement fault parallels the principal part of the thin-skinned thrust belt for a long distance, but there is no direct indication that the basement trend intersects the thrust belt in the Precordillera. Farther to the north, other basement uplifts intersect the thrust belt, but their geometry and timing are at present poorly described.

The age of the deformation of the thin-skinned Central Precordillera is constrained to be Miocene and younger, and the deformation of the basement-involved Sierra Pampeanas, though less constrained, is probably Mio-Pliocene to Recent in age. The northern portion of the Eastern Precordillera was a depositional basin until less than 2.3 m.y. ago, implying that interacting thin- and thick-skinned deformation did not characterize earlier stages of the thin-skinned thrust belt history. This suggests that the thin- and thick-skinned systems may have evolved independently until they impinged upon one another, forming the Eastern Precordillera. Given the current uncertainty of the ages of deformation in the Sierras Pampeanas and the possibility that the age of deformation varies along strike in the Eastern Precordillera, the event that triggered west-verging deformation in the Eastern Precordillera remains highly speculative at this time.

Given the presently available data, we can suggest that paleogeographic differences, including the presence of a thick Paleozoic sedimentary section and possible terrane boundaries in the Precordillera, are one control on the location of the transition between the thin- and thick-skinned deformational provinces of the Precordillera and Sierras Pampeanas. The contribution of other controlling factors, such as the depth of the brittle-ductile transition and the effect of Miocene volcanism in the Precordillera, is less certain, but future studies should shed more light on the material properties and thermal state of the crust and lithosphere.

ACKNOWLEDGMENTS

We thank Apolo Ortiz for many helpful discussions of the geology of the Eastern Precordillera and surrounding areas, and Victor Ramos, Rick Allmendinger, Noye Johnson, and Bob Smalley for their collaboration on this study. Muawia Barazangi, Hugo Bastias, Jim Beer, Peter Flemings, Bryan Isacks, and Dave Snyder provided helpful comments, David Kraig provided encouragement and a preprint of his paper in this volume, and Rex Pilger and James Lowell provided helpful reviews. We thank Chris Schmidt for very helpful editorial suggestions and encouragement, Eniko Farkas and Pamela Bishop for drafting figures, and Cities Service/Occidental Petroleum of Bakersfield for providing data. This study was supported by National Science Foundation Grants EAR-8206787 and EAR-84-18131 and by the Petroleum Research Fund of the American Chemical Society (grant 13297-AC2). E. J. Fielding was supported under NASA Graduate Student Research Training Grant NGT 33-010-801 during 1985–1987. INSTOC contribution no. 57.

REFERENCES CITED

Allmendinger, R. A., Jordan, T. E., Ramos, V. A., and Strecker, M., 1983a, Foreland structures associated with flat subduction, Argentine Andes: Geological Society of America Abstracts with Programs, v. 15, p. 514.

Allmendinger, R. A., Ramos, V. A., Jordan, T. E., Palma, M., and Isacks, B. L., 1983b, Paleogeography and Andean structural geometry, northwest Argentina: Tectonics, v. 2, p. 1–16.

Andreis, R. R., Spalletti, L. A., and Mazzoni, M. M., 1975, Estudio geológico del Subgrupo Sierra de Maz (Paleozoico Superior), Sierra de Maz, Provincia de la Rioja, República Argentina: Revista Asociación Geológica Argentina, v. 30, p. 247–273.

Armstrong, F. C., and Oriel, S. S., 1965, Tectonic development of Idaho-Wyoming thrust belt: American Association Petroleum Geologists Bulletin, v. 49, p. 1847–1866.

Baldis B., and Bordonaro, O., 1984, Cámbrico y Ordovícico de la Sierra Chica de Zonda y Cerro Pedernal, Provincia de San Juan, Genesis del margen continental en la Precordillera: 9th Congreso Geológico Argentina, v. 4, p. 190–207.

Baldis, B. A., and Chebli, G. A., 1969, Estructura profunda del area central de la Precordillera Sanjuanina: 4th Jornadas Geológicas Argentinas, v. 1, p. 47–65.

Baldis, B. A., Uliarte, E. R., and Vaca, A., 1979, Análisis estructural de la comarca Sísmica de San Juan: Revista Asociación Geológica Argentina, v. 34, p. 294–310.

Baldis, B. A., Beresi, M. S., Bordonaro, O., and Vaca, A., 1982, Síntesis evolutiva de la Precordillera Argentina: 5th Congreso Latinoamericano de Geología, Argentina, Actas, v. 1, p. 399–445.

Bastias, H. E., Weidmann, N. E., and Perez, A. M., 1984, Dos zonas de fallamiento Pliocuaternario en la Precordillera de San Juan: 9th Congreso Geológico Argentina, v. 2, p. 329–341.

Barazangi, M., and Isacks, B. L., 1976, Spatial distribution of earthquakes and subduction of the Nazca plate beneath South America: Geology, v. 4, p. 686–692.

Bally, A. W., 1981, Thoughts on the tectonics of folded belts, *in* McClay, K. R., and Price, N. J., eds., Thrust and nappe tectonics: Oxford, Blackwell Scientific Publications, p. 13–32.

Beer, J. A., Jordan, T. E., and Johnson, N. M., 1986, Sedimentary characteristics as a function of sedimentary accumulation rate; A study of Miocene fluvial sediments, Bermejo Basin, Argentina: Society of Economic Paleontologists and Mineralogists Annual Midyear Meeting Abstracts, p. 8.

Bercowski, F., Berenstein, L. R., Johnson, N. M., and Naeser, C., 1986, Sedimentologia, magnetoestratigrafía y edad isotópica del Terciario en Lomas de las Tapias, Ullum, Provincia de San Juan: Primer Reunión Argentina de Sedimentología, La Plata, p. 169–172.

Berg, R. R., 1962, Mountain flank thrusting in Rocky Mountain foreland, Wyoming and Colorado: American Association of Petroleum Geologists Bulletin, v. 46, p. 2019–2032.

Bevis, M., and Isacks, B., 1984, Hypocentral trend surface analysis; Probing the geometry of Benioff zones: Journal of Geophysical Research, v. 89, p. 6153–6170.

Bird, P., 1984, Laramide crustal thickening event in the Rocky Mountain foreland and Great Plains: Tectonics, v. 3, p. 741–758.

Blackstone, D. L., Jr., 1963, Development of geologic structure in central Rocky Mountains: American Association Petroleum Geologists Memoir 2, p. 160–179.

—— , 1979, Geometry of the Prospect-Darby and La Barge faults at their junction with the La Barge platform, Lincoln and Sublette counties, Wyoming: Geological Survey of Wyoming Report of Investigations no. 18, 34 p.

Cahill, T., and Isacks, B. L., 1985, Shape of the subducted Nazca plate [abs.]: EOS Transactions of the American Geophysical Union, v. 66, p. 1088.

Caminos, R., Cingolani, C. A., Herve, F., and Linares, E., 1982, Geochronology of the pre-Andean metamorphism in the Andean Cordillera between latitudes 30° and 36°S: Earth-Science Reviews, v. 18, p. 339–352.

Castellanos, A., 1945, El terremoto de San Juan, in Cuatro Lecciones Sobre Terremotos: Asociación Cultural de Conferencias de Rosario, Argentina, p. 79–242.

Chapin, C. E., and Cather, S. E., 1981, Eocene tectonics and sedimentation in the Colorado Plateau; Rocky Mountain area, in Dickinson, W. R., and Payne, W. D., eds., Relations of tectonics to ore deposits in the southern Cordillera: Arizona Geological Society Digest, v. 14, p. 173–198.

Chinn, D. S., and Isacks, B. L., 1983, Accurate source depths and focal mechanisms of shallow earthquakes in western South America and in the New Hebrides island arc: Tectonics, v. 2, no. 6, p. 529–563.

Cingolani, C. A., Varela, R., and Leguizamón, M. A., 1981, Las vulcanitas alcalinas Cretácicas del Cerro Morado, Sierra de Mogna, Provincia de San Juan y su implicancia estratigráfica: Asociación Argentina de Petrología Sedimentaría, v. 12, p. 53–70.

Coney, P. J., 1976, Plate tectonics and the Laramide orogeny: New Mexico Geological Society Special Publication 6, p. 5–10.

Contreras, V. H., 1981, Características bioestratigráficas del Terciario de Lomas de las Tapias, Departamento Ullún, Provincia de San Juan: 8th Congreso Geológico Argentino, v. 4, p. 813–822.

Cuerda, A. J., Cingolani, C. A., Varela, R., and Schauer, O. C., 1981, Geología de la Sierra de Mogna, Precordillera de San Juan: Actas 8th Congreso Geológico Argentino, v. 3, p. 139–158.

Cuerda, A. J., Cingolani, C. A., Varela, R., and Schauer, O. C., 1984, Descripción geológica de la Hoja 19d-Mogna, Provincia de San Juan: Servicio Geológico Nacional, Buenos Aires, Argentina, Boletín. 192, 86 p.

De Alba, E., 1954, Descripción geológica de la Hoja 16c, Villa Union, Provincia de La Rioja: Dirección Nacional de Minería, Boletín 82, 81 p.

Dickinson, W. R., and Snyder, W. S., 1978, Plate tectonics of the Laramide orogeny, in Matthews, V., III, ed., Laramide folding associated with basement block faulting in the western United States: Geological Society of America Memoir 151, p. 355–366.

Dixon, J. S., 1982, Regional structural synthesis, Wyoming salient of western Overthrust belt: American Association Petroleum Geologists Bulletin, v. 66, p. 1560–1580.

Fletcher, R. C., 1984, Instability of lithosphere undergoing shortening; A model for Laramide foreland structures: Geological Society of America Abstracts with Programs, v. 16, p. 83.

Furque, G., 1963, Descripción geológica de la Hoja 17b-Guandacol, Provincias de San Juan y La Rioja: Servicio Geológico Nacional, Buenos Aires, Argentina, Boletín. 92, 110 p.

—— , 1972, Descripción geológica de la Hoja 16-b-Cerro la Bolsa, Provincias de La Rioja y San Juan: Servicio Geológico Nacional, Buenos Aires, Argentina, Boletín. 125, 70 p.

—— , 1979, Descripción geológica de la Hoja 18c-Jáchal, Provincia de San Juan: Servicio Geológico Nacional, Buenos Aires, Argentina, Boletín. 164, 79 p.

—— , 1983, Descripción geológica de la Hoja 19c-Ciénaga de Gualilán, Provincia de San Juan: Servicio Geológico Nacional, Buenos Aires, Argentina, Boletín. 193, 111 p.

Garing, J. D., and Tainter, P. A., 1985, Greater Green River basin regional seismic line, in Gries, R. R., and Dyer, R. C., Seismic exploration of the Rocky Mountain region: Rocky Mountain Association of Geologists and Denver Geophysical Society, v. 233–238.

Gentili, C. A., 1972, Descripción geológica de la Hoja 17c-Cerro Rajado, Provincias de La Rioja y San Juan: Servicio Geológico Nacional, Buenos Aires, Argentina, Boletín. 131, 62 p.

Gray de Cerdan, N. A., 1969, Bosquejo geomorfológico del Bolsón de Tulum, San Juan, Argentina: Mendoza, Boletín de Estudios Geograficos, v. 17, p. 215–250.

Gries, R., 1981, Oil and gas prospecting beneath the Precambrian of foreland thrust plates in the Rocky Mountains: Mountain Geologist, v. 18, p. 1–18.

—— , 1983, North-south compression of Rocky Mountain Foreland structures, in Lowell, J. D., ed., Rocky Mountain foreland basins and uplifts: Rocky Mountain Association of Geologists, p. 9–32.

Heim, A., 1952, Estudios tectónicos en la Precordillera de San Juan: Revista Asociación Geológica Argentina, v. 7, p. 11–70.

Heller, P. L., Bowdler, S. S., Chambers, H. P., Coogan, J. C., Hagen, E. S., Shuster, M. W., Winslow, N. S., and Lawton, T. F., 1986, Timing of initial thrusting in the Sevier orogenic belt, Idaho-Wyoming and Utah: Geology, v. 14, v. 388–391.

Johnson, N. M., Jordan, T. E., Johnsson, P. A., and Naeser, C. W., 1986, Magnetic polarity stratigraphy, age, and tectonic setting of sediments in the eastern Andean foreland basin, San Juan Province, Argentina: Special Publication on Foreland Basins, International Association of Sediment, p. 63–75.

Johnsson, P. A., Johnson, N. M., Jordan, T. E., and Naeser, C. W., 1984, Magnetic polarity stratigraphy and age of the Quebrada del Cura, Río Jáchal, and Mogna Formations near Huaco, San Juan Province, Argentina: 9th Congreso Geológico Argentino, v. 3, p. 81–96.

Jones, P. B., 1983, Oil and gas beneath east-dipping underthrust faults in the Alberta Foothills, Canada, in Powers, R. B., ed., Geologic studies of the Cordilleran thrust belt, 1982: Rocky Mountain Association of Geologists, v. 1, p. 61–74.

Jordan, T. E., 1981, Thrust loads and foreland basin evolution: American Association Petroleum Geologists Bulletin, v. 65, p. 2506–2520.

Jordan, T. E., and Allmendinger, R. W., 1986, The Sierras Pampeanas of Argentina; A modern analogue of Laramide deformation: American Journal of Science, v. 286, p. 737–764.

Jordan, T. E., and Gardeweg, M., 1988, Tectonic evolution of the late Cenozoic Central Andes, in Ben-Avraham, Z., ed., Mesozoic and Cenozoic evolution of the Pacific Margin: Oxford University Press (in press).

Jordan, T. E., Isacks, B. L., Allmendinger, R. W., Brewer, J. A., Ramos, V. A., and Ando, C. J., 1983a, Andean tectonics related to geometry of subducted Nazca plate: Geological Society of America Bulletin, v. 94, p. 341–361.

Jordan, T. E., Isacks, B. L., Ramos, V. A., and Allmendinger, R. W., 1983b, Mountain building in the Central Andes: Episodes, v. 1983, no. 3, p. 20–26.

Jordan, T. E., Naeser, C. W., Johnson, N. M., Johnsson, P. A., Johnson, A., Reynolds, J., Reynolds, S. A., and Fielding, E. J., 1985, Foreland basin evolution in the Central Andes, Bermejo basin, San Juan Province, Argentina: Geological Society of America Abstracts with Programs, v. 17, p. 621.

Jordan, T. E., Flemings, P. B., and Beer, J. A., 1988, Dating thrust fault activity by use of foreland basin strata, in Kleinspehn, K., and Paola, C., eds., New perspectives in basin analysis: New York, Springer-Verlag, p. 307–330.

Kadinsky-Cade, K., 1985, Seismotectonics of the Chile margin and the 1977 Caucete earthquake of western Argentina [Ph.D. thesis]: Ithaca, New York, Cornell University, 253 p.

Kadinsky-Cade, K., Reilinger, R., and Isacks, B., 1985, Surface deformation associated with the November 23, 1977, Caucete, Argentina, earthquake sequence: Journal of Geophysical Research, v. 90, no. B14, p. 12691–12700.

Kay, S. M., Maksaev, V., Mpodozis, C., Moscoso, D. R., Nasi, C., and Gordillo, C., 1988, Tertiary Andean magmatism in Argentina and Chile between 28°–33°S; Correlation of magmatic chemistry with a changing Benioff Zone:

Journal of South American Geology, v. 1, no. 1, p. 21–38.

King, P. B., and Beikman, H. M., 1974, Geologic map of the United States: U.S. Geological Survey, scale 1:2,500,000.

Lawton, T. F., 1985, Style and timing of frontal structures, Thrust Belt, central Utah: American Association of Petroleum Geologists Bulletin, v. 69, p. 1145–1159.

Lowell, J. D., 1985, Structural styles in petroleum exploration: Tulsa, Oil and Gas Consultant Institute Publications, 460 p.

Mirre, J. C., 1976, Descripción geológica de la Hoja 19e-Valle Fértil, Provincias de San Juan y La Rioja: Servicio Geológico Nacional, Buenos Aires, Argentina, Boletín. 147, 70 p.

Ortiz, A., 1968, Los denominados estratos de Ichichusca como sección media de Formación Los Rastros: 3rd Jornadas Geológica Argentina, v. 1, p. 333–339.

Ortiz, A., and Zambrano, J. J., 1981, La provincia geológica Precordillerana Oriental: Actas 8th Congreso Geologico Argentino, v. 3, p. 59–74.

Price, R. A., 1981, The Cordilleran foreland thrust and fold belt in the southern Canadian Rocky Mountains, *in* McClay, K. R., and others, eds., Thrust and nappe tectonics: Geological Society of London Special Publication 9, p. 427–448.

Polanski, J., 1970, Carbónico y Pérmico de la Argentina: Universidad de Buenos Aires, 216 p.

Ramos, V. A., Jordan, T. E., Allmendinger, R. W., Kay, S. M., Cortés, J. M., and Palma, M., 1984, Chilenia; Un terreno alóctono en la evolución Paleozoica de los Andes centrales: 9th Congreso Geológico Argentino Actas, v. 2, p. 84–106.

Ramos, V. A., Jordan, T. E., Allmendinger, R. W., Kay, S. M., Mpodozis, C., Cortés, J. M., and Palma, M., 1986, Paleozoic terranes of the central Argentine–Chilean Andes: Tectonics, v. 5, no. 6, p. 855–880.

Rapela, C. W., Heaman, L. M., and McNutt, R. H., 1982, Rb-Sr geochronology of granitoid rocks from the Pampean Ranges, Argentina: Journal of Geology, v. 90, p. 574–582.

Reynolds, J. H., Jordan, T. E., and Johnson, N. M., 1987, Cronología Neogenica y velocidad de sedimentación en la cuenca de La Troya, La Rioja: 10th Congreso Geológico Argentino, Túcuman, v. 2, p. 109–112.

Rolleri, E. O., 1969, Rasgos tectónicos generales del Valle de Matagusanos y de la zona entre San Juan y Jocoli, provincia de San Juan, República Argentina: Asociació Geológica Argentina, Revista, v. 24, p. 408–412.

Royse, F., 1985, Geometry and timing of the Darby-Prospect-Hogsback thrust fault system, Wyoming: Geological Society of America Abstracts with Programs, v. 17, p. 263.

Royse, F., Jr., Warner, M. A., and Reese, D. L., 1975, Thrust belt structural geometry and related stratigraphic problems Wyoming–Idaho–Northern Utah: Rocky Mountain Association of Geologists, p. 41–54.

Sales, J. K., 1968, Crustal mechanics of Cordilleran foreland deformation; A regional and scale-model approach: American Association of Petroleum Geologists Bulletin, v. 52, p. 2016–2044.

Schmidt, C. J., Evans, J. P., Fletcher, R. C., and Spang, J. H., 1985, Spacing of Rocky Mountain foreland arches and Laramide magmatic activity: Geological Society of America Abstracts with Programs, v. 17, p. 710.

Sharry, J., Langan, R.T., Jovanovich, D. B., Jones, G. M., Hill, N. R., and Guidish, T. M., 1986, Enhanced imaging of the COCORP seismic line, Wind River Mountains, *in* Barazangi, M., and Brown, L., eds., Reflection seismology; A global perspective: American Geophysical Union Geodynamics series, v. 13, p. 223–236.

Sibson, R. H., 1983, Continental fault structure and the shallow earthquake source: Journal of the Geological Society of London, v. 140, p. 741–767.

Smalley, R. F., Jr., 1988, Two earthquake studies; (1) Seismicity of the Argentine Andean Foreland and (2) A renormalization group approach to earthquake mechanics [Ph.D. thesis]: Ithaca, New York, Cornell University.

Smalley, R. F., Jr., and Isacks, B. L., 1986, Crustal seismicity of the Precordillera and Sierras Pampeanas, N.W. Argentine Andes, from local network data [abs.]: EOS Transactions of the American Geophysical Union, v. 67, p. 1102.

—— , 1987, A high-resolution local network study of the Nazca plate Wadati-Benioff zone under western Argentina: Journal of Geophysical Research, v. 92, no. B13, p. 13,903–13,912.

Smalley, R. F., Jr., Isacks, B. L., and Castano, J. C., 1985, Preliminary results on thickness of Benioff zone in the San Juan Province of Argentina from digital local network data [abs.]: EOS Transactions of the American Geophysical Union, v. 66, p. 299.

Snyder, D. B., Ramos, V. A., and Allmendinger, R. W., 1986, Deep seismic reflection profiles of the crust beneath the Sierras Pampeanas, Andean foreland of Argentina [abs.]: EOS Transactions of the American Geophysical Union, v. 67, p. 1102.

Spang, J. H., Evans, J. P., and Berg, R. R., 1985, Balanced cross sections of small fold-thrust structures: Mountain Geologist, v. 22, no. 2, p. 41–46.

Spinelli, R. O., 1983, Edades potasio-argón de algunas rocas de la Sierra de Valle Fértil, provincia de San Juan: Asociación Geológica Argentina, v. 38, p. 405–411.

Stauder, W., 1973, Mechanism and spatial distribution of Chilean earthquakes with relation to subduction of the oceanic plate: Journal of Geophysical Research, v. 78, p. 5033–5061.

Stockton, S. L., and Hawkins, C. M., 1985, Southern Green River Basin/Moxa Arch, *in* Gries, R. R., and Dyer, R. C., Seismic Exploration of the Rocky Mountain Region: Rocky Mountain Association of Geologists and Denver Geophysical Society, p. 73–78.

Suppe, J., 1983, Geometry and kinematics of fault-bend folding: American Journal of Science, v. 283, p. 684–721.

Suppe, J., and Medwedeff, D. A., 1984, Fault-propagation folding: Geologicl Society of America Abstracts with Programs, v. 16, p. 670.

Uliarte, E. R., and Lendaro de Gianni, S., 1982, Fenómenos de neotectónica en la Provincia de San Juan, Argentina: 5th Congreso Latinoamericano de Geología, Argentina, v. 4, p. 265–276.

Vásquez, J. and Gorroño, R., 1982, Límite de la faja plegada en la República. Argentina: Revista Asociación Geológica Argentina, v. 35, no. 4, p. 582–585.

Wiltschko, D. V., and Dorr, J. A., Jr., 1983, Timing of deformation in Overthrust Belt and foreland of Idaho, Wyoming, and Utah: American Association of Petroleum Geologists Bulletin, v. 67, no. 8, p. 1304–1322.

Whitney, R. A., and Bastias, H., 1984, The Pre-Cordilleran active overthrust belt, San Juan province, Argentina (Field Trip 17): Geological Society of America, p. 354–386.

Woodward, N. B., Boyer, S. E., and Suppe, J., 1985, An outline of balanced cross-sections: University of Tennessee Department of Geological Sciences Studies in Geology no. 11, 2nd edition, 170 pp.

MANUSCRIPT ACCEPTED BY THE SOCIETY FEBRUARY 9, 1988

Printed in U.S.A.

Geological Society of America
Memoir 171
1988

Two major thrust slabs in the west-central Montana Cordillera

James W. Sears
Geology Department, University of Montana, Missoula, Montana 59812

ABSTRACT

Large Precambrian-cored thrust slabs dominate the west-central Montana thrust belt. Near Missoula, a western slab was emplaced over a thick eastern slab along an imbricate thrust zone in Campanian time, with development of a wide zone of cleavage in the footwall. Plunge projections suggest that the eastern slab is more than 25 km thick, with biotite zone rocks at depth and unmetamorphosed, syntectonic clastic deposits on top. It was thrust about 65 km to the northeast, forming a major anticlinorium above a large footwall ramp and an imbricate thrust fan in the Montana disturbed belt during Paleocene time. The slabs are comparable in dimensions to other cratonal margin thrust plates and to some uplifts of the neighboring Rocky Mountain foreland province.

INTRODUCTION

Many uplifts of the Rocky Mountain foreland are thick, Precambrian-cored plates that were thrust over foreland basins along gently dipping faults during late Cretaceous to Eocene orogenesis (Gries, 1983a, b). The Wind River Mountains of Wyoming, for example, may comprise a 20-km-thick thrust plate emplaced over the Green River basin (Smithson and others, 1979). Where the Rocky Mountain foreland intersects the Cordilleran thrust and fold belt in west-central Montana, the pattern of thick, Precambrian-cored thrust plates continues: the Middle Proterozoic Belt Supergroup forms the core of major thrust plates that were emplaced over narrow imbricate thrust systems in late Cretaceous to late Paleocene time.

This chapter discusses two of these thrust plates, which dominate the thrust and fold belt near Missoula, Montana. These plates are informally called the eastern and western slabs to differentiate them from the more typical, thinner thrust plates that characterize the Cordilleran thrust and fold belt in Alberta and Wyoming.

EASTERN SLAB

The eastern slab is more than 100 km wide, lying between the Montana disturbed belt on the northeast, and a thrust system passing through Missoula, Montana, on the southwest (Figs. 1, 2). It is a broad, northeasterly tapering wedge, primarily molded by thickness variations in the Belt Supergroup. Along its southwestern edge, the Belt Supergroup has a 20-km structural thickness (Harrison, 1972), whereas along its northeastern edge, it is less

than 4 km thick (Mudge and others, 1982). Paleozoic shelf sediments maintain a fairly consistent thickness of 1 to 2 km (Kauffman, 1963; Mudge and others, 1982) across the slab. Mesozoic rocks thin from a thickness in excess of 6 km near Drummond (Gwinn, 1961) to less than 4 km in the disturbed belt (Mudge and others, 1982).

The thin northeastern edge of the slab is carried by the interleaved Lewis, Hoadley, Eldorado, and other thrust faults, and is tilted to the southwest by an underlying wedge of imbricate thrust slices in the disturbed belt. Paleozoic and Mesozoic rocks form duplexes beneath the Precambrian rocks of the slab at least as far as 18 km southwest of its leading edge near Rogers Pass, as interpreted from seismic data (Dolberg, 1986). Horizontal shortening in the disturbed belt shows that the slab has moved a minimum of 40 to 50 km toward the foreland (Mudge, 1970; Dolberg, 1986), with rocks as young as Paleocene caught up in the leading imbricate fan (Mudge and others, 1982).

Mesoscopic fabric

The eastern slab has a distinctive cleavage that increases in strength with increased structural depth and with proximity to the western slab: it is strongest in the area labeled "cleavage zone" in Figure 2. The cleavage is present in pelitic layers from the deepest levels of the slab upward into Upper Cretaceous (Campanian) strata.

In the deepest levels of the slab, pelitic schists in the lowermost part of the Belt Supergroup contain the assemblage biotite-

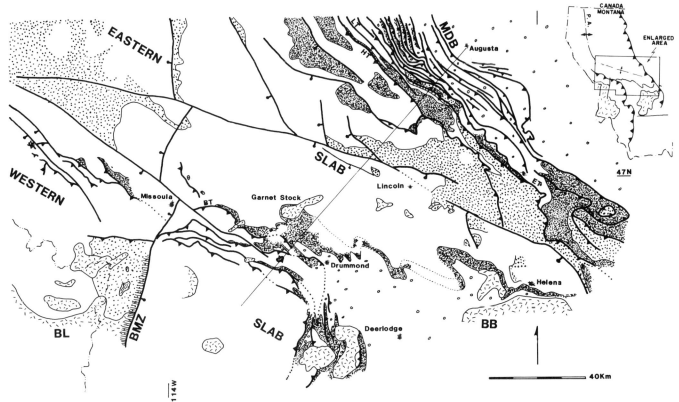

Figure 1. Geologic map of west-central Montana showing major thrust slabs. Cross-section line shown in Figure 4c. Symbols: wavy lines = Precambrian crystalline rocks; light stipple = lower Belt Supergroup; no pattern = upper Belt Supergroup; heavy stipple = Paleozoic strata; open circles = Mesozoic strata; chicken tracks = late Cretaceous granitic plutons. Tertiary and Quaternary deposits not shown. MDB = Montana disturbed belt; BB = Boulder batholith; BL = Bitterroot lobe of Idaho Batholith; HT = Hoadley thrust; LT = Lewis thrust; ET = Eldorado thrust; BMZ = Bitterroot mylonite zone; P.A. = Purcell anticlinorium (on inset map). Compiled and generalized from Mudge and others, 1982; Hall, 1968; Harrison and others, 1981; Hyndman, 1980; Nold, 1968; Wallace and others, 1981; Woodward, 1982.

muscovite-plagioclase-quartz, which is stable above 450° (see Winkler, 1976). The schistosity passes upward into a phyllitic cleavage in the middle parts of the Belt Supergroup. In the upper part of the Belt Supergroup, flexural-slip folding dominates, with abundant slickenfibers on bedding and thrust surfaces. Folds are associated with thrusts, and fans of spaced cleavage characterize pelitic layers. A shear zone in a diabase sill in the upper part of the Belt Supergroup has the assemblage chlorite-actinolite-epidote-plagioclase. Actinolite fibers form a lineation normal to associated southeast-plunging folds. This assemblage is stable above 350°C (Winkler, 1976).

The cleavage passes across the Precambrian-Cambrian unconformity, and is a slaty cleavage in Cambrian pelites. Upward in the Paleozoic and Mesozoic section the cleavage becomes weaker, passing into a spaced, pressure-solution cleavage apparent only in pelitic and micritic rocks. As cleavage diminishes, thrust faults and small disharmonic folds become more abundant.

The Golden Spike Formation is the highest level in which cleavage is found. This Campanian-aged syntectonic clastic unit contains mudflow and landslide deposits (Gwinn and Mutch, 1965), in which broken sandstone layers are contorted, rolled, and boudinaged in a pebbly mudstone matrix. Pebbles and cobbles of distinctive Paleozoic and Proterozoic lithologies were probably derived from tectonic uplifts to the west (Gwinn and Mutch, 1965).

Cordierite porphyroblasts grew coevally with the cleavage in the contact aureole of the Garnet stock (Minnich, 1984), which has a hornblende K-Ar date of 82 Ma (Ruppel and others, 1981).

The mesoscopic fabric defines a consistent southeasterly plunge across the stippled band in Figure 2. Figure 3 shows fabric data from all structural levels exposed in the western part of this band. Bedding poles (Fig. 3a) define a distinct girdle about an axis plunging gently to the southeast. The girdle's monoclinic symmetry shows that bedding folds are dominantly northeast-facing. Cleavage poles (Fig. 3b) define a diffuse partial girdle about a gently southeast-plunging axis. The maximum represents relatively uniform southwesterly dipping cleavage found at deeper structural levels, whereas dispersion about the girdle is caused by fans of cleavage found at shallow levels. The mean orientation of bedding-cleavage intersections (Fig. 3c, stippled cluster), matches poles to the bedding and cleavage girdles. Stretching lineations on cleavage planes at deeper levels and

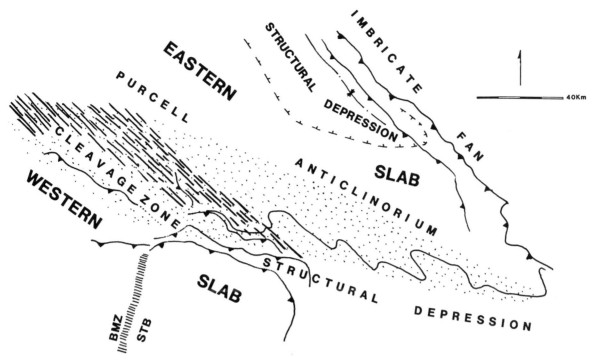

Figure 2. Sketch map showing major structural features of Figure 1 discussed in text. Dashed lines = zone of strong cleavage; stippled zone = region of proposed footwall ramp. BMZ = Bitterroot mylonite zone; STB = Sapphire tectonic block of Hyndman, 1980.

slickenfiber lineations at shallower levels define a diffuse girdle normal to the southeast-plunging axis (Fig. 3c).

Thickness of the Eastern Slab

In the western part of the stippled band in Figure 2, the slab has a relatively consistent plunge of 10°/135° for a length of 150 km in the downplunge direction, except near some Tertiary block faults. While this distance is rather large for ideal plunge projection, the thickness of the slab derived trigonometrically (25.5 km) is close to the cumulative reported thickness of the strata in this part of the slab (28 km). Furthermore, the increase in metamorphic grade and change in structural style with depth are consistent with a thick structural interval. As noted above, the deepest rocks were deformed at more than 450°C. By comparison, along a typical geotherm in continental crust, rocks at 25 km are at 300°C (Turcotte and Schubert, 1982, p. 148).

A major footwall ramp

If the eastern slab tapers from approximately 25 km thick in the southwest to 4 km in the northeast, as the above discussion implies, there should be a matching step in the footwall from which it emerged. In the Montana disturbed belt, near Augusta, autochthonous rocks are at a depth of less than 3 km below the surface (Mudge and others, 1982; Dolberg, 1986). Near Drummond, a thick section of Upper Cretaceous rocks is preserved at

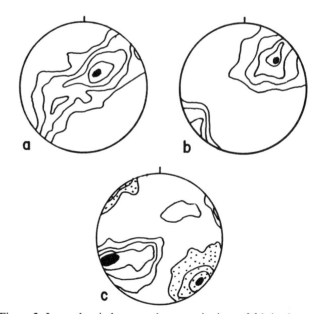

Figure 3. Lower hemisphere equal area projections of fabric elements from the southwestern part of the eastern slab. Contours in percent population per 1 percent area. a, Poles to bedding; n = 837; contours at 0.4, 1.2, 3, and 5 percent, maximum 10.3 percent at 65/042. b, Poles to cleavage; n = 731; contours at 1, 2, 4, and 5 percent, maximum 5.5 percent at 30/042. c, Stippled area: bedding-cleavage intersection lineatins; n = 234, contours at 1, 7, and 14 percent, maximum 24.44 percent at 10/135. Unpatterned area: stretching lineations on cleavage and slickenfibers on bedding and thrust fault planes; n = 259; contours at 1, 3, and 5 percent, maximum 12 percent at 09-248.

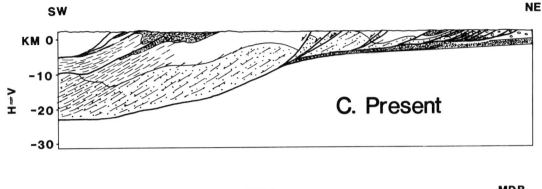

SW   NE

C. Present

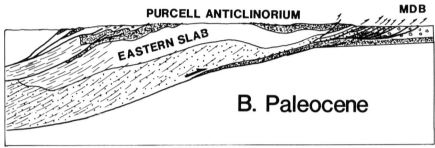

PURCELL ANTICLINORIUM   MDB

EASTERN SLAB

B. Paleocene

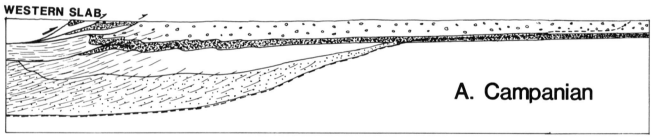

WESTERN SLAB

A. Campanian

Figure 4. Kinematic model for emplacement of western and eastern slabs. A, Campanian (Late Cretaceous): Western slab thrust over eastern slab along imbricate fault zone. Strong cleavage zone develops beneath western slab. Strain decreases to northwest. B, Paleocene: Eastern slab thrust up ramp and over imbricate fault zone along Montana disturbed belt. C, Present: Tertiary block-faults disrupt earlier structure. Western area of section controlled by downplunge projections.

the surface on the eastern slab. Northeast of Drummond, near Lincoln, the slab carries a thick section of lower Belt Supergroup rocks, exposed along a Tertiary faultblock. Since most thrust faults cut into younger rocks toward their leading edges, the base of the eastern slab should lie in or below the lower Belt Supergroup near Drummond. If estimates of stratigraphic thickness are correct, the base of the eastern slab must lie about 25 km below the surface near Drummond, and the footwall must step upward toward the northeast across a major ramp, between Drummond and Augusta.

The likely location for this major footwall ramp is the stippled band in Figure 2. This band marks a zone across which the structural level of the slab steps down to the southwest, from levels in the lower to middle parts of the Belt Supergroup in the north to levels in Upper Cretaceous rocks and structurally high allochthons in the south. Figure 4c shows the suggested footwall

ramp along a transect passing through Augusta (see Fig. 1 for location of cross section). The western part of the section is based on downplunge projections.

The stippled band is essentially the southwestern limb of the Purcell anticlinorium, a complex, regionally significant structure extending to British Columbia (see Fig. 1, inset map). The thickest sections of the Belt Supergroup are along this anticlinorium. Price (1981) and Bally (1984) modeled the anticlinorium as a large hanging-wall ramp anticline carried on the Purcell and Lewis thrusts in British Columbia and northern Montana. In Price's model, the northeastern limb of the anticlinorium corresponds to the northeasterly truncation of the Purcell (Belt) Supergroup, and the southwestern limb drapes a large, southwest-facing footwall ramp (Price, 1981). Note the similar interpretation offered in Figure 4b. Matching of the suggested footwall ramp with the wedging-out of the Belt Supergroup in the slab indicates approximately 65 km of displacement for the slab along this cross section. This value is consistent with associated horizontal shortening in the disturbed belt.

WESTERN SLAB

The western slab lies in a structural depression southwest of the Purcell anticlinorium. Its thickness is not known because of structural complexities in the Idaho batholith border zone, but it contains the entire Belt Supergroup and possibly pre-Belt crystalline rocks. It is bordered by a southwest-dipping imbricate thrust fan. Regional plunge reveals hanging-wall and footwall truncations of stratigraphic units, indicating as much as 12 km of displacement along individual faults, although total displacement of the system has not been determined.

The rocks along the leading edge of the western slab contrast strikingly with those in the structurally underlying eastern slab. Stratigraphic units that are strongly cleaved in the eastern slab are uncleaved in the overlying western slab. This may mean that the eastern slab was under greater burial depth during deformation than was the western slab. Apparently, the leading edge of the western slab was uplifted and denuded, whereas the eastern slab was buried by the western slab as well as by debris eroded from it.

The imbricate thrusts gather westward into the middle part of the Belt Supergroup, and root beneath lower Belt Supergroup and possible pre-Belt Supergroup crystalline rocks that emerge in a large antiform adjacent to the Bitterroot lobe of the Idaho batholith. Farther southwest, structural relationships are obscured by the batholith and its metamorphic border zone, and it is uncertain how far the western slab extends. However, Belt Supergroup lithologies extend to the region of the western Idaho suture zone, where terranes were accreted in Late Cretaceous time (Fleck and Criss, 1985).

A distinctive mylonite zone trends north across the western slab, separating the Bitterroot lobe from the Sapphire tectonic block (Hyndman, 1980). The mylonite zone formed within the amphibolite facies rocks and associated batholithic rocks, possibly in late Cretaceous time (Hyndman, 1980), although Chase and others (1983) have proposed that the mylonite is of Eocene age. As the thrust system that defines the leading edge of the western slab and the associated cleavage zone extends far beyond the northern end of the mylonite zone, I consider the mylonite zone to be an integral feature of the western slab, rather than the fundamental root zone of the imbricate thrust system.

KINEMATIC MODEL

The western slab was thrust in a northeasterly direction over an imbricate fan between about 82 and 75 Ma, and shed clastic debris into a foreland basin (Fig. 4a). The overridden rocks deformed ductilely as horizontal shortening continued, and a wide zone of strong cleavage formed. Deformation progressed toward the northeast, producing a wave train of folds at shallow levels and weak cleavage at deeper levels.

The eastern slab was emplaced after deposition of Paleocene units in the foreland basin (Fig. 4b). The earlier formed fabric was carried passively along as the slab moved northeastward up a major footwall ramp and overrode an imbricate thrust fan along its leading edge in the Montana disturbed belt. Following emplacement of the eastern slab, Tertiary block-faults disrupted the region (Fig. 4c).

DISCUSSION

The scale of the thrust slabs proposed in the model is compatible with that of other cratonal margin thrust systems whose geometry is inferred from deep seismic reflection profiles (Ando and others, 1984). In the Alps, the Italian-Austrian thrust plate is 35 km thick and 150 km wide (Giese and others, 1982). In Oman, the Semail ophiolite thrust sheet is 15 km thick and 100 km wide (Hopson and others, 1981). Ando and others (1984) have reported footwall thrust ramps from the Appalachians, Ouachitas, and Alps ranging from 10 to more than 20 km in structural relief.

ACKNOWLEDGMENTS

University of Montana Grant 1117 funded parts of this research. Discussions with colleagues and students at the university helped develop the ideas contained in this chapter. Ian Watson helped gather and plot the data for Figure 3. I am grateful for the reviews of an earlier draft of the manuscript by Raymond Price, Paul Hoffman, Warren Hamilton, and Ronald Chase, and I appreciate the careful work of the symposium organizers, Christopher Schmidt and William Perry.

REFERENCES CITED

Ando, C. J., Czuchra, B. L., Klemperer, S. L., Brown, L. D., Cheadle, M. J., Cook, F. A., Oliver, J. E., Kaufman, S., Walsh, T., Thompson, J. B., Jr., Lyons, J. B., and Rosenfeld, J. L., 1984, Crustal profile of mountain belt; COCORP deep seismic reflection profiling in New England Appalachians and implications for architecture of convergent mountain chains: American Association of Petroleum Geologists Bulletin, v. 68, p. 819–837.

Bally, A. W., 1984, Tectogenese et sismique reflexion: Bulletin Societe Geologique de France, v. 26, p. 279–286.

Chase, R. L., Bickford, M. E., and Arruda, E. C., 1983, Tectonic implications of

Tertiary intrusion and shearing within the Bitterroot dome, northeastern Idaho batholith: Journal of Geology, v. 91, p. 462–470.

Dolberg, D. M., 1986, A duplex beneath a major overthrust plate in the Montana disturbed belt; Surface and subsurface data [M.S. thesis]: Missoula, University of Montana, 57 p.

Fleck, R. J., and Criss, R. E., 1985, Strontium and oxygen isotope variations in Mesozoic and Tertiary plutons of central Idaho: Contributions to Mineralogy and Petrology, v. 90, p. 291–308.

Giese, P., Ruetter, K., Jacobshagen, V., and Nicolich, R., 1982, Explosion seismic crustal studies in the Alpine Mediterranean region and their implications to tectonic processes, *in* Berckhemer, H., and Hsu, K., eds., Alpine-Mediterranean geodynamics: American Geophysical Union Geodynamics series, v. 7, p. 39–74.

Gries, R., 1983a, Oil and gas beneath Precambrian of foreland thrust plates in the Rocky Mountains: American Association of Petroloeum Geologists Bulletin, v. 67, p. 1–28.

—— , 1983b, North-south compression of Rocky Mountain foreland basins and uplifts, *in* Lowell, J. D., and Gries, R., eds., Rocky Mountain foreland basins and uplifts: Denver, Colorado, Rocky Mountain Association of Geologists, p. 9–32.

Gwinn, V. E., 1961, Geology of the Drummond area, central-western Montana: Montana Bureau of Mines and Geology Geologic Map 4.

Gwinn, V. E., and Mutch, T. A., 1965, Intertongued Upper Cretaceous volcanic and nonvolcanic rocks, central-western Montana: Geological Society of America Bulletin, v. 76, p. 1125–1144.

Hall, F. W., 1968, Bedrock geology, north half of Missoula 30-minute Quadrangle, Montana [Ph.D. thesis]: Missoula, University of Montana, 253 p.

Harrison, J. E., 1972, Precambrian Belt Basin of the northwestern United States; its geometry, sedimentation, and copper occurrences: Geological Society of America Bulletin, v. 83, p. 1215–1240.

Harrison, J. E., Griggs, A. B., and Wells, J. D., 1981, Generalized geologic map of the Wallace 1° by 2° Quadrangle, Montana and Idaho: U.S. Geological Survey Miscellaneous Field Studies Map MF-1354-A, scale 1:250,000.

Hopson, C. A., Coleman, R. G., Gregory, R. T., Pallister, J. S., and Bailey, E. H., 1981, Geologic section through the Semail ophiolite and associated rocks along a Muscat-Ibra transect, southeastern Oman Mountains: Journal of Geophysical Research, v. 86, p. 2527–2544.

Hyndman, D. W., 1980, Bitterroot dome–Sapphire block, an example of a plutonic-core gneiss-dome complex with its detached suprastructure, *in* Crittenden, M. D., Coney, P. J., and Davis, G. H., eds., Cordilleran metamorphic core complexes: Geological Society of America Memoir 153, p. 427–443.

Kauffman, M. E., 1963, Geology of the Garnet-Bearmouth area, western Montana: Montana Bureau of Mines and Geology Memoir 39, 40 p.

Minnich, G., 1984, The timing of metamorphism relative to rock fabric in the Silver Hill Formation near the Garnet stock [B.S. thesis]: Missoula, University of Montana, 11 p.

Mudge, M. R., 1970, Origin of the disturbed belt in northwestern Montana: Geological Society of America Bulletin, v. 81, p. 377–392.

Mudge, M. R., Earhart, R. L., Whipple, J. W., and Harrison, J. E., 1982, Geologic and structure map of the Choteau 1° by 2° Quadrangle, western Montana: U.S. Geological Survey Miscellaneous Investigations Map I-1300, scale 1:250,000.

Nold, J. L., 1968, Geology of the northeastern border zone of the Idaho Batholith, Montana and Idaho [Ph.D. thesis]: Missoula, University of Montana, 159 p.

Price, R. A., 1981, The Cordilleran thrust and fold belt in the southern Canadian Rocky Mountains, *in* McClay, K. R., and Price, N. J., eds., Thrust and nappe tectonics: Geological Society of London Special Publication 9, p. 427–448.

Ruppel, E. T., Wallace, C. A., Schmidt, R. G., and Lopez, D. A., 1981, Preliminary interpretation of the thrust belt in southwest and west-central Montana and east-central Idaho: Montana Geological Society Field Conference Guidebook, p. 139–159.

Smithson, S. B., Brewer, J. A., Kaufman, S., Oliver, J. E., and Hurich, C. A., 1979, Structure of the Laramide Wind River uplift, Wyoming, from COCORP deep reflection data and from gravity data: Journal of Geophysical Research, v. 84, p. 5955–5972.

Turcotte, D. L., and Schubert, G., 1982, Geodynamics: New York, John Wiley & Sons, 450 p.

Wallace, C. A., Schmidt, R. G., Waters, M. R., Lidke, D. J., and French, A. B., 1981, Preliminary geologic map of the Butte 1° by 2° Quadrangle, central Montana: U.S. Geological Survey Open-File Report 81-1030, scale 1:250,000.

Winkler, H.G.F., 1976, Petrogenesis of metamorphic rocks, 4th ed.: New York, Springer-Verlag, 334 p.

Woodward, L. A., 1982, Tectonic map of the fold and thrust belt and adjacent areas, west-central Montana: Montana Bureau of Mines and Geology Geologic Map series, no. 30, scale 1:250,000.

MANUSCRIPT ACCEPTED BY THE SOCIETY FEBRUARY 9, 1988

Geological Society of America
Memoir 171
1988

Influence of Rocky Mountain foreland uplifts on the development of the frontal fold and thrust belt, southwestern Montana

Christopher J. Schmidt
Department of Geology, Western Michigan University, Kalamazoo, Michigan 49008
J. Michael O'Neill
U.S. Geological Survey, MS 913, Box 25046, Denver Federal Center, Denver, Colorado 80225
William C. Brandon
Stone and Webster Engineering Corporation, 245 Sumner Street, Boston, Massachusetts 02107

ABSTRACT

A distinct structural style is present in southwestern Montana where the Cordilleran frontal fold and thrust belt encountered basement surface irregularities in the adjacent cratonic foreland. This structural style is characterized by footwall thrust ramps that have a close spatial and genetic relationship to the basement surface irregularities. These basement irregularities are normal fault blocks, of Proterozoic ancestry, oriented parallel to the direction of tectonic transport on the décollement, and southwest-facing fault blocks, bounded by steeply northeast-dipping reverse faults, oriented obliquely to the direction of tectonic transport, that acted as buttresses to thrust propagation. A major east-trending Late Cretaceous and Paleocene structural boundary is the southwest Montana transverse zone that separates a terrane composed of "thin-skinned" thrusts in the Middle Proterozoic and younger rocks on the north in the Helena salient from basement-involved "thick-skinned" thrusts and reverse faults of the Rocky Mountain foreland on the south. This first-order structural boundary is interpreted to be superimposed on a down-to-the-north normal fault zone that marked the southern margin of the Proterozoic Belt basin. West-to-east shortening in the salient was manifested in right-reverse slip movements on the faults of the transverse zone. The principal fault of the zone is interpreted as a major oblique-to-lateral ramp formed over one or more normal-fault steps.

Second-order features, produced when thrust sheets impinged upon abrupt basement surface irregularities, include strongly anastomosing patterns of thrusts, younger-over-older thrust relations, and the localization of small, convex-eastward thrust salients. These features are directly controlled by Late Cretaceous, northwest-trending, left-reverse slip faults of Middle Proterozoic ancestry. Basement-cored anticlines on the hanging-wall sides of these faults deflected frontal thrust sheets into zones of oblique ramps that locally place younger rocks over older rocks. The convex-eastward shape of the McCartney Mountain salient is probably the result of local changes of the direction of west-southwest–east-northeast principal shortening adjacent to two northwest-trending en-echelon foreland blocks along the northeastern side of the salient.

The principal sets of foreland structures and thrust belt structures along the front of the thrust belt in southwestern Montana overlap closely in time. Both structures are interpreted to have been produced by the same, dominantly eastward- or east-northeastward–directed forces during Late Cretaceous and early Paleocene time. Structures in the foreland probably continue for some distance into and beneath the thin-skinned structures of the thrust belt.

INTRODUCTION

The frontal margin of the Cordilleran thrust belt in southwestern Montana reflects several types of interaction with basement-involved uplifts of the Rocky Mountain foreland. The principal aspect of this interaction is the control that previously formed foreland structures, either Laramide or much older, exerted on the trend and position of the fold and thrust belt.

The trend of the frontal margin is characterized by a pronounced eastward convex-salient, the Helena salient, and a broadly concave-eastward and less pronounced reentrant, the southwest Montana reentrant (Fig. 1). A first-order structural feature connects the reentrant and the salient; this feature is a narrow east- to northeast-trending zone of faults that composes the southwest Montana transverse zone (Schmidt and O'Neill, 1983). This zone is superimposed over the ancient east-trending crustal break that defines the southern margin of the Proterozoic Belt basin and exerted profound control on the geometry and kinematic evolution of structures within the transverse zone.

Second-order changes in trend of the frontal thrust belt in this part of southwestern Montana are marked by the small, convex-eastward McCartney Mountain salient and by a pronounced anastomosing pattern of thrust faults both in this small salient and in the transverse zone. These second-order features appear to be directly related to the intersection of the frontal fold and thrust belt with a set of evenly spaced, northwest-trending, basement-involved reverse faults which have foreland-style anticlines on their uplifted hanging walls (Schmidt and Garihan, 1983, 1986; Brown, 1983). The nature of the controls of these structures on the second-order geometry has been addressed only in a general way (Schmidt and Garihan, 1983).

This chapter focuses on discussions of the control that the southern margin of the Belt basin has had on the geometry and kinematics of the structures within the transverse zone, and the details of the geometry and kinematics of the thrust belt structures as they relate to the northwest-trending foreland structures.

FORELAND STRUCTURES

The Rocky Mountain foreland of southwestern Montana is characterized by differentially uplifted and tilted basement fault blocks (Fig. 2). Three sets of faults are largely responsible for the complex structural pattern that exists in this region: (1) an east-trending set of north-dipping normal faults that show Middle Proterozoic ancestry; (2) a northwest-trending set of predominantly northeast-dipping reverse faults of Late Cretaceous and Paleocene age that locally show Neogene reactivation and also show evidence of Middle Proterozoic ancestry; and (3) faults of various trends (from northeast to northwest) that dip westwardly and compose the principal first-order Rocky Mountain foreland structures of the region.

East-trending faults

Major east-trending fault zones or single faults of Proterozoic age are inferred to be either buried beneath thrusts or reactivated by thrusting along the southwest Montana transverse zone (Berry, 1943, p. 25; Harris, 1957, p. 23; McMannis, 1955, p. 1420; Robinson, 1963, p. 103; Ruppel and others, 1981, Fig. 1). The east-trending transverse thrust zone may be traced for more than 120 km; it is composed of several major structural features that include, from west to east, the Camp Creek thrust, Mayflower Mine thrust, Jefferson Canyon thrust, Pass fault, and Battle Ridge monocline (locations 1, 2, 3, 5, and 6, respectively, Fig. 2). Collectively, these structures mark the southern limit of Proterozoic Belt Supergroup rocks in this portion of southwestern Montana. Portions of the footwall sides of each of the faults also mark the northern limit of exposed Archean basement rocks in the region. Furthermore, the entire transverse thrust zone essentially separates coarse clastic sedimentary rocks of the Proterozoic LaHood Formation to the north from their inferred Archean source terrain to the south.

These facts have led to the interpretation that the transverse thrust zone must have coincided with, or have been controlled by, a major structure or structures that marked the southern margin of the Belt basin in Proterozoic time. Based on the abrupt change in lithologies across the zone, Thom (1957, p. 13) and Harris (1957, p. 29) suggested that the southern margin of the Belt basin was a "major crustal rift" and a "line of basement faulting," respectively; Harris named the feature the "Perry line." Alexander (1955), Lowell (1956), and McMannis (1955, 1963) interpreted the Perry line as a steep shoreline that was partly fault-controlled; the work of Hawley and others (1982) and O'Neill and others (1986) has largely substantiated this view. The part of the Perry line that is located in the Jefferson Canyon area of the Tobacco Root Mountains was named the Willow Creek fault by Robinson (1963, p. 103).

The interpretation of the original geometry and position of this important Proterozoic structure, or structures, depends on several factors: (1) the inferences that can be drawn from the coarse clastic nature of the LaHood Formation and the rapid lateral changes in facies within the formation; (2) the identification of other Proterozoic structural elements, such as northwest-trending fault sets; and (3) the structural interpretation of the various thrusts that have overprinted it. Studies of the LaHood Formation clearly indicate an elevated Archean source terrain on the south and a depositional basin on the north. This evidence has led most authors to conclude that the Perry line was a normal fault or a series of normal faults (Alexander, 1955; McMannis, 1955, 1963; Hawley and others, 1982; Schmidt and Garihan, 1986). Studies of the rapid east-west facies changes in the LaHood indicate that the lateral continuity of the shoreline may have been interrupted (O'Neill and others, 1986; Schmidt and Garihan, 1986). Regional structural studies (discussed in the following section) indicate that northwest-trending basement faults offset, or intersected, the Perry line in Proterozoic time (Schmidt and Garihan, 1986). Interpretations that the thrusts of the transverse zone are reactivated normal faults (McMannis, 1963; Robinson, 1963) imply that the position of the thrusts is near the original position of the normal faults, whereas interpretations that

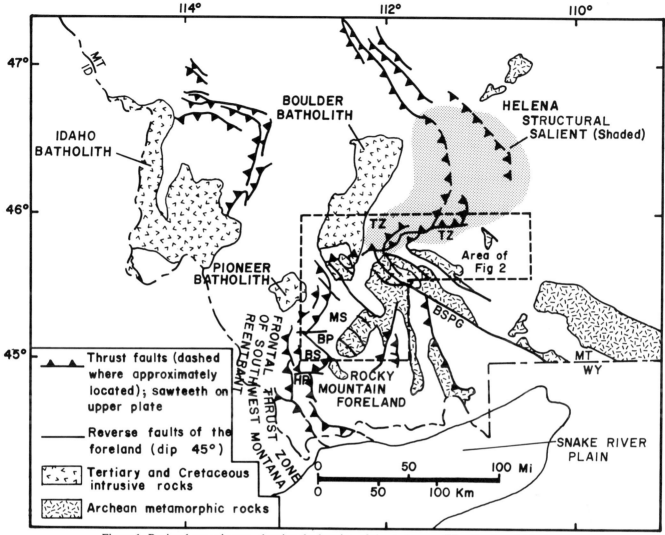

Figure 1. Regional tectonic map showing the location of the study area. TZ = Southwest Montana transverse thrust zone; MS = McCartney Mountain salient; BS = Blacktail salient; BP = Badger Pass fault; HP = Horse Prairie fault; BSPG = Bismark-Spanish Peaks-Gardiner fault zone. Location of Figure 2 is shown. Except for Snake River Plain, only Montana geology is shown.

the thrusts are controlled by the basement-normal fault steps (Garrett, 1972; Schmidt, 1975) imply that the position of the normal faults may be several kilometers north of the traces of the thrusts and buried beneath the thrust sheets.

Based on the present position of the principal thrusts of the transverse zone, Winston (1986) suggested that the Perry line comprised two or more normal faults in an en-echelon arrangement. Harrison and others (1974, Figs. 2, 3) depicted the line as a single, continuous normal fault in Proterozoic time. However, because of the uncertainties about the exact nature of the Late Cretaceous deformation, the Proterozoic configuration of the Perry line remains obscure.

Other east-trending faults of inferred Proterozoic age in the region of thrust belt–foreland interaction in southwestern Montana include the Horse Prairie and Badge Pass faults (Scholten, 1983, p. 127–128; Ruppel and Lopez, 1984, Fig. 3) (Fig. 1).

Northwest-trending faults

Northwest-trending faults in the foreland of southwestern Montana compose a closely spaced network of more than 30 structures, most of which were active in Late Cretaceous and early Tertiary time and some of which are important range-marginal faults today (Fig. 2). All but two of these faults dip steeply northeast (Schmidt and Garihan, 1983). Cutting both Archean metamorphic and Phanerozoic sedimentary rocks, they are spaced 6 to 10 km apart, and have separations, measured on the Archean-Cambrian unconformity, that range from tens of meters to several kilometers. A Middle Proterozoic ancestry of these faults is demonstrated by the presence of diabase dikes dated at 1,455 and 1,130 Ma in the fault zones (Wooden and others, 1978); by separations of Archean rock units along the faults, which differ from separations of the Archean-Cambrian

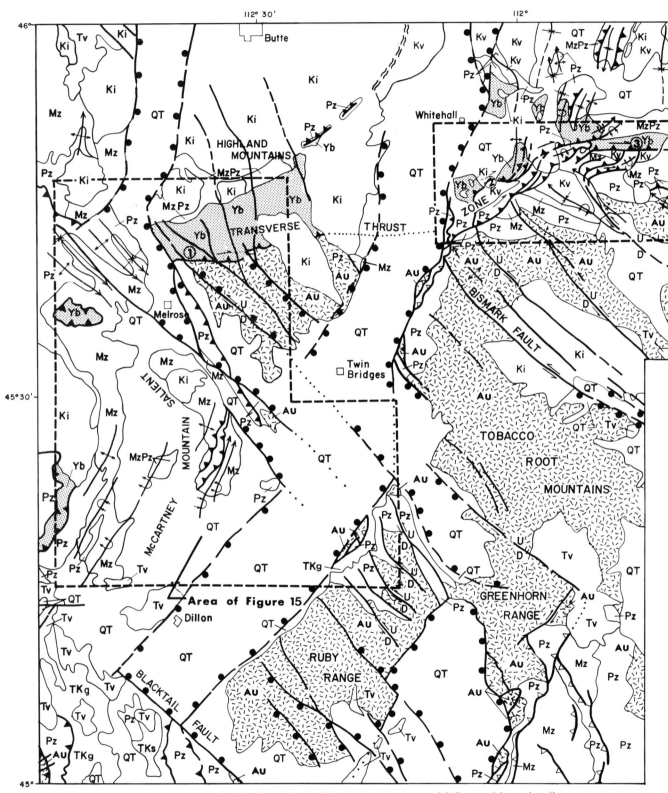

Figure 2. Tectonic map showing the southwest Montana transverse zone, McCartney Mountain salient and adjacent Rocky Mountain foreland. Locations of Figures 4 and 15 are shown.

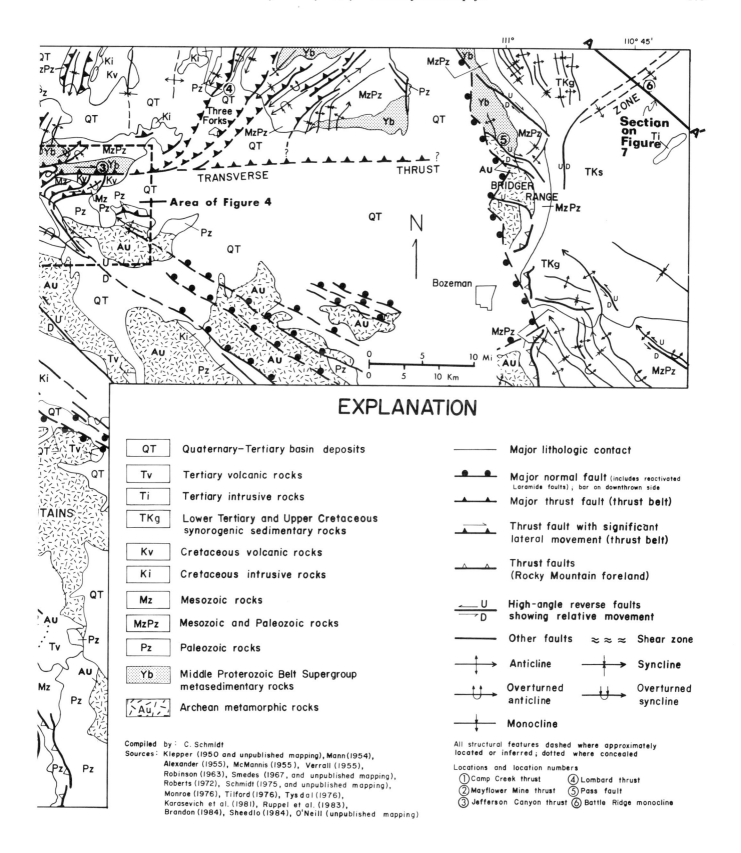

EXPLANATION

QT	Quaternary-Tertiary basin deposits
Tv	Tertiary volcanic rocks
Ti	Tertiary intrusive rocks
TKg	Lower Tertiary and Upper Cretaceous synorogenic sedimentary rocks
Kv	Cretaceous volcanic rocks
Ki	Cretaceous intrusive rocks
Mz	Mesozoic rocks
MzPz	Mesozoic and Paleozoic rocks
Pz	Paleozoic rocks
Yb	Middle Proterozoic Belt Supergroup metasedimentary rocks
Au	Archean metamorphic rocks

———— Major lithologic contact

●—●—● Major normal fault (includes reactivated Laramide faults); bar on downthrown side

▲—▲—▲ Major thrust fault (thrust belt)

▲—→ Thrust fault with significant lateral movement (thrust belt)

△—△ Thrust faults (Rocky Mountain foreland)

⊢U/→D High-angle reverse faults showing relative movement

———— Other faults   ≈ ≈ ≈ Shear zone

↔ Anticline   ⊣→ Syncline

⊔ Overturned anticline   ⊓ Overturned syncline

⊣ Monocline

All structural features dashed where approximately located or inferred; dotted where concealed

Locations and location numbers
① Camp Creek thrust   ④ Lombard thrust
② Mayflower Mine thrust   ⑤ Pass fault
③ Jefferson Canyon thrust   ⑥ Battle Ridge monocline

Compiled by: C. Schmidt
Sources: Klepper (1950 and unpublished mapping), Mann (1954),
Alexander (1955), McMannis (1955), Verrall (1955),
Robinson (1963), Smedes (1967, and unpublished mapping),
Roberts (1972), Schmidt (1975, and unpublished mapping),
Monroe (1976), Tilford (1976), Tysdal (1976),
Karasevich et al. (1981), Ruppel et al. (1983),
Brandon (1984), Sheedlo (1984), O'Neill (unpublished mapping)

unconformity (Reid, 1957; Schmidt and Garihan, 1979, 1983, 1986); and by control of depositional patterns of the Proterozoic sedimentary rocks along the southern margin of the Belt basin (O'Neill and others, 1986; Schmidt and Garihan, 1986). Recurrent movement on all but two of the northwest-trending faults in Late Cretaceous and early Tertiary time was oblique slip, with roughly equal components of left-lateral and reverse movement (Schmidt and Garihan, 1983). The reverse component of movement on the faults produced a series of elevated Archean blocks that faced toward the southwest.

The Proterozoic Perry line fault zone may have been significantly affected by this later movement on the northwest-trending faults. If, in Proterozoic time, the Perry line was a single east-trending zone, as depicted by Harrison and others (1974), the present en-echelon relationship between the Camp Creek thrust in the Highland Mountains and the Jefferson Canyon thrust in the northern Tobacco Root Mountains may have been produced by the dominant left-reverse oblique slip on the northwest-trending fault set. The principal offset of this Proterozoic boundary would have occurred along the Bismark fault, the northwestern extension of the Spanish Peaks–Gardiner fault zone. This fault zone, which can be traced from the Tobacco Root Mountains 150 km to the southeast into Wyoming, is the largest fault in the northwest-trending set (Figs. 1, 2).

The geometry of the folds associated with the northwest-trending faults closely resembles that of fold-thrusts described elsewhere in the foreland (Berg, 1962; Brown, 1983). However, their development is clearly associated with movement on preexisting faults of Proterozoic ancestry, and therefore, faulting and folding were coeval from the beginning of the Late Cretaceous deformation (Schmidt and Garihan, 1983). The anticlines that formed on the hanging walls of the northwest-trending faults are cored by Archean metamorphic rocks in which the foliation is often folded locally in concordance with the cover rocks. Anticlines that overlap with thrust belt structures generally plunge gently northwest between 15° and 40° (Schmidt and Garihan, 1983, Fig. 11). The folds are significantly asymmetrical; the gentle limbs dip 20° to 60° northeast; the southwestern limbs are steep to overturned. Net horizontal east-west shortening by faulting and associated folding on all these structures is estimated to be 10 to 20 km.

Other major Laramide foreland structures

The third fault pattern within the foreland is a group of variously oriented Laramide structures that differ in trend and spacing from the aforementioned northwest-trending reverse faults. We include these as a set not so much because of orientation, but because of similarities in size, deformation style, and age. The faults are thrusts involving Archean metamorphic and younger sedimentary rocks. They are generally Late Cretaceous structures for which the timing is reasonably well documented by examination of associated synorogenic conglomerates (Nichols and others, 1985; Tysdal, 1986; DeCelles and others, 1987). On

the southwest they strike northeast and dip northwest; on the north they strike north and dip west; and on the southeast they strike northwest and dip to the southwest (Fig. 3). Some of these faults, most notably the northeast-trending ones, were probably strongly influenced by earlier structural trends. For example, the Snowcrest-Greenhorn thrust system (see Perry and others, this volume) was probably strongly controlled by a Paleozoic depositional trend (the Snowcrest trough) that may itself have a Precambrian ancestry (Maughan and Perry, 1986, and references therein). In most places the thrusts are truncated by or merge with late Cenozoic range-marginal normal faults with the same trends and are therefore incompletely exposed along the flanks of some of the major ranges within the foreland of southwestern Montana. The geometry of these structures has been interpreted in two ways: as gently dipping mountain-flank thrusts (Perry and others, 1981; Perry and others, 1983; Schmidt and Garihan, 1983; Tysdal, 1986; DeCelles and others, 1987); and as upthrusts that steepen with depth (Ruppel and others, 1981; Ruppel and Lopez, 1984). At the surface, many of the faults dip west 25° to 40°.

At least four regional uplifts or arches, two of which were originally described by Scholten (1967), are located on the hanging walls of the thrusts and reverse faults (Fig. 3); these broad uplifts are inferred to have been directly associated with the faulting. Although not generally as large as first-order features elsewhere in the Rocky Mountain foreland, such as the Wind River uplift, they are nevertheless significant first-order features in the Montana foreland, and have an average wavelength of 45 km and an inferred structural relief of as much as 7 km. They can be shown to have interacted with thrust belt structures in several places outside of the immediate study area in the Lima region (Perry and others, this volume) and in the Bridger Range (Lageson and others, 1984). The hinge regions of the uplifts have been dropped by late Cenozoic normal faults and are therefore buried below the younger basins (Fig. 2).

THRUST BELT STRUCTURES

The leading edge of the frontal fold and thrust belt in Montana is defined by the Disturbed Belt in northwestern Montana and by the east-bulging Helena salient in west-central Montana. The belt merges to the south with the east-trending zone of oblique-slip faults of the southwest Montana transverse zone, and then turns south in the Highland Mountains and continues into the McCartney Mountain salient of southwestern Montana. The frontal zone is again deflected where it intersects the northwest-trending Blacktail fault (Ruppel and Lopez, 1984, Fig. 3), and then continues into Idaho where it is intersected by the Snake River Plain (Fig. 1).

Most structures in the frontal fold and thrust belt are similar in style to the frontal parts of thrust belts in other regions of the Cordillera (Dahlstrom, 1970; Royce and others, 1975). These similarities include: (1) major décollement horizons that follow weak, predominantly shaley formations and cut up-section in the direction of transport across stronger rocks; (2) zones of closely

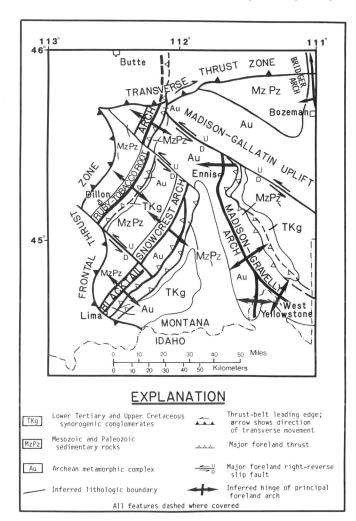

Figure 3. Paleotectonic map (Paleocene time) showing the principal Laramide thrusts and associated arches in southwestern Montana.

spaced imbricate thrusting that are separated by wide zones of relatively little deformation; (3) deformation that is generally brittle, with comparatively little homogeneous strain within thrust sheets; (4) folding that is concentric; and (5) strain by both folding and faulting that decreases in magnitude toward the direction of transport. Important additional structural complications are present in the southwestern Montana portion of the thrust belt; many of these anomalous structural features are related to the unique interaction between thrust belt and foreland structures. The two areas where structural elements of both the frontal fold and thrust belt and the Rocky Mountain foreland are particularly well developed are the southwestern Montana transverse zone that marks the northernmost exposures of basement rocks, and the McCartney Mountain salient along the western edge of the basement exposures.

Southwestern Montana transverse zone

Evidence for the existence of an east-trending Middle Proterozoic fault (or faults) along at least a part of the southern

margin of the Belt basin seems compelling because of the position and extreme thickness of the coarse-grained Belt clastic and overlying sedimentary rocks north of the margin, and the lack of Belt sedimentary rocks south of the margin. The southwest Montana transverse zone closely follows this margin of the basin. The zone is about 10 km wide and 120 km long and can be traced from the southwestern Highland Mountains near Melrose, Montana, eastward across the northern part of the Tobacco Root Mountains, to the Bridger Range near Bozeman, Montana (Fig. 2). Structures in the zone, best developed along the northern part of the Tobacco Root Mountains, are characterized by an anastomosing system of thrusts that change trend frequently from east-west to north-south, forming a wide, imbricate fan-and-horse system (Fig. 2) (Schmidt and Hendrix, 1981; Schmidt and O'Neill, 1983). The thrusts dip west and north, with comparatively steep dips at the surface (35 to 75°). Slip on north-trending segments is generally reverse dip-slip, whereas the more east-trending segments show a strong component of dextral slip (Schmidt, 1975). The aggregate eastward transport of the principal thrust sheet and several minor sheets was at least 15 km (Schmidt and O'Neill, 1983, p. 214).

The principal thrust faults of the transverse zone mainly juxtapose the LaHood Formation of the Proterozoic Belt Supergroup in the hanging wall, with rocks ranging in age from Archean to Cretaceous. In the Highland Mountains on the west, the principal fault is the Camp Creek thrust (Fig. 2, location 1). It is a gently north-dipping thrust with an anomalous younger-on-older structural relationship. The hanging-wall rocks are Belt Supergroup, and the footwall consists of Archean basement rocks.

The central portion of the transverse zone is located in the northern Tobacco Root Mountains and in Jefferson Canyon. The principal fault is named the Mayflower Mine thrust in the northern Tobacco Root Mountains (Schmidt, 1975) (Fig. 2, location 2; Fig. 4), the Cave fault in the western part of Jefferson Canyon (Alexander, 1955) (Fig. 4), and the Jefferson Canyon thrust in the eastern part of Jefferson Canyon (Robinson, 1963) (Fig. 2, location 3). This fault mainly juxtaposes Belt Supergroup rocks on the hanging wall against rocks as young as Upper Cretaceous (Elkhorn Mountains Volcanics) on the footwall. In two places, blocks of Archean metamorphic rocks about 1.5 km long and 0.5 km wide are located on the hanging wall of the fault between the Belt rocks and the Cretaceous volcanic rocks (Fig. 4, locations A and B). These anomalous blocks are important to the alternative explanations of the relationship between the Proterozoic Willow Creek fault and the transverse thrust zone (Fig. 5, B and C). Several major splays branch from the Mayflower Mine–Cave–Jefferson Canyon thrust zone and cut younger rocks south of this principal fault (Fig. 4). These splays make the transverse zone locally more than 5 km wide in the northern Tobacco Root Mountains. Because they can be seen to branch from the principal fault, we believe that they also are important to the interpretation of the relationship between the Proterozoic Willow Creek fault and the transverse thrust zone.

In the Bridger Range the Pass fault (Fig. 2, location 5) may be the eastward continuation of the principal fault of the transverse thrust zone. It trends northwest and dips very steeply north-east. It juxtaposes very coarse Proterozoic LaHood Formation and overlying Paleozoic rocks against moderately deformed Archean rocks (McMannis, 1955; Lageson and others, 1984). McMannis (1955, 1963) and Schmidt and O'Neill (1983) interpreted the Pass fault to be a reactivated Proterozoic, northwest-trending normal fault, similar to northwest-trending faults present in the Highland Mountains (O'Neill and others, 1986). The Pass fault loses displacement to the southeast, however, and cannot be traced into the craton. Lageson and others (1984) have suggested that the Pass fault was originally a gently north-dipping, east-trending thrust much like the Camp Creek thrust in the Highland Mountains, and that it was folded into its present northwest trend by foreland uplift of the Bridger Range on a north-trending axis that we have called the Bridger arch (Fig. 3). The Pass fault shows significant right separation (McMannis, 1955), a fact that

Lageson and others (1984) have interpreted to reflect earlier right-lateral thrust movement.

The easternmost portion of the transverse zone coincides with the northeast-trending, southeast-verging Battle Ridge monocline (Fig. 2, location 6). This fold is exposed in Cretaceous rocks but is believed to be subtended by a blind thrust that has some right-lateral slip and that has Belt Supergroup on the hanging wall (Garrett, 1972).

McCartney Mountain salient

Well-developed folds and thrusts define a convex-eastward salient within the frontal fold and thrust belt directly south of the western end of the southwest Montana transverse zone and just west of the Archean exposures of the foreland (Fig. 2) (Brumbaugh, 1973). The westernmost thrusts of the salient make up the

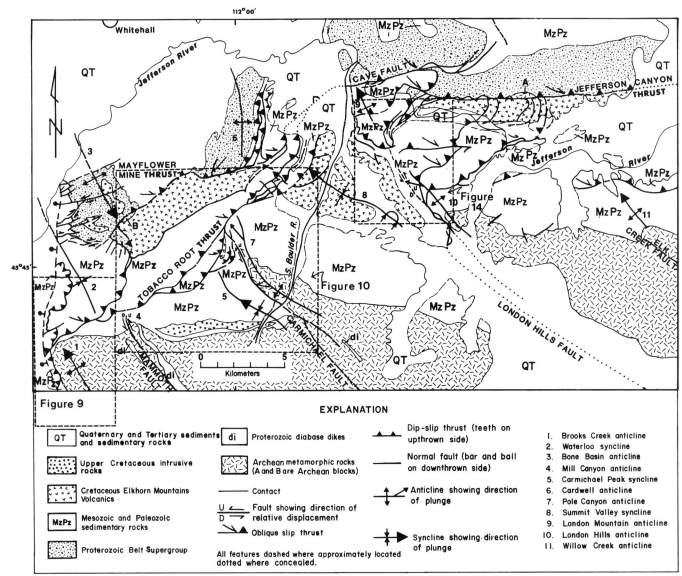

Figure 4. Tectonic map showing the northern Tobacco Root Mountains and Jefferson Canyon area (modified from Schmidt and Hendrix, 1981). Locations of Figures 9, 10, and 14 are shown.

leading edge of the Grasshopper thrust plate (Ruppel and others, 1981; Ruppel and Lopez, 1984) that places Proterozoic Belt Supergroup over Paleozoic and Mesozoic rocks. The northern limit of the salient is directly north of Melrose, and the southern part has been interpreted as being terminated by the Badger Pass fault (Ruppel and Lopez, 1984). The southeastern margin of the salient is obscured by Tertiary and Quaternary valley fill. Archean crystalline rocks of the foreland bound the salient along its northeastern and eastern edges.

The structural style of the salient is dominated by typical "thin-skinned" thrusting. Major thrust faults beneath the Grasshopper thrust plate (Ruppel and others, 1981; Ruppel and Lopez, 1984) give way to thrust faults of smaller displacement to the east, in the McCartney Mountain area (Brumbaugh, 1973; Brumbaugh and Dresser, 1976) and along the southwestern edge of the Highland Mountains. Thrust faults in the McCartney Mountain area appear to sole into a décollement between Mississippian and Pennsylvanian rocks (Brandon, 1984).

TIMING OF FORELAND AND THRUST BELT STRUCTURES

The development of foreland structures and thrust belt structures in southwestern Montana began in Late Cretaceous (Coniacian-Maastrichtian) and ended in early Tertiary (Paleocene–early Eocene) time. Although the structural relationships between foreland structures and thrust belt structures indicate that many of the foreland basement uplifts were developing before frontal folding and thrusting, there is also evidence indicating that foreland uplifts postdated thrust belt structures. Both the foreland structures and the thrust belt structures appear to be oldest on the west and become progressively younger eastward (Schmidt and O'Neill, 1983; Schmidt and Garihan, 1983).

The relative ages of foreland and thrust belt structures can generally be inferred from cross-cutting relationships, although such relationships can usually be interpreted only in terms of the final movements in the foreland or thrust belt. On the west, in the McCartney Mountain salient, frontal folds and thrust faults truncate several northwest-trending, basement-involved foreland structures (Brandon, 1984; Lopez and Schmidt, 1985). In the Tobacco Root Mountains, northwest-trending foreland faults are cut by the thrust faults of the east-trending transverse zone, although a few, presumably earlier, thrusts are folded in the foreland anticlines associated with the northwest-trending faults (Schmidt and Hendrix, 1981). Outside the immediate study area, in the Blacktail Range south of the McCartney Mountain salient, the principal northwest-trending foreland fault appears to be younger than the thrusts of the Blacktail salient (Tysdal, this volume).

If the interpretation is correct that the Pass fault in the Bridger Range was originally a thrust that was folded by the Bridger arch, then the north-trending foreland thrusts were the latest features to form in the study area. This conclusion is supported by our own observations along the western Tobacco Root

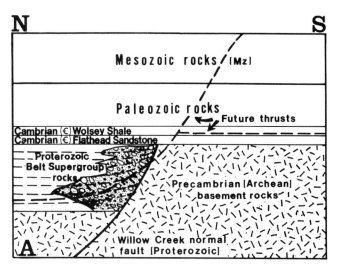

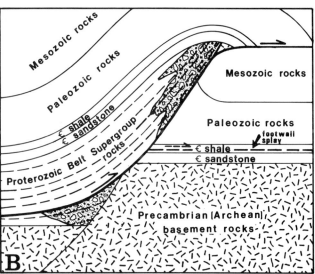

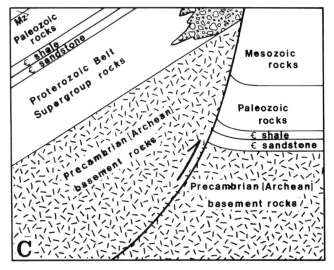

Figure 5. Diagrammatic sections depicting two hypotheses for control of Willow Creek normal fault on thrust geometry. A = Inferred pre-thrust configuration; B = thrust-ramp hypothesis; C = reactivated normal fault hypothesis.

Mountains, where a north-trending thrust zone, locally involving basement rocks, transects the northwest-trending Bismark Fault and thin-skinned thrusts of the transverse thrust zone (Figs. 2, 3). Outside the immediate study area, in the Snowcrest Range and adjacent Tendoy Mountains, northeast-trending foreland thrusts (Snowcrest thrust system) appear to have formed earlier than the thin-skinned structures of the thrust belt and overlap the Cretaceous movement on the northwest-trending fault set (Sheedlo, 1984; Perry and others, this volume).

These apparently conflicting observations on the relative timing of the two sets of foreland structures and the thrust belt structures seem to indicate that their development was mutually overlapping in time. The fact that the principal conclusions of this chapter differ somewhat from those of Perry and others (this volume) and of Tysdal (this volume) reflects this overlapping development of the different structures.

The absolute age for the northwest-trending foreland structures and the thrust belt structures within the study area is constrained partly by the ages of igneous rocks and partly by stratigraphic bracketing. In the southern Highland Mountains, small granitic stocks, satellitic to the 70.1-Ma Hell Canyon pluton (Tilling and others, 1968), intrude northwest-trending faults associated with foreland uplift, but in the Tobacco Root Mountains, northwest-trending faults cut the 75-Ma Tobacco Root batholith. Outside the immediate study area to the east (Madison and Gallatin Ranges), folding associated with northwest-trending faults involves rocks as young as the Late Cretaceous to late Paleocene Fort Union Formation (Roberts, 1972) and the Maastrichtian Sphinx Conglomerate (Tysdal and others, 1986; DeCelles and others, 1987). Thus it appears that on the west the northwest-trending faults show recurrent movement after 75 Ma but before about 70 Ma, which constrains their latest pre-Neogene displacements principally to the latest Cretaceous (Maastrichtian), whereas on the east, much of the deformation was post-Maastrichtian. This supports the general west-to-east younging of movement on the northwest-trending faults suggested by Schmidt and Garihan (1983).

The thrust faults also appear to become younger from west to east, from the McCartney Mountain salient eastward along the transverse zone. Thrust faults in the McCartney salient are intruded by the McCartney stock, dated at 70 ± 1.5 Ma (Brumbaugh, 1973, p. 48; Ruppel and Lopez, 1984, p. 33). The Camp Creek thrust fault in the Highland Mountains is also intruded by the 70.1-Ma Hell Canyon pluton (Schmidt and O'Neill, 1983). Eastward along the transverse zone in the Bridger Range, rocks about 70 m.y. old are cut by thrusts (Skipp and McGrew, 1977, p. 321).

STYLES OF INTERACTION BETWEEN FORELAND AND THRUST BELT

Basement surface irregularities have produced a distinct structural style within the thrusts of the leading edge of the thrust belt in southwestern Montana. The structural style is character-

ized by footwall thrust ramps that have a close spatial and genetic relationship to the basement surface irregularities. Two types of irregularities of the basement surface have controlled the position of these ramps: normal faults of Proterozoic ancestry and foreland anticlines cored by basement rocks (Wiltschko and Eastman, 1983, p. 178, and this volume). The types of structures resulting from the variety of interactions between thrusts and normal faults and between thrusts and foreland anticlines have been discussed in a general way by Kulik and Schmidt (this volume). Some specific examples of these interactions present in the study area are discussed below.

Thrust fault–normal fault interaction

Highland Mountains. The Camp Creek thrust fault trends east through the central Highland Mountains (Fig. 2). It places the Proterozoic LaHood Formation on the north against Archean metamorphic rocks on the south. The fault was described by McMannis (1963, p. 424) as dipping 60°N in one location and somewhat less elsewhere; current mapping along this zone by J. M. O'Neill indicates that it dips as gently as 20°, averaging about 30° along much of its trace; Belt metasedimentary rocks on the hanging wall dip to the north at about the same angle as the fault. Locally, the Belt rocks are folded into northwest-plunging folds that, when unfolded, also yield a gentle northerly homoclinal dip. The Archean rocks on the footwall are highly sheared only where the Camp Creek fault is intersected by northwest-trending high-angle faults (O'Neill and others, 1986). Where the Camp Creek fault is well exposed, neither the Archean rocks nor the Belt rocks near the fault are strongly deformed. Latest movement on the fault appears to be mainly reverse slip, accommodated along a frontal ramp, bringing younger, structurally deeper Proterozoic Belt Supergroup rocks up and over an Archean basement block elevated during Proterozoic time. The Belt rocks on the hanging wall appear to have originally dipped subparallel to the fault.

Tobacco Root Mountains. The principal faults of the central transverse zone in the northern Tobacco Root Mountains thrust coarse Belt metasedimentary and Paleozoic sedimentary rocks over Archean to Cretaceous rocks (Fig. 4). On the hanging wall of the Mayflower Mine and the Jefferson Canyon thrusts, long narrow tectonic slivers of Archean metamorphic rocks, overlain by north-dipping Belt rocks, are juxtaposed against Cretaceous volcanic rocks on the footwall. Belt rocks strike nearly parallel to the fault and dip northward at about the same angle as the fault plane. The Cretaceous volcanic rocks are locally turned up steeply against the faults in a south-verging footwall syncline. The Mayflower Mine–Cave–Jefferson Canyon thrust system generally dips 45 to 75°N. Although its trend is mainly east, it has several north-trending segments. Movement along the Mayflower Mine–Cave–Jefferson Canyon thrust system is demonstrably oblique, with nearly equal components of reverse slip and dextral slip (Schmidt and Hendrix, 1981). The first-order structure on the hanging wall is a north-dipping homocline that is somewhat obscured by folding associated with the dextral movement component along the fault system; the structure is reasonably clear on the east-trending Jefferson Canyon segment of the fault where the Belt rocks and overlying Paleozoic section dip 45 to 55°N, which is nearly parallel to the fault plane. Along the other segments of the fault system the principal structures on the hanging wall are north-plunging folds that, when unfolded, yield the same north homoclinal dip seen on the Jefferson Canyon segment.

The structural geometry and the hanging-wall/footwall relationships have been interpreted to have been controlled by preexisting structures. Robinson (1963, p. 107) suggested that the Jefferson Canyon thrust could be the Proterozoic Willow Creek fault reactivated with opposite throw (Fig. 5C). This is a reasonable interpretation in that it explains the anomalous occurrence of Archean metamorphic rocks in the hanging wall of the Jefferson Canyon thrust and a similar occurrence of Archean rocks in the hanging wall of the Mayflower Mine thrust (Schmidt, 1975). Robinson (1963, p. 108), however, suggested that the Jefferson Canyon thrust may bend northward near the town of Three Forks and connect with the Lombard thrust (Fig. 2), a suggestion supported by magnetic data (Davis and others, 1965). If this connection exists, the Jefferson Canyon–Lombard thrust probably flattens above the Archean basement and does not continue into it, as required by the reactivated normal-fault interpretation (Fig. 5B). The observation that the bedding in the hanging-wall rocks roughly parallels the dip of the Jefferson Canyon thrust also is not compatible with the reactivated normal fault interpretation.

Berry (1943, p. 23), Alexander (1955, p. 99), and Robinson (1963, p. 108) suggested that Archean crystalline rocks south of the Proterozoic margin of the Belt basin acted as a buttress to thrust movements in the Belt basin. Following this concept, Schmidt (1975, p. 346–347; 1976, p. 142), Schmidt and Hendrix (1981, p. 177), and Schmidt and O'Neill (1982, p. 213) suggested that the Belt rocks on the downthrown side of the Proterozoic Willow Creek fault were detached along a décollement at or near the base of the Belt section and were translated up and to the east along this horizon (Fig. 5B). The décollement interpretation implies that a major east-trending lateral ramp developed in the thrust system where it encountered the old elevated Archean crystalline rocks along the Willow Creek fault (Fig. 6). The anomalous outcrops of Archean rocks along the Jefferson Canyon fault and Mayflower Mine fault may be explained as pieces of the upper edge of the footwall of the Proterozoic normal-fault boundary broken off during ramping (Fig. 5B).

The lateral-thrust–ramp hypothesis helps to explain the imbricate thrust faults associated with the Mayflower Mine–Cave–Jefferson Canyon thrust system. The faults occur south of the principal ramp and are interpreted as footwall splays that propagated from the ramp at different stratigraphic horizons. The lowest splay, the Tobacco Root thrust, occurs in Cambrian rocks; its branch point with the Mayflower Mine thrust is well exposed in the western Tobacco Root Mountains (Fig. 4). Movement on this and other splays in front of the principal thrust ramp is responsible for a zone of oblique thrust faulting about 5 km wide super-

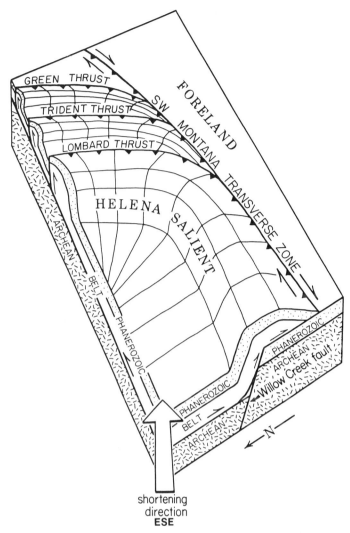

Figure 6. Interpretive structural block diagram showing the inferred relationship between the Proterozoic Willow Creek fault, the southwest Montana transverse zone lateral ramp, and the frontal ramps of the Helena salient (after Schmidt and Garihan, 1986).

imposed on the footwall of the Proterozoic normal-fault block. Therefore, the Proterozoic rocks on the hanging wall of the principal thrust have been translated several kilometers south from their original position along the southern margin of the Belt basin in addition to their eastward transport of at least 10 km (Schmidt and Hendrix, 1981).

Bridger Range. The Pass fault in the central Bridger Range places Proterozoic LaHood Formation on the hanging wall against Archean basement rocks on the footwall. Lageson and others (1984) have suggested that the Pass fault was originally a north-dipping thrust that formed as a lateral ramp over the eastward extensions of the Proterozoic Willow Creek fault zone. The Pass fault and the Cross Range fault directly to the north of it both show significant right separation (McMannis, 1955), a fact that Lageson and others (1984) attributed to earlier right-lateral

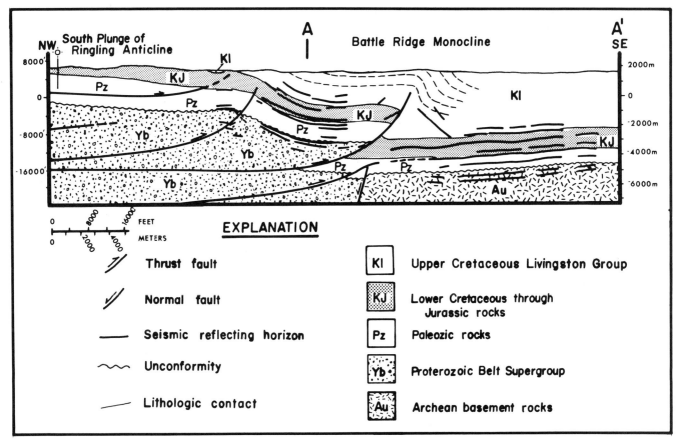

Figure 7. Cross section across the Battle Ridge monocline based on seismic data. Position of blind thrust ramp is inferred to be above the Willow Creek normal fault (after Garrett, 1972).

thrust movement prior to the folding of these thrusts by foreland uplift of the Bridger arch.

A lateral ramp over a normal-fault step seems likely in the easternmost part of the transverse thrust zone in the Crazy Mountain Basin directly east of the Bridger Range. The northeast-trending Battle Ridge monocline (Fig. 2, location 6), as interpreted from seismic data, is a fold above a blind thrust that ramped upward over an obliquely oriented normal-fault step in the subsurface (Garrett, 1972, p. 113) (Fig. 7). The resulting ramp monocline represents a fold developed at the highest structural level in the transverse thrust zone. The formation of the monocline may have been facilitated by strike-slip movement on the northwest-trending Cross Range fault (directly north of Pass fault, Fig. 2) in the central part of the Bridger Range, which ". . . functioned as a tear, probably connecting at depth with a thrust which almost certainly subtends the monocline" (McMannis, 1955, p. 1419).

The above interpretation of the transverse zone as a ramp above a basement fault step applies to the entire zone from the Highland Mountains on the west to the Battle Ridge monocline on the east. At each position along the transverse zone the ramp is exposed at a different structural level. In the Highland Mountains and Bridger Range, we see it at its deepest level; in the northern

Tobacco Root Mountains, we see it at the intermediate level, and in the Battle Ridge area, it is exposed at its highest level. Most of the available evidence suggests that it is a lateral ramp with a strong right-lateral component. The evidence for the Camp Creek thrust, however, is inconclusive, as this fault shows no clear evidence of strike-slip movement.

Thrust fault–foreland fold interaction

Tobacco Root Mountains. The frontal thrusts of the transverse zone are deflected over the hinges of three large foreland anticlines associated with the northwest-trending faults. These are, from west to east, the Brooks Creek anticline, the Pole Canyon anticline, and the London Hills anticline (Fig. 4). The interaction produces strongly sinuous outcrop patterns of the thrusts. A ramp in the thrust surface occurs where thrusts change from an easterly trend to a more northerly trend. Thus the Mayflower Mine–Cave–Jefferson Canyon thrust system is not only a large lateral ramp above a normal-fault step, but it also has several secondary ramps developed along its trace that are located precisely where northwest-trending foreland anticlines intersect the transverse zone (Fig. 8). Northwest-trending rootless anticlines and synclines in the hanging-wall rocks of this thrust system formed above these secondary ramps (folds numbered 2, 3, and 6; Fig. 4).

Each of the three cases of interaction of the frontal thrusts of the transverse zone in the Tobacco Root Mountains with foreland anticlines is somewhat different, but in general the hanging-wall rocks are middle and upper Paleozoic, most notably limestones of the Mississippian Madison Group. The ages of the footwall rocks, where the thrusts cut across the hinges of the foreland anticlines, vary from Cambrian on the west (Brooks Creek anticline), to Mississippian in the central region (Pole Canyon anticline), to Cretaceous on the east (London Hills anticline).

Brooks Creek anticline–Mayflower Mine thrust. The Brooks Creek anticline is located on the northwestern flank of the Tobacco Root Mountains. It is a major foreland anticline on the uplifted hanging wall of the Bismark fault and plunges beneath the thrust belt at about 40°. The frontal oblique slip thrusts of the transverse zone (the Mayflower Mine thrust at this location) and the westernmost foreland thrusts (Beall Canyon thrust) of the Tobacco Root Mountains intersect here and are overlapped by a Neogene normal fault (Fig. 9A). The Mayflower Mine thrust strikes generally northeast and dips about 40° to 50°NW, roughly the same inclination as the plunge of Brooks Creek anticline. The thrust transects the hinge of this anticline, placing the Mississippian Lodgepole Limestone over the Cambrian Meagher Lime-

stone and Wolsey Shale (Fig. 9A). To the east it changes to a more northerly strike, ramps up-section across the footwall rocks, and branches to produce the Tobacco Root thrust, an important splay in the Cambrian section.

The younger-over-older thrust fault relationship along the Mayflower Mine thrust at the hinge of the Brooks Creek anticline is significant because it is one of two places where faults with younger rocks on older rocks exist along the transverse thrust zone and clearly indicates that the Brooks Creek foreland anticline was present before thrusting. Furthermore, the fault follows the bedding in the Cambrian rocks of the footwall around the anticline from its steep western limb to its hinge and then into the gentle limb, suggesting that the steep limb deflected the fault in a ramp over the foreland fold. The hanging-wall rocks have a rootless anticline and syncline formed above the ramp (Fig. 9B). The alternative explanation, that the fault was folded by the foreland anticline, is less tenable because the thrust places younger rocks on older rocks. It is possible, however, that some of the development of the Brooks Creek anticline continued after thrusting.

South of where the Mayflower Mine thrust transects the anticlinal hinge, the Archean rocks on the steep limb of the anticline are sheared along a north-trending fault zone (Fig. 9A). We are not certain whether this fault is part of the "thin-skinned" structures of the transverse zone, as suggested by Schmidt (1975), or whether it is related to the system of foreland thrusts and reverse faults (Beall Canyon thrust of Samuelson and Schmidt, 1981), which follows the west flank of the range farther south. Currently we favor the latter interpretation.

Pole Canyon anticline–Tobacco Root thrust. The Tobacco Root thrust is the principal footwall splay of the Mayflower Mine thrust. It cuts obliquely acrss two foreland structures, the Carmichael syncline and Pole Canyon anticline (Fig. 10A). It cuts up-section across the syncline and down-section across the anticline. The principal splay of the Tobacco Root thrust (Pole Canyon thrust) places Mississippian Mission Canyon Limestone over Cretaceous volcanic rocks in the core of the Carmichael syncline (stratigraphic throw of about 1,300 m); 1,500 m to the east, where it rejoins the Tobacco Root thrust and crosses the Pole Canyon anticline, the stratigraphic throw is less than 300 m (base of the Mission Canyon Limestone over uppermost Mission Canyon). This abrupt eastward loss of throw of about 1 km is a reflection of ramping of the Pole Canyon thrust over the hinge of the Pole Canyon foreland anticline.

A single thrust crosses the hinge region of the Pole Canyon anticline, but an imbricate stack of at least four, and probably several more, thrusts occurs in the adjacent Carmichael syncline. The structurally lower thrusts are sharply curved over the steep foreland fold limb and show only minor displacements. The structurally higher thrusts show more displacement and are less affected by the foreland anticline. The structurally highest Tobacco Root thrust shows very little deflection or curvature related to the anticline (Fig. 10B). Schmidt (1983) interpreted these relationships as an overstep sequence in which the higher thrusts

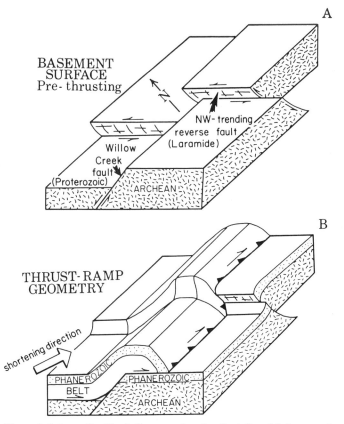

Figure 8. Interpretive block diagrams showing the inferred influence of the Willow Creek normal fault and the northwest-trending foreland blocks on thrust-fault geometry in the transverse zone (after Schmidt and Garihan, 1986).

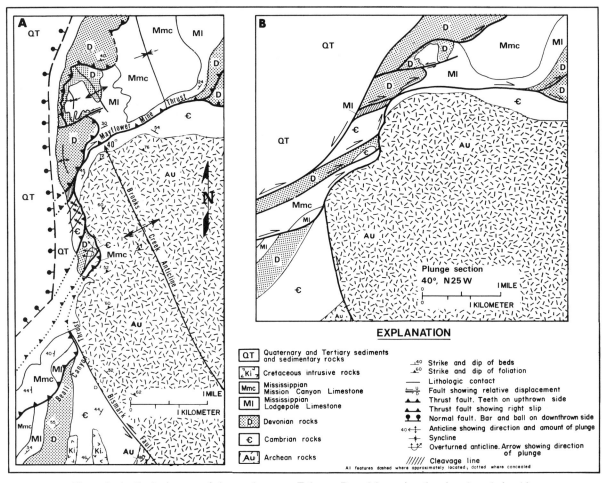

Figure 9. A, Geologic map of the northwestern Tobacco Root Mountains showing the relationship between the Bismark fault–Brooks Creek foreland anticline and the Mayflower Mine–Beall Canyon thrust system. B, Down-plunge profile of the map in A based on the trend and plunge (40°, N25°W) of the Books Creek foreland anticline. Location of area shown in Figure 4.

moved later in the sequence, similar to that described by Serra (1977, mode 1). In this structural mode, imbricate thrusts splay from the main décollement, become successively shallower going up-section in the upper plate, and are assumed to develop out of sequence because of the initial steepness of the ramp. Movement on the lower thrusts became locked due to the steepness of the ramp; the structurally higher thrusts developed farther back from the steep foreland fold limb, moving over the structurally lower thrusts. An alternative explanation is that folding of the foreland structure was coeval with thrusting so that the earliest splays on the southeast were more folded than the later formed splays. This alternative also favors an overstep imbrication sequence, as the frontal splays are more folded than those to the northwest.

Minor structures within the Lodgepole Limestone of the Pole Canyon thrust sheet indicate a considerable amount of shortening of the thrust sheet against the foreland buttress prior to and during thrusting. Biosparite units near the top of the Lodgepole are tightly folded for a distance of 2.2 km west of the Pole

Canyon anticline (Fig. 11). Shortening by folding over this distance was determined by direct measurement on a distinct limestone bed and averages about 32 percent. Shortening nearer the foreland anticline is greatest (36 percent), and that farthest away is least (27 percent). The more micritic units near the base of the Lodgepole are also folded, but folds are much more open and represent an estimated (i.e., not directly measured) strain of about 10 percent. However, in terms of modern rock-fabric classification schemes (such as Borradaile and others, 1982; Engelder and Marshak, 1985), these rocks are strongly cleaved with a narrowly to closely spaced (0.3 to 1 cm) disjunctive cleavage (Fig. 12). Cleavage seams are nonsutured to slightly undulatory, generally continuous, and wavy to slightly anastomosing. Shortening by cleavage formation is probably about 22 percent, the difference between shortening by folding in the uncleaved upper units and the cleaved lower units.

An equal-area plot of these minor structures (Fig. 13, A and B) shows that the maximum concentration of 60 fold hinges is

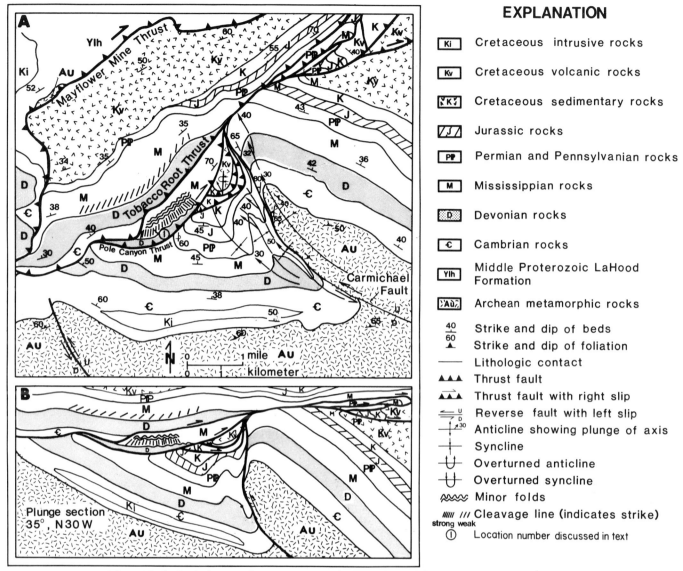

EXPLANATION

Ki	Cretaceous intrusive rocks
Kv	Cretaceous volcanic rocks
K	Cretaceous sedimentary rocks
J	Jurassic rocks
PP	Permian and Pennsylvanian rocks
M	Mississippian rocks
D	Devonian rocks
€	Cambrian rocks
Ylh	Middle Proterozoic LaHood Formation
Au	Archean metamorphic rocks

40/60 Strike and dip of beds
▲ Strike and dip of foliation
——— Lithologic contact
▲▲▲ Thrust fault
▲▲→ Thrust fault with right slip
⇌ U/D Reverse fault with left slip
┼30 Anticline showing plunge of axis
┼ Syncline
⊔ Overturned anticline
⊔ Overturned syncline
〰 Minor folds
▥ /// Cleavage line (indicates strike)
strong weak
① Location number discussed in text

Figure 10. A, Geologic map of the Pole Canyon foreland anticline and impinging Tobacco Root and Pole Canyon thrust sheets. B, Down-plunge profile of the map in A based on the trend and plunge (35°, N30°W) of the Pole Canyon anticline. Location of area shown in Figure 4 (after Schmidt and Geiger, 1985).

oriented 38°, N35°W, and is therefore roughly parallel to the Pole Canyon thrust plane. Calcite-filled extension veins are normal to cleavage seams at each measurement location (for example, Fig. 13A). The mean cleavage orientation is roughly north-south with a steep westerly dip (Fig. 13B). Both the hinges of the minor folds and the cleavage planes show a change in orientation along the thrust sheet. The folds are dispersed from their mean trend and spread out along a crude great-circle girdle through an angle of about 45°. This spread may reflect somewhat nonuniform deformation and/or measurement error, but it may also reflect postfolding warping of the thrust sheet in which the folds are located. Cleavage changes from N10° to 20°E, 75° to 90°NW on the west, to N40° to 50°W, vertical on the east. The change of orientation of the cleavage is associated with a change

of strike of the thrust from nearly east-west on the west, where it branches from the Tobacco Root thrust, to N45°E where it crosses the hinge of the Carmichael syncline and begins to be deflected over the adjacent Pole Canyon anticline. Rotation of cleavage planes appears to have taken place around a steeply plunging, northwest-trending axis (Fig. 13B), but data are not sufficient to prove that this axis lies in the thrust plane.

We interpret the presence and orientation of minor structures on the Pole Canyon thrust sheet as having been formed by west-northwest–east-southeast shortening of the rocks against the uplifted Pole Canyon anticlinal buttress. After initial layer-parallel shortening by folding and cleavage development, the Pole Canyon thrust formed as a footwall splay from the Tobacco Root thrust. As it propagated eastward, it was deflected from an east to

Figure 11. Photo showing minor fold in biosparite units of the Lodgepole Limestone on the Pole Canyon thrust sheet near location 1 in Figure 10. Hammer for scale is left of center. View is to the northwest.

Figure 12. Photo showing cleavage in micritic lower portion of the Lodgepole Limestone in the Pole Canyon thrust sheet near location 1 in Figure 10. Scale is in inches. View is to the north.

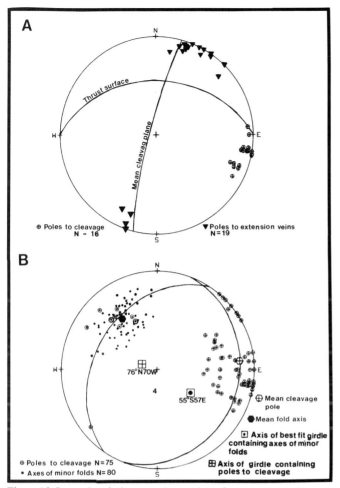

Figure 13. Lower hemisphere equal-area plots of structural data from the Lodgepole Limestone on the Pole Canyon thrust sheet. A, Cleavage and extension veins at one station (location 1, Fig. 10). B, Cleavage and fold axes of minor folds for all stations in the Lodgepole Limestone on the Pole Canyon thrust sheet (after Schmidt and Geiger, 1985).

a northeast trend by the Pole Canyon foreland anticline. The deflection of the hanging-wall rocks in the Pole Canyon sheet caused the initial N10° to 20°E cleavage orientations and northerly trends of minor folds to be rotated counterclockwise (westerly) more than 45°. The Pole Canyon thrust rejoined the Tobacco Root thrust after being deflected over the hinge of the foreland anticline. An alternative, though less likely, explanation is that variations in the stress field due to the local effect of the foreland anticline produced the observed variation in fold hinges and cleavage orientation.

The Lodgepole Limestone on the next higher Tobacco Root thrust sheet is not folded and is only weakly cleaved. Cleavage seams are anastomosing and more widely spaced (average spacing greater than one centimeter). Considerably less homogeneous strain was apparently developed in this sheet because it formed higher in the imbricate stack and was much less deflected by the Carmichael anticline.

London Hills anticline–London Mountain thrust system. The London Mountain thrust system, named for the prominent peak between the Jefferson Canyon and the South Boulder River valley, is probably the eastward continuation of the Tobacco Root–Pole Canyon thrust system. It is very similar to that system in its inferred relationship to the major foreland folds except that the footwall rocks of the London Mountain thrust system are generally the structurally highest, and are therefore the youngest rocks of the foreland folds. The London Mountain thrust system consists of five thrust sheets that cut across the northern portion of the Summit Valley syncline and the London Hills foreland anticline and then over the hinge of the anticline (Fig. 14A). The thrust system rejoins the main Jefferson Canyon thrust at the east end of Jefferson Canyon (Fig. 14A).

Except for a minor splay at the top of the thrust system, the London Mountain thrust is the structurally highest thrust in this system. It is a folded thrust, and its trace encircles the southern half of London Mountain (Fig. 14A). It places limestones of the Mississippian Madison Group over rocks as young as the Jurassic Morrison Formation. The hanging-wall rocks are broadly arched above the thrust in the northwest-plunging London Mountain anticline. This fold was originally interpreted as a structurally deeper part of the London Hills foreland anticline brought to the surface by thrusting (Schmidt, 1975). However, because the thrust dips more gently than the plunge of the anticline and because the two anticlines have different senses of asymmetry, we believe that it is probably a rootless hanging-wall anticline above the thrust. It may, however, have been modified by postthrust folding of the foreland structure.

As in the case of the Pole Canyon thrust, successively lower thrust sheets are splays from the London Mountain thrust. They show progressively less displacement but are progressively more folded than the structurally higher thrusts. This indicates either that folding in the London Hills foreland anticline was coeval with thrusting or that the structurally lower thrusts were more strongly influenced by the steep west-facing limb of the London Hills anticline. The evidence that the London Hills anticline was at least partly formed before thrusting, besides the apparent deflection of the thrusts by the steep limb of the structure, may be found in the change in throw of the structurally lowest splays. These thrusts place Jurassic rocks on the middle part of the Upper Cretaceous Elkhorn Mountains Volcanics in the Summit Valley syncline. At the hinge region of the London Hills anticline, the same thrusts place Jurassic rocks on the top of the Lower Cretaceous Kootenai Formation. This represents a loss of throw of several hundred meters due to ramping over the anticline.

Three other, earlier formed thrusts are folded by the London Hills foreland anticline (Fig. 14). These thrusts are clearly cut by the London Hills fault and thus are interpreted as having formed earlier than the London Mountain thrust system.

McCartney Mountain salient. The eastern and northeastern margins of the McCartney Mountain salient coincide with the southwestern edge of the Highland Mountains foreland uplift. This uplift apparently extended farther to the southeast, beyond

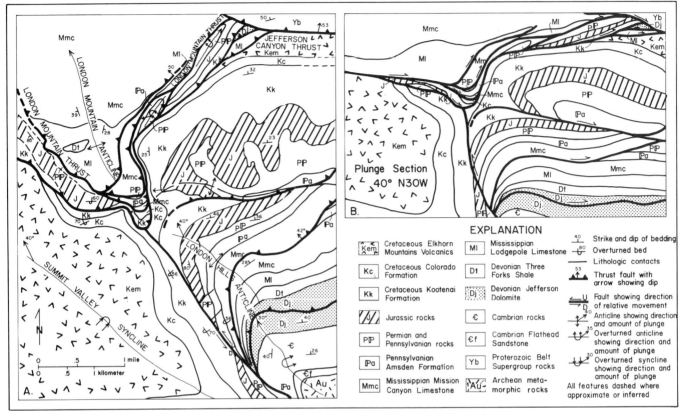

Figure 14. A, Geologic map of the northern London Hills foreland anticline and folded thrusts on London Mountain. B, Down-plunge profile of the map in A based on the trend and plunge (40°, N30°W) of the London Hills anticline. Location of area shown in Figure 4.

the salient, and was once continuous with the Ruby Range; a seismic reflection profile (Lopez and Schmidt, 1985) and gravity and magnetic data (W. F. Hanna, 1986, personal communication) indicate that shallowly buried crystalline basement rocks are present in the lower Beaverhead Valley, between the Highland and Ruby Mountains. The edge of this north-northwest–trending uplift is defined by the outcrop and inferred subcrop contact between the Archean crystalline rocks and the Paleozoic cover, as shown by the dotted line in Figure 15. At the surface this contact ranges in dip from vertical to about 20°SE.

The Archean basement rocks east of the Archean-Paleozoic boundary are cut by several northwest-trending, high-angle faults that show Precambrian, Late Cretaceous, and Neogene movement (O'Neill and others, 1986). One of the faults, the South Rochester fault (Figs. 15 and 16), intersects the Paleozoic sedimentary rocks along the western edge of the range in the vicinity of Camp Creek. North of Camp Creek, the South Rochester fault shows evidence of pre-thrusting reverse movement; Paleozoic sedimentary rocks are folded over the edge of this uplifted Archean block and define a northwest-plunging anticline, the Rochester anticline, locally overturned to the southwest. The anticline is poorly exposed except between Camp Creek and Soap Gulch where part of the hinge and vertical southwest limb are exposed in Cambrian rocks. The northeast limb of the fold is not exposed

in the Phanerozoic sedimentary section, as it was eroded down to its Archean metamorphic core prior to Neogene normal faulting. Most of the Paleozoic rocks on the southwest side of the Highland Mountains dip gently southwest and are inferred to form the syncline adjacent to the Rochester anticline. The Rochester anticline is cut by the Camp Creek thrust just north of the Soap Gulch (Fig. 16).

Another important fault of the northwest-trending set is the Biltmore fault, which bounds the Biltmore foreland anticline ad-

Figure 15. Tectonic map of the McCartney Mountain salient showing locations of Figures 16 and 22 and line of cross section A-A′ (Fig. 23) (modified from Ruppel and others, 1983). Structures referred to in text are: BA = Biltmore anticline; BF = Biltmore fault; CCF = Camp Creek fault; MF = McCartney fault; MMS = McCartney Mountain stock; RA = Rochester anticline; SRF = South Rochester fault; SHFZ = Southern Highlands fault zone; SHT = Sandy Hollow thrust. Other labeled features are: BMK = Beal's Mountain klippe; CCA = Canyon Creek anticline; DMA = Dutchman Mountain anticline; FCT = French Creek thrust; FPB = Frying Pan Basin; HCF = Hinch Creek fault; HCA = Hinch Creek anticline; HT = Hogback thrust; LCF = Lost Creek fault; MCA = McHessor Creek anticline; MCF = McHessor Creek fault; PB = Pioneer batholith; RCF = Rock Creek fault; NRF = North Rochester fault. Location of area shown in Figure 2. Locations of Figures 16 and 22 are shown.

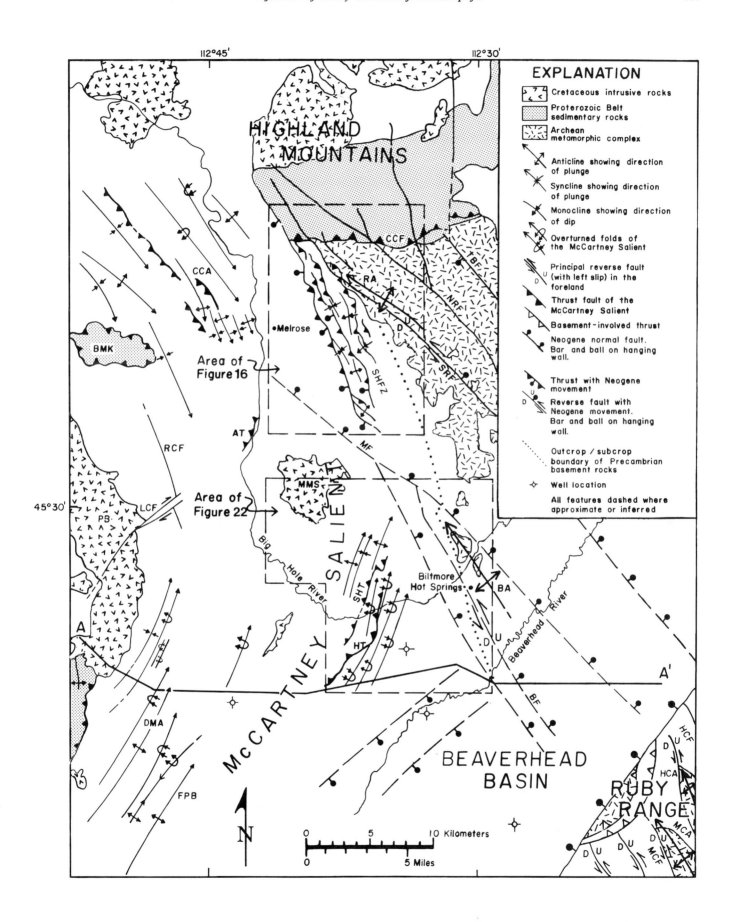

joining the central part of the McCartney Mountain salient (Fig. 15). Although the Biltmore anticline is also poorly exposed, the structure is inferred from reasonably good exposures of its vertical southwest limb near Biltmore Hot Springs and from a seismic profile along the line A-A', which intersects it on the southeast (Fig. 15). The McCartney fault is slightly oblique to the Biltmore fault and shows well-defined Neogene movement; however, it may have a Laramide or even Precambrian ancestry, as do many of the other northwest-trending faults in the region (Schmidt and Garihan, 1983). Seismic data from the west-central part of the McCartney Mountain salient west of the basement-cover outcrop/subcrop boundary indicate the presence of at least one reverse fault and associated fold involving basement rocks (Lopez and Schmidt, 1985). It seems probable that this fault also has a northwest trend.

Southern Highlands fault zone–Rochester anticline. The Pa-

leozoic sedimentary rocks along the southern margin of the Highland Mountains directly east of Melrose are deformed by small, northeast-directed thrust faults and northeast-verging folds that make up the Southern Highlands fault zone (SHFZ) (Fig. 16) of Schmidt and Geiger (1985). The fault zone was discussed by Brumbaugh (1973) and mapped in part by H. W. Smedes (unpublished mapping). Brandon (1984) also mapped this zone and identified younger-over-older thrust fault relationships important to its interpretation.

Asymmetrical folds and monoclines are present in the Paleozoic cover rocks along this fault zone. The monoclinal flexures are long, semi-continuous, southwest-facing structures. Their sense of asymmetry is opposite to that of the northeast-verging folds in the fault zone. Their origin is uncertain: they may be related to small offsets in the underlying basement rocks, or they may also be synclinal crowd structures (Brown, this volume)

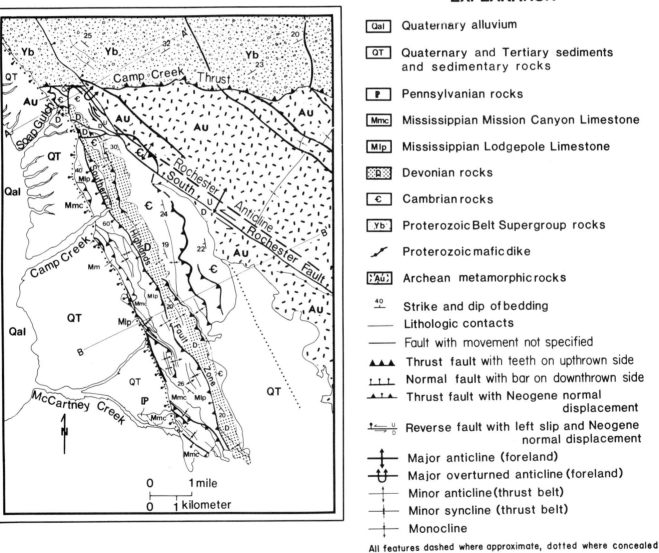

EXPLANATION

Qal — Quaternary alluvium

QT — Quaternary and Tertiary sediments and sedimentary rocks

P — Pennsylvanian rocks

Mmc — Mississippian Mission Canyon Limestone

Mlp — Mississippian Lodgepole Limestone

D — Devonian rocks

€ — Cambrian rocks

Yb — Proterozoic Belt Supergroup rocks

⟋ — Proterozoic mafic dike

Au — Archean metamorphic rocks

40 ⊥ — Strike and dip of bedding

——— — Lithologic contacts

——— — Fault with movement not specified

▲▲▲ — Thrust fault with teeth on upthrown side

⊥⊥⊥ — Normal fault with bar on downthrown side

▲⊥▲ — Thrust fault with Neogene normal displacement

⇄ U/D — Reverse fault with left slip and Neogene normal displacement

┼ — Major anticline (foreland)

⊎ — Major overturned anticline (foreland)

┼ — Minor anticline (thrust belt)

┼ — Minor syncline (thrust belt)

┼ — Monocline

All features dashed where approximate, dotted where concealed

Figure 16. Geologic map of the southern Highland Mountains near Melrose, Montana. Sections A-A' and B-B' are shown in Figure 17. Location of area shown in Figure 15.

related to the formation of the adjacent Rochester foreland anticline. The faults and folds of this zone trend north-northwest (Fig. 16), increasing in number and intensity from southeast to northwest. The increase in deformation corresponds to the decrease in distance between the leading edge of thin-skinned thrusts of the Southern Highlands fault zone and the South Rochester fault and Rochester anticline (Figs. 16, 17) and to an increase in the dip of the basement/cover contact. On the south, near McCartney Creek, Paleozoic rocks are weakly folded into northeast-verging anticline-syncline pairs with amplitudes and wavelengths measured in tens of meters. Locally, the anticlinal bend is missing, and the syncline is bounded on the southwest by a forelimb thrust fault. Most of the folding and faulting is in the Mississippian carbonate rocks. In the central part of the area, south of Camp Creek (Fig. 16), thrust faults and related folds are found in Cambrian through Mississippian sedimentary rocks. The thrust faults in the lowest unit, the uniformly southwest-dipping Cambrian limestone, thicken and repeat the sedimentary sequence. However, thrust faults west of the thickened limestones thin the Upper Cambrian limestone (Pilgrim) and overlying shale. These thrusts are bounded on the east by southwest-facing monoclinal flexures; the thinning of the sedimentary sequence

occurs where the faults impinge on the preexisting monoclines and cut down-section (Fig. 17).

Directly south of Camp Creek, thrust faults show greater displacement, and low-amplitude, northeast-verging folds become tighter in Mississippian rocks. At Soap Gulch (Fig. 16) the SHFZ intersects the South Rochester fault and the associated northwest-plunging Rochester anticline. In this area the South Rochester fault and Rochester anticline juxtapose Archean rocks against Cambrian shale and limestone that are vertical to overturned and dip northwest; northeast-directed thrust faults of the SHFZ have detached tectonic slivers of Archean rocks and lower Paleozoic rocks and stacked these slices in imbricate fashion against the preexisting structure (Fig. 17). Possible late movement on the Cretaceous south Rochester fault has also truncated these slivers (H. Dresser, written communication, 1986). The geologic relationshps in this area are extremely complex, not only because of the intersection of foreland faults and folds with thrust belt structures, but also because the north-dipping Camp Creek fault and numerous basin-range normal faults also intersect these structures (Fig. 16).

The increase in intensity of deformation from southeast to northwest, measured by number and intensity of minor folds and

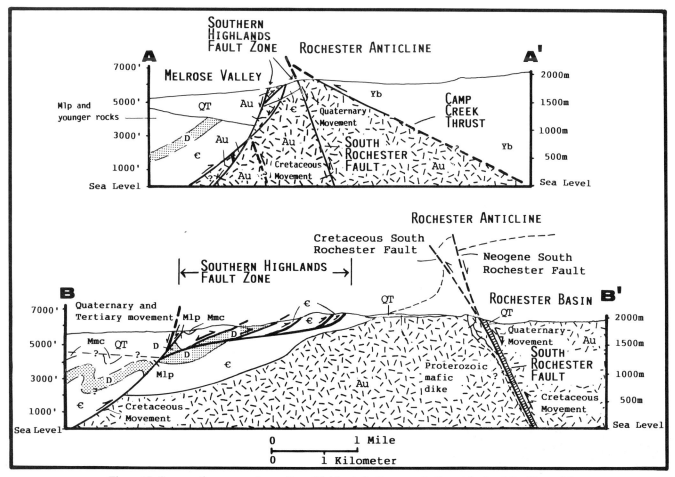

Figure 17. Cross sections across the southern Highlands fault zone and adjacent foreland. See Figure 16 for section locations and map symbols.

Figure 18. Veins and tectonic stylolites in the Lodgepole Limestone in the southern part of the southern Highlands fault zone near McCartney Creek. Scale is in inches. View is to the northeast.

thrusts, is accompanied by a progressive northwestward change in the shortening fabric of the Mississippian Lodgepole and Mission Canyon Limestones (Schmidt and Geiger, 1985). At the south end of the SHFZ near McCartney Creek (Fig. 16), the Lodgepole Limestone displays no penetrative fabric. Cleavage is present within the limestones, but the cleavage domains are generally sutured to undulatory and widely spaced (about 1 cm), even in the most micritic units. In most places the micrite units have very weak cleavages or widely spaced tectonic stylolites (sutured domains) (Fig. 18).

Farther to the north, roughly midway between McCartney Creek and Camp Creek, cleavage is ubiquitous in the micrites and is closely spaced, undulatory, continuous, and wavy to anastomosing. It is also locally present in the biosparite units of both the Lodgepole Limestone and overlying more massive Mission Canyon Limestone. Where folds are present, cleavage fans around the fold hinges, indicating that it developed prior to folding (Fig. 19). In this area the distance between the SHFZ and the South Rochester fault is less than 5 km.

From Camp Creek northward, where the South Rochester fault intersects the southwest-dipping rocks along the edge of the Highland Mountains uplift (Fig. 16), cleavage seams are narrowly spaced (<0.5 cm) to penetrative (Fig. 20). Cleavage domains are very narrow and do not occur as distinct seams. Locally, bedding does not match across cleavage domains, indicating considerable solution within the domains. There is no evidence of shear along the cleavage. In many places, some of the domains are widened and filled by calcite, indicating that the

shortening represented by cleavage development was followed by local extension and opening of cleavage seams.

Like the cleavage in the Pole Canyon thrust sheet adjacent to the Pole Canyon foreland anticline, the cleavage in the Mississippian carbonates of the SHFZ was probably formed by pre-thrust shortening of these rocks against a foreland buttress (i.e., the steep basement-cover contact on the southwest limb of the Rochester anticline). The northward intensification of cleavage, folding, and thrusting in the zone appears to be related to the degree of shortening of these rocks against this boundary. The principal shortening direction in the zone is N65° to 70°E, interpreted from dominant cleavage, fold-axis, and extension-fracture orientations (Fig. 21). This direction is approximately normal to the orientation of the basement-cover outcrop/subcrop boundary. The northern portion of the SHFZ was considerably more shortened against this boundary than the southern portion because of the northward steepening of dip of the basement-cover contact.

The fabric elements show a reasonably well constrained sequence of development. An early extension(?) vein set is transected by tectonic stylolites, and a later set clearly cuts both stylolites and cleavage seams. The folds are younger than the cleavage, as indicated by the fact that the cleavage fans across folds and maintains a nearly constant angle to bedding. The steep limbs of folds are cut by thrusts indicating that thrusting occurred during or after folding. Along the southern portion of the SHFZ near McCartney Creek (Fig. 16), these sets of structures have distinctly different orientations. The early extension veins are ori-

Figure 19. Fold in Lodgpole Limestone between McCartney Creek and Camp Creek showing fanning of cleavage around the fold. Pack and hammer are on outcrop right of center for scale. View is to the northwest.

Figure 20. Narrowly spaced cleavage in the Lodgepole Limestone north of Camp Creek. Hammer above center for scale. View is to the southeast.

ented east-west (Fig. 21) and may indicate an early east-west shortening. The cleavage directions are parallel to the major N20°W trend of cleavage for the entire zone and are perpendicular to the second extension vein set (N70°E) (Fig. 21). This indicates a period of shortening in a N70°E direction. The later folds and minor thrusts are oriented about N45°W, suggesting a N45°E direction of shortening (Fig. 16). It is probable, therefore, that the direction of maximum shortening changed progressively from easterly to N45°E in this area (also recently indicated by Geiger, 1986). Although a connection between this hypothesized change in shortening direction and the foreland buttress cannot be demonstrated, it may be related to a progressive refraction of directions of maximum compression with time as the foreland buttress gradually developed across the path of the frontal thrusts.

Sandy Hollow thrust system–Biltmore anticline. The Biltmore foreland anticline is located 10 to 15 km east and southeast of McCartney Mountain and is transected by the Big Hole River (Fig. 22A). It is similar to the Rochester anticline in orientation

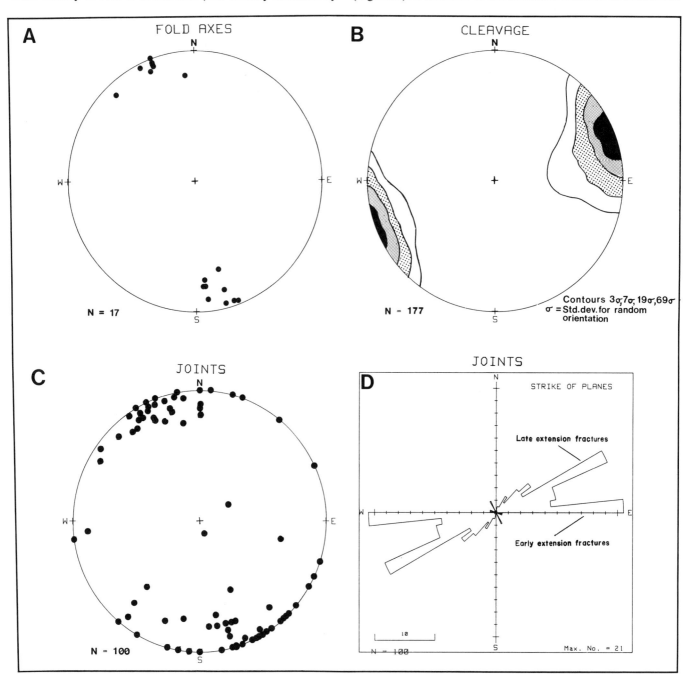

Figure 21. Lower hemisphere equal-area plots of folded axes (A), poles of cleavage (B), and poles to joints in Lodgepole Limestone along the southern Highlands fault zone (C). Inset D is a rose diagram of strikes of principal extension fracture sets (after Schmidt and Geiger, 1985).

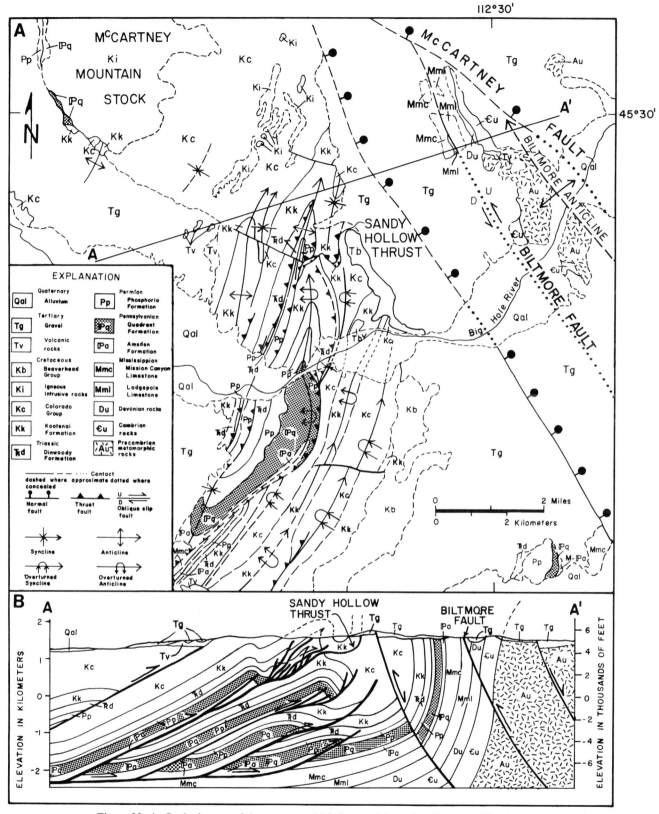

Figure 22. A, Geologic map of the east-central McCartney Mountain salient (modified from Brumbaugh, 1973; Brandon, 1984; and H. Dresser, unpublished mapping); B, Cross section A-A′ based on down-plunge projections of Brandon (1984) and seismic line interpretation of Lopez and Schmidt (1985). Location of area shown in Figure 15.

and size and is inferred to have a relationship to the Biltmore fault similar to that which the Rochester anticline has to the Laramide South Rochester fault; that is, the fold developed on the hanging wall of a northeast-dipping reverse fault in basement rocks, and, like the Rochester anticline, the northeast limb of the fold has been dropped by Neogene movement. The Neogene McCartney fault intersects the Biltmore fault obliquely. If there was Laramide movement on the McCartney fault, as suggested by Ruppel and Lopez (1984), then the Biltmore fault may originally have been a splay of the McCartney fault.

Excellent exposures of thin-skinned folds and thrusts of the McCartney Mountain salient are located 4 km west of the Biltmore foreland anticline. These structures consist of imbricate thrusts and folds in upper Paleozoic and Mesozoic rocks with thrusts merging in a décollement within the Pennsylvanian Amsden Formation (Brumbaugh and Dresser, 1976; Brandon, 1984; Schmidt and others, 1984; Lopez and Schmidt, 1985) (Fig. 22B). At least one folded thrust, the Sandy Hollow thrust, and an intensely deformed duplex zone within the uppermost limestone units of the Cretaceous Kootenai Formation characterize the strong shotening in this region (Brumbaugh and Dresser, 1976; Hendrix and Porter, 1980; Brandon, 1984). Closely spaced cleavage within the Kootenai micritic limestone units is also associated with the frontal thrusts in this part of the McCartney Mountain salient (Brumbaugh and Hendrix, 1981; Brandon, 1984; Geiger, 1986).

The shortening within the thrust belt decreases abruptly just west of the Biltmore anticline, and the spacing of major imbricate splays becomes shorter toward the frontal edge of the McCartney Mountain salient. Brandon (1984) interpreted this abrupt change in shortening and spacing to be the result of "buttressing" by the Biltmore anticline. This is not a testable hypothesis at present because of lack of exposures between the northern limit of the Sandy Hollow thrust system and the steep western flank of the Biltmore anticline (Fig. 22A). There is no obvious change in the general northeasterly trend of the thrust system at its northerly end, where it is only 3.5 km from the steep flank of the anticline, and the 50° discordance in strike between the thrust system and the anticline does not change significantly (Fig. 22A).

South of the Big Hole River the frontal thrusts appear to be progressively farther away from Biltmore anticline (Fig. 15), but seismic reflection and well data along an east-west line in this portion of the salient indicate that the frontal thrusts are blind or buried and that they do continue to the western edge of the Beaverhead River Valley (Lopez and Schmidt, 1985) (Fig. 23A). These data also show that below the easternmost thrusts the contact between Archean basement rocks and the Paleozoic cover dips steeply (30° to 45°) to the west. Several of the normal faults below the northern Beaverhead River Valley, which appear on the seismic section interpreted by Lopez and Schmidt (1985), are probably continuous with the McCartney and Biltmore faults, and with similar northwest-trending Laramide faults in the Ruby Range to the east (Figs. 15, 23A). Restoration of the inferred Neogene movement on the faults in the Beaverhead Valley

indicates the presence of an anticlinal structure that may be the continuation of the Biltmore anticline below the valley (Fig. 23B). This observation provides an explanation for the steep dip of the basement-cover contact inferred from the seismic data. The cross section alone does not indicate whether this inferred foreland structure noticeably affected the frontal thrusts of the salient or even that it was a prethrust structure. However, here too, the close-spaced imbrication in the thrust sheets immediately west of the steeply dipping basement-cover contact may be the result of crowding of the thrust sheets against a northwest-trending foreland structure. This interpretation is equivocal.

Another interpretation apparent from examination of the cross section north of the Big Hole River (Fig. 22B) and the restored seismic interpretation (Fig. 23B) is that the Biltmore foreland anticline formed after the movement on the frontal thrusts and that the uplifting of the basement and the sedimentary cover produced the concave upward curvature of the thrust front. A similar interpretation is presented by Tysdal (this volume) for a nearly identical geometry in the Blacktail salient 45 km to the south. In both cases, the foreland structures and thrust belt structures formed so near the same time that it is not possible to resolve the relative timing of the two styles. We favor the notion of impingement because it can be demonstrated with reasonable certainty in the Tobacco Root Mountains, and because it is a better—although less certain—explanation for the structures in the southern Highlands fault zone.

CONCLUSIONS

At least three sets of structures involving Archean basement rocks of the Rocky Mountain foreland influenced the geometry and kinematics of thrust belt structures at the leading edge of the fold and thrust belt in southwestern Montana. Along the generally east-trending southwestern Montana transverse zone and the convex eastward McCartney Mountain salient, two of the three sets of foreland structures, an east-trending zone and a northwest-trending set, have most significantly influenced the thrust belt structures.

The east-trending structure that is responsible for the inferred major geometry of the southwestern Montana transverse zone is a normal fault or normal fault zone of Middle Proterozoic ancestry. This normal fault zone, the Perry line, strongly influenced both the geometry and kinematics of the transverse thrust zone by providing both a southern limit to décollement thrusting in Belt Supergroup rocks of the Proterozoic Belt basin and a north-facing mechanical impediment of basement rocks that effectively translated the east-west shortening in the Belt rocks of the Helena salient into a major lateral ramp with right-reverse oblique movement. Approximately 15 to 25 km of right slip has occurred on this transverse zone, which is compatible with the west-east thrusting in the Helena salient to the north. As much as 10 km of dip-slip movement has also occurred along the transverse zone, implying an important component of north-south shortening. This is somewhat surprising, given the easterly trend of the zone

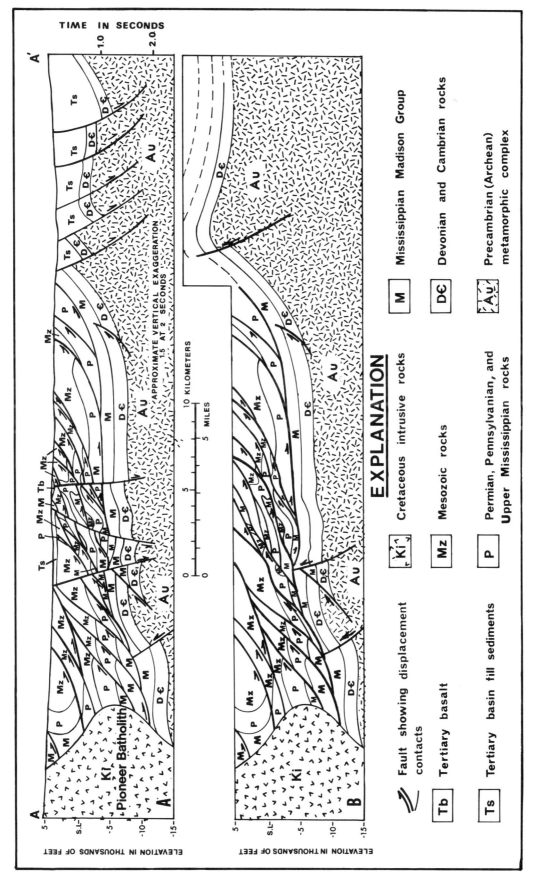

Figure 23. A, Cross section interpretation of A-A' Figure 15, based on a seismic reflection line (after Lopez and Schmidt, 1985); B, Cross section restored for Neogene movement showing Biltmore anticline (on east) and other foreland structures.

and the west-east and west-southwest–east-northeast shortening of the rocks in the salient to the north. One possible explanation for this component of north-south shortening, resulting in demonstrably oblique thrust movement, is that the trajectories of west-east maximum compression were refracted somewhat toward the north-facing foreland block, so that the resulting shortening was in a southeast direction (Beutner, 1977; Schmidt and O'Neill, 1983).

The northwest-trending foreland structures, likewise, are of Proterozoic ancestry. Left-reverse oblique movement on these northeast-dipping faults produced southwest-verging foreland anticlines prior to and during thrusting. These basement-cored folds have modified the basic east-west trend of the southwestern Montana transverse zone and have produced changes in the minor thrust sheets in the Paleozoic rocks of this zone south of the major lateral ramp. These northwest-trending foreland anticlines have also been largely responsible for the geometry and kinematics of the second-order McCartney Mountain salient.

Where thrusts of the transverse thrust zone interact with the northwest-trending foreland anticlines, minor deflections in the thrust surfaces occur over the hinges of the foreland structures. In at least one case these deflections have resulted in a younger-on-older thrust fault relationship, and in two other cases they have resulted in a local overstep or break-back hanging-wall imbrication sequence. Minor structures such as cleavage in micritic Mississippian limestones and small folds are found on the hanging-wall side of thrust sheets ahead of the foreland anticlines, indicating shortening against these foreland structures prior to and during thrusting.

The evidence that northwest-trending foreland anticlinal buttresses have influenced thrust sheets in the northern and central McCartney Mountain salient includes the curved geometry of the salient itself, the well-developed cleavage within the Mississippian limestones of the thrust sheets in front of the anticlines, increased imbrication toward the anticlines, local younger-over-older thrusts, and seismically verified, steep basement-surface dips. Eldridge and Van der Voo (this volume) have indicated strong rotations of the Cretaceous pole positions in this area, which they ascribe to thrust-sheet rotations against a foreland buttress.

We interpret the curvature of the McCartney Mountain salient to be largely the result of a changing direction of shortening from roughly west-east to southwest-northeast as the foreland anticlinal buttresses are approached from the thrust belt side. A similar salient, the Blacktail salient (Ruppel and Lopez, 1984; Perry and others, 1985), is located immediately to the south of the McCartney Mountain salient and owes its existence to similar circumstances; that is, the northwest-trending Blacktail fault (Fig. 2) is part of the regional set of northwest-trending faults and is believed to have moved up on the northeast in Late Cretaceous time forming a foreland anticline. Like the Rochester and Biltmore anticlines of the McCartney Mountain salient, this foreland feature may have caused the frontal thrusts to be deflected to the northwest. The leading edges of several of the

thrusts were subsequently folded by recurrent movement on the foreland fault, as described by Tysdal (this volume).

The third set of foreland structures, the west-dipping basement-involved thrusts and reverse faults, has influenced the thrust belt in nearby areas. For example, an inferred north-trending thrust below the Bridger Range may have been responsible for folding the east-trending thrust of the eastern portion of the transverse thrust zone (Lageson and others, 1984). In addition, the northwest-dipping Snowcrest thrust system intersects the frontal Tendoy sheet near Lima at nearly right angles to the thrust belt, causing changes in the geometry of the Tendoy and adjacent Four Eyes Canyon thrust sheets (Perry and Sando, 1983; Perry and others, this volume).

In this chapter we have cited examples of thrust belt–foreland interaction at the leading edge of the thrust belt, where interaction is most easily seen and interpreted. But foreland structures do not end at the leading edge of the thrust belt, and the overlap between the two styles of deformation extends westward well beyond the frontal thrusts (Kulik and Schmidt, this volume). The complex thrust sheet geometry of the more westerly thrusts in southwestern and west-central Montana may ultimately be better understood in terms of interaction with foreland structures that extend westward beneath the thrust belt (Kulik, 1984; Ruppel and Lopez, 1984; Skipp, this volume).

It is interesting to note that our 15-km estimate of minimum displacement in the thrust belt north of the southwest Montana transverse zone is in the range of the shortening estimated for the cratonic foreland to the south. One way to interpret this is that crustal shortening in the foreland and thrust belt were essentially the same in the region of overlap; one region involved basement, whereas the other did not. Our preference, however, is to view the deformation in the thrust belt as the product of three superimposed events. The first was movement along northwest-trending basement faults; the second was thin-skinned décollement thrusting involving principally Proterozoic and younger rocks; and the third was movement on north-trending basement-involved thrusts. Viewed in this way the actual crustal shortening within the Helena salient north of the transverse zone and in the McCartney Mountain salient southwest of it may be considerably greater than our estimates of shortening represented by the thin-skinned thrust belt structures alone.

In light of several regional syntheses of thrust belt and foreland structures presented in this volume, it is worth noting that the sets of overlapping and roughly coeval foreland and thrust belt structures discussed in this chapter are most compatible with a nearly west-east direction of shortening. The northwest-trending foreland faults have nearly equal components of reverse-dip slip and left-lateral strike-slip movement (Schmidt and Garihan, 1983). The generally north-trending and west-dipping foreland thrusts and reverse faults are chiefly dip-slip (Sheedlo, 1984; Young, 1985). Where these faults trend northeasterly, as in the Snowcrest Range and western Tobacco Root Mountains, they have minor components of right-lateral strike-slip (Sheedlo, 1984; McBride, 1988). Therefore, these two sets of foreland structures and observed variations in the sets are most likely the result of west-east shortening.

In the southwestern Montana transverse zone, the right-reverse slip movement is most compatible with a northwest-southeast direction of shortening. A slight southeastward deflection of trajectories of maximum compression oriented generally west-east could account for this observed movement on the faults of the transverse zone (Schmidt and O'Neill, 1983). The radial path of principally dip-slip movement directions on the thrusts in the McCartney Mountain salient (Brumbaugh and Hendrix, 1981) is also compatible with principal shortening in a west-east direction with local changes due to foreland interference (Beutner, 1977; Brandon, 1984).

Several syntheses in this volume propose that the regional shortening direction for foreland structures or for thrust-belt structures, or for both, was oriented southwest-northeast in northern Wyoming, western Montana, and eastern Idaho (see chapters by Brown, Hamilton, and Sears, this volume). This direction is not compatible with structures we have observed in the thrust belt and the foreland in the vicinity of the southwest Montana transverse zone. It is possible that the shortening direction shifted to a southwest-northeast orientation in Paleocene and Eocene time, as has been suggested by Gries (1983), and that the pattern of structures is a product of a range of shortening directions between west-east and southwest-northeast. This suggestion cannot be tested at present because of a lack of precise data on the relative timing of structures produced by different shortening directions. What is reasonably clear in the region we have discussed is that both the thrust belt and foreland structures are manifestations of a Late Cretaceous to early Paleocene direction of principally west-east shortening with a minor component of northwest-southeast shortening in the southwestern Montana transverse zone and a minor component of southwest-northeast shortening in the northern McCartney Mountain salient.

ACKNOWLEDGMENTS

We thank Nancy Arnold, Carol Harkness, and Beverly Britt for typing the manuscript, Bob Havira for assistance in the photography work, and Pete Haff, Barry McBride, Jeff Brown, Bob Versical, and Bob Havira for help with drafting. We have learned much from discussions about this area with other geologists, including Dave Brumbaugh, Ed Ruppel, Jack Garihan, Hugh Dresser, Dave Lopez, Bill Thomas, Dave Lageson, Harry Smedes, Beth Geiger, and Bill Perry. W.C.B. also thanks Jim Sears and Dave Ault for their help and advice. Bruce Bryant, Bill Johnson, Dave Brumbaugh, Hugh Dresser, and Bill Perry read earlier versions of this chapter and collectively provided a thorough review. A portion of this work was supported by National Science Foundation Grant EAR-7926380 (to C.S. and J. M. Garihan) and by a Western Michigan University Faculty Research Fund Grant (to C.S.).

REFERENCES CITED

Alexander, R. G., Jr., 1955, Geology of the Whitehall area, Montana: Yellowstone-Bighorn Research Association Contribution 195, 111 p.

Berg, R. R., 1962 Mountain flank thrusting in Rocky Mountain foreland, Wyoming and Colorado: American Association of Petroleum Geologists Bulletin, v. 46, p. 2019–2032.

Berry, G. W., 1943, Stratigraphy and structure at Three Forks, Montana: Geological Society of America Bulletin, v. 54, p. 1–30.

Beutner, E. C., 1977, Causes and consequences of curvature in the Sevier orogenic belt, Utah to Montana: Wyoming Geological Association 29th Annual Field Conference Guidebook, p. 353–365.

Borradaile, G. J., Bayly, M. C., and Powell, C. McA., eds., 1982, Atlas of deformational and metamorphic rock fabrics: New York, Springer-Verlag, 551 p.

Brandon, W. C., 1984, An origin for the McCartney's Mountain salient of the southwestern Montana fold and thrust belt [M.S. thesis]: Missoula, University of Montana, 128 p.

Brown, W. G., 1983, Sequential development of the fold-thrust model of foreland deformation, *in* Lowell, J. D., ed., Rocky Mountain foreland basins and uplifts: Denver, Colorado, Rocky Mountain Association of Geologists, p. 57–64.

Brumbaugh, D. S., 1973, Structural analysis of the complexly deformed Big Hole area, Beaverhead, Madison and Silver Bow Counties, Montana [Ph.D. thesis]: Bloomington, Indiana University, 96 p.

Brumbaugh, D. S., and Dresser, H. W., 1976, Exposed step in Laramide thrust fault, southwest Montana: American Association of Petroleum Geologists Bulletin, v. 60, no. 12, p. 2142–2150.

Brumbaugh, D. S., and Hendrix, T. E., 1981, The McCarthy Mountain structural salient, southwestern Montana, *in* Tucker, T. E., ed., Southwest Montana: Montana Geological Society Field Conference and Symposium Guidebook, p. 201–209.

Dahlstrom, C.D.A., 1970, Structural geology in the eastern margin of the Canadian Rocky Mountains: Bulletin of Canadian Petroleum Geology, v. 18, p. 332–406.

Davis, W. E., Kinoshita, W. T., and Robinson, G. D., 1965, Bouger gravity, aeromagnetic, and generalized geologic map of the western part of the Three Forks Basin, Jefferson, Broadwater, Madison, and Gallatin Counties, Montana: U.S. Geological Survey Geophysical Investigations Map GP-497, scale 1:62,500.

DeCelles, P. G., Tolson, R. B., Graham, S. A., Smith, G. A., Ingersoll, R. V., White, J., Schmidt, C. J., Rice, T., Moxon, I., Lemke, L., Handschy, J. W., Follo, M. F., Edwards, D. P., Cavazza, W., Caldwell, M., and Bargar, E., 1987, Laramide thrust-generated alluvial-fan sedimentation, southwestern Montana: American Association of Petroleum Geologists Bulletin, v. 71, p. 135–155.

Engelder, T., and Marshak, S., 1985, Disjunctive cleavage formed at shallow depths in sedimentary rocks: Journal of Structural Geology, v. 7, no. 3/4, p. 3.

Garrett, H. L., 1972, Structural geology of the Crazy Mountain basin: Montana Geological Society 21st Annual Field Conference Guidebook, p. 113–118.

Geiger, B. C., 1986, Ductile strain in the overlap zone between the Cordilleran thrust belt and the Rocky Mountain foreland near Melrose, Montana: [M.S. thesis]: Missoula, University of Montana, 47 p.

Gries, R. R., 1983, North-south compression of Rocky Mountain foreland structures, *in* Lowell, J. R., ed., Rocky Mountain foreland basins and uplifts: Denver, Colorado, Rocky Mountain Association of Geologists, p. 9–32.

Harris, S. A., 1957, The tectonics of Montana as related to the Belt Series: Billings Geological Society 8th Annual Field Conference Guidebook, p. 22–33.

Harrison, J. E., Griggs, A. G., and Wells, J. D., 1974, Tectonic features of the Precambrian Belt basin and their influence on post-Belt structures: U.S. Geological Survey Professional Paper 866, 15 p.

Hawley, D., Bonnett-Nicoloyson, A., and Coppinger, W., 1982, Stratigraphy, depositional environments, and paleotectonics of the LaHood Formation: Montana State University Department of Earth Sciences Publication 2, 20 p.

Hendrix, T. E., and Porter, E., 1980, Sandy Hollow collision structure, *in* Miller, M., ed., Guidebook of the Drummond-Elkhorn areas, west-central Montana: Montana Bureau of Mines and Geology Special Publication 82, p. 25–34.

Karasevich, L. P., Garihan, J. M., Dahl, P. S., and Okuma, A. F., 1981, Summary of Precambrian Metamorphic and structural history, Ruby Range, southwest Montana, *in* Tucker, T. E., ed., Southwest Montana: Montana Geological Society Field Conference and Symposium Guidebook, p. 225–237.

Klepper, M. R., 1950, A geologic reconnaissance of parts of Beaverhead and Madison counties, Montana: U.S. Geological Survey Bulletin 969–C, p. 53–85.

Kulik, D. M., 1984, A structural model for the overlap zone between the Rocky Mountain foreland and the Cordilleran thrust belt in southwestern Montana: Geological Society of America Abstracts with Programs, v. 16, p. 227.

Lageson, D. R., Kelly, M. C., and Zim, J. C., 1984, Superimposed styles of deformation in the Bridger Range, southwestern Montana: Geological Society of America Abstracts with Programs, v. 16, no. 6, p. 567.

Lopez, D. A., and Schmidt, C. J., 1985, Seismic profile across the leading edge of the fold and thrust belt in southwestern Montana, *in* Gries, R. R., and Dyer, R. C., eds., Seismic exploration of the Rocky Mountain region: Rocky Mountain Association of Geologists and Denver Geophysical Society, p. 45–50.

Lowell, W. R., 1956, Unconformity between Belt Series and Archean metamorphic rocks, Montana [abs.]: Geological Society of America Bulletin, v. 67, no. 12, p. 1717.

Mann, J. A., 1954, Geology of part of the Gravelly Range, Montana: Yellowstone-Bighorn Research Association Contribution 190, 92 p.

Maughan, E. K., and Perry, W. J., Jr., 1986, Lineaments and their tectonic implications in the Rocky Mountains and adjacent plains region, *in* Peterson, J. A., ed., Paleotectonics and sedimentation in the Rocky Mountain region: American Association of Petroleum Geologists Memoir 41, p. 41–53.

McBride, B. C., 1988, Effects of Late Cretaceous compression in southwestern Montana: Implications of thrust motions and Rocky Mountain foreland deformation: Geological Society of America Abstracts with Programs, v. 20, no. 6, p. 431.

McMannis, W. J., 1955, Geology of the Bridger Range, Montana: Geological Society of America Bulletin, v. 66, p. 1385–1430.

—— , 1963, LaHood Formation; A coarse facies of the Belt Series in southwestern Montana: Geological Society of America Bulletin, v. 74, p. 407–436.

Monroe, J. S., 1976, Vertibrate paleontology, stratigraphy, and sedimentation of the Upper Ruby River Basin, Madison County, Montana [Ph.D. thesis]: Missoula, University of Montana, 301 p.

Nichols, D. J., Perry, W. J., Jr., and Haley, J. C., 1985, Reinterpretation of the palynology and age of Laramide syntectonic deposits, southwestern Montana, and revision of the Beaverhead Group: Geology, v. 13, p. 149–153.

O'Neill, J. M., Ferris, D. C., Hanneman, D. L., and Schmidt, C. J., 1986, Recurrent movement along northwest-trending faults, Southern Highland Mountains, southwestern Montana, *in* Roberts, S. M., Belt Supergroup: Montana Bureau of Mines and Geology Special Publication 94, p. 209–216.

Perry, W. J., Jr., and Sando, W. J., 1983, Sequence of deformation of Cordilleran thrust belt in Lima, Montana region, *in* Powers, R. B., ed., Geologic studies of the Cordilleran thrust belt–1982: Denver, Colorado, Rocky Mountain Association of Geologists, v. 1, p. 137–144.

Perry, W. J., Jr., Ryder, R. T., and Maughan, E. K., 1981, The southern part of the southwest Montana thrust belt, *in* Tucker, T. E., ed., Southwest Montana: Montana Geological Society 1981 Field Conference and Symposium Guidebook, p. 261–273.

Perry, W. J., Jr., Wardlaw, B. R., Bostick, N. H., and Maughan, E. K., 1983, Structure, burial history, and petroleum potential of the frontal thrust belt and adjacent foreland, southwest Montana: American Association of Petroleum Geologists Bulletin, v. 67, no. 5, p. 725–743.

Perry, W. J., Jr., Sando, W. J., and Sandberg, C. A., 1985, Structural geometry of newly defined Blacktail salient of Montana thrust belt [abs.]: American Association of Petroleum Geologists Bulletin, v. 69, no. 5, p. 858–859.

Reid, R. R., 1957, Bedrock geology of the north end of the Tobacco Root Mountains, Madison County, Montana: Montana Bureau of Mines and Geology Memoir 36, 25 p.

Roberts, A. E., 1972, Cretaceous and early Tertiary depositional and tectonic history of the Livingston area, southwestern Montana: U.S. Geological Survey Professional Paper 526–C, 119 p.

Robinson, G. D., 1963, Geology of the Three Forks Quadrangle, Montana: U.S. Geological Survey Professional Paper 370, 143 p.

Royce, F., Jr., Warner, M. A., and Reese, D. L., 1975, Thrust belt structural geometry and related stratigraphic problems, Wyoming, Idaho-northern Utah, *in* Bolyard, D. W., ed., Symposium on deep drilling in the central Rocky Mountains: Denver, Colorado, Rocky Mountain Association of Geologists, p. 41–54.

Ruppel, E. T., and Lopez, D. A., 1984, The thrust belt in southwest Montana and east-central Idaho: U.S. Geological Survey Professional Paper 1278, 41 p.

Ruppel, E. T., Wallace, C. A., Schmidt, R. G., and Lopez, D. A., 1981, Preliminary interpretation of the thrust belt in southwest and west-central Montana and east-central Idaho, *in* Tucker, T. E., ed., Southwest Montana: Montana Geological Society Field Conference and Symposium Guidebook, p. 139–159.

Ruppel, E. T., O'Neill, J. M., and Lopez, D. A., 1983, Preliminary geologic map of the Dillon 1° by 2° Quadrangle, Montana: U.S. Geological Survey Open-File Report 83–168, scale 1:250,000.

Samuelson, K. J., and Schmidt, C. J., 1981, Structural geology of the western Tobacco Root Mountains, southwestern Montana, *in* Southwest Montana: Montana Geological Society Field Conference and Symposium Guidebook, p. 191–199 with map, scale 1:24,000.

Schmidt, C. J., 1975, An analysis of folding and faulting in the northern Tobacco Root Mountains, southwest Montana [Ph.D. thesis]: Bloomington, Indiana University, 480 p.

—— , 1976, Structural development of the Lewis and Clark Cavern State Park area, southwest Montana: Montana Bureau of Mines and Geology Special Publication 73, p. 141–150.

—— , 1983, Factors which control the trend and position of transverse thrust ramps, southwestern Montana: Geological Society of America Abstracts with Programs, v. 15, no. 1, p. 10.

Schmidt, C. J., and Garihan, J. M., 1979, A summary of Laramide basement faulting in the Ruby, Tobacco Root, and Madison Range and its possible relationship to Precambrian continental rifting: Geological Society of America Abstracts with Programs, v. 11, no. 6, p. 301.

—— , 1983, Laramide Tectonic development of the Rocky Mountain foreland of southwestern Montana, *in* Lowell, J. D., ed., Rocky Mountain foreland basins and uplifts: Denver, Colorado, Rocky Mountain Association of Geologists, p. 271–294.

—— , 1986, Middle Proterozoic and Laramide tectonic activity along the southern margin of the Belt basin, *in* Roberts, S. M., Belt Supergroup: Montana Bureau of Mines and Geology Special Publication 94, p. 217–235.

Schmidt, C. J., and Geiger, B., 1985, Nature of deformation in foreland anticlines and impinging thrust belt; Tobacco Root and southern Highland Mountains, Montana: Tobacco Root Geological Society 10th Annual Field Conference Guidebook, p. 41–65.

Schmidt, C. J., and Hendrix, T. E., 1981, Tectonic controls for thrust belt and Rocky Mountains foreland structures in the northern Tobacco Root Mountains-Jefferson Canyon area, southwestern Montana, *in* Tucker, T. E., ed., Southwest Montana: Montana Geological Society Field Conference and Symposium Guidebook, p. 167–180.

Schmidt, C. J., and O'Neill, J. M., 1983, Structural evolution of the southwest Montana transverse zone, *in* Powers, R. W., ed., Geologic studies of the Cordilleran thrust belt–1982: Denver, Colorado, Rocky Mountain Association of Geologists, v. 1, p. 193–218.

Schmidt, C. J., O'Neill, J. M., and Brandon, W. C., 1984, Influence of foreland structures on the geometry and kinematics of the frontal thrust belt, southwestern Montana: Geological Society of America Abstracts with Programs, v. 16, no. 6, p. 647.

Scholten, R., 1967, Structural framework and oil potential of extreme southwestern Montana: Montana Geological Society 18th Annual Field Conference Guidebook, p. 7–19.

—— , 1983, Continental subduction in the northern U.S. Rockies; A model for back-arc thrusting in the western Cordillera, *in* Powers, R. B., ed., Geologic studies of the Cordilleran thrust belt–1982: Denver, Colorado, Rocky Mountain Association of Geologists, v. 1, p. 123–136.

Serra, S., 1977, Styles of deformation in the ramp regions of overthrust faults; Wyoming Geological Society 29th Annual Field Conference Guidebook, p. 487–498.

Sheedlo, M. K., 1984, Structural geology of the northern Snowcrest Range, Beaverhead and Madison Counties, Montana [M.S. thesis]: Kalamazoo, Western Michigan University, 131 p.

Skipp, B., and McGrew, L. W., 1977, The Maudlow and Sedan Formations of the Upper Cretaceous Livingston Group on the west edge of the Crazy Mountains basin, Montana: U.S. Geological Survey Bulletin 1422-B, p. B1–B68.

Smedes, H. W., 1967, Preliminary geologic map of the Butte South Quadrangle, Montana: U.S. Geological Survey Open-File Report, scale 1:48,000.

Tilford, M. J., 1976, Structural analysis of the southern and western Greenhorn Range, Madison County, Montana, and magnetic beneficiation of Montana talc ores [M.S. thesis]: Bloomington, Indiana University, 143 p.

Tilling, R. I., Klepper, M. R., and Obradovich, J. D., 1968, K-Ar ages and time span of emplacement of the Boulder batholith, Montana: American Journal of Science, v. 266, p. 671–689.

Thom, W. T., Jr., 1957, Tectonic relationships, evolutionary history, and mechanics of origin of the Crazy Mountain Basin, Montana: Billings Geological Society 8th Annual Field Conference Guidebook, p. 9–21.

Tysdal, R. G., 1976, Geologic map of the northern part of the Ruby Range, Madison County, Montana: U.S. Geological Survey Miscellaneous Geologic Investigations Map I–951, scale 1:24,000.

—— , 1986, Thrust faults and back thrusts in Madison Range of southwestern Montana foreland: American Association of Petroleum Geologists Bulletin, v. 70, no. 4, p. 360–376.

Tysdal, R. G., Marvin, R. F., and DeWitt, E., 1986, Late Cretaceous stratigraphy, deformation, and intrusion in the Madison Range of southwestern Montana: Geological Society of America Bulletin, v. 97, p. 851–868.

Verrall, P., 1955, Geology of the Horseshoe Hills area, Montana [Ph.D. thesis]: Princeton University, 261 p.

Wiltschko, D. V., and Eastman, D. B., 1983, Role of basement warps and faults in localizing thrust fault ramps, *in* Contributions to tectonics and geophysics of mountain chains: Geological Society of America Memoir 158, p. 177–190.

Winston, D., 1986, Sedimentation and tectonics of the Middle Proterozoic Belt Basin and their influence on Phanerozoic compression and extension in western Montana and northern Idaho, *in* Peterson, J., ed., Paleotectonics and sedimentation: American Association of Petroleum Geologists Memoir 41, p. 87–118.

Wooden, J. L., Vitaliano, C. J., Koehler, S. W., and Ragland, P. C., 1978, The late Precambrian mafic dikes of the southern Tobacco Root Mountains, Montana; Geochemistry, Rb-Sr geochronology, and relationship to Belt tectonics: Canadian Journal of Earth Sciences, v. 15, p. 467–479.

Young, S. W., 1985, Structural history of the Jordan Creek area, northern Madison Range, Madison County, Montana [M.S. thesis]: Austin, University of Texas, 112 p.

MANUSCRIPT ACCEPTED BY THE SOCIETY FEBRUARY 9, 1988

Geological Society of America
Memoir 171
1988

Deformation along the northeast side of Blacktail Mountains salient, southwestern Montana

Russell G. Tysdal
U.S. Geological Survey, MS 905, Box 25046, Denver Federal Center, Denver, Colorado 80225

ABSTRACT

The Blacktail Mountains salient is a convex-eastward area of stacked Laramide-age thrust faults that trend north and dip west at moderate angles. The thrusts occur in Mississippian to Cretaceous strata above a basement of Archean metamorphic rocks. The northern margin of the salient is delimited by the Jake Canyon fault, a northwest-trending, northeast-dipping Laramide reverse fault. During the Laramide orogeny, the fault formed a common boundary of the present-day Blacktail Mountains and a structural high that existed in the area of the present-day valley of Blacktail Deer Creek. The fault juxtaposed Archean metamorphic rocks upon Phanerozoic strata in the northwestern half of its extent, and against other Archean metamorphic rocks in the southeastern half. General structural relationships and study of small-scale structures in local areas show that movement along the Jake Canyon fault caused deformation of the north-trending thrust faults and associated folds. During Cenozoic extensional faulting, the Blacktail fault developed northeast of the Jake Canyon fault, and generally delimits the southwestern side of the basin of sedimentary rocks that lies beneath the valley of Blacktail Deer Creek.

INTRODUCTION

The Blacktail Mountains are a northwest-trending range in the Rocky Mountains of southwestern Montana, about 20 km (12 mi) south of Dillon (Fig. 1). They are flanked on the northeast by a basin from which they are separated by the Blacktail fault, a basin-and-range normal fault. The mountains were uplifted along this fault during the mid- to late Cenozoic and now display a northeast face that rises abruptly from alluvial fans at about the 1,825-m (6,000-ft) elevation, to the range crest at about 2,900 m (9,500 ft). To the southwest, the mountains slope gently beneath Cenozoic volcanic and sedimentary rocks. The mountain range is tilted to the northwest, such that erosion has exposed progressively older rocks to the southeast. The Blacktail Mountains lie in a zone of overlap of the Cordilleran thrust belt and the crystalline basement of the Rocky Mountain foreland.

Sevier-style (thin-skin) thrust faults of Laramide age are present within the northwestern part of the Blacktail Mountains and were first recognized and mapped by Pecora (1981). The thrusts strike northward, dip westward at low angles, and are accompanied by north-trending, east-verging overturned mesoscopic folds. The faults and folds are confined to Mississippian

and younger Paleozoic strata; they have not been recognized in the underlying Paleozoic strata or Archean metamorphic rocks. The thrusts form part of a convex-eastward zone that Ruppel and Lopez (1984) named the Blacktail Mountains salient (Fig. 1). The present-day expression of the salient is, at least in part, a pattern reflecting erosion of sedimentary strata from above the Archean rocks.

During the Laramide orogeny, the foreland in the region east of Dillon was deformed into a large southwest-plunging basement-involved arch called the Blacktail-Snowcrest uplift (Fig. 1) (Scholten and others, 1955; Scholten, 1967). Basin-and-range faults later segmented the uplift into individual mountain ranges, including the Blacktail Mountains and the Ruby Range. The area of the uplift is delimited on the southeast by the northwest-dipping Snowcrest-Greenhorn system of thrust faults, some of which juxtaposed Archean metamorphic rocks over Phanerozoic strata (Klepper, 1950; Heinrich, 1960; Hadley, 1969; Berg, 1979; Sheedlo, 1984; Perry and others, this volume). Northwest of the Ruby Range (Fig. 1), the uplift is delimited by the Beaverhead Valley, the eastern, normal fault–bounded edge of which probably formed along the leading part of a basement-involved thrust fault that Schmidt and Garihan (1983) showed is exposed locally along the northwestern edge of the Ruby Range. In the Blacktail Mountains, the northwestern limit of the uplift is concealed by thrusted strata of the Blacktail Mountains salient.

Several faults active during the Laramide orogeny trend northwest across western ranges of the Blacktail-Snowcrest uplift, and are part of a system of such faults present in the southwestern Montana foreland. The faults dip steeply and, where Phanerozoic strata are preserved on top of the Archean metamorphic rocks, are flanked by an anticline on the upthrown side and a syncline on the downthrown side. Characteristics of the northwest-trending faults and folds in southwestern Montana were recently summarized in a regional synthesis by Schmidt and Garihan (1983). Similar faults and folds present elsewhere in the Rocky Mountain foreland, as well as these of Montana, have been attributed to either vertical tectonic movements, as advocated by Prucha and others (1965), Stearns (1971), and many subsequent workers, or to compressional forces, as advocated by Berg (1962), Sales (1968), and many other workers. In the Ruby Range area of the Blacktail-Snowcrest uplift, some of the northwest-trending faults have a throw of more than 2,000 m (6,500 ft) (Tysdal, 1976, 1981), and display a strike-slip component of movement as well (Schmidt and Garihan, 1983, 1986). One of the faults in the Ruby Range and several in the Tobacco Root Mountains (Fig. 1) were shown by Schmidt and Garihan (1983, 1986) to have originated during Precambrian time and to have been reactivated during the Laramide orogeny. In a later paper, Schmidt and Garihan (1986) discussed the role of recurrent movement along the northwest-trending faults.

The Jake Canyon fault is a major northwest-trending fault of the Blacktail Mountains area of the Blacktail-Snowcrest uplift. The fault displaced Archean metamorphic rocks against Phanerozoic strata along a zone that later became the northeast flank of the Blacktail Mountains (Fig. 2) (Tysdal and others, 1987). Phanerozoic strata immediately southwest of the fault were folded to form the northwest-plunging Blacktail syncline. This chapter describes the structures associated with the Jake Canyon fault and shows that the thrust faults and associated folds of the Blacktail Mountains salient were deformed by subsequent movement along the steeply dipping Jake Canyon fault.

In general, for the southwestern Montana foreland, the north-trending thrust faults and the Sevier-style thrusts where they encountered the foreland were emplaced after movement had ceased on the steeply dipping northwest-trending faults (Schmidt and Garihan, 1983). However, both sets of faults may have been active concurrently earlier in their Laramide histories. Specific examples of thrust plates impinging against uplifted blocks (buttresses) that flanked the northwest-trending faults have been described by Samuelson and Schmidt (1981), Tysdal and others (1986), and Schmidt and others (this volume). The relative sequence of movement observed along the Jake Canyon fault and the thrust faults of the Blacktail Mountains salient does not fit the general pattern. It is not the only exception, however, as Schmidt

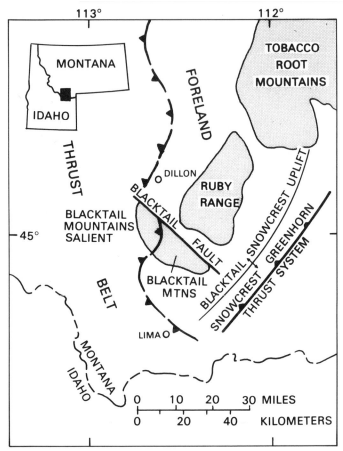

Figure 1. Index map of southwestern Montana showing location of thrust belt, foreland, and Blacktail Mountains salient.

and others (this volume) cite an example about 45 km (28 mi) north of the Blacktail Mountains where thrust faults apparently were deformed along the Biltmore anticline; Schmidt and Hendrix (1981) gave other examples.

PREVIOUS WORK

Previous work in or near the study area in the Blacktail Mountains includes the regional geologic mapping studies of Klepper (1950), and Scholten and others (1955). More detailed mapping was undertaken by Lowell (1949), at the northern end of the mountains, and by Tysdal (1988) along the entire length of the mountain front. Thesis mapping studies were conducted in parts of the mountains by Mannion (1948), Beard (1949), Keenmon (1950), Achuff (1981a,b), Pecora (1981, 1987), and Zeigler (1954). Topical work related to regional studies was conducted by Heinrich (1960), who examined Archean metamorphic rocks near Jake Canyon, about 5 km (3 mi) south of the study area; by Giletti (1966), who radiometrically dated metamorphic rocks from several localities within the Blacktail Mountains; and by Pardee (1950), who examined the Blacktail fault along the mountain front. Other topical work related to regional studies was concerned primarily with measurement of stratigraphic sections in the Blacktail Mountains and includes that of Hanson (1952) for Cambrian rocks; Huh (1967), and Wardlaw and Pecora (1985), for Mississippian strata; several papers concerning phosphate in the Permian Phosphoria Formation, but particularly Cressman and Swanson (1964), Yochelson (1968), Swanson (1970), and Schock and others (1981); Sloss and Moritz (1951), concerning several Paleozoic formations; and Moritz (1951), concerning Triassic strata. Mineral resource studies include a brief comment by Sinkler (1942), concerning mineral deposits near Jake Canyon; and mineral resource studies on lands being considered for inclusion in the nation's wilderness system, conducted by Benham (1986) and Tysdal and others (1987). Gravity data obtained in support of mineral resource studies were collected by Hassemer and others (1986).

STRATIGRAPHY

Rock units present in the Blacktail Mountains study area shown in Figure 2 are described briefly, in ascending order, in this section. The sequence and thicknesses of units are shown in the stratigraphic column of the figure. Archean metamorphic rocks underlie the study area and constitute most of the exposed rocks of the Blacktail Mountains south of the study area. The rocks, chiefly of the amphibolite grade of metamorphism, are mainly gneisses of intermediate to felsic composition. Paleozoic strata unconformably overlie the Archean rocks and aggregate 1,050 to 1,375 m (3,500 to 4,500 ft) thick, depending on structural interpretations. Middle and Late Cambrian formations, chiefly limestone and dolomite, make up the lower part of the Paleozoic sequence (Hanson, 1952). They are overlain by rubbly dolomite of the Late Devonian Jefferson Formation, and siltstone, limestone, and evaporite-solution breccia of the Three Forks Formation. Limestone strata of the Early and Late Mississippian Madison Group, made up of the Lodgepole and Mission Canyon Formations, constitute as much as 610 m (2,000 ft) of the Paleozoic section (Huh, 1967; Pecora, 1981).

The Late Mississippian Kibbey Sandstone, Lombard Formation, and Conover Ranch Formation (formerly assigned to the Amsden Formation), were first recognized in the Blacktail Mountains by Pecora (1981), constitute the Snowcrest Range Group of Wardlaw and Pecora (1985). The Lombard is composed of thin limestone beds that deformed readily during thrust faulting in the Blacktail Mountains salient and required that Pecora (1981) reconstruct Lombard stratigraphy from three tectonic sequences. Depending on structural assumptions, its thickness is 91 to 183 m (350 to 600 ft). The remaining Paleozoic rocks are assigned to the Quadrant Sandstone, composed entirely of quartz sandstone, and the Phosphoria Formation, composed of sandstone, dolomite, chert, and phosphatic mudstone.

The lower part of the Mesozoic sequence, about 460 m (1,500 ft) thick, is composed of mudstone and dolomite of the Triassic Dinwoody Formation; nonmarine sandstone, siltstone, and mudstone of the Morrison and Kootenai Formations; and

about 30 m (100 ft) of marine shale assigned to the Cretaceous Blackleaf Formation. In nearby areas of southwestern Montana, the sequence of Blackleaf and younger marine and marginal marine strata is much thicker, indicating extensive erosion within the study area prior to deposition of younger Cretaceous rocks.

The upper part of the Mesozoic sequence comprises several hundred meters of synorogenic conglomerate of the Cretaceous Beaverhead Group, which unconformably overlies older Phanerozoic formations. Some of the conglomerate, particularly limestone clasts derived from Mississippian formations, probably is detritus eroded from an arching Blacktail-Snowcrest uplift, as suggested by Scholten (1967). Other clastics of the conglomerate are composed of material shed eastward from thrust sheets advancing from the west. Some of this conglomerate is rich in pebbles and cobbles eroded from Proterozoic Belt Supergroup strata, which crop in the thrust belt several kilometers west of the Blacktail-Snowcrest uplift. In the northwestern part of the Blacktail Mountains, clasts derived from Belt Supergroup strata are mixed with clasts derived from Phanerozoic rocks. No outcrops composed wholly of Belt clasts were observed.

Cenozoic rocks make up only a small part of the map area and are mainly rhyolitic and basaltic volcanic rocks, basin-fill sedimentary strata, and alluvium. The basin flanking the mountains on the northeast contains Cenozoic rocks that are largely concealed by Quaternary alluvial deposits.

JAKE CANYON FAULT

The northwest-trending Jake Canyon fault was named for a zone of jasperoid and tectonic breccia in Archean gneiss (Tysdal and others, 1987). The zone is especially prominent near the mouth of Jake Canyon, along the northeast face of the Blacktail Mountains, 5 km (3 mi) southeast of the map area in Figure 2. Northwestward toward Small Horn Canyon (Fig. 2), the fault can be delimited locally by Archean gneiss that has been juxtaposed against Paleozoic limestone, by jasperoid that has replaced the gneiss, and by reddish brown, hydrothermally altered and oxidized breccia.

The Jake Canyon fault dips 45° to 75° to the northeast, where the footwall is Paleozoic sedimentary rocks, but southeastward, where the fault is entirely in Archean metamorphic rocks, the dip ranges from about 40° to 60°. Within the area of Archean rocks, southeast of the area in Figure 2, the fault may have been reactivated during Cenozoic extensional faulting. Near Price's Canyon, 18 km (11 mi) southeast of the area in Figure 2, Zeigler (1954) reported that Miocene volcanic rocks were downdropped basinward along part of the fault, which he considered to be a strand of the Blacktail fault.

During the Laramide orogeny, the Jake Canyon fault formed the mutual boundary of the area of the present-day Blacktail Mountains and a structurally high block, hereinafter called the Blacktail Valley block, that occupied the present area of the valley of Blacktail Deer Creek northeast of the mountains. Later, during Cenozoic extension, the Blacktail Valley block was

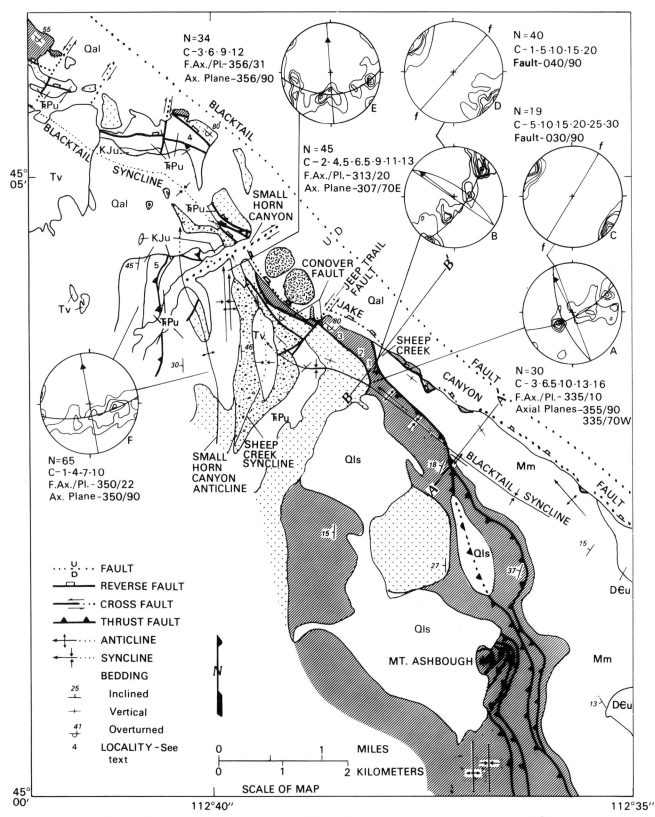

Figure 2. Geologic map of northern margin of Blacktail Mountains salient, showing stereographic plots of poles to bedding of folded strata (plots A, B, E, F) and cross faults (plots C, D). N = Number of measurements; C = contour intervals (in percentage per 1 percent area); F. Ax./Pl. = fold axis/plunge; Ax. Plane = axial plane. Stereo plot F represents the entire area shown of the Small Horn anticline.

SYMBOL	SYSTEM	ROCK UNIT	THICK-NESS METERS (FEET)	SYMBOL	SYSTEM		ROCK UNIT	THICK-NESS METERS (FEET)
	MISSISSIPPIAN	LOMBARD LIMESTONE	91-183 (350-600)	Qal	QUAT.		ALLUVIUM	
		KIBBEY SANDSTONE	30-49 (100-160)	Qls			LANDSLIDE DEPOSIT	
Mm		MISSION CANYON LIMESTONE	305 (1000)	QTb			CENOZOIC BASIN DEPOSITS	?
		LODGEPOLE LIMESTONE	305 (1000)	Tv	TERTIARY		VOLCANIC ROCKS	
	DEV.	THREE FORKS FORMATION	18 (60)				RHYOLITE—44.0±1.6 m.y.	
		JEFFERSON FORMATION	30-37 (100-120)		CRET.		BEAVERHEAD GROUP	?
DЄu	CAMBRIAN	PILGRIM LIMESTONE	30-38 (100-125)				BLACKLEAF FORMATION	30 (100)
		PARK SHALE	30-61 (100-200)	KJu			KOOTENAI FORMATION	305 (1000)
		MEAGHER LIMESTONE	175 (575)			JU.	MORRISON FORMATION	61 (200)
		WOLSEY SHALE	15-46 (50-150)	ЂPu	PN.PERTRI.		DINWOODY FORMATION	152 (500)
		FLATHEAD SANDSTONE	9-30 (30-100)				PHOSPHORIA FORMATION	91 (300)
	ARCHEAN	GNEISS, UNDIVIDED	— —			PN.	QUADRANT SANDSTONE	221 (725)
						M.	CONOVER RANCH FORMATION	30 (100)

downdropped along the Blacktail fault, within the zone of structural weakness associated with the Jake Canyon fault. A few outcrops of Archean gneiss are preserved along the mountain front in the area of Phanerozoic strata (for example, at the mouth of Sheep Creek), severed from the Blacktail Valley block by the Blacktail fault. Existence of the structurally high block during Laramide time, and later isolation of Archean outcrops during Tertiary normal faulting, was recognized originally by Pecora (1981). Achuff (1981b) also recognized these features but considered them to be of late Tertiary and Recent origin. Northwest of Ashbough Canyon (Fig. 2), Archean gneiss is here inferred to exist between the Blacktail fault and the Jake Canyon fault, but is concealed by Quaternary alluvial fan deposits. Southeast of Ashbough Canyon and the area of Phanerozoic strata, the Jake Canyon fault curves into the mountains about 1.5 km (1 mi) before continuing southeastward, and a larger area of Archean rocks is preserved between the two faults.

The original age of the Jake Canyon fault is uncertain; it may have formed during the Precambrian, as has been demonstrated by Schmidt and Garihan (1983) for several other northwest-trending faults in the crystalline foreland of southwestern Montana. However, no evidence was found to confirm the possibility for the Jake Canyon fault. The fault likely was active throughout the Laramide orogeny, but the data presented here bear only on its latest Laramide movement relative to that of the thrust faults and associated folds of the Blacktail Mountains salient.

RELATIVE AGE OF MOVEMENT OF THRUST FAULTS AND JAKE CANYON FAULT

The east-directed thrust faults and associated folds of the Blacktail Mountains were interpreted by Pecora (1981) as forming during a time in which the Blacktail Valley block existed. The interpretation favored here, however, is that the structurally high Blacktail Valley block was uplifted after the east-directed thrusting, as indicated by several general lines of evidence. The low-angle, westward-dipping thrust faults mapped by Pecora (1981) occupy about the same stratigraphic horizon; from south to north, as the thrusts approach the northeastern flank of the mountains (Fig. 2), their curvature in plan view is only apparent and is a result of steep topography. The thrust faults steepen abruptly adjacent to the Jake Canyon fault, in concert with upturning of strata along the mountain front. Had the Blacktail Valley block existed at the time of thrusting, the Phanerozoic rocks presently preserved in the Blacktail Mountains would have been flanked on the northeast by Archean metamorphic rocks of the uplifted block. Thrust faults, subsequently developed within the Phanerozoic strata of the then relative downthrown block of the present Blacktail Mountains, likely would have had to climb a lateral ramp at the margin of the Blacktail Valley block. Further, because the lateral ramp would have been flanked on the northeast by metamorphic rocks within which the thrusts did not develop, the steep to vertical (northwest-striking) northeastern

edges of the thrusts should be tear faults that display features of eastward-directed movement. The tear faults would have formed at the margin of the thrust plates of Phanerozoic strata as they moved eastward past the upthrown, rigid, Archean metamorphic rocks of the Blacktail Valley block. No evidence for lateral ramping or tear faulting was found.

The southwestern margin of the upthrown Blacktail Valley block trends northwest, about 45° to the eastward movement direction of the thrusts within the Phanerozoic strata. As thrusting took place, impingement of the Phanerozoic strata against the buttress of metamorphic rocks would have taken place at this oblique angle. The strata likely would have tended to curl back upon themselves and create a complex structural pattern of folds, tear faults, and probably back-thrusts; the fold and fault pattern observed contains neither tear nor back-thrust faults, nor a complex pattern of folding. A further complication may have existed due to overhang of metamorphic rocks above the Phanerozoic strata. Remnants of Archean metamorphic rocks now preserved only along the northeast flank of the Blacktail Mountains reveal that the Jake Canyon fault dips from about 45° to 75° northeast, as shown in cross section B–B'. Down-structure viewing to the northwest shows that, if the Blacktail Valley block had existed at the time of thrusting, the uplifted metamorphic rocks of the block would have formed an overhang above the Phanerozoic strata of the Blacktail Mountains. If this overhang had existed at the time of thrusting, the thrust faults likely would have overstepped the upturned strata beneath the overhang and would not be located within the upturned strata as they are now.

STRUCTURE ALONG NORTHEAST FLANK OF RANGE

Structures along the northeast flank of the Blacktail Mountains show a continuous pattern of features that resulted from shortening in a northeast-southwest direction. The shortening is related to uplift of the Blacktail Valley block and is localized along the mountain flank. Upturned Phanerozoic strata along the mountain flank make up the steeply dipping northeast limb of the Blacktail syncline, which extends for most of the length of the outcrop of Phanerozoic strata (Fig. 2). Phanerozoic strata become progressively more deformed northwestward, as evidenced by an increase in the number of faults, complexity of the fault pattern, overturning of strata, and brecciation of rocks. Progressively younger strata were deformed toward the northwest where the highest structural level is exposed. The structures are described here from southeast to northwest.

Ashbough Canyon to Sheep Creek

The effects of reverse movement along the Jake Canyon fault are evident in the southeasternmost area of Phanerozoic strata (Fig. 2). As pointed out by Pecora (1981), strike of Cambrian through Mississippian strata along the northeastern margin of the mountains changes abruptly from north, near Ashbough

Canyon, to northwest about 2.5 km (1.5 mi) to the northwest. In this area, dips are 10° to 20° west and southwest. Farther northwest, dips on the flank of the northwest-trending Blacktail syncline increase to near vertical. Pecora attributed this change in orientation to strike-slip movement along the Blacktail fault, but no significant drag features are associated with the changes in strike, as might be expected from strike-slip movement. The change in strike could be the result of reverse faulting along the Jake Canyon fault, accompanied by a component of lateral movement.

Near cross section A-A′, the Blacktail syncline crosses a thrust fault that it folded, which indicates that the syncline is younger than the thrust fault. But the existence of a landslide and talus do not permit physically tracing the fault across the fold, thus leaving the interpretation with less certainty than desired. Nevertheless, folding of the thrust fault can be demonstrated.

A series of thrust faults is present in the Mt. Ashbough area in the southernmost part of Figure 2, although only two of them have been mapped north of there. The westernmost one is the fault that is folded by the Blacktail syncline. Between Mt. Ashbough and cross section A-A′, the fault is covered by a landslide beneath which it must exist because the Lombard Limestone of the area would otherwise be too thick. Further, overturned mesoscopic folds commonly associated with the thrust faults of the area occur right up to the edge of the landslide. From the north end of the landslide to where the thrust fault turns northwest (near section A-A′), the fault must lie within a talus-covered zone that is about 75 m (250 ft) thick.

The north-trending, concealed segment of the fault must dip west at a moderate angle, but the northwest-trending segment is nearly vertical. This change in character could reflect either that the thrust is folded by the Blacktail syncline, or that the fault cut up-section as it approached an already uplifted Blacktail Valley block. Folding of the fault is more likely for the following reasons. (1) The vertical segment of the thrust fault (northwest of cross section A-A′) shows no evidence of strike-slip movement, which it should, if the segment had been vertical during eastward-directed thrusting. Folds adjacent to the vertical northwest-trending segment are parallel to that segment; they do not curve into it as would be the case for drag folds formed during strike-slip movement. (2) Folds immediately southwest of the vertical segment are in the upper plate of the thrust. They are on strike with, and have the same orientation as, the macroscopic folds shown in cross section A-A′ through the lower plate. The folds of the lower plate maintain the same orientation where they are both beneath the north-trending, westward-dipping part of the thrust fault, and beneath the upturned, vertical part of the thrust. If the folds beneath the north-trending part of the thrust had been generated by east-directed thrusting, their axes should trend northward as do the axes of thrust-related folds farther south along the system of thrusts. (3) The same general northwest strike characterizes both the lower plate beds of the macroscopic folds and the nearly vertical beds northeastward to the Jake Canyon fault at the range front. These nearly vertical beds form the north-

east limb of the throughgoing Blacktail syncline, which is present along the range front both northwest and southeast of the area of the cross section. The macroscopic folds beneath the thrust fault thus lie within the axial area of the much larger Blacktail syncline.

The north-trending segment of the thrust fault caused repetition of Lombard strata. But along the northwest-trending vertical segment of the fault, some of the Lombard Limestone has been cut out: upper beds of the Lombard are juxtaposed against Kibbey Sandstone (not shown in Fig. 2). This thinning of the Lombard is believed to have occurred during folding of the fault as the Blacktail Valley block was uplifted. The northwest-trending segment thus would have undergone southwest-directed movement subsequent to east-directed thrusting. The basis for this belief is presented in the following section on the contiguous structures of the Sheep Creek area to the northwest. There, folding of strata to form the upturned limb of the Blacktail syncline was accompanied by development of the Conover fault (Fig. 2), which was formed during folding that produced the Blacktail syncline. Southwest-directed movement along the northwest-trending segment of the thrust fault is considered analogous to movement along the Conover fault, for which much more structural data are available.

Sheep Creek

Strata exposed near the mouth of Sheep Creek yield data that show that major movement on the Jake Canyon fault and related faults took place after that on the east-directed thrust faults. Axes of three folds on the southeast side of the creek plunge northwest at 10° to 15°, and the axial planes of these folds (measured in the field) dip 70° to 90° southwest (stereographic plot A, Fig. 2). Axes of three folds on the northwest side of the creek plunge at about 10° to 15° northwest and strike at about 310° (stereographic plot B, Fig. 2). Axial planes of these latter folds are inclined about 70° northeast. The strike of both sets of axial planes is about parallel to the trace of the Jake Canyon fault and reflects shortening in a southwestward direction. The change in dip direction of the axial planes from south of the creek to north of it may be related to their distance from the Jake Canyon fault. The measured folds on the northwest side of the creek are closer to the Jake Canyon fault than those on the southeast and reflect greater appression, producing southwest vergence of axial planes (i.e., up-dip direction of planes is to the southwest). Orientations of the measured folds on both sides of Sheep Creek are similar to orientations of the adjacent segments of the nearby Blacktail syncline. The change in axial vergence from south to north across Sheep Creek may have been accompanied by a tear fault (cross fault) along the creek valley, normal to the fold axes. The possible fault, which would have a small amount of left-lateral offset, could not be confirmed because of a lack of outcrops in the valley bottom.

The general structure on the northwest side of Sheep Creek is illustrated in cross section B-B′ (Fig. 2). Four faults are shown in the cross section, including the previously discussed unnamed

Figure 3. Approximate position of Conover detachment fault, which is necessitated by contrasting deformation of the tightly folded Lombard Limestone on the northeast (right side of photo) and the upturned strata of the Quadrant Sandstone on the southwest. Shale and mudstone of the Conover Ranch Formation thin and pinch out upward. Planes of cross faults are vertical and about parallel to plane of photograph. View is to the northwest, on the northwest side of Sheep Creek, near its mouth. Vertical dimension is about 125 m (400 ft).

folded thrust fault near the center of the section. The southwest-ernmost fault, the Conover fault, is believed to have formed during southwest-directed shortening. It strikes parallel to the Jake Canyon fault, dips westward in the lower exposures, and steepens upward. The Conover fault is covered by a landslide southeast of Sheep Creek (Fig. 2).

The Conover fault has many of the characteristics of a detachment fault, as the term is used by Dahlstrom (1969) and Brown (1984), wherein a sequence (panel) of concentrically folded strata is separated by a fault from more resistant (competent) overlying rocks that behaved differently from the panel of strata during deformation. These characteristics are shown in cross section B-B′ (Fig. 2), where a triangle-shaped area (wedge) of folded Lombard Limestone is overstepped by younger strata of the Conover Ranch Formation and resistant Quadrant Sandstone above the Conover fault. Strata southwest of (and above) the Conover fault are upturned sharply, whereas strata northeast of (and below) the fault form a panel that displays several folds (shown diagramatically in cross section B-B′) in addition to being

upturned. Figure 3 shows these folds and the trace of a marker bed, rich in *Siphonophyllia* sp. corals (identified by W. J. Sando, written communication, 1985), in the upper part of the Lombard Limestone below the Conover fault. As can be seen in the figure, the thickness of strata between the marker bed and the Conover Ranch Formation is greater where the beds are folded into a syncline, necessitating that the folded strata be detached from the upturned strata farther southwest.

Dahlstrom's (1969) illustrations show that once a detachment fault has overstepped the panel, it tends to flatten to a subhorizontal fault above the panel. The Conover fault differs in that, northwest of Sheep Creek, it steepens and then becomes overturned to the southwest. This fact reflects the continuing southwest-directed shortening as the fault developed. At a larger scale, Figure 2 shows that the Conover fault extends from the axial area of the Blacktail syncline and could be considered an out-of-the-syncline fault (Brown, 1984), but one that propagated up the steep limb of the fold. In essence, then, the fault developed in the core of the syncline; upward tightening of the syncline as folding proceeded caused a volume problem of decreasing space available for folding, and the detachment fault developed to resolve the problem.

The detachment fault is actually a zone, because the red beds of the Conover Ranch Formation are sheared as they thin and pinch out upward, as shown in Figure 3. Thinning of the Conover Ranch Formation is shown by two limestone beds (not indicated in Fig. 3), each about 0.3 m (1 ft) thick, that occur within it. In the lower part of Figure 3, where the formation is about 30 m (100 ft) thick, the limestone beds are separated by several meters of shale and mudstone. As the formation thins upward (upper center in Fig. 3), the two limestone beds become closer together and, where the formation is only about 6 m (20 ft) thick, they are only about 3 m (10 ft) apart. The mudstone and shale between the two beds have been thinned by shearing and cataclastic flow.

Cross faults. Vertical and near-vertical faults are very common throughout the strata on both sides of Sheep Creek. The faults strike about 030° on the southeast side of the creek, and about 040° on the northwest side (stereographic plots C and D, Fig. 2). These orientations are about normal to strike of beds and axial planes on both sides of Sheep Creek, and to the trend of the Jake Canyon fault. The 10° difference in strike corresponds with the difference in orientations of bedding and folds on opposite sides of the creek. The continual map pattern of left-lateral offset from southeast to northwest indicates an additive increase in total offset to the northwest, which corresponds with increased appression of folds and overturning of beds northwestward.

The cross faults display left-lateral offsets that range from nearly nil to a few meters, and locally several meters. Striations and chatter marks on the surfaces of the cross faults (that is, on fault planes normal to bedding) confirm the left-lateral offsets. Striations of the slickensides on the fault planes show inclinations that range from 27° to 80°. They indicate that, relative to strata southeast of a particular cross fault, rocks on the northwest side moved upward and to the southwest in some cases, and downward and to the southwest in other cases. None of the cross faults curve into the major northwest-trending faults, nor into folded thrust faults, as would be expected if they formed under a stress regime that included a component of east-directed transport. Cross faults were not observed to offset the Conover fault in the Sheep Creek area, but the Conover fault occurs in a poorly exposed zone of shaly material. Local offset of the Conover fault is likely, however, because both it and the cross faults were active concurrently. Figure 4 is a closeup view of the axial area of one of the northwest-plunging anticlines, and displays a cross fault that has a small amount of left-lateral offset of the fold hinge.

Cross faults are present on both sides of the upturned red shale and mudstone of the Conover Ranch Formation (Fig. 3), but none of the faults could be traced across the red beds themselves. Cross faults clearly offset the basal and upper strata of the upturned red-bed sequence, but well within the red beds, no offset is evident. This probably is a result of the greater ductility of the red beds as opposed to that of the limestone and sandstone on either side of the red beds. Under the regime of southwestward

shortening, as the red beds were being upturned, they deformed by flowing (flexural flow). The direction of flow was upward, and the red beds flowed around the ends of limestone or sandstone beds offset a meter or two by the cross faults.

Bedding surfaces. Structures on bedding surfaces, best preserved on the bottoms of steeply dipping beds, indicate flexural slip movement that accommodated fold development was consistent with forces that produced the cross faults. Striations and

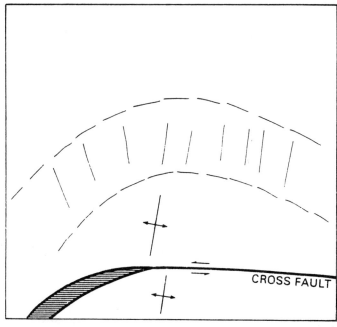

Figure 4. Photo and sketch of cross fault that shows about 8 cm (3 in) of left-lateral offset of core area of an anticline. View is to the northwest, along fold axis that plunges 15° to 20° to the northwest, and is about normal to plane of the cross fault. The anticline is on the northwest side of Sheep Creek, its location is shown to Figure 3. Scale in upper middle of photograph is 18 cm (7 in.) long.

grooves are the most common structures and only locally are accompanied by polished, slickensided rock. This probably is due to the fact that the interbed material is shaly and that it deformed by flexural flow during folding of the sequence. Insufficient friction was generated to cause widespread development of glassy slickensides on the bottom of most beds. Without exception, each striation on the bottom of a bedding plane is parallel to the direction of dip of the bed or within 10° of it. Each striation thus lies within a plane that is perpendicular to bedding and is vertical or within 10° of vertical. Such planes are about parallel with the cross faults because both are normal to the bedding. Chatter marks of slickensides associated with the striations indicate that the beds moved upward and to the northeast relative to the stratigraphically lower beds.

Sheep Creek to Small Horn Canyon

Northwestward along the mountain front from Sheep Creek to Small Horn Canyon, structures near the Jake Canyon and Conover faults show progressively more deformation. Near point 1 (Fig. 2) (Sec.18,T.9S., R.8W.), the Conover fault steepens; strata of the Mississippian Lombard Limestone, Conover Ranch Formation, and the Pennsylvanian Quadrant Sandstone on the southwest are upthrown relative to Lombard strata on the northeast. The Conover Ranch Formation is sheared, thins, and pinches out to the northwest and upward (cross section B-B', Fig. 2), leaving Quadrant Sandstone juxtaposed against Lombard strata. At point 2 (Sec.7,T.9S., R.8W.), the Conover fault dips about 65° southwest, as measured by dips of flanking strata. Northwest from point 3 (Sec.12,T.9S.,R.9W.) to the northeast-trending Jeep Trail fault, the Conover fault steepens to vertical, then becomes slightly overturned. It is offset by the Jeep Trail fault, northwest of which it becomes further overturned and dips about 60° northeast.

The Jeep Trail fault is parallel to the cross faults present in Sheep Creek and is interpreted to have formed under the same stress regime. It has about 100 m (325 ft) of left-lateral offset, much more than the offset on the cross faults to the southeast. The Jeep Trail fault may be more correctly considered a tear fault because northwest of it, increased overturning of the Conover fault and associated strata reflects greater shortening than is present southeastward. The Jeep Trail fault is not well exposed along much of its length, but its location and offset are narrowly delimited by outcrops on opposite sides of it. The southwest end of the fault splays, and one strand cuts the conglomerate of the Beaverhead Group. Northwest of the Jeep Trail fault, small cross faults trend parallel to it or are oriented at a small angle to it.

Beds northwest of the Jeep Trail fault (Fig. 2) contain north-trending fractures that dip moderately to the west and contain slickenside striations and chatter marks that indicate hanging-wall strata were displaced upward and to the northeast relative to footwall strata. This movement direction, similar to that found in Sheep Creek, suggests strata northwest of the tear fault were shortened in a southwestward direction, became overturned to

the southwest (now dip northeast), and adjusted to the shortening by moving upward.

Northwest of the Jeep Trail fault, and several tens of meters southwest of the Conover fault, is another northwest-trending, northeast-dipping fault (Fig. 2). It juxtaposed Quadrant Sandstone on the northeast against Cretaceous Beaverhead Group strata on the southwest. The unnamed fault, which is accompanied by breccia, abuts the Jeep Trail fault on the southeast, its existence probably reflects the greater shortening of strata northwest of the Jeep Trail fault.

Small Horn Canyon

Stratigraphic and structural relationships on opposite sides of Small Horn Canyon require that a northeast-trending fault exists within the canyon, although the fault is concealed by alluvium. It cannot be determined with certainty, however, if the fault is one of the Laramide cross faults related to the Jake Canyon fault, or if it is an extensional structure formed during Cenozoic basin-and-range faulting. No evidence was found for an extensional origin of other northeast-trending faults, however, and the fault within the canyon is considered to be a right-lateral tear formed by compression.

Small Horn Canyon anticline, and the associated Sheep Creek syncline to the east (Fig. 2) were mapped initially by Lowell (1949) and were studied subsequently by Achuff (1981a, b). Achuff pointed out that the anticline displays megascopic folds with west vergence reflecting west-directed shortening, and that it and the Sheep Creek syncline have nearly vertical axial planes. He interpreted these major folds as having formed during east-directed shortening, and called on back-thrusting to account for the west-shortened structures and steep axial planes of the folds.

A plan view shows that the north end of the axial trace of the Sheep Creek syncline curves to the northwest and becomes about parallel to the Jake Canyon fault and related faults. Although the curvature appears to be due to drag during east-directed thrusting, it actually is caused by steep topography. In a similar manner, the northern end of the Small Horn Canyon anticline previously was shown by Lowell (1949) to curve to the northwest, but detailed mapping and stereographic plots of structural data (Fig. 2) show that the axis maintains a northerly trend. An abrupt change from north to northwest trends for these and related folds of the Small Horn Canyon area takes place only very near (within about 150 m [500 ft]) the northwest-trending Jake Canyon fault or related faults. These observations suggest the actual swing in plunge direction of the folds is due to southwest shortening movement along the northwest-trending reverse faults near the range front.

Achuff (1981a, b) interpreted the northwest-trending Jake Canyon and nearby northwest-trending reverse faults as back-thrusts developed concurrently with the Small Horn Canyon anticline. The interpretation is kinematically untenable because the Jake Canyon structures trend about 45° to those of the thrust related folds. Moreover, the Jake Canyon fault formed the southwestern margin of the uplifted Blacktail Valley block, a much larger structure than the Small Horn Canyon anticline or any other of the folds related to the thrust faults preserved within the Phanerozoic strata. Study of the entire front of the Blacktail Mountains shows that structures related to the Jake Canyon fault, and hence to the southwest margin of the block, form a continuous pattern of southwest-shortened structures that are younger than the thrust faults and related folds.

Northwest of Small Horn Canyon

The general pattern of structures caused by shortening in a southwest direction southeast of Small Horn Canyon also is present northwest of the canyon. The Jake Canyon fault itself is not visible because no exposures of Archean metamorphic rocks juxtaposed against Phanerozoic strata exist to define it. The fault must lie northeast of the range front, concealed by Quaternary sediments. But a series of northwest-striking, northeast-dipping faults closely related to the Jake Canyon fault form a zone as much as 1.5 km (1 mi) wide along the range front. They are accompanied by Phanerozoic strata that are overturned to the southwest (dips are to northeast).

The pattern of cross faulting is more complex than to the southeast; some of the faults strike north, as opposed to the northeast strikes farther south. The reason for this is uncertain, but the area displays a complex interference pattern of east-directed thrust structures that are overprinted by structures associated with the Jake Canyon fault. One example to illustrate this is made evident by contrasting the area near point 4 in Figure 2 (S½,Sec.35,T.8S.,R.9W.) with part of the Small Horn Canyon anticline near point 5 (NW¼,Sec.11,T.8S.,R.9W.) on the north wall of the canyon. Near point 5, almost the entire section of Triassic Dinwoody Formation is repeated by a thrust fault that Achuff (1981a, b) determined was folded during thrusting. Near point 4, a double thickness of the Dinwoody Formation is present, repeated by a fault that presumably is a segment of the same thrust as occurs at Small Horn Canyon. The fault-repeated section near point 4 has been deformed within the Jake Canyon fault system; its beds are overturned and now trend northwest in concert with the other structures along the range front.

BLACKTAIL FAULT

The northwest-trending Blacktail fault separates the Blacktail Mountains from the basin of Cenozoic sedimentary strata that underlies the valley of Blacktail Deer Creek, northeast of the mountains (Fig. 2). No offset of Holocene alluvial fans was found along the 35-km-long (22 mi) fault segment that extends southeast from the Beaverhead River (Fig. 1), confirming the observation of Pardee (1950). In the southeastern 8 km (5 mi) of this segment, the fault trace is delimited by Archean gneiss and by aligned springs marked by abundant vegetation. The position of this part of the fault coincides with the northeastern limit of a

steep gravity gradient (Tysdal and others, 1987, Fig. 3; Hassemer and others, 1986). The remainder of the fault segment to the northwest was drawn to coincide with the continuation of this gravity gradient.

The dip of the Blacktail fault cannot be ascertained from ground observation because the fault is either covered, or, in its southeasternmost extent, the trace does not cross terrain with sufficient relief to determine its inclination. Although no modeling of the gravity data has been done, the pattern of contours on the gravity map (Fig. 3 in Tysdal and others, 1987) indicates that the fault is nearly vertical or dips steeply to the northeast. During my studies, no evidence was found to suggest that the Blacktail fault dips to the southwest, as believed by Pecora (1981). The fault is a Cenozoic extensional feature that formed after Laramide deformation, as originally shown by Pardee (1950).

TIMING OF DEFORMATION

The timing of Laramide deformation within the study area is not tightly constrained. The minimum age of deformation is middle Eocene, based on a K-Ar age of 44.0 ± 1.6 Ma obtained on biotite from the rhyolite body at the mouth of Small Horn Canyon (Fig. 2) (R. F. Marvin, written communication, 1985). The rhyolite was emplaced after overturning of strata along the Jake Canyon fault. The maximum age of deformation must be sought from the conglomerate of the Beaverhead Group, which is the youngest rock unit deformed during thrusting. No dates were obtained from the Beaverhead within the study area; its age is inferred from studies of Nichols and others (1985), who worked in the region northeast and northwest of Lima (Fig. 1), about 40 km (25 mi) south of the study area. Their palynological dating showed that the Beaverhead ranges from Coniacian through at least mid-Campanian, and probably includes strata no younger than Maastrichtian. However, Perry and others (this volume) state that thrusting in the Lima region may have been active into the early Tertiary. Ruppel and Lopez (1984) indicated that thrust plates west of the Blacktail Mountains ceased movement by the end of the Cretaceous. Hence, movement along the Jake Canyon fault could have occurred during Cretaceous or early Tertiary time.

DISCUSSION

The pattern of deformation indicated by features observed in the Phanerozoic strata along the front of the Blacktail Mountains reflects shortening in a southwest direction, coincident with uplift of the Blacktail Valley block. But a strike-slip component of movement along the Jake Canyon fault is not ruled out. Such movement could have preceded the pronounced vertical component of movement now so evident in the Phanerozoic strata. The observed structures also are not inconsistent with a small component of lateral movement that could have been present during uplift. In their summary paper on the northwest-trending faults in the foreland of southwestern Montana, Schmidt and Garihan

(1983) reported that many of the faults exhibit a component of Laramide-age strike-slip movement that is equally as large as the vertical component of movement. In this volume, Schmidt and others show a Laramide-age strike-slip fault along the front of the Blacktail Mountains in their model for the development of northwest-trending faults in the foreland. And Ruppel and Lopez (1984) interpreted the Blacktail fault as an oblique tear fault that developed during Laramide-age thrusting. The front of the Blacktail Mountains is a structurally weak zone that is not fully exposed; part of it is concealed beneath sediments of the basin in front of the mountains. Laramide faults northeast of the Jake Canyon fault could be concealed beneath the basin deposits, and the (concealed) Blacktail fault itself could be a reactivated Laramide-age fault. Any or all of these faults could have experienced a significant strike-slip component of movement early in their Laramide hsitory.

CONCLUSIONS

The Blacktail Mountains lie in a zone of overlap of the Cordilleran thrust belt and the crystalline foreland of the Rocky Mountains. The Cordilleran thrust belt is represented in the northwestern part of the mountains by low-angle thrust faults and associated folds. The foreland is represented by the Blacktail-Snowcrest uplift, a southwest-plunging basement-involved arch

that underlies the Blacktail Mountains, and by the Jake Canyon fault and adjacent northwest-plunging Blacktail syncline, one of a series of steeply dipping faults and associated folds that trend northwest across the uplift. The thrust-belt structures of the salient were deformed by subsequent movement along the Jake Canyon fault. This conclusion is suggested by relationships of macroscopic folds and faults, and is confirmed by movement directions determined from chatter marks associated with slickensides, striations of slickensides, striations on the bottoms of beds that lack slickensides, cross faults, and fold orientations. The events that formed these Laramide-age structures ceased before the middle Eocene, indicated by a date of 44 Ma from a rhyolite body that intruded the Jake Canyon fault zone. The Cenozoic Blacktail normal fault, which delimits the common boundary of the mountains and the basin to the northeast, developed along the zone of weakness associated with the Jake Canyon fault.

ACKNOWLEDGMENTS

I thank R. F. Marvin for making available the K-Ar date, W. J. Sando for identification of Mississippian fossils, and W. J. Perry for discussions of structure during the early stages of the investigation. W. C. Day, J. M. Garihan, D. A. Lindsey, R. C. Pearson, and C. J. Schmidt reviewed the manuscript and offered suggestions for its improvement.

REFERENCES CITED

Achuff, J. A., 1981a, Folding and faulting in the northern Blacktail Range, Beaverhead County, Montana [M.S. thesis]: Missoula, University of Montana, 64 p.

—— , 1981b, Structural analysis of faulting and folding in Small Horn Canyon, Beaverhead County, Montana, in Tucker, T. E., ed., Montana Geological Society Field Conference and Symposium Guidebook to southwest Montana: Montana Geological Society 1981 Guidebook, p. 239–243.

Beard, T., 1949, Geology of part of the Blacktail Range, Beaverhead County, Montana [M.S. thesis]: Ann Arbor, University of Michigan, 46 p.

Benham, J. R., 1986, Mineral resources of the Blacktail Mountains study area, Beaverhead County, Montana: U.S. Bureau of Mines Mineral Lands Assessment Open-File Report 86-26, 14 p.

Berg, R. B., 1979, Precambrian geology of the west part of the Greenhorn Range, Madison County, Montana: Montana Bureau of Mines and Geology Geologic Map 6, scale 1:28,000.

Berg, R. R., 1962, Mountain flank thrusting in Rocky Mountain foreland, Wyoming and Colorado: American Association of Petroleum Geologists Bulletin, p. 2019–2032.

Brown, W. G., 1984, Basement involved tectonics; Foreland areas: American Association of Petroleum Geologists Continuing Education Course Notes no. 26, 92 p.

Cressman, E. R., and Swanson, R. W., 1964, Stratigraphy and petrology of the Permian rocks of southwestern Montana: U.S. Geological Survey Professional Paper 313-C, p. 275–569.

Dahlstrom, C.D.A., 1969, The upper detachment in concentric folding: Bulletin of Canadian Petroleum Geology, v. 17, p. 326–346.

Giletti, B. J., 1966, Isotopic ages from southwestern Montana: Journal of Geophysical Research, v. 71, p. 4019–4036.

Hadley, J. B., 1969, Geologic map of the Varney Quadrangle, Madison County, Montana: U.S. Geological Survey Geologic Quadrangle Map GQ-814, scale 1:62,500.

Hanson, A. M., 1952, Cambrian stratigraphy in southwestern Montana: Montana Bureau of Mines and Geology Memoir 33, 46 p.

Hassemer, J. H., Kaufmann, H. E., and Hanna, W. F., 1986, Description magnetic tape containing the principal facts for the gravity stations in and adjacent to the Dillon 1° × 2° Quadrangle, Montana and Idaho: National Technical Information Service PB 86-197407/AS, 6 p.

Heinrich, E. W., 1960, Geology of the Ruby Mountains and nearby areas in southwestern Montana, in Pre-Beltian geology of the Cherry Creek and Ruby Mountains areas, southwestern Montana: Montana Bureau of Mines and Geology Memoir 38, p. 15–40.

Huh, O. J., 1967, The Mississippian system across the Wasatch line, east central Idaho, and extreme southwestern Montana, in Centennial basin of southwest Montana: Montana Geological Society 18th Annual Field Conference Guidebook, p. 31–62.

Keenmon, K. A., 1950, The geology of the Blacktail-Snowcrest region, Beaverhead County, Montana [Ph.D. thesis]: Ann Arbor, University of Michigan, 207 p.

Klepper, M. R., 1950, A geologic reconnaissance of parts of Beaverhead and Madison Counties, Montana: U.S. Geological Survey Bulletin 969-C, p. 55–85.

Lowell, W. R., 1949, Geology of the Small Horn Canyon, Daly's Spur, Cedar Creek, and Dell areas, southwestern Montana; Preliminary report: U.S. Geological Survey Open-File Report, 7 p., two maps, 1:24,000 scale.

Mannion, L. E., 1948, Geology of a part of the Blacktail Range, Beaverhead County, Montana [M.S. thesis]: Ann Arbor, University of Michigan, 41 p.

Moritz, C. A., 1951, Triassic and Jurassic stratigraphy of southwestern Montana: American Association of Petroleum Geologists Bulletin, v. 35, p. 1781–1814.

Nichols, D. J., Perry, W. J., Jr., and Haley, J. C., 1985, Reinterpretation of the palynology and age of Laramide syntectonic deposits, southwestern Montana, and revision of the Beaverhead Group: Geology, v. 13, p. 149–153.

Pardee, J. T., 1950, Late Cenozoic block faulting in western America: Geological Society of America Bulletin, v. 61, p. 359–406.

Pecora, W. C., 1981, Bedrock geology of the Blacktail Mountains, southwestern Montana [M.A. thesis]: Middletown, Connecticut, Wesleyan University, 203 p.

——, 1987, Geologic map of the central part of the Blacktail Mountains, Beaverhead County, Montana: U.S. Geological Survey Open-File Report 87-0079, scale 1:24,000.

Perry, W. J., Jr., Wardlaw, B. R., Bostick, N. H., and Maughan, E. K., 1983, Structure, burial history, and petroleum potential of frontal thrust belt and adjacent foreland, southwest Montana: American Association of Petroleum Geologists Bulletin, v. 67, p. 725–743.

Prucha, J. J., Graham, J. S., and Nickelsen, R. P., 1965, Basement controlled deformation in Wyoming province of Rocky Mountain foreland: American Association of Petroleum Geologists Bulletin, v. 49, p. 966–992.

Ruppel, E. T., and Lopez, D. A., 1984, The thrust belt in southwest Montana and east-central Idaho: U.S. Geological Survey Professional Paper 1278, 41 p.

Sales, J. K., 1968, Crustal mechanics of Cordilleran foreland deformation; A regional and scale-model approach: American Association of Petroleum Geologists Bulletin, v. 52, p. 2061–2064.

Samuelson, K. J., and Schmidt, C. J., 1981, Structural geology of the western Tobacco Root Mountains, southwestern Montana, *in* Tucker, T. E., ed., Field Conference and Symposium Guidebook to Southwest Montana: Montana Geological Society 1981 Guidebook, p. 191–199.

Schmidt, C. J., and Garihan, J. M., 1983, Laramide tectonic development of the Rocky Mountain foreland of southwestern Montana, *in* Lowell, J. D., and Gries, R., eds., Rocky Mountain foreland basins and uplifts: Denver, Colorado, Rocky Mountain Association of Geologists, p. 271–294.

——, 1986, Middle Proterozoic and Laramide tectonic activity along the southwestern margin of the Belt basin, *in* Roberts, S. M., ed., Belt Supergroup; A guide to Proterozoic rocks of western Montana and adjacent areas: Montana Bureau of Mines and Geology Special Publication 94, p. 217–235.

——, 1986, Role of recurrent movement on northwest-trending basement faults in the tectonic evolution of southwestern Montana, *in* Aldrich, M. J., and Laughlin, A. W., eds., Proceedings of the 6th International Conference on Basement Tectonics: Salt Lake City, Utah, International Basement Tectonic Association, p. 1–15.

Schmidt, C. J., and Hendrix, T. E., 1981, Tectonic controls for the thrust belt and Rocky Mountain foreland structures in the northern Tobacco Root Mountains; Jefferson Canyon area, southwestern Montana, *in* Tucker, T. E., ed., Field Conference and Symposium Guidebook to southwest Montana: Montana Geological Society 1981 Guidebook, p. 167–180.

Schock, W. W., Maughan, E. K., and Wardlaw, B. R., 1981, Permian-Triassic boundary in southwestern Montana and western Wyoming, *in* Tucker, T. E., ed., Field Conference and Symposium Guide to southwestern Montana: Montana Geological Society 1981 Guidebook, p. 59–69.

Scholten, R., 1967, Structural framework and oil potential of extreme southwestern Montana: Montana Geological Society 18th Annual Field Conference Guidebook, p. 7–19.

Scholten, R., Keenmon, K. S., and Kupsch, W. O., 1955, Geology of the Lima region, southwestern Montana and adjacent Idaho: Geological Society of America Bulletin, v. 66, p. 345–404.

Sheedlo, M. K., 1984, Structural geology of the northern Snowcrest Range, Beaverhead and Madison Counties, Montana [M.S. thesis]: Kalamazoo, Western Michigan University, 132 p.

Sinkler, H., 1942, Geology and ore deposits of the Dillon nickel prospect, southwestern Montana: Economic Geology, v. 31, p. 136–152.

Sloss, L. L., and Moritz, C. A., 1951, Paleozoic stratigraphy of southwestern Montana: American Association of Petroleum Geologists Bulletin, v. 35, p. 2135–2169.

Stearns, D. W., 1971, Mechanics of drape folding in the Wyoming province: Wyoming Geological Association 23rd Field Conference Guidebook, p. 149–158.

Swanson, R. W., 1970, Mineral resources in Permian rocks of southwest Montana: U.S. Geological Survey Professional Paper 313-E, p. 661–771.

Tysdal, R. G., 1976, Geologic map of the northern part of the Ruby Range, Montana: U.S. Geological Survey Miscellaneous Investigations Map I-0951, scale 1:24,000.

——, 1981, Foreland deformation in the northern part of the Ruby Range of southwestern Montana, *in* Tucker, T. E., ed., Field Conference and Symposium Guidebook to Southwest Montana: Montana Geological Society 1981 Guidebook, p. 215–224.

——, 1988, Geologic map along the northeast side of the Blacktail Mountains, Beaverhead County, Montana: U.S. Geological Survey Miscellaneous Field Studies Map MF-2041, scale 1:24,000.

Tysdal, R. G., Marvin, R. F., and DeWitt, Ed, 1986, Late Cretaceous stratigraphy, deformation, and intrusion in the Madison Range of southwestern Montana: Geological Society of America Bulletin, v. 97, p. 859–868.

Tysdal, R. G., Lee, G. K., Hassemer, J. H., Hanna, W. F., and Benham, J. R., 1987, Mineral resources of the Blacktail Mountains Wilderness Study Area, Beaverhead County, Montana: U.S. Geological Survey Bulletin 1724B, p. B1–B21.

Wardlaw, C. C., and Pecora, W. C., 1985, New Mississippian-Pennsylvanian stratigraphic units in southwest Montana and adjacent Idaho, *in* Sando, W. J., ed., Mississippian and Pennsylvanian stratigraphy in southwest Montana and adjacent Idaho: U.S. Geological Survey Bulletin 1656, p. B1–B9.

Yochelson, E. L., 1968, Biostratigraphy of the Phosphoria, Park City, and Shedhorn Formations: U.S. Geological Survey Professional Paper 313-D, p. 571–660.

Zeigler, J. M., 1954, Geology of the Blacktail area, Beaverhead County, Montana [Ph.D. thesis]: Cambridge, Harvard University, 147 p.

MANUSCRIPT ACCEPTED BY THE SOCIETY FEBRUARY 9, 1988

Printed in U.S.A.

Geological Society of America
Memoir 171
1988

Structural geology of the Armstead anticline area, Beaverhead County, Montana

J. J. Coryell*
ARCO Exploration Company, P.O. Box 51408, Houston, Texas 70508
J. H. Spang
Center for Tectonophysics and Department of Geology, Texas A&M University, College Station, Texas 77843

ABSTRACT

The Armstead anticline is an Archean-cored, asymmetrical anticline located within the hanging wall of the leading edge thrust along the central portion of the southwestern Montana reentrant. Structural analysis, consisting of detailed mapping of megascopic structures, was undertaken to determine the extent and effects that the foreland deformation had on subsequent thrusting. Based on this analysis, the structural history of the area is interpreted to be the result of a dominantly horizontal compressive mode of deformation involving a model of overthrusting. In this model, uplift of the Precambrian-cored Armstead anticline and thrusting are genetically related through the development of a "Rich-Model" anticline, thus indicating the presence of a subsurface thrust ramp that is structurally lower and westward of the Armstead anticline. Other structural features that point to the existence of a subsurface ramp include backthrusts (Serra, 1977, Mode III) along the eastern edge of Hans Peterson Flats, listric normal faults along the western edge of the Armstead anticline, and the Cedar Creek syncline. Additionally, a previously unmapped duplex structure involving layered Precambrian rocks is identified along the eastern limb of the Armstead anticline. The duplex structure, which probably records earliest thrusting, has been rotated along with bedding by later thrusting.

INTRODUCTION

The Armstead anticline is located along the eastern edge of the Cordilleran thrust belt, a feature that can be traced from southern California to northern British Columbia. In western Montana, the trace of the leading edge of the thrust belt turns abruptly westward near Bozeman, Montana, forming the transverse zone between the central Montana salient and the southwestern Montana reentrant (Fig. 1). South of the transverse zone, the thrust belt has an eastward concave trace and continues southward to the Snake River Plain. The style of footwall deformation, from disturbed belt structures (Woodward, 1981; Alpha, 1955) to foreland structures (Prucha and others, 1965), also changes in this region. Southwestern Montana may be a region where the Rocky Mountain Foreland and the frontal part of the Cordilleran thrust belt interact.

In southwestern Montana, the foreland is characterized by long, asymmetric, basement-cored uplifts. There are at least two sets of these uplifts: a northwest-trending set of predominantly southwest-verging anticlines cored by northeast-dipping reverse faults (Schmidt and Garihan, 1983; Schmidt and others, this volume; Tysdal, this volume), and a set of major fault-bounded uplifts that trend generally north to northwest and verge eastward (Kulik and Perry, this volume).

In contrast, the frontal part of the Cordilleran thrust belt is characterized by tightly folded, partly overturned rocks that are cut by numerous imbricate thrust faults (Ruppel and others, 1981). Movement of the major thrust sheets is commonly interpreted as being along subhorizontal faults. Basement rocks are not generally interpreted to be involved in thrusting, and thick Phanerozoic or Proterozoic Belt Supergroup rocks form the backbone of the thrust ranges.

The Armstead anticline, located about 25 km southwest of

---
*Present address: Sun Exploration and Production Co., Southeast District, Campbell Centre II, P.O. Box 2880, Dallas, Texas 75221-2880.

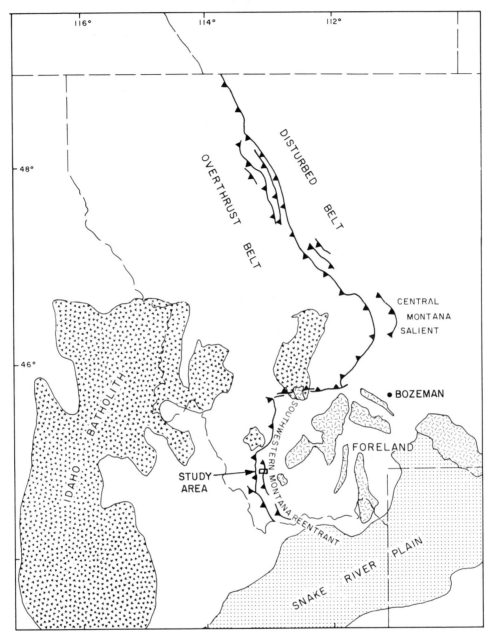

Figure 1. Location of Rocky Mountain Foreland and easternmost extent of frontal fold and thrust belt (modified from Schmidt and Hendrix, 1981). (Square indicates study area.)

Dillon, Montana, is at the northernmost end of the Tendoy Range but is separated from the main range by Horse Prairie Creek (Fig. 2). Although the structural framework of the Armstead anticline seems to include features characteristic of both foreland and thrust belt deformation, our detailed examination suggests that the observed structural features can best be explained by a Rich (1934) Model anticline formed during eastward thrusting, followed by listric normal faulting.

STRATIGRAPHY

The Henneberry Ridge area is underlain by 2,100 m (6,100 ft) of unmetamorphosed Paleozoic and Mesozoic sedimentary rocks (Hildreth, 1981), deposited with angular unconformity over Archean metamorphic and intrusive igneous rocks (Fig. 3). The stratigraphic units are essentially the same as autochthonous foreland rocks, but distinctive changes occur in almost every system.

The generalized stratigraphic column (Fig. 3) represents measurements and descriptions taken in or near the study area using a Jacob Staff and a standard Brunton compass.

REGIONAL GEOLOGIC FRAMEWORK

Early regional studies of southwestern Montana in the vicinity of the study area were completed by Klepper (1950) and

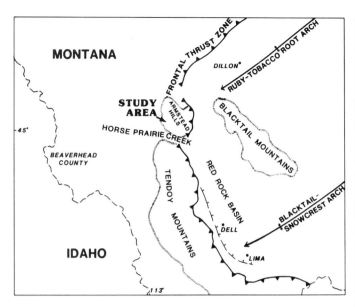

Figure 2. Generalized map showing location of study area, major ranges, and regional structural features (adapted from Schmidt and others, this volume).

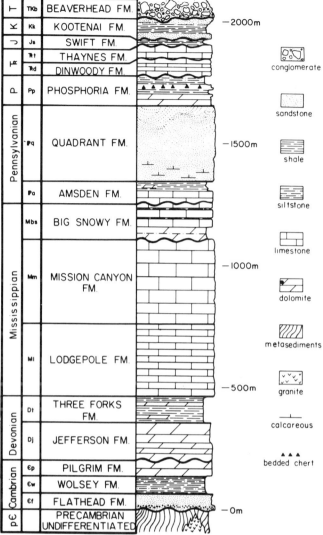

Figure 3. Generalized stratigraphic column of study area (from Coryell, 1983).

Scholten and others (1955). At that time, the Armstead anticline was considered to be the northernmost extension of the Tendoy thrust (Fig. 2). Scholten and others (1955) interpreted the Tendoy thrust to be a high-angle thrust fault, which cut earlier structures and tilted portions of overlying thrust plates during the final stages of the Laramide orogeny. Tanner (1963), studying pitted and sheared cobbles in the Beaverhead Formation along the Tendoy thrust, proposed that the fault movement was left-lateral with slip on the order of tens of kilometers. This view was rejected by Scholten (1964), who suggested that the dip of the Tendoy thrust was shallow at high elevations and steep at low elevations, and thus was an upthrust.

Skipp and Hait (1977) have interpreted the Tendoy thrust to be the structurally lowest thrust in a series of stacked allochthons. Lowell (1965) mapped in detail north of Horse Prairie Creek, including the Armstead anticline, and in a cross section he suggested it is underlain by a low-angle thrust. Hammons (1981), in the southern Tendoy Range, suggested that the Tendoy thrust does not steepen with depth, but instead is a flat thrust. Conodont CAI (coloration alteration index) values by Perry and others (1981) support relatively shallow depths of burial for rocks in the hanging wall of the Tendoy thrust.

In the transverse thrust zone of southwest Montana, Schmidt and O'Neill (1982) and Schmidt and others (this volume) have described the spatial and temporal overlap of thrust belt and foreland "styles" and suggested that, where thrust sheets impinge against basement blocks, a series of imbrications formed such that at least one involved Archean basement rocks. In each of these locations the main thrust sheet ramped over the uplifted basement block. Stratigraphic and radiometric age data suggest that many

of the faults formed during Precambrian time and were reactivated by Laramide tectonics (Sloss, 1950; Wooden and others, 1978; Schmidt, 1976).

Ruppel (1982) reported a definite sequence of thrusting followed by vertical uplift along high-angle faults in east-central Idaho. He interpreted the uplifts as flat-topped with monoclinal drape-folded flanks. Folded thrust planes provide the necessary slip plane for gravity sliding of material into intermontane valleys. The orientation and nature of these fault-bounded uplifts are similar to foreland deformation east of the thrust belt. Based on this, Ruppel (1982) suggested that the foreland deformation extends westward into Idaho.

Other large-scale structural features of southwestern Montana include Tertiary block faults and listric(?) normal faults. Variably oriented block faults have down-dropped large parts of the thrust belt and adjacent foreland (Scholten and others, 1955). Faceted spurs and fault scarps are associated with some of the block faults, such as along the north-northwest–trending Red Rock fault west of Dell, Montana, immediately south of the study area (Fig. 2). Scholten and others (1955) described the East Muddy Creek fault as a normal fault bounding the western portion of the Tendoy Range. They also pointed out that the Tertiary basin beds steepen into the fault, attaining dips as much as 35°. This relationship is indicative of listric normal faulting elsewhere in the thrust belt (Royse and others, 1975; Bally and others, 1966; Constenius, 1982) and adjacent foreland (Schmidt and Garihan, 1986).

LOCAL STRUCTURAL GEOLOGY

The structure of the area is controlled by three major northwest-trending faults (Fig. 4). The easternmost and westernmost faults are thrust faults that carry Pennsylvanian and Mississippian rocks upon Cretaceous syntectonic deposits of the Beaverhead Formation. The middle fault is a normal fault that places Mississippian rocks against Archean rocks.

The Armstead thrust (Johnson and Sears, this volume), which is the structurally lowest mapped thrust, is located along the eastern part of the study area (Figs. 4A, 5A). The thrust cuts up-section in the hanging wall from Mississippian carbonates to Pennsylvanian sandstones. The footwall rocks commonly consist of the Beaverhead Formation, but also include Upper Paleozoic rocks (Lowell, 1965), suggesting that stratigraphic separation is relatively small. Consequently, the Armstead thrust is considered separate from the Tendoy thrust. The dip of the fault was calculated to be 32° to 37° southwest.

The structurally highest mapped thrust fault is along the extreme western margin of the study area (see Fig. 4D), where Pennsylvanian carbonates and sandstones are in fault contact with the Beaverhead Formation. To the south, the thrust fault ends against a dextral tear fault, which places the Thaynes Formation against the Beaverhead Formation. Erosion near the southern end of the thrust exposes the three-dimensional geometry of the thrust plane as "sledrunner"-shaped, with dips to the southwest at about 12°.

The middle fault (Figs. 4B, 5B) places Mississippian carbonates against Archean gneisses. The fault is not well exposed but apparently dips southwest at 60° to 80°. The trace of the fault is subparallel to the axial surface trace of the major folds. An apparent synthetic fault is located about 660 m (2,000 ft) farther west.

A reverse fault is found along the eastern edge of Hans Peterson Flats (Fig. 4C). Field evidence supporting faulting is best exposed at two locations. At the northeast corner of Hans Peterson Flats, where 330 m (1,000 ft) of Pennsylvanian and Permian strata along the western limb of Madigan Gulch anticline have been removed by faulting, the fault plane dips 80° to 85° northeast and trends N15W. About 3.2 km (2 mi) north of Hans Peterson Flats, along the western limb of Madigan Gulch anticline, the Quadrant Formation is in fault contact with the Bea-

verhead Formation. Additional evidence for high-angle faulting is suggested by geometric constructions; they show the exposed Quadrant Formation is consistently thinned along the western limb of the Madigan Gulch anticline and suggest that faulting is continuous along the eastern edge of Hans Peterson Flats.

Along the eastern limb of the Armstead anticline south of the Tertiary gravels (Fig. 4E), blocks of Precambrian gneiss are bordered on two sides by relatively undeformed, linear ridges of Flathead Formation. The relationship between bedding orientation and fault angle, the fact that fault movement is dominantly within the Wolsey shale, and the continuity of bedding orientations within the Cambrian sandstones bounding the Precambrian gneisses all point toward the development of a duplex (Boyer and Elliott, 1982).

Locally, the duplex was rotated with bedding during the development of the Armstead anticline, and subsequent erosion

EXPLANATION

Qt	TALUS
Qal	ALLUVIUM
UNCONFORMITY	
Tg	TERRACE GRAVELS
UNCONFORMITY	
Tv	VOLCANICS (UNDIFFERENTIATED)
Tkb	BEAVERHEAD FORMATION
ANGULAR UNCONFORMITY	
Kk	KOOTENAI FORMATION
UNCONFORMITY	
Jsw	SWIFT FORMATION
UNCONFORMITY	
Tt	THANES FORMATION
Td	DINWOODY FORMATION
UNCONFORMITY	
Pp	PHOSHORIA FORMATION
Pp	QUADRANT FORMATION
Pa	AMSDEN FORMATION
UNCONFORMITY	
Mbs	BIG SNOWY FORMATION
UNCONFORMITY	
Mm	MISSION CANYON FORMATION
Ml	LODGEPOLE FORMATION
Dt	THREE FORKS FORMATION
Dj	JEFFERSON FORMATION
UNCONFORMITY	
Cp	PILGRAM FORMATION
UNCONFORMITY	
Cw	WOLSEY FORMATION
Cf	FLATHEAD FORMATION
ANGULAR UNCONFORMITY	
pC	PRECAMBRIAN (UNDIFFERENTIATED)

exposed an end-on view (Figs. 4E, 6B). In the southern part of the study area, only Archean rocks are involved in thrusting, but isolated linear ridges of Cambrian sandstone present in the foot-wall help to define the thrust trace. Young (1982) reported a distinct compositional change in the Archean gneisses coincident with the proposed thrust trace. Farther north, the thrust becomes bedding-plane-parallel in the upper part of the Jefferson Formation, and part of the Jefferson Formation is duplicated. Immediately south of the Tertiary gravels, the thrust truncates against a series of vertical tear faults, providing a mechanism for displacement transfer. North of the Tertiary gravels, a normal unfaulted stratigraphic sequence is present. As expected, a very small amount of mesoscopic deformation is observed in the duplex structure. The overlying Mississippian carbonates do not appear to be involved in faulting. However, a large-scale, slightly conical fold is developed in the Mississippian carbonates above the duplex structure. The axial surface trace of this fold makes an oblique angle to the implied transport direction.

Four major northwest-trending folds are present within the study area from east to west: the Grayling syncline, the Armstead anticline, the Cedar Creek syncline, and the Madigan Gulch anticline. All of the folds are in the hanging wall of the structurally lowest thrust fault. Analysis using tangent diagrams suggests that the folds are cylindrical, and, except for the Madigan Gulch anticline, have a mean plunge of about 8°, N19W. The Madigan Gulch anticline plunges 7°, S18E.

The Grayling syncline is an eastward-verging, asymmetrical syncline with a steep west limb and a flat east limb. The east limb contains several low-amplitude minor folds roughly parallel to the major folds; these minor structures are possibly related to thrusting. The syncline is covered by Tertiary volcanics to the north and truncated against the Armstead thrust to the south.

The Armstead anticline, an arcuate asymmetrical anticline, is the central structural feature in the study area (Fig. 4). Erosion has breached the anticline, exposing an Archean core. The southern extension of the fold is covered by the Clark Canyon Reservoir.

The Cedar Creek syncline is separated from the Armstead

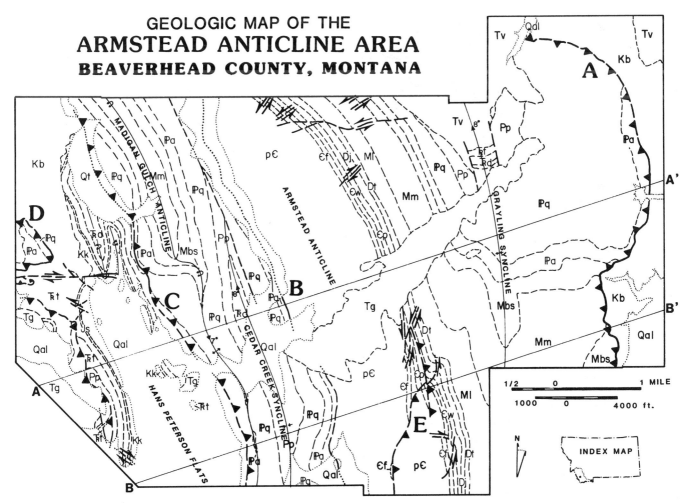

Figure 4. Geologic map of study area showing location of leading edge thrust (A), listric normal fault (B), backthrusts (C), structurally highest thrust (D), duplex structure (E), and major folds. Explanation on facing page.

Figure 5. Photographs showing major faults in study area. A, North-facing view of structurally lowest thrust fault along eastern edge of study area (apparent offset of fault trace is due to topography); Mm = Mission Canyon Formation, Kb = Beaverhead Formation. B, North-facing view of listric normal fault along western edge of Armstead anticline; Mbs = Big Snowy Formation, PC = Precambrian gneisses. C, North-facing aerial view of Cedar Creek syncline, foreground to midground. D, South-facing view of Hans Peterson Flats; foreground is small-scale Kootenai Formation fold; background shows linear, tree-covered Quadrant Formation ridges.

anticline by north-northwest–trending faults (Figs. 4, 5C). The limbs of the syncline are well defined by linear ridges of the Quadrant Formation. In the core of the syncline, the Phosphoria Formation is exposed. The northern terminus of the syncline is fault-bounded, and to the south, the fold extends beyond the map area for an unknown distance.

The Madigan Gulch anticline (Fig. 4) is an eastward-verging, asymmetrical anticline with an overturned east limb and a steep west limb. Reverse faults along the eastern edge of Hans Peterson Flats offset major parts of the fold, suggesting that the fold is dying out southward. The fold is most easily recognized at its north end, where Mississippian carbonates are well exposed in the anticlinal core.

Several smaller folds at the northwest corner of Hans Peterson Flats (Figs. 4, 5D) appear to continue southward beneath alluvium. Farther north, the folds are cut off by faulting, while to

the south an east-west fault cuts across the folds. Analysis of the largest anticline suggests that it is cylindrical and that the fold hinge plunges steeply (45°) southward. The trace of the axial surface is roughly parallel to those of the major folds. The greater development of folds north of an east-west fault (Fig. 4) strongly suggests an interaction between eastward thrusting and westward backthrusting.

HYPOTHESES FOR THE ORIGIN OF THE ARMSTEAD ANTICLINE

Three possible models can be formulated for the structural development of the Henneberry Ridge area: Model I: a cut-off portion of a preexisting structure (Fig. 7A, B); Model II: a block uplift flanked by monoclinal fold(s) (Fig. 7C, D); and Model III: a hanging wall anticline involving Archean rocks (Fig. 7E).

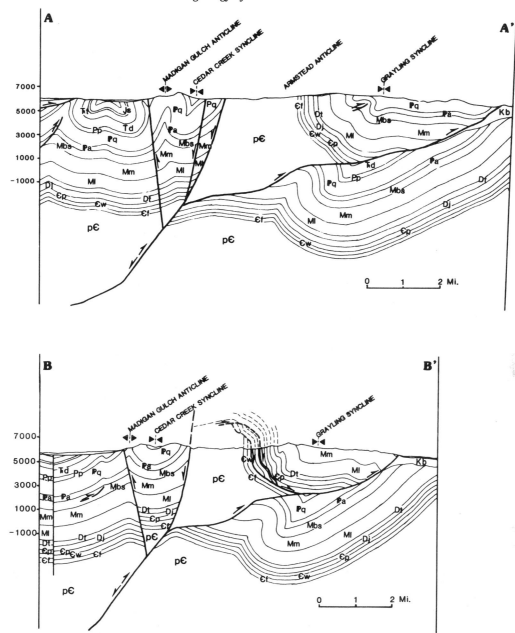

Figure 6. Cross sections A-A′ and B-B′ across study area. Footwall rocks are interpreted from scattered outcrops at Daly's Spur and Clark Canyon Dam (Lowell, 1965). Section B-B′ cuts through duplex structure and shows proposed pre-erosion structure. (Location of cross sections is shown in Fig. 4.)

Model I can be broken into two slightly different geometries based on the mechanical response of the Archean rocks and the amount of stratigraphic displacement. The first involves the decapitation of an Archean-cored "high" by eastward migrating thrusts (Fig. 7A). The continued movement results in the passive transport of the decapitated basement high. Scholten and others (1955) suggested somewhat similar relations along the Tendoy thrust. Allmendinger (1981) inferred a similar situation for the Meade plate in southeastern Idaho.

Model Ib, suggested by C. J. Schmidt (1983, personal communication), suggests dynamic overlap of foreland and thrust belt tectonics, such as those suggested along the transverse region between the southwestern Montana reentrant and the central Montana salient (Schmidt and Hendrix, 1981). In this model, eastward moving thrusts encounter the steep west-facing side of a foreland block uplift (Fig. 7B). To circumvent the block uplift and maintain the detachment within the same stratigraphic level, the thrust cuts off the triangular corner of the uplift (Serra, 1977). The now allochthonous Archean block is rotated during transport to a position superposed on the block uplift. The area where the triangular corner was removed from the autochthonous Archean block would then represent a subsurface thrust ramp.

Model II involves the development of monoclinal folds associated with movement along vertical block uplifts. Two slightly different kinematic variations can be envisioned, based on the position of the leading edge thrust at depth. In Model IIa, surficial thrusting is interpreted to have been generated by dominantly vertical movement at depth (Fig. 7C). This implies that the structurally lowest fault would steepen from 35° to near-vertical at depth. The steepening of the fault and the change from horizontal to vertical movement with depth make the presence of Archean rocks in the Armstead anticline understandable. This structure would most likely represent a transitional structure between the high-angle foreland structures and the low-angle thrust belt structures.

Model IIb suggests that vertical movement of crystalline basement blocks could be responsible for the drape folding of the east limb of the Armstead anticline, as well as uplift of the Archean core of the anticline (Fig. 7D). The earlier thrust faults would be drape-folded along with the allochthonous Paleozoic strata during uplift. Normal faulting or gravitational sliding along the western edge of the Armstead anticline would be facilitated by the steeply dipping bedding on the western limb of the drape fold. Ruppel (1982, p. 11–14) proposed a similar mechanism for folding of thrusts in the ranges of east-central Idaho.

Model III (Fig. 7E) suggests that eastward thrusting and uplift are related through the development of a ramp anticline as a thrust fault cuts up-section from basement into the Paleozoic cover rocks. The Armstead anticline would be related to eastward thrusting through the development of a ramp (or Rich Model)

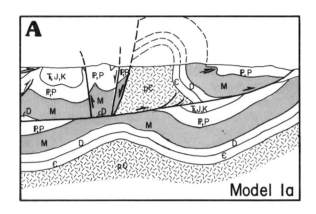

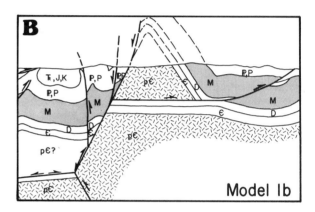

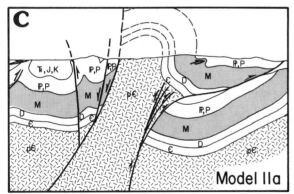

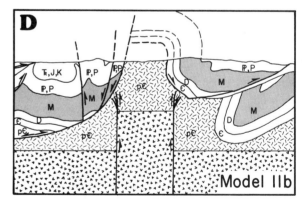

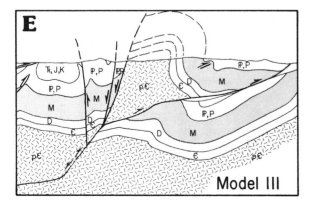

Figure 7. Diagrammatic cross sections through models. A, Diagram Model Ia, a "cut-off" portion of a preexisting structure. B, Diagram Model Ib, rotated corner of a reverse fault. C, Diagram Model IIa, an upthrust. D, Diagram Model IIb, a crystalline block uplift. E, Diagram Model III, a ramp anticline.

anticline (Rich, 1934) by the continued displacement of alloch-thonous material over a ramp (or step) in the footwall.

DISCUSSION

Each of the models represents a possible explanation for the structural development of the study area that would be compati-ble with regional observations.

Model Ia requires a preexisting basement high. Also, this model implies that the mechanical response to thrusting of the Archean rocks is similar to the overlying Paleozoic strata, in order for the thrust to cut through the basement high rather than be deflected over it. This suggests that the prethrust structure was relatively free of major structural anisotropies. The model does

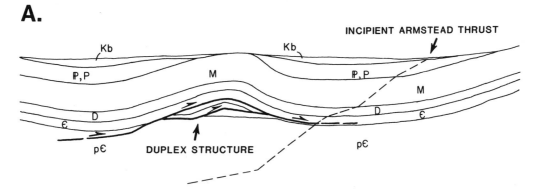

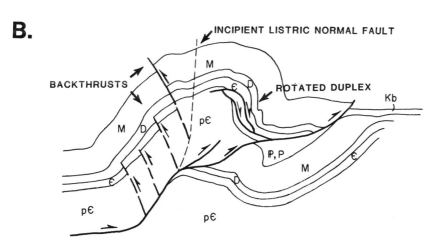

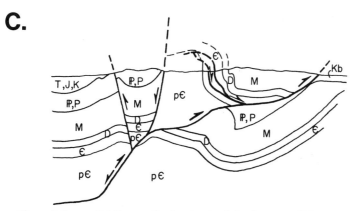

Figure 8. Sequential diagram for the structural development of the present-day structural configuration of the Armstead anticline. A, Development of duplex structure, causing localized topographic relief. B, Thrusting along Armstead thrust, resulting in ramp anticline, backthrusting, and rotation of duplex structure. C, Listric normal faulting over ramp results in present-day structures.

not provide a reasonable explanation for the development of major folds in the sedimentary rocks and high-angle normal faults along the western edge of the Armstead anticline. Additionally, all movement along the normal faults must have postdated thrusting in order to avoid reactivation. The faults must then either cut the sole fault or merge with it at depth. If the normal faults cut the major thrust, then the resulting geometry is indistinguishable from Model III. Conversely, the normal faults rapidly flatten and merge with the major thrust fault at depth (i.e., listric). In this case, the tight curvatures of the normal faults would mean that the stratigraphic displacement of several thousand feet would most certainly result in a larger degree of rotation than is observed along the western margin of the Armstead anticline.

The dimensions of the triangular mass of Archean rocks (Fig. 7B) dictate the dip and displacement on the fault. This also fixes the structural relief between Archean rocks in the hanging wall and the footwall. However, based on surface exposures, reasonable stratigraphic reconstructions show that the base of the Cambrian is ±6,000 ft (1,830 m) above the top of the Archean rocks on the footwall (left side in Fig. 7B). This discrepancy, or void, between the base of the Cambrian rocks and top of the Archean rocks is indicated by question marks in Figure 7B. The void must be filled by either Archean rocks or imbricate thrust slices (Serra, 1977, Mode I). Additionally, the fact that the ramps are localized above the basement highs (Schmidt and O'Neill, 1982; Schmidt and others, this volume) indicates that the Archean rocks are mechanically more competent than the overlying Paleozoic strata. Model studies using photoelastic material (Wiltschko and Eastman, this volume) suggest that stresses induced by the advancing thrust would be concentrated at the tip of the reverse fault in the Archean rocks. This would imply that thrusts in the Paleozoic rocks would be deflected up over the tip of the mechanically more competent Archean rocks rather than cutting off the tip of these rocks.

The absence of extensional features tends to render Models IIa and IIb (block uplifts) less attractive. Model studies by Sanford (1959) and Friedman and others (1976) suggest that extensional features along the crest of the uplift may develop due to the lateral expansion of material. The only extensional features observed along the crest of the structure are the normal faults along the western edge of the Armstead anticline. Finally, if the model involves a folded thrust plane (Ruppel, 1982), no evidence of mass wasting of material was observed along the east flank of the Armstead anticline.

Model III represents our preferred model for the structural history of the Armstead anticline. In this model the development of the Archean-cored Armstead anticline is genetically related to overthrusting through the development of a Rich Model anticline

over a subsurface ramp (Fig. 8). The presence of the thrust ramp triggers the development of the other major structural features of the area. The high-angle reverse faults along the western limb of the Madigan Gulch anticline can be interpreted to be backthrusts caused by the movement of allochthonous material over the ramp. The high-angle normal faults separating the Madigan Gulch anticline and the Cedar Creek syncline from the Armstead anticline are interpreted as listric normal faults, which were localized over the thrust ramp as eastward thrusting waned (Royse and others, 1975). The development of the Madigan Gulch anticline and Cedar Creek syncline between the backthrusts and the listric normal faults, as well as its being parallel to the Grayling syncline and the Armstead anticline, suggest a common compressional development. The east-west faults at the northern end of Hans Peterson Flats and the northern end of the Armstead anticline strongly suggest that these faults are related to the fault in the Archean rocks cutting up-section rapidly toward the north (i.e., a transverse ramp).

CONCLUSIONS

The structural development of the Armstead anticline is interpreted to be the result of eastward thrusting forming a Rich-Model anticline over a subsurface ramp. Thrusting was originally concentrated around the duplex area, possibly forming localized highlands. Continued thrusting incorporated larger amounts of Archean rocks via a lower detachment zone. Displacement of this allochthonous material over a ramp resulted in the formation of the Armstead anticline and the development of backthrusts along the eastern edge of Hans Peterson Flats. As backthrusting progressed, it impinged against the westernmost thrust and caused the development of several smaller folds along the northern end of Hans Peterson Flats. Later, listric normal faulting localized over the footwall ramp, cut the western limb of the Armstead anticline, and placed rotated Mississippian carbonates in the hanging wall against Archean rocks in the footwall.

ACKNOWLEDGMENTS

This manuscript is based on a master's thesis completed at Texas A&M University, College Station. Constructive criticism from Chris Schmidt and reviewers Ed Ruppel, Ned Stearns, and Jerry Bartholomew greatly improved the manuscript.

Support from the Arco Oil and Gas Company, Shell Oil Company, Conoco Oil Company, and the American Association of Petroleum Geologists for the original thesis work is acknowledged and appreciated.

REFERENCES CITED

Allmendinger, R. N., 1981, Structural geometry of Meade Thrust Plate in northern Blackfoot Mountains, southeastern Idaho: American Association of Petroleum Geologists Bulletin, v. 65, p. 509–525.

Alpha, A. G., 1955, Tectonic history of north central Montana: Billings Geological society 6th Annual Field Conference Guidebook, p. 129–142.

Bally, A. W., Gordy, P. L., and Stewart, G. A., 1966, Structure, seismic data, and orogenic evolution of southern Canadian Rocky Mountains: Bulletin of Canadian Petroleum Geology, v. 14, p. 337–381.

Boyer, S. E., and Elliot, D., 1982, Thrust systems: American Association of Petroleum Geologists Bulletin, v. 66, p. 1196–1230.

Constenius, K., 1983, Relationship between the Kisherln Basin and the Flathead listric normal fault and Lewis thrust salient, *in* Powers, R. B., ed., Geologic studies of the Cordilleran thrust belt, 1982: Denver, Colorado, Rocky Mountain Association of Geologists, p. 817–830.

Coryell, J. J., 1983, Structural geology of the Henneberry Ridge area, Beaverhead County, Montana [M.S. thesis]: Texas A&M University, 126 p.

Friedman, M., Handin, J., Logan, J. M., Min, K. D., and Stearns, D. W., 1976, Experimental folding of rocks under confining pressure; Part III, Faulted drape folds in multilithologic layered specimens: Geological Society of America Bulletin, v. 87, p. 1049–1066.

Hammons, P. M., 1981, Structural observations along the southern trace of the Tendoy Fault, southern Beaverhead County, Montana, *in* Tucker, T. E., ed., Montana Geological Society Field Conference and Symposium Guidebook to southwest Montana: Montana Geological Society 1981 Guidebook, p. 253–260.

Hildreth, G. D., 1981, Stratigraphy of the Mississippian Big Snowy Formation of the Armstead Anticline, Beaverhead County, Montana, *in* Tucker, T. E., ed., Montana Geological Society Field Conference and Symposium Guidebook to southwest Montana: Montana Geological Society 1981 Guidebook, p. 49–57.

Klepper, M. R., 1950, A geologic reconnaissance of parts of Beaverhead and Madison Counties, Montana: U.S. Geological Survey Bulletin 969-C, 85 p., 1 map, scale 1:250,000.

Lowell, W. R., 1965, Geologic map of the Bannock-Grayling area, Beaverhead County, Montana: U.S. Geological Survey Miscellaneous Geologic Investigations Map, I-433, scale 1:31,680.

Perry, W. F., Ryder, R. T., and Maughan, E. K., 1981, The southern part of the Montana thrust belt; A preliminary reevaluation of structure, thermal maturation, and petroleum potential, *in* Tucker, T. E., ed., Montana Geological Society Field Conference and Symposium Guidebook to southwest Montana: Montana Geological Society 1981 Guidebook, p. 261–273.

Prucha, J. J., Graham, J. A., and Nickelsen, R. P., 1965, Basement controlled deformation in Wyoming Province of Rocky Mountains Foreland: American Association of Petroleum Geologists Bulletin, v. 49, p. 966–992.

Rich, J. L., 1934, Mechanics of low-angle overthrust faulting as illustrated by Cumberland thrust block, Virginia, Kentucky, and Tennessee: American Association of Petroleum Geologists Bulletin, v. 18, p. 1584–1596.

Royse, F., Jr., Warner, M. A., and Reese, D. L., 1975, Thrust belt structural geometry and related stratigraphic problems Wyoming–Idaho–northern Utah: Denver, Colorado, Rocky Mountain Association of Geologists 1985 Symposium, p. 41–54.

Ruppel, E. T., 1982, Cenozoic block uplifts in east-central Idaho and southwest Montana: U.S. Geological Survey Professional Paper 1224, 24 p.

Ruppel, E. T., Wallace, C. H., Schmidt, C. J., and Lopes, D. A., 1981, Preliminary interpretation of the thrust belt in southwest and west-central Montana and east-central Idaho, *in* Tucker, T. E., ed., Montana Geological Society Field Conference and Symposium Guidebook to southwest Montana: Montana Geological Society 1981 Guidebook, p. 139–159.

Sanford, A. R., 1959, Analytical and experimental study of simple geologic structures: Geological Society of America Bulletin, v. 70, p. 19–52.

Schmidt, C. J., 1976, The influence of Precambrian structural trends on Laramide faulting in the northern Tobacco Root Mountains, southwestern Montana: Geological Society of America Abstracts with Programs, v. 8, p. 627.

Schmidt, C. J., and Garihan, J. M., 1983, Laramide tectonic development of the Rocky Mountain foreland of southwestern Montana, *in* Lowell, J. D., ed., Rocky Mountain foreland basins and uplifts: Denver, Colorado, Rocky Mountain Association of Geologists, p. 271–294.

——— , 1986, Role of recurrent movement on northwest-trending basement faults in the tectonic evolution of southwestern Montana: Proceedings of the 6th International Symposium on Basement Tectonics, p. 1–15.

Schmidt, C. J., and Hendrix, T. E., 1981, Tectonic controls for thrust belt and Rocky Mountain foreland structures in northern Tobacco Root Mountains, Jefferson Canyon area, southwestern Montana, *in* Tucker, T. E., ed., Montana Geological Society Field Conference and Symposium Guidebook to southwest Montana: Montana Geological Society 1981 Guidebook, p. 167–180.

Schmidt, C. J., and O'Neill, J. M., 1983, Structural evolution of the southwest Montana transverse zone, *in* Powers, R. B., ed., Geologic studies of the Cordilleran thrust belt, 1982: Denver, Colorado, Rocky Mountain Association of Geologists, p. 193–218.

Scholten, R., 1964, Crushed pebble conglomerate; A discussion: Journal of Geology, v. 72, p. 486–489.

Scholten, R., Keenmon, K. A., and Kupsch, W. O., 1955, Geology of the Lima region, southwestern Montana and adjacent Idaho: Geological Society of America Bulletin, v. 66, p. 345–404.

Serra, S., 1977, Styles of deformation in the ramp regions of overthrust faults: Wyoming Geological Association 29th Annual Field Conference Guidebook, p. 487–498.

Skipp, B., and Hait, M. H., Jr., 1977, Allochthons along the northeast margin of the Snake River Plain, Idaho: Wyoming Geological Association 29th Annual Field Conference Guidebook, p. 499–515.

Sloss, L. L., 1950, Paleozoic sedimentation in Montana area: American Association of Petroleum Geologists Bulletin, v. 34, p. 423–451.

Tanner, W. F., 1963, Crushed pebble conglomerate of southwestern Montana: Journal of Geology, v. 71, p. 637–641.

Woodward, L. A., 1981, Tectonic framework of disturbed belt of west-central Montana: American Association of Petroleum Geologists Bulletin, v. 65, p. 291–203.

Wooden, J. L., Vitaliano, C. J., Koehler, S. W., and Ragland, P. C., 1978, The late Precambrian mafic dikes of the southern Tobacco Root Mountains, Montana; Geochemistry, Rb-Sr geochronology, and relationship to Belt tectonics: Canadian Journal of Earth Sciences, v. 15, p. 467–479.

Young, M. L., 1982, Petrology and origin of Archean rocks in the Armstead anticline of southwest Montana [M.S. thesis]: Missoula, University of Montana, 66 p.

MANUSCRIPT ACCEPTED BY THE SOCIETY FEBRUARY 9, 1988

Geological Society of America
Memoir 171
1988

Cordilleran thrust belt–Rocky Mountain foreland interaction near Bannack, Montana

L. M. Johnson and J. W. Sears
Department of Geology, University of Montana, Missoula, Montana 59812

ABSTRACT

Near Bannack, Montana, the Cordilleran thrust belt overlaps a Laramide Rocky Mountain foreland structure. The Precambrian-cored Armstead anticline formed along a steep, basement-rooted fault. Erosion breached the anticline, and Upper Cretaceous Beaverhead Group rocks, including distinctive conglomerates and tuffs, overlapped the truncated structure with angular unconformity. The Ermont thrust and associated structures then advanced into the area, disrupted the preexisting foreland structure, and tightly folded the Beaverhead Group.

The interaction between thrust structures and the Rocky Mountain foreland structure resulted in younger-over-older thrust faults and thrusts that cut down-section in the direction of transport.

INTRODUCTION

Near Bannack, Montana (Fig. 1), Upper Cretaceous synorogenic conglomerate and volcanic rock provide time constraints on the evolution of the overlap zone between the overthrust belt and the Rocky Mountain foreland. We studied this area to determine the geometry and structural history of the overlap zone where the Precambrian basement-cored Armstead anticline intersects the Ermont thrust system.

Lowell (1965) published the first detailed map of the Bannack area. Thomas (1981) and Coryell (1983) completed structural studies to the north and south, respectively. De la Tour-du-Pin (1983), Ruppel and Lopez (1984), Skipp and Hait (1977), and Scholten (1968) provided regional structural interpretations. Perry and others (1981, 1983) studied the detailed structural history of the nearby Blacktail-Snowcrest arch. Coryell and Spang (this volume) have interpreted the Armstead anticline as a large fold above a thrust ramp rather than as a foreland uplift.

Regional structural setting

Southwestern Montana is the meeting ground of two structural provinces: the largely allochthonous rocks of the Cordilleran thrust belt and the relatively autochthonous rocks of the Rocky Mountain foreland (Scholten, 1968; Dubois, 1983; Beutner, 1977). Following the lead of Armstrong (1968) and Beutner (1977), Perry and others (1983) adopted the terms "Sevier-style"

for the western allochthonous province, and "Laramide" for the eastern parautochthonous province.

The Tendoy thrust (Fig. 1) defines the leading edge of the frontal fold and thrust zone as defined by Ruppel and Lopez (1984) from near Lima, Montana, northward to a point approximately 20 km south of the study area (Fig. 1). This zone of imbricate thrusts marks the boundary between the Rocky Mountain foreland province to the east and the thrust belt to the west. The Tendoy fault carries Mississippian rocks over Upper Cretaceous Beaverhead conglomerate along much of its exposed length (Hammons, 1981). Lowell (1965) and Coryell (1983) mapped a thrust in the Bannack area, which also carries Mississippian and Pennsylvanian rocks over Beaverhead conglomerate. This thrust is on trend with the Tendoy thrust to the south. However, the McKenzie thrust system, which W. J. Perry and W. J. Sando are currently analyzing (W. J. Perry, written communication, 1987) interrupts the trend so that the thrust in the Bannack area cannot be directly traced into the Tendoy thrust (Fig. 1). Following De la Tour-du-Pin (1983), we refer to the thrust in the Bannack area as the Armstead thrust.

Geologic setting of the Bannack area

Three major structures underlie the hills south of Bannack: the Armstead thrust, the Precambrian-cored Armstead anticline, and the Ermont thrust (Fig. 1).

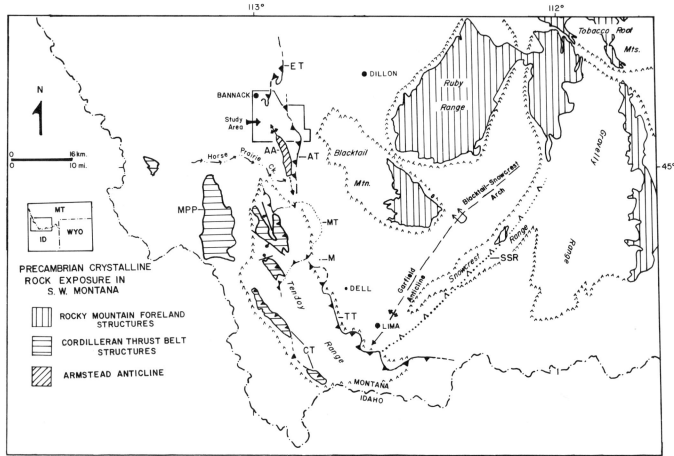

Figure 1. Regional map showing Bannack area, selected tectonic features, and distribution of Precambrian basement rocks. AA = Armstead anticline; AT = Armstead thrust; CT = Cabin thrust; ET = Ermont thrust; M = McKnight Canyon; MPP = Maiden Peak Prong; MT = McKenzie thrust system (based on work in progress by W. J. Sando and W. J. Perry); SSR = sub–Snowcrest Range thrust; TT = Tendoy thrust.

The Armstead thrust (Fig. 1) places Mississippian limestone over Upper Cretaceous (middle-Campanian to late-Maastrichtian) Beaverhead conglomerate (southeast corner Fig. 2). South of Grasshopper Creek (Fig. 2), the fault crosses the Beaverhead unconformity and places Upper Cretaceous andesitic agglomerate over Beaverhead conglomerate.

The Armstead anticline is a broad, asymmetric fold with a steep eastern limb and a gentle north plunge. Precambrian crystalline rocks, including marble, schist, gneiss, and amphibolite, crop out in its core. The Armstead anticline is cut on both flanks by faults. The Armstead thrust cuts Paleozoic rocks that form the east limb of this fold and the adjacent Grayling syncline (Lowell, 1965; Coryell, 1983) (Fig. 2). A steep fault cuts the west limb. The Armstead thrust is one of a large number of Precambrian-cored structures in southwest Montana (Fig. 1). Precambrian crystalline basement rocks crop out in large areas of Late Cretaceous to Tertiary uplifts (Scholten and others, 1955; Perry and others, 1983; Schwartz, 1983). Precambrian crystalline rocks also crop out along the eastern edge of the thrust belt. West of the

Tendoy thrust, the Cabin thrust carries Precambrian crystalline rock over Mississippian and older rocks (Dubois, 1983; Scholten and others, 1955) (Fig. 1).

The Ermont thrust (Figs. 1, 2) places Mississippian limestone over Upper Cretaceous Beaverhead conglomerate and associated volcanic rocks. Its sinuous trace extends 25 km north of Bannack (Thomas, 1981; Lowell, 1965; Myers, 1952), where it apparently passes into north-plunging folds that are cut by the Late Cretaceous Pioneer batholith complex (Brandon, 1984). To the south, the Ermont thrust is replaced by a complex set of thrusts and folds west of the Armstead anticline. One of these folds, the Madigan Gulch anticline, was active both before and after deposition of the Beaverhead conglomerate.

SYNTECTONIC DEPOSITS

Beaverhead conglomerate and associated volcanic rocks formed during growth of the structures in the Bannack area. The Beaverhead conglomerate has two distinct lithotypes, which are

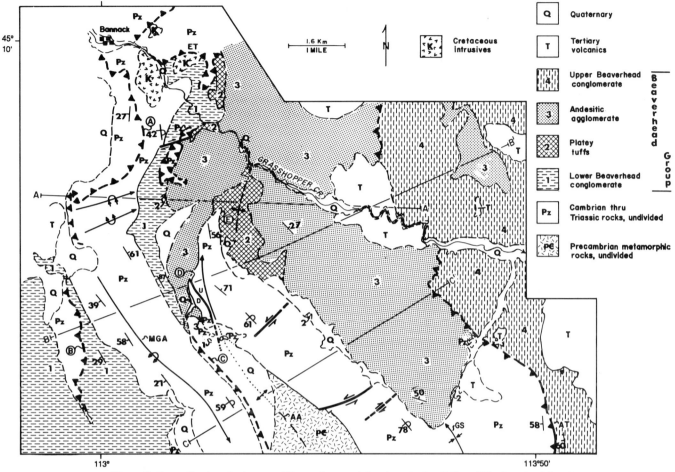

Figure 2. Generalized geologic map of Bannack area. AA = Armstead anticline; AT = Armstead thrust; ET = Ermont thrust; GS = Grayling syncline; MGA = Madigan Gulch anticline. Circled letters are locations referred to in the text.

stratigraphically separated by a thick volcanic rock sequence. Descriptions of the Beaverhead Group (Lowell and Klepper, 1953; Nichols and others, 1985; Ryder and Scholten, 1973; Ryder and Ames, 1970) do not mention volcanic rock. Since the Beaverhead conglomerate stratigraphically bounds the volcanic rocks, we include them in the Beaverhead Group. We have divided the Beaverhead Group into four informal units in the Bannack area. From oldest to youngest these units are: limestone-clast conglomerate, bedded tuff, andesitic agglomerate, and quartzite+limestone-clast conglomerate.

Unit 1 of the Beaverhead Group crops out in the western part of the map area (Fig. 2). It is a limestone-clast conglomerate with minor coarse- to medium-grained sandstone beds. The conglomerate is clast-supported and forms beds that are 0.5 to 10 m thick. Clasts are subangular to rounded, range from <1 to >20 cm in diameter, and appear to be exclusively derived from Paleozoic strata. Eighty to 90 percent are limestone, many containing crinoid stems; 10 to 20 percent are quartzite and chert, apparently derived from Upper Paleozoic formations. The conglomerate matrix is medium- to coarse-grained carbonate-cemented sand. Sand grains are predominately chert and quartz. Reddish brown to maroon sandstone beds form lenses within the conglomerates. Haley (1983) interpreted similar deposits in the Beaverhead Group as perennial braided-stream deposits.

Unit 2 overlies unit 1 with angular unconformity and is a distinctive bedded tuff unit more than 30 m thick. The tuff is white, tan, or reddish brown, fine-grained to aphanitic, and has a well-developed platey parting in the lower part of the unit. The platey parting is subparallel to bedding, which is defined by differences in color and/or grain size. Thin sections show the platey tuff is composed of alternating beds (0.5 to 2 cm thick) of fine-grained matrix and pumice fragments. Thin bedding, platey parting, and grading of pumice fragments indicate the tuff may have been deposited as air-fall tuff in a lacustrine environment (Thomas, 1981). Planar zones of platey tuff are intercalated with massive tuff, which may represent subaerially deposited ash.

Unit 3 is an andesitic agglomerate that overlies unit 2 with local angular unconformity. The rock matrix is green, brown, and purple andesite that is medium- to fine-grained with 5 to 30 percent plagioclase phenocrysts, 1 to 5 percent hornblende phenocrysts, and less than 1 percent biotite phenocrysts. Clasts are of similar composition and mineralogy, ranging from 1 to 20 cm long, and are well rounded to subangular. The thickness of the unit in the Bannack area is unknown, due to the lack of distinct bedding, but Thomas (1981) estimated a minimum thickness of 300 m.

Unit 4 is a quartzite+limestone-clast conglomerate that unconformably overlies unit 3. The stratigraphic contact between units 3 and 4 is exposed in the northeastern corner of the map area. Clasts in unit 4 are predominately red to maroon quartzite that is medium- to coarse-grained with internal cross-stratification, probably derived from the Proterozoic quartzites of the thrust belt to the west (Ryder and Scholten, 1973; Ruppel and Lopez, 1984). Exposures of this unit along the north side of Grasshopper Creek, 13 km downstream from Bannack, also contain highly weathered andesite clasts derived from the underlying andesite agglomerate unit. Visual estimates of the number of andesite clasts range from 3 to 5 percent; however, clast-shaped voids in the conglomerate, which most likely represent weathered-out andesite clasts, account for another 3 to 5 percent. Gray limestone and white quartzite clasts probably derived from Paleozoic formations make up about 30 percent of the clasts. The conglomerates are clast-supported with a matrix of medium- to coarse-grained, carbonate-cemented sands. The conglomerate is interbedded with sandstone that is fine- to coarse-grained, tan to reddish brown, and carbonate-cemented. South of Grasshopper Creek, conglomerate pebbles are notably smaller, and sandstone is more prevalent in unit 4.

The conglomerates and volcanic rocks assigned herein to the Beaverhead Group define a stratigraphic sequence. The stratigraphic contacts within this sequence of rocks all have local angular unconformities, indicating that this sequence of rocks was deposited while structures were forming in the area.

Correlations

The Beaverhead type section at McKnight Canyon (Fig. 1) contains two clastic units, ranging from conglomerate to sandstone, and an intervening lacustrine limestone unit (Lowell and Klepper, 1953). The sequence of conglomerate and volcanic rock in the Bannack area is similar to the Beaverhead type section in that it also contains upper and lower conglomerate, but with an intervening volcanic sequence that was in part also deposited in a lacustrine environment. This overall similarity between the two sections allows for lithostratigraphic correlations.

Ryder and Scholten (1973) mapped our unit 4 of the Beaverhead Group as the Kidd Quartzite conglomerate. The Kidd Quartzite conglomerate unit is younger than the Lima Conglomerate unit of Ryder and Scholten (1973). As unit 1 is older than the Kidd Quartzite conglomerate (unit 4), it is most easily correlated with either the Lima Conglomerate unit in the Dell or Lima areas or the McKnight limestone-conglomerate unit of Ryder and Scholten (1973). Ryder and Scholten (1973) reported that both the Lima Conglomerate unit in the Dell area and the McKnight

limestone-conglomerate unit contain significant percentages of Belt quartzite clasts; recent investigations, however, have revealed that these two basal conglomerate units do not contain Belt clasts (W. J. Perry, personal communication, 1987). Member 1 of the Beaverhead Group in the Bannack area contains no Belt clasts; we have tentatively correlated it with the Lima Conglomerate. Thomas (1981) also correlated the limestone-clast conglomerate north of the map area with the Lima Conglomerate. Palynologic data suggest the Lima conglomerate is of middle Campanian (78 to 81 Ma) age (Nichols and others, 1985).

Lowell (1965) assigned a Tertiary age to the bedded tuff (unit 2) and andesitic agglomerate (unit 3) in the Bannack area. More recently, Thomas (1981) assigned a Cretaceous age to this volcanic sequence, based on Late Cretaceous dates of 67 to 71 Ma (Snee and Sutter, 1981). Units 2 and 3 in the map area are continuous with the sequence mapped to the north by Thomas (1981).

The sequence of two lithologically distinct conglomerates and stratigraphically intervening volcanic rocks records an episode of volcanism that is bracketed in time by the two conglomerate units. Unit 4 is probably Maastrichtian or upper Campanian (Nichols and others, 1985) and overlies unit 3. Unit 1 may be 78 to 81 m.y. old if it is coeval with the lithologically similar Lima conglomerate. Thus this sequence of rocks likely represents deposition between 81 and perhaps 65 Ma (Fig. 3).

As mentioned above, the Late Cretaceous sequence in the Bannack area is similar to the Beaverhead Group type section at McKnight Canyon. Further lithostratigraphic correlation can be made in Clark Canyon, located about 20 km southeast of the Bannack area, where Lowell (1965) found andesite clasts in conglomerate overlying the middle limestone unit of the Beaverhead Group. Lowell's sequence of rock correlates with the stratigraphic

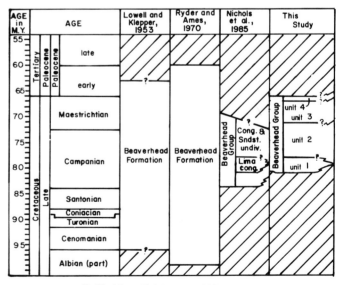

Modified from Nichols et al., 1985

Figure 3. Correlation chart of Beaverhead Group. Unit 1 = limestone-clast conglomerate; unit 2 = bedded tuff; unit 3 = andesitic agglomerate; unit 4 = quartzite+limestone-clast conglomerate.

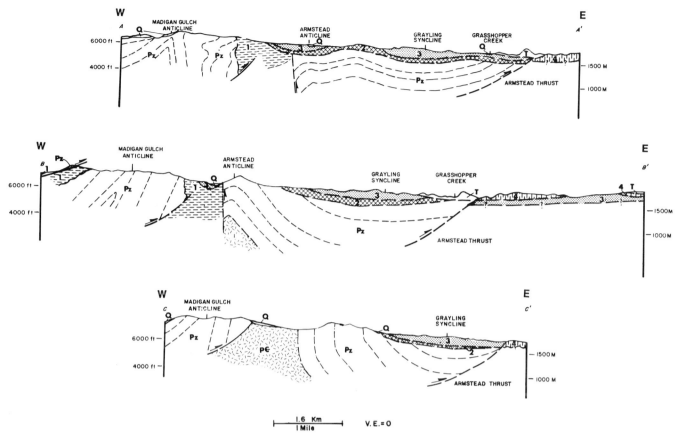

Figure 4. Cross sections (vertical scale = horizontal scale).

sequence in the map area, in which conglomerate with andesite clasts overlie the stratigraphically intermediate volcanic rock. Therefore the limestone unit in the Beaverhead Group type section and Beaverhead unit 2 in the Bannack area appear to occupy the same stratigraphic position and may represent deposition in a foreland basin lake. The platey tuff (unit 2) gave way to subaerially deposited tuff as the lake was filled, and then units 3 and 4 covered the area.

THRUST BELT–FORELAND INTERACTION

Two distinct episodes of deformation occurred in the Bannack area. Structures created during the first deformation were eroded and overlapped by Beaverhead conglomerate and volcanic rock. Structures formed during the second episode of deformation then cut the Beaverhead Group rocks. We suggest that the earlier deformation was related to development of Laramide Rocky Mountain foreland structures. Structures that cut rocks of the Beaverhead Group are part of the Cordilleran thrust belt.

The Ermont thrust transported Mississippian limestones eastward over Beaverhead conglomerate and volcanic rock (Fig. 2); thus, it is an older-over-younger thrust. In the north wall of Grasshopper Creek, 3 km east of Bannack, however, the fault cuts downsection through the Lodgepole Limestone from west to east in the hanging wall. This shows that the hanging-wall limestone was deformed prior to formation of the Ermont thrust.

The Armstead thrust is exposed or inferred for approximately 8 km of strike length in the eastern part of the map area (Fig. 2). Where the fault truncates the Grayling syncline, it carries Mississippian and Pennsylvanian rocks over Beaverhead Group unit 4. Previous maps (Lowell, 1965; Coryell, 1983) have indicated that the fault ends where the Grayling syncline plunges beneath unit 3 of the Beaverhead Group (Fig. 2). However, the contact between units 3 and 4 is on the same trend as the Armstead thrust. Examination of this contact immediately north of the point where the Grayling syncline plunges beneath unit 3 reveals that unit 3 structurally overlies unit 4 along a westward dipping fault (Fig. 4, A-A', B-B').

Most of the contact between the Beaverhead volcanic rocks and Paleozoic rocks on the east limb of the Armstead anticline is covered by colluvium. However, this contact is well exposed on the north-plunging nose of the Armstead anticline and shows that unit 2 overlaps the fold (Fig. 2, loc. E). Unit 2 also overlies Triassic rocks exposed in the core of the Grayling syncline. Because unit 2 lies unconformably on Paleozoic rocks on the east limb of the Armstead anticline and in the core of the Grayling syncline (near the southwest corner of Fig. 2), the Paleozoic rocks

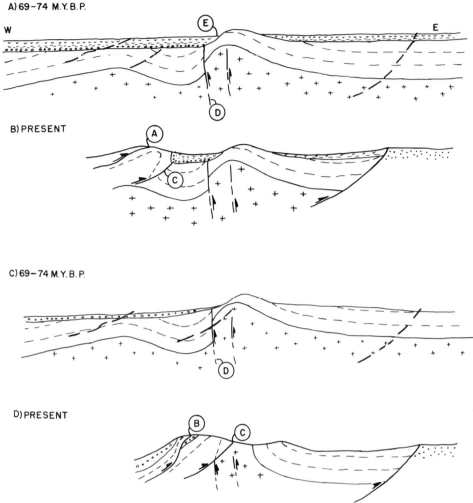

Figure 5. Schematic cross sections through Bannack area. Sections are arranged from south (C and D) to north (A and B), down plunge on the Armstead anticline. Circled letters correspond to locations in Figure 2. Location E is projected into line of section. Dashed lines curring up-section in A and C represent trace of future thrusts shown in B and D.

must have been deformed before deposition of unit 2. Since the Ermont thrust cuts units 2 and 3, we know that thrusting occurred after the deformation mentioned above. We believe that this pre-Beaverhead Group deformation was related to Laramide events of the Rocky Mountain foreland.

Further evidence for pre-Beaverhead Group deformation is found where unit 1 unconformably overlies Paleozoic rock exposed on both limbs of the Madigan Gulch anticline. Beds in unit 1 on the west limb of the fold dip moderately to the west, and beds on the east limb dip steeply to the east, forming an eastward-verging fold that is the same type of structure formed by the underlying pre-Beaverhead rocks (Fig. 4, B-B′). However, the Beaverhead rocks do not dip as steeply as the unconformably underlying Paleozoic rocks. This indicates the unconformity beneath the Beaverhead was involved in the folding, and therefore predates the later folding. The unconformity is on top of Mississippian limestones on the west limb of the fold, and rocks as

young as Permian are overlain by unit 1 on the east limb, showing that the Paleozoic rocks were tilted and eroded prior to deposition of unit 1.

The cross-cutting and overlapping relationships indicate that considerable folding and some faulting had taken place before deposition of the Beaverhead Group. Specifically, the Madigan Gulch anticline, the Armstead anticline, and the Grayling syncline had developed, perhaps as portions of a larger structure. Because thrusts cut the Beaverhead Group, these anticlines and synclines predate thrusting. We interpret the Precambrian-cored Armstead anticline as a Rocky Mountain foreland structure. A steep fault exposed on the west limb of the Armstead anticline does not cut unit 3 (Fig. 2, loc. D) and is therefore older than unit 3. This also shows that deformation occurred prior to deposition of the Beaverhead volcanic sequence and before Sevier-style thrusting in the Bannack area.

The Ermont thrust advanced into the area, cutting Beaverhead Group rocks. A possible southern extension of the Ermont thrust is exposed south of Bannack (Fig. 2, loc. A). This thrust carries uppermost Mississippian and Pennsylvanian rocks in the hanging wall. A small klippe east of location A (Fig. 2) also has uppermost Mississippian and Pennsylvanian rocks in the hanging wall and is interpreted as the same thrust. Where the thrust underlies the klippe, it is an older-over-younger thrust fault; however, where the fault is exposed west of the klippe, it is a younger-over-older thrust fault. The former type of thrust fault, located in the southwestern corner of the area (Fig. 2, loc. B), may also be the southward extension of the Ermont thrust, as it carries nearly the same part of the Paleozoic section in the hanging wall. The Madigan Gulch anticline is interpreted as a hanging-wall anticline which involved Paleozoic rocks, the Paleozoic-Late Cretaceous unconformity, and the Ermont(?) thrust. This anticline formed above the younger-over-older thrust fault that cuts the west limb of the Armstead anticline (Fig. 2, loc. C). This thrust turns into a blind thrust along its northern trace (Fig. 5, B; Fig. 4, A-A′, B-B′). The Armstead thrust cut the east limb of the preexisting Laramide structure and gently folded this limb into the Grayling syncline. This is similar to the interpretation Lowell (1965) implied in his cross sections. The Armstead thrust also cut the Paleozoic–Late Cretaceous unconformity and carried the Beaverhead unit 3 over unit 4. Steepening and overturning of the east limb of the preexisting Armstead anticline also probably accompanied displacement along the thrust.

The amount of displacement along each of the thrust faults is unknown because data necessary for balancing cross sections is not available. Efforts to balance sections are also hindered by the anomalous nature of the thrust structures.

An anticline within volcanic rocks of the Beaverhead Group, just north of the nose of the Armstead anticline (Fig. 2), may be a ramp anticline associated with the Armstead thrust. If this is the case, displacement along this thrust may be 3 or 4 km.

Displacement along the thrust that carries the Madigan Gulch anticline over the Armstead anticline must be considerably more, as it has juxtaposed two large-scale folds. Mapping indicates that displacement on this thrust gradually dies out northward. At the southern end of the map area the fault places

Mississippian rocks over Precambrian rocks. Farther north, a small outcrop of Mississippian limestone is exposed in the footwall (0.6 km north of loc. C, Fig. 2). Another small nearby outcrop exposes Beaverhead conglomerate, which is interpreted as being in depositional contact with the Mississippian limestone. If so, the thrust was cutting up-section in the footwall, evidently up through the pre–Upper Cretaceous unconformity.

Temporal relationships between the thrust faults are not clear. The southern extension of the Ermont(?) thrust (Fig. 2, loc. A, B) may have preceded the thrust, cutting the west limb of the Armstead anticline. The Ermont(?) thrust dips to the east, where it underlies the klippe, but dips to the west, where it cuts the Madigan Gulch anticline. This indicates the thrust was folded along with the Madigan Gulch anticline. This folding may have also involved the Ermont thrust north of Grasshopper Creek. No evidence is available to determine whether the Armstead thrust formed before or after the more western thrusts.

SUMMARY

Cross-cutting and overlapping relationships between the Upper Cretaceous Beaverhead Group and fold and thrust structures define two Late Cretaceous structural events in the Bannack area. The earlier event created a Precambrian-cored foreland bulge that was subsequently eroded and overlapped by Beaverhead conglomerate and volcanic rock. Sevier-style thrusts then cut the preexisting structure and overlying Beaverhead Group. The interaction of these structures resulted in younger-over-older thrust faults, thrust faults that cut down-section in the direction of transport, and thrust faults that cut through and displace stratigraphic unconformities.

ACKNOWLEDGMENTS

We thank W. J. Perry, Jr., for suggesting publication of this work. His knowledge of regional structures and Beaverhead stratigraphy has been of great value to us. We also thank E. T. Ruppel, H. W. Dresser, and B. Pearson for their valuable reviews.

REFERENCES CITED

Armstrong, R. L., 1968, Sevier orogenic belt in Nevada and Utah: Geological Society of America Bulletin, v. 79, p. 427–458.

Beutner, E. C., 1977, Causes and consequences of curvature in the Sevier orogenic belt, Utah to Montana, *in* Heisey, E. L., and others, eds., Rocky Mountain thrust belt geology and resources: Wyoming Geological Association 29th Field Conference Guidebook, p. 353–365.

Brandon, W. C., 1984, An origin for the McCartney's Mountain salient of the southwestern Montana fold and thrust belt [M.S. thesis]: Missoula, University of Montana, 110 p.

Coryell, J. J., 1983, Structural geology of the Henneberry Ridge area, Beaverhead County, Montana [M.S. thesis]: College Station, Texas A&M University, 125 p.

De la Tour-du-Pin, H., 1983, Contribution a l'etude geologique de l'Overthrust Belt du Montana (U.S.A.); Stratigraphie et Tectonique des Rocky Hills et du

Tendoy Range (Sud-Ouest du Montana) [Ph.D. thesis]: Brest, France, Universite' de Bretagne Occidentale, 256 p.

Dubois, D. P., 1983, Tectonic framework of basement thrust terrane, northern Tendoy Range, southwestern Montana, *in* Powers, R. B., ed., Geologic studies of the Cordilleran thrust belt, 1982: Denver, Colorado, Rocky Mountain Association of Geologists, v. 1, p. 145–158.

Haley, J. C., 1983, Depositional processes in Beaverhead Formation, southwestern Montana and northeastern Idaho, and their tectonic significance [abs.]: American Association of Petroleum Geologists Bulletin, v. 67, p. 1340.

Hammons, P. M., 1981, Structural observations along the southern trace of the Tendoy Fault, southern Beaverhead County, Montana: Montana Geological Society 1981 Field Conference Guidebook, p. 253–260.

Lowell, W. R., 1965, Geologic map of the Bannock-Grayling area, Beaverhead County, Montana: U.S. Geological Survey Miscellaneous Geologic Investigations Map, I-433, scale 1:31,680.

Lowell, W. R., and Klepper, M. R., 1953, Beaverhead Formation, a Laramide deposit in Beaverhead County, Montana: Geological Society of America Bulletin, v. 64, p. 235–244.

Myers, W. B., 1952, Geology and mineral deposits of the northwest quarter of the Willis Quadrangle and adjacent Brown's Lake area, Beaverhead County, Montana: U.S. Geological Survey Trace Element Investigations Report 259, 46 p.

Nichols, D. J., Perry, W. J., Jr., and Haley, J. C., 1985, Reinterpretation of palynology and age of Laramide syntectonic deposits, southwestern Montana, and revisions of the Beaverhead Group: Geology, v. 13, p. 149–153.

Perry, W. J., Ryder, R. T., and Maughn, E. K., 1981, The southern part of the southwest Montana thrust belt; A preliminary reevaluation of structure, thermal maturation, and petroleum potential, *in* Tucker, T. E., ed., Montana Geological Society Field Conference and Symposium Guidebook to Southwest Montana: Montana Geological Society 1981 Guidebook, p. 261–273.

Perry, W. J., Jr., Wardlaw, B. R., Bostick, N. H., and Maughan, E. K., 1983, Structure, burial history, and petroleum potential of frontal thrust belt and adjacent foreland, southwest Montana: American Association of Petroleum Geologists Bulletin, v. 67, no. 5, p. 725–743.

Ruppel, E. T., and Lopez, D. A., 1984, The thrust belt in southwest Montana and east-central Idaho: U.S. Geological Survey Professional Paper 1278, 41 p.

Ryder, R. T., and Ames, H. T., 1970, Palynology and age of Beaverhead Formation and their paleotectonic implications in Lima region, Montana-Idaho: American Association of Petroleum Geologists Bulletin, v. 54, p. 1155–1171.

Ryder, R.T., and Scholten, R., 1973, Syntectonic conglomerates in southwestern Montana; Their nature, orogen, and tectonic significance: Geological Society of America Bulletin, v. 84, p. 773–796.

Scholten, R., 1968, Model for evolution of Rocky Mountains east of Idaho Batholith: Tectonophysics, v. 6, p. 109–126.

Scholten, R., Keenmon, K. A., and Kupsch, W. O., 1955, Geology of the Lima region, southwestern Montana and adjacent Idaho: Geological Society of America Bulletin, v. 66, p. 345–403.

Schwartz, R. K., 1983, Broken Early Cretaceous foreland basin, *in* Powers, R. B., ed., Geologic studies of the Cordilleran thrust belt, 1982: Denver, Colorado, Rocky Mountain Association of Geologists, v. 1, p. 159–183.

Skipp, B., and Hait, M. H., 1977, Allochthons along the northeast margin of the Snake River Plain, Idaho, *in* Heisey, E. L., and others, eds., Rocky Mountain thrust belt geology and resources: Wyoming Geological Association 29th Annual Field Conference Guidebook, p. 499–515.

Snee, L. W., and Sutter, J. F., 1981, K-Ar geochronology and major element geochemistry of plutonic and associated volcanic rocks from the southeastern Pioneer Mountains, Montana: Geological Society of America Abstracts with Programs, v. 11, p. 302.

Thomas, G. M., 1981, Structural geology of the Badger Pass area southwestern Montana [M.S. thesis]: Missoula, University of Montana, 58 p.

MANUSCRIPT ACCEPTED BY THE SOCIETY FEBRUARY 9, 1988

Geological Society of America
Memoir 171
1988

Cordilleran thrust belt and faulted foreland in the Beaverhead Mountains, Idaho and Montana

Betty Skipp
U.S. Geological Survey, Box 25046, Denver Federal Center, Denver, Colorado 80225

ABSTRACT

The Idaho-Wyoming segment of the Cordilleran thrust belt is characterized by west-dipping folded thrusts that place older strata over younger, by thrust plates that have lateral continuity and distinctive stratigraphic sequences, and by a gently west-dipping uninvolved basement beneath the thrust plates. Northwestward across the Snake River Plain, frontal thrusts and thrust plates of the Idaho-Montana segment of the Cordilleran belt exhibit the first two characteristics, but differ in that basement rocks locally are involved in the thrusts, indicating that these Idaho-Montana thrust plates overrode a previously faulted foreland.

Distribution of basement rocks indicates that the faulted foreland consisted of west-northwest– and east-northeast–trending faults of probable Proterozoic ancestry in the area of the shelf west of the Montana craton, and northeast-trending, northwest-dipping, basement-rooted Cretaceous thrust faults of the southwestern Montana craton to the east. The hanging wall of the Cordilleran Cabin thrust contains Archean(?) rocks in a fragment of the Cabin block, a regional Proterozoic basement uplift cut by the thrust as it propagated northeastward. Hanging walls of structurally lower Cordilleran thrusts contain segments of northeast-trending Cretaceous foreland thrusts and fold structures, such as the Snowcrest Range thrust system and the Little Water syncline. Renewed movement on foreland thrusts subsequently locally folded Cordilleran thrusts. Available paleontological data and radiometric age determinations indicate that major movements on both foreland and Cordilleran thrusts took place in Late Cretaceous time in the Beaverhead Mountains and vicinity.

Major Cordilleran thrust plates in the Beaverhead Mountains are, from west to east: the Hawley Creek, Fritz Creek, Cabin, Medicine Lodge, Four Eyes Canyon, and Tendoy. A west-to-east deformational sequence is assumed for all of the plates except part of the Cabin. Diagrammatic cross sections of the southern Beaverhead Mountains suggest that locally the Cabin may have overridden the Medicine Lodge, and is out of sequence.

The redefined Cabin thrust plate is thick and more than 200 km in length. It has been thinned secondarily by several younger-over-older Cenozoic normal faults, some of which were mapped previously as thrusts. Archean(?) through Triassic rocks make up the plate in the central and southern Beaverhead Mountains, and Proterozoic Yellowjacket Formation and Lemhi Group rocks make up the plate in the northern Beaverhead Mountains. There, Proterozoic rocks are thrust over Belt Supergroup strata of the Grasshopper thrust plate and are part of a structural culmination in the position of the Salmon River Arch. A large lateral ramp in the hanging wall of the Cabin thrust marks the northern margin of the 75-km-long transported segment of the Proterozoic Cabin block. Structural and stratigraphic throw diminish to the south near Bannack Pass, but increase north of the ramp near latitude 45°, where the Cabin thrust cuts down section with respect to the hanging wall to include several thousand meters of Proterozoic Yellowjacket Formation.

The northern margin of the Cabin block may compose the northern margin of Archean basement beneath the thrust belt in south-central Idaho. Northeastward translation of the Cabin and Medicine Lodge thrust plates is about 40 km in the southern Beaverhead Mountains; thus, Archean(?) crystalline basement rocks of the block originally were at least as far southwest as the present Lemhi Range. These old crystalline rocks constitute a western projection of the southwestern Montana reentrant.

INTRODUCTION

Continuity of thrusts across the Snake River Plain (Fig. 1) was first suggested by Kirkham (1927), who mapped the Medicine Lodge overthrust fault (Fig. 2), a structure that juxtaposes upper Paleozoic carbonates and Mesozoic conglomerates in the southern Beaverhead Mountains; Kirkham suggested that the fault might be coextensive with the Bannock thrust zone south of the plain. For the next half century, interpretations of faulting in the Beaverhead Mountains characterized the area as a distinct structural province with few similarities to the Idaho-Wyoming belt (Scholten and Ramspott, 1968; Scholten, 1983; Ruppel, 1978; Ruppel and Lopez, 1984). The suggestion was even made that thrust belt segments north and south of the Snake River Plain were never coextensive, and that the northern extension of the Idaho-Wyoming belt is offset laterally 145 km east along the axis of the plain (Pratt, 1983).

Three apparent dissimilarities—extension faults, younger-over-older thrust faults, and older-over-younger faults involving basement crystalline rocks—distinguish the fold and thrust belt segments north and south of the plain. North of the plain, numerous Cenozoic extension (normal) faults offset Mesozoic thrust plates and obscure their lateral continuity (Skipp and Hait, 1977; Bond, 1978), whereas south of the plain, thrusts and thrust plates are somewhat less disrupted by younger faults (Armstrong and

Oriel, 1965; Royse and others, 1975; Dixon, 1982; Oriel and Moore, 1985). North of the plain, several structures mapped as thrusts place younger strata over older strata and thin the stratigraphic section (Scholten and others, 1955; Scholten and Ramspott, 1968; Skipp and Hait, 1977; Ruppel, 1978; Scholten, 1983; Ruppel and Lopez, 1984), whereas southeast of the plain, thrusts juxtapose older strata over younger strata (Armstrong and Cressman, 1963; Armstrong and Oriel, 1965; Royse and others, 1975; Dixon, 1982; Oriel and Moore, 1985). North of the plain, Precambrian crystalline rocks are brought to the surface along thrust faults in the Beaverhead and Tendoy Mountains (Scholten and others, 1955; Skipp and Hait, 1977; Dubois, 1983; Scholten, 1983), whereas southeast of the plain, basement is uninvolved in the frontal thrusts of the fold-thrust belt (Armstrong and Oriel, 1965; Royse and others, 1975; Dixon, 1982; Oriel and Moore, 1985). Basement rocks, however, are involved in thrust sheets in the central Wasatch Range (Fig. 1, this chapter) in northeastern Utah (Eardley, 1944; Bell, 1952; Royse and others, 1975).

Tectonic models proposed for the Beaverhead Mountains segment of the Cordilleran thrust belt include Kirkham's (1927), various models of Scholten (Scholten and others, 1955; Scholten, 1968, 1973, 1983; Scholten and Ramspott, 1968), the Medicine Lodge thrust system of Ruppel (Ruppel, 1978; Ruppel and Lopez, 1984), and one of Skipp and Hait (1977). Kirkham (1927) considered the Medicine Lodge thrust to be the eastern frontal thrust of a two-sided tectonic wedge that was bounded on the west by east-dipping Lost River, Lemhi, and Hawley Mountain overthrusts. Scholten (Scholten and others, 1955) considered the Tendoy thrust the eastern limit of the thrust belt and characterized the Medicine Lodge fault as a major, southwest-dipping, low-angle thrust with displacement of 16 km (10 mi) or more, broken by subsequent high-angle thrusts such as the Nicholia and Cabin (Fig. 2). All of these faults, with the exception of a splay of the Medicine Lodge, were shown to juxtapose older rocks over younger rocks. The hanging wall of the Cabin thrust consisted of Precambrian crystalline rocks. Subsequently, Scholten reinterpreted the previously mapped structures as upthrusts, growing steeper with depth, overlain by low-angle younger-over-older gravity slide sheets of folded Paleozoic carbonate rocks, such as the Willow Creek and Tex Creek "thrusts" that were shed eastward or radially off adjacent western uplifts (Scholten, 1968, 1973; Scholten and Ramspott, 1968; Ryder and Scholten, 1973) (see Fig. 2, this chapter). Most recently, Scholten (1983) returned

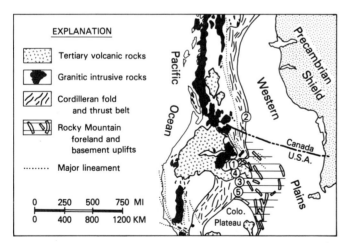

Figure 1. Geologic sketch map of western North America showing generalized location of: 1, the Beaverhead Mountains; 2, Foothills and Front Range structural provinces of the Canadian Rocky Mountains; 3, Idaho-Wyoming thrust belt; 4, Snake River Plain; 5, thrust belt in northeastern Utah. Adapted from Bally and others (1966).

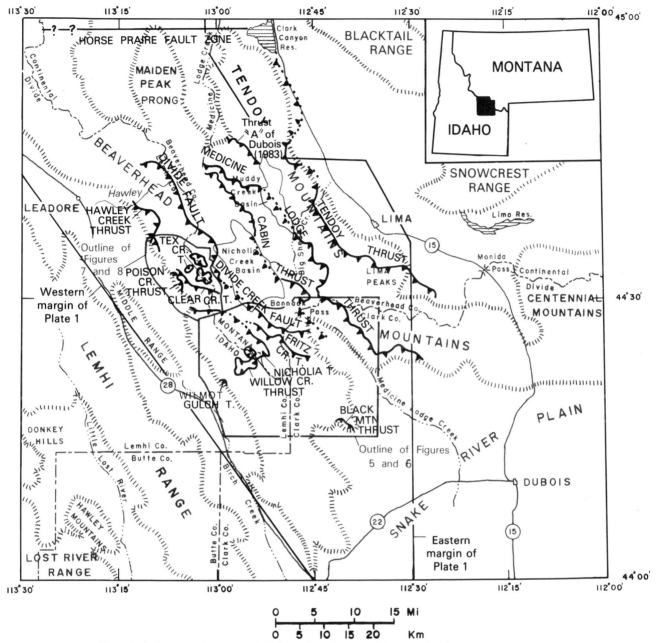

Figure 2. index map of east-central Idaho and southwestern Montana showing locations of Figures 5 through 8, and Plate 1, and generalized locations of selected previously mapped faults discussed in text. Faults interpreted to be thrusts in the earlier literature have teeth on upper plates and are dotted where concealed. Locations of faults are from Kirkham (1927); Scholten and others (1955); Lucchitta (1966); Scholten and Ramspott (1968); Scholten (1983); Dubois (1983); Skipp, Prostka, and Schleicher (1979). Outlines of mountain ranges shown by hachures.

to the concept of low-angle west-dipping thrust plates and proposed that they formed as a result of westward continental subduction in a back-arc setting. In this interpretation, he chose the Cabin thrust as the major thrust dipping westward beneath the Beaverhead Mountains. He extended the Cabin thrust northward to connect with a thrust having a hanging wall of cratonic basement (thrust "A" of Dubois, 1983; see Fig. 2, this chapter), and terminated the structure at the east-trending Horse Prairie fault

zone (Fig. 2). Basement rocks were suggested by Scholten (1983) to possibly have been cut by other faults, including the Divide Creek, which places younger strata on older. The Medicine Lodge thrust itself was still considered a possible gravity-slide feature.

The Medicine Lodge thrust system (Ruppel, 1978; Ruppel and Lopez, 1984) is presumed to be a major flat thrust sheet in the Beaverhead Mountains extending at least as far west as the

Lemhi Range. The thrust system juxtaposes miogeoclinal rocks from the west—but not crystalline basement—against cratonal rocks, along a trace that includes the Medicine Lodge thrust of Kirkham (1927) and Scholten (Scholten and others, 1955) (Fig. 2), and younger-over-older faults in Proterozoic rocks in the central and northern Beaverhead Mountains (Ruppel, 1978; Ruppel and Lopez, 1984). In this interpretation, the Proterozoic Yellowjacket Formation is autochthonous beneath the thrust system in the northern Beaverhead Mountains (Ruppel, 1978).

Skipp and Hait (1977) proposed a series of west-dipping thrust slabs offset by listric normal faults in the southern Beaverhead Mountains. In this interpretation, basement crystalline rocks were involved in the frontal thrusts, but some thrusts were shown to place younger strata over older.

Southeast of the Snake River Plain, most structural interpretations of the Idaho-Wyoming thrust belt in the last 20 yr (Armstrong and Oriel, 1965; Royse and others, 1975; Dixon, 1982; Oriel and Moore, 1985) have been based on observed thrust geometries similar to those recognized in the Canadian Cordillera and summarized by Dahlstrom (1970). The basic premises of these geometries are that thrusts cut up-section in the direction of propagation, and consist of flats and frontal ramps. The order of a stratigraphic section need not be changed by thrusting, but if it is, beds are repeated, not omitted, and the stratigraphic section is thickened, not thinned. Lateral ramps that form at an angle to the direction of thrust propagation may cut either up- or down-section. In the Idaho-Wyoming overthrust belt and in the Canadian Foothills and Front Ranges structural provinces, thrusts have formed above a gently west-dipping, uninvolved crystalline basement. Subsequent extension was common in these thrust terranes, and in some cases, normal faults utilized older thrust zones. Application of these thrust concepts has resulted in the successful search for hydrocarbons in southwestern Wyoming.

The tectonic interpretation of the Beaverhead Mountains presented here uses the same empirical thrust concepts recognized in other parts of the Cordilleran frontal thrust belt insofar as possible, and is based on detailed mapping of about 1,000 km^2 (400 mi^2) in the southern Beaverhead Mountains (Skipp, 1984; Skipp and others, 1984), and compilation of the work of many workers in regions to the north and south (Plate 1, in pocket inside back cover). In this interpretation, most major west-dipping thrusts propagated from southwest to northeast, and, in all cases, placed older strata over younger. One thrust is described as locally out of sequence, because it appears to have broken through and overridden a segment of its own former leading edge after that segment was locked in place. The thrust plates, which are bounded by major thrust faults, include numerous smaller subsidiary thrusts that are called imbricates in this report. Most plates are later extended by Cenozoic normal faults, some of which formed along former thrust zones. Primary tear faults or large lateral ramps are more commonly observed contraction structures in the Beaverhead Mountains segment of the Cordilleran thrust belt than in the Canadian Foothills province and the Idaho-Wyoming thrust belt (Fig. 1). Distribution of geologic map

units, differences in thicknesses of upper Paleozoic rock units, ages and stratigraphic relations of Cretaceous synorogenic deposits, the alignment of gravity highs, and the distribution of aeromagnetic contours indicate that the foreland in southwestern Montana was faulted before the Cordilleran thrusts moved across it (Kulik and Perry, 1982; Kulik and others, 1983; Perry and others, 1981; Perry and others, 1983; Ryder and Scholten, 1973; Nichols and others, 1985; Perry, 1986). Positions of these foreland faults appear to have had a Precambrian ancestry (Schmidt and O'Neill, 1983; Schmidt and Garihan, 1983). The Beaverhead Mountains, therefore, are a segment of the Cordilleran fold-thrust belt that has impinged upon a previously folded and faulted foreland, a deformational sequence recognized earlier by Scholten (Scholten and others, 1955).

REGIONAL STRATIGRAPHIC SETTING

Rocks ranging in age from Archean(?) through Late Cretaceous are involved in Cordilleran fold-and-thrust structures of the Beaverhead Mountains. High-rank granitic gneisses, marbles, schists, and quartzites of the Cabin thrust plate in the southern Beaverhead Mountains are lithologically similar to metasedimentary and metaigneous rocks, including the Dillon Granite Gneiss, of the southwestern Montana craton (Scholten and others, 1955) that subsequently have been radiometrically dated as Archean (Giletti, 1966; James and Hedge, 1980; Peterman, *in* Perry, 1982). Thus the metasedimentary and metaigneous rocks in the Beaverheads probably also are Archean, although no reliable radiometric ages are available.

Proterozoic and Paleozoic sedimentary rocks in the southern and central Beaverhead Mountains above Archean(?) basement were deposited on a western outer cratonic shelf (miogeoclinal sequences) and an eastern inner cratonic platform (cratonal sequences), as recognized by many authors. During Mesozoic thrusting, rocks deposited on the outer shelf were moved eastward over cratonic rocks (Skipp and Hait, 1977; Ruppel, 1978; Ruppel and Lopez, 1984). Paleozoic and thick Mesozoic sedimentary rocks of the Tendoy thrust plate (Scholten and others, 1955; Plate 1, this chapter) are cratonic rocks (Fig. 3), and Proterozoic, Paleozoic, and minor Triassic sedimentary rocks west of the overlying Cabin and Medicine Lodge thrusts (Scholten and others, 1955; Plate 1, this chapter) constitute the western shelf sequence (Fig. 4). Most Paleozoic formations and lithologies of the inner craton margin are distinct from those of the outer shelf, or miogeocline, but recently Mississippian strata transitional between the miogeoclinal rocks of the Cabin and Medicine Lodge thrust plates and those of the Tendoy plate have been identified in the northern Tendoy Mountains (Sando and others, 1985).

Marine rocks of the Lower Triassic Dinwoody Formation are the only Mesozoic sedimentary rocks known in the western outer shelf sequences (Lucchitta, 1966; Skipp, Hoggan, and others, 1979). Thick, more complete, Mesozoic marine and nonmarine sedimentary sequences are present on the craton (Fig. 3, Plate 1). Synorogenic conglomerates and sandstones of the Upper

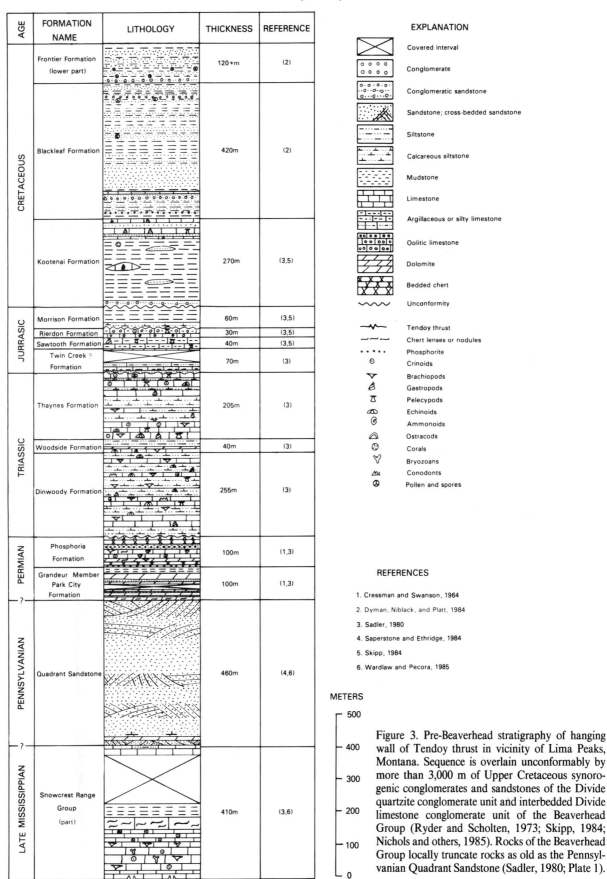

EXPLANATION

Symbol	Description
	Covered interval
	Conglomerate
	Conglomeratic sandstone
	Sandstone; cross-bedded sandstone
	Siltstone
	Calcareous siltstone
	Mudstone
	Limestone
	Argillaceous or silty limestone
	Oolitic limestone
	Dolomite
	Bedded chert
	Unconformity
	Tendoy thrust
	Chert lenses or nodules
	Phosphorite
	Crinoids
	Brachiopods
	Gastropods
	Pelecypods
	Echinoids
	Ammonoids
	Ostracods
	Corals
	Bryozoans
	Conodonts
	Pollen and spores

REFERENCES

1. Cressman and Swanson, 1964
2. Dyman, Niblack, and Platt, 1984
3. Sadler, 1980
4. Saperstone and Ethridge, 1984
5. Skipp, 1984
6. Wardlaw and Pecora, 1985

METERS

— 500
— 400
— 300
— 200
— 100
— 0

Figure 3. Pre-Beaverhead stratigraphy of hanging wall of Tendoy thrust in vicinity of Lima Peaks, Montana. Sequence is overlain unconformably by more than 3,000 m of Upper Cretaceous synorogenic conglomerates and sandstones of the Divide quartzite conglomerate unit and interbedded Divide limestone conglomerate unit of the Beaverhead Group (Ryder and Scholten, 1973; Skipp, 1984; Nichols and others, 1985). Rocks of the Beaverhead Group locally truncate rocks as old as the Pennsylvanian Quadrant Sandstone (Sadler, 1980; Plate 1).

Figure 4. Generalized stratigraphic sequences of Hawley Creek, Fritz Creek, Cabin, and Medicine Lodge thrust plates in southern and central Beaverhead Mountains (Figs. 5 through 8). Thicknesses given in meters. Question marks indicate uncertainties resulting from poor exposures or faulting. References used for the columns include Hawley Creek: Scholten and Ramspott, 1968; Skipp, 1984; Fritz Creek: Scholten and Ramspott, 1968; Skipp, 1984, 1985; Sandberg and Poole, 1977; Huh, 1967; Skipp and others, 1985; Cabin: Scholten and Ramspott, 1968; Skipp, 1985; Huh, 1967; Wardlaw and Pecora, 1985; Lucchitta, 1966; Medicine Lodge: Skipp, Prostka, and Schleicher, 1979; Skipp, 1984. Age and/or formation assignments of Proterozoic rocks have been revised as discussed in text.

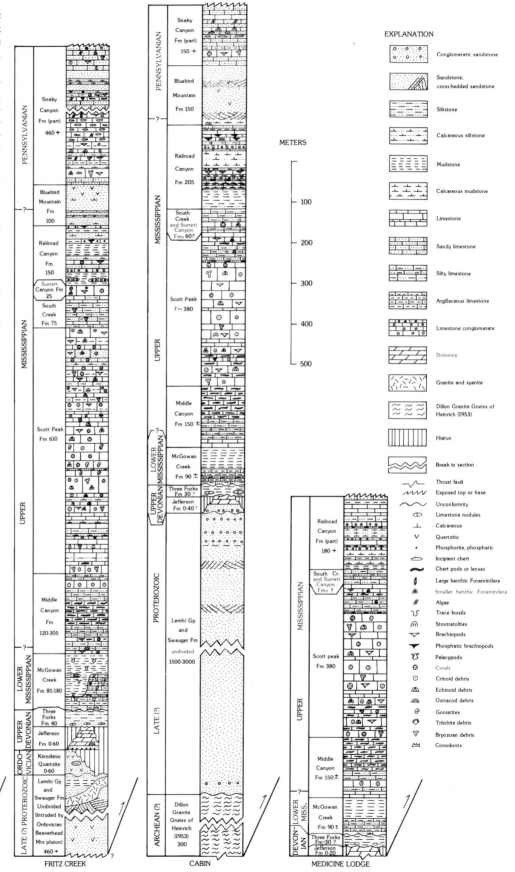

Cretaceous Beaverhead Group are the youngest rocks involved in Cordilleran thrust belt deformation in southwestern Montana.

THRUST FAULTS AND THRUST PLATES IN THE SOUTHERN BEAVERHEAD MOUNTAINS

Major thrust faults (those that have lateral continuity for tens of kilometers and stratigraphic offsets of about a thousand meters or more) in the southern Beaverhead Mountains include, from structurally highest to lowest: the Hawley Creek, the Fritz Creek, the Cabin, and the Medicine Lodge (Figs. 5 through 8). Rocks of the Tendoy thrust plate compose the footwall of the Medicine Lodge thrust. Several unnamed subsidiary thrusts or imbricates, including the Black Mountain thrust, are present also, but they lack the continuity of the major thrusts. Thrust plates are named for their lower boundary thrusts, and each has a distinctive stratigraphy (Fig. 4).

Absent in this listing are several "thrusts" previously mapped in this area (Scholten and Ramspott, 1968): Willow Creek, Tex Creek, Nicholia, Clear Creek, Poison Creek, and Divide Creek (Fig. 2). Parts of these "faults" were found to be unrecognized complete stratigraphic sequences that have no structural breaks (Willow Creek, Tex Creek, Nicholia, and Clear Creek), or normal faults (Nicholia and Divide Creek), or valid thrust fault segments (Tex Creek, Nicholia, and Poison Creek) (Figs. 5 through 8). Part of the Tex Creek "thrust" is a well-exposed segment of the Fritz Creek thrust at the head of Tex Creek (Figs. 7, 8). A part of the Nicholia thrust between Chamberlain and Eighteenmile Creeks (Fig. 7) and the Poison Creek thrust at Poison Creek (Figs. 7, 8) are segments of the Hawley Creek thrust. The Divide Creek "thrust" (Fig. 6), which juxtaposes younger rocks over older and thins the stratigraphic section, is instead an extension fault within the Cabin thrust plate that probably formed partly along a preexisting lateral thrust ramp (Skipp, 1985).

Hawley Creek thrust plate

The Hawley Creek plate includes at least 100 m of Proterozoic sandstone of the Lemhi Group and/or Swauger Formation (on Wilmot Gulch thrust), a minimum of 305 m of Ordovician Kinnikinic Quartzite, an indeterminate thickness of syenite and granite of the Ordovician Beaverhead Mountains pluton, 23 to 62 m of dolomite, limestone, and sandstone of the Devonian Jefferson Formation, 25 to 40 m of siltstone and mudstone of the Devonian Sappington Member of the Three Forks Formation, and about 90 m of limestone, siltstone, and mudstone of the Mississippian McGowan Creek Formation (Skipp, 1984; Fig. 4, this chapter).

The Beaverhead Mountains pluton constitutes a large part of the plate and consists of granite and syenite or leucosyenite and dikes and irregular masses of aplite (Ramspott, 1962; Scholten and Ramspott, 1968). Major element chemical analyses, one of granite and one of syenite (Skipp, 1985), confirm the earlier

petrographic classifications. The syenite has low initial strontium ratios of 0.7025 to 0.7030 (C. E. Hedge, written communication, 1980); this indicates little crustal contamination. Radiometric ages suggest the syenite is younger (450 to 470 m.y. old) than the granite (481 to 484 m.y. old) and that all intrusive bodies are no younger than Middle Ordovician (Skipp, 1984).

The Hawley Creek thrust, the lower boundary thrust of the plate, was first mapped and named in the central Beaverhead Mountains by Lucchitta (1966), who recognized the allochthonous nature of the Beaverhead Mountains pluton. No upper boundary thrust for the plate is present in the Beaverhead Mountains, because the plate is truncated on the west by the Beaverhead normal fault zone and other basin-range faults (Figs. 6, 8; Plates 1, 2). The Hawley Creek thrust fault appears to be folded; the trace of the fault is nearly flat on the Continental Divide, and steep south of Willow Creek (Fig. 5).

The Hawley Creek plate crops out along the western margin of the Beaverhead Mountains for a distance of at least 45 km (Figs. 6, 8; Plates 1, 2). The plate also is offset in a right-lateral sense by a probable tear fault along Willow Creek (Fig. 6) and a possible left-lateral tear north of Eighteenmile Creek (Fig. 8). Two hanging-wall imbricates, the Wilmot Gulch thrust and one that places Kinnikinic Quartzite over Mississippian and Devonian rocks south of the Wilmot Gulch thrust, are present within southern outcrops of the plate (Figs. 5, 6). Rocks of the thrust plate are folded into large, northwest-trending symmetrical or northeast-verging asymmetrical folds that subsequently have been offset by a swarm of extension faults trending northwest to northeast.

Sheared and tightly folded thin- to thick-bedded limestones of the Upper Mississippian Middle Canyon and Scott Peak Formations, on the Continental Divide just east of the trace of the Hawley Creek thrust, make up the deformed footwall of the Hawley Creek thrust.

In the southern and central Beaverhead Mountains (Figs. 5 through 7), the Hawley Creek thrust brings Ordovician plutonic rocks and sedimentary quartzites over Upper Mississippian limestones, a stratigraphic offset of not less than 610 meters. East of the Wilmot Gulch thrust, apparent stratigraphic throw on the Hawley Creek thrust diminishes to near zero, although the Kinnikinic Quartzite of the hanging wall is much thicker than the Kinnikinic of the subjacent footwall (Fig. 5). In the central Beaverhead Mountains to the north, stratigraphic throw on the Hawley Creek thrust exceeds 1,830 m (Lucchitta, 1966).

An east-northeastward minimum transport distance of 1.1 km is shown on cross-section A-A' (Fig. 5) relative to the Fritz Creek plate. Diminished stratigraphic throw on the Hawley Creek thrust from north to south suggests decreasing eastward transport to the south.

Fritz Creek thrust plate

Rocks of the Fritz Creek thrust plate (Fig. 4) differ from those of the Hawley Creek thrust plate in that: (1) the Ordovician

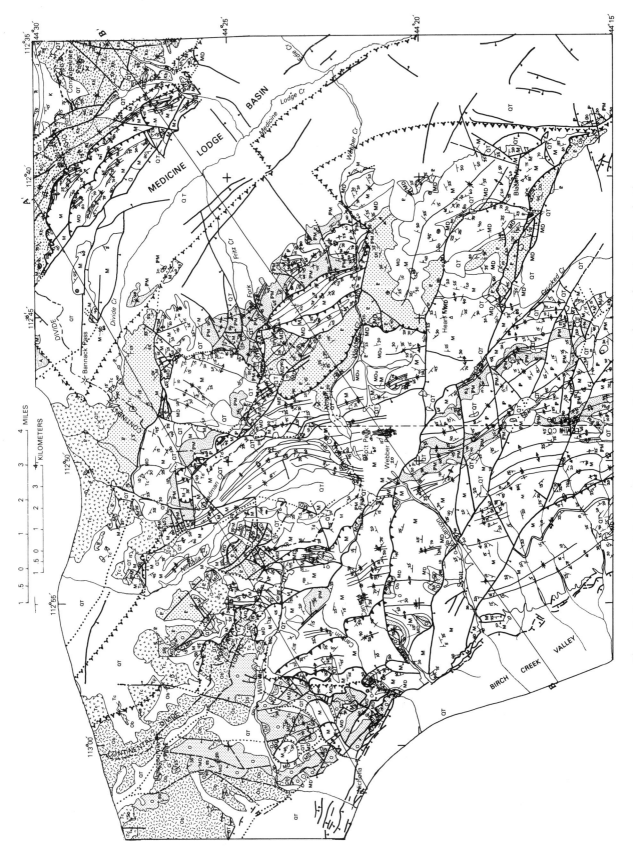

Figure 5. Geologic map (above) and cross sections (facing page) of part of southern Beaverhead Mountains, Lemhi and Clark Counties, Idaho, and Beaverhead County, Montana. Simplified from Skipp (1984).

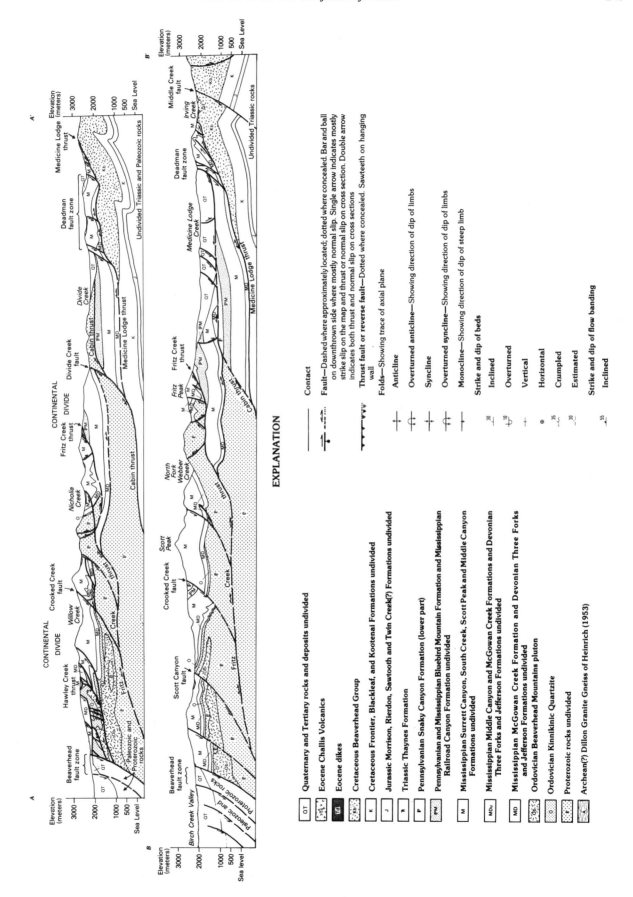

EXPLANATION

Kinnikinic Quartzite is thin or missing due to Silurian or Devonian erosion; (2) only small apophyses of the Beaverhead Mountains pluton crop out, although geophysical studies suggest the pluton is a major component of the rocks beneath the surface near Scott Canyon (Fig. 5, cross section B-B'; Skipp and others, 1983); (3) the McGowan Creek Formation is thicker, as much as 180 m, and the basal limestone of that formation is as thick as

122 m in eastern parts of the thrust sheet; and (4) 1,525 m of Upper Mississippian and Pennsylvanian Formations, dominantly carbonate bank deposits, make up most of the outcrop area (Figs. 5, 7).

The Fritz Creek thrust plate makes up a large part of the southern Beaverhead Mountains and has a minimum length of 60 km (Plate 2; Figs. 6, 8). The lower Fritz Creek boundary thrust

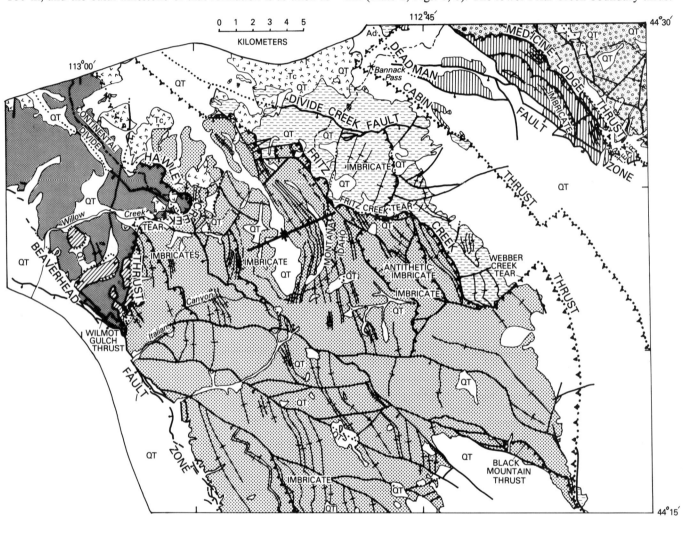

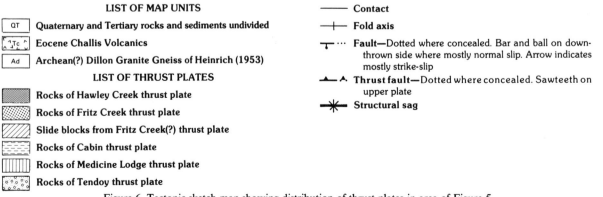

LIST OF MAP UNITS

QT	Quaternary and Tertiary rocks and sediments undivided
Tc	Eocene Challis Volcanics
Ad	Archean(?) Dillon Granite Gneiss of Heinrich (1953)

LIST OF THRUST PLATES

Rocks of Hawley Creek thrust plate

Rocks of Fritz Creek thrust plate

Slide blocks from Fritz Creek(?) thrust plate

Rocks of Cabin thrust plate

Rocks of Medicine Lodge thrust plate

Rocks of Tendoy thrust plate

——— Contact

—+— Fold axis

—⊤··· Fault—Dotted where concealed. Bar and ball on downthrown side where mostly normal slip. Arrow indicates mostly strike-slip

—▲—▲ Thrust fault—Dotted where concealed. Sawteeth on upper plate

—✳— Structural sag

Figure 6. Tectonic sketch map showing distribution of thrust plates in area of Figure 5.

was first recognized by Scholten and Ramspott (1968). The upper boundary thrust is the Hawley Creek. Numerous hanging-wall imbricates, a possible horse, an antithetic imbricate, and a klippe are parts of the thrust sheet (Figs. 6, 8; Skipp, 1984). Folded Ordovician Kinnikinic Quartzite and Devonian and Mississippian carbonate rocks locally overlie sheared Mississippian Scott Peak and Middle Canyon Formations on the Continental Divide along a subsidiary thrust at the head of Italian Canyon (Fig. 5). The Black Mountain thrust in the southeastern corner of the map area, also an imbricate, places Proterozoic sandstone and Beaverhead Mountain plutonic rocks over Upper Mississippian carbonate rocks. An antithetic east-dipping thrust fault, also an imbricate, brings Proterozoic rocks over Proterozoic through Mississippian rocks east of the North Fork of Webber Creek (Fig. 5, cross section B-B'; Skipp, 1984).

Proterozoic and Ordovician terrigenous rocks and Paleozoic carbonate rocks all are folded (Fig. 5). Fold types include large, open symmetrical concentric folds in thick-bedded limestone (Fig. 9A); chevron or kink folds in relatively thinner bedded limestones above subhorizontal detachments (Fig. 9B); asymmetrical concentric folds above thrust detachment surfaces (Fig. 9C); and flattened concentric folds (Ramsay, 1967) (Fig. 9D). Folds are disharmonic and are not laterally continuous over long distances. A single fold axis could not be traced for a distance of more than 8 km. Fold axes trend from northwest to north-northwest, and variations in orientation seem to be related to differential movement between segments of the thrust sheet.

Stratigraphic separations along the exposed length of the leading edge of the Fritz Creek thrust plate decrease slightly to the northwest, where thin-bedded cherty limestone of the Middle Canyon Formation overrides mudstone and limestone of the Railroad Canyon Formation (Figs. 7, 8). Elsewhere, thick-bedded limestone of the Scott Peak Formation is thrust over folded limestone, sandstone, and mudstone of the Railroad Canyon, Bluebird Mountain, and Snaky Canyon Formations, a stratigraphic offset of about 305 to 914 m. Minimum eastward transport relative to the Cabin plate of 2.4 km (1.5 mi) is shown in cross section A-A', Figure 5, and 4.3 km (2.7 mi) on cross section B-B', Figure 5, indicating increased displacement on the Fritz Creek thrust to the southeast.

East-trending tear faults divide the eastern part of the Fritz Creek plate into three lobes, each of which has accommodated increased southeastward shortening by different mechanisms. Tight overturned folds are the primary shortening mechanism north and west of the Fritz Creek tear where the thrust plate advanced the least; moderately tight folds and imbricate thrusts are dominant between the Fritz Creek and Webber Creek tear faults, and broad open folds characterize the segment south of the Webber Creek tear where the thrust plate traveled farthest northeastward (Fig. 6).

Frontal ramp anticlines of the three lobes of the sheet have been offset progressively northeastward from northwest to southeast. Proterozoic rocks of the core of a frontal ramp anticline are exposed along the Continental Divide west of Nicholia Creek in the northern part of the area of Fig. 5 (cross section A-A'). Similar relations are present east of the North Fork of Webber Creek in the central part, and near the mouth of Webber Creek in the southeastern part of the area of Fig. 5 (cross section B-B'). A northeast-trending structural saddle or sag (Fig. 6), in which no Proterozoic rocks are exposed west of the tear fault along Fritz Creek near the head of Nicholia Creek, may be a hanging-wall syncline produced over a lateral ramp in the footwall.

Cabin thrust plate

Rocks of the Cabin thrust plate include Archean(?) Dillon Granite Gneiss, Proterozoic sandstone, Devonian Jefferson and Three Forks Formations, Mississippian McGowan Creek, Middle Canyon, Scott Peak, South Creek, Surrett Canyon, and Railroad Canyon Formations, the Bluebird Mountain Formation of Mississippian and Pennsylvanian age, and the Lower Pennsylvanian part of the Snaky Canyon Formation (Fig. 4). These formations crop out south of Nicholia Creek Basin and along the western margin of the valley of Medicine Lodge Creek (Figs. 2, 5).

Basement crystalline rocks in the southern Beaverhead Mountains have been correlated with the Dillon Granite Gneiss by Scholten and Ramspott (1968). The gneiss was assigned a pre-Belt age (Scholten and Ramspott, 1968) and, more recently, an Early Proterozoic age (Skipp and Hait, 1977; Ruppel, 1978; Scholten, 1983). The Dillon Granite Gneiss in the Ruby Range of southwestern Montana, just north of the Blacktail Range (Fig. 2), has been dated as Archean (James and Hedge, 1980), as has cataclastic gneiss about 10 km (6 mi) northeast of the town of Lima, Montana, in the Snowcrest Range (Perry, 1982). These dates make an Archean age probable, but unproven, for the granite gneiss and associated high-rank metasedimentary rocks of the Beaverhead Mountains.

Proterozoic sandstone north of the Divide Creek fault (Figs. 5, 6) is partly conglomeratic, containing clasts of chert, quartzite, quartz, and gneiss, as much as 2 cm in diameter. Mudchip conglomerates also are present. Conglomeratic sandstones as coarse as these were not found in Proterozoic rocks of the higher thrust sheets. An outcrop of Proterozoic light-colored, medium-grained quartzite in the north-central edge of Figure 5 that is surrounded by volcanics, was assigned to the Ordovician Kinnikinic Quartzite by Scholten and Ramspott (1968). The quartzite, however, has argillaceous cement that is more characteristic of Proterozoic sandstone (Lucchitta, 1966) than the Kinnikinic Quartzite. I have not recognized Ordovician rocks anywhere on the Cabin plate.

Rocks of the Devonian Jefferson Formation were not found in the southern part of the thrust plate, but are known to be a part of the plate to the north (Lucchitta, 1966). The Upper Mississippian Railroad Canyon Formation is about 55 m thicker (about 205 m) in the Cabin plate than in the Fritz Creek plate. The Bluebird Mountain Formation is about 50 m thicker (150 m) and is coarser grained in the Cabin plate than in the overlying Fritz Creek plate.

Rocks of the Cabin thrust plate are exposed on all sides of

Figure 7. Geologic map of Eighteenmile area, Lemhi County, Idaho, and Beaverhead County, Montana. Modified from Skipp and others (1984). Explanation same as for Figure 5, except for addition of Permian rocks of the Phosphoria Formation (Pp) and the Snaky Canyon Formation (ℙP).

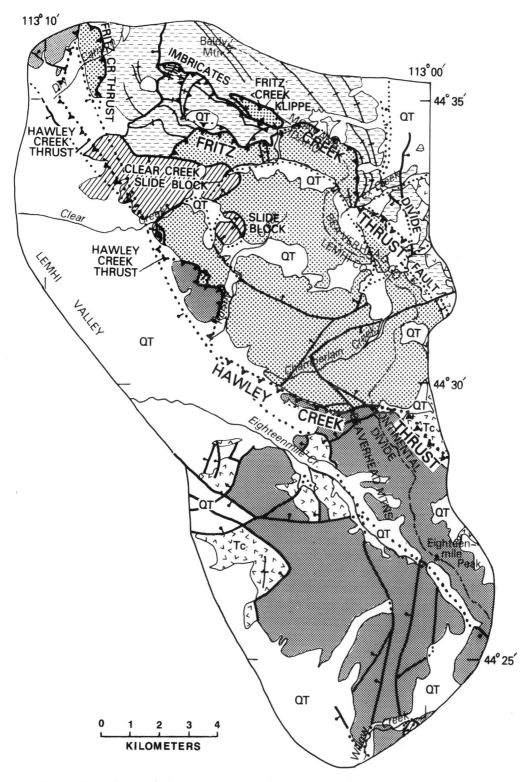

Figure 8. Tectonic map of Eighteenmile area showing distribution of major thrust plates. Explanation same as for Figure 6.

Figure 9. Typical structures in upper Paleozoic limestones of Fritz Creek thrust plate (Figs. 5, 6). A, Large, symmetric concentric fold in thick-bedded limestones of the Scott Peak Formation on the north side of Continental Divide at head of Deadman Creek, showing detachment and kink folds in thinner bedded limestones in adjacent syncline (right center). One-half wave length of fold approximately 460 m. View looking south-southeast. B, East-verging kink folds in medium-bedded limestones of Scott Peak and Surrett Canyon Formations above subhorizontal detachments on east flanks of Scott and Webber Peaks in Lemhi County, Idaho. View looking west of south. C, East-verging asymmetric concentric fold formed by eastward translation along several slip planes. Author (arrow) is standing less than 1 m above a prominent detachment surface in Scott Peak Formation just west of fork near head of Italian Canyon. View looking north-northwest. D, Flattened concentric folds (Ramsay, 1967) in limestones of Scott Peak Formation at head of south fork of Italian Canyon in footwall of imbricate just below Continental Divide in Lemhi County, Idaho. Fold axes appear to trend north-northeast subparallel to thrust transport directions. Folds probably the result of local northwest-southeast–directed compression within the Fritz Creek thrust plate. View looking east-northeast.

Nicholia Creek Basin (Fig. 2, Plate 1), and along the western margin of the Medicine Lodge Creek Basin (Figs. 5, 6; Plate 1). Tear faults, hanging-wall imbricates, and a deformed footwall are all associated with the plate (Skipp, 1985).

The Cabin thrust, the eastern lower boundary thrust of the Cabin plate, was named for hanging-wall exposures of granite gneiss and metasedimentary rocks that extend from the north-central border of the area of Figure 5 northward several kilometers (Fig. 2, Plate 2; Scholten and others, 1955). The western boundary thrust in the southern Beaverhead Mountains is the Fritz Creek. Stratigraphic throw on the Cabin thrust fault ranges from more than 3,000 m to about 760 m from north to south.

North of Bannack Pass, Archean(?) basement crystalline rocks are thrust over Upper Mississippian limestones and shales of the Railroad Canyon(?) Formation. Near Bannack Pass, Proterozoic detrital rocks and, south of the Divide Creek fault, Upper Mississippian limestones are thrust over folded silicified sandstone of the Mississippian-Pennsylvanian Bluebird Mountain Formation. The differences in stratigraphic throw along the Cabin thrust are due largely to decreasing stratigraphic separation southward along the fault. The presence of basement crystalline rocks on the thrust plate, however, requires either that the thrust cut down-section in the direction of propagation or encountered a north-northwest–trending upraised block of basement as it moved northeastward. The latter explanation is more geometrically sound, and fits into the patterns of basement faulting described for the southwestern Montana craton (Schmidt and Garihan, 1983; Schmidt and O'Neill, 1983). In addition, Proterozoic conglomeratic sandstone west of Bannack Pass contains clasts of gneiss that suggest a faulted basement source. A model in which the Cabin thrust fault encountered an upraised basement block and carried basement rocks on one segment of the thrust is diagrammed in Figure 10. Late normal movement on the Divide Creek fault probably removed the Paleozoic formations that are present elsewhere between the Proterozoic sandstone and the Mississippian Scott Peak Formation (Fig. 5).

Contractional features such as small-scale tight folds that have dominant north-northwest vergence and local shear zones in the hanging wall of the Divide Creek fault adjacent to the fault, combined with the southwest dip of the hanging wall panel (Fig. 5) suggest that this segment of the Divide Creek fault zone may have originated as an oblique-slip tear fault or ramp during compression. The juxtaposition of younger strata over older and the deletion of beds (Fig. 5) indicate later normal movement. Western parts of the Divide Creek fault are buried beneath unfaulted Eocene Challis Volcanics (Fig. 5; Skipp, 1984), and thus, extension along this fault is older than about 50 Ma, but younger than the Cabin thrust, probably early Eocene.

The Cabin thrust plate has a large stratigraphic throw that diminishes to the southeast, and lateral continuity for a minimum of 56 km. An estimate of minimum local out-of-sequence northeastward horizontal transport of the Cabin plate over the Medicine Lodge thrust plate is 8.8 km (5.5 mi) south of Bannack Pass (Fig. 5, cross sections).

Medicine Lodge thrust plate

Strata making up the Medicine Lodge plate range in age from Late Devonian to Late Mississippian and include the Jefferson(?), Three Forks, McGowan Creek, Middle Canyon, Scott Peak, South Creek and Surrett Canyon, and Railroad Canyon Formations (Fig. 4). Rocks of the plate are too deformed to allow determination of thicknesses, but in general, lithologies and faunas resemble those of the rocks of the overlying Cabin thrust plate. Basement crystalline rocks probably are not a part of the Medicine Lodge plate in the southern Beaverhead Mountains, as suggested earlier by Skipp and Hait (1977) and Scholten (1983).

The Medicine Lodge thrust, the lower boundary thrust of the Medicine Lodge plate, was named for the segment of the surface trace present in the southern Beaverhead Mountains (Fig. 5; Kirkham, 1927), along which Mississippian carbonate rocks override Upper Cretaceous synorogenic conglomerates, a stratigraphic throw of at least 2,740 m. The thrust was traced to the northwest about 37 km into the northern Medicine Lodge Valley of Montana, and to the southeast about 19 km to a point where it is buried beneath Cenozoic sediments and volcanics (Fig. 2; Scholten and others, 1955). Similar interpretations of the thrust trace were shown in subsequent reports (Scholten, 1967,

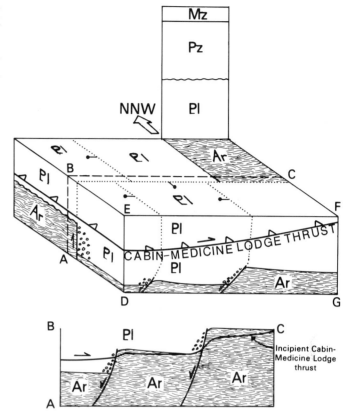

Figure 10. Block diagram showing proposed propagation path of Cabin thrust across blocks of Archean crystalline basement (Ar) upraised along east-northeast- and north-northwest-trending Precambrian normal faults unconformably overlain by Proterozoic (P̶l) and younger rocks (Pz = Paleozoic, Mz = Mesozoic). Arrow indicates transport direction. Sequence of faults is hypothetical.

1968, 1973, 1983; Ryder and Scholten, 1973; M'Gonigle, 1965; Lucchitta, 1966; Skipp and Hait, 1977; Ruppel, 1978; Sadler, 1980; Dubois, 1983). Recently, new mapping identified the Four Eyes Canyon thrust between the Medicine Lodge and the Tendoy thrusts north of the Continental Divide and locally changed the configuration of the trace of the Medicine Lodge thrust (Perry and Sando, 1983; Plate 2). The upper boundary thrust of the Medicine Lodge plate is the Cabin thrust.

Rocks of the Medicine Lodge plate are present on the northeast side of the Medicine Lodge Creek Basin of Idaho (Fig. 5, Plate 1). Limestones are tightly folded and broken and veined with calcite along the present leading edge. Folds are disharmonic and verge northeast, and fold axes are vertical to southwest-dipping and trend northwest. The plate is folded, imbricated, offset by tear faults, and has been extended along the Deadman normal fault zone (Figs. 5, 6). The thrust dips about 20° just south of the Continental Divide near the northern border of Figure 5 (see Fig. 11A), and is nearly vertical northwest of Irving Creek (Fig. 11B). One hanging-wall imbricate has been identified, although others may be present (Fig. 6). The buried trace of a short, right-stepping, northeast-trending tear fault is present along Irving Creek, and another tear fault is present just east of the area of Figure 6 (Plate 1), indicating increased northeastward transport of southern parts of the plate much like the southern lobes of the Fritz Creek plate.

I interpret the Medicine Lodge and Cabin thrust plates to have been originally part of a single, far-traveled plate. A part of the leading edge of the Medicine Lodge ceased movement, and the Cabin broke through and locally overrode the Medicine Lodge as shown on the cross sections of Figure 5, becoming an out-of-sequence thrust with respect to its original leading edge. Transport on the Medicine Lodge thrust is linked with that of the Cabin, and on the interpretive cross sections of Figure 5, the combined movement is a minimum of 40 km. Whereas the Cabin thrust loses throw to the southeast, the Medicine Lodge thrust gains throw in that direction, indicating that major parts of the thrust plates moved nearly simultaneously.

Tendoy thrust plate

The Tendoy thrust, the lower boundary thrust of the Tendoy plate, was first mapped and named for exposures of Mississippian limestone resting on Upper Cretaceous or younger synorogenic conglomerates along a fault trace northeast of the present map area (Fig. 2; Scholten and others, 1955). As originally mapped, the Tendoy thrust extended from the southern Beaverhead Mountains northward to beyond Clark Canyon Reservoir (Fig. 2).

Recently, however, the fault was shown to terminate south of the Horse Prairie fault zone of Scholten (1983) (Fig. 2). The upper boundary thrust of the Tendoy plate in the southern Beaverhead Mountains (Fig. 6) is the Medicine Lodge.

Rocks ranging in age from Triassic through Late Cretaceous constitute the Tendoy plate in the map area of Figures 5 and 6. Immediately to the northeast, rocks as old as Late Mississippian are present, and include the upper part of the Upper Mississippian Snowcrest Range Group, Pennsylvanian Quadrant Sandstone, Permian Grandeur Member of the Park City Formation and Phosphoria Formation, Triassic Dinwoody and Woodside Formations, and locally, possibly the Gypsum Springs Member of the Twin Creek Formation (Fig. 3).

Immediately northeast of the area of Figure 5, the Tendoy plate is folded and imbricated (Hammons, 1981; Perry and others, this volume) (Plate 1). Stratigraphic offset on the Tendoy thrust may be as much as 5,000 m.

NEW INTERPRETATIONS OF STRUCTURES IN THE SOUTHERN BEAVERHEAD MOUNTAINS

The assemblage of contraction structures associated with Mesozoic compression in the southern Beaverhead Mountains is similar to the assemblage in the Canadian Rocky Mountains, as summarized by Dahlstrom (1970). Concentric folds bounded by upper and lower detachments, folded low-angle thrust faults that juxtapose older strata over younger, and transverse tear faults are

Figure 11. Medicine Lodge thrust. A, Gently southwest-dipping (20°) thrust (dashed line) along northern border of Figure 5 just south of Continental Divide. View looking northwest. Limestones of Scott Peak Formation (M) in thrust contact above conglomerates of Beaverhead Group (K). B, Steeply dipping folded thrust. Lighter limestones of Scott Peak Formation of Medicine Lodge plate to left. Relatively darker east-dipping or tightly folded conglomerates of Beaverhead Group to right of thrust in middle ground. About 3 km northwest of Irving Creek, Clark County, Idaho. View looking northwest.

present. Transverse tear faults and lateral ramps, however, appear to be more common components of the thrust belt in the southern Beaverhead Mountains than in the Canadian Rockies.

Five major thrust faults in the area—the Hawley Creek, Fritz Creek, Cabin, Medicine Lodge, and Tendoy—are the lower boundary thrusts of thrust plates bearing their names. Each thrust fault has a minimum stratigraphic throw of about a thousand meters and lateral continuity for tens of kilometers, and, with the possible exception of the Cabin and Medicine Lodge plates, each thrust plate has a distinctive stratigraphic sequence.

A major departure from the structural characteristics of the Canadian Rockies and the Idaho-Wyoming thrust belts is the presence of basement crystalline rocks in the southwest-to-northeast-transported thrust plates in the southern Beaverhead Mountains. The Cabin thrust plate locally contains Archean(?) crystalline basement rocks, as do other thrust plates in the region (Plate 1), whereas crystalline basement is not involved in thrusting in the Foothills and Front Range provinces of the Canadian Rocky Mountains or the Idaho-Wyoming thrust belt. The crystalline rocks on the Cabin thrust probably are part of a regional raised basement block encountered by the thrust as it propagated northeastward.

Geologic sketch maps (Figs. 5 through 8) show the locations of the thrusts and associated faults that bound the major plates, and the locations of cross sections A-A′ and B-B′. The interpretation of the subsurface geology illustrated on these cross sections incorporates thrust concepts, and is constrained by the surface geology of Figures 5 and 7, material balance, and the results of a gravity survey by D. M. Kulik (unpublished data, 1983) that suggests the presence of thick, low-density rocks beneath the Medicine Lodge, Cabin, and probably the Fritz Creek thrust plates. The interpretation resulting from new mapping (Figs. 6, 8) differs from earlier ones (Scholten and others, 1955; Scholten and Ramspot, 1968) in the following ways: (1) faults surrounding the Beaverhead Mountains pluton and associated Paleozoic rocks are folded low-angle thrust faults at the leading edge of the Hawley Creek thrust plate, rather than high-angle reverse faults along which the pluton was raised; (2) Proterozoic rocks along the middle part of Nicholia Creek are part of a folded and faulted normal stratigraphic sequence that forms the core of a frontal ramp anticline above the Fritz Creek thrust, rather than part of a Nicholia thrust plate in fault contact with underlying Paleozoic rocks; (3) upper Paleozoic rocks in the position of the Willow Creek and Tex Creek "thrusts" of Scholten and Ramspott (1968) (Fig. 2) are part of a tightly folded normal stratigraphic sequence; (4) the Fritz Creek thrust is a low-angle folded thrust rather than a high-angle reverse fault; (5) the Divide Creek fault zone is a normal fault zone probably formed along an earlier oblique tear fault or lateral ramp rather than a thrust fault zone; (6) silicified sandstone in the vicinity of Bannack Pass is in the Pennsylvanian-Mississippian Bluebird Mountain Formation south of the pass, and is Proterozoic sandstone north of the pass, rather than the Ordovician Kinnikinic Quartzite; (7) Paleozoic rocks, rather than Proterozoic sandstone, underlie Tertiary deposits in both the Medicine Lodge and Birch Creek valleys (Fig. 5); (8) irregular trends in fold axes probably are the result of differential movement between segments of the thrust sheets, rather than late doming of the Beaverhead Mountains pluton; (9) Proterozoic and Ordovician sandstones are tightly folded and faulted on the thrust plates along with the upper Paleozoic carbonate complex, and do not make up a relatively uninvolved infrastructure different from that of the overlying carbonates—this is true even though the Mississippian and Devonian siltstones and shales are far less competent than stratigraphic units above and below, and formed zones along which fault movements were concentrated; and (10) rocks of the Cabin, Medicine Lodge, and Tendoy plates all continue westward beneath the southern Beaverhead Mountains. The folded, west-dipping Medicine Lodge thrust plate constitutes a thrust slab, locally overridden by the Cabin thrust, rather than a separate gravity glide plate derived from the west, as was suggested earlier by Scholten (1983). The westward extension of the Cabin thrust plate beneath the Beaverhead Mountains was recognized previously (Scholten, 1983).

Estimates of transport distances along the four major thrust faults in the Beaverhead Mountains range from about 1 km (Hawley Creek) to more than 40 km (Medicine Lodge), and displacement transfer took place between pairs of faults. As throw on one fault diminished, displacement was transferred to an adjacent structure, indicating simultaneous movement. Apparent stratigraphic throw on the Hawley Creek thrust diminishes southward to near zero in the west-central part of the map area, whereas throw increases to the southeast on the subjacent Fritz Creek thrust. In a similar way, stratigraphic throw on the Cabin thrust diminishes to the south, whereas stratigraphic throw on the Medicine Lodge thrust is large within the area, but diminishes to the northwest.

Ages of thrust emplacement are poorly constrained. One sample of carbonaceous shale from 3,000 m or more below the exposed top of the Divide quartzite conglomerate unit of the Beaverhead Group in the footwall of the Medicine Lodge thrust (Skipp, Prostka, and Schleicher, 1979) yielded pollen and spores identified by R. H. Tschudy (written communication, 1983) as post-Santonian Cretaceous (Campanian or Maastrichtian). The Divide quartzite conglomerate unit conformably overlies the Lima Conglomerate (Beaverhead Group) of Coniacian to middle Campanian age in the footwall of the Tendoy thrust (Nichols and others, 1985). Because the Divide quartzite conglomerate unit is no older than middle Campanian, and because there is no evidence for an early Tertiary age for any part of the synorogenic conglomerates in southwestern Montana (Nichols and others, 1985), final movement on the Medicine Lodge thrust in the southern Beaverhead Mountains probably took place in Late Cretaceous (post-middle Campanian) time. No other evidence for the ages of thrusting in the southern Beaverhead Mountains is presently available.

Cenozoic, postthrusting, extension faults offset and extend all of the thrust plates, and range in age from early Eocene to late Pleistocene or Holocene (Skipp, 1985). Extension faults of early

Eocene age, such as the Divide Creek fault, appear to have formed soon after compression ceased. Parts of the faults are buried beneath unfaulted, approximately 50-m.y.-old, Eocene Challis Volcanics, or are intruded by dikes of similar age. Several of these faults are interpreted to have listric geometries. The Divide Creek fault seems to have formed initially as an oblique lateral ramp or tear fault during Mesozoic compression, and subsequently was reactivated as a normal fault in pre-Challis time (Skipp, 1984). Further extension of the Beaverhead Mountains was accomplished along additional extension faults that locally offset till and outwash deposits of Pinedale age (late Pleistocene) within the area of Figure 5 (Scott, 1982). The elongate Lost River and Lemhi Ranges, and the southern Beaverhead Mountains have been raised and tilted to the northeast along northwest-trending basin-range faults. Hanging walls of the range front faults are down to the southwest.

INTERACTION BETWEEN CORDILLERAN THRUSTS AND FORELAND FAULTS

Interactions of the Cordilleran thrust plates and the faulted foreland are treated here within the framework of individual thrust plates newly recognized in the southern Beaverheads, and the interpretations of their northward and southward continuations shown in Plate 2. The interpretation of the full extent of the thrust plates (Plate 2) includes a reinterpretation of many previously mapped structures, based on thrust concepts applied to geologic maps of the Beaverhead Mountains (Figs. 12, 13; Plate 1). Figure 13, the geologic map of the Beaverheads north of latitude 45°, is an excerpt from the preliminary geologic map of the Dillon 1° × 2° quadrangle by Ruppel and others (1983), and Plate 1 is a compilation of the geology of the Beaverheads south of latitude 45°.

All of the thrust plates of the southern Beaverhead Mountains, plus the Four Eyes Canyon thrust plate of Perry and Sando (1983), are present to the north. The Blue Dome block of Skipp and Hait (1977) in the southernmost part of the mountains (Plate 2) tentatively is considered part of the Hawley Creek thrust plate. Most of the thrust sheets are confined to the central and southern Beaverhead Mountains. Only the Cabin thrust sheet is interpreted to extend into the northern Beaverhead Mountains where the present eastern limit of rocks belonging to the plate is interpreted to coincide with the eastern limit of the Medicine Lodge thrust system of Ruppel (Ruppel and others, 1983; Ruppel and Lopez, 1984). All of the thrust plates have undergone extension by Cenozoic normal faults, some of which have been identified previously as younger-over-older thrusts. In some cases, Cenozoic normal displacement is shown to have taken place on segments of the older Mesozoic thrusts.

Discussions of the regional interaction of individual thrust plates include: (1) an expanded description or definition of the plate; (2) a brief review of stratigraphy with emphasis on stratigraphic units not previously described in the southern Beaverhead

Mountains; (3) a description of the interpreted interaction, if any, of the thrust plate with the foreland; and (4) a discussion of regional structural and stratigraphic implications resulting from such interaction.

Hawley Creek plate

Rocks of the Hawley Creek plate can be traced northward into the Railroad Canyon area northeast of Leadore, Idaho, and southward along the southwestern margin of the Beaverhead Mountains to the Snake River Plain, a minimum distance of 95 km. Rocks of the plate constitute the Lemhi Range south and west of the Beaverheads, and part of the mountains northwest of Leadore where Ordovician plutonic rocks (Evans and Zartman, 1981) have been identified near Leesburg, west of Salmon, Idaho. Major portions of the plate have been downdropped to the southwest into the Birch Creek and Lemhi River Valleys along northwest- and east-trending basin-range faults.

In the Leadore area, rocks of the plate include at least 1,000 m of Proterozoic Lemhi Group rocks, 350 m of the Ordovician Saturday Mountain Formation (Ruppel, 1968), and more than 300 m of the Devonian Jefferson Formation (Lucchitta, 1966), in addition to thick sections of the Ordovician Kinnikinic Quartzite and rocks of the Beaverhead Mountains pluton found farther south. The presence of thick sections of Proterozoic rocks north of Leadore (Plate 1) suggests that the Hawley Creek thrust ramps laterally down section to the northwest with respect to the hanging wall.

Thick sections of Mississippian through Permian rocks including, in ascending order, the Scott Peak, South Creek, Surrett Canyon, Arco Hills, Bluebird Mountain, and Snaky Canyon Formations, total about 1,034 m in the Blue Dome block and are similar in lithology and thickness to the same sequences in the Lemhi Range (Skipp and Hait, 1977; Skipp, Hoggan, and others, 1979).

Within the limited area of exposure, no interaction with the foreland was identified in this plate.

Fritz Creek plate

Rocks of the Fritz Creek thrust plate make up most of the southern Beaverhead Mountains and are exposed for a distance of about 70 km from north to south. The plate branches off from the Hawley Creek plate south of Hawley Creek (Plates 1, 2), and increases in both structural and stratigraphic displacement from the northwest to the southeast, where it is buried beneath lavas of the Snake River Plain. Permian rocks of the Snaky Canyon and Phosphoria Formations and a thin remnant of Triassic Dinwoody Formation are present in the plate in the southernmost Beaverheads in addition to the Proterozoic through Pennsylvanian rocks already described (Fig. 4).

Structures within the Fritz Creek plate do not appear to involve basement, and interaction with the foreland has not been detected.

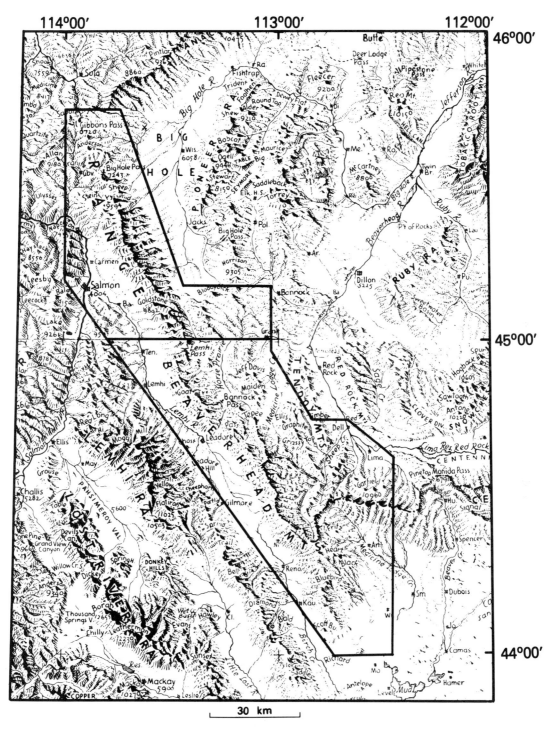

Figure 12. Map showing outlines of areas of Plate 1 south of 45°00′, and Figure 13 north of 45°00′ that together make up the area of Plate 2 in the Beaverhead Mountains and Bitterroot Range of Idaho and Montana. Base from Raisz (1968).

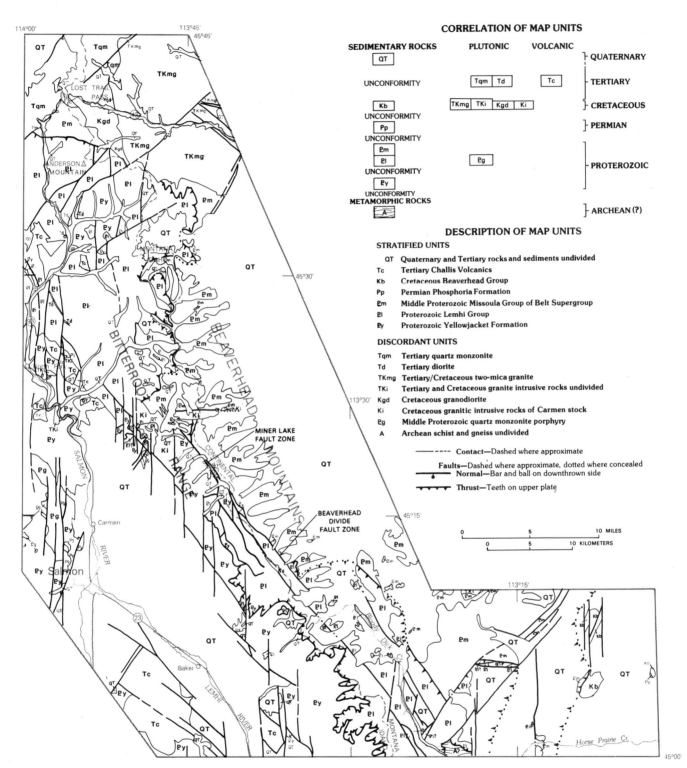

CORRELATION OF MAP UNITS

DESCRIPTION OF MAP UNITS

STRATIFIED UNITS

QT   Quaternary and Tertiary rocks and sediments undivided
Tc   Tertiary Challis Volcanics
Kb   Cretaceous Beaverhead Group
Pp   Permian Phosphoria Formation
Pm   Middle Proterozoic Missoula Group of Belt Supergroup
Pl   Proterozoic Lemhi Group
Py   Proterozoic Yellowjacket Formation

DISCORDANT UNITS

Tqm   Tertiary quartz monzonite
Td   Tertiary diorite
TKmg Tertiary/Cretaceous two-mica granite
TKi   Tertiary and Cretaceous granite intrusive rocks undivided
Kgd   Cretaceous granodiorite
Ki   Cretaceous granitic intrusive rocks of Carmen stock
Pg   Middle Proterozoic quartz monzonite porphyry
A   Archean schist and gneiss undivided

------   Contact—Dashed where approximate
          Faults—Dashed where approximate, dotted where concealed
          Normal—Bar and ball on downthrown side
          Thrust—Teeth on upper plate

Figure 13. Geologic map of northern Beaverhead Mountains, Montana and Idaho. Modified from Ruppel and others (1983).

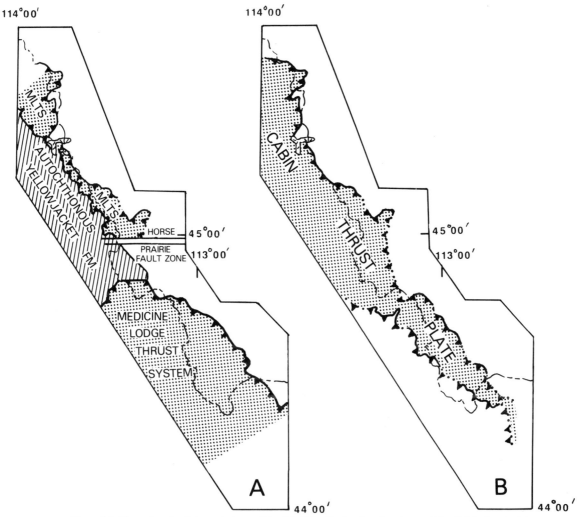

Figure 14. Maps showing interpretations of the Medicine Lodge thrust system and the Cabin thrust plate in area of Plate 2: A, Medicine Lodge thrust system (MLTS) and underlying autochthonous Yellowjacket—interpretation by Ruppel (Ruppel, 1978; Ruppel and Lopez, 1984). B, Distribution of rocks of Cabin thrust plate—interpretation by Skipp (1985; this chapter).

Cabin plate

Rocks of the redefined Cabin thrust plate extend from the Snake River Plain northwestward for about 200 km to the Tertiary and Cretaceous plutonic rocks of the Idaho batholith complex near Lost Trail Pass (Plate 2) and may continue northward (Skipp, 1987). This definition is based on the reinterpretation of several previously mapped structures in the central and northern Beaverhead Mountains.

Basement crystalline rocks at the present eroded leading edge of the thrust plate in the southern and central Beaverheads are overlain by thick Proterozoic sandstones, below the Phanerozoic succession. West of the Maiden Peak area, no crystalline rocks are present (Plates 1, 2). To the northwest, however, along latitude 45°, crystalline rocks reappear in structural contact with the overlying Lemhi Group near Bloody Dick Creek (Fig. 13, Plate 1), a relationship similar to that recognized in the central

Beaverheads in the Maiden Peak area. For this reason, I have included the crystalline rocks at the mouth of Bloody Dick Creek in the Cabin plate and have located the buried thrust east of these outcrops (Plates 1, 2). This construction uses thrusting to explain juxtaposition of Archean(?) crystalline rocks and overlying Proterozoic rocks against both Archean(?) crystalline rocks with only Phanerozoic cover of the Maiden Peak area and the Middle Proterozoic Belt Supergroup rocks of the Grasshopper thrust plate (Fig. 14), instead of the east-trending Horse Prairie normal fault zone (Scholten, 1983; Ruppel and Lopez, 1984). North of Bloody Dick Creek no crystalline basement is present, and the Lemhi Group structurally overlies the Proterozoic Yellowjacket Formation (Fig. 13). Both the Lemhi Group and Yellowjacket Formation in this area are faulted against Belt Supergroup rocks for a distance of about 75 km (Fig. 13). This fault has been interpreted by Ruppel (Ruppel and others, 1983; Ruppel and Lopez, 1984) to be the eastern edge of a large klippe of Lemhi

Group rocks of the Medicine Lodge system thrust over both autochthonous Yellowjacket Formation and allochthonous Belt Supergroup strata (Fig. 14A, this chapter). Because the contact between the Yellowjacket Formation and Belt rocks is a steep west-dipping fault along the Beaverhead Divide and Miner Lake fault zones (Ruppel and Lopez, 1984, p. 36), and because those faults place older Yellowjacket Formation against younger Belt Supergroup strata, I have interpreted the Proterozoic Yellowjacket Formation and overlying Lemhi Group to be allochthonous and in thrust contact with the Belt rocks of the Grasshopper plate (Plates 1, 2). Subsequent normal movement along the Cabin thrust in the positions of the Beaverhead Divide and Miner Lake fault zones locally has dropped the Cabin plate down to the west (Plate 2). In this interpretation, the Yellowjacket is not a block of autochthonous basement rocks in the middle of a thrust belt (Fig. 14A), but is Proterozoic basement brought to the surface on a major west-dipping thrust, the Cabin (Fig. 14B).

The fault that bounds the western margin of the northern klippe of the Medicine Lodge thrust system of Ruppel (Ruppel, 1978) is a low-angle fault that places younger Lemhi Group rocks over older Yellowjacket Formation (Figs. 13, 14A); this fault has the characteristics of a detachment fault within the Cabin plate rather than a major thrust. The Hawley Creek thrust is the western boundary thrust of the west-dipping Cabin plate in the northern Beaverhead Mountains (Skipp, 1987).

Several younger-over-older faults formerly mapped as thrusts that delete stratigraphic section in the Goat Mountain and Grizzly Hill areas west of Horse Prairie Creek (Ruppel, 1978; Staatz, 1973, 1979) are reinterpreted in this report as normal faults that thin the Cabin plate (Plates 1, 2). Two of the faults drop Paleozoic rocks down against Proterozoic rocks much as the Divide and Divide Creek faults do in the central and southern Beaverhead Mountains (Fig. 2, Plate 1), indicating that a regional extensional detachment probably separates the Proterozoic and Phanerozoic successions in much of the Beaverhead Mountains (Plates 1, 2).

In the central Beaverhead Mountains, the Cabin plate consists of 4,500 to 9,600 m of rocks ranging in age from Archean(?) to Early Triassic. A minimum of 305 m of the Triassic Dinwoody Formation and 260 m of the Permian Park City and Phosphoria Formations are present above the Permian rocks of the Snaky Canyon Formation in the Hawley Creek area (Lucchitta, 1966), in addition to stratigraphic units previously described in southern parts of the mountains (Fig. 4).

Proterozoic rocks that exceed 12,000 m in thickness (Ruppel and Lopez, 1984) are interpreted to constitute the hanging wall of the Cabin plate in the northern Beaverhead Mountains where the plate is thickest and northeastward transport of the plate probably was greatest. These Proterozoic rocks constitute the Yellowjacket Formation and the overlying Lemhi Group and Swauger Formation, considered to be of Middle Proterozoic age by most workers and correlative with some part of the Middle Proterozoic Belt succession (Ruppel, 1975). The Late(?) Proterozoic age attributed to the Lemhi Group and Swauger Formation

in this chapter (Fig. 4) is based on lithologic correlation with Late Proterozoic rocks in southeastern Idaho and northern Utah. Diamictites that are present in the lower part of the Lemhi Group in the Lemhi Range (Tietbohl, 1986) are characteristic components of the Late Proterozoic succession south of the Snake River Plain (Crittenden and others, 1983). Recent (for example, see Skipp, 1987) field examination, however, confirms that diamictites and adjacent rocks of the Lemhi Group in the Lemhi Range are Middle Proterozoic (Ruppel, 1975; Tietbohl, 1986), not Late Proterozoic as suggested here. Some of the Proterozoic rocks in the Beaverhead Mountains, however, appear to be younger than rocks of the Lemhi Group and Swauger Formation and may correlate with part of the Wilbert Formation which is known to be Early Cambrian (Derstler and McCandless, 1981), and may be as old as Late Proterozoic (Ruppel, 1975).

The distribution of hanging-wall rocks of the Cabin thrust suggests that this Cordilleran thrust encountered a faulted foreland as it propagated northeastward. Hanging-wall rocks just above the basal Cabin thrust range from upper Paleozoic miogeoclinal sedimentary rocks and Proterozoic sandstone to Archean(?) crystalline rocks from south to north within the southern and central Beaverhead Mountains. Crystalline rocks remain at the present leading edge of the Cabin thrust as far north as the mouth of Bloody Dick Creek (Fig. 13, Plate 2). From this locality northward along the Continental Divide, the Cabin thrust is interpreted to have Proterozoic Lemhi Group and structurally underlying Proterozoic Yellowjacket Formation in the hanging wall. The Yellowjacket is exposed on the leading edge of the plate along the Beaverhead Divide and Miner Lake fault zones (Fig. 13). All of these formations—Archean(?) basement crystalline rocks, the Middle Proterozoic Yellowjacket Formation, and the Middle Proterozoic Lemhi Group including the overlying Middle Proterozoic Missoula Group (Belt Supergroup) rocks, and a thin Phanerozoic cover, of the southwestern part of the Grasshopper thrust sheet (Fig. 13, Plate 2) in the northern Beaverhead Mountains.

The presence of basement crystalline rocks on a 75-km-long, partly covered segment of the present leading edge of the hanging wall of the Cabin plate suggests that the Cabin thrust encountered an upraised rectangular fault block of Archean(?) basement, the Cabin block (Fig. 10), approximately 40 km west of the Beaverhead Mountains in the miogeocline, and incorporated a segment of that block into the Cabin plate. The long northwest-trending dimension of the block is a minimum of 75 km, the length of outcrop of crystalline rocks on the Cabin plate. The northeast-trending dimension of the rectangular block may be 40 km, the estimated transport distance of the combined Cabin–Medicine Lodge thrust plate. A minor northeast-trending fault in the block may be present near Bannack Pass in the southern Beaverhead Mountains (Figs. 6, 10; Plates 1, 2). The faults that separate crystalline rocks from Proterozoic Yellowjacket Formation in the central Beaverheads are not exposed, but probably lie not far north of the outcrop of crystalline rocks at the mouth of Bloody Dick Creek near 45°00′ latitude (Fig. 13), and west of Horse

Prairie Creek between the Archean(?) crystalline rocks and the Yellowjacket outcrops south of latitude 45°00′ (Plate 1).

The fact that Archean(?) crystalline rocks do not reappear north of the mouth of Bloody Dick Creek near 45° latitude suggests that the northern margin of the Cabin block may represent a segment of the northern margin of Archean basement in Idaho and the western projection into Idaho of the northern edge of the southwestern Montana reentrant of Beutner (1977). It is possible that Archean basement is present at depth across all of south-central Idaho adjacent to the Snake River Plain where xenoliths from lavas exhibit an Archean ancestry (Leeman and others, 1985).

Proterozoic rocks overlie both the crystalline rocks of the Cabin block and the Middle Proterozoic sedimentary rocks of the Yellowjacket Formation, indicating that the block has a Proterozoic or older ancestry.

The distribution of rocks within the footwall of the Cabin thrust also suggests that as the Cabin thrust moved northeastward out of the miogeocline it encountered northeast-trending thrusts on the Montana craton. Precambrian crystalline rocks of the craton in the footwall of the Cabin thrust in the Maiden Peak area may have been thrust southeastward by a largely buried and queried foreland thrust in the valley of Medicine Lodge Creek of Montana east of Maiden Peak shown in Plate 1, before the arrival of the northeast-directed Cabin. Though both interpretations are tentative, it is also possible that a proto-Grasshopper thrust north of Maiden Peak had some southeast-directed movement prior to emplacement of the Cabin, and subsequent northeastward transport of the Grasshopper plate.

Medicine Lodge plate

The Medicine Lodge thrust plate has been traced northward about 60 km from exposures in the southern Beaverhead Mountains to the Medicine Lodge Creek area in Montana (Fig. 2, Plates 1, 2; Scholten and others, 1955). In the Medicine Lodge Creek area the thrust joins the Cabin thrust, and the Medicine Lodge plate, the former leading edge of the combined Cabin–Medicine Lodge thrust plate locally appears to have been overridden by the out-of-sequence Cabin thrust plate. The Medicine Lodge plate consists of poorly studied lower and upper Paleozoic western shelf-facies strata that appear to be similar to those of the Cabin plate (Fig. 4).

The thrust plate appears to have encountered a faulted foreland in the footwall. South of Bannack Pass, the Medicine Lodge plate lies above strata of the Tendoy plate, and northeast of Bannack Pass, above rocks of the Four Eyes Canyon thrust sheet. The Four Eyes Canyon sheet emerges abruptly from beneath the Medicine Lodge plate at the position of the southwestward extension of the northeast-trending sub-Snowcrest Range thrust (Perry and others, 1981), and the northeast-trending segment at the southern limit of the present leading edge of the Four Eyes Canyon thrust may be a reactivated part of the older northeast-trending thrust.

Four Eyes Canyon plate

The Four Eyes Canyon thrust plate (Perry and Sando, 1983) can be traced with certainty for a distance of a little over 5 km from northeast of Bannock Pass to Muddy Creek near Big Sheep Creek (Plate 1).

Rocks of the plate consist of upper Paleozoic cratonic sequences of the Lower Mississippian Lodgepole and Lower and Upper Mississippian Mission Canyon Limestones and post–Mission Canyon limestones, shales, and siltstones that may include rocks as young as Permian.

Known map relationships (Plate 1) allow for a northwestern extension of the plate that contains Mesozoic strata on the east side of Muddy Creek (Dunlap, 1982) and crystalline rocks of thrust "A" of Dubois (1983) (Fig. 2; Plates 1, 2). In this interpretation, the Archean(?) crystalline rocks and Paleozoic cover on the northwest side of Muddy Creek are part of the hanging-wall sequence of the Four Eyes Canyon thrust plate that earlier was transported from the northwest to the southeast on a buried foreland thrust that crosses the Muddy Creek Basin (Plates 1, 2). The present trace of the Four Eyes Canyon thrust may include thrust "A" (Dubois, 1983) as shown in Plate 2 (see Fig. 2), or one of the structurally lower thrusts that cut crystalline basement.

An alternate interpretation of the northern continuation of the Four Eyes Canyon thrust sheet is given by Perry and others (this volume) in which no basement is involved.

Tendoy plate

The Tendoy thrust plate extends with certainty only from the Lima Peaks area on the south to the area north of Big Sheep Creek and west of Dell (Plate 1), where it contains the east-northeast–trending Little Water syncline (Plate 2) and is cut by the Cenozoic Red Rock extension fault, a distance of about 35 km. From here to the northwest, the thrust has been interpreted to extend in several directions (Kupsch, 1950; Lowell and Klepper, 1953; Scholten and others, 1955; Scholten, 1960; Williams, 1984). The interpretation of this chapter is similar to that of Williams and Bartley (this volume) in which the northwest-trending Tendoy plate contains a segment of an earlier northeast-trending foreland thrust just south of 44°45′ latitude (Plate 1) and the northeast-trending Little Water syncline southeast of the foreland thrust segment. A similar interpretation is made by Perry and others (this volume).

Summary of the interaction between the thrust belt and the foreland

Interaction between the Cordilleran thrust belt and the foreland in southwestern Montana and east-central Idaho is evident in the Cabin, Medicine Lodge, Four Eyes Canyon, and Tendoy northeast-directed thrust sheets. To the west, structurally higher thrust plates, such as the Fritz Creek and Hawley Creek apparently were unaffected, or the effects of the interaction are undetected. A series of hanging-wall sequence diagrams (Fig. 15)

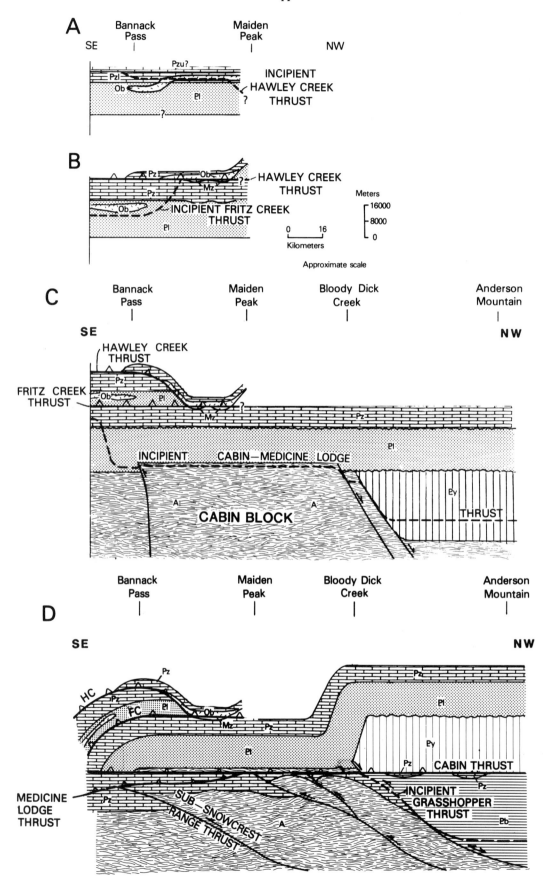

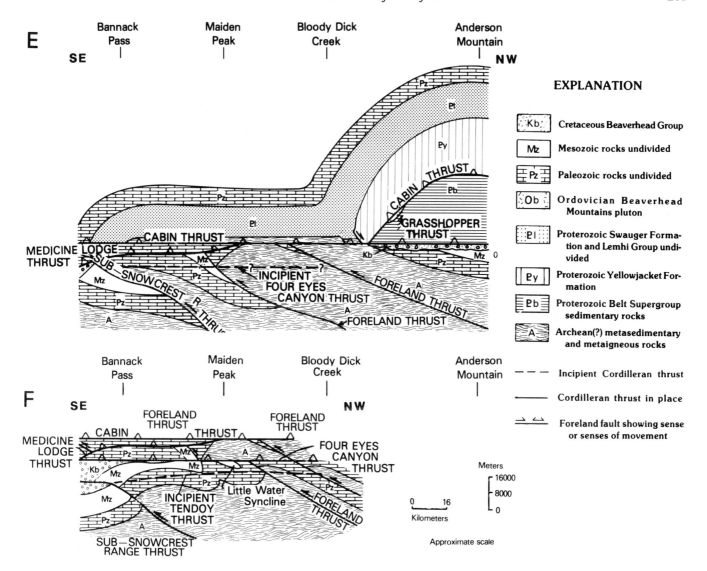

Figure 15. Hanging-wall sequence diagrams showing hypothetical evolution of Cordilleran thrust belt in Beaverhead Mountains and adjacent areas, viewed to the southwest, from the approximate latitude of Bannack Pass on the southeast to the approximate latitude of Anderson Mountain near Lost River Pass on the northwest (Plates 1, 2). Diagrams depict sequence of events discussed in text. Diagrams are oriented perpendicular to direction of transport, which is out of page. Distances and thicknesses are approximate. Vertical exaggeration, ×5. A, Position of incipient Hawley Creek thrust in miogeocline. Hanging wall of thrust ramps down-section to north, up-section to south. B, Hawley Creek thrust plate in place over miogeoclinal sequence, and position of incipient Fritz Creek thrust. C, Hawley Creek and Fritz Creek thrust plates in place over miogeocline sequence. Position of incipient Cabin–Medicine Lodge thrust plate is shown. Position of Cabin block in miogeocline and local faulted southern limit of Yellowjacket Formation are indicated. Age of basement beneath Yellowjacket Formation may be Early Proterozoic rather than Archean. D, Medicine Lodge thrust in place over faulted foreland. Cabin thrust has broken through and overridden the Medicine Lodge plate. Belt sediments are thrust southeastward over Archean craton and Phanerozoic cover on proto-"Grasshopper thrust." E, Grasshopper thrust beneath Cabin thrust emplaced over cratonic sequences forming a structural culmination of Proterozoic rocks. Position of incipient Four Eyes Canyon thrust is shown to follow trace of sub-Snowcrest Range foreland fault near Bannack Pass, and to incorporate at least one other foreland thrust. F, Four Eyes Canyon thrust in place over Archean craton and incorporated thrust segments. Position of incipient Tendoy thrust and included Little Water Canyon syncline and foreland thrust segments indicated.

summarize the hypothetical development presented in this chapter of the Cordilleran thrust plates of the Beaverhead Mountains as they propagated northeastward across the western shelf and miogeocline onto the Montana craton. The diagrams are oriented perpendicular to the direction of transport and cover a northwest-southeast distance of about 120 km from a latitude 15 km south of Bannack Pass on the south to the latitude of Anderson Mountain and Lost Trail Pass on the north. They are patterned after hanging-wall sequence diagrams showing the development of the complex structures at the north end of the Glencoul thrust in Scotland (Elliot and Johnson, 1980, Fig. 14), a concept first developed by Harris (1970), in which the reader views the emplacement of thrusts head-on. All of the diagrams are consistent with the known distribution of stratigraphic units and structures depicted on the geologic maps of Figure 13 and Plate 1.

The sequence begins with the incipient Hawley Creek thrust (Fig. 15A) an unknown distance west of the Beaverhead Mountains on the western shelf. In the second diagram (Fig. 15B) the Hawley Creek thrust plate is in place above the western shelf strata in which the position of the incipient Fritz Creek thrust is shown. In the third diagram (Fig. 15C), the Hawley Creek and Fritz Creek plates are in place above a footwall section also in western shelf strata in which the position of the incipient combined Cabin–Medicine Lodge thrust is shown. A large lateral ramp near the mouth of Bloody Dick Creek formed in the hanging wall of the thrust in response to the encounter with the upraised Proterozoic Cabin block in the miogeocline. The northern edge of the Cabin block may be the local southern limit of Middle Proterozoic Yellowjacket Formation as shown in this diagram, and thus, the local northern extent of continental Archean rocks in Idaho. Younger Proterozoic rocks have been deposited across both the crystalline rocks of the Cabin block and the adjacent Yellowjacket Formation. In the fourth diagram (Fig. 15D), the Cabin–Medicine Lodge thrust plate has moved into place, and the Cabin plate locally has been transported over its former leading edge, the Medicine Lodge thrust plate. Both thrust plates moved into place above a footwall deformed by three major northeast-trending thrust plates, two of which transported Archean basement rocks of the Montana craton with a cover of Paleozoic cratonal sequences. The southeasternmost of these is identified as the sub-Snowcrest Range fault. The third footwall plate is shown to consist of Belt Supergroup rocks, with a thin eroded Phanerozoic cover, that were thrust to the southeast over Archean crystalline basement rocks and Phanerozoic cover along a hypothetical proto-Grasshopper thrust. The inferred position of the incipient Cordilleran Grasshopper thrust is shown. In the fifth diagram (Fig. 15E), the Cordilleran Grasshopper thrust has moved into place above Archean rocks and Phanerozoic cover including synorogenic conglomerates of the Montana craton, creating a structural culmination of Proterozoic rocks in the position of the northern Beaverhead Mountains. This diagram indicates that the Salmon River arch of Armstrong (1975) is a tectonically thickened sequence of Proterozoic rocks transported

from the southwest rather than a western extension of the craton. The position of the incipient Four Eyes Canyon thrust plate shows the faulted foreland to be cut by the northeast-directed thrust, containing a northeast-trending thrust that transported Paleozoic and basement crystalline rocks from the northwest over Mesozoic strata to the southeast. Figure 15E also demonstrates how the southern terminus of the Four Eyes Canyon thrust may be a reactivated segment of the sub-Snowcrest Range foreland thrust. The sixth hanging-wall sequence diagram (Fig. 15F) shows the Four Eyes Canyon thrust plate containing a segment of a foreland thrust in place above a faulted foreland in which the position of the incipient Tendoy thrust is shown. This diagram shows how the Tendoy thrust plate incorporates the Little Water syncline and the thrust northwest of the syncline and also utilizes a segment of the earlier northeast-trending sub-Snowcrest Range fault.

Northeast-trending foreland thrusts shown in the diagrams are the sub-Snowcrest Range thrust, an unnamed foreland thrust across Muddy Creek Basin, an unnamed and queried thrust in the vicinity of Medicine Lodge Valley of Montana east of Maiden Peak, and a hypothetical proto-Grasshopper thrust. All of these structures are presumed to dip to the northwest and to have moved from the northwest to the southeast as depicted on the diagrams.

The cutting of the northeast-trending structures on the craton by the Cordilleran thrusts indicates that the foreland structures were in place before the arrival of the northeast-directed thrusts. However, postthrust reactivation of the northeast-trending Snowcrest thrust system folded the northwest-trending Tendoy thrust along an east-northeast axis (Perry and others, this volume), demonstrating that thrust belt and foreland deformation took place in pulses overlapping in time.

Available paleontologic data and radiometric ages do not clearly define discrete periods of movement. Synorogenic conglomerates derived from the Snowcrest Range thrust system have been palynologically dated as Coniacian to Middle Campanian or Late Cretaceous (Nichols and others, 1985). Conglomerates derived primarily from Cordilleran thrust sheets overlie the foreland-derived detritus. Palynomorphs recovered from western-derived synorogenic deposits in the footwall of the Medicine Lodge thrust have been dated as post-Santonian Cretaceous (Campanian or Maastrichtian) by R. H. Tschudy (written communication, 1983). Quartz diorite of the Carmen stock (Plate 2) that intrudes both the Cabin and Grasshopper plates, has been dated radiometrically ($^{40}Ar/^{39}Ar$) as 82.4 ± 1.2 Ma and 80.9 ± 1.9 Ma (Kilroy, 1984) or early Campanian.

At best, these dates suggest geologic contemporaneity for the Medicine Lodge, Cabin, Grasshopper, and Snowcrest Range thrusts, even though syntectonic conglomerates derived from the Snowcrest terrane lie stratigraphically below conglomerates derived from thrusts of the Cordilleran terrane. The evidence is consistent, however, in indicating that all of these thrusts moved in Late Cretaceous time.

CONCLUSIONS

The Beaverhead Mountains and vicinity in east-central Idaho and southwestern Montana comprise six major west-dipping Cordilleran thrust plates named after laterally continuous lower boundary thrusts that place older rocks over younger. The plates generally have distinctive stratigraphic sequences, and are characterized by northeast-verging folds, frontal and lateral ramps, and transverse tear faults. From southwest to northeast, the major thrust plates are the Hawley Creek, Fritz Creek, Cabin, Medicine Lodge, Four Eyes Canyon, and Tendoy. A west-to-east deformational sequence has been demonstrated locally (Perry and Sando, 1983) and is assumed for all of the thrusts except parts of the Cabin and the Medicine Lodge. Cross sections in the southern Beaverhead Mountains constrained by surface mapping, material balance, and a gravity survey (Skipp, 1985) suggest that the western Cabin thrust overrode the eastern Medicine Lodge thrust plate and locally is out of sequence. Eocene to Holocene extension faults have thinned the thrust plates. Some extension faults have introduced normal movement along former thrust zones.

Cordilleran thrust plates north of the Snake River Plain differ from those of the Idaho-Wyoming belt south of the plain in that they propagated northeastward across a previously faulted foreland and locally incorporated upraised basement rocks and northeast-trending folds and faults. As the combined Cabin–Medicine Lodge thrust plate was translated northeastward, it encountered the northwest-trending Proterozoic Cabin block in the midgeocline, and farther northeastward, the northeast-trending structures of the Montana craton. The thrust transported segments of these preexistent structures farther to the northeast. The 75-km-long western edge of the Cabin block, which was transported 40 to 50 km in the Cabin–Medicine Lodge thrust plate is a fragment of Archean(?) basement that was detached from its source located at least as far west as the Lemhi Range. Northeast-trending faults and folds of the Montana craton transported by the Cordilleran thrusts include the sub-Snowcrest Range thrust and the Little Water syncline. Both foreland structures and Cordilleran thrusts of the Beaverhead Mountains were emplaced in Cretaceous time.

Five of the west-dipping Cordilleran thrust slabs are present only in the southern and central Beaverhead Mountains. The redefined Cabin thrust plate is the major plate of the northern Beaverhead Mountains. The eastern boundary of the west-dipping Cabin thrust, as interpreted here, coincides with the eastern boundary of a flat-lying klippe of the Medicine Lodge thrust system of Ruppel (1978). Allochthonous Yellowjacket Formation and overlying Lemhi Group rocks are interpreted to constitute the hanging wall of the Cabin plate in the northern Beaverheads. Archean(?) crystalline basement, overlying Proterozoic sedimentary rocks, and an incomplete Phanerozoic section make up the Cabin plate in the southern and central Beaverhead Mountains. In the northern Beaverheads, the Yellowjacket Formation and Lemhi Group are thrust over Belt Supergroup rocks of the Grasshopper thrust plate in a structural culmination of Proterozoic rocks in the position of the Salmon River Arch of Armstrong (1975); this suggests these thickened Proterozoic sections have been transported from the southwest, and are not western extensions of the craton. Stratigraphic and structural throw increase laterally to the northwest with respect to the hanging wall of the Cabin thrust in the northern Beaverhead Mountains, and farther north, the Cabin may ramp down-section into pre-Belt Proterozoic basement rocks (Skipp, 1987).

ACKNOWLEDGMENTS

This study is an outgrowth of part of my Ph.D. dissertation completed at the University of Colorado, Boulder. I thank my committee members, Don L. Eicher, Steven S. Oriel, Erle G. Kauffman, Allison R. Palmer, and Roy G. Kligfield for their helpful suggestions. The study incorporates mapping completed for several USGS projects, including a study of the eastern Snake River Plain coordinated by S. S. Oriel, and two wilderness studies cited in the chapter.

Most of all, I thank my USGS colleagues, M. H. Hait, Jr., W. J. Perry, Jr., and D. M. Kulik for their stimulating discussions concerning local and regional structures in adjacent areas of Idaho and southwestern Montana. Ms. Kulik provided the invaluable, though at times unsettling, geophysical constraints on the structural interpretation of the area of Figure 5. Robert Scholten kindly has indicated that he believes the interpretations presented herein are improvements on the work he initiated in this area years ago. This chapter has benefited greatly from reviews by J. M. O'Neill, S. E. Boyer, and T.L.T. Grose.

REFERENCES CITED

Anderson, A. L., 1961, Geology and mineral resources of the Lemhi Quadrangle, Lemhi County [Idaho]: Idaho Bureau of Mines and Geology Pamphlet 124, 111 p.

Armstrong, F. C., and Cressman, E. R., 1963, The Bannock thrust zone, southeastern Idaho: U.S. Geological Survey Professional Paper 374-J, 22 p.

Armstrong, F. C., and Oriel, S. S., 1965, Tectonic development of Idaho-Wyoming thrust belt: American Association of Petroleum Geologists Bulletin, v. 19, no. 11, p. 1847–1866.

Armstrong, R. L., 1975, Precambrian (1500 m.y. old) rocks of central Idaho; The Salmon River Arch and its role in Cordilleran sedimentation and tectonics: American Journal of Science, v. 275-A, p. 437–467.

Bally, A. W., Gordy, P. L., and Stewart, G. A., 1966, Structure, seismic data, and orogenic evolution of southern Canadian Rocky Mountains: Bulletin of Canadian Petroleum Geology, v. 14, p. 337–381.

Bell, G. L., 1952, Geology of the northern Farmington Mountains, *in* Guidebook to the geology of the central Wasatch Mountains, Utah: Utah Geological Society Guidebook 8, p. 38–51.

Beutner, E. C., 1977, Causes and consequences of curvature in the Sevier orogenic belt, Utah to Montana: Wyoming Geological Association 29th Annual Field Conference Guidebook, p. 353–365.

Bond, J. G., 1978, Geologic map of Idaho: Idaho Department of Lands, Bureau of Mines and Geology, with contributions from U.S. Geological Survey, scale 1:500,000.

Cressman, E. R., and Swanson, R. W., 1964, Stratigraphy and petrology of the Permian rocks of southwestern Montana: U.S. Geological Survey Professional Paper 313-C, 569 p.

Crittenden, M. D., Jr., Christie-Blick, N., and Link, P. K., 1983, Evidence for two pulses of glaciation during the later Proterozoic in northern Utah and southeastern Idaho: Geological Society of America Bulletin, v. 94, no. 4, p. 437–450.

Dahlstrom, C.D.A., 1970, Structural geology in the eastern margin of the Canadian Rocky Mountains: Bulletin of Canadian Petroleum Geology, v. 18, no. 3, p. 332–406.

Derstler, K., and McCandless, D. O., 1981, Cambrian trilobites and trace fossils from the southern Lemhi Range, Idaho; Their stratigraphic and paleotectonic significance: Geological Society of America Abstracts with Programs, v. 13, no. 4, p. 194.

Dixon, J. S., 1982, Regional structural synthesis, Wyoming salient of western overthrust belt: American Association of Petroleum Geologists Bulletin, v. 66, no. 10, p. 1560–1580.

Dubois, D. P., 1983, Tectonic framework of basement thrust terrane, northern Tendoy Range, southwest Montana, in R. B. Powers, ed., Geologic studies of the Cordilleran thrust belt, 1982: Denver, Colorado, Rocky Mountain Association of Geologists, v. 1, p. 145–158.

Dunlap, D. G., 1982, Tertiary geology of the Muddy Creek Basin, Beaverhead County, Montana [M.S. thesis]: Missoula, University of Montana, 135 p.

Dyman, T. S., Niblack, R., and Platt, J. E., 1984, Measured stratigraphic section of Lower Cretaceous Blackleaf Formation and lower Upper Cretaceous Frontier Formation (lower part) near Lima, in southwestern Montana: U.S. Geological Survey Open-File Report 84-838, 25 p.

Eardley, A. J., 1944, Geology of the north-central Wasatch Mountains, Utah: Geological Society of America Bulletin, v. 55, p. 819–894.

Elliot, D., and Johnson, M.R.W., 1980, Structural evolution in the northern part of the Moine thrust belt, northwest Scotland: Transactions of the Royal Society of Edinburgh, Earth Sciences, v. 71, p. 69–96.

Embree, G. F., Hoggan, R. D., and Williams, E. J., 1983, Preliminary reconnaissance geologic map of the Copper Mountain Quadrangle, Lemhi County, Idaho: U.S. Geological Survey Open-File Report 83-599, scale 1:24,000.

Evans, K. V., and Zartman, R. E., 1981, Evidence from U-Th-Pb Zircon ages for Cambrian-Ordovician plutonism in east-central Idaho: Geological Society of America Abstracts with Programs, v. 13, no. 4, p. 195.

Garmezy, L., 1981, Geology and tectonic evolution of the southern Beaverhead Range, east-central Idaho [M.S. thesis]: University Park, Pennsylvania State University, 155 p., map scale 1:24,000.

Giletti, B. J., 1966, Isotopic ages from southwestern Montana: Journal of Geophysical Research, v. 71, p. 4029–4036.

Hammons, P. M., 1981, Structural observations along the southern trace of the Tendoy fault, southern Beaverhead County, Montana, in Tucker, T. E., ed., Southwest Montana: Montana Geological Society Field Conference and Symposium Guidebook, p. 253–260.

Hansen, P. M., 1983, Structure and stratigraphy of the Lemhi Pass area, Beaverhead Range, southwest Montana, and east-central Idaho [M.S. thesis]: University Park, Pennsylvania State University, 112 p., map scale, 1:24,000.

Harris, L. D., 1970, Details of thin-skinned tectonics, in parts of Valley and Ridge and Cumberland Plateau provinces of the southern Appalachians, in Fischer, G. W., Pettijohn, F. J., Read, J. C., and Weaver, K. N., eds., Studies of Appalachian geology; Central and southern: New York, Interscience, p. 161–173.

Heinrich, E. W., 1953, Pre-Beltian geologic history of Montana: Geological Society of America Bulletin, v. 64, p. 1432.

Huh, O. K., 1967, The Mississippian System across the Wasatch line, east-central Idaho and extreme southwestern Montana, in Centennial basin of southwest Montana: Montana Geological Society 18th Annual Field Conference Guidebook, p. 31–62.

James, H. L., and Hedge, C. E., 1980, Age of the basement rocks of southwest Montana: Geological Society of America Bulletin, v. 91, no. 1, p. 11–15.

Kilroy, K. C., 1984, ^{40}Ar/^{39}Ar geochronology and structural relationships of some intermediate intrusions in the northern Beaverhead Mountains, Idaho-Montana: Geological Society of America Abstracts with Programs, v. 16, no. 4, p. 226.

Kirkham, V.R.D., 1927, A geologic reconnaissance of Clark and Jefferson, and parts of Butte, Custer, Fremont, Lemhi, and Madison Counties, Idaho: Idaho Bureau of Mines and Geology Pamphlet 19, 47 p.

Kulik, D. M., 1984, A structural model for the overlap zone between the Rocky Mountain foreland and Cordilleran thrust belt in southwestern Montana: Geological Society of America Abstracts with Programs, v. 16, no. 4, p. 227.

Kulik, D. M., and Perry, W. J., Jr., 1982, Gravity modeling of the steep southern limb of the Blacktail-Snowcrest uplift: Geological Society of America Abstracts with Programs, v. 14, no. 6, p. 318.

Kulik, D. M., Perry, W. J., Jr., and Skipp, B., 1983, A model for Rocky Mountain foreland and overthrust belt development; Geophysical and geological evidence for spatial overlap: Geological Society of America Abstracts with Programs, v. 15, no. 5, p. 318.

Kupsch, W. O., 1950, Geology of the Tendoy-Beaverhead area, Beaverhead County, Montana [Ph.D. thesis]: Ann Arbor, University of Michigan, 163 p.

Landis, C. A., Jr., 1963, Geology of the Graphite Mountain–Tepee Mountain area, Montana-Idaho [M.S. thesis]: University Park, Pennsylvania State University, 153 p.

Leeman, W. P., Menzies, M. A., Matty, D. J., and Embree, G. F., 1985, Strontium, neodymium, and lead isotope compositions of deep crustal xenoliths from the Snake River Plain; Evidence for Archean basement: Earth and Planetary Science Letters, v. 75, no. 4, p. 354–368.

Lopez, D. A., 1981, Stratigraphy of the Yellowjacket Formation of east-central Idaho: U.S. Geological Survey Open-File Report 81-1088, 203 p.

Lowell, W. R., and Klepper, M. R., 1953, Beaverhead Formation, a Laramide deposit in Beaverhead County, Montana: Geological Society of America Bulletin, v. 64, p. 235–244.

Lucchitta, B. K., 1966, Structure of the Hawley Creek area, Idaho-Montana [Ph.D. thesis]: University Park, Pennsylvania State University, 203 p.

M'Gonigle, J. W., 1965, Structure of the Maiden Peak area, Montana-Idaho [Ph.D. thesis]: University Park, Pennsylvania State University, 146 p.

Nichols, D. R., Perry, W. J., Jr., and Haley, J. C., 1985, Reinterpretation of the palynology and age of Laramide syntectonic deposits, southwestern Montana, and revision of the Beaverhead Group: Geology, v. 13, no. 2, p. 149–153.

Oriel, S. S., and Moore, D. W., 1985, Geologic map of the west and east Palisades Roadless areas: U.S. Geological Survey Miscellaneous Field Studies Map MF-1619-B, scale 1:50,000.

Perry, W. J., Jr., 1982, The thrust belt in the Lima-Dell, Montana area, in Beaver, P., ed., The overthrust province in the vicinity of Dillon, Montana, and how this structural framework has influenced mineral and energy resources accumulation: Tobacco Root Geological Society 7th Annual Field Conference Guidebook, p. 69–78.

—— , 1986, Critical deep drill holes and indicated Paleozoic paleogeography north of the Snake River downwarp in southern Beaverhead County, Montana, and adjacent Idaho: U.S. Geological Survey Open-File Report 86–413, 16 p.

Perry, W. J., Jr., and Sando, W. J., 1983, Sequential deformation in the thrust belt of southwestern Montana, in Powers, R. B., ed., Geologic studies of the Cordilleran thrust belt, 1982: Denver, Colorado, Rocky Mountain Association of Geologists, v. 1, p. 137–144.

Perry, W. J., Jr., Ryder, R. J., and Maughan, E. K., 1981, The southern part of the southwest Montana thrust belt; A preliminary reevaluation of structure, thermal maturation, and petroleum potential, in Tucker, T. E., ed., Southwest Montana: Montana Geological Society Field Conference and Symposium Guidebook, Southwest Montana, p. 261–273.

Perry, W. J., Jr., Wardlaw, B. R., Bostick, N. H., and Maughan, E. K., 1983, Structure, burial history, and petroleum potential of the frontal thrust belt and adjacent foreland, southwest Montana: American Association of Petroleum Geologists Bulletin, v. 67, no. 5, p. 725–743.

Perry, W. J., Jr., Haley, J. C., and Nichols, D. J., 1986, Interactions of Rocky Mountain foreland and Cordilleran thrust belt in Lima region, southwest Montana: Geological Society of America Abstracts with Programs, v. 18, no 5, p. 402.

Pratt, R. M., 1983, The case for lateral offset of the overthrust belt along the Snake River Plain, *in* Powers, R. B., ed., Geological studies of the Cordilleran thrust belt, 1982: Denver, Colorado, Rocky Mountain Association of Geologists, v. 1, p. 235–245.

Raisz, E., 1968, Landforms of the northwestern states (3rd ed.): Boston, Massachusetts, Erwin Raisz, map scale 1:1,350,000.

Ramsay, J. G., 1967, Folding and fracturing of rocks: New York, McGraw-Hill, 568 p.

Ramspott, L. D., 1962, Geology of the Eighteenmile Peak area and petrology of the Beaverhead pluton [Ph.D. thesis]: University Park, Pennsylvania State University, 215 p.

Ross, C. P., Andrews, D. A., and Witkind, I. J., 1955, Geologic map of Montana: U.S. Geological Survey, in cooperation with Montana Bureau of Mines and Geology, scale 1:500,000.

Royse, F., Jr., Warner, M. A., and Reese, D. L., 1975, Thrust belt structural geometry and related stratigraphic problems, Wyoming–Idaho–northern Utah, *in* Symposium on deep drilling frontiers in central Rocky Mountains: Denver, Colorado, Rocky Mountain Association of Geologists, p. 41–54.

Ruppel, E. T., 1968, Geologic map of the Leadore Quadrangle, Lemhi County, Idaho: U.S. Geological Survey Geologic Quadrangle Map GQ-733, scale 1:62,500.

—— , 1975, Precambrian Y sedimentary rocks in east-central Idaho: U.S. Geological Survey Professional Paper 889-A, p. 1–23.

—— , 1978, The Medicine Lodge thrust system, east-central Idaho and southwest Montana: U.S. Geological Survey Professional Paper 1031, 23 p.

—— , 1980, Geologic map of the Patterson Quadrangle, Lemhi County, Idaho: U.S. Geological Survey Geologic Quadrangle Map GQ-1529, scale 1:62,500.

—— , 1982, Cenozoic block uplifts in east-central Idaho and southwest Montana: U.S. Geological Survey Professional Paper 1224, 24 p.

Ruppel, E. T., and Lopez, D. A., 1984, The Thrust Belt in southwest Montana and east-central Idaho: U.S. Geological Survey Professional Paper 1278, 41 p.

Ruppel, E. T., Wallace, C. A., Schmidt, R. G., and Lopez, D. A., 1981, Preliminary interpretation of the Thrust Belt in southwest and west-central Montana and east-central Idaho, *in* Tucker, T. E., ed., Southwest Montana: Montana Geological Society Field Conference and Symposium Guidebook, Southwest Montana, p. 139–159.

Ruppel, E. T., O'Neill, J. M., and Lopez, D. A., 1983, Preliminary geologic map of the Dillon 1° by 2° Quadrangle, Montana: U.S. Geological Survey Open-File Report 83–168, scale 1:250,000.

Ryder, R. T., and Scholten, R., 1973, Syntectonic conglomerates in southwestern Montana; Their nature, origin, and tectonic significance: Geological Society of America Bulletin, v. 84, no. 3, p. 773–796.

Sadler, R. K., 1980, Structure and stratigraphy of the Little Sheep Creek area, Beaverhead County, Montana [M.S. thesis]: Corvallis, Oregon State University, 294 p.

Sandberg, C. A., and Poole, F. G., 1977, Conodont biostratigraphy and depositional complexes of Upper Devonian cratonic-platform and continental-shelf rocks in the Western United States, *in* Murphy, M. A., Berry, W.B.N., and Sandberg, C. A., eds., Western North America; Devonian: Riverside, University of California, Campus Museum Contributions 4, p. 144–182.

Sando, W. J., Sandberg, C. A., and Perry, W. J., Jr., 1985, Revision of Mississippian stratigraphy, northern Tendoy Mountains, southwest Montana: U.S. Geological Survey Bulletin 1656-A, p. A1–A10.

Saperstone, H. I., and Ethridge, F. G., 1984, Origin and paleotectonic setting of the Pennsylvanian Quadrant Sandstone, southwestern Montana: Wyoming Geological Association 35th Annual Field Conference Guidebook,

p. 309–332.

Schmidt, C. J., and Garihan, J. M., 1983, Laramide tectonic development of the Rocky Mountain foreland of southwestern Montana, *in* Lowell, J. D., ed., Rocky Mountain foreland basins and uplifts: Denver, Colorado, Rocky Mountain Association of Geologists, p. 271–294.

Schmidt, C. J., and Hendrix, T. E., 1981, Tectonic controls for thrust belt and Rocky Mountain foreland structures in the northern Tobacco Root Mountains-Jefferson Canyon area, southwestern Montana, *in* Tucker, T. E., ed., Southwest Montana: Montana Geological Society Field Conference and Symposium Guidebook, p. 167–180.

Schmidt, C. J., and O'Neill, J. M., 1983, Structural evolution of the southwest Montana transverse zone, *in* Powers, R. B., ed., Geologic studies of the Cordilleran thrust belt, 1982: Denver, Colorado, Rocky Mountain Association of Geologists, v. 1, p. 193–218.

Scholten, R., 1960, Sedimentation and tectonism in the thrust belt of southwestern Montana and east-central Idaho: Wyoming Geological Association 13th Annual Field Conference Guidebook, p. 73–83.

—— , 1967, Structural framework and oil potential of extreme southwestern Montana: Montana Geological Society Guidebook no. 18, p. 7–19.

—— , 1968, Model for evolution of Rocky Mountains east of Idaho batholith: Tectonophysics, v. 6, p. 109–126.

—— , 1973, Gravitational mechanisms in the northern Rocky Mountains of the United States, *in* deJong, K. A., and Scholten, R., eds., Gravity and tectonics: New York, Wiley-Interscience, p. 473–489.

—— , 1983, Continental subduction in the northern Rockies; A model for back-arc thrusting in the western Cordillera, *in* Powers, R. B., ed., Geologic studies of the Cordilleran thrust belt, 1982: Denver, Colorado, Rocky Mountain Association of Geologists, v. 1, p. 123–136.

Scholten, R., and Ramspott, L. D., 1968, Tectonic mechanisms indicated by structural framework of central Beaverhead Range, Idaho-Montana: Geological Society of America Special Paper 104, 71 p., map scale 1:62,500.

Scholten, R., Keenman, K. A., and Kupsch, W. O., 1955, Geology of the Lima region, southwestern Montana and adjacent Idaho: Geological Society of America Bulletin, v. 66, no. 4, p. 345–404, map scale 1:125,000.

Skipp, B., 1984, Geologic map and cross-sections of the Italian Peak and Italian Peak Middle Roadless areas, Beaverhead County, Montana, and Clark and Lemhi Counties, Idaho: U.S. Geological Survey Miscellaneous Field Studies Map MF-1061-B, with text, scale 1:62,500.

—— , 1985, Contraction and extension faults in the southern Beaverhead Mountains, Idaho and Montana: U.S. Geological Survey Open-File Report 545, 170 p.

—— , 1987, Basement thrust sheets in the Clearwater orogenic zone, central Idaho and western Montana: Geology, v. 15, p. 220–224.

Skipp, B., and Hait, M. H., Jr., 1977, Allochthons along the northeast margin of the Snake River Plain, Idaho, *in* Heisey, E. L., ed., Rocky Mountain thrust belt; Geology and resources: Wyoming Geological Association 29th Annual Field Conference Guidebook, p. 499–515.

Skipp, B., Hoggan, R. D., Schleicher, D. L., and Douglass, R. C., 1979, Upper Paleozoic carbonate bank in east-central Idaho; Snaky Canyon, Bluebird Mountain, and Arco Hills Formations and their paleotectonic significance: U.S. Geological Survey Bulletin 1486, 78 p.

Skipp, B., Prostka, H. J., and Schleicher, D. L., 1979, Preliminary geologic map of the Edie Ranch Quadrangle, Clark County, Idaho, and Beaverhead County, Montana: U.S. Geological Survey Open-File Report 79-845, scale 1:62,500.

Skipp, B., Antweiler, J. C., Kulik, D. M., Lambeth, R. H., and Mayerle, R. T., 1983, Mineral resource potential of the Italian Peak and Italian Peak Middle Roadless areas, Beaverhead County, Montana, and Clark and Lemhi Counties, Idaho: U.S. Geological Survey Miscellaneous Field Studies Map MF-1601-A, scale 1:62,500.

Skipp, B., Hassemer, J. R., and Detra, D. E., 1984, Geology, geochemistry, and mineral resource potential of the Eighteenmile Wilderness Study area (ID-43-3), Lemhi County, Idaho: U.S. Geological Survey Open-File Report 84-279, 55 p., map scale 1:62,500.

Skipp, B., Baesemann, J. F., and Brenckle, P. L., 1985, A reference area for the

B. Skipp

Mississippian-Pennsylvanian (Mid-Carboniferous) boundary in east-central Idaho: Compte Rendu X International Carboniferous Congress, Madrid, Spain, v. 4, p. 403–428.

Staatz, M. H., 1972, Geology and description of the thorium-bearing veins, Lemhi Pass Quadrangle, Idaho and Montana: U.S. Geological Survey Bulletin 1351, 94 p.

—— , 1973, Geologic map of the Goat Mountain Quadrangle, Lemhi County, Idaho, and Beaverhead County, Montana: U.S. Geological Survey Geological Quadrangle Map GQ-1097, scale 1:24,000.

—— , 1979, Geology and mineral resources of the Lemhi Pass thorium district, Idaho and Montana: U.S. Geological Survey Professional Paper 1049-A, p. A1-A90, map scale 1:31,680.

Tietbohl, D., 1986, Middle Proterozoic diamictite beds in the Lemhi Range, east-central Idaho, *in* Roberts, S. M., ed., Belt Supergroup; A guide to Proterozoic rocks of western Montana and adjacent areas: Montana Bureau of Mines and Geology Special Publication 94, p. 197–207.

Wardlaw, B. R., and Pecora, W. C., 1985, New Mississippian-Pennsylvanian stratigraphic units in southwest Montana and adjacent Idaho: U.S. Geological Survey Bulletin 1656–B, p. B1–B9.

Williams, N. S., 1984, Stratigraphy and structure of the east-central Tendoy Range, southwestern Montana [M.S. thesis]: Chapel Hill, University of North Carolina, 91 p.

MANUSCRIPT ACCEPTED BY THE SOCIETY FEBRUARY 9, 1988

Geological Society of America
Memoir 171
1988

Interactions of Rocky Mountain foreland and Cordilleran thrust belt in Lima region, southwest Montana

W. J. Perry, Jr.
U.S. Geological Survey, Box 25046, Denver Federal Center, Denver, Colorado 80225
J. C. Haley*
Conoco, Inc., 907 North Poplar, Casper, Wyoming 82601
D. J. Nichols
U.S. Geological Survey, Box 25046, Denver Federal Center, Denver, Colorado 80225
P. M. Hammons
P.O. Box 441, Lakewood, Colorado 80215
J. D. Ponton
Shell Western Exploration and Production, Inc., P.O. Box 831, Houston, Texas 77001

ABSTRACT

Laramide-style deformation of the Rocky Mountain foreland began in the Lima region of southwest Montana in Coniacian to Santonian (Late Cretaceous) time with the growth of the Blacktail-Snowcrest uplift. The Lima Conglomerate of the Beaverhead Group locally onlaps its deformed source terrane, the Laramide-style (thick-skin) Snowcrest-Greenhorn thrust-fault system of the foreland, along the southeastern margin of this uplift. Associated sandstones as old as Coniacian to Santonian, also derived from this uplift, are here reinstated into the Beaverhead Group. Northeast of Lima, the Snowcrest thrust transported Archean gneiss, marble, and schist southeastward over deformed Phanerozoic rocks. These Phanerozoic rocks are locally overturned and intensely fractured, and they exhibit many cross-faults. The Archean rocks exhibit locally intense cataclasis, microfaults, and pressure solution at grain boundaries.

The first incursion of Sevier-style (thin-skin) thrusting into the Lima region followed Campanian erosion of the Blacktail-Snowcrest uplift, locally to Archean basement. This thrusting shed thick quartzite-roundstone conglomerates eastward. These are placed in a new informal stratigraphic unit, the Little Sheep Creek conglomerate unit, which appears to conformably overlie the fining-upward sequence at the top of the Lima Conglomerate, palynologically dated as mid-Campanian. Quartzite clasts in the Little Sheep Creek conglomerate unit were probably recycled from proximal fans adjacent to deeply eroded hinterland thrust sheets to the west. However, this unit contains large slide blocks of Mississippian limestone from the front of the closer Four Eyes Canyon sheet, the lower bounding thrust of which reached the land surface, probably in late Campanian time. The Little Sheep Creek conglomerate unit is overridden by the Tendoy thrust. Consequently, the Tendoy is younger than the Four Eyes thrust to the west. Complex structural imbrication of upper Paleozoic and Triassic through Lower Cretaceous rocks of the Tendoy thrust sheet occurs in the Lima Peaks area, above the inferred southwestern extension of the older Snowcrest-Greenhorn thrust system. This imbricate stack, transported east-northeast on the Tendoy thrust, subsequently was folded about a N70°E axis, together with the Tendoy thrust and Lima Conglomerate of its footwall, by possible later reactivation of Snowcrest-Greenhorn thrust system.

*Present address: Route 2, Box 176, Leesburg, Virginia 22075.

Structural relationships within the Little Water Canyon and McKnight Canyon
areas northwest of Lima indicate that northeast-trending structures of probable foreland
origin developed in these areas prior to emplacement of the Tendoy thrust sheet, but
subsequent to emplacement of the Four Eyes Canyon thrust sheet. Therefore, these
northeast-trending structures are younger than the Snowcrest-Greenhorn thrust system
east of Lima and may be Maastrichtian, based on structural involvement of Beaverhead
rocks palynologically dated as late Campanian to early Maastrichtian in the northern
part of the McKnight Canyon area. Cessation of thrusting in the Lima region is still
poorly dated. The youngest Beaverhead conglomerates, those derived in part from the
Tendoy thrust sheet, underlie middle to upper Eocene basin beds northeast of Dell.

INTRODUCTION

The Lima region in extreme southwestern Montana is centered about the town of Lima (Fig. 1), which lies at an elevation
of about 1,890 m (6,200 ft) in southern Beaverhead County,
approximately 128 km (80 mi) west of Yellowstone National
Park. The region lies in a zone of overlap between the northeast-
trending Blacktail-Snowcrest uplift of the Rocky Mountain foreland and the northwest-trending Cordilleran thrust belt, first
studied by Scholten and others (1955). The Tendoy thrust sheet
(Hammons, 1981; Perry and others, 1981), at the frontal margin
of the thrust belt several miles south and west of Lima, displays
impressive imbricates of Pennsylvanian Quadrant Sandstone in
the southwestern part of the Lima Peaks. These mountains reach
an elevation of 3,350 m (~11,000 ft), some 11 km (7 mi) south
of Lima, providing nearly 1.5 km (5,000 ft) of topographic relief
in the region. Southeast of the Lima Peaks, complexly deformed
Cretaceous rocks lie in a generally southwest-dipping structural
panel that defines the southwestern limb of the Lima anticline
(Fig. 2). This anticline is underlain by a system of blind thrusts
(Perry and others, 1983a) that trend southeastward beneath the
Snake River downwarp.

Less than 9.6 km (6 mi) northeast of Lima, an intensely
deformed northeast-striking belt of chiefly Paleozoic rocks
emerges from beneath Tertiary and Quaternary cover, as well as
Cretaceous Beaverhead cover, and extends northeastward into
and beyond the Snowcrest Range (Figs. 1, 2). This Snowcrest
structural terrane forms the southeastern margin of the Blacktail-
Snowcrest uplift and contains several northwest-dipping thrust
faults, one of which, the Snowcrest thrust (Klepper, 1950; Perry
and others, 1981; Perry, 1982), places Archean crystalline rocks
over Paleozoic limestones. This structural terrane also exhibits
many folds and cross-faults and has been recently studied by
Sheedlo (1984) in the higher part of the Snowcrest Range, east of
the Lima region. In the Lima region, this belt is bounded on the
southeast and onlapped by Lima Conglomerate, composed
chiefly of limestone clasts and associated distal sandstones of the
Cretaceous Beaverhead Group. These clastic deposits are only
gently deformed compared to the shattered, locally overturned,
and intensely faulted older rocks.

Preliminary geological and geophysical data, compiled by
Perry and others (1981, 1983a), suggest that the Blacktail-
Snowcrest uplift and bounding Snowcrest-Greenhorn thrust system extend beneath the frontal zone of the Cordilleran thrust belt
near Lima and are responsible for the arcuate geometry of this
zone, particularly the Tendoy thrust sheet. Gravity-supported
structural models and additional geophysical documentation are
provided by Kulik and Perry (this volume). Definitive evidence
includes (1) cross-strike discontinuities in thrust stacking and development of lateral ramps in the Tendoy, Four Eyes Canyon,
Medicine Lodge, and Cabin thrusts (see Skipp, this volume)
along the projected extension of the Snowcrest-Greenhorn thrust
system beneath the thrust belt, and (2) the warped configuration
of the sub-Beaverhead erosion surface along the rear exposed
portion of the Tendoy thrust sheet southwest of the Lima Peaks
(Perry and others, 1981, 1983a; also Kulik and Perry, this volume). The alignment of structural discontinuities forms a
cross-strike discontinuity in the sense of Wheeler and others
(1979) and Wheeler (1980). This discontinuity is part of the
Greenhorn lineament of Maughan (1983). Continuation of the
Sage Creek normal fault southwestward across the Tendoy sheet,
discussed herein, provides additional evidence. This Tertiary
normal fault is inferred to be listric to the basal thrust of the
Campanian (Cretaceous) Snowcrest-Greenhorn thrust system of
the Rocky Mountain foreland.

The Four Eyes Canyon thrust sheet (Fig. 1), a Sevier-style
(thin-skin) sheet composed primarily of Mississippian carbonate
rocks, lies west of and structurally above the Tendoy sheet and
east of and structurally beneath the Medicine Lodge thrust sheet
(Perry and Sando, 1983). The Four Eyes Canyon thrust sheet is
obscured to the north by Tertiary deposits of the Muddy Creek
basin. Work in progress by Perry and W. J. Sando indicates that
Upper Mississippian and possibly Lower Pennsylvanian carbonate rocks of the Four Eyes Canyon sheet emerge on the north side
of the basin. Here, these rocks are footwall to Devonian and
Lower Mississippian rocks of the McKenzie thrust system of
Perry and others (1985), the lower bounding thrust of which
trends northeastward into the northern part of the McKnight
Canyon area (Figs. 1B, 2). Upper Mississippian carbonate rocks
in the western part of the McKnight Canyon area mapped by
Williams (1984; see Williams and Bartley, this volume) and
thrust slices of similar rocks in the western part of the Little
Water syncline (Fig. 2) structurally overlie the Tendoy sheet and
also appear to belong to the Four Eyes Canyon sheet. At the

southern end of the Four Eyes Canyon sheet, the lower bounding Four Eyes Canyon thrust merges with the Medicine Lodge thrust (Fig. 1) at a branch point. Structural implications of the implied branch line (a term defined by Boyer and Elliot, 1982) were pointed out by Perry and Sando (1983, p. 143): "Structural linkage of these two sheets [Four Eyes and Medicine Lodge], i.e., movement of both together as a structural unit during Four Eyes Canyon thrusting, is strongly suggested by mapped relations." Skipp (this volume) discusses structural relationships to the west and considers the McKenzie thrust system to the north a part of the Four Eyes Canyon sheet. Based on work in progress, Perry and W. J. Sando recognize two quite different Mississippian carbonate successions, one on the Four Eyes sheet (Madison Group), another in the McKenzie thrust system (Tendoy Group, briefly described by Sando and others, 1985).

The Lima region also includes the Quaternary extension-fault-bounded Red Rock valley graben (Fig. 2), which extends northwestward from Lima to Clark Canyon reservoir (Johnson, 1981a). The Centennial Valley, which extends eastward from Lima toward Yellowstone Park, is a Quaternary lake basin bounded on the south by the Centennial fault (Witkind, 1975, 1977). The Centennial Mountains south of the fault occupy the upthrown block and separate the Lima region from the Snake River volcanic plain and downwarp to the south (Fig. 1). Pliocene(?) basalts, of probable Snake River plain origin, extend to the southern outskirts of Lima, where they form isolated hill-capping outliers (Scholten and others, 1955, p. 377). These basalts have been uplifted in the Centennial Mountains, indicating the very young age of the Centennial Mountains and Centennial fault (Witkind, 1975). Near Lima, basalt rests with angular unconformity on lower to mid-Campanian (Cretaceous) Lima Conglomerate of the Beaverhead Group (Nichols and others, 1985). The elevation of these hill-capping basalts provides evidence of the level and extent of a late Tertiary erosion surface (Alden, 1953) as well as relative elevation changes due to later (Quaternary) extension faulting.

Major questions concerning the region include: (1) the nature and extent of thrust belt/Rocky Mountain foreland interactions; (2) the nature, timing, and sequence of development of Cordilleran thrust faulting; (3) the nature of Tertiary block faulting; and (4) the relation of Tertiary faulting to the older Laramide uplifts and thin-skinned thrusts of the Cordilleran thrust belt. This chapter focuses on the first question, and also sheds some light on the other structural questions.

Previous work

Considerable previous work in the Lima region includes general studies of areal geology (Klepper, 1950; Scholten and others, 1955), numerous additional studies by Robert Scholten and his students at Pennsylvania State University (Scholten, 1957, 1967, 1983; Ryder, 1967, 1968; Ryder and Scholten, 1973; Dubois, 1983), and Harvard University doctoral disserta-

tions (Gealy, 1953; Zeigler, 1954) concerning the geology of the Snowcrest Range. Geologic studies of the Tendoy Mountains include Oregon State University master's theses (Klecker, 1981; Sadler, 1980) and Texas A&M structural studies (Hammons, 1981; Ponton, 1983). The structure of the northern Tendoy Mountains and adjoining areas to the north and east was the subject of a French Ph.D. dissertation by de la Tour-du-Pin (1983). University of Montana theses deal with the Tertiary stratigraphy and structure of the Muddy Creek basin (Dunlap, 1982), neotectonics and gravity modeling of the Red Rock graben (Johnson, 1981a,b), and the stratigraphy and sedimentology of the Triassic Thaynes Formation (Sikkink, 1984). Stratigraphic studies include older general reports (Moritz, 1951; Sloss and Moritz, 1951; Sandberg and Mapel, 1967; Swanson, 1970) and more recent summaries (Dyman, 1985a; Dyman and others, 1984; Perry and others, 1983b; Peterson, 1981, 1985; Sandberg and others, 1983, 1985; Sando and others, 1985; Saperstone and Ethridge, 1984, and Wardlaw and Pecora, 1985). Studies of Laramide synorogenic sedimentation include those by Lowell and Klepper (1953), Wilson (1967, 1970), Ryder and Scholten (1973) and Haley (1983a,b 1986). Palynostratigraphic age relations of synorogenic deposits have been discussed by Ryder and Ames (1970) and Nichols and others (1985). Recently, the sedimentology and petrology of Lower Cretaceous rocks have been thoroughly investigated (Dyman, 1985b). Recent structural studies include those by Skipp and Hait (1977), Perry and others (1981, 1983a, 1985), Perry and Sando (1983), Perry and Hossack (1984), Ruppel and Lopez (1984), Skipp (1984, 1985, 1987, this volume), Williams (1984), and Williams and Bartley (1983, this volume). Sheedlo (1984, Pl. 3) provided a comprehensive and thought-provoking tectonic map of the Snowcrest, Greenhorn, and Gravelly Ranges.

STRATIGRAPHY

Paleozoic through Jurassic rocks

Abrupt changes in the thickness and character of Paleozoic rocks in the Lima region define important Paleozoic paleotectonic features that have affected later structural patterns (Perry, 1986). The Paleozoic stratigraphy of the Tendoy sheet includes, from base to top: more than 457 m (1,500 ft) of Upper Mississippian to Lower Pennsylvanian Snowcrest Range Group (Wardlaw and Pecora, 1985; formerly assigned to the Big Snowy and Amsden Formations), 457 m (1,500 ft) of Pennsylvanian Quadrant Sandstone, and more than 244 m (800 ft) of Permian Park City and Phosphoria Formations. More than 610 m (2,000 ft) of Triassic rocks, chiefly limestones, are assigned to the Dinwoody, Woodside, and Thaynes Formations. Jurassic rocks are assigned to the thin Ellis Group, chiefly limestone, and overlying gray and red mudstones constitute the Morrison Formation.

The Paleozoic and lower Mesozoic sequence of the Snowcrest Range to the east is comparable to, but slightly thinner than, that of the Tendoy sheet. In the Snowcrest Range the Jurassic

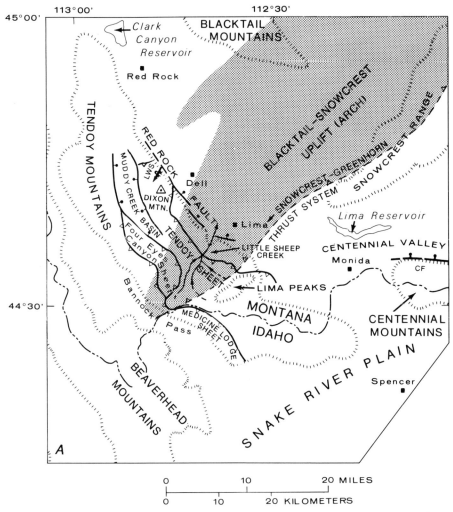

Figure 1. Index maps of Lima, Montana, region. A, Map showing prominent physiographic features, place names, and generalized tectonic features; map modified from Perry and Sando (1983). Abbreviations: CF = Centennial fault; LWS = Little Water syncline. B, More detailed tectonic map of region, with Cenozoic normal faults and basins removed to show better the configuration of Cordilleran thrust sheets. Inferred position of thrust faults beneath Tertiary and Quaternary basins is dotted. AA' is line of cross section of Figure 12. Explanation of structural symbols is given in Figure 2.

sequence is very thin and locally absent (Sikkink, 1984). Most Paleozoic and lower Mesozoic units thin northward in the Tendoy Mountains. An exception is the Kinderhookian through lower Meramecian (Mississippian) Tendoy Group defined by Sando and others (1985). This group, present in the McKenzie thrust system (Fig. 2) in the northern Tendoy Mountains (Perry and others, 1985) north of and structurally above the Four Eyes Canyon and Tendoy sheets, is a unique shelf-to-basin carbonate sequence correlative with and partly younger than the Madison shelf sequence of areas to the north and east (Sandberg and others, 1985). Rocks of the Madison Group are absent in exposures of the Tendoy sheet but are inferred to exist at depth in both the hanging wall and footwall. In aggregate, the upper Paleozoic and lower Mesozoic sequence in the Blacktail Range (Pecora, 1981) 48 km (30 mi) north of Lima is less than half its thickness in the Lima Peaks area.

Deep exploratory test-holes drilled in the Centennial Valley and Centennial Mountains east of the Lima Peaks (Fig. 2) contain an upper Paleozoic stratigraphic section (Fig. 3) very different from that of the Tendoy sheet and Snowcrest terrane (Perry and others, 1983a, p. 728–729, Fig. 1; Perry, 1986). The recently drilled Amoco No. 1 Snowline Grazing dry hole on the Lima anticline (drill-hole 1, Fig. 2) and Exxon No. 1 Myers Federal dry hole (drill-hole 2, Fig. 2) contain no Snowcrest Range Group rocks and 50 ft (15 m) or less of Quadrant Sandstone below very thin Permian formations. The area of these drill-holes was a part of the late Paleozoic Wyoming shelf termed the Monida high (Saperstone, 1986; Perry, 1986). During late Paleozoic time a rather sharp depositional boundary, possibly a system of down-to-the-northwest normal faults, separated the Monida high from the Snowcrest trough to the north (Maughan and Perry, 1982; Saperstone and Ethridge, 1984; Perry, 1986). The keel (axial

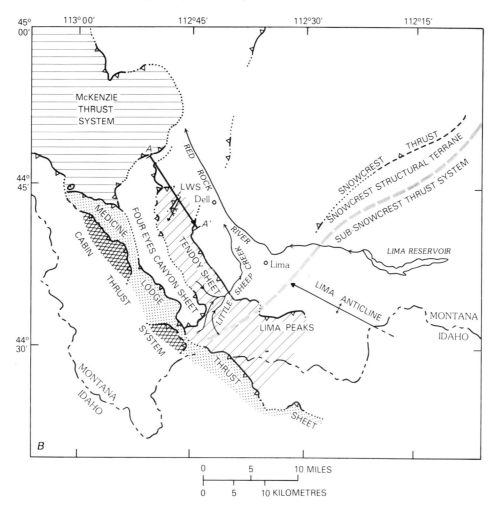

part) of the Snowcrest trough is represented by rocks exposed in the southern part of the Tendoy sheet and in the Snowcrest and Greenhorn Ranges to the northeast. In Cretaceous time, the keel of the Snowcrest trough became the axis of the Blacktail-Snowcrest Laramide uplift, and the sharp hinge or normal fault system along the southeastern margin of the Snowcrest trough became a northwest-dipping Laramide thrust system of crustal dimensions (Kulik and Perry, this volume).

Cretaceous rocks

Cretaceous rocks exposed south of Lima Peaks consist of two depositional sequences: (1) Lower Cretaceous Kootenai and Blackleaf Formations are overlain by an imprecisely known but variable thickness of Cenomanian to Turonian Frontier Formation (Perry and others, 1983a; Dyman, 1985a,b) and (2) the younger synorogenic conglomerates of the Beaverhead Group (Divide quartzite and limestone conglomerate units of the Beaverhead Formation of Ryder and Scholten, 1973) rest with angular unconformity on rocks as old as Permian on the southern flank of the southwestern Lima Peaks. The unconformity decreases southeastward, such that the Beaverhead may rest con-

formably on older Cretaceous rocks southwest of locality D6600 (Fig. 2).

The Beaverhead Group, as defined by Nichols and others (1985), contains at least two depositional suites: (1) the Lima Conglomerate and associated distal sandstones derived from the Blacktail-Snowcrest uplift, and (2) overlying conglomerates and sandstones of the Beaverhead Group southwest, west, and northwest of Lima, chiefly derived from the Cordilleran thrust belt. However, limestone conglomerates very similar to, and perhaps originally continuous with, the Lima Conglomerate occur at the base of the Beaverhead Group in the McKnight Canyon area (Fig. 2), as well as northeast of Dell (Haley, 1986). Conglomerates of the Beaverhead Group commonly have a red siliciclastic matrix. The associated gray-brown to buff sandstones, siltstones, and mudrocks weather buff and impart a buff color to overlying soils. These finer grained rocks generally are poorly exposed.

Foreland-derived syntectonic deposits. Palynostratigraphic methods were used by Nichols and others (1985) to show that Laramide-style deformation began in the Lima region in Coniacian to Santonian (Late Cretaceous) time with emergence of the Blacktail-Snowcrest uplift, from which sands containing Pennsylvanian spores were shed southward (locality D6597,

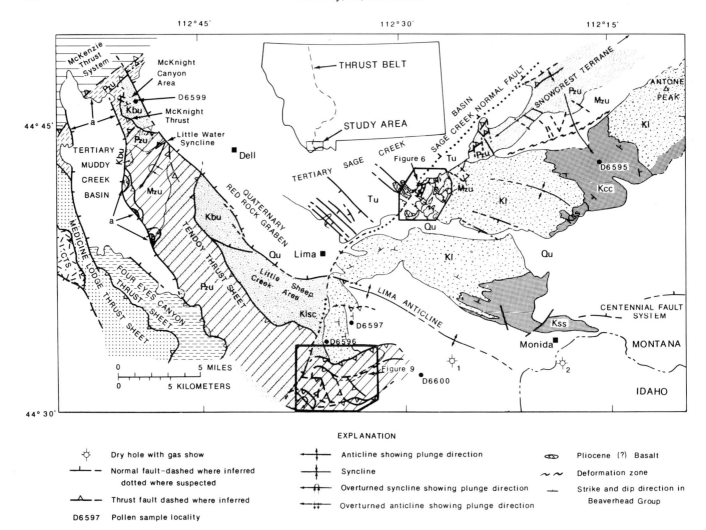

Figure 2. Generalized geologic map of Lima region, modified from Ziegler (1954), Scholten and others (1955), and Ryder and Scholten (1973). Grouped map units: Qu = Quaternary sediments, undivided; Tu = Tertiary rocks, undivided; Mzu = Lower Cretaceous through Triassic rocks, undivided; Pzu = Paleozoic rocks, undivided. Different stratigraphic units of the Beaverhead Group: Kbu = Beaverhead Group, undivided, including McKnight Canyon units; Kbl = Lima Conglomerate; Klsc = Little Sheep Creek conglomerate unit of this report. The following are informal map units proposed by Ryder and Scholten (1973), reinstated into the Beaverhead Group in this report: Kcc = Clover Creek sandstone unit; Kss = Snowline sandstone unit of their Beaverhead Formation; these sandstones of the Antone Peak depositional sequence of Haley (1986) are shown with a common screen pattern. "D"-numbered localities yielded datable pollen and spores, described by Nichols and others (1985). Different Sevier-style thrust sheets are labeled and are shown in separate patterns. Arrows from "a" point to segments of the Four Eyes Canyon thrust sheet separated by Tertiary deposits of the Muddy Creek basin. CTS = Cabin thrust sheet.

Truax Creek, Fig. 2). These sands coarsen upward into the Lima Conglomerate of the Beaverhead Group (Fig. 4; Nichols and others, 1985), formerly the Lima conglomerate unit of the Beaverhead Formation of Ryder and Scholten (1973). Where these sands can be clearly differentiated from the older Frontier Formation, they are herein formally included in the Beaverhead Group, as discussed in the Appendix. Beds from the fining-upward sequence near the top of the Lima Conglomerate (locality D6596, Alder Creek, Fig. 2) are "middle Campanian (*Aquilapollenites senonicus* Interval Zone; estimated absolute age 78–81 Ma)"

(Nichols and others, 1985, p. 149). To date, the Lima Conglomerate represents the youngest Laramide deposit known to be derived entirely from the Blacktail-Snowcrest uplift (Ryder, 1967; Wilson, 1970; Ryder and Scholten, 1973). The Rocky Mountain foreland near Lima appears to have reached nearly its present structural relief by 78 Ma, although limestone conglomerate deposition may have continued later to the east in the Antone Peak area of the Snowcrest Range (Fig. 2).

Thrust-belt derived syntectonic deposits. At Alder Creek (locality D6596, Fig. 2) in the footwall of the Tendoy thrust, the

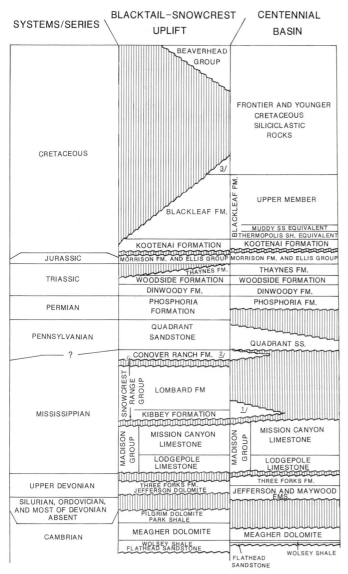

Figure 3. Correlation chart for Paleozoic and Mesozoic rocks of the Blacktail-Snowcrest uplift and adjacent Centennial basin, modified from Perry and others (1983b). Stratigraphy of the Tendoy thrust sheet is that of the middle column, except that beds older than upper Lombard Formation are not exposed on the Tendoy sheet as restricted herein. 1 = Lower part of Amsden Formation (of Wyoming); 2 = "Amsden Formation" of Lima region of older literature. 3 = lower part of Frontier Formation.

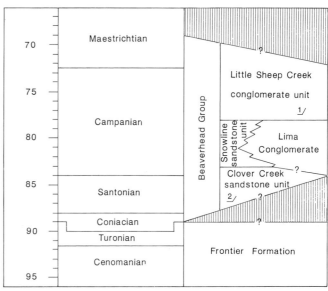

Figure 4. Correlation chart for rocks of the Beaverhead Group of the Little Sheep Creek area north of Lima Peaks east to Antone Peak (Fig. 2) and Frontier Formation near locality D6600 (Fig. 2) studied by Dyman and others (1984) and Dyman (1985b). 1 = Little Sheep Creek conglomerate unit may be correlative with the upper part of the Divide quartzite conglomerate unit of Ryder and Scholten (1973) southwest of the Lima Peaks. It is also correlative, at least in part, with the following informal units of Ryder and Scholten (1973) north of Lima: upper McKnight conglomerate unit, McKnight limestone and siltstone unit, Kidd conglomerate unit, and possibly the Chute Canyon sandstone unit. 2 = Clover Creek sandstone unit appears correlative with the Monida sandstone unit of Ryder and Scholten (1973).

palynologically dated middle Campanian (78–81 Ma) sandstone, siltstone, mudrock, and lignite in the top of the Lima Conglomerate are overlain with apparent conformity by quartzite-roundstone conglomerate (Divide quartzite conglomerate unit of Ryder and Scholten, 1973; informal Little Sheep Creek conglomerate unit of this chapter as discussed in the Appendix) derived from the Cordilleran thrust belt. In consequence, 78 to 81 Ma is a maximum age for thrust-belt derived conglomerates of the Beaverhead Group near Lima, as well as the minimum age for conglomerates derived entirely from the Blacktail-Snowcrest uplift.

A few limestone clasts are present in the lower part of the quartzite conglomerate at the foot of Lima Peaks several hundred meters southwest of locality D6596 (Fig. 2). This suggests a continued modest contribution of material from the Blacktail-Snowcrest uplift after the major shift in source area indicated by the quartzite conglomerate. Limestone clasts higher in the Little Sheep Creek conglomerate unit are uncommon; those present may have been derived from emergent thrust sheets to the west.

In the Little Sheep Creek area to the north (Fig. 2), the Little Sheep Creek conglomerate unit consists of highly polished and rounded quartzite and siltite clasts derived chiefly from the Proterozoic Lemhi Group (E. T. Ruppel, oral communication, 1981) and some Phanerozoic clasts as discussed in the Appendix. These quartzite and siltite clasts, which reach boulder size, were ultimately derived from deeply eroded hinterland thrust sheets now exposed in east-central Idaho and in the Beaverhead Mountains (Fig. 1; Ryder and Scholten, 1973). Their presence in the Lima region is probably the result of multiple episodes of uplift, recycling, and deposition as thrust-belt deformation proceeded from west to east.

The Little Sheep Creek conglomerate unit now dips steeply westward (45° to 65°) at a slightly lower angle than the dip of the Tendoy fault in the Little Sheep Creek area. Because of possible

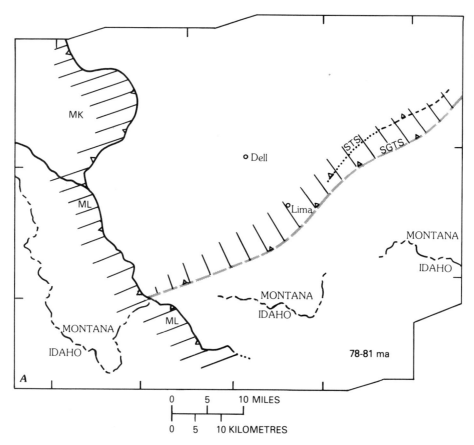

Figure 5. Sequence of development of Laramide-style Snowcrest-Greenhorn thrust system and Sevier-style Cordilleran thrust sheets in Lima region, based in part on work in progress with W. J. Sando and Betty Skipp. Transport direction of Cordilleran thrust sheets is assumed to be N70°E for purposes of palinspastic restoration. Absolute values of displacements are unknown. Total shortening of frontal zone (Tendoy and inferred sub-Tendoy thrust sheets) is assumed to be slightly less than 11 km (7 mi), and shortening associated with emplacement of Four Eyes Canyon thrust sheet is assumed to be 8 km (5 mi), for purposes of restoration. Diagonal parts of map borders represent direction and magnitude of palinspastic restoration. A, restored configuration at approximately 78 to 81 Ma of inferred active Cordilleran thrust front (composite Medicine Lodge [ML]–McKenzie Canyon [MK] thrust complex) and early to middle Campanian Snowcrest-Greenhorn thrust system [SGTS] including the Snowcrest thrust [STS]; no thrust-belt derived conglomerates reached as far east as Lima at this time. B, Restored configuration at approximately 70 to 75 Ma (late Campanian to early Maastrichtian time). Active Sevier-style thrusting along inferred Cordilleran thrust front of composite Medicine Lodge–Four Eyes

structural imbrication and generally poor exposure, the thickness of this unit has not been determined. This conglomerate unit contains large exotic blocks of Mississippian limestone (Ryder and Scholten, 1973; 2 and 3 of Fig. 5b). Perry and Sando (1983) determined that these were slide blocks from the Four Eyes Canyon thrust sheet just west of and structurally above the Tendoy sheet. Evidence for this determination included the lithostratigraphy, biostratigraphy, and internal deformation of the blocks examined. CAI values from conodonts (C. A. Sandberg, written communication, 1983) obtained from the blocks are greater than 1 and are consistent with those obtained from the front of the Four Eyes Canyon sheet, but not the Tendoy sheet or Blacktail-Snowcrest uplift.

South of the branch line between the Medicine Lodge and Four Eyes Canyon thrusts, the Medicine Lodge sheet rests di-

rectly on the Tendoy sheet (Fig. 1), thus sharing a common footwall (Beaverhead limestone-clast conglomerate at the exposed western margin of the Tendoy sheet) with the Four Eyes Canyon sheet to the north. The Little Sheep Creek conglomerate unit with its slide blocks was later overridden by the Tendoy sheet, requiring a break-forward, west-to-east sequence of first Medicine Lodge (Fig. 5A), then composite Four Eyes Canyon–Medicine Lodge (Fig. 5B), and finally Tendoy and sub-Tendoy thrusting.

Perry and others (1981, 1983a) discussed structural implications of the sub-Beaverhead erosion surface on the rear of the Tendoy sheet. The geometry of the rocks beneath this unconformity is believed to reflect the shape of the downplunge portion of the Blacktail-Snowcrest uplift and Little Water syncline prior to Tendoy thrusting. This conglomerate commonly includes Missis-

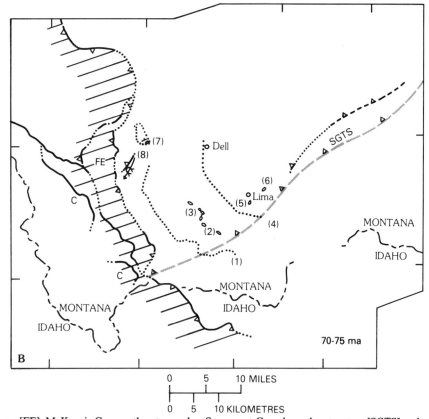

Canyon [FE]–McKenzie Canyon thrust complex. Snowcrest-Greenhorn thrust system [SGTS] no longer active. The Cabin thrust sheet [C], here a break-back imbricate of the Medicine Lodge thrust system. Numbered features: 1, dotted present trace of later Tendoy thrust plotted with respect to restored position of the Four Eyes and Medicine Lodge thrusts; 2 and 3, exotic blocks derived from Four Eyes Canyon thrust sheet—both 2 and 3 plotted in restored position assuming subequal partitioning of shortening in frontal zone between Tendoy and sub-Tendoy thrust sheets; 4, inferred position of later sub-Tendoy thrust, required by steeply west-dipping structural panel of Beaverhead quartzite-roundstone conglomerate (Little Sheep Creek unit) containing exotic blocks 2 and 3, plotted with respect to Lima and Dell, the autochthon; 5, exotic block or thrust slice south of Lima in Lima Conglomerate derived from Blacktail-Snowcrest uplift; 6, exotic block of Lodgepole Limestone in Lima Conglomerate; 7, McKnight Canyon area plotted in hypothetical restored position—exotic block shown near base (southern end) of Beaverhead sequence is probably derived from Blacktail-Snowcrest uplift; 8, Little Water syncline—eastern exposed edge of axial trace appears rotated counterclockwise due to deformation associated with later emplacement of Tendoy sheet.

sippian limestone boulders and smaller clasts, Proterozoic quartzite clasts, and, at its base, upper Paleozoic and Mesozoic clasts derived locally from the subjacent erosion surface. Some of this conglomerate was derived from erosion of the frontal Four Eyes–Medicine Lodge thrust system, after the branching Four Eyes Canyon thrust had developed (Fig. 5B). West of Lima, this conglomerate locally contains large limestone boulders derived from the hanging wall of this composite thrust system and is overridden by the lower bounding thrust of this system. This composite thrust system was emplaced after formation of the Blacktail-Snowcrest uplift, during late Campanian to Maastrichtian time, based on the inferred age of the Little Sheep Creek conglomerate unit with its slide blocks derived from this system. Therefore, the sub-Beaverhead erosion surface on the rear of the Tendoy sheet

west of Lima is probably of Campanian age, although it could be slightly older.

North of Lima, the Beaverhead Group is rather widely distributed in isolated outcrop areas (Ryder and Scholten, 1973; Pecora, 1981; Haley, 1986). Stratigraphic correlations between these Beaverhead outcrop areas are subject to debate. Only one palynostratigraphic date (locality D6599, Fig. 2), discussed by Nichols and others (1985), is available for rocks north of Lima and south of Clark Canyon reservoir (Fig. 1), in spite of extensive sampling.

Dell sequence. As described in detail by Haley (1986), the Dell area contains the stratigraphically youngest conglomerate of the Beaverhead Group recognized in the Lima region. This conglomerate, recognized at Red Butte by Haley ("Red Butte Formation" of Haley, 1986), has been overridden by the Tendoy thrust sheet southwest of Dell (Fig. 2). Northeast of Dell, this conglomerate, herein informally termed the Red Butte unit, rests with locally profound angular unconformity on older conglomerates (Haley, 1986). These older conglomerates include a limestone-pebble conglomerate unit and overlying quartzite-roundstone conglomerate unit closely similar respectively to the Lima Conglomerate and overlying Little Sheep Creek conglomerate unit near Lima. The Dell sequence, as described herein, includes from base to top the limestone-pebble conglomerate unit, quartzite conglomerate unit, and Red Butte conglomerate unit, which unconformably overlies both.

The proximal facies of the Red Butte conglomerate unit is exposed adjacent to the Tendoy thrust west of Dell. Here it contains large boulders of Upper Mississippian, Pennsylvanian, Permian and Triassic rocks derived from the adjacent Tendoy plate as well as boulders of limestone-pebble conglomerate, boulders of probable McKnight Canyon limestone unit, and clasts from the quartzite conglomerate (Haley, 1986). Some of these reworked quartzite clasts were sheared and recemented prior to being deposited in this youngest conglomerate (Haley, 1986). Sheared quartzite clasts were found elsewhere only in the Little Sheep Creek conglomerate unit and (the probably correlative) quartzite conglomerate northeast of Dell. The Red Butte unit is palynologically undated. It underlies middle to upper Eocene sediments and volcanics northeast of Dell (A. R. Tabrum, oral communication, 1987) and thus may be early Tertiary in age. It appears to be the only extant conglomerate derived from the Tendoy thrust sheet, which has locally overridden it. It shows that the Tendoy sheet is younger than thrust sheets farther west in the Lima region.

McKnight Canyon sequence. The McKnight Canyon area (Fig. 2) was designated the type area of the Beaverhead Formation, now Group, by Lowell and Klepper (1953) with the type section "near the mouth of McKnight Canyon." Here the Beaverhead is approximately 2,955 m (9,700 ft) thick and can be subdivided into four mappable units (Lowell and Klepper, 1953). This homoclinally northwest-dipping Beaverhead sequence is fault-separated from all other Beaverhead exposures by the Quaternary Red Rock fault on the east and a thrust complex on the south, west, and north, which is discussed by Williams and Bartley (this volume). The basal unit, a limestone-clast conglomerate at least 820 m (2,700 ft) thick, exposed in the southern part of the area, is composed almost entirely of limestone clasts derived from the Mississippian Madison Group, as first observed by Lowell and Klepper (1953). It contains a large exotic block of Woodhurst Limestone, the upper member of the Lodgepole Limestone of the Madison Group (W. J. Sando, oral communication, 1983; (7) of Fig. 5b), very similar to exotic blocks of Lodgepole observed in the Lima Conglomerate south and east of Lima, mapped by Ryder and Scholten (1973, Fig. 3). We found no indigenous quartzite clasts in this conglomerate. Lithologically, it appears to be closely similar to the Lima Conglomerate and to the limestone-pebble conglomerate at the base of the Dell sequence

described by Haley (1986); that is also composed almost exclusively of Mississippian limestone clasts. We have no palynostratigraphic dates from either this unit or the overlying freshwater limestone (about 305 m; 1,000 ft thick) but are reasonably confident of the correlation of this basal conglomerate with the Lima Conglomerate based on stratigraphic position as well as clast composition. The sequence above the limestone unit was subdivided by Lowell and Klepper (1953), from base to top (and south to north), into a siltstone dominated unit, with "interbedded sandstone, conglomerate, limestone, and arkose" approximately 490 m (1,600 ft) thick, and an overlying limestone-clast conglomerate about 1,100 m (3,600 ft) thick at the top of the sequence, the latter studied by Haley (1986).

Upper Campanian to lower Maastrichtian palynomorphs were recovered from lignitic beds in sandstone near the base of this limestone-clast conglomerate (locality D6599, Fig. 2; Nichols and others, 1985), approximately 1,100 m (3,600 ft) beneath the faulted top of the sequence. This upper limestone conglomerate contains an inverted clast stratigraphy in which carbonate clasts from Triassic and Permian formations predominate in the basal part of the unit, and Upper Mississippian Lombard Limestone clasts predominate higher in the unit to the north. Although sedimentologically similar to the upper conglomerate of the Dell sequence (Haley, 1986), this upper unit of the McKnight sequence lacks any boulders of the older limestone-pebble conglomerate or any other clasts obviously reworked from older Beaverhead deposits. It rests with apparent conformity on the siltstone unit and thus is probably older than the Red Butte conglomerate unit of the Dell sequence. This conglomerate at the top of the McKnight sequence is indicated by Ryder and Scholten (1973) and Haley (1986) to have had a northwest to western source, based on clast imbrication. The presence of large limestone boulders suggests a proximal source. The indicated source of this conglomerate is the McKenzie thrust system of Perry and others (1985) to the northwest and possibly the Four Eyes Canyon sheet as well (see Fig. 5A and 5B). Therefore, the McKenzie thrust system and possibly the Four Eyes Canyon sheet had developed significant structural relief by late Campanian to early Maastrichtian time, based on the palynological results obtained by Nichols from locality D6599. The underlying limestone and siltstone were combined into one unit by Ryder and Scholten (1973). The siltstone unit of Lowell and Klepper (1953), above the freshwater limestone and beneath the limestone-boulder conglomerate at the top of the sequence, contains lenses of quartzite conglomerate, which Ryder and Scholten termed Kidd quartzite conglomerate unit, based on the abundance of red and green Proterozoic quartzite and siltite clasts. Both we and Ryder and Scholten (1973) have correlated this quartzite conglomerate unit with the quartzite conglomerate of the Dell sequence.

The McKnight sequence of the Beaverhead Group dips homoclinally 25° to 80° northwest. It appears to have been rotated northwestward prior to being cut and overridden by the McKnight thrust of Williams and Bartley (this volume) to the west.

FORELAND STRUCTURAL PATTERNS

Klepper (1950) was the first to investigate and map the complex structural patterns in the northeast-trending Snowcrest Range northeast of Lima. This deformed belt of Paleozoic and lower Mesozoic rocks, with Archean metamorphic rocks locally exposed along the northwest margin, forms the generally southeast-dipping cross-faulted Snowcrest structural terrane of

Perry and others (1983a; southwestern part shown in Fig. 2). It is bounded on the northwest by Miocene rocks of the Tertiary Sage Creek basin ("Blacktail Deer Creek formation" of Scholten and others, 1955). The Sage Creek normal fault, a down-to-northwest Tertiary fault bounding the southeast margin of the Sage Creek basin, is poorly exposed and chiefly defined by geophysical data. In the Lima region, the Sage Creek fault is generally covered by Quaternary alluvium and colluvium or onlapped by Miocene

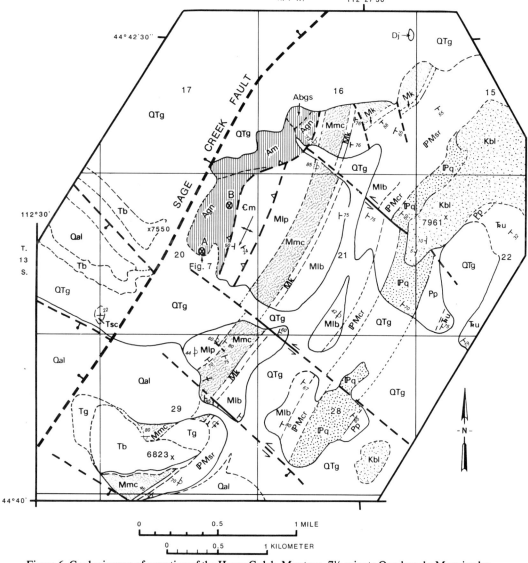

Figure 6. Geologic map of a portion of the Henry Gulch, Montana, 7½-minute Quadrangle. Mapping by W. J. Perry and Stephen M. Richard. Abbreviations: Qal = Quaternary alluvium; QTg = Quaternary to Tertiary colluvium and gravel; Tb = Pliocene(?) basalt; Tg = Pliocene(?) reworked Beaverhead quartzite conglomerate; Tsc = Miocene(?) sediments of the Sage Creek basin beds; Kbl = Cretaceous (early to middle Campanian) Lima Conglomerate of Beaverhead Group; Ru = Triassic rocks, undivided; Pp = Permian Phosphoria Formation and Park City Group; Pq = Pennsylvanian Quadrant Sandstone; PMcr = Pennsylvanian and Mississippian Conover Ranch Formation; PMsr = Snowcrest Range Group (Lombard and Conover Ranch Formations), undivided; Mississippian rocks: Mlb = Lombard Formation; Mk = Kibbey Sandstone; Mmc = Mission Canyon Limestone; Mlp = Lodgepole Limestone; Dj = Devonian Jefferson? Dolomite; €m = Cambrian Meagher Formation; Agn = Archean gneiss; Abgs = Archean biotite garnet schist; Am = Archean marble. A indicates collection locality of Archean rock sample shown in Figure 7; B indicates collection locality of dated Archean gneiss.

sediments as mapped by Zeigler (1954); its position is inferred. The southeast margin of the Snowcrest terrane is unconformably overlapped by the early to middle Campanian (Cretaceous) Lima Conglomerate, which laps northwestward onto the intensely deformed older rocks of the Snowcrest terrane, the source area for the Lima Conglomerate (Ryder and Scholten, 1973).

The Snowcrest terrane extends southwestward from the

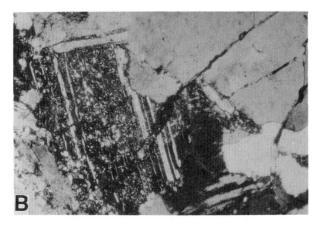

Figure 7. Photomicrographs of microfaults (A and B), cataclasis (A and C), and associated pressure solution (A and B) under crossed nicols; thin section of Archean gneiss from locality A in Figure 6, SW¼NE¼ of section 20. Scale bar = 1 mm.

Snowcrest Range along a line of hills to within 8.9 km (5.5 mi) of Lima, in the western part of the Henry Gulch 7½-minute Quadrangle. Here (Fig. 6, sections 15, 21, and 22, T.13S.,R.7W.), Lima Conglomerate rests unconformably on rocks as old as the upper part of the Mississippian to Pennsylvanian Snowcrest Range Group. Not far southwest of the map area (Fig. 6), clasts of Archean metamorphic rocks are present in the Lima Conglomerate in a small roadside quarry, indicating that the Snowcrest terrane was locally eroded to basement by middle Campanian time. In section 21 (Fig. 6), the Quadrant dips 50° to 70° southeast on the west and southwest flanks of hill 7961. Lapping northwestward onto the Quadrant, the Lima Conglomerate dips 10° to 15° west and strikes N5 to 10°E near the crest of the hill, resulting in an angular unconformity of 60° to 85°. Near the unconformity, the Lima Conglomerate contains large boulders of Quadrant Sandstone on the northwest flank of hill 7961, where it rests on Quadrant. The present gentle northwest dip of the Beaverhead rocks at the crest of the hill is attributed to postdepositional warping, possibly Tertiary to Quaternary northwest tilting. Similar warping also tilted Pliocene(?) basalt that caps hill 6823 in the southern half of section 29. Because beds of the Lima Conglomerate on hill 7961 dip into the angular unconformity yet fine southeastward away from the unconformity, we conclude that the erosion surface originally dipped southeastward at a steeper angle than the onlapping conglomerate. Between this area and Clover Creek to the northeast (locality D6595, Fig. 2), the Lima Conglomerate dips southeast at generally less than 20°. In the latter area, a broad northwest-trending anticline, probably very late Cretaceous to early Tertiary in age, warps both the Lima Conglomerate and the earlier deformed Snowcrest terrane. On the northwest flank of Antone Peak (Fig. 2), the conglomerate is locally rotated to southeast dips in excess of 40°, apparently tilted by late movement of the Blacktail-Snowcrest uplift itself.

The oldest rocks exposed in this part of the Snowcrest terrane are Archean gneiss, marble, and biotite garnet schist (Fig. 6). The gneiss is intensely shattered and, with the exception of two small exposures, is primarily grus. Both Keenmon (1950) and Zeigler (1954) mapped the "quartz monzonite" (gneiss) as a Tertiary intrusive. However, Klepper (1950) mapped these as "gneissic rocks of probable pre-Cambrian age," and Z. E. Peterman (written communication, 1982) obtained a Rb-Sr whole-rock date of 2.9 Ga from this biotite-quartz-microcline-oligoclase gneiss. The gneiss contains abundant evidence of brittle deformation: microfaulting, cataclasis, and associated pressure solution (Fig. 7). It is separated from Cambrian dolostones to the southeast (Perry, 1982) by a shear zone, which dips about 45° to the northwest. These Cambrian dolostones, which contain interbedded glauconitic quartzite, were identified as lower Meagher Formation by C. J. Schmidt (oral communication, 1982). Both Keenmon (1950) and Zeigler (1954) assigned these rocks to the Pennsylvanian Quadrant Sandstone and the underlying Pennsylvanian Amsden Formation. We have interpreted the shear zone as a thrust (Fig. 6), a southwestern extension of the Snowcrest thrust (Perry and others, 1981, Fig. 2) possibly reactivated in

Cenozoic time as a normal fault. The shear zone contains crush breccia of Archean gneiss, Flathead Sandstone, and Meagher Formation, all heavily iron-oxide stained. It also contains a large, irregular pod of undeformed hydrothermal-vein quartz. The Meagher dolostones occupy a small anticlinally folded horse (imbricate slice), separated by a reverse fault from Mississippian Lodgepole Limestone to the southeast (NW¼ of section 21 and adjacent parts of section 20, Fig. 6). Reverse faults of the Snowcrest thrust system bounding this horse merge northeastward, placing Archean marble and schist directly against Mississippian rocks (SW¼ of section 16, Fig. 6).

A set of three N50°W–trending faults with 100 to 300 m (330 to 980 ft) of left separation (here termed set 1) cut the Paleozoic sequence in sections 20, 21, 28, and 29 (Fig. 6). A second set (set 2) located in the SE¼ of section 16, with right separation, strikes N15 to 19°W. Unlike similarly oriented normal faults to the south and west, set 1 cannot have a significant down-to-the-southwest dip-slip component because the beds adjacent to these faults dip steeply southeast, yet from northeast to southwest across the faults of set 1, the strata are offset to the east. Counterclockwise rotation of the strike of beds adjacent to the southern fault of set 1 indicates that the separation direction is also the slip direction (left-lateral slip). The map pattern of beds adjacent to the middle fault of set 1 also suggests left-slip. The northern fault of set 1 is overlapped by apparently unfaulted Lima Conglomerate (Fig. 6) and thus is older than the conglomerate, pre-Campanian Cretaceous or older (possibly late Paleozoic, as suggested by Maughan and Perry, 1982), and it was not reactivated during Tertiary time. Similarly oriented faults in sections 19 and 20, west of the inferred position of the buried Sage Creek normal fault, were active following extrusion of Pliocene(?) basalt because they offset the basalt, but they may be reactivated Laramide faults as suggested by their orientation. Map relations here also require late Tertiary to Quaternary reactivation of the Sage Creek fault. The wrench faults of set 1 do not form a conjugate system with the two smaller faults of set 2 because the shear sense is incorrect; sets 1 and 2 could have been formed at different times. The small faults of set 2 may not be strike-slip faults. The right separation may be due to vertical displacements in the steeply dipping beds.

The presence of closely spaced northwest-trending extension fractures (Fig. 8A) provides evidence that the principal compression direction was oriented northwest-southeast, consistent with the folds observed and with the results obtained by Sheedlo (1984) to the northeast.

At the southwestern end of the Snowcrest terrane, intensely shear-fractured overturned Mississippian rocks (Fig. 8B) disappear under Quaternary alluvium along the south side of hill 6823 along the southern edge of and just south of section 29. The attitude of bedding and shear fractures shown in Figure 8B supports the interpretation of northwest-southeast compression derived from the analysis of extension fractures (above). The Pliocene(?) basalt-capping hill 6823 is tilted 7° to the northwest, such that, prior to tilting of the basalt, the Mississippian Mission

Canyon and structurally underlying Kibbey Sandstone and Lombard Limestone of the Snowcrest Range Group were more overturned than at present. The tilted basalt also suggests that some late Tertiary to Quaternary movement took place on the southernmost of the three Laramide left-slip faults of set 1, discussed above.

The presence of the intensely shear-fractured and inverted Upper Mississippian rocks just south of section 29 (Figs. 6, 8B), much more deformed and overturned than those to the north, suggests proximity to a major subsurface thrust, the subjacent sub-Snowcrest thrust of previous reports by Perry (1982) and Perry and others (1981,1983a). This is inferred from gravity data and gravity modeling to be a major northwest-dipping buried foreland thrust beneath the Snowcrest structural terrane, on which the deformed Paleozoic and lower Mesozoic rocks of the Snowcrest terrane—the hanging wall—moved southeastward over Cretaceous footwall rocks (Kulik, 1982; Kulik and Perry, 1982 and this volume; Perry and Kulik, 1982, 1983). Subsurface geological data are insufficient to draw well-constrained cross sections across the Snowcrest structural terrane or Snowcrest-Greenhorn thrust system. Gravity-structural models are presented by Kulik and Perry (this volume). A diagrammatic cross section across the Snowcrest-Greenhorn thrust system northeast of Figure 6, based in large part on D. M. Kulik's work (written communication, 1982) was given in an earlier report (Perry and others, 1983a, Fig. 12).

Sage Creek normal fault. The Sage Creek basin (Fig. 2) represents the middle Eocene to Miocene partial collapse of the Blacktail-Snowcrest Laramide uplift. The Sage Creek normal fault forms the southeastern margin of this basin. Gravity modeling (Kulik, 1982; Kulik and Perry, this volume) suggests that this Tertiary fault is listric and merges at depth with the sub-Snowcrest thrust, dipping somewhat more steeply northwest than the latter, as indicated by Perry and others (1983a, Fig. 12). Schmidt and Garihan (1983, p. 286) suggested that normal faults of the Rocky Mountain foreland are generally listric and merge at depth with the adjacent foreland thrusts rather than cut them, a pattern long recognized with respect to thin-skin thrusts in the Cordilleran thrust belt (Dahlstrom, 1970; Royse and others, 1975). Therefore, the western extent of the Sage Creek normal fault provides suggestive evidence of the westward continuation of the buried thrust-faulted southeast margin of the Blacktail-Snowcrest uplift.

Approximately 4.8 km (3 mi) southwest of the map area (Fig. 6), Lima Conglomerate to the south is separated from topographically lower Miocene rocks to the north, by a narrow gorge along the inferred trace of the Sage Creek normal fault. On the hill south of this gorge, Perry and Haley observed very large slide(?) blocks of Mississippian Lodgepole Limestone in the Lima Conglomerate. Ryder and Scholten (1973, Fig. 3) also mapped an exotic block of Mississippian limestone at this locality (locality 6 of Fig. 5B) in the Lima Conglomerate which they show to be derived from the Blacktail-Snowcrest uplift. The deformed Paleozoic rocks of the Snowcrest source terrane are not exposed in

Figure 8. Mesoscopic deformational features in Paleozoic rocks of map area (Fig. 6). A, Northwest-trending, closely spaced, anastomose extension fractures (center) and cataclasis (to right) in Mission Canyon Limestone in NE¼ section 29. Minor faults dip to left; extension fractures dip steeply to right. Azimuth of view 105°, oblique to 75° SE-dipping massive beds. B, Closely (1 to 10 cm) spaced, N 30 to 40° E–striking, subvertical shear fractures (extension faults) at high angles to nearly flat northwest-dipping overturned lower Lombard Limestone in NW¼ section 32 (just south of section 29, Fig. 6). View to northeast.

this area, but are inferred to underlie the Sage Creek basin to the north, consistent with the southwest plunge of the Blacktail-Snowcrest uplift inferred by Perry and others (1981, 1983a). No clasts of Archean basement rocks were observed by Perry and Haley in the Lima Conglomerate at this locality or farther west, suggesting that here and farther west the adjacent Blacktail-

Snowcrest uplift was *not* eroded to Archean basement during Campanian (Cretaceous) time.

Approximately 4 km (2.5 mi) farther southwest along the inferred trace of the Sage Creek normal fault, another patch of Lodgepole Limestone is present at the northwest end of the low hills of Lima Conglomerate west of I-15, 2 km (1.3 mi) south-

southeast of Lima (locality 5 of Fig. 5b). It may be a slide block from the Snowcrest terrane, but it could also be a thrust slice from the Snowcrest thrust system. At this locality, a low, northwest-facing scarp separates a large exposure of Mississippian Lodgepole Limestone from a low pavement of Beaverhead quartzite roundstone conglomerate to the northwest (the informal Little Sheep Creek conglomerate unit of this report). The Lodgepole exposure extends the length of the scarp, roughly 80 m (260 ft), and a somewhat greater distance to the southeast, where it is bounded by limestone (sharpstone) conglomerate. If this is a thrust slice of the Snowcrest thrust system, it has locally overridden its debris and then has been separated from the remainder of the Snowcrest terrane by the Sage Creek normal fault. Although the fault scarp is low, down-to-north displacement may be quite large, as this locality represents the southern end of the north-northwest–trending Quaternary Red Rock Valley graben, superposed on the southwestern end of the Tertiary Sage Creek basin (Fig. 2). Johnson's (1981a) gravity map indicates that a gravity low, possibly representing the deepest part of the Red Rock Valley graben, lies between this locality and Lima 1.6 km (1 mi) to the northwest.

Nearly 10 km (6 mi) south-southwest of Lima, an inferred extension of the Sage Creek normal fault system cuts the leading edge of the Tendoy thrust sheet in sec.32,T.14S.,R.8W. This normal fault strikes N15 to 20°E and displays down-to-the-northwest displacement of more than 200 m (650 ft). This fault can be traced south-southwestward into the NE¼ of Sec.18,T.15S.,R.8W. (Fig. 9), where it appears to merge with or die out against a detachment (bed-parallel thrust) in the upper part of the Snowcrest Range Group at the base of Garfield Mountain, the southwesternmost of the Lima Peaks.

EVIDENCE OF FORELAND STRUCTURAL PATTERNS IN CORDILLERAN THRUST-BELT

Lima Peaks area

One of the most striking features in the Cordilleran thrust belt of southwestern Montana occurs in the Lima Peaks area: the Tendoy thrust abruptly changes from a generally north-northwest strike to an east-northeast strike (Fig. 2). This change occurs along a low-angle hanging-wall ramp in which the Tendoy hanging-wall cutoff rises stratigraphically southward from upper Lombard Formation in the southern part of the Little Sheep Creek area (less than 4.8 km (3 mi) north of Fig. 9) to Pennsylvanian Quadrant Sandstone just beyond the bend (section 9, northwestern part of Fig. 9). The sharpness of the bend is partly due to the crosscutting Sage Creek normal fault. The actual eastward bend begins farther north (Fig. 2). The hanging-wall relations immediately east of the bend, along the northeastern edge of Lima Peaks (northern part, Fig. 9) are as follows: Here, for a distance of 4.6 km (3 mi) east of the bend, the hanging-wall cutoff remains in the lower Quadrant (a hanging-wall flat or conceivably a lateral ramp). Farther east a frontal or oblique hanging-wall ramp is indeed present in the front of the Tendoy thrust sheet as it

cuts up-section with respect to the hanging wall, through the Triassic limestones, before bending southeastward around the east end of Lima Peaks (Hammons, 1981).

Evidence summarized by Perry and others (1981, 1983a, p. 732–733, Fig. 8) indicates that the Tendoy propagated across the southeastern margin of the Blacktail-Snowcrest uplift, such that the hanging wall of the Tendoy sheet in the Lima Peaks area mirrors the original shape of this part of the uplift, displaced eastward.

The western part of the Lima Peaks area (Fig. 9) is cut by a group of southwest-dipping, generally northwest-trending, imbricate thrusts on which the Pennsylvanian Quadrant Sandstone is repeated or partially repeated three times. The peak labeled 10,441 (ft) and West Lima Peak (Fig. 9) represent southwest- to east-tilted slabs of Quadrant Sandstone, approximately 457 m (1,500 ft) thick in section 17. These imbricates, first observed by E. K. Maughan in 1983, climb section southeastward; they bring Pennsylvanian Quadrant Sandstone over Permian Phosphoria Formation in the higher part of the peaks, Mississippian and basal Pennsylvanian limestones of the Snowcrest Range Group over Quadrant along the northwest side of the peaks in sections 8 and 17, and Permian Phosphoria Formation over Triassic rocks along the southeast side of the Peaks in sections 20 and 21. This imbricate pattern is oblique to the inferred east-northeast transport direction for the Tendoy thrust system in the Lima Peaks area. Most of the imbricate faults gather southward into an east-west–trending fault with left separation. Perry has interpreted this fault as the roof thrust for the imbricate stack just to the north. The Lima Peaks area thus represents a southward-inclined duplex fault zone. The absence of subsurface geologic data in this area prevents us from constructing an adequately constrained balanced cross section.

The steep aeromagnetic gradient on the southeast flank of the Blacktail-Snowcrest uplift (Perry and others, 1983a) extends southwestward beneath the Tendoy thrust system just north of the Lima Peaks. Gravity data (D. M. Kulik, personal communication, 1984) indicates that the Lima Peaks are underlain by low-density material, presumably Cretaceous rocks. As more data accumulate, it becomes clearer that the front of the Tendoy sheet in the area of Lima Peaks is underlain by the same major northwest-dipping thrust fault system as the Snowcrest structural terrane to the northeast (Kulik and Perry, this volume). From the Lima Peaks westward to the Beaverhead Mountains, an east-west interference pattern affects Sevier-style thrust sheets (Fig. 1); the Four Eyes Canyon sheet (Perry and Sando, 1983) ends abruptly southward in the steep aeromagnetic gradient zone. The abrupt south end of involvement of Archean(?) gneissic basement in the Cabin thrust sheet, just west of the southern end of the Four Eyes Canyon sheet, also occurs along this zone (see Skipp, this volume). This steep aeromagnetic gradient is associated with the southern margin of the Blacktail-Snowcrest uplift and the predicted continuation of this uplift beneath the Cordilleran thrust belt in the Lima region (Perry and others, 1983a; see also Kulik and Perry, this volume).

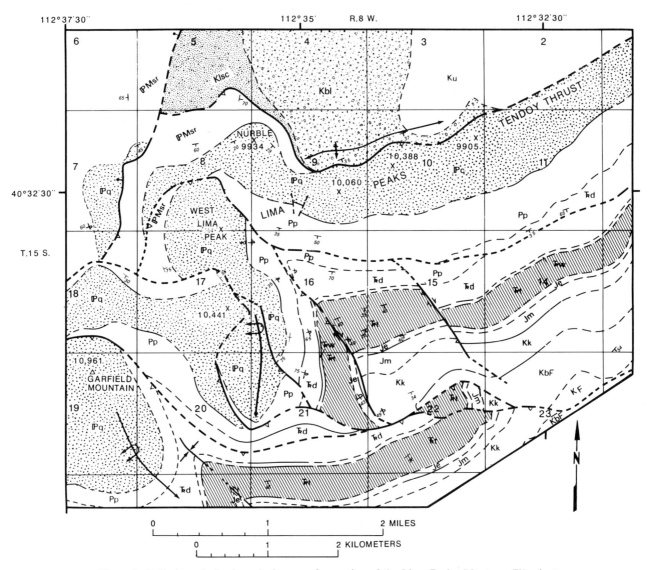

Figure 9. Preliminary bedrock geologic map of a portion of the Lima Peaks, Montana, 7½-minute Quadrangle. Mapping by C. J. Haley, Phil Hammons, W. J. Perry, Betty Skipp, and H. I. Saperstone. Abbreviations: Cretaceous rocks: Kf = Frontier Formation; Kbf = Blackleaf Formation; Kk = Kootenai Formation; Kbl = Lima Conglomerate of Beaverhead Group; Klsc = Little Sheep Creek conglomerate unit of Beaverhead Group of this report; Ku = undivided rocks beneath Lima Conglomerate. Jurassic rocks: Jm = Morrison Formation; Je = Ellis Group, undivided. Triassic rocks: Ṝt = Thaynes Formation; Ṝw = Woodside Formation; Ṝd = Dinwoody Formation. ℙq = Quadrant Sandstone; ℙMsr = Pennsylvanian and Mississippian Snowcrest Range Group, undivided; additional abbreviations as in Figure 6.

The northeastern part of the Lima Peaks area underwent folding along a N70°E structural trend (Fig. 10; anticlinal axial trace shown in the NE¼ of section 9, and NW¼ of section 10, Fig. 9) subsequent to emplacement of the Tendoy thrust plate, as suggested by Hammons (1981, p. 259). Beaverhead rocks of the footwall, the overlying Tendoy thrust sheet, and the Quadrant of the hanging wall are equally affected. Northeast of peak 9905 in section 10, the elevation of the exposed Tendoy thrust drops gradually eastward along the plunging nose of this late fold. The south flank of the Lima Peaks in this area represents the steeply dipping south limb of this anticline. An aerial view westward

from the eastern edge of the Lima Peaks (Fig. 11) provides a view along the axis of this late fold. The Tendoy thrust clearly ramps upward to the north with respect to the Lima Conglomerate of the footwall.

The southern flank of the Lima Peaks in the foreground and middleground in Figure 11A approximates a dip slope in the Pennsylvanian Quadrant Sandstone. The beds actually dip about 10° more steeply than the slope (about 45°S), so that the Tendoy thrust must also steepen southward to avoid cutting up-section southward in the Quadrant Sandstone. This late N70°E–trending fold has placed the entire panel of rocks exposed on the southern

Figure 10. Aerial view of front of Tendoy thrust on north side of Lima Peaks (center, east half of section 9, Fig. 9) showing Lima Conglomerate of the footwall, Tendoy thrust, and Paleozoic rocks of the hanging wall, all folded concentrically about axis of late northeast-trending anticline. White line on photograph marks boundary between Pennsylvanian Quadrant Sandstone (above) and limestones of the Pennsylvanian Conover Ranch Formation of Snowcrest Range Group (below) in the hanging wall. Black line marks position of Tendoy thrust. View to southeast.

flank of the Lima Peaks on its side, including imbricates and kink folds, rotating all these elements southward, adding to the inferred pre-Tendoy dip of this panel discussed by Perry and others (1983a, p. 732–733).

It is tempting to compare this late folding with the late Laramide homoclinal 25° to 80° northwest warping of the Beaverhead panel in the McKnight Canyon area mentioned above in the stratigraphic discussion. However, if the latter warping occurred prior to emplacement of the Tendoy sheet, it is clearly older than this anticline. Also there is no evidence that this anticline is basement-involved, whereas there is some evidence from gravity data (D. M. Kulik, oral communication, 1983) that northeast-trending structures in the McKnight and Little Water Canyon areas are basement-involved.

Little Water Canyon area

The asymmetric Little Water syncline trends northeast, within the northern part of the Tendoy thrust sheet as restricted by Perry and others (1985), 18 to 19 km (11 to 12 mi) northwest of Lima (Fig. 2). The syncline has long been considered a foreland structure (Scholten and others, 1955; Scholten, 1967; Ryder and Scholten, 1973; Perry and others, 1981, 1983a). However, its origin has not been explored until recently (Ponton, 1983). The axial trend of the Little Water syncline roughly parallels minor N25–35° E–trending anticlines and synclines within the Beaverhead in the footwall of the Tendoy thrust to the southeast,

mapped by Ryder and Scholten (1973, Fig. 3; T.13S.,R.9W.). This axial trend also coincides with the general strike of the northwest-dipping panel of Beaverhead rocks in the McKnight Canyon area just to the north. We are suspicious of such parallelism, because northeast trends in the Lima region may be inherited from the northeast-trending upper Paleozoic Snowcrest trough (Perry, 1986) and may be as old as Archean (Erslev, 1982), and because the original northwest limb of the Santonian to Campanian Blacktail-Snowcrest uplift may have influenced later thrust-belt structural patterns in the area between Dell and McKnight Canyon.

Ponton (1983) has provided a wealth of structural data in his analysis of the Little Water syncline, the axis of which he shows to plunge 18°SW,S28°W. This structure extends the width of the exposed Tendoy sheet, preserving Jurassic and Cretaceous rocks along its hinge, downplunge to the southwest. As discussed by Ponton (1983, p. 72), the northwest limb is overturned in Little Water Canyon, dipping 45° to the northwest near the upplunge end of this structure against the Quaternary Red Rock fault. Here a 61° northwest-dipping reverse fault, "axial planar to the concentrically folded Little Water syncline," truncates and displaces the northwest limb southeastward against the southeast limb (Ponton, 1983, p. 67).

Perry and others (1981) indicated that the Little Water syncline was an inherited structure, formed during the development of the Blacktail-Snowcrest uplift and later transported northeastward on the Tendoy sheet, as originally concluded by Scholten

Figure 11. Aerial view of Lima Peaks, facing west. A, View showing steep dip slopes in the Quadrant Sandstone and Phosphoria Formation on south flank of Lima Peaks to the left and south-dipping Tendoy thrust above Lima Conglomerate of the footwall to the right. B, View to west along north side of Lima Peaks showing south-dipping Tendoy thrust and axis of late northeast-trending fold that warps the Beaverhead of the footwall, as well as Paleozoic rocks of the hanging wall of the Tendoy thrust. t = toward; a = away. Photographs by H. I. Saperstone.

and others (1955). This was based chiefly on the occurrence of an exposure of Beaverhead conglomerate in the northwestern part of the Little Water Canyon area resting with apparent angular unconformity on older Mesozoic rocks, thereby indicating that the syncline was present and rather deeply eroded prior to Beaverhead deposition at this locality. However, the base of the conglomerate is not exposed, and this body of conglomerate could

have been emplaced by thin-skin thrusting from the west, an alternative suggested by M. J. Bartholomew (oral communication, 1986) and E. J. Sterne (written communication, 1986). T. E. Dill (oral communication, 1987) observed that Beaverhead clasts within this exposure were probably of local derivation; they consist primarily of Triassic and younger rocks which occur within the syncline. This supports the inference by Perry and others (1981) that this conglomerate was deposited on a sub-Beaverhead erosion surface developed on previously folded rocks, later incorporated into the Tendoy thrust sheet. Ponton (1983, p. 125) indicated that the average strike and dip of this Beaverhead conglomerate is N33°E,50°NW, and that the subjacent rocks unfold "to a mean orientation of N80°W, 62°SW" by rotation of the Beaverhead conglomerate to horizontal about its strike. By comparing this to the present orientation of subjacent beds, Ponton (1983, p. 127–128) concluded that "Post-Beaverhead deformation accounts for a maximum [counterclockwise] rotation of 40° of the strike direction of the Little Water syncline, supporting the hypothesis of a pre-existing syncline predating Beaverhead deposition."

To Perry, one of the most compelling arguments for the existence of the Little Water syncline prior to Tendoy thrusting is provided by Ponton's (1983) analysis of calcite twin lamellae from widely spaced oriented samples of Thaynes Limestone in the Little Water Canyon area. Two vertical thin sections were cut from each sample, one oriented parallel and the other perpendicular to the N70°E transport direction. None of the resolved principal strain axes were bed-parallel in any of the samples. Principal compression axes in two of the samples were within a few degrees of parallel to the N70°E transport direction of the Tendoy thrust; however, three of the five samples analyzed show nearly east-west compression axes. These appear to represent the strain field imposed by Tendoy thrusting, shortening associated with thrusting, but not the development of the Little Water syncline. Compression axes consistent with the formation of the syncline would be oriented northwest, at nearly 90° to those resolved by Ponton (1983). In four of the five samples, the principal extension direction was vertical irrespective of the attitude of bedding, consistent only with strain lamellae development during Tendoy thrusting subsequent to formation of the Little Water syncline; in a fifth, the intermediate strain axis was nearly vertical. In all cases the intermediate strain axes were also extensional (of the same sign as the principal extension), hardly consistent with the development of an overturned cross-fold. If any significant rotation of bedding had taken place during or subsequent to development of this calcite-strain imprint of Tendoy thrusting, the results would have been significantly different; none of the principal strain axes would be vertical, except those in the hinge of the fold (R. H. Groshong, oral communication, 1987).

The asymmetry of the Little Water syncline suggests a component of northwest to southeast transport, possibly basement involved, as suggested by gravity data (D. M. Kulik, oral communication, 1983). The conclusions by Perry and others (1981, 1983a) that the Little Water syncline originated as a result of deformation of the Rocky Mountain foreland prior to Tendoy thrusting still appears sound. The syncline also appears to have formed prior to at least the final phase of Four Eyes Canyon thrusting.

An alternate hypothesis, presented by E. J. Sterne (written communication, 1986), is that folding of the Little Water syncline was subsequent to the emplacement of the Tendoy thrust. He based this hypothesis on inferred extraordinary structural relief developed on the Tendoy thrust where it crosses the hinge of the Little Water syncline. However, Scholten and others (1955) and Ryder and Scholten (1973), and subsequent mapping (Klecker, 1981; Ponton, 1983), have indicated that the front of the Tendoy sheet is downdropped to the east by the Quaternary Red Rock fault; its position with respect to beds in the hinge area of the Little Water syncline is unknown. The Tendoy thrust beneath the hinge area of the Little Water syncline is neither exposed nor drilled, nor to our knowledge is it resolved by seismic data. Therefore we have seen no evidence that the Tendoy thrust was folded by warping of the Little Water syncline after emplacement of the Tendoy sheet. This alternate hypothesis is not consistent with the strain field revealed by calcite twin lamellae (Ponton, 1983).

A second alternative was preferred by Ponton (1983): that folding of the syncline was synchronous with emplacement of the Tendoy sheet over an inferred lateral footwall ramp by a process analogous to convergent flow. This one-step model is appealing in its simplicity but does not now appear consistent with the strain field revealed by the calcite twin lamellae nor the timing evidence from the Beaverhead conglomerates, particularly those of the Dell sequence.

On the basis of the available evidence, we suggest the following model: (1) the northwest-dipping Beaverhead panel to the north of the Little Water syncline was warped during Late Cretaceous basement-involved thrusting from northwest to southeast, as part of the hanging wall of the inferred Kidd foreland thrust system (Fig. 12); and (2) The Little Water syncline represents the syncline southeast of this Laramide-style thrust, detached and incorporated into the later Tendoy thrust sheet. In this model, curvature of the Tendoy thrust (as shown in Fig. 12) was the original shape, an attempt by the thrust to follow already folded multilayers. Additional deformation of the Little Water syncline during emplacement of the Tendoy thrust should be expected, because the indicated transport direction on the Tendoy thrust is less than 45° to the axial trend of the Little Water syncline. The exposed eastern edge of the Little Water syncline appears to have been rotated counterclockwise, toward parallelism with the trend of the Tendoy sheet between Little Sheep Creek and Little Water Canyon, consistent with our model. Structures just to the north are analyzed by Williams and Bartley (this volume).

SUMMARY AND CONCLUSIONS

Studies of synorogenic deposits of the Beaverhead Group in the Lima region discussed in this chapter reveal the following.

1. Laramide-style deformation began in the Lima region in Coniacian to Santonian (Late Cretaceous) time with emergence of the Blacktail-Snowcrest uplift, from which sands containing Pennsylvanian spores were shed southward, based on palynostratigraphic studies by Nichols and others (1985). These sands coarsen upward into the Lima Conglomerate of the Beaverhead Group.

2. Beds from the fining-upward sequence near the top of the

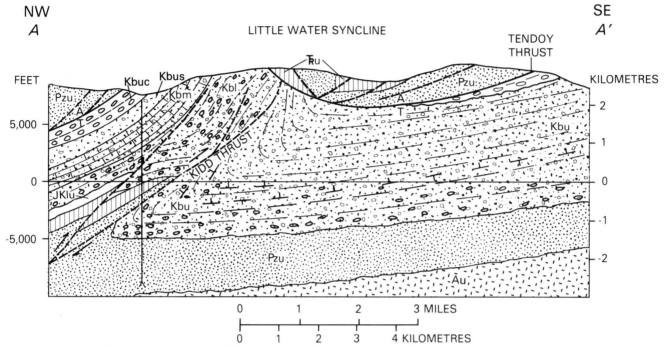

Figure 12. Cross section AA'; location shown in Figure 1B. Line of section, topography, and surficial geology from northern 15 km (9.3 mi) of section AA', Figure 4 of Ryder and Scholten (1973). Dips of rocks at the surface modified from Ryder and Scholten (1973, Fig. 4), modifications based on mapping by Williams (1984) and observations by Perry. Abbreviations: Cretaceous Beaverhead Group: Kbuc = upper conglomerate unit; Kbus = siltstone unit with lenses of sandstone and conglomerate; Kbm = McKnight limestone unit; Kbl = Lima(?) Conglomerate; Kbu = Beaverhead Group, undivided. Other rocks: JKlu = Jurassic and Lower Cretaceous rocks, undivided; Ťu = Triassic rocks, undivided; Pzu = Paleozoic rocks, undivided; Au = Archean(?) rocks, undivided. Projection of the well-bore of the Amoco no. 1 McKnight Canyon Unit, which encountered the Kidd thrust at a depth of 2,830 m (9,285 ft) is shown in the northwestern part of section AA'. The McKnight Canyon drill-hole is projected 122 m (400 ft) southwest onto the line of section.

Lima Conglomerate are middle Campanian (Late Cretaceous), with an estimated absolute age of 78 to 81 Ma. Because the Lima Conglomerate represents the youngest synorogenic deposit known to be derived entirely from the Blacktail-Snowcrest uplift in the Lima region, the uplift near Lima appears to have ceased its growth by 78 Ma.

3. The middle Campanian (78 to 81 Ma) beds in the top of the Lima Conglomerate are overlain with apparent conformity by the Little Sheep Creek conglomerate unit, composed primarily of highly rounded clasts of Proterozoic quartzite and siltite derived from proximal fans adjacent to hinterland thrust sheets in the Cordilleran thrust belt, recycled into lag deposits atop the Medicine Lodge and Four Eyes Canyon thrust sheets. Consequently, an age of 78 to 81 Ma is also a maximum age for thrust-belt–derived conglomerates of the Beaverhead Group near Lima.

4. The Little Sheep Creek conglomerate unit west of Lima contains large slide blocks derived from the Medicine Lodge–Four Eyes Canyon thrust system. The composite Medicine Lodge–Four Eyes Canyon plate, bounded below by the Four Eyes Canyon thrust, probably surfaced west of Lima in late Campanian to Maastrichtian time.

5. The composite McKenzie Canyon–Four Eyes Canyon

thrust system of the McKnight Canyon area to the north (Fig. 2) surfaced by late Campanian to early Maastrichtian time, based on palynostratigraphic dating.

6. Conglomerates at the exposed rear of the Tendoy sheet west of Lima are composed in part of large limestone clasts derived from the Medicine Lodge–Four Eyes Canyon thrust system and therefore are probably Campanian to early Maastrichtian in age as well. These commonly include Proterozoic quartzite clasts and rest on a sub-Beaverhead erosion surface, probably of Campanian age. Conglomerates derived from this surface form the basal deposits of the conglomerates at the exposed rear of the Tendoy sheet.

7. The youngest conglomerate of the Beaverhead Group so far studied in the Lima region is exposed near Dell, where it is overridden by the Tendoy sheet. This conglomerate contains boulders and cobbles reworked from the Lima Conglomerate and overlying Little Sheep Creek conglomerate unit, as well as from the Tendoy sheet. The composition and structural setting of this conglomerate require that the Tendoy sheet acquired structural relief subsequent to the deposition of the Campanian to Maastrichtian Little Sheep Creek conglomerate unit. Therefore, the Tendoy thrust is younger than the Medicine Lodge–McKenzie

Canyon–Four Eyes Canyon thrust complex to the west. This conglomerate is palynologically undated. It underlies middle to upper Eocene sediments and volcanics northeast of Dell (A. R. Tabrum, oral communication, 1987) and may be early Tertiary in age.

Structural studies described in this chapter are as follows.

1. A detailed investigation of the southwestern tip of the Snowcrest structural terrane on the southeastern margin of the Blacktail-Snowcrest uplift indicates that this area underwent compressional deformation, including Archean basement-involved thrusting with associated strike-slip faulting and folding and locally intense mesoscopic deformation prior to erosional beveling, in places to Archean basement. Upper Paleozoic rocks are here overlain unconformably by middle Campanian Lima Conglomerate. Reactivation of some of these older contraction and strike-slip faults occurred during Tertiary to Quaternary time.

2. An analysis of the Lima Peaks area indicates a complex sequence of events: the development of structural relief on the southeastern margin of the Blacktail-Snowcrest uplift; the emplacement and imbrication of the Tendoy sheet, carrying the southwestern extension of this margin eastward to its present location; and the warping of the southern margin of the Tendoy sheet about a N70°E anticlinal axis.

3. A review of structural investigations in the Little Water Canyon area indicates that primary formation of the Little Water syncline preceded final emplacement of the Tendoy thrust sheet. This syncline is inferred to be a foreland structure, originally a footwall syncline associated with the buried northeast-trending Kidd thrust system beneath the McKnight Canyon area. The northwest-dipping homocline represented by the type Beaverhead synorogenic deposits of the McKnight Canyon area is the hanging wall of this inferred northwest-dipping thrust and indicates its presence. The late Campanian to Maastrichtian age of the youngest rocks involved in this homocline indicate that this feature postdated the development of the Blacktail-Snowcrest uplift.

The geometry of both the southern and northern parts of the very late Cretaceous to early Tertiary(?) Tendoy thrust system in the frontal zone of the Cordilleran thrust belt in the Lima region is controlled by preexisting structures of the Rocky Mountain foreland. The Lima Peaks in the southern part of the Tendoy thrust system were deformed after emplacement by folding apparently associated with late Laramide-style deformation. The mid-Late Cretaceous (Santonian to Campanian) Blacktail-Snowcrest uplift, which may have been a positive element even earlier, formed a buttress that controlled the shape of the Cordilleran thrust belt in southwestern Montana. The thick-skin, thrust-faulted southeastern margin of this uplift is inferred to extend southwest of the Lima region into east-central Idaho beneath the Cordilleran thrust belt. Subsequent to emplacement of the composite McKenzie–Four Eyes Canyon thrust system, but prior to development of the Tendoy thrust, northwest to southeast Laramide-style? thrusting of probable Maastrichtian (very late Cretaceous) age is inferred for the Little Water syncline and McKnight Canyon areas.

ACKNOWLEDGMENTS

We acknowledge the helpful reviews of preliminary versions of this report by T. S. Dyman, M. E. MacLachlan, R. T. Ryder, Betty Skipp, and R. G. Tysdal. Intensive constructive reviews of a later version of the manuscript by John M. Garihan, Edward J. Sterne, and William A. Thomas were most helpful and are greatly appreciated, as were additional comments by C. J. Schmidt. The alternate structural model presented to us by E. J. Sterne caused us to reevaluate some of our original conclusions, which, though basically unchanged, are now supported by considerably more observations than originally presented. Careful reviews of the revised manuscript by Betty Skipp and R. L. Wheeler are appreciated.

APPENDIX

STRATIGRAPHIC NOMENCLATURE OF THE CRETACEOUS BEAVERHEAD GROUP

By raising the Beaverhead to group rank, Nichols and others (1985) had no intention of overturning the useful informal unit designations of Ryder (1968) and Ryder and Scholten (1973); it was simply a matter of raising one of the most significant and mappable units, the Lima Conglomerate, to formation status. These previous studies, along with that by Wilson (1970), form the basis of all subsequent work on syntectonic conglomerates in southwestern Montana. However, a recent thorough investigation of Beaverhead limestone conglomerates and associated synorogenic deposits by Haley (1986), ongoing studies of older Cretaceous rocks by Dyman (1985a), and ongoing studies of the structural development of the Lima region by Perry have required additional changes in the stratigraphic nomenclature of the Cretaceous Beaverhead Group.

Restoration of sandstone units into Beaverhead Group

Because of correlation problems among Cretaceous siliciclastic rocks southeast of Lima and recognition that some rocks assigned to the Beaverhead south of Lima Peaks were more closely related to the Frontier Formation of Wyoming (Perry and others, 1983a), clearly belonging to a previous depositional cycle (Dyman, 1985a,b), Nichols and others (1985) removed the Clover Creek, Monida, and Snowline sandstone units of the Beaverhead of Ryder and Scholten (1973) from the Beaverhead Group, pending further study. Haley (1986) has shown that the Clover Creek, Monida, and Snowline sandstone units are coextensive with, and part of, the same depositional sequence as the Lima Conglomerate, which together form his Antone Peak depositional sequence. Therefore, we herein reinstate the Clover Creek, Monida, and Snowline as informal sandstone units within the lower part of the Beaverhead as mapped by Ryder and Scholten (1973, Fig. 3; see Figs. 2, 4, this chapter). As a consequence of reinstating these sandstone units into the Beaverhead, the age of the basal Beaverhead Group is now determined as Coniacian to earliest Campanian.

Wilson (1970) considered the sandstone-dominated Monida and conglomerate-dominated Beaverhead (Lima Conglomerate of present usage) as separate, laterally equivalent formations. He placed the boundary between these two formations about 8 km (5 mi) west-northwest of Monida, his Monida Formation to the east and his Beaverhead Formation to the northwest. Here, the limestone conglomerate beds become "so reduced in thickness [eastward] that sandstone becomes the dominant lithologic type" (Wilson, 1970, p. 1846). The lower (sandstone) member of Wilson's Beaverhead Formation plus the lower member of his Monida Formation make up the Monida sandstone unit of the Beaverhead Formation of Ryder and Scholten (1973). Wilson (1967, and oral communication, 1987) characterized underlying Cretaceous rocks as "salt-and-pepper" sandstones with interbedded shale and mudrock, in contrast to the quartzose, virtually plagioclase-free, sandstone beds of the Monida sandstone unit of Ryder and Scholten (1973). Examination of the Monida sandstone unit by Perry, Haley, and Dyman in its type area shows it to be a nearly white quartz arenite with small chert clasts and occasional leaf impressions, which is well cemented in part and very similar in appearance to the Pennsylvanian Quadrant sandstone from which it is undoubtedly derived. This interpretation is supported by the palynologic evidence. Nichols and others (1985) reported the presence of spores of Pennsylvanian age in these beds that probably were reworked from the Quadrant Sandstone. The base of the Monida was covered where mapped (M. D. Wilson, oral communication, 1987). However, it is distinctly different from the mudstone-dominated Frontier Formation. Dyman (1985b) has shown that sandstones of the underlying Frontier Formation contain varying amounts of feldspar, primarily plagioclase, but did not study the upper part of the Frontier Formation. Work in progress by Dyman, Haley, and Perry shows distinctive differences between the "salt-and-pepper" grits of the upper Frontier and the Quadrant-like Monida sandstone unit.

Little Sheep Creek conglomerate unit

The quartzite roundstone conglomerate that rests with apparent conformity on the Lima Conglomerate beneath the Tendoy thrust at the northern foot of Lima Peaks (locality D6596, Fig. 2) was assigned by Ryder and Scholten (1973) to their Divide quartzite conglomerate unit of the Beaverhead Formation. This conglomerate, northeast of Lima Peaks, is continuous with that of the Little Sheep Creek area (Fig. 2); the type Divide unit is not. As stated above in the main body of this report

(discussion of thrust-belt–derived synorogenic deposits), this quartzite conglomerate is probably late Campanian to early Maastrichtian in age, younger than the mid-Campanian fining-upward sequence at the top of the Lima Conglomerate. This conglomerate consists of highly polished and rounded quartzite and siltite clasts derived chiefly from the Proterozoic Lemhi Group (E. T. Ruppel, oral communication, 1981). Other quartzite clasts are present and probably represent Paleozoic units, including the Ordovician Kinnikinnic Quartzite (Ryder and Scholten, 1973). Clasts from the Ordovician Beaverhead Mountains pluton are also present. It would appear that the Hawley Creek and Fritz Creek thrust plates of Skipp (this volume), which together carry the detached Ordovician Beaverhead Mountains pluton, were being eroded at the time of deposition of the Little Sheep Creek conglomerate unit.

The thick quartzite conglomerate of the Little Sheep Creek area is significantly different in clast composition and age from roundstone conglomerates south of Lima Peaks now assigned to the Frontier Formation, exposed near locality D6600 (Fig. 2). These were also included in the Divide quartzite conglomerate unit by Ryder and Scholten (1973), as discussed by Perry and others (1983a) and Nichols and others (1985). Outside of the study area, the Beaverhead Group southwest of the Lima Peaks consists of the Divide quartzite and limestone conglomerate units of Ryder and Scholten (1973, Fig. 3; mapped by Skipp and others, 1979), which cannot be readily correlated with those in the footwall of the Tendoy plate. These units, named for that part of the Continental Divide, have been only broadly dated as Late Cretaceous (Coniacian to Maastrichtian: D. J. Nichols, unpublished data, 1986) and may be correlative with the entire Beaverhead Group (of Fig. 4). For this reason it is appropriate to withdraw the informal designation "Divide quartzite conglomerate unit" for the quartzite conglomerates north of Lima Peaks in the footwall of the Tendoy thrust, including the Little Sheep Creek area, and give them an informal local name, Little Sheep Creek conglomerate unit (Fig. 4), pending further study. The distribution of the Little Sheep Creek conglomerate unit, as well as Clover Creek sandstone and Snowline sandstone units (of Ryder and Scholten, 1973) of the Beaverhead Group, is shown in Figure 2.

REFERENCES CITED

Alden, W. C., 1953, Physiography and glacial geology of western Montana and adjacent areas: U.S. Geological Survey Professional Paper 231, 200 p.

Boyer, S. E., and Elliot, D., 1982, Thrust systems: American Association of Petroleum Geologists Bulletin, v. 66, p. 1196–1230.

Dahlstrom, C.D.A., 1970, Structural geology in the eastern margin of the Canadian Rocky Mountains. Bulletin of Canadian Petroleum Geology, v. 10, p. 332–406.

De la Tour-du-Pin, H., 1983, Contribution a l'etude geologique de l'Overthrust Belt du Montana (U.S.A.); Stratigraphie et Tectonique des Rocky Hills et du Tendoy Range (Sud-Ouest du Montana) [Ph.D. thesis]: Brest, France, Universite de Bretagne Occidentale, 256 p.

Dubois, D. P., 1983, Tectonic framework of basement thrust terrane, northern Tendoy Range, southwestern Montana, in Powers, R. B., ed., Geologic studies of the Cordilleran thrust belt, 1982: Denver, Colorado, Rocky Mountain Association of Geologists, v. 1, p. 145–158.

Dunlap, D. G., 1982, Tertiary geology of the Muddy Creek basin, Beaverhead County, Montana [M.S. thesis]: Missoula, University of Montana, 133 p.

Dyman, T. S., 1985a, Measured stratigraphic sections of Lower Cretaceous Blackleaf Formation and lower Upper Cretaceous Frontier Formation (lower part) in Beaverhead and Madison Counties, Montana: U.S. Geological Survey Open-File Report 85-431, 72 p.

—— , 1985b, Stratigraphic and petrologic analysis of the Lower Cretaceous Blackleaf Formation and the Upper Cretaceous Frontier Formation (lower part), Beaverhead and Madison Counties, Montana [Ph.D. thesis]: Pullman, Washington State University, 230 p.

Dyman, T. S., Niblack, R., and Platt, J. E., 1984, Measured stratigraphic section

of Lower Cretaceous Blackleaf Formation and lower Upper Cretaceous Frontier Formation (lower part) near Lima, in southwest Montana: U.S. Geological Survey Open-File Report 84-838, 25 p.

Erslev, E. A., 1982, The Madison mylonite zone; A major shear zone in the Archean basement of southwestern Montana: Wyoming Geological Association 33rd Annual Field Conference Guidebook, p. 213–221.

Gealy, W. J., 1953, Geology of the Antone Peak Quadrangle, southwestern Montana [Ph.D. thesis]: Cambridge, Massachusetts, Harvard University, 143 p.

Haley, J. C., 1983a, Depositional processes in Beaverhead Formation, southwestern Montana and northeastern Idaho, and their tectonic significance [abs.]: American Association of Petroleum Geologists Bulletin, v. 67, p. 1340.

—— , 1983b, The sedimentology of a synorogenic deposit; The Beaverhead Formation of Montana and Idaho: Geological Society of America Abstracts with Programs, v. 16, no. 6, p. 589.

—— , 1986, Upper Cretaceous (Beaverhead) synorogenic sediments of the Montana-Idaho thrust belt and adjacent foreland; Relationships between sedimentation and tectonism [Ph.D. thesis]: Baltimore, Maryland, Johns Hopkins University, 542 p.

Hammons, P. M., 1981, Structural observations along the southern trace of the Tendoy fault, southern Beaverhead County, Montana, in Tucker, T. E., ed., Southwest Montana: Montana Geological Society Field Conference and Symposium Guidebook, p. 253–260.

Johnson, P. P., 1981a, Geology of the Red Rock fault and adjacent Red Rock valley, Beaverhead County, Montana [M.S. thesis]: Missoula, University of Montana, 88 p.

——, 1981b, Geology along the Red Rock fault and adjacent Red Rock basin, Beaverhead County, Montana, *in* Tucker, T. E., ed., Southwest Montana: Montana Geological Society Field Conference and Symposium Guidebook, p. 245–251.

Keenmon, K. A., 1950, The geology of the Blacktail-Snowcrest region, Beaverhead County, Montana [Ph.D. thesis]: Ann Arbor, University of Michigan, 207 p.

Klecker, R. A., 1981, Lower Triassic strandline deposits in the Tendoy Range near Dell, Montana, *in* Tucker, T. E., ed., Southwest Montana: Montana Geological Society Field Conference and Symposium Guidebook, p. 71–81.

Klepper, M. R., 1950, A geologic reconnaissance of parts of Beaverhead and Madison Counties, Montana: U.S. Geological Survey Bulletin 969-C, 85 p., 1 map, scale 1:250,000.

Kulik, D. M., 1982, Illustrations of gravity models of the southeast limb of the Blacktail-Snowcrest uplift, southwest Montana: U.S. Geological Survey Open-File Report 82-823, 7 p.

Kulik, D. M., and Perry, W. J., Jr., 1982, Gravity modeling of the steep southeast limb of the Blacktail-Snowcrest uplift: Geological Society of America Abstracts with Programs, v. 14, no. 6, p. 318.

Lowell, W. R., and Klepper, M. R., 1953, Beaverhead Formation; A Laramide deposit in Beaverhead County, Montana: Geological Society of America Bulletin, v. 64, p. 235–244.

Maughan, E. K., 1983, Tectonic setting of the Rocky Mountain region during the late Paleozoic and early Mesozoic, *in* Tucker, T. E., ed., Proceedings of the symposium on the genesis of Rocky Mountain ore deposits; Changes with time and tectonics: Denver Colorado, Denver Regional Exploration Geologists Society, p. 39–50.

Maughan, E. K., and Perry, W. J., 1982, Paleozoic tectonism in southwest Montana: Geological Society of America Abstracts with Programs, v. 14, no. 6, p. 341.

Moritz, C. A., 1951, Triassic and Jurassic stratigraphy of southwestern Montana: American Association of Petroleum Geologists Bulletin, v. 35, no. 8, p. 1781–1814.

Nichols, D. J., Perry, W. J., Jr., and Haley, J. C., 1985, Reinterpretation of the palynology and age of Laramide syntectonic deposits, southwestern Montana, and revision of the Beaverhead Group: Geology, v. 13, p. 149–153.

Pecora, W. C., 1981, Bedrock geology of the Blacktail Mountains, southwestern Montana [M.A. thesis]: Middletown, Connecticut, Wesleyan University, 203 p.

Perry, W. J., Jr., 1982, The thrust belt in the Lima-Dell, Montana, area, *in* Beaver, P., ed., The overthrust province in the vicinity of Dillon, Montana, and how this structural framework has influenced mineral and energy resources accumulation: Tobacco Root Geological Society 7th Annual Field Conference Guidebook, p. 69–78.

——, 1986, Critical deep drillholes and indicated Paleozoic paleotectonic features north of the Snake River downwarp in southern Beaverhead County, Montana, and adjacent Idaho: U.S. Geological Survey Open-File Report 86-413, 16 p.

Perry, W. J., Jr., and Hossack, J. R., 1984, Structure of the frontal zone, southwest Montana sector of Cordilleran thrust belt: Geological Society of America Abstracts with Programs, v. 16, no. 6, p. 622.

Perry, W. J., Jr., and Kulik, D. M., 1982, Laramide deformation in extreme southwestern Montana: Geological Society of America Abstracts with Programs, v. 14, no. 6, p. 345.

——, 1983, Laramide foreland thrust faulting in southwestern Montana [abs.]: American Association of Petroleum Geologists, v. 67, no. 3, p. 532.

Perry, W. J., Jr., and Sando, W. J., 1983, Sequence of deformation of Cordilleran thrust belt in Lima, Montana, region, *in* Powers, R. B., ed., Geologic studies of the Cordilleran thrust belt, 1982: Denver, Colorado, Rocky Mountain Association of Geologists, v. 1, p. 137–144.

Perry, W. J., Jr., Ryder, R. T., and Maughan, E. K., 1981, The southern part of the southwest Montana thrust belt, *in* Tucker, T. E., ed., Southwest Montana: Montana Geological Society 1981 Field Conference Guidebook, p. 261–273.

Perry, W. J., Jr., Wardlaw, B. R., Bostick, N. H., and Maughan, E. K., 1983a, Structure, burial history, and petroleum potential of the frontal thrust belt and adjacent foreland, southwest Montana: American Association of Petroleum Geologists Bulletin, v. 67, no. 5, p. 725–743.

Perry, W. J., Jr., Rice, D. D., and Maughan, E. K., 1983b, Petroleum potential of wilderness lands in Montana: U.S. Geological Survey Circular 902-G, 23 p.

Perry, W. J., Jr., Sando, W. J., and Sandberg, C. A., 1985, Structural geometry of newly defined Blacktail salient of Montana thrust belt [abs.]: American Association of Petroleum Geologists Bulletin, v. 69, no. 5, p. 858–859.

Peterson, J. A., 1981, General stratigraphy and regional paleostructure of the western Montana overthrust belt, *in* Tucker, T. E., ed., Southwest Montana: Montana Geological Society Field Conference and Symposium Guidebook, p. 5–35.

——, 1985, Regional stratigraphy and general petroleum geology of Montana and adjacent areas *in* Montana Oil and Gas Fields Symposium 1985: Montana Geological Society, p. 5–45.

Ponton, J. D., 1983, Structural analysis of the Little Water syncline, Beaverhead County, Montana [M.S. thesis]: College Station, Texas A&M University, 165 p.

Royse, F., Jr., Watner, M. A., and Reese, D. L., 1975, Thrust belt of Wyoming, Idaho, and northern Utah; Structural geometry and related problems, *in* Symposium on deep drilling frontiers in the central Rocky Mountains: Denver, Colorado, Rocky Mountain Association of Geologists, p. 41–54.

Ruppel, E. T., and Lopez, D. A., 1984, The thrust belt in southwest Montana and east-central Idaho: U.S. Geological Survey Professional Paper 1278, 41 p.

Ryder, R. T., 1967, Lithosomes in the Beaverhead Formation, Montana-Idaho; A preliminary report: Montana Geological Society 18th Annual Field Conference Guidebook, p. 63–70.

——, 1968, The Beaverhead Formation; A Late Cretaceous–Paleocene syntectonic deposit in southwestern Montana and east-central Idaho [Ph.D. thesis]: University Park, Pennsylvania State University, 143 p.

Ryder, R. T., and Ames, H. T., 1970, The palynology and age of the Beaverhead Formation and their paleotectonic implications in the Lima Region, Montana-Idaho: American Association of Petroleum Geologists Bulletin, v. 54, p. 1155–1171.

Ryder, R. T., and Scholten, R., 1973, Syntectonic conglomerates in southwest Montana; Their nature, origin, and tectonic significance: Geological Society of America Bulletin, v. 84, p. 773–796.

Sadler, R. K., 1980, Structure and stratigraphy of the Little Sheep Creek area, Beaverhead County, Montana [M.S. thesis]: Corvallis, Oregon State University, 294 p.

Sandberg, C. A., and Mapel, W. J., 1967, Devonian of the northern Rocky Mountains and Plains, *in* Oswald, D. H., ed., International Symposium on the Devonian System, Calgary, Alberta, September 1967: Calgary, Alberta Society of Petroleum Geologists, v. 1, p. 843–877.

Sandberg, C. A., Gutschick, R. C., Johnson, J. G., Poole, F. G., and Sando, W. J., 1983, Middle Devonian to Late Mississippian history of the overthrust belt region, western United States, *in* Powers, R. B., ed., Geologic studies of the Cordilleran thrust belt, 1982: Denver, Colorado, Rocky Mountain Association of Geologists, v. 2, p. 691–719.

Sandberg, C. A., Sando, W. J., and Perry, W. J., Jr., 1985, New biostratigraphic and paleotectonic interpretation of Devonian and Mississippian rocks in southwestern Montana thrust belt [abs.]: American Association of Petroleum Geologists Bulletin, v. 69, no. 5, p. 865.

Sando, W. J., Sandberg, C. A., and Perry, W. J., Jr., 1985, Revision of Mississippian stratigraphy, northern Tendoy Mountains, southwest Montana: U.S. Geological Survey Bulletin 1656-A, p. A1–A10.

Saperstone, H. I., 1986, Sedimentology and paleotectonic setting of the Pennsylvanian Quadrant Sandstone, southwest Montana [M.S. thesis]: Fort Collins, Colorado State University, 178 p

Saperstone, H. I., and Ethridge, F. G., 1984, Origin and paleotectonic setting of the Pennsylvanian Quadrant Sandstone, southwestern Montana: Wyoming Geological Association 35th Annual Field Conference Guidebook, p. 309–331.

Schmidt, C. J., and Garihan, J. M., 1983, Laramide tectonic development of the Rocky Mountain foreland of southwestern Montana, *in* Lowell, J. D., ed., Rocky Mountain foreland basins and uplifts: Denver, Colorado, Rocky Mountain Association of Geologists, p. 271–294.

Scholten, R., 1957, Paleozoic evolution of the geosynclinal margin north of the Snake River Plain: Geological Society of America Bulletin, v. 68, p. 151–170.

——, 1967, Structural framework and oil potential of extreme southwestern Montana: Montana Geological Society 18th Annual Field Conference Guidebook, p. 7–19.

——, 1983, Continental subduction in the northern Rockies; A model for back-arc thrusting in the western Cordillera, *in* Powers, R. B., ed., Geologic studies of the Cordilleran thrust belt, 1982: Denver, Colorado, Rocky Mountain Association of Geologists, v. 1, p. 123–137.

Scholten, R., Keenmon, K. A., and Kupsch, W. O., 1955, Geology of the Lima region, Montana-Idaho: Geological Society of America Bulletin, v. 66, p. 345–404.

Sheedlo, M. K., 1984, Structural geology of the northern Snowcrest Range, Beaverhead and Madison Counties, Montana [M.S. thesis]: Kalamazoo, Western Michigan University, 132 p.

Sikkink, P.G.L., 1984, Depositional environments and biostratigraphy of the Lower Triassic Thaynes Formation, southwestern Montana [M.S. thesis]: Missoula, University of Montana, 161 p.

Skipp, B., 1984, Geologic map and cross-sections of the Italian Peak and Italian Peak Middle Roadless Areas, Beaverhead County, Montana, and Clark and Lemhi Counties, Idaho: U.S. Geological Survey Miscellaneous Field Studies Map MF-1601-B with text, scale 1:62,500.

——, 1985, Contraction and extension faults in the southern Beaverhead Mountains, Idaho and Montana [Ph.D. thesis]: Boulder, University of Colorado 169, p., and U.S. Geological Survey Open-File Report 85-845, 170 p.

——, 1987, Basement thrust sheets in the Clearwater orogenic zone, central Idaho and western Montana: Geology, v. 15, p. 220–224.

Skipp, B., and Hait, M. H., Jr., 1977, Allochthons along the northeast margin of the Snake River Plain, Idaho, *in* Heisey, E. L., and others, eds., Rocky Mountain thrust belt geology and resources: Wyoming Geological Association 19th Annual Field Conference with Montana Geological Society and Utah Geological Society, p. 499–522.

Skipp, B., Prostka, H. J., and Schleicher, D. C., 1979, Preliminary geologic map of the Edie Ranch Quadrangle, Clark County, Idaho, and Beaverhead County, Montana: U.S. Geological Survey Open-File Report 79-845, with text, scale 1:62,500.

Sloss, L. L., and Moritz, C. A., 1951, Paleozoic stratigraphy of southwestern Montana: American Association of Petroleum Geologists Bulletin, v. 35, no. 10, p. 2135–2169.

Swanson, R. W., 1970, Mineral resources in Permian rocks of southwest Montana: U.S. Geological Survey Professional Paper 313-E, p. 661–773.

Wardlaw, B. R., and Pecora, W. C., 1985, New Mississippian-Pennsylvanian stratigraphic units in southwest Montana and adjacent Idaho: U.S. Geological Survey Bulletin 1656-B, p. B1–B9.

Wheeler, R. L., 1980, Cross-strike structural discontinuities; Possible exploration tool for natural gas in detached Appalachian foreland, *in* Dean, C. S., and Wheeler, R. L., eds., Western limits of detachment and related structures in the Appalachian foreland: Morgantown, West Virginia, Morgantown Energy Technology Center, DOE/METC/SP-80/23, p. 41–55.

Wheeler, R. L., Winslow, M., Horne, R. R., Dean, S., Kulander, B., Drahovsal, J. A., Gold, D. P., Gilbert, O. E., Jr., Werner, E., Sites, R., and Perry, W. J., Jr., 1979, Cross-strike structural discontinuities in thrust belts, mostly Appalachian: Southeastern Geology, v. 20, p. 193–204.

Williams, N. S., 1984, Stratigraphy and structure of the east-central Tendoy Range, southwestern Montana [M.S. thesis]: Chapel Hill, University of North Carolina, 94 p.

Williams, N. S., and Bartley, J. M., 1983, Stratigraphy and structure of the northeastern Tendoy Range, southwestern Montana: Geological Society of America Abstracts with Programs, v. 15, p. 375.

Wilson, M. D., 1967, The stratigraphy and origin of the Beaverhead Group in the Lima area, southwestern Montana [Ph.D. thesis]: Evanston, Illinois, Northwestern University, 171 p.

——, 1970, Upper Cretaceous-Paleocene synorogenic conglomerates of southwestern Montana: American Association of Petroleum Geologists Bulletin, v. 54, p. 1843–1867.

Witkind, I. J., 1975, Geology of a strip along the Centennial fault, southwestern Montana and adjacent Idaho: U.S. Geological Survey Miscellaneous Investigations Series Map I-890, scale 1:62,500.

——, 1977, Structural pattern of the Centennial Mountains, Montana-Idaho, *in* Heisey, E. L., and others, eds., Rocky Mountain thrust belt geology and resources: Wyoming Geological Association 29th Annual Field Conference with Montana Geological Society and Utah Geological Society, p. 531–536.

Zeigler, J. M., 1954, Geology of the Blacktail area, Beaverhead County, Montana [Ph.D. thesis]: Cambridge, Massachusetts, Harvard University, 147 p.

MANUSCRIPT ACCEPTED BY THE SOCIETY FEBRUARY 9, 1988

Geological Society of America
Memoir 171
1988

The Blacktail-Snowcrest foreland uplift and its influence on structure of the Cordilleran thrust belt—Geological and geophysical evidence for the overlap province in southwestern Montana

Dolores M. Kulik
U.S. Geological Survey, MS 964, Box 25046, Denver Federal Center, Denver, Colorado 80225
William J. Perry, Jr.
U.S. Geological Survey, MS 940, Box 25046, Denver Federal Center, Denver, Colorado 80225

ABSTRACT

The Blacktail-Snowcrest uplift in Beaverhead County, Montana, is a northeast-trending structure of the Rocky Mountain foreland. Models of a detailed gravity traverse across the steep southeastern limb of the structure require the presence of a major thrust-fault system, only subsidiary parts of which are exposed at the surface. Gravity models, consistent with mapped surface structure, are based on density logs and thicknesses of Paleozoic and Mesozoic stratigraphic intervals penetrated in nearby drillholes. Interpretation of the models requires a thicker sequence of low-density Cretaceous rocks southeast of the uplift than was encountered in the wells, and also suggests that the thrust system beneath the uplift involves rocks of both the sedimentary sequence and the crystalline basement with at least 3,700 m (12,000 ft) of vertical separation. The models require the assumption of unusually low densities for some of the Precambrian and Paleozoic rocks; these densities are interpreted as being related to pervasive fracturing of these rocks during thrust deformation.

Gravity and aeromagnetic trends associated with the Snowcrest-Greenhorn fault system extend westward beneath the Cordilleran thrust belt, indicating that the fault system is present there in the subsurface. A reentrant in the Medicine Lodge thrust sheet, the termination of the Four Eyes Canyon thrust sheet, and a change in strike of the Cabin thrust sheet, all in the frontal thrust belt, overlie the inferred westward extension of the Snowcrest-Greenhorn fault system, and probably are caused by the impingement of east-directed Cordilleran thrust faults on the older Rocky Mountain foreland structure. Cordilleran thrust sheets appear not only to overlap but also to crosscut older foreland faults, uplifts, and basins. Where crosscutting occurs, both upper and lower plates may exhibit rapid changes in stratigraphic level along strike, and these changes may be used as field evidence of overlap in the subsurface.

INTRODUCTION

The study area in southwestern Montana (Fig. 1) is located where the Cordilleran thrust belt adjoins the Rocky Mountain foreland within the area of the Overlap Province (Kulik and Schmidt, this volume). Until recently, structures of the thrust belt and foreland have been considered mutually distinct (Prucha and others, 1965), and to have developed at different times (Armstrong, 1968), within separate spatial domains, with different deformational styles, and under different regional stress regimes.

Within the last decade, however, gravity modeling (Kulik, 1981, 1982; Hurich and Smithson, 1982) and seismic and drill-hole data (Smithson and others, 1979; Gries, 1983; Brown, this volume) have indicated that many structures of the Rocky Mountain foreland are underlain by low-angle thrust faults. For purposes of this paper, we define a Rocky Mountain foreland structure as one that involves significant deformation of the Precambrian basement of the craton, possibly involving the entire thickness of

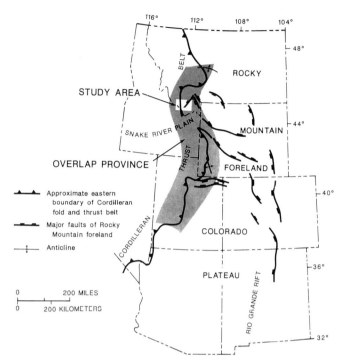

Figure 1. Index map showing the study area in southwestern Montana, the Cordilleran thrust belt, Rocky Mountain foreland, and the Overlap Province.

brittle cratonic continental crust. We do not discuss detachment structures limited to the sedimentary cover of the foreland as in Petersen (1983).

The Blacktail-Snowcrest uplift within the study area has been interpreted as a basement massif cored by Archean rocks and bounded on its southeast flank by moderate- to high-angle reverse faults (Klepper, 1950; Eardley, 1951, 1960; Scholten and others, 1955; Scholten, 1967). These early workers, particularly Eardley, considered the Blacktail-Snowcrest uplift to be Paleocene to Eocene in age—classical Laramide. The first breach in this basic misunderstanding came with the palynological dating reported by Ryder and Ames (1970) and Wilson (1970), who showed the Blacktail-Snowcrest uplift to be Cretaceous to Paleocene in age. Further refinement in palynological dating of the youngest sediments derived from the uplift indicate that the main phase of uplift was completed by 78 Ma (Nichols and others, 1985), before thin-skinned thrusting had occurred in the frontal part of the adjacent Cordilleran thrust belt (Perry and others, this volume). Perry and others (1981) named the Snowcrest-Greenhorn fault system for the system of thrust faults exposed (mapped by Klepper, 1950; Zeigler, 1954; Hadley, 1969) and inferred from preliminary geophysical data along the southeastern margin of the uplift. They named the master fault, which they inferred to lie beneath the rest, the sub-Snowcrest Range thrust. Perry and others (1981, 1983) indicated that the sub-Snowcrest thrust is concealed beneath synorogenic and younger cover of the Centennial Valley southeast of the uplift. Geological mapping by Klepper (1950), Keenmon (1950), Gealy (1953), Scholten and

others (1955), Flanagan (1958), and Perry and others (this volume) has indicated the structural complexity and compressional style of deformation exhibited by Archean and Phanerozoic rocks exposed on the hanging wall of this inferred thrust. Recent mapping by Sheedlo (1984) in the northeastern Snowcrest Range tends to support the inferred thrusting; he correlated the sub-Snowcrest thrust with the Greenhorn thrust mapped by Hadley (1969) farther northeast.

Scholten and others (1955), Ryder and Scholten (1973), and Perry and others (1981, 1983) indicated that the Blacktail-Snowcrest uplift and its bounding faults extend westward beneath the Tendoy Mountains, first recognized to be the front of the Cordilleran thrust belt by Skipp and Hait (1977). A gravity study was undertaken in 1981 and 1982 to determine if the inferred low-angle sub-Snowcrest Range fault might indeed underlie the uplift, to define the subsurface geometry of the uplift, and to determine the possible westward extent of the uplift beneath the thrust belt (Kulik and others, 1983; Kulik, 1984). Subsequently, Skipp (1985, this volume) has interpreted a westward extension of the uplift beneath the thrust belt, to the vicinity of the Beaverhead Mountains. The results of the gravity study are presented herein.

GRAVITY SURVEY

Data collection

The gravity measurements on profile A-A' (Plate 1, Fig. 2) were obtained in 1981, and additional measurements were made in 1982 to supplement regional gravity data and to provide sufficient data for modeling. The gravity stations were established using Worden gravimeter W-177. The data were tied to the International Gravity Standardization Net 1971 (U.S. Defense Mapping Agency Aerospace Center, 1974) at base station ACIC 3945-1 at Grant, Montana. Station elevations were obtained from benchmarks, spot elevations, and estimates from topographic maps (scale, 1:24,000), and are accurate to approximately ±5 m (±10 to 20 ft). The error in the Bouguer gravity anomaly is approximately ±1 mGal for errors in elevation control.

Gravity reduction

Gravity data were reduced using an unpublished digital computer program of the U.S. Geological Survey. Gravity meter readings were converted to observed gravity using the 1971 base values of the International Gravity Standardization Net. Corrections were made for earth tides and linear instrument drift which averaged less than 1 mGal over 12 hr. The Geodetic Reference System 1967 formula (International Association of Geodesy, 1967) was used to compute theoretical gravity. The data were reduced to Bouguer gravity values using an assumed average rock density of 2.67 g/cm³. A description of the gravity-reduction equations is given by Cordell and others (1982). Terrain corrections were based on digitized terrain elevations spaced at 15-sec intervals, and were made from the station to a distance of 167 km

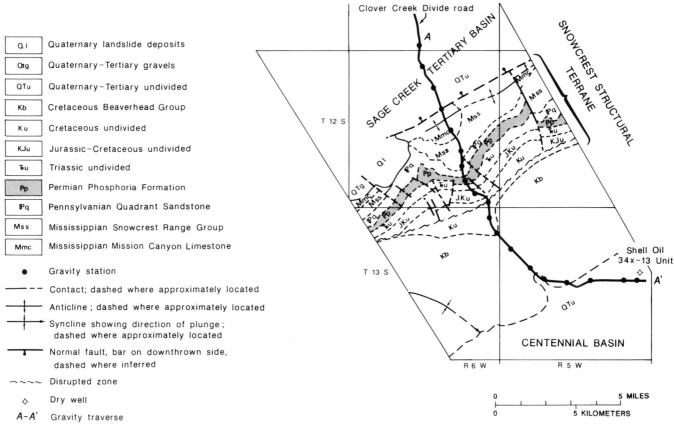

Qsl	Quaternary landslide deposits
QTg	Quaternary-Tertiary gravels
QTu	Quaternary-Tertiary undivided
Kb	Cretaceous Beaverhead Group
Ku	Cretaceous undivided
KJu	Jurassic-Cretaceous undivided
Tͬu	Triassic undivided
Pp	Permian Phosphoria Formation
Pq	Pennsylvanian Quadrant Sandstone
Mss	Mississippian Snowcrest Range Group
Mmc	Mississippian Mission Canyon Limestone

● Gravity station

— — — Contact; dashed where approximately located

Anticline ; dashed where approximately located

Syncline showing direction of plunge ; dashed where approximately located

Normal fault, bar on downthrown side, dashed where inferred

~~~~ Disrupted zone

◇ Dry well

A-A' Gravity traverse

Figure 2. Geological map of the Snowcrest structural terrane showing location of gravity profiles and well control; geological map modified from Zeigler (1954).

(100 mi) using the method of Plouff (1977). The data are shown in Plate 1 as a complete Bouguer anomaly map.

Regional interpretation

Low gravity values at the western edge of the map are caused by a thick sequence of Tertiary sedimentary rocks in the Nicholia and Horse Prairie Creek basins. Local gravity lows occur over the basins of Divide Creek, Muddy Creek, and Alkali and Meadow Creeks in the Beaverhead Mountains, the Red Rock River valley south of Clark Canyon Reservoir, the valley of Blacktail Deer Creek in the northeast corner of the map, and the Summit Creek–Dry Creek basin in the southwest corner. High Bouguer gravity values in the southeast part of the map are associated with basalts near the Snake River Plain. Elongate northwest-trending highs occur over Paleozoic and Proterozoic rocks on thrust sheets of the Beaverhead Mountains and Lemhi Range. A local gravity high west of Red Conglomerate Peaks is coincident with outcrops of limestone conglomerate (B. Skipp, oral communication, 1985). A gravity high in the northeast corner of the map is associated with the basement-cored Blacktail-Snowcrest uplift, and lower gravity values occur to the south of the uplift over the Centennial basin. The belt of local high anomalies, which extends from west of the Alkali–Meadow Creek basin northeasterly across the map (see also Fig. 3), may be

caused by Paleozoic and Archean rocks of the Snowcrest-Greenhorn fault system, which is discussed in detail in the section on gravity modeling. Other gravity highs to the north (Plate 1, in pocket inside back cover, and Fig. 3) suggest that there are imbricate faults of the Snowcrest-Greenhorn system within the Blacktail-Snowcrest massif. East of the frontal Cordilleran thrusts in the Tendoy Mountains, the northeast-trending contours associated with structures of the Rocky Mountain foreland are interrupted by northwest trends associated with crosscutting structures. In particular, the gravity gradient in the northeastern corner of the map indicates that the bounding fault of the northwest-trending Blacktail Mountains continues southward, is offset to the west where it crosscuts the northeast-trending Snowcrest-Greenhorn fault system, and extends across the northeast-trending Centennial basin (Kulik, 1985).

WELL CONTROL

Two wells have been drilled in the immediate vicinity of the gravity profile. Shell Oil No. 34X-13 Unit in NE¼SW¼SE¼, Sec.13,T.13S.,R.5W., is shown in Figure 2 at the southeast end of gravity profile A-A'. The American Quasar Petroleum Company No. 29-1 Peet Creek-Federal well is in SW¼NE¼,Sec.29,T.14S., R.4W., eight miles south of the Shell well.

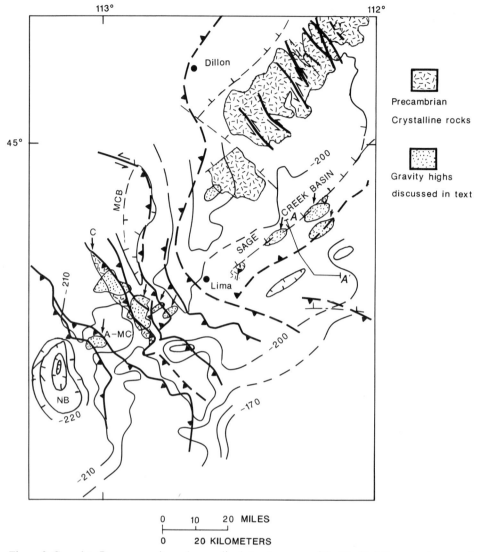

Figure 3. Complete Bouguer gravity and generalized structure map of the Blacktail-Snowcrest area and the frontal thrust belt. Contour interval = 10 mGal. C = Cabin plate; MCB = Muddy Creek basin; A-MB = Alkali–Meadow Creek basin; NB = Nicholia basin. High anomalies indicated with arrows are associated with Precambrian and Paleozoic rocks in leading edge of Snowcrest-Greenhorn fault system. A-A′, location of gravity profile.

Borehole velocity (sonic) logs were available for both the Shell and Peet Creek wells, and a borehole compensated-density log was also available for the Peet Creek well (Fig. 4). Stratigraphic thicknesses were determined from the well logs and are represented graphically on the velocity and density logs in Figure 4. These thicknesses are discussed in greater detail by Perry (1986). No significant facies changes occur between the two wells. The velocity logs and stratigraphic columns for the two wells are markedly similar, although they are located 13 km (8 mi) apart and were drilled on different structures. We assume a reasonable correlation between velocity and density, and therefore, because of the similarity in velocity logs, extrapolated the densities derived from the Peet Creek well log to the gravity models, which are actually nearer the Shell well. The average

densities shown in Figure 4b were used to calculate the models that will be described. In addition, alternate models were calculated using the alternate average densities shown in Figure 4c; there was no significant variation from the previous set of models.

GRAVITY MODELS

It is appropriate to consider the limitations of gravity modeling. Because neither the mass distribution (the subsurface geometry) nor the density values are known with certainty, a gravity model provides only a nonunique solution. Other variations of geometry and assumed densities may provide an equally satisfactory computed profile. Any model must be evaluated in terms of reasonable density assumptions, realistic geometries, and appro-

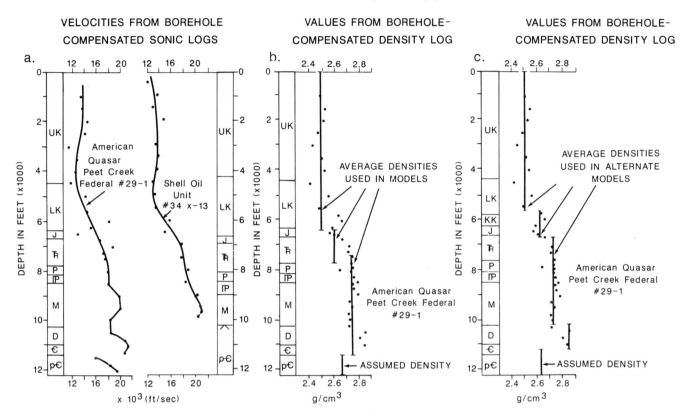

Explanation: UK – Upper Cretaceous rocks; LK–Lower Cretaceous rocks; Kk – Lower Cretaceous Kootenai Formation; J – Jurassic rocks; Ƭ̵ – Triassic rocks;

P – Permian rocks; ƖP – Pennsylvanian rocks; M – Mississippian rocks; D – Devonian rocks; ∈ – Cambrian rocks; p∈ – Precambrian rocks.

Figure 4. Plots of values of velocity and density from sonic logs (a) and compensated density log (b and
c). Average densities in b were used for gravity models described in this chapter; those in c were used for
alternate models with similar results.

priate structural style. It is our opinion that simplistic models
based on generalized polygons are of little practical value in
testing the potential validity of geologic cross sections. The
amount of geologic detail in the models derived here is possible
because of the integration of stratigraphic, seismic, drill hole, and
surface map data, although it is dependent on the accuracy of the
gravity and density measurements. The geological map data used
are from Zeigler (1954), field-checked and modified by Perry. The
models were computed using a 2½ D profile adaptation of a
program by Cordell and Henderson (1968). The profile was modeled in two sections, the first from A to the bend in section, and
the second from the bend in section to A′. Computed values were
corrected for the angle at which the modeled profile crosses the
trend of the contoured data. Regional and isostatic factors were
not considered because of the local scale of the models. Model 1
(Fig. 5) was based on the simplest configuration that would incorporate the known geologic relationships mapped at the surface
(Fig. 2), including, from north to south: Tertiary deposits in the
Sage Creek basin, a mid-Tertiary normal fault, shallowly dipping
Paleozoic rocks with a surface anticline, a steeply dipping (40° to
80°S) panel of Paleozoic through Lower Cretaceous rocks, a
disrupted zone, and essentially flat-lying Cretaceous rocks in the

Centennial basin. The Shell Oil 34X-13 Unit well was used as a
control point; its location is indicated in Figure 2 and on the
model profiles.

If the computed values are considered controlled and fixed
at the well location and the rest of the profile is free to deviate, it
is clear that the geologic section assumed for the model includes a
major mass excess at all points west and north of the control
point.

We must consider the possibility, however, that the stratigraphic control from the well logs is itself in error. If it is assumed
that the computed values match those observed for the profile,
with the exception of being 8 to 10 mGal too low at the well
control point, we must then assume that a greater thickness of
high density material—an additional thick Paleozoic section, for
instance—underlies the Precambrian (Archean) rocks drilled in
the Peet Creek well and must also be present in the Shell well.
We must also assume that the Archean unit is structurally thin in
order for underlying high-density Paleozoic rocks to be near
enough to the surface to cause an additional anomaly of 8 to 10
mGal. If such a situation exists, the geologic section as drawn
may be approximately correct, and the inferred sub–Snowcrest
Range fault may have little horizontal offset, although the vertical

displacement of the fault and associated fold would exceed 2,400 m (8,000 ft). In this case, the stratigraphic changes reported by Perry and others (1981) would have to be explained by rapid thickening of the section across very short distances during deposition. Available seismic data, however, show no reflectors indicative of high-velocity/high-density layered rocks beneath the interpreted Precambrian unit in the area of the Shell and Peet Creek wells. On that basis we assumed that the control section at the well is accurate, and investigated other geologically feasible subsurface relationships that would remove the mass excess assumed on cross section 1 and thereby provide a better fit to the observed gravity profile.

Several general adjustments are immediately required for model 2 (Fig. 6):

1. Because there is a 2,100 m (7,000 ft) section of Cretaceous rocks in the Shell well and an observed gravity decrease of 5 to 8 mGal between the station at the well and the stations measured in the basin west of the well, the low-density Cretaceous and Tertiary rocks west of the well must be much thicker than 2,100 m (7,000 ft) to cause the decrease in gravity values. Quaternary silts, sands, and gravels are present near the well, but outcrops west and north along the gravity traverse are predominantly sandstones of the Cretaceous Beaverhead Group (Fig. 2;

Perry and others, this volume, Fig. 2). It is reasonable geologically to assume that the Cretaceous section might be thicker here because of either deposition of thick syntectonic deposits from the rising Blacktail-Snowcrest uplift (Ryder and Scholten, 1973; Haley, 1986) or tectonic thickening of the Cretaceous section by thrust repetition, as seen nearby in the Farmers Union Lima State wells no. 9-31 and no. 2-33, which lie 40 km (25 mi) to the southwest (Perry and others, 1983).

2. The gravity gradient between the station measured at the Shell well and the next station immediately to the west is steep, decreasing 3.5 mGal in only 0.8 km (0.5 mi), indicative of a near-surface, fault-bounded low-density body. A Tertiary body bounded by a listric normal fault similar to that mapped near the northern end of the profile has therefore been included in model 2. Surficial Tertiary and Quaternary beds (Fig. 2), mapped near the eastern end of the gravity profile, are assumed to be thin and are not included in the models. In the Shell Oil 34X-13 drillhole (Fig. 2), Cretaceous rocks were encountered at a depth of 12 m (40 ft). The inferred fault may be related to the northwest-trending Blacktail fault interpreted from the regional gravity data to extend into this area.

3. A mass excess has also been assumed in model 1 for the section north of the steeply dipping panel (left part of Fig. 5) and

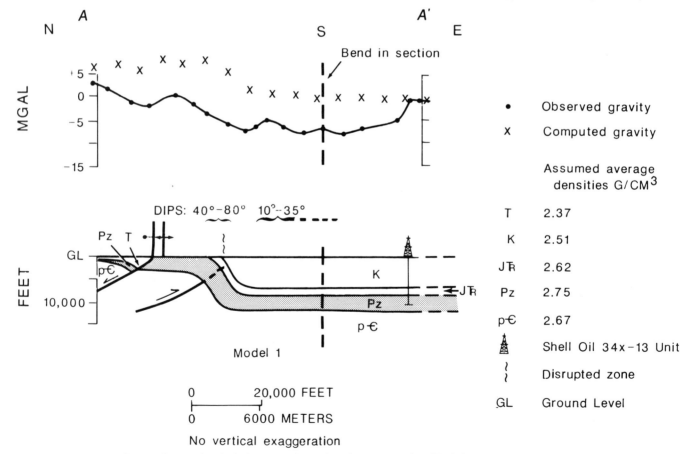

Figure 5. Assumed geological cross section and gravity model 1 of profile A-A'. T = Tertiary rocks; K = Cretaceous rocks; JT̄ = Jurassic and Triassic rocks; Pz = Paleozoic rocks; other abbreviations as in Figure 4.

the disrupted zone (Fig. 2), as the computed values are 8 to 12 mGal higher than the observed values. Since the Paleozoic rocks occur in outcrop here, it is likely that a section of high-density Paleozoic rocks occurs at or near the surface across the interval shown. The most logical interpretation that will introduce low-density, presumably Cretaceous, rocks beneath this area of the model is to assume that a shallow-dipping (approximately 20°) thrust fault, whose leading edge is concealed beneath surface deposits in the northern Centennial basin, underlies the Paleozoic rocks and a thin section of Precambrian crystalline basement rocks. The steeply dipping panel is thus interpreted to be a result of rollover of the hanging wall at the toe of the main thrust, which is the sub–Snowcrest Range fault, possibly a southwestern extension of the Greenhorn thrust as indicated by Sheedlo (1984).

Compared to model 1, a better fit is obtained on model 2 (Fig. 6) by the addition of the thicker Cretaceous section in the Centennial basin and an assumed density of 2.45 g/cm³ for the Upper Cretaceous rocks, although the fit in the northern part of the model has not been much improved.

In model 3 (Fig. 7), an even shallower angle, about 16°, has been assumed for the main sub–Snowcrest Range fault, reducing the cross-sectional area and mass of high-density material. The Snowcrest Range thrust fault, mapped by Zeigler (1954) along the northwestern margin of the Snowcrest structural terrane, is interpreted here to be a hanging-wall imbricate of the inferred

sub-Snowcrest Range thrust. The beds of the footwall have been flexed downward beneath the inferred major thrust in order to place low-density Upper Cretaceous rocks beneath the entire northern part of the profile. A reasonably good fit has been obtained with these assumptions, although the computed values at the northern end are now slightly lower and the computed values over the small anticline and the toe of the thrust (arrows) are slightly higher than the observed values. As the rocks here have been fractured, their densities have presumably been lowered somewhat from the densities assumed, which would account for the minor deviations. The type of fracturing is probably similar to that seen in thin sections of Archean metamorphic rocks from outcrops adjacent to the Snowcrest thrust fault system approximately 13 km (8 mi) to the southwest in the Henry Gulch 1:24,000 quadrangle (Perry and others, this volume, Fig. 6); these sections show rocks that are highly fractured and have cataclastic textures (Fig. 8). Density and porosity measurements from three samples within 460 m (1,500 ft) of the bounding thrust were calculated by Clark Grose of the U.S. Geological Survey, using the technique of Chleborad and others (1975), and are summarized in Table 1. Clearly, these Archean rocks near the fault zone are shattered and dilated and have higher than normal porosities and lower than normal densities. Model 4 (Fig. 9) incorporates these inferred reduced densities as well as a more sophisticated cross-sectioned model of the foot wall.

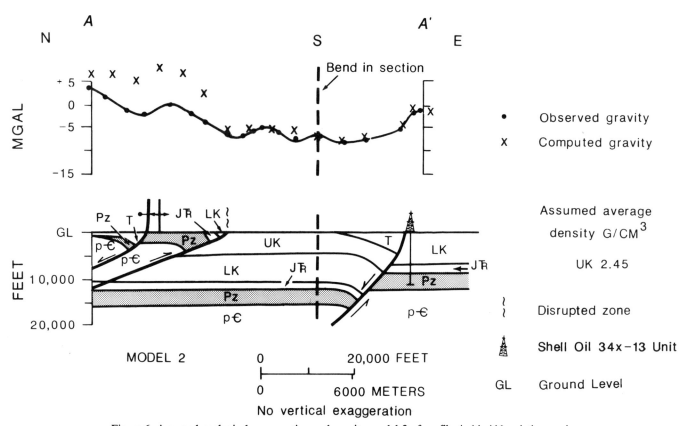

Figure 6. Assumed geological cross section and gravity model 2 of profile A-A'. Abbreviations as in Figures 4 and 5.

Model 5 (Fig. 10) shows an alternative subsurface rock distribution. The Phanerozoic rocks of the lower plate extend only as far north as the Tertiary basin. The Paleozoic section of the upper plate previously assumed to underlie the Tertiary rocks is omitted, and the Tertiary rocks are increased in thickness to provide the needed low-density material. Model 5 produces computed values that also match the observed profile A-A′.

The modeling sequence applied here to the Blacktail-Snowcrest uplift demonstrates not only some of the inherent problems in gravity modeling of deformed structural terranes, but also the desirability of making integrated analyses incorporating surface mapping, stratigraphic and structural studies, geophysical modeling, seismic data, and drill-hole measurements. Although we cannot determine whether model 4 or model 5 is more nearly correct on the basis of the gravity data and minimal well control available, it is clear that the deformed Archean and Paleozoic rocks along the southeastern margin of the Blacktail-Snowcrest uplift must be underlain by low-density material. The modeling indicates that the uplift is bounded by a major thrust system including at least one, and possibly several, faults that do not reach the surface. It also indicates that the Snowcrest thrust of Klepper (1950), the Snowcrest Range thrust of Zeigler (1954), and the Greenhorn thrust-fault system of Hadley (1969) are imbricates of the more extensive system that has at least 4,000 to 5,000 m (14,000 to 16,000 ft) of vertical offset. The frontal part of the Blacktail-Snowcrest uplift traversed by profile A-A′ is separated by the Sage Creek Tertiary basin from the main mass of the uplift that lies to the northwest,

TABLE 1. DENSITY AND POROSITY MEASUREMENTS FOR THREE SAMPLES OF ARCHEAN GNEISS

Sample Number	Bulk Density (g/cm³)	Grain Density (g/cm³)	Porosity (%)
P3	2.53	2.61	3.06
P33	2.44	2.59	5.79
P34	2.51	2.62	4.20

where the crystalline rocks of its core are exposed in the Blacktail Mountains and Ruby Range.

Overlap of foreland and thrust-belt structures

Several lines of geological and geophysical evidence indicate that this entire basement-cored foreland uplift extends westward and is overlapped by the frontal faults of the Cordilleran thrust belt. Beutner (1977) suggested that the Blacktail-Snowcrest uplift acted as a buttress to eastward-directed faults of the southwest Montana thrust belt, based on structural relations outlined by Ryder and Scholten (1973). Kulik and Schmidt (this volume) have described various types of interaction between structures of the Cordilleran thrust belt and Rocky Mountain foreland and the structural complexities that result in the overlap zone. Because unusual field relationships may be caused and/or controlled by overlap interaction, it is vital to recognize structural, stratigraphic,

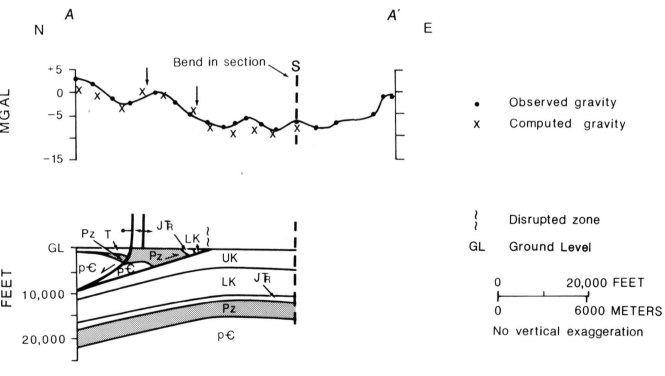

MODEL 3

Figure 7. Assumed geological cross section and gravity model 3 of profile A-A′. Abbreviations as in Figures 4 and 5.

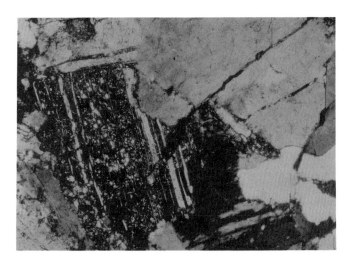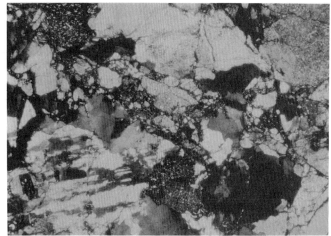

Figure 8. Photomicrographs with crossed nicols of thin sections of Archean gneiss of the Snowcrest-Greenhorn fault system, showing highly fractured nature and cataclastic texture of these rocks. Scale bar = 1 mm.

and geophysical clues by which areas of overlap may be identified.

Both gravity and aeromagnetic data indicate that the uplift extends in the subsurface as far west as the Beaverhead Range. Aeromagnetic data (Zietz and others, 1980) show a northeast-trending magnetic high over the Blacktail-Snowcrest uplift (Fig. 11). The anomaly extends westward beyond the frontal fault of the thrust belt, and the gradient associated with the anomaly extends southward to the area of the Snowcrest-Greenhorn fault

system. Regional gravity data obtained in 1981–1983 also show a high anomaly associated with the main part of the uplift (Fig. 3; Plate 1. Local high anomalies, identified with the stippled pattern in Figure 3, are superimposed on the regional pattern and extend southwestward along the same trend as far as the Beaverhead Mountains within the Cordilleran thrust belt. Some local high anomalies, identified with arrows in Figure 3, including those that appear on the northern end of profile A-A' (Figs. 5, 6, 7, 9, 10) are associated with the Precambrian and Paleozoic rocks

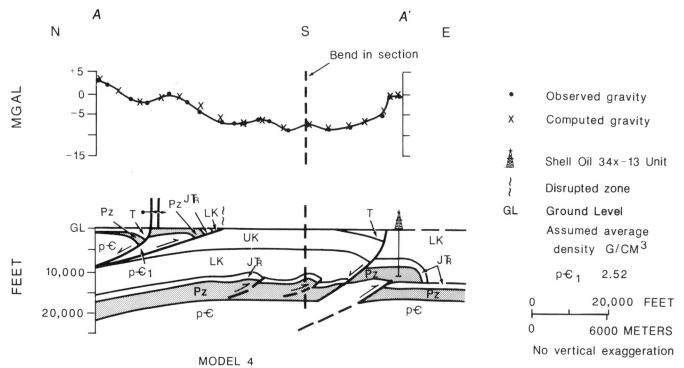

Figure 9. Assumed geological cross section and gravity model 4 of profile A-A'. $p\mathcal{C}_1$ = Fractured Precambrian rocks; other abbreviations as in Figures 4 and 5.

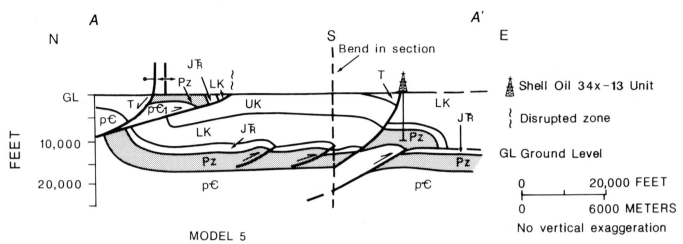

Figure 10. Assumed geological cross section for alternate model 5, of profile A-A'. Abbreviations as in Figure 9.

in the leading edge of the Snowcrest-Greenhorn fault system and also extend westward to the Beaverhead Mountains.

The gravity and magnetic trends are easily traced here because the foreland structure and the subsequent thrust-belt faults were oriented perpendicular to each other so that the geophysical anomalies were augmented rather than obscured by thrust-belt deformation, as illustrated schematically in Figure 12. Linear anomalies in the magnetic (Fig. 12b) and gravity (Fig. 12c) patterns are associated with a simplified section of Precambrian, Paleozoic, and Mesozoic rocks (Fig. 12a) similar to the relationships in the Blacktail-Snowcrest uplift. The trace of a potential fault is shown by the dashed line in Figure 12a, and two possible directions of motion on the fault are indicated by the arrows identified as A and B. Field relations after faulting in the A direction are shown in Figure 12d, with the Precambrian, Paleozoic, and Mesozoic units superimposed. The magnetic (Fig. 12e) and gravity (Fig. 12f) expressions that would be expected over the faulted section have been augmented by the doubled units. Field relations are different after faulting in the B direction, as shown in Figure 12g, with the Precambrian, Paleozoic, and Mesozoic units both superposed and offset by the oblique motion of the fault. The linear magnetic and gravity anomaly patterns are obscured; the magnetic (Fig. 12h) and gravity (Fig. 12i) expressions expected in this case would be dominated more by the strike of the upper plate units. These expressions would be more difficult to interpret, particularly if the simple Precambrian-Paleozoic-Mesozoic section had been obscured by sediment deposition, as was the case in the Tendoy area.

Perry and others (1983) indicated that, prior to development of the Tendoy thrust, rocks later incorporated into the Tendoy sheet had been differentially eroded down to the Triassic (Fig. 13), due to foreland-thrust uplift of the southwest-plunging nose of the Blacktail-Snowcrest uplift. Perry and others (this volume) have shown that this uplift occurred before middle Campanian time (78 to 81 Ma), and that development of the Tendoy thrust could not have occurred before late Maastrichtian time (70 Ma).

Beaverhead Group conglomerate was deposited unconformably over this erosion surface prior to Tendoy thrusting, leading to locally rapid lateral changes in stratigraphic relationships between Beaverhead Group rocks and subjacent Triassic through Early Cretaceous rocks, due to Cretaceous structural relief across the southwest-plunging nose of the Blacktail-Snowcrest uplift. The angular unconformity is inferred to be greatest over the southeast flank of the Blacktail-Snowcrest uplift (Fig. 13).

In our model, subsequent lateral ramping of the Tendoy thrust along the preexisting Snowcrest-Greenhorn fault system occurred as the Tendoy thrust emplaced the previously deformed rocks now incorporated into the Tendoy sheet higher onto the uplift from their original, more westerly position on its southwest-plunging nose (Fig. 13 and Perry and others, 1983). Such rapid lateral changes along strike within thrust sheets provide field evidence for the recognition of areas where foreland and thrust-belt structures overlap and complicate subsurface relationships. In an area of west-to-east basin-to-shelf transition (Fig. 14a), Rocky Mountain foreland faults such as the Snowcrest-Greenhorn system may deform the section, transporting rocks of the upper plate southward (Fig. 14b). Cross sections drawn successively from north to south prior to faulting would show the potential low-angle foreland fault cutting the section at various levels (Fig. 14c). Similar cross sections drawn after movement of the foreland fault (Fig. 14d) would show a range of stratigraphic assemblages resulting from transport of the upper plate over the lower plate at a low angle. A later-developing east-directed fault of the Cordilleran thrust belt (indicated by the dashed line in Fig. 14, b and d) would encounter an already deformed and rearranged stratigraphic section that would be incorporated into the Cordilleran thrust sheet and transported eastward. Dramatic changes in the stratigraphy of both upper and lower plates would result from such sequential deformation.

This model contrasts markedly with that presented by N. B. Woodward (oral communication, 1986; this volume); he has suggested that lateral ramps in thrust sheets are sited where abrupt

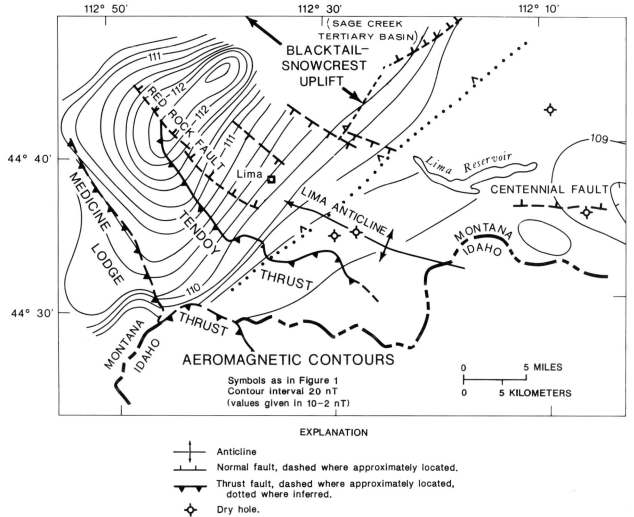

Figure 11. Aeromagnetic (Zietz and others, 1980) and generalized structure map of the Blacktail-Snowcrest area and the frontal thrust belt from Perry and others (1983).

facies changes occur laterally, independent of foreland events. Abrupt facies changes are nearly always controlled by abrupt changes in paleotopography or abrupt paleotectonic hingelines related to differential subsidence, a likely result of basement-involved faulting. Within the exposed part of the Tendoy sheet, no major facies changes take place.

Major thickness changes in upper Paleozoic strata are described east of the thrust belt (Perry and others, 1983) between the hanging wall and the footwall of the Snowcrest-Greenhorn thrust system. These are clearly due to Paleozoic paleotectonic events associated with the growth of the ancestral Rocky Mountains farther south (Maughan and Perry, 1982). Perry (1986) showed that this abrupt upper Paleozoic thickness change parallels the Snowcrest-Greenhorn Laramide fault system, and indicated that this abrupt change was associated with a down-to-the-north, late Paleozoic normal fault zone that bounded the southeast margin of an asymmetric sedimentary basin, the Snowcrest trough. The deepest part of this precursor

basin was structurally inverted during the development of the Snowcrest-Greenhorn thrust system as the hanging wall of that system. The Paleozoic platform south of the Snowcrest trough is now represented by the Cretaceous foredeep southeast of the Snowcrest-Greenhorn thrust system, as indicated by wells discussed by Perry and others (1981, 1983). This paleotectonic boundary undoubtedly persists some distance to the west, beneath the Tendoy sheet, where it controlled the position of the southwestern extension of the Snowcrest-Greenhorn fault (Fig. 13). Thickness contrasts across this fault zone are discussed by Maughan and Perry (1982) and Perry (1986). They are *not* directly responsible for the lateral ramp or other lateral structural changes within the Tendoy thrust sheet (Figs. 13, 14).

The Blacktail-Snowcrest uplift projects westward beneath the frontal thrust belt, based on the associated gravity and magnetic anomalies (Fig. 15). In the area of overlap there is an embayment and change of strike of the Tendoy thrust sheet, a small reentrant in the Medicine Lodge thrust sheet (Scholten and

302

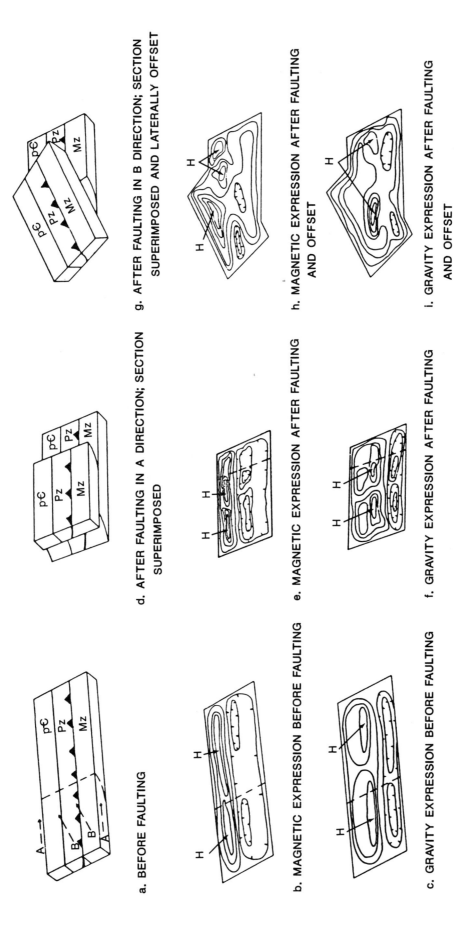

a. BEFORE FAULTING

d. AFTER FAULTING IN A DIRECTION; SECTION SUPERIMPOSED

g. AFTER FAULTING IN B DIRECTION; SECTION SUPERIMPOSED AND LATERALLY OFFSET

b. MAGNETIC EXPRESSION BEFORE FAULTING

e. MAGNETIC EXPRESSION AFTER FAULTING

h. MAGNETIC EXPRESSION AFTER FAULTING AND OFFSET

c. GRAVITY EXPRESSION BEFORE FAULTING

f. GRAVITY EXPRESSION AFTER FAULTING

i. GRAVITY EXPRESSION AFTER FAULTING AND OFFSET

Figure 12. Block diagram of a simplified section of Precambrian (pC), Paleozoic (Pz), and Mesozoic (Mz) units, and associated magnetic and gravity anomalies. Units before faulting (a). Dashed lines labeled A show direction of faulting assumed in (d). Dashed lines labeled B show direction of faulting assumed in (g). Magnetic (b) and gravity (c) expression before faulting. Units after faulting in A direction (d). Magnetic (e) and gravity (f) expression after faulting in A direction. Units after faulting in B direction (g). Magnetic (h) and gravity (i) expression after faulting in B direction. High anomalies indicated by H.

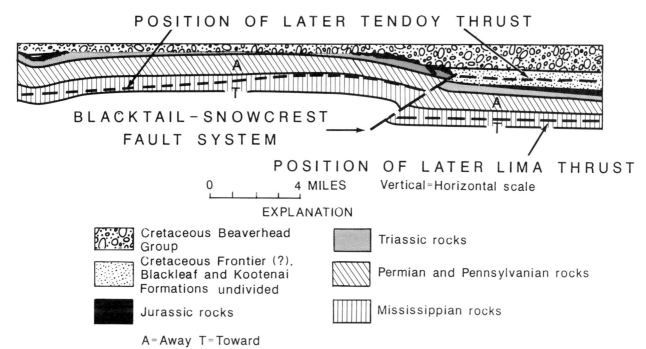

Figure 13. Hypothetical northwest-southeast section of the southern Tendoy area prior to Sevier-type thrusting, showing position of later Tendoy and Lima thrust faults.

others, 1955; Ryder and Scholten, 1973), and a southward termination of the Four Eyes Canyon thrust sheet (Perry and Sando, 1983). Archean gneisses are present in the leading edge of the Cabin sheet where it intersects the Blacktail-Snowcrest trend; these rocks were incorporated into the sheet as it encountered the plunging nose of the Blacktail-Snowcrest uplift (Kulik and others, 1983) possibly as illustrated in Figure 14d on sections A/B-A′/B′ and B/C-B′/C′. Alternatively, the basement rocks may have been incorporated into the plate as it encountered previously formed normal faults along the craton-to-miogeocline transition (Fig. 16). Although the Cabin sheet may sole in crystalline basement rocks farther west where movement on the fault was initiated, the crystalline rocks exposed in its leading edge are interpreted as discontinuous segments from the hanging wall(s) of preexisting faults (see Skipp, this volume).

Perry and others (1983) described other lines of evidence for the incorporation of strata from the pre-existing Blacktail-Snowcrest uplift into the Tendoy sheet of the frontal Cordilleran thrust belt. In particular, the low vitrinite reflectance values (R_o = 0.28 to 0.35) and TAI (Thermal Alteration Index) values indicate burial depths of no more than 6,500 ft (2,000 m) for any length of time of Mississippian rocks on the central Tendoy sheet, along the projected axis of the Blacktail-Snowcrest uplift. If the paleogeothermal gradient had exceeded 1°F/100 ft (18°C/km) for any length of time, the estimated burial depths would be less (Perry and others, 1983). A burial of 2,000 m (6,500 ft) represents only Pennsylvanian to Lower Cretaceous cover. More than 1,500 m

(5,000 ft) of upper Paleozoic cover is estimated for the southern part of the Tendoy sheet along the original trough axis of the Snowcrest trough (Perry, 1986). This supports the contention that the central Tendoy sheet includes the original southwest-plunging nose of the Blacktail-Snowcrest uplift (see Perry and others, this volume).

CONCLUSIONS

Gravity models of the steep southeast limb of the Blacktail-Snowcrest uplift require that the leading edge of the uplift be underlain by low-density material either as autochthonous or para-autochthonous Cretaceous strata. The models are consistent with an uplift bounded by a major low-angle thrust system, including one or more reverse faults that are concealed beneath deposits in the Centennial basin south of the uplift. The models indicate that the Snowcrest and other minor thrusts exposed in the Snowcrest structural terrane are imbricates of the more extensive Snowcrest-Greenhorn thrust fault system on which primary movement may shift from fault to fault along the length of the uplift. Although the gravity data alone do not provide a unique solution, the preferred model presented here is consistent with the style of deformation partially exposed and mapped along the Snowcrest Range, as well as with the stratigraphic, seismic, and drillhole data.

Gravity and aeromagnetic anomalies associated with the Blacktail-Snowcrest uplift extend westward to the Beaverhead

304

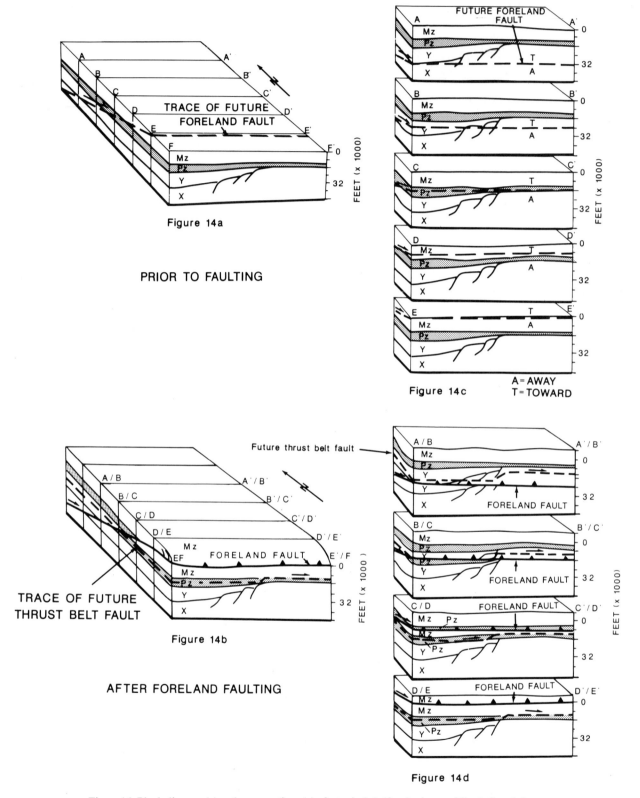

Figure 14. Block diagram (a) and cross sections (c) of a typical shelf-to-basin transition before deformation, showing trace of future foreland-type fault, with future north-to-south–transported hanging wall. Mz = Mesozoic rocks; Pz = Paleozoic rocks; Y = Middle Proterozoic rocks; X = Early Proterozoic rocks. Block diagram (b) and cross sections (d) after foreland faulting, showing trace of future west-to-east–transported thrust-belt fault block and resulting changes in stratigraphy of upper and lower plates.

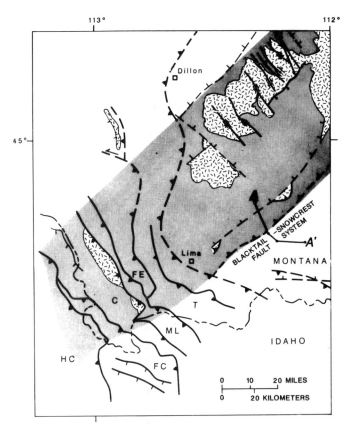

Figure 15. Westward-projected trend of the Blacktail-Snowcrest uplift (shaded) and its overlap by the frontal faults of the Cordilleran thrust belt. HC = Hawley Creek plate; FC = Fritz Creek plate; C = Cabin plate; ML = Medicine Lodge plate; FE = Four Eyes Canyon plate; T = Tendoy plate. Outcrops of crystalline basement rocks shown by random hachure. A-A′, location of gravity profile.

Mountains well beyond the frontal thrusts of the southwest Montana segment of the Cordilleran thrust belt. Structural complexities such as lateral ramps, termination of Cordilleran thrust sheets, changes in stratigraphic thicknesses, and rapid changes in stratigraphic relationships along strike of the sheets identify areas where the faults of the Cordilleran thrust belt overlap and interact with the previously formed Blacktail-Snowcrest uplift. This uplift controlled the shape of much of the southwest Montana recess of the Cordilleran thrust belt, one of the largest such recesses in North America.

ACKNOWLEDGMENTS

We gratefully acknowledge the use of gravity data collected by Viki Bankey and Joseph M. Mancinelli of the U.S. Geological Survey for the regional Bouguer anomaly map. The manuscript has benefited from reviews by Lindreth Cordell and William F. Hanna of the U.S. Geological Survey; William E. Bonini, Princeton University; an anonymous reviewer; and additional comments by C. J. Schmidt. Our thanks also to Freddy Thorsten for typing numerous versions of the manuscript, and to Tom Kostick, who prepared the final illustrations.

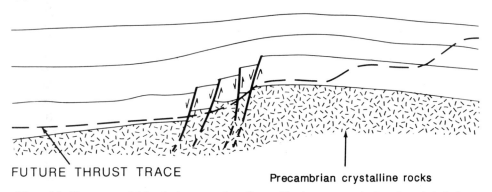

FUTURE THRUST TRACE   Precambrian crystalline rocks

Figure 16. Alternate model for the incorporation of crystalline basement rocks into thrust belt faults.

REFERENCES CITED

Armstrong, R. L., 1968, Sevier Orogenic belt in Nevada and Utah: Geological Society of America Bulletin, v. 79, p. 429–458.

Beutner, E. C., 1977, Causes and consequences of curvature in the Sevier orogenic belt, Utah to Montana, *in* Heisey, E. L., and others, eds., Rocky Mountain thrust belt geology and resources: Wyoming Geological Association 29th Annual Field Conference Guidebook, p. 353–365.

Chleborad, A. F., Powers, P. S., and Farrow, R. A., 1975, A technique for measuring bulk volume of rock materials: Bulletin of the Association of Engineering Geologists, v. 12, p. 317–322.

Cordell, L., and Henderson, R. G., 1968, Iterative three-dimensional solutions of gravity anomaly data using a digital computer: Geophysics, v. 33, p. 596–601.

Cordell, L., Keller, G. R., and Hildenbrand, T. G., 1982, Bouguer gravity map of the Rio Grande Rift, Colorado, New Mexico, and Texas: U.S. Geological Survey Geophysical Investigations Map GP-949, scale 1:1,000,000.

Eardley, A. J., 1951, Structural geology of North America: New York, Harper and Brothers, 624 p.

——, 1960, Phases of orogeny in the deformed belt of southwestern Montana and adjacent areas of Idaho and Wyoming: Billings Geological Society, 11th Annual Field Conference Guidebook, p. 86–91.

Flanagan, W. H., 1958, Geology of the southern part of the Snowcrest Range, Beaverhead County, Montana [M.A. thesis]: Bloomington, Indiana University, 41 p.

Gealy, W. J., 1953, Geology of the Antone Peak Quadrangle, southwestern Montana [Ph.D. thesis]: Cambridge, Massachusetts, Harvard University, 143 p.

Gries, R., 1983, Oil and gas prospecting beneath the Precambrian of foreland thrust plates in the Rocky Mountains: American Association of Petroleum Geologists Bulletin, v. 67, p. 1–28.

Hadley, J. B., 1969, Geologic map of the Varney Quadrangle, Madison County, Montana: U.S. Geological Survey Map GO-814, scale 1:62,500.

——, 1980, Geology of the Varney and Cameron Quadrangles, Madison County, Montana, with a chapter on paleontology and correlation of the Madison group on Baldy Mountain by W. J. Sando and J. T. Dutro, Jr.: U.S. Geological Survey Bulletin 1459, 108 p.

Haley, J. C., 1986, Upper Cretaceous (Beaverhead) synorogenic sediments of the Montana-Idaho thrust belt and adjacent foreland; Relationships between sedimentation and tectonism [Ph.D. thesis]: Baltimore, Maryland, Johns Hopkins University, 542 p.

Hurich, C. A., and Smithson, S. B., 1982, Gravity interpretation of the southern Wind River Mountains, Wyoming: Geophysics, v. 47, no. 11, p. 1550–1561.

International Association of Geodesy, 1967, Geodetic reference system, 1967: International Association of Geodesy Special Publication 3, 74 p.

Keenmon, K. A., 1950, The geology of the Blacktail-Snowcrest region, Beaverhead County, Montana [Ph.D. thesis]: Ann Arbor, University of Michigan, 207 p.

Klepper, M. R., 1950, A geologic reconnaissance of parts of Beaverhead and Madison Counties, Montana: U.S. Geological Survey Bulletin 969-C, 85 p.

Kulik, D. M., 1981, Gravity interpretation of subsurface structures in overthrust and covered terrains; Sedimentary tectonics, principles and applications, *in* Spring Conference, University of Wyoming, 1981 [abs.]: Wyoming Geological Association and Geological Survey of Wyoming.

——, 1982, Illustrations of gravity models of the southeast limb of the Blacktail-Snowcrest uplift, southwest Montana: U.S. Geological Survey Open-File Report 82-823, 8 p.

——, 1984, A structural model for the overlap zone between the Rocky Mountain foreland and Cordilleran thrust belt in southwestern Montana: Geological Society of America Abstracts with Programs, v. 16, p. 227.

——, 1985, Structural and tectonic significance of gravity interpretations and modeling in the overlap province of southwestern Montana and east-central Idaho: Geological Society of America Abstracts with Programs, v. 17, p. 250.

Kulik, D. M., and Perry, W. J., Jr., 1982, Gravity modeling of the steep southeast limb of the Blacktail-Snowcrest uplift: Geological Society of America Abstracts with Programs, v. 14, p. 318.

Kulik, D. M., Perry, W. J., Jr., and Skipp, B., 1983, A model for Rocky Mountain foreland and overthrust belt development; Geophysical and geological evidence for spacial overlap: Geological Society of America Abstracts with Programs, v. 15, p. 318.

Maughan, E. K., and Perry, W. J., 1982, Palezoic tectonism in southwest Montana: Geological Society of America Abstracts with Programs, v. 14, p. 341.

Nichols, D.J., Perry, W. J., Jr., and Haley, J. C., 1985, Reinterpretation of the palynology and age of Laramide syntectonic deposits, southwestern Montana, and revision of the Beaverhead Group: Geology, v. 13, p. 149–153.

Perry, W. J., Jr., 1982, The thrust belt in the Lima-Dell, Montana area, *in* Beaver, P., ed., The overthrust province in the vicinity of Dillon, Montana, and how this structural framework has influenced mineral and energy resources accumulation: Tobacco Root Geological Society 7th Annual Field Conference Guidebook, p. 69–78.

——, Critical deep drillholes and indicated Paleozoic paleontologic features north of the Snake River downwarp in southern Beaverhead County, Montana, and adjacent Idaho: U.S. Geological Survey Open-File Report 86-413, 16 p.

Perry, W. J., Jr., and Sando, W. J., 1983, Sequence of deformation of Cordilleran thrust belt in Lima, Montana, region, *in* Powers, R. B., ed., Geologic studies of the Cordilleran thrust belt, 1982: Denver, Colorado, Rocky Mountain Association of Geologists, v. 1, p. 137–144.

Perry, W. J., Jr., Ryder, R. T., and Maughan, E. K., 1981, The southern part of the southwest Montana thrust belt; A preliminary re-evaluation of structure, thermal maturation, and petroleum potential, *in* Tucker, T. E., ed., Southwest Montana: Montana Geological Society 1981 Field Conference Guidebook, p. 261–273.

Perry, W. J., Jr., Wardlaw, B. R., Bostick, N. H., and Maughan, E. K., 1983, Structure, burial history, and petroleum potential of frontal thrust belt and adjacent foreland, southwest Montana: American Association of Petroleum Geologists Bulletin, v. 67, p. 725–743.

Petersen, F. A., 1983, Foreland detachment structures, *in* Lowell, J. D., and Gries, R., eds., Rocky Mountain foreland basins and uplifts: Denver, Colorado, Rocky Mountain Association of Geologists, p. 65–77.

Plouff, D., 1977, Preliminary documentation for a FORTRAN program to compute gravity terrain corrections based on topography digitized on a geographic grid: U.S. Geological Survey Open-File Report 77-535, 45 p.

Prucha, J. J., Graham, J. A., and Nickelsen, R. P., 1965, Basement controlled deformation in the Wyoming province of the Rocky Mountains foreland: American Association of Petroleum Geologists Bulletin, v. 49, p. 966–992.

Ryder, R. T., and Ames, H. T., 1970, The palynology and age of the Beaverhead Formation and their paleotectonic implications in the Lima Region, Montana-Idaho: American Association of Petroleum Geologists Bulletin, v. 54, p. 1155–1171.

Ryder, R. T., and Scholten, R., 1973, Syntectonic conglomerates in southwest Montana; Their nature, origin, and tectonic significance: Geological Society of America Bulletin, v. 84, p. 773–796.

——, 1967, Structural framework and oil potential of extreme southwestern Montana: Montana Geological Society 18th Annual Field Conference Guidebook, p. 7–19.

Scholten, R., Keenmon, K. A., and Kapsch, W. O., 1955, Geology of the Lima region, southwestern Montana and adjacent Idaho: Geological Society of America Bulletin, v. 66, p. 345–404.

Sheedlo, M. K., 1984, Structural geology of the northern Snowcrest Range, Beaverhead and Madison Counties, Montana [M.S. thesis]: Kalamazoo, Western Michigan University, 132 p.

Skipp, B., 1985, Contraction and extension faults in the southern Beaverhead Mountains, Idaho and Montana [Ph.D. thesis]: Boulder, University of Colorado, 169 p., and U.S. Geological Survey Open-File Report 85-845, 170 p.

Smithson, S. B., Brewer, J., Kaufman, S., and Oliver, J., 1979, Nature of the Wind River thrust, Wyoming from COCORP deep-reflection data and from gravity data: Geology, v. 6, p. 648–652.

U.S. Defense Mapping Agency Aerospace Center, 1974, World Relative Gravity Reference Network, North America, part 2: Defense Mapping Agency Aerospace Center Reference Publication 25, with supplement updating gravity values to the International Gravity Standardization Net 1971, 1635 p.

Wilson, M. D., 1970, Upper Cretaceous–Paleocene synorogenic conglomerates of south-western Montana: American Association of Petroleum Geologists Bulletin, v. 54, p. 1843–1867.

Zeigler, J. M., 1954, Geology of the Blacktail area, Beaverhead County, Montana [Ph.D. thesis]: Cambridge, Massachusetts, Harvard University, 147 p.

Zietz, I., Gilbert, F. P., and Snyder, S. L., 1980, Aeromagnetic map of Montana: U.S. Geological Survey Geophysical Investigations Map GP-934, scale 1:1,000,000.

MANUSCRIPT ACCEPTED BY THE SOCIETY FEBRUARY 9, 1988

Geological Society of America
Memoir 171
1988

Geometry and sequence of thrusting, McKnight and Kelmbeck Canyons, Tendoy Range, southwestern Montana

Nancy S. Williams
P.O. Box 84, Jamestown, Colorado 80455
John M. Bartley
Department of Geology and Geophysics, University of Utah, Salt Lake City, Utah 84112

ABSTRACT

The central Tendoy Range lies within a northwest-trending transition zone across which changes occur in both Paleozoic stratigraphy and Laramide structural style. (The term "Laramide" is used in this chapter in its classical temporal sense, i.e., orogenesis of Late Cretaceous to Eocene age.) To the east, Paleozoic strata have cratonal affinities, whereas miogeoclinal facies lie to the west. Mississippian strata in the study area compose a facies transitional between craton and miogeocline. This transition was telescoped by Laramide thrusting. The miogeocline was shortened by thin-skinned "Cordilleran-type" thrusts, whereas the craton was affected by Rocky Mountain "foreland-type" basement uplifts. Mapping and geophysical data from the transition zone have been interpreted to indicate that Cordilleran-type thrusts overrode and truncated thrusts and folds related to the Snowcrest foreland thrust system. Chronologic constraints indicate that Snowcrest-system thrusts were active before Cordilleran-type thrusts, but the two structural styles overlap both in time and space in the Tendoy Range.

Field relationships in the McKnight–Kelmbeck Canyon area of the Tendoy Range support this interpretation of overlapping deformation. The earliest deformation phase in this area is manifest in Cordilleran-type folds and thrusts (Kelmbeck and Timber Butte thrusts) that emplaced transitional-facies Mississippian rocks eastward. The age of Late Cretaceous Beaverhead Group rocks in the footwall of the Kelmbeck thrust clearly shows that these thrusts are younger than much of the uplift along the Snowcrest foreland thrust system. However, the Kelmbeck thrust was then rotated to a moderate northwestward dip about a northeast-trending axis. This rotation probably reflects resurgence of activity along the Snowcrest trend. This rotation was followed by emplacement of the north-northwest–trending, east-directed McKnight thrust, which probably correlates with the Tendoy thrust farther south in the range. The McKnight thrust cut through and locally rotated the Kelmbeck and Timber Butte thrusts, truncated structures in both its hanging wall and footwall, and locally reactivated the Timber Butte thrust.

INTRODUCTION

During much of the Paleozoic, western North America was characterized by a subsiding, Atlantic-type continental margin (Burchfiel and Davis, 1975; Armin and Mayer, 1983). In southwestern Montana, the transition between the craton to the east and the subsiding miogeocline to the west is most clearly reflected in Mississippian strata within a zone that passes north-westward through the Tendoy Range (Fig. 1; Rose, 1976; Sandberg and others, 1983). This transition is also expressed in contrasting Laramide thrust styles, from thin-skinned "Cordilleran-type" thrusts to the west of the transition zone (Skipp and Hait, 1977) to basement-involved "foreland-type" thrusts to the east (Scholten and others, 1955; Perry and others, 1983, this

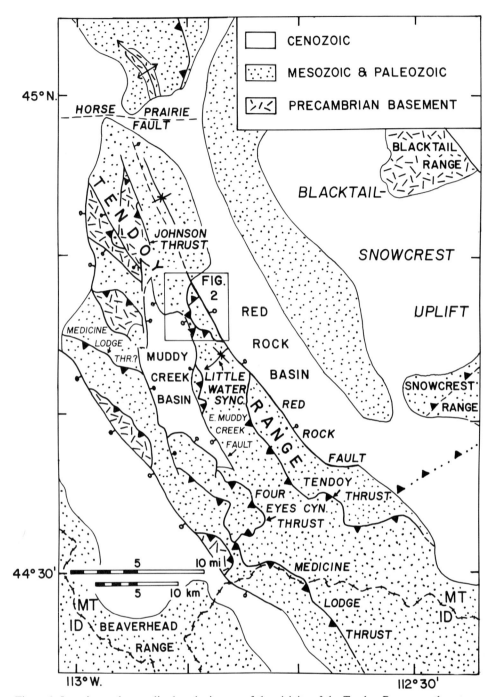

Figure 1. Location and generalized geologic map of the vicinity of the Tendoy Range, southwestern Montana and adjacent Idaho. Geology after DuBois (1983), Perry and Sando (1983), Perry and others (1983), Scholten (1983), Scholten and others (1955), and Williams (1984).

volume). In this chapter, we present results of mapping within the transition zone on the eastern flank of the Tendoy Range. Based on these data, we propose a new interpretation of the intersecting faults in the area of McKnight and Kelmbeck Canyons of the central Tendoy Range. This interpretation bears on regional thrust correlations in southwestern Montana, and on the interaction of Cordilleran- and foreland-type structural styles in this region.

REGIONAL GEOLOGY

Stratigraphic changes across the transition zone include both a general westward thickening of the section and facies changes, particularly within rocks of the Mississippian System (Huh, 1967; Rose, 1976). Mississippian strata in the northern Tendoy Range make up a recently distinguished lithofacies that is transitional between the craton and miogeocline (Sando and others, 1985).

Structures in southwestern Montana reflect both Laramide shortening and late Cenozoic Basin-Range extension. Laramide thrusts and folds may be separated into two major sets that differ in trend and structural style: the Snowcrest thrust system includes mainly northeast-trending foreland-type structures, whereas the Medicine Lodge and Tendoy thrust systems comprise thin-skinned Cordilleran-type structures that trend north or northwest (Scholten and others, 1955; Perry and others, 1983, this volume).

The Snowcrest thrust system is manifested by folds and basement-involved foreland-type thrusts (Perry and others, this volume). Remnants of a major foreland massif (Blacktail-Snowcrest uplift) are exposed in the Blacktail and Snowcrest Ranges east of the Tendoy Range (Fig. 1; Scholten and others, 1955). This massif probably is thrust-bounded on its southeast side (Perry and Kulik, 1983; Perry and others, 1983). Perry and others (1983) suggested that the Blacktail-Snowcrest uplift continues to the southwest into the Cordilleran thrust belt and affected younger thrust-belt structures now exposed in the Tendoy Range. On the eastern flank of the Tendoy Range, northeast-trending structures that are probably related to the Blacktail-Snowcrest uplift are refolded and cut by thrusts of the second phase of Laramide deformation (for example, the Little Water syncline; see Perry and others, this volume, for discussion). Sedimentological data from the oldest synorogenic clastic rocks of the Beaverhead Group show that the Blacktail-Snowcrest uplift supplied some of this detritus (Ryder, 1967), indicating that foreland-type structures were active before Cordilleran-type thrusting began in this area. Palynological results of Nichols and others (1985) indicate a Late Cretaceous age (Coniacian to Santonian) for these deposits.

Perry and others (1985) recently distinguished the McKenzie thrust system in the northern Tendoy Range, which is composed of a northeast-trending stack of imbricated upper Paleozoic rocks of the transitional facies. The lowest exposed thrust of the stack may occur in the study area. Upper Campanian or younger Beaverhead Group conglomerate in the study area was derived from sheets of the McKenzie system; thus the McKenzie system is younger than the early activity along the Snowcrest system (Perry and others, this volume). However, fault geometries indicate that the McKenzie system is older than the Tendoy thrust system (see below).

The easternmost exposed thin-skinned Cordilleran-type thrust is the Tendoy thrust, which trends northwest along the eastern flank of the Tendoy Range. For most of its length, the Tendoy thrust places upper Paleozoic rocks upon Upper Cretaceous syntectonic deposits of the Beaverhead Group. At least some of the rocks cut by the Tendoy thrust were already deformed before the Tendoy sheet was emplaced: both the hanging wall and the footwall of the Tendoy thrust include structures that are probably related to the older Blacktail-Snowcrest uplift (Scholten and others, 1955). Thin-skinned thrusts emplaced the Tendoy and related thrust sheets eastward to a higher position on the flank of the Blacktail-Snowcrest uplift (Perry and others, 1983).

Along the western flank of the southern Tendoy Range, the Four Eyes Canyon thrust, which structurally overlies the Tendoy thrust plate (Fig. 1), emerges from beneath the Medicine Lodge thrust (as restricted by Perry and Sando, 1983). Erosional debris from the Four Eyes Canyon plate was cut by the Tendoy thrust, thus documenting earlier movement on the higher Four Eyes Canyon thrust (Perry and Sando, 1983).

The Medicine Lodge thrust juxtaposes Mississippian miogeoclinal and cratonal facies, and is at least partly responsible for the present abrupt craton-miogeocline transition (Scholten and others, 1955; Ruppel, 1978). Associated with the Medicine Lodge thrust are thrusts that carry Precambrian basement, both between the Medicine Lodge and Tendoy thrusts (Johnson thrust system; DuBois, 1983), and above the Medicine Lodge thrust (Cabin thrust; Scholten and others, 1955).

The Tendoy thrust has been inferred by all previous workers to crop out within the study area. However, controversy exists regarding the actual trace of the Tendoy thrust, its relationship to other faults in the Tendoy Range, and possible correlations of these other faults to the Medicine Lodge or other thrusts (see discussion of relationships of Kelmbeck and Timber Butte thrusts). As detailed below, we interpret the structure of the northern Tendoy Range to reflect overprinting of structures related to the Blacktail-Snowcrest uplift by later Cordilleran-type thrusts.

ROCK UNITS

Rocks exposed in the study area range from Early Mississippian to Tertiary ages, and include parts of the Mississippian Tendoy Group, the Mississippian-Pennsylvanian Snowcrest Range Group, the Pennsylvanian Quadrant Sandstone, the Triassic Thaynes Formation, and the Upper Cretaceous Beaverhead Group. Tertiary rocks include conglomerate, rhyolitic ashflow and airfall tuffs, andesite flows and volcanic breccia, and basalt (Dunlap, 1982; Williams, 1984). The Tendoy, Snowcrest Range, and Beaverhead Groups are of principal concern here because their stratigraphic interpretation carries significant structural and tectonic implications. The characteristics of these units in the study area are discussed below.

Tendoy Group

The Tendoy Group was recently defined based on exposures in the northern Tendoy Range (Sando and others, 1985). This sequence represents a transitional facies between the miogeocline to the west and the craton to the east. The present study in the central Tendoy Range was completed before the Tendoy Group was proposed. Rocks of this age in the study area were mapped as members of the Mission Canyon Limestone, but stratigraphic and petrologic characteristics summarized below indicate that they correspond to the Middle Canyon Formation, Mission Canyon Limestone, and McKenzie Canyon Limestone of Sando and others (1985).

The Middle Canyon Formation in the study area comprises at least 160 m of thin-bedded, medium gray to grayish black limestone that contains zones of up to 70 percent dusky brown chert in irregular beds, stringers, and nodules. Nodules and stringers of light gray chert are also present, but are much less abundant. The limestone is fine grained except for coarse-grained, medium light gray crinoidal zones with less chert. In thin section, the limestone is an intraclast-bearing micrite or pelmicrite with sparse fossil fragments.

The Mission Canyon Limestone is composed of 200 m of massive, light gray, medium- to coarse-grained limestone that rarely contains chert. Patches of very light gray sparry calcite are commonly visible in hand sample. The limestone is a poorly washed intrasparite or poorly washed intraclast-bearing echinoid-bryozoan pelsparite, with some replacement of micrite by fine-grained dolomite along fractures and stylolites. Beds of pelmicrite similar to that in the Middle Canyon Formation are scattered throughout the Mission Canyon Limestone.

The McKenzie Canyon Limestone comprises more than 40 m of extremely weathered limestone and limestone breccia with minor dolomite. The light gray to light brownish gray, porous, laminated dolomite occurs in beds 10 to 30 cm thick.

Snowcrest Range Group

The name Snowcrest Range Group was recently introduced by Wardlaw and Pecora (1985) for rocks in southwestern Montana that lie above the Tendoy Group (and correlative Madison Group), and beneath the Pennsylvanian Quadrant Sandstone. The Snowcrest Range Group replaces the Big Snowy and Amsden Groups, and includes, in ascending order, the Kibbey Sandstone, the Lombard Limestone, and the Conover Ranch Formation. The corresponding rock units in the study area were referred to as unnamed Mississippian limestone "A" and Big Snowy Formation in Williams (1984), but correspond well to the lower and upper members of the Lombard Limestone of Wardlaw and Pecora (1985).

Beaverhead Group

Conglomerate, siltstone, and fresh-water limestone in the McKnight Canyon area crop out in a northwest-dipping, essentially homoclinal section. The stratigraphically lowest unit is limestone-clast conglomerate that Perry and others (this volume) suggest may correlate with the Lima Conglomerate of Nichols and others (1985), which was derived from the Blacktail-Snowcrest uplift. This conglomerate is overlain by an informal member of limestone and siltstone, which is in turn overlain by a limestone-clast conglomerate that lithologically resembles that below. However, the provenance of this higher conglomerate indicates that it was derived from thrust sheets of the McKenzie system in the northern Tendoy Range during their emplacement (Perry and others, this volume).

THRUST FAULTS

Kelmbeck thrust

At Kelmbeck Canyon, a major northwest-dipping thrust places Lombard Limestone upon the upper conglomerate of the Beaverhead Group (Fig. 2). Although the fault surface is unexposed, outcrops of limestone and conglomerate on the southern slope of Kelmbeck Canyon closely constrain the fault trace. Bedding in both the hanging wall and footwall dips concordantly 35° to 45° to the north-northwest (Fig. 3, section A-A'; Fig. 4). The relationships suggest that the Kelmbeck thrust is approximately bedding-parallel and also dips approximately 40° to the northwest. We therefore suggest that the Kelmbeck thrust is an upper flat; that is, two segments of bedding-parallel detachment along the thrust have been juxtaposed by displacement of the hanging wall up an intervening ramp. Late Campanian–early Maastrichtian pollen from the middle of the Beaverhead in the footwall (Nichols and others, 1985) constrains this thrust to be no older than latest Cretaceous.

Timber Butte thrust

Near the southern end of the study area on the west flank of Timber Butte (section 33), a west-dipping fault places Lombard Limestone upon Pennsylvanian Quadrant Sandstone (Fig. 2). Northward, the fault forks into two branches that isolate a horse of Lombard Limestone, at the north end of which the Timber Butte thrust intersects the McKnight thrust (see below). The actual fault contact is not exposed, but a three-point solution on the western branch of the Timber Butte thrust indicates that this fault strikes N30E and dips 70° to the northwest, parallel to hanging-wall bedding (Fig. 2; Fig. 3, C-C'); the attitude of the eastern branch is not well constrained, but the map pattern suggests that it dips even more steeply. For reasons discussed below, we do not believe that the fault was active with its present steep dip, but rather the fault has been rotated to its present attitude by later deformation. Bedding within the horse is almost perpendicular to both branches of the Timber Butte thrust. Bedding in the Quadrant Sandstone that forms the footwall is commonly obscure, but where recognizable near the thrust is nearly parallel to the contact, defining a footwall syncline (Fig. 3, C-C').

McKnight thrust

Much of the thrust here called the McKnight thrust was correlated with the Tendoy thrust by previous authors (Fig. 5; Kupsch, 1950; Scholten and others, 1955; Scholten, 1960; Williams, 1984), because both faults have Beaverhead conglomerate in their footwalls, and southeast of (structurally below) the Timber Butte thrust, each fault bounds the same hanging-wall block. However, the correlation ultimately depends on the structure beneath Red Rock Basin (Fig. 1), and the connection as yet cannot be demonstrated. Therefore, we have adopted the conservative alternative of a local name.

In the study area, the McKnight thrust cuts both hanging-wall and footwall bedding at a significant angle (Figs. 2, 6) and intersects the Kelmbeck and Timber Butte thrusts at high angles (70° to 90°). The Kelmbeck thrust cannot be a part of the McKnight thrust that has been reoriented by folding because there is no fold of the appropriate scale and geometry in Beaverhead Group rocks of the footwall. Based on this and other considerations detailed below, the McKnight thrust appears to truncate both the Timber Butte and Kelmbeck thrusts, and is therefore younger.

On the north and east flanks of Timber Butte, the McKnight thrust is concealed by talus derived from hanging-wall Quadrant Sandstone, but its location can be estimated based on the topographically highest outcrops of Beaverhead Group rocks. Where exposed, the fault contact is sharp and brecciation is rare. The thrust plane locally dips gently to moderately to the southwest,

and is steepest near its intersection with the Timber Butte thrust. Three-point solutions on the trace of the McKnight thrust throughout the study area average about N20W, 20SW (Fig. 6). No slickensides were identified on exposures of the main thrust surface, but striae that plunge 18° toward N80E were found on a hanging-wall splay of the McKnight thrust exposed 30 m up the north wall of McKnight Canyon.

North of its intersection with the Kelmbeck thrust, the McKnight thrust places Lombard Limestone and Tendoy Group rocks upon Lombard Limestone, making the fault difficult to trace. On the north wall of Kelmbeck Canyon, the fault is expressed as a zone of discontinuous outcrop of faulted and locally brecciated limestone, across which strike of bedding changes from east-northeast on the east to north-northeast on the west (Figs. 2, 4d,e). This fault apparently corresponds to part of that which Kupsch (1950) mapped as the Limekiln thrust (Fig. 5a,b). However, this fault strikes to the north, not northwest. Furthermore, north of Kelmbeck Canyon, no single through-

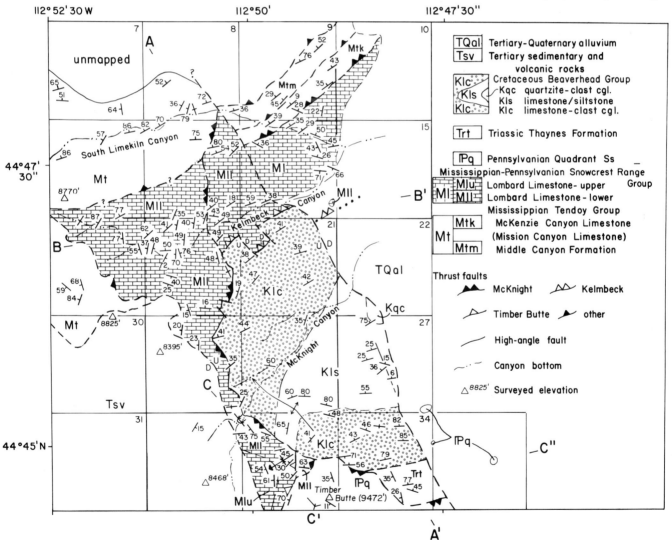

Figure 2. Geologic map of the Kelmbeck Canyon–McKnight Canyon area (T12S, R10W) of the central Tendoy Range, simplified from Williams (1984).

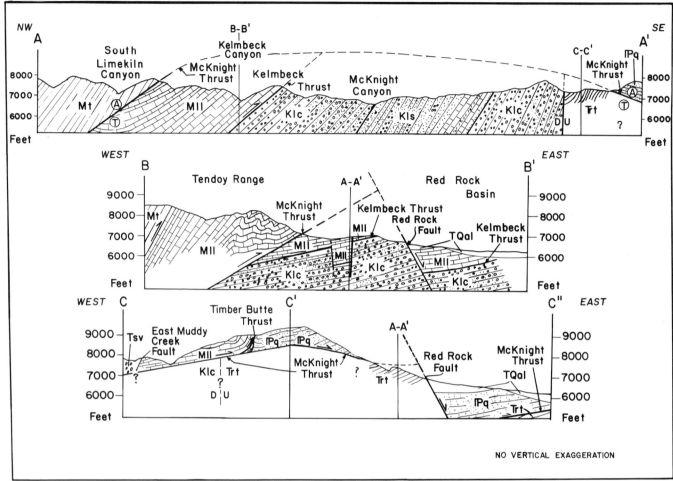

Figure 3. Geologic cross sections through the study area; Figure 2 shows locations. A and T along McKnight thrust in section A-A′ indicate "away" and "toward," respectively.

going fault is present that matches the Limekiln thrust as mapped by Kupsch (Witte, 1965; DuBois, 1982). The complex imbricate structure in that area is now interpreted to form part of the McKenzie thrust system of Perry and others (1985).

Both hanging-wall and footwall bedding locally were folded about north-northwest–trending axes near the McKnight thrust (Figs. 2, 4d). Above the thrust, a large mesoscopic, east-vergent overturned syncline is exposed in the narrows of McKnight Canyon (Fig. 2, NE¼,NE¼,Sec.32). North-plunging east-vergent folds in the Lombard Limestone in Kelmbeck Canyon (Fig. 2, NW¼,Sec.20) also appear to be related to movement on the McKnight thrust. The outcrop pattern of the Beaverhead limestone-siltstone member defines a steeply northwest-plunging anticline that trends roughly parallel to the thrust trace (Fig. 2, S½,Sec.28). However, poles to bedding in the Beaverhead as a whole define a statistical best-fit axis oriented 29, N73W (Fig. 4f), significantly different from that suggested by the map. The diffuse pattern in Figure 4f probably reflects superposition of the McKnight thrust-related folding with deformation related to the overall northward dip of the Beaverhead. Unfortunately,

neither exposure nor dispersion of the structural measurements allow discrimination of these deformations in this area.

Minor thrusts above the McKnight thrust

Along the Kelmbeck Canyon–South Limekiln Canyon divide (Fig. 2) and south of Kelmbeck Canyon, stratigraphic repetitions and inversions suggest the presence of two thrusts that imbricate Lombard Limestone and Tendoy Group. Rocks in this area are poorly exposed and were not studied in detail, so the traces of these inferred thrusts are not well constrained.

DISCUSSION

Bedding-fault geometries of the thrusts, and the geometries of the fault intersections at McKnight and Kelmbeck Canyons, lead us to conclude that the McKnight thrust is a through-going thrust that carries the older Timber Butte thrust in its hanging wall, and truncates the older Kelmbeck thrust in its footwall. The following discussion details the basis of this interpretation.

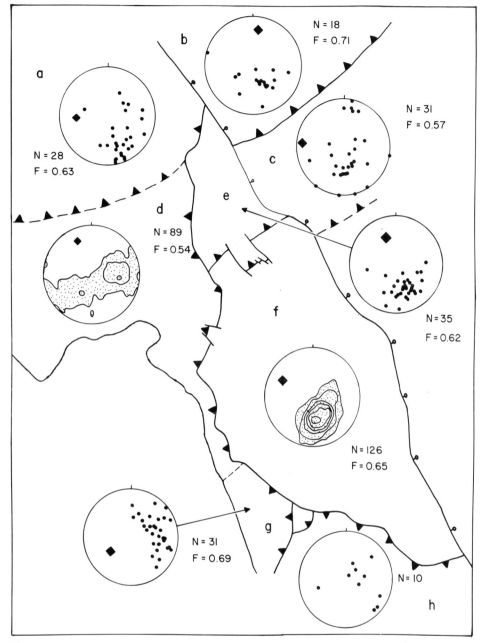

Figure 4. Equal-area plots of poles to bedding in the study area. Where the data are contoured, the Kamb (1959) method was used; contours are integral multiples of random concentration. Diamond symbol is the pole to the best-fit great circle through the data, found by extracting the eigenvectors of the orientation tensor (for example, Woodcock and Naylor, 1983). N is the number of measurements. F is the maximum eigenvalue of the inverse of the orientation tensor, divided by the sum of the eigenvalues; F ranges from 0.33 to 1, and is an estimate of the fraction of the variation of the measurements that is explained by rotation around the best-fit axis.

Relationship between the McKnight and Timber Butte thrusts

North of the intersection of the Timber Butte and McKnight thrusts on the north flank of Timber Butte, it appears to be the Timber Butte thrust that continues northward across McKnight Canyon. On the south wall of McKnight Canyon, the strike of hanging-wall bedding is generally parallel to this thrust. South of the intersection, hanging-wall bedding bends into parallellism with the Timber Butte thrust, defining a syncline that plunges 47° toward S55W (Fig. 2, W½,Sec.33; Fig. 4g). This syncline appears to be a fault-bend fold (Suppe, 1983), that is, a fold formed by

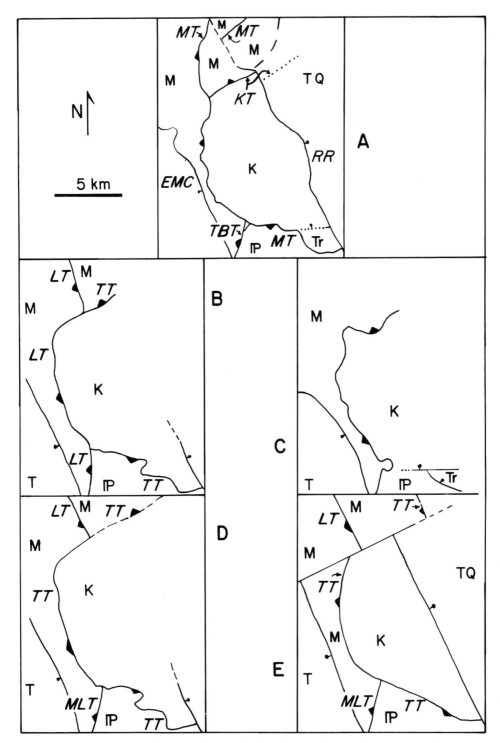

Figure 5. Alternate interpretations of the intersecting faults in the Kelmbeck Canyon–McKnight Canyon area: A, this study; B, Kupsch (1950); C, Lowell and Klepper (1953); D, Scholten and others (1955); E. Scholten (1960). Abbreviations: M = Mississippian limestones; P = Quadrant Sandstone; Tr = Thaynes Formation; K = Beaverhead Group; T = Tertiary rocks; TQ = Tertiary and Quaternary basin fill; MT = McKnight thrust; KT = Kelmbeck thrust; EMC = East Muddy Creek fault; TBT = Timber Butte thrust; LT = Limekiln thrust; TT = Tendoy thrust; MLT = Medicine Lodge thrust.

bending of the fault block as it rode over a nonplanar fault surface. Specifically, the Lombard Limestone was folded at the base of a northeast-trending footwall ramp of the Timber Butte thrust through the Quadrant Sandstone (Fig. 3, section C-C′; compare Suppe, 1983, Fig. 3).

Three possible interpretive models for this geometry can be considered:

1. South of the junction, the McKnight thrust may carry the Timber Butte thrust "piggy-back" in its hanging wall. North of the junction, the McKnight thrust has reactivated a hanging-wall flat within the Lombard Limestone along the Timber Butte thrust. In this case, the Timber Butte thrust is older than the McKnight thrust, and the two need not be kinematically related.

2. The Timber Butte and McKnight thrusts might be part of a single thrust system. The two thrusts on Timber Butte would be interpreted as branch lines from a single basal thrust exposed in McKnight Canyon. In this case, the two thrusts would have moved at nearly the same time, but the upper branch would probably be the older.

3. The thrust north of the junction of the two thrusts may be strictly the Timber Butte thrust, which has truncated the McKnight thrust beneath it. This would require the Timber Butte thrust to be the younger fault.

The first model is favored for three reasons, which are discussed further below: (a) it best explains the steep dip of the Timber Butte thrust, (b) it accommodates the large angle between the two thrusts on Timber Butte, and (c) it best explains the horse of Lombard Limestone at the intersection of the thrusts.

The thrust north of the junction lies above a footwall ramp. If the Timber Butte thrust is younger than the McKnight thrust (model 3 above), then this ramp simply steepens upward (passing southward) where it crosses the older McKnight thrust and intersects the Quadrant Sandstone. However, unless the entire range has been rotated toward the west since thrusting, this model requires the Timber Butte thrust to have been emplaced with its present 70° dip. This is improbably steep for a thrust ramp; if ramps form by shear failure at the leading edge of a detached sheet (for example, see Bombolakis, 1986), they should be initiated with dips of 30° or less. Actual observations worldwide support this prediction (Boyer and Elliot, 1982; Suppe, 1983; and many others). There are no data to suggest that any large rotation of the entire range has occurred. On these grounds alone, model 3 seems unlikely.

The steep dip of the Timber Butte thrust is explained in models 1 and 2 as a result of rotation of the thrust after it was no longer active. This would be a result of fault-bend rotation like that described for the Timber Butte thrust ramp, but above the north-trending footwall ramp of the McKnight thrust. Thus, slip on the steep part of the Timber Butte thrust need not have occurred after dip on the older segment had increased to more than about 35° to 45°. Passive rotation of inactive thrusts to steep dips is common in imbricate thrust stacks (Boyer and Elliot, 1982).

The large angle between the Timber Butte and McKnight thrusts seems excessive for two kinematically related strands of the same thrust. This favors model 1, in which the thrusts are not kinematically related, but the data are not compelling in this regard.

Models 1 and 2 also better explain the geometry of the horse of Lombard Limestone at the thrust intersection. The McKnight thrust east of the junction does not involve rocks as old as Mississippian; therefore, in model 3, the horse would have to have been emplaced along the later Timber Butte thrust. This requires the horse to have been wedged into the footwall, coincidentally where the Timber Butte thrust joins the McKnight thrust. By contrast, in models 1 and 2, the horse reached its position between the Lombard Limestone and Quadrant Sandstone during movement of the Timber Butte thrust; then the horse and the overlying Timber Butte thrust were carried along the McKnight thrust to their present position.

Relationship of the McKnight and Kelmbeck thrusts

Our thrust nomenclature for this area (Fig. 5a) differs from previous publications. For the sake of clarity, we briefly review previous interpretations and names. Kupsch (1950) mapped the

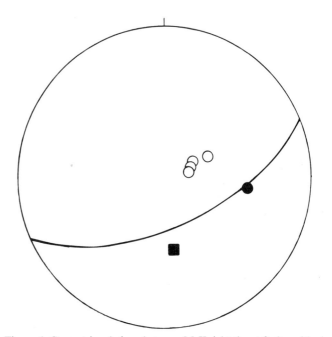

Figure 6. Geometric relations between McKnight thrust fault and bedding in its hanging wall and footwall. Open circles indicate poles to the McKnight thrust between Kelmbeck and McKnight Canyons, determined by three-point solution. Filled square indicates mean pole to 126 bedding measurements in footwall of the McKnight thrust between Kelmbeck and McKnight Canyons. Significance of this mean pole is quantified using the strength parameter C defined by Woodcock and Naylor (1983). In this case, C = 2.2, which indicates significance at the 99 percent confidence level (see Woodcock and Naylor, 1983, Table 1). Great circle and dot indicate best-fit girdle and mode of 89 poles to bedding in the hanging wall of the McKnight thrust. Hanging-wall bedding data are rather scattered (C = 1.0, which indicates a weak preferred orientation). However, the preferred orientation is significant at the 99 percent confidence level (C = 0.48 is the cutting value).

western half of what we call the Kelmbeck thrust as part of the Limekiln thrust, and the remaining eastern part as the Tendoy thrust emerging from beneath the Limekiln thrust (Fig. 5b). Later workers interpreted the entire Kelmbeck thrust as part of the Tendoy thrust (Fig. 5c,d; Lowell and Klepper, 1953; Scholten and others, 1955), or as a high-angle fault that cuts the Tendoy thrust (Fig. 5e; Scholten, 1960; Ryder and Scholten, 1973).

As described in previous sections, the northeast-trending Kelmbeck thrust is parallel to upper and lower plate bedding, and probably is an upper flat. This implies that, after emplacement at a shallow dip, the thrust and its footwall and hanging wall were tilted to the present 40° northwest dip by rotation about a northeast-trending axis. This tilting may relate to northeast-trending folds farther south in the Tendoy Range, which Scholten and others (1955) and Perry and others (this volume) have interpreted as older than the Tendoy thrust. The tilt could also reflect rotation above blind thrusts suspected to be present in the subsurface beneath Red Rock Basin (Perry and others, 1983); in fact, the two are not mutually exclusive.

South of Kelmbeck Canyon, the McKnight thrust dips to the southwest and truncates the northwest-dipping panel beneath the Kelmbeck thrust at a high angle (Figs. 2, 6). This geometry permits two alternatives: either the McKnight is younger than and truncates the Kelmbeck thrust, or the McKnight is a steep ramp adjacent to the flat of the Kelmbeck thrust. The latter seems unlikely. If the McKnight thrust is restored along with the Kelmbeck thrust to the Kelmbeck's unrotated state, the McKnight thrust assumes a steep southward dip. The overlying Timber Butte thrust is further steepened, as is the plunge of the fault-bend syncline above it. In short, the geometric problems associated with the McKnight and Timber Butte thrusts are exacerbated by this interpretation.

The north-trending fault zone exposed on the north wall of Kelmbeck Canyon therefore appears to be a more logical choice for the northward continuation of the McKnight thrust, leading to our view that the McKnight thrust cuts off the top of the Kelmbeck thrust. (Section B-B′ in Fig. 3 appears to show the McKnight thrust cutting off the Kelmbeck thrust from behind; this is because the cross section was drawn parallel to the strike of the Kelmbeck thrust. In fact, this is simply a different view of the same cutoff line shown in section A-A′; such problems emphasize the fundamentally three-dimensional nature of the structure in this area.) The abrupt loss of stratigraphic throw across the McKnight thrust is a result of it cutting across the older Kelmbeck thrust. This relationship is corroborated by relations of the presumably correlative Tendoy thrust farther south, which truncates preexisting northeast-trending structures (Fig. 1; Scholten and others, 1955; Hammons, 1981; Perry, 1982; Perry and others, this volume).

Relationships of the Timber Butte and Kelmbeck thrusts

To the south of the study area, Klecker (1980) mapped short thrust segments along the east side of Muddy Creek Basin.

Klecker assigned the hanging-wall rocks of these fault segments to the Middle Canyon Formation, correlating these fault segments and the Timber Butte thrust of the present study with the Medicine Lodge thrust. We support the correlation of the thrust segments with the Timber Butte thrust, but not their correlation with the Medicine Lodge. Much of the limestone above these thrust segments closely resembles the Lombard Limestone in the study area, and is included in the Four Eyes Canyon sheet by Perry and others (this volume).

Both the Timber Butte and Kelmbeck thrusts are northeast-striking thrusts interpreted to be older than the McKnight thrust. It is possible that the two thrusts are the same, offset by movement on the McKnight thrust. The hanging wall is composed of Lombard Limestone in both cases; both are considered part of the Four Eyes Canyon thrust system by Perry and others (this volume). However, the rock unit immediately beneath each of the thrusts differs greatly, so that correlation of the thrusts would require a major footwall structure between them.

SUMMARY

1. In latest Cretaceous time, the Kelmbeck and Timber Butte thrusts emplaced transitional-facies upper Paleozoic rocks upon a footwall ranging from Pennsylvanian Quadrant Sandstone to Upper Cretaceous (upper Campanian or Maastrichtian) Beaverhead Group conglomerate. The slip direction of these faults is not well constrained in the study area, although the Timber Butte thrust must have had a significant reverse component up a ramp that strikes N30E. While this is the earliest structural phase distinguished in the area, age constraints from the Beaverhead clearly indicate that these thrusts are younger than the principal period of shortening that formed the Blacktail-Snowcrest uplift.

2. The Kelmbeck thrust and its footwall of Beaverhead Group rocks were tilted to the northwest. This deformation is most likely related to other northeast-trending structures in the Tendoy Range, and probably reflects late northwest-southeast shortening along the Blacktail-Snowcrest trend.

3. The McKnight thrust was emplaced, cutting across and locally reactivating older structures. Folding of Mississippian limestones in the hanging wall and footwall Beaverhead Group around north- to northwest-plunging axes suggests that the thrust was emplaced to the east or northeast. The Tendoy-McKnight thrust(s) commonly are not stratigraphically controlled, presumably because earlier deformation had distorted potential stratigraphic detachment horizons. The presence of basement in higher thrust sheets (for example, DuBois, 1982) may imply that the Tendoy thrust also involves basement at depth.

Structures in the study area reflect two contrasting styles of Laramide crustal shortening that overlapped in time and space in the Tendoy Range. The earlier Kelmbeck and Timber Butte thrusts are of the Cordilleran type, and may represent the earliest phase of thin-skinned thrusts in the area. By analogy with adjacent areas, the tilting of the Kelmbeck thrust may reflect ongoing activity along northeast-trending foreland-style thrusts of the Snowcrest system during development of the thin-skinned thrust belt. These older structures caused the McKnight, Tendoy, and related thrusts to depart from stratigraphic control, and resulted in the complex pattern of intersecting faults and folds within the Tendoy Range.

ACKNOWLEDGMENTS

The ideas presented here benefited from discussions with M. J. Bartholomew, D. P. DuBois, W. J. Perry, Jr., B. Skipp, and W. J. Sando, among others. Bill Perry was particularly generous with unpublished data and hypotheses. Reviews of the manuscript by Bartholomew, Perry, and two anonymous reviewers led to substantial improvement in both content and presentation. Financial support for fieldwork to N.S.W. was provided by grants from the American Association of Petroleum Geologists, the Geological Society of America, the Society of Sigma Xi, and the Martin Trust Fund of the University of North Carolina. The U.S. Geological Survey provided field equipment and supplies. Assistance from the University Research Council of the University of North Carolina (to J.M.B.) is acknowledged.

REFERENCES CITED

Armin, R. A., and Mayer, L., 1983, Subsidence analysis of the Cordilleran miogeocline: Geology, v. 11, p. 702–705.

Bombolakis, E. G., 1986, Thrust-fault mechanics and origin of a frontal ramp: Journal of Structural Geology, v. 8, p. 281–290.

Boyer, S. E., and Elliot, D., 1982, Thrust systems: American Association of Petroleum Geologists Bulletin, v. 66, p. 1196–1230.

Burchfiel, B. C., and Davis, G. A., 1975, Nature and controls of Cordilleran orogenesis, western United States; Extensions of an earlier synthesis: American Journal of Science, v. 275-A, p. 363–396.

DuBois, D. P., 1983, Tectonic framework of basement thrust terrane, northern Tendoy Range, southwest Montana, *in* Powers, R. B., ed., Geologic studies of the Cordilleran thrust belt, 1982: Denver, Colorado, Rocky Mountain Association of Geologists, p. 145–158.

Dunlap, D. G., 1982, Tertiary geology of the Muddy Creek basin, Beaverhead County, Montana [M.S. thesis]: Missoula, University of Montana, 133 p.

Hammons, P. M., 1981, Structural observations along the southern trace of the Tendoy fault, southern Beaverhead County, Montana, *in* Tucker, T. E., ed., Southwestern Montana: Montana Geological Society Field Conference and Symposium Guidebook, p. 253–260.

Huh, O. K., 1967, The Mississippian system across the Wasatch line, east-central Idaho, extreme southwestern Montana, *in* Henderson, L. B., ed., Centennial Basin of southwestern Montana: Montana Geological Society 18th Annual Field Conference Guidebook, p. 31–62.

Kamb, W. B., 1959, Theory of preferred orientation developed by crystals under stress: Journal of Geology, v. 67, p. 153–170.

Klecker, R. A., 1980, Stratigraphy and structure of the Dixon Mountain–Little Water Canyon area, Beaverhead County, Montana [M.S. thesis]: Corvallis, Oregon State University, 233 p.

Kupsch, W. O., 1950, Geology of the Tendoy-Beaverhead area, Beaverhead County, Montana [Ph.D. thesis]: Ann Arbor, University of Michigan, 251 p.

Lowell, W. R., and Klepper, M. R., 1953, Beaverhead Formation, a Laramide deposit in Beaverhead County, Montana: Geological Society of America Bulletin, v. 64, p. 235–243.

Nichols, D. J., Perry, W. J., Jr., and Haley, J. C., 1985, Reinterpretation of the palynology and age of Laramide syntectonic deposits, southwestern Montana, and revision of the Beaverhead Group: Geology, v 13, p. 149–153.

Perry, W. J., Jr., 1982, The thrust belt in the Lima-Dell, Montana, area, *in* Beaver, P., ed., The overthrust province in the vicinity of Dillon, Montana, and how this structural framework has influenced mineral and energy resources accumulation: Tobacco Root Geological Society 7th Annual Field Conference Guidebook, p. 69–78.

Perry, W. J., Jr., and Kulik, D. M., 1983, Laramide foreland thrust faulting in southwestern Montana: Geological Society of America Abstracts with Programs, v. 67, p. 532–533.

Perry, W. J., Jr., and Sando, W. J., 1983, Sequence of deformation of Cordilleran thrust belt in Lima, Montana region, *in* Powers, R. B., ed., Geologic studies of the Cordilleran thrust belt, 1982: Denver, Colorado, Rocky Mountain Association of Geologists, p. 137–144.

Perry, W. J., Jr., Wardlaw, B. R., Bostick, N. H., and Maughan, E. K., 1983, Structure, burial history, and petroleum potential of frontal thrust belt and adjacent foreland, southwest Montana: American Association of Petroleum Geologists Bulletin, v. 67, p. 725–743.

Perry, W. J., Jr., Sando, W. J., and Sandberg, C. A., 1985, Structural geometry of newly defined Blacktail salient of Montana thrust belt: American Association of Petroleum Geologists, v. 69, p. 858–859.

Rose, P. R., 1976, Mississippian carbonate shelf margins, western United States: U.S. Geological Survey Journal of Research, v. 4, p. 449–466.

Ruppel, E. T., 1978, Medicine Lodge thrust system, east-central Idaho and southwest Montana: U.S. Geological Survey Professional Paper 1031, 23 p.

Ryder, R. T., 1967, Lithosomes in the Beaverhead Formation, Montana-Idaho; A preliminary report: Montana Geological Society 18th Annual Field Conference Guidebook, p. 63–70.

Ryder, R. T., and Scholten, R., 1973, Syntectonic conglomerates in southwestern Montana; Their nature, origin, and tectonic significance: Geological Society of America Bulletin, v. 84, p. 773–796.

Sandberg, C. A., Gutschick, R. C., Johnson, J. G., Poole, F. G., and Sando, W. J., 1983, Middle Devonian to Late Mississippian geologic history of the overthrust belt region, western United States, *in* Powers, R. B., ed., Geologic studies of the Cordilleran thrust belt, 1982: Denver, Colorado, Rocky Mountain Association of Geologists, p. 691–719.

Sando, W. J., Sandberg, C. A., and Perry, W. J., Jr., 1985, Revision of Mississippian stratigraphy: U.S. Geological Survey Bulletin 1656A, 10 p.

Scholten, R., 1960, Sedimentation and tectonism in the thrust belt of southwestern Montana and east-central Idaho, *in* McGookey, D. P., and Miller, D. N., Jr., ed., Overthrust belt of southwestern Wyoming and adjacent areas: Wyoming Geological Association, p. 73–83.

—— , 1983, Continental subduction in the northern U.S. Rockies; A model for back-arc thrusting in the western Cordillera, *in* Powers, R. B., ed., Geologic studies of the Cordilleran thrust belt, 1982: Denver, Colorado, Rocky Mountain Association of Geologists, p. 123–136.

Scholten, R., Keenmon, K. A., and Kupsch, W. O., 1955, Geology of the Lima region, southwestern Montana and adjacent Idaho: Geological Society of America Bulletin, v. 66, p. 345–403.

Skipp, B., and Hait, M. H., Jr., 1977, Allochthons along the northeast margin of the Snake River Plain, Idaho, *in* Heisey, E. L., Lawson, D. E., Norwood, E. R., Wach, P. H., and Hale, L. A., eds., Rocky Mountain thrust belt geology and resources: Wyoming Geological Association 29th Annual Field Conference Guidebook, p. 499–515.

Suppe, J., 1983, Geometry and kinematics of fault-bend folding: American Journal of Science, v. 283, p. 684–721.

Wardlaw, B. R., and Pecora, W. C., 1985, New Mississippian-Pennsylvanian stratigraphic units in southwest Montana and adjacent Idaho: U.S. Geological Survey Bulletin 1656B, 9 p.

Williams, N. S., 1984, Stratigraphy and structure of the east-central Tendoy Range, southwestern Montana [M.S. thesis]: Chapel Hill, University of North Carolina, 94 p.

Witte, H. C., 1965, Geology of the Limekiln Canyon and Four Eyes Canyon areas, southwesternmost Montana [M.S. thesis]: University Park, Pennsylvania State University, 85 p.

Woodcock, N. H., and Naylor, M. A., 1983, Randomness testing in three-dimensional orientation data: Journal of Structural Geology, v. 5, p. 539–548.

MANUSCRIPT ACCEPTED BY THE SOCIETY FEBRUARY 9, 1988

Geological Society of America
Memoir 171
1988

Paleomagnetic study of thrust sheet rotations in the Helena and Wyoming salients of the northern Rocky Mountains

Sarah Eldredge and Rob Van der Voo
Department of Geological Sciences, University of Michigan, Ann Arbor, Michigan 48109-1063

ABSTRACT

Paleomagnetic investigations throughout the overthrust belt in the Wyoming and Helena salients show that buttressing effects of the Rocky Mountain foreland have caused local rotations of thrust sheets along the margins of the salients. Two previous studies of Triassic, Upper Jurassic, and Lower Cretaceous rocks in the Wyoming-Idaho overthrust belt involved rocks from the Prospect, Bear, Darby, and Absaroka thrust sheets. These studies documented as much as 60° counterclockwise rotation in the northern edge, and as much as 30° clockwise rotation in the southeastern edge of the Wyoming salient. It has been suggested that these rotations were buttressing edge effects, since the rotations do not appear to have been transferred back into the interior of the Wyoming salient.

New work in the southern portion of the Helena salient in southwestern Montana has documented a similar situation. Here, samples from the Lower Cretaceous Kootenai Formation show a maximum of 54° clockwise rotation in the region of the McCarthy Mountain salient, 23° clockwise rotation within the southwest Montana transverse zone, and 35° clockwise and 30° counterclockwise rotations in the nose of the salient. These rotations vary greatly from site to site, suggesting that the thrust sheets were not deformed in a coherent fashion, but rather, they broke and rotated as individual pieces where the effects of buttressing against the Rocky Mountain foreland were the greatest.

INTRODUCTION

Although the overthrust belt of the northern Rocky Mountains remains roughly linear for thousands of kilometers, it shows some significant deviations from its north-south trend in Montana, Idaho, and Wyoming (Beutner, 1977). In the Helena salient of southwestern Montana, the trends of the thrust traces change from northwest to east-northeast (Figs. 1, 2), and back to north again in the smaller McCarthy Mountain salient in the region of the southwest Montana reentrant. The thrust traces disappear beneath the Snake River Plain volcanics near the Idaho-Montana border, and reappear again in the Wyoming salient. In the Wyoming salient, the thrust traces change direction abruptly from northwest to north (Fig. 1).

Determination of thrust sheet rotations, or the lack thereof, in anomalous sections of thrust belts such as these can be very useful for large-scale structural and tectonic interpretations. Paleomagnetic techniques can be used to quantify postulated horizontal thrust sheet rotations in these anomalous areas, and in doing so, the mechanism causing rotations may be better under-

stood. Before any rotations can be detected, it must be established that the age of magnetization predates deformation. By sampling rocks of similar age from a number of sites throughout the area of interest, the paleomagnetic declinations of the site means can be compared to each other and to a stable reference direction, either measured or calculated, to determine postdepositional rotation of thrust sheets. A certain amount of scatter in the data is inherent to any paleomagnetic study, and minor amounts of rotation are difficult to detect. Only declinations that differ significantly from the reference direction can truly be called rotated (Beck, 1980; Demarest, 1983; Schwartz and Van der Voo, 1983, 1984).

Many curved thrust belts have been the subject of paleomagnetic investigation, including the Sicilian-Calabrian and the Umbrian Arcs of Italy, the Jura Mountains, portions of the Appalachians, and the Wyoming salient of the western overthrust belt (Eldredge and others, 1985, and references therein). These studies have demonstrated the usefulness of paleomagnetism as a tool for the determination of horizontal rotations in thrust sheets.

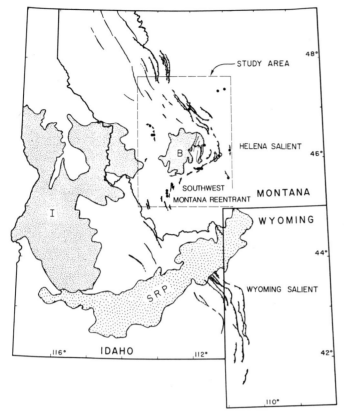

Figure 1. Map of the Northern Rocky Mountains, showing the fault traces of the overthrust belt. I = Idaho batholith, B = Boulder batholith, SRP = Snake River Plain volcanics. The dots indicate the locations of the sampling sites.

The present study of the Helena salient in Montana may be considered an extension of the earlier work done in the Wyoming salient. Grubbs and Van der Voo (1976) measured paleomagnetic directions in Triassic red beds from 15 sites throughout the Prospect, Bear, Darby, and Absaroka thrust sheets. Most sites are concentrated near the margin of the salient where the thrust sheets are buttressed against the ancestral Teton and Gros Ventre ranges to the north and the Game Hill Reverse Fault to the east. Their results (Table 1; Fig. 3) showed a clear 60° counterclockwise rotation relative to the stable foreland reference Triassic direction (site G) in the northern portion of the salient, and a few clockwise rotations up to 30° in the southeastern portion of the salient. These rotations are found in the easternmost Prospect thrust sheet, which is the youngest and lowermost thrust fault to reach the surface in the Wyoming salient. If the Prospect thrust sheet rotated as a unit, then it should have carried the previously faulted, overlying thrust sheets in a similar rotation. Schwartz and Van der Voo (1984) sampled seven sites in Upper Jurassic strata from the more westerly Darby and Absaroka thrust sheets (Table 2; Fig. 3) and found no systematic rotation of these thrust sheets. Thus, these workers have concluded that the rotations measured in the Prospect thrust sheet are simply buttressing edge effects that

were not transmitted back into the interior of the salient. The success of these two studies in determining the nature of thrust sheet motion in the well-mapped region of the Wyoming salient prompted the present work in the Helena salient of Montana. Thus, this chapter documents our work on the nature and extent of thrust sheet rotations along the frontal portions of the thrust belt in the Helena salient.

GEOLOGY OF THE HELENA SALIENT

Western Montana has had a complicated structural and depositional history since the formation of the Belt Basin in the Proterozoic. An east-trending embayment, the Helena embayment, of the Belt Basin (Fig. 2) underlies the region now known as the Helena salient (Harrison and others, 1974). North and east of the salient is the disturbed belt, where the thrusts trend north-northwest and are very highly imbricated (Mudge, 1970; Woodward, 1981). The thrusting advanced from west to east approximately 72 to 56 Ma (Hoffman and others, 1976). The salient itself is bounded on the north by the west-northwest-trending Lewis and Clark line. These faults are thought to be tear thrusts with some left-lateral component (Smith, 1965; Smeedes and Schmidt, 1979; Woodward, 1981; Birkholz, 1967). The southwest Montana transverse zone, also known as the Perry line, is a 120-km-long, east-trending fault zone that defines the southern boundary of the Helena salient (Schmidt and O'Neill, 1983). The faults of this transverse zone dip to the north-northwest, the motion along them is right-lateral and reverse, and a net slip of 20 to 50 km has been calculated (Schmidt and O'Neill, 1983; Meyers, 1981). The transverse zone has been interpreted as a lateral ramp over a Proterozoic normal fault step (Schmidt and Garihan, 1986). There is close interaction along this zone between the thrust structures of the salient and the northwest-trending structures (faults) in the Precambrian crystalline rocks that make up the Rocky Mountain foreland. These northwest-trending faults in the foreland have been present since the Proterozoic, and were reactivated during the Laramide orogeny before thrusting took place. Movement along these foreland faults was oblique and left-reverse (Schmidt and O'Neill, 1983).

The nose of the Helena salient lies between the Lewis and Clark line and the transverse zone, and is characterized by west-dipping, imbricated thrusts. The thrust traces change direction from northwest-trending in the north to northeast-trending in the south. The Lombard thrust (Fig. 2) is a major thrust that underlies the Elkhorn plate (Ruppel and others, 1981) in the central portion of the salient. Motion along the thrust faults here is largely dip slip, and is of a smaller magnitude than farther west in the thrust belt (Woodward, 1981).

There are three batholiths and numerous satellite plutons in the overthrust belt of western Montana. The largest of these is the Idaho batholith (Fig. 2), which is intruded well to the west of the Helena salient. The Boulder batholith was intruded synthrusting (78 to 68 Ma) in the center of the salient (Tilling and others, 1968). The Sapphire plate is a major thrust plate or "tectonic

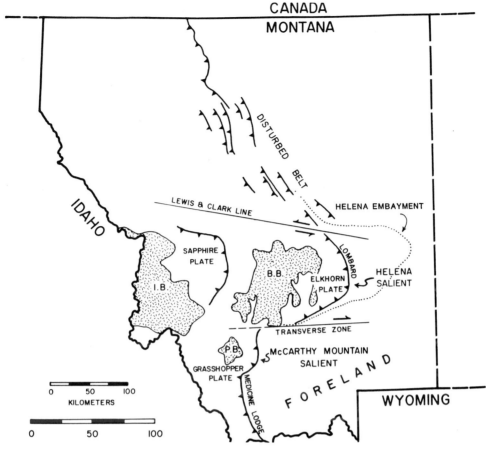

Figure 2. Schematic map of western Montana showing the major structural and geological features. I.B. = Idaho batholith, B.B. = Boulder batholith, P.B. = Pioneer batholith. The dotted line indicates the approximate margin of the Helena embayment of the Belt basin. Dashed line marks eastern edge of the study area.

TABLE 1. PALEOMAGNETIC RESULTS FROM TRIASSIC ROCKS IN THE WYOMING SALIENT*

Site	Age	Site Location	N/N_0	k	α_{95}	Characteristic Direction D/I
A	L.Tr.	43°18'N111°14'W	6/7	56	9.0	341.7/+22.8
B	L.Tr.	43°13'N110°36'W	7/7	149	5.0	9.2/+23.1
C	L.Tr.	42°51'N110°40"W	8/11	18	13.5	162.8/-11.0
D	L.Tr.	43°15'N110°47'W	5/5	126	6.8	145.9/-16.2
E	L.Tr.	43°15'N110°49'W	6/8	139	5.7	320.9/+13.4
F	L.Tr.	43°22'N110°45'W	11/11	55	6.2	336.0/+19.0
G	L.Tr.	43°38'N110°33'W	28/28	34	4.8	158.0/-11.4
H	L.Tr.	43°16'N110°31'W	8/8	19	12.9	193.4/-8.1
I	L.Tr.	43°08'N110°34'W	7/10	40	9.6	157.4/-17.3
J	E.Tr.	43°20'N110°35'W	10/10	37	8.1	154.7/-25.0
K	E.Tr.	43°22'N110°46'W	8/10	28	10.6	156.6/-8.4
S	L.Tr.	43°27'N110°57'W	6/6	18	16.2	268.0/+29.9
T	L.Tr.	43°31'N111°00'W	10/11	48	70	111.3/-17.4
V	L.Tr.	43°33'N111°18'W	12/12	64	5.5	316.8/+22.8
X	L.Tr.	43°24'N110°41'W	9/10	15	13.8	131.0/-10.6

*k = Fisher precision parameter. α_{95} = half-angle of 95 percent confidence cone;
N/N_0 = number of samples used in site mean calculations vs. number of analyzed samples;
D/I indicates declination and inclination. From Grubbs and Van der Voo, 1976.

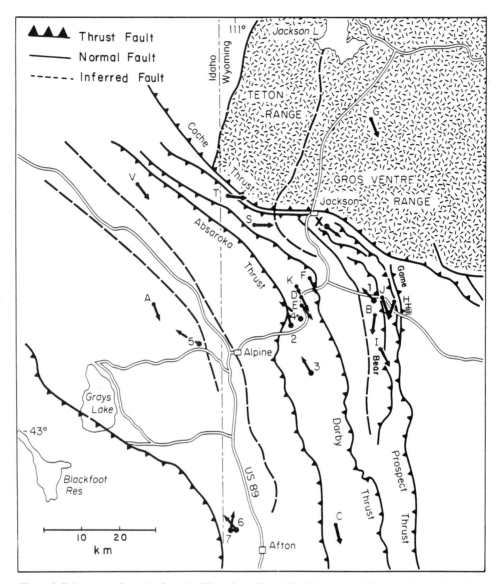

Figure 3. Paleomagnetic results from the Wyoming salient (after Schwartz and Van der Voo, 1984). The lettered sites are Triassic sampling localities (Grubbs and Van der Voo, 1976); the numbered sites are Jurassic sampling localities (Schwartz and Van der Voo, 1984). The arrows are mean site declinations; the lettered sites are reversed relative to the numbered sites. The stippled region is the ancestral Teton–Gros Ventre block. Site G is the Triassic reference site in the stable foreland. A declination of 330° (not shown) was used as a reference for the Jurassic sites. This direction was derived from the Upper Morrison pole (Steiner and Helsley, 1975).

block" between the Idaho and Boulder batholiths. The emplacement of the Boulder batholith and its satellite plutons may be related to the motion of the Sapphire thrust plate (Hyndman and others, 1975). The third and smallest major batholith is the Pioneer batholith, which is intruded into the Grasshopper plate (Ruppel and others, 1981) southwest of the transverse zone in the McCarthy Mountain salient (Fig. 2). This smaller salient is characterized by imbricated west-dipping thrusts that have been buttressed against the syntectonically rising foreland just to the east (Schmidt and others, this volume). The frontal thrusts in the southwest Montana reentrant, south of the Pioneer batholith (Fig.

2), dip to the west and trend south until they disappear beneath the Snake River Plain in Idaho.

MODELS

Paleomagnetic data may be used to test kinematic models of thrust sheet emplacement, particularly those models that involve rotation of thrust sheets. At least three kinematic models may be applied to the general geometry of the Helena salient. The simplest model for development of the curved thrust front involves only differential translation along strike, with no rotations (Fig.

4-I). If the Helena salient had such a deformational history, then there should be several east-west–trending strike-slip faults and no rotations found within the salient.

The second model predicts the greatest amount of rotation in the regions where the thrust belt deviates most from the regional trend (Fig. 4, II). In the Helena salient this would be near the transverse zone and the Lewis and Clark line. In this scenario, the thrust sheets would act in a coherent fashion, wrapping around the foreland, and there would be a one-to-one correlation between the change in trend of the thrust traces and the deviations in paleomagnetic declinations from the reference direction (Beutner, 1977; Eldredge and others, 1985). If a thrust sheet acts coherently without breaking into smaller pieces, then the rotations near the edge of the salient would be transmitted back into the interior of the salient.

The third model requires a different mechanism than the first and second, and the role of the foreland becomes more important. The maximum rotations are predicted where the buttressing effect of the foreland is the greatest (Figure 4, III). In southwestern Montana, this would be in the region of the McCarthy Mountain salient and in the nose of the Helena salient. Where there is little impedance to the west-to-east translation of the thrust sheets, such as near the transverse zone and the Lewis and Clark line, the rocks would move with little or no rotation. Where the thrust sheets impinge on the uplifted foreland, they would not act coherently, but would break apart and have local rotations that are not transmitted back into the interior of the salient.

STRATIGRAPHY AND SAMPLING

The study area (Fig. 1) includes a very thick section of sedimentary rocks beginning with the Proterozoic Beltian sediments. These sediments form a sequence of rocks about 7,000 m thick (Nelson, 1963), which are now found at the surface in much of the northern portion of the study area. The Precambrian rocks are overlain by a thick Paleozoic sequence dominated by carbonates, followed by a predominantly clastic Mesozoic section that is capped by the Upper Cretaceous Elkhorn Mountain volcanics.

There are four formations in southwestern Montana that have significant red-bed sequences: the Mississippian Big Snowy, Pennsylvanian Amsden, Jurassic Morrison, and Cretaceous Kootenai Formations. The Lower Cretaceous Kootenai proved to be the only formation suitable for this investigation. The fact that only a relatively short period of time elapsed between the Early Cretaceous deposition and Late Cretaceous and Paleocene folding and thrusting of the Kootenai Formation is quite useful. If it can be proved that the magnetization in the rocks predates deformation, then the age of magnetization is closely constrained, even if it is diagenetic (chemical), and not detrital, in origin.

The Kootenai is a nonmarine deposit (DeCelles, 1984; Suttner, 1969; James, 1977) consisting of conglomerate, coarse sand, silt, mud, and limestone (Fig. 5). It varies from 100 to 420 m in

TABLE 2. PALEOMAGNETIC RESULTS FROM THE UPPER JURASSIC STUMP FORMATION IN THE WYOMING SALIENT*

Site	N/N$_0$	k	α_{95}	Characteristic Direction D/I Before Tilt Correction	After Tilt Correction
1	8/9	43	9	278/11	310/56
2	4/7	—	—	270/15	343/60
3	8/8	16	14	354/43	329/47
4	9/9	105	5	10/47	310/57
5	6/8	22	13	334/40	298/61
6	8/9	168	4	32/49	318/73
7	9/9	32	9	276/31	7/63

*k = Fisher precision parameter. α_{95} = half-angle of 95 percent confidence cone; N/N$_0$ = number of samples used in site mean calculations vs. number of analyzed samples; D/I indicates declination and inclination. From Schwartz and Van der Voo, 1984.

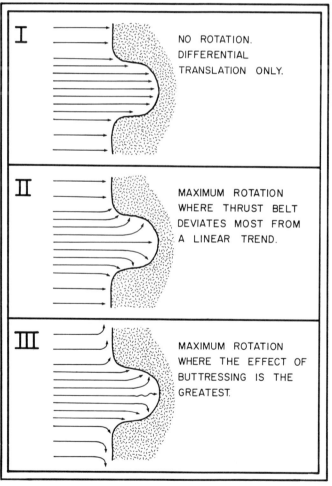

Figure 4. Three possible models of thrust sheet movement in the Helena salient of Montana. The arrows represent the thrust sheet transportation direction from west to east. The stippled area is the Rocky Mountain foreland. See text for further explanation.

thickness in the study area. Between the two sandstone beds (see Fig. 5), and above the second sand, there are thick sequences of red muds, silts, fine sands, and some nodular limestones from levee and overbank deposits. Paleomagnetic sampling was restricted to the fine-grained red horizons.

Sampling was carried out in the field with a hand-held drill, with a minimum of 9 and a maximum of 17 cores drilled per site. Hand samples were taken from a few sites and drilled later in the laboratory. Approximately 400 cores from 23 sites were drilled in the Kootenai. The 23 sites were chosen first by general locality, and then specifically by availability of lithified redbeds. These lithified outcrops were very rare in the northern portion of the Helena salient, so sampling concentrated in the region of the nose of the salient, the transverse zone, and the McCarthy Mountain salient. Two sites were drilled east of the thrust belt in the northeast part of the study area (Fig. 1) in the nearly horizontal undeformed rocks of the stable foreland. These sites serve as the reference against which the possibly rotated sites within the overthrust belt were compared.

To maximize the chances that secular variation is averaged out in our site-mean directions, individually oriented samples were taken from different beds, distributed over a minimum of 2 m and a maximum of 8 m per site.

PALEOMAGNETIC TECHNIQUES

Alternating field treatments of up to 100 mT were unsuccessful in removing the magnetization of the Kootenai samples. The paleomagnetic directions for 225 samples were determined after thermal demagnetization. Of these 225 individual samples, 159 were used in the final evaluation (Table 3). The directions of 66 samples were discarded because their magnetic behavior was unstable during demagnetization and it was impossible to determine magnetic directions from them. Weathering of the rocks appears to play a role with many, if not all, of these unstable samples. All samples were treated with a minimum of 7 and a maximum of 20 demagnetization steps. The sample directions and intensities were measured with a cryogenic magnetometer. For most samples the magnetizations were unblocked continuously in treatments of as much as 690°C, implying that hematite is the predominant magnetic carrier. Hematite can also be seen in thin section (Suttner, 1969), and appears to be a late stage modification (DeCelles, 1984) of ferrous precursors. Characteristic directions from individual samples were determined using vector subtraction, and the site means were calculated by averaging the sample directions within a single site. Fisher statistical parameters, k and α^{95}, were calculated for every site (Table 3).

PALEOMAGNETIC RESULTS

The calculated expected Early Cretaceous direction (D/I = 327°/67°) for southwestern Montana (Van Alstine and de Boer, 1978) is quite similar to the present-day axial dipole field (D/I = 360°/64°), as shown in Figure 6. The Kootenai reference direc-

LOWER CRETACEOUS KOOTENAI FORMATION

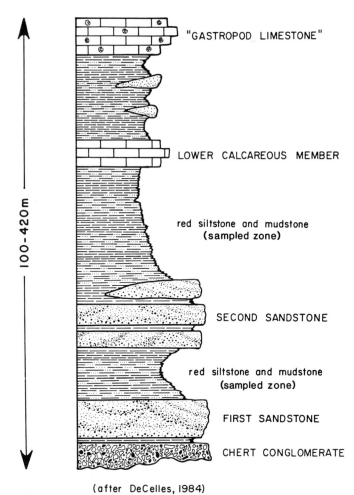

(after DeCelles, 1984)

Figure 5. Generalized stratigraphic section of the Lower Cretaceous Kootenai Formation in Montana (after DeCelles, 1984). The Kootenai thins from west to east.

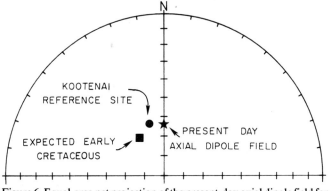

Figure 6. Equal-area net projection of the present-day axial dipole field for western Montana, the expected Early Cretaceous direction for western Montana (calculated from Van Alstine and de Boer, 1978), and the Kootenai reference site, which is the average of two sites (5 and 6) from the stable foreland near Great Falls, Montana.

**TABLE 3. PALEOMAGNETIC RESULTS FROM THE LOWER CRETACEOUS
KOOTENAI FORMATION IN MONTANA**

Site	N/N$_0$	k	α_{95}	Declination Deviation*		Characteristic Direction D/I	
				a	b	Before Tilt Correction	After Tilt Correction
1	10/10	61	6.2	17	34	230/82	1/61
2	9/11	37	8.6	20	37	288/64	4/60
3	8/9	119	5.1	1	18	6/71	345/57
2 and 3[†]	17/20	21/46	8/5.3	11	28	318/72	355/58
4	11/11	58	6.0	-27‡	-10	11/43	317/52
5[§]	11/11	64	5.7	—	25	348/61	352/61
6[§]	12/12	74	5.1	—	10	333/69	337/64
5 and 6[§]	23/23	61	3.9	—	17	335/65	344/63
7	10/10	26	9.7	22	39	262/-13	6/63
8	10/10	39	7.9	13	30	35/47	357/42
9	9/9	66	6.4	10	27	256/-7	354/55
7, 8, and 9[†]	29/29	2/26	27/5	15	32	278/16	359/53
10	12/12	122	4.0	35‡	52	329/67	19/76
11	(remagnetized)						
12	8/9	30	10.2	24‡	41	6/43	8/75
13	10/10	24	10.1	-29‡	-12	8/57	315/56
14, 15, and 16	(random directions)						
17	10/10	68	5.9	39‡	56	93/49	23/42
18	5/2	135	6.6	80	97	28/37	64/20
19	8/10	47	8.2	54‡	71	321/26	38/51
20	10/2	264	3.0	- 4	13	29/63	340/39
21	10/10	280	2.9	29‡	46	83/20	13/69.3
22	(random directions)						
23	10/12	49	6.9	23‡	40	159/61	7/56

Table headings:
k = Fisher precision parameter; α_{95} = half-angle of 95 percent confidence cone;
N/N$_0$ = number of samples used in site mean calculations vs. number of analyzed samples
(sides 18 and 20 are exceptions); D/I indicates declination and inclination; Positive
declination deviations are in a clockwise sense from the reference direction, negative
declinations are in a counterclockwise sense.

*Declination deviation (a) relative to stable foreland sites 5 and 6 reference direction (D/I =
344/63); these numbers are used in the text, and (b) relative to the calculated expected Early
Cretaceous direction (D/I = 327/67) of Van Alstine and De Boer (1978). Too few samples (2 for
each site) to be considered statistically significant (site 18 consists of 5 specimens drilled
from two hand samples, and site 20 consists of 10 specimens from two hand samples).

[†]Sites that are averaged together. The two fold tests show k and α_{95} before and after tilt
correction.

[‡]Indicates statistically significant deviation from the stable foreland reference direction
(D/I = 344/63).

[§]Sites 5 and 6 from the stable foreland are averaged together to give a reference direction
(D/I = 344/63) against which other sites are compared.

tion (D/I = 344°/63°) was averaged from sites 5 and 6 in the stable foreland (Fig. 1, Table 3), and falls between the calculated Cretaceous direction and the present-day field. The similarity in these directions, which are typically of normal polarity and north-northwesterly in declination, necessitated careful work in the interpretation of magnetic results, and increased the importance of a positive fold test to rule out the possibility of recent remagnetizations. A fold test is a statistical test that compares magnetic directions before and after tilt correction (McElhinny, 1964; Collinson, 1983). If the magnetic directions scatter before tilt correction, and closely cluster after tilt correction, then the fold test is positive, indicating that the age of the magnetization predates deformation. It is crucial to have predeformational magnetization in the rocks in order to quantify rotations.

Using directions obtained through demagnetization analysis (described below), we have performed three fold tests in the study area, one on a regional and two on a local scale. The regional fold test (Fig. 7) is a compilation of the 16 site means with precision parameters (α^{95}) of 10° or less (Table 3) that have sample sizes of N ≥ 8. The two reference sites, 5 and 6, are averaged and included as a triangle (Fig. 7). Comparing the site means before and after tilt correction, the resulting k2 to k1 ratio is 7.9, giving a positive regional fold test that is significant at the 99 percent confidence level (Collinson, 1983). This regional test does include possibly rotated sites, and is thus subject to second-order perturbations of the fold test. In addition to this regional fold test, there are two local fold tests (Fig. 8): the first is from sites 7, 8, and 9, near Drummond in the Sapphire plate in the northwestern por-

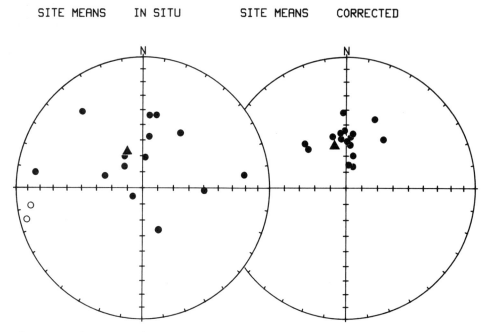

Figure 7. Equal-area net projection of the regional fold test for 16 sites from the Kootenai Formation, shown before, and after, tilt correction. The closed circles are lower hemisphere projections and the open circles are upper hemisphere projections. The triangle is the stable foreland Kootenai reference direction (sites 5 and 6 averaged). Notice that the site means cluster much better after tilt correction, giving a positive fold test significant at the 99 percent confidence level (Collinson, 1983), suggesting that the magnetization in the rocks predated deformation.

tion of the study area, and the second is from sites 2 and 3, in the region between the McCarthy Mountain salient and the transverse zone (Table 3). The first local test has a k ratio of 13.2, based on specimen directions, and is significant at the 99 percent confidence level. The second test has a ratio of 2.24 and is significant at the 95 percent confidence level. These three positive tests indicate that the magnetization in the Kootenai predates the Late Cretaceous to Paleocene deformation.

The Kootenai redbeds behave well during demagnetization, as can be seen in the orthogonal demagnetization diagrams in Figure 9. Nearly all samples were of normal polarity. The first two examples (Fig. 9a) are representative of the bulk of the collection, being univectorial toward the origin and very stable. The magnetization of both of these samples decayed continuously during stepwise thermal demagnetization at temperatures as much as 680°, and the tilt-corrected directions are northwesterly and steeply down, which corresponds well to the expected Early Cretaceous direction.

Some samples do show two components of magnetization, as exemplified by the sample in Figure 9b. Before tilt correction (top), the early removed component (NRM to 200°) of this sample is northerly and steeply down, and is probably of recent origin. The second removed component passes the fold test, proving that it is predeformational in age. In tilt-corrected coordinates (bottom), this second removed component of magnetization is northerly and steeply down, which corresponds to a slightly rotated Cretaceous direction.

The results of the paleomagnetic investigation in the Kootenai are summarized in Table 3, and their declinations are plotted in Figure 10. The individual site means of 18 of the sites cluster well, giving an α^{95} of 10° or less. Of these 18 sites, sites 20 and 18 cannot be considered fully representative, for site 20 consists of 10 specimens drilled from only two large hand samples, and site 18 consists of only 5 drilled specimens from two hand samples. Consequently, we consider the characteristic directions for these sites to be preliminary. A minimum of eight samples was measured from each of the other 16 sites. The directions from site 11 clustered well, but the magnetic behavior of the samples was viscous, and very different from all other samples. The rocks from this site were highly weathered, and it seems likely that these rocks have been totally remagnetized. When the directions from site 11 and nearby site 10 are compared to each other, they do not pass the fold test. Thus it seems likely that site 10 may carry a predeformational magnetization, but site 11 probably does not. For the reasons listed above, site 11 is not included in this study. Four sites (14, 15, 16, and 22) have an α^{95} above 25° and thus do not have reliable characteristic directions. Sites such as these are useless for determining rotations, and thus are not included in this study. Unfortunately, two of these sites, 14 and 15, are found in the northern portion of the study area, with the remaining significant sites mostly concentrated in the southern portion of the salient and in the Sapphire plate. Reliable site mean declinations have been plotted on a map of the Helena salient (Fig. 10). The average declinations for the two local fold tests are plotted as heavy arrows instead of the individual site directions.

DISCUSSION

Before discussing the individual site rotations and their significance, there are two issues that must be addressed.

The first issue deals with the effects of strain at the site level and whether this can influence our paleomagnetic directions. Cleavage has been observed in the Kootenai Formation, but no systematic study was undertaken by us to evaluate the relationship, if any, between cleavage and the magnetic behavior or the magnetic declinations. It therefore must be acknowledged that strain remains a source of unevaluated error. In studies of similar rocks in the Western Alps, however, the effects of strain could be tested because of the occurrence of deformed reduction spots. The observations in that area, relevant to the magnetic directions, were threefold: (1) moderate strain (pencil cleavage) has no effect on the remanence directions, (2) higher strain (oblate and triaxial reduction spots) caused a non-Fisherian distribution of directions in the sites with cones of 95 percent confidence generally exceeding 10°, and (3) these directions failed a simple fold test because they had been deflected significantly from what they were originally (Kligfield and others, 1983; Cogné and Perroud, 1985). We note that in our study, sample directions in the sites are well grouped and apparently Fisherian, and that the fold tests are reassuringly positive, implying that the strain levels in the Kootenai Formation did not reach levels sufficient to influence the paleomagnetic directions.

The second issue deals with the possibility that secular variation has not been averaged out and that our site-mean directions may be deviating from a "norm" because of this. To assess this possibility, one ideally would like to know how much time lapsed during the acquisition of the magnetization in a typical site of, on average, a 5-m section of hematite-bearing rocks. Estimates of the time it takes for such a section to become stably magnetized, however, are extremely difficult to make and have led to controversial debates (e.g., Elston and Purucker, 1979; Larson and others, 1982); it is clear that we cannot hope to resolve the question in this chapter. While sedimentation rates in such a section can be very rapid, we argue that it is very likely that it takes tens of thousands of years for the hematite to grow through the critical grain sizes necessary for stable magnetizations to be acquired. If that assumption is correct, it is nearly certain that secular variation has been averaged out.

The 18 site means have been compared to two reference directions (Table 3), the stable foreland Kootenai reference direction and the calculated expected Early Cretaceous direction of Van Alstine and De Boer (1978). The declination deviations cited within the text are those calculated using the Kootenai reference direction obtained from sites 5 and 6. In all but two cases (sites 4 and 13), the use of the Kootenai reference gives more conservative declination deviations (possible rotations).

Determination of which sites are rotated significantly rela-

tive to the reference direction is difficult. Using the more conservative declination deviations (Table 3), and taking the statistical accuracies (cones of 95 percent confidence) into account, 8 sites of the 18 have been rotated significantly ($\geq 23°$) relative to the Kootenai reference direction. These are site 4 (27° counterclockwise), site 10 (35° clockwise), site 12 (24° clockwise), site 13 (29° counterclockwise), site 17 (39° clockwise), site 19 (54° clockwise), site 21 (29° clockwise), and site 23 (23° clockwise).

The eight sites with significant rotations are distributed throughout the study area (Fig. 10), but the maximum rotations are seen just east of the Pioneer batholith (Fig. 2) in the northern portion of the McCarthy Mountain salient near the transverse zone (sites 17 and 19). The site mean directions vary considerably from site to site, but the sense of rotation here is consistently clockwise. The thrusts are anastomosing and imbricated, and the motion along these faults is largely dip slip to the east. Immediately to the east of these sites is the syntectonically faulted and

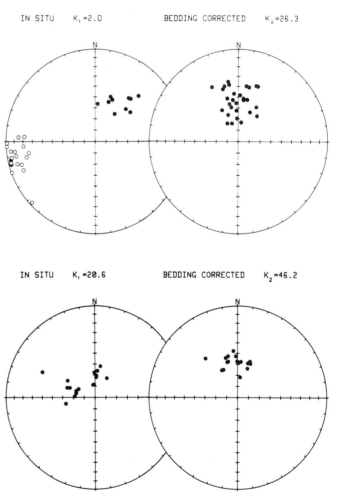

Figure 8. Equal-area net projections for two local fold tests, shown before and after tilt correction. Filled circles are lower hemisphere projections, and open circles are upper hemisphere. k = Fisher precision parameter. The upper example is from sites 7, 8, and 9, and is positive at the 99 percent confidence level; the lower example, from sites 2 and 3, is positive at the 95 percent confidence level (Collinson, 1983).

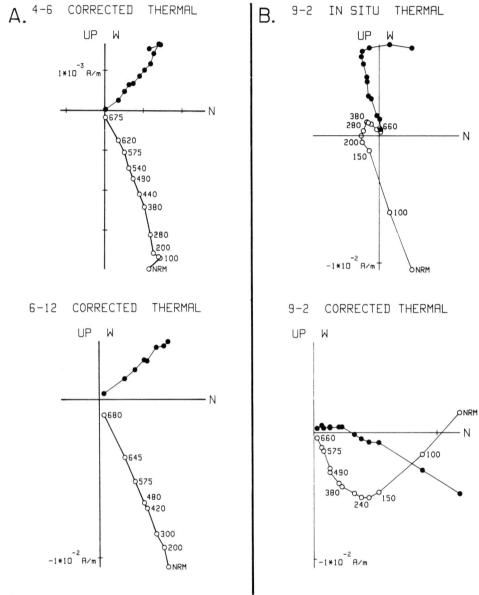

Figure 9. Zijderveld diagrams for three thermally demagnetized samples. The filled circles are a projection onto the horizontal plane, with north to the right of the figure. The open circles are a projection onto the north-south vertical plane. Temperatures are in degrees Centigrade; NRM = natural remanent magnetization. The two samples in Figure 9a are both shown after tilt correction and are univectorial toward the origin. Their directions are both northwesterly and steeply down. Figure 9b is a single sample both before (top) and after (bottom) tilt correction, which displays two components of magnetization. The early removed component (NRM = 200°) is probably of recent origin; the second removed component passes the fold test and is predeformational in age.

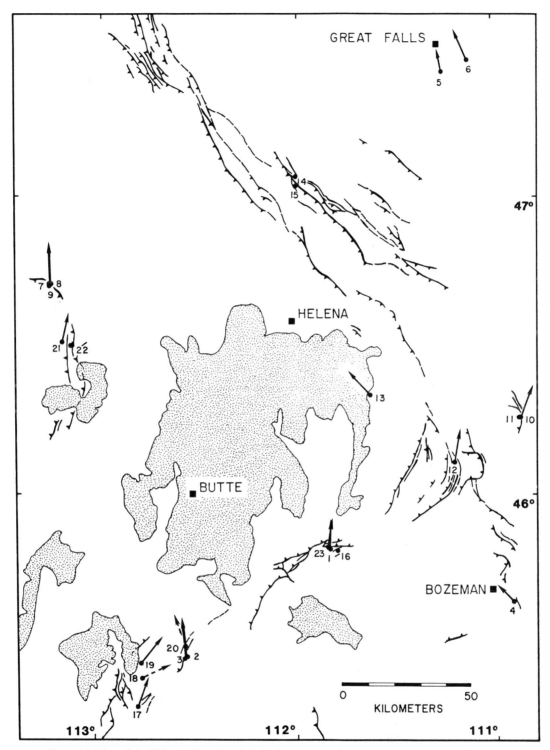

Figure 10. Map of the Helena salient showing the site mean declination directions. Sites 5 and 6 are the reference sites drilled in the stable foreland. The two heavy arrows are the averaged declination directions at the site of the two local fold tests (sites 7, 8, 9, and 2, 3). The dashed arrows (sites 18 and 20) are from sites with a small sample size, and thus are not statistically significant. Sites without arrows are sites where the samples were remagnetized or the directions were random and not interpretable. The stippled regions are igneous intrusives, the largest of which is the Boulder batholith.

uplifted Rocky Mountain foreland (Schmidt and O'Neill, 1983; C. J. Schmidt, personal communication), which may have acted as a buttress to the oncoming thrust sheets, causing them to stack up, break apart, and rotate.

To the northeast, site 23 in the transverse zone has rotated 23° clockwise. The clockwise sense of rotation is consistent with the right-lateral oblique slip seen on the north-northwest–dipping faults of this area. In this region there was some interference from foreland structures (Schmidt and O'Neill, 1982), but not to the extent found to the southwest. There was less impedance to the forward motion of the thrusts in the transverse zone than there was in the McCarthy Mountain salient or in the easternmost nose of the Helena salient. Field mapping north of Helena (Sheep Creek quadrangle) in the northern portion of the salient (Bregman, 1976) suggests a similar, but mirror-image, structural situation, with foreland buttressing and imbricate thrusting in the north giving way to décollement thrusting to the south.

Three sites within the apex of the Helena salient are rotated. Site 10 is rotated 35° clockwise, site 12 is rotated 24° clockwise, and site 13 is rotated 29° counterclockwise. The faults dip to the west, are highly imbricated and anastomosing, and show dip slip motion to the east. The thrust sheets in the nose of the salient may have been constricted by the narrowing eastern portion of the Helena embayment, causing them to break apart and rotate. Site 4, which is rotated 27° counterclockwise, is located within the Rocky Mountain foreland and may have been rotated along a northwest-trending basement-controlled fault.

A single site within the Sapphire plate, site 21, has been rotated 29° clockwise, perhaps by interference with the syntectonically emplaced Boulder batholith. The clockwise sense of rotation is consistent with possible deviations noted in the measurements of trough cross sets in the Kootenai Formation (P. G. DeCelles, written communication).

CONCLUSIONS

Figure 11 is a highly schematic sketch that summarizes the rotations found within the Helena and Wyoming salients. In the Helena salient, the rotated thrusts are found where the effect of buttressing against the Rocky Mountain foreland is the greatest. There is relatively little rotation in the transverse zone where the thrust traces run east-west, nearly perpendicular to the regional north-south trend. This pattern of rotations matches the third model of thrust sheet motion (Fig. 4, III) put forth earlier. Interference with the simultaneously faulted and uplifted Rocky Mountain foreland, particularly in the stippled regions of Figure 11, has caused local crumpling and rotation of thrust sheets. Because the rotations vary greatly from site to site, it is very unlikely that the thrust sheets deformed in a coherent fashion. Therefore, it is also unlikely that these rotations were ever transferred back into the interior of the Helena salient. Unavailability of outcrop due to the presence of the Boulder batholith prevents absolute proof of this hypothesis.

Paleomagnetic studies by Schwartz and Van der Voo (1984)

and Grubbs and Van der Voo (1976) have documented a similar situation in the Wyoming salient (Figs. 3, 11; Tables 1, 2). There, rotations of 60° counterclockwise and 30° clockwise have been ascribed to buttressing edge effects that were not transmitted back to the west into the thrust sheets. In Wyoming the buttressing was against the ancestral Gros Ventre and Teton Mountain ranges.

Perhaps it is best not to think of this region in the Northern Rockies as consisting of two independent and unrelated salients, but rather as a large foreland promontory where Montana meets Idaho and Wyoming. This promontory is characterized by buttressing and right-lateral shear rotating thrust sheets to the north,

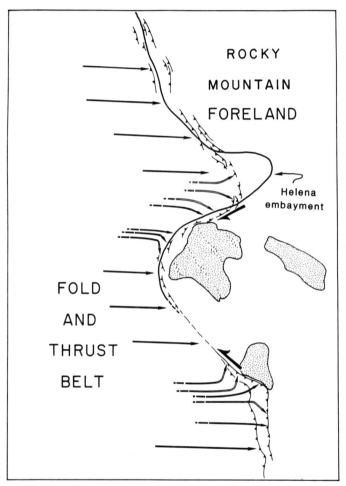

Figure 11. Schematic sketch of the Northern Rockies showing the Helena (north) and Wyoming (south) salients. The stippled regions are uplifted regions in the Rocky Mountain foreland, the southernmost being the ancestral Gros Ventre–Teton uplift. The heavy line delineates the approximate margin of the Helena embayment. The two heavy half-arrows show the sense of shear present in the southern portion of the Helena salient and the northern portion of the Wyoming salient. The long, straight arrows schematically show the thrust sheet transportation direction from west to east. The shorter, and locally bent, arrows represent the rotated declinations measured in the Cretaceous Kootenai Formation in the Helena salient and in Triassic rocks (Grubbs and Van der Voo, 1976) in the Wyoming salient. The Boulder batholith (not shown) is in the middle of the Helena salient. There is no evidence for rotation in the interior of either salient.

and buttressing and left-lateral shear to the south. The Snake River Plain volcanics preclude any further paleomagnetic investigations to connect these two regions.

ACKNOWLEDGMENTS

Our thanks to Susan Schwartz for advice and support with this project, and to Jack Dorr for critical comments on the manuscript. We also thank Neil Opdyke, Myrl Beck, Dave Symons, Chris Schmidt, and Dave Wiltschko for extremely thorough and helpful reviews. Chris Schmidt, Peter DeCelles, and Ed Ruppel provided invaluable information regarding outcrop location and general geology in the field in Montana. We are very grateful to Lee J. Suttner from Indiana University's Geologic Field Station in Cardwell, Montana, for allowing the use of the station as a base camp. Niels Wolter proved to be a fantastic field assistant who kept us sane when outcrops refused to materialize. Financial support was provided by an American Association of Petroleum Geologists grant-in-aid, a Geological Society of America research grant, a Sigma-Xi grant-in-aid of research, an Explorers Club Award for Research, and grants from Mobil Oil Corporation, Shell Oil Company, and Champlin Petroleum Company.

REFERENCES CITED

Beck, M. E., 1980, Paleomagnetic record of plate-margin tectonic processes along the western edge of North America: Journal of Geophysical Research, v. 85, p. 7115–7131.

Beutner, E. C., 1977, Causes and consequences of curvature in the Sevier orogenic belt, Utah to Montana: Wyoming Geological Association 29th Annual Field Conference Guidebook, p. 353–365.

Birkholz, D. O., 1967, Geology of the Lamas Creek area, Meagher County, Montana [M.Sc. thesis]: Butte, Montana College of Mineral Science and Technology, 68 p.

Bregman, M. L., 1976, Change in tectonic style along the Montana thrust belt: Geology, v. 4, p. 775–778.

Cogné, J.-P., and Perroud, H., 1985, Strain removal applied to paleomagnetic directions in an orogenic belt; The Permian red slates of the Alpes Maritimes, France: Earth and Planetary Science Letters, v. 72, p. 125–140.

Collinson, D. W., 1983, Methods in rock magnetism and paleomagnetism; Techniques and instrumentation: New York, Chapman and Hall, 503 p.

DeCelles, P. G., 1984, Sedimentation and diagenesis in a tectonically partitioned foreland basin; The Kootenai Formation (Lower Cretaceous) of southwestern Montana [Ph.D. thesis]: Bloomington, Indiana University, 422 p.

Demarest, H. H., 1983, Error analysis for the determination of tectonic rotation from paleomagnetic data: Journal of Geophysical Research, v. 88, p. 4321–4328.

Eldredge, S., Bachtadse, V., and Van der Voo, R., 1985, Paleomagnetism and the orocline hypothesis: Tectonophysics, v. 119, p. 153–179.

Elston, D. P., and Purucker, M. E., 1979, Detrital magnetization in red beds of the Moenkopi Formation (Triassic), Gray Mountain, Arizona: Journal of Geophysical Research, v. 84, p. 1653–1665.

Grubbs, K. L., and Van der Voo, R., 1976, Structural deformation of the Idaho-Wyoming overthrust belt (U.S.A.), as determined by Triassic paleomagnetism: Tectonophysics, v. 33, p. 321–336.

Harrison, J. E., Griggs, A. B., and Wells, J. D., 1974, Tectonic features of the Precambrian Belt basin and their influence on post-Belt structures: U.S. Geological Survey Professional Paper 866, 15 p.

Hoffman, J., Hower, J., and Aronson, J. L., 1976, Radiometric dating of time of thrusting in the disturbed belt of Montana: Geology, v. 4, p. 16–20.

Hyndman, D. W., Talbot, J. L., and Chase, R. B., 1975, Boulder Batholith; A result of emplacement of a block detached from the Idaho batholith infrastructure?: Geology, v. 3, p. 401–404.

James, W. C., 1977, Origin of nonmarine-marine transitional strata at the top of the Kootenai Formation, southwestern Montana [Ph.D. thesis]: Bloomington, Indiana University, 433 p.

Kligfield, R., Lowrie, W., Hirt, A., and Siddans, A.W.B., 1983, Effect of progressive deformation on remanent magnetization of Permian red beds from the Alpes Maritimes (France): Tectonophysics, v. 97, p. 59–85.

Larson, E. E., Walker, T. R., Patterson, P. E., Hoblitt, R. P., and Rosenbaum, J. G., 1982, Paleomagnetism of the Moenkopi Formation, Colorado Plateau; Basis for long-term model of acquisition of chemical remanent magnetization in red beds: Journal of Geophysical Research, v. 87, p. 1081–1106.

McElhinny, M. W., 1964, Statistical significance of the fold test in paleomagnetism: Geophysical Journal of the Royal Astronomy Society, v. 8, p. 338–340.

Meyers, J. H., 1981, Carbonate sedimentation in the Ellis Group (Jurassic) on the southern flank of Belt Island, southwestern Montana, *in* Tucker, T. E., ed., Southwest Montana, Montana Geologic Society Field Conference and Symposium Guidebook, p. 83–91.

Mudge, M. R., 1970, Origin of the disturbed belt in northwestern Montana: Geological Society of America Bulletin, v. 81, p. 377–392.

Nelson, W. H., 1963, Geology of the Duck Creek Pass Quadrangle, Montana: U.S. Geological Survey Bulletin, v. 1121–J, 56 p.

Ruppel, E. T., Wallace, C. A., Schmidt, R. G., and Lopez, D. A., 1981, Preliminary interpretation of the thrust belt in southwest and west-central Montana and east-central Idaho, *in* Tucker, T. E., ed., Southwest Montana: Montana Geologic Society Field Conference and Symposium Guidebook, p. 139–159.

Schmidt, C. J., and Garihan, J., 1986, Middle Proterozoic and Laramide tectonic activity along the southern margin of the Belt Basin: Montana Bureau of Mines and Geology Special Publication, v. 94.

Schmidt, C. J., and O'Neill, J. M., 1983, Structural evolution of the southwest Montana transverse zone, *in* R. B. Powers, ed., Geologic studies of the Cordilleran thrust belt, 1982: Denver, Colorado, Rocky Mountain Association of Geologists, v. 1, p. 193–218.

Schwartz, S. Y., and Van der Voo, R., 1983, Paleomagnetic evaluation of the orocline hypothesis in the central and southern Appalachians: Geophysical Research Letters, v. 10, p. 505–508.

—— , 1984, Paleomagnetic study of thrust sheet rotation during foreland impingement in the Wyoming-Idaho overthrust belt: Journal of Geophysical Research, v. 89, p. 10077–10086.

Smeedes, H., and Schmidt, C. J., 1979, Regional geologic setting of the Boulder batholith, Montana: Penrose Conference Guidebook [Granite II], p. 1–36.

Smith, J. G., 1965, Fundamental transcurrent faulting in northern Rocky Mountains: American Association of Petroleum Geologists Bulletin, v. 49, p. 1398–1409.

Steiner, M. B., and Helsley, C. E., 1975, Reversal pattern and apparent polar wander for the Late Jurassic: Geological Society of America Bulletin, v. 86, p. 1537–1543.

Suttner, L. J., 1969, Stratigraphic and petrographic analysis of Upper Jurassic–Lower Cretaceous Morrison and Kootenai Formations, southwest Montana: American Association of Petroleum Geologists Bulletin, v. 53, p. 1391–1410.

Tilling, R. I., Klepper, M. R., and Obradovich, J. D., 1968, K-Ar ages and time span of emplacement of the Boulder Batholith, Montana: American Journal of Science, v. 266, p. 671–689.

Van Alstine, D., and de Boer, J., 1978, A new technique for constructing apparent polar wander paths and the revised Phanerozoic path for North America: Geology, v. 6, p. 137–139.

Woodward, L. A., 1981, Tectonic framework of disturbed belt in west-central Montana: Amcrican Association of Petroleum Geologists Bulletin, v. 65-2, p. 291–302.

MANUSCRIPT ACCEPTED BY THE SOCIETY FEBRUARY 9, 1988

Geological Society of America
Memoir 171
1988

Interaction between the northern Idaho–Wyoming thrust belt and bounding basement blocks, central western Wyoming

John P. Craddock*
Department of Geological Sciences, University of Michigan, Ann Arbor, Michigan 48109-1063
Andrew A. Kopania*
Champlin Petroleum, P.O. Box 1257, Englewood, Colorado 86105
David V. Wiltschko
Center for Tectonophysics and Department of Geology, Texas A&M University, College Station, Texas 77843-3115

ABSTRACT

The curved east-facing salient of the Idaho-Wyoming thrust belt is a prime location to study well-dated interactions of foreland basement-cored uplifts and thrust belt development. Both field and fabric data, as well as analyses of twinned calcite, have been used to infer the deformation paths of rocks within the Absaroka, Darby, and Prospect thrust sheets as they approached the bounding foreland basement-cored uplifts. Each thrust sheet has a specific fracture pattern that maintains a constant orientation relative to the curvilinear strike of each thrust fault. Mean shortening directions computed from twinned calcite are layer-parallel, except in samples taken from sedimentary cover rocks of the basement uplifts, and mean compression and shortening axes are normal to local thrust strike. The joint and calcite fabric data indicate that the stress, strain, and presumably, deformation paths of each thrust sheet were normal to both the strike of the thrust fault, where it is exposed, and the base of the thrust ramp. Similarly, these data suggest that thrust sheet rotation, as much as 40° in a counterclockwise sense, took place as these thrust sheets approached the salient-bounding basement uplifts. South of Hoback Canyon, where there is no nearby basement uplift, a clockwise rotation of 36° is suggested. Interpretation of the thrust belt and Teton–Gros Ventre buttress tectonic history is based on deformation paths, cross sections, palinspastic maps, and well-documented timing relationships (Wiltschko and Dorr, 1983) of both terranes. Differential rotation and frontal imbrication are the primary responses of these thrust sheets to accommodate rotation into parallelism with the bounding basement uplifts.

INTRODUCTION

As early as 1949 it was suggested that deformation in the northern Idaho-Wyoming Overthrust belt was complicated by interaction between eastward-moving thrust sheets and neighboring basement-cored uplifts (Horberg and others, 1949; Beutner, 1977). Horberg and others (1949) noticed that both fold wavelength and fault spacing decreased toward the basement uplifts to the north and east. Beutner (1977, p. 358–360) showed that the thickest synorogenic deposits are found near regions of apparent impingement of the thrust belt and basement uplifts, thus arguing for increased tectonic uplift and erosion in these areas. The seismic studies of Royse and others (1975) and, more recently, by Dixon (1982) clearly show the proximity, and presumed mechanical interactions, of subthrust structural basement variations (e.g., the Moxa Arch) as well as the foreland basement uplifts (ancestral Teton–Gros Ventre Range) to thrust ramps. There is also some direct evidence of interaction. Grubbs and Van der Voo (1976) showed that the paleomagnetic poles from Triassic red beds within the distal thrust sheets of the Idaho-Wyoming thrust belt have rotated into parallelism with bounding basement

*Present addresses: Craddock, 100 Kinross Dr., #56, Walnut Creek, California 94598; Kopania, 11514 Sogrell Way, Culver City, California 90230.

blocks. They interpreted these results to indicate that thrust-sheet motion was "buttressed," or inhibited in its motion by impingement upon foreland basement uplifts. In contrast, Schwartz and Van der Voo (1984) found no rotations of paleomagnetic poles from the Upper Jurassic and Lower Cretaceous rocks of the Absaroka and Darby thrust sheets, suggesting that the younger Prospect sheet rotated locally and independent of the overlying thrust sheets. Beutner (1977) and Gwinn (1967), however, suggested that the change in trend of the thrust belt is due to differential thrust motion without rotation.

Our purpose in undertaking the present study was to collect rock fabric and other structural data in the allochthonous sedimentary rocks of the Absaroka, Darby, and Prospect thrust sheets both to see if the fabrics of these rocks were affected by superimposed impingement by bounding basement uplifts and to use the

rocks' fabric data to reconstruct the deformation paths of these thin-skinned thrust sheets. With the deformation paths determined, it is possible to construct balanced, restorable cross sections that minimize the amount of material moving in and out of each cross section (i.e., non-plane strain). With this information, we then present a tectonic and palinspastic model that displays the areal geometry of the thrust salient relative to dated thrusting events. In general, only two points in the development of a thrust sheet are known. One is the present position; the second is the unrestored ramp position, if sufficient subsurface control is available to draw restorable cross sections. These two points form the basis for the deformation path between the two points. To draw the deformation path between these two points, fracture patterns and compression and strain axes from mechanically twinned calcite have been used as the markers, which sweep out the path as

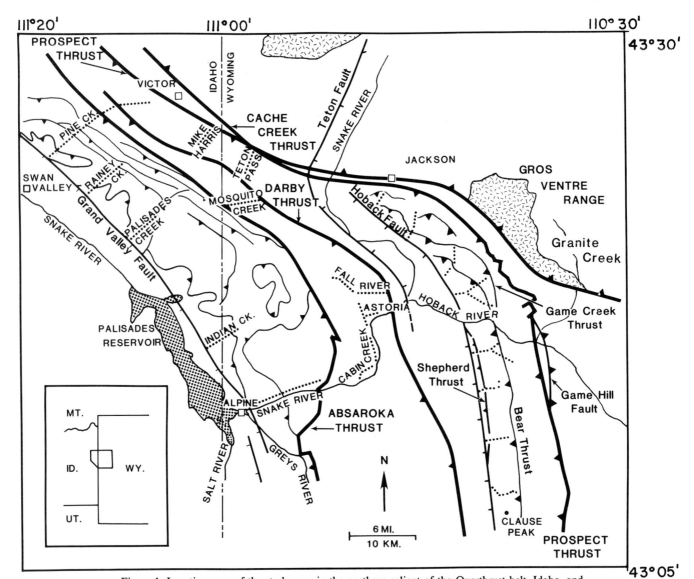

Figure 1. Location map of the study area in the northern salient of the Overthrust belt, Idaho, and Wyoming. Dotted lines are traverses. Stippled pattern is exposed crystalline basement rock. Faults from Blackstone (1980) and Woodward (1986).

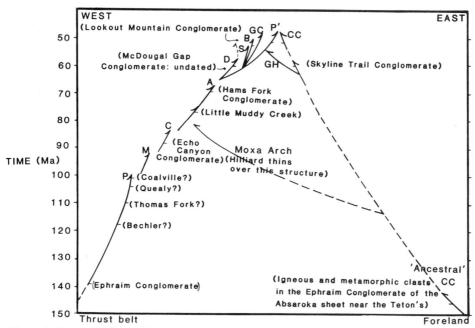

Figure 2. Cross-cutting and timing relations of major thrust faults in the Idaho-Wyoming thrust belt (adapted from Wiltschko and Dorr, 1983, Fig. 3) and foreland. P = Paris thrust; M = Meade thrust; C = Crawford thrust; A = Absaroka thrust; D = Darby thrust; S = Shepherd thrust; B = Bear thrust; GC = Game Creek thrust; P′ = Prospect thrust; CC = Cache Creek thrust; GH = Game Hill fault; MA = Moxa arch. Associated synorogenic conglomerates are in parentheses. We have omitted the LaBarge and Calpet thrusts (Eocene) in the Green River basin, and the Pass Peak Conglomerate (Eocene), due to space in this figure.

the thrust sheets are restored from their present positions. The major assumption to be made, backed up by some evidence, is that the calcite twin fabrics and fracture orientations are largely imposed early in the deformation history (Craddock and van der Pluijm, 1987; Jackson and others, 1988) and are later passively rotated with thrust sheet motion (e.g., Engelder and Geiser, 1980; Wiltschko and others, 1985). There are, of course, an infinite number of paths that can be drawn between two points. We have chosen one intermediate between a line connecting the two points and a wide arc. There are no data that we can bring to bear on the *exact* path of motion.

The following sections concern regional geology, local geology, joint measurements, calcite twin analysis data, a synthesis of these data with deformation path maps and restorable cross sections, and a discussion of possible mechanisms used to arrive at the final present-day geometry.

REGIONAL GEOLOGY

The Paris, Meade, Crawford, Absaroka, Darby, and Prospect thrust faults, from west to east, comprise the major structural features of the Idaho-Wyoming Overthrust belt (Fig. 1; Blackstone, 1980). The ages of fault initiation of these thrust sheets decrease to the east. Likewise, they cut up stratigraphic section along décollements in the Precambrian Big Cottonwood Group, Cambrian Gros Ventre Group, and Triassic Dinwoody shales

from west to east (Royse and others, 1975), and generally maintain fault displacement along strike (see however, Dixon, 1982). These tectonic features as well as the Cache Creek thrust, which brings Precambrian crystalline rocks to the surface in the foreland, are attributed to the Sevier-Laramide orogenic events of late Jurassic through Paleocene time (Rubey and Hubbert, 1959; Armstrong and Cressman, 1963; Armstrong and Oriel, 1965; Royse and others, 1975; Dorr and others, 1977; Wiltschko and Dorr, 1983).

Throughout the study area, deformation of the sedimentary cover rocks is characterized by predominantly concentric folding, brittle fracturing, thrust imbrication, and an absence of any metamorphism or regionally pervasive solution cleavage. Fold amplitudes generally decrease eastward toward the craton, whereas thrust fault imbrication spacing increases (Dorr and others, 1977).

Within the Absaroka thrust sheet there are numerous imbricate thrust faults (Oriel and others, 1985; Oriel and Moore, 1985). Woodward (1981, p. 107; 1986) and Woodward and others (1983, p. 318) suggested that these imbricates predate the main movement of the Absaroka thrust because they have been folded, presumably by movement on the Absaroka thrust. He also referred to these imbricate faults as a frontal imbricate fan (Woodward, 1981, p. 105; 1986) and cited Dahlstrom (1970, p. 353–355) that frontal imbricates are younger in the direction of transport. According to Dahlstrom's (1970, p. 351–353) terminology, however, frontal imbricates are structurally lower than the main thrust. The imbricates above the Absaroka are, in fact, "hindward" imbricates, and therefore may be younger *away* from the direction of transport (Dahlstrom, 1970, p. 353), although these sorts of timing arguments are, by their nature, ambiguous. In addition, the Absaroka thrust has also been folded; this folding parallels the folding in the overlying imbricates (see Figs. 7 through 10). This relationship is clearly visible on proprietary seismic lines and is most likely caused by a younger footwall imbrication. This relationship is shown by Dixon (1982, Figs. 5, 6) and, interestingly, also by Woodward (1981, Fig. III: 4-1-4c; 1986, Fig. 5e). It has also been observed by Lageson (1984, p. 407–412) immediately south of the area of this study. Publicly available well data and U.S. Geological Survey mapping (for example, Jobin, 1965, 1971; Staatz and Albee, 1966) show that the oldest rock cut is progressively younger to the east, indicating that these imbricates all root into the main thrust at the crest of the ramp. All of this evidence makes a case for these imbricates postdating major movement on the Absaroka thrust.

Along Hoback Canyon in the Prospect sheet, the approximate junction between buttressed and unbuttressed thrusting, are a number of structural anomalies, including (1) east-west trending tear faults with folds of different trend, plunge, and style on opposite sides of a fault; (2) anomalous east-west trending folds; and (3) numerous examples of thrust imbrication (Dorr and others, 1977, 1987; Hunter, this volume). Thrust imbrication in the Prospect sheet near Teton Pass is spaced approximately ca. every 10 m and has been mapped by Schroeder (1969). The Prospect thrust, near the Gros Ventre Range, may be underlain by the older, west-dipping Granite Creek thrust (Royse, 1985; Hunter, this volume).

Much of the thrust belt and foreland has been overprinted by younger Basin and Range extension and uplift. The Plio-Pleistocene Teton fault is an obvious example, as are the Grand Valley and Hoback listric normal faults that localized above the Absaroka and Prospect (and Bear) thrust ramps, respectively. Offset on each of these normal faults is at least 2,500 m (Dorr and others, 1977). Slide blocks of Triassic red beds resting on Mississippian Madison Group and Tertiary Camp Davis Formation in southern Jackson Hole are the result of uplift of the Hoback Range on the Hoback fault (Dorr and others, 1977).

TIMING OF TECTONIC AND STRUCTURAL EVENTS

A necessary first step is to review available data on both thrust sheet motion and timing of uplift of the bounding basement blocks. The timing of thrust fault motion here is relatively well established relative to other fold and thrust belts (Fig. 2). Major motion on the Absaroka thrust fault occurred in latest Cretaceous time, although motion may have begun in the Santonian (85 to 80 Ma). The Darby thrust is not well dated, but must be younger than middle Late Cretaceous. Dixon (1982) suggested that the Darby thrust may be younger than the Prospect thrust, at least north of the Snake River Canyon.

The Prospect thrust sheet moved between 56 and 58 m.y. ago (Dorr and others, 1977), truncated the east-dipping Game Hill fault, and deformed the Skyline Trail Conglomerate, which was shed from the Gros Ventre Range to the northeast (see also Schroeder, 1973). The Prospect thrust is folded and cut by imbricate thrust faults. The Game Creek, Bear, and Shepherd thrusts, from east to west, are these younger imbricate thrust faults (Dorr and others, 1977; Craddock and others, 1985).

In the foreland, the Cache Creek thrust extends from the Snake River Plain in Idaho to the Wind River front in Wyoming. It lies along the southwest margin of the Gros Ventre Range and the south and west ends of the Teton Range. Precambrian crystalline rocks and Paleozoic sedimentary beds are thrust southwestward over Cretaceous strata, resulting in deposition of the Skyline Trail synorogenic conglomerate (Schroeder, 1969; Love and Albee, 1972; Dorr and others, 1977; see, however, Oriel and Moore, 1985). Seismic and well data from Teton Valley and the extreme north end of the Green River Basin, where the Cache Creek thrust is buried by sediments, show that this fault does not cut the Gannett Group (Fig. 3). Therefore, the "ancestral" Cache Creek thrust had a major phase of movement during Early Cretaceous (Aptian) time, prior to movement on the Prospect, Darby, and Absaroka thrusts (Kopania, 1984). An Early Cretaceous or Late Jurassic episode of motion is further supported by subangular igenous and metamorphic clasts in the Ephraim Conglomerate along North Rainey and Mike Harris Creeks in the Absaroka sheet. The Cache Creek thrust was reactivated one or more times subsequent to early Cretaceous time (Dorr and others, 1977), although fault displacement clearly varied along strike (Fig. 3 vs. Fig. 10). Restoring the Plio-Pleistocene Teton fault (Love, 1973) shows that the Teton and Gros Ventre Ranges were once part of a larger Laramide-type basement-cored uplift along the "ancestral" Cache Creek thrust (Fig. 3), equivalent to the ancestral Teton–Gros Ventre and Targhee uplifts of Love and Albee (1972) and Love and others (1973).

The Cache Creek and Prospect thrusts are in contact at Teton Pass (Schroeder, 1969). The relationship between these two faults has been addressed by several authors. Dunn (1983) and Corbett (1982) showed the Cache Creek thrust overlying the Prospect thrust, whereas Schroeder (1969) and Dixon (1982) suggested the opposite relationship. The well-established ages of both faults farther south along strike make the former interpretation seem unlikely because the Prospect thrust is latest Paleocene to earliest Eocene in age, and the Cache Creek thrust is Early Cretaceous in age, where they are dated. Therefore, where the two faults are in contact, the Prospect must overlie the Cache Creek. This also demonstrates that a basement-cored uplift formed along the present trace of the Cache Creek thrust prior to movement on the Prospect, Darby, and Absaroka thrust, and that the Cache Creek fault was later truncated by the Prospect thrust sheet (Dorr and others, 1977; Dixon, 1982). The shape of the embayment that would become the thrust belt salient was established by uplift on the Cache Creek thrust system in Early Cretaceous time (Figs. 1, 3) or earlier (Craddock, 1988).

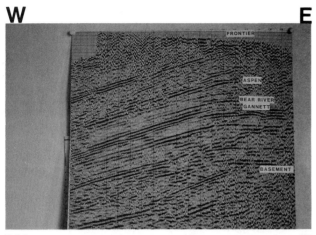

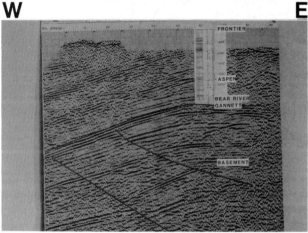

Figure 3. Proprietary west-east synthetic seismic section (top) and interpretation (bottom) of the Teton uplift showing overlap of Cretaceous Gannett sediments on Precambrian basement faults. See text for timing of this uplift. Depth and time can be inferred from the grid.

Possible modes of thrust sheet motion near nonparallel bounding blocks

There seem to be at least three modes by which the Absaroka, Darby, and Prospect thrust sheets could conform to this structural embayment: (1) rotation and strike-parallel stretching of each or all three thrust sheets, (2) fault imbrication as, or after, major thrust sheet motion ends; and/or (3) thrust sheet rotation (around vertical axes) accommodated by strike-varying fault displacement on the major thrust fault (Grubbs and Van der Voo, 1976; Beutner, 1977). Whether a thrust sheet rotates, imbricates, or "spreads" should be reflected by the deformation paths, strain markers, and timing relations. Thrust sheet rotation should be reflected in the rocks by rotation of early formed features. Stretching should be seen in either the intragranular strains or the orientations of small faults at low angles to the transport direction.

JOINTS

The geologic origin of joint partings and the relationship between joints and fracture systems and compressive tectonic events has long been debated (Parker, 1942; Meuhlberger, 1961; Secor, 1965; Price, 1966; Nickelson and Hough, 1967; Engelder and Geiser, 1980). In the most detailed study to date, Engelder and Geiser (1980) documented along the Central Appalachian salient in New York and northern Pennsylvania one joint set perpendicular to the maximum shortening strain axis, as recorded by deformed fossil fabric (set Ia), and a second oblique joint set (Ib) interpreted by them to be associated with an early imposed penetrative rock fabric, even though the actual joint surfaces did not form until removal of overburden and thermal cooling occurred (see also Engelder and Marshak, 1985). Engelder and Geiser (1980), using field cross-cutting relations, interpreted joint set Ia as having been formed early; joint set Ib, which formed as a result of strain relaxation associated with a penetrative fabric, formed late but followed the early fabric. Following the insights of Engelder and Geiser, and having observed no field evidence to the contrary, we have assumed that the systematic joint sets in the northern Wyoming salient of the Overthrust belt were formed early (pre-thrust translation) or followed an early formed rock fabric.

The methods for measuring joint and fracture orientations were as follows. In each outcrop the major joint sets were identified. For most outcrops, there were two to five different joint sets. Ten to fifteen individual joints of each set were measured, and the mean orientation of these was taken as the orientation of each set at that location. The validity of this method has been confirmed by Reches (1976) and Perry and Colton (1981).

Joint fractures are best developed in Jurassic and Cretaceous sandstones and Paleozoic carbonates and sandstones. The systematic joints were approximately normal to bedding in every location visited, whether bedding was at a steep angle or not. In these stratigraphic units, both filled and unfilled joints occur. In the filled joints, the mineralization may be either euhedral, blocky, or fibrous calcite. There is not a consistent relationship between the type of filling and either the areal distribution or orientation of a joint set.

Figure 4 is a map showing the orientation of the systematic joint sets, after bedding is locally rotated to horizontal around bedding strike. The patterns on each traverse represent data collected at a minimum of three outcrops, but in most cases more than four. See Table 1 for details of the joint data.

Thrust belt

The joint data are summarized in Table 1. Within the Absaroka sheet, there appears to be a consistent relationship between the orientation of the nearest thrust trace and both the bisector of joint sets 1 and 2 and the orientation of joint set 3. With the exception of the data from the Snake River canyon, the acute bisector of joint sets 1 and 2 is nearly normal to the nearest

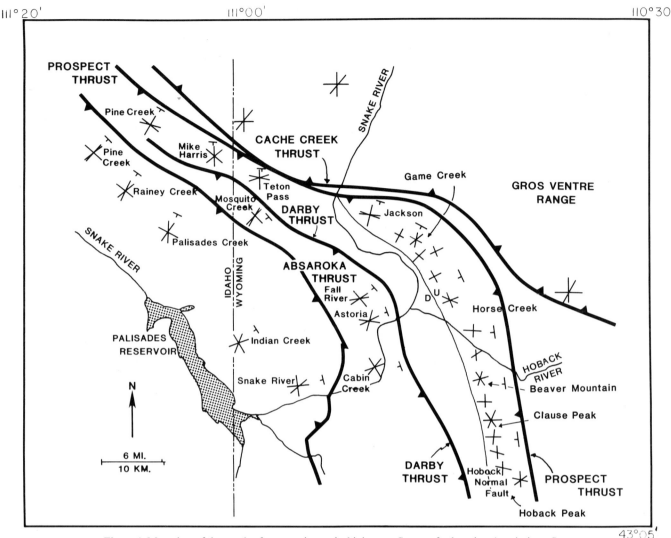

Figure 4. Map view of the trends of systematic, vertical joint sets. See text for location descriptions. See Table 1 for data.

thrust trace, although the thrust trace is as much as 14 km distant in one case (Indian Creek). In addition, joint set 3 appears to be parallel to the nearest thrust trace, again excepting the Snake River canyon data. On the Darby sheet, there is significantly more divergence between the bisector of sets 1 and 2 and the normal-to-the-thrust trace. For Cabin Creek, the worst case, the divergence is 27°. Joint set 3 is also nearly parallel to the nearest thrust trace, the worst case being at Astoria Springs where there is a 20° difference between the two. North of Jackson, Wyoming, the joint data for the Prospect thrust sheet show a relationship distinctly different from that shown by those in the Absaroka and Darby sheets. For the Prospect sheet, the acute bisectors of sets 1 and 2 parallel the nearest trace of the Prospect thrust fault to within 6°. Joint set 3 is nearly normal to the nearest thrust trace (see Table 1). South of Jackson in the Prospect sheet, the divergence of the acute bisectrix of sets 1 and 2 with the normal-to-the-fault trace is everywhere less than 26°, the worst example being Clause Peak.

Elsewhere, only sets 1 and 3 are present, set 1 being consistently normal to the Prospect thrust trace, and ranging in strike from N42°E near Jackson to N76°W near Hoback Peak. Set 3 is consistently parallel to the Prospect thrust trace and varies in strike from N27°W near Jackson, to N3°W near Hoback Peak. It is somewhat surprising that the apparent systematic relationship between joint orientations and the nearest thrust trace exists at all, because, as shown on Figure 1 and in more detail by Woodward (1981, 1986), the rocks containing the joints are imbricated and folded, and in places highly so (see Woodward, 1986, Fig. 5). In any event, on the basis of the data presented here, each thrust sheet appears to have an internally consistent joint pattern, which, in the case of the Absaroka and Darby sheets vs. the Prospect sheet, is distinctive.

Craton

The joint system in the Paleozoic sedimentary rocks in the Teton–Gros Ventre Range consists of three vertical sets: N-S,

TABLE 1. DETAILS OF JOINT DATA FOR EACH THRUST SHEET

Location	Joint Sets 1	2	3	Thrust Trace	Comments*
Absaroka Thrust Sheet					
Snake River Canyon	N55E	N86E	N08W	N14W-N30E	Thrust trace swings through 30°. Sets 1 and 2 bisector lies 6° CCW from thrust normal in southern segment. No consistent relationship to N30°E segment of thrust.
Indian Creek	N24E	N72E	N30W	N30W	Sets 1 and 2 bisector lies 12° CCW from thrust normal. Set 3 parallel to thrust trace.
Palisades Creek	N03E	N38E	N60W	N62W	Sets 1 and 2 bisector lies 9° CCW from thrust normal to thrust trace. Set 3 is parallel to thrust trace.
Rainey Creek	N52E	N25E	N50W	N51W	Sets 1 and 2 bisected by thrust normal. Set 3 parallel to thrust trace.
Pine Creek	N42E	N53E	N46W	N43W	Sets 1 and 2 bisected by thrust normal. Set 3 parallel to thrust trace.
Darby Thrust					
Cabin Creek	N40E	N69E	N32W	N28W	Sets 1 and 2 bisector lies 27° CW from thrust normal. Set 3 is 4° CCW from thrust trace.
Astoria Springs	N50E	N70W	N10E	N10W	Sets 1 and 2 bisector normal to thrust.
Fall River	N60E	N81E	N38W	N35W	Sets 1 and 2 bisector lies 15° CW from thrust normal. Set 3 lies 3° CW from thrust trace.
Mosquito Creek	N32E	N44E	N41W	N38W	Sets 1 and 2 bisector lies 14° CW from thrust normal. Set 3 lies 3° CW from thrust.
Prospect Thrust					
Pine Creek	N51W	N72W	N30E	N60W	Sets 1 and 2 bisector parallel to thrust. Set 3 is normal to thrust.
Mike Harris Canyon	N50W	N55E	N01W	N81W	Sets 1 and 2 bisector is 6° CCW from thrust trace. Set 3 is 10° CCW from thrust normal.
Teton Pass	N77W	N74E	N03E	N83W	Sets 1 and 2 bisector is 6° CW from thrust trace. Set 3 is 4° CCW from thrust normal.
Jackson	N69W	N82W	N11E	N75W	Sets 1 and 2 bisector is parallel to thrust trace. Set 3 is 4° CW from thrust normal.
Game Creek	N10E	N45E	N30W	N30W	Sets 1 and 2 bisector is 0° from thrust trace normal. Set 3 is parallel to thrust.
Horse Creek	N70E	N21W	N18W	N22W	Sets 1 and 2 bisector is 12° CCW from thrust trace normal. Set 3 is 4° CW from being thrust parallel.
Beaver Mountain	N76E	N42W	N20E	N24W	Sets 1 and 2 bisector is 14° CW from thrust trace normal. Set 3 is 44° CW from being thrust parallel.
Clause Peak	N88E	N34W	N22E	N21W	Sets 1 and 2 bisector is 26° CW from thrust trace normal. Set 3 is 43° CW from being thrust parallel.
Hoback Peak	N79W	N36E	N03W	N10W	Sets 1 and 2 bisector is 0° from thrust trace normal. Set 3 is 7° CW from being thrust parallel.

*CW = clockwise; CCW = counterclockwise.

N40°E, and N90°E (Fig. 4). These data are from three locales, and it is unknown whether these joint sets are also developed in the underlying crystalline rocks.

PETROFABRICS

The preponderance of carbonate twinning strain and compression axis (Turner, 1953) data from upper crustal deformed rocks may be interpreted as indicating that the twinning fabric was imposed early in the deformation history. Whether in folds (Groshong, 1975; Chapple and Spang, 1974) or thrust sheets (Spang and others, 1981; Ballard and Wiltschko, 1983; Craddock and Wiltschko, 1983; Wiltschko and others, 1985), the maximum shortening direction as well as the mean compression axis direction in most cases is parallel to both the transport direction

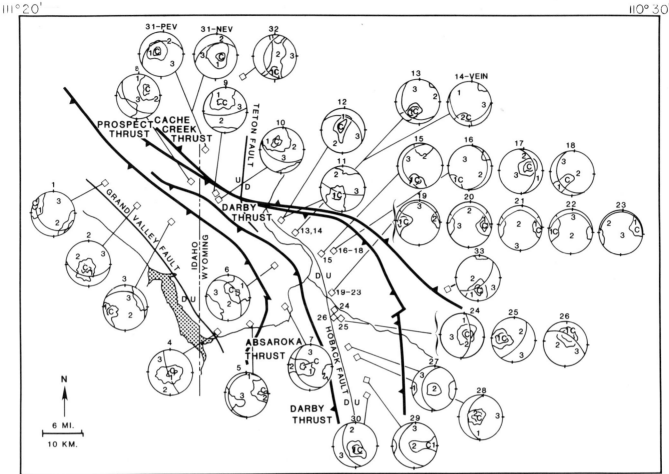

Figure 5. Locations of oriented carbonate rock specimens and their corresponding calcite twin analyses, plotted on lower hemisphere stereonets. 1 = maximum shortening strain axis; 2 = intermediate shortening strain axis; 3 = minimum strain axis. Turner (1953) compression axes are contoured per 1 percent area starting with the third standard deviation; "C" is the maxima. The great circle is bedding for each specimen. See Table 2.

and bedding. As an extreme example, in several samples studied by Ballard and Wiltscko (1983), the maximum shortening direction within nearly vertical beds, when rotated back to the horizontal around an axis parallel to bedding strike, was both transport- and bedding-parallel. The only exceptions to the layer- and transport-parallel fabric observation occur in overturned folds (Allmendinger, 1982), within layers that have high curvature (Spang and others, 1981), within veins that formed part way through the transport history of the thrust sheet (Spang and Groshong, 1981; Kilsdonk and Wiltschko, 1985; Wiltschko and Budai, 1985; Craddock, 1986). Groshong (1975), Ballard and Wiltschko (1983), Wiltschko and others (1985), and Kilsdonk and Wiltschko (1985) have interpreted these observations to indicate that calcite twinning occurs early in the stress history to the point that a later, and perhaps differently oriented, maximum principal stress direction does not significantly alter the earlier formed fabric; there is a strain hardening associated with calcite twinning, the exact mechanism for which is not known.

Although this monotonous fabric poses a problem for interpreting the mechanics of thrust ramp motion, it instead turns into a tool for interpreting thrust rotations. *If* the strains are imposed early, as we contend based on the above data, and *if* the maximum principal stress direction was largely the same from point to point (east-west) before significant motion on the Absaroka, Darby, and Prospect thrust sheets, *then* the present difference in the orientation of both the maximum principal shortening strains as well as the mean compression axes around the salient should be a measure of thrust sheet rotation.

To document principal strain orientations and magnitudes in the foreland and thrust belt, oriented specimens were collected for calcite twin analysis (Groshong, 1972; Groshong and others, 1984; Fig. 5). All samples were taken from either the Mission Canyon or Lodge Pole members of the Mississippian Madison Group, or the Jurassic Twin Creek Limestone. Both units are fossiliferous and contain fecal pellets and ooids. Dolomite is present in the Mississippian rocks, but dolomite twins were not

TABLE 2. DETAILED RESULTS OF THE CALCITE TWIN ANALYSIS STUDY

Specimen/ Thrust Sheet*	e_1[†] (%)	e_2[†] (%)	e_3[†] (%)	No. of Grains	No. of Grains Cleaned	No. of NEVs	No. of NEVs Cleaned	Rock Type[‡]
1-A	-1.8	-1.1	3.0	50	41	18	9	Mm
2-A	-4.2	1.3	3.0	50	40	20	14	Mm
3-A	-4.2	0.9	3.3	50	40	20	17	Mm
4-A	-4.7	0.2	4.4	51	40	21	15	Mn
5-A	-2.8	1.1	1.7	50	40	20	31	Mn
6-D	-4.0	-0.9	4.8	49	40	18	16	Jtc
7-D	-3.5	-2.4	5.9	50	40	20	19	Jtc
8-P	-3.5	0.6	2.9	50	40	20	1	Mm
9-P	-5.2	1.7	3.5	52	42	19	14	Mm
10-P	-3.2	-1.6	4.9	50	40	20	5	Mm
11-P	-3.5	0.8	2.7	50	40	20	3	Mm
12-P	-2.6	-1.1	3.7	50	35	30	0	Mm
13-P	-1.1	-0.21	1.2	50	35	37	17	Mm
14-P	-5.5	2.0	3.5	50	35	37	30	Mm
15-P	-6.0	-5.4	11.4	50	35	37	29	Mm
16-P	-2.0	0.25	1.7	50	35	31	0	Mm
17-P	-1.9	-0.05	1.9	50	35	36	14	Mm
18-P	-2.4	-0.02	2.4	50	35	26	5	Mm
19-P	-7.5	-4.7	12.1	50	35	28	5	Mm
20-P	-7.3	2.3	5.0	50	35	33	16	Mm
21-P	-6.1	-2.4	8.5	50	35	25	0	Mm
22-P	-3.1	0.07	2.3	50	35	0	0	Mm
23-P	-2.6	0.36	2.3	50	35	25	9	Mm
24-P	-1.4	-0.19	7.5	50	35	37	26	Mm
25-P	-3.0	-0.83	3.1	50	35	25	12	Mm
26-P	-4.1	-0.45	4.5	50	35	32	8	Mm
27-P	-3.8	0.26	3.6	50	35	14	0	Mm
28-P	-3.5	0.15	3.3	50	35	22	3	Mm
29-P	-4.2	-0.32	4.5	50	35	26	7	Mm
30-P	-3.1	0.76	2.3	50	35	8	0	Mm
31-C	-8.2	2.6	5.6	44	28	37	7	Mm
Z	-2.9	-1.2	4.1	44	16	37	100	Mm
32-C	-6.3	0.38	5.9	50	36	12	3	Mm
33-C	-2.5	0.37	2.2	28	20	8	0	Mm

*A = Absaroka, D = Darby, P = Prospect, C = Cache Creek thrust sheet.

[†] e_1 = Maximum shortening axis, e_2 = intermediate shortening axis, e_3 = maximum extension axis; shortening is negative, extension is positive.

[‡] Mm = Mississippian Madison Group; Jtc = Jurassic Twin Creek Limestone.

Z = Negative expected value (NEV) split.

common enough to permit a separate strain analysis (see Allmendinger, 1982).

The 34 specimens analyzed for twinning strains had fewer than 40 percent negative expected values (NEVs) so that multiple deformations were not indicted (see Teufel, 1980). Our technique was to remove those grains with the largest deviations, as much as 10 percent, in the total original data set (Groshong, 1972; 1974), along with at least five NEVs, so that a minimum of 35 twin sets from each specimen remained to contour for Turner (1953) compression axis densities (Kamb, 1959). In Figure 5 the three principal strain axes are plotted (shortening is negative), along with contoured compression axes; Table 2 presents the details of the calcite data.

Thrust belt

Oriented carbonate rock specimens were collected from five locations within the Absaroka thrust sheet. All samples collected are Madison Group rocks and are labeled 1 through 5 (Fig. 5).

Both compression and maximum principal shortening axes intersect with bedding great circles, except in sample 5. In this specimen, the shortening axis (e_1) trends north and intersects with bedding, but the compression axis ("C") trends east-west and the contour maximum nearly intersects with bedding. The low strains from this specimen (see Table 1) could be small measurement errors that could cause large strain ellipse rotation. The four specimens with layer-parallel shortening show a systematic counterclockwise compression-axis rotation from south to north (specimens 4 to 1) of nearly 150°.

Only two carbonate rock specimens were collected from the Darby thrust sheet for calcite twin analysis, both of which are Jurassic Twin Creek Limestone from near the Snake River (Fig. 5). Both specimens 6 and 7 show maximum principal shortening directions parallel to bedding. The compression axis trend for the southern one, no. 7, is N90°E, whereas the more northern one trends N50°E; both are normal to the local trace of the Darby thrust.

The Prospect thrust sheet is in contact with the foreland basement, from Teton Pass in the northern part of the study area to as far south as Granite Creek in the Gros Ventre Range. Twenty-three oriented Madison Group carbonate rocks were collected from just west of Teton Pass, south to Granite Creek, and also toward Clause Peak where the effects of buttressing are presumably absent (Fig. 1).

Three samples from the Teton Pass area—8, 9, and 10—show reasonable correlation between the maximum shortening and compression axes, but they were shortened at a high angle to bedding. The range of shortening and compression axis trends perhaps indicates small rotations on small, younger imbricate faults.

Of the remaining 20 Prospect specimens, only three deviate from the above layer-parallel, thrust-normal shortening; these are numbered 14, 24, and 28. Specimen 14 is a calcite vein within a micritic unit and records a presumably younger twinning strain. Kilsdonk and Wiltschko (1985) found nonlayer-parallel shortening directions in calcite veins within a similar structure in the Pine

Mountain block, Tennessee. Specimens 26 and 28 are from the hinge and the limb of an overturned, east-verging anticline. Allmendinger (1982) found similar, nonlayer-parallel shortening directions in overturned folds within the Meade sheet.

Craton

Three Madison Group specimens were collected from the allochthonous foreland: two from the Teton Range and one from Granite Creek in the Gros Ventre Range (Fig. 5).

Specimen 31 is from Glory Mountain, within a few hundred meters of the Prospect–Cache Creek fault intersection at Teton Pass. A high percentage of NEVs was found, and the data were separated into positive and negative expected-value groups. In both groups the maximum shortening and compression axes coincided; neither group displayed shortening directions within 20° of bedding, although the positive and negative shortening trends were 90° to each other. Specimen 32 is from farther north and was shortened parallel to bedding but in a north-south direc-

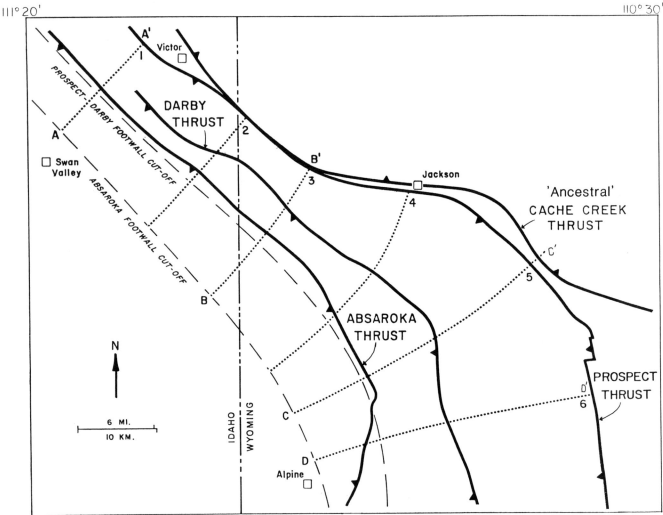

Figure 6. Calculated deformation paths, labeled 1 through 6, corresponding to cross sections A-A', B-B', and C-C', D-D'. See Table 3.

tion (present coordinates). Contours of the compression axes also display a girdle across the stereonet, indicating either a changing stress field during deformation, or calcite twinning associated with bending.

The rollover anticline associated with the Cache Creek thrust near Granite Creek is the location of specimen 33. Unlike the previous specimen, layer-parallel shortening is evident here, but in a north-south direction, not directed normal to the thrust trace nearby.

Summary

Calcite twinning within carbonate rocks of the thrust belt indicates that early layer-parallel shortening was prevalent throughout each of the three thrust sheets studied. Maximum shortening strains range from 0.2 to 7.9 percent, averaging 3.5 percent. No obvious patterns in variation of strain magnitude exist between separate thrust sheets or along strike. The trends of maximum principal shortening strain axes and compression axes are normal to the trace of the nearest thrust fault, even where associated with small-scale structures such as fold (specimens 16–18; see also Craddock, 1983) and complicated fault imbricate structures (specimens 19–23; see also Craddock, 1983), except for the southern, unbuttressed specimens (24, 26–30), which are from along a single north-south–trending anticline (Dorr and others, 1977) and show evidence of layer-parallel slip during folding. The only area of nonlayer-parallel shortening is near Teton Pass where the Prosepct and Cache Creek thrust moved intermittently and overlapped.

Limited sampling in the Teton–Gros Ventre Ranges indicates that the maximum shortening directions were not layer-parallel, but that the maximum principal shortening was oriented north-south, and not normal to the present trace of the Cache Creek thrust. These data also had more NEVs and a higher average shortening strain (4.6 percent).

CROSS SECTIONS AND PALINSPASTIC RECONSTRUCTIONS

In order to reconstruct the subsurface geometry and tectonic history of the study area, balanced restorable cross sections have been made (Figs. 6 through 10) according to the principles set forth by Elliott (1983). Data from several different sources are incorporated into these sections. Published U.S. Geological Survey maps were used for surface control. Overall thrust geometry and depth to basement were determined from well and seismic data, the same data used by Dixon (1982). The basic assumption in constructing and restoring balanced cross sections, other than conservation of volume, is that the thrust sheets, or any types of transported rock, were displaced parallel to the lines of section (Elliott, 1983). If this were not the case, a cross section could not be accurately restored because some parts, or even all, of the original section would not lie in the plane of the restored section. In essence, cross sections are only restorable if they have been

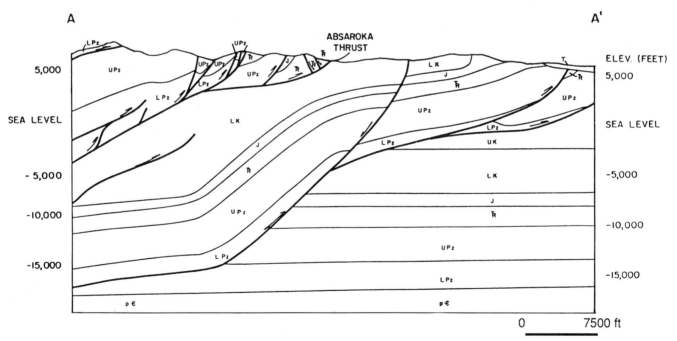

Figure 7. Cross section A-A′. T = Tertiary (Camp Davis Formation, Frontier-Harebell, Skyline Trail Conglomerate); UK = Upper Cretaceous (Aspen Formations); LK = Lower Cretaceous (Gannett-Aspen Formations); J = Jurassic (Nugget-Stump Formations); Tr = Triassic (Dinwoody-Thaynes Formations); UPz = Upper Paleozoic (Amsden-Phosphoria Formations); LPz = Lower Paleozoic (Flathead Sandstone–Madison Group); PC = Precambrian crystalline basement rocks. Well data are projected onto sections. See Dorr and Wiltschko, 1983, for more stratigraphic details.

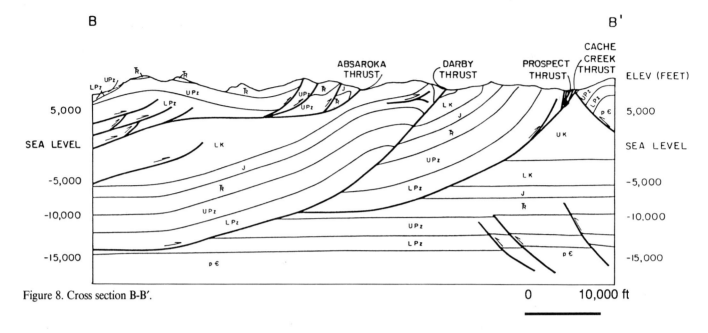

Figure 8. Cross section B-B′.

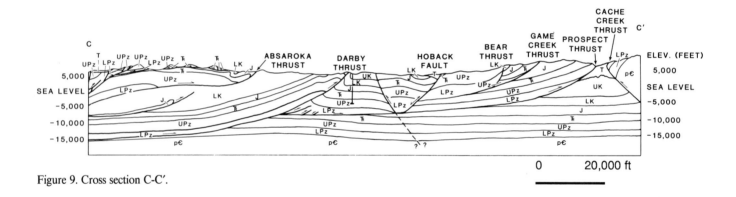

Figure 9. Cross section C-C′.

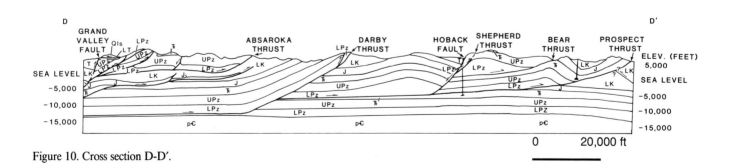

Figure 10. Cross section D-D′.

constructed along deformation paths. Therefore, we have restored our cross sections along the curved deformation paths of Figure 6 in order to facilitate accurate restoration.

The tectonic history of the salient is reconstructed in Figures 11 through 14 based on relative and absolute timing information, the deformation paths, and the restored cross sections. Table 3 shows the amount of displacement and degree of rotation used in the reconstruction along the deformation paths (Fig. 6). Several cultural features are also plotted on the maps in their present and palinspastic positions for reference markers.

The Absaroka thrust sheet was emplaced in Late Cretaceous time. Prior to this, the contiguous Teton–Gros Ventre block had been uplifted along the Cache Creek thrust. It is not possible to determine if the Teton–Gros Ventre block caused any rotation of the Absaroka sheet as it was emplaced because the Absaroka was subsequently carried by the Darby and Prospect thrusts. However, it does not appear likely that the Absaroka sheet would have rotated much after ramping, because its ramp and leading edge do

not diverge or converge noticeably. The tectonic reconstruction begins just after major movement on the Absaroka had ceased (Fig. 11).

By early Paleocene time, movement had begun on the Darby thrust (Fig. 12). The effect of the Teton–Gros Ventre uplift is unknown, but the fact that offset on the Darby dies out to zero north of Teton Pass is evidence that the thrust sheet probably rotated as it was being emplaced. By late Paleocene time, movement had ceased on the Darby and begun on the Prospect. Some time before the earliest Eocene the Prospect sheet was impinging upon the Teton–Gros Ventre uplift from Teton Pass northward (Fig. 13). As the northern part of the thrust sheet was impeded, the part south of Teton Pass was transported farther into the salient, resulting in an even greater counterclockwise rotation. At about this time, several major imbricates formed in the Prospect sheet in the southern part of the salient (Fig. 12; Wiltschko and Dorr, 1983, p. 1313, Fig. 2).

As the Prospect sheet was rotated further into the salient,

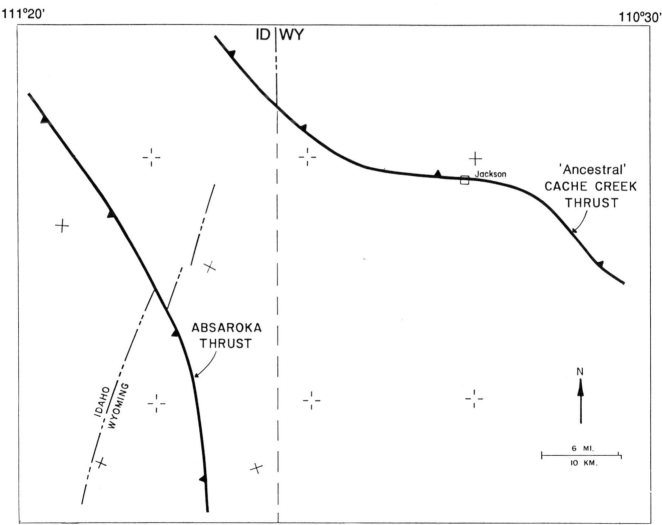

Figure 11. Palinspastic map during Late Cretaceous time. Dashed crosses are present day latitude and longitude markers. Solid crosses are palinspastic latitude and longitude markers. Long-dashed line is the present day Idaho-Wyoming border. Dash and dot line is the palinspastic Idaho-Wyoming border.

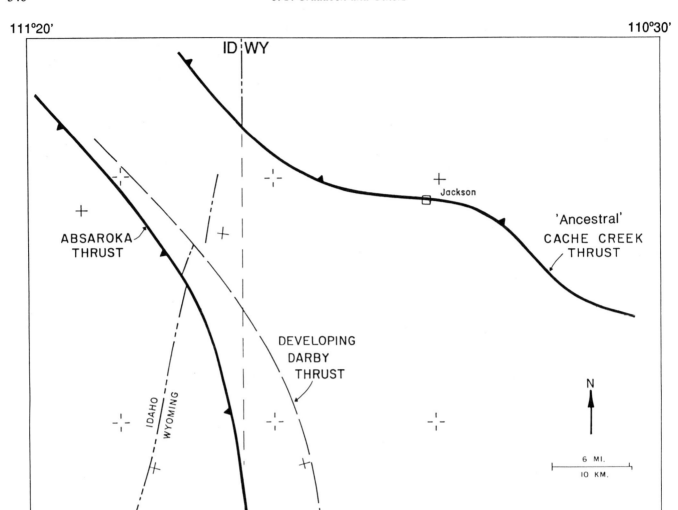

111°20'

110°30'

43°05'

Figure 12. Palinspastic map during Early Paleocene time. Dark dashed line shows the subsurface leading edge of the incipient Darby Thrust. Other symbols same as in Figure 11.

deformation at the initial area of impingement would be expected to increase. This is reflected in the imbricate wedges at Teton Pass (Schroeder, 1969). The strain and compression axes of calcite specimens 8, 9, and 10 (Fig. 5) indicate that compression occurred at a high angle to bedding. This implies that the rotation of the beds to a steep dip preceded the last major compression in the area, compression of the Prospect sheet against the immovable Teton–Gros Ventre buttress.

As the Prospect and Darby thrusts moved into the salient, they also carried the Absaroka thrust in piggyback fashion. As the thrust sheets beneath the Absaroka began to rotate, they would force the uppermost sheet to rotate some as well. Because the displacements and rotations of the Darby and Prospect are not constant from north to south, the Absaroka sheet would have been forced to rotate different amounts along strike and probably different amounts than the underlying thrust sheets. The differential rotations would result in an along-strike component of either extension or compression. This extension or compression normal

to the local transport direction, or deformation path, must have been accommodated by a mechanism that would allow some parts of the Absaroka thrust sheet to rotate more or less than other parts.

STRATIGRAPHIC EFFECTS ON THRUST SHEET ROTATION

In addition to the possible effects of basement-cored buttresses on thrust geometry, it is also important to consider the potential effects of strike-parallel and strike-normal stratigraphic changes as influences on thrust initiation and thrust sheet motion (Wiltschko and Eastman, 1983; Woodward, this volume). There are, however, two major difficulties with this latter approach. First, although stratigraphic variations almost certainly have some influence on thrust geometry (Woodward and others, 1983), their importance is very difficult to quantify due to a lack of modelling and fabric work on known "impingement" or "strat-

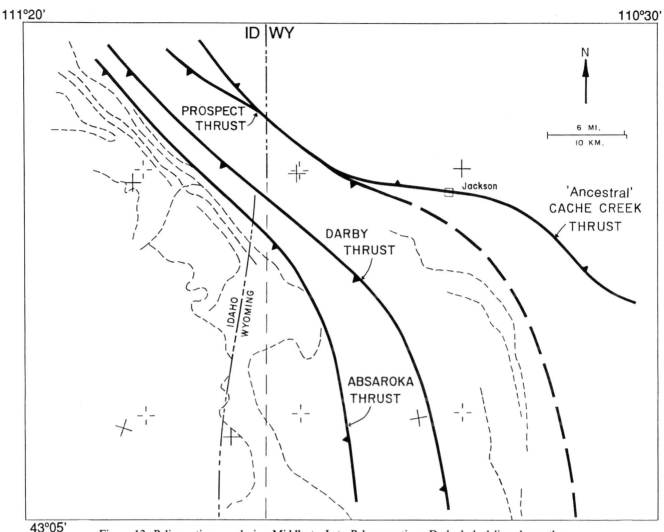

Figure 13. Palinspastic map during Middle to Late Paleocene time. Dark dashed line shows the subsurface leading edge of the incipient Prospect Thrust south of Jackson. Small dashed lines are incipient upper plate imbricates above the Prospect and Absaroka thrusts. Other symbols same as in Figure 11.

igraphic" structures. Detailed measured sections of each imbricate and major thrust sheet would have to be compared before the degree of structural significance can be postulated. Second, observations of stratigraphic thickness variations provide no information about fault rotation, transport direction, or deformation paths. Without structural data from which these kinematic parameters can be inferred, one can only guess as to which cross section lines to use to restore the stratigraphic data. Therefore, except by serendipity, the restoration will be incorrect, and this will most likely produce an apparent stratigraphic perturbation which actually does not exist.

A recent study of the southern part of the Idaho-Wyoming-Utah thrust belt (Kopania, 1985) compares the effect of a major stratigraphic change on thrust geometry with structural measurements. Just north of the Uinta Mountains the entire Cambrian through Devonian section has been removed beneath a major

unconformity. This has resulted in decreasing thrust displacement on the Absaroka thrust at its southern end (Dixon, 1982), which is manifested by its curvilinear surface trace. However, structural data from this area do not indicate any rotation of the Absaroka thrust (Kopania, 1985). It is also important to note that the Uinta North Flank fault postdates the Absaroka and Hogsback thrusts, so the Uinta Mountains were not present as a formidable buttress to Sevier thrust movement (Kopania, 1985). Thus, in this example, a very major stratigraphic break has affected thrust displacement and geometry but has not caused any perceptible rotations.

In the northern segment of the Idaho-Wyoming-Utah thrust belt there is a general paucity of complete measured stratigraphic sections on a local scale. This lack of data prevents us from being able to compare stratigraphic thickness variations between various imbricate sheets since measuring stratigraphic sections is beyond the scope of this study. We believe that lithologic and thickness changes almost certainly played some role in the structural complexity of this area. However, there is no evidence that stratigraphic variations could have contributed significantly to the rotations detected by us or others (e.g., Grubbs and Van der Voo, 1976). It seems more plausible that these stratigraphic variations acted as a catalyst for imbrication and the associated duplexes and lateral ramps during buttress-induced rotation rather than as the actual cause of rotation. Improved knowledge about lateral variations in fault zone strength and the mechanical controls on thrust sheet motion by stratigraphic variations could significantly alter these conclusions.

DISCUSSION AND CONCLUSIONS

Do the along-strike changes in both the maximum principal shortening direction computed from twinned calcite and joint orientations reflect an along-strike change in the maximum principal compressive stress direction or rotation of the thrust sheets?

TABLE 3. DETAILS OF CROSS SECTION RESTORATIONS AND THRUST ROTATIONS ALONG CHOSEN TRAVERSES (FIG. 6)

Deformation Path	Cross Section	— Displacements — Darby + Prospect (km)	Darby (km)	Rotations*
North				
1	A-A'	10.4	0	10° CW
2	none	14.7 (est.)	1.4 (est.)	7° CW
3	B-B'	19.2	3.1	19° CCW
4	none	22.4 (est.)	2.6 (est.)	40° CCW
5	C-C'	37.4	1.9	33° CCW
6	D-D'	36.8	9.4	18° CW
South				

*CW = clockwise; CCW = counterclockwise.

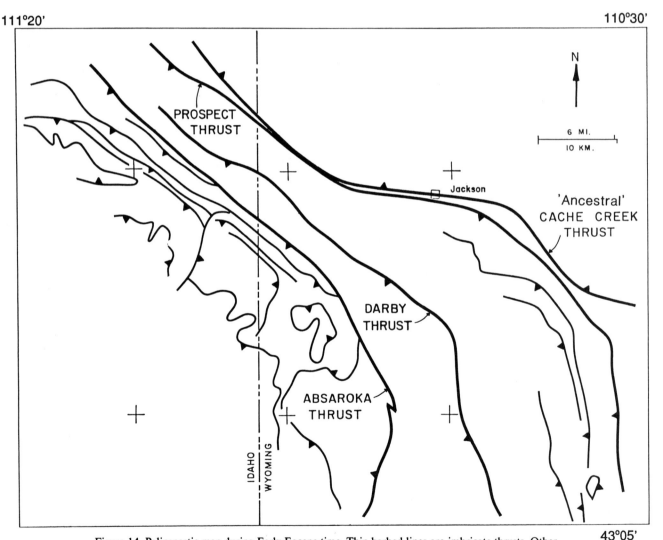

111°20'   110°30'

43°05'

Figure 14. Palinspastic map during Early Eocene time. Thin barbed lines are imbricate thrusts. Other symbols same as in Figure 11.

TABLE 4. DETAILS OF THRUST SHEET ROTATIONS*

Sedimentary Strata Sampled	Absaroka Sheet	Darby Sheet	Prospect Sheet
Cretaceous[†]	No rotation[§] (Samples 8-14)	No data	No data
Jurassic[‡]	No rotation (samples 5, 6, 7)	No rotation (samples 2, 3, 4)	No rotation (sample 1)
Triassic**	No rotation (sample A)	No rotation (samples C, D, E, F, K)	Rotated (samples B, I, J, S, T, X)

*Based on the paleomagnetic results of Grubbs and Van der Voo (1976) and Schwartz and Van der Voo (1984).

[†]Ephraim Conglomerate, Peterson Limestone, Smith's Formation, Wayan Formation.

[§]Cretaceous synfolding chemical remagnetization

[‡]Stump Formation

**Woodside/Chugwater Formation

That is, do the strains and joints reflect a curvilinear stress field at the time of thrusting, or were they imposed in a rectilinear stress field and then rotated in various degrees into parallelism with a curvilinear boundary?

There are conflicting results that bear on both sides of this question. On the one hand, Grubbs and Van der Voo (1976) and Schwartz and Van der Voo (1984) have shown that thrust sheet rotation, possibly large, has occurred within the Absaroka and more eastward thrusts. However, there is little evidence of strike-parallel stretching, such as would be evidenced by transverse structures or oblique slip on the same thrust faults as would be required to accommodate this rotation. On the other hand, a model for the stress trajectories within the Wyoming salient by Beutner (1977) shows that curvilinear stress trajectories approximately similar to the orientations of our joint and calcite data are produced. We favor a combination of the two models. The original stress trajectories were most likely curvilinear (see also Angelier and others, 1986; Huchon and others, 1986) to some extent because, even though the Absaroka thrust sheet has been little rotated according to the paleomagnetic data, the calcite and joint orientations change trends significantly around the salient. However, significant rotations in the Prospect thrust sheet seem to have taken place, as indicated by the paleomagnetic data, although the amounts of rotation indicated by the two data sets differ (Table 4) and both are different from rotations implied by the fabric data. We conclude, therefore, that the stress effects of the bounding basement uplifts were felt as far west as the Absaroka thrust sheet, whereas the constraints on motion were experienced only by the most frontal thrust sheet, which also presumably rotated the older, overlying thrust sheets. We have no explanation for why the rotations implied by the fabric data should not match the rotations found by paleomagnetic techniques.

As stated earlier, it would seem that the motion of thrust sheets near nonparallel bounding blocks could be by rotation and stretching, fault imbrication, or "spreading." The paleomagnetic study of Triassic red beds in the Prospect sheet indicates Prospect rotations that differ on opposite sides of the east-west–trending Hoback Canyon (Fig. 1). Hoback Canyon also is the approximate junction between impinged thrusting to the north and unimpinged thrusting to the south. Surface geologic features along Hoback Canyon are unique and closely spaced—tear faults, east-west–trending folds, and the contorted Red Creek outcrop (see Craddock and others, 1985; Dorr and others, 1987). Some of the Triassic paleomagnetic data (sites B, J, and H of Grubbs and Van der Voo, 1976; and site 1 of Schwartz and Van der Voo, 1984) are from these areas, and the Triassic cratonic pole is from the allochthonous Gros Ventre Block. Following Grubbs and Van der Voo (1976), Schwartz and Van der Voo (1984) concluded that the older Absaroka and Darby sheets did not rotate, and that the younger Prospect thrust sheet rotated 60° in a counterclockwise sense north of Hoback Canyon and 30° in a clockwise sense south of Hoback Canyon (see Table 4). This implies several facts: (1) that the undated Darby thrust is younger than the Prospect thrust (see Kraig and others, 1985; Craddock, 1988), (2) that the presumably younger Prospect thrust sheet decoupled along the overlying Darby thrust plane and rotated in simple shear, (3) that rotation of the Absaroka and Darby was too small for paleomagnetism to detect accurately (R. Van der Voo, 1984, personal communication), or (4) that the allochthonous Triassic pole in the Gros Ventre Range rotated in the same sense and magnitude above the Cache Creek thrust as the Absaroka and Darby sheets did above their respective detachments.

Our fabric data and deformation-path maps suggest that all three thrust sheets responded to the shape of the ancestral basement uplift embayment to the north and northeast, and rotated in a counterclockwise sense north of Hoback Canyon and in a clockwise sense south of Hoback Canyon. Thrust imbrication was also important in shortening the Prospect sheet where it encountered the basement uplift. These imbrications mimic the shape of the salient and the older thrust faults. This interpretation also implies that the calcite and joint fabrics formed uniquely in each thrust sheet in a regional horizontal curvilinear stress field, which changed slightly from an east-west trend in the west to a northeasterly trend near the buttress. Rock strains, fabrics, and the direction of thrust sheet motion in the foreland are less clear.

ACKNOWLEDGMENTS

We gratefully acknowledge the field assistance of John A. Dorr, Jr., Patti P. Craddock, Jean Kopania, and Greg Miller, and the financial support of Champlin Petroleum Company, Sigma Xi, ARCO Exploration Company, the Scott Turner Fund and the University of Michigan, and National Science Foundation Grant EAR 82-12714 (to D.V.W.). We also thank Champlin Petroleum for allowing us to use proprietary seismic data. Earlier versions of this chapter were greatly improved by Chris Schmidt, Don Blackstone, Nick Woodward, Ben van der Pluijm, and an anonymous reviewer.

REFERENCES CITED

Allmendinger, R., 1982, Analysis of microstructures in the Meade plate of the Idaho-Wyoming foreland thrust plate, U.S.A.: Tectonophysics, v. 85, p. 221–251.

Angelier, J., Barrier, E., and Chu, H. T., 1986, Plate collision and paleostress trajectories in a fold-thrust belt; The foothills of Taiwan: Tectonophysics, v. 125, p. 161–178.

Armstrong, F. C., and Cressman, E. R., 1963, The Bannock thrust zone, southeast Idaho: U.S. Geological Survey Professional Paper 374-J, p. J1–J22.

Armstrong, F. C., and Oriel, S. S., 1965, Tectonic development of the Idaho-Wyoming thrust belt: American Association of Petroleum Geologists Bulletin, v. 49, p. 1848–1866.

Ballard, S., and Wiltschko, D. V., 1983, Strain directions and structural style at the northeast end of the Powell Valley anticline, Pine Mountain Block, southwestern Virginia: Geological Society of America Abstracts with Programs, v. 15, p. 520.

Beutner, E. C., 1977, Causes and consequences of curvature in the Sevier orogenic belt, Utah to Montana: Wyoming Geological Association 19th Annual Field Conference Guidebook, p. 353–365.

Blackstone, D. L., Jr., compiler, 1980, Tectonic map of the Overthrust Belt, western Wyoming, southeast Idaho, and northeast Utah showing current oil and gas drilling and development: Geological Survey of Wyoming, scale 1:316,800.

Chapple, W. M., and Spang, J. S., 1974, Significance of layer-parallel slip during folding of layered sedimentary rocks: Geological Society of America Bulletin, v. 84, p. 1523–1534.

Corbett, M. K., 1983, Superimposed tectonism in the Idaho-Wyoming thrust belt, *in* Powers, R. B., ed., Geologic studies of the Cordilleran thrust belt, 1982: Denver, Colorado, Rocky Mountain Association of Geologists, v. 1, p. 341–355.

Craddock, J. P., 1983, Deformation history of the Prospect thrust sheet, overthrust belt, Wyoming [M.S. thesis]: Ann Arbor, University of Michigan, 33 p.

—— , 1986, Calcite strain and rock fabric variations across the Idaho-Wyoming

thrust belt: Geological Society of America Abstracts with Programs, v. 18, p. 573.

—— , 1988, Geologic map, cross section, and mesostructures across the Idaho-Wyoming fold-and-thrust belt at latitude 43°45′: Geological Society of America Map and Chart MCHO67.

Craddock, J. P., and van der Pluijm, B., 1987, Migration of late Paleocene brines through cratonic carbonates by calcite twin "pumping"; A hypothesis: Geological Society of America Abstracts with Programs, v. 19, no. 4, p. 194.

Craddock, J. P., and Wiltschko, D. V., 1983, Strains in the Prospect thrust sheet, Overthrust belt, Wyoming: Geological Society of America Abstracts with Programs, v. 15, p. 549.

Craddock, J. P., Eastman, D. B., and Wiltschko, D. V., 1985, Sequence of deformation events beneath the Bear thrust, Hoback Canyon, western Wyoming: Earth Science Bulletin, v. 18, p. 31–44.

Dahlstrom, C.D.A., 1970, Structural geology of the eastern margin of the Canadian Rocky Mountains: Bulletin of Canadian Petroleum Geology, v. 18, p. 332–406.

Dixon, J. S., 1982, Regional structural synthesis, Wyoming salient of the western overthrust: American Association of Petroleum Geologists Bulletin, v. 66, no. 10, p. 1560–1580.

Dorr, J. A., Jr., Spearing, D. R., and Steidtmann, J. R., 1977, Deformation and deposition between a foreland uplift and an impinging thrust belt; Hoback Basin, Wyoming: Geological Society of America Special Paper 177, 82 p.

Dorr, J. A., Spearing, D. R., Steidtmann, J., Wiltschko, D. V., and Craddock, J. P., 1987, Hoback River Canyon, Wyoming, *in* Beus, S. S., ed., The Rocky Mountain Section of the Geological Society of America: Boulder, Colorado, Geological Society of America Centennial Field Guilde, v. 2, p. 197–200.

Dunn, S.L.D., 1983, Timing of foreland and thrust belt deformation in an overlap area, Teton Pass, Idaho and Wyoming, *in* Lowell, J. D., ed., Rocky Mountain foreland basins and uplifts: Denver, Colorado, Rocky Mountain Association of Geologists, p. 263–269.

Elliott, D., 1983, The construction of balanced cross sections: Journal of Structural Geology, v. 5, p. 101.

Engelder, T., and Geiser, P., 1980, On the use of regional joint sets as trajectories of paleostress field during development of the Appalachian Plateau, New York: Journal of Geophysical Research, v. 85, p. 6319–6341.

Engelder, T., and Marshak, S., 1985, Disjunctive cleavage formed at shallow depths in sedimentary rocks: Journal of Structural Geology, v. 7, no. 3/4, p. 327–343.

Groshong, R. H. Jr., 1972, Strain calculated from twinning in calcite: Geological Society of America Bulletin, v. 83, p. 2025–2038.

—— , 1974, Experimental test of least-squares strain calculations using twinned calcite: Geological Society of America Bulletin, v. 85, p. 1855–1864.

—— , 1975, Strain, fractures, and pressure solution in natural single-layer folds: Geological Society of America Bulletin, v. 86, p. 1363–1376.

Groshong, R. H., Teufel, L. W., and Gasteiger, C., 1984, Precision and accuracy of the calcite strain-gage technique: Geological Society of America Bulletin, v. 95, p. 357–363.

Grubbs, K. L., and Van der Voo, R., 1976, Structural deformation of the Idaho-Wyoming overthrust belt, as determined by Triassic paleomagnetism: Tectonophysics, v. 33, p. 321–336.

Gwinn, V., 1967, Curvature of marginal folded belts flanking major mountain ranges; Accentuated or caused by lateral translation of epidermal stratified cover?: Geological Society of America Abstracts with Programs, New Orleans, p. 87.

Horberg, L., Nelson, V., and Church, V., 1949, Structural trends in central western Wyoming: Geological Society of America Bulletin, v. 60, p. 183–216.

Huchon, P., Barrier, E., DeBremaecher, T.-C., and Augelier, J., 1987, Collision and stress trajectories in Taiwan; A finite element model: Tectonophysics, v. 125, p. 179–191.

Jackson, M., Craddock, J. P., Ballard, M., Van der Voo, R., and McCabe, C., 1988, Anhysteretic magnetic anisotropy and calcite strains in Devonian carbonates from the Appalachian Plateau. Tectonophysics, (in press).

Jobin, D. A., 1965, Preliminary geologic map of the Palisades Peak Quadrangle,

Bonneville County, Idaho and Teton County, Wyoming: U.S. Geological Survey Open-File Report no. 2, scale 1:24,000.

——, 1971, Geologic map of the Ferry Peak Quadrangle, Lincoln County, Wyoming, U.S. Geological Survey Quadrangle Map GQ-1027, scale 1:24,000.

Kamb, W. B., 1959, Ice petrofabric observations from Blue Glacier, Washington, in relation to theory and experiment: Journal of Geophysical Research, v. 64, p. 1891–1901.

Kilsdonk, M. W., and Wiltschko, D. V., 1985, Deformation mechanisms in the southwest part of the Pine Mountain block: Geological Society of America Abstracts with Programs, v. 17, p. 97.

Kopania, A. A., 1984, Deformation consequences of the impingement of the foreland and northern thrust belt (Palisades-Jackson Hole area), eastern Idaho and western Wyoming [abs.]: American Association of Petroleum Geologists Bulletin, v. 68, p. 939.

——, 1985, The effects of basement-cored buttresses and major stratigraphic changes on thrust sheets; An example from the Idaho-Wyoming-Utah thrust belt: Geological Society of America Abstracts with Programs, v. 17, p. 249.

Kraig, D. H., Wiltschko, D. V., and Spang, J. H., 1985, Emplacement of the Moxa Arch and related imitation of the ancestral Prospect thrust, southwestern Wyoming: Geological Society of America Abstracts with Programs, v. 17, p. 364.

Lageson, D. R., 1984, Structural geology of Stewart Peak culmination, Idaho-Wyoming thrust belt: American Association of Petroleum Geologists Bulletin, v. 68, p. 401–416.

Love, J. D., 1973, Harebell Formation (Upper Cretaceou) and Pinyon Conglomerate (uppermost Cretaceous and Paleocene), northwestern Wyoming: U.S. Geological Survey Professional Paper 734-A, p. A1–A54.

Love, J. D., and Albee, H. F., 1972, Geological map of the Jackson Quadrangle, Teton County, Wyoming: U.S. Geological Survey Miscellaneous Investigations Series Map I-769-A, scale 1:24,000.

Love, J. D., Reed, J. C., Christiansen, R. L., and Stacy, R. L., 1973, Geologic block diagram and tectonic history of the Teton region; Wyoming-Idaho: U.S. Geological Survey Miscellaneous Investigations Series Map I-730.

Muehlberger, W. R., 1961, Conjugate joint sets of small dihedral angle: Journal of Geology, v. 69, p. 211–219.

Nickelson, R. P., and Hough, V.N.D., 1967, Jointing in the Appalachian Plateau of Pennsylvania: Geological Society of America Bulletin, v. 78, p. 609–630.

Oriel, S. S., and Moore, D. W., 1985, Geologic map of the west and east Palisades roadless areas, Idaho and Wyoming: U.S. Geological Survey Miscellaneous Field Studies Map M-16198, scale 1:50,000.

Oriel, S. S., Antweiler, J. C., Moore, D. W., Benhem, J. R., and Maley, D. R., 1985, Mineral resource potential of the west and east Palisades roadless areas, Idaho and Wyoming: U.S. Geological Survey Miscellaneous Field Studies Map MF-1619A, scale 1:50,000.

Parker, J. M., III, 1942, Regional systematic jointing in slightly deformed sedimentary rocks: Geological Society of America Bulletin, v. 53, p. 381–408.

Perry, W. J., Jr., and Colton, G. W., 1981, A summary of the methodology and results of regional joint-studies in the central and northern Appalachian basin: U.S. Geological Survey Open-File Report 81-1342, 17 p.

Price, N. J., 1966, Fault and joint development in brittle and semi-brittle rock: Oxford, Pergamon Press, 176 p.

Reches, Z., 1976, Analysis of joints in two monoclines in Israel: Geological Society of America Bulletin, v. 87, p. 1654–1662.

Royse, F., Jr., 1985, Geometry and timing of the Darby-Prospect-Hogsback thrust fault system, Wyoming: Geological Society of America Abstracts with Programs, v. 17, p. 263.

Royse, F., Jr., Warner, M. A., and Reese, D. L., 1975, Thrust belt structural geometry and related stratigraphic problems, Wyoming–Idaho–northern Utah: Denver, Colorado, Rocky Mountain Association of Geologists Symposium, p. 41–54.

Rubey, W. W., and Hubbert, M. K., 1959, Role of fluid pressure in the mechanics of overthrust faulting, II: Geological Society of America Bulletin, v. 70, p. 167–206.

Schroeder, M. L., 1969, Geologic map of the Teton Pass Quadrangle, Teton County, Wyoming: U.S. Geological Survey Geologic Quadrangle Map GQ-793, scale 1:24,000.

——, 1973, Geologic map of the Clause Peak Quadrangle, Lincoln, Sublette, and Teton Counties, Wyoming: U.S. Geological Survey Geologic Quadrangle Map GQ-1092, scale 1:24,000.

Schwartz, S. Y., and Van der Voo, R., 1984, Paleomagnetic study of thrust sheet rotation during foreland impingement in the Wyoming-Idaho overthrust belt: Journal of Geophysical Research, v. 89, no. B12, p. 10077–10086.

Secor, D. R., Jr., 1965, Role of fluid pressure in joints: American Journal of Science, v. 263, p. 633–646.

Spang, J. H., and Groshong, R. H., Jr., 1981, Deformation mechanisms and strain history of a minor fold from the Appalachian Valley and Ridge province: Tectonophysics, v. 72, p. 323–342.

Spang, J. H., Wolcott, T. L., and Serra, S., 1981, Strain in the ramp regions of two minor thrusts, southern Canadian Rocky Mountains, *in* Carter, N. L., and others, eds., Mechanical behavior of crustal rocks; The Handin volume: Geophysical Monograph 24, p. 243–250.

Staatz, M. H., and Albee, H. F., 1966, Geology of the Garns Mountain Quadrangle, Bonneville, Madison, and Teton Counties, Idaho: U.S. Geological Survey Bulletin 1205, 122 p.

Teufel, L. W., 1980, Strain analysis of experimental superposed deformation using calcite twin lamellae: Tectonophysics, v. 65, p. 291–309.

Turner, F. J., 1953, Nature and dynamic interpretation of deformation lamellae in calcite of marbles: American Journal of Science, v. 251, p. 276–298.

Wiltschko, D. V., and Budai, J., 1985, Structural controls on fluid migration; An example from the Absaroka sheet, Idaho-Wyoming thrust belt: Geological Society of America Abstracts with Programs, v. 17, p. 754.

Wiltschko, D. V., and Dorr, J. A., Jr., 1983, Timing of deformation in Overthrust belt and foreland of Idaho, Wyoming, and Utah: American Association of Petroleum Geologists Bulletin, v. 67, no. 8, p. 1304–1322.

Wiltschko, D. V., and Eastman, D. B., 1983, Role of basement warps and faults in localizing thrust fault ramps: Geological Society of America Memoir 158, p. 177–190.

Wiltschko, D. V., Medwedeff, D. A., and Millson, H. E., 1985, Distribution and mechanisms of strain within rocks on the northwest ramp of Pine Mountain blocks, southern Appalachian foreland; A field test of of theory: Geological Society of America Bulletin, v. 96, p. 426–435.

Woodward, N. B., 1981, Structural geometry of the Snake River Range, Idaho and Wyoming [Ph.D. thesis]: Baltimore, Maryland, Johns Hopkins University, 401 p.

——, 1986, Thrust geometry of the Snake River Range, Idaho and Wyoming: Geological Society of America Bulletin, v. 97, p. 178–193.

Woodward, N. B., Walker, K. R., and Simmons, W. A., 1983, Facies controls on structural trends; Examples from the southern Appalachians: Geological Society of America Abstracts with Programs, v. 15, p. 723.

MANUSCRIPT ACCEPTED BY THE SOCIETY FEBRUARY 9, 1988

Printed in U.S.A.

Geological Society of America
Memoir 171
1988

Primary and secondary basement controls on thrust sheet geometries

Nicholas B. Woodward
Department of Geological Sciences, University of Tennessee, Knoxville, Tennessee 37996-1410

ABSTRACT

Active buttressing of thin-skinned structures by simultaneous thick-skinned structures is a primary basement control for thrust belt geometries. Stratigraphic variations in the sedimentary cover are a form of secondary basement control that can explain many changes in thrust geometry better than primary controls. Thin-skinned structural style changes related to secondary basement control lack the precise temporal and geographic proximities that provide the critical evidence for primary control. Secondary controls, however, are ubiquitous throughout orogenic belts, not just near present basement uplifts, and they provide a powerful mechanism to understand regional and local changes in thrust geometries. Secondary controls are derived from the downwarp behavior of the basement surface when loaded by sediments. Variable subsidence produces different stacking sequences of lithic units (and structural lithic units for later deformation). When deformed by thrusting, lateral ramps and changes in duplex and imbricate geometries result from the regionally variable stratigraphic package being folded and faulted.

An unexposed Snake River fault zone has been proposed previously to explain apparent offsets of stratigraphic and structural trends across the Snake River Plain. This feature is often considered to involve foreland basement rocks as well, and to be part of a foreland structure that affected the thrust belt's evolution. On a palinspastic map, isopachs and many facies boundaries south of the plain trend northeast-southwest. Once these stratigraphic variations within thrust sheets of the Idaho-Wyoming-Utah thrust belt are understood, the need for any such fault zone is removed because correlative structures across the plain carry different stratigraphic sections.

Basement asperities as the cause of thrust ramps are examined in two field examples in which basement and sedimentary strata are involved in the same thrust sheet at the surface. In both the Ogden, Utah, and the Mountain City, Tennessee, areas, the presence of basement seems to have no effect on the structural geometries developed above them, although stratigraphic layering does. As a result, basement faulting in general seems a less likely direct cause for thrust ramp locations than does stratigraphic control. The inference is that, because different stratigraphic packages vary at different rates and in different directions, they are the most likely control on the areal and vertical locations of thrust ramp positions.

INTRODUCTION

Horberg and others (1949) suggested that the Sevier fold-thrust belt directly impinged on the Teton basement uplift in the vicinity of Teton Pass in Wyoming (Fig. 1). Their evidence was: (1) changing thrust belt structural geometries near the buttress; (2) changing structural trends near the buttress; and (3)

overlap in timing between the thrust belt structures and the basement uplifts. These factors are still the primary arguments for the thrust belt–foreland uplift interactions described in this volume.

This chapter examines two aspects of the general problem of possible structural interactions between basement-involved and cover structures. The first is the question of whether foreland uplifts or basement trends are necessary to explain offsets in thrust trends (such as those seen in the northern Idaho–Wyoming–Utah thrust belt). Another part of the same question is the suggested presence of a basement-involved fault parallel to the eastern Snake River Plain. The Snake River fault has never been observed, but is postulated based on a presumed lack of continuity of stratigraphy and structure across the Plain (Pratt, 1983; Sandberg and others, 1983). The second aspect involves the question of whether basement faults are necessary or sufficient conditions for the formation of thrust ramps (Jacobeen and Kanes, 1974, 1975; Wiltschko and Eastman, 1983). If basement block–thrust belt interactions are not necessary, what is the origin of the many trend changes and geometric variations? This chapter offers the hypothesis that stratigraphic variations are both necessary and sufficient causes for regional and local changes in thrust belt geometries.

The essential contrast in views between this chapter and many of the others in this volume lies in which of two major parameters cause the changing map patterns and structural geometries. The buttress hypothesis is based on modification of regional stress distributions associated with thrusting by small or large basement irregularities or fault blocks. The hypothesis of stratigraphic controls on thrust geometries presented here and elsewhere (Woodward and Rutherford, 1988), is based on regionally variable material properties in the rocks being deformed in a relatively constant stress field. The stratigraphic variability is derived from irregular subsidence during sedimentation, either because of differential flexural rigidity of the basement or because the basement surface is broken by earlier fault trends. These earlier basement faults, if they are present, need not be very large. The thrust structures do not ever necessarily approach the basement faults, nor are the regional stress patterns modified; rather, the ramps in the thrusts are controlled by the facies and thickness changes of the stratigraphy.

THE ALTERNATIVE HYPOTHESIS AND EXAMPLE

How can stratigraphic controls on thrust geometries work? Basement faulting or basement flexural properties can relate directly to sedimentation (Jordan, 1981). Where basement subsides uniformly, stratigraphic facies changes and lithologic contrasts will gradually reflect the change from cratonal to miogeoclinal to deeper water sedimentation. Where basement properties are regionally nonuniform, more abrupt stratigraphic changes should be common. The changes in stratigraphy (loss of a glide horizon for example) and thickness will have a major impact on the origin and evolution of subsequent thrust structures. Areal and vertical locations of ramps and flats in the stratigraphic section are proposed to be controlled more by stratigraphic packaging as structural lithic units than by basement-fault proximity or geometry. The vertical position of ramps within the stratigraphic section is a major part of the question. Commonly there are several major ramps in thrust paths. Although a basement fault might conceivably localize the ramp upward from the lowest glide zone into an intermediate level flat horizon, it is difficult to use that explana-

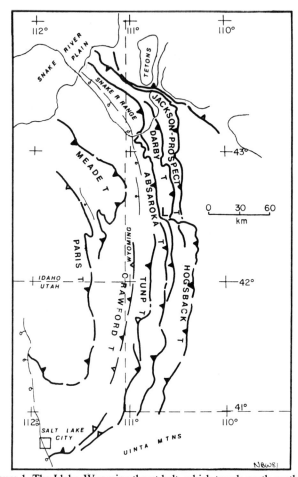

Figure 1. The Idaho-Wyoming thrust belt, which trends north-south for most of its length. It changes trend both at the north and south ends. The spacing of thrusts and the dominant stratigraphy seen on the surface changes roughly at the latitude of LaBarge Meadows (L; 42°30′). There are several significant reentrants in the thrust traces, especially at the south end of the Snake River Range, at LaBarge Meadows and at the south end of the Meade thrust.

tion alone to explain ramps across higher stratigraphic units. Some stratigraphic changes are almost certainly related to sea level, and those do not involve basement at all.

Woodward (1983) and Woodward and Rutherford (1988) discussed the role of structural lithic units in the evolution of thrust structures in the northern Idaho–Wyoming thrust belt. Four units were recognized: Lower Paleozoic, Upper Paleozoic, Lower Mesozoic, and Cretaceous (Fig. 2). The units were first described from the Snake River Range, where nine imbricate sheets of the Absaroka thrust system are well exposed in several canyons (Woodward, 1986). Major ramps were recognized through parts of each structural lithic unit. To extend the structural lithic unit analysis to a larger area, two problems had to be resolved: the deformed distribution of initial stratigraphic data points, as shown by the present geography, and the amount of regional stratigraphic information.

A palinspastic map of the northern Idaho–Wyoming thrust

belt was constructed based on five local and two regional balanced sections. Three additional regional balanced sections were prepared for the thrust belt south of the Snake River Range and north of LaBarge Meadows (L in Fig. 1). Stratigraphic information was derived from published maps and papers, unpublished theses, the author's unpublished measured sections, and from thicknesses used in published cross sections (especially those of Rubey, 1973; Rubey and others, 1980; Lamerson, 1983).

The regional variations in structural lithic units for the northern Idaho–Wyoming thrust belt are shown in Figure 3. For this first approximation, changing structural styles are correlated solely with regional thickness changes. Regional facies changes in each stratigraphic horizon and each structural lithic unit are too poorly documented to be conclusively correlated with detailed structural changes except in a few places. The Lower Paleozoic structural lithic unit primarily thickens westward, although there are no surface data on it in the Crawford-Meade thrust system. The Upper Paleozoic structural lithic unit thickens to the west and to the northwest. Isopach trends are significantly rotated in a clockwise direction away from parallelism with the regional thrust trends. For the well-documented Mississippian (Fig. 4) and Pennsylvanian rocks, stratigraphic units become more distal and thicker from south to north along individual thrust sheets, as well

as from east to west from one thrust sheet to another (Sando, 1977; Rose, 1977; N. B. Woodward, unpublished measured sections).

The Lower Mesozoic structural lithic unit has a nearly constant thickness along strike in the northern Absaroka thrust system, but thickens dramatically from the northern Absaroka sheet southward and westward. Fold amplitudes and wavelengths in the Lower Mesozoic unit increase from north to south and from east to west as it thickens. The Cretaceous structural lithic unit is poorly preserved in frontal imbricate thrust structures in the northern Idaho–Wyoming thrust belt, so it is difficult to reach conclusions about its possible impact on observed structural geometries there.

Overall, the closely spaced imbricate thrust style of the northern thrust belt is related to the thickness and mostly massive nature of the Upper Paleozoic structural lithic unit. It is about 50 percent of the pre-Cretaceous section there. As the Lower Mesozoic unit becomes a larger and larger percentage of the section from north to south (75 percent of the pre-Cretaceous section south of LaBarge Meadows), it is structurally most important and probably controls the more broadly spaced faults and major folds that have become the target of major oil exploration. Currie and others (1962) demonstrated that in any folded sequence the spacing and relative thicknesses of strong and weak layering controlled the thickness of fold trains. This was the origin of their concept of structural lithic units. The regional changes in thrust spacing and in the amplitude and wavelength of folds are both inferred to reflect areally variable structural lithic units that were mechanically significant during thrust deformation. The inference is also that because the different stratigraphic packages—which are recognized as individual structural lithic units—vary at different rates and in different directions, they are the most likely cause of areal and vertical variability in thrust ramp position.

On a finer scale (hundreds of meters), stratigraphic variations can also be correlated with specific structural changes. The northern Absaroka thrust system is typified by several large lateral ramps in thrust surfaces. The faults generally cut up-section to the south (Fig. 4). These lateral structures align on the palinspastic map with thickness changes and facies boundaries (reconstructed from Sando, 1976; Rose, 1976) in the Mississippian part of the Upper Paleozoic structural lithic unit. The Mississippian becomes thinner and more representative of on-shelf sedimentation from northwest to southeast. Evaporites have been reported from several localities southeast of the 400-m isopach but not northwest of it. Other stratigraphic changes in the upper Paleozoic are that the well-developed (>100 m) Late Mississippian paleokarst observed in the Idaho part of the Snake River Range thins greatly (to less than 10 m) in Wyoming parts of the Absaroka thrust sheet. The Permian Phosphoria Formation shales that form the boundary zone between the Upper Paleozoic and Lower Mesozoic structural units also thicken significantly from north to south within the thrust sheets.

Other types of changes within stratigraphic packages include the internal stacking sequence of massive and thinly bedded in-

FORMATION		STRUCTURAL LEVEL	STYLE
ASPEN	K	CRETACEOUS UNIT 1800 m	LARGE AMPLITUDE FOLDS
BEAR RIVER			
GANNETT			
STUMP+PREUSS	J	LOWER MESOZOIC UNIT	LARGE KINK-FOLDS
TWIN CREEK			
NUGGET			
ANKAREH	Ŧ	1300 m	
THAYNES			
WOODSIDE			
DINWOODY			
PHOSPHORIA	P	UPPER PALEOZOIC UNIT 1150 m	MAJOR THRUSTS WITH FOLDS RELATED TO RAMPS
WELLS	₱		
AMSDEN			
MISSION CANYON	M		
LODGEPOLE			
DARBY	D	LOWER PALEOZOIC UNIT 600m	MAJOR DECOLLEMENT IMBRICATE AND BLIND THRUSTS, HORSES
BIGHORN	O		
GALLATIN	€		
GROS VENTRE			

Figure 2. Four structural lithic units in the Snake River Range that are used to explain changes in structural styles for the northern Idaho–Wyoming thrust belt (Woodward, 1981; Woodward and others, 1988). The units are based on changes in ramp-flat geometry for the thrust surfaces and on changing folding styles in different parts of the section, as described by Currie and others (1962).

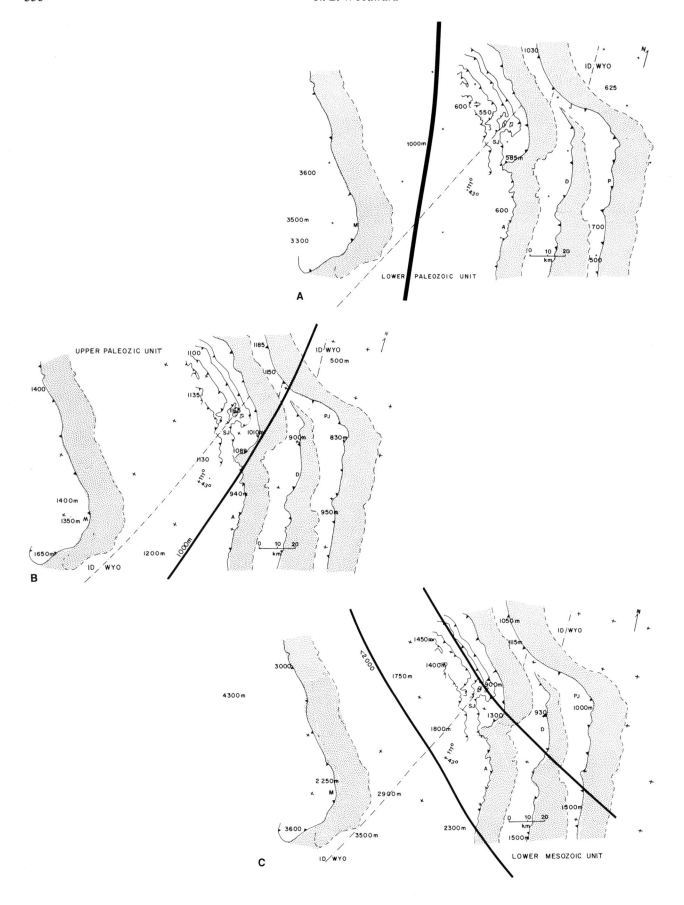

tervals within a structural lithic unit (Woodward and Rutherford, 1988), as well as the stacking sequence of separate structural lithic units. Probably the most important variable in controlling the ramp-flat paths is the critical taper of mechanically dominant parts of the structural lithic units, such as major décollement horizons or massive ramp units (Rutherford, 1985).

The lateral ramps have been easier to study because both the hanging wall and footwall parts of the ramps are exposed, but normal frontal ramps also seem to be controlled by similar stratigraphic changes. Stratigraphic controls on thrust shapes are not generally well documented beyond the usual statement that ramps cross strong units and flats are in weak units. Unfortunately this statement is frequently wrong, and glide zones are commonly found in massive carbonates where cataclastic flow promotes the ease of sliding (Wojtal and Mitra, 1986; Paul, 1986; Paul and Woodward, 1985; Coleman and Lopez, 1986). Stratigraphic changes provide a reasonable origin for localizing thrust ramps both in map pattern (via facies or thickness changes) and in vertical position within the stratigraphic section (via regionally changing stacks of structural lithic units).

Why are changing stratigraphic packages not more easily correlated with changes in thrust geometries? Two reasons are probably most important. Dahlstrom (1969) noted that without palinspastic maps, most stratigraphic trends plot everywhere as roughly parallel to thrust trends. This is the result of the 50 to 75

Figure 3. A through C, All of the four structural lithic units originally recognized in the Snake River Range; they vary in thicknesses regionally (1,000-m isopach shown to illustrate thickness trends). Facies patterns within many units follow the thickness trends, but sections measured for many units are too sparse to make more detailed facies maps reliable at this time. The stratigraphic data were plotted on a palinspastic map derived from serial balanced cross sections. The thrusts restored on the map are generalized insofar that individual fault lines lump all of the displacements in one fault system. For example, the single "Prospect-Jackson" (J-P) thrust lumps all of the displacements in the frontal imbricates of that major sheet; therefore, the sequence of thrusting within the imbricates is not a problem. Only the major imbricates in the Snake River Range are shown also. The rotation of thrust trends and the Idaho-Wyoming border with respect to the foreland is primarily the result of the unfolding of structures within the Absaroka (A) thrust sheet, and secondarily the result of the loss of Darby (D) thrust displacement from south to north. Variations in displacements, or identification of new previously unknown faults such as the sub-Prospect Granite Creek thrust (Royse, 1985), will alter the palinspastic map of thrust belt trends very little. It may affect the amount of rotation of the thrust belt trends relative to the foreland. The Lower Paleozoic structural lithic unit is well exposed only in the eastern thrusts and in the Paris-Willard-Putnam thrust sheet to the west of the palinspastic map. Its westward thickening trend is the only one identifiable. The isopach trends in both the Upper Paleozoic and Lower Mesozoic structural lithic units cross structural trends on the palinspastic map at oblique angles. The isopach trends for the two intervals indicate that the subsidence history for the thrust belt area varied regionally over time with maximum subsidence during the upper Paleozoic being to the northwest, but during the Triassic and Jurassic being to the southwest. Crosses mark longitude-latitude at 15-minute quadrangle corners.

percent horizontal thrust shortening and the discontinuous exposures of stratigraphic horizons (most of any unit in a thrust sheet is covered by younger units or is buried beneath the trailing thrust sheet). This is the major drawback to nonpalinspastic paleogeographic maps such as those of Rose (1976, 1977) or Koch (1976).

A second reason is that stratigraphic nomenclature tends to remain consistent in structural provinces and change dramatically where major faults are crossed. In many ways this latter approach follows the traditional European (especially Alpine) tradition that emphasized that "facies realms" were unique to particular thrust nappes. If the facies realm was identified, then the exposure could be classified according to the nappe from which it was derived. Trümpy (1969) summarized the earlier arguments and challenged their validity on the basis of newer mapping. He pointed out that even in the type areas, the nappes and the facies realms were not necessarily linked. Several facies realms could be found in a single thrust nappe. Insofar as our stratigraphic nomenclature chooses convenient boundaries (thrusts, or covered areas) to separate regions of one formation from another formation of the same age, we are perpetuating the "facies realms concept."

Stratigraphic nomenclature in the Idaho-Wyoming-Utah thrust belt has many examples of map units from distant, well-defined type areas being used despite significant changes in almost all aspects of their internal composition. The upper Paleozoic Wells Formation is a good example. In Wells Canyon, Utah, the Wells is defined with a lower sandstone member and an upper carbonate member. According to the findings of most U.S. Geological Survey mapping in the northern Absaroka thrust system (100 km away on the present geographic base), the Upper Wells is dominantly sandstone and the Lower Wells is dominantly carbonate. The foreland nomenclature of Tensleep Formation (upper sandstone) and Amsden Formation (lower carbonate) from only 25 km away in the Teton Range is clearly more suited to the rocks involved. More recent workers (Woodward, 1981; Moore and others, 1984; Oriel and Moore, 1985) have reintroduced the foreland nomenclature in this part of the thrust belt.

A reexamination of stratigraphic variations based on the physical description of units rather than distant names is improving the correlation of structural changes with the changing material properties of the rock package (Woodward and Rutherford, 1988). Woodward and others (1983, 1988) have documented similar types of changes for the better subdivided stratigraphy of the Tennessee thrust belt.

SNAKE RIVER FAULT

The Snake River fault (Fig. 5) has been postulated as one influence of basement-type structure on thrust belt geometries. Pratt (1983) argued that 145 km (90 mi) of right-lateral offset separated the Montana thrust belt from that in Wyoming. Gutschick and others (1980) and Sandberg and others (1983) did not discuss the Snake River fault, although they showed it offsetting major facies trends in their figures. Sandberg and others (1983)

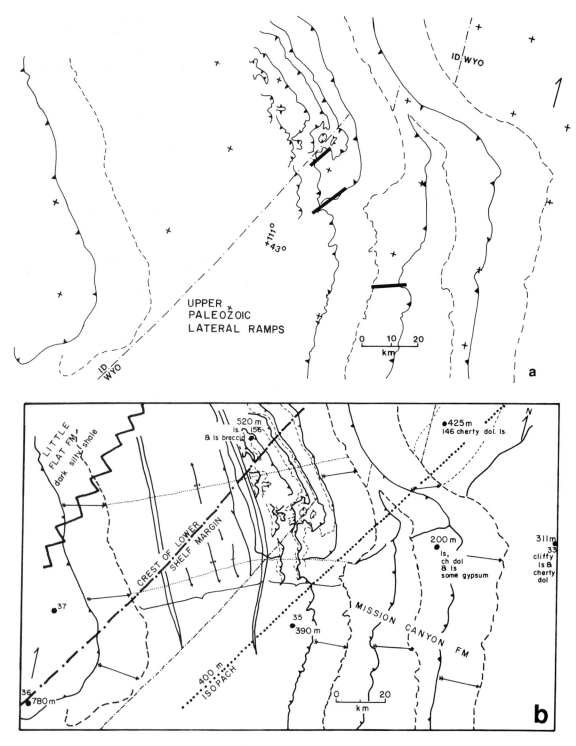

Figure 4. a, Reentrants in the thrusts of the Absaroka and Darby systems, which coincide with lateral ramps in the Upper Paleozoic structural lithic unit and roughly parallel its isopach trend (black bars). b, Mississippian isopach and facies trends, which are replotted from Sando (1976, 1977) and Rose (1976, 1977) are shown on the palinspastic base. The on-shelf Madison Limestone becomes the thicker Madison Group both from east to west and from south to north within the Prospect. Darby, and Absaroka thrust sheets. Shelf-margin facies found in the northern Snake River Range are much more similar to those found in the Meade thrust sheet (Sando and others, 1981) than they are to the rest of the Madison Group in the Absaroka sheet.

had different stratigraphic intervals offset in both a right-lateral and a left-lateral sense across the same fault in different figures. Skipp (1976) and Skipp and Hall (1980) recognized some offset in stratigraphic trends but argued against the presence of a single fault zone. They explained the offset trends by 75 percent less Tertiary extensional faulting north of the Snake River Plain than south of it. All of these authors plotted or discussed their stratigraphic data on nonpalispastic base maps. They all sought an explanation of why thrust sheets along strike from one another across the plain, such as the Medicine Lodge and Absaroka thrusts, do not contain correlative stratigraphic sequences.

The problem of the Snake River fault disappears without the assumption that correlative thrust systems must contain the same stratigraphic section ("facies realm"). Palinspastically restored isopach and facies trends (Fig. 3) south of the plain are north- or northeast-trending, depending on the displacement of the Granite Creek or other minor thrusts of uncertain displacement. The stratigraphic trends cannot have the thrust-parallel trends shown by Rose (1977) or Sando (1977). Stratigraphic trends in the thrust sheets north of the Plain are uncertain because the complex structures there are only now being systematically studied (Perry and Sando, 1983; Skipp, 1985; Ruppel and Lopez, 1984). If the north-northeast trends continue across plain, then "correlative" thrust sheets will contain more distal, thicker facies. The thinner, shallower water facies will be in more easterly thrust sheets or the foreland. There is no reason to postulate major changes in Tertiary extension either. The Snake River Plain "offsets" facies or isopach trends little more than they are displaced from west to east over a similar distance within the Idaho-Wyoming segment of the thrust belt.

The trend of the eastern Snake River Plain today cuts at a high angle across the facies trends and does not mark any fundamental part of the original continental margin. On the other hand, there are onshore to offshore trends in the palinspastic maps here from southeast to northwest for many stratigraphic horizons. Precambrian rocks in the Paris-Willard-Putnam allochthon discussed by Crittenden and others (1971) show the dramatic northward thickening, although they are not exposed on any other sheet, so that palinspastic paleogeographic maps such as those of Figure 3 are not possible. Similar or deeper water Precambrian strata (such as the Yellowjacket Formation(?); Ruppel and Lopez, 1984) should occur within more easterly thrust sheets north of the Snake River Plain. The Fritz Creek, Divide Creek, and Medicine Lodge thrust sheets all include such Precambrian sediments. This suggests that the original continental margin had a relative reentrant in the area now beneath central Idaho.

BASEMENT CONTROLS ON THRUST RAMPS

As noted by Beutner (1977) and Pratt (1983), a simple change in thrust-map pattern orientation is insufficient to prove the existence of an active buttressing mechanism. Similar salients and reentrants can be caused by later foreland uplifts occurring beneath thrust belt structures folding them. The salient and reen-

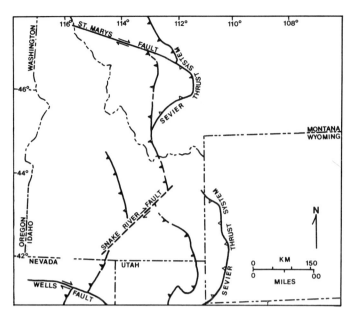

Figure 5. The Snake River fault, which is not exposed. It is proposed to explain offset facies and isopach trends across the 100-km-wide Snake River Plain. The length of the fault varies in different references. The offset shown here is for the first thrust sheets carrying Precambrian rocks, which therefore were considered correlative, but which do not line up along strike across the plain (after Gutschick and others, 1980; Sandberg and others, 1983).

trant pattern is the result of erosion of the uplifted parts of previously linear sheets. Woodward (1986) and Oriel and Moore (1985) documented that in the Snake River Range–Teton region the later rise of the Teton block had uplifted and warped the Sevier thrust belt. The thrust fault geometries in the Snake River Range attributed by Horberg and others (1949) to a Teton buttress are primarily within the Absaroka thrust system of late Cretaceous age, whereas the Teton uplift seen today is Pliocene (Wiltschko and Dorr, 1983). The thrust structures developed west of their present position and were separated from any possible "foreland uplift" by the width of the later Jackson-Prospect thrust sheet. The out-of-sequence thrust geometries suggested for buttress areas by Kulik and Schmidt (this volume) do not exist in the Snake River Range anywhere near the Tetons, based on the mapping of Woodward (1981, 1986), Moore and others (1984), or Oriel and Moore (1985). Kopania's (1983) discussion of out-of-sequence thrusts in the area was based entirely on microstructural evidence that ignored map-scale and outcrop-scale complexities.

The critical evidence for primary basement control of thrust belt structures via a buttress lies in the timing overlap of both sets of structures. Love (1977, 1983) and Wiltschko and Dorr (1983) discussed relative thrust and foreland-uplift timing. Love's argument for the existence of an Ancestral Teton or Targhee Uplift during thrusting is mainly stratigraphic. Love (1983) acknowledged that the comglomerates, which are the main evidence for this basement uplift, could possibly have come from Precambrian quartzite-bearing thrust sheets west of the Absaroka thrust system and thus may not be evidence for a basement uplift of this age. Wiltschko and Dorr (1983) have not presented any new data on the Teton region, although they repeated the arguments of Love (1977, 1983) and Grubbs and Van der Voo (1976).

Primary basement influences on the geographic location of thrust ramp positions were reported by Jacobeen and Kanes (1974, 1975) and Thomas (1985). Wiltschko and Eastman (1983) discussed a theoretical and modeling approach to how and why stress trajectories could be reoriented by the presence of basement normal faults. This is another example of the proposed importance of changing stress fields as a major control on thrust belt geometry. Seismic investigations demonstrate that there are many (most?) thrust ramps that cannot be related to any proximity to basement faults (Royse and others, 1975; Bally and others, 1966; Dixon, 1982; Lamerson, 1983). Schmidt and others (this volume) and many other chapters presented here examine areas where surficial thrusts and basement are both exposed on the surface and argue that the presence of basement modified the thrust geometries. To further explore this problem, two well-mapped areas were chosen for reexamination. In each case, thrusts at the surface have both basement and cover rocks in the upper plate of the fault. The geometries of thrust sheets carrying basement are interesting in themselves, but the purpose here is also to examine the thrust sheets that overlie the first sheet carrying basement. If any primary deflections occur in overlying structures or in the basal thrust, they should be visible in these two areas.

What sort of structures should be observed? Kulik and Schmidt (this volume) list five macroscopic structural changes: (1) crowding or convergence of fold hinges; (2) deflection of fold hinges parallel to the buttress; (3) increased stacking or imbrication of faults; (4) out-of-sequence thrust imbrications; and (5) rotation of thrust sheets against the buttress. Schmidt and others (this volume) also mention anastomosing thrust patterns, younger-on-older thrust geometries, and lateral folding and tear faulting as evidence suggesting buttressing. These are similar to the types of evidence used by Horberg and others (1949).

The two areas of discussion are the Taylor thrust area near Ogden, Utah (Eardley, 1944; Crittenden and others, 1971), and the Holston Mountain thrust system in northeastern Tennessee (King and Ferguson, 1960). Both areas are in unmetamorphosed thrust sheets at the trailing edges of foreland fold-thrust belts. The Ogden area (Fig. 6) is already partially involved in Basin and Range extensional faulting, so the Tennessee example (Fig. 7) provides a case study without later deformation superimposed on it. These areas are considered applicable to the problem because they are the first areas where basement is present in the respective thrust belts. If basement faulting is an important control of thrust ramps within thrust belts, then the uplifted basement asperities are the most likely areas to be incorporated within thrust sheets (Cook and others, 1983).

Crittenden and others (1971) discussed stratigraphic variations of upper Precambrian and Cambrian sequences from Pocatello, Idaho, to Huntsville, Utah, in the Paris-Willard-Putnam allochthon. These sediments thicken greatly from south to north along the length of the major thrust sheet. Link (1983) documented that the thickest northern exposures were tectonically thinned, after thrusting, so that present thicknesses are minima. Crittenden (1972a) discussed the Willard and Ogden thrusts east of Ogden, Utah, and the Farmington Canyon Complex basement that underlies them by only a few hundred meters. The Ogden and Taylor thrusts (the latter is not exposed in the area but carries Precambrian Farmington Canyon complex crystalline rocks) are short distances beneath the Willard thrust and they may be parts of the same thrust system. Alternatively, the Taylor thrust sheet carrying basement rocks is part of the trailing edge of the Crawford thrust system (Crittenden and Sorensen, 1985). In any case, the question is whether the Willard or Ogden thrusts change geometry where they approach the basement beneath them.

Bryant (1979), Sorensen and Crittenden (1972, 1976, 1979), Crittenden and Sorensen (1985), and Crittenden (1972b) documented the structures of the Wasatch Mountains around the Farmington Canyon complex exposures. There is no exceptional thrust crowding, out-of-sequence thrusting, thrusts cutting down-section, or other indication (Fig. 6) of unusual geometries in the overlying thrust sheets or deflection of stresses into lateral folds or tear faults. Extra imbrications could have been carried farther east by motion on the Willard or Ogden thrusts after they formed, although there is no evidence for them there either (Mullens, 1969; Mullens and Cole, 1972; Mullins and Laraway, 1964, 1973). Lateral tear faults in overlying sheets at an asperity such as a basement high should have continued to form as overlying rocks moved over the asperity and have the best chance of preservation. The lack of any such indicators of stress concentration by the basement surface suggests that it was a minor influence. Where the Taylor thrust cuts down-section into basement from north to south, there is a lateral fold related to the extra section of basement being carried on the planar thrust, but that does not reflect any deflection of transport directions. Certainly, the thrust structures in the area are complex, but again, they can be rather easily explained as normal thrust imbrications, folded thrusts, or duplexes.

An example of similar basement involvement in thrusts from the Appalachians is included here, primarily because of its excellent exposure and because it is not complicated by the Basin and Range deformation. The Holston Mountain thrust system is exposed along the front of Holston Mountain and as the framing faults of the Mountain City Window 15 km farther east (Fig. 7; Hardeman and others, 1966; King and Ferguson, 1960). On the west side of the window, the bounding fault is called the Iron Mountain thrust and on the east side of the window it is called the Stone Mountain thrust. The Holston Mountain thrust carries upper Unicoi Formation of Cambrian Age in its hanging wall opposite the north end of the window, and cuts up-section through the Cambrian Shady and Rome Formations and the Cambrian Conasauga Group to the southwest and flattens into the Cambrian-Ordovician Knox Group (Fig. 7b). This lateral thrust ramp connecting two flat parts of the thrust path occurs

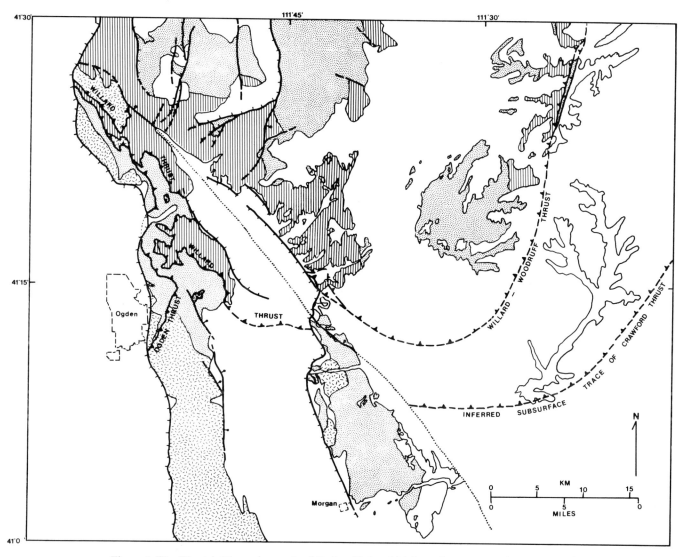

Figure 6. The Wasatch Mountains north of Ogden, Utah, which have the most easterly exposures of Precambrian basement rocks brought up by thrusts of the Sevier orogenic belt. The overlying thrust sheets are also well exposed. Dashed pattern indicates crystalline basement; lined pattern, younger Precambrian sediments; dotted pattern, Paleozoic rocks; unpatterned, Mesozoic and Cenozoic rocks (from Crittenden and Sorensen, 1985).

opposite the middle of the window. The Holston Mountain thrust has a regular stair-stepped thrust path, controlled by stratigraphic layers, laterally along its trace.

The Stone Mountain part of the thrust (on the east side of the window) carries basement rocks and is involved in a basement-cover duplex structure at the south end of the window (Boyer and Elliott, 1982; Diegel, 1986). The Iron Mountain part of the thrust (on the west side of the window) occurs where the fault cuts up-section from basement into cover rocks (Fig. 7b). The cutoff-line is slightly sinuous, and the thrust trace cuts back and forth from lower Unicoi Formation into basement. The thrust cuts down into basement completely at the north end of the window and at the Little Pond Mountain thrust in the middle of the window (Diegel, 1986). The mapping of King and Ferguson (1960) shows several slight lateral tear faults in the basement-

cover contact in the largest basement block involved in the Iron Mountain thrust hanging wall. These do not penetrate any substantial distance into the upper plate. There are no lateral folds or tears in the Shady Valley thrust sheet, which can be related to the presence of basement in the hanging wall.

There is only a single thrust imbricate shown in the Shady Valley thrust sheet near the largest basement block in the hanging wall; otherwise, the Shady Valley sheet is remarkably unaffected by the presence of basement. Based on bedding dips and structure contours on the fault surface, the fault is planar where it passes from sediments into basement. The fault does not even cause the lateral folding of the bedding seen at a lateral ramp. Thus, the basement in the thrust sheet most likely was a topographic irregularity in the basement surface overlapped by flat bedding. It would seem an ideal basement-warp type of asperity. Over the 15

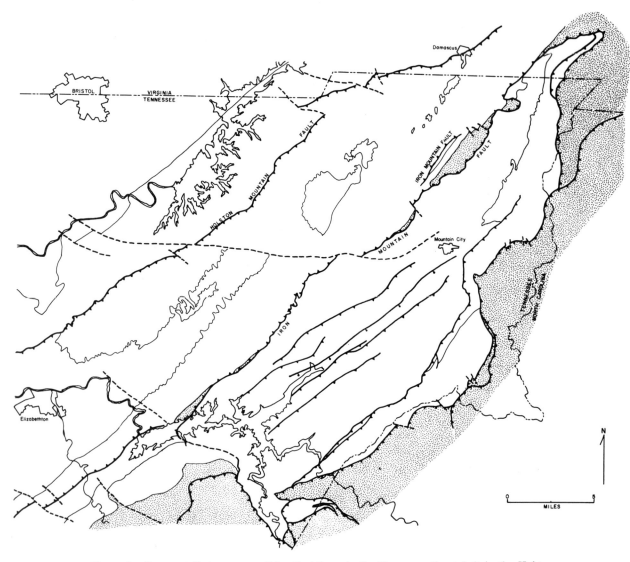

Figure 7a. Basement first appears within allochthons in the Tennessee thrust belt in the Holston Mountain–Iron Mountain–Stone Mountain thrust sheet (H-I-S thrust) around Mountain City, Tennessee (from King and Ferguson, 1960). Convergent structural trends and unusual structural geometries are not associated in any way with basement involvement in this sheet. Stipple marks indicate basement rock.

km between the Iron Mountain thrust and the Holston Mountain thrust the fault cuts up-section forward from the lower Unicoi to the upper Unicoi. The Holston Mountain thrust cuts upward in a lateral ramp opposite the southern part of the window. Both forward and laterally, the stratigraphic packaging controls the thrust's stair-step path, but there is no indication of basement influences near where a basement high was present.

Both of the examples discussed are from the internal parts of the foreland thrust belts. The deformation probably occurred at higher temperatures and pressures than in more external thrust sheets. The deformation was still controlled, in both places, more by the stratigraphic anisotropy on a fine scale (hundreds of meters) than by the presence or absence of basement. Basement asperities at this scale do not seem to nucleate thrust ramps or

lateral tears—where the situation is exposed on the surface—and therefore they seem unnecessary for the formation of thrust ramps at depth.

DISCUSSION

Basement influences on thrust belt geometries generally are represented as modifying the stress fields responsible for deformation. These modified regional or local stress fields cause thrust ramping or localize more intense deformation at a buttress. The thrusts are always deflected around the basement-cored structures. It is suspicious that only thrust belt structures are purported to have had their geometries modified, because presumably the altered stress-field would effect both sets of structures. The pres-

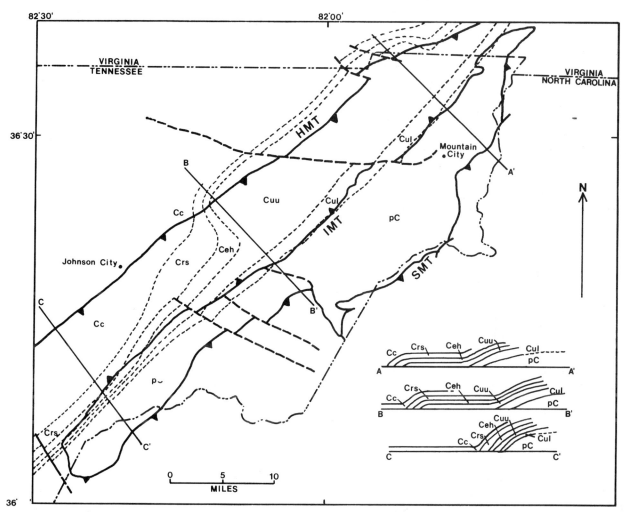

Figure 7b. The H-I-S thrust sheet, which shows ramps and flats in its three-dimensional geometry. It is controlled by stratigraphic layering in the Cambrian-Precambrian quartzites of the Chilhowee Group. Cross sections A-A′, B-B′, and C-C′ trend northwest-southeast across the H-I-S thrust sheet and show the changing frontal ramp position from northeast to southwest (after King and Ferguson, 1960).

ent geographic distribution of foreland uplifts adjacent to the Sevier orogenic belt gives a convenient and probably partially correct model of direct basement uplift–thrust belt interactions, as documented by some other chapters in this volume. The direct influences may cause changing fault geometries, out-of-sequence thrusts, lateral tears, lateral or frontal ramps, and trend changes. However, except for the few possible cases of thrust interactions with much older basement structures, the interaction of thrust belt and Rocky Mountain foreland structures is critically dependent on assumed simultaneity in timing. Each piece of evidence for buttresses alone is neither necessary nor sufficient to prove a foreland–thrust belt interaction, because each alone or in limited combinations can arise from different causes.

On a fine scale, basement is involved in several thrust sheets in the Cordillera and the Appalachians, with no concurrent influence on geometries or trends. Seismic investigations show little evidence to relate most thrust ramps to basement fault blocks. As discussed, lateral thrust ramps in Wyoming can be related both

geographically and vertically to along-strike stratigraphic change much more easily than they can be to any "basement involvement." The critical taper and internal composition of stacked structural lithic units is far more important for the evolution of thrust geometries than are the few basement faults presently identified with ramps. Changes in thrust trends and geometries east of LaBarge Meadows (Oriel and Platt, 1980) occur where the stratigraphic section is becoming dominated by the Lower Mesozoic structural unit. They do not need to be explained by a special undocumented extension of the poorly dated Moxa Arch (Lageson, 1984; Kraig and others, 1986) into the thrust belt. F. Royse (1985; personal communication, 1986) suggested that much of the basement relief beneath the northern part of the thrust belt was caused by early Eocene uplift after all of the thrusts were emplaced. Although both basement faults and stratigraphic changes can occur separately or together, once the obvious and the subtle stratigraphic controls begin being recognized, it is probably unnecessary to worry about basement influences in most areas. It is unclear how basement faults or warps could control the vertical position of ramps through middle or upper parts of the stratigraphic section. Stratigraphic variations in the middle or upper horizons themselves, or changing stacking sequences of adjacent units, are direct explanations of upper-level ramps.

On a still more regional scale, any postulated Snake River fault zone is based on offset stratigraphic packages tied to individual thrust sheets, such as Precambrian sediments first appearing in the Paris sheet south of the Plain, but within the Fritz Creek or Medicine Lodge sheets north of the Plain (Skipp and Hait, 1977; Bond and others, 1978). After the stratigraphic relations within the individual thrust sheets south of the Snake River Plain are recognized on a palinspastic map, the need for the fault zone disappears. The Paleozoic stratigraphic package in each thrust sheet thickens along strike and becomes more like that in western sheets. Upper Paleozoic rocks have palinspastically restored isopachs that trend north-south or northeast-southwest. If these regional trends continue north across the covered interval of the Snake River Plain, the shelf sediments typical of the Absaroka thrust sheet will occur in a more easterly thrust sheet or in the foreland, as they do. Although thick Precambrian and Cambrian clastic rocks are typical only of the Paris-Willard-Putnam sheet on the surface south of the plain, they will be found in more easterly sheets north of the plain. These observations could not disprove the existence of a well-documented fault zone. The Snake River fault, however, is entirely a hypothesis used to explain the apparent offsets of "correlative" stratigraphic or structural trends. The alternate hypothesis offered here both explains why apparent trends do not correlate easily and why such a major structure is never exposed, namely, that it does not exist.

CONCLUSIONS

The need for regional interactions between foreland uplifts and the Sevier thrust belt is critically dependent on data indicating the timing of deformation. The interaction proposed by Horberg and others (1949) for Teton Pass was in error because of inadequately understood structural geometries (Woodward, 1986; Moore and others, 1984; Oriel and Moore, 1985) and errors in timing. Other proposed interactions need to be judged on the basis of the whole set of criteria discussed above, because any one or two pieces of evidence can be the result of much different processes. Stratigraphic controls on thrust shapes, both ramps and flats, and regional changes in thrust trends and styles seem far more important for structural evolution than are locally variable stress trajectories caused by primary basement influ-

ences. The stratigraphic controls will operate everywhere as the thrusts propagate, and therefore are far more general controls than a few basement uplifts or basement fault blocks.

The need for basement faults at depth to control the geographic position of thrust ramps is in serious question in the Idaho-Wyoming-Utah thrust belt, based on several observations: (1) there is no deflection of structures at basement highs where both basement and cover are exposed in several thrust sheets; (2) most seismic sections do not show basement faults underlying thrust ramps in their present positions; (3) seismic sections do not show basement ramps beneath the trailing edge of thrust sheets where they should be located after the thrust ramp has moved toward the foreland on later lower thrusts; and (4) it is unclear how a basement fault could directly control the geographic position of ramps through middle or upper parts of the stratigraphic section. This does not mean that an irregular basement surface is not important in the evolution of thrust belt structures, only that it is not the best explanation in many areas.

The stratigraphic packaging and sequences of structural lithic units are proposed here to reflect the downwarp of the basement surface during evolution of the continental margin throughout pre-Jurassic time and are therefore evidence of secondary basement influence on structural style. The downwarp mechanism may include either bending or spaced faulting during sedimentation. The critical distinction of secondary basement controls is that the basement surface configuration is passive during deformation, rather than active as in the buttress models. This does not mean that an irregular basement surface is not important in the evolution of thrust belt structures, only that it is not the best explanation in many areas.

ACKNOWLEDGMENTS

I thank Drs. C. J. Schmidt and W. J. Perry, Jr., for their invitation to participate in this symposium volume, despite the fact that my research has led me to conclusions somewhat divergent from others expressed here. Charles Lutz, Peter Regan, Frank Royse, Lucien Platt, William Thomas, Steven S. Oriel, and Christopher Schmidt provided careful, insightful reviews of various drafts of the manuscript. The late David Elliott, David Moore, and the late Steven S. Oriel provided lively discussions on the nature of thrust belt–buttress interactions. Oriel also provided help in gaining access to field notes and stratigraphic data collected by W. W. Rubey. This research was funded by a Professional Development Grant from the University of Tennessee and by National Science Foundation Grant EAR-8312872.

REFERENCES CITED

Bally, A. W., Gordy, P. L., and Stewart, G. A., 1966, Structure, seismic data, and orogenic evolution of southern Canadian Rocky Mountains: Bulletin of Canadian Petroleum Geology, v. 14, p. 337–381.

Beutner, E., 1977, Causes and consequences of curvature in the Sevier Orogenic Belt, Utah and Montana, *in* Heisey, E. L., ed., Rocky Mountain thrust belt; Geology and resources: Wyoming Geological Association 29th Annual Field Conference Guidebook, p. 353–366.

Bond, J. G., Kauffman, J. D., Miller, D. A., and Venkatakrishnan, R., 1978, Geologic map of Idaho: Idaho Department of Lands, Bureau of Mines and Geology, scale, 1:500,000.

Boyer, S. E., and Elliott, D., 1982, Thrust systems: American Association of Petroleum Geologists Bulletin, v. 66, p. 1196–1230.

Bryant, B., 1979, Reconnaissance geologic map of the Precambian Farmington Canyon complex and surrounding rocks in the Wasatch Mountains between Ogden and Bountiful, Utah: U.S. Geological Survey Open-File Report 79-709, scale 1:50,000.

Coleman, J. L., Jr., and Lopez, J. A., 1986, Dolomite décollements; Exception or rule?: American Association of Petroleum Geologists Bulletin, v. 70, no. 5, p. 576.

Cook, F. A., Brown, L. D., Kaufman, S., and Oliver, J. E., 1983, The COCORP seismic reflection traverse across the Southern Appalachians: American Association of Petroleum Geologistss Studies in Geology no. 14, 61 p.

Crittenden, M. D., Jr., 1972a, Willard thrust and the Cache allochthon, Utah: Geological Society of American Bulletin, v. 83, p. 2871–2880.

——, 1972b, Geologic map of the Browns Hole Quadrangle, Utah: U.S. Geological Survey Geologic Quadrangle Map GQ-968, scale 1:24,000.

Crittenden, M. D., Jr., and Sorensen, M. L., 1985, Geologic map of the North Ogden Quadrangle and part of the Ogden and Plain City Quadrangles, Box Elder and Weber Counties, Utah: U.S. Geological Survey Miscellaneous Investigation Map I-1606, scale 1:24,000.

Crittenden, M. D., Jr., Schaeffer, F. E., Trimble, D. E. and Woodward, L. E., 1971, Nomenclature and correlation of some upper Precambrian and basal Cambrian sequences in western Utah and southeastern Idaho: Geological Society of America Bulletin, v. 82, p. 581–602.

Currie, J. B., Patnode, A. W., and Trump, R. P., 1962, Development of folds in sedimentary strata: Geological Society of America Bulletin, v. 73, p. 461–472.

Dahlstrom, C. D. A., 1969, Balanced cross-sections: Canadian Journal of Earth Sciences, v. 6, p. 743–757.

Diegel, F. A., 1986, Topological constraints on imbricate thrust networks; Examples from the Mountain City Window, Tennessee, U.S.A.: Journal of Structural Geology, v. 8, no. 3/4, p. 269–280.

Dixon, J. S., 1982, Regional structural synthesis, Wyoming salient of western overthrust belt: American Association of Petroleum Geologists Bulletin, v. 66, p. 1560–1580.

Eardley, A. J., 1944, Geology of the north-central Wasatch Mountains, Utah: Geological Society of America Bulletin, v. 55, p. 819–894.

Grubbs, K. L. and Van der Voo, R., 1976, Structural deformation of the Idaho-Wyoming overthrust belt (U.S.A.) as determined by Triassic paleomagnetism: Tectonophysics, v. 33, p. 321–336.

Gutschick, R. C., Sandberg, C. A., and Sando, W. J., 1980, Mississippian Shelf margin and carbonate platform from Montana to Nevada, *in* Fouch, T. D., and Magathan, E. R., eds., Paleozoic paleogeography of west-central United States, Rocky Mountain Section, Society of Economic Paleontologists and Mineralogists Paleogeography Symposium 1, p. 111–128.

Hardeman, W. D., Miller, R. A., and Swingle, G. D., 1966, Geologic map of Tennessee: Tennessee Division of Geology, four sheets, scale 1:250,000.

Horberg, C. L., Nelson, V. E., and Church, V., 1949, Structural trends in central western Wyoming: Geological Society of America Bulletin, v. 60, p. 193–215.

Jacobeen, F., Jr., and Kanes, W. H., 1974, Structure of the Broadtop Synclinorium and its implications for Appalachian structural style: American Association of Petroleum Geologist Bulletin, v. 58, p. 362–375.

——, 1975, Structure of Broadtop Synclinorium Wills Mountain Anticlinorium, and Allegheny frontal zone: American Association of Petroleum Geologists Bulletin, v. 59, p. 1136–1150.

Jordan, T., 1981, Thrust loading and foreland basin evolution, Cretaceous, Western United States: American Association of Petroleum Geologists Bulletin, v. 65, p. 2506–2520.

King, P. B., and Ferguson, W. H., 1960, Geology of northeasternmost Tennessee: U.S. Geological Survey Professional Paper 311, 136 p.

Koch, W. J., 1976, Lower Triassic facies in the vicinity of the Cordilleran hingeline; Western Wyoming, southeastern Idaho, and Utah: Denver, Colorado, Rocky Mountain Association of Geologists 1976 Symposium Guidebook, p. 203–218.

Kopania, A. A., 1983, Deformation consequences of the impingement of the foreland and northern thrust belt, eastern Idaho and western Wyoming: Geological Society of America Abstracts with Programs, v. 15, p. 296.

Kraig, D. H., Wiltschko, D. V., and Spang, J. H., 1986, Interaction of the La Barge Platform with the Western Overthrust Belt, southwestern Wyoming: Geological Society of America Abstracts with Programs, v. 18, p. 367.

Lageson, D. R., 1984, Structural geology of the Stewart Peak culmination Idaho-Wyoming thrust belt: American Association of Petroleum Geologists Bulletin, v. 8, p. 401–416.

Lamerson, P. R., 1983, The Fossil Basin area and its relationship to the Absaroka thrust fault system, *in* Powers, R. B., ed., Geologic studies of the Cordilleran thrust belt, 1982: Denver, Colorado, Rocky Mountain Association of Geologists, v. 1, p. 279–341.

Link, P. K., 1983, Structural geology of the Oxford and Malad Summit Quadrangles, Bannack Range, southeastern Idaho *in* Powers, R. B., ed., Geologic studies of the Cordilleran thrust belt: Denver, Colorado, Rocky Mountain Association of Geologists, p. 851–858.

Love, J. D., 1977, Summary of Upper Cretaceous and Cenozoic stratigraphy and of tectonic and glacial events in Jackson Hole, northwestern Wyoming, *in* Heisey, E. L., ed., Rocky Mountain thrust belt; Geology and resources: Wyoming Geological Associaiton 29th Annual Field Conference Guidebook, p. 585–593.

——, 1983, A possible gap in the western thrust belt in Idaho and Wyoming, *in* Powers, R. B., ed., Geologic studies of the Cordilleran thrust belt: Denver, Colorado, Rocky Mountain Association of Geologists, v. 1, p. 247–260.

Moore, D. W., Woodward, N. B., and Oriel, S. S., 1984, Preliminary geologic map of the Mount Baird Quadrangle, Bonneville County, Idaho, and Teton and Lincoln Counties, Wyoming: U.S. Geological Survey Open-File Report 84-776, 12 p., map scale 1:24,000.

Mullens, T. E., 1969, Geologic map of the Causey Dam Quadrangle, Weber County, Utah: U.S. Geological Survey Quadrangle Map GQ-790, scale 1:24,000.

Mullens, T. E., and Cole, T. H., 1972, Geologic map of the northeast quarter of the Morgan 15-minute Quadrangle, Morgan and Weber Counties, Utah: U.S. Geological Survey Miscellaneous Field Studies Map MF-304, scale 1:24,000.

Mullens, T. E., and Laraway, S. H., 1964, Geology of the Devils Slide Quadrangle, Morgan and Summit Counties, Utah: U.S. Geological Survey Mineral Investigations Field Studies Map MF-290, scale 1:24,000.

——, 1973, Geologic map of the Morgan 7½-minute Quadrangle, Morgan County, Utah: U.S. Geological Survey Miscellaneous Field Studies Map MF-318, scale 1:24,000.

Oriel, S. S. and Moore, D. W., 1985, Mineral resource potential map (A) and geologic map (B) of the west and east Palisades Roadless area, Idaho and Wyoming: U.S. Geological Survey Miscellaneous Field Studies Map MF-1619 A and B, scale 1:50,000.

Oriel, S. S., and Platt, L. B., 1980, Geologic map of the Preston 1° by 2° Quadrangle, southeastern Idaho and western Wyoming: U.S. Geological

Survey Miscellaneous Investigations Map I-1127, scale 1:250,000.

Paul, J. B., 1986, Geometry and fabrics of the Saltville Fault in Knoxville, Tennessee [M.S. thesis]: Knoxville, University of Tennessee, 143 p.

Paul, J. B., and Woodward, N. B., 1985, Brittle and ductile evolution of a thrust zone; Thin and thick cataclasites along the Saltville fault: Geological Society of America Abstracts with Programs, v. 17, p. 685–686.

Perry, W. J., and Sando, W. J., 1983, Sequential deformation in the thrust belt of southwestern Montana, *in* Powers, R. B., ed., Geologic studies of the Cordilleran thrust belt, 1982: Denver, Colorado, Rocky Mountain Association of Geologists, v. 1, p. 137–144.

Pratt, R. M., 1983, The case for lateral offset of the overthrust belt along the Snake River Plain: in Powers, R. B., ed., Geologic studies of the Cordilleran thrust belt, 1982: Denver, Colorado, Rocky Mountain Association of Geologists, v. 1, p. 235–245.

Rose, P. R., 1976, Mississippian carbonate shelf margins, western United States, *in* Hill, J. G., ed., Geology of the Cordilleran hingeline: Denver, Colorado, Rocky Mountain Association of Geologists, p. 135–152.

—— , 1977, Mississippian carbonate shelf margins, western United States: Wyoming Geological Association 29th Annual Field Conference Guidebook, p. 155–172.

Royse, F., 1985, Geometry and timing of the Darby-Prospect-Hogsback thrust fault system, Wyoming: Geological Society of America Abstracts with Programs, v. 17, p. 263.

Royse, F., Jr., Warner, M. A., and Reese, D. L., 1975, Thrust belt structural geometry and related stratigraphic problems, Wyoming–Idaho–northern Utah, *in* Symposium on deep drilling frontiers in central Rocky Mountains: Denver, Colorado, Rocky Mountain Association of Geologists, p. 44–54.

Rubey, W. W., 1973, Geologic map of the Afton Quadrangle and part of the Big Piney Quadrangle, Lincoln and Sublette Counties, Wyoming: U.S. Geological Survey Miscellaneous Investigations Map I-686, scale 1:62,500.

Rubey, W. W., Oriel, S. S., and Tracey, J. L., Jr., 1980, Geologic map and structure sections of the Cokeville 30-minute Quadrangle, Lincoln and Sublette Counties, Wyoming: U.S. Geological Survey Miscellaneous Investigations I–1129, scale 1:62,500.

Ruppel, E. T, and Lopez, D. A., 1984, The thrust belt in southwest Montana and east-central Idaho: U.S. Geological Survey Professional Paper 1278, 41 p.

Rutherford, E., 1985, Stratigraphic controls of thrust faulting and the structural evolution of the Wartburg Basin, Tennessee [M.S. thesis]: Knoxville, University of Tennessee, 145 p.

Sandberg, C. A., Gutschick, R. C., Johnson, J. G., Poole, F. G., and Sando, W. J., 1983, Middle Devonian to Late Mississippian geologic history of the Overthrust Belt region, Western United States, *in* Powers, R. B., ed., Geologic studies of the Cordilleran thrust belt, 1982: Denver, Colorado, Rocky Mountain Association of Geologists, v. 2, p. 691–720.

Sando, W. J., 1976, Mississippian history of the northern Rocky Mountains region: U.S. Geological Survey Journal of Research, v. 4, p. 317–338.

—— , 1977, Stratigraphy of the Madison Group (Mississippian) in the northern part of the Wyoming-Idaho Overthrust Belt and adjacent areas: Wyoming Geological Association 29th Annual Field Conference Guidebook, p. 173–177.

Sando, W. J., Sandberg, C. A., and Gutschick, R. C., 1981, Stratigraphic and economic significance of Mississippian sequence at North Georgetown Canyon, Idaho: American Association of Petroleum Geologists Bulletin, v. 65, p. 1433–1443.

Skipp, B. L., 1976, Eastward bulge of the Antler Highland across the Snake River Plain: Geological Society of America Abstracts with Programs, v. 8, p. 1109–1110.

—— , 1985, Contraction and extension faults in the southern Beaverhead Mountains, Idaho and Montana: U.S. Geological Survey Open-File Report 85-545, 170 p.

Skipp, B. L., and Hait, M. M., Jr., 1977, Allochthons along the northwest margin of the Snake River Plain, Idaho, *in* Heisey, E. L., ed., Rocky Mountain thrust belt; Geology and resources: Wyoming Geological Association 29th Annual Field Conference Guidebook, p. 449–515.

Skipp, B. L., and Hall, W. E., 1980, Upper Paleozoic paleotectonics and paleogeography of Idaho, *in* Fouch, T. D., and Magathan, E. R., Paleozoic paleogeography of west-central United States: Rocky Mountain Section, Society of Economic Paleontologists and Mineralogists Paleogeography Symposium #1, p. 287.422.

Sorensen, M. L., and Crittenden, M. D., Jr., 1972, Preliminary geologic map of part of the Wasatch Range near north Ogden, Utah: U.S. Geological Survey Miscellaneous Field Studies Map MR–428, scale 1:24,000.

—— , 1976, Preliminary geologic map of the Mantua Quadrangle and part of the Willard Quadrangle, Box Elder, Weber, and Cocke Counties, Utah: U.S. Geological Survey Miscellaneous Field Studies Map MF-720, scale 1:24,000.

—— , 1979, Geologic map of the Huntsville Quadrangle, Weber and Cache Counties, Utah: U.S. Geological Survey Geologic Quadrangle Map GQ-1503, scale 1:24,000.

Thomas, W. A., 1985, Northern Alabama sections (29-32), *in* Woodward, N. B., ed., and Appalachian Basin Industrial Associates, Valley and Ridge thrust belt; Balanced structural sections, Pennsylvania to Alabama: Knoxville, University of Tennessee Studies in Geology, no. 12, p. 54–60.

Trümpy, R., 1969, Die helvetischen Decken der Ostschweiz: Versuch einer palinspastichen Korrelation und Ansatze zu einer kinematischen analyse: Eclogae Geologicae Helveticae, v. 62/1, p. 105–142.

Wiltschko, D. V., and Dorr, J. A., Jr., 1983, Timing of deformation in Overthrust Belt and foreland of Idaho, Wyoming, and Utah: American Association of Petroleum Geologists Bulletin, v. 67, p. 1304–1322.

Wiltschko, D., and Eastman, D., 1983, Role of basement warps and faults in localizing thrust fault ramps: Geological Society of America Memoir 158, p. 177–190.

Wojtal, S., and Mitra, G., 1986, Strain hardening and strain softening in fault zones from foreland thrusts: Geological Society of America Bulletin, v. 97, p. 674–687.

Woodward, N. B., 1981, Structural geometry of the Snake River Range, Idaho and Wyoming [Ph.D. thesis]: Baltimore, Maryland, Johns Hopkins University, 261 p.

—— , 1983, A balanced view of the northern Idaho–Wyoming thrust belt: Geological Society of America Abstracts with Programs, v. 15, p. 318.

—— , 1986, Thrust fault geometry of the Snake River Range, Idaho and Wyoming: Geological Society of America Bulletin, v. 97, p. 178–193.

Woodward, N. B., and Rutherford, E., Jr., 1988, Structural lithic units in external orgenic zones, *in* Ord, A., ed., Conference on Deformation of Crustal Rocks: Special issue of Tectonophysics (in press).

Woodward, N. B., Walker, K. R., and Simmons, W. A., 1983, Facies controls on structural trends; Examples from the southern Appalachians: Geological Society of America Abstracts with Programs, v. 15, p. 723.

Woodward, N. B., Walker, K. R., and Lutz, C. T., 1988, Relationships between lower Paleozoic facies patterns and structural trends in the Southern Appalachians: Geological Society of America Bulletin (in press).

Manuscript Accepted by the Society February 9, 1988

Geological Society of America
Memoir 171
1988

Timing and structural interaction between the thrust belt and foreland, Hoback basin, Wyoming

R. B. Hunter*

University of Wyoming, Department of Geology and Geophysics, P.O. Box 3006, University Station, Laramie, Wyoming 82071

ABSTRACT

Detailed geologic mapping and structural analysis along the northeast margin of the Wyoming overthrust belt reveals a complex interaction between the thrust belt and foreland faults and folds. Palynologic dates and structural overprinting provide the primary age control for the timing of these events: (1) late Cretaceous to early Paleocene motion on the east-directed Granite Creek thrust; (2) middle to late Paleocene movement on the east-directed Granite Creek blind thrust and the genetically related (by triangle zone) west-directed Game Hill thrust; (3) possibly early to late Paleocene motion on the foreland Cache Creek fault system on the Cache Creek "blind" fault; (4) late Paleocene to early Eocene motion on the out-of-sequence, east-directed Prospect thrust system; (5) early Eocene motion on the foreland Cache Creek subfault and Cache Creek fault of the Cache Creek fault system; and (6) late normal faulting, which truncates the above structures. Thrusts within the out-of-sequence Prospect thrust system include, from east to west, the westward-younging Cliff Creek, Little Granite Creek, Bull Creek, Game Creek, and Bear thrusts. The evolving Gross Ventre foreland uplift provided a buttress against further eastward thrusting, thus primarily causing this westward-younging thrust sequence.

INTRODUCTION

The Hoback Basin area in western Wyoming (Figs. 1, 2, 3) is a structurally complex thrust zone where structures of the thin-skinned, Sevier-style fold and thrust belt impinge upon contemporaneous structures of the thick-skinned, Laramide-style foreland uplift province. The primary objectives of this study were (1) to recognize and differentiate structures formed by these two distinct and overlapping styles of deformation, (2) to determine the complex timing relations of deformation within and between each structural province, and (3) to determine the development history of a structural triangle zone within the thrust belt.

Methods

Methods of study were geologic mapping combined with interpretations of drill hole and seismic subsurface data, structural analysis, and palynologic sampling and dating of Cretaceous and Paleocene rocks. Unless otherwise stated, all data, discussions,

and interpretations refer to the study area of Figure 3 (in pocket inside back cover). Locations of 50 previously unpublished palynologic sample sites are plotted in Figures 3 and 4. Twenty-eight pollen samples were collected, and Chevron, Inc., provided 22 additional samples and analyzed all samples to determine their age.

Previous studies

Previous stratigraphic and structural studies in the Hoback Basin area contributed significantly to an understanding of the complex geology in this region. Nelson and Church (1943) and Horberg and others (1949) differentiated structures of the Gros Ventre Range foreland uplift from the Hoback Range thrust belt, recognized that the Gros Ventre foreland uplift may have created a buttress that caused the dramatic changes in structural trend in the thrust belt near their areas of impingement, and noted that the age of some thrusting decreased from east to west. Love (1956a, b, 1977) interpreted the Cenozoic history of the region. The regional work of Armstrong and Oriel (1965) and Blackstone (1971,

*Present Address: Standard Oil Production Co., 5151 San Felipe, P.O. Box 4587, Houston, Texas 77210

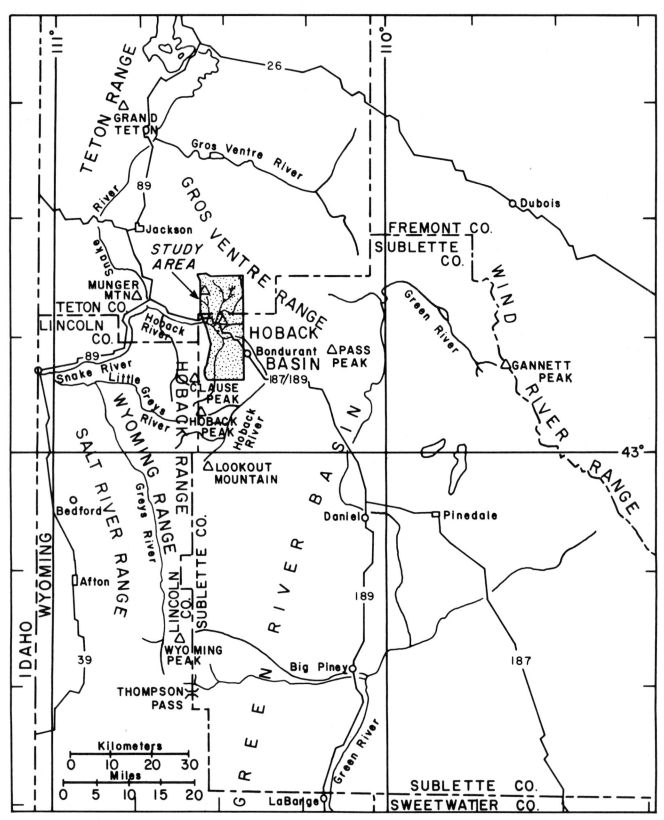

Figure 1. Index map of the study area (modified from Froidevaux, 1977; from Hunter, 1987).

1977) provided a foundation for thrust belt studies. Dorr and others (1977), Blackstone (1977), and Love (1977) acknowledged many other important references.

Pertinent geologic maps include Eardley (1944) of the Camp Davis area, Froidevaux (1968, 1977) for the Hoback Peak area, Schroeder (1973, 1976) for the Bull Creek and Clause Peak Quadrangles, Dorr and others (1977) for the Hoback Basin region, and Simons and others (1980) for the Gros Ventre Wilderness area (Fig. 5). A crucial recent discovery was the recognition in seismic and well data of the Granite Creek thrust in the subsurface (Royse, 1985), which played a critical role in the development of folds and faults in the frontal part of the thrust belt (Figs. 6, 7, 8). This chapter is expanded and modified from Hunter (1987).

Development of a triangle zone

The term triangle zone, introduced by Gordy and others (1977, p. 14) in the Alberta foothills, denotes a triangle-shaped zone of intense folding and thrust imbrication bounded on three sides by thrust faults (Fig. 9). The bounding faults include: (1) an initial thrust directed in the primary transport direction; (2) a blind thrust at the base directed in the primary transport direction, structurally below the initial thrust; and (3) a "back thrust" (oppositely vergent thrust) genetically and temporally related to the blind thrust, on the side opposite the initial thrust. To balance displacements, the structurally lower blind thrust must have propagated just before and during the development of the back thrust. If the back thrust propagated first, it would either have to root into the basement or another thrust to maintain structural balance.

Seismic information may not detect the blind thrust of the triangle zone or the cratonward subsurface termination of the back thrust, because these features usually parallel bedding planes. Therefore, in areas with little or no drillhole data, the blind thrust critical to the development of the hinterland-directed triangle zone back thrust(s) could be very difficult to detect. Before seismic data became available, a triangle zone was commonly misinterpreted as an anticline at the end of a fold and thrust belt. The Turner Valley Field in Alberta was discovered in 1913 on this false premise (Jones, 1983).

Elliott (1981) noted the common spatial association of prominent blind thrusting below triangle zones. Price (1986) also recognized this critical genetic relation between the blind thrust and the associated oppositely-vergent thrust that together form a tectonic wedge into the foreland basin strata (Fig. 10). Thompson (1981) also emphasized the necessity for a blind thrust to cause triangle-zone development. However, Thompson's (1981) model required a nearby major thrust ramp to induce the propagation of a "hanging-wall detachment" from the primary thrust that becomes blind after ramping (Fig. 11). Butler (1982) also included a nearby ramp in his triangle-zone model (Fig. 12). A ramp does not necessarily induce the formation of all triangle zones (Figs. 8, 9), although it may be a passive tectonic element in some triangle zones.

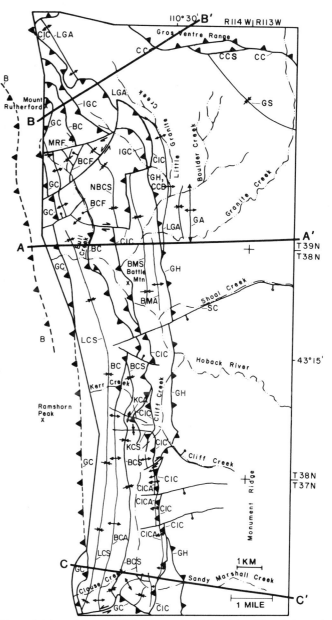

Figure 2. Tectonic map of Hoback area (see Table 4 for abbreviations of structural names; from Hunter, 1987).

Alternatively, Jones (1983) proposed that folding of the upper detachment of Dahlstrom (1969b, 1970) by younger, structurally lower thrusting could form an oppositely vergent thrust wedge (Fig. 13). However, in the frontal thrust belt where triangle zones form, the upper "detachment" is commonly the contact between rock and air or water above these structurally high thrusts. Therefore, the upper detachment model of triangle zone formation is also unnecessary. Dahlstrom (1969b) admitted that the upper detachment "does not and never did exist" if the folded panel of rocks reached the surface during deformation. Therefore, the upper "detachment" becomes the interface between rock and air or rock and water at the erosional surface.

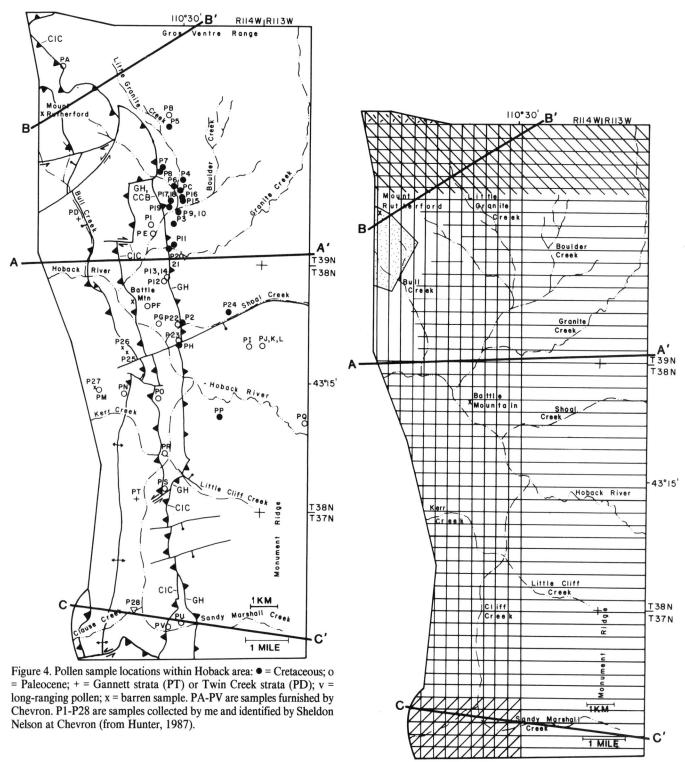

Figure 4. Pollen sample locations within Hoback area: ● = Cretaceous; o = Paleocene; + = Gannett strata (PT) or Twin Creek strata (PD); v = long-ranging pollen; x = barren sample. PA–PV are samples furnished by Chevron. P1–P28 are samples collected by me and identified by Sheldon Nelson at Chevron (from Hunter, 1987).

Figure 5. Index map showing locations of previous mapping within the Hoback area. Horizontally ruled area mapped by Dorr and others (1977); vertically ruled area mapped by Schroeder (1973, 1976); diagonally ruled area with southeast-trending lines mapped by Simons and others (1980); diagonally ruled area with southwest-trending lines mapped by Froidevaux (1968, 1977); dotted area mapped by Moulton (1980), and short-dashed area, at top of map, represents area mapped by Love and Love (1978) (from Hunter, 1987).

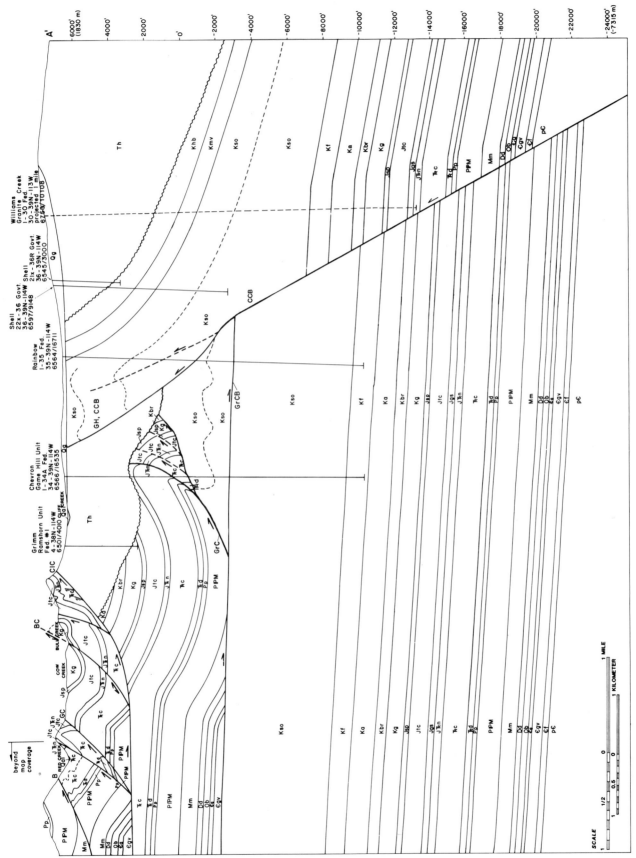

Figure 6. Cross section A-A'. Location, stratigraphic units, and well control shown in Figure 3. Structure west of Bear thrust (B) interpreted from geologic mapping by Schroeder (1976). Scale, 1:53,300 (from Hunter, 1987).

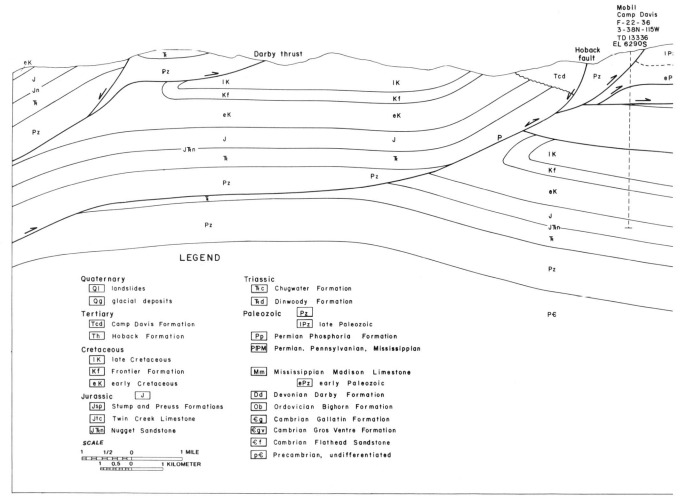

Figure 7. Regional cross section. West half modified from Royse and others (1975); right quarter modified from Simons and others (1980). Middle portion is B-B' noted in Figure 3. Scale, 1:158,400 (from Hunter, 1987).

Banks and Warburton (1986) introduced the term passive roof duplex for a triangle zone where a hinterland-directed upper detachment forms within each duplex during progressive thrusting toward the foreland.

STRATIGRAPHIC FRAMEWORK

The stratigraphic units observed in this study are summarized in Table 1. This table provides a summary of the age, thickness range, and dominant lithology of each unit. Symbols given in Table 1 provide a key to the units shown on the geologic map (Fig. 3), cross sections (Figs. 6 through 8), and subsequent figures. In summary, 1,311 m (4,300 ft) of Paleozoic rocks, 5,029 m (16,500 ft) of Mesozoic rocks, and 3,810 m (12,500 ft) of Tertiary rocks occur in the study area.

Syntectonic sedimentation

The Cretaceous Sohare Formation (Love and Christiansen,

1985; Hilliard Formation equivalent) and Paleocene to early Eocene Hoback Formation were probably semi-consolidated before their deformation. Therefore, water-saturated shales within these formations may have accommodated substantial bedding plane slip and internal flow during thrusting and folding. These palynologically dated formations tightly constrain the timing of deformation, as discussed below. The Tertiary Skyline Trail Conglomerate (Tstc) of Dorr and others (1977) consists of alluvial fans in the upper part of the Paleocene to early Eocene Hoback Formation, which coalesced into the basin from a Gros Ventre Range uplifted source. Shales of the late Paleocene Hoback Formation, dated by palynology, underlie the Tstc. Probable early Eocene molluscs (J. D. Love, personal communication, 1986) within the Hoback Formation near the center of the Granite syncline (GS) south of the Gros Ventre Range stratigraphically overlie and bracket the age of the Tstc (Fig. 3). The Tertiary Eocene(?) red conglomerate, unfortunately, is yet undated. Accurate dating of this unit would provide an even more detailed timing history of fault movements in this region.

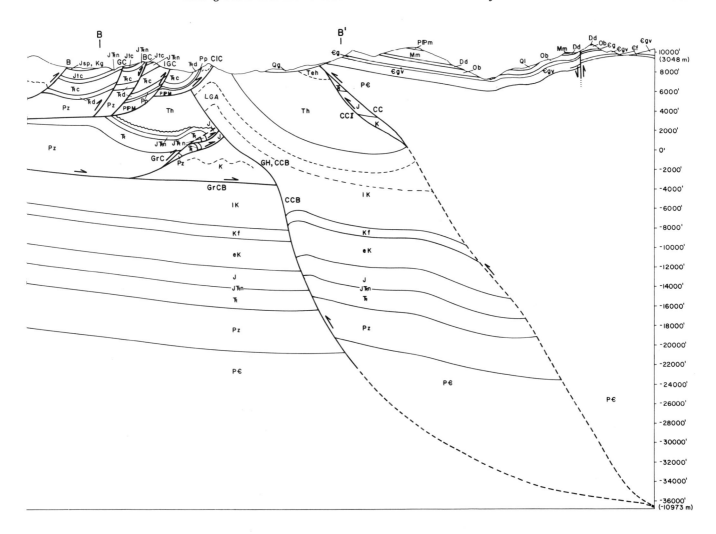

Palynological data

Palynology provides the only reliable means to stratigraphically differentiate the lithologically and environmentally similar Paleocene to early Eocene Hoback Formation and late Cretaceous Sohare Formation fluvial sandstones and shales. Tables 2 and 3 summarize the age results and palynomorph assemblages from the pollen samples studied.

STRUCTURAL GEOLOGY

Outcrops and subsurface data document a specific family of structures in the Hoback Basin area. This family of structures includes: (1) parallel folding (i.e., both kink and concentric geometries); (2) minor conical folding in the Twin Creek and Chugwater shales; (3) basal detachment faults; (4) low-angle thrust faults; (5) steeper thrust faults; (6) transverse faults, such as tear faults and lateral ramps; (7) compartmental faults; (8) medium-angle faults of the foreland province involving basement rocks; and (9) high-angle and listric normal faults. These structures of the thrust belt and foreland provinces account

for all the observed geometries depicted on the geologic map (Fig. 3) and the cross sections (Figs. 6, 7, 8).

Generally, the basic rules of thrusting outlined by Rich (1934), Dahlstrom (1969a, b, 1970), and Royse and others (1975) apply to local thrust fault geometry. The evident characteristics of thrust faulting include: (1) thrust faults cut stratigraphically upsection in the transport direction, (2) thrust faults parallel bedding in incompetent rocks and cut obliquely through bedding in competent rocks, (3) folds commonly steepen or overturn in the direction of transport, (4) fault-bend folds (Suppe, 1983) commonly form a hanging-wall anticline along some thrust traces, and (5) fault-propagation folds (Suppe and Medwedeff, 1984) commonly form above the tip of blind thrusts as an expression of the shortening accommodated below on the blind thrust. Exceptions to these rules are apparent on the map (Fig. 3) and cross sections (Figs. 6, 7, 8). Contemporaneous interaction of the thick-skinned foreland province with the thin-skinned thrust belt is probably primarily responsible for these exceptions.

Table 4 lists the abbreviations used to identify the major structures on the geologic map (Fig. 3), the tectonic map (Fig. 2), and the cross sections (Figs. 6, 7, 8).

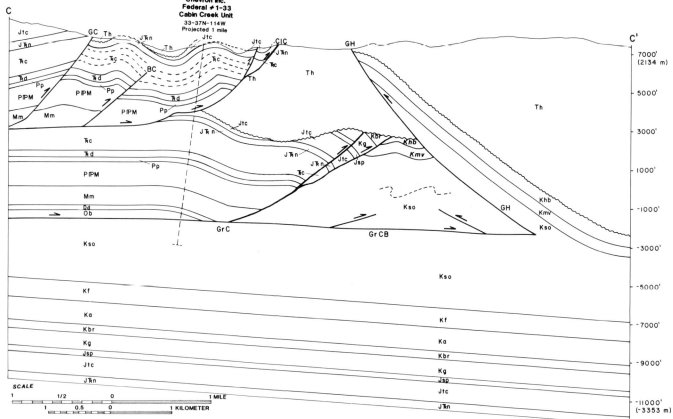

Figure 8. Cross section C-C′. Location and stratigraphic units shown in Figure 3. Scale, 1:48,000 (from Hunter, 1987).

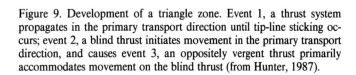

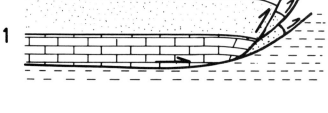

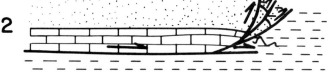

Figure 9. Development of a triangle zone. Event 1, a thrust system propagates in the primary transport direction until tip-line sticking occurs; event 2, a blind thrust initiates movement in the primary transport direction, and causes event 3, an oppositely vergent thrust primarily accommodates movement on the blind thrust (from Hunter, 1987).

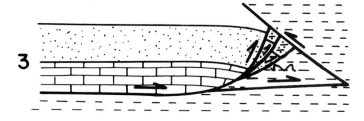

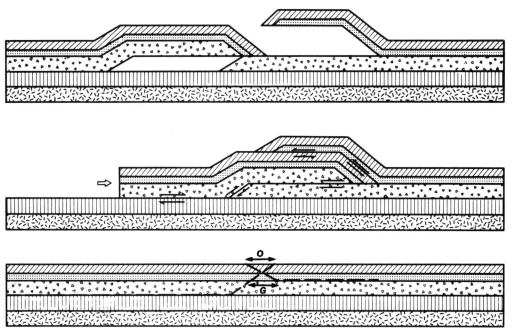

Figure 10. Simplified geometric and kinematic model for tectonic wedging and delamination along the eastern edge of the Cordilleran thrust and fold belt. Gap (G) and overlap (O) in this palinspastic reconstruction can be accounted for by stretching and shortening in folds. This reconstruction is based on the assumption that bed length remains constant (from Price, 1986, reproduced by permission of the Canadian Government).

Figure 11. A diagrammatic representation of the blind thrust model. The patterns define mechanically incompetent strata separated by a rigid carbonate unit with no pattern. A. Illustration of the onset of displacement across the thrust, accompanied by development of a hanging-wall detachment(s) (hwd), which allows the incompetent strata within the hanging-wall plate to deform disharmonically and absorb displacement on the underlying thrust. The thrust ceases to exist at the point where shortening due to folding in the hanging wall equals displacement on the thrust—hence the pin on the right side of the section. B, Illustration of the continued thrust fault displacement that increases the width of disharmonically deformed hanging-wall succession. C, Illustration of the difficulty involved in deciphering the detached nature of the mountain front anticline using surface exposures. The major thrust remains "blind," and much of the shortening within the disharmonically deformed incompetent unit may be difficult to assess unless good stratigraphic markers are present. Reprinted by permission of the Geological Society of London (Thompson, R. I., 1981, The nature and significance of large "blind thrusts" within the northern Rocky Mountains of Canada, *in* Thrust and nappe tectonics, v. 9).

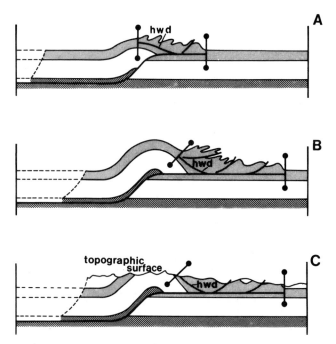

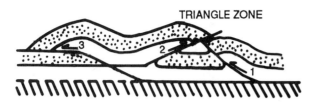

Figure 12. Development of a triangle zone where a pop-up back-thrust (2) and a forward-directed imbricate thrust (1) converge. The thrusts are numbered in order of their relative displacement, and the sequence continues with the development of a frontal ramp (3) at the leading edge of the pop-up. Reprinted by permission of Pergamon Press (Butler, R. H.W., 1982, The terminology of structures in thrust belts).

Thrust belt structures

Thrust belt structures can be divided into one major thrust, the Granite Creek thrust, and one major thrust system, the Prospect thrust system. The Granite Creek thrust is the oldest thrust-belt structure, and the Prospect thrust system is the youngest.

A thrust system is a series of thrust faults related to a common sole detachment fault (Boyer and Elliott, 1982). Royse and others (1975) used the term thrust zone to apply to this linking system of thrust faults. West of the Hoback Basin area, seismic and well data show that the Granite Creek thrust and Prospect thrust system ramp together to compose a single thrust system (i.e., Darby thrust zone of Royse and others, 1975; Fig. 5).

Granite Creek thrust. The Granite Creek thrust (GrC) is not exposed at the surface. Interpretations of its geometry and trend are thus limited to well data and proprietary seismic information. These data indicate that the thrust generally parallels the north-south surface trace of the Prospect thrust system. However, the data do not constrain its position north of the Chevron, Inc., No. 1-34 Game Hill Unit well (Sec.34,T.39N.,R.114W.) near the Gros Ventre foreland uplift. The Chevron Game Hill Unit well (Figs. 3, 6) penetrated a thickened, upright section of Triassic Chugwater Formation. One possible explanation for this thickened, unoverturned strata is that it represents a series of imbricate slices of Triassic rocks that are part of the frontal Granite Creek thrust. Triassic Chugwater rocks are analogously imbricated in the Prospect thrust system on the surface. The Chevron Game Hill Unit well penetrated the primary Granite Creek thrust below the thickened hanging-wall Triassic section (Figs. 3, 6, 7). The Granite Creek thrust emplaced Paleozoic and Mesozoic strata over the Maastrichtian Sohare Formation. Middle Paleocene rocks dated by pollen unconformably overlie the concealed Granite Creek thrust plate (Royse, 1985), thus bracketing and proving the early age of this thrust.

The Chevron, Inc., Federal No. 1-33 Cabin Creek Unit well (Sec.33,T.37N.R.114W.) also penetrated the Granite Creek thrust (Fig. 8). This well data and seismic data farther south indicate that the Granite Creek thrust continues in the subsurface until it loses displacement near T.34N. (F. Royse, Jr., personal communication, 1986). An interpretive regional cross section

(Fig. 7) illustrates the possible configuration of the Granite Creek thrust from its western connection with the Prospect thrust system to form the Darby thrust to its eastern extent in the subsurface. The concealed trace of the Granite Creek thrust below the Hoback Formation essentially parallels the surface trace of the related Game Hill thrust.

The Game Hill thrust (GH) is a west-vergent fault in the Hoback Basin area (Figs. 2, 3, 6, 7, 8). Guennel and others (1973) first identified and named the "Game Hill fault" based on their palynological studies of the "type section" of the Hoback Formation as defined by Dorr (1952). The palynologic data indicated that generally eastward-dipping late Cretaceous Sohare Formation lies between two generally eastward-dipping panels of Paleocene Hoback Formation. Therefore, the Game Hill thrust brought the Sohare Formation up from east to west over the Hoback Formation (Figs. 2, 3, 6, 7, 8). Schroeder (1973, 1976) called this fault the Battle Mountain normal fault, for its position 2 km east of Battle Mountain (Figs. 2, 3). However, without the benefit of additional palynology to further constrain the fault's trace, he mapped it west of my location of the fault, lost its trace beneath glacial debris, and thus misinterpreted its timing south of the Hoback River. Dorr and others (1977) better constrained the position of the Game Hill thrust to the north with additional palynological data to differentiate the juxtaposed Late Cretaceous and Paleocene rocks. However, north of Granite Creek, they also lost the fault's trace beneath glacial debris. The pollen-sample age data (Tables 2, 3; Figs. 3, 4) refine this earlier data and thus better constrain the position and timing of the Game Hill thrust. The fault continues northward beneath the glacial debris near Granite Creek and crops out in Section 22 (Fig. 3) just before an overriding lateral ramp of the Cliff Creek thrust conceals its trace (Fig. 14). New structural data (Fig. 3) support this position and timing of the Game Hill thrust. South of Little Cliff Creek, Sec.34,T.38N.,R.114W., the southernmost tear fault of the Cliff Creek thrust also truncated the Game Hill thrust (Fig. 3). The Game Hill thrust trace reappears on the surface structurally beneath the eroded Cliff Creek thrust plate, in Sec.15,T.37N., and continues south (Figs. 2, 3). Seismic and well data indicate that the Game Hill thrust terminates in a fold approximately 26 km south in T.34N. (F. Royse, Jr., personal communication, 1986).

Prospect thrust system. The Prospect thrust system lies structurally above the Granite Creek thrust (Figs. 6, 7, 8). Five exposed imbricate thrust faults define the system. From east to west, oldest to youngest, and structurally lowest to highest, these faults include the Cliff Creek (C1C), Little Granite Creek (1GC), Bull Creek (BC), Game Creek (GC), and Bear (B) thrusts.

Cliff Creek thrust. Horberg and others (1949) first identified the Cliff Creek thrust. Prominent exposures of this thrust continue from the southern to the northern border of the area for 30 km (Fig. 3). The Cliff Creek thrust throughout most of its extent emplaced Jurassic Twin Creek, Jurassic-Triassic Nugget, and/or Triassic Chugwater formations over the middle–upper Paleocene Hoback Formation in the footwall of the Game Hill thrust or over the Cretaceous Sohare Formation in the hanging wall of the Game Hill thrust (Figs. 2, 3). Pollen dates constrain the ages of the Hoback and Sohare formations in this area (Figs. 3, 4; Tables 2, 3).

Little Granite Creek thrust. The Little Granite Creek thrust (1GC) lies structurally above and west of the Cliff Creek thrust and may have truncated the hanging-wall anticline of the Cliff Creek thrust 1 km north of the oblique lateral ramp of the Cliff Creek thrust, just southwest of Little Granite Creek (Sec.22,T.39N.,R.114W; Figs. 3, 7). The thrust emplaced Triassic Chugwater over Chugwater and Jurassic-Triassic Nugget formations (Figs. 3, 7). To the northwest, the thrust is poorly defined within the bedding planes of the Chugwater Formation.

Bull Creek thrust. The Bull Creek thrust (BC) is structurally above the Little Granite Creek and Cliff Creek thrusts (Figs. 2, 3). Three zones characterized by major differences in offset define the Bull Creek thrust plane. The northern Bull Creek thrust is exposed on the east face of Mount Rutherford, peak "10,013" (Sec.7,T.39N.,R.114W.; Fig. 3), terminated against the Mount Rutherford compartmental fault (MRF), and emplaced the Chugwater and Nugget Formations over the Twin Creek Limestone. The Mount Rutherford fault exhibits all the characteristics of compartmental deformation noted by Bell (1956) and Brown (1983), including finite ends; fold and other fault termination against the fault; and abrupt changes in structural style, which occur across the fault.

The Middle Bull Creek thrust plane, the Bull Creek fault (BCF), originates south of the Mount Rutherford compartmental fault and extends southward to terminate against the middle tear fault (Sec.33,T.39N.,R.114W.) of the Cliff Creek thrust (Figs. 3, 14). The Bull Creek fault shows normal displacement and emplaced Triassic Chugwater strata on the east against Cretaceous Bear River strata on the west. The fault, therefore, attains a minimum of 460 m of stratigraphic separation.

South of the middle tear fault of the Cliff Creek thrust, thrust motion resumed on the southern Bull Creek thrust that emplaced Jurassic Twin Creek and Jurassic-Triassic Nugget over the Twin Creek (Figs. 2, 3). However, normal drag on some folds east of Bull Creek indicates possible later Tertiary extensional motion on the fault plane for 1 km to the south. Southward, the Bull Creek thrust locally truncated palynologically dated Paleocene Hoback strata that lie unconformably on the Jurassic Twin Creek Limestone (Tables 2, 3; Fig. 3). Some 2 to 3 km south of Kerr Creek, the thrust most likely became blind and probably terminated below a prominent fault-propagation anticline, the Bull Creek anticline (BCA; Figs. 2, 3, 8).

Game Creek thrust. Nelson and Church (1943) first identi-

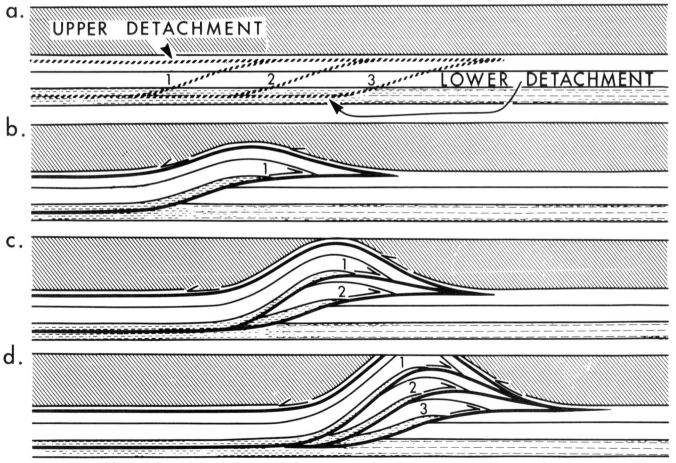

Figure 13. Computer-synthesized model of a triangle zone (from Jones, 1983, reprinted by permission of the Rocky Mountain Association of Geologists).

R. B. Hunter

TABLE 1. HOBACK BASIN AREA STRATIGRAPHIC UNITS, AGE, THICKNESS, AND LITHOLOGY[1]

Age	Formation or Group	Thickness Range (ft)	Dominant Lithology	Age	Formation or Group	Thickness Range (ft)	Dominant Lithology
Quaternary	Qls slumps/ landslides	0-200*	Debris from higher source	Permian	Pp Phosphoria Formation	220	Shale, sandstone, limestone, phosphorite
	Qt Talus	0-200*	Blocky debris from higher source	to			
	Qal alluvium	1-100*	Stream and river gravels	Pennsylvanian and Mississippian	PPM Wells, Amsden, Tensleep Formations	1,200-1,400	Limestone, shale, sandstone
	Qaf alluvial fan	0-50*	Water-laid debris in fan		Mm Madison Limestone	1,000	Limestone
	Qg glacial debris	0-800*	Moraine and out-wash debris	Devonian	Dd Darby Formation	420	Siltstone, shale, dolomite
	Qc colluvium	0-300*	Cover debris	Ordovician	Ob Bighorn Dolomite	270	Dolomite
Tertiary				Cambrian	Cg Gallatin Formation	200	Limestone, dolomite
Eocene(?)	Tr red conglomerate	0-2,000*	Red siltstone and conglomerate		Cgv Gros Ventre Formation	600	Shale, limestone
	Tb basalt dikes	0-50*	Mafic basalt dikes intruding Kg		Cf Flathead Sandstone	300	Qaurtzitic sandstone
Paleocene	Th Hoback Formation	8,000-15,000	Shale, sandstone, and conglomerate	Archean	pC undifferentiated		Granitic gneisses
Cretaceous	Khb Harebell Formation	0-1,000*	Shale, lenticular sandstone				
	Kmv Mesaverde Formation	0-1,000*	Sandstone, shale				
	Kso Sohare Formation	8,000-10,000	Shale, lenticular sandstone				
	Kf Frontier Formation	1,000-1,500[†]	Sandstone, shale				
	Ka Aspen Formation	1,000-1,500[†]	Shale, sandstone				
	Kbr Bear River Formation	500-600	Shale, sandstone				
	Kg Gannett Group	800-1,000	Limestone, shale sandstone, conglomerate				
Jurassic	Jsp Stump and Preuss Formations	150-300	Siltstone, shale				
	Jtc Twin Creek Limestone	1,000-1,100	Limestone, shale				
	Jus Upper Sundance Formation	500[§]	Sandy limestone, shale				
	Jls Lower Sundance Formation	500[§]	Limestone, shale				
	Jgs Gypsum Spring Formation	50-300*,[‡]	Collapse breccia, limestone				
Triassic	JTRn Nugget Sandstone	300-400*	Sandstone				
	TRc Chugwater Formation	1,250-1,500*	Shale, sandstone, limestone, dolomite				
	TRd Dinwoody Formation	330	Siltstone, shale, limestone				

[1]Data primarily adapted from Wanless and others (1955), Froidevaux (1968, 1977), Imlay (1967), Love; (1956, 1977), Dorr and others (1977), Love and Christiansen (1985), and unpublished data of this study.
*Thickness estimated in field.
[†]Not exposed on surface.
[§]Twin Creek equivalent foreland facies.
[‡]Mapped with Twin Creek where not tectonically significant.

TABLE 2. POLLEN SAMPLE AGE DATA FROM THIS STUDY IDENTIFIED BY SHELDON NELSON OF CHEVRON, INC.*

Sample	Age	Pollen Genera, Species, or Types	Sample	Age	Pollen Genera, Species, or Types
P1	Paleocene 2 - 6	*Momipites wyomingensis*, undifferentiated bisaccate sp.	P16	Upper Cretaceous, probably Hilliard Formation	*Cyathidites* sp., *Foraminisporis* sp., *Quadripollis krempii, Lycopodiumsporites* sp., *Classopollis classoides*, undifferentiated bisaccate sp., undifferentiated tricolpate sp.
P2	Upper Cretaceous Hilliard-Evanston	*Cyathidites* sp., *Vitreisporites* sp., *Proteacidites* sp., undifferentiated bisaccate sp.	P17	Unknown	Barren
P3	Cretaceous	*Cyathidites* sp., *Cicatricosisporites*, sp., *Appendicisporites* sp., *Gleicheniidites* sp., *Acanthotriletes* sp.	P18	Upper Cretaceous Hilliard-Evanston	*Cyathidites* sp., *Foraminisporis* sp., *Proteacidites* sp., undifferentiated bisaccate sp.
P4	Upper Cretaceous Hilliard Formation equivalent	*Quadripollis krempii, Cicatricosisporites*, sp., *Lycopodiumsporites*, sp., *Cyathidites*, sp., *Laevigatisporites*, sp., undifferentiated bisaccate sp., undifferentiated tricolpate sp.	P19	Cretaceous, probably upper	*Quadripollis krempii, Appendicisporites* sp., undifferentiated bisaccate sp., undifferentiated tricolpate sp.
P5	Upper Cretaceous Hilliard-Evanston	*Proteacidites* sp., undifferentiated bisaccate sp.	P20	Upper Cretaceous Adaville-Evanston equivalent	*Cyathidites* sp., *Proteacidites* sp., *Aequitriradites ornatus, Aquilapollenites spinulosus, Cicatricosisporites* sp., *Zlivisporis* sp., *Foveasporis* sp., undifferentiated bisaccate sp.
P6	Upper Cretaceous Hilliard-Evanston	*Gleicheniidites* sp., *Laevigatisporites* sp., undifferentiated tricolpate sp.	P21	Upper Cretaceous probably Hilliard-Formation equivalent (Sohare Fm.)	*Cyathidites* sp., *Quadripollis krempii, Veryhachium* sp., *Cicatricosisporites* sp., *Laevigatisporites* sp., *Lycopodiumsporites* sp., *Appendicisporites* sp., undifferentiated bisaccate sp., *Normapolles* type
P7	Upper Cretaceous Hilliard	*Quadripollis krempii, Veryhachium* sp., *Proteacidites* sp., undifferentiated bisaccate sp.			
P8	Upper Cretaceous Hilliard-Evanston	*Proteacidites* sp., *Cyathidites* sp., *Foraminisporis* sp., undifferentiated bisaccate sp., undifferentiated tricolpate sp.	P22	Paleocene 3	*Quadripollis krempii, Deflandrea* sp., *Momipites ventifluminus, Momipites wyomingenesis, M. anellus, Cyathidites* sp., *Ulmipollenites* sp., *Tilia* sp., undifferentiated bisaccate sp.
P9	Upper Cretaceous	*Proteacidites* sp., *Cyathidites* sp. undifferentiated bisaccate sp., undifferentiated tricolpate sp.	P23	Paleocene 3	*Cyathidites* sp., *Momipites wyomingensis, Momipites ventifluminis, M. anellus, Deflandrea* sp., undifferentiated bisaccate sp.
P10	Essentially barren	*Classopollis classoides*, undifferentiated bisaccate sp.			
P11	Paleocene, probably 3	*Cicatricosisporites* sp., *Cyathidites* sp., *Polyposiidites* sp., *Foraminisporis* sp., undifferentiated bisaccate sp., undifferentiated tricolpate sp.	P24	Upper Cretaceous Evanston Formation equivalent	*Cyathidites* sp., *Cicatrisporites* sp., *Proteacidites* sp., *Gleicheniidites* sp., *Appendicisporites* sp., *Camarozonosporites* sp., *Cranwellia striatus, Classopollis classoides, Foraminisporis* sp., undifferentiated bisaccate sp.
P12	Paleocene, probably 3	*Ulmipollenites* sp., *Deflandrea* sp., *Momipites ventifluminis, Monipites wyomingensis*, undifferentiated bisaccate sp.	P25	Unknown	Barren
			P26	Unknown	Barren
P13	Paleocene 3	*Momipites wyomingensis, Momipites annelus, M. leffingwellii, Alnipollenites* sp., *Deflandrea* sp., undifferentiated bisaccate sp.	P27	Unknown	Barren
			P28	Long-range species, fluvial	*Cyathidites* sp., *Chomotriletes* sp., undifferentiated bisaccate sp.
P14	Paleocene, probably 3	*Deflandrea* sp., *Cicatricosisporites* sp., *Chatangiella victoriensis, Appendicisporites* sp., *Gleicheniidites* sp., *Momipites annelus, Momipites ventifluminis, Quadripollis krempii, Ulmipollites* sp., *Classopollis classoides*, undifferentiated bisaccate sp.			
P15	Upper Cretaceous Hilliard-Adaville	*Proteacidites* sp., undifferentiated tricolpate sp.			

*P1-P28 marked by triangles in Figures 3 and 7. Paleocene time is divided into 6 even time intervals, with 1 the oldest and 6 the youngest. Upper Cretaceous strata are divided into Frontier, Hilliard, Evanston, and Adaville Formation equivalents.

TABLE 3. POLLEN SAMPLE AGE DATA FROM CHEVRON, INC.*

Sample		Age
PA	—	Paleocene 3
PB	—	Paleocene 2 - 6
PC	—	Late Cretaceous, Frontier Formation or younger
PD	—	Jurassic (Jtc)
PE	—	Paleocene 3 - 4
PF	—	Paleocene 3 - 6
PG	—	Paleocene 4 - 6
PH	—	Cretaceous, Hilliard-Evanston Formation equivalent
PI	—	Paleocene 2 - 6
PJ	—	Paleocene 3
PK	—	Paleocene 3 - 4
PL	—	Paleocene 3
PM	—	Paleocene 4 - 6
PN	—	Paleocene 5 - 6
PO	—	Paleocene 5 - 6
PP	—	Upper Cretaceous, Maastrichtian
PQ	—	Paleocene 5 - 6
PR	—	Paleocene 5 - 6
PS	—	Paleocene 5
PT	—	Cretaceous, upper Frontier to Hilliard Formations
PU	—	Paleocene 3
PV	—	Paleocene 4 - 5

*PA-PV marked by squares in Figures 3 and 7. Paleocene time is divided into 6 even time intervals, with 1 the oldest and 6 the youngest. Upper Cretaceous strata are divided into Frontier, Hilliard, Evanston, and Adaville Formation equivalents.

TABLE 4. ABBREVIATIONS OF MAJOR STRUCTURES AND THEIR ORIGINS ON THE GEOLOGIC MAP (FIG. 3), THE TECTONIC MAP (FIG. 2), AND THE CROSS-SECTIONS (FIGS. 6, 7, AND 8)

Thrust Belt
Thrust Faults
Granite Creek thrust system: GrC
- GrC — Granite Creek thrust
- GrCB — Granite Creek blind thrust
- GH — Game Hill thrust

Prospect thrust system: P
- CIC — Cliff Creek thrust
- IGC — Little Granite Creek thrust
- BC — Bull Creek thrust
- GC — Game Creek thrust
- B — Bear thrust

Other
- S — Shepard thrust
- D — Darby thrust

Thrust belt-associated faults
- MRF* — Mount Rutherford compartmental fault
- BCF* — Bull Creek fault

Major thrust belt-associated folds
- BMA — Battle Mountain anticline
- BMS — Battle Mountain syncline
- BCA — Bull Creek anticline
- BCS — Bull Creek syncline
- LCS — Lime Creek syncline
- NBCS — Northern Bull Creek syncline
- CICA — Cliff Creek anticline
- GA* — Granite anticline
- LGA* — Little Granite anticline

Foreland
Foreland faults
Cache Creek fault system
- CCB — Cache Creek "blind" fault
- CCI — Cache Creek subfault
- CC — Cache Creek fault

Foreland-associated faults
- SC* — Shoal Creek fault
- MRF* — Mount Rutherford compartmental fault

Major foreland-associated folds
- GS — Granite syncline
- KCA — Kerr Creek anticline
- KCS — Kerr Creek Syncline
- GA* — Granite anticline
- LGA* — Little Granite anticline

Other
Late Basin and Range province-associated faults
- BCF* — Bull Creek fault
- SC* — Shoal Creek fault

*Alternate origin possible.

fied and named the Game Creek thrust where the Nugget Sandstone had been thrust over the Twin Creek Limestone on the east flank of Mount Rutherford in Sec.8,T.39N.,R.114W., structurally above the Cliff Creek, Little Granite Creek, and Bull Creek thrusts to the east (Fig. 7). Approximately 24 km south of the Gros Ventre foreland uplift, the Cliff Creek, Bull Creek, and Game Creek thrusts merge into the Cliff Creek thrust plane (Figs. 2, 3). A large tear fault or very high-angle oblique lateral ramp transferred the displacement and truncated the Bull Creek anticline and several folds on the Cliff Creek thrust plate before merging with the Cliff Creek thrust 1 km south of Sandy Marshall Creek (Figs. 2, 3).

Bear thrust. Schroeder (1976) mapped the north-south–trending Bear thrust that crops out structurally above and west of the Game Creek thrust. Dorr and others (1977) interpreted the thrust to terminate a few kilometers north of the Hoback River. Alternatively, Schroeder (1976) showed the thrust to continue north-northwest. Southward, the Bear thrust may have terminated in an easterly overturned anticline near Clause Creek just east of Clause Peak, and displacement may have transferred eastward into the Lookout Mountain thrust (Dorr and others, 1977). Alternatively, it may continue south, west of Clause Peak (Froidevaux, 1977, Plate 1).

Foreland structures

Cache Creek fault system. The Cache Creek fault system represents the major family of foreland structures. From southwest to northeast, faults composing the Cache Creek fault system

include the Cache Creek "blind" fault (CCB), the Cache Creek subfault (CCI), and the Cache Creek fault (CC).

Cache Creek blind fault. Seismic data from Dixon (1982; cross sections 8, 9) and Chevron (F. Royse, Jr., personal communication, 1985) constrain the position and amount of offset of the Cache Creek blind fault (Figs. 2, 3, 6, 7, 15). The fault generally parallels the southeast-to-northwest trend of the Gros Ventre foreland uplift and dips steeply to the northeast. The Williams No. 1-30 Granite Creek–Federal well (Sec.30,T.39N., R.113W.) penetrated the Nugget Sandstone on an anticline that was generated by movement on this fault (Fig. 6). Correlations between this well and the Chevron No. 1-35 Federal well (Sec.35,T.39N.,R.114W.) and the Game Hill Unit well (Sec.34,

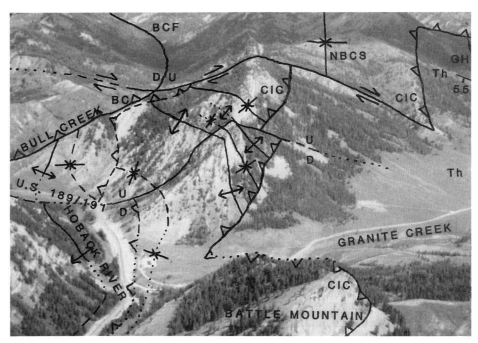

Figure 14. View north of the Cliff Creek thrust (C1C). Covered Hoback Formation and red conglomerate on right are overthrust by Chugwater and Nugget Formations on the Cliff Creek thrust plate. Note the prominent tear fault in the Cliff Creek thrust on the upper right and the lateral ramp on the extreme upper right where the Cliff Creek thrust overrode the Game Hill thrust. Battle Mountain lies on the lower right (east). Figure 19 views the Cliff Creek thrust to the west from Battle Mountain. Aerial photograph by F. Royse (from Hunter, 1987).

T.39N.,R.114W.) indicate an increase in stratigraphic separation of 600 m (2,000 ft) across the fault to the northeast (Fig. 6). This fault is referred to as "blind" because only subsurface data reveal its possible relation to foreland deformation. The fault affected only the northern, more foreland-influenced, half of the area. Here, it ramped toward the surface and most likely merged with the Game Hill thrust plane because it does not outcrop elsewhere (Figs. 2, 3, 6). Offset on the Game Hill thrust correspondingly increased in this area (Fig. 3).

Cache Creek subfault. The Cache Creek subfault (CCI) emplaced an overturned section of Jurassic Sundance (Twin Creek equivalent) through Chugwater Formations over Paleocene to early Eocene Hoback strata folded within the Granite syncline (GS) (Figs. 2, 3).

Cache Creek fault. The primary Cache Creek fault (CC) truncated the Cache Creek subfault (CCI) to the east and west (Figs. 2, 3, 7) and emplaced Paleozoic rocks as young as the Mississippian Madison Limestone over the Paleocene to early Eocene Hoback Formation and the Cache Creek subfault (Figs. 3, 7).

Other structures

Other faults include the generally east-west–trending normal faults that truncate the Game Hill thrust, Prospect thrust system, and probably the Granite Creek thrust at depth. The larger faults are dominantly down to the south and dip at very high angles near the surface. The Shoal Creek fault (SC; Sec.11,T.38N., R.114W.) is an excellent example of this type of fault (Figs. 2, 3). Similar normal faults truncate thrusts and stratigraphy south of Little Cliff Creek near Sec.35,T.38N.,R.114W. (Figs. 2, 3). Other, smaller, southwest-to-northeast–trending normal faults occur between the Game Creek and Bull Creek thrusts north of the Hoback River (Figs. 2, 3). Several unnamed folds trend generally north-south to N30°W, are asymmetric in the tectonic transport direction, and likely formed during thrusting as fault-bend or fault propagation folds.

STRUCTURAL INTERPRETATIONS

The probable history of the major tectonic and stratigraphic events from the Late Cretaceous through the present in the Hoback Basin area is schematically illustrated in Figure 16. This chronology and the discussion demonstrate the spatial and temporal interaction of Sevier and Laramide styles of deformation.

Development of the Granite Creek thrust–Game Hill thrust triangle zone

The east-directed Granite Creek thrust (GrC), the east-directed Granite Creek blind thrust (GrCB), and the west-directed Game Hill thrust (GH) make up a triangle zone in the

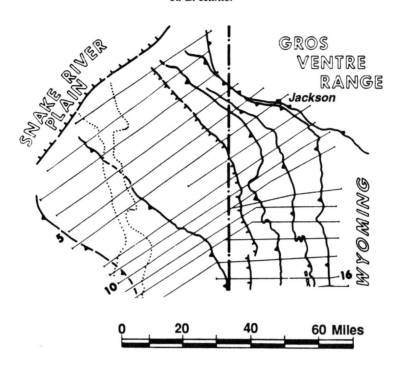

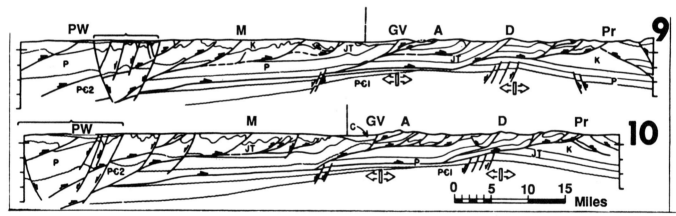

Figure 15. Location map and cross sections showing an interpretation of the Cache Creek thrust and Cache Creek blind thrust on the right (northeast) side (after Dixon, 1982, reprinted by permission of the American Association of Petroleum Geologists).

Hoback area (Figs. 5, 6, 8, 16d). The Granite Creek thrust likely propagated through the upper Cretaceous Sohare Formation with no real upper detachment (Fig. 16, a and b). Erosional truncation of the thrust by an early(?) Paleocene unconformity shortly after or even during emplacement (Figs. 6, 7, 8, 16, a and b) illustrates that the lower detachment intersected the erosional surface during or shortly after its propagation. Therefore, the thrust probably did not have an upper detachment.

As the Granite Creek thrust moved eastward upon Paleozoic rocks, complex Paleozoic and Mesozoic facies changes may have induced ramping. These complex Paleozoic and Mesozoic facies changes occurred near the ancient sedimentary axis between the eastern platform sequence and the thinned, eastern miogeocline sequence near the present-day Hoback Basin (Dorr, 1956; Stokes, 1976). The thrust plate likely encountered more resistance as it moved eastward through these changing hangingwall strata. Increased resistance to eastward thrust propagation may have resulted in ramping, tip-line sticking, imbrication, and later folding of upper thrusts by younger, structurally lower thrusts (Fig. 16a). Eventually, the Granite Creek thrust plate may have imbricated and formed an antiformal stack that became structurally locked in very Late Cretaceous time (Fig. 16a).

Erosion of the uplifted thrust belt to the west initiated syntectonic deposition of the Paleocene to early Eocene Hoback Formation (Spearing, 1969) unconformably over the Granite Creek thrust system (Fig. 16, b and c). Therefore, movement of the Granite Creek thrust occurred between Maastrichtian and early to middle Paleocene. Further compression in middle to late Paleocene time probably initiated the propagation of the subhorizontal Granite Creek blind thrust (GrCB) within the Cretaceous Sohare Formation beneath the structurally locked antiformal stack (Fig. 16d). Folding and/or faulting of the Sohare Formation above this blind bedding-plane thrust (F. Royse, Jr., personal communication, 1986) likely accommodated some of the shortening on the blind thrust. The Chevron Game Hill Unit well (Sec.34,T.39N.,R.114W.) penetrated these deformed Sohare strata and the Granite Creek blind thrust below them (Fig. 6). The contemporaneous, west-directed Game Hill thrust (GH) accommodated the remainder of this shortening and formed the triangle zone with the Granite Creek thrust (Figs. 8, 16d). The Game Hill thrust is, therefore, genetically related to movement on the Granite Creek thrust.

The Game Hill thrust truncated middle to late Paleocene Hoback strata dated by pollen analysis (Figs. 3, 4; Tables 2, 3). The Cliff Creek thrust truncated both the Game Hill thrust and late Paleocene Hoback strata in Sec.22, T.39N.,R.114W., Sec. 34,T.38N.,R.114W., and Sec.10,T.37N.,R.114W. (Fig. 3). Early Eocene Wasatch strata overlie the Cliff Creek thrust to the south (Dorr and others, 1977). Therefore, the Game Hill thrust and associated Granite Creek blind thrust probably propagated during late Paleocene through early Eocene time.

The Game Hill thrust was considered a foreland fault by Dorr and others (1977) and Corbett (1983). *Three critical relations* indicate that the Game Hill thrust is neither an out-of-the-basin thrust (see Brown, 1983; Sacrison, 1978, Fig. 15) nor a southward extension of the Cache Creek fault system.

First and foremost, frontal thrust-belt triangle zones worldwide do not all interact with foreland, Laramide-style deformation (Jones, 1983; Teal, 1983; Morley, 1986; Price, 1986; Banks and Warburton, 1986). Preexisting foreland Moxa Arch–type basement warps may have localized Sevier-style thrust ramping in the front of the Wyoming thrust belt (Wiltschko and Eastman, 1983). However, this mechanism cannot dominantly control ramping of thrust-belt thrusts and triangle zones worldwide because the basement is not arched or deformed beneath most triangle zones associated with thrust belts (Jones, 1983; Teal, 1983; Morley, 1986; Price, 1986; Banks and Warburton, 1986). For example, thin-skinned thrusting and deformation in the Alberta foothills did not involve the complex interaction with foreland, Laramide-style uplifts. Bally and others (1966), Spang and Brown (1981), Price (1981), and Jones (1983) reported only basement dipping at low angles beneath the Canadian thrust belt and associated triangle zones. Therefore, by inference of like processes producing triangle zones, the Granite Creek thrust–Game Hill thrust triangle zone probably formed originally by thrust-initiated processes and only later interacted with foreland

deformation. Furthermore, during propagation of the Granite Creek thrust, the basement beneath the Hoback Basin was probably flat or had a slight west dip (F. Royse, Jr., personal communication, 1986). The regional basement arch interpreted from seismic data probably formed in Eocene time and tilted the Granite Creek thrust system to the east (Figs. 6, 7, 8, 16k): Paleocene strata are tilted by this basement arching, and Eocene strata overlie the tilted strata in an angular unconformity observed in seismic data from the Hoback Basin (F. Royse, Jr., personal communication, 1985).

Second, the Game Hill thrust trends north-south from the Hoback area, southward to T.34N., where seismic and well data indicate it terminates in a concealed fold beneath younger deposits (F. Royse, Jr., personal communication, 1986). This trend diverges markedly from the southeast-northwest trend of the Cache Creek fault system. Simons and others (1980) showed a small imbricate of the north-south–trending Cache Creek fault system that emplaced Cretaceous Frontier through Harebell Formations over Hoback strata 6 km east of the eastern border of the area. However, this fault does not persist to the south. Gravity data summarized by Pattridge (1976) indicate that the Cache Creek fault system continues to the southeast beneath Quaternary deposits and merges with the Wind River thrust near New Fork Lakes. Also, Skinner (1960), Keefer (1964), and Cutler (1984) interpreted the Cache Creek fault system to continue several kilometers to the southeast beyond the Hoback area. These authors implied that the Cache Creek fault continues west of the Green River below younger deposits toward the Wind River thrust.

Third, seismic data reveal that the genetically and temporally related Granite Creek thrust and Game Hill thrust both terminate in folds beneath younger deposits in T.34N. (F. Royse, Jr., personal communication, 1986). The termination of these thrusts in the same area implies their genetic and temporal association. Here, thrust displacement may have transferred westward into the Granite Creek thrust from the Darby thrust (Royse, 1985).

Together, these three major points illustrate that thrust processes primarily caused the formation of the Granite Creek thrust–Game Hill thrust triangle zone.

Timing and interaction of thrust belt and foreland structures

Cache Creek blind fault and Granite Creek thrust. The foreland, Laramide-style, Cache Creek blind fault is interpreted to have propagated after the Game Hill thrust in the late Paleocene (Fig. 16e), remobilizing the northern part of the Game Hill thrust north of the Hoback River (Figs. 2, 3, 6, 7). This fault or its fault-propagation anticline may have originated earlier, during the propagation of the Granite Creek thrust and associated triangle zone (Fig. 16, b-d). However, since overlap in time only constrains the final movement on this fault, direct evidence of its earlier history is unavailable. Seismic and well data reveal that fault-propagation folding associated with movement of the Cache

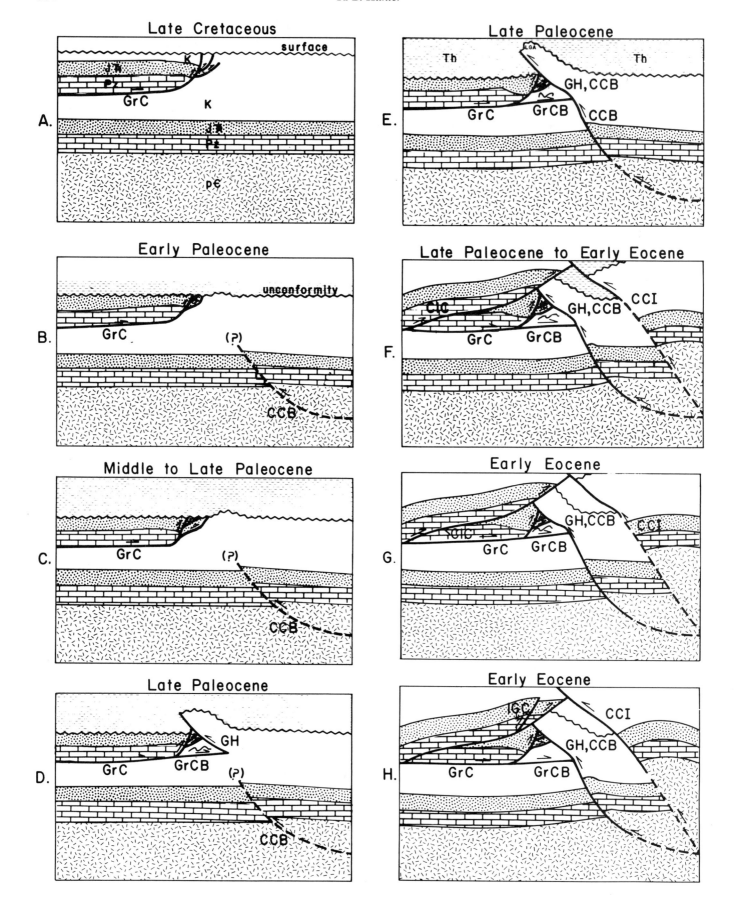

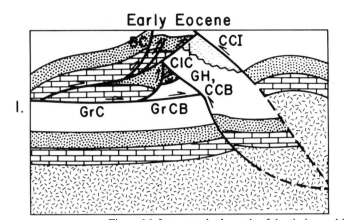
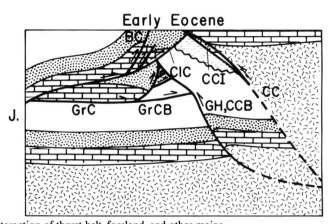

Figure 16. Interpreted schematic of the timing and interaction of thrust belt, foreland, and other major tectonic and stratigraphic events from the late Cretaceous through present in the Hoback basin area. A, The Granite Creek thrust (GrC) truncates the Sohare Formation and is overlain by an early(?) Paleocene unconformity. B, Early(?) Paleocene erosion bevels into the Granite Creek thrust plate. The Cache Creek blind fault (CCB) may have initiated at this time. However, it does not significantly fold the Granite Creek thrust. C, The middle to late Paleocene Hoback Formation, dated by pollen analysis, is deposited over the unconformity. D, The Granite Creek blind thrust (GrCB) propagates, initiating movement on the Game Hill thrust (GH) in middle to late Paleocene time. The Game Hill thrust truncates middle Paleocene Hoback strata. E, Further movement on the foreland Cache Creek blind fault remobilizes the Game Hill thrust plane north of the Hoback River. The Little Granite anticline (LGA) may have formed from movement of this thrust. F, The Prospect thrust system (Cliff Creek thrust, C1C) overrides the Game Hill thrust and the Cache Creek blind fault. Displacement on the foreland Cache Creek blind fault transfers into the foreland Cache Creek subfault (CCI). The Cache Creek subfault truncates early Eocene upper Hoback strata. G, Motion on the Cache Creek subfault continues. H, The Little Granite Creek thrust (1GC) propagates and truncates the hanging-wall anticline of the Cliff Creek thrust. Motion continues on the Cache Creek subfault. I, The Bull Creek thrust (BC) propagates and truncates folds formed by movement on the Cliff Creek thrust. Cache Creek subfault displacement increases. Early Eocene strata are deposited over the Cliff Creek thrust to the south. J, Major foreland thrusting continues on the Cache Creek subfault and transfers into the Cache Creek fault, which propagates over it. Motion on the Cache Creek subfault and Cache Creek fault rotate and overturn a section of Triassic through Cretaceous rocks between them. (K, L, and M are on the next page.) K, The Game Creek thrust (GC) propagates and truncates the Bull Creek anticline, the Bull Creek blind thrust, and the Cliff Creek thrust to the south (Fig. 3). Major basement arching tilts all previously formed structures and strata to the east. L, Foreland fault motion rates on the Cache Creek fault system decrease. The Bear thrust (B), and probably also the Shepard thrust (S), propagate as the last out-of-sequence thrusts in the Prospect thrust system. Latest Prospect thrust motion folds the Eocene(?) red conglomerate. Deposition of the red conglomerate continues and overlaps the Game Creek, Bull Creek, Little Granite Creek, and Cliff Creek thrusts. M, Thrust belt and foreland tectonism has halted. The north-south–trending Hoback normal Fault (HF) and associated faults have developed in response to extension associated with the development of the Basin and Range province. East-west–trending normal faults also developed in response to these forces or possibly isostatic adjustment associated with the load of the Gros Ventre foreland uplift (from Hunter, 1987).

Creek blind fault did not significantly deform the Granite Creek and Game Hill thrusts. This provides indirect evidence that the Cache Creek blind fault propagated before and/or contemporaneously with the Granite Creek thrust (Fig. 16b). Otherwise, movement of the initial anticlinal stage of the Cache Creek blind fault would have significantly folded the Granite Creek and Game Hill thrusts.

The Granite Creek thrust may have transferred displacement into the Jackson thrust to the northwest (Royse, 1985). However, the Jackson thrust, or northern Prospect thrust, truncated Paleocene Hoback strata (Simons and others, 1980), and these same Paleocene strata unconformably overlie the Granite Creek thrust in the subsurface just to the south. Therefore, to satisfy these

timing constraints, the Granite Creek and Game Hill thrusts probably continue to the northwest beneath the Jackson thrust of the Prospect thrust system.

Final movements on the Cache Creek blind fault where it remobilized the northern portion of the Game Hill thrust may have formed the Little Granite anticline (LGA; Figs. 2, 3, 7). Indirect evidence implying this genetic association between the Cache Creek blind fault and the Little Granite anticline includes the following observations: (1) the Little Granite anticline terminates just 1.3 km south of Granite Creek in Sec.3,T.38N., R.114W. near where the interpreted Cache Creek blind fault also terminates; (2) the Little Granite anticline continues to the northwest parallel to the strong, nearby foreland structural trends

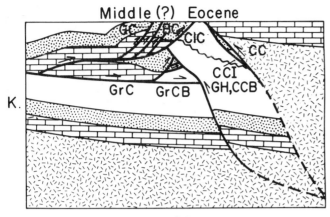

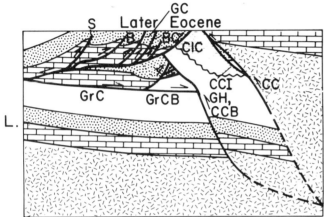

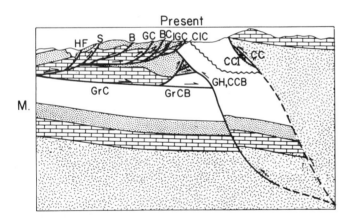

Figure 17. View to the northwest of the very low-angle Cliff Creek thrust, which is within the Phosphoria Formation, parallel to bedding, and view of the overridden Hoback strata folded in the Little Granite anticline 3 km north of Mount Rutherford. Aerial photograph by F. Royse (from Hunter, 1987).

The Cache Creek blind fault may, alternatively, represent an out-of-the-basin thrust generated by uplift of the basement-cored Cache Creek foreland fault system.

The smaller, doubly plunging Granite anticline (GA) north of Granite Creek may be a fault-propagation fold that formed by movement on a small, blind back-limb imbricate of the Game Hill thrust (Figs. 3, 6). Alternatively, it may have formed by local structural rotation in a transfer zone from the decreasing displacement on the Cache Creek blind fault to the Cache Creek subfault (Fig. 16g). The Cache Creek blind fault may, alternatively, represent an out-of-the-basin thrust generated by initial uplift of the basement-cored Cache Creek fault system to the southeast.

Prospect thrust system. The Prospect thrust system represents an out-of-sequence thrust system composed of later back-limb imbrication of the older Granite Creek thrust plate by the Cliff Creek thrust (ClC; Figs. 7, 16f). Paleocene Hoback strata unconformably overlie the Granite Creek thrust plate, and the Prospect thrust system (ClC) truncated these Paleocene strata. Individual thrusts within the Prospect thrust system are also out of sequence, or westward younging, with respect to each other. The younger thrust imbricates to the west consistently truncated structures on the older thrust plates to the east (Fig. 3). Thus, the entire Prospect thrust system represents an out-of-sequence or break-back thrust system derived from the structurally lower and older Granite Creek thrust plate (Fig. 5).

Two major causes probably contributed to the out-of-sequence thrusting of the Prospect thrust system in the Hoback area. First, the structurally locked Granite Creek thrust system and the changing hanging-wall sedimentary facies would probably not allow any structurally lower detachment during further deformation. Therefore, further compression had to deform rocks in other areas—such as structurally above the Granite Creek

(Simons and others, 1980); and (3) the Cliff Creek thrust truncated both the Little Granite anticline in the northwest corner of the map area (Figs. 2, 3, 17) and the Cache Creek blind fault where it coincides with the Game Hill thrust in Sec.22,T.39N., R.114W. This latter relation demonstrates the foreland and thrust-belt interaction through time. Alternatively, movement on the Game Hill thrust plate could have formed the Little Granite anticline. However, anticlines as large as the Little Granite anticline are not commmonly associated with the formation of the oppositely vergent thrusts of triangle zones. The Little Granite anticline may have been initiated during the formation of the triangle zone and amplified during later foreland deformation.

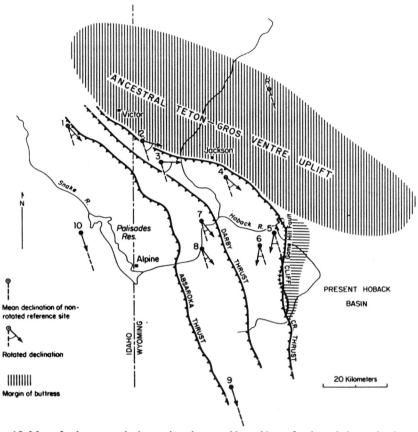

Figure 18. Map of paleomagnetic data points that provides evidence for thrust belt rotation in response to foreland buttress effect. Shown are major thrust faults, margins of buttresses, mean declination of nonrotated reference site (R), and rotated declination points in thrust belt (after Grubbs and Van der Voo, 1976, reprinted by permission of Elsevier Science Publishers).

thrust—as a major out-of-sequence thrust system. Morley (1986) discussed similar facies changes as a possible cause of antiformal stacking in the thrust front of the internal and external Rides, Moroccan Rif. Such changes in lithology can significantly affect the pore-water pressures and resulting plasticity of a detachment zone (Morley, 1986).

Second, the initial Cache Creek fault system, the Cache Creek blind fault (CCB), was an evolving structural high that created a buttress against further eastward thrusting after and possibly during propagation of the Granite Creek thrust (Fig. 16, b-e). Therefore, the Prospect thrust system was forced to imbricate the Granite Creek thrust plate as a major out-of-sequence thrust system. Grubbs and Van der Voo (1976) presented paleomagnetic data that demonstrate that the Cache Creek fault system foreland buttress caused the westward tectonic rotation of the Prospect thrust system (Fig. 18). Two prominent tear faults and a lateral ramp in the northern Cliff Creek thrust (Figs. 2, 3) may have propagated in response to this buttress. Further compression likely caused consecutively younger out-of-sequence thrusts to initiate west of the Cliff Creek thrust; these include the Little Granite Creek, Bull Creek, Game Creek, and Bear thrusts, from east to west and oldest to youngest (Figs. 2, 3).

In the Hoback region, the foreland buttress primarily provided the tectonic setting to cause the out-of-sequence thrusting. However, the effects of the foreland buttress on out-of-sequence thrusting rapidly decreased southward until the Cliff Creek, Bull Creek, and Game Creek thrusts all combined into a single thrust (Fig. 3). However, Dorr and others (1977, p. 53) documented some significant out-of-sequence thrusting farther to the south. Structurally locked thrusts and/or facies changes probably impeded further, structurally lower, eastward thrust movement south of significant foreland buttressing.

Cliff Creek thrust. The Cliff Creek thrust (C1C), the major out-of-sequence imbricate of the Granite Creek thrust plate, propagated between the late Paleocene and early Eocene (Fig. 16f). To demonstrate its out-of-sequence nature, the Cliff Creek thrust truncated the early(?) Paleocene unconformity and middle to upper Paleocene Hoback Formation that overlie the Granite Creek thrust, folds that may originally have formed from movement of the Granite Creek thrust, and the Game Hill thrust that propagated after the main Granite Creek thrust (Figs. 3, 6, 7, 8; Tables 2, 3). North of the junction of the Hoback River and Granite Creek, in Sec.4,T.38N.,R.114W., the Cliff Creek thrust cuts down-section for a short distance through the Triassic

Chugwater (Figs. 3, 6, 19), probably because it truncated and refolded folds that originally formed on the older Granite Creek thrust plate.

Little Granite Creek thrust. The Little Granite Creek thrust (1GC) is interpreted to have formed due to more foreland buttressing on the thrust belt structures very near the Cache Creek fault system (Fig. 16h). The Little Granite Creek thrust solves a space problem between the Bull Creek and Cliff Creek thrusts (Fig. 3) and propagated out-of-sequence after the structurally lower Cliff Creek thrust, as demonstrated by its apparent truncation of the Cliff Creek thrust's hanging-wall anticline just north of the Cliff Creek thrust's northernmost lateral ramp (Fig. 3).

Bull Creek thrust, Bull Creek fault, and Mount Rutherford compartmental fault. The Bull Creek thrust (BC) formed the next-youngest out-of-sequence thrust of the Prospect thrust system after the Little Granite Creek and Cliff Creek thrusts (Fig. 16i). Two kilometers south of Battle Mountain, the Bull Creek thrust demonstrates out-of-sequence thrusting, where it truncated an anticline that probably formed during movement of the Cliff Creek thrust (Fig. 3).

Late normal faulting may have remobilized the middle Bull Creek thrust plane. Royse and others (1975) documented a similar multiple history of movement where the north-south–trending Hoback normal fault remobilized the Shepard thrust plane 9 km to the west (Figs. 1, 7).

Alternatively, the middle Bull Creek fault may have thrust younger rocks over older rocks by truncating an earlier, lower angle thrust fault. Fox (1969) has suggested that this commonly occurs during out-of-sequence thrusting (Fig. 20). Map and cross-section relations (Figs. 3, 6, 7, 8, 21) show that the Bull Creek thrust would have had to truncate the nearby Game Creek thrust to conform to the improbable relations illustrated in Figures 20 and 21. However, the Game Creek thrust truncated the Bull Creek thrust to the south, indicating that the alternative and improbable relations illustrated in Figures 20 and 21 probably did not actually occur.

The Mount Rutherford compartmental fault (MRF) and middle Cliff Creek tear fault provide nearly vertical fault barriers to confine the Bull Creek normal fault (BCF; Fig. 3). The Mount Rutherford fault probably propagated after the Cliff Creek thrust and before the Game Creek thrust in late Paleocene to early Eocene times. Along its approximately 3-km length, it truncated structures on the Cliff Creek, Little Granite Creek, and Bull Creek thrust plates and terminated just east of the Game Creek thrust to the west and against the northernmost Cliff Creek thrust to the east (Figs. 2, 3). Alternatively, the Mount Rutherford fault may be a steep lateral ramp (D. L. Blackstone, personal communication, 1987), which would account for the large displacement discrepancies across it (Fig. 3).

The decrease of displacement on the Bull Creek thrust south of the Hoback River until its termination beneath the Bull Creek anticline (BCA) demonstrates the decrease in foreland buttressing effects 14 km south of the Cache Creek fault system (Fig. 3). However, some foreland-related compression still affects the Bull

Figure 19. View west-northwest from Battle Mountain. Twin Creek, Nugget, and Chugwater strata are deformed into kink and concentric folds at the leading edge of the Cliff Creek thrust. This thrust truncates these folds at a high angle. These folds are commonly refolded, probably from modification by the Cliff Creek thrust of folds, which may have originally formed due to motion on the Granite Creek thrust (from Hunter, 1987).

Creek anticline area. The Cliff Creek thrust and the Bull Creek anticline and syncline (BCA, BCS) are folded in the Kerr Creek anticline-syncline pair (KCA, KCS; Fig. 3). Southward-directed compression from the evolving Cache Creek subfault and Cache Creek fault at this time likely formed the Kerr Creek anticline-syncline pair (Fig. 16j).

Game Creek thrust. The Game Creek thrust (GC) locally forms the next youngest out-of-sequence thrust (Fig. 16k). As a response to diminished foreland buttressing, the Game Creek thrust likely truncated the Bull Creek blind thrust in a transfer zone along a high-angle tear fault or oblique lateral ramp (Secs. 20, 21, 22-T.37N.-R.114W.) and transferred displacement into the Cliff Creek thrust 24 km south of the Gros Ventre uplift (Fig. 3). Dahlstrom (1970), Spang and Brown (1981), and O'Keefe and Stearns (1983) noted that similar tear faults can commonly transfer displacement between thrust faults within a thrust system. Displacement and stratigraphic separation of the Cliff Creek thrust increase accordingly where these thrusts join (Fig. 3). Southward, the hanging-wall cutoff of the Cliff Creek thrust changes from the Twin Creek Limestone (Fig. 3) to the Nugget Sandstone and Chugwater Formation (Froidevaux, 1968, 1977, map) to accommodate the increased displacement from the Game Creek thrust transfer zone.

Where the tear fault or lateral ramp turns to trend southeast, Hoback strata unconformably overlie the underlying Twin Creek Limestone to the northeast. Hoback beds here strike and dip depositionally over the unconformable contact between the Hoback and Twin Creek formations (Figs. 3, 8). This is the same unconformity as that 8 km (5 mi) to the north where Hoback strata unconformably overlie the Twin Creek Limestone on the Bull Creek thrust plate (Fig. 3).

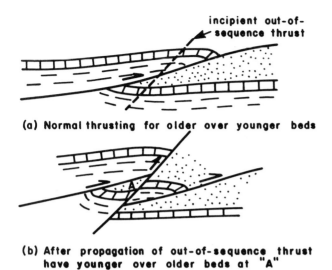

(a) Normal thrusting for older over younger beds

(b) After propagation of out-of-sequence thrust have younger over older beds at "A"

Figure 20. Out-of-sequence thrusting can cause both older-over-younger and younger-over-older thrust geometries where a steeper, younger thrust offsets an older, flatter thrust. Reproduced by permission of the Geological Society of London (Fox, F. G., 1969, Some principles governing interpretation of structure in the Rocky Mountain orogenic belt, *in* Time and place in orogeny, v. 3).

Bear thrust. The Bear thrust probably forms the youngest thrust of the Prospect thrust system (Fig. 16l). A crucial unsolved problem in the Hoback area concerns the actual age of the Tertiary Eocene(?) red conglomerate (Table 1) that unconformably overlies the Hoback Formation and the Cliff Creek, Little Granite Creek, Bull Creek, and Game Creek thrusts (Fig. 3). Schroeder (1976) showed that the Bear thrust truncated the red conglomerate. The uplifting Bear thrust plate may have provided some of the Triassic sedimentary source rocks that give the conglomerate its distinctive red color. However, most of the clasts are derived from the Gros Ventre Range (J. D. Love, written communication, 1986). Folds caused by movement on the thrusts of the Prospect thrust system deformed the red conglomerate. For example, the red conglomerate and the underlying strata were folded in the Northern Bull Creek syncline (NBCS; Sec.28, T.39N.,R.114W.) during the propagation of the Cliff Creek thrust (Fig. 3). However, the red conglomerate unconformably overlies the Cliff Creek thrust 2 km west-northwest of the Northern Bull Creek syncline (Fig. 3). Therefore, the Prospect thrust system probably propagated during the deposition of the syntectonic red conglomerate. However, the Cliff Creek, Little Granite Creek, Bull Creek, and Game Creek thrusts ceased movement before cessation of the deposition of the red conglomerate that locally buried their surface traces (Fig. 3). Reliable dating of the red conglomerate would thus very tightly constrain the timing of and within the Prospect thrust system. Pollen samples taken within the red conglomerate unit, unfortunately, were barren (Table 2, P25-P27).

Cache Creek fault system. Uplift on the Cache Creek fault system or the related Ancestral Teton–Gros Ventre positive area

may have begun as early as the Late Cretaceous (Love, 1977). However, structural evidence in the Hoback area proves only that the last movement on an interpreted portion of the Cache Creek fault system, the Cache Creek blind fault, occurred before the last movement on the overriding Cliff Creek thrust (Fig. 16, b-f). Movement on the Cache Creek blind fault where it coincided with the northernmost Game Hill thrust had ceased by the time the Cliff Creek thrust's northernmost lateral ramp propagated over it in the late Paleocene to early Eocene (Figs. 2, 3, 12f). Cache Creek fault system displacement probably transferred into the Cache Creek subfault (CCI) to the northeast at this time (Figs. 2, 3, 16f and g). Propagation of the Cache Creek subfault and Cache Creek fault likely continued until the deposition of the Eocene Pass Peak conglomerate which overlies these faults to the east (Fig. 16, i and j; Simons and others, 1986). Contemporaneous motion of these two faults probably rotated and overturned the strata between them (Fig. 16, i and j). The Cache Creek subfault overrode the earliest Eocene part of the Hoback Formation, which is folded along the Granite syncline (GS; Sec.13, T.39N.,R.114W.; Figs. 2, 3, 7). This relation illustrates the large amount of overhang that resulted from the extended displacement history of the fault.

Love (1977) estimated that part of the Cache Creek fault system may have remained active until the Miocene, based on the Miocene age of the syntectonic Camp Davis Formation. However, no overlap deposits older than Pleistocene glacial debris bracket movement on the Cache Creek fault system in the map area (Fig. 3).

Later deformation

Late north-south–trending normal faulting is probably associated with the overprinting of regional Basin and Range extension upon the earlier deformation (Fig. 16m). Alternatively, these normal faults may have accommodated isostatic crustal response to the load of the Gros Ventre foreland uplift, similar to the initial Miocene-Pliocene Teton fault movement, or collapse along or near the foreland fault margin. Love (1977) interpreted the beginning of this isostatic adjustment or collapse as occurring near the Miocene-Pliocene boundary, as it has in adjacent foreland mountains.

CONCLUSIONS

The documented and interpreted timing history between foreland and thrust-belt faulting and folding in the Hoback Basin area illustrates the definite spatial and temporal interaction of these contrasting styles of deformation. Figure 16 schematically illustrates the probably history of the major tectonic and stratigraphic events from the Late Cretaceous through the present.

Tectonic Event I

The Granite Creek thrust (GrC) truncated the late Cretaceous Sohare Formation, and was beveled by an early(?) Paleocene unconformity (Fig. 16, a and b).

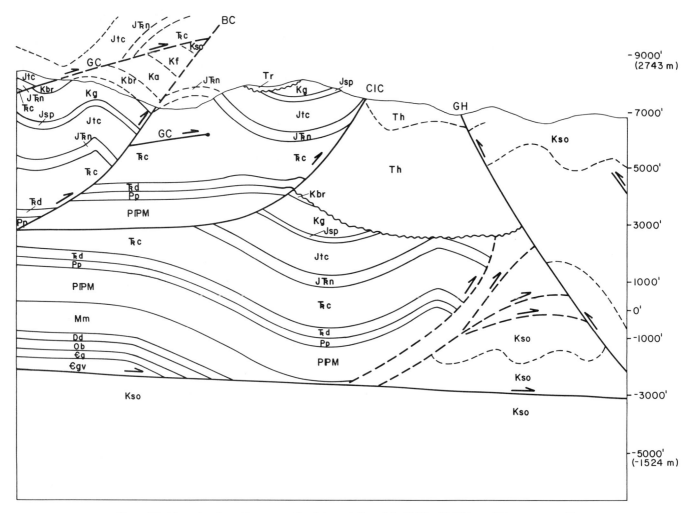

Figure 21. Alternate schematic cross section interpretation of A-A' (Fig. 6). This could have occurred in out-of-sequence thrusting similar to the sequence illustrated in Figure 20. However, map relations do not support this alternate and improbable interpretation (see text).

Depositional Event I

Erosion of the uplifted thrust belt to the west initiated deposition of the syntectonic Paleocene to early Eocene Hoback Formation unconformably over the Granite Creek thrust system (Fig. 16c).

Tectonic Event II

The subhorizontal Granite Creek blind thrust (GrCB) propagated in the middle to late Paleocene below the inferred imbricated antiformal stack at the tip of the Granite Creek thrust (Fig. 16d). Folding of Upper Cretaceous Sohare strata above this blind thrust accommodated some of the shortening on the blind thrust, and the west-directed Game Hill thrust (GH) accommodated the remainder of the shortening. These thrusts formed a structural triangle zone. The Game Hill thrust truncated middle Paleocene Hoback strata (Figs. 3, 4; Tables 2, 3).

Tectonic Event III

The foreland Cache Creek fault system may have been emplaced as early as the Late Cretaceous on the Cache Creek blind fault (CCB; Fig. 16b). Movement on the Cache Creek blind fault likely caused the formation of the Little Granite anticline (LGA; Figs. 16e, 17). Final movement of the Cache Creek blind fault occurred in late Paleocene time before the last movement of the Cliff Creek thrust that overrode it and the Little Granite anticline (Fig. 17). Cache Creek fault-system displacement likely transferred into the Cache Creek subfault (CCI) at this time (Fig. 16, f and g).

Tectonic Event IV

The out-of-sequence Cliff Creek thrust (C1C) of the Prospect thrust system truncated late Paleocene Hoback strata, the Game Hill thrust, and the Cache Creek blind fault (Figs. 3, 4;

Tables 2, 3). Early Eocene Wasatch strata overlie it to the south (Dorr and others, 1977). Therefore, Cliff Creek thrust movement occurred between the late Paleocene and early Eocene (Fig. 16f).

Tectonic Event V

In latest Paleocene time, the Little Granite Creek (1GC) and Bull Creek (BC) thrusts likely consecutively imbricated the Cliff Creek thrust plate as out-of-sequence, westward-younging, thrusts (Fig. 16, h and i). The Little Granite Creek and Bull Creek thrusts truncated folds formed by movement on the Cliff Creek thrust. The Mount Rutherford compartmental fault (MRF) truncated folds on the Cliff Creek, Little Granite Creek, and Bull Creek thrust plates, and likely formed during the propagation of these thrusts to accommodate differential movements between them and the evolving foreland uplift.

Tectonic Event VI

The Cache Creek fault system continued to evolve from late Paleocene through early Eocene times into a significant structural high, leading to dramatic "break-back" or out-of-sequence thrusting of and within the Prospect thrust system (Fig. 16j). Foreland compression refolded some folds initially caused by movement of the Prospect thrust system. The Cache Creek subfault (CCI) and Cache Creek fault (CC) were probably active during this time period because they truncated early Eocene Hoback strata folded within the Granite syncline (GS; Fig. 3). The basement beneath the Hoback area probably arched in Eocene time, possibly as a response to the foreland compression and/or load. This arch tilted all previously formed structures (Fig. 16j and k). Eocene strata unconformably overlie these tilted structures and strata (F. Royse, Jr., personal communication, 1985).

Tectonic Event VII

The Game Creek thrust (GC) occurs west of the Bull Creek thrust and probably propagated in late Paleocene to early Eocene time (Fig. 16k). It truncated the Bull Creek and Cliff Creek thrusts on a large tear fault or oblique lateral ramp south of the junction of Cliff Creek and Sandy Marshall Creek (Figs. 2, 3).

Tectonic Event VIII/Depositional Event II

The Bear thrust (B) probably formed the last out-of-sequence thrust within the Prospect thrust system, after the Cliff Creek, Little Granite Creek, Bull Creek, and Game Creek thrusts, respectively, from east to west. It probably propagated in the early Eocene (Fig. 16l). Dating of the Tertiary early(?) Eocene(?) red conglomerate would further constrain the timing of the out-of-sequence motion between the Prospect thrust-system imbricates. The red conglomerate was folded by motion of the Prospect thrust system. However, it also unconformably overlies all of these thrusts except the Bear thrust. According to Schroeder (1976), the Bear thrust truncated the red conglomerate. If this interpretation is substantiated, the Prospect thrust system must have moved during the deposition of the red conglomerate. Yet, thrust motion on all faults, except possibly the westernmost and youngest Bear thrust, ceased before the cessation of the deposition of the syntectonic red conglomerate.

Tectonic Event IX

All earlier tectonic structures are truncated by later normal faulting (Fig. 16m). The normal faults likely formed in the Miocene to Pliocene and developed in response to (1) regional extension associated with the development of the Basin and Range province, and/or possibly (2) isostatic crustal adjustment associated with the load of the Gros Ventre foreland uplift, or (3) collapse along or near the foreland thrust overhang margin.

ACKNOWLEDGMENTS

I express thanks to my thesis advisor, Arthur Snoke, who provided advice in the field, discussed various problems in the research, and edited many drafts of the manuscript. The facilities and financial support of the University of Wyoming are gratefully acknowledged, as are the significant contributions of previous workers, who set the stage for the present study.

Special thanks also to Frank Royse, Jr., and Chevron, U.S.A., who suggested this project, contributed financial support, provided access to invaluable seismic and well data, and processed shale samples for the palynologic data used in the research. The advice and research of Chevron geologists Frank Royse, M. A. Warner, Paul Lamerson, and palynologist Sheldon Nelson were instrumental in the completion of this study.

The research benefited greatly from the comments and interpretations of J. David Love and D. L. Blackstone, Jr. The helpful reviews of Arthur Snoke, James Steidtmann, J. David Love, Donald Blackstone, the late Steven Oriel, Dave Moore, and Bill Perry significantly improved the manuscript. The dedication of Bill Perry and Chris Schmidt to the entire memoir is admirable.

REFERENCES CITED

Armstrong, F. C., and Oriell, S. S., 1965, Tectonic development of Idaho-Wyoming thrust belt: American Association of Petroleum Geologists Bulletin, v. 49, p. 1847–1866.

Bally, A. W., Gordy, P. L., and Stewart, G. A., 1966, Structure, seismic data, and orogenic evolution of southern Canadian Rockies: Bulletin of Canadian Petroleum Geology, v. 14, p. 337–381.

Banks, C. J., and Warburton, F., 1986, Passive-roof duplex geometry in the frontal structures of the Kirthar and Sulaiman mountain belts, Pakistan: Journal of Structural Geology, v. 8, no. 3/4, p. 229–237.

Bell, W. G., 1956, Tectonic setting of Happy Springs and nearby structures in the Sweetwater uplift area, central Wyoming: Rocky Mountain Section American Association of Petroleum Geologists Geological Record, p. 81–86.

Blackstone, D. L., Jr., 1971, Plate tectonics and its possible role in the Rocky Mountains, *in* Symposium on Wyoming tectonics and their economic significance: Wyoming Geological Association 23rd Annual Field Conference Guidebook, p. 11–17.

—— , 1977, The overthrust belt salient of the Cordilleran fold belt, western Wyoming–southeastern Idaho–northeastern Utah, *in* Heisey, E. L., and others, eds., Rocky Mountain thrust belt; Geology and resources: Wyoming Geological Association 29th Annual Field Conference Guidebook, p. 367–384.

Boyer, S. E., and Elliott, D., 1982, Thrust systems: American Association of Petroleum Geologists Bulletin, v. 66, p. 1196–1230.

Brown, W. G., 1983, Rocky Mountains foreland structure; Compressional basement tectonics: American Association of Petroleum Geologists Structural School, 43 p.

Butler, R.H.W., 1982, The terminology of structures in thrust belts: Journal of Structural Geology, v. 4, p. 239–245.

Corbett, M. R., 1983, Superposed tectonism in the Idaho-Wyoming thrust belt, *in* Powers, R. B., ed., Geological studies of the Cordilleran thrust belt, 1982: Denver, Colorado, Rocky Mountain Association of Geologists, v. 1, p. 341–356.

Cutler, E. R., 1984, Geology of the upper Green River area, between the Gros Ventre and Wind River Mountains, Sublette County, Wyoming [M.S. thesis]: Laramie, University of Wyoming, 103 p.

Dahlstrom, D.C.A., 1969a, Balanced cross sections: Canadian Journal of Earth Sciences, v. 6, p. 743–757.

—— , 1969b, The upper detachment in concentric folding: Bulletin of Canadian Petroleum Geology, v. 17, p. 326–347.

—— , 1970, Structural geology in the eastern margin of the Canadian Rocky Mountains: Bulletin of Canadian Petroleum Geology, v. 18, p. 332–406.

Dixon, J. S., 1982, Regional structural synthesis, Wyoming salient of western overthrust belt: American Association of Petroleum Geologists Bulletin, v. 66, p. 1560–1580.

Dorr, J. A., Jr., 1952, Early Cenozoic stratigraphy and vertebrate paleontology of the Hoback Basin, Wyoming: Geological Society of America Bulletin, v. 63, p. 59–94.

—— , 1956, Post-Cretaceous geologic history of the Hoback basin area, central western Wyoming, *in* Jackson Hole area, Wyoming: Wyoming Geological Association 11th Annual Field Conference Guidebook, p. 99–108.

Dorr, J. A., Jr., Spearing, D. R., and Steidtmann, J. R., 1977, Deformation and deposition between a foreland uplift and an impinging thrust belt: Hoback basin, Wyoming: Geological Society of America Special Paper 177, 82 p.

Eardley, A. J., 1944, Geologic map of Camp Davis area prepared for Hoback–Gros Ventre–Teton Range, Wyoming: Augustana Library Publication 23, p. 1–82.

Elliott, D., 1981, The strength of rocks in thrust sheets [abs.]: EOS Transactions of the American Geophysical Union, v. 62, p. 397.

Fox, F. G., 1969, Some principles governing interpretation of structure in the Rocky Mountain orogenic belt, *in* Kent, P. E., and others, eds., Time and place in orogeny: Geological Society of London Special Publication 3, p. 23–42.

Froidevaux, C. M., 1968, Geology of the Hoback Peak area in the overthrust belt, Lincoln and Sublette Counties, Wyoming [M.S. thesis]: Laramie, University of Wyoming, 126 p.

—— , 1977, Geology of the Hoback Peak area in the overthrust belt, Lincoln and Sublette Counties, Wyoming, *in* Heisey, E. L., and others, eds., Rocky Mountain thrust belt; Geology and resources: Wyoming Geological Association 29th Annual Field Conference Guidebook, p. 563–584.

Gordy, P. L., Frey, F. R., and Norris, D. K., 1977, Geological guide for the Canadian Society of Petroleum Geologists and 1977 Waterton-Glacier Park field conference: Canadian Society of Petroleum Geology, 93 p.

Grubbs, K. L., and Van der Voo, R., 1976, Structural deformation of the Idaho-Wyoming overthrust belt (U.S.A.), as determined by Triassic paleomagnetism: Tectonophysics, v. 33, p. 321–336.

Guennel, G. D., Spearing, D. R., and Dorr, J. A., Jr., 1973, Palynology of the Hoback basin, *in* Geology and mineral resources of the greater Green River basin, Wyoming: Wyoming Geological Association 25th Annual Field Conference Guidebook, p. 173–185.

Horberg, L., Nelson, V., and Church, V., 1949, Structural trends in central western Wyoming: Geological Society of America Bulletin, v. 60, p. 183–216.

Hunter, R. B., 1986, Timing and structural relations between the Gros Ventre foreland uplift, the Prospect thrust system, and the Granite Creek thrust, Hoback basin area, Wyoming [M.S. thesis]: Laramie, University of Wyoming, 111 p.

—— , 1987, Timing and structural relations between the Gros Ventre foreland uplift, the Prospect thrust system, and the Granite Creek thrust, Hoback basin, Wyoming, *in* The thrust belt revisited: Wyoming Geological Association 38th Annual Field Conference Guidebook, p. 109–131.

Imlay, R. W., 1967, Twin Creek Limestone (Jurassic) in the western interior of the United States: U.S. Geological Survey Professional Paper 540, 105 p.

Jones, P. B., 1983, Oil and gas beneath east-dipping underthrust faults in the Alberta foothills, Canada, *in* Powers, R. B., ed., Geologic studies of the Cordilleran thrust belt, 1982: Denver, Colorado, Rocky Mountain Association of Geologists, v. 1, p. 61–74.

Keefer, W. R., 1964, Preliminary report on the structure of the southeast Gros Ventre Mountains, Wyoming, *in* Geological Survey research 1964: U.S. Geological Survey Professional Paper 501-D, p. D22–D27.

Love, C. M., and Love, J. D., 1978, Geologic map of the Turquoise Lake Quadrangle, Teton County, Wyoming: U.S. Geological Survey Open-File Report 78-481, scale 1:24,000.

Love, J. D., 1956a, Cretaceous and Tertiary stratigraphy of the Jackson Hole area, northwestern Wyoming, *in* Jackson Hole area, Wyoming: Wyoming Geological Association 11th Annual Field Conference Guidebook, p. 76–94.

—— , 1956b, Summary of geologic history of Teton County, Wyoming, during late Cretaceous, Tertiary, and Quaternary times, *in* Jackson Hole area, Wyoming: Wyoming Geological Association 11th Annual Field Conference Guidebook, p. 140–150.

—— , 1977, Summary of Upper Cretaceous and Cenozoic stratigraphy, and of tectonic and glacial events in Jackson Hole, northwestern Wyoming, *in* Heisey, E. L., and others, eds., Rocky Mountain thrust belt; Geology and resources: Wyoming Geological Association 29th Annual Field Conference Guidebook, p. 585–593.

Love, J. D., and Christiansen, A. C., 1985, Geologic map of Wyoming: U.S. Geological Survey, scale 1:500,000.

Morley, C. K., 1986, A classification of thrust fronts: American Association of Petroleum Geologists Bulletin, v. 70, p. 12–25.

Moulton, D. R., 1981, Geology of the upper Bull Creek area, northern Hoback Range, Teton County, Wyoming [M.S. thesis]: Pocatello, Idaho State University, 53 p.

Nelson, V. E., and Church, V., 1943, Critical structures of the Gros Ventre and northern Hoback ranges, Wyoming: Journal of Geology, v. 51, p. 143–166.

O'Keefe, F. S., and Stearns, D. W., 1983, Characteristics of displacement transfer zones associated with thrust faults, *in* Powers, R. B., ed., Geologic studies of the Cordilleran thrust belt, 1982: Denver, Colorado, Rocky Mountain Association of Geologists, v. 1, p. 219–233.

Pattridge, K. A., 1976, The Gannett Peak Lineament; A passive element during Laramide uncoupling of the Wyoming foreland, *in* Podwysocki, M. H., and Earle, J. L., eds., Proceedings of the 2nd International Conference on Basement Tectonics: Denver, Colorado, Basement Tectonics Committee, p. 145–156.

Price, R. A., 1981, The Cordilleran foreland thrust and fold belt in the southern Canadian Rocky Mountains, *in* McClay, K. R., and Price, N. J., eds., Thrust and nappe tectonics: Geological Society of London Special Publication 9, p. 427–488.

—— , 1986, The southeastern Canadian Cordillera; Thrust faulting, tectonic wedging, and delamination of the lithosphere: Journal of Structural Geology, v. 8, no. 3/4, p. 239–254.

Rich, J. L., 1934, Mechanics of low-angle overthrust faulting illustrated by Cumberland thrust block, Virginia, Kentucky, and Tennessee: American Association of Petroleum Geologists Bulletin, v. 18, p. 1584–1596.

Royse, F., Jr., 1985, Geometry and timing of the Darby-Prospect-Hogsback thrust fault system, Wyoming: Geological Society of America Abstracts with Programs, v. 17, p. 263.

Royse, F., Jr., Warner, M. A., and Reese, D. L., 1975, Thrust belt structural geometry and related stratigraphic problems, *in* Bolyard, O. W., ed., Deep drilling frontiers in the central Rocky Mountains: Denver, Colorado, Rocky Mountain Association of Geologists, p. 41–54.

Sacrison, W. R., 1978, Seismic interpretation of basement block faults and associated deformation, *in* Matthews, V., ed., Laramide folding associated with basement block faulting in the Western United States: Geological Society of America Memoir 151, p. 39–50.

Schroeder, M. L., 1973, Geologic Map of the Clause Peak Quadrangle, Lincoln, Sublette, and Teton Counties, Wyoming: U.S. Geological Survey Geologic Quadrangle Map GQ-1092, scale 1:24,000.

—— , 1976, Geologic map of the Bull Creek Quadrangle, Teton and Sublette Counties, Wyoming: U.S. Geological Survey Geologic Quadrangle Map GQ-1300, scale 1:24,000.

Simons, F. S., Keefer, W. R., Harwood, D. S., Love, J. D., and Bieniewski, C. L., 1980, Mineral resources of the Gros Ventre Wilderness study area, Teton and Sublette Counties, Wyoming: U.S. Geological Survey Open-File Report 81-510, 94 p. (superceded by U.S. Geological Survey Bulletin 1591, 1986).

Skinner, R. E., 1960, Tectonic elements of the northern Green River area of Wyoming, *in* Overthrust belt in southwestern Wyoming and adjacent areas: Wyoming Geological Association 15th Annual Field Conference Guidebook, p. 85–88.

Spang, J. H., and Brown, S. P., 1981, Dynamic analysis of a small imbricate thrust and related structures, Front Ranges, southern Canadian Rocky Mountains, *in* McClay, K. R., and Price, N. J., eds., Thrust and nappe tectonics: Geological Society of London Special Publication 9, p. 449–462.

Spearing, D. R., 1969, Stratigraphy and sedimentation of the Paleocene-Eocene Hoback Formation, western Wyoming, *in* Symposium on Tertiary rocks of Wyoming: Wyoming Geological Association 21st Annual Field Conference Guidebook, p. 763–767.

Stokes, W. L., 1976, What is the Wasatch Line?, *in* Hill, G. J., ed., Geology of the Cordilleran hingeline: Denver, Colorado, Rocky Mountain Association of Geologists, p. 11–27.

Suppe, J., 1983, Geometry and kinematics of fault-bend folding: American Journal of Science, v. 283, p. 684–721.

Suppe, J., and Medwedeff, D. A., 1984, Fault-propagation folding [abs.]: Geological Society of America Abstracts with Programs, v. 16, p. 670.

Teal, P. R., 1983, The triangle zone at Cabin Creek, Alberta, *in* Bally, A. W., ed., Seismic expression of structural styles: American Association of Petroleum Geologists Studies in Geology 15, v. 3, p. 3.4-1-48–3.4-1-53.

Thompson, R. I., 1981, The nature and significance of large "blind thrusts" within the northern Rocky Mountains of Canada, *in* McClay, K. R., and Price, N. J., eds., Thrust and nappe tectonics: Geological Society of London Special Publication 9, p. 449–462.

Wanless, H. R., Belknap, R. L., and Foster, H., 1955, Paleozoic and Mesozoic rocks of Gros Ventre, Teton, Hoback, and Snake River Ranges, Wyoming: Geological Society of America Memoir 63, 90 p.

Wiltschko, D. V., and Eastman, D., 1983, Role of basement warps and faults in localizing thrust fault ramps: Geological Society of America Memoir 158, p. 177–190.

MANUSCRIPT ACCEPTED BY THE SOCIETY FEBRUARY 9, 1988

Geological Society of America
Memoir 171
1988

The interaction of the Moxa Arch (La Barge Platform) with the Cordilleran thrust belt, south of Snider Basin, southwestern Wyoming

David H. Kraig,* David V. Wiltschko, and John H. Spang
Center for Tectonophysics and Department of Geology, Texas A&M University, College Station, Texas 77843

ABSTRACT

Interaction of the Rocky Mountain foreland and the Cordilleran thrust belt has taken place in the Snider Basin area, west of Big Piney, Wyoming. Here, the central segment (La Barge Platform) of the Moxa Arch, a Late Cretaceous, basement-cored uplift, plunges northwestward beneath, and disrupts the continuity of, the Darby, Hogsback, and Prospect thrusts. Although to the north and south of the La Barge Platform, basement shortening appears to have been along low-angle thrust faults, this was probably not the case for the platform. The 2,600 m of west-verging structural relief along the southwest limb of the La Barge Platform occurs over about 5 km of horizontal distance and might be the result of shortening of the basement across a zone of discrete, closely spaced reverse faults, generally restricted to basement. This shear zone (here termed the La Barge shear zone) dips about 60°NE. Shortening in the basement appears to have been matched by shortening of the cover rocks along a pair of west-dipping reverse faults, the upper of which is the Tip-Top thrust. According to our interpretation, Tip-Top thrusting was synchronous with the emplacement of the La Barge Platform and thus predated the Hogsback thrust. Our work confirms earlier interpretations that the Darby and Prospect thrusts link in the subsurface below Snider Basin and continue to the south as the Hogsback thrust. According to our interpretation, Hogsback thrusting is a composite of Paleocene Prospect thrust movement and later Darby thrusting. In the area of the La Barge Platform, the Hogsback thrust was localized by following west-dipping Cretaceous beds on the monocline above the La Barge shear zone.

INTRODUCTION

There are few places where mechanical interaction of the Rocky Mountain foreland and the Cordilleran thrust belt is so apparent as the area immediately west and north of La Barge, in southwestern Wyoming. Here, the Moxa Arch, a Late Cretaceous (Kreuger, 1960; Thomaidis, 1973; Wach, 1977) basement-cored uplift, trends northwestward and clearly disrupts the north-south continuity of the Darby, Prospect, and Hogsback thrusts (Fig. 1). The central, northwest-trending segment of the Moxa Arch is termed the La Barge Platform (Kreuger, 1960). North of Big Piney, Wyoming, the Moxa Arch trends north, remaining near the eastern edge of the Cordilleran thrust belt, beneath the Darby and

Prospect thrusts (Royse and others, 1975; Dixon, 1982). Although it seemed to early workers that the Moxa Arch had localized the ramps of the Darby and Prospect thrusts, there was little evidence to indicate how this localization could have been accomplished. The prevailing thought was that the Moxa Arch, uplifted prior to thrusting, had somehow acted as a buttress, forcing the thrusts to the surface (Blackstone, 1979; Dixon, 1982; Wiltschko and Dorr, 1983) and/or deflecting their trends (Wach, 1977). The nature of the mechanical link between the uplift and the overlying thrusts was studied further by Wiltschko and Eastman (1983), who modeled the effects of preexisting basement structure on later thrusting.

F. Royse (personal communication, 1986) believes that north of La Barge, Wyoming, the uplift that continues north

---

*Present address: Los Alamos Technical Associates, P.O. Box 410, Los Alamos, New Mexico 87544.

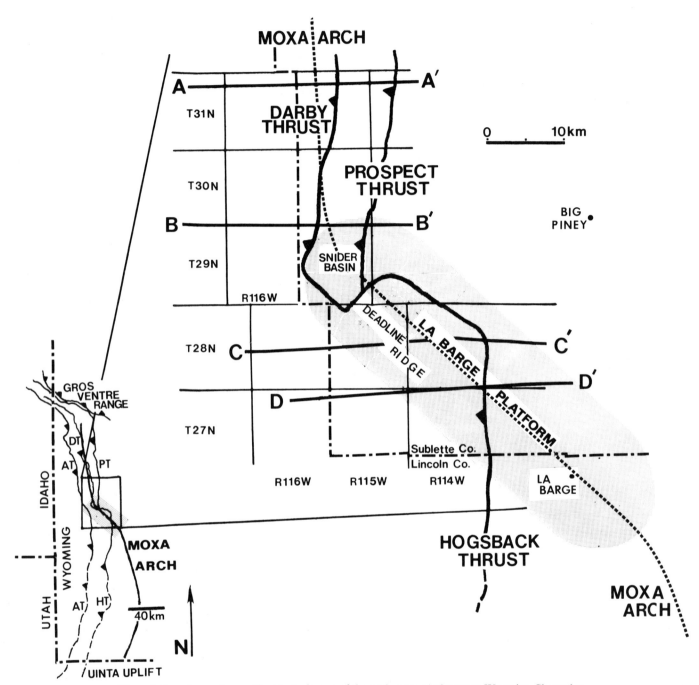

Figure 1. Location and generalized tectonic map of the study area, southwestern Wyoming. Shown by shading, the La Barge Platform is the central, northwest-trending segment of the Moxa Arch, which is shown as a thick dotted line in the blowup. The approximate bounds of Snider Basin are section BB′ on the north and the major eastern swing of the Darby thrust to the south. Deadline Ridge is a northwest-trending raised region south of Snider Basin. AT, PT, DT, and HT are the Absaroka, Prospect, Darby, and Hogsback thrusts, respectively. Figure modified after Dixon's Figure 4 (1982).

beneath the Darby and Prospect thrusts is post-Paleocene, and therefore should not be included as the Moxa Arch. His prime basis for this interpretation is the "coaxial folding" of the thrusts with the basement along the crest of the uplift. We suggest that the primary uplift of the basement occurred prior to the main episode of Darby and Prospect thrusting and that the entire suite was deformed further during the Eocene.

This chapter is concerned with the kinematics of the uplift of the Moxa Arch–La Barge Platform and with the mechanical interaction of the uplift with the thrust belt both during and subsequent to the time of the basement uplift. Although this study deals primarily with the La Barge Platform, to understand this area we must consider its northern and southern extensions. The relationship between the uplift and the thrust belt is more apparent north of Snider Basin than in the area of the La Barge Platform. Therefore, we first summarize our model of the mechanical interaction just north of Snider Basin and then examine how that model might be extended to the area of the La Barge Platform.

UPLIFT OF THE NORTHERN SEGMENT OF THE MOXA ARCH AND ITS RELATION TO THE PROSPECT THRUST

Configuration of basement

Earlier workers have shown the northern Moxa Arch (north of Big Piney) as the crest of a regional fold (Royse and others, 1975; Blackstone, 1979), or as uplifted along its western margin by a series of normal faults (Dixon, 1982). Recent seismic data suggest that one may instead interpret a low-angle, east-dipping thrust below the Moxa Arch, north of La Barge. The interpretation of thrust uplift of the northern segment of the Moxa Arch has several distinct advantages over previous models. First, a thrust origin for the Moxa Arch is consistent with much work that suggests that the upper crust was in compression at this time. Failure of the basement of the Rocky Mountain foreland along north- or northwest-trending thrust faults has been documented elsewhere for the Laramide uplift of the Wind River Mountains (e.g., Coffin, 1946; Eardley, 1951; Love, 1950; Berg, 1961a,b, 1962; Zawislak and Smithson, 1981), the Casper Arch (Montecchi, 1981; Skeen and Ray, 1983), the Medicine Bow Mountains along the Arlington thrust (Houston and others, 1968; Mitchell and Pritchett, 1981), and the Pacific Creek Anticline along the Pacific Creek thrust (Lynne and others, 1981). Second, a thrust interpretation has the advantage of providing a geologically consistent link of the northern and southern segments of the Moxa Arch, the latter having been at least in part uplifted along a thrust fault (see CGG advertisement, 1985), although in the southern segment, the thrust is west-dipping. Finally, the interpretation is advantageous in that a thrust hypothesis for the uplift of the northern segment of the Moxa Arch leads to balanced, sequentially restorable cross sections that encompass all

the surface and subsurface data and provide explanations for features that heretofore were not interpretable.

Geometry of the Moxa Thrust. The model (Fig. 2) that the northern segment of the Moxa Arch was emplaced along a low-angle, east-dipping thrust that becomes bedding-plane parallel to the west along a detachment in middle Triassic rocks is summarized below. Other interpretations are considered by Kraig and others (1987).

The data base used to constrain our model for the emplacement of the Moxa Arch north of Snider Basin is composed primarily of the following points:

1. F. Royse (personal communication, 1986) has observed large offset of the near-basement reflector at least as far north as T.31N., indicating a thrusted basement. Our proposal of a thrust fault uplift for the northern Moxa Arch is based on this data, regional considerations discussed above, and by analogy to the southern Moxa Arch, which was at least in part uplifted along a thrust fault.

2. The structural relief on basement is about 1,850 m just north of Snider Basin. The seismic data shown in Dixon's Figure 14 (1982) were used in determining basement relief. The location of this seismic line is the same as our section AA′. The assumption of a thrust below the Moxa Arch dictates the appropriate method of measuring the basement relief. The basement relief is found by measuring straight down from the near basement reflector at the crest of the uplift, to the projected cutoff of this reflector in the footwall. This point is found by projecting the near-basement reflector about 10 km to the east, to the point where it intersects with the basement fault. Although this method of measuring the relief is dependent on the dip of the basement fault, varying the fault over a wide range of dip angles only very slightly affects the measured basement relief.

3. The depth to basement was determined using stratigraphic reconstructions (Rubey and others, 1980; Blackstone, 1979) and interpretations from seismic sections (Dixon, 1982).

4. Much of the geometry of the Darby and Prospect thrusts is known and is shown on the seismic section of Dixon's Figure 14 (1982), which is the same line of section as our section AA′. The Prospect thrust apparently ramps from a basal detachment in the Cambrian (J. S. Dixon, 1982, personal communication, 1985; Blackstone, 1979) to a detachment in the middle of the Triassic section, and breaks to the surface along a ramp just east of the Lincoln-Sublette county line (Blackstone, 1979; Royse, 1985; Dixon, 1982). The geometry we assumed for the Prospect thrust (Fig. 2) is similar to that shown by Dixon (1982) with the exception of our showing slight eastern dip of the Darby and Prospect thrusts just east of the Moxa Arch, in order to better coincide with the seismic data of Dixon's Figure 14 (1982), and the Eocene folding discussed by Royse (1985).

5. The Prospect thrust utilizes a detachment within the Triassic Thaynes Formation (Rubey and others, 1980). We generally refer to this detachment as the Thaynes detachment.

6. The CGG advertisement (May 1985) shows a thrust fault below the Moxa Arch, south of the La Barge Platform.

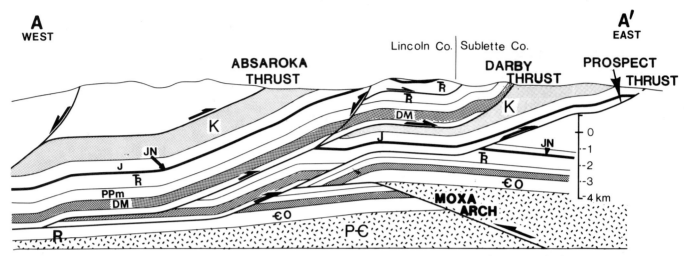

Figure 2. Cross section 2 (AA′), our interpretation of the present geology north of Snider Basin. The significance of the slight eastward dip of the Darby and Prospect thrusts just west of the county line is discussed in the text. Total Prospect thrust displacement is about 10.4 km, of which 5.3 km occurred during the emplacement of the Moxa Arch. Darby thrust displacement is about 28 km. No scale exaggeration. Explanation of the symbols used in all cross sections: *Faults:* PT = Prospect thrust, DT = Darby thrust, HT = Hogsback thrust; AT = Absaroka thrust; faults are dashed where hypothetical. *Stratigraphy:* P€ = Precambrian rocks, undivided; €O = Cambrian through the Ordovician section; DM = Devonian through the Mississippian section; PPm = Pennsylvanian and Permian section; T = Triassic rocks, lower and upper Triassic rocks are divided by a dotted line; J = Jurassic rocks undivided except for JN; JN = Jurassic Nugget Formation; K = Cretaceous rocks, undivided; T = Tertiary rocks. *Other:* MA = Moxa Arch; LBP = La Barge Platform. *Scale:* No vertical exaggeration in any of the sections.

Although not strictly part of the data base, the constraints and limitations imposed on a model by drawing cross sections that are both balanced and restorable sequentially are exceedingly important in developing a realistic model. The balanced and sequentially restorable cross sections presented here (2, 3, 4, 5) were drawn using some of the methods for drawing locally balanced cross sections as outlined by Cook (1985), Spang and others (1985), and Spang and Evans (1984a,b). These cross sections (Figs. 2 through 5) show our interpretation of the sequence of basement–cover rock interaction immediately north of the La Barge Platform.

Figure 3 is our restoration of the geometry of Figure 2 to the time of the emplacement of the Moxa Arch. The Moxa thrust flattens to the west along the Thaynes detachment in the footwall. Where the Moxa thrust flattens, the Paleozoic and lower Triassic rocks in the hanging wall form a ramp anticline that conforms to the footwall flat of the Moxa thrust.

Our interpretation of the geometry at this time requires that during motion on the Moxa thrust, the leading (western) edge of the ramp anticline (labeled N on Fig. 3) wedged westward, peeling back the rocks above the detachment and thrusting them relatively east along what we earlier termed the ancestral Prospect thrust (Kraig and others, 1985). The Prospect thrust was required in order to shorten the rocks above the Thaynes detachment as the Moxa thrust was shortening the basement and the sedimentary section below the detachment.

Balancing displacement above and below the Moxa thrust in section 3 leads to the conclusion that the Prospect thrust moved

twice. First motion of about 5.3 km was initiated by the emplacement of the Moxa Arch during the Late Cretaceous, and subsequent offset of about 5.1 km (Fig. 4) occurred as the ancestral Prospect thrust was reactivated when thrust belt deformation progressed east to the Moxa Arch. Figure 5 shows the geometry following the emplacement of the Moxa Arch, Prospect, and Darby thrusts, but prior to the Eocene, when the frontal thrusts were tilted (Royse, 1985). As shown in Figure 2, this Eocene deformation resulted in the slight (4°) eastward dip of the Darby and Prospect thrusts along with the basement surface just east of the crest of the Moxa Arch.

UPLIFT OF THE LA BARGE PLATFORM

Structural differences north and south of Snider Basin

There are four fundamental differences in the geology north and south of Snider Basin such that, without significant alteration, the model outlined above cannot be extended to explain the geology south of Snider Basin.

1. Rather than parallel the thrusts, as the Moxa Arch does to the north, the La Barge Platform intersects the thrust belt at about 45°. This impingement in the subsurface coincides with a 30-km swing toward the east of the surface trace of the Darby thrust. From here south (Fig. 1), it resumes its southerly trend, and south of Snider Basin, the Darby thrust is renamed the Hogsback thrust (Armstrong and Oriel, 1965).

2. The structural relief along the steep southwest limb of the

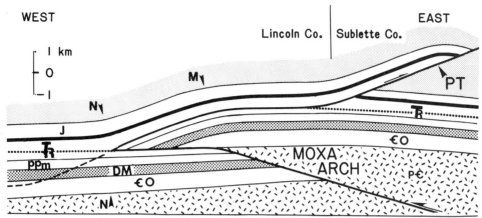

Figure 3. Cross section 3 (AA′), which is restored to the time of the emplacement of the Moxa Arch and illustrates the geometry required as the Moxa thrust flattened to the west along a detachment in middle Triassic rocks. The ancestral Prospect thrust shortened the stratigraphic section above the Triassic detachment (dotted line) as the Moxa thrust shortened the rocks below this detachment. At cessation of motion on the Moxa thrust, there had been no movement west of the leading edge (N) of the ramp anticline. The dashed line indicates the most likely path for the ultimate linking of this ancestral Prospect thrust and the regional detachment in Cambrian rocks. Explanation of symbols is given in caption of Figure 2. No scale exaggeration.

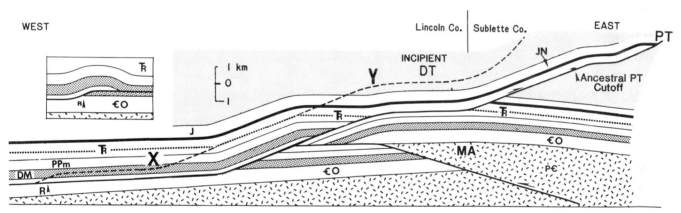

Figure 4. Cross section 4 (AA′) which shows the geometry after the second motion on the Prospect thrust (Fig. 3 shows the geometry prior to this time). For this section we assumed that the Prospect thrust extended its early ramp (Fig. 3) directly down from N to the detachment in the Cambrian rocks and that the late Prospect thrust motion preceded the movement of the Darby thrust. Explanation of symbols is given in caption of Figure 2. No scale exaggeration.

northwest-trending La Barge Platform is in excess of 2,600 m (Dixon, 1982; Royse, 1985), which is at least 700 m greater than the relief of the Moxa Arch just north of Snider Basin (Fig. 2). Consequently, the top of the uplifted basement of the La Barge Platform is at least 700 m above the Thaynes detachment of the relatively lower section to the southwest.

3. Immediately north of Snider Basin the Jurassic Nugget Formation has more than 10 km of dip separation along the Prospect thrust (Fig. 2). About half of this shortening of the cover rocks was the direct consequence of shortening of the basement along the Moxa thrust (Fig. 3). Based on drilling data (Blackstone, 1979; Dixon, 1982) immediately south of Snider Basin, the Nugget Formation has only 1 or 2 km of shortening; this shortening is not related to the Hogsback thrust. As explained

below, this places an upper limit of shortening of the basement at about 2 km.

4. There is no surface expression of the Prospect thrust (Fig. 1) south of Snider Basin (Royse and others, 1975; Blackstone, 1979; Oriel and Platt, 1980).

In the following discussion, we explain the development of a model to account for the kinematics of the uplift of the La Barge Platform and the interaction of the La Barge Platform with the frontal part of the Cordilleran thrust belt immediately south of Snider Basin. This model addresses the following points: (1) the kinematics of the emplacement of the La Barge Platform; (2) the reason for the 30-km eastern swing in the surface trace of the Darby (Hogsback) thrust; (3) the subsurface linkage of the Prospect, Darby, and Hogsback thrusts; (4) the disappearance of the Prospect thrust trace and the geometry of the Prospect thrust south of Snider Basin; and (5) the reason for the marked change in the trend of the Moxa Arch through its central segment (La Barge Platform).

METHOD OF AND CONSTRAINTS ON RECONSTRUCTIONS SOUTH OF SNIDER BASIN

In general, we follow Dahlstrom's (1969) guidelines (see also Table 1) for drawing balanced cross sections; additionally, we use some of the methods of Cook (1985), Spang and Evans (1984a,b), and Spang and others (1985).

Our cross sections (Figs. 6, 7) are drawn east-west to coincide with what appears, on the basis of strain data from the Darby thrust sheet, to have been the regional transport direction (Kraig and Wiltschko, 1987). However, as discussed below, the possibility that there was significant strike-slip motion in basement along the southwest margin of the La Barge Platform cannot be ruled out. Dahlstrom's (1969) requirement of preservation of volume is generally violated by motion that is not parallel to the plane of the section. However, if we assume that in the immediate vicinity of the southwest limb of the La Barge Platform the strike of stratigraphic units and faults parallels the strike of the basement structure of about N40° to 45°W, and, additionally, that through the length of the platform, stratigraphic units maintain relatively constant thickness, then volume should be conserved in a properly drawn section even though there may be transport into or out of the plane of the section.

Support for the assumption that, locally, the strike of the stratigraphic units and faults is about N45°W is found in Plates 2, 3, and 4 of Blackstone (1979). Plate 2 shows structural contours on top of the Nugget Formation; Plates 3 and 4 show structural contours on the Prospect and Darby thrusts. These plates show that the Nugget Formation, Darby, and Prospect thrusts strike

TABLE 1. GENERAL GUIDELINES IN DEVELOPING CROSS SECTIONS

• Cross sections must not only balance, but be restorable. By undoing the effects of deformation on the rocks shown in the cross sections, we should be able to work backward to their undeformed state, with every intermediate stage being geometrically possible.

• During construction of models and cross sections, the mechanical behavior of the rocks must be considered. Processes that were active in the deformation of the sedimentary rocks are likely to have differed from those that acted on the crystalline basement.

• Adjacent cross sections should tie in a geologically reasonable manner. Large thrusts do not generally die out over short distances along strike unless displacement transfer allows the shortening to be taken up by other faults or folding.

northwest along the southwest limb of the La Barge Platform. The northwest trend of the basement structure is well documented by seismic and drill data (Blackstone, 1979; Dixon, 1982). We are unable to evaluate fully the assumption of constant stratigraphic thickness through the area. It is necessary to recognize that the cross sections presented here (Figs. 6, 7) are balanced, assuming constant stratigraphic thickness, and that the greater the local variation in the thickness of the units, the greater will be the error introduced into these cross sections.

RECONSTRUCTIONS

Configuration of basement

Several mechanisms have been forwarded to account for the uplift of the La Barge Platform. Dixon (sections 21 through 23, 1982) has shown the southwest margin of the platform as a series of large-displacement, high-angle normal faults. Normal faults do not seem to be the most reasonable mechanism for uplift of the La Barge Platform in light of much work suggesting that,

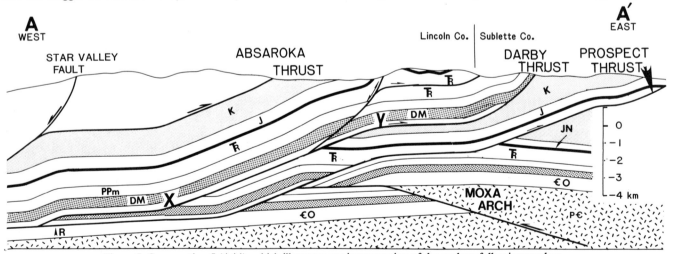

Figure 5. Cross section 5 (AA'), which illustrates our interpretation of the geology following emplacement of the Moxa Arch, Prospect, and Darby thrusts, but prior to the Eocene folding described in the text and shown in Figure 2. Explanation of symbols is given in caption of Figure 2. No scale exaggeration.

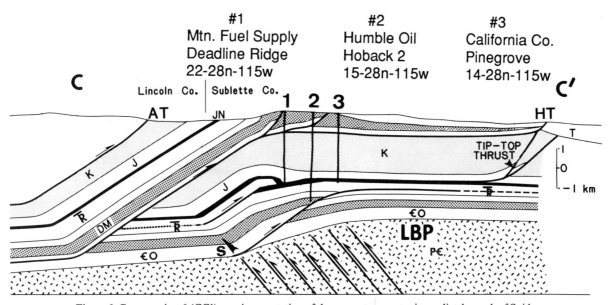

Figure 6. Cross section 6 (CC′), our interpretation of the present geometry immediately south of Snider Basin. The number of faults in the La Barge shear zone is strictly a diagramatic representation of distributed shearing of the basement. The paired reverse faults (the upper of which is the Tip-Top thrust) shortened the cover rocks as the La Barge shear zone shortened the basement and therefore predate the Hogsback thrust. Tertiary rocks are generalized here. Explanation of symbols is given in caption of Figure 2. No scale exaggeration.

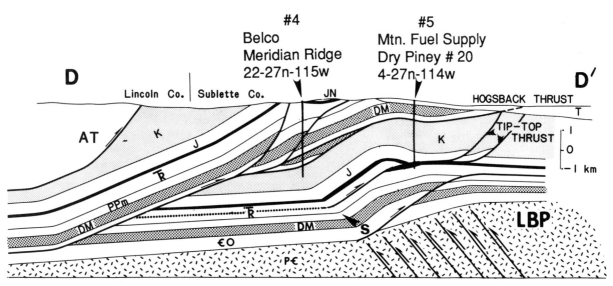

Figure 7. Cross section 7 (DD′), which shows our interpretation south of Snider Basin. As in section 6 (CC′), west-dipping Cretaceous beds of the monocline formed above the La Barge shear zone, localized the ramp of the Hogsback thrust. Explanation of symbols is given in caption of Figure 2. No scale exaggeration.

regionally, the basement was in compression with the principal shortening axis oriented east-northeast (Armstrong and Oriel, 1965; Brown, 1981). Royse (1985) has suggested that the platform was raised both by folding and by faulting of the basement related temporally to the uplift of the Wind River Mountains. Presumably, this uplift was caused both by regional folding and by localized asymmetric folding and faulting of the basement, which would have been required to preferentially uplift the platform.

Based on our model for the emplacement of the Moxa Arch north of Snider Basin, our early attempts at restorations (not presented here) south of Snider Basin showed that the La Barge Platform was uplifted along a low-angle, east-dipping thrust, analogous to the Moxa thrust. *We assume that shortening of the basement requires equal shortening of the cover rocks.* Therefore, the shortening of the cover rocks below the Hogsback thrust places an upper limit on the amount of shortening in the basement. The reason we consider only sub-Hogsback thrust shortening is that, by drawing analogy to the northern Moxa Arch, we initially concluded—incorrectly—that shortening of basement south of Snider Basin was compensated in the cover rocks through initiation of an ancestral Hogsback thrust. The problem with this interpretation is that it is incompatible with the fact that the Hogsback thrust soles to the west in Cambrian rocks. By analogy with the northern segment of the Moxa Arch, the proposed basement thrust would have flattened to the west along the detachment in the Cambrian rocks, delaminating the layers above. This model compounds the problem of explaining the origin of the structural relief on basement. Because the detachment in the Cambrian rocks is only about 400 m above the upper basement surface, and because the proposed basement thrust would sole along this horizon, the other 2,200 m of basement relief would have to be explained by some process other than the proposed fault. The remaining 2,000$^+$ m of basement relief would have to have resulted from folding of the upper basement over a horizontal distance of less than 7 km. Fletcher (1984) demonstrated that, under appropriate flow laws, the shallow crust can fold at wavelengths of 100 to 200 km. Based on rock-mechanics experiments, Stearns (1975) concluded that it is unlikely that homogeneous and isotropic Precambrian crystalline rocks can fold at wavelengths as short as 7 km under shallow crustal conditions.

Yet, the upper basement surface *appears* to be folded at some scale of observation (Blackstone, 1979; Royse, 1985). One of the problems in describing the deformation here is the use of the terms fold and folding. The upper basement surface appears folded in that it is a curved surface that was presumably once planar. Matthews (1986) has shown that, wherever visible, the surface of the basement is planar, and that only through interpretation is a tightly folded basement indicated. On the basis of synthetic seismic sections he concluded that normal-faulted, reverse-faulted, or folded basement would yield indistinguishable seismic responses, and that an interpretation of folded basement is at the expense of other, equally valid, interpretations.

We believe that this apparent folding is not due to buckling (folding) of the crust, but rather to distributed shearing of the basement across a zone as wide as 4 km (Fig. 6). Distributed shearing could arise from motion along discrete, closely spaced faults, as is described for basement-involved structures elsewhere by Houston and others (1968), Young (1985), Young and others (1983), Evans (1985), Spang and others (1985), and Schmidt and Garihan (1988). Folding of the basement can also occur by movement along a myriad of preexisting joints (Blackstone, 1983) or along foliation surfaces (Schmidt and O'Neill, 1983).

We envision the La Barge Platform as uplifted along its southwest margin by a zone, here termed the La Barge shear zone, of high-angle reverse faults generally restricted to basement (Kraig and others, 1986).

The cross sections presented here for the area south of Snider Basin are based on this model of basement deformation and our added assumptions of locally constant stratigraphic thickness and a N45°W strike for the La Barge shear zone, stratigraphic units, and faults in cover rocks above the shear zone in basement.

Determination of the dip of the shear zone. To determine the dip of the shear zone, it is necessary to know the structural relief on basement and the line length of some stratigraphic unit that presumably has not changed length during deformation. The Jurassic Nugget Formation is a well-indurated sandstone; it has been chosen for this purpose as it would presumably most closely approximate the requirement that its length did not change appreciably during deformation. The relief of basement was taken directly from the appropriate cross sections of Dixon (1982).

Using a constant line length of Nugget Formation and the method outlined in Figure 3 of Spang and others (1985), the apparent dip in the east-west direction for the shear zone is determined to be about 50° east (Fig. 6). In calculating this dip, it was first necessary to determine the maximum possible shortening of the Nugget Formation beneath the Hogsback thrust. This shortening was accomplished both by folding and thrusting of the Nugget Formation (Figs. 6, 7). The presence of folded and thrusted Nugget Formation above the basement shear zone in sections CC′ and DD′ is a necessary consequence of basement shortening. Blackstone (1979) and Dixon (1982) have presented evidence supporting the existence of this fold/thrusting; it is discussed further in the following section. The amplitude and western extent of the fold are limited by the geometry of the overlying Hogsback thrust sheet. Furthermore, drill data that indicate subhorizontal Nugget Formation beneath a slightly thickened Jurassic section limits the extent of the fold to the east. The geometry of the folded Nugget Formation conforms to the overlying thrust sheet and to the available drill data. The 60° northeastern dip determined for the shear zone is based on the maximum possible shortening of the Nugget Formation, and is therefore the maximum possible dip for the shear zone.

Figures 6 and 7 show the La Barge shear zone as a series of parallel faults in basement, although the number of faults shown here is strictly diagrammatic. If there were only a few discrete faults in the basement, the upper basement surface would appear stepped, not smoothly folded. The greater the number of faults, the smoother the upper basement surface would appear. To achieve a smoothly folded upper basement surface as shown (Figs. 6, 7), the faulting would presumably have to be pervasive. This series of faults has the same vertical and horizontal displacement as would a single fault (Spang and others, 1985). However, the possibility that such a fault exists can be eliminated since drilling records show no indication that an east-dipping fault of such magnitude has penetrated the sedimentary section beneath what is now Deadline Ridge, just south of Snider Basin (Blackstone, 1979; Dixon, 1982).

Configuration of the cover rocks over the La Barge shear zone

Dixon showed a small ramp anticline that formed above a small-displacement, sub-Prospect thrust (dashed thrust immediately beneath the Prospect thrust, cross section 20, Fig. 8, Dixon, 1982). This thrust is not shown in adjacent sections and it was apparently included in his section 20 on the basis of well control. Blackstone's sections DD' and EE' (1979) showed this same anticline and underlying small-displacement thrust that he calls the Deadline Ridge fault. We suggest that this is the upper of two west-dipping reverse faults that accommodated the shortening of the sedimentary section (Fig. 6), as the basement shortened during the Late Cretaceous uplift of the La Barge Platform. According to our interpretation, this upper fault originates along the Thaynes detachment out of the synclinal hinge (labeled S in Figs. 6, 7), and follows the detachment eastward up through the west-dipping monoclinal section. At the crest of the monocline, the fault cuts up-section through upper Triassic rocks and the Nugget Formation, and flattens to the east along the top of the Nugget Formation. Farther east, this thrust cuts up-section and is termed the Tip-Top thrust (Blackstone, 1979; Dixon, 1982). The fold and fault shortening of the Nugget Formation was used to calculate the dip of the La Barge shear zone as discussed above.

The lower of these two reverse faults, shown in cross sections 6 and 7, ramps from basement, cuts directly up-section to the east, and flattens along the Thaynes detachment. Displacement on this bedding-parallel fault decreases gradually to the east. This lower fault shortened the section below the Thaynes detachment equal to the amount of shortening by the Tip-Top thrust.

During the Late Cretaceous, the Tip-Top thrust shortened upper Triassic and higher rocks as the basement was being shortened by the La Barge shear zone. Therefore, according to our interpretation, the Tip-Top thrust must predate the Hogsback thrust, which is dated as Paleocene (Dorr and Gingerich, 1980; Dorr, 1981; Wiltschko and Dorr, 1983). In that the Tip-Top lies beneath the Hogsback thrust, the conclusion that the Tip-Top predated the Hogsback thrust is not in accord with the supposition that thrusts of the Cordilleran thrust belt young progressively eastward (Armstrong and Oriel, 1965), but the interpretation is in

agreement with previous work (Blackstone, 1979) showing that the Tip-Top thrust is older than the Hogsback thrust and is truncated by it.

The combined effect of this pair of reverse faults is to shorten the sedimentary section commensurate with the shortening of the basement. These reverse faults are limited to the area immediately above the La Barge shear zone and do not extend much beyond it.

DISCUSSION

Geologic continuity through Snider Basin

Transition in the basement from the Moxa Arch to the La Barge Platform. According to our interpretation, east-west horizontal shortening of the basement decreases from north to south in the area of Snider Basin. East-west shortening on the Moxa thrust, just north of Snider Basin (Fig. 3), is about 4.8 km. Just south of Snider Basin, east-west shortening across the La Barge shear zone is about 1.8 km (Fig. 6). To explain the major difference in horizontal shortening north and south of Snider Basin, we consider three scenarios that could have acted individually or in concert:

1. Coincident with the decrease in horizontal shortening to the south is a marked increase in vertical displacement from about 1,850 m of basement relief on the Moxa Arch (Fig. 2) to about 2,600 m on the La Barge Platform (Fig. 6). It is likely that some of the horizontal shortening associated with the Moxa thrust was converted to vertical displacement along the La Barge shear zone through upward rotation of the leading edge of the La Barge Platform. Hennings and Spang (1988) have proposed similar conversion of lateral shortening to vertical uplift, by motion along a curved reverse fault, for the uplift of the Bighorn Mountains. The La Barge shear zone had to have acted as a curved fault zone, concave to the northeast, to have generated this proposed rotation.

Major vertical rotation of the La Barge Platform relative to the Moxa Arch would presumably require some structural discontinuity between the two. This discontinuity could be a lateral ramp or a high-angle normal or reverse fault. Structural contouring on the Moxa thrust and top of the La Barge shear zone (Fig. 8) shows that the Moxa thrust curves east and sweeps into the La Barge shear zone beneath southernmost Snider Basin. Other than this, we find no evidence for major discontinuity between the Moxa Arch and the La Barge Platform. It is possible that the discontinuity is restricted to a narrow zone that cannot be resolved between the sections. The full 3 km of unresolved lateral shortening cannot be accounted for by lateral-to-vertical conversion.

2. Substantial east-west shortening south of Snider Basin could have occurred by strike-slip motion along the La Barge shear zone. Blackstone (1979) believed that cover rocks above the La Barge shear zone are offset in a left-lateral sense by at least 5 km along the Thompson fault. We are not aware of any direct

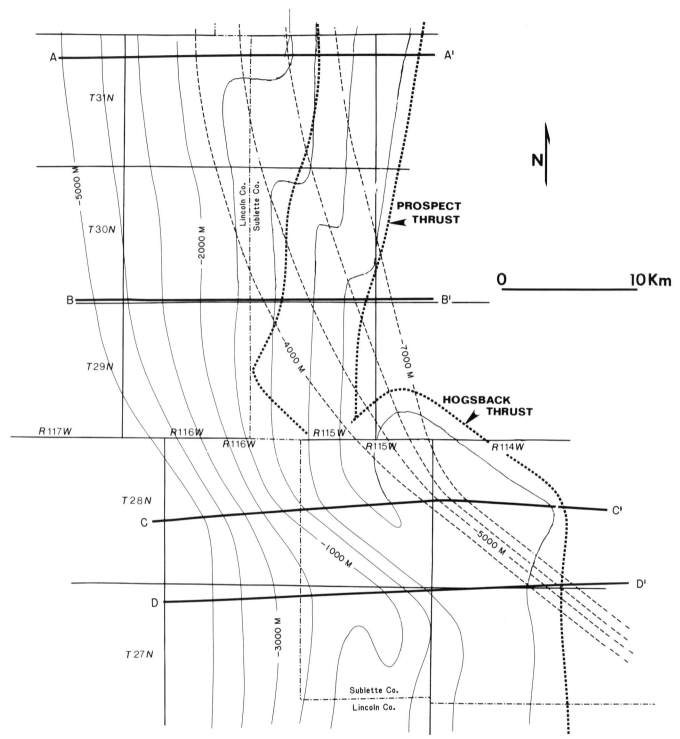

Figure 8. Structure contour map based on sections 2, 6, 7, and 9. Solid contours are drawn on the Prospect-Hogsback thrust. Dashed contours are on the Moxa thrust and on the top of the La Barge shear zone. Thick dotted line shows the surface trace of the Prospect and Hogsback thrusts. Contour interval = 1,000 m.

TABLE 2. SUMMARY OF THE DISPLACEMENTS OF THE PROSPECT, DARBY, AND HOGSBACK THRUSTS

Cross Section	Displacement (km)					Total Thrust Shortening (Prospect, Darby, and Hogsback)
	Ancestral Prospect Thrust	Late Prospect Thrust	Total Prospect Thrust	Darby Thrust	Hogsback Thrust	
AA'	5+	5	10+	28	0	38
BB'	5+	2	7+	27	0	34
CC'	1	*	1	*	29*	30
DD'	0	*	*	*	26*	26

*Hogsback thrust displacement includes that of the Darby and late (Paleocene) Prospect thrusting.

evidence for strike offset of the basement along the margin of the La Barge Platform. However, Schmidt and O'Neill (1983) and Schmidt and others (this volume) have documented large strike offset along a similar northwest-trending transverse zone in Montana. East-west shortening of the La Barge shear zone by an additional 3 km, to match the shortening of the Moxa thrust, would require 3 km of oblique-slip motion along the Moxa thrust. Large oblique displacements are not well documented along thrust faults, although they might be possible. Provided that the basement was not detached from the cover rocks, strike-slip motion along the La Barge shear zone would have required an equal amount of strike-slip motion along the paired reverse faults in the cover rocks above the La Barge shear zone.

3. Anticlockwise rotation of the overriding (eastern) crustal block relative to the western block would result in greater shortening to the north. The regional implications of such crustal rotations would be considerable but are not easy to evaluate. Although relative rotation of basement blocks might have been important in determining basement geometries, an evaluation of the magnitude and geological implications of these rotations is beyond the scope of this chapter.

It seems that a combination of a conversion of lateral shortening to vertical uplift and considerable strike-slip motion along the La Barge shear zone could best account for the apparent decrease in basement shortening to the south.

Subsurface linkage of the Darby-Hogsback-Prospect thrust system. The radically different styles of deformation of basement and cover rocks north and south of Snider Basin converge beneath Snider Basin. The structure of this area must be very complex and it might not be possible to follow individual faults through this area. It seems likely that folding, small-scale faulting, and internal deformation of the rocks are pervasive through this area.

The geometry of the deformed cover rocks is dependent on the style of deformation of the basement. North of Snider Basin, the ancestral Prospect thrust might have formed in response to the out-of-basement Moxa thrust that became bedding-parallel along the Thaynes detachment. This ancestral Prospect thrust was not

required south of Snider Basin, where a pair of reverse faults locally shortened the cover rocks in response to shortening of the basement along the La Barge shear zone. Royse (1985) and Royse and others (1975) have suggested that the Prospect thrust cut up-section stratigraphically toward the south, ultimately linking with the Darby thrust. According to their interpretation, the Darby and Prospect thrusts merged to become the Hogsback thrust. Blackstone (1979) showed that the Prospect thrust dies out south of Snider Basin by passing into a plunging fold beneath the Darby (Hogsback) thrust. We believe this is the southernmost extension of the ancestral Prospect thrust. However, as explained below, we also agree with the interpretations of Royse (1985) and Royse and others (1975) that the Hogsback thrust is a composite of Prospect and Darby thrusting. Therefore, regarding the geometry of the Prospect thrust south of Snider Basin, our model is generally compatible with the models of Royse (1985), Royse and others (1975), and Blackstone (1979).

Prospect thrust continuation to the south. Blackstone (1979) suggested that the Prospect thrust lost its displacement by passing into a plunging fold south of Snider Basin. Comparison of his sections BB' and DD' shows a marked decrease in Prospect thrust offset over a comparatively short distance. This displacement loss appears to be too abrupt in light of the supposition that thrusts can only lose displacement gradually along the strike of the thrust. Dixon's (1982) approach to this problem was to show the Prospect thrust as overridden by the Darby thrust, south of Snider Basin. Comparison of his section 17–23 shows abrupt changes in displacement over relatively short distances along strike.

According to our model north of Snider Basin, the total displacement on the Prospect thrust occurred in two distinct deformation episodes. This fact is crucial in explaining the apparently abrupt decrease in Prospect thrust offset. Table 2 summarizes the displacements, according to our interpretation, on the Darby, Hogsback, and ancestral and late Prospect thrusts north and south of Snider Basin. Because the Prospect thrust displacement occurred during two phases, each deformation should be considered separately in terms of evaluating a reasonable decrease

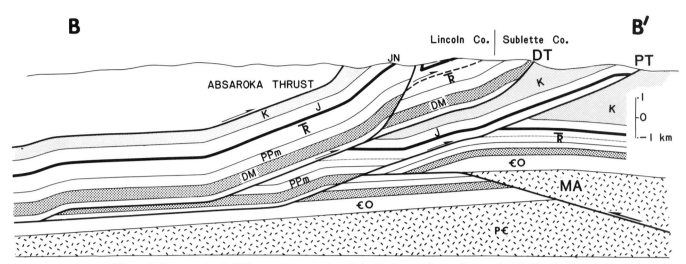

Figure 9. Cross section 9 (BB′), our interpretation of the geology at the northern end of Snider Basin. Total Prospect thrust offset is about 7 km, of which 5+ km occurred during the emplacement of the Moxa Arch. Explanation of symbols is given in caption of Figure 2. No scale exaggeration.

of offset relative to distance along the strike of the fault. Taking this into account, for each deformation episode there is a much more gradual decrease in the Prospect thrust displacement to the south, relative to distance along strike.

Southward continuation of the ancestral Prospect thrust. As the interpreted deformation in basement changed to the south, from a single thrust to a shear zone, the ancestral Prospect thrust was not required to the south to shorten the sedimentary section. Because thrusts generally do not lose displacement abruptly, the ancestral Prospect thrust must have either continued a short distance south of Snider Basin or have lost its displacement through intensive deformation of the rocks beneath Snider Basin, or some combination of the two. South of Snider Basin, drilling records show that the Prospect thrust continued through the area of Blackstone's (1979) section CC′ but terminated north of section DD′. According to our reconstructions, the pre–thrust belt shortening south of here was solely by the paired reverse faults above the La Barge shear zone.

Southward continuation of the late Prospect thrust. Late offset along the Prospect thrust decreases from about 5 km on section 2 to about 2 km on section 9. Dixon's section 20 (1982) shows the transitional geometry from cover rocks shortened over the Moxa Arch to those shortened over the La Barge shear zone. The northernmost extent of the Tip-Top thrust (the Tip-Top thrust is the upper of the reverse faults as proposed here and is shown as a dashed sub-Prospect thrust on Dixon's section 20, 1982) shares a small section of ramp with the Prospect thrust. We suggest that the offset of 2 km along the Prospect thrust here is a result of the late phase of Prospect thrusting that occurred during Paleocene time.

Figure 8 shows our interpretation that the Prospect thrust continues to the south. South of Snider Basin, the Prospect thrust is coincident with the Hogsback thrust, and we suggest that latest motion on the Prospect thrust here initiated the earliest, though

minor, motion on the Hogsback thrust. This probably resulted in about 2 km of offset on the Hogsback thrust. We have no way of determining how far south the Hogsback thrust extended at this time.

We believe that much of the confusion as to whether the Prospect thrust dies out south of Snider Basin (Blackstone, 1979) or links up with the Darby thrust (Royse and others, 1975) results from a lack of recognition of the two phases of motion of the Prospect thrust. According to our interpretation, the ancestral Prospect thrust does continue a short distance south of Snider Basin, which we believe is what Blackstone (1979) detailed. On the other hand, the younger (Paleocene) Prospect thrust linked to the south with the Darby, as described by Royse and others (1975) and Royse (1985).

Continuation of the Darby thrust to the south

North of Snider Basin, the geometry, as interpreted, of the Moxa and Prospect thrusts localized the later Darby thrust (Kraig and others, 1987). The situation appears to be analogous to the south. Figure 6 shows that south of Snider Basin, the Hogsback thrust climbs from its basal detachment in upper Cambrian rocks, through the Paleozoic and Mesozoic rocks, to slide along a west-dipping detachment in the Cretaceous rocks. The position and orientation of this detachment were determined by the underlying basement shear zone. It appears that west-dipping beds above the La Barge shear zone provided zones of relatively easy slip that subsequently localized the Hogsback thrust.

Structural contouring on the Darby and Hogsbcack thrusts (Fig. 10) indicates that these are one fault plane (also Blackstone, Plate 4, 1979; Dixon, Fig. 18, 1982). The Darby thrust curved east, south of Snider Basin, to follow the west limb of the monocline. The monocline appears to die out to the southeast as relief on the underlying basement uplift decreases (see sections 21–24,

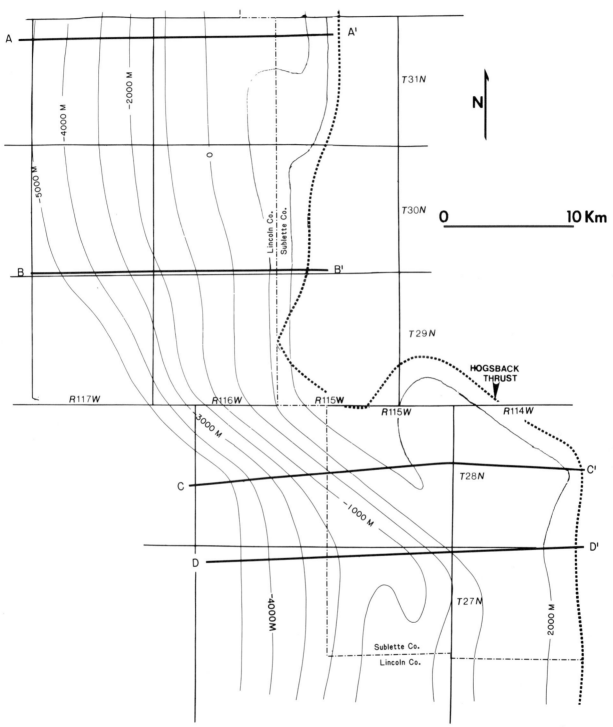

Figure 10. Structure contour map of the Darby-Hobsback thrust in the area of Snider Basin. Data base consisted of sections 2, 6, 7, and 9. Thick dotted line shows the surface trace of the Darby-Hogsback thrust. Contour interval = 1,000 m.

Dixon, 1982). We recommend (as do Royse and others, 1975) continuing the usage of the term Hogsback thrust south of Snider Basin, as the thrust appears to be a composite of both Prospect and Darby thrusting.

Summary of deformation in the Snider Basin area

We envision the following sequence of events in the Snider Basin area: the basement yielded to regional eastward compression by failing along an east-dipping thrust from Snider Basin northward, along a series of east-dipping reverse faults along the margin of the La Barge Platform, just south of Snider Basin, and along a west-dipping thrust along part of the southern segment of the Moxa Arch. Shortening of the cover rocks above the northern segment of the Moxa thrust was accommodated through the formation of the ancestral Prospect thrust, which moved about 5.3 km at this time. In the area of the La Barge Platform, the cover rocks were shortened through the formation of a pair of west-dipping reverse faults, the upper of which is the Tip-Top thrust. During the Paleocene, when deformation of the thrust belt reached this area, the ancestral Prospect thrust was reactivated north of Snider Basin, moving an additional 5 km. To the south, the Prospect thrust following west-dipping beds of the monocline formed above the La Barge shear zone. This late Prospect thrusting south of Snider Basin is the first, although minor, motion on what is now known as the Hogsback thrust. Continued motion on the Paleocene Prospect thrust north of Snider Basin localized the Darby thrust as a back-limb imbricate. Once formed, the Darby thrust accomplished all additional shortening of the cover rocks. To the south, the Darby thrust utilized the fault plane established by early Hogsback thrusting, and south of Snider Basin, the Darby is called the Hogsback thrust. *According to this scenario, the Hogsback thrust had two closely timed movements: an early minor offset that coincided with the period of late Prospect thrusting, and a later, major offset that was synchronous with Darby thrusting.* As described by Royse (1985), the gentle eastern dip of the frontal thrusts was established during Eocene compression associated temporally with the uplift of the Wind River Mountains.

Possible cause of the northwest trend of the La Barge Platform

Blackstone (1979) observed that the La Barge Platform is aligned with a northwest-trending zone of structural discontinuity. Major north-trending structures such as the Darby, Hogsback, and Absaroka thrusts and most major folds are diverted to follow this northwest trend (Blackstone, 1979, 1981; Oriel and Platt, 1980). At least 60 km of the surface trace of the Meade thrust also lies along this trend. Additionally, the Moxa Arch, which trends generally north from the Uinta Mountains, turns abruptly northwest near La Barge, Wyoming (Fig. 1) and follows this northwest trend for about 30 km, at which point it resumes

its northerly course beneath the frontal thrusts of the Cordilleran thrust belt.

South of the La Barge Platform, the trend appears to continue into the Green River Basin, where it is followed by major present-day drainages such as the Green River and La Barge Creek and is also paralleled locally by Pliocene terraces (Oriel and Platt, 1980). Regionally, the southwest margin of the La Barge Platform and its north and southward extensions are subparallel to other major northwest-trending features such as the Gros Ventre and Wind River Ranges (Blackstone, 1979).

The underlying reason for this pronounced northwest alignment of structural features is unclear. However, as we showed, it is unreasonable to extend the Moxa thrust south from Snider Basin to account for the uplift of the La Barge Platform. By including a consideration of a probable rheology of basement in the construction of our cross sections CC' and DD', we have concluded that the most reasonable model for the uplift of the La Barge Platform is by distributed shearing along its southwest margin. This shear zone trends N40° to 45°W and dips about 60° NE. At this time, it is not possible to say whether the dip and the width in the area of the La Barge shear zone are fundamentally characteristic of the more extensive northwest-trending shear zone. However, the coincidence of the uplifted margin of the La Barge Platform along this extensive shear zone may provide insights as to the pervasively deformed nature of the zone.

CONCLUSIONS

The cross sections presented here encompass all published data, are balanced and sequentially restorable, and are based on assumed rheologic properties of the deforming rocks. These sections show the La Barge platform as uplifted along its southwest margin by a zone of reverse faults generally restricted to basement. Shortening of the sedimentary rocks above this shear zone appears to have been accommodated by a pair of west-dipping reverse faults that shortened the cover rocks commensurate with shortening of basement.

The west-dipping detachment on the monocline above this shear zone localized the late Prospect-Hogsback and Darby-Hogsback thrusts. The Hogsback thrust is linked to both the Darby and Prospect thrusts in the subsurface, although during motion, only one moved with the Hogsback at a time. Earliest Hogsback thrusting of about 2 km was initiated where the late (Paleocene) Prospect thrust broke along the west-dipping sediments above the La Barge shear zone. The majority of Hogsback thrust offset, about 28 km, occurred soon after the late Propsect thrusting, as the Darby thrust (north of Snider Basin) broke along the west-dipping sediments of the Prospect thrust sheet, and linked to the south with the Hogsback thrust. During the Eocene, the Prospect, Darby, and Hogsback thrusts were broadly folded together with the basement (Royse, 1985) along the trend of the Moxa Arch.

ACKNOWLEDGMENTS

This work was partially funded by the Center for Tectono-physics and the Department of Geology at Texas A&M University, and by the Sigma Xi Foundation. For helpful discussions we are indebted to Robert Berg, Ray Fletcher, Joe Dixon, Frank Royse, Jr., Don Erickson, and James Evans, and for essential logistical help we are grateful to Ellen Kraig. For critical reviews we are indebted to Frank Royse, Jr., and D. L. Blackstone, and for the forum to present these ideas and their continued encouragement and constructive criticism, we are most indebted to Chris Schmidt and Bill Perry.

REFERENCES CITED

Armstrong, F. C., and Oriel, S. S., 1965, Tectonic development of Idaho-Wyoming thrust belt: American Association of Petroleum Geologists Bulletin, v. 49, p. 1847–1886.

Berg, R. R., 1961a, Laramide sediments along the Wind River thrust, Wyoming [abs.]: American Association of Petroleum Geologists Bulletin, v. 45, p. 416.

—— , 1961b, Laramide tectonics of the Wind River mountains, *in* Symposium on Late Cretaceous rocks: Wyoming Geological Association 16th Annual Field Conference Guidebook, p. 70–80.

—— , 1962, Mountain flank thrusting in Rocky Mountain foreland, Wyoming and Colorado: American Association of Petroleum Geologists Bulletin, v. 46, p. 2019–2032.

Blackstone, D. L., Jr., 1979, Geometry of the Prospect-Darby and La Barge faults at their junction with the La Barge Platform, Lincoln and Sublette Counties, Wyoming: Wyoming Geological Survey Report of Investigations no. 18, 29 p.

—— , 1981, Tectonic map of the Western Overthrust Belt, western Wyoming, southeastern Idaho, and northeastern Utah, 4th ed.: Wyoming Geological Survey Map Series 8A.

—— , 1983, Laramide compressional tectonics, southeastern Wyoming: University of Wyoming Contributions to Geology, v. 22, no. 1, p. 1–38.

Brown, W. G., 1981, Surface and subsurface examples from the Wyoming foreland as evidences of a regional compressional origin for the Laramide Orogeny: Wyoming Geological Survey Public Information Circular no. 13, p. 7–10.

CGG Advertisement, May, 1985, Moxa Arch, Wyoming, Sublette and Sweetwater Counties: American Association of Petroleum Geologists Explorer, p. 10.

Coffin, R. C., 1946, Recent trends in geological-geophysical exploration: American Association of Petroleum Geologists Bulletin, v. 30, p. 2031–2032.

Cook, D. G., 1985, Balancing basement-cored folds of the Wyoming Province type-A unique solution: Geological Society of America Abstracts with Programs, v. 17, p. 552.

Dahlstrom, C.D.A., 1969, Balanced cross-sections: Canadian Journal of Earth Sciences, v. 6, no. 4, p. 743–757.

Dixon, J. S., 1982, Regional structural synthesis, Wyoming salient of Western Overthrust Belt: American Association of Petroleum Geologists Bulletin, v. 66, p. 1560–1580.

Dorr, J. A., Jr., 1981, Timing of tectonic activity in the Overthrust Belt, western Wyoming and southeastern Idaho, *in* Sedimentary tectonics principles and applications: University of Wyoming Department of Geology, Wyoming Geological Survey, and Wyoming Geological Association Conference Notes, May 3–5, p. 9–10.

Dorr, J. A., and Gingerich, P. D., 1980, Early Cenozoic mammalian paleontology, geologic structure, and tectonic history in the Overthrust Belt near La Barge, Wyoming: University of Wyoming Contributions to Geology, v. 18, no. 2, p. 101–115.

Eardley, A. J., 1951, Structural geology of North America: New York, Harper and Brothers, Figure 203, p. 348.

Evans, J. P., 1985, Deformation mechanisms and textures in feldspar-rich rocks; Examples from Laramide fault zones: EOS Transactions of the American Geophysical Union, v. 66, p. 83.

Fletcher, R. C., 1984, Instability of lithosphere undergoing shortening; A model for Laramide foreland structures: Geological Society of America Abstracts with Programs, v. 16, p. 83.

Hennings, P. H., and Spang, J. H., 1988, A method for determining fault geometry from rotated basement blocks using slip lines: Mountain Geologist (in press).

Houston, R. S., and others, 1968, A regional study of rocks of Precambrian age in that part of the Medicine Bow Mountains lying in southeastern Wyoming, with a chapter on the relationship between Precambrian and Laramide structure: Geological Survey of Wyoming Memoir 1, 167 p.

—— , 1986, Interaction of the La Barge Platform with the Western Overthrust Belt, southwestern Wyoming: Geological Society of America Abstracts with Programs, v. 18, no. 5.

Kraig, D. H., and Wiltschko, D. V., 1987, Effects on the calcite fabric (Madison Formation) of the impingement of the Darby/Hogsback thrust sheet and La Barge Platform, Snider Basin area, *in* Baugh, R., ed., Contributions to the geology of the Utah-Wyoming-Idaho thrust belt: Wyoming Geological Association 38th Annual Field Conference Guidebook.

Kraig, D. H., Wiltschko, D. V., and Spang, J. H., 1985, Emplacement of the Moxa Arch and related initiation of the ancestral Prospect thrust, southwestern Wyoming: Geological Society of America Abstracts with Programs, v. 17, no. 7.

—— , 1987, Interaction of basement uplift and thin-skinned thrusting, Moxa Arch and the Western Overthrust Belt, Wyoming; A hypothesis: Geological Society of America Bulletin, v. 99, p. 654–662.

Kreuger, M. L., 1960, Occurrence of natural gas in the western part of the Green River Basin, *in* Overthrust Belt of southwestern Wyoming: Wyoming Geological Association 15th Annual Field Conference Guidebook, p. 194–209.

Love, J. D., 1950, Paleozoic rocks on the southwest flank of the Wind River Mountains near Pinedale, Wyoming: Wyoming Geological Association 5th Annual Field Conference Guidebook, p. 25–27.

Lynn, H. B., Cape, C. D., and MacLeod, M. K., 1981, The Pacific Creek Anticline; Buckling above a basement thrust fault: Wyoming Geological Survey Public Information Circular 13, p. 18.

Matthews, V., III, 1986, A case for brittle deformation of the basement during the Laramide revolution in the Rocky Mountain foreland province: Mountain Geologist, v. 23, no. 1, p. 1–5.

Mitchell, G. C., and Pritchett, R. W., 1981, New exploration concepts and observations along the western margin of the Laramide Basin: Wyoming Geological Survey Public Information Circular 13, p. 21–22.

Montecchi, P., 1981, Some tectonic details of the Casper Arch, as seen on a regional reflection seismic line: Wyoming Geological Survey Public Information Circular 13, p. 23.

Oriel, S. S., and Platt, L. B., 1980, Geological map of the Preston 1° by 2° Quadrangle, southeastern Idaho and western Wyoming: U.S. Geological Survey Miscellaneous Investigations Map I-1127, scale 1:250,000.

Royse, F., Jr., 1985, Geometry and timing of the Darby-Prospect-Hogsback thrust fault system, Wyoming: Geological Society of America Abstracts with Programs, v. 17, p. 683.

Royse, F., Jr., Warner, M. A., and Reese, D. L., 1975, Thrust belt structural geometry and related stratigraphic problems, Wyoming, Idaho, northern Utah, *in* Symposium on deep drilling frontiers in central Rocky Mountains: Denver, Colorado, Rocky Mountain Association of Geologists, p. 41–54.

Rubey, W. W., Oriel, S. S., and Tracey, J. I., 1980, Geological map and structure sections of the Cokeville 30-minute Quadrangle, Lincoln and Sublette Counties, Wyoming: U.S. Geological Survey Miscellaneous Investigations Map I-1129, scale 1:62,500.

Schmidt, C. J., and Garihan, J. M., 1983, Laramide tectonic development in the Rocky Mountain foreland of southwestern Montana, *in* Lowell, J. D., ed.,

Rocky Mountain foreland basins and uplifts: Denver, Colorado, Rocky Mountain Association of Geologists, p. 271–294.

——, 1988, Role of recurrent movement on northwest-trending basement faults in the tectonic evolution of southwestern Montana: Proceedings of 6th Annual Conference on Basement Tectonics, Santa Fe, New Mexico (in press).

Schmidt, C. J., and O'Neill, J. M., 1983, Structural evolution of the southwestern Montana transverse zone, *in* Powers, R. B., ed., Geologic studies of the Cordilleran thrust belt, 1982: Denver, Colorado, Rocky Mountain Association of Geologists, v. 1, p. 193–218.

Skeen, R. C., and Ray, R. R., 1983, Seismic models and interpretation of the Casper Arch and thrust; Application to Rocky Mountain foreland structure, *in* Lowell, J. D., ed., Rocky Mountain foreland basins and uplifts: Denver, Colorado, Rocky Mountain Association of Geologists, p. 99–125.

Spang, J. H., and Evans, J. P., 1984a, Regioanlly balanced cross sections for Laramide foreland structures, Wyoming and Montana: Geological Society of America Abstracts with Programs, v. 16, p. 663.

——, 1984b, Basement fault configurations, Wyoming Province: American Association of Petroleum Geologists Bulletin, v. 58, p. 950.

Spang, J. H., Evans, J. P., and Berg, R. R., 1985, Balanced cross sections of small fold-thrust structures: Mountain Geologist, v. 22, no. 2, p. 41–46.

Stearns, D. W., 1975, Laramide basement deformation in the Bighorn Basin; The controlling factors for structures in the layered rocks: Wyoming Geological Association 27th Annual Field Conference Guidebook, p. 149–158.

Thomaidis, N. D., 1973, Church Buttes arch, Wyoming and Utah: Wyoming Geological Association 25th Annual Field Conference Guidebook, p. 35–39.

Wach, P. H., 1977, The Moxa Arch, An Overthrust model?: Wyoming Geological Association 25th Annual Field Conference Guidebook, p. 651–664.

Wiltschko, D. V., and Dorr, J. A., 1983, Timing of deformation in Overthrust Belt and Foreland of Idaho, Wyoming, and Utah: American Association of Petroleum Geologists Bulletin, v. 67, no. 8, p. 1304–1322.

Wiltschko, D. V., and Eastman, D., 1983, Role of basement warps and faults in localizing thrust fault ramps: Geological Society of America Memoir 158, p. 177–190.

Young, S. W., 1985, Structural history of Jordan Creek area, northern Madison range, Madison County, Montana [M.S. thesis]: Austin, University of Texas, 125 p.

Young, S. W., Werkema, M., and Sheedlo, M. K., 1983, Mechanisms of rock deformation in basement-involved thrusts of southwestern Montana: Geological Society of America Abstracts with Programs, v. 15, p. 725.

Zawislak, R. L., and Smithson, S. B., 1981, The Wind River COCORP profile; Sedimentary deformation and deep reflection interpretation problems: Wyoming Geological Survey Public Information Circular 13, p. 29.

MANUSCRIPT ACCEPTED BY THE SOCIETY FEBRUARY 9, 1988

Geological Society of America
Memoir 171
1988

Late Mesozoic and early Tertiary reactivation of an ancient crustal boundary along the Uinta trend and its interaction with the Sevier orogenic belt

Bruce Bryant and D. J. Nichols
U.S. Geological Survey, MS 913, Box 25046, Denver Federal Center, Denver, Colorado 80225

ABSTRACT

The junction between Archean and Proterozoic crust forms a zone of weakness near the north margin of the Uinta trend that extends west from Colorado to the edge of Precambrian continental crust in central Nevada. In the vicinity of the Wasatch Mountains of central Utah, areas north and south of this crustal boundary differ markedly in thicknesses of Middle and Late Proterozoic sedimentary rocks and in the degree of involvement of basement rocks in thrusting in the Sevier orogenic belt. North of the crustal boundary, where Proterozoic sedimentary rocks are absent and the total thickness of the section is less than half of that directly south of the crustal boundary, a large area of Archean crust was uplifted above and west of the Farmington ramp.

Stratigraphic and sedimentological data show that rock in the thrust belt northwest of the Uinta Mountains reflects deformation in older parts of the belt to the west in Early Cretaceous time. Palynological dating and stratigraphic correlations in the upper East Canyon area, north of the Uinta trend, indicate deformation less far to the west in Cenomanian, Turonian, Coniacian, and Santonian times. Paleocurrent data from the Echo Canyon Conglomerate and the position of its proximal facies on upturned rocks of the east margin of the northern Utah highland suggest that deposition of the Echo Canyon was concurrent with formation of the Farmington ramp and the overlying fold, chiefly in late Coniacian and Santonian time. Similar conglomerates interbedded with the underlying Frontier Formation suggest that the ramp and fold may have begun to form as early as Cenomanian time. By the time the fold was completely formed, early movements on the Absaroka thrust in southwestern Wyoming had occurred.

South of the Uinta uplift, an anticline that formed in Campanian time during movement associated with the Charleston thrust is unconformably overlain by the basal beds of the Currant Creek Formation that were deposited in late Campanian or early Maastrichtian time. East of the anticline the uppermost beds of the Mesaverde Formation are of Santonian age; this suggests Campanian uplift along part of the south flank of the Uinta Mountains at the same time that the Charleston thrust was being emplaced. Dips in the Currant Creek Formation are moderately steep in its basal part and decrease upsection, suggesting that it was deposited during a major pulse of uplift of the Uinta Mountains. No ages have been obtained more than 100 m above the base that would date the main body of the formation and thus the uplift.

In the Neil Creek area at the northwest corner of the Uinta Mountains, the North Flank fault zone splays out and cuts the Absaroka thrust. Rocks in the footwall of that thrust have been overturned and sliced by deformation along that fault zone. The youngest rocks involved are the late Campanian–early Maastrichtian Hams Fork Member of the Evanston Formation, and the Wasatch Formation of late Paleocene age overlies several of the splays of the North Flank fault zone.

Time of major movement along the Hogsback thrust 150 km north of the Uinta Mountains is between early Campanian and middle Paleocene. No information is available on time of movement on that fault near the Uintas, because it is entirely in the subsurface. Seismic data are said to show that the North Flank fault zone overrides the Hogsback thrust at the margin of the Uintas.

Major movements on the Uinta uplift occurred in late Paleocene and early Eocene time and continued into Oligocene time.

Structural relief on the Cottonwood uplift is mainly, but not entirely, the result of Neogene faulting.

Data on timing of structural movements are interpreted to show that the major movement along the Sevier thrusts did not overlap times of major uplift of the western Uinta Mountains, but many events are not closely dated.

INTRODUCTION

In the Uinta Mountains in northern Utah and northwestern Colorado, Middle Proterozoic rocks and a small area of late Archean and Early Proterozoic rocks are exposed in the 250-km-long west-trending Uinta uplift (Figs. 1, 2). West on trend with the Uinta Mountains, in the Wasatch Mountains, the Cottonwood uplift exposes Early, Middle, and Late Proterozoic rocks. These uplifts are impinged upon by the N25°E–trending Sevier orogenic belt (Figs. 1, 2). Major thrust sheets of that belt crop out both north and south of the Cottonwood uplift and extend 80 km to the east along the north side of the Uinta Mountains and 40 km to the east south of the Cottonwood uplift.

The relations between structural events in the Sevier orogenic belt and those in the Uinta Mountains and the Cottonwood uplift have been discussed only sparsely in the literature. Armstrong (1968a), who named the Sevier orogenic belt, thought that major movements in it ceased before the formation of the foreland uplifts, such as the Uintas, but Crittenden (1969, 1976) found that thrusting in the Sevier belt and uplift of the Uinta Mountains overlapped in a confusing fashion. Beutner (1977) considered the area of the Uinta Mountains and the Cottonwood uplift as a buttress in the path of the eastward-advancing thrust sheets of the Sevier orogenic belt. Bruhn and others (1983, 1986) constructed a model to explain the interplay between the thrust-belt structures and the Uinta Mountain structures that involved simultaneous movement on thrust faults and reactivation of older structures along the Uinta Mountains. An ancient west-trending discontinuity in the crust (Fig. 1) coincides with the north flank of the Uinta Mountains that was in existence by at least 1,800 Ma (Bryant, 1985), and formed the south margin of the Archean craton. Here, we discuss the relationship between this ancient discontinuity and the structure of the Uintas and the Sevier orogenic belt. We also review the known time constraints on thrusting in the Sevier orogenic belt in the Uinta region, the timing of the uplift of the Uintas, and the relations between these structures.

THE EFFECT OF AN ANCIENT CRUSTAL DISCONTINUITY ON SEDIMENTATION

In Middle Proterozoic time the margin of the Archean craton formed the north margin of an east-trending basin in which a clastic sequence, the Uinta Mountain Group, accumulated to thicknesses of as much as 7 km. Source area for the sediments was an uplift on the Archean craton northeast of the basin, and the sediments were dispersed westward (Hansen, 1965; Wallace, 1972). In the Cottonwood uplift, a sequence of clastic rocks about 5 km thick, the Big Cottonwood Formation, is probably correlative with the Uinta Mountain Group (Crittenden, 1976). These rocks are absent on the Archean craton to the north in exposures in the Mill Creek area northeast of Salt Lake City, Utah, and on Antelope Island in Great Salt Lake (Larsen, 1957); they thin southward to 120 m in the Charleston thrust sheet near Santaquin, 70 km south of the Cottonwood uplift. Some of that thinning is erosional, for the overlying Cambrian Tintic Quartzite cuts into the Big Cottonwood Formation and decreases its thickness from 400 m to 120 m in a distance of only 6 km in the exposure at Santaquin (Brady, 1965).

The north-trending margin of the North American continent was established by Late Proterozoic time probably by rifting of the older Proterozoic continent normal to the Archean crustal margin (Fig. 1), and a thick north-trending clastic sequence was deposited on the new continental margin (Stewart, 1972). A major embayment in the depositional margin of this Late Proterozoic clastic sequence west of the Uinta Mountains was probably controlled by the ancient east-trending Archean continental margin (Fig. 1). In the Cottonwood uplift, as much as 1.2 km of late Precambrian quartzite and tillite is exposed (Crittenden, 1976). Within the Cottonwood uplift, the Late Proterozoic beds pinch out to the east and south within short distances because of unconformities within the sequence and below overlying Cambrian quartzite. Only 20 km north of the Cottonwood uplift and north of the ancient crustal boundary, the Late Proterozoic beds are missing, and Cambrian quartzite overlies Archean crystalline rocks. About 30 km to the west on Antelope Island in Great Salt Lake, about 100 m of Late Proterozoic rocks overlie basement rock and are overlain by Cambrian quartzite (Larsen, 1957; Crittenden, 1972). This area where Proterozoic sedimentary rocks are thin or absent north of the crustal boundary was called the northern Utah highland by Eardley (1939, p. 1285–1289). These rocks have been transported some kilometers to the east in relation to

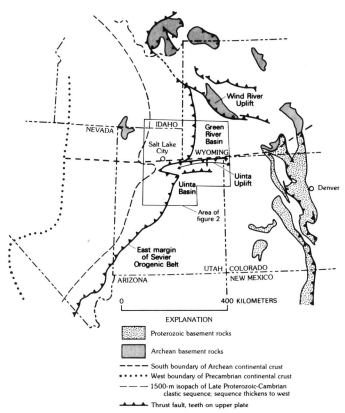

Figure 1. Tectonic map of the east-central part of the Cordilleran belt in the United States. West margin of Precambrian continental crust after Farmer and DePaolo (1984); isopach of Late Proterozoic to Cambrian clastic sequence modified from Stewart (1972).

EXPLANATION

Proterozoic basement rocks

Archean basement rocks

– – – South boundary of Archean continental crust

• • • • • West boundary of Precambrian continental crust

– – – 1500-m isopach of Late Proterozoic-Cambrian clastic sequence; sequence thickens to west

▲▲▲ Thrust fault, teeth on upper plate

0   400 KILOMETERS

those in the Cottonwood uplift; so the margin of deposition of Late Precambrian clastic rocks immediately north of the ancient boundary was even farther west in relation to autochthonous rocks in the Cottonwood uplift than at present. Southward in the Charleston thrust sheet the Late Proterozoic sequence is about 700 m thick in the American Fork area (Baker and Crittenden, 1961), 45 m thick near Springville, Utah (Baker, 1973), and is missing near Santaquin 70 km south of the Cottonwood uplift. The Charleston sheet has moved tens of kilometers eastward in relation to the Cottonwood uplift (Crittenden, 1961), so the presence of a 700-m-thick section of Late Proterozoic rocks immediately south of the Cottonwood uplift suggests another west-trending discontinuity in sedimentation patterns. One fault of this age and trend, the Hoyt Canyon fault, is exposed in the southwestern Uinta Mountains (Wallace, 1972). Thus, the crustal discontinuity that controlled the deposition of the Uinta Mountain Group in Middle Proterozoic time also affected the depositional pattern of the Late Proterozoic clastic sequence west of the Uinta Mountains.

In early Paleozoic time the block along the south margin of the Archean craton containing a thick section of Precambrian clastic rock acted as a positive structural element, and less sedi-

ment was deposited there than to the north or south (for example, see Lochman-Balk, 1972).

In late Paleozoic time, the Oquirrh Group was deposited in a northwest-trending basin that crossed the ancient crustal discontinuity. These rocks, which are as much as 8 km thick, were probably deposited in a fault-bounded basin (Jordan and Douglass, 1980, p. 231); we suspect that west-trending faults at and south of the discontinuity helped define the basin as suggested by Armstrong (1968b, p. 33), but until a comprehensive study of the Oquirrh is made, we reserve judgment on the details of that interaction. Palinspastic isopachs in western Utah show that Mississippian rocks are twice as thick in an east-trending basin that was on the south side of the ancient crustal discontinuity as they are north of the discontinuity (Hintze, 1973, p. 35). Much of the increased thickness in the Mississippian rocks is in the Upper Mississippian Great Blue Limestone. A palinspastic map of the Pennsylvanian and Permian isopachs in the whole basin suggests that it was divided into two subbasins. The southern and deeper subbasin trended to the east and was south of the ancient crustal discontinuity (Roberts and others, 1965).

In summary, the discontinuity at the margin of the Archean craton affected both Proterozoic and Paleozoic sedimentation in the area. North of the margin, Cambrian rocks rest on basement rocks at the longitude of the Wasatch Mountains. Immediately south of the Archean craton, Proterozoic rocks exposed in the Cottonwood uplift are 6 km thick. West of there, the thickness of the Middle Proterozoic rocks probably decreases and that of the Late Proterozoic rocks increases, but few data on their thicknesses are available. The late Paleozoic rocks of the Oquirrh basin are thicker south of the crustal discontinuity than north of it. Conservative, but very approximate, calculations for the Phanerozoic, based on the summaries of Hintz (1973), and for the Proterozoic, on extrapolations of available data, indicate that, by the end of Triassic time, the stratigraphic section overlying basement rock north of the discontinuity was about 8 km thick, compared to 16 km south of it.

STRUCTURAL EVENTS

Sevier orogenic belt

North of the Archean continental margin, crust lacking a thick Middle or Late Proterozoic sedimentary sequence is directly juxtaposed against crust having several kilometers of rocks of those ages. Thicker sections of late Paleozoic rocks south of the margin resulted in a cross-strike structural discontinuity (Wheeler and others, 1979) in the thrust sheets formed during the Sevier orogenic event. This discontinuity, which is controlled by the margin of the Archean craton, was the site where lateral ramps formed in the thrust strata in late Mesozoic time. Because the sedimentary section on the north sidde was half as thick as that on the south, a large amount of Archean crust was involved in the thrusting on the north side of the discontinuity. Where the sole thrust ramped upward from deep in the basement into Cambrian

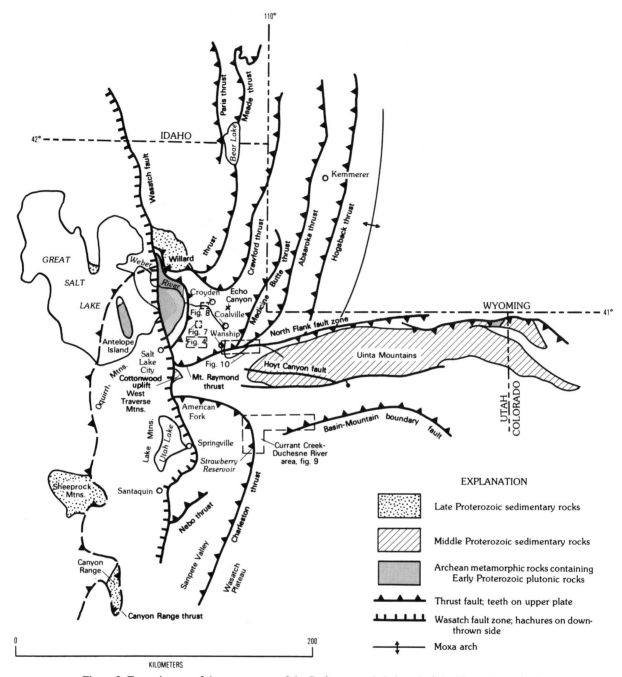

Figure 2. Tectonic map of the eastern part of the Sevier orogenic belt and of the Uinta Mountains in northern Utah and southwestern Wyoming showing major structural features and locations of areas of more detailed maps.

rocks, a large ramp uplift was formed, and in it are now exposed Archean basement rocks (Royse and others, 1975). The cross-strike structural discontinuity occurs along the south terminus of the ramp uplift (Bruhn and others, 1985; Smith and Bruhn, 1984).

North of the Uinta Mountains and Cottonwood uplift. In north-central Utah, the earliest suggestion of Sevier orogeny to the west is the disconformity between the marine Preuss Sand-

stone of late Middle Jurassic (Callovian) age (Imlay, 1980, p. 69) and the nonmarine Kelvin Formation of Early Cretaceous age (Fig. 3). Rocks of Late Jurassic age were either not deposited or were eroded before Early Cretaceous time west of the Uinta Mountains. Below the Absaroka thrust, the Kelvin overlies the Stump Sandstone and Morrison Formation of Late Jurassic age near Peoa, Utah (Morris, 1953; Crittenden, 1963), indicating that the disconformity diminished eastward. No fossils have been

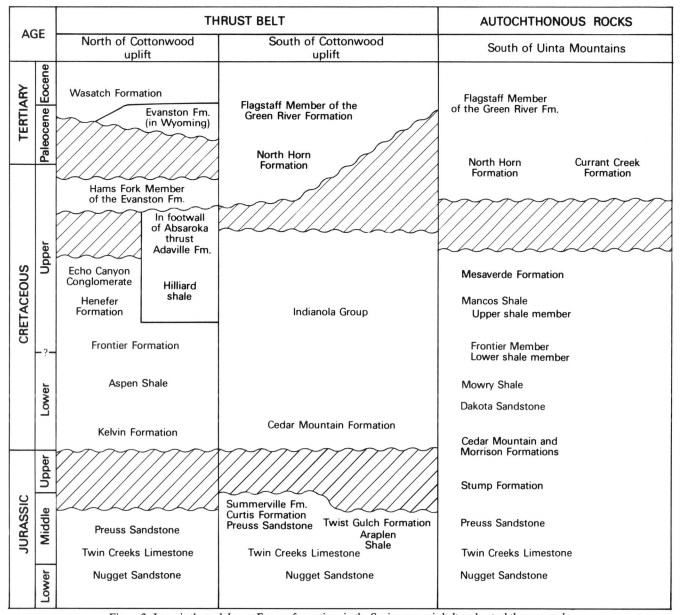

Figure 3. Jurassic through lower Eocene formations in the Sevier orogenic belt and autochthonous rocks to the south near the west end of the Uinta Mountains.

reported from the Kelvin in Utah, but in southwestern Wyoming it intertongues with fossiliferous Lower Cretaceous rocks. In its westernmost exposures near Salt Lake City, the Kelvin contains beds of cobble conglomerate as much as 25 m thick derived from Mesozoic and Paleozoic rocks to the west (Granger, 1953). This suggests uplift in that direction, uplift that may have been associated with movements on thrust systems in the Sevier orogenic belt.

The next activity in the Sevier orogenic belt north of the Archean continental margin occurred from late Cenomanian to middle Santonian time, as evidenced by the following stratigraphic relations. In the upper East Canyon Creek area east of Salt Lake City, tongues of cobble and boulder conglomerate occur in the Frontier Formation (Figs. 3, 4). The middle Turonian ammo-

nite *Collignoniceras woollgari* has been found in a marine sandstone along upper East Canyon (E. A. Merewether and C. M. Molenaar, written communication, 1980). This ammonite also occurs in the Allen Valley Shale and Oyster Ridge Sandstone Members of the Frontier Formation near Coalville (Cobban and Reeside, 1952, p. 1936–1937) and furnishes a key for correlating the two sections. Large inoceramids occur in a marine sandstone higher in the upper East Canyon Creek section in strata probably correlative with the Judd Shale or Upton Sandstone Members of the Frontier at Coalville. The correlation of the section of Frontier in upper East Canyon with that in Coalville (Fig. 5) indicates that westward-thickening tongues of conglomerate are of late Cenomanian, late Turonian, and middle Coniacian age, and sug-

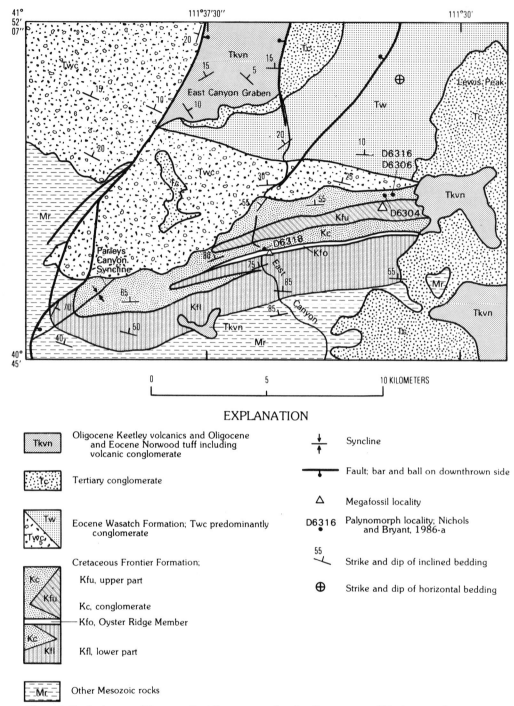

Figure 4. Geologic map of the upper East Canyon area showing Cretaceous and Tertiary conglomerates, and fossil localities in the Frontier Formation.

gests that these were times of uplift and probably thrusting in areas not far to the west (Bryant and Nichols, 1985; Fig. 13).

In late Coniacian and Santonian time, a thick sequence of conglomerate, the Echo Canyon Conglomerate, was deposited near Coalville, where it conformably overlies the Henefer Formation, a transitional unit between the Frontier and the Echo Canyon. A belt of coarse-grained, crudely bedded conglomerate

between East Canyon Reservoir and Croyden has been correlated with the Echo Canyon Conglomerate by Mullens (1971) and Crawford (1979). Nichols and Warner (1978), however, considered this conglomerate to be the basal conglomerate of the Hams Fork Member of the Evanston Formation because of the identification of late Campanian–early Maastrichtian palynomorphs (Fig. 6) in overlying siltstone. Reexamination of the conglomerate suggests that both interpretations may be partly correct in that this unit consists of two conglomerates: a well-cemented conglomerate of angular pebbles and cobbles (Kec in Fig. 7), and an overlying poorly cemented conglomerate containing round cobbles and pebbles of quartzite (Kehc in Fig. 7). The areal distribution of the round cobble conglomerate and steep dips in the well-cemented conglomerate indicate that there is an unconformity between the two in the Rocky Canyon area north of East Canyon dam (Fig. 7). Southwest of Croyden, Utah, 1 to 2 km south of the Weber River, the poorly cemented conglomerate truncates the underlying well-cemented conglomerate, which dips gently, and rests on steeply dipping Jurassic rocks (Fig. 8). If the well-cemented conglomerate is the Echo Canyon Conglomerate of late Coniacian-Santonian age (Jacobson and Nichols, 1983), this indicates that important structural movements took place at that time in the Sevier orogenic belt in rocks that have been thrusted close to the Cottonwood uplift. The well-cemented conglomerate in the East Canyon Creek–Croyden belt unconformably overlies steeply dipping Jurassic rock that forms the east flank of a large basement-cored fold above a ramp in the thrust system (Royse and others, 1975). We call this ramp the Farmington ramp, after the Farmington Canyon Complex that forms the core of the structurally high area above and west of the ramp. That structurally high area makes up the northern Utah highland.

The time at which the Farmington ramp started to form is not precisely known. The Echo Canyon Conglomerate has been correlated with uplift and movement on the Crawford thrust that lies to the north (Royse and others, 1975, p. 50). Paleocurrent data from the Echo Canyon Conglomerate indicate derivation from the west (Crawford, 1979), the direction of the Farmington ramp and associated uplift, and the proximal facies conglomerate unconformably overlies turned-up rocks on the east flank of that uplift. This suggests that the uplift formed in late Coniacian or Santonian time. Another possible interpretation is that the conglomerate mapped in the East Canyon Reservoir–Croyden area (Kec on Fig. 7) is not correlative with the Echo Canyon, but is a younger conglomerate, although older than the unconformably overlying late Campanian–early Maastrichtian Hams Fork Member of the Evanston Formation, and that the Echo Canyon was derived from rocks in the Crawford thrust sheet when it overlay the area now occupied by the northern Utah highland. No precise dating of the time of movement of the Crawford thrust, which crops out only north of the northern Utah highland (Fig. 2), is available. It cuts the Lower Cretaceous Sage Junction Formation in T.10N.,R.8E, about 100 km north of the Uintas (Dover, 1985), and is overlain by the early Campanian–late Maastrichtian Hams Fork Member of the Evanston Formation in T.4N.,R.4E., 40 km north of the Uinta trend and about 15 km northwest of Echo Canyon. These data indicate that the Farmington ramp and associated fold may have formed in late Coniacian or Santonian time or between Santonian and late Campanian to early Maastrichtian time, but we favor the earlier time based on correlation of the lower conglomerate in the East Canyon Reservoir–Croyden area with the Echo Canyon Conglomerate.

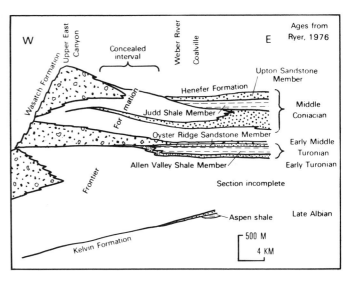

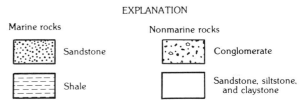

Figure 5. Diagram showing stratigraphic relations in the Frontier Formation between Coalville, Utah, and upper East Canyon.

On the north flank of the Cottonwood uplift, the Mt. Raymond thrust cuts up-section in an easterly direction and is apparently continuous with the Absaroka thrust of southwestern Wyoming (Crittenden, 1974). Near Wanship, Utah, rocks north of the Absaroka thrust and faults branching from it are unconformably overlain by the Hams Fork Member of the Evanston Formation of late Campanian or early Maastrictian age (Nichols and Warner, 1978; Jacobson and Nichols, 1983), but the Hams Fork does not overlie the main strand of the Absaroka thrust in that area (Fig. 10). North of Coalville the Hams Fork unconformably overlies the Echo Canyon Conglomerate and older rocks. Thus the major deformation of the rocks now directly northwest of the Uinta Mountains took place in Santonian and Campanian time (Fig. 13).

South of the Uinta Mountains and Cottonwood uplift. Southwest of the Uinta Mountains and south of the Cottonwood uplift, major movement of the Charleston thrust sheet took place before late Campanian or early Maastrichtian time. Pulses of uplift, probably associated with thrusting to the west, occurred in late Albian, Cenomanian, middle Turonian, Santonian, and early Campanian time.

South-southwest of the Uinta Mountains, a nonmarine sequence of sandstone and siltstone formerly called "Morrison(?)" (Spieker, 1946, p. 125–126) has been dated as Early Cretaceous and identified as the Cedar Mountain Formation (Fig. 3) (Witkind and others, 1986). The first indication of uplift relatively

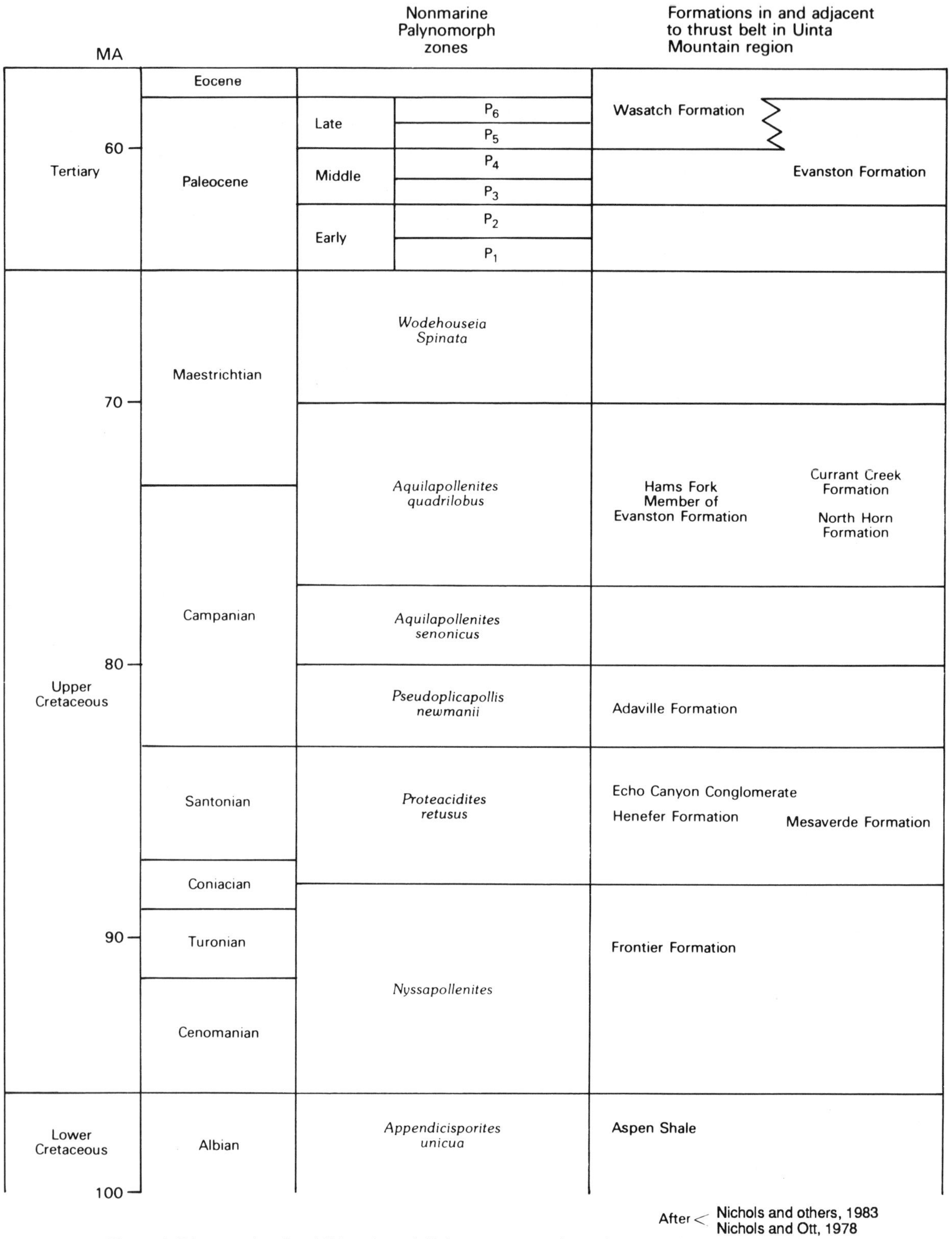

Bryant and Nichols

MA		Nonmarine Palynomorph zones			Formations in and adjacent to thrust belt in Uinta Mountain region	
		Eocene				
60	Tertiary	Paleocene	Late	P_6	Wasatch Formation	
				P_5		
			Middle	P_4		Evanston Formation
				P_3		
			Early	P_2		
				P_1		
70	Upper Cretaceous	Maestrichtian	*Wodehouseia Spinata*			
		Campanian	*Aquilapollenites quadrilobus*		Hams Fork Member of Evanston Formation	Currant Creek Formation / North Horn Formation
80			*Aquilapollenites senonicus*			
			Pseudoplicapollis newmanii		Adaville Formation	
		Santonian	*Proteacidites retusus*		Echo Canyon Conglomerate / Henefer Formation	Mesaverde Formation
		Coniacian				
90		Turonian	*Nyssapollenites*		Frontier Formation	
		Cenomanian				
100	Lower Cretaceous	Albian	*Appendicisporites unicua*		Aspen Shale	

After Nichols and others, 1983
Nichols and Ott, 1978

Figure 6. Diagram showing Albian through Paleocene nonmarine palynomorph zones and the formations in which these zones have been identified near the intersection of the Sevier orogenic belt with the Uinta uplift in northern Utah and southwestern Wyoming.

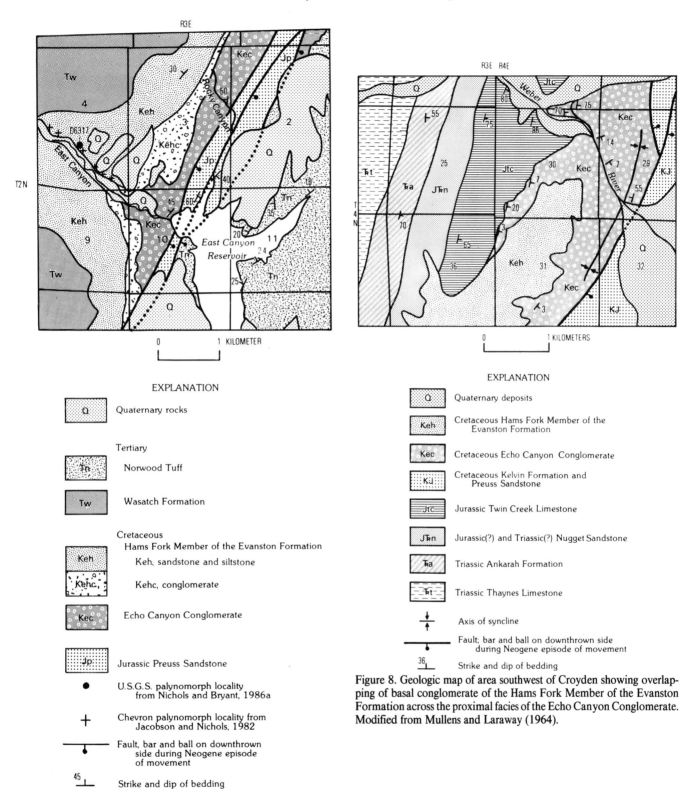

EXPLANATION

Q — Quaternary rocks

Tertiary

Tn — Norwood Tuff

Tw — Wasatch Formation

Cretaceous
Hams Fork Member of the Evanston Formation

Keh, sandstone and siltstone

Kehc, conglomerate

Kec — Echo Canyon Conglomerate

Jp — Jurassic Preuss Sandstone

● — U.S.G.S. palynomorph locality from Nichols and Bryant, 1986a

+ — Chevron palynomorph locality from Jacobson and Nichols, 1982

⊢•— Fault, bar and ball on downthrown side during Neogene episode of movement

45⌐ — Strike and dip of bedding

Figure 7. Geologic map of East Canyon Reservoir area showing basal conglomerate of the Hams Fork Member of the Evanston Formation and underlying proximal facies of the Echo Canyon Conglomerate and palynomorph localities.

EXPLANATION

Q — Quaternary deposits

Keh — Cretaceous Hams Fork Member of the Evanston Formation

Kec — Cretaceous Echo Canyon Conglomerate

KJ — Cretaceous Kelvin Formation and Preuss Sandstone

Jtc — Jurassic Twin Creek Limestone

JTͤn — Jurassic(?) and Triassic(?) Nugget Sandstone

Tͤa — Triassic Ankarah Formation

Tͤt — Triassic Thaynes Limestone

⊥ — Axis of syncline

⊢•— Fault; bar and ball on downthrown side during Neogene episode of movement

36⌐ — Strike and dip of bedding

Figure 8. Geologic map of area southwest of Croyden showing overlapping of basal conglomerate of the Hams Fork Member of the Evanston Formation across the proximal facies of the Echo Canyon Conglomerate. Modified from Mullens and Laraway (1964).

nearby is in the basal conglomerate of the Indianola Group, which is of Albian age and grades downward into sandstone and siltstone of the Cedar Mountain (Witkind and others, 1986). Stratigraphy of the Indianola Group (Lawton, 1982; Jefferson, 1982) suggests pulses of uplift to the west, probably associated with movement on the Canyon Range and Nebo, and to the south, beyond this area, on the Pavant (Lawton, 1985, p. 1156–1157) thrust systems, in Cenomanian, middle Turonian, Santonian, and early Campanian time (Fig. 13).

The principal angular unconformity in this region is between rocks of the Indianola Group and older formations and conglomerate in the basal part of the North Horn Formation, which has been assigned to the Price River Formation by some workers. Conglomerate and sandstone mapped as Price River Formation unconformably overlie Indianola Group rocks in the Sanpete valley area (Spieker, 1946, p. 131–132; I. J. Witkind, oral communication, 1985) and have been dated as late Campanian and early Maastrichtian by palynomorphs (Fouch and others, 1983, Fig. 3). The Price River grades upward into continental mudstones of the North Horn Formation. Palynomorphs of an unspecified Maastrichtian zone have been found in the lower part of the North Horn (Standlee, 1983). In the Wasatch Plateau to the east, the lower part of the North Horn contains dinosaur remains of latest Cretaceous age (Spieker, 1946, p. 134–135), and in Price Canyon some 50 km east of the Sevier belt, the formation contains palynomorphs of late Campanian and early Maastrichtian age (Fouch and others, 1983, Fig. 3). However, in the Wasatch Mountains north of Spanish Fork Canyon, the base of the North Horn is probably younger than to the south and east, because the North Horn lapped against highlands that existed in Paleocene time. In that area the Flagstaff Member of the Green River Formation of late Paleocene age oversteps the North Horn and rests on Paleozoic rocks of the Charleston thrust plate (Baker, 1976). The available evidence indicates major deformation during Campanian time in the region south and immediately east of the southern end of the Wasatch Mountains, which occupies the southern part of the Charleston thrust sheet.

Tertiary structural movements in the Sanpete valley area were recognized by Spieker (1946, p. 155), who attributed formation of a large fold to compressive stress in Paleocene time. The role of diapirism of a thick sequence of Jurassic evaporite deposits in the Arapien Shale in the deformation of the area was first suggested by Stokes (1952, 1956), and has been emphasized by Witkind (1982) based on comprehensive 1:100,000–scale mapping of the region. However, proprietary seismic and drill hole information suggest that the thrusting extended along the Arapien Shale east of the Nebo thrust and died out in and east of a triangle zone underlying the Sanpete valley along trend of the Charleston thrust south-southwest of Strawberry Reservoir (Standlee, 1983; Lawton, 1985). Complex structural and stratigraphic relations adjacent to linear valleys in this region underlain by Arapien Shale are probably the result of a combination of thrusting in latest Mesozoic time, diapiric movement of evaporite deposits during and after Mesozoic thrusting, and of Neogene

regional extension. The evaporite deposits tended to become tectonically concentrated in cores of anticlines and in triangle zones during thrusting to thicknesses great enough for the deposits to become gravitationally unstable. North of the linear valleys underlain by Arapien Shale, unconformities within the lower Tertiary section have not been detected; we conclude that the early Tertiary deformation was confined to the belts of tectonically thickened Arapien Shale rather than related to more regional movement on thrusts.

The last major movement on the Charleston thrust immediately southwest of the Uinta Mountains was in the Campanian. In the Racetrack Creek area west of Currant Creek, the Currant Creek Formation rests on folded Jurassic and older Cretaceous rocks in front of the thrust (Fig. 9). On Red Creek 15 km east of the fold in the Racetrack Creek area, palynomorphs from a coal bed and adjacent strata in the Mesaverde Formation are Santonian, and palynomorphs from the "transitional strata" (Walton, 1944) of the Currant Creek Formation are late Campanian or early Maastrichtian (Fig. 6; Nichols and Bryant, 1986b). Palynomorphs of the same age have been obtained from the same stratigraphic interval in the Currant Creek from 5 km east of the fold and from east of the Duchesne River more than 30 km to the east (Fig. 9).

Charophytes and ostracodes have been found, in addition to palynomorphs, in the Currant Creek Formation at a locality east of the Duchesne River. The sample is from the lowet siltstone interval containing some pinkish red beds and is located at 7,220 ft altitude in a gulley 1.7 km S61.5°E of road intersection 6939 in the Farm Creek Peak 7½-minute Quadrangle in SE¼T.1S.,R.7W. According to R. C. Forester (written communication, 1980), the following organisms occur in the sample: the charophytes *Stellatochara mundula* (Peck), *Mesochara* (two new species), *Strobitochara* sp., and a new genus and species, and the ostracodes *Timiriasevia* sp., *Cypridea* sp., and a new genus and species. Forester stated that ". . .charophytes and ostracodes in this sample have only been found in Upper Cretaceous rocks. Some are known from the lower North Horn, Harebell, and Willow Creek Formations in North America. . . . My own work in the stratigraphic distribution of these organisms suggests that this sample may be late Campanian to early Maastrichtian in age." We conclude that major movement on the Charleston thrust occurred in Campanian time (Fig. 13), before deposition of the "transitional strata" of the Currant Creek Formation.

Uinta Mountains

The Uinta Mountains are bounded on the north by a series of discontinuous, overlapping, south-dipping thrust faults (Ritzma, 1969; Gries, 1981), and on the south by a north-dipping thrust fault overlapped by Tertiary deposits (Forrester, 1937; Hansen, 1957; Ritzma, 1969; Garvin, 1969; Campbell, 1975). Tertiary deposits of the Green River Basin, adjacent to the mountains on the north, and of the Uinta Basin, adjacent on the south, are generally alluvial sandstones and conglomerates; they are dif-

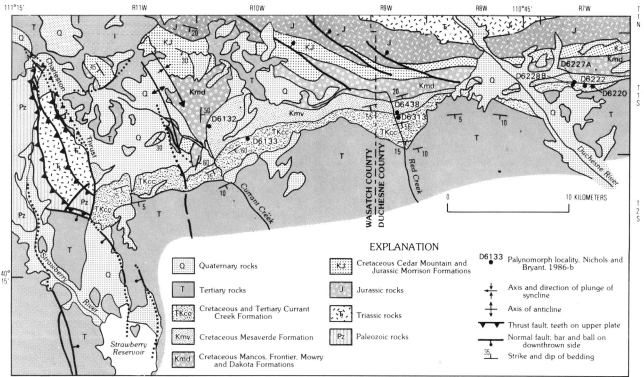

Figure 9. Geologic map of a part of the south flank of the Uinta uplift just east of the Charleston thrust showing fossil localities and the extent of the Currant Creek Formation.

ficult to date precisely and in many places crop out poorly. Also, younger Tertiary and Quaternary rocks conceal or overstep the older Teritary rocks in many places, obscuring stratigraphic and structural relations.

The structural history of the Uinta Mountains has been summarized by Forrester (1937), Walton (1944), and Hansen (1965). Recent studies have served primarily to refine the earlier ones.

The first uplift of part of the Uintas probably occurred in late Campanian to early Maastrichtian time. Drainage in the region was reorganized, and one or more small lakes were ponded in the Uinta Basin (Fouch and others, 1983, p. 322). Additional evidence of uplift at that time is found in the Currant Creek Formation. The Currant Creek is 1,460 m thick at its type locality and thins to less than 500 m east of the Duchesne River, due to some extent, to overlap by younger Tertiary conglomerate and sandstone. Paleocurrent studies show that the sediments of the Currant Creek were derived from the north and northwest (Isby and Picard, 1983). Clasts in conglomerate beds, especially in the lower part of the formation, were derived from Late Proterozoic quartzites such as those in the Cottonwood uplift and the Willard thrust sheet to the north (Isby, 1984). This indicates that the thrust belt, rather than the Uinta uplift, was the principal source for detritus in that part of the formation. However, clasts of Mesozoic rock are numerous in the upper part of the Currant Creek in the eastern part of its outcrop and were probably derived from nearby parts of the Uinta uplift (Isby, 1984). At the

west end of the south flank of the Uintas, the Currant Creek Formation unconformably overlies the Mesaverde Formation and cuts down-section in an eastward direction (Walton, 1944; Garvin, 1969; Fig. 9). At the base the Currant Creek beds dip as much as 50° to the south, subparallel to the underlying Mesaverde. Up-section in the Currant Creek, dips decrease to as little as 15°, suggesting that the Currant Creek was deposited during a period of uplift of the Uintas (Walton, 1944). Late Campanian–early Maastrichtian palynomorphs and Maastrichtian ostracodes (Nichols and Bryant, 1986b; R. C. Forrester, written communication, 1980) that are present in the basal 100 m of the Currant Creek do not date major uplift of the Uintas, and fossils that might help to date the time of dip change and the influx of clasts of Mesozoic rock were not found higher in the Currant Creek. A reasonable inference of the time of uplift during deposition of the upper part of the Currant Creek is late Maastrichtian or Paleocene.

On the north side of the western Uintas, evidence for late Campanian to early Maastrichtian uplift is lacking. There, the Hams Fork Member of the Evanston Formation unconformably overlies the Frontier Formation and at least some faults of the Absaroka thrust system (Fig. 10). Farther east, near the western terminus of the North Flank fault zone, the Hams Fork is overturned along splays of that fault zone. Based on limited exposures, the Hams Fork reveals no evidence of uplift of the Uinta arch during Hams Fork deposition. If uplift occurred at that time, it affected only a small area compared to the present area of the

Uinta uplift, and was located in the southern part of the structure. Although the basal part of the Currant Creek Formation is the same age as the Hams Fork, the upper part is probably significantly younger than the Hams Fork.

On the northwest flank of the Uintas, the Hams Fork is unconformably overlain by gently dipping conglomerate and sandstone of the Wasatch Formation (Fig. 10). The base of the Wasatch has been dated as late Paleocene in the Chalk Creek drainage east of Coalville (Nichols and Bryant, 1986a, sample D6104) and just east of the Weber River north of the Uintas (Nichols and Bryant, 1986a, samples D6305 and D6308). The age of the base of the Wasatch where it overlies the North Flank fault zone is not known, but it may be somewhat younger than late Paleocene because the formation overlaps the Uinta uplift. Consequently, the major movement on the North Flank fault zone in the western Uintas where it intersects the thrust belt predates the deposition of the Wasatch, and therefore, took place possibly in late Maastrichtian or more probably in early or middle Paleocene time. Farther east on the north flank of the Uintas, the Ericson Sandstone, which predates the initial major uplift of the Uintas and is the same age as the Hams Fork (Jacobson and Nichols, 1983), is unconformably overlain by the Fort Union Formation (Hansen, 1965). Palynomorphs of middle Paleocene age have been obtained from a sample collected by W. R. Hansen 50 m above the base of the Fort Union in SE¼,Sec.19,T.12N.,R.106W. This indicates a late Maastrichtian or early Paleocene age for the initial deformation in the Uintas about 100 km east of the thrust belt.

On the south flank of the Uinta Mountains, the Currant Creek Formation is overlapped by much younger alluvial deposits of the Duchesne River Formation of late Eocene and Oligocene age, which conceal older Tertiary stratigraphic units and structural relations. Many wells penetrate deep into the Tertiary section in the central part of the Uinta Basin. Data from wells in the deepest part of the basin, only 20 km south of the Uinta Mountains, show that a tongue of alluvial facies rocks of late Paleocene and early Eocene age overlies early and middle Paleocene lacustrine rocks (Fouch, 1981). The deposition of this tongue probably represents a period of erosion that accompanied movement on the buried Basin-Mountain boundary fault. The alluvial facies rocks are overlain by about 1,000 m of middle Eocene lacustrine facies rocks that represent the most extensive phase of Lake Uinta and a time of less uplift of the Uinta Mountains. Renewed uplift of the Uinta Mountains occurred in late Eocene and Oligocene time, producing the flood of clastic debris that buried the older Tertiary rocks in the north-central and northwestern parts of the Uinta Basin (see Fig. 13).

Relations between Uinta structures and structures of the Sevier orogenic belt

Data from surface studies bearing on relations between Uinta structures and Sevier orogenic belt structures are sparse. The data available allow the interpretation that the principal structural events in the Sevier belt occurred before those along the Uinta uplift.

A key area for interpreting the relations between the North Flank fault zone and the thrusts of the Sevier orogenic belt is north of the Weber River on the northwest flank of the Uinta Mountains in the Neil Creek–Crandall Canyon area. Figure 10 is a geologic map of the area and shows our interpretation of the stratigraphy and structure. Other workers have described the area somewhat differently (Lamerson, 1983, Pl. 12; Bradley, 1985). In our opinion, splays from the North Flank fault zone cut a section of Late Cretaceous rocks in the footwall of the Absaroka thrust; these rocks have been overturned by movement along the North Flank fault zone. The Oyster Ridge Sandstone Member of the Frontier and probably the upper (Coniacian) part of the Frontier are missing in the overturned section in the North Flank fault zone. Below the Absaroka thrust, rocks as young as the Frontier Formation are cut by the main splay of the North Flank fault zone. In the fault zone, a considerable thickness of interbedded marine and nonmarine rocks that contain beds of pebbly sandstone is equivalent to the Hilliard Shale, a marine unit of late Coniacian and Santonian age in southwestern Wyoming (Fig. 3). These beds are an intermediate facies between that of the Hilliard and the entirely nonmarine Henefer Formation and Echo Canyon Conglomerate in the Absaroka thrust sheet north of Coalville. Northward and up-section in the overturned rocks, conglomerate beds increase in abundance, and strata containing definitive palynomorphs decrease; some of the rocks may represent proximal facies of the Adaville Formation of early Campanian age. Coarse conglomerates forming the northern exposures of steeply dipping to overturned rocks constitute the Hams Fork Member of the Evanston Formation, as shown by the palynomorphs from a sample in upper Crandall Canyon (Nichols and Bryant, 1986a, sample D6592). The Hilliard, Adaville, and Hams Fork beneath the Absaroka thrust have been bent up, overturned, and faulted during movements along the North Flank fault zone sometime after deposition of the Hams Fork Member in late Campanian-early Maastrichtian time and before deposition of the Wasatch Formation in late Paleocene time (Fig. 11).

The time of movement on the North Flank fault zone may be further restricted. About 100 km to the north-northeast in southwestern Wyoming, some movement occurred along the Absaroka thrust in late Maastrichtian or early Paleocene time (Oriel and Armstrong, 1966). We infer that movement also occurred at this time just north of the Uinta Mountains along the Absaroka thrust. The gross structural concordance between the Frontier, Adaville-Hilliard, and Hams Fork units in the footwall of the Absaroka thrust suggests that the North Flank fault zone became active after the movement on the Absaroka thrust so initial movement on the North Flank fault zone was probably in middle Paleocene time.

To the west, in Crandall Canyon, west of the boundary between R.6E. and R.5E., movement on the North Flank fault zone was along the Absaroka thrust, which has been steepened for at least 3 km west by deformation related to movement on the

North Flank fault zone. Relations between the belt of Hams Fork Member that overlies the Dry Canyon fault at the north edge of Sec.26,T.1N.,R.5E. and the Absaroka fault in Crandall Canyon (Crittenden, 1974) are not exposed in the critical area in Sec.30,T.1N.,R.6E. In this covered area we have drawn a strand of the North Flank fault zone between steeply dipping to overturned sandstone, siltstone, and shale that have been mapped as undifferentiated Hilliard-Adaville and rocks covered by debris from the Wasatch Formation that forms the slope above. In the southwest corner of Sec.21,T.1N.,R.6E., marine shale contains *Baculites yokyamai* and *Inoceramus altersdorfensis* that indicate a very early Coniacian age (W. A. Cobban, written communication, 1982), and palynomorphs that indicate Coniacian age (Nichols and Bryant, 1986a, samples D6589, and D6591). We interpret this shale and associated sandstone to be in the upper part of the Frontier Formation and to occur in a slice along the Absaroka fault zone that is cut by the North Flank fault zone just south of the exposure. South of the Absaroka fault are vertical to

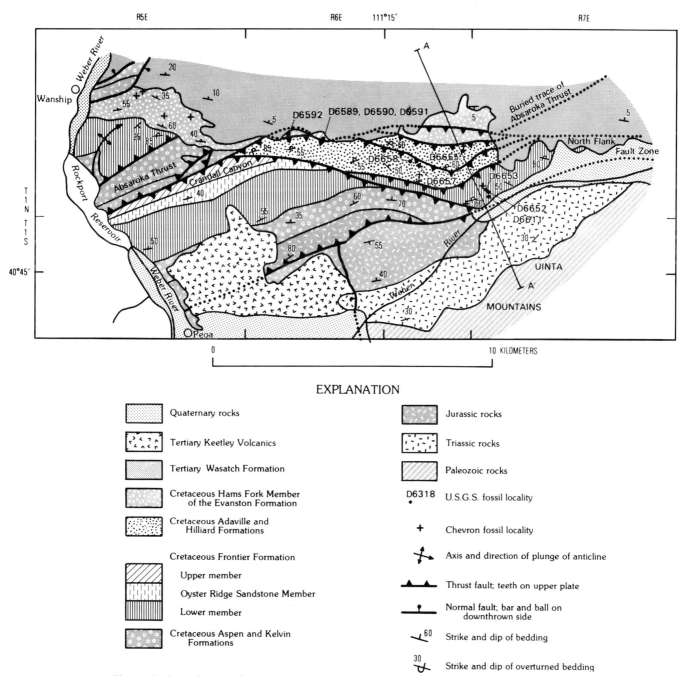

EXPLANATION

Figure 10. Geologic map of the Crandall Canyon–Neil Creek area showing palynomorph localities. Chevron fossil localities from Lamerson (1982). U.S. Geological Survey localities described by Nichols and Bryant (1986a). A-A′ line of cross section shown in Figure 11.

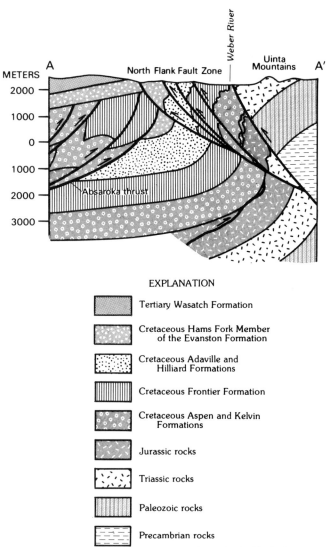

EXPLANATION

Tertiary Wasatch Formation

Cretaceous Hams Fork Member
of the Evanston Formation

Cretaceous Adaville and
Hilliard Formations

Cretaceous Frontier Formation

Cretaceous Aspen and Kelvin
Formations

Jurassic rocks

Triassic rocks

Paleozoic rocks

Precambrian rocks

Figure 11. Cross section through area where North Flank fault zone intersects the Absaroka thrust. Line of section shown on Figure 10.

overturned south-dipping beds of pebble conglomerate, sandstone, and siltstone of the Adaville-Hilliard unit. These data form the basis for the interpretations shown in Figure 10. Additional data are needed before these interpretations can be proved.

Another critical area for relations between the Uinta uplift and the thrust belt is where the Hogsback thrust intersects the Uinta uplift (Fig. 2). North of the Paleozoic rocks exposed along the north margin of the Uintas, conglomerates and sandstones of Eocene and Oligocene age conceal the Hogsback thrust and parts of the North Flank fault zone. Well and seismic data indicate that the Hogsback thrust is overridden by the North Flank fault zone (Blackstone, 1977; Kopania, 1985). About 150 km to the north, some movement on the Hogsback thrust was synchronous with deposition of the middle to early late Paleocene Hoback Formation and earlier than deposition of the late Paleocene Chappo Member of the Wasatch Formation (Oriel, 1969;

Dorr and Gingerich, 1980). A widespread unconformity between middle Paleocene and middle Upper Cretaceous rocks has been interpreted by Oriel (1969, p. M26) to mean that much of the movement may have been in the early to middle Paleocene, but movement could have occurred earlier in the Maastrichtian or late Campanian, younger than the Adaville Formation of early Campanian age but older than the Hoback Formation of middle and late Paleocene age.

The time of movement on the Hogsback thrust at the margin of the Uinta Mountains is not known, but the relations between the Hogsback thrust and the North Flank fault zone indicate that the North Flank fault is younger (Blackstone, 1977). The time of movement on the North Flank fault zone is inferred, from evidence in the Neil Creek–Perdue Creek area 40 km to the west of intersection with the Hogsback thrust, to be early or middle Paleocene. About 90 km to the east in Sweetwater County, Wyoming (SE¼,Sec.19,T.12N.,R.106W.), middle Paleocene palynomorphs were collected by W. R. Hansen 50 m above the base of the Fort Union Formation that overlies the Ericson Sandstone of late Campanian–early Maastrichtian age. These palynomorphs date the first uplift of the Uintas in that area as late Maastrichtian or early Paleocene. The relations cited above indicate that movement on the Hogsback thrust at the margin of the Uinta Mountains was before either early or middle Paleocene time.

We infer that the main movements in the Sevier belt took place before the principal episode of northward thrusting along the north flank of the western Uintas but not necessarily before some important deformation farther east in the range. Middle Paleocene or younger movements in the Sevier belt 100 km or less north of the Uintas are minor, although at least locally both the Medicine Butte and Absaroka thrusts were reactivated and had 1 to 2 km of movement after deposition of the Hams Fork Member of late Campanian–early Maastrichtian. The Medicine Butte thrust south of Evanston, Wyoming (T.14N.,R.120W.), had about 1 km of movement after deposition of the Hams Fork Member in late Campanian or early Maastrichtian time and before deposition of middle Paleocene rocks of the main body of the Evanston Formation. The middle Paleocene rocks were tipped up along another splay of the Medicine Butte fault but not overridden by the hanging-wall rocks (Lamerson, 1983, Pl. 10). The displacement of the Hams Fork Member by the Medicine Butte thrust near Evanston may represent the maximum displacement of that thrust. Farther south, displacement appears to be less (Lamerson, 1983, Pl. 12, unlabeled fault in the Preuss and Stump Sandstones above the Absaroka thrust). The post–Hams Fork movement on the Absaroka thrust may be relatively minor, compared to the movement that occurred after deposition of the Adaville in earliest Campanian time and before deposition of the Hams Fork in latest Campanian or early Maastrichtian time. Earliest movements on the Absaroka thrust system took place in Santonian time, as indicated by the age and location of the conglomerate at Little Muddy Creek (Royse and others, 1975; Jacobson and Nichols, 1983) in front of an early splay of that thrust fault system.

Displacement on the thrusts impinging on the Uinta uplift from the north shows no systematic relation with proximity to that uplift (Dixon, 1982). Displacement on the Absaroka thrust decreases quite fast south of Kemmerer, Wyoming, but more slowly as one approaches the Uinta uplift. Displacement on the Hogsback thrust is quite uniform from north of Kemmerer to the margin of the Uinta uplift. The Absaroka sheet is not bent around the Uinta uplift, but its displacement decreases rapidly to the south (Kopania, 1985). Cross sections based on seismic and well data (Lamerson, 1983) show that the Absaroka thrust rises stratigraphically in the footwall toward the Uintas. This relation may indicate a lateral ramp is present in the Absaroka thrust at the ancient crustal discontinuity at and west of the north flank of the Uinta Mountains. Little information is available on whether the Hogsback thrust cuts up-section to the south in the area where it is overridden by the North Flank fault zone. The absence of the Hogsback thrust in exposed Paleozoic rocks on the northwest flank of the Uintas led to the hypothesis that the Hogsback went down-section into a south-dipping thust ramp along the north margin of the Uintas and the Cottonwood uplift to the west. Later movements on this ramp may have formed the North Flank fault zone that cuts the Hogsback thrust (Bruhn and others, 1983, 1986).

The Cottonwood uplift

In the structural saddle between the Uinta uplift and the Cottonwood uplift, the late Eocene and early Oligocene Keetley volcanics unconformably overlie Pennsylvanian and younger rocks. A broad anticline existed here, and by the end of Eocene time, Cretaceous rocks had been eroded from its crest (Fig. 12). Where the late Eocene and early Oligocene rocks overlap rocks on the Absaroka thrust sheet to the north, they are unconformable on the Wasatch Formation of late Paleocene–early Eocene age. This relation suggests that some uplift occurred in middle or late Eocene time. Whether any of the structural relief on the Cottonwood uplift is related to uplift of the Uintas during early or middle Paleocene time is difficult to prove, but we believe that some uplift may have occurred then (Fig. 13).

Synorogenic deposits that can be related to the uplift of the Cottonwood area are scarce. In the upper East Canyon area north of the uplift, the youngest rocks deformed by movements associated with thrusting are Coniacian in age. They are unconformably overlain by the Wasatch Formation, the basal part of which is probably late Paleocene, judging by extrapolation of palynological data from east of the Weber River (Nichols and Bryant, 1986a, samples D6305, D6308; Figs. 4, 12). Paleocurrent data indicate that the Wasatch Formation north of the Cottonwood uplift was derived from the west rather than the south (Mann, 1974), so the part of the Cottonwood uplift east of the Wasatch fault apparently was not a source of the conglomerates and sandstones of the Wasatch Formation and was not high in late Paleocene and early Eocene time compared to land to the west. Conglomerates underlying and interbedded with the lower part of the

Keetley volcanics of latest Eocene and Oligocene age contain clasts that were derived from Mesozoic rocks exposed in the Cottonwood uplift. These conglomerates were deposited in broad valleys leading north and south away from the structural saddle between the Uinta and Cottonwood uplifts. Much of the present structural relief on the Cottonwood uplift was imposed on it by northeastward tilting of a block in the Wasatch Mountains during Neogene time, for Oligocene plutonic rocks now exposed in the Cottonwood uplift were emplaced several kilometers deeper on the west side than on the east side of the block (Fig. 12; Lawton and others, 1980; Bruhn and others, 1986).

The Cottonwood uplift or any uplift along trend with the Uinta Mountains is not apparent in the Oquirrh Mountains just to the west. No uplift occurred there after emplacement of the thrust sheets of Paleozoic rock now forming that range.

Folds mapped in the thrust sheets composing the Oquirrh Mountains, the Lake Mountains, and the West Traverse Range form an arcuate pattern around the projection of the west end of the Uinta axis (Beutner, 1977; Moore and Sorensen, 1979), suggesting that the thrust sheet impinged on a resistant high along that axis and was not folded after emplacement (Beutner, 1977).

RELATIONS BETWEEN THRUST SHEETS ACROSS THE ANCIENT CRUSTAL DISCONTINUITY

The Charleston thrust fault, where it separates the Cottonwood uplift from the thrust belt to the south, is inferred to be downthrown to the west side by the Wasatch fault. As a result of this offset, its trace is shifted north 10 to 15 km and is concealed under the Salt Lake valley (Crittenden, 1959, 1976). The trace of the fault is inferred to jog west around the north end of the Oquirrh Mountains along the ancient margin of the Archean craton.

Geologic relations in the subsurface at the south boundary of the northern Utah highland where it abuts the Charleston sheet are unknown. The relation of the Absaroka sheet, north of the Cottonwood uplift, with the Charleston is also uncertain. The Absaroka sheet has a similar, but probably not identical, history of movement to that of the Charleston sheet but contains a markedly different Proterozoic and Late Paleozoic stratigraphic section. This difference is primarily due to the origin of the Absaroka thrust sheet north of the ancient crustal discontinuity, which controlled the sedimentation during the Proterozoic and late Paleozoic.

Correlation between the Willard and Charleston thrust sheets, once inferred by Crittenden (1972, Fig. 4), no longer appears valid, because the Willard contains 5 km of Late Proterozoic clastic rocks, whereas the Charleston has a maximum of a few hundred meters. The Willard sheet is more comparable from a stratigraphic point of view to the Canyon Range sheet that lies above the Charleston, and that contains as much as 7.2 km of Late Proterozoic clastic rocks in the Sheeprock Mountains (Christie-Blick, 1982) (see Fig. 2).

The times of movement on the Willard and Charleston

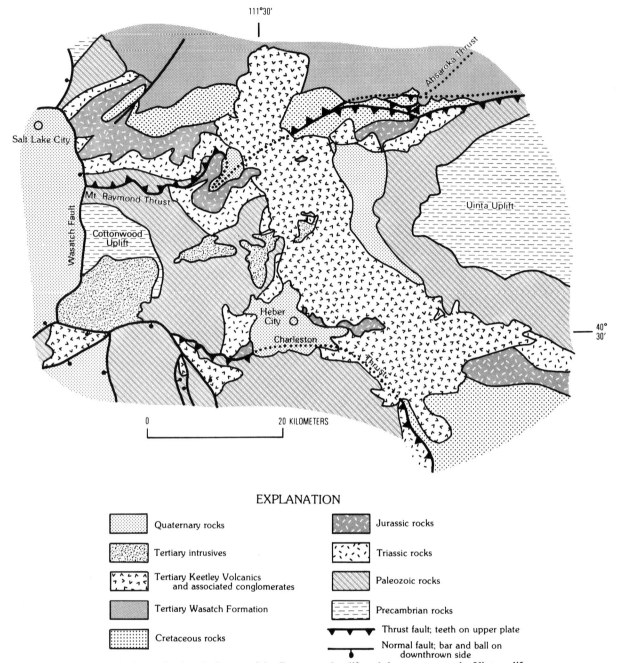

EXPLANATION

Quaternary rocks

Tertiary intrusives

Tertiary Keetley Volcanics
and associated conglomerates

Tertiary Wasatch Formation

Cretaceous rocks

Jurassic rocks

Triassic rocks

Paleozoic rocks

Precambrian rocks

Thrust fault; teeth on upper plate

Normal fault; bar and ball on
downthrown side

Figure 12. Generalized geologic map of the Cottonwood uplift and the area east to the Uinta uplift.

thrusts are different. As mentioned above, evidence favors a Campanian age of movement on the Charleston. The Willard thrust has been connected under many kilometers of cover with the Paris thrust (Fig. 2) of southeastern Idaho by numerous workers, beginning with Richards and Mansfield (1912) and continuing to the present. However, recent mapping by Dover (1985) has supported the conclusion of Armstrong and Cressman (1963, p. J18) that the Paris thrust, as mapped west of Bear Lake, dies out southward. The Willard may connect either with the Meade thrust (Dover, 1983, 1985) or with a lower splay of the

Paris thrust that is apparent on seismic surveys conducted north of Bear Lake (F. Royse, oral communication, 1985). In either case, movement on the Willard is probably older than that on the Charleston. If the Willard correlates with the Paris, Early Cretaceous movement is indicated, because erosion of the hanging wall of the Paris thrust furnished sediment to the Ephraim Conglomerate and other formations of the Gannet Group of that age (Mansfield, 1927; Armstrong and Cressman, 1963, p. J9-14). Conversely, if the Willard correlates with the Meade thrust, which cuts rocks of the Gannet Group, then a late Early Cretaceous or

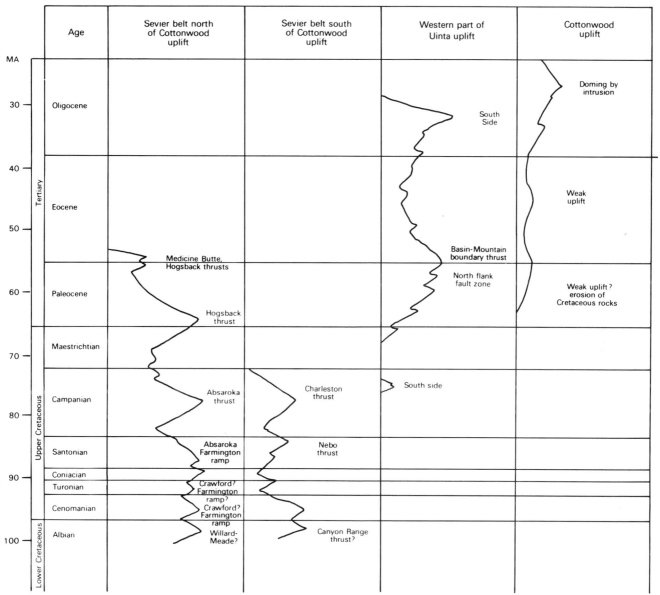

Figure 13. Summary of interpreted times of orogenic movements in the western part of the Uinta uplift, the Cottonwood uplift, and the nearby parts of the Sevier orogenic belt. Line indicates times and relative intensities of deformation; intensity of deformation increases to the right.

younger age is indicated. The Wayan Formation of Albian age may be the synorogenic product of major movement on the Meade thrust (Oriel and Armstrong, 1986), indicating that movement on the Meade was earlier than that on the Crawford thrust, rather than being closely related to movement on the Crawford thrust, as suggested by Royse and others (1975).

CONCLUSION

The ancient crustal boundary at the south margin of the Archean craton was an intermittently active feature that influenced sedimentation in Precambrian and Paleozoic time. Marked differences in stratigraphic thicknesses of Middle and Late Proter-

ozoic rocks north and south of this discontinuity in and west of the Wasatch Mountains affected the patterns of later deformation in the Sevier orogenic belt on either side. In Middle and Late Proterozoic time the area immediately north of the discontinuity was positive in relation to the area immediately south, and by Cambrian time, 5 or 6 km of sedimentary rocks had been deposited just south of it, whereas none has survived on the north side. Rocks of the late Paleozoic Oquirrh basin are thicker on the south side of the discontinuity than the north side. The thinner section of sedimentary rocks north of the discontinuity may have led to greater involvement of basement rocks in the thrusting in that area as reflected by uplift of the northern Utah highland along the Farmington ramp. To the south, where the Proterozoic and Paleozoic section is thicker, no such ramp affecting a large volume of basement rock is known, although 50 to 100 km south of the discontinuity, Precambrian sedimentary and basement rocks are involved in the Charleston thrust sheet. The ancient crustal discontinuity was an important cross-strike discontinuity in the Sevier orogenic belt.

The timing of movements on the various structures in the Uinta uplift and the nearby Sevier orogenic belt is poorly constrained in much of the area. A summation of the interpretations presented here is shown in Figure 13. The data available can be interpreted to show that the earliest uplift in the vicinity of the Uinta Mountains occurred before movement on the Hogsback thrust (Fig. 13), and that the main thrusting in this part of the Sevier orogenic belt took place before the main uplift of the western Uinta Mountains. The main deformation along the Uinta uplift was overlapped in time by minor movements in the Sevier belt as close as 70 km from the Uinta Mountains.

ACKNOWLEDGMENTS

Over the years of our work in the Salt Lake City 1° × 2° quadrangle, many people have contributed to our knowledge and understanding of the complexities of the region. We particularly thank the late M. D. Crittenden, Jr., for his advice and for the legacy of fine geologic maps and reports he left our profession. We thank Frank Royse, Jr., P. R. Lamerson, and S. R. Jacobson of Chevron USA, R. L. Bruhn, S. L. Beck, J. S. Isby, and M. J. Bradley of the University of Utah, Lehi Hintze of Brigham Young University, and S. S. Oriel, J. D. Dover, I. J. Witkind, E. A. Merewether, C. M. Molenaar, W. A. Cobban, T. D. Fouch, W. R. Hansen, W. J. Cashion, C. W. Naeser, R. F. Marvin, C. A. Wallace, W. J. Moore, and M. L. Sorensen of the U.S. Geological Survey for their help and advice during this work. We also thank R. L. Wheeler, E. R. Cressman, W. C. Swadley, and R. L. Bruhn for helpful informal and formal reviews.

REFERENCES CITED

Armstrong, F. C., and Cressman, E. R., 1963, The Bannock thrust zone, southeastern Idaho: U.S. Geological Survey Professional Paper 347-J, 22 p.

Armstrong, R. L., 1968a, Sevier orogenic belt in Nevada and Utah: Geological Society of America Bulletin, v. 79, no. 4, p. 429–458.

—— , 1968b, The Cordilleran miogeosyncline in Nevada and Utah: Utah Geological and Mineralogical Survey Bulletin 68, 58 p.

Baker, A. A., 1973, Geologic map of the Springville Quadrangle, Utah County, Utah: U.S. Geological Survey Geological Quadrangle Map GQ-1103, scale 1:24,000.

—— , 1976, Geologic map of the west half of the Strawberry Valley Quadrangle, Utah: U.S. Geological Survey Miscellaneous Investigations Map I-931, scale 1:63,360, 11 p. text.

Baker, A. A., and Crittenden, M. D., Jr., 1961, Geology of the Timpanogos Cave Quadrangle, Utah: U.S. Geological Survey Geologic Quadrangle Map GQ-132, scale 1:24,000.

Blackstone, D. L., Jr., 1977, The overthrust belt salient of the Cordilleran fold belt, western Wyoming–southeastern Idaho–northeastern Utah, *in* Heisey, E. L., and others, eds., Rocky Mountain thrust belt; Geology and resources: Wyoming Geological Association 29th Annual Field Conference Guidebook, p. 367–384.

Beutner, E. C., 1977, Causes and consequences of curvature in the Sevier orogenic belt, Utah to Montana, *in* Heisey, E. L., and others, eds., Rocky Mountain thrust belt; Geology and resources: Wyoming Geological Association 29th Annual Field Conference Guidebook, p. 353–365.

Bradley, M. D., 1985, Geometry and kinematics of deformation along the intersection of the Absaroka thrust system and the Uinta axis, Summit County, Utah: Geological Society of America Abstracts with Programs, v. 17, p. 210.

Brady, M. J., 1965, Thrusting in the southern Wasatch Mountains, Utah: Brigham Young University Geology Studies, v. 12, p. 3–53.

Bruhn, R. L., Picard, M. D., and Beck, S. L., 1983, Mesozoic and early Tertiary structure and sedimentology of the central Wasatch Mountains, Uinta Mountains and Uinta Basin, *in* Gurgel, K. D., ed., Geologic excursions in the overthrust belt and metamorphic core complexes of the intermountain region: Utah Geological and Mineral Survey Special Studies 59, p. 63–105.

Bruhn, R. L., Picard, M. D., and Isby, J. S., 1986, Tectonics and sedimentology of Uinta arch, western Uinta Mountains, and Uinta Basin, *in* Peterson, J. A., ed., Paleotectonics and sedimentation in the Rocky Mountain region, United States: American Association of Petroleum Geologists Memoir 32, p. 333–352.

Bryant, B., 1985, Structural ancestry of the Uinta Mountains, *in* Picard, M. D., ed., Geology and energy resources, Uinta Basin, Utah: Utah Geological Association Publication 12, p. 115–120.

Bryant, B., and Nichols, D. J., 1985, Synorogenic conglomerate east of Salt Lake City; New data and interpretations: Geological Society of America Abstracts with Programs, v. 17, p. 210.

Campbell, J. A., 1975, Structural geology and petroleum potential of the south flank of the Uinta Mountain uplift, northeastern Utah: Utah Geology, v. 2, p. 129–132.

Christie-Blick, N., 1982, Upper Proterozoic and Lower Cambrian rocks of the Sheeprock Mountains, Utah: Regional correlation and significance: Geological Society of America Bulletin, v. 93, p. 735–750.

Cobban, W. A., and Reeside, J. B., Jr., 1952, Frontier Formation, Wyoming, and adjacent areas: American Association of Petroleum Geologists Bulletin, v. 36, p. 1913–1961.

Crawford, K. A., 1979, Sedimentology and tectonic significance of the Late Cretaceous-Paleocene Echo Canyon and Evanston synorogenic conglomerates of the north-central Utah thrust belt [M.S. thesis]: Madison, University of Wisconsin, 143 p.

Crittenden, M. D., Jr., 1959, Mississippian stratigraphy of the central Wasatch and western Uinta Mountains, Utah: Intermountain Association of Petroleum Geologists 10th Annual Field Conference Guidebook, p. 63–74.

—— , 1961, Magnitude of thrust faulting in northern Utah, *in* Short papers in the geologic and hydrologic sciences: U.S. Geological Survey Professional Paper 424-D, Art. 335, p. D128–D131.

—— , 1963, Emendation of the Kelvin Formation and Morrison Formation near Salt Lake City, Utah: U.S. Geological Survey Professional Paper 475-B, p. B95–B98.

—— , 1969, Interaction between Sevier orogenic belt and Uinta structures near Salt Lake City, Utah: Geological Society of America Abstracts with Programs, v. 1, pt. 5, p. 8.

—— , 1972, Willard thrust and the Cache autochthon, Utah: Geological Society of America Bulletin, v. 83, p. 2871–2880.

—— , 1974, Regional extent and age of thrusts near Rockport Reservoir and relation to possible exploration targets in northern Utah: American Association of Petroleum Geologists Bulletin, v. 58, p. 2428–2435.

—— , 1976, Stratigraphic and structural setting of the Cottonwood area, Utah, *in* Hill, J. G., ed., Symposium on geology of the Cordilleran hingeline: Denver, Colorado, Rocky Mountain Association of Geologists, p. 363–379.

Dixon, J. S., 1982, Regional structural synthesis, Wyoming salient of western overthrust belt: American Association of Petroleum Geologists Bulletin, v. 66, p. 1560–1580.

Dorr, J. A., Jr., and Gingerich, P. B., 1980, Early Cenozoic mammalian paleontology, geologic structure, and tectonic history in the overthrust belt near LaBarge, western Wyoming: University of Wyoming Contributions to Geology, v. 8, p. 101–115.

Dover, J. H., 1983, New data on thrusts in northeastern Utah and southwestern Wyoming: Geological Society of America Abstracts with Programs, v. 15, p. 318–19.

—— , 1985, Geologic map and structure sections of the Logan 30′ by 60′ Quadrangle, Utah and Wyoming: U.S. Geological Survey Open-File Report 85-0216, scale 1:100,000.

Eardley, A. J., 1939, Structure of the Wasatch–Great Basin region: Geological Society of America Bulletin, v. 50, p. 1277–1310.

Farmer, G. L., and DePaolo, D. J., 1984, Origin of Mesozoic and Tertiary granite in the western United States and implications for pre-Mesozoic crustal structure; Part 2, Nd and Sr isotopic studies of unmineralized and Cu and Mo-mineralized granite in the Precambrian craton: Journal of Geophysical Research, v. 89, no. B12, p. 10141–10160.

Forrester, J. D., 1937, Structure of the Uinta Mountains: Geological Society of America Bulletin, v. 48, p. 631–666.

Fouch, T. D., 1981, Distribution of rock types, lithologic groups, and interpreted depositional environment for some lower Tertiary and Upper Cretaceous rocks from outcrops at Willow Creek–Indian Canyon through the subsurface of Duchesne and Altamont oil fields, southwest to north-central part of the Uinta Basin, Utah: U.S. Geological Survey Oil and Gas Investigations Chart OC-81.

Fouch, T. D., Lawton, T. F., Nichols, D. J., Cashion, W. B., and Cobban, W. A., 1983, Patterns and timing of synorogenic sedimentation in Upper Cretaceous rocks of central and northeast Utah, *in* Reynolds, M. W., Dolly, E., and Spearing, D. R., eds., Symposium on Mesozoic paleogeography of west-central United States: Society of Economic Paleontologists and Mineralogists, Rocky Mountain section, p. 305–336.

Garvin, R. F., 1969, Stratigraphy and economic significance, Currant Creek Formation, northwest Uinta Basin, Utah: Utah Geological and Minerological Survey Special Studies 27, 62 p.

Granger, A. E., 1953, Stratigraphy of the Wasatch Range near Salt Lake City, Utah: U.S. Geological Survey Circular 296, 14 p.

Gries, R., 1981, Oil and gas prospecting beneath the Precambrian of foreland thrust plates in the Rocky Mountains: The Mountain Geologist, v. 8, no. 1, p. 1–18.

Hansen, W. R., 1957, Structural features of the Uinta arch: Intermountain Association Petroleum Geologists 8th Annual Field Conference Guidebook, p. 35–39.

—— , 1965, Geology of the Flaming Gorge area, Utah-Colorado-Wyoming: U.S. Geological Survey Professional Paper 490, 196 p.

Hintze, L., 1973, Geologic history of Utah: Brigham Young University Geology Studies, v. 20, pt. 3, 181 p.

Imlay, R. W., 1980, Jurassic paleobiogeography of the conterminous United States in its continental setting: U.S. Geological Survey Professional Paper 1062, 134 p.

Isby, J. S., 1984, The petrology and tectonic significance of the Currant Creek Formation, north-central Utah [M.S. thesis]: Salt Lake, University of Utah, 134 p.

Isby, J. S., and Picard, M. D., 1983, Currant Creek Formation; Record of tectonism in Sevier-Laramide orogenic belt, north-central Utah: University of Wyoming Contributions to Geology, v. 22, p. 91–100.

Jacobson, S. R., and Nichols, D. J., 1983, Palynological dating of syntectonic units in the Utah-Wyoming thrust belt; The Evanston Formation, Echo Canyon Conglomerate, and Little Muddy Creek Conglomerate, *in* Powers, R. B., ed., Geologic studies of the Cordilleran thrust belt, 1982: Denver, Colorado, Rocky Mountain Association of Geologists, p. 735–750.

Jefferson, W. S., 1982, Structural and stratigraphic relations of Upper Cretaceous to lower Tertiary orogenic sediments in the Cedar Hills, Utah, *in* Neilson, D. L., ed., Overthrust belt of Utah: Utah Geological Association Publication 10, p. 65–80.

Jordan, T. E., and Douglass, R. C., 1980, Paleogeography and structural development of the Late Pennsylvanian to Early Permian Oquirrh Basin, northwestern Utah, *in* Fouch, T. D., and Magathan, E. R., eds., Paleozoic paleogeography of the west-central United States, Rocky Mountain paleogeography symposium 1: Denver, Colorado, Society of Economic Paleontologists and Mineralogists, Rocky Mountain Section, p. 217–237.

Kopania, A. A., 1985, The effects of basement-cored buttresses and major stratigraphic changes on thrust sheets; An example from the Idaho-Wyoming-Utah thrust belt: Geological Society of America Abstracts with Programs, v. 17, p. 249.

Lamerson, P. R., 1983, The Fossil Basin and its relationship to the Absaroka thrust system, Wyoming and Utah, *in* Powers, R. B., ed., Geologic studies of the Cordilleran thrust belt, 1982: Denver, Colorado, Rocky Mountain Association of Geologists, p. 279–340.

Larsen, W. N., 1957, Petrology and structure of Antelope Island, Davis County, Utah [Ph.D. thesis]: Salt Lake City, University of Utah, 142 p.

Lawton, T. F., 1982, Lithofacies correlations within the Upper Cretaceous Indianola Group, central Utah, *in* Nielson, D. L., ed., Overthrust belt of Utah: Utah Geological Society Publication 10, p. 199–213.

—— , 1985, Style and timing of frontal structures, thrust belt, central Utah: American Association of Petroleum Geologists Bulletin, v. 69, p. 1145–1159.

Lawton, T. F., John, D. A., and Moore, W. J., 1980, Levels of emplacement of mid-Tertiary plutons in the central Wasatch Mountains, Utah: Geological Society of America Abstracts with Programs, v. 12, p. 278.

Lochman-Balk, C., 1972, Cambrian system, *in* Geologic atlas of the Rocky Mountain region: Denver, Colorado, Rocky Mountain Association of Geologists, p. 60–75.

Mann, D. C., 1974, Clastic Laramide sediments of the Wasatch hinterland; Northwestern Utah [M.S. thesis]: Salt Lake City, University of Utah, 112 p.

Mansfield, G. R., 1927, Geography, geology, and mineral resources of part of southeastern Idaho: U.S. Geological Survey Professional Paper 152, 453 p.

Moore, W. J., and Sorensen, M. L., 1979, Geologic map of the Tooele 1° by 2° Quadrangle, Utah: U.S. Geological Survey Miscellaneous Investigation Map I-1132, scale 1:250,000.

Morris, E. C., 1953, Geology of the Big Piney area, Summit County, Utah [M.S. thesis]: Salt Lake City, University of Utah, 66 p.

Mullens, T. E., 1971, Reconnaissance study of the Wasatch, Evanston, and Echo Canyon Formations in part of northern Utah: U.S. Geological Survey Bulletin 1311-A, 31 p.

Mullens, T. E., and Laraway, W. A., 1964, Geology of the Devils Slide Quadrangle, Morgan and Summit Counties, Utah: U.S. Geological Survey Mineral Investigations Field Studies Map MF-290, scale 1:24,000.

Nichols, D. J., and Bryant, B., 1986a, Palynological data from Cretaceous and early Tertiary rocks in the Salt Lake City 30′ by 60′ Quadrangle, Utah: U.S Geological Survey Open-file Report 86–116, 18 p.

—— , 1986b, Palynology of the Currant Creek and Mesaverde Formations in the Currant Creek-Duchesne River area, Duchesne and Wasatch Counties, Utah: U.S. Geological Survey Open-file Report 86-160, 7 p.

Nichols, D. J., and Ott, H. L., 1978, Biostratigraphy and evolution of the *Momipites-Carypollenites* lineage in the early Tertiary in the Wind River Basin, Wyoming: Palynology, v. 2, p. 93–112.

Nichols, D. J., and Warner, M. A., 1978, Palynology, age, and correlation of the Wanship Formation and their implication for the tectonic history of northeastern Utah: Geology, v. 6, p. 430–433.

Nichols, D. J., Jacobson, S. R., and Tschudy, R. H., 1983, Cretaceous palynomorph biozones for the central and northern Rocky Mountains region of the United States, *in* Powers, R. B., ed., Geologic studies of the Cordilleran thrust belt, 1982: Denver, Colorado, Rocky Mountain Association of Geologists, p. 721–733.

Oriel, S. S., 1969, Geology of the Fort Hill Quadrangle, Lincoln County, Wyoming: U.S. Geological Survey Professional Paper 594-M, 39 p.

Oriel, S. S., and Armstrong, F. C., 1966, *Times* of thrusting in Idaho-Wyoming thrust belt; Reply: American Association of Petroleum Geologists Bulletin, v. 50, p. 2614–2621.

——, 1986, Tectonic development of Idaho-Wyoming thrust belt: Authors' commentary, *in* Peterson, J. A., ed., Paleotectonics and sedimentation in the Rocky Mountain region: American Association of Petroleum Geologists Memoir, p. 267–279.

Richards, R. W., and Mansfield, G. R., 1912, The Bannock overthrust; A major fault in southeastern Idaho: Journal of Geology, v. 20, p. 681–707.

Ritzma, H. R., 1969, Tectonic resume, Uinta Mountains: Intermountain Association of Geologists 16th Annual Field Conference Guidebook of the Uinta Mountains, p. 57–63.

Roberts, R. J., Crittenden, M. D., Jr., Tooker, E. W., Morris, H. T., Hose, R. K., and Cheney, T. M., 1965, Pennsylvanian and Permian basins in northwestern Utah, northeastern Nevada, and south-central Idaho: American Association of Petroleum Geologists Bulletin, v. 49, p. 1926–1956.

Royse, F., Jr., Warner, M. A., and Reese, D. L., 1975, Thrust belt structural geometry and related stratigraphic problems, Wyoming–Idaho–northern Utah, *in* Bolyard, D. W., ed., Deep drilling frontiers of the central Rocky Mountains: Denver, Colorado, Rocky Mountain Association of Geologists Symposium, p. 41–54.

Smith, R. B., and Bruhn, R. L., 1984, Intraplate extensional tectonics of the eastern Basin-Range; Inferences on structural style from seismic reflection data, regional tectonics, and thermal-mechanical models of brittle-ductile deformation: Journal of Geophysical Research, v. 89, no. B7, p. 5733–5762.

Spieker, E. M., 1946, Late Mesozoic and early Cenozoic history of central Utah: U.S. Geological Survey Profssional Paper 205-D, p. 117–161.

Standlee, L. A., 1983, Structure and stratigraphy of Jurassic rocks in central Utah; Their influence on tectonic development of the Cordilleran foreland thrust belt, *in* Powers, R. B., ed., Geologic studies of the Cordilleran thrust belt, 1982: Denver, Colorado, Rocky Mountain Association of Geologists, p. 357–382.

Stewart, J. H., 1972, Initial deposits in the Cordilleran geosyncline; Evidence of a late Precambrian (850 m.y.) continental separation: Geological Society of America Bulletin, v. 83, p. 1345–1360.

Stokes, W. L., 1952, Salt-generated structures of the Colorado Plateau and possible analogies [abs.]: American Association of Petroleum Geologists Bulletin, v. 36, p. 961.

——, 1956, Tectonics of the Wasatch Plateau and near-by areas [abs.]: American Association of Petroleum Geologists Bulletin, v. 40, p. 790.

Wallace, C. A., 1972, A basin analysis of the upper Precambrian Uinta Mountain Group [Ph.D. thesis]: Santa Barbara, University of California, 412 p.

Walton, P. T., 1944, Geology of the Cretaceous of the Uinta Basin, Utah: Geological Society of America Bulletin, v. 55, p. 91–130.

Wheeler, R. L., Winslow, M., Horne, R. R., Dean, S., Kulander, B., Drahavzal, J. A., Gold, D. P., Gilbert, O. E., Jr., Werner, E., Sites, R., and Perry, W. J., Jr., 1979, Cross-strike structual discontinuities in thrust belts, mostly Appalachian: Southeastern Geology, v. 20, p. 193–203.

Witkind, I. J., 1982, Salt diapirism in central Utah, *in* Nielson, D. L., ed., Overthrust belt of Utah: Utah Geological Association Publication 10, p. 13–30.

Witkind, I. J., Standlee, L. A., and Maley, K. F., 1986, Age and correlation of Cretaceous rocks previously assigned to the Morrison(?) Formation, Sanpete–Sevier Valley area, central Utah: U.S. Geological Survey Bulletin 1584, 9 p.

Manuscript Accepted by the Society February 9, 1988

Geological Society of America
Memoir 171
1988

Structural interactions between the Uinta arch and the overthrust belt, north-central Utah; Implications of strain trajectories and displacement modeling

Michael D. Bradley* and Ronald L. Bruhn
Department of Geology and Geophysics, University of Utah, Salt Lake City, Utah 84112

ABSTRACT

Analysis of mesoscopic structures in the Jurassic Twin Creek Formation reveals two major periods of deformation in the central Wasatch and westernmost Uinta Mountains during Late Cretaceous through early Eocene time. Spaced cleavage, extension veins, and tension gash bands developed early in the evolution of the Mount Raymond thrust fault and were subsequently folded around first-phase folds as deformation progressed. First-phase folds occur as trains of northeast-plunging, asymmetric anticlines and synclines, with an overall eastward vergence. A second spaced cleavage and associated extension veins and tension gash bands developed after the first-phase folding and prior to the development of second-phase folds. The first-phase and early second-phase structures were subsequently folded into east-northeast–trending second-phase anticlines and synclines during evolution of the Uinta arch.

The Uinta arch in the central Wasatch and westernmost Uinta Mountains formed during Late Cretaceous to early Eocene time, partly in response to movement on the Hogsback thrust. Two possible models, which are consistent with the field data for the evolution of the Uinta arch, are (1) dextral wrench strain along the southern termination of the Hogsback thrust, and (2) dextral transpression along a south-dipping ramp where the Hogsback thrust cut down along the northern boundary of the basin in which the Middle Proterozoic Uinta Mountain Group was deposited.

INTRODUCTION

The geometric and kinematic relations between décollement-controlled overthrusts of the Sevier orogenic belt and fault-bounded foreland uplifts of Laramide age in the Rocky Mountains of northcentral Utah and southwestern Wyoming have been long-standing problems (Roberts and others, 1965; Hansen, 1965, 1984; Sales, 1968; Beutner, 1977; Crittenden, 1976; Bruhn and others, 1983, 1986). In north-central Utah, there was a spatial and temporal overlap between the two types of structures. Here, a complex history of structural interference occurred between the north-trending overthrusts that developed above regional décollement during Late Cretaceous and early Tertiary time, and the east-trending basement uplift, the Uinta arch (Crittenden, 1976; Beutner, 1977; Bruhn and others, 1983, 1986).

This study documents and analyzes the orientation of the regional incremental strain field during the period of structural interaction between the overthrusts and the Uinta arch. We have utilized the orientations of spaced cleavage planes, extension veins, and tension gash bands in the Jurassic Twin Creek Formation to determine the spatial and sequential distribution of bulk shortening and extension. The Twin Creek Formation was chosen for this topical study because of its widespread outcrop and the frequent occurrence of syntectonic spaced cleavage and vein arrays (Mitra and others, 1984). The results of the incremental strain orientation analysis are then used to discuss regional tectonic models for the evolution of the overthrust belt and Uinta Mountains.

*Present address: Mobil Exploration and Producing U.S. Inc., P.O. Box 5444, Denver, Colorado 80217.

REGIONAL GEOLOGY

The Uinta arch is a major east-trending anticlinorium extending from western Colorado through the Wasatch Mountains in north-central Utah (Fig. 1). The western part of the Uinta arch, which includes the western end of the Uinta Mountains and the Cottonwood segment of the Uinta arch (Cottonwood arch) in the central Wasatch Mountains, divides the north-trending overthrust belt into two structural segments. These segments are marked by abrupt changes in stratigraphy within allochthons and by differences in the age of deformation and amount of thrust displacement (Royse and others, 1975; Crittenden, 1976; Beutner, 1977; Bruhn and others, 1983, 1986).

The Uinta Mountains are separated by a structural and physiographic depression from the main exposures of the Uinta arch in the Wasatch Mountains. This depression, named Rhodes Valley, is marked on its eastern side by a west-plunging closure of strata at the western end of the Uinta Mountains (Fig. 1). A similar, east-plunging closure occurs in strata along the western margin of the saddle. However, steeply north-dipping Mesozoic strata in the north limb of the Uinta arch can be traced almost continuously along strike to the west, cutting directly across the north end of Rhodes Valley and continuing into the steeply dipping limb of the Cottonwood arch in the Wasatch Mountains. This is clear evidence that the Uinta arch and Cottonwood arch were originally part of the same large, north-vergent anticlinorium.

The structural saddle may have evolved partly in two separate phases. Separation on the North Flank thrust fault in the Uinta Mountains decreases westward, and the surface trace of the fault ends adjacent to the west-plunging closure in the mountain range. Here, structural closure may owe its origin to westward-decreasing separation on this thrust system. If so, the closure presumably developed during the Paleogene, when the North Flank thrust was last active.

The east-plunging structural closure in the Uinta arch may be partly Late Cenozoic in age. The southwestern end of the arch has been uplifted at least 5 km with respect to the northern end as the result of normal faulting in the Wasatch normal fault zone during the last 17 m.y. (Bruhn an others, 1986; Parry and Bruhn, 1986). This differential uplift was accommodated by eastward tilting of the Uinta arch, which locally may be as great as 20°. This rotation may account for much of the eastward-plunge of the arch into Rhodes Valley.

The Uinta Mountains evolved over an extended period of time, beginning in the Late Cretaceous and ending in the Eocene or earliest Oligocene. In the Flaming Gorge area, a latest Maastrichtian to early Paleocene rise of the eastern Uinta Mountains is recorded in the Fort Union Formation. Hansen (1965) estimated that 2.4 to 3.4 km of uplift and erosion was necessary for pebbles of Cretaceous Mowry Shale to be deposited as clasts in the Paleocene Fort Union Formation. Evidence for a Late Cretaceous rise in the western Uinta Mountains is less obvious, but Isby and Picard (1983) and Bruhn and others (1986) believe that part of the northerly derived conglomerates in the Maastrichtian-Paleocene(?) Currant Creek Formation, along the southwestern flank of the Uintas, was eroded from the Uinta Mountains. Crittenden (1976) suggested that the rotation of the Mount Raymond thrust about an east-trending fold axis occurred in Late Cretaceous; Bruhn and others (1986) have suggested that the Uinta arch may have been initiated at this time, but they considered the main period of deformation to be Paleocene to early Eocene, coinciding with displacement on the Hogsback thrust system. Consequently, between latest Cretaceous and early Eocene, the Uinta arch may have extended from northwestern Colorado to at least the central Wasatch Mountains.

A major Eocene to earliest Oligocene rise of the Uinta Mountains is recorded by the thick synorogenic sediments deposited in the Uinta and Green River basins. Paleocurrent analysis and inverted cobble stratigraphy in the Green River Formation show that the deposits resulted from progressive unroofing of the Uinta Mountains. Presumably, much of the uplift of the Uinta Mountains occurred at this time (Hansen, 1965, 1984; Bruhn and others, 1983; Gries, 1983). This period of uplift is not considered here.

Thrust faulting immediately north of the Uinta arch on the Absaroka and Hogsback thrust systems was partly concurrent with movement on the Charleston thrust system south of the Uinta arch (Royce and others, 1975; Dixon, 1982; Lamerson, 1983). However, crystalline basement in the upper sheet of the Absaroka thrust system is directly overlain by a thin section of Lower Paleozoic strata, and Upper Paleozoic strata are only 2 km thick. In contrast, the base of the Late Cretaceous (Bryant and Nichols, this volume) Charleston allochthon, located along the southern edge of the Uinta arch, consists of Upper Proterozoic strata overlain by a thin section of Lower Paleozoic rocks. The Upper Paleozoic section is as much as 10 km thick, consisting mostly of shallow marine Pennsylvanian and Permian strata deposited in the ancient Oquirrh basin. These Upper Paleozoic rocks are more than twice the thickness of equivalent strata in the Absaroka allochthon immediately to the north (Hintze, 1973).

The Absaroka thrust in southwestern Wyoming has two major splays: An older splay active in pre–middle Santonian time, and a younger splay active during Campanian-Maastrichtian time (Lamerson, 1982). Southeast of Evanston, Wyoming, Eocene-age Wasatch Formation overlaps both splays of the Absaroka thrust, but the two splays can be traced on seismic reflection profiles and in boreholes southward from Wyoming into north-central Utah. The older splay emerges near Rockport Lake, Utah, where it has been rotated to steep dips within the north-dipping limb of the Uinta arch. Here, the fault is mapped as the Crandall Canyon thrust (Crittenden, 1974; Bradley, 1984, 1985). West of Rockport Lake, the Crandall Canyon thrust is buried under Oligocene-age Keetley volcanic rocks but emerges farther west in the northern limb of the Cottonwood arch, where it is mapped as the Mount Raymond thrust (Fig. 1; Mount, 1952; Crittenden, 1974; Lamerson, 1983; Bradley, 1986). Folding of the Mount Raymond and Crandall Canyon thrusts and the subse-

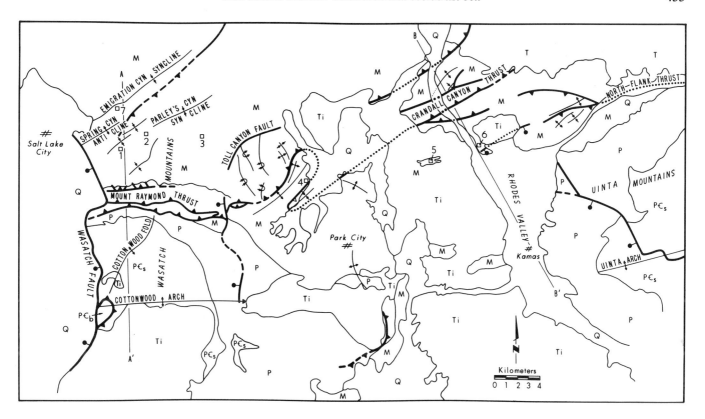

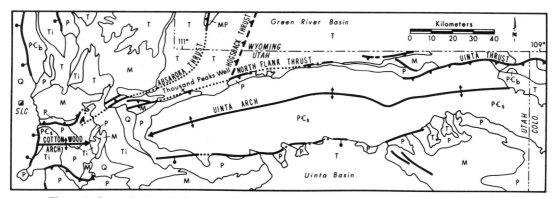

Figure 1. Generalized geologic maps of northeastern Utah and the western end of the Uinta arch.
Modified from Lamerson (1982) and Bruhn and others (1983).

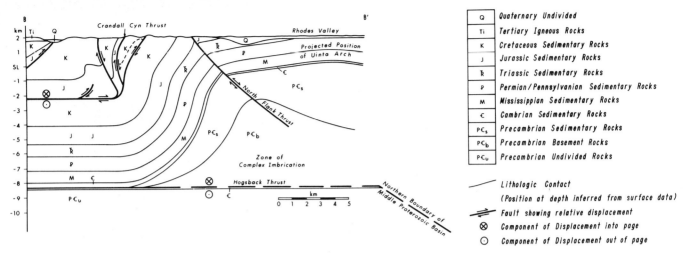

Figure 2. Northwest-southeast structure section along the Weber River from Wanship, Utah to Rhodes Valley. See Figure 1: B-B′. Note that the Hogsback thrust does not remain in Cambrian strata but cuts down stratigraphic section to the south. The Hogsback thrust cuts deeper into the crust along the northern boundary of the Middle Proterozoic basin in which the Uinta Mountain Group was deposited, thus forming a south-dipping ramp in the Hogsback décollement.

quent erosion of the Uinta arch have exposed the system of fault ramps and folds composing the southern end of the Absaroka (Crandall Canyon and Mount Raymond) thrust system.

The Hogsback thrust system was active during Late Cretaceous to early Eocene time (Royse, 1985; Bryant and Nichols, this volume). West of the Wasatch Front, the basal décollement of this fault system was located in crystalline basement, perhaps occupying the same décollement as the earlier Absaroka thrust system in that area. The Hogsback décollement stepped upsection toward the east, ramping through Paleozoic and Mesozoic rocks and carrying the Absaroka thrust system about 24 km eastward in its hanging wall. The southern edge of the Hogsback thrust system has not been mapped on the surface either within the Uinta Mountains or in the central Wasatch Mountains. Therefore, we assume the southern edge of the thrust system is located in the subsurface, in the footwall of the North Flank thrust of the Uinta Mountains.

Detailed mapping and cross-section construction in the westernmost Uinta Mountains, done by one of us (M. B.), places constraints on the structural position of the Hogsback décollement in this area (Fig. 2). Projection of borehole data in the Thousand Peaks well (Fig. 1), Moffit Basin, Utah, 70 km east of the Wasatch Front, shows that the Hogsback thrust lies within Precambrian/Cambrian strata. Therefore, in the Wasatch Mountains the Hogsback thrust does not lie any higher than Cambrian strata. The thrust between the Early Proterozoic Little Willow Series and the Middle Proterozoic Big Cottonwood Formation exposed in the Cottonwood arch (Fig. 1) cannot be the Hogsback thrust because this thrust is folded into the Cottonwood fold (not arch), which is older than the Hogsback thrust. Because the Hogsback thrust is not exposed in the Cottonwood arch, the décollement must lie deeper than the exposed section of the metamorphic rocks of the Precambrian Little Willow Series. The observa-

tion that the Hogsback thrust system is apparently not exposed in the core of the Uinta arch led Bruhn and others (1983) to speculate that it may have rooted downward, toward the south, into crystalline basement beneath the arch. In their structural model, Precambran and younger rocks exposed in the Uinta arch occupy the hanging wall of the Hogsback thrust system, above an east-striking, south-dipping ramp that penetrated deep into the crust (Fig. 3). The east-directed translation on the Hogsback thrust sheet contained a northward component of crustal shortening at the western end of the Uinta arch where the Hogsback thrust sheet was forced up a south-dipping ramp formed along the northern boundary of the basin in which the Middle Proterozoic Uinta Mountain Group was deposited. This north-directed crustal shortening resulted in the formation of the Uinta arch (second-phase deformation), which folded the ramp developed in the Absaroka thrust in the Wasatch Mountains (Fig. 4) and Rockport Lake region.

STRUCTURAL ANALYSIS

Topical Study

Tectonic models evaluating the structural evolution of this region tend to be based on displacement fields inferred either from plate tectonic models (Sales, 1968; Hamilton, 1981; Gries, 1983) or from the orientations and apparent displacement of fold trains (Hansen, 1965, 1984; Crittenden, 1976; Beutner, 1977). We decided that documenting the orientation and sequential history of formation of tectonic stylolites and extension veins throughout the area encompassing the western end of the Uinta Arch might provide new information on the evolution of the regional strain field. In this study, we interpret mesoscopic structures preserved in the Jurassic Twin Creek Formation because the formation outcrops throughout the area of interest, and carbonate strata in the formation, particularly micrite, contain abundant spaced cleavage (tectonic stylolites) and extension veins (Fig. 5).

Procedure

Field Observations. We selected a wide distribution of outcrops of the Twin Creek Formation within the western Uinta arch. Each outcrop was treated as a structural domain and its position on folds noted. The orientations of spaced cleavage planes, extension veins, tension gash bands, and fibers on fault surfaces and bedding planes were measured at each outcrop. Each outcrop was inspected to ensure that the measurements represented the average orientation of discrete sets of structures. Special effort was made to determine temporal relations between the various types of mesoscopic structures and between multiple sets of each type of structure.

The spaced cleavage is generally stylolitic, oriented at a high angle to bedding, and occurs in two distinct sets. The cleavage is defined by zones of clay-rich insoluble material concentrated by the preferential removal of calcite during deformation (Mitra and others, 1984). Material dissolved along the spaced cleavage planes was presumably precipitated as calcite in adjacent extension veins and tension gash bands.

We interpreted the relation between the strain field and mesoscopic structures as follows. The shortening direction was presumably perpendicular to the spaced cleavage planes, paralleling the long axis of stylolitic columns. The incremental extension

axis was assumed to parallel the long axes of mineral fibers in extension veins, or to be approximately perpendicular to the vein walls where fibers were not developed. The shortening and extension axes of tension gash bands were plotted to bisect the angles between conjugate sets of bands, with the two strain axes plotted in the appropriate quadrant for the sense of slip on the shear zones containing the gashes. Shortening and extension axes of single tension gash bands were plotted at 45° to the gash band boundary.

The mesoscopic structures formed during two phases of deformation, based on the observed cross-cutting relationships between structures of the same type. We considered sets of spaced cleavage planes, extension veins, and tension gash bands within an outcrop to belong to a discrete deformation phase if the shortening and/or extension directions indicated by the various structures were all consistent. That is, the extension axis indicated by vein-filling material should be essentially perpendicular to the shortening axis indicated by associated spaced cleavage planes, and the strain axes inferred from the orientation and slip directions of tension gash band sets should be subparallel to those inferred from the coexisting extension veins and spaced cleavage.

Two phases of deformation were recognized. The first-phase spaced cleavage, extension veins and tension gash bands formed throughout the study region and are present in all outcrops of the Twin Creek Formation that contain these types of structures. The second-phase mesoscopic structures cross-cut the first set. This second set occurs more sporadically than the first, both throughout the study area and within individual outcrops.

Structural Corrections. The field data were plotted on lower hemisphere projections to show both the orientation of the mesoscopic structures and the attitudes of inferred strain axes

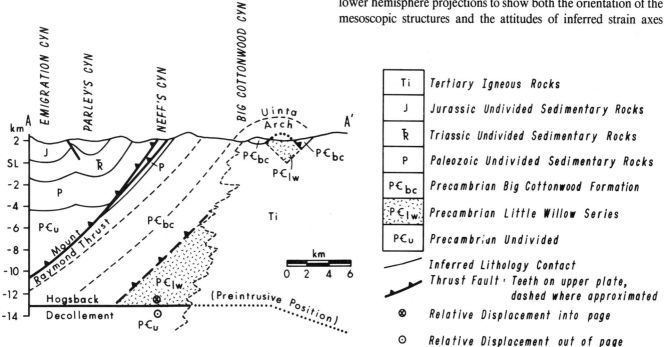

Figure 3. North-south structure section in the Wasatch Mountains from Emigration Canyon to Little Cottonwood Canyon. See Figure 1: A-A'. Note that the Hogsback décollement ramps down to the south. Modified from Bruhn and others (1986).

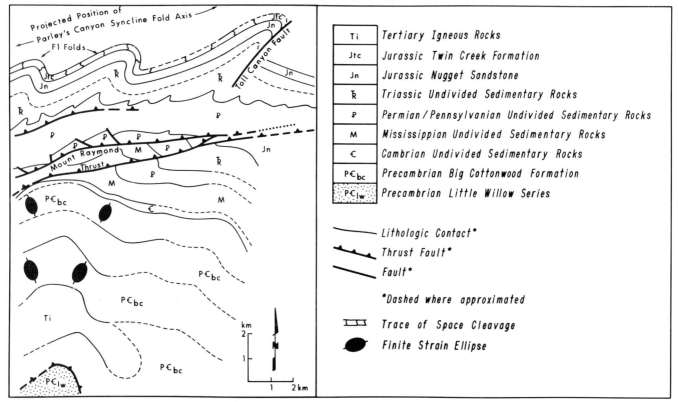

Figure 4. Down-plunge projection of the Cottonwood fold. Note that the Mount Raymond thrust is a back-limb thrust fault in the fold and that crystalline basement is deformed in the fold core. Projection was constructed using mapping of Crittenden (1965a,b).

uncorrected for any structural rotations. A second set of stereo-plots was then constructed in which the strain axes were rotated back to their original positions, based on inferences concerning the folding history of the study area. No correction was applied for regional rotations in the western Wasatch Mountains caused by Late Cenozoic displacement on the Wasatch normal fault zone (Parry and Bruhn, 1986; Bruhn and others, 1987). This correction would add an additional, poorly defined rotation to the data set. In the area of this study the correction is probably less than 20° about a northeast-trending axis. Trials using rotations up to the maximum estimate of 20° indicated that neglecting it would not significantly affect our results.

The study area was affected by two phases of folding: an early phase (F1) that developed during movement on the Mount Raymond thrust fault, and a later (F2) phase associated with formation of the Uinta arch (Crittenden, 1976). The earliest folds (F1) occur as trains of northeast-plunging, asymmetric anticlines and synclines with a variable, but overall eastward vergence (Fig. 4). These folds die out structurally downward into the Mount Raymond thrust, which is their décollement. The Cottonwood fold, in the footwall of the Mount Raymond thrust, is also attributable to F1 deformation. The F1 folds must have developed between middle Turonian (truncation of the Oyster Ridge Sandstone Member of the Frontier Formation by the

Crandall Canyon thrust) and late Maastrichtian (overlap of the Crandall Canyon thrust by the Hams Fork Conglomerate Member of the Evanston Formation), based on the regional correlation of the Mount Raymond and Crandall Canyon thrusts.

The first-phase folds and Mount Raymond thrust were subsequently folded into a set of east-northeast–trending anticlines and synclines during the latest folding phase (F2). Three large folds of this set occur in the study area: the Emigration Canyon syncline, the Spring Canyon anticline, and Parley's Canyon syncline (Fig. 1). Folds of this phase presumably formed during the evolution of the Uinta arch (Crittenden, 1976), and strata folded into the Spring Canyon anticline and Emigration Canyon syncline are unconformably overlain by the Paleocene to early Eocene Wasatch Formation. Therefore, the second-fold phase developed prior to middle Eocene and presumably after late Maastrichtian. This time period overlaps with the time of regional eastward displacement on the Hogsback thrust system, which may underlie the western end of the Uinta arch (Bruhn and others, 1983, 1986), and late-stage movement on the Absaroka thrust.

The relation of the first- and second-phase sets of mesoscopic structures to these fold phases is evident in the field. The first-phase spaced cleavage, extension veins, and tension gash band boundary planes are perpendicular to subperpendicular to bedding, and folded about the first phase folds. The spaced cleavage planes are oriented subparallel to the fold hinges, but not parallel to the folds' axial planes. Rather, the cleavage is folded with bedding about the first-phase fold hinges. These structural relations imply that the first set of mesoscopic structures formed prior to, or early synkinematically to, the earliest phase of folding. Notably, the orientation of the spaced cleavage planes and extension veins indicates (1) bedding plane–parallel shortening approximately perpendicular to the F1 hinges; (2) extension subparallel to the axes prior to folding; and locally, (3) a component of layer parallel shear, with the shearing direction toward the east-southeast.

The second spaced cleavage and associated extension veins and tension gash bands developed after the first (F1) folding and prior to, or early in the development of, second-phase (F2) folds. Evidence for this timing is as follows: (1) the second-phase cleavage cuts across first-phase fold hinges at a high angle, and (2) the second-phase mesoscopic structural planes are folded along with their enveloping bedding planes into the F2 folds. The orientation of the strain axes relative to bedding indicates that shortening and extension were approximately bedding plane parallel.

The rotations of strain axes and mesoscopic structures to their original orientation was done as follows. Second-phase folds were "unfolded" by one of two procedures. In those areas where no first-phase folds were present, the rotations were accomplished solely about second-phase fold axes. Bedding and mesoscopic structures were first rotated by an amount needed to bring the second-phase fold axes to horizontal. Then, an appropriate rotation was applied such that bedding was restored to horizontal. In these outcrops, both first- and second-phase structures were restored to their estimated original attitudes by this procedure.

A more complicated procedure was required for those outcrops where first- and second-phase folds were both present. In this case, the orientation data were rotated by bringing the second-phase fold axis to horizontal and removing the effects of bed rotation due to that folding, which was followed by rotation of the first-phase fold axis to horizontal. On completion of this procedure, the second-phase structures and inferred strain axes were considered as rotated to their original orientation. A third

Figure 5. Well-developed spaced cleavage and extension veins in the Jurassic Twin Creek Formation exposed in Parley's Canyon. The planar surfaces are bedding planes. Note camera lens cap for scale.

rotation about the "corrected" F1 fold axes was then applied to first-phase structures and strain axes by rotating all data the amount required to bring bedding planes back to horizontal.

Shortening directions at each field station (domain) are given in Table 1. The combined results from field stations 1 through 5 and 7 are indicated in stereoplots (Fig. 6), which show average shortening directions of 298° and 010° for first- and second-phase deformations, respectively. The shortening directions at station 6 are 285° and 343°, which may reflect errors in the assumed rotations or a change in the shortening directions.

First-phase shortening axes were originally subhorizontal, oriented east to southeast, and extension axes were subhorizontal, oriented north to northeast. Presumably, this strain field developed either pre- or synkinematically to the first-phase folds; that is, during the early phase of development of the Mount Raymond thrust.

Second-phase shortening and extension axes were also subhorizontal, but their orientations are markedly different than those of the first phase. A clockwise rotation in the strain field of 45° to 60° is indicated. We do not know if this rotation resulted from a progressive and temporally continuous change in principal

TABLE 1. PRINCIPAL SHORTENING DIRECTIONS DETERMINED AT EACH FIELD STATION FOR THE TWO PHASES OF DEFORMATION

Field Station Number	Phase 1	Phase 2
1	295°	010°
2	296°	008°
3	288°	010°
4	298°	*
5	300°	*
6	285°	343°
7	085°	353°

*Second-phase structures not well developed.

strain directions, or whether it reflects two discrete, temporally separated events. At a few locales in Parley's Canyon syncline, first-phase cleavage planes are sigmoidal in shape, with the tips of the stylolitic surfaces deflected toward the strike of coexisting second-phase cleavage planes. Such geometry is consistent with rotational strain during cleavage formation (Ramsay and Huber, 1983), but this geometry is not ubiquitous throughout the study area. In most outcrops the second- and first-phase cleavages are confined to distinct and separate orientation ranges, with first-phase cleavage planes truncated or apparently offset by removal of material during formation of the second-phase spaced cleavage.

STRUCTURAL INTERPRETATION AND MODELING

First-phase strain field

The original orientation of the first-phase spaced cleavage, extension veins, and tension gash bands in the Twin Creek Formation is consistent with deformation during evolution of the Mount Raymond thrust fault at the southern end of the regional Absaroka system of thrust faults. Notably, spaced cleavage formation preceded development of the F1 folds. Similar conclusions were reached by Mitra and others (1984) in their study of spaced cleavage in the Twin Creek Formation in an adjacent part of the overthrust belt. They concluded that the spaced cleavage commonly originated in the hanging wall, either pre- or early synkinematically with the formation of ramp anticlines. The hanging-wall rocks of the Mount Raymond thrust were located in a similar position prior to thrusting, in that the Mount Raymond thrust ramped toward the east, climbing section out of the back limb of the Cottonwood fold in the western Wasatch Mountains (Fig. 4). Note that the shortening axis in the footwall of the Mount Raymond thrust is folded about the Cottonwood fold.

In the easternmost domains, the Twin Creek Formation is located in the footwall of the Crandall Canyon thrust (the eastern end of the Mount Raymond Thrust), structurally below oblique-slip ramps that originally cut upsection from the Twin Creek Formation to Cretaceous rocks in the eastern edge of the thrust system. These ramps originally had a northeast strike and dipped northwest (Bradley, 1985, 1986).

Second-phase deformation model

A satisfactory model for the second phase of deformation must account for: (1) a clockwise rotation in strain axes of 45° to 60° between the first and second phase of deformation, (2) formation of second-phase spaced cleavage and tension gash bands, and (3) subsequent buckling of the rocks into a series of east-northeast–trending folds. Temporally, this period of deformation was probably latest Cretaceous to early Eocene in age, directly overlapping in space and time with (1) late-stage movement on the Absaroka thrust, (2) the early period of formation of the Uinta Mountains to the east, and (3) thrusting on the Hogsback thrust system.

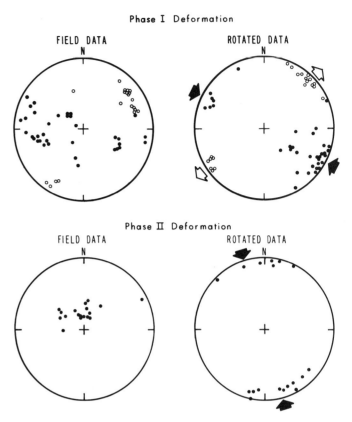

Figure 6. Stereoplots of poles to spaced cleavage (solid) and extension veins (open) for first- and second-phase deformations. Arrows show shortening (shaded) and extension directions. Combined data from field stations 1 through 5 and 7.

A progressive southward decrease in displacement within the Absaroka thrust sheet (Mount Raymond thrust) could be accommodated by distributed shear. The principal shortening direction for such a distributed shear zone would be subparallel to the shortening direction for second-phase deformation, and could explain some of the second-phase deformation features. Indeed, angular unconformities within the core of the Parley's Canyon syncline suggest that this fold initially formed in Late Cretaceous, and was later tightened by coaxial deformation during rise of the Uinta arch. However, we conclude that second-phase deformational features are attributable to the building of the Uinta arch, which was the major regional deformational event that folded the Mount Raymond thrust.

Several hypotheses have been proposed for the evolution of the Uinta arch. Here, we briefly review these hypotheses in order to establish the predicted displacement fields of crustal rocks during deformation. Simple strain factorization models are then constructed. The results of the strain modeling are compared with the observed strain orientations at the western end of the Uinta arch to constrain and partially test the various tectonic hypotheses for the evolution of the arch.

Two plate tectonic models proposed for the Uinta arch require a significant component of sinistral slip parallel to the structural axis of the arch. Sales (1968) interpreted the Uinta arch as a crust-thick drag fold formed in a sinistral shear couple. In his model, the sinistral shear was generated between an eastward moving Colorado Plateau subplate on the south and a counterclockwise-rotating Wyoming subplate to the north.

Hamilton (1981) hypothesized that the Uinta arch formed during a 2° to 4° clockwise rotation of the Colorado Plateau subplate relative to the North American interior, the Euler pole for this rotation being in northern Texas. In the Uinta arch, the rotation resulted in sinistral transpression. Hamilton attributed the rotation of the Colorado Plateau to a landward transfer of stress from the western continental margin due to a change in the convergence rate and angle of subduction of the Farallon plate beneath the North American plate.

On a smaller scale, several authors have emphasized the problems of structural interaction between eastward-moving thrust sheets and the Uinta arch. Crittenden (1976) proposed several episodes of east-directed shortening, alternating with episodes of north-south shortening in the Uinta arch during Middle to Late Cretaceous. He emphasized the conceptual difficulty with this model, which invoked rapid fluctuations in principal stress orientation, and suggested that the Uinta arch may have lain within a dominantly north-south compressive regime that was occasionally influenced by thrust sheets gravity-sliding eastward in response to uplift in western Utah and Nevada.

An alternate proposal by Beutner (1977) viewed the Uinta arch as a rigid structural buttress to eastward thrust propagation. In this model, the eastward-advancing thrust sheets were refracted about the Uinta reentrant or "buttress" in a manner similar to the refraction of ocean waves about a promontory.

Subsequently, Bruhn and others (1983, 1986) suggested that the Uinta arch formed during latest Cretaceous to Eocene, when the Hogsback décollement cut down-section along strike, merging into a south-dipping thrust ramp that extended beneath the region of the Uinta arch. They noted that the early phase of uplift in the east-central Uinta Mountains also occurred during this interval and inferred that the south-dipping ramp system extended along the entire length of the Uinta arch, well east of the overthrust belt. The regional displacement field for this model is potentially complex. Two possible scenarios predict significantly different strain and displacement fields in the arch. In the first model, all of the eastward displacement on the Hogsback thrust system is accommodated by discrete slip on the south-dipping ramp beneath the Uinta arch. In this case, the crust south of the arch moved ≈24 km eastward with respect to the footwall of the Hogsback thrust to the north of the Uinta arch. An alternative, and perhaps more realistic model, is that part of the 24 km of displacement on the Hogsback thrust was distributed as strain within the Uinta arch. This model has the intriguing result of creating dextral strain within the arch and sinistral slip along the south-dipping sidewall ramp at depth.

Strain factorization modeling

Strain factorization modeling (dividing strain into pure and simple shear components) is a useful procedure for comparing hypothetical strain and displacement fields with those inferred from structural data (Sanderson, 1982). The results provide a guide for identifying tectonic histories that are compatible with the natural deformation, but the results are not unique. The modeling predicts the orientation and magnitudes of the finite strain, and is therefore most powerful when field and laboratory measurements of both these parameters are available for direct comparison with the strain factorization. However, structural orientation data alone, when interpreted in terms of finite strain orientations, are useful in constraining potential deformation histories. This is the approach taken here.

A three-dimensional block diagram illustrating potential deformation components in the Uinta arch is given in Figure 7. Details of the stratigraphy and structure have been omitted to allow us to concentrate on modeling regional displacement and strain fields. The model is based partly on the inferred relation between the Hogsback thrust décollement and the Uinta arch during latest Cretaceous to early Eocene time. The Hogsback décollement is shown in the northern half of the diagram, where it occupies a flat in the Lower Paleozoic section, just above the crystalline basement. The décollement dips southward at some unknown angle (ρ) beneath the Uinta structural axis (the arch), occupying an east-striking and south-dipping fault ramp that cuts deeply into crystalline basement. Presumably, this ramp developed because of reactivation of the Precambrian Uinta aulacogen(?), and it may have continued far to the east of the diagram, throughout the entire length of the Uinta Mountains. It is only in the westernmost Uinta Mountains and the Cottonwood arch that the Hogsback thrust could have terminated southward into this ramp, and that is the area to which we confine our discussion.

In general, several components of strain and displacement can be accommodated in the model (Fig. 7). Displacement within the arch is accommodated by net slip on the south-dipping fault ramp, with an eastward component (δ_W) and a reverse (northward) component (δ_R). Strain is partitioned into several components: (1) $\gamma_W = \tan \Psi_W$, a horizontal wrench strain caused by angular shear (Ψ_W); (2) $\gamma_T = \tan \Psi_t$, which arises from angular shear Ψ_t; and (3) $\gamma_R = \tan \Psi_r$, which results from angular shear Ψ_r. These components of horizontal shortening and angular shear could lead to three pure shear strains, α_x and α_y, parallel and perpendicular to strike, respectively, and α_z in the vertical direction.

We consider only the possible role of the horizontal angular shear (Ψ_W) and pure shear components ($\alpha_{x,y,z}$) in the formation of the Uinta arch. This approach is motivated by our desire to test proposed tectonic models, which infer either sinistral slip and/or strain along the trend of the arch combined with a shortening component perpendicular to its trend (Sales, 1968; Hamilton, 1981; Bruhn and others, 1983, 1986), or dextral shear due to

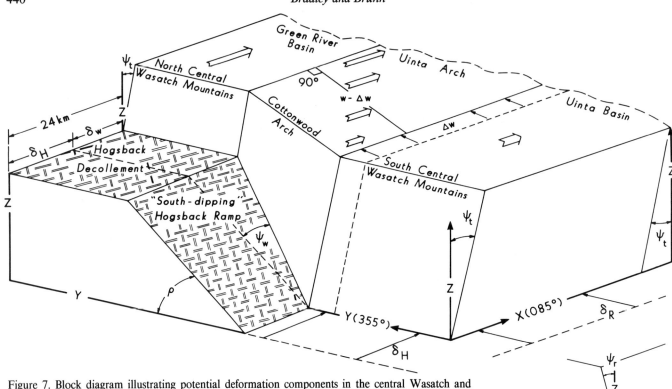

Figure 7. Block diagram illustrating potential deformation components in the central Wasatch and western Uinta Mountains during Late Cretaceous to early Eocene time. ρ = dip of Hogsback ramp; δ_W = component of eastward translation of the Uinta arch; δ_H = component of eastward translation south of the Uinta arch; δ_R = component of northward translation of the Uinta arch; Ψ_w = horizontal wrench-type angular shear; Ψ_t = thrust-type (east-directed) angular shear; Ψ_r = reverse-type (north directed) angular shear (inset); Δw = component of shortening across the Uinta arch (w = original width of the structural axis); X, Y, Z = cartesian reference axes; $\Rightarrow$ = hanging wall displacement directions and relative magnitudes.

thrust sheet curvature (Beutner, 1977). Consequently, we arbitrarily set Ψ_t and Ψ_r equal to zero. Potential effects of these latter strain components will be briefly discussed, but quantitative modeling is deferred. The displacements, δ_H and δ_R, are not necessarily zero, and we will briefly discuss their relations to the deformation after developing and discussing a simple strain factorization model. The reader is reminded that, in general, there need be no relation, a priori, between displacement and strain.

Two simple, two-dimensional strain models involving pure shear strain and simple shear strain are introduced first. We then proceed to the more general, three-dimensional transpression model, which allows us to mix components of pure and simple shear (Fig. 8; Sanderson and Marchini, 1984). The key features of this latter model are horizontal shortening (S) in an angular direction β to the boundary of the deformed zone, no volume loss during deformation, and homogeneous strain.

Three cartesian reference axes are chosen: X = horizontal and oriented parallel to the long axis of the deformed zone, Y = horizontal and oriented perpendicular to X, and Z = oriented vertically (Fig. 7). Deformation is modeled by factorizing the strain into the two components γ_w (simple shear) and $\alpha^{-1} = \alpha_y$ (pure shear). The desired results are the orientation and magnitudes of the three principal finite stretches, Λ_1, Λ_2, and Λ_3.

The plane containing Λ_1 and Λ_2 is interpreted physically as equivalent to the plane of second-phase spaced cleavage, or the axial planes of F2 folds. These structural planes are not principal planes of total finite strain in the rock, because the second-phase cleavage and F2 folds developed during only part of the total strain history. The magnitudes of principal stretches are not discussed because we have not reported strain measurements in this study.

The strain field within the transpression zone is controlled by the angle β and shortening component S (Fig. 8). At $\beta = 90°$, the deformation is two-dimensional pure shear, with shortening (α^{-1}) parallel to Y and vertical extension (α_z) parallel to Z. Alternatively, $\beta < 90°$ results in both simple and pure shear strain components within the deformed zone, with the amount of simple shear increasing as β decreases at constant α^{-1}. The sense of shear varies from dextral to sinistral, depending on the sign of β. If β = zero, the strain field is no longer transpressional and the model degenerates into a two-dimensional simple shear zone of either dextral or sinistral type.

One strain axis is always vertical in the transpressional model, and for most combinations of S and β, this is the greatest extension axis (Λ_1). This characteristic of the model has a significant implication concerning deformation on the inferred south-

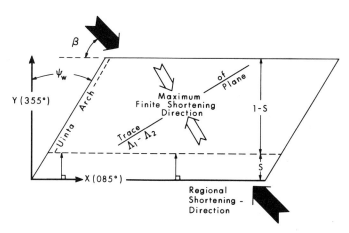

Figure 8. General transpression model. Horizontal shortening (S) occurs at angle, β, to the boundary of the deformed zone; Ψ_w = horizontal angular shear. X and Y are horizontal reference axes. See text for discussion.

dipping ramp beneath the Uinta arch (Fig. 7), in that we are assuming that any movement on this ramp was confined to displacement (slip on a discrete fault zone) and not distributed as strain in the hanging wall. The structural implications of this assumption are discussed below.

Case 1: Two-dimensional pure shear (β = 90°, S > 0)

The X-axis is chosen parallel with the estimated trend of the Uinta arch, about 085°. The deformation history is coaxial, with α^{-1} parallel to Y. The shortening across the axis is accommodated by vertical extension (Λ_1). The strike of the Λ_1–Λ_2 plane is then 085°, parallel to the structural axis (Fig. 9A).

The strike of second-phase spaced cleavage predicted by this model (085°) lies in the southeastern margin of the structurally corrected strike distribution of second-phase spaced cleavage measurements (060° to 100°). The fact that most of the corrected cleavage strikes lie counterclockwise with respect to 085° could simply reflect errors in removing the effects of F2 folding or could be a potentially significant discrepancy between observation and model. However, the model is not compatible with observed horizontal extension (Fig. 6) and F2 axial plane strikes, lying 15° to 25° counterclockwise of the predicted strike (085°). Also, F2 folds, which postdate the second-phase cleavage, have steep axial planes; their hinges trend 060° to 070°. The axial planes of the folds dip steeply south, not consistent with horizontal, coaxial shortening.

Case 2: Vertical simple shear zone (β = 0°, S = 0)

Ideal simple shear deformation is two-dimensional, with shortening and extension confined to the plane perpendicular to the shear zone boundary (Ramsay and Graham, 1970). In Figure 9B,C, the shear zone boundary is assumed to dip vertically and strike parallel to the Uinta structural axis at 085°. The strike of the Λ_1–Λ_2 plane is totally different for dextral vs. sinistral

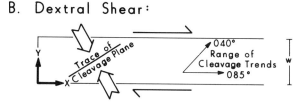

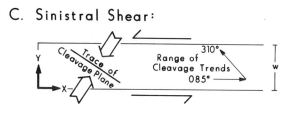

Figure 9. A, Two-dimensional pure shear model. The strike of the Λ_1-Λ_2 plane is parallel to the Uinta structural axis, 085°. B and C, Vertical simple shear models. The shear zone boundary is vertical with strike parallel to the Uinta structural axis. The predicted strike of the Λ_1-Λ_2 plane differs for dextral (B) vs. sinistral (C) shear. The field data support a dextral shear model; w is the original width of the zone (Uinta arch); Δw is the amount of shortening; X and Y are horizontal reference axes.

shear. The plane must strike between 040° and 085° in dextral shear, but between 085° and 130° (310°) for sinistral shear. The corrected second-phase cleavage strikes between 060° and 100° (280°), with the preponderance of strikes lying in the range 060° to 080°. Clearly, if a vertical shear zone is used to model deformation in the Uinta arch, the model must involve dextral rather than sinistral shear. Notice that the F2-fold axial planes also strike in a manner compatible with dextral simple shear, but not with sinistral shear. This model is also consistent with subhorizontal extension as reflected in rotated measurements of extension axes.

Case 3: Transpression ($0°$ < β < $90°$, S > 0)

Finite strain in a zone of transpressive deformation is uniquely defined by the orientation (β) of the shortening axis and the fractional shortening (S) parallel to β (Fig. 8; Sanderson and Marchini, 1984). The wrench strain (γ_W) and shortening strain (α^{-1}) are directly related to β and S through the following equations:

$$\alpha^{-1} = (1-S) \quad (1)$$

$$\gamma_W = \left(\frac{S}{1-S}\right)\cot\beta \quad (2)$$

The variation of γ_W with α^{-1} is plotted in Figure 10 for various values of contstant β to illustrate the relation between wrench strain and stretch in the transpression model. Notice that γ_W increases rapidly as α^{-1} decreases (shortening increases) for small β.

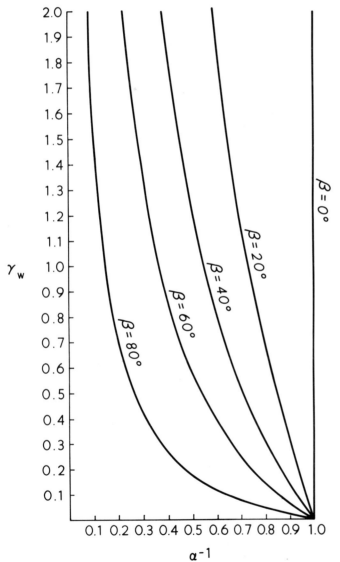

Figure 10. The variation of γ_W and α^{-1} is plotted for various values of constant β to illustrate the relation between wrench and stretch in the transpression model. Notice that γ_W increases rapidly as α^{-1} decreases (shortening increases) for small β.

The deformation gradient matrix is written as:

$$D = \begin{bmatrix} 1 & \gamma_W\,\alpha^{-1} & 0 \\ 0 & \alpha^{-1} & 0 \\ 0 & 0 & \alpha \end{bmatrix} \quad (3)$$

This matrix represents a wrench strain (γ_W) superimposed on a pure shear strain (α and α^{-1}), and is not a unique combination of these two strains (Sanderson and Marchini, 1984). However, the general characteristics of transpressive deformation are preserved in this matrix, and further discussions of the variations caused by a more complicated procedure of strain factorization are not warranted here. The reader is referred to Sanderson and Marchini (1984) for additional details.

The principal stretches and their orientations are found by taking $D \cdot D^T$, and finding the eigenvalues and eigenvectors of this tensor. In general, the strain is three-dimensional, with none of the principal stretches equal to 1.

The strike of the Λ_1–Λ_2 plane for various amounts of shortening (S) over a range of orientations (β) is plotted in Figure 11. The bulk of the spaced cleavage strike data falls well within the field of dextral transpression, as does the strike of F2 axial planes. No unique transpression history is implied, because the available data can fit a broad range of dextral transpression models. However, with the exception of those few outcrops where corrected cleavage planes strike between 085° and 100° (280°), sinistral transpression is ruled out.

IMPLICATIONS FOR REGIONAL TECTONICS

The orientations of second-phase spaced cleavage and F2-fold axial planes in the Uinta arch are not compatible with a regional component of sinistral shear strain, although several regional tectonic models imply or explicitly state that sinistral deformation was important in the evolution of the arch (Sales, 1968; Hamilton, 1981; Bruhn and others, 1983, 1986). This implies that either the models are wrong or that sinistral deformation was accomplished by discrete slip on fault planes at depth and not transferred as strain into the upper crust. Certainly, the latter suggestion is plausible, in that displacement and strain are not necessarily related.

Bruhn and others (1983, 1986) have cited the spatial and temporal overlap in the evolution of the Uinta arch and Hogsback thrust system. Here, we expand on that model and consider its potential implications for strain distributions within the Uinta arch.

First, we consider wrench strains that may have developed at the southern end of the Hogsback thrust sheet if the displacement on the décollement north of the Uinta arch was dissipated as shear strain within the Uinta arch (Fig. 12). Eastward displacement on the Hogsback thrust immediately north of the Uinta arch is estimated as about 24 km by Dixon (1982) and Lamerson (1983). The Uinta arch is about 30 km wide. If the 24 km of displacement were partitioned into the arch as dextral simple shear, the shear strain is γ_W = 24 km/30 km = 0.8. The predicted strike of spaced cleavage due to this wrench strain is 34° north of the shear zone boundary, taken as 085°. That is, the cleavage should strike about 050°, well within the corrected strike distributions of spaced cleavage from the study area and about 10° to 20° north of the F2-fold trends. Consequently, the structures we have measured in the Uinta arch are consistent with a model in which simple shear strains were caused by the southward decreasing displacement gradient of the Hogsback thrust.

Dextral transpression models are also viable. Possible solutions involving factorization of α^{-1} and γ_W are given by the dashed line in Figure 11, which traces out the γ_W = 0.8 field in a dextral transpression model. Figure 13 shows an example for β = −40°.

At this point it is important to consider the geometry of deformation in the Uinta arch and its constraints on thrust-type shear strain components. Typically, the axial planes of folds and cleavage planes will dip toward the interior of a thrust sheet at its termination, and in the direction of dip of the underlying sidewall ramp. This dip direction is the result of superposition of (1) a thrust-type simple shear strain (γ_T) that parallels the direction of thrust displacement, and (2) the horizontal wrench strain (γ_W). If γ_T was a significant strain component compared to (γ_W), then the axial planes of F2 folds and the earlier, corrected second-phase spaced cleavage in the Uinta arch should dip to the northwest. Instead, the F2 folds and corrected spaced cleavage planes both dip nearly vertical, or, in the case of the folds, steeply to the south. The south-dipping F2 axial planes could reflect a component of north-directed simple shear, possibly caused by shortening across the hypothetical south-dipping ramp at the southern end of the Hogsback décollement (Fig. 7). This potential strain component was not included in the transpression strain model.

Finally, we note an important geometric aspect of the Uinta arch model (Fig. 7) with respect to displacement. If, as we imply here, a significant amount of dextral wrench strain was applied in the Uinta arch, then the crystalline basement in the hanging wall of the south-dipping ramp may have become decoupled from that

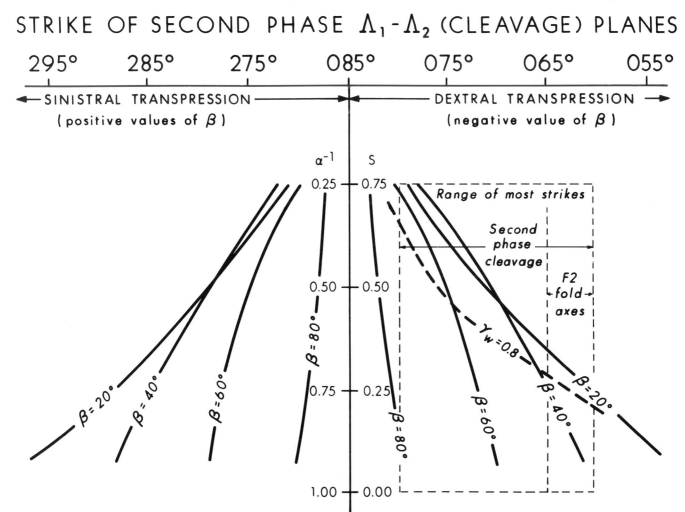

Figure 11. Plot of the strike of second phase Λ_1-Λ_2 planes for various amounts of shortening (S) over a range of orientations (β). Note that the spaced cleavage data support dextral transpression but not sinistral transpression.

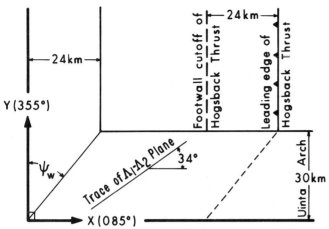

Figure 12. An eastward displacement of 24 km on the Hogsback thrust, distributred as dextral simple shear strain across the 30-km width of the Uinta arch at the southern termination of the Hogsback thrust, results in the formation of spaced cleavage (Λ_1-Λ_2 plane) at 34° north of the shear zone boundary (085°).

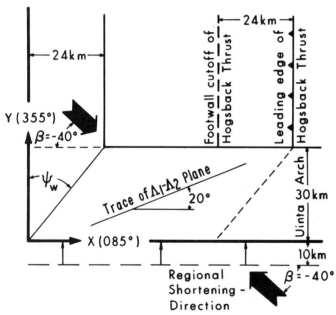

Figure 13. Dextral transpression model of the Uinta arch. Example for β = 40° and γ_W = 0.8. The predicted strike of the Λ_1-Λ_2 plane lies 20° north of the Uinta structural axis.

in the footwall to the north. This decoupling to accommodate dextral simple shear, or more likely, dextral transpression, in the overlying hanging wall, would have resulted in sinistral slip (displacement, not strain) of the basement in the arch with respect to that in the footwall of the ramp.

If decoupling was concentrated on a single south-dipping ramp as shown, the amount of sinistral slip deep within the

basement at the northern edge of the arch would have been 24 km, the estimated eastward displacement on the Hogsback décollement to the north. More likely, the "ramp" consisted of a series of splayed faults, and the total slip was partitioned among the various splays.

SUMMARY

The central Wasatch and westernmost Uinta Mountains have undergone at least two major periods of deformation during Late Cretaceous to early Eocene time. During the early phase of each deformation, spaced cleavage and associated extension veins and tension gash bands developed, and were subsequently folded as deformation progressed.

The first cleavage-forming event recognized in the Twin Creek Formation was layer-parallel shortening directed east-southeast with associated subhorizontal extension at a high angle to the shortening axis. Locally, there is evidence for a component of layer-parallel shear, with the shearing direction toward the east-southeast. The first-phase cleavages were rotated into the first-phase folds. We attribute first-phase deformation to the development of the Mount Raymond thrust fault.

The azimuth of the shortening axis rotated clockwise 45° to 60° between the development of the first- and second-phase cleavages. The early second-phase cleavages were subsequently folded during formation of the Uinta arch into the east-northeast–trending fold train comprising the Parley's Canyon and Emigration Canyon synclines and the Spring Canyon anticline.

Noting the spatial and temporal overlap between movement on the Hogsback thrust and the building of the Uinta arch, we have considered several models that genetically link the two structures. Field data support dextral shear strain within the arch, but not sinistral shear strain. Two possible models for the evolution of Uinta arch are (1) a simple model of dextral wrench strain along the southern termination of the Hogsback thrust, and (2) a more complex model of dextral transpression along a south-dipping ramp where the Hogsback thrust cut down along the northern boundary of the basin in which the Middle Proterozoic Uinta Mountain Group was deposited.

ACKNOWLEDGMENTS

This research was supported in part by grants from Exxon Company, USA; Tenneco Oil Company; Chevron, USA; Marathon Oil Company; Amoco Production Company; and Phillips Petroleum Company (to M.D.B.), and by National Science Foundation Grant EAR-8420774 (to R.L.B. and W. T. Parry). We thank Kristina Moran, who performed a structural analysis of the Emigration Canyon syncline as part of an undergraduate special project. We also thank B. Bryant, N. B. Woodward, C. R. Sanders, W. A. Yonkee, W. J. Taylor, and R. R. Reid for critically reviewing the manuscript.

REFERENCES CITED

Beutner, E. C., 1977, Causes and consequences of curvature in the Sevier orogenic belt, Utah to Montana, *in* Heisey, E. L., and others, eds., Rocky Mountain thrust belt; Geology and resources: Wyoming Geological Association 29th Annual Field Conference Guidebook, p. 353–365.

Bradley, M. D., 1984, Demarcation of a duplex zone; Rockport Lake area, Utah [abs.]: American Association of Petroleum Geologists Bulletin, v. 68, no. 7, p. 932.

—— , 1985, Geometry and kinematics of deformation along the intersection of the Absaroka thrust system and the Uinta axis, Summit County, Utah: Geological Society of America Abstracts with Programs, v. 17, p. 210.

—— , 1986, Thrust splay correlation in the Absaroka thrust system of north-central Utah: Geological Society of America Abstracts with Programs, v. 18, p. 343.

Bruhn, R. L., Picard, M. D., and Beck, S. L., 1983, Mesozoic and early Tertiary structure and sedimentology of the central Wasatch Mountains, Uinta Mountains and Uinta Basin: Utah Geological and Mineral Survey Special Studies no. 59, p. 63–105.

Bruhn, R. L., Picard, M. D., and Isby, J. S., 1986, Tectonics and sedimentology of Uinta arch, western Uinta Mountains and Uinta basin, *in* Petersen, J. A., ed., Paleotectonics and sedimentation in Rocky Mountain region, United States: American Association of Petroleum Geologists Memoir 32, p. 333–352.

Bruhn, R. L., Gibler, P. R., and Parry, W. T., 1987, Rupture characteristics of normal faults; An example from the Wasatch Fault zone, Utah, *in* Coward, M. P., Dewey, J. F., and Hancock, P. L., eds., Continental extension tectonics: Geological Society of London Special Publication, p. 337–353.

Crittenden, M. D., Jr., 1965a, Geology of the Mount Aire Quadrangle: U.S. Geological Survey Quadrangle Map GQ-379, scale 1:24,000.

—— , 1965b, Geology of the Sugarhouse Quadrangle: U.S. Geological Survey Quadrangle Map GQ-380, scale 1:24,000.

—— , 1974, Regional extent and age of thrusts near Rockport Reservoir and relation to possible exploration targets in northern Utah: American Association of Petroleum Geologists Bulletin, v. 58, no. 12, p. 2428–2435.

—— , 1976, Stratigraphic and structural setting of the Cottonwood area, Utah, *in* Hill, J. G., ed., Symposium on geology of the Cordilleran Hingeline: Denver, Colorado, Rocky Mountain Association of Geologists, p. 363–379.

Crittenden, M. D., Jr., Calkins, F. C., and Sharp, B. J., 1966, Geologic map of the Park City West Quadrangle: U.S. Geological Survey Quadrangle Map GQ-535, scale 1:24,000.

Dixon, J. S., 1982, Regional structural synthesis, Wyoming salient of western overthrust belt: American Association of Petroleum Geologists Bulletin, v. 66, no. 10, p. 1560–1580.

Gries, R., 1983, North-south compression of Rocky Mountain foreland structures, *in* Lowell, J. D. (ed.), Symposium on Rocky Mountain foreland basins and uplifts: Denver, Colorado, Rocky Mountain Association of Geologists, p. 9–32.

Hamilton, W., 1981, Plate tectonic mechanism of Laramide deformation: University of Wyoming Contributions to Geology, v. 19, p. 87–92.

Hansen, W. R., 1965, Geology of the Flaming Gorge area, Utah-Colorado-Wyoming: U.S. Geological Survey Professional Paper 490, 196 p.

—— , 1984, Post-Laramide tectonic history of the eastern Uinta Mountains, Utah, Colorado, Wyoming: Mountain Geologist, v. 21, p. 5–29.

Hintze, L., 1973, Geologic history of Utah: Brigham Young University Geology Studies, v. 20, pt. 3, 181 p.

Isby, H. S., and Picard, M. D., 1983, Currant Creek Formation; Record of tectonism in Sevier-Laramide orogenic belt, north-central Utah: University of Wyoming Contributions to Geology, v. 22, p. 91–108.

Lamerson, P. R., 1983, The Fossil Basin and its relationship to the Absaroka thrust system, Wyoming and Utah, *in* Powers, R. B., ed., Geologic studies of the Cordilleran thrust belt, 1982: Denver, Colorado, Rocky Mountain Association of Geologists, p. 279–340.

Mitra, G., Yonkee, W. A., and Gentry, D. J., 1984, Solution cleavage and its relationship to major structures in the Idaho-Utah-Wyoming thrust belt: Geology, v. 12, p. 354–358.

Mount, D. L., 1952, Geology of the Wanship Park City region, Utah [M.S. thesis]: Salt Lake City, University of Utah, 35 p.

Parry, W. T., and Bruhn, R. L., 1986, Pore fluid and seismogenic characteristics of fault rock at depth of the Wasatch fault, Utah: Journal of Geophysical Research, v. 91, p. 730–744.

Ramsay, J. G., and Graham, R. H., 1970, Strain variation in shear belts: Canadian Journal of Earth Sciences, v. 7, p. 786–813.

Ramsay, J. G., and Huber, M. I., 1983, The techniques of modern structural geology; Vol. 1, Strain analysis: New York, Academic Press, 307 p.

Roberts, R. J., Crittenden, M. D., Tooker, E. W., Morris, H. T., Hose, R. K., and Cheney, T. M., 1965, Pennsylvanian and Permian basins in northwestern Utah, northeastern Nevada, and south-central Idaho: American Association of Petroleum Geologists Bulletin, v. 49, p. 1926–1956.

Royse, F., 1985, Geometry and timing of the Darby-Prospect-Hogsback thrust fault system, Wyoming: Geological Society of America Abstracts with Programs, v. 17, p. 263.

Royse, F., Jr., Warner, M. A., and Reese, D. L., 1975, Thrust belt structural geometry and related stratigraphic problems, Wyoming-Idaho-northern Utah, *in* Symposium on deep drilling frontiers in the central Rocky Mountains: Denver, Colorado, Rocky Mountain Association of Geologists, p. 41–54.

Sales, J. K., 1968, Crustal mechanics of Cordilleran foreland deformation; A regional and scale-model approach: American Association of Petroleum Geologists Bulletin, v. 52, p. 2016–2044.

Sanderson, D. J., 1982, Models of strain variation in nappes and thrust sheets; A review: Tectonophysics, v. 88, p. 201–233.

Sanderson, D. J., and Marchini, W.R.D., 1984, Transpression: Journal of Structural Geology, v. 6, no. 5, p. 449–458.

MANUSCRIPT ACCEPTED BY THE SOCIETY FEBRUARY 9, 1988

Geological Society of America
Memoir 171
1988

Development of the foreland zone and adjacent terranes of the Cordilleran orogenic belt near the U.S.-Mexican border

Harald Drewes
U.S. Geological Survey, Box 25046, Denver Federal Center, Denver, Colorado 80225

ABSTRACT

Rocks across the Cordilleran orogenic belt between El Paso, Texas, and Las Vegas, Nevada, show the systematic changes in deformational style, age, and cover thickness found along other transects of the belt. Along the northern part of the El Paso–Las Vegas region, continuity of the tectonic zones—foreland, fold and thrust, intermediate, and hinterland—is disrupted by strike-slip, oblique-slip, and other kinds of structures, as well as by some areas in which erosion has removed overriding plates.

Typical fold and thrust deformation occurs in Mesozoic rocks of the Sierra Juárez, southwest of El Paso, where folds are abundant, large, and disharmonic to large thrust faults and small backthrusts. Paleocene-Eocene fold and thrust zone and foreland zone deposits occur in small continental basins. Late-orogenic Eocene igneous rocks are sparse. Deformation at exposed levels occurred beneath 2 to 3 km of cover and was of relatively short duration.

In the foreland zone, folds are few, widely dispersed, and associated with reverse faults whose downdip continuity with the fold and thrust zone faults seems unlikely. This Paleocene-Eocene deformation involves the continental basin deposits. Similar mild deformation probably occurred in a subfold and thrust terrane, now exposed through erosion of fold and thrust zone rocks, and possibly is exemplified in the Florida Mountains of central southern New Mexico.

In southwestern New Mexico and southeastern Arizona the intermediate tectonic zone (or zones) contains more intensely deformed Mesozoic to Precambrian rocks, voluminous and varied orogenic igneous rocks, and older foreland basin deposits partly of marine origin. Folds are smaller, tighter, and subparallel to shingled thrusts and large backthrusts. Deformation occurred beneath 6 to 8 km of cover during early Late Cretaceous–Paleocene time. This zone(s) contains remnants of earlier and shallower fold and thrust zone and foreland zone structures that were overprinted by the more intense, deeper seated, longer lasting deformation characteristic of this zone.

INTRODUCTION

The features along a transect of the Cordilleran orogenic belt near the Mexican border have many similarities to features of other transects of the belt, as well as a few differences. The fact of these similarities has led me to propose that the orogenic belt extends between Las Vegas, Nevada, and El Paso, Texas (Fig. 1), much as it is continuous from Las Vegas to Alaska and from El Paso to Guatemala (Drewes, 1978, 1980, 1981a). The differences have required explanation and may have influenced others (for example, Dickinson, 1984) to deny this hypothesis, but thus far have not produced any alternate hypothesis to attempt to explain

more than a few local features along this 800-km-long transect. Part of the difficulty is due to the fact that the orogenic belt developed in a region already strongly deformed and one that subsequently was deformed during the Basin-and-Range extensional event.

For example, the northwest-aligned, three-range-wide, basement-cored-uplift model of Davis (1979) attempts to explain certain low-angle faults as having formed through gravity-impelled tectonic denudation off the northeast and southwest flanks of the uplift. This model, however, attempts to explain features of only a county-sized area, rather than of the entire orogenic belt. Furthermore, the model is not supported by mapping data: (1) bounding faults to the uplift are not identified; (2) the proposed uplifted area is not the most deeply eroded, rather, the thickest sequences of youngest preorogenic rocks, the Bisbee Group, occur on that "uplift"; (3) there is no sedimentary record of such an "uplift" preserved along its flanks; and (4) low-angle faults also occur within the "uplift," and resemble those on the supposed flanks.

These complications in development are nowhere more apparent than along the frontal part of the orogenic belt. Clearly, some enigmas remain. If the orogenic belt is continuous across the El Paso–Las Vegas segment of the belt, where is the frontal fault? Why is there no fold and thrust tectonic zone across Arizona? What happens to divide a compressionally deformed terrane west-northwest of El Paso from a similar terrane trending northward along the Rocky Mountain front, as emphasized by King (1969)? While resolutions to these enigmas are necessary to a regional synthesis, now in preparation, they are not critical to the present objective of offering a comparison of the structural styles and the environment of development of the rocks in the fold and thrust zone and the foreland zone. Therefore, major problems are only briefly discussed herein, after an explanation of some terminology.

Some fundamental tectonic terms used in this chapter that have been variously applied in the literature require attention at the outset. The orogenic belt, as I view it, includes the entire continuously deformed terrane, extending from the frontal line in the east or northeast to the orogenic core in the west or southwest (Fig. 2). Typically, and also along the El Paso–Las Vegas transect, a foreland fold and thrust zone is distinguished from one or more intermediate zones, and from a hinterland zone that is characterized by metamorphic features and a flow fabric. These orogenic zones have in common a known or implied continuous basal fault or faults, above which is concentrated the deformational response to the regional compressional stress. Lesser deformational responses, without assured continuity to the orogenic belt, may occur in front of the belt in a foreland zone, and may also occur beneath the fold and thrust zone, or the subfold and thrust terrane.

Along those segments of an orogenic belt where the compressed rocks are uniform or systematically changing in style of deformation, the belt is straight; in map view its various zones form bands of regular width parallel to the frontal line. Such is the case in parts of Alberta and northern Montana. Along other segments, in which particularly incompetent rocks underlie competent ones, the eastward- or northeastward-propagating stress field may advance more rapidly than in adjacent regions and thereby develop a lobate bulge, concave toward the orogenic core, in which the fold and thrust zones and its frontal line are arcuate. Such lobes occur in parts of the Yukon and also in Chihuahua. Still other segments of the orogenic belt may encounter transverse stresses, perhaps caused by differential rates of movement between the converging North American plate and the

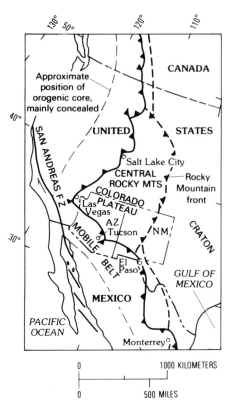

Figure 1. Cordilleran orogenic belt between Canada and Mexico, showing the main Cordilleran orogenic front and the subordinate Rocky Mountain front. Broken line indicates eastern margn of foreland zone. Absence of sawteeth northwest of Tucson indicates presence of many structural complications.

various northeast Pacific plates or perhaps through encountering a particularly resistant cratonic salient. Such complications have been proposed for part of southern Montana, and I suggest that they also have influenced the particularly irregular development of the normally parallel tectonic zones of the Cordilleran orogenic belt across southern New Mexico and Arizona.

In essence, beginning in the Triassic or Jurassic, the convergence of the North American plate with the northeast Pacific plates resulted in a partly collisional margin of western North America. While the Pacific plates were subducted beneath North America, the sedimentary wedge along the continental margin was compressed and tectonically transported northeastward farther onto the craton. The southwestern margin of the craton, essentially the area of the Colorado Plateau and Central Rocky Mountains, formed a salient against and around which the mobile belt was molded. Although the strength characteristics of this salient and that of the contiguous Rocky Mountain terrane was mainly like that of the craton, its present crustal thickness is only 50 instead of 60 km, common for the craton. A similar difference may have existed 60 m.y. ago, resulting in a break between the two as the salient was placed under stress, and in the development of a minor belt of adjustment in response to that portion of compressional stress that was transmitted across the Colorado

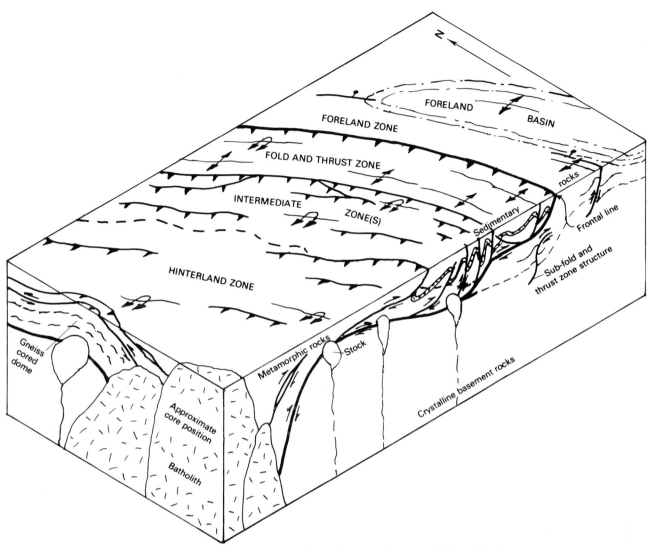

Figure 2. Diagram showing terminology used for main tectonic features of El Paso–Las Vegas transect of the Cordilleran orogenic belt.

Plateau–Rocky Mountain block. As a result, the frontal line to the fold and thrust zone and other strongly deformed zones extends west-northwest toward Las Vegas and the Wasatch front; the zone of minor foreland deformation becomes broad and develops its own front extending northward from some point northeast of and near El Paso along the eastern edge of the Rocky Mountains. Although there is no assurance that the structures of the foreland zone along this minor eastern split of the frontal line are physically continuous with the major frontal line beneath the semi-rigid Colorado Plateau–Rocky Mountain block (and its western salient near Las Vegas), that option should not yet be dismissed. In any case, the following analysis focuses on the major branch of the frontal line that has been impressed around the southwestern side of the salient, where the mobile belt developed in the face of two particular structural features.

Two key features or circumstances, which may be related to one another and largely predate the Cordilleran orogeny, have

disrupted the regular development of tectonic zones in the otherwise continuous orogenic belt. The mobile belt along the El Paso–Las Vegas transect was generally transported N60°–70°E during its main phase of deformation, whereas the southwest margin of the plateau salient trends N60°–80°W across southern New Mexico and Arizona. Collision thus was oblique rather than head-on, with all the attendant complications that commonly result from such a case. Also, the mobile belt encountered a set of preorogenic northwest-trending strike-slip basement faults, such as those described by Drewes (1981a, p. 16–21). Along some fault segments the crystalline basement was offset in such a way as to form barriers to northeast-moving thrust plates developing along the interface between basement and supracrustal rocks, or even to plates moving within these rocks. The responses to oblique collision with such scattered obstacles probably varied from accommodation as a strike-slip plate margin, to an oblique-slip fault and ramp combination, to the truncation of a part of the

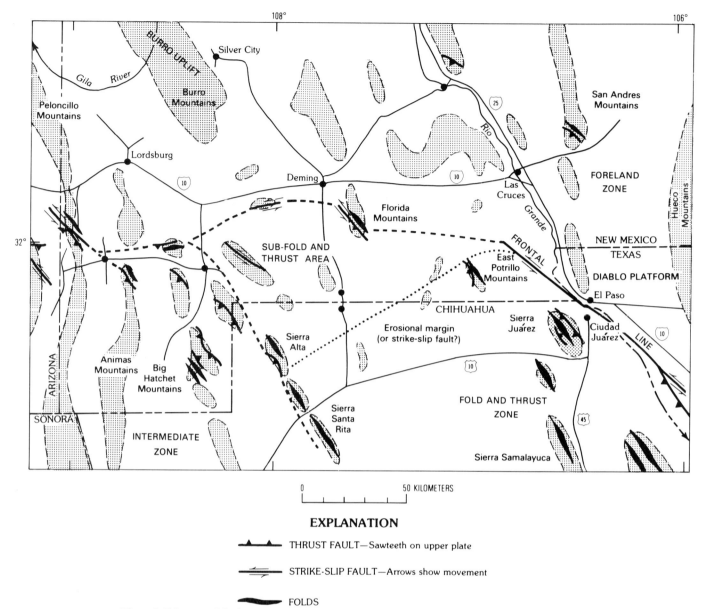

Figure 3. Diagram of the key geographic localities and tectonic features of the fold and thrust zone and foreland zone near El Paso, Texas.

barriers, and possibly even to some northeast-directed underthrusting. Most of these collision features of the major frontal line along the southwestern side of the Colorado Plateau are not germane to this chapter because they involve other parts of the orogenic belt than those of the fold and thrust zone and foreland zone. In the instance of the interaction of the Mesilla Valley fault and the basal décollement at El Paso, this collision factor is discussed more fully in the section on the frontal line. In summary, I believe that along the El Paso–Las Vegas transect the truncation of some of the tectonic zones of the orogenic belt, but not of the belt itself, reflects the oblique collision with ancient faults or raised blocks of the cratonic margin.

After compressional shortening in the orogenic belt, the re-

gion underwent an extensional deformation known as the Basin-and-Range event. This tectonic event of middle and late Tertiary age resulted in widespread block faulting and block tilting, and in a voluminous outpouring of rhyolitic to andesitic magma. Much of the geologic record of the Cordilleran orogeny was buried by the volcanic rocks, as well as by the sedimentary rocks that accumulated in the down-faulted basins. Consequently, the continuity of individual structural features from range to range is difficult to demonstrate, and inevitably, issues of the regional extent of any geologic feature invite skepticism.

Systematic studies of tectonic features from range to range have provided a basis for proposing the presence of regional thrust faults and an orogenic belt mainly of Cretaceous-Paleocene age (Drewes, 1981a; in preparation). Unpublished deep seismic profiles provide additional support. This chapter focuses on a comparison of the structural features and development of the fold and thrust zone, the foreland zone, and the frontal fault between them (Fig. 2).

FOLD AND THRUST ZONE

The fold and thrust zone of the Cordilleran orogenic belt along the El Paso–Las Vegas transect, as that of other transects, is characterized by a broad band of large folds and by genetically related thrust faults, all developed in some of the youngest deformed rocks of the belt. The Chihuahuan fold and thrust zone forms an arcuate pattern, concave to the southwest, crossing southwestern Texas and extending at least as far northwest as the Sierra Juárez, just across the Rio Grande from El Paso (Fig. 3), and possibly as far northwest as the East Potrillo Mountains. This fold and thrust zone is covered to the northwest by extensive younger deposits beneath which it is either cut by a northeast-trending strike-slip fault, such as the case north of the Dragoon Mountains (Drewes, 1980), or, more likely, it is eroded back from the original frontal fault position where that fault swings more westward under the influence of several northwest- to west-trending reactivated basement faults. This concealed northwestern end of the fold and thrust zone trends west or southwest near the international boundary to a point near where that boundary turns southward around the "boot heel" of New Mexico, from which it swings south along the west side of the Sierra Alta–Sierra Santa Rita group of ranges in northwestern Chihuahua.

The ranges in the boot heel, or southwestern corner, of New Mexico—such as the Big Hatchet Mountains (Fig. 3)—are in an intermediate tectonic zone of the orogenic belt (Fig. 2), in which shingled thrust faults and swarms of small folds that are strongly inclined toward the subjacent faults are the common structural features (Zeller, 1970, 1975; Drewes, in preparation).

The deformed rocks in the Sierra Juárez and some nearby hills are mainly marine carbonate and clastic rocks of Aptian-Albian age but include some of early Late Cretaceous age and of early Early Cretaceous–Jurassic age (Cordoba, 1969; Wacker, 1972; Nodeland, 1977; Lovejoy, 1980). To the south and southeast of the Sierra Juárez, these rocks, as well as slightly younger and older rocks, are similarly deformed. A widespread unit of Jurassic gypsum or anhydrite is of particular interest there because it commonly is the locus of a major décollement, above which rocks are folded either in the style described in the Sierra Juárez or in a box fold style (De Cserna, 1960; Weide and Murray, 1967).

Many folds of the fold and thrust zone (Figs. 4, 5) are both long and of large amplitude. Fold axes trend northwest and plunge gently either northwest or southeast; commonly, plunge directions alternate to produce culminations and sags. Near the frontal line (to the northeast of Fig. 4), folds have limbs that dip 60° to 80°. Away from the frontal line (to the southwest), folds are more open and their limbs dip only 20° to 40°. (Folds along

the proximal side of the fold and thrust zone in the Sierra Alta–Sierra Santa Rita group of ranges are also open [Brown, 1985; Muela, 1985].) The tighter folds of the Sierra Juárez verge to the northeast (axial planes dip steeply southwest), but among them a few small folds have the opposite vergence. Some folds are demonstrably disharmonic with respect to underlying thrust faults, and thereby show their genetic association to the folds. In such situations, the orientation of folds and faults indicates a northeast vergence of the folds; therefore, tectonic transport of the upper thrust plates was northeast relative to the lower plates.

Faults of the fold and thrust zone include thrust faults, back thrusts, and assorted transverse faults. The main thrust faults in the Sierra Juárez commonly strike northwest parallel to the fold axes. They typically follow the incompetent shale formations or the bases of massive limestone formations. Thrust faults emplacing younger rocks over older ones are as common as those that bring older rocks over younger ones. Most segments of these faults are concealed by extensive colluvium and talus deposits. Where faults are exposed, the shales are strongly contorted, commonly to such an intensity that bedding features are obliterated. Along some fault segments, bedding near the main faults is truncated by the fault, and along other segments, bedding seems undisturbed. Locally, drag folds and other small folds oblique to faults occur; however, breccia zones are rare.

Back thrusts abut some of the major thrust faults. They are local features that grade upward into an anticline-syncline pair or into a monocline. Between the master, southwest-dipping thrust fault and a subordinate, northeast-dipping back thrust, the rocks have, in effect, been thickened and thereby have gained strength. Such back thrusts form a zone along some of the small ranges between the Sierra Alta and Sierra Santa Rita, as well as at scattered localities in the intermediate tectonic zones.

Transverse faults in the Sierra Juárez are probably small normal and strike-slip faults. They typically trend northeast, are vertical or dip steeply, and offset bedding and folds alike. Some transverse faults cut small thrust faults; others abut large thrust faults and thus are disharmonic strike-slip faults that formed concurrently with the nearby folds and thrust faults. Their northeast trend, like trajectory lines drawn normal to fold axes, indicates the sense of tectonic transport to either the northeast or the southwest.

The style of deformation in the Sierra Juárez, and in much of the Chihuahuan fold and thrust terrane, indicates a development under thin cover. The thickness of cover I estimate through projection into the area of the Late Cretaceous and Paleocene sequence now only found far to the southeast, a sequence that probably was present during deformation but was eroded in post-orogenic time. About 100 to 200 km to the southeast, as well as to the northwest of the Sierra Juárez, a minimum of 2 km of such young rocks are present. The remaining sequence in the range is also about this thick. Therefore, the basal décollement, which is nowhere exposed, developed beneath at least 2 to 4 km of cover. Additional thickness would be gained by early deformation itself; for example, the exploratory oil well Pozo Juárez No. 1 (D. V.

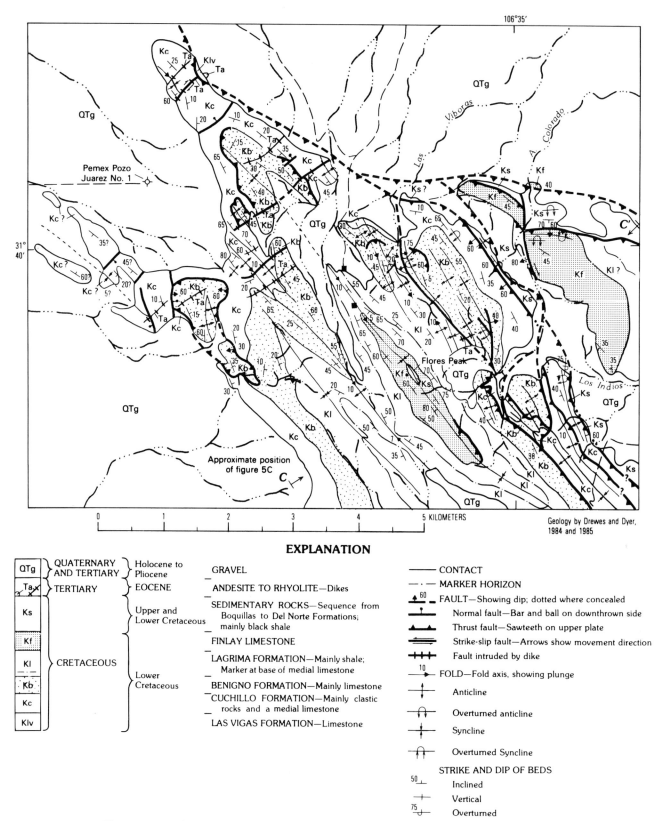

Figure 4. Map of the northwestern part of the Sierra Juárez, northeastern Chihuahua, showing the tectonic style of the foreland zone of the Cordilleran orogen. A and B after Drewes and others (1982, Fig. 5); C, after mapping by Dyer, Drewes, and others.

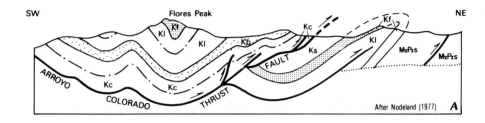

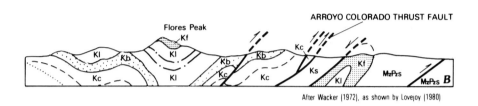

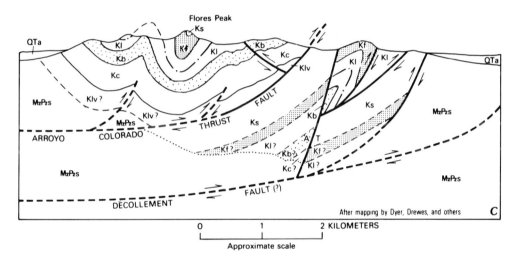

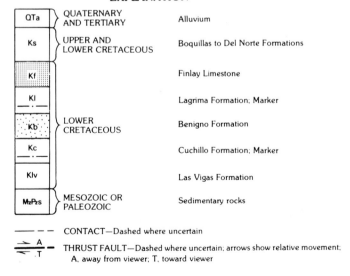

EXPLANATION

QTa	QUATERNARY AND TERTIARY	Alluvium
Ks	UPPER AND LOWER CRETACEOUS	Boquillas to Del Norte Formations
Kf		Finlay Limestone
Kl		Lagrima Formation; Marker
Kb	LOWER CRETACEOUS	Benigno Formation
Kc		Cuchillo Formation; Marker
Klv		Las Vigas Formation
MzPzs	MESOZOIC OR PALEOZOIC	Sedimentary rocks

— — — CONTACT—Dashed where uncertain

THRUST FAULT—Dashed where uncertain; arrows show relative movement; A, away from viewer; T, toward viewer

Figure 5. Structure sections of the Sierra Juárez, northeastern Chihuahua, showing the tectonic style of the foreland zone of the Cordilleran orogen. A and B, After Drewes and others (1982, Fig. 5); C, generalized from Figure 4, line A-A'.

LeMone, oral communication, 1984) penetrated three structural repetitions of one formation (Fig. 4).

The direction of tectonic transport in the Sierra Juárez is N45°E, about 30° more northerly than is typical along most of the transect. This change in direction reflects the lobate pattern of the Chihuahuan fold and thrust zone, a pattern possibly inherited from a greater forward mobility and thus lesser lateral confinement of the fold and thrust terrane over the Jurassic gypsum base. The bases for inferring the transport direction are the orientation of folds and of strike-slip faults. The amount of tectonic transport is probably a few tens of kilometers, a value estimated by Nodeland (1977) through reconstructions from cross sections.

The age of deformation near the frontal line at El Paso is established as post–early Late Cretaceous and pre–early Eocene. The Cretaceous age limit is set by the Boquillas Formation, the youngest deformed unit. Andesitic dikes dated at 48 Ma (R. F. Marvin, H. H. Mehnert, and E. L. Brandt, 1985, written communication) intrude the disharmonic strike-slip fault and cut the folds, and therefore constrain the upper age limit of deformation. These andesitic rocks are probably magmatic-tectonic correlatives of the late orogenic to early post-orogenic andesites found along much of the transect. I therefore place the actual age of deformation in the late Paleocene, closer to the age of the andesite than to the age of the Boquillas Formation.

FORELAND ZONE AND SUBFOLD-AND-THRUST TERRANE

Since the time this chapter was first in preparation, a deep hole, the Phillips No. Sunland Park Unit, located about 60 km northwest of the Sierra Juárez, penetrated 1,000 m of combined Maastrichtian, Paleocene, and Eocene marine rocks. The slightly deformed terranes contiguous with the fold and thrust zone include the foreland zone, north and east of El Paso, and the subfold and thrust terrane, inferred to lie northwest of El Paso and the East Potrillo Mountains, where it is exposed as a result of erosion of the overlying fold and thrust nappe (Fig. 2). The two terranes are described together because their structural characteristics are similar and perhaps distinguishable only through detailed control on the development of the orogen. For the present purpose, it suffices to generate an awareness that these two tectonic environments may be present near the frontal line; hereafter, I use the term "foreland zone" to cover both environments unless specifically stated to the contrary.

The foreland zone is underlain mainly by a Paleozoic sequence chiefly composed of carbonate formations. A thick Late Cretaceous marine and nonmarine clastic sequence overlies the Paleozoic rocks and laps against preorogenic uplifted areas, such as the Burro Uplift of New Mexico and the Diablo Platform of Texas (Fig. 3). These rocks are capped by Paleocene-Eocene coarse clastic deposits preserved in only a few ranges. The clastic deposits show a deformational response to northeast-southwest-oriented compressional stress of the latest Cordilleran time. Late Eocene and especially Oligocene volcanic rocks overlie these

clastic sequences and postdate the orogenic deformation but not the Basin-and-Range block faulting nor the development of the Rio Grande graben north of El Paso (not shown in Fig. 3 because they are postorogenic features).

In the foreland area, then, the rocks are mostly flat-lying or gently tilted, but at scattered localities they, too, are folded and cut by thrust or reverse faults. The locally disturbed areas to the west, the possible subfold and thrust terrane, are associated with northwest-trending, strike-slip basement structures. Three cases are reviewed—the San Andres, the Florida Mountains of the foreland zone, and the East Potrillo Mountains (Fig. 3), which provisionally are considered to belong to the fold and thrust zone, but are considered here for easier comparison.

The Bear Peak fold and fault system of the southern San Andres Mountains (Fig. 6) is typical of the widely scattered disturbed areas of the foreland zone. A large northeastward-overturned anticline and syncline pair and a reverse faulted or thrust faulted anticlinal axial plane are described in the San Andres by Seager (1981). The fold axes trend northwest, with the southwestern mass, in effect, raised against the northeastern mass. The axial plane fault dips 40 to 45° southwest and extends deep into the basement rocks in the core of the anticline without a sign of downward flattening. Therefore, the fault is inferred to die out in a ductile zone at greater depth without an obvious tie to the faults of the fold and thrust zone.

Thick deposits of the Eocene Love Ranch Formation are preserved in the core of the syncline. A strong angular unconformity separates an upper member from a lower member of this formation, whose coarse conglomerate deposits were probably derived from the adjacent uplifted core of the anticline. Apparently sedimentation and deformation were contemporaneous in the Bear Peak area of the San Andres Mountains. In a sense, this basin of deposition represents a most distal foreland basin of a series of such basins or shifting depocenters of a single basin. This far in front of the main deformed terrane, the downwarped areas are probably just a group of small disconnected basins on the cratonic margin that are unlike the larger, longer-lived, and partly destroyed basins or depocenter stages of the more interior part of the orogenic belt. The San Andres area is most noteworthy for the evidence that the last compressional stress of the foreland zone was probably early Eocene, similar to the youngest features of the Cordilleran orogen along other transects.

In the Florida Mountains (Fig. 3), compressionally deformed Paleozoic rocks interact with a northwest-trending basement fault that cuts diagonally across the range. This major fault dips moderately to steeply southwest and separates mainly lower Paleozoic formations, thickest in the hanging wall, from a crystalline basement (Clemons, 1985; Clemons and Brown, 1983). Small folds and thrust faults deform the Paleozoic rocks, apparently as subordinate structures to oblique-slip movement on the major fault. During an earlier stage, compressional stress generated a small, ramp-like flap of thrust plates across a raised basement-rock obstacle. Later, a reversal of movement across the northwest-trending fault brought the Paleozoic formations down

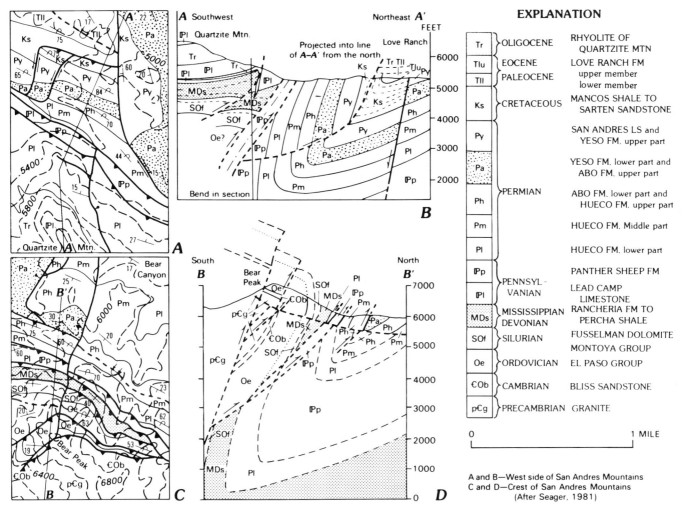

Figure 6. Maps and structure sections of parts of the Bear Peak fold and thrust zone, southern San Andres Mountains, New Mexico (after Seager, 1981, as shown by Drewes and others, 1982, Fig. 11).

against the raised northeastern block of Precambrian granite and a thin cap of Paleozoic rocks. The local evidence fails to distinguish a possible foreland zone situation from one of the possible exposure of the terrane underlying a larger overriding thrust plate by subsequent erosion. Such enigmas are typical of other regions where Cordilleran compressional effects mix with structural barriers in the basement rocks, and are not simply an exceptional occurrence in this area.

Structures in the East Potrillo Mountains (Fig. 3) represent either another variant of the foreland area, or are a remnant of the fold and thrust zone of the main part of the deformed belt. Although I provisionally favor the latter interpretation on illustrations where commitment is necessary, I describe them here so that comparisons are easier to make with both alternatives. Permian and Early Cretaceous formations underlie the range (Figs. 7, 8), and plugs of hornblende andesite (or latite?) porphyry underlie some hills 1 to 3 km northwest of the range. In the southeastern part of the range, the Cretaceous rocks, correlative with the Aptian-Albian limestone, shale, and sandstone of the

Sierra Juárez, lie conformably on the Permian limestone and dolomite. In the northwestern part of the range, where this contact is covered by surficial deposits, a second sheet of the Permian rocks is thrust- or reverse-faulted upon the Cretaceous rocks in a manner resembling the Bear Peak structures, except for their smaller size. The Permian rocks of this plate are partly recrystallized and have scattered clusters of small folds and thrust faults. The underlying Cretaceous rocks are warped into tight asymmetric folds of moderate size that are disharmonic to internal thrust faults, and are vergent to the northeast, a style typical of the foreland zone. A weak metamorphism, southwest-dipping fracture cleavage, and some lineation mark the Cretaceous rocks of the middle of the range.

The assortment of intriguing features of this narrow and isolated range are difficult to equate with those of other ranges. The signs of higher pressure and temperature during deformation may suggest a situation like that which could underlie the Sierra Juárez, or, alternatively, it may reflect complications of compressional deformation near a basement barrier along an unexposed,

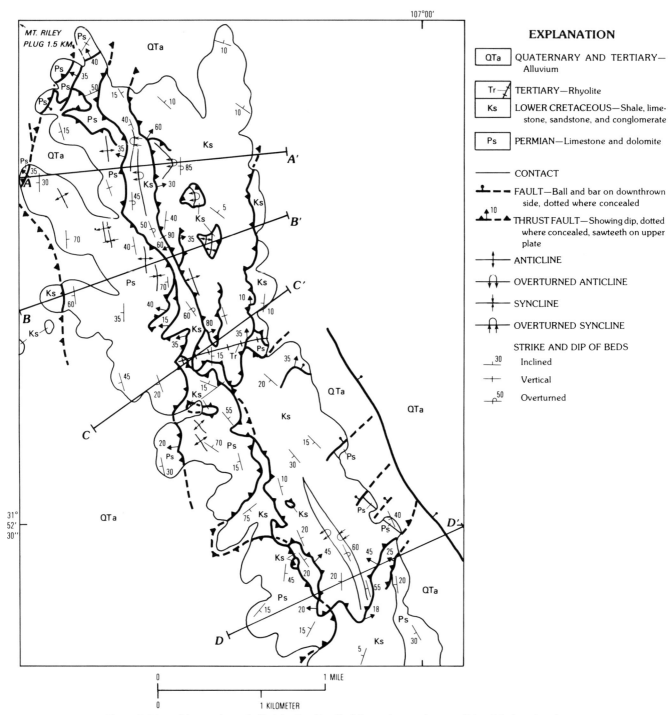

Figure 7. Map of the northwest half of the East Potrillo Mountains, south-central New Mexico, showing only generalized stratigraphic units and key structural features (after unpublished map by Drewes, 1984, 1985).

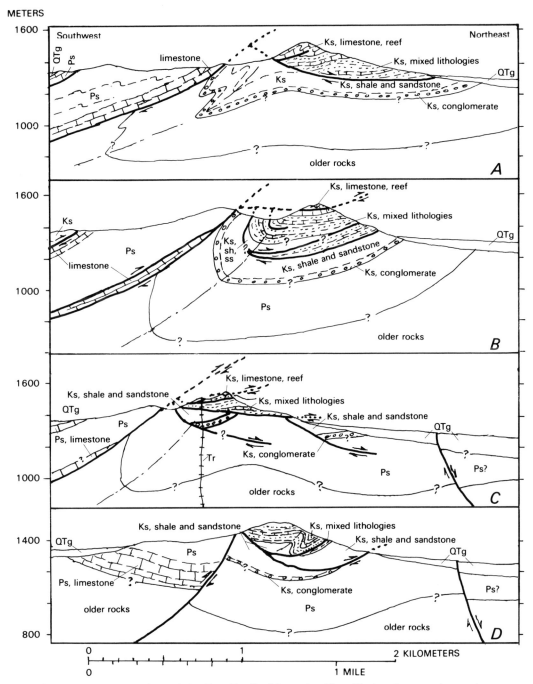

Figure 8. Structure sections of the East Potrillo Mountains, New Mexico, from northwest, A, to southeast, D, showing style of Cordilleran deformation. Unit symbols explained in Figure 7.

northwest-trending strike-slip fault. Although the age of deformation is not known exactly, the hornblende andesite of the nearby
plugs is is possibly correlative with the early Eocene andesite
plugs of El Paso and dikes of the Sierra Juárez; thus deformation
is probably pre-Eocene.

FRONTAL LINE

The leading edge of the more highly deformed part, or mobile belt, is herein referred to as the main frontal line. In the El
Paso area, this line is entirely concealed by alluvium, but farther
to the west, adjacent to the intermediate tectonic zones, the line is
exposed in places where it crosses the uplifted Basin-and-Range
blocks. A variety of conditions are shown along a 300-km-long
segment of the frontal line between El Paso and southeastern
Arizona (Fig. 9).

At El Paso (Fig. 9A, site 1) a major northwest-trending fault
known as the Texas lineament separates folded and thrust-faulted
Cretaceous rocks of the Sierra Juárez from the tilted fault block
underlain by Precambrian and Paleozoic rocks of the Franklin
Mountains (Fig. 10). Both geophysical and drill-hole data help to
fix the position and attitude of this essentially vertical fault. Various ages and directions of strike-slip movements have been attributed to this lineament; some attempts have been made to
project it, or a broader zone of northwest-trending faults, across
New Mexico and Arizona or even farther (Albritton and Smith,
1957; Kelly, 1975; Drewes, 1981a). At El Paso the folded and
thrust-faulted terrane of northern Chihuahua abuts the lineament
and is more intensely deformed near it than farther away from it.
The tectonic transport direction, as determined from the orientation of folds and small strike-slip faults within the plate system,
shows that the mobile terrane approached the lineament at nearly
right angles. This suggests that the encroaching plates, here near
their distal edge and thus responding under a dwindling stress
condition, abutted any barrier along the lineament, such as a
raised mass of deeper level stronger rock, jammed together and
possibly moved up a ramp and over the edge of the barrier. The
possible ramp situation can no longer be checked, for this area
was relatively high during late orogenic time, and signs of such
structures would have been removed before the subsequent alluviation along the Rio Grande Valley and the extensive bolson east
of El Paso. Downstream, to the southeast of El Paso, however,
where the frontal line does appear, there is a little overthrusting of
Cretaceous rocks that might suggest either a minor ramp or an
absence of a barrier situation.

West and northwest of El Paso, in the subfold and thrust
belt terrane, a blend of strike-slip movement and minor thrust
faulting has already been described in the situation of the Florida
Mountains. While Clemons and Brown (1983) and Clemons
(1985) have inferred a right-lateral component of movement on a
major northwest-trending fault there, I suggest that the local data
are not clear-cut and that projections from the west rather than
the southeast indicate at least a late(?) orogenic phase of left-
lateral movement. In any case, across this part of southern New

Mexico, the mobile belt rocks are believed to have been removed
by erosion, and the northern edge was then covered by alluvium
and volcanic rocks, so that the frontal line forms part of the base
rather than the edge of thrust plates (Fig. 9B, site 2; Fig. 11). That
original edge of major plates may have extended as far north as
the Cedar and Victorio Mountains (Thorman and Drewes, 1980,
1981), which offer more evidence of strike-slip and/or thrust
faulting. To the southwest the eroded and buried segment of the
frontal line merges with a thrust-fault system that marks the
concealed eastern margin of the intermediate tectonic zones (Fig.
9C, site 3), characterized by the shingled thrust faults of the Sierra
Rica and Little Hatchet Mountains (Zeller, 1970).

In the Brockman Hills (Fig. 9D, site 4), an east-
west–trending high-angle fault separates a folded terrane of
Lower Cretaceous rocks to the south from a terrane of Upper
Cretaceous rocks and a klippe of Paleozoic rocks to the north
(Thorman, 1977). The frontal line is projected either to this fault,
or just north of these hills, with the southern terrane assigned to
the eastern intermediate tectonic zone and the northern terrane to
the foreland zone. In any case, the upended fault is mapped as a
left-lateral strike-slip fault, and the folds just south of the fault
trend anomalously east-west, possibly reflecting a local drag on
the strike-slip fault. These hills are surrounded by postorogenic
deposits. In the north end of the Little Hatchet Mountains, the
next major range south of the Brockman Hills, Zeller (1970)
shows northwest-striking shingled thrust plates. Apparently, then,
the frontal line follows a segment of the eastern margin of the
eastern intermediate zone northwest to the strike-slip fault at the
Brockman Hills, from which it trends west beneath extensive
cover separating the strongly deformed rocks of the northern
Animas Mountains (Drewes, 1986a) and the little-deformed
rocks near Lordsburg.

Across southwesternmost New Mexico and southeasternmost Arizona, block-faulted linear basins and ranges are well
developed, and several sets of northwest-trending, reactivated
basement faults are well exposed in the ranges, as summarized by
Drewes (1981a). One such set of faults appears in the Peloncillo
Mountains, where it separates less deformed rocks to the northeast from more deformed ones to the southwest (Drewes and
Thorman, 1980a,b). The trace of the frontal line apparently extends west to the intersection of this reactivated basement flaw
and then follows that fault set 5 to 10 km before resuming a
westward trace beneath the next alluviated basin. The Peloncillo
Mountains leg of the frontal line, then, was either a reactivated,
left-lateral strike-slip fault or an oblique-slip ramp. The traces of a
few fold axes are arcuate and converge gradually with one branch
of this set of faults, suggesting such lateral or oblique movement,
up and southeastward, of the southwestern or more mobile
terrane.

In the Chiricahua Mountains (Fig. 9E, site 6), the next range
to the west, deformed terrane generally to the south or west is
separated from undeformed terrane to the north and east. To the
east in this range, the frontal line is seen to lie north of a cluster of
east-west–trending shingled thrust plates of alternating Paleozoic

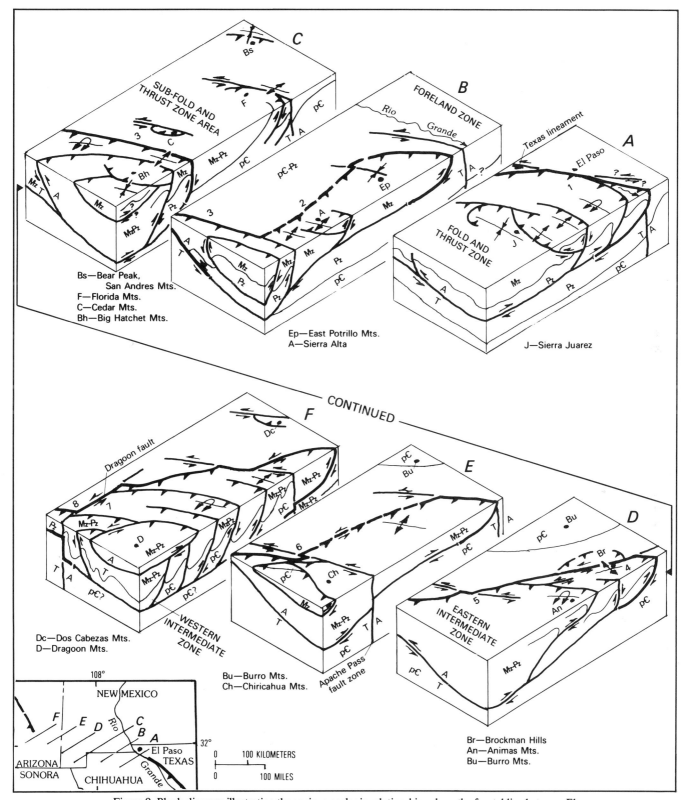

Figure 9. Block diagram illustrating the various geologic relationships along the frontal line between El Paso, Texas, and southeastern Arizona.

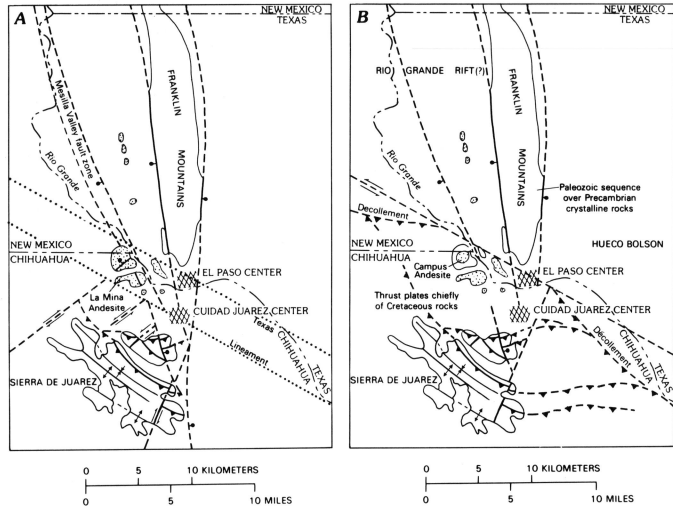

Figure 10. Diagrammatic maps showing frontal line of the Cordilleran orogenic belt at El Paso, Texas, and two interpretations differing more in nomenclature and dynamics than in geometric relationships. A, After Nodeland (1977), modified by Lovejoy (1980); B, alternate view reflecting a Mesilla Valley fault or Texas lineament, largely predating the frontal zone décollement fault.

and Mesozoic rocks (Sabins, 1957; Drewes, 1982). These plates and this segment of the frontal line are offset left-laterally 2 km along a branch fault of the next set of northwest-trending, reactivated basement faults. A bit of the folded and thrust-faulted terrane is caught up along the main part of the northwest-trending fault set; once again, the frontal line is seen to diverge from the influence of such faults and trend more westerly beneath an alluviated basin (Sabins, 1957; Drewes, 1981b, 1984). It is noteworthy that the southwestern terrane of mobile-belt rocks here has the easternmost plate of Precambrian crystalline rocks emplaced among plates of Cretaceous rocks. Here, too, the northeastward-moving, strongly deformed, western intermediate–zone rocks appear to have shifted left laterally along the northwest-trending fault set or to have ramped obliquely over a part of the obstacle presented by the northeastern basement rocks.

Next to the west, the frontal fault is believed to separate highly deformed terrane in the Dragoon Mountains (Fig. 9F,

site 7) from nearly undeformed rocks in the hills to the northeast, with this segment of the frontal line offset a few kilometers along a northeast-trending strike-slip fault. This fault is cogenetic with the intensive deformation to the south and west, and splay faults off it have drag-fold evidence of left-lateral offset. The terrane to the southeast, in the main part of the Dragoon Mountains, comprises three major thrust plates (Gilluly, 1956; Cooper and Silver, 1964; Drewes, 1986b). These have evidence of major involvement of crystalline basement rocks, and of telescoping of sedimentary, as well as metamorphic facies. They contain small folds with imbricate thrust platelets, as well as part of a major overturned fold, all features of the western intermediate tectonic zone. The terrane to the northwest is also thrust faulted, but not so that to the northeast. The trace of the frontal zone, thus, continues northwestward from Figure 9F and approaches a region containing other geologic enigmas related to the hinterland tectonic zone and not herein reviewed.

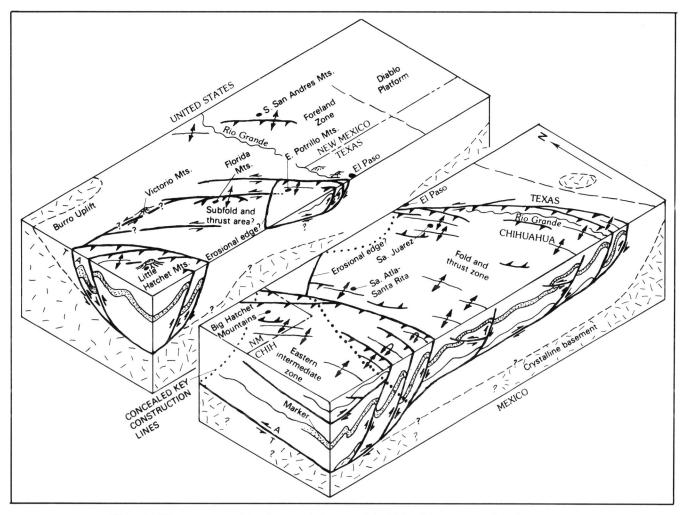

Figure 11. Diagram summarizing the tectonic features of the fold and thrust zone and the foreland zone of the Cordilleran orogenic belt near El Paso, Texas.

The dating of movement along the various structures of frontal line is largely dependent on dating of adjacent terranes. In only a few places, such as at sites of Figure 9F and near site 1 of Figure 9A, are postorogenic intrusive igneous rocks found nearby, to set minimum ages of Paleocene and Eocene, respectively, on frontal structures. However, using data obtained along tectonic strike and farther from the frontal line, the development of areas represented by Figure 9, F and E is about Late Cretaceous, by Figure 9, D and C about early Paleocene, and that by Figure 9, B and A about late Paleocene–early Eocene. By implication of this progressive development of the various tectonic zones across the orogenic belt, the development of the adjacent foreland zone also spans considerable time and is generally older to the west than to the east.

FOLD AND THRUST ZONE AND FORELAND ZONE IN EARLIER CORDILLERAN TIMES

Thus far, the discussions of the structural features of the fold and thrust zone and foreland zone have been directed toward the

tectonic record impressed on the rocks at the close of orogenic time. This conventional approach to describing an orogen, in effect, freezes the tectonic action at that point of development that provides the most comprehensive record. However, the orogenic development is a dynamic, rather than a static, event, and so a paleoforeland zone may be expected.

The compressional stress field propagated from the orogenic core to the distal frontal line, and in a small and probably disconnected way even into the foreland zone. Consequently, the frontal line and the various tectonic zones also migrated through the orogenic belt, as it is now fixed in the geologic record. Indeed, the characteristics by which the several intermediate and hinterland tectonic zones may be recognized are the composite results of an earlier fold and thrust stage of development plus another (or other) deeper-seated kinds of development. The zone we recognize at present as the hinterland zone, for example, is a composite of an early, shallow fold and thrust tectonic zone; a later, deeper intermediate zone; and a still later, still deeper, hinterland zone tectonic environment. Naturally, in the hinterland zone particularly, the effects of the latest, deepest development probably nearly obliterated evidence of the earlier stages of development. In the intermediate zones, however, such obliteration is likely to have been less severe. Thus, along the El Paso–Las Vegas transect, remnants of a paleofold and thrust zone style of deformation may be preserved. There are even possible remnants of a paleoforeland style found in the western intermediate zone.

In the Big Hatchet Mountains (Fig. 3), two styles of deformation occur literally side-by-side. Shingled thrust faults and small folds strongly inclined toward these faults occur in the southwestern part of the mountains (Zeller, 1970; Drewes, in preparation). In the foothills adjacent to the southwestern flank, and probably separated from the mountains by a reverse fault or backthrust, are large, moderately open folds in Cretaceous rocks like those of the fold and thrust zone. I suggest that these large folds are remnants of a fold and thrust stage of deformation, and that the structures of the main mountains developed during a later stage at a deeper tectonic level indicative of the eastern intermediate zone.

Still farther west of the present position of the frontal zone, in the Dragoon Mountains of southeastern Arizona (Fig. 9F), some tectonic and sedimentary features suggest a Cordilleran development with several stages of overprinting, possibly beginning with a foreland stage. The area contains a wide variety of Precambrian, Paleozoic, and Mesozoic sequences, abundantly fold, faulted, and intruded (Gilluly, 1956; Drewes, 1980, 1981a, 1986b). In the lowest of three major thrust plates, the Early Cretaceous Bisbee Group is present in multiple shingled thrust platelets and includes a basal conglomerate hundreds of meters thick, comprising very coarse boulder and cobble detritus and landslide masses. Similar occurrences of thick conglomerate are widely scattered in southeastern Arizona; they are known to be a local facies that is time-transgressive, extending as high as the Mural Limestone horizon, two formations above the Glance Conglomerate. Typically, sections in adjacent ranges show the conglomerate to be only a few meters thick, finer grained, and overlain by a thick sequence of shale, siltstone, and some limestones that were deposited in estuarine and lagoonal environments not influenced by local high relief. Such a more normal Bisbee sequence occurs in the Dragoon Mountains, in the uppermost of the three major thrust plates that was tectonically telescoped to within 1 km of the coarse Glance facies (Drewes, 1981, Pl. 2).

The relations thus far explained are indicative simply of the presence during Bisbee time of scattered local areas of high relief (Ransome, 1904; Hayes and Landis, 1964; Finnell, 1971; Drewes and others, 1988). Whereas Bilodeau (1982) offered the opinion that this local relief is the result of tensional stress and consequent block faulting, consideration of the regional development of the orogenic belt favors an interpretation of initial effects of Cordilleran compression and consequent reverse faulting in a paleoforeland zone.

The Bisbee rocks are probably part of a broad, time-transgressive depocenter, a foreland basin filled largely with black or gray shale and silt whose ultimate source must have been to the west because the terrane to the north and east was (and still is) covered mainly by Paleozoic carbonate rocks that do not make such clastic deposits and because the terrane to the southeast was the site of an arm of the sea. A western provenance is attractive because the orogen had already formed there and the deformed rocks were widely covered by late-orogenic andesitic volcanic rocks whose remnants include various units of greenstone, metavolcanic rock, graywacke, and metadiorite. These rocks were cannibalized to fill the Bisbee foreland basin lying to the east during an earlier stage of the orogen; the Bisbee basin itself was overwhelmed by the tectonism of a later stage. However, before the inception of this later tectonic stage, the foreland kind of mild deformation possibly generated some reverse faults, raised some blocks, and produced local coarse deposits, such as those of the Love Ranch Formation, in a region still predominantly being flooded by estuarine-fluvial mud. This Dragoon Mountains situation must still be adjusted palinspastically to accommodate the tectonic telescoping between the three plates and the overall northeastward tectonic transport relative to the underlying cratonic mass.

CONCLUSIONS

In the foregoing resume of the distal part of the Cordilleran orogen, I have illustrated the tectonic styles and development of rocks of the folds and thrust zone and of the foreland zone. Structures of the fold and thrust zone are large, numerous, and closely associated with thrust faults. Those of the foreland zone are isolated cases closely associated with a reverse fault that extends into the basement, rather than to the frontal line. The interaction of backthrusts with thrust faults is clearer in the fold and thrust zone than in the intermediate zones.

From the basis of a more broadly regional study than of these frontal terranes, several other deductions are offered. The individual tectonic zones terminate northward against a zone of strike-slip faults inherited from a set of basement structures, oblique-slip ramp structures, and other complex features. Along this termination zone, already a positive area during orogenic time, greater uplift and deeper erosion have probably resulted in the removal of a part of the foreland zone, to expose a subfold and thrust zone terrane having structural characteristics like those of the foreland zone but modified by strike-slip and oblique-slip interaction with the basement faults.

Remnants of structural features characteristic of more distal parts of the orogen may be recognized in more proximal zones. An example of paleofold and thrust zone folds occurs in the eastern intermediate zone of southwestern New Mexico. Another example of possible paleoforeland area structures is deduced for scattered localities in southeastern Arizona from the Early Cretaceous sedimentary record and from concurrent conditions in more proximal parts of the orogen. These paleotectonic terranes were subsequently incorporated into the more intensively deformed intermediate zones as the orogen was propagated eastward to its termination near El Paso by Eocene time.

REFERENCES CITED

Bilodeau, W. L., 1982, Tectonic models for early Cretaceous rifting in southeastern Arizona: Geology, v. 10, no. 9, p. 466–470.

Brown, M. L., 1985, Geology of Sierra de los Chinos-Cierro La Cueva area, northwest Chihuahua, Mexico [M.S. thesis]: University of Texas at El Paso, 162 p.

Clemons, R. E., 1985, Geology of South Peak Quadrangle, Luna County, New Mexico: New Mexico Bureau of Mines and Mineral Resources Geologic Map 59, scale 1:24,000.

Clemons, R. E., and Brown, G. A., 1983, Geology of Gym Peak Quadrangle, Luna County, New Mexico: New Mexico Bureau of Mines and Mineral Resources Geologic Map 58, scale 1:24,000.

Cooper, J. C., and Silver, L. T., 1964, Geology and ore deposits of the Dragoon Quadrangle, Cochise County, Arizona: U.S. Geological Survey Professional Paper 416, 196 p.

Cordoba, D. A., 1969, Mesozoic stratigraphy of northeastern Chihuahua, Mexico, *in* Guidebook of the border region: New Mexico Geological Society 20th Field Conference Guidebook, p. 91–96.

Davis, G. H., 1979, Laramide folding and faulting in southeastern Arizona: American Journal of Science, v. 279, no. 5, p. 543–569.

De Cserna, Z., 1960, Orogenesis in time and space in Mexico: Geologische Rundschau, v. 50, p. 595–605.

Dickinson, W. R., 1984, Reinterpretation of Lime Peak thrust as a low-angle normal fault; Implications for the tectonics of southeastern Arizona: Geology, v. 12, p. 610–613.

Drewes, H., 1978, The Cordilleran orogenic belt between Nevada and Chihuahua: Geological Society of America Bulletin, v. 89, p. 641–657.

—— , 1980, Tectonic map of southeastern Arizona: U.S. Geological Survey Miscellaneous Geologic Investigations Map I-1109, scale 1:125,000.

—— , 1981a, Tectonic synthesis of southeastern Arizona: U.S. Geological Survey Professional Paper 1144, 96 p.

—— , 1981b, Geologic map and sections of the Bowie Mountain South Quadrangle, Cochise County, Arizona: U.S. Geological Survey Miscellaneous Geologic Investigations Map I-1363, scale 1:24,000.

—— , 1982, Geologic map and sections of the Cochise Head Quadrangle and adjacent areas: U.S. Geological Survey Miscellaneous Geologic Investigations Map I-1312, scale 1:24,000.

—— , 1984, Geologic map and structure sections of the Bowie Mountain North Quadrangle, Cochise County, Arizona: U.S. Geological Survey Miscellaneous Investigations Series Map I-1492, scale 1:24,000.

—— , 1986a, Geologic map of the northern part of the Animas Mountains, Hidalgo County, New Mexico: U.S. Geological Survey Miscellaneous Investigations Series Map I-1686, scale 1:24,000.

—— , 1986b, Geologic map and cross sections of the Dragoon Mountains, southeastern Arizona: U.S. Geological Survey Miscellaneous Geologic Investigations Map I-1662, scale 1:24,000.

Drewes, H., and Thorman, C. H., 1980a, Geologic map of the Steins and part of the Vanar Quadrangles, New Mexico and Arizona: U.S. Geological Survey Miscellaneous Geologic Investigations Series Map I-1220, scale 1:24,000.

—— , 1980b, Geologic map of the Cotton City and part of the Vanar Quadrangles, New Mexico and Arizona: U.S. Geological Survey Miscellaneous and Geologic Investigations Series Map I-1221, scale 1:24,000.

Drewes, H., Keith, S. B., LeMone, D. V., Seager, W. R., Clemons, R. E., and Thompson, S., III, 1982, Styles of deformation in the southern Cordillera, U.S.A., *in* Drewes, H., ed., Cordilleran overthrust belt, Texas to Arizona field conference: Denver, Colorado, Rocky Mountain Association of Geologists, Field trip, symposium, and articles, 156 p.

Drewes, H., Klein, D. P., and Birmingham, S., 1988, Tectonic and volcanic controls of mineralization in the Dos Cabezas Mountains, southeastern Arizona: U.S. Geological Survey Bulletin 1676.

Finnell, T. L., 1971, Preliminary geologic map of the Empire Mountains Quadrangle, Pima County, Arizona: U.S. Geological Survey Open-File Report OF71-106, scale 1:48,000.

Gilluly, J., 1956, General geology of central Cohise County, Arizona, *with sections on* Age and correlation by Palmer, A. R., Williams, J. S., and Reeside, J. B., Jr.: U.S. Geological Survey Professional Paper 281, 169 p.

Hayes, P. T., and Landis, E. R., 1964, Geologic map of the southern part of the Mule Mountains, Cochise County, Arizona: U.S. Geological Survey Miscellaneous Geologic Investigations Map I-418, scale 1:48,000.

King, P. B., 1969, Tectonic map of North America: U.S. Geological Survey, scale 1:5,000,000.

Lovejoy, E. M., ed., 1980, Sierra Juarez, Chihuahua, Mexico, structure and stratigraphy: El Paso Geological Society Guidebook, 59 p.

Muela, P., 1985, Geology of northern Sierra Santa Rita, northwest Chihuahua, Mexico [M.S. thesis]: University of Texas at El Paso, 101 p.

Nodeland, S. K., 1977, Cenozoic tectonics of Cretaceous rocks in the northeast Sierra de Juarez, Chihuahua, Mexico [M.S. thesis]: University of Texas at El Paso, 79 p.

Ransome, F. L., 1904, Geology and ore deposits of the Bisbee Quadrangle, Arizona: U.S. Geological Survey Professional Paper 21, 167 p.

Sabins, F. F., Jr., 1957, Geology of the Cochise Head and western part of the Vanar Quadrangles, Arizona: Geological Society of America Bulletin, v. 68, p. 1315–1342.

Seager, W. R., 1981, Geology of Organ Mountains and southern San Andres Mountains, New Mexico: New Mexico Bureau of Mines and Mineral Resources Memoir 36, 97 p.

Thorman, C. H., 1977, Geologic map of the Coyote Peak and Brockman Quadrangles, Hidalgo and Grant Counties, New Mexico: U.S. Geological Survey Miscellaneous Field Studies Map MF-924, scale 1:24,000.

Thorman, C. H., and Drewes, H., 1980, Geologic map of Victorio Mountains, Luna County, New Mexico: U.S. Geological Survey Miscellaneous Field Studies Map MF-1175, scale 1:24,000.

—— , 1981, Geologic map of the Gage SW Quadrangle, Grant and Luna Counties, New Mexico: U.S. Geological Survey Miscellaneous Geologic Investigations Map I-1231, scale 1:24,000.

Wacker, H. J., 1972, The stratigraphy and structure of the Cretaceous rocks in north-central Sierra de Juarez, Chihuahua, Mexico [M.S. thesis]: University of Texas at El Paso, 82 p.

Wiede, A. E., and Murray, G. A., 1967, Geology of the Parras basin and adjacent areas of northeastern Mexico: American Association of Petroleum Geologists Bulletin, v. 51, no. 5, p. 678–695.

Zeller, R. A., 1970, Geology of the Little Hatchet Mountains, Hidalgo and Grant Counties, New Mexico: New Mexico Bureau of Mines and Mineral Resources Bulletin 96, 23 p.

—— , 1975, Structural geology of the Big Hatchet Peak Quadrangle Hidalgo County, New Mexico, *with* commentary by Thompson, S., III: New Mexico Bureau of Mines and Mineral Resources Circular 146, 23 p.

MANUSCRIPT ACCEPTED BY THE SOCIETY FEBRUARY 9, 1988

Geological Society of America
Memoir 171
1988

Syntectonic sedimentation and Laramide basement thrusting, Cordilleran foreland; Timing of deformation

Richard A. Beck,* Carl F. Vondra, Jeffrey E. Filkins, and Jon D. Olander
Department of Earth Sciences, Iowa State University, Ames, Iowa 50011

ABSTRACT

Recent seismic and drilling data from the Laramide-style basement-cored uplifts of the central Rocky Mountains suggest that thick-skinned basement thrusting due to horizontal compression, rather than block uplift due to vertical forces, is responsible for their origin. Interpretation of these structural uplifts as basement thrusts requires a new sedimentary-tectonic model for the region. Sedimentary facies associations within the Upper Cretaceous and lower Tertiary strata of Laramide-style intermontane basins are best understood as a response of sedimentation to thick-skinned basement-thrusting.

Laramide-style structural features of the central Rocky Mountains include asymmetric basins and arcuate, basement-cored thrust sheets. Sedimentary facies of the basins reflect a common history of asymmetric subsidence due to thrust loading and a consistent pattern of depositional environments. These facies have a depositional polarity similar to the structural asymmetry of their underlying basement. Characteristic syntectonic sedimentary facies of these basins include a narrow, coarse conglomerate facies adjacent to the thrust, a narrow to absent sandstone/mudstone/coal facies just basinward, a basinal thrustward-thickening mudstone/coal/carbonate/evaporite facies above the depositional axis, and finally, a wide distal sandstone/mudstone/coal facies. The wide distal sandstone/mudstone/coal facies depositionally thins above the shallowing basement opposite the impinging thrust or above the hanging wall of yet another thrust, as in the Wind River Basin.

Episodes of rapid Laramide-style basement thrusting caused rapid tectonically induced asymmetric basin subsidence that equaled or exceeded the rate of sedimentation. Major sediment sources were the gently dipping basin margins opposite each thrust. The frontal edges of the hanging walls of basement thrusts provided coarse but volumetrically minor quantities of clastic sediment during thrust movement. Areally extensive, thick, coarse-grained, fluvial clastic wedges derived from impinging basement thrusts developed only after thrusting had greatly slowed or ceased.

INTRODUCTION

Major Laramide-style upper crustal features of the Cordilleran foreland (Figs. 1, 2) of Wyoming, northeastern Utah, and northwestern Colorado include arcuate basement thrusts and large, structurally asymmetric basins (Berg, 1962, 1981, 1983; Blackstone, 1981, 1983; Brown, 1983, 1984; Bruhn and others, 1983; Chapin and Cather, 1981; Foose and others, 1961; Gries, 1983a, b; Hamilton, 1978, 1981; Hennier and Spang, 1983; Kan-

ter and others, 1981; Keefer and Love, 1963; Love, 1939, 1940, 1960, 1970, 1977, 1978). Penetration by drilling of the frontal edges of several basement-thrust sheets (Gries, 1983a, b) coupled with structural and seismic evidence (Allmendinger and others, 1982; Berg, 1962, 1981, 1983; Blackstone, 1981, 1983; Brewer and others, 1982; Brown, 1983; Erslev, 1986; Johnson and others, 1983; Lowell, 1983; Petersen, 1983; Skeen and Ray, 1983; Smithson and others, 1979) indicate that the question of block uplift vs. basement-thrust origin has been resolved for most of the Laramide-style uplifts of the Rocky Mountain foreland.

---

*Present address: Department of Geological Sciences, University of Southern California, Los Angeles, California 90089-0740.

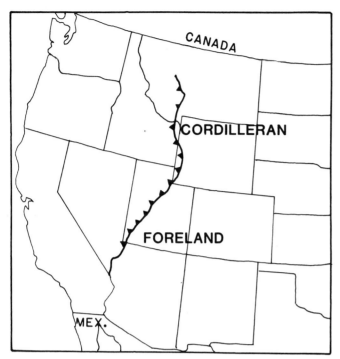

Figure 1. Location map of Cordilleran foreland, western United States. Modified after Prucha and others, 1965.

Late Cretaceous and Paleogene strata in the intermontane basins of the central Rocky Mountains record the tectonic evolution of the region and corroborate the structural, seismic, and borehole evidence for Laramide-style basement thrusting. Application of the following model for sedimentation adjacent to Laramide-style basement thrusts provides a sedimentary-tectonic framework for reconstructing the history of basement thrusting in the Wyoming region of the Cordilleran foreland.

Coeval displacement on both Sevier- and Laramide-style thrusts occurred during deposition of Upper Cretaceous and Lower Cenozoic nonmarine strata in the Cordilleran foreland basin (Dorr and others, 1977; Wiltschko and Dorr, 1983; Gries, 1983b; Beck, 1985). Basement thrusting within the Cordilleran foreland with corresponding thrust-loading overprinted the large-scale facies associations that characterized the basin during most of the Jurassic and Cretaceous. Imbrication along the margins of large, relatively coherent sheets of Precambrian basement 10 to 26 km thick (or more) and 100 to 300 km in width gradually divided the Cordilleran foreland into a mosaic of smaller Laramide-style foreland basins with intervening mountain ranges during latest Cretaceous through Eocene time.

Contemporaneous deformation in the Cordilleran Thrust Belt and Cordilleran foreland throughout the latest Cretaceous and early Tertiary (Armstrong, 1968) indicates that the terms Sevier and Laramide refer to different styles of deformation rather than temporally distinct orogenies. Deformation during this period reflects the end of an eastward-migrating Cordilleran orogeny that spanned the Mesozoic and early Cenozoic (Burchfiel

and Davis, 1975; Lageson, 1982). Recent work by Schwartz (1982), DeCelles (1984), and Kvale (1986) indicates that an early episode of Laramide-style deformation occurred in the Montana-Wyoming portion of the Cordilleran foreland during the Early Cretaceous. This is further evidence for considering the terms Sevier and Laramide as styles, rather than periods, of deformation.

FACIES MODEL FOR SYNTECTONIC SEDIMENTATION ADJACENT TO LARAMIDE BASEMENT THRUSTS

Laramide-style basement thrusting caused asymmetric subsidence of the footwall of each thrust. This pattern of thrusting and tectonically induced subsidence caused the formation of structurally and depositionally asymmetric basins adjacent to the frontal edges of each hanging wall. Asymmetric subsidence led to near-coincidence of structural and depositional axes during syntectonic sedimentation. The coincidence of these axes is recorded by marked intraformational thickening of facies representing low-energy depositional environments *toward* each basement-thrust (Beck, 1985; Beck and Vondra, 1985). Similar models have been proposed by Jordan (1981) and Wiltschko and Dorr (1983) for syntectonic sedimentation in the Cordilleran thrust belt adjacent to Sevier-style (predominantly thin-skinned) deformation.

The following sedimentary-tectonic model for syntectonic and posttectonic sedimentation adjacent to the impinging hanging walls of Laramide basement thrusts are described below in four phases: early thrusting, rapid thrusting, slow thrusting, and post-thrusting (Fig. 3,a,b,c,d). Variation in the rate of basement thrusting caused the vertical and horizontal distribution of syntectonic facies to vary accordingly.

Early thrusting phase

Isopach data for the Laramide intermontane basins of the Rocky Mountain foreland suggest that they were characterized by both structural and depositional asymmetry from the beginning of their development (Fig. 3a) (Keefer, 1965a,b; Keefer and Love, 1963; McDonald, 1972; Ryder and others, 1976; Skeen and Ray, 1983). Early uplift associated with initially blind basement thrusting caused development of erosional unconformities within upper Cretaceous and lower Paleocene strata (Curry, 1973; Johnson, 1985; Lawton, 1983; Ray, 1982; Rea and Barlow, 1975). Conglomerate consisting of clasts derived from Mesozoic strata was preferentially deposited in front of the impinging hanging walls of incipient basement-thrusts (Berg, 1963; Flueckinger, 1971; Love, 1978; Obernyer, 1978, 1980).

Thick-skinned basement thrusting caused the contemporaneous asymmetric uplift and subsidence at basin margins documented by Keefer (1965a,b; 1970), Keefer and Love (1963), and Love (1960). Uplift above the initially blind basement thrusts was manifest as asymmetric arching (force or drape folding) of Mesozoic and Paleozoic strata (Keefer, 1965b; Keefer and Love,

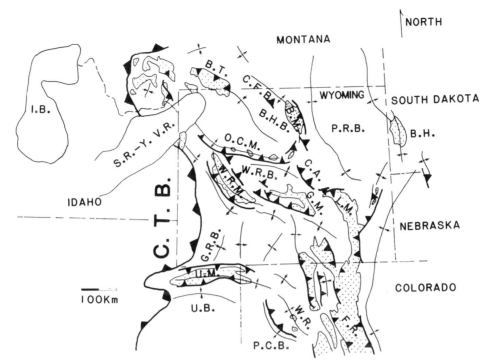

Figure 2. Major structural features of the Wyoming region showing predominance of arcuate Laramide basement thrusts and asymmetric basins. Precambrian outcrops are stippled. B.H. = Black Hills; B.H.B. = Bighorn basin; B.M. = Bighorn Mountains; B.T.M. = Beartooth Mountains; C.A. = Casper arch; C.F.B. = Clark's Fork Basin; C.T.B. = Cordilleran thrust belt; F.R. = Front Range; G.M. = Granite Mountains; G.R.B. = Green River basin; I.B. = Idaho batholith; L.M. = Laramie Mountains; O.C.M. = Owl Creek Mountains; P.C.B. = Piceance Creek basin; P.R.B. = Powder River basin; S.R.-Y.V.R. = Snake River–Yellowstone volcanic rift; U.B. = Uinta basin; U.M. = Uinta Mountains; W.R. = White River uplift; W.R.B. = Wind River basin; W.R.M. = Wind River Mountains. Modified after Hamilton (1978).

1963). Asymmetric basin subsidence due to thrust-loading along one basin margin tilted the pre-basin Mesozoic strata toward the rising foreland uplifts and caused erosional reworking of this sediment into thrustward thickening wedges of latest Cretaceous and Paleocene strata. Low-gradient fluvial and paludal depositional environments characterized the basins during this early phase of syntectonic sedimentation (Berg, 1963; Ethridge and others, 1981; Flores, 1981; Gingerich, 1983; Hickey, 1980; Keefer, 1965b, 1969; Rea and Barlow, 1975).

Rapid thrusting phase

This phase of Laramide basin evolution was characterized by increased rates of thrusting, during which the rate of subsidence exceeded or equalled the rate of sedimentation, causing the structural and depostional axes of the basins to converge (Fig. 3b). Characteristic syntectonic facies of each basin included a narrow, coarse conglomeratic facies adjacent to the impinging hanging wall of each thrust, a narrow sandstone/mudstone/coal facies immediately basinward, a mudstone/coal/carbonate/evaporite facies above the depositional axis, and finally, a wide distal sandstone/mudstone/coal facies. Conglomerate lithologies predictably change upward, consisting of clasts derived from Mes-

ozoic strata, Paleozoic strata, and Precambrian basement. This reflects sequential unroofing of the rising thrust-bounded basement blocks (Berg, 1963; Brown, 1948; Flueckinger, 1971, 1972; Keefer, 1965b, 1969; Love, 1978; Sharp, 1948).

Basement thrusting caused tectonically induced subsidence of the footwall of each thrust. Rapid subsidence adjacent to the frontal edge of the hanging wall of each thrust relative to the rate of sedimentation is recorded by the intraformational thickening of strata representing low-energy depositional environments *toward* each impinging thrust. Localization of these low-gradient, low-energy environments near the thrusts (Berg, 1963; Gingerich, 1983; Hickey, 1980; Keefer, 1965a,b, 1969; McDonald, 1972; Obernyer, 1978, 1980; Ryder and others, 1976; Surdam and Stanley, 1980b) suggests that the depositional axes of the Laramide intermontane basins were well defined near their respective structural axes, and that the frontal edges of impinging hanging-wall blocks did not supply the majority of sediment deposited in the basins during episodes of rapid thrusting.

Continued asymmetric subsidence during this phase maintained a thrustward-dipping depositional gradient within each basin during rapid thrust movement. Paleocurrent and sediment provenance data, coupled with isochronous facies associations, indicate that the large areas of Mesozoic and Paleozoic strata

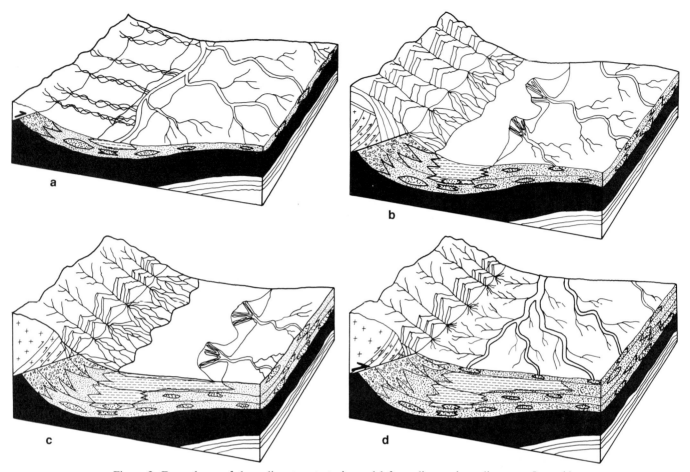

Figure 3. Four phases of the sedimentary-tectonic model for sedimentation adjacent to Laramide basement thrusts. These phases include early thrusting (a), rapid thrusting (b), slow thrusting (c), and postthrusting (d). Irregular oval outline pattern indicates conglomeratic facies; fine stippling indicates sandstone/mudstone/coal facies; coarse stippling indicates isolated sandstone bodies; dashed line pattern indicates mudstone/coal/carbonate/evaporite facies; dark patterned areas in cross section indicate pre–Late Cretaceous strata; crosses indicate Precambrian basement. See text for discussion. Structure is schematic only.

above thrustward-dipping monoclines were the major sources of sediment deposited in Laramide-style intermontaine basins of the Cordilleran foreland (Berg, 1963; Courdin and Hubert, 1969; Denson and Pipiringos, 1969; Gingerich, 1983; Hickey, 1980; Ryder and others, 1976; Seeland, 1976, 1978). Areas above the frontal ramps of basement thrusts provided coarse but volumetrically minor quantities of clastic sediment during thrust movement (Seeland, 1976, 1978).

Slow thrusting phase

Thrusting slowed or ceased during the transition phase between syntectonic and posttectonic sedimentation, allowing the rate of sedimentation to equal or exceed the rate of thrust-load–induced subsidence adjacent to the frontal edge of each hanging wall (Fig. 3c). Low-energy depositional environments were no longer localized near the frontal ramp areas of each basement thrust (Eugster and Hardie, 1975; Eugster and Surdam,

1973; Ryder and others, 1976). Tectonically induced subsidence was no longer sufficient to maintain thrustward-dipping depositional gradients. Clastic sediment supply from the gently dipping basin margins opposite the thrusts decreased. The structural and depositional axes of the basins diverged, and the depositional axes became poorly defined. Low-energy paludal, playa, and lacustrine depositional environments expanded to their greatest areal extent during this time. Low-gradient conditions were widespread during the transition from syntectonic to posttectonic sedimentation unless followed by another episode of more rapid thrusting.

Post-thrusting phase

The late or post-thrusting phase of basin evolution (Fig. 3d) was characterized by rates of sedimentation that greatly exceeded the rate of subsidence. The structural and depositional axes diverged. Higher gradient, higher energy alluvial plain and fluvial environments expanded in area (Ryder and others, 1976; Surdam and Stanley, 1980b), and the frontal edges of hanging-wall basement-thrust blocks became more important as sediment source areas (Andersen and Picard, 1974). Thick, areally extensive fluvial clastic wedges developed adjacent to the leading edges of impinging hanging walls, and the depositional asymmetry of each basin decreased. Fluvial environments dominated the basins as a whole, with trunk streams and small areas of paludal and lacustrine deposition occupying poorly defined depositional axes. Thrust collapse (Sales, 1983; Winterfeld and Conard, 1983) or minor thrusting at the thrusted margins may have occurred, but overall facies associations were not affected.

The model described above is derived from areas of proven basement thrusting, such as the northern Green River Basin, and accurately predicts the facies patterns found in other Laramide intermontane basins of the Central Cordilleran foreland. The following discussion compares the model with the histories of the Clark's Fork, Bighorn, Powder River, Wind River, northern Green River, southern Green River, Uinta, and Piceance Creek Basins.

BIGHORN AND CLARK'S FORK BASINS

Late Cretaceous

Late Cretaceous events in the Bighorn Basin of Wyoming included the arching of Mesozoic strata, shoreline sedimentation, and regression of the Lewis Sea (Bown, 1980). The Lewis Sea, part of the Cretaceous Interior Seaway, retreated from the region now occupied by the Bighorn Basin before the deposition of the fluvial, paludal, and lacustrine sediments of the Lance Formation during Maastrichtian time (Bown, 1980). Keefer and Love (1963) noted that the downwarping of basins kept pace with or exceeded sedimentation from rising source areas. Late Cretaceous sediment in central Wyoming was deposited in two troughs that were segmented by perpendicular upwarps during and soon after Paleocene time (Keefer and Love, 1963).

Rea and Barlow (1975) attributed westward thickening of the uppermost Cretaceous Meeteetse and Lance Formations within the Bighorn Basin to an early phase of Laramide deformation. Structure contour data for the top of the underlying Mesaverde Formation indicate that this thickening was structurally controlled and is not an artifact of erosion at the overlying Cretaceous-Tertiary unconformity near the basin margins (Fig. 4) (Rea and Barlow, 1975). Eastward thrusting beneath the present axis of the Bighorn Basin (Hausel and others, 1979) may have controlled the westward thickening of uppermost Cretaceous strata—a thrust referred to herein as the Meeteetse thrust. Southwestward thrusting of the Washakie Range, which lies southwest of the present Bighorn Basin (Fig. 2), created a northwest-trending arch (Love, 1977; Winterfeld and Conard, 1983) during latest Cretaceous time. The Washakie Range was eroded to its Paleozoic strata by the end of the Cretaceous (Love, 1977). Contemporaneous thrusting and uplift of the Washakie, Beartooth, and northern Bighorn Mountains during the Late Cre-

taceous and their subsequent denudation provided clasts derived from Precambrian basement during the Paleocene (Bown, 1980; Van Houten, 1952).

Paleocene

Paleontological and paleobotanical research completed on the Paleogene strata of the Bighorn Basin, Clark's Fork Basin and adjacent basins (Fig. 2) has resulted in the delineation of isochrons (Bown, 1980; Gingerich, 1983; Hickey, 1980). These studies have allowed detailed basin analysis with respect to time. The Paleocene Fort Union Formation overlies the Lance with angular unconformity at the western and southeastern margins of the Bighorn Basin and with erosional unconformity to the north and south. These relationships were interpreted by Bown (1980) as defining an open-ended, north-south–trending basin downwarped during the Paleocene.

Southwestward thrusting of the northern Bighorn Mountains (Foose and others, 1961; Hamilton, 1978, 1981) may have localized the Paleocene Puercan, Torrejonian, and early Tiffanian terrestrial deposits of the Fort Union Formation (Fig. 5) along the

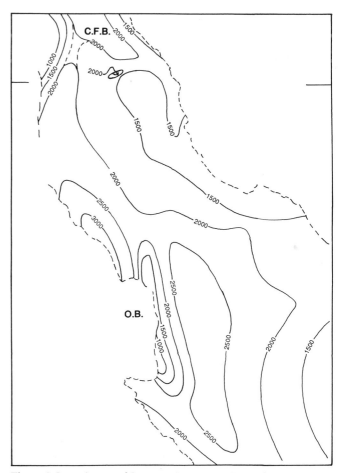

Figure 4. Isopach map of Lance and Meeteetse Formations in Bighorn basin. O.B. = Oregon Basin uplift; C.F.B. = Clark's Fork basin. Modified after Rea and Barlow (1975).

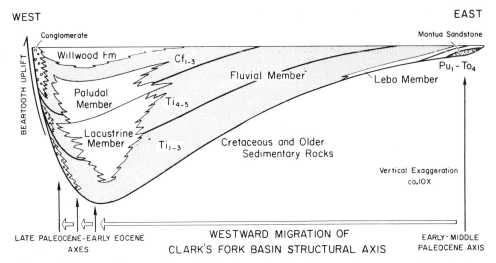

Figure 5. Diagrammatic cross section of the Clark's Fork basin as it appeared at the end of Clarkforkian time (earliest Eocene). Upper Paleocene sediments (Ti_1 – Cf_3) reflect asymmetric subsidence induced by northeastward movement of the Beartooth Thrust. Note localization of low-gradient conditions adjacent to the thrusted margin. From Gingerich (1983). Reproduced by permission of the Wyoming Geological Association.

northeast margin of the Bighorn and Clark's Fork Basins adjacent to the rising Pryor and northern Bighorn Mountains (Bown, 1980; Gingerich, 1983; Hickey, 1980; Oswald and Kraus, 1986). These deposits constitute the fluvial Mantua Sandstone (Gingerich, 1983; Oswald and Kraus, 1986) and overlying carbonaceous shale, mudstone, sandstone, and lignite of the Lebo Member (Hickey, 1980).

The Beartooth basement-thrust sheet (Fig. 1) (Foose and others, 1961) moved northeastward above a southwest-dipping shear plane from middle Paleocene to early Eocene time. It appears to have loaded the western margin of the Clark's Fork Basin (Fig. 5), and reversed the asymmetry of the basin during the middle Tiffanian (Gingerich, 1983) north of the Clark's Fork Fault. Subsidence on the western margin of the Bighorn Basin due to loading by thrusting was not as great as subsidence along the western margin of the Clark's Fork Basin. The structural and depositional asymmetry of the Bighorn Basin south of the Clark's Fork Fault was correspondingly less, although the structural and depositional axes of the Bighorn Basin did migrate westward (Bown, 1980; Gingerich, 1983; Hausel and others, 1979; Rea and Barlow, 1975). Kraus (1985) found paleosol sequences in the northern Bighorn Basin to be less mature than those to the south, reflecting a northward increase in rates of accumulation and subsidence. Inferred eastward thrusting of the central segment of the Bighorn Mountains (Berg, 1981; Blackstone, 1981; Fanshawe, 1971; Peterson, 1983) and development of the Bighorn Monocline on their western flank by middle Paleocene continued into the early Eocene (Brown, 1948; Sharp, 1948). This enhanced the structural and depositional asymmetry of the Bighorn Basin while providing a large, west-dipping sediment source area composed of Mesozoic and Paleozoic strata.

Facies developed within the Clark's Fork Basin during the middle and late Paleocene (Fig. 5) intraformationally thickened to the west after middle Tiffanian time, when the structural and depositional axes shifted to the west (Gingerich, 1983). The following facies occur from west to east: (1) a narrow, coarse conglomerate facies adjacent to the tip of the Beartooth Thrust, which is indicative of alluvial fan and coarse braided stream environments (Bredall, 1971; Flueckinger, 1972; Neasham and Vondra, 1972); (2) a narrow sandstone/mudstone facies, which reflects streams with basinward decreasing gradients (Gingerich, 1983; Hickey, 1980); (3) a basinal mudstone/coal facies, which was deposited under paludal to lacustrine conditions (Gingerich, 1983; Hickey, 1980); and (4) a wide sandstone/mudstone/coal facies, which is indicative of fluvial conditions (Gingerich, 1983; Hickey, 1980) that spanned the eastern two-thirds of the basin opposite the Beartooth thrust.

The depositional axis of the Clark's Fork Basin did not diverge significantly eastward from the structural axis during late Paleocene time. Low-gradient paludal and lacustrine conditions remained localized along the western margin of the basin (Fig. 5) (Gingerich, 1983). We interpret the restricted middle to late Paleocene development of a fluvial clastic wedge on the western margin of the Clark's Fork Basin (Figs. 2, 5) as being due to rapid, thick-skinned basement-thrusting; rapid, thrust-load–induced asymmetric subsidence; and the southwestward dip of the Beartooth thrust sheet away from the Clark's Fort Basin. The leading edge of the Beartooth thrust sheet provided a coarse but volumetrically minor quantity of sediment to the Clark's Fork Basin (Gingerich, 1983).

Topographic expression of the South Owl Creek Thrust (Fanshawe, 1939; Hamilton, 1978; Keefer and Love, 1963; Wise, 1963) occurred by early Eocene time. Maximum elevation of the Precambrian basement of the South Owl Creek thrust occurs in the western portion of the thrust (Love and others, 1955).

Early Eocene sediment input from the Washakie Range therefore diverged about the Owl Creek Mountains and provided conglomerate reworked from the Harebell Formation via braided streams to the southwest Bighorn Basin (Young, 1972) and northwest Wind River Basin (Seeland, 1978). Eocene roundstone conglomerate deposits overlie the conglomerate facies of the Paleocene Fort Union Formation with angular unconformity in the southwestern Bighorn Basin (Young, 1972; Kraus, 1984).

POWDER RIVER BASIN

Paleocene

Isopach data by Curry (1971) from the Powder River Basin (Fig. 6a,b,c) adjacent to the central and southern Bighorn Mountains (Figs. 1, 2, 6a) show little evidence of Laramide deformation in that area until the deposition of the early Paleocene Fort Union Tullock Sandstone (Curry, 1971).

We infer that middle Paleocene development of the east-directed Bighorn thrust (Fig. 2) caused subsidence of the western margin of the Powder River Basin. This subsidence is recorded by the westward thickening of the mudstones of the Lebo Member of the Fort Union Formation (Fig. 6b) (Curry, 1971), and by a narrow conglomerate facies deposited adjacent to the leading edge of the Bighorn thrust within the Fort Union Formation (Obernyer, 1980). Isopach and structure contour data show that, from the middle Paleocene through at least the early Eocene, the Powder River Basin was strongly asymmetric, with its structural and depositional axes near the frontal edge of the east-directed Bighorn thrust (Fig. 6, b and c) (Curry, 1971; Obernyer, 1978, 1980; Seeland, 1976). The structural asymmetry of the Powder River Basin was probably enhanced by eastward thrusting of the Black Hills and by development of the west-dipping Black Hills monocline. The Black Hills display a pattern of differential uplift similar to that of the Bighorn Mountains to the west (Lisenbee, 1978; Shapiro, 1971). Relationships between Early Tertiary intrusives and structural features such as the Fanny Peak Lineament (Shapiro, 1971) suggest thrusting of the Black Hills occurred during the late Paleocene and early Eocene.

Rapid subsidence of the western margin of the Powder River Basin during the late Paleocene (Fig. 6c) (Curry, 1971) resulted in low-gradient fluvial and paludal depositional environments in which the thick coals of the late Paleocene Tongue River Member of the Fort Union Formation were deposited (Ethridge and others, 1981; Flores, 1981; Glass, 1976). East of Sheridan, Wyoming, early Wasatchian-age strata lack significant coal deposits (Culbertson and Mapel, 1976), possibly reflecting lower rates of subsidence relative to sedimentation.

Early Eocene

Initiation of a second phase of terrestrial coal deposition during the middle Wasatchian in the western Powder River Basin (Culbertson and Maple, 1976; Glass, 1976) is interpreted to have resulted from renewed early to middle Wasatchian eastward movement on the Bighorn thrust. Obernyer (1978, 1980) attributed Wasatchian subsidence of the western portion of the Powder River Basin to faulting. Kraus (1980) attributed deposition of the Clark's Fork sheet sandstone of the Willwood Formation to decreased rates of basinal subsidence and decreased rates of sedimentation in the Clark's Fork Basin at the end of Clarkforkian and the beginning of Wasatchian time. Therefore, rates of thrust-loading for both the Beartooth and Bighorn thrusts are inferred to have decreased during latest Clarkforkian and earliest Wasatchian time.

Lower Eocene conglomerate was deposited along the structural axes of the Wind River, Bighorn, Clark's Fork, and Powder River Basins (Fig. 2) above angular unconformities that separated them from older Paleocene conglomerate or tilted Mesozoic strata. Paleocene conglomerate deposits consist predominantly of clasts derived from Mesozoic strata. Eocene conglomerate deposits are dominated by clasts derived from Paleozoic strata near their base and grade upward to clasts derived predominantly from Precambrian basement (Brown, 1948; Flueckinger, 1971, 1972; Keefer, 1965a,b; Love, 1978; McDonald, 1972; Sharp, 1948). These Paleogene conglomerate deposits record the unroofing of adjacent, initially blind basement thrusts, and have a depositional polarity similar to that of their associated structurally asymmetric basins (Figs. 7a, b).

Seeland (1976, 1978) studied the early Eocene paleocurrent patterns and sediment provenance of the Powder River Basin. His studies showed that the depositional axes of these basins lay near to the frontal edges of the Southern Bighorn and South Owl Creek thrusts (Fig. 2), respectively. The frontal edges of these basement-thrust sheets provided clasts for coarse deposits of conglomerate and sandstone, but they contributed only a fraction of the total sediment that was deposited in the Powder River and Wind River Basins (Seeland, 1976, 1978). In the Powder River Basin, these conglomerate deposits are designated as the Wasatchian (lower Eocene) Kingsbury Conglomerate (Brown, 1948; Darton, 1906; Hose, 1955; Sharp, 1948), which is overlain unconformably by the upper Eocene(?) Moncrief Gravel (Sharp, 1948). Paleozoic limestone has been locally thrust over the Moncrief Gravel along the eastern flank of the Bighorn Mountains (Hose, 1955; Sharp, 1948).

Paleocurrent studies by Seeland (1976, 1978) from the Powder River and Wind River Basins indicate that the Wind River of early Eocene time flowed eastward just south of the structural axis of the Wind River Basin before crossing the Casper Arch (Fig. 2) and turning northward to flow just east of the structural axis of the Powder River Basin. This drainage system deposited narrow bands of fluvial sandstone within the predominantly fine-grained facies characteristic of their depositional axes (Ethridge and others, 1981; Flores, 1981; Seeland, 1976, 1978). Paleocurrent and sediment provenance data for the eastern three-fourths of the Powder River Basin indicate that early Eocene sediment in this area was deposited by streams flowing westward from the Black Hills and Black Hills monocline (Seeland, 1976).

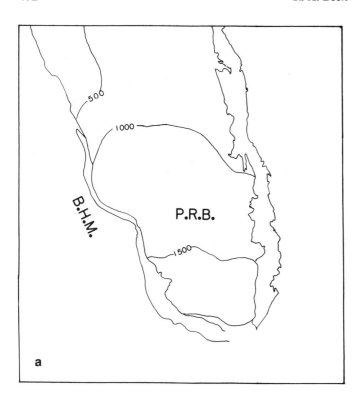

Figure 6. Isopach maps of lower Tertiary strata in the Powder River basin. a, Isopach map of Tullock member of Paleocene Fort Union Formation. b, Isopach map of Lebo member of Paleocene Fort Union Formation. c, Isopach map of Tongue River member of Fort Union Formation plus Wasatch Formation. B.H.M. = Bighorn Mountains; P.R.B. = Powder River basin. Modified after Curry (1971).

Furthermore, Seeland (1976, p. 53) stated, "In contrast, the streams flowing eastward off the Bighorns had a relatively minor effect on sedimentation patterns of the basin and contributed relatively little to the sediment now preserved in the basin."

WIND RIVER BASIN

Late Cretaceous

Love (1960) and Keefer (1965a, b) noted that the uppermost Cretaceous Lance Formation of the Wind River Basin was significantly influenced by local tectonic movements. Isopach data for the Lance indicate pronounced thickening from southwest to northeast within the basin, to a maximum of more than 2,000 m adjacent to the southern margin of the Southern Bighorn Mountains and western margin of the Casper Arch. Curry (1971) presented isopach data for the southern Powder River Basin, which show southwestward thickening of the uppermost Cretaceous Fox Hills and Lance Formations toward a maximum of 1,000 m adjacent to the eastern margin of the Casper Arch (Fig. 5a). Thickening of the Lance Formation toward each margin of the Casper Arch suggests either tectonic disruption of previously deposited strata in a common depocenter or syntectonic sedimentation influenced by thrust-load–induced subsidence due to basement thrusting on both margins of the Casper Arch. Recent seismic data presented by Gries (1983b) and Skeen and Ray (1983) show southward thrusting of the Owl Creek and Southern Bighorn Mountains (Demorest, 1941) and southwestward thrusting of the Casper Arch relative to the Wind River Basin. Drill penetration of 3,000 m of a thrusted slab of Precambrian base-

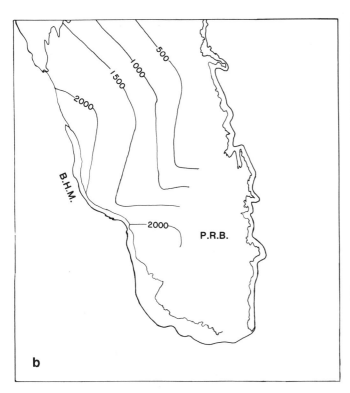

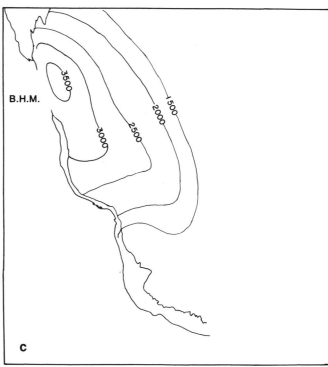

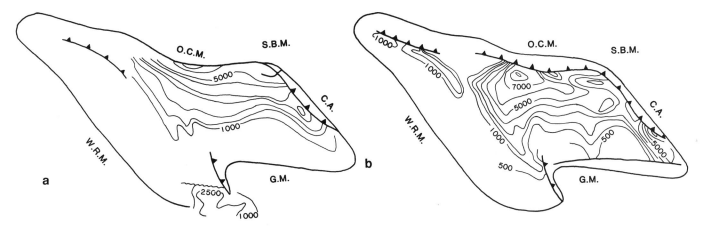

Figure 7. Isopach maps of lower Tertiary strata in the Wind River basin. a, Isopach map of Paleocene Fort Union Formation. b, Isopach map of lower Eocene strata. C.A. = Casper arch; G.M. = Granite Mountains; O.C.M. = Owl Creek Mountains; S.B.M. = southern Bighorn Mountains; W.R.M. = Wind River Mountains. After Gries (1983b), modified from Keefer (1965b) and Love (1970).

ment on the western margin of the Casper Arch, with gas production from underlying Cretaceous strata, proved the existence of a basement thrust (Gries, 1983a, b).

Maximum thrust displacement of the southern Bighorn Mountains and of the western margin of the Casper Arch occurs at the northeastern margin of the Wind River Basin where they intersect (Fig. 7b) (Gries, 1983a, b; Skeen and Ray, 1983). This point coincides with the isopach maximum for the uppermost Cretaceous Lance Formation (Fig. 6), and suggests that thrusting of one or both structures was active during its deposition.

Paleocene

The uppermost Cretaceous Lance Formation in the Wind River Basin is overlain by the Paleocene Fort Union Formation. Fort Union strata are divided into two members, the lower unnamed member (Keefer, 1961) and the overlying Waltman Member (Phillips, 1983). The former consists of conglomerate, sandstone, and shale deposited in fluvial environments. This unit thickens northeastward to a maximum of about 300 m (Keefer, 1965b). Strata of the Waltman Member thicken northeastward to a maximum of 2,260 m (Fig. 7a) adjacent to the southern Bighorn Mountains (Keefer, 1965b) at the northeastern margin of the Wind River Basin.

Phillips (1983) summarized the basinward sequence of facies as fan plain, braided stream channel, distal fan, and prodelta-lacustrine. Lithologies of the basin margin facies of the Waltman Member include conglomerate, sandstone, dull-colored claystone, and noncarbonaceous shale. Carbonaceous shale and coal are minor constituents (Keefer, 1965b; Phillips, 1983). The prodelta-lacustrine facies of the Waltman Member is characterized by dark, silty micaceous shale, and intercalated, rare, thin, fine-grained sandstones deposited in Waltman Lake (Keefer, 1965b; Phillips, 1983). The depositional axis of Waltman Lake was located near the overthrust northern and northeastern margins of the Wind River Basin (Fig. 7a) (Keefer, 1965b; Phillips, 1983; Skeen and Ray, 1983).

Within the Waltman Member, Phillips (1983) distinguished a lower and an upper sequence separated by a thin, calcareous siltstone marker bed. During deposition of the lower sequence, coarse clastics were restricted to narrow belts along the basin margins. The majority of these coarse clastics were deposited along the southern margin of the Wind River Basin and were derived from the gently northward-dipping monocline of the Granite Mountains (Keefer, 1965b; Love, 1970; Phillips, 1983). The overlying thin calcareous siltstone marker bed was attributed to a period of tectonic quiescence (Phillips, 1983). The upper sequence indicates a major influx of coarse clastics that were deposited in extensive fan-delta complexes (Phillips, 1983) along the basin margins.

The above stratigraphic relationships indicate that the structural and depositional axes of the Wind River Basin converged during deposition of the lower sequence of the middle to late Paleocene (Fig. 7a) (Keefer, 1965b) Waltman Member of the Fort Union Formation. We interpret this convergence to represent rapid basement thrusting of the western Casper Arch toward the southwest and of the Owl Creek and Southern Bighorn Mountains to the south. Inferred lower rates of thrusting, or perhaps changes in basin drainage or climate, resulted in deposition of the thin, laterally extensive middle Waltman siltstone. Development of laterally extensive fan deltas during deposition of the upper sequence of the Waltman Member suggests divergence of the structural and depositional axes, possibly due to decreased rates of thrusting.

Skeen and Ray (1983) developed isochron maps of the Lance, lower Fort Union, and upper Fort Union adjacent to the thrusted western margin of the Casper Arch (Gries, 1983a, b; Skeen and Ray, 1983). Their isochron synclinal thicks indicate a shift of the depositional axis westward during deposition of the above strata (Skeen and Ray, 1983). Skeen and Ray (1983) attributed westward migration of the depositional axis to westward thrusting of the Casper Arch.

Ray (1982) recognized five unconformities from seismic data associated with Paleocene Fort Union strata near the southwestern margin of the Wind River Basin. These unconformities are probably directly related to folding and thrusting in the southwestern Wind River Basin (Ray, 1982) and southwestward thrusting and northeastward tilting of the Wind River Mountains (Berg, 1962, 1963).

Early Eocene

Lower Eocene strata of the Wind River Basin include the Indian Meadows Formation and overlying Wind River Formation. Both units thicken from the southwestern margin toward the northeastern margin of the basin (Fig. 7b) (Keefer, 1961, 1965b, 1969; Love, 1978). Two major facies associations exist within early Eocene strata of the Wind River Basin and consist of mountainward and basinward facies associations (Keefer, 1969). Strata of the mountainward facies association are relatively thin and conglomeratic with unconformable contacts, whereas strata of the basinward facies association are thicker and finer grained with conformable or nearly conformable contacts (Keefer, 1965, 1969). Near the north-central portion of the basin, deposition in low-energy depositional environments was probably continuous, or nearly so, throughout Paleocene and early Eocene time (Keefer, 1965b, 1969; Love, 1978).

The Indian Meadows Formation (Love, 1939), as redefined by Keefer (1965b), is Graybullian (middle Wasatchian) in age (Keefer, 1965b; Winterfeld and Conard, 1983). It consists of vari-colored claystone, siltstone, and conglomerate (Keefer, 1965b). A narrow conglomeratic facies outcrops along the northwestern (Winterfeld and Conard, 1983), northern (Keefer, 1965b) and northeastern (Love, 1978) margins of the Wind River Basin. Clasts of the conglomeratic facies were derived from rocks of Mesozoic, Paleozoic, and Precambrian ages (Keefer 1965). Large allochthonous blocks of Mesozoic and Paleozoic strata are locally present within the formation along the northwestern (Winterfeld and Conard, 1983) and northern (Keefer, 1965b) margins of the basin. Lower Eocene Indian Meadows strata are separated from steeply dipping upper Paleocene strata of the Waltman Member of the Fort Union Formation by an angular unconformity along the northern and northeastern margins of the Wind River Basin (Keefer, 1965b; Love, 1978; Winterfeld and Conard, 1983).

This unconformity indicates that major thrust movement occurred before Graybullian (middle Wasatchian) time. The allochthonous masses of Mesozoic and Paleozoic strata were emplaced soon after this phase of thrusting (Winterfeld and Conard, 1983).

Upturned Paleocene strata of the Waltman Member along the western margin of the Casper Arch are overlapped by strata of the late Wasatchian Wind River Formation and locally by strata of the middle Wasatchian Indian Meadows Formation (Keefer, 1965b, 1970; Phillips, 1983). Therefore, major thrusting occurred along the western Casper Arch prior to late Wasatchian, and probably before mid-Wasatchian, time.

The late Wasatchian (early Eocene) Wind River Formation overlies the middle Wasatchian Indian Meadows Formation unconformably along the northern and northeastern margins of the Wind River Basin (Keefer, 1965b, 1970; Love, 1978; Winterfeld and Conard, 1983). Strata of the Wind River Formation are divided into two members, the Lysite Member and the Lost Cabin Member. These members are defined on the basis of lithology and vertebrate faunal content (Granger, 1910; Keefer, 1965b; Sinclair and Granger, 1911). They have been differentiated from each other only along the northern and northeastern margins of the Wind River Basin where they are separated by an erosional or angular unconformity (Keefer, 1965b; Love, 1978).

The Lysite Member was deposited in response to southward thrusting of the southern margins of the South Owl Creek Mountains and Southern Bighorn Mountains on the South Owl Creek thrust fault system, which tilted Indian Meadows strata as much as 35° and initiated erosion of much of the formation adjacent to the Southern Bighorn Mountains (Love, 1978). In the northwestern portion of the Wind River Basin, thrusting was transferred northeastward from the latest Cretaceous through middle Wasatchian (early Eocene) Goose Lake anticline–EA–North EA thrust system to the Waynes Hole anticline–Diamond Ridge thrust system before being overlapped by the late Wasatchian Wind River Formation (Winterfeld and Conard, 1983). The Lysite Member consists of clasts derived from predominantly Precambrian sources (Keefer, 1965b; Winterfeld and Conard, 1983), except in the Badwater area adjacent to the Southern Bighorn Mountains where it is dominated by clasts derived from Paleozoic strata (Love, 1978).

Renewed southward and southwestward thrusting of the South Owl Creek Mountains and Southern Bighorn Mountains tilted the Lysite Member before deposition of the Lost Cabin Member above an erosional to angular unconformity (Keefer, 1965b, 1969; Love, 1978). This episode of thrusting displaced the southernmost portion of the Southern Bighorn Mountains and northwestern Casper Arch as a discrete block (Love, 1978). The Lost Cabin Member is distinguished from the underlying Lysite Member in the Badwater area by its composition of Precambrian vs. Paleozoic rock fragments and by the presence of *Lambdotherium* in the Lost Cabin Member (Keefer, 1965b; Love, 1978; Sinclair and Granger, 1911).

North- to south-changing facies within the fluvial lower sequence of the Paleocene Fort Union and Eocene Wind River Formations were described by Courdin and Hubert (1969), Keefer (1965a,b), and Seeland (1975, 1978). Coarse conglomerate was deposited adjacent to the South Owl Creek thrust. A wide sandstone/mudstone facies dominated the basin. Along the depositional axis, the sandstone and mudstone facies resulted from depositional in flood plains, lakes, and swamps. Major trunk streams deposited channel sandstones within the low-energy environment. The sandstone to mudstone ratio *increases* to the south of the depositional axis, *away* from the South Owl Creek thrust. This increase reflects the gradual increase in gradient from the depositional axis to the north-dipping southern margin of the Wind River Basin (Seeland, 1975, 1978).

Paleocurrent data presented by Courdin and Hubert (1969) and by Seeland (1975, 1978) for the Wind River Basin indicate that the ancestral Wind River flowed adjacent to the northern margin of the basin, with many north-northeast–flowing tributaries joining it from the south. This drainage pattern characterized the Wind River Basin during deposition of the lower member of the Paleocene Fort Union Formation and during deposition of most lower Eocene strata (Courdin and Hubert, 1969; Keefer, 1965b, 1969; Seeland, 1975, 1978). Therfore, during this style of deposition the north- and northeast-dipping basin margins *opposite* the thrusts were the dominant sediment source regions in terms of basin area and possibly in terms of total volume of sediment deposited.

GREEN RIVER BASIN

Paleocene

Berg (1963) and Curry (1973) described the Paleocene sedimentary facies of the Fort Union Formation in the subsurface along the southwestern margin of the Wind River Thrust (Fig. 1). The Wind River basement-thrust sheet lies above a fault plane that dips approximately 35° northeastward (Brewer and Turcotte, 1980; Smithson and others, 1979). Approximately 15 km of vertical and 32 km of horizontal displacement have occurred on the fault (Gries, 1983a; Smithson and others, 1979).

Paleocene sedimentary facies in the Green River (Bridger) Basin (Figs. 2, 9) include, from northeast to southwest, a narrow conglomerate and sandstone facies adjacent to the leading edge of the thrust, which abruptly interfingers with a thick mudstone/ coal facies above the depositional axis and a wide distal sandstone/mudstone/coal facies. The conglomerate facies consists of a vertical sequence of clasts derived from Mesozoic shale; Paleozoic limestone, dolomite, chert, and quartzite; and Precambrian crystalline basement (Berg, 1963). Paleocene conglomerate lithologies of the northeastern Green River Basin record unroofing of the Wind River basement-thrust sheet by the end of Paleocene time. The mudstone/coal facies consists of drab shale with thin beds of carbonaceous shale and coal (Berg, 1963). The wide distal sandstone/mudstone/coal facies contains more sandstone and less coal with increasing distance from the depositional axis. Low-energy Paleocene sediments in the Green River Basin thicken toward the Wind River thrust (Fig. 8) (Curry, 1973).

The depositional axis of the Green River Basin was nearly coincident with its structural axis during the Paleocene (McDonald, 1972). Low-energy depositional environments were localized adjacent to the structural axis throughout Paleocene time (Fig. 9). Maintenance of these conditions during the Paleocene is attributed to rapid thrust-load–induced subsidence that equalled or exceeded the rate of sedimentation. This subsidence resulted from

Paleocene southwestward displacement of the Wind River thrust. Early Eocene development of a thick, extensive fluvial clastic wedge (Wasatch Formation) adjacent to the frontal edge of the Wind River thrust (McDonald, 1972; Steidtmann and others, 1983) is attributed to decreased rates of thrusting near the end of the Paleocene. Steidtmann and others (1983) demonstrated minor displacement on the Wind River thrust during latest early Eocene time and displacement on the Continental Fault to the north during late early Eocene time.

Eocene

During earliest Eocene time, the structural and depositional polarity of the Green River Basin was reversed (Fig. 9). Isopach data indicate that the depositional axis shifted from the northern to the southern part of the Green River Basin (Fig. 2, McDonald, 1972). We attribute this reversal to late Paleocene through middle Eocene northward thrusting of the Uinta Mountains (Bruhn and others, 1983; Gries, 1983a; Hamilton, 1978, 1981; Ritzma, 1971). This thrust system is referred to herein as the North Uinta thrust.

Thrusting along the northern margin of the Uinta Mountains is inferred to have caused the rate of subsidence to exceed the rate of sedimentation along the southern margin of the Green River Basin during early Eocene time. Facies developed in the Wasatch Formation during the early Eocene (Fig. 9), from southwest to northeast, consisted of the Richard's Mountain Fanglomerate adjacent to the North Uinta thrust, a narrow fluvial sandstone/mudstone/coal facies just basinward, a palaudal to lacustrine facies above the depositional axis, and a wide distal sandstone/mudstone/coal facies (McDonald, 1972). Early Eocene strata of the Green River Basin depositionally thicken toward the North Uinta thrust (Fig. 9) (McDonald, 1972). Anderson (1985, p. 5) noted that strata of dominantly Uintan provenance in the Green River Basin occur within 20 km of the Uinta Mountains, and that "the contribution of the eastern Uinta Mountains to synorogenic basin fill evidently was volumetrically minor during the Early Eocene."

The predominantly fluvial and lacustrine deposits of the Wasatch Formation of the Green River Basin are intercalated with and overlain by the playa and lacustrine deposits of the Green River Formation (Eugster and Hardie, 1975; Surdam and Stanley, 1980b). Facies and depositional environments of the Green River Formation in the Green River Basin were summarized by Surdam and Stanley (1980b).

Deposition of the Wasatch Formation was followed by deposition of the thin Luman Tongue Member of the Green River Formation. Strata of the Luman Tongue consist of mudstone, coal, coquinoidal limestone, and sandstone. Some of the mudstone is low-grade oil shale. These sediments were deposited under shallow lacustrine and paludal conditions (Surdam and Stanley, 1980b). The Luman Tongue Member is overlain by fluvial sandstone and mudstone of the Niland Tongue Member of the Wasatch Formation (McDonald, 1972).

Rates of thrusting and thrust-load–induced subsidence rela-

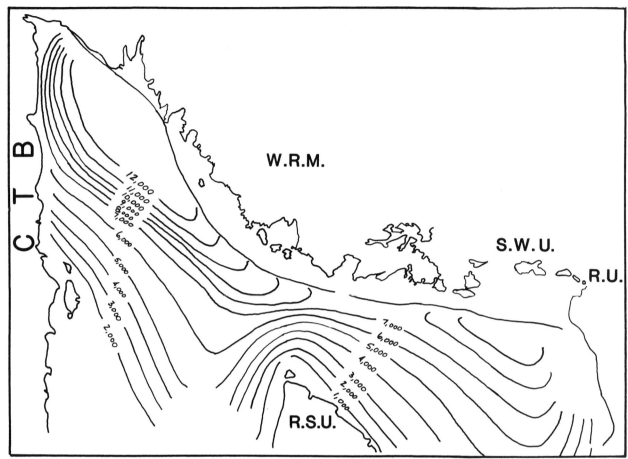

Figure 8. Isopach map of Fort Union and Wasatch Formations in the northern Green River Basin. C.T.B. = Cordilleran thrust belt; R.S.U. = Rock Springs uplift; R.U. = Rawlins uplift; S.W.U. = Sweetwater uplift; W.R.M. = Wind River Mountains. After Curry (1973).

tive to the rate of sedimentation are inferred to have decreased until they were no longer sufficient to localize low-gradient conditions adjacent to the North Uinta thrust during late Wasatchian time. Low-energy, paludal, and lacustrine depositional environments of the Wasatch Formation expanded, resulting in deposition of the Luman Tongue. Near the end of early Eocene time, the rate of sediment accumulation exceeded the rate of subsidence, resulting in the fluvial sandstone and mudstone of the Niland Tongue of the Wasatch Formation.

During latest early or early-middle Eocene time, renewed northward movement of the hanging wall of the North Uinta thrust is inferred to have caused thrust-load–induced subsidence that equalled or slightly exceeded the rate of sedimentation in the southern Green River Basin. This balance between subsidence and sedimentation resulted in deposition of the areally extensive oil shale and dolostone of the Tipton Shale Member of the Green River Formation. Surdam and Stanley (1980b) interpreted these strata to represent deposition in the shallow fresh water of Lake Gosiute within a closed hydrographic basin. Increasing aridity coupled with restricted drainage caused the alkalinity and salinity of Lake Gosiute to increase during deposition of the overlying

Wilkins Peak Member (Surdam and Stanley, 1980b). Facies deposited in the Green River Formation during Wilkins Peak time consisted from south to north of a narrow conglomerate facies adjacent to the North Uinta thrust, a narrow sandstone/mudstone facies, a basinal mudstone/carbonate/evaporite facies above the depositional axis, and a wide distal sandstone/mudstone facies (Bradley, 1964; Eugster and Hardie, 1975; McDonald, 1972; Smoot, 1978).

Interpretation of the Wilkins Peak Member as a playa-lake deposit (Bradley, 1973; Eugster and Hardie, 1975; Eugster and Surdam, 1973; Smoot, 1978) implies that low-gradient conditions were maintained near the structural axis for several million years (Gazin, 1965; Wolfbauer, 1971). Furthermore, a thick, areally extensive, syntectonic fluvial clastic wedge did not develop adjacent to the leading edge of the North Uinta thrust (Bradley, 1964; Eugster and Hardie, 1975). The lack of a permanent, large, stratified lake during deposition of the Wilkins Peak Member indicates that ponding did not cause the restriction of middle Eocene fluvial depositional environments to the extreme southern margin of the Green River Basin. Evaporite deposits of trona and halite localized along the southern margin of the basin

SOUTH   **NORTH**

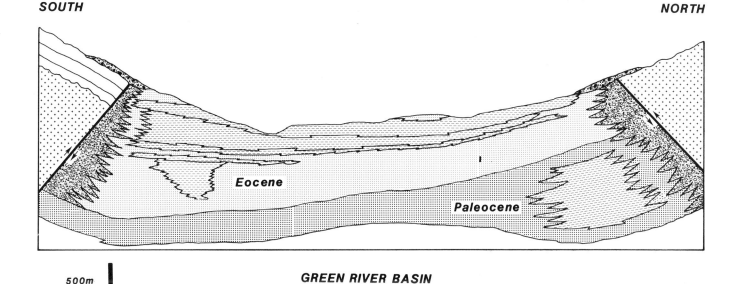

500m

10km

GREEN RIVER BASIN

Figure 9. Paleocene and Eocene facies of the Green River basin. Note localization of Paleocene low-gradient conditions adjacent to the Wind River thrust (north) and of Eocene low-energy environments adjacent to the North Uinta thrust (south). Maximum expansion of low-energy depositional environments occurred as displacement on the North Uinta thrust slowed. Coarse stippling indicates Paleocene sandstone/mudstone/coal facies; fine stippling indicates Eocene sandstone/mudstone/coal facies; finely dashed pattern indicates basinal mudstone/coal/carbonate/evaporite facies regardless of Paleocene or Eocene age; open circle pattern indicates Paleocene through middle Eocene conglomerate; closed circle pattern indicates late Tertiary gravels; crosses indicate Precambrian basement; unpatterned areas equal pre-Tertiary strata. Structure is schematic only. Modified after McDonald (1972).

(Culbertson, 1971; Surdam and Stanley, 1980b; Wolfbauer, 1971) are evidence that variation in climatic conditions and/or drainage patterns (Surdam and Stanley, 1979, 1980a, b) within a subsiding, structurally asymmetric basin controlled the distribution of sedimentary facies within the Green River Basin during deposition of the Wilkins Peak Member.

Displacement on the North Uinta thrust and consequent thrust-load–induced subsidence of the southern margin of the Green River Basin is inferred to have decreased during deposition of the Laney Shale Member. Subsidence adjacent to the thrust was no longer sufficient to maintain a southerly gradient in the northern portion of the Green River Basin. Low-energy depositional environments adjacent to the North Uinta thrust expanded rapidly in response to decreases in subsidence and clastic sediment supply from the north. Maximum expansion of Lake Gosiute (Bradley, 1964) and of low-gradient conditions represent the transition from syntectonic to posttectonic sedimentation. A similar scenario of opposite polarity caused maximum expansion of Lake Uinta and of low-gradient conditions in the Green River Formation of the Uinta Basin to the south.

Increased rainfall and the advent of an open-basin hydrologic regime caused a return to fresh-water lacustrine conditions during deposition of the Laney Shale Member of the Green River Formation (Surdam and Stanley, 1980a, b). The rate of sedimen-

tation exceeded the rate of thrust-load–induced subsidence along the southern margin of the Green River Basin during Bridgerian (middle Eocene) time. Fluvial sediments of the Bridger Formation were deposited above the oil shale, evaporite, carbonate, tuff, mudstone, and sandstone of the Green River Formation (Surdam and Stanley, 1980b).

UINTA BASIN AREA

Late Cretaceous

Laramide-style deformation in northeastern and east-central Utah began in late Campanian time and caused the eastward regression of the Cretaceous Seaway (Fouch and others, 1983; Lawton, 1983). Upper Mesaverde Group strata of late Campanian age erosionally thin over the San Rafael Swell. Sedimentary rocks west of the San Rafael Swell were derived from the Cordilleran thrust belt and deposited in eastward- and northeastward-flowing braided rivers (Lawton, 1983). Sediment deposited east of the San Rafael Swell coarsens upward from fluvial and marginal marine deposits through channelized meanderbelt deposits to sediments reflecting deposition in pebbly braided rivers (Lawton, 1983). Mesaverde Group strata east of the San Rafael Swell reflect two sediment source areas; the first was the Cordilleran thrust belt to the west, and the second was a volcanic arc terrane to the southwest (Lawton, 1983). This arc terrane ceased to supply sediment during deposition of strata higher in the sequence (Lawton, 1983).

Development of a large internal drainage system by latest Campanian time (Fouch and others, 1983; Lawton, 1983) and sediment provenance studies for contemporaneous strata (Lawton, 1983) indicate prominence of the Circle Cliffs, San Rafael, Monument, Uncompahgre, and Sawatch Laramide-style structures by that time. Maastrichtian-age strata deposited within the newly formed isolated basin or basins indicate deposition in warm, shallow, alkaline lakes surrounded by low-energy marginal lacustrine environments (Fouch and others, 1983). This style of nonmarine sedimentation continued into the Paleocene and Eocene (Fouch, 1976; Fouch and others, 1983; Ryder and others, 1976). Paleocene strata of the North Horn Formation and Flagstaff Limestone were deposited above a major erosional unconformity developed on latest Cretaceous strata (Fouch and others, 1983; Lawton, 1983; Stanley and Collinson, 1979), indicating major uplift of the San Rafael Swell by early Paleocene (Lawton, 1983).

Bruhn and others (1983, p. 70) suggested that southerly paleocurrent directions in the conglomeratic Current Creek Formation (Isby and Picard, 1983), and indications from structural studies raise the possibility that the Uintas may have begun to rise in latest Cretaceous time. The base of the Current Creek Formation was dated as Maastrictian on the basis of ostracodes and pollen (B. Bryant, personal communication, 1982; *in* Bruhn and others, 1983). Their paleogeographic reconstruction shows the Uintas to have risen by early Paleocene time (Fig. 8 *in* Bruhn and others, 1983).

Paleocene and early Eocene

The Paleocene and early Eocene depositional axis of the Uinta Basin (Figs. 2, 10) of northeastern Utah parallels its structural axis along the southern margin of the Uinta uplift (Ryder and others, 1976). Isopach and cross-section data show gradual depositional thickening of Eocene strata to the north (Osmond, 1964; Fig. 2 *in* McDonald, 1972; Ryder and others, 1976). Porter (1963) and Ryder and others (1976) reviewed the sedimentary facies and depositional environments of the early Tertiary sediments of the Uinta Basin. The following summary is derived largely from their work. A simplified facies diagram for the Uinta Basin during the early middle Eocene is presented in Figure 10.

The following sedimentary facies existed in the Uinta Basin from north to south from at least middle Paleocene to early Eocene time. A narrow conglomerate facies with minor sandstone, mudstone, and carbonate is indicative of braided streams on alluvial fans. Just basinward, a narrow band of mudstone, localized sandstone, and minor carbonate was deposited. It reflects fluvial, high mud-flat and lower delta-plain environments. Sediments consisting of drab mudstone, channel sandstone, and grain- or mud-supported carbonate were deposited in a marginal

lacustrine environment of low relief. Mud-supported, often kerogenic, carbonates, together with minor amounts of mudstone and sandstone, were deposited in an open lacustrine environment above the depositional axes of Lakes Flagstaff and Uinta. Similar fine-grained facies and low-energy depositional environments existed south and east of the lakes, although they were considerably wider (Fig. 10). The greater width of the marginal lacustrine muddy sandstone facies on the southern margin of Lake Uinta was attributed to a lower gradient relative to the northern margin of the lake (Bruhn and others, 1983; Ryder and others, 1976).

Bruhn and others (1983), Gries (1983a,b) and Hamilton (1978, 1981) discussed the existence of a basement thrust along the southern margin of the Uinta Mountains (Fig. 2). Ryder and others (1976) showed a southward-directed thrust on this margin in their paleogeographic reconstructions. These authors stated that "the orientation of Lake Uinta clearly reflects structural control by the adjacent uplift." The existence of a basement-thrust on the southeast margin of the Uinta Mountains has been proven by drilling through a sheet of Precambrian basement into overturned Paleozoic and Mesozoic strata (Gries, 1983a,b). We will refer to this basement-thrust system as the South Uinta thrust.

Localization of low-energy depositional environments from middle Paleocene until middle Eocene time adjacent to the structural axis of the Uinta Basin (Ryder and others, 1976) is attributed to basement thrusting and rapid subsidence due to thrust-loading. Climatic variation and/or changes in basin hydrology are suggested by the presence of evaporite deposits of

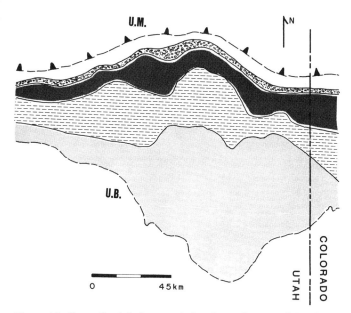

Figure 10. Generalized facies association for sediments of the Green River Formation in the Uinta Basin (U.B.), Utah, during early-middle Eocene time. The South Uinta thrust dips beneath the Uinta Mountains (U.M.) to the north. Open circle pattern indicates conglomerate; dark stipple indicates sandstone; dashed line pattern indicates oil shale; light stipple indicates muddy sandstone and sandy mudstone. After Porter (1963) and Picard and High (1981).

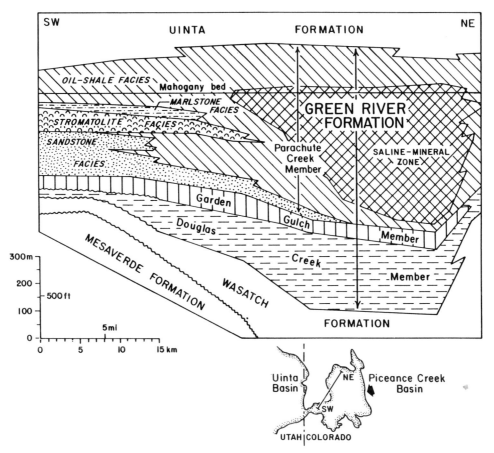

Figure 11. Southwest-northeast cross section from the Douglas Creek arch to just northeast of Piceance Creek basin depositional axis, Colorado. Note northwestward intraformational thickening of Eocene upper Wasatch and Green River Formations toward the overthrust eastern margin. Low-energy depositional environments were localized near the White River thrust until just before deposition of the Mahogany bed. After Roehler (1974) from Cole and Picard (1981).

middle Eocene age (Ryder and others, 1976; Surdam and Stanley, 1980b).

Lake Uinta attained its greatest areal extent during middle Eocene time (Bruhn and others, 1983; Ryder and others, 1976). The areally extensive kerogeneous silty dolomicrite of the Mahogany Bed (oil shale) (Cashion and Donnell, 1974; Cole and Picard, 1981) was deposited during the transition from clastic input from the northward-dipping southern margin to coarse clastic input derived from the Uinta Mountains (Andersen and Picard, 1974). Decreased asymmetric subsidence and loss of clastic input from the south allowed the depositional axis of the Uinta Basin to diverge southward from the structural axis. Late-middle and late Eocene alluvial sediments derived from the Uinta Mountains (Andersen and Picard, 1974; Bruhn and others, 1983; Ryder and others, 1976) were deposited in the Uinta Basin as Lake Uinta waned. Infilling by coarse clastics from the north suggests that displacement on the South Uinta thrust and consequent tectonically induced subsidence were no longer sufficient to localize low-energy depositional environments along the structural axis or maintain a northward-dipping gradient in the southern Uinta Basin.

PICEANCE CREEK BASIN

Paleocene and Eocene

Sedimentary facies in the Piceance Creek Basin (Fig. 11) of northwestern Colorado reflect a depositional and structural history very similar to that of the Uinta Basin to the west (Cole and Picard, 1981; Donnell, 1961, 1969; Johnson, 1985; Johnson and May, 1980; Roehler, 1974; Ryder and others, 1976).

Donnell (1961) described the Piceance Creek Basin as a large northwest-trending asymmetric structural downwarp. The southwest limb of the basin dips gently to the northeast, whereas the northeast limb dips more steeply to the southwest. Structural asymmetry is more pronounced in older sedimentary strata, although strata of the Eocene Green River Formation along the northeast margin dip as much as 27° to the southwest (Donnell, 1961). Older strata of the Mesaverde Group (Upper Cretaceous) are vertical to overturned along the northeast margin of the basin. These steeply dipping strata form the Grand Hogback (Donnell, 1961).

Gries (1983a, b) and Meissner (1984) showed a southwest-directed basement-thrust on the northeast margin of the Piceance Creek Basin. This thrust fault forms the southwestern margin of the White River Uplift (Tweto, 1975). This basement-thrust system and its hanging wall are referred to herein as the White River thrust. Isopach data by McDonald (1972, Fig. 2) indicate that Paleocene and Eocene strata depositionally thicken northeastward toward a maximum thickness adjacent to the thrusted margin. Southwestward movement of the White River thrust is inferred to have caused the structural and depositional asymmetry of the Piceance Creek Basin.

The Upper Cretaceous Ohio Creek Member of the Hunter Canyon Formation is unconformably overlain by the Paleocene and Eocene Wasatch Formation (Johnson and May, 1980). Donnell (1969) subdivided the Wasatch Formation into three members. From oldest to youngest, they are the Atwell Gulch Member, the Molina Member, and the Shire Member. The Atwell Gulch Member contains carbonaceous shale, lignite, gray claystone, gray siltstone, lenticular brown sandstone, and thin fresh-water limestones. Sandstone and siltstone content increases *away* from the thrusted margin (Donnell, 1969). The dominantly fine-grained Atwell Gulch Member depositionally thickens from 230 m in the southwestern part of the basin to 615 m in the east-central part (Donnell, 1969) toward the White River thrust.

The Molina Member of the Wasatch Formation overlies the Atwell Gulch Member. The Molina Member consists mainly of massive variegated claystone and some sandstone in the southwestern Piceance Creek Basin. Sandstone gradually replaces mudstone to the southwest. The Molina Member depositionally thickens from southwest to northeast (Donnell, 1969) toward the White River thrust.

The Shire Member consists of variegated claystone, siltstone, and lenticular sandstone. These lithologies reflect deposition in predominantly low-gradient, low-energy fluvial environments (Donnell, 1961, 1969; Johnson and May, 1980). Marked depositional thickening of this unit toward the thrust (Donnell, 1969; Johnson and May, 1980) suggests relatively rapid thrust-load–induced subsidence and southwestward displacement of the White River thrust. Conglomerate containing large boulders and cobbles are present in fanglomerate and coarse braided stream deposits in the Wasatch Formation adjacent to the Grand Hogback (Roehler, 1974). The Grand Hogback lies adjacent to the impinging White River thrust and forms the eastern margin of the Piceance Creek Basin.

The structural and depositional asymmetry that characterized the Piceance Creek Basin during the Paleocene and early Eocene (Donnell, 1961, 1969; Johnson and May, 1980, McDonald, 1972) continued into the middle Eocene (Cole and Picard, 1981; Roehler, 1974). Facies that existed in the Piceance Creek Basin during deposition of the lower Parachute Creek Member of the Green River Formation (Fig. 11) are described below from northeast to southwest.

Along the northeastern margin of the basin, moderate to high-energy fluvial depositional environments yielded the narrow sandstone and mudstone facies of the Anvil Points Member of the Green River Formation (McDonald, 1972). Southwestward, lower energy marginal lacustrine to fluvial environments resulted in deposition of the narrow, fine-grained sandstone and mudstone facies of the Douglas Creek Member of the Green River Formation (Cole and Picard, 1981; McDonald, 1972; Roehler, 1974). Closer to the depositional axis, oil shale, mudstone, carbonate, and tuff were deposited in open lacustrine conditions (Cole and Picard, 1981; Roehler, 1974). Along the depositional axis of the basin, evaporite minerals intercalated with oil shale suggest the influence of climatic or hydrologic variation within the subsiding basin.

Low-energy depositional environments were no longer localized adjacent to the White River thrust during deposition of the upper Parachute Creek Member (Cole and Picard, 1981; Moncure and Surdam, 1980; Roehler, 1974). Inferred thrusting and consequent subsidence were insufficient to prevent divergence of the structural and depositional axes. Moncure and Surdam (1980) stated that lacustrine deposition was continuous across the Douglas Creek Arch during deposition of the Mahogany Bed and sediments assigned to the overlying uppermost strata of the Parachute Creek Member. Lake Uinta extended from the Uinta Basin to the Piceance Creek Basin at this time (Cashion and Donnell, 1974; Moncure and Surdam, 1980).

Successive infilling of the Wind River, Green River, Piceance Creek, and Uinta Basins during the middle Eocene by volcaniclastic sediments from the Absaroka volcanic field has been documented by Surdam and Stanley (1980a). High lake-level stands of Lakes Gosiute and Uinta, with deposition of the Laney Shale Member and Mahogany Bed in their respective basins, preceded the volcaniclastic influx (Surdam and Stalney, 1979, 1980a). These high stands were attributed to increased water supply due to expansion and integration of previously closed hydrographic basins. Tectonic stability caused basin infilling and enlargement of the hydrographic limits of the basins (Surdam and Stanley, 1980a). The diachronous existence of the high stands of Lakes Gosiute and Uinta is further evidence that successive enlargement of hydrographic basins, rather than climatic change, was responsible for lake-level rise (Surdam and Stanley, 1980a). The lag time required to fill each successive basin with fluvial volcaniclastic sediments was responsible for the diachroneity of high lake-level stands. We correlate the end of major basement-thrust movement with the expansion of low-energy depositional environments, but not necessarily with high lake-level stands. Since tectonic stability was a prerequisite for the expansion of hydrographic basins (Surdam and Stanley, 1980a), Laramide basement thrusting in Wyoming, northeastern Utah, and northwestern Colorado must have slowed considerably by middle Uintan time.

TIMING OF DEFORMATION

Cordilleran Thrust Belt vs. foreland basement thrusts

Figure 12 summarizes the timing of deformation and uplift of the major Laramide structural features described in the text.

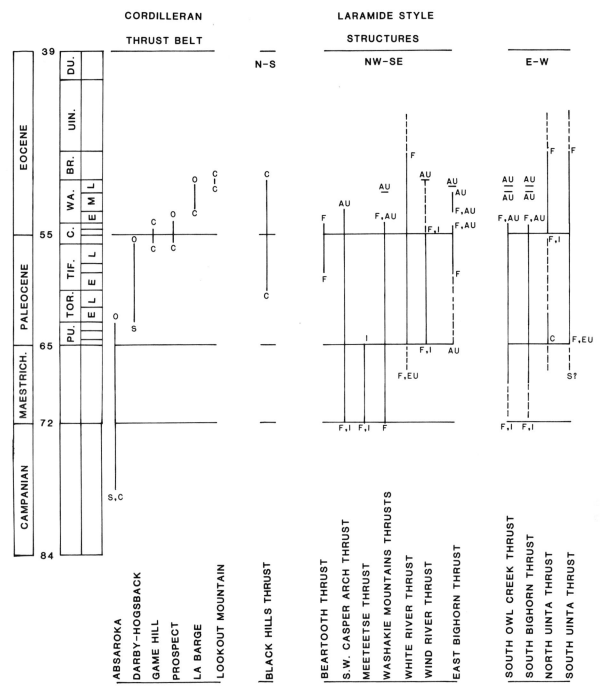

Figure 12. Timing of basement thrusting and uplift of some of the major basement-cored structural features within the Wyoming region of the Cordilleran foreland. Major Laramide uplifts and their associated basement-thrusts are grouped according to their trend. Data for the Cordilleran thrust belt from Dorr and others (1977) and Wiltschko and Dorr (1983) are shown for comparison purposes. AU, C., E.U., F., I., O. and S. represent criteria for determining episodes of basement-thrusting. AU = Angular unconformity; C = cross-cutting relationship; F = facies associations (this model); EU = erosional unconformity; I = isopach data, especially thrustward thickening of facies representing low-energy depositional environments; O = depositional overlap of faults or folds; S = syntectonic conglomerate adjacent to thin-skinned structures in the Cordilleran thrust belt (see Wiltschko and Dorr, 1983).

The timing of deformation in the Cordilleran foreland is compared with that of the Cordilleran Thrust Belt to the west. Major Laramide-style uplifts and their bounding basement thrusts are grouped according to their trend.

Dorr and others (1977) documented contemporaneous deformation in the Cordilleran Thrust Belt and the western portion of the Cordilleran foreland. They suggested that this contemporaneous deformation was due to a single causal mechanism. Recent drilling, seismic, and structural data from basement-cored uplifts throughout the Cordilleran foreland strongly support a thick-skinned basement-thrust origin for Laramide structures (Gries, 1983a,b; Lowell, 1983; Petersen, 1983; Smithson and others, 1979).

Application of the preceding sedimentary-tectonic model to the sediments deposited adjacent to the above basement thrusts indicates that deformation throughout the Wyoming portion of the Cordilleran foreland was largely contemporaneous with deformation in the Cordilleran Thrust Belt. Horizontal compression was the common agent of deformation in each region. Simultaneous thrusting in both regions due to horizontal compression requires a plate tectonic model that is compatible with the geologic histories of each.

Timing of deformation within the foreland

The timing of basement thrusting within the Wyoming region of the Cordilleran foreland (Fig. 12) reveals no simple correlation between the trend of uplifts bounded by basement thrusts and the timing of displacement on their margins. East-west–trending Laramide structures such as the Uinta and Owl Creek Mountains may have begun to rise during the latest Cretaceous, causing asymmetric subsidence in adjacent basins (Bruhn and others, 1983; Keefer, 1965b, 1969, 1970; Phillips, 1983; Ryder and others, 1976). Contemporaneous basement thrusting of the northwest-southeast–trending, southwestern margin of the Casper Arch and east-west–trending southern margins of the Southern Bighorn and Owl Creek Mountains suggests that the timing of displacement was independent of the orientations of these basement-thrusts.

Development of marked structural and depositional asymmetry in the Uinta, northern Green River and northeastern Wind River Basins by middle Paleocene (Berg, 1963; Keefer, 1965b, 1970; Phillips, 1983; Ryder and others, 1976) is better explained by blind, low-angle basement thrusting rather than by a basement fold-thrust model. During blind basement thrusting, the rising basement localized folding in the overlying ductile sedimentary strata (Stearns, 1971), while regional crustal shortening supplied the additional strata necessary to cover the rising hanging walls of basement thrusts (Brown, 1984). Thick-skinned basement thrusting provides a mechanism for simultaneous mountain range uplift and asymmetric basin subsidence due to thrust-loading and isostatic compensation (Hagen and others, 1985).

Gries (1983b) emphasized the differences in the timing of uplift of Laramide-style basement thrusts in the Cordilleran fore-

land; in contrast, we emphasize the similarities. Note that Gries (1983b) considered more uplifts in the Colorado region than does this study. Within the Wyoming region, both interpretations are largely based on the same data. Gries (1983b) interpreted the northward intraformationally thickening wedge of fine-grained Paleocene sediments in the Wind River Basin (Fig. 7a) to be nonsynorogenic and to indicate quiescence on the southern margin of the Owl Creek Mountains. Similar wedges adjacent to the southwestern margins of Wind River Mountains and the Casper Arch, and those adjacent to the southern margins of the Uinta and Granite Mountains, were also interpreted to indicate a Late Paleocene lull in basement-thrust activity (Fig. 7). Alternatively, according to the proposed sedimentary-tectonic model, we suggest that these thrustward-thickening fine-grained clastic wedges represent a relative maximum of basement-thrust activity. Consequently, basement-thrust activity, although episodic, appears to us to have been relatively continuous throughout the Paleocene in the Wyoming region. We interpret basin starvation with respect to areally extensive coarse-grained clastic sedimentation to have been due to rapid thrust-load–induced subsidence rather than to quiescence and lack of suitable source areas. Therefore we interpret the progradation of coarse-grained thrust-derived clastic wedges as indicating a relative decrease in basement-thrust activity, in contrast to Gries (1983b) who interpreted them to indicate a relative increase. We note that many positive and negative feedback relationships between rates of uplift, erosion, subsidence, and sedimentation require quantitative evaluation. Recently, Hagen and others (1985) have taken the first step by computer modeling the relationship between Laramide-style thrust-loading, lithospheric flexure, and asymmetric basin subsidence.

Although we disagree with Gries (1983b) concerning the timing of uplift of the Laramide-style structures discussed above, the possibility of systematic changes in regional strain patterns through time remains. Such patterns may be manifest as variations in the degree of development of structures with different trends, as suggested by Gries (1983b). More accurate dating of Cretaceous and Paleocene strata seems necessary to refine the timing of Laramide-style uplift and subsidence.

SPECULATIVE MODELS FOR LARAMIDE BASEMENT-THRUSTING

The overall pattern of basement-thrusting in the Cordilleran foreland (Gries, 1983a, b; Hamilton, 1981; Lowell, 1983; Petersen, 1983) and timing of basement-thrust displacement—coupled with recent drilling, structural, and seismic data—suggests that Laramide-style deformation was caused by imbrication about the margins of relatively coherent, lobate, basin-scale sheets of Precambrian basement. Thick-skinned basement thrusting at imbricate margins produced large, asymmetric uplifts and structural basins with relatively low values of regional crustal shortening (Kanter and others, 1981). These low values of regional crustal shortening indicate that rates of Laramide-style basement thrusting should be thought of in terms of the rate at which mass was tectonically added to basin margins by crustal imbrication rather than in terms of thrust displacement per unit time.

Back-thrusting behind the imbricate margins complicated the structure of the basement-cored uplifts (Lageson, 1982). A dominant direction of basement thrusting, however, may usually be determined from the structural polarity of the adjacent asymmetric basins, as in the case of the Bighorn Mountains. In the case of the Uinta Mountains, displaced basement thrusts on each side of the uplift attained roughly equal value, although the South Uinta thrust apparently became well developed before the North Uinta thrust (see Bruhn and others, 1983, for a contrasting viewpoint). Basement-thrusting on the northern and southern margins of the Uinta Mountains is strong evidence for regional compressive stresses. The apparent absence of a strong regional correlation between basement-thrust trend and the temporal evolution of Laramide structures (Fig. 12) is consistent with imbrication along the margins of large, irregular lobate sheets of basement. Overall compression was *probably* northeast-southwest (Brown, 1984). Frontal ramps developed preferentially on either northeast- or southwest-dipping conjugate shear planes. Lateral ramps and left- and right-lateral strike-slip fault systems, such as the Lake Basin, Nye Bowler, and Badwater Fault Zones (Foose and others, 1961; Love and others, 1955; Osterwald, 1961), developed to allow relative movement between the large, irregular sheets of basement. Ductile deformation at depth allowed brittle deformation and crustal shortening above.

Subduction of the Farallon plate beneath western North America and convergence of the two plates during latest Cretaceous, Paleocene, and early Eocene, with the accompanying eastward wave of magmatism (Dickinson, 1979), may have increased the ductility of the lower crust. Drag between the subducted slab of oceanic lithosphere and the overriding slab of continental lithosphere may have produced the horizontal compression that caused simultaneous thrusting in the Cordilleran Thrust Belt and Cordilleran foreland (Dickinson and Snyder, 1978; Hamilton, 1981). The role of the Colorado Plateau as a "rigid indentor" in Laramide deformation (Chapin and Cather, 1981; Hamilton, 1981; Sales, 1968) deserves further study.

Recent research has led to variations on the above Farallon subduction–Laramide orogeny model. Livaccari and others (1981) suggested that the Laramide orogeny was due to the subduction of a buoyant oceanic plateau, a Farallon analogue of the Hess Rise on the Pacific Plate. This model was in turn refined by Henderson and others (1984), who envisioned the subduction of a north-northeast–trending aseismic ridge. In their model, the point of convergence between the Farallon aseismic ridge and the western margin of North America migrated progressively southward. The buoyant aseismic ridge was subducted progressively southward, accounting for the southward migration of the late Cretaceous–early Tertiary magmatic lull.

Engebretson and others (1984) attributed Laramide compression to the acceleration of the rate of convergence between the Farallon and North American Plates rather than more rapid sea-floor spreading and subduction of young buoyant crust. They

maintained that the age of subducted Farallon Plate had not decreased greatly at the subduction zone until after the beginning of Laramide-style deformation. In fact they correlated the end of Laramide deformation with difficult subduction of very young, warm, buoyant Farallon material.

Bird (1984) modeled crustal thickening in the Cordilleran foreland during the late Mesozoic and early Cenozoic. Bird attributed crustal thickening to the transport of ductile lower crust from southwest to northeast due to shear stresses exerted by the Farallon Plate on the base of the North American lithosphere. In summary, several plate tectonic models for Laramide-style deformation exist and complement the diversity of structural and tectonic models for deformation within the craton and indicate that further research is needed.

SUMMARY

Sedimentary facies of Laramide style intermontane basins in the Cordilleran foreland of Wyoming, northeastern Utah, and northwestern Colorado reflect a common history of asymmetric subsidence due to basement-thrust loading and a consistent pattern of depositional environments. These facies have a depositional polarity similar to the structural asymmetry of their underlying basement. The structural and depositional axes of these basins were nearly coincident during periods of rapid basement-thrusting and syntectonic sedimentation. Characteristic syntectonic sedimentary facies in these basins include a narrow conglomerate facies adjacent to the thrust, a narrow sandstone/mudstone/coal facies immediately basinward, a basinal mudstone/coal/carbonate/evaporite facies along the depositional axis, and finally, a wide distal sandstone/mudstone/coal facies. The wide distal sandstone/mudstone/coal facies depositionally thins against the shallowing basement or above the back of the hanging wall of yet another thrust, as in the case of the Wind River Basin. Periods of basement thrusting caused tectonically induced subsidence of the footwall of each thrust. Asymmetric basinal subsidence caused marked syntectonic intraformational thickening of low-gradient facies adjacent to each thrust.

As long as the rate of thrusting and consequent asymmetric subsidence exceeded the rate of sedimentation, low-gradient depositional environments were localized adjacent to the structural axis of each basin. The frontal edges of impinging hanging walls of basement thrusts provided coarse but volumetrically minor clastic input during rapid basement-thrust movement. Major sediment sources were large areas of Mesozoic and Paleozoic strata above gently thrustward-dipping homoclines opposite impinging hanging walls. Large quantities of sediment were transported across lateral ramps and along major trunk streams above the depositional axes.

Lower rates of thrusting and thrust-load–induced subsidence caused the thrustward gradients above the shallowly dipping margins opposite the thrusts to decrease. Areally extensive low-gradient depositional environments represent the transition from syntectonic to posttectonic sedimentation. Only after the rate of thrust-load–induced subsidence decreased relative to the rate of sedimentation were thick and extensive fluvial clastic wedges able to develop adjacent to the impinging hanging walls of Laramide-style basement thrusts.

The above model for sedimentation adjacent to Laramide basement thrusts provides a method for distinguishing between syntectonic and late- or posttectonic clastic strata in the Cordilleran foreland. Its application allows the reconstruction of a regional sedimentary-tectonic history. Episodic basement thrusting dominated the Wyoming region of the Cordilleran foreland during the latest Cretaceous, Paleocene, and early Eocene, and was in large part contemporaneous with late Mesozoic and Cenozoic deformation in the Cordilleran Thrust Belt (Dorr and others, 1977; Wiltschko and Dorr, 1983). Episodes of basement thrusting during this period divided the Cordilleran foreland into a mosaic of asymmetric intermontane basins. Laramide basement thrusting in Wyoming, northeastern Utah, and northwestern Colorado effectively ceased by middle Uintan time.

ACKNOWLEDGMENTS

This research was funded in part by grants from Standard Oil of California (Chevron) and the Graduate College of Iowa State University. This manuscript benefited from discussions with B. Barnes, D. L. Biggs, T. M. Bown, R. D. Cody, T. Elliott, R. M. Flores, R. Gries, J. Hanley, K. M. Hussey, C. E. Jacobson, M. Kraus, E. Kvale, K. S. Noggle, R. H. Osborne, W. J. Perry, C. Postlewaite, C. Shaw, L. J. Suttner, and D. M. Uhlir. We thank W. L. Bilodeau, W. C. James, J. B. Conard, W. R. Keefer, and T. A. Bigbee for constructive reviews. V. G. Beck and L. Olberding prepared early versions of this manuscript, S. Turnbow and D. Moton typed the final manuscript, and M. Oschner drafted some of the figures.

REFERENCES CITED

Allmendinger, R. W., Brewer, J. A., Brown, L. D., Kaufman, S., Oliver, J. E., and Houston, R. S., 1982, COCORP profiling across the Rocky Mountain front in southern Wyoming; Part 2, Precambrian basement structure and its influence on Laramide deformation: Geological Society of America Bulletin, v. 93, p. 1253–1263.

Andersen, D. W., 1985, Provenance of Lower Eocene sandstone on the south flank of the Rock Springs uplift, southwestern Wyoming: Society of Economic Paleontologists and Mineralogists Annual Midyear Meetng Abstracts, v. 2, p. 5.

Andersen, D. W., and Picard, M. D., 1974, Evolution of synorogenic clastic deposits in the intermontane Uinta Basin of Utah, in Dickinson, W. R., ed., Tectonics and sedimentation: Society of Economic Paleontologists and Mineralogists Special Publication 22, p. 167–189.

Armstrong, R. L., 1968, Sevier orogenic belt in Nevada and Utah: American Association of Petroleum Geologists Bulletin, v. 79, no. 4, p. 429–458.

Beck, R. A., 1985, Syntectonic sedimentation adjacent to Laramide basement thrusts, Rocky Mountain foreland; Timing of deformaiton [M.Sc. thesis]: Ames, Iowa State University, 88 p.

Beck, R. A., and Vondra, C. F., 1985, Syntectonic sedimentation and Laramide basement thrusting, Rocky Mountain foreland, Wyoming, Utah, and Colorado [abs.]: Society of Economic Paleontologists and Mineralogists 2nd Annual Midyear Meeting, v. 2, p. 9.

Berg, R. R., 1962, Mountain flank thrusting in Rocky Mountain foreland, Wyoming and Colorado: American Association of Petroleum Geologists Bulletin, v. 46, p. 2019–2032.

—— , 1963, Laramide sediments along the Wind River Thrust, Wyoming, in Childs, O. E., and Beebe, B. W., eds., Backbone of the Americas: American Association of Petroleum Geologists Memoir 2, p. 220–230.

—— , 1981, Review of thrusting in the Wyoming foreland: University of Wyoming Contributions to Geology, v. 19, no. 2, p. 93–104.

—— , 1983, Geometry of the Wind River Thrust, Wyoming, in Lowell, J. D., ed., Rocky Mountain foreland basins and uplifts: Denver, Colorado, Rocky Mountain Association of Geologists, p. 257–262.

Bird, P., 1984, Laramide crustal thickening event in the Rocky Mountain foreland and Great Plains: Tectonics, v. 3, no. 7, p. 741–758.

Blackstone, D. L., 1981, Compression as an agent in deformation of the east-central flank of the Bighorn Mountains, Sheridan and Johnson Counties: Wyoming: University of Wyoming Contributions to Geology, v. 19, no. 2, p. 105–122.

—— , 1983, Laramide compressional tectonics, southeastern Wyoming: University of Wyoming Contributions to Geology, v. 22, no. 1, p. 1–38.

Bown, T. M., 1980, Summary of latest Cretaceous and Cenozoic sedimentary, tectonic, and erosional events, Bighorn Basin, Wyoming, in Gingerich, P. D., ed., Early Cenozoic paleontology and stratigraphy of the Bighorn Basin, Wyoming: University of Michigan Papers on Paleontology no. 24, p. 25–32.

Bradley, W. H., 1964, Geology of the Green River Formation and associated Eocene rocks in southwestern Wyoming and adjacent parts of Colorado and Utah: U.S. Geological Survey Professional Paper 496–A, 86 p.

—— , 1973, Oil shale formed in desert environment: Green River Formation, Wyoming: Geological Society of America Bulletin, v. 84, p. 1121–1124.

Bredall, S. R., 1971, Early Eocene fanglomerate, northwestern Bighorn Basin, Wyoming [M.Sc. thesis]: Ames, Iowa State University, 73 p.

Brewer, J. A., and Turcotte, D. L., 1980, On the stress system that formed the Laramide Wind River Mountains, Wyoming: Geophysical Research Letters, v. 7, no. 6, p. 449–452.

Brewer, J. A., Allmendinger, R. W., Brown, L. D., Oliver, J. E., and Kaufman, S., 1982, COCORP profiling across the Rocky Mountain Front in southern Wyoming; Part 1, Laramide structure: Geological Society of America Bulletin, v. 93, p. 1242–1252.

Brown, R. W., 1948, Age of Kingsbury Conglomerate is Eocene: Geological Society of America Bulletin, v. 59, p. 1165–1172.

Brown, W. G., 1983, Sequential development of the fold-thrust model of foreland deformation, in Lowell, J. D., ed., Rocky Mountain foreland basins and uplifts: Denver, Colorado, Rocky Mountain Association of Geologists, p. 57–64.

—— , 1984, Basement involved tectonics foreland areas: American Association of Petroleum Geologists Continuing Education Course Note Series 26, 92 p.

Bruhn, R. L., Picard, M. D., and Beck, S. L., 1983, Mesozoic and early Tertiary structure and sedimentology of the central Wasatch Mountains, Uinta Mountains, and Uinta Basin: Utah Geological and Mineralogical Survey Special Studies no. 59, p. 63–105.

Burchfiel, B. C., and Davis, G. A., 1975, Nature and controls of Cordilleran orogenesis, western United States; Extensions of an earlier synthesis: American Journal of Science, v. 275–A, p. 363–396.

Cashion, W. B., and Donnell, J. R., 1974, Revision of nomenclature of the upper part of the Green River Formation, Piceance Creek Basin, Colorado, and eastern Uinta Basin, Utah: U.S. Geological Survey Bulletin 1394–G, p. 1–9.

Chapin, C. E., and Cather, S. M., 1981, Eocene tectonics and sedimentation in the Colorado Plateau–Rocky Mountain Area: Arizona Geological Society Digest, v. 14, p. 173–198.

Cole, R. D., and Picard, M. D., 1981, Sulfur-isotope variations in marginal-lacustrine rocks of the Green River Formation, Colorado and Utah, in

Ethridge, F. G., and Flores, R. M., eds., Recent and ancient nonmarine depositional environments; Models for exploration: Society of Economic Paleontologists and Mineralogists Special Publication 31, p. 2161–2175.

Courdin, J. L., and Hubert, J. F., 1969, Sedimentology and mineralogical differentiation of sandstones in the Fort Union Formation (Paleocene), Wind River Basin, Wyoming: Wyoming Geological Association 21st Annual Field Conference Guidebook, p. 29–37.

Culbertson, W. C., 1971, Stratigraphy of the trona deposits in the Green River Formation, southwest Wyoming: University of Wyoming Contributions to Geology, v. 10, p. 15–23.

Culbertson, W. C., and Mapel, W. J., 1976, Coal in the Wasatch Formation, northwest part of Powder River Basin near Sheridan, Sheridan County, Wyoming: Wyoming Geological Association 28th Annual Field Conference Guidebook, p. 193–201.

Curry, W. H., III, 1971, Laramide structural history of the Powder River Basin, Wyoming: Wyoming Geological Association 23rd Annual Field Conference Guidebook, p. 49–60.

——— , 1973, Late Cretaceous and Early Tertiary rocks, southwestern Wyoming: Wyoming Geological Association 25th Annual Field Conference Guidebook, p. 79–86.

Darton, N. H., 1906, Geology of the Bighorn Mountains: U.S. Geological Survey Professional Paper No. 51, p. 1–129.

DeCelles, P. G., 1984, Sedimentation and diagenesis in a tectonically partitioned, nonmarine foreland basin; Lower Cretaceous Kootenai Formation, southwestern Montana [Ph.D. thesis]: Bloomington, Indiana, University of Indiana, 423 p.

Demorest, M., 1941, Critical structural features of the Bighorn Mountains, Wyoming: Geological Society of America Bulletin, v. 52, p. 161–176.

Denson, N. M., and Pipiringos, G. N., 1969, Stratigraphic implications of heavy-mineral studies of Paleocene and Eocene rocks of Wyoming: Wyoming Geological Association 21st Annual Field Conference Guidebook, p. 9–18.

Dickinson, W. R., 1979, Cenozoic plate tectonic setting of the Cordilleran region in the United States, *in* Armentrout, J. M., Cole, M. R., and Terbest, H., eds., Cenozoic paleogeography of the western United States: Society of Economic Paleontologists and Mineralogists, Pacific Section, Pacific Coast Paleogeography Symposium 3, p. 1–13.

Dickinson, W. R., and Snyder, W. S., 1978, Plate tectonics of the Laramide orogeny, *in* Matthews, V., III, ed., Laramide folding associated with basement block faulting in the western United States: Geological Society of America Memoir 151, p. 355–366.

Donnell, J. R., 1961, Tertiary geology and oil-shale resources of the Piceance Creek basin between the Colorado and White Rivers, northwestern Colorado: U.S. Geological Survey Bulletin 1081–L, p. 835–887.

——— , 1969, Paleocene and lower Eocene units in the southern part of the Piceance Creek Basin, Colorado: U.S. Geological Survey Bulletin 1274–M, 18 p.

Dorr, J. A., Jr., Spearing, D. R., and Steidtmann, J. R., 1977, Deformation and deposition between a foreland uplift and an impinging thrust belt: Geological Society of America Special Paper 177, 82 p.

Engebretson, D. C., Cox, A., and Thompson, G. A., 1984, Correlation of plate motions with continental tectonics; Laramide to Basin-Range: Tectonics, v. 3, no. 2, p. 115–119.

Erslev, E. A., 1986, Basement balancing of Rocky Mountain foreland uplifts: Geology, v. 14, p. 259–262.

Ethridge, F. G., Jackson, T. J., and Youngberg, A. D., 1981, Floodbasin sequence of a fine-grained meander belt subsystem; The coal-bearing Lower Wasatch and Upper Fort Union formations, southern Powder River Basin, Wyoming, *in* Ethridge, F. G., and Flores, R. M., eds., Recent and ancient nonmarine depositional environments; Models for exploration: Society of Economic Paleontologists and Mineralogists Special Publication 31, p. 191–209.

Eugster, H. P., and Hardie, L. A., 1975, Sedimentation in an ancient playa lake complex; The Wilkins Peak Member of the Green River Formation of Wyoming: Geological Society of America Bulletin, v. 86, p. 319–334.

Eugster, H. P., and Surdam, R. C., 1973, Depositional environments of the Green River Formation of Wyoming; A preliminary report: Geological Society of America Bulletin, v. 84, p. 1115–1120.

Flueckinger, L. A., 1971, Stratigraphy, petrography, and origin of the Tertiary sediments off the front of the Beartooth Mountains, Montana-Wyoming [Ph.D. thesis]: State College, Pennsylvania State University, 249 p.

Flueckinger, L. A., and Dutcher, R. R., 1972, Stratigraphy, petrography, and origin of the Tertiary sediments off the front of the Beartooth Mountains, Wyoming-Montana: Geological Society of America Abstracts with Programs, v. 4, p. 320–321.

Flores, R. M., 1981, Coal deposition in fluvial paleoenvironments of the Tongue River Member of the Fort Union Formation, Powder River area, Powder River Basin, Wyoming and Montana, *in* Ethridge, F. G., and Flores, R. M., eds., Recent and ancient nonmarine depositional environments; Models for exploration: Society of Economic Paleontologists and Mineralogists Special Publication 31, p. 169–190.

Foose, R. M., Wise, D. U., and Garbarini, G. S., 1961, Structural geology of the Beartooth Mountains, Montana and Wyoming: Geological Society of America Bulletin, v. 72, p. 1143–1172.

Fouch, T. D., 1976, Revision of the lower part of the Tertiary System in the central and western Uinta Basin, Utah: U.S. Geological Survey Bulletin 1405–C, p. C1–C7.

Fouch, T. D., Lawton, T. F., Nichols, D. J., Cashion, W. B., and Cobban, W. A., 1983, Patterns and timing of synorogenic sedimentation in Upper Cretaceous rocks of central and northeast Utah, *in* Reynolds, M. W., and Dolly, E. D., eds., Symposium 2, Mesozoic paleogeography of west-central United States: Rocky Mountain Section Society of Economic Paleontologists and Mineralogists, p. 305–327.

Gazin, C. L., 1965, Early Eocene mammalian faunas and their environment in the vicinity of the Rock Springs uplift, Wyoming: Wyoming Geological Association 19th Annual Field Conference Guidebook, p. 205–221.

Gingerich, P. D., 1983, Paleocene-Eocene faunal zones and a preliminary analysis of Laramide structure deformation in the Clark's Fork Basin, Wyoming: Wyoming Geological Association 34th Annual Field Conference Guidebook, p. 185–195.

Glass, G. B., 1976, Update on the Powder River Coal Basin: Wyoming Geological Association 28th Annual Field Conference Guidebook, p. 209–220.

Granger, W., 1910, Tertiary faunal horizons in the Wind River Basin, Wyoming, with descriptions of new Eocene mammals: American Museum of Natural History Bulletin, v. 28, p. 235–251.

Gries, R., 1983a, Oil and gas prospecting beneath Precambrian of foreland thrust plates in the Rocky Mountains: American Association of Petroleum Geologists Bulletin, v. 67, no. 1, p. 1–28.

——— , 1983b, North-south compression of Rocky Mountain foreland structures, *in* Lowell, J. D., ed., Rocky Mountain foreland basins and uplifts: Denver, Colorado, Rocky Mountain Association of Geologists, p. 9–32.

Hagen, E. S., Shuster, M. W., and Furlong, K. P., 1985, Tectonic loading and subsidence of intermontane basins; Wyoming foreland province; Geology, v. 13, p. 585–588.

Hamilton, W., 1978, Mesozoic tectonics of the western United States, *in* Howell, D. G., and McDougall, K. A., eds., Mesozoic paleogeography of the western United States: Pacific Section, Society of Economic Paleontologists and Mineralogists Pacific Coast Paleogeography Symposium 2, p. 33–70.

——— , 1981, Plate-tectonic mechanism of Laramide deformation: University of Wyoming Contributions to Geology, v. 19, no. 2, p. 87–92.

Hausel, W. D., and others, 1979, Structural index map; Wyoming mines and minerals, Geological Survey of Wyoming: Wyoming Geological Association 31st Annual Field Conference Guidebook, frontispiece.

Henderson, L. J., Gordon, R. G., and Engebretson, D. C., 1984, Mesozoic aseismic ridges on the Farallon plate and southward migration of shallow subduction during the Laramide Orogeny: Tectonics, v. 3, no. 2, p. 121–132.

Hennier, J., and Spang, J. H., 1983, Mechanisms for deformation of sedimentary strata at Sheep Mountain Anticline, Bighorn Basin, Wyoming: Wyoming Geological Association 34th Annual Field Conference Guidebook, p. 96–112.

Hickey, L. J., 1980, Paleocene stratigraphy and flora of the Clark's Fork Basin, *in* Gingerich, P. D., ed., Early Cenozoic paleontology and stratigraphy of the Bighorn Basin, Wyoming: University of Michigan Papers on Paleontology, no. 24, p. 25–32.

Hose, R. K., 1955, The geology of the Crazy Woman Creek area, Johnson County, Wyoming: U.S. Geological Survey Bulletin 1027-B, 118 p.

Isby, J. S., and Picard, M. D., 1983, Current Creek Formation: Record of tectonism in Sevier-Laramide orogenic belt, north-central Utah: University of Wyoming Contributions to Geology, v. 22, p. 91–108.

Johnson, R. A., Smithson, S. B., Huntoon, P. W., and Frost, B. R., 1983, Interpretation of foreland structure in the Laramie Range from reprocessed CO-CORP deep crustal reflection data [abs.]: Geophysics, v. 48, no. 4, p. 425.

Johnson, R. C., 1985, Early Cenozoic history of the Uinta and Piceance Creek Basins, Utah and Colorado, with special reference to the development of Eocene Lake Uinta, *in* Flores, R. M., and Kaplan, S. S., eds., Cenozoic paleogeography of west-central United States: Rocky Mountain Section, Society of Economic Paleontologists and Mineralogists, p. 247–276.

Johnson, R. C., and May, F., 1980, A study of the Cretaceous-Tertiary unconformity in the Piceance Creek Basin, Colorado; The underlying Ohio Creek Formation (Upper Cretaceous) redefined as a member of the Hunter Canyon or Mesaverde Formation: U.S. Geological Survey Bulletin 1482-B, 27 p.

Jordan, T. E., 1981, Thrust loads and foreland basin evolution, Cretaceous, western United States: American Association of Petroleum Geologists Bulletin, v. 65, no. 12, p. 2506–2520.

Kanter, L. R., Dyer, R., and Dohmen, T. E., 1981, Laramide crustal shortening in the northern Wyoming Province: University of Wyoming Contributions to Geology, v. 19, no. 2, p. 135–142.

Keefer, W. R., 1961, Waltman Shale and Shotgun Members of Fort Union Formation (Paleocene) in Wind River Basin, Wyoming: American Association of Petroleum Geologists Bulletin, v. 45, p. 1310–1323.

——, 1965a, Geologic history of Wind River Basin, central Wyoming: American Association of Petroleum Geologists Bulletin, v. 49, p. 1878–1892.

——, 1965b, Stratigraphy and geologic history of the uppermost Cretaceous, Paleocene, and lower Eocene rocks in the Wind River Basin, Wyoming: U.S. Geological Survey Professional Paper 495-A, p. 1–77.

——, 1969, General stratigraphy and depositional history of the Fort Union, Indian Meadows, and Wind River Formations, Wind River Basin, Wyoming: Wyoming Geological Association 21st Annual Field Conference Guidebook, p. 19–28.

——, 1970, Structural geology of the Wind River Basin, Wyoming: U.S. Geological Survey Professional Paper 495-D, 35 p.

Keefer, W. R., and Love, J. D., 1963, Laramide vertical movements in central Wyoming: University of Wyoming Contributions to Geology, v. 2, p. 47–54.

Kraus, M. J., 1980, Genesis of a fluvial sheet sandstone, Willwood Formation, northwest Wyoming, *in* Gingerich, P. D., ed., Early Cenozoic paleontology and stratigraphy of the Bighorn Basin, Wyoming: University of Michigan Papers on Paleontology, no. 24, p. 25–42.

——, 1984, Sedimentology and tectonic setting of early Tertiary quartzite conglomerates, northwest Wyoming, *in* Koster, E. H., and Steel, R. J., eds., Sedimentology of gravels and conglomerates: Canadian Society of Petroleum Geologists Memoir 10, p. 203–216.

——, 1985, Changes in sediment accumulation rates determined from lower Eocene alluvial paleosols: 3rd International Fluvial Sedimentology Conference, Fort Collins, Colorado, Abstracts Volume, p. 25.

Kvale, E. P., 1986, Paleoenvironments and tectonic significance of the Upper Jurassic Morrison and Lower Cretaceous Cloverly Formations, Bighorn Basin, Wyoming [Ph.D. thesis]: Ames, Iowa State University, 191 p.

Lageson, D. R., 1982, Regional tectonics of the Cordilleran fold and thrust belt: American Association of Petroleum Geologists Continuing Education Short Course Notes, 66 p.

Lawton, T. F., 1983, Late Cretaceous fluvial systems and the age of foreland uplifts in central Utah, *in* Lowell, J. D., ed., Rocky Mountain foreland basins and uplifts: Denver, Colorado, Rocky Mountain Association of Geologists, p. 181–199.

Lisenbee, A. L., 1978, Laramide structure of the Black Hills uplift, South Dakota-Wyoming-Montana, *in* Matthews, V., ed., Laramide folding associated with basement block faulting in the western United States: Geological Society of America Memoir 151, p. 165–169.

Livaccari, R. F., Burke, K., and Sengor, A.M.C., 1981, Was the Laramide orogeny related to subduction of an oceanic plateau?: Nature, v. 289, p. 276–278.

Love, J. D., 1939, Geology along the southern margin of the Absoroka Range, Wyoming: Geological Society of America Special Paper 20, 134 p.

——, 1940, Thrust faulting at the southern end of the Bighorn Mountains, Wyoming [abs.]: Geological Society of America Bulletin, v. 51, no. 12, pt. 2, p. 1934.

——, 1960, Cenozoic sedimentation and crustal movement in Wyoming: American Journal of Science, Bradley Volume, p. 258-A, p. 204–214.

——, 1970, Cenozoic geology of the Granite Mountain area, central Wyoming: U.S. Geological Survey Professional Paper 495-C, 153 p.

——, 1977, Summary of Upper Cretaceous and Cenozoic stratigraphy, and of tectonic and glacial events in Jackson Hole, northwestern Wyoming: Wyoming Geological Association 29th Annual Field Conference Guidebook, p. 585–593.

——, 1978, Cenozoic thrust and normal faulting, and tectonic history of the Badwater area, northeastern margin of Wind River Basin, Wyoming: Wyoming Geological Association 30th Annual Field Conference Guidebook, p. 235–238.

Love, J. D., Weitz, J. L., and Hose, R. K., 1955, Geologic map of Wyoming: U.S. Geological Survey Map Series 7-A, scale 1:500,000.

Lowell, J. D., 1983, Foreland deformation, *in* Lowell, J. D., ed., Rocky Mountain foreland basins and uplifts: Denver, Colorado, Rocky Mountain Association of Geologists, p. 1–8.

McDonald, R. E., 1972, Eocene and Paleocene rocks of the southern and central basins, *in* Mallory, W. W., ed., Geologic atlas of the Rocky Mountain region: Denver, Colorado, Rocky Mountain Association of Geologists, p. 243–256.

Meissner, F. F., 1984, Cretaceous and lower Tertiary coals as sources for gas accumulations in the Rocky Mountain area, *in* Woodward, J., and others, eds., Hydrocarbon source rocks of the greater Rocky Mountain region: Denver, Colorado, Rocky Mountain Association of Geologists, p. 401–431.

Moncure, G., and Surdam, R. C., 1980, Depositional environment of the Green River Formation in the vicinity of the Douglas Creek Arch, Colorado and Utah: University of Wyoming Contributions to Geology, v. 19, no. 1, p. 9–24.

Neasham, J. W., and Vondra, C. F., 1972, Stratigraphy and petrology of the lower Eocene Willwood Formation, Bighorn Basin, Wyoming: Geological Society of America Bulletin, v. 83, p. 2167–2180.

Obernyer, S. L., 1978, Basin margin depositional environments of the Wasatch Formation in the Buffalo-Lake De Smet Area, Johnson County, Wyoming, *in* Hodgson, H. E., ed., Proceedings of the second symposium on the geology of Rocky Mountain Coal, 1977: Colorado Geological Survey Resource Series 4, p. 49–65.

——, 1980, The Lake De Smet coal seam; The product of active Basin-margin sedimentation and tectonics in the Buffalo–Lake De Smet area, Johnson County, Wyoming, during Eocene Wasatch time, *in* Glass, G. B., ed., Guidebook to the coal geology of the Powder River coal basin, Wyoming: Geological Survey of Wyoming Public Information Circular 14, p. 31–70.

Osmond, J. C., 1964, Tectonic history of the Uinta Basin, Utah: Intermountain Association of Petroleum Geologists 13th Annual Field Conference, Guidebook p. 47–58.

Oswald, E. B., and Kraus, M. J., 1986, Depositional setting of Mantua Lentil Sandstone, earliest Paleocene, Bighorn Basin, Wyoming: Geological Society of America Abstracts with Programs, v. 18, p. 401.

Petersen, F. A., 1983, Foreland detachment structures, *in* Lowell, J. D., ed., Rocky Mountain foreland basins and uplifts: Denver, Colorado, Rocky Mountain Association of Geologists, p. 65–78.

Phillips, S. T., 1983, Tectonic influence on sedimentation, Waltman Member, Fort Union Formation, Wind River Basin, Wyoming, *in* Lowell, J. D., ed.,

Rocky Mountain foreland basins and uplifts: Denver, Colorado, Rocky Mountain Association of Geologists, p. 149–160.

Picard, M. D., and High, L. R., 1981, Physical stratigraphy of ancient lacustrine deposits, *in* Ethridge, F. G., and Flores, R. M., eds., Recent and ancient nonmarine depositional environments; Models for exploration: Society of Economic Paleontologists and Mineralogists Special Publication 31, p. 233–259.

Porter, L., Jr., 1963, Stratigraphy and oil possibilities of the Green River Formation in the Uinta Basin, Utah, *in* Crawford, A. L., ed., Oil and gas possibilities of Utah, Re-evaluated: Utah Geological and Mineralogical Survey Bulletin, v. 54, p. 193–198.

Prucha, J. J., Graham, J. A., and Nickelsen, R. P., 1965, Basement-controlled deformation in Wyoming Province of Rocky Mountains foreland: American Association of Petroleum Geologists Bulletin, v. 49, p. 966–992.

Ray, R. R., 1982, Seismic stratigraphic interpretation of the Fort Union Formation, western Wind River Basin; Example of subtle trap exploration in a nonmarine sequence, *in* Halbouty, M. T., ed., The deliberate search for the subtle trap: American Association of Petroleum Geologists Memoir 32, p. 169–180.

Rea, B. D. and Barlow, J. A., 1975, Upper Cretaceous and Tertiary rocks, northern part of Bighorn Basin, Wyoming and Montana: Wyoming Geological Association 27th Annual Field Conference Guidebook, p. 63–71.

Ritzma, H. R., 1971, Faulting on the north flank of the Uinta Mountains, Utah and Colorado: Wyoming Geological Association 23rd Annual Field Conference Guidebook, p. 145–150.

Roehler, H. W., 1974, Depositional environments of rocks in the Piceance Creek basin, Colorado, *in* Murray, D. K., ed., Energy resources of the Piceance Creek Basin, Colorado: Denver, Colorado, Rocky Mountain Association of Geologists, p. 57–69.

Ryder, R. T., Fouch, T. D., and Elison, J. H., 1976, Early Tertiary sedimentation in the western Uinta Basin: Geological Society of America Bulletin, v. 87, p. 496–512.

Sales, J. K., 1968, Crustal mechanics of Cordilleran foreland deformation; A regional and scale-model approach: American Association of Petroleum Geologists Bulletin, v. 52, p. 2016–2044.

—— , 1983, Collapse of Rocky Mountain Basement Uplifts, *in* Lowell, J. D., ed., Rocky Mountain foreland basins and uplifts: Denver, Colorado, Rocky Mountain Association of Geologists, p. 79–97.

Schwartz, R. K., 1982, Broken Early Cretaceous foreland basin in southwestern Montana; Sedimentation related to tectonism, *in* Powers, R. P., and Geologic studies of the Cordilleran Thrust Belt: Denver, Colorado, Rocky Mountain Association of Geologists, p. 159–183.

Seeland, D. A., 1976, Relationships between Early Tertiary sedimentation patterns and uranium mineralization in the Powder River Basin, Wyoming: Wyoming Geological Association 28th Annual Field Conference Guidebook, p. 53–64.

—— , 1978, Eocene fluvial drainage patterns and their implications for uranium and hydrocarbon exploration in the Wind River Basin, Wyoming: U.S. Geological Survey Bulletin 1446, 21 p.

Shapiro, L. H., 1971, Structural geology of the Fanny Peak Lineament, Black Hills, Wyoming–South Dakota: Wyoming Geological Association 23rd Annual Field Conference Guidebook, p. 61–64.

Sharp, R. P., 1948, Early Tertiary fanglomerate, Bighorn Mountains, Wyoming: Journal of Geology, v. 57, p. 175–195.

Sinclair, W. J., and Granger, W., 1911, Eocene and Oligocene of the Wind River and Bighorn Basins: American Museum of Natural History, v. 30, p. 83–117.

Skeen, R. C., and Ray, R. R., 1983, Seismic models and interpretation of the Casper Arch Thrust; Application to Rocky Mountain foreland structure, *in* Lowell, J. D., ed., Rocky Mountain foreland basins and uplifts: Denver, Colorado, Rocky Mountain Association of Geologists, p. 99–124.

Smithson, S. B., Brewer, J. A., Kaufman, S., Oliver, J. E., and Hurich, C. A., 1979, Structure of the Laramide Wind River Uplift, Wyoming, from CO-CORP deep reflection data and from gravity data: Journal of Geophysical Research, v. 84, no. B-11, p. 5955–5972.

Smoot, J. P., 1978, Origin of the carbonate sediments in the Wilkins Peak Member of the lacustrine Green River Formation (Eocene) Wyoming, *in* Matter, A., and Tucker, M. E., eds., Modern and ancient lake sediments: International Association of Sedimentologists Special Publication 2, p. 109–127.

Stanley, K. O., and Collinson, J. W., 1979, Depositional history of Paleocene-lower Eocene Flagstaff Limestone and coeval rocks, central Utah: American Association of Petroleum Geologists Bulletin, v. 63, p. 311–323.

Stearns, D. W., 1971, Mechanisms of drape folding in the Wyoming province: Wyoming Geological Association 23rd Annual Field Conference Guidebook, p. 125–144.

Steidtmann, J. R., McGee, L. C., and Middleton, L. T., 1983, Laramide sedimentation, folding, and faulting in the southern Wind River Range, Wyoming, *in* Lowell, J. D., ed., Rocky Mountain foreland basins and uplifts: Denver, Colorado, Rocky Mountain Association of Geologists, p. 161–168.

Surdam, R. C., and Stanley, K. O., 1979, Lacustrine sedimentation during the culminating phase of Eocene Lake Gosiute, Wyoming (Green River Formation): Geological Society of America Bulletin, part 1, v. 90, p. 93–110.

—— , 1980a, Effects of changes in drainage basin boundaries on sedimentation in Eocene Lakes Gosiute and Uinta of Wyoming, Utah, and Colorado: Geology, v. 8, p. 135–139.

—— , 1980b, The stratigraphic and sedimentologic framework of the Green River Formation, Wyoming: Wyoming Geological Association 31st Annual Field Conference Guidebook, p. 205–221.

Tweto, O., 1975, Laramide (Late Cretaceous–early Tertiary) orogeny in the southern Rocky Mountains: Geological Society of America Memoir 144, p. 1–44.

Van Houton, F. B., 1952, Sedimentary record of Cenozoic orogenic and erosional events, Bighorn Basin, Wyoming: Wyoming Geological Association 7th Annual Field Conference Guidebook, p. 74–79.

Wiltschko, D. V., and Dorr, J. A., Jr., 1983, Timing of deformation in Overthrust Belt and Foreland of Idaho, Wyoming, and Utah: American Association of Petroleum Geologists Bulletin, v. 67, no. 8, p. 1304–1322.

Winterfeld, G. F., and Conard, J. B., 1983, Laramide tectonics and deposition, Washakie Range and northwestern Wind River Basin, Wyoming, *in* Lowell, J. D., ed., Rocky Mountain foreland basins and uplifts: Denver, Colorado, Rocky Mountain Association of Geologists, p. 137–148.

Wolfbauer, C. A., 1971, Geologic framework of the Green River Formation in Wyoming: University of Wyoming Contributions to Geology, v. 10, p. 3–8.

Young, M. A., 1972, Willwood metaquartzite conglomerate in a southwestern portion of the Bighorn Basin, Wyoming [M.Sc. thesis]: Ames, Iowa State University, 71 p.

MANUSCRIPT ACCEPTED BY THE SOCIETY FEBRUARY 9, 1988

Geological Society of America
Memoir 171
1988

Cordilleran Foreland Basin evolution in response to interactive Cretaceous thrusting and foreland partitioning, southwestern Montana

Robert K. Schwartz
Department of Geology, Allegheny College, Meadville, Pennsylvania 16335
Peter G. DeCelles
Department of Geological Sciences, University of Rochester, Rochester, New York 14627

ABSTRACT

Cretaceous strata of southwestern Montana indicate that the large, first-order Cordilleran Foreland Basin was tectonically partitioned by a complex of second-order intraforeland uplifts that occupied sites of eventual classic Laramide intraforeland uplifts. The intraforeland uplifts and intervening basins formed a block-like surficial pattern throughout the evolving Cretaceous foreland. Preliminary stratigraphic and sedimentary petrologic evidence suggests that some of the same structures were active during Jurassic time. Thus, the Laramide orogeny in southwestern Montana can be viewed as the structural culmination of a long (at least 100 m.y.) history of basement-involved deformation.

The developmental history of the Cordilleran Foreland in southwestern Montana is divisible into three stages: (1) an early stage of embryonic foreland development in Late Permian–Late Jurassic time, characterized by carbonate shallow-marine sedimentation with local coarse siliciclastic input from intraforeland structural elements; (2) a middle stage of fully developed, first-order foreland-basin subsidence in Early–early Late Cretaceous time, characterized by siliciclastic-dominated nonmarine and shallow-marine sedimentation; major reactivated intraforeland uplift (and subsidence); and eastward encroachment of the Cordilleran (Sevier) thrust belt; and (3) a late stage, during latest Cretaceous–early Eocene time, characterized by impingement of the frontal Cordilleran thrust belt upon major intraforeland uplifts (Laramide foreland uplifts) and nonmarine-dominated synorogenic sedimentation.

The early stage (Late Permian–Late Jurassic) of foreland development was temporally associated with terrane accretion and other tectonic events in the Cordillera. The onset of first-order basin subsidence and a coeval increase in intraforeland tectonism were temporally associated with a second phase of Cordilleran tectonism and eastward migration of the Cordilleran thrust belt. Deposition of the Cretaceous Kootenai, Blackleaf, and lower Frontier Formations in southwestern Montana occurred during this middle stage of foreland-basin evolution. Source areas consisted of the Cordilleran fold-thrust upland, intraforeland uplifts, and the unstable craton. Thus, the Cretaceous stratigraphic sequence in southwestern Montana was produced by the interaction of Cordilleran and intraforeland tectonic events.

The entire Kootenai-Blackleaf-lower Frontier sequence developed during a single cycle bounded by tectonic maxima (Cordilleran and intraforeland) with an intervening period of tectonic quiescence and continued foreland-basin subsidence. However, this longer term (~20 m.y.) sequence was punctuated by higher frequency (~3 to 4 m.y.) events, most clearly signalled by intraforeland reactivation. The first-order behavior of the Cordilleran Foreland Basin in southwestern Montana is partly explained as the flexural response to thrust-sheet loading of a viscoelastic lithosphere. However, explanation of foreland-basin evolution in Montana requires a model that incorporates an additional, interactive mechanism for broad-scale reactivation of second-order (i.e., intraforeland) elements.

INTRODUCTION

During Mesozoic–early Cenozoic time, the lithosphere of western interior North America was depressed into a broad (several hundred kilometers wide) foreland basin that extended from northwestern Canada to at least as far south as northern New Mexico (Fig. 1; Dickinson, 1976). This basin, referred to as the Cordilleran Foreland Basin, was bordered on the east by the stable craton and on the west by the North American Cordillera, a complicated, linear orogenic belt of thrust sheets, accreted terranes, batholiths, and local basins (Coney, 1972; Burchfiel and Davis, 1972; Davis and others, 1978; Monger and others, 1982). Geodynamic models by Beaumont (1981), Jordan (1981), and Schedl and Wiltschko (1984) have demonstrated that, as suggested by Price (1973), the Cordilleran Foreland Basin was produced by downward flexure of the lithosphere in response to loading by stacked thrust sheets in the Cordilleran orogenic belt. These and similar (e.g., Quinlan and Beaumont, 1984) models predict that the sedimentary fill of a foreland basin should be wedge-shaped and gradually attenuated toward the craton interior in cross sections oriented perpendicular to the orogenic belt. Although this geometry is an effective first-order approximation of the shape of the Cordilleran Foreland Basin-fill in Montana and Wyoming (McGookey, 1972), significant local variations in stratigraphic thickness (see Jordan's [1981] palinspastic isopach maps) and facies indicate that distinct, second-order topographic basins and highs existed within the large, first-order foreland basin. We refer to these second-order features as intraforeland basins and uplifts (Schwartz, 1983; DeCelles, 1986).

The question of whether Cordilleran thrusting ("Sevier style") and basement-involved intraforeland deformation ("Laramide style") were interactive and influential upon sedimentation during incipient to middle stages of foreland-basin evolution has been a central issue in our work. Previous stratigraphic studies in the Wyoming foreland have suggested that major thrust activation and related sedimentation *preceded* intraforeland uplift (e.g., the Moxa, Wind River, and Gros Ventre uplifts; Wiltschko and Dorr, 1983; Shuster and Steidtmann, this volume). A cursory examination of some evidence in southwestern Montana might suggest a similar relationship. For example, structural evidence indicates that initial thrusting of the Sapphire and Medicine Lodge plates (Ruppel and Lopez, 1984; Perry and Sando, 1983) preceded coarse synorogenic sedimentation associated with large-scale intraforeland (Laramide) uplift (e.g., Lima Conglomerate, Golden Spike Formation, Elkhorn Mountains Volcanics, Sphinx Conglomerate; Fig. 2). Thus, without the diagnosis of older, and perhaps more subtle, sedimentary patterns, which may have been associated with developmental intraforeland uplift, the most popular contention has been that Cordilleran (or Sevier) thrusting and its effects on sedimentation largely preceded and outweighed the effects of intraforeland (Laramide) uplift (Suppe, 1985).

The developmental history of the Cordilleran Foreland Basin in southwestern Montana can be crudely subdivided into three stages (Fig. 2): (1) an early, embryonic stage (Late Permian–Jurassic or earliest Cretaceous), which was characterized by marine carbonate and mixed carbonate-terrigenous sedimentation, and incipient localized uplift within the unstable craton or "embryonic foreland"; (2) a middle stage (Early Cretaceous–early Late Cretaceous), which was dominated by nonmarine and shallow-marine terrigenous sedimentation, development of first-order basin subsidence, and tectonic partitioning of the foreland; and (3) a late stage (Late Cretaceous–Early Eocene), which was dominated by proximal, synorogenic, nonmarine terrigenous sedimentation and volcanism, and during which the first-order basin became severely partitioned by large Laramide uplifts (Wilson, 1970; Ryder and Scholten, 1973; DeCelles and others, 1987). Recent discussions of the stratigraphy of the Cordilleran Foreland Basin (e.g., Suttner and others, 1981; Jordan, 1981; Wiltschko and Dorr, 1983; DeCelles, 1986; Heller and others, 1986) have attempted to correlate individual stratigraphic units with specific tectonic episodes in the Cordilleran fold-thrust belt (e.g., Nevadan, Columbian, and Sevier orogenies). Although these attempts are essential to build a temporally and geographically broader framework, they have resulted in misconceptions concerning the duration and geographic distribution of the Cordilleran Foreland Basin. We view the Mesozoic and early Cenozoic stratigraphic sequence in western Montana and Wyoming as the sedimentary response to a prolonged (~100 m.y.) history of development of the Cordilleran Foreland Basin as it evolved through its various stages (early, middle, late).

In this chapter we summarize recent findings (Schwartz, 1972, 1983; Suttner and others, 1981; Thompson, 1984; DeCelles, 1984, 1986) and new sedimentological and sedimentary petrological information from the Cretaceous Kootenai, Blackleaf, and lower Frontier Formations of southwestern Montana (Fig. 3). These three formations were deposited in the Montana portion of the Cordilleran Foreland Basin during its middle stage of evolution, a period during which the basin experienced nascent tectonic partitioning of the foreland basin and the eastward impingement of the Cordilleran fold-thrust belt. We suggest that Cordilleran and intraforeland tectonics exerted an interactive control on foreland sedimentation. We further contend that development of the Cordilleran Foreland Basin was inextricably linked to processes of subduction, terrane accretion, plutonism,

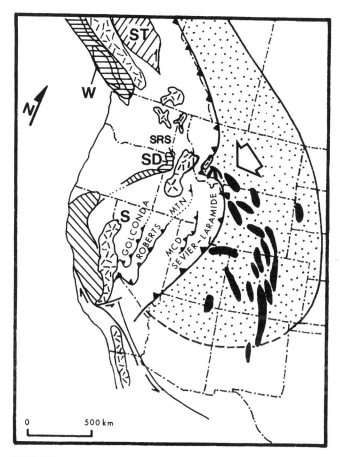

 CORDILLERAN FORELAND BASIN

 LARAMIDE UPLIFTS

 LATE MESOZOIC BATHOLITHS

 STIKINIAN SUPER-TERRANE

 WRANGELLIAN/SEVEN DEVILS SUPER-TERRANE

 JURASSIC TERRANES

Figure 1. Generalized map showing the Cordilleran Foreland Basin and some Cordilleran and Laramide tectonic elements pertinent to this study, including the Golconda, Roberts Mountain, Sevier, and Manning Canyon (MCD) thrust zones. Important accreted terranes are Wrangellia (W), Stikinia (ST), Seven Devils (SD), and Sonomia (S). SRS indicates position of Salmon River Suture zone of Lund and Snee (1988). Arrow points to the location of the study area in western Montana. Modified from Dickinson (1976), Davis and others (1978), Hamilton (1978), and Monger and others (1982).

and thrusting in the westward adjacent Cordillera. Although the present state of knowledge is insufficient to allow precise mechanical and/or temporal correlations between tectonic events in the Cordillera and possible tectonic and stratigraphic responses in the foreland basin, we present preliminary evidence in support of a broad temporal correlation between major Cordilleran and foreland events.

APPROACH AND METHODS

As discussed by Jordan and others (1988), attempts to decipher the tectonic history of a foreland basin and its adjacent thrust belt on the basis of foreland-basin strata can be plagued by circular reasoning. Only with independent dates for tectonic events (e.g., thrusting, subsidence) and corresponding foreland strata can true cause-effect relationships be ascertained. The Lower Cretaceous section of Wyoming and Montana has historically proven difficult to date in any detail because it is dominantly nonmarine (and hence lacks a continuous fossil record) and was deposited during the Cretaceous paleomagnetic quiet zone. Nevertheless, sufficient biostratigraphic data exist to bracket deposition of the Kootenai–lower Frontier sequence within Aptian-Cenomanian time (~118 to 95 Ma; Suttner, 1969; James, 1977; Burden, 1984; Dyman and Nichols, 1988). In contrast to the lack of high-resolution dates for the foreland strata, recent work by Lund and Snee (1988) documented a series of tightly constrained dates on deformational and thermal events in the adjacent Cordillera of Idaho. With these broad constraints on the ages of tectonic events in the Cordillera and strata in the foreland basin, we attempt to analyze the stratigraphic sequence in terms of depositional systems and petrologic composition to determine in as much detail as possible the tectonic-sedimentologic evolution of the Early Cretaceous foreland basin in southwestern Montana.

This approach is potentially risky in that the composition of foreland sediments and the character of depositional systems are strongly influenced by eustatic sea level, composition of source terranes, and climate (e.g., Baker, 1978; Graham and others, 1986; DeCelles and others, 1987; Posamentier and Vail, 1988; Jordan and others, 1988). However, rather than make the blanket assumption that, because of these possible nontectonic influences, the depositional systems and sediment compositions of foreland-basin strata are useless for determining tectonic history, we attempt to deal with individual cases as they arise. For example, because much of the Kootenai Formation in southwestern Montana was deposited in internally drained basins and the Cretaceous sea was located several hundred kilometers to the north, it is probably safe to assume that eustatic sea level did not exert much, if any, control on Kootenai fluvial systems. On the other hand, much of the Blackleaf Formation was deposited in marine environments or flanking nonmarine systems, so relative sea level must be taken into account.

Our interpretations are based on data gathered from approximately 100 localities throughout southwestern Montana. These data include more than 60 measured stratigraphic sections, ap-

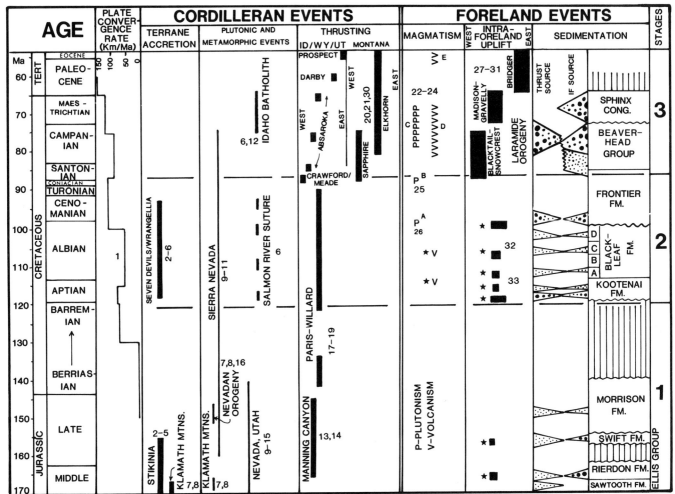

Figure 2. Chart showing correlations between some important Cordilleran tectonic events and episodes of tectonism and sedimentation in the Mesozoic–early Cenozoic foreland of western Montana. The three postulated stages of foreland evolution are shown on the right. The lengths of the black bars represent possible temporal ranges of events, not necessarily the duration of events. In the column labeled "intraforeland uplift," the widths of black bars represent relative magnitudes of events. Stars indicate events postulated in this chapter. Numbered references are: 1, Engebretson and others (1984); 2, Davis and others (1978); 3, Coney and others (1980); 4, Monger and others (1982); 5, Saleeby (1983); 6, Lund and Snee (1988); 7, Harper and Wright (1984); 8, Wright and Miller (1986); 9, Armstrong and others (1977); 10, Armstrong and Suppe (1973); 11, Evernden and Kistler (1970); 12, Robinson and others (1968); 13, Allmendinger and Jordan (1981); 14, Allmendinger and Jordan (1984); 15, Miller and others (1987); 16, Ingersoll and Schweickert (1986); 17, Wiltschko and Dorr (1983); 18, Jordan (1981); 19, Royse and others (1975); 20, Ruppel and others (1981); 21, Ruppel and Lopez (1984); 22, Tilling and others (1968); 23, Zen and others (1975); 24, Klepper and others (1957); 25, Young (1985); 26, Daugherty and Vitaliano (1969); 27, Ryder and Scholten (1973); 28, Nichols and others (1985); 29, DeCelles and others (1987); 30, Schmidt and Hendrix (1981); 31, Lageson (1985); 32, Schwartz (1983); 33, DeCelles (1986).

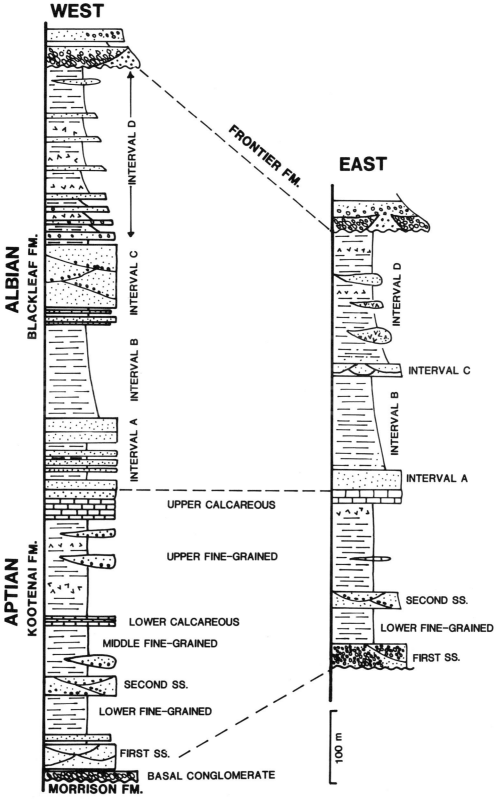

Figure 3. Generalized, composite stratigraphic columns of the Kootenai, Blackleaf, and lower Frontier Formations in the western and eastern study area. Random "v" pattern represents volcaniclastic or tuffaceous strata. Thicknesses are approximate.

proximately 3,600 paleocurrent measurements, and petrographic analyses of 266 thin sections. Several isopach maps shown in this chapter are based on thickness data from Peterson (1981), which were recontoured using facies and paleocurrent data that independently indicate the presence of intraforeland uplifts and basins within the study area. However, Peterson (1981) combined data from the Morrison Formation (Jurassic) with data from the Kootenai and data from the Blackleaf Formation with data from the Marias River Formation (and other Colorado Group equivalents). Although Peterson's (1981) isopach maps do not convey the level of detail obtainable from isopach maps of individual formation members, they nevertheless clearly exhibit thickness patterns for the Kootenai and Blackleaf Formations that reflect the paleotopographic elements discussed in this chapter. Other methodological details and raw data can be found in Schwartz (1972, 1983), DeCelles (1984, 1986), and in Appendix 1 (in pocket inside back cover).

REGIONAL STRUCTURAL SETTING AND PALEOGEOGRAPHY

Foreland-basin development in southwestern Montana

The Cordilleran Foreland Basin in southwestern Montana is characterized by the presence of the frontal fold-thrust belt, eastward- to southeastward-trending transverse faults, an eastward-trending salient of Mesozoic batholiths and plutons, and basement-cored uplifts of the northern end of the Laramide structural province (Figs. 1, 4). Summaries of literature pertinent to these various structural and plutonic elements are available in Schwartz (1983) and DeCelles (1986). Paleogeographic elements related to each of these structural systems exerted variable degrees of control on Mesozoic foreland-basin development and sedimentation (Schwartz, 1983; DeCelles, 1986). In addition, a wealth of stratigraphic data indicates that the structure of the pre-Mesozoic western continental margin was inherently complex, having experienced a long history (dating back to Proterozoic time) of rifting, differential subsidence, and local uplift (Harrison and others, 1974; Peterson, 1981; Winston and others, 1984). Thus, the Cordilleran Foreland Basin in western Montana was superimposed upon a structurally complex continental margin.

The stratigraphy of southwestern Montana indicates three significant steps in sedimentary responses to tectonism leading up to Kootenai sedimentation. Prior to the Permian, sedimentation in southwestern Montana predominantly occurred in shallow-marine carbonate and marine quartz-rich systems. However, rapid westward thickening of the Snaky Canyon Formation (Quadrant Formation equivalent, Pennsylvanian) into central Idaho, and its interfingering with graywackes of the Wood River Formation (Scholten, 1957; Skipp and Hall, 1980), indicate tectonic activity farther to the west. During deposition of the Phosphoria Formation (Permian) in western Montana, differential basin subsidence increased, and lithic sand and gravel, including clasts of chert, limestone, quartz-arenite, phosphatic chert, and

volcanic material, were supplied in various amounts to a previously carbonate-dominant setting (R. K. Schwartz and P. G. DeCelles, unpublished data). Clast sizes and compositions suggest that at least some of the detritus was locally (intrabasinally) derived from intraformational and subjacent lithologies, and not from a distal fold-thrust upland. Farther south, in southeastern Idaho, western Utah, and Nevada, Late Paleozoic–Early Triassic sedimentary rocks also record synorogenic and postorogenic sedimentation in a differentially subsiding foreland or back-arc setting (Collinson and Hasenmueller, 1978; Speed, 1978; Poole and Wardlaw, 1978).

The unconformably overlying Ellis Group (Jurassic), which includes the Sawtooth, Rierdon, and Swift Formations, represents a second major change in sedimentary style. Coarse, chert-rich sandstone and angular chert- and quartzite-clast conglomerates occur in separate major lithosomes within carbonate shoreface and shallow-carbonate platform deposits of the Ellis Group (Peterson, 1972; Fox, 1982; J. H. Meyers, 1981, personal communication, 1986). Facies and petrologic data provide strong evidence that, although a marine carbonate setting persisted where terrigenous influx was minor, basin topography was quite irregular, and much of the detritus was locally derived and transported offshore (westward) from upper-Paleozoic-cored, tectonically active positive elements (Belt Arch complex) within the embryonic Cordilleran Foreland Basin (J. H. Meyers, 1981, personal communication, 1986; Hayes, 1984; Schwartz and DeCelles, unpublished data).

The overlying Morrison Formation consists of mudstone, lenticular fluvial sandstone, and lacustrine limestone (Suttner, 1969; Walker, 1974). It represents the onset of nonmarine-dominated siliciclastic sedimentation in the incipient Cordilleran Foreland Basin of western Montana (Suttner and others, 1981). In addition, Morrison framework mineralogy, isopach trends, and unconformity relationships with the overlying Kootenai strongly suggest the occurrence of, and derivation of sediment from, Late Jurassic tectonic elements within the foreland basin of southwestern Montana (Suttner, 1969; Walker, 1974; Schwartz, 1983; DeCelles, 1986). In particular, Morrison isopach patterns in southwestern Montana (Suttner, 1969, Fig. 5) show zones of thickening and thinning (or local absence), reflecting zones of differential subsidence within the foreland. However, Morrison isopachs in northwestern Montana, north of the central Montana trough (which includes terminal elements of the Laramide structural province), exhibit a less complex second-order thickness pattern, which is superimposed upon a first-order westward-thickening trend (Fig. 5; Peterson, 1981; Schwartz, 1983).

Isopach patterns of the Ellis Group display similar variability (Peterson, 1981). The Ellis isopach pattern in northwestern Montana is suggestive of simple clastic-wedge geometry, with subdued intrabasinal (second-order) control on sedimentation, whereas Ellis isopach patterns in southwestern Montana exhibit thickness variations more typical of a structurally partitioned and differentially subsiding foreland region. Similar to northwestern Montana, a first-order pattern of basin subsidence was initiated in

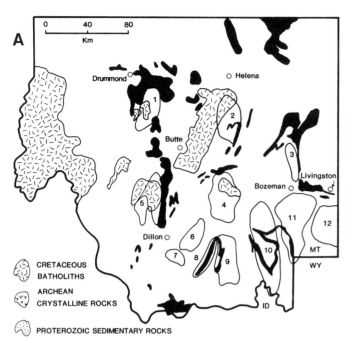

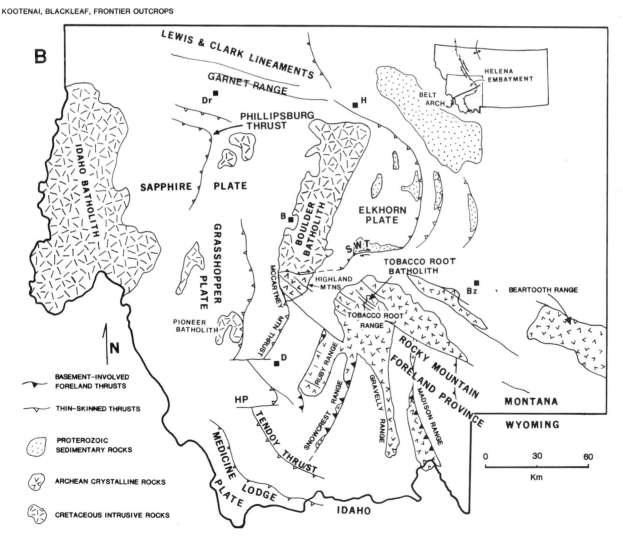

Figure 4. A, Map of the study area, showing outcrop patterns of Kootenai, Blackleaf, and Frontier Formations. Numbered mountain ranges referred to in text are: 1, Flint Creek; 2, Elkhorn; 3, Bridger; 4, Tobacco Root; 5, Pioneer; 6, Ruby; 7, Blacktail; 8, Snowcrest; 9, Gravelly; 10, Madison; 11, Gallatin; 12, Beartooth. Modified from DeCelles (1986). B, Map showing the generalized structural, igneous, and metamorphic geology of the study area (after Ruppel and others, 1981, and Schmidt and O'Neill, 1983). HP = Horse Prairie fault zone; SWT = southwest Montana transverse zone. City symbols: D = Dillon; B = Butte; Dr = Drummond; H = Helena; Bz = Bozeman.

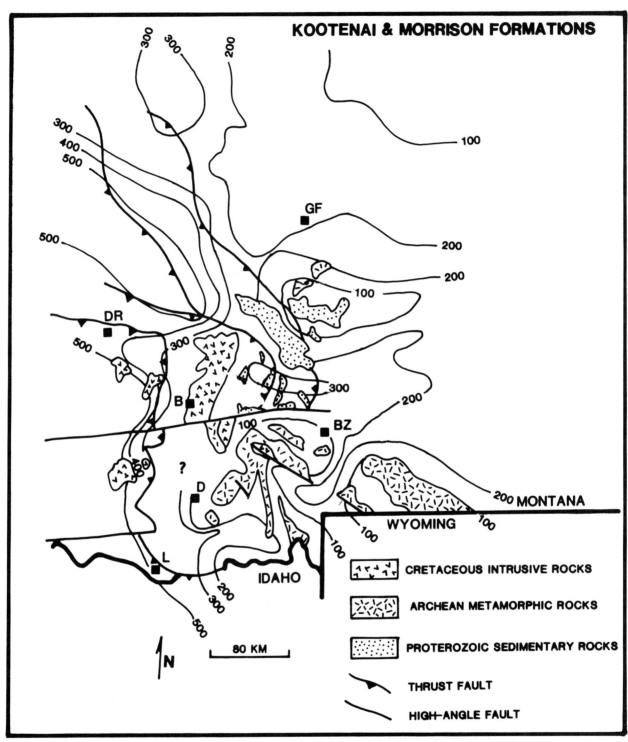

Figure 5. Composite isopach map of the Kootenai and Morrison Formations in western Montana. Contours are in meters. Major thrust plates have been palinspastically restored according to Peterson (1981). GF = Great Falls; L = Lima. Other city symbols are the same as in Figure 4. Modified from Peterson (1981) and Schwartz (1983).

the westernmost Wyoming–Idaho portion of the foreland basin during deposition of the lower Gannett Group (Morrison time-equivalent; Jordan, 1981; Heller and others, 1986). Preliminary data, however, suggest roughly coeval basin partitioning to the east in west-central Wyoming (L. J. Suttner, personal communication, 1985) and north-central Wyoming (Kvale, 1986).

Thus, a first-order basin, or "moat," apparently did not develop in southwestern Montana during Late Jurassic time, but did develop in western Wyoming and eastern Idaho and in northwestern Montana. Based on known relationships between crustal loading by thrust plates and basin subsidence (e.g., Walcott, 1970; Jordan, 1981; Quinlan and Beaumont, 1984), regional first-order subsidence is expected in areas adjacent to a thrust belt. Therefore, during Ellis and Morrison deposition, it is only reasonable that another locus of major foreland-basin subsidence, and the location of a hinge zone separating a first-order basin from a cratonward region of differentially subsiding second-order features were located to the west of southwestern Montana.

As discussed below, the positions of partitioning Jurassic and Cretaceous paleogeographic elements in southwestern Montana closely correspond with positions of Late Cretaceous Laramide uplifts. Schwartz (1983) and DeCelles (1984, 1986) have suggested that the Jurassic and Cretaceous uplifts were structurally inherited and later reactivated again during the Laramide orogeny. If this is true, the areal distribution of Jurassic-Cretaceous intraforeland tectonic elements should overlap the Laramide structural province, which extends south-southeastward from its northern terminus in southwestern Montana (Fig. 1). It is noteworthy that first-order foreland-basin geometry developed to the north and south of, but not within, southwestern Montana during the Late Jurassic. This suggests that the Gannett Group of western Wyoming and eastern Idaho may have been deposited west of the zone of active intraforeland elements, while correlative rocks in southwestern Montana were deposited within the realm of active intraforeland structures. Similarly, Jurassic and Cretaceous rocks of northwestern Montana may have been deposited north of the terminus of active intraforeland structures, as marked by the distribution of later Laramide uplifts. Alternatively, intraforeland uplifts may have been more pervasive in the Jurassic-Cretaceous Cordilleran Foreland Basin, and the Laramide structural province may simply comprise a relatively localized group of intraforeland uplifts that were again reactivated during the Laramide orogeny.

In summary, we submit that: (1) localized, but relatively minor, intraforeland uplift and subsidence occurred in southwestern Montana from Late Permian through middle Late Jurassic time; (2) siliciclastic-dominated sedimentation was initiated during Ellis deposition, in association with eastward encroachment of the Cordilleran thrust belt, increased intraforeland deformation within southwestern Montana, and first-order foreland-basin subsidence in eastern Idaho and northwestern Montana; and (3) first-order basin subsidence was subsequently superimposed upon an already incipiently partitioned basin in southwestern Montana during deposition of the Lower Cretaceous Kootenai Formation.

Foreland evolution in context of Cordilleran tectonism

A clearer perspective of Mesozoic tectonics and sedimentation within southwestern Montana is derived by considering the timing of regional tectonic and thermal events in the evolving Cordillera. The Cretaceous events of southwestern Montana may be viewed as later stage, eastward-migrated tectonism associated with the overall evolution and growth of the Cordillera. Although current knowledge is insufficient to specifically link mechanical aspects of subduction and continental-margin accretionary events in the Cordillera with distal inboard events, such as thrusting, subsidence, and basement reactivation in the foreland, some causation has been suggested (e.g., Coney and others, 1980; Oldow and others, 1984; Cant, 1985; Suttner and others, 1985; Sears and Schmitt, 1987).

Figure 2 presents a summary—by no means complete—of the temporal and paleogeographic relationships between important Cordilleran tectonic events and events in the foreland basin. The chart is not meant to imply specific mechanical relationships; rather, it is intended to highlight the apparent contemporaneity of certain Cordilleran and foreland events. Also, the proposed three stages of evolution of the Jurassic–Cretaceous Cordilleran foreland region are shown. The lengths of the black bars representing times of accretion of Stikinia and Wrangellia indicate the ranges of possible dates of accretion, not the actual durations of accretion events.

Accretion of the Stikinian super-terrane occurred during the Middle to Late Jurassic (Coney and others, 1980; Monger and others, 1982). Although this terrane presently lies entirely north of the United States–Canada border, paleomagnetic data suggest that it, as well as the Wrangellia–Seven Devils super-terrane which accreted later, experienced significant northward translation after accretion (Davis and others, 1978; Irving and others, 1980).

The onset of Jurassic deformation in the Cordillera, initial intraforeland uplift, and Ellis-Morrison siliciclastic-rich sedimentation in the foreland of southwestern Montana roughly coincided with accretion of Stikinia (Suttner and others, 1985). In addition, widespread arc magmatism occurred in the Cordillera during the Middle and Late Jurassic (Evernden and Kistler, 1970; Armstrong and Suppe, 1973; Armstrong and others, 1977; Hamilton, 1978; Allmendinger and Jordan, 1981; Allmendinger and others, 1984). Allmendinger and Jordan (1981, 1984) suggested that Middle to Late Jurassic eastward thrusting of the Hansel allochthon on the Manning Canyon detachment of northern Utah and southern Idaho may have been the first major episode of Mesozoic Cordilleran thrusting in the western United States (Fig. 2). Although direct correlation between Manning Canyon thrusting and foreland-basin sedimentation has not been demonstrated, geohistory analysis of Middle Jurassic strata in Wyoming by Heller and others (1986) suggests that a major episode of foreland subsidence occurred simultaneously in eastern Idaho and/or western Wyoming. This episode of subsidence may have been related to distal lithospheric flexure owing to loading by the

Hansel thrust plate. We suggest that Middle to Late Jurassic intraforeland reactivation and deposition of the Ellis Group and Morrison Formation in southwestern Montana were related to coeval Cordilleran tectonism farther north in Idaho. However, Jurassic tectonic events along the eastern margin of the Cordillera in Idaho have not been demonstrated (Lund and Snee, 1988). Moreover, the work of Miller and others (1987) in east-central Nevada indicates that Jurassic shortening occurred in an east-to-west direction. Clearly, the nature and extent of Jurassic tectonism on the inboard side of the Cordillera remains poorly understood, rendering tectonic-sedimentologic interpretations of the Jurassic strata in the foreland region speculative at best.

Late-Early to early–Late Cretaceous accretion of the Wrangellia–Seven Devils super-terrane (Coney and others, 1980; Monger and others, 1982) coincided with Paris-Willard thrusting, local intraforeland uplift, and igneous activity, and deposition of the Kootenai-Frontier sequence in the foreland basin (Fig. 2). In addition, Engebretson and others (1984) showed a roughly synchronous seven-fold increase in the rate of convergence between the Farallon and North American plates (Fig. 2). Recent work by Lund (1984), Sutter and others (1984), and Lund and Snee (1988) has documented a series of middle and Late Cretaceous thermal and metamorphic events along the Salmon River suture of west-central Idaho. Lund and Snee (1988) suggested the Salmon River suture formed by right-lateral transpressive accretion of the Seven Devils arc and related exotic rocks to the western continental margin over a period of ~25 m.y. A major dynamothermal event at ~118 Ma was followed by two other tectonic events—at ~109 and ~101–99 Ma—which may not have involved thermal activity. A second major thermal event was accompanied by the emplacement of tonalite plutons of the Idaho batholith at ~93 Ma (Fig. 2; Lund and Snee, 1988).

Lund and Snee (1988) suggested that the Cretaceous fold-thrust belt in eastern Idaho and western Montana resulted from large-scale crustal thickening and compression in response to transpressional tectonism along the Salmon River suture. Their hypothesis is supported by the approximate correlation of the synorogenic basal conglomerates of the Kootenai and Frontier Formations with the two major thermal events at ~118 and ~101 to 99 Ma in the Salmon River suture (Fig. 2). Thus, sedimentological data from the Kootenai–lower Frontier sequence; radiometric dates from intraforeland igneous rocks; and the work of Lund (1984), Sutter and others (1984), and Lund and Snee (1988) all suggest that Cordilleran transpressive accretion, major thrusting episodes, and intraforeland uplifts occurred roughly synchronously during the second stage of foreland-basin evolution (Fig. 2). Work in the hinterland of Nevada (Miller and others, 1987) and the adjacent frontal fold-thrust belt and foreland basin of Utah (Lawton, 1985) suggests a similar temporal relationship between Cordilleran tectonism and foreland-basin sedimentation farther south.

The third and final stage of foreland-basin evolution in southwestern Montana witnessed the complete break-up of the foreland during the Laramide orogeny. Cordilleran thrust sheets impinged upon fully developed intraforeland (Laramide) uplifts, and coarse, synorogenic conglomerate was deposited in intermontane basins (Fig. 2; Schmidt and Hendrix, 1981; Schmidt and Garihan, 1983; Nichols and others, 1985; DeCelles and others, 1987). A discussion of the Laramide orogeny, the causes of which remain controversial, is beyond the scope of our work (cf. Cross and Pilger, 1978; Dickinson and Snyder, 1978; Bird, 1984; Henderson and others, 1984; Engebretson and others, 1984). Because it apparently involved a combination of anomalous tectonic driving mechanisms (e.g., flat-slab subduction, an increase in plate velocities, subduction of an oceanic aseismic ridge), the Laramide orogeny and its related sedimentary deposits probably are not fully representative of typical later stages of foreland-basin evolution.

KOOTENAI, BLACKLEAF, AND LOWER FRONTIER FORMATIONS

Basin configuration

Regional isopach maps of southwestern Montana indicate that Morrison through lower Frontier deposition was not laterally continuous across a geometrically simple foreland basin. The classical concept of a cratonward-thinning clastic wedge does not apply to this portion of the Cordilleran Foreland Basin. Although integrated sets of data are necessary to convincingly demonstrate a complex basin geometry and intraforeland control on sedimentation, the regional distribution of total formation thickness does reflect the presence of several elongated, second-order (intraforeland) highs and basins within the region.

Both the Kootenai and Blackleaf Formations show marked first-order thickening west of a hinge zone located east of the Boulder batholith (Figs. 5, 6). Local isopach patterns indicate intraforeland thinning of the Kootenai and Blackleaf in the areas of present-day Archean-cored structures (Beartooth, Tobacco Root–Ruby, Madison-Gravelly, Blacktail-Snowcrest, Highland uplifts); a Proterozoic-cored region (Big Belt and Little Belt Mountains); the Boulder batholith; and two areas to the north of Great Falls and Drummond. Corresponding intraforeland paleogeographic elements, which apparently controlled Cretaceous sediment thickness in southwestern Montana, are referred to as the Beartooth, Tobacco Root–Ruby, Madison-Gravelly, Blacktail-Snowcrest, Belt, Lewis-and-Clark, Boulder-Highland, and the Sweetgrass–Milk River highs (Fig. 7). Not shown, but also a part of the Cordilleran Foreland Basin configuration, was the Central Montana high, located within the Central Montana embayment farther to the east (Peterson, 1981), as well as other elements of subtle relief in eastern Montana and northern Wyoming.

Zones of relatively great Kootenai-Blackleaf thickness between the intraforeland highs define areas of maximum relative subsidence, or second-order intraforeland basins (Fig. 7). These second-order basins included: (1) north- to northwest-oriented basins parallel to positive elements of similar orientation; (2) the somewhat discontinuous, eastward-oriented Central Montana–

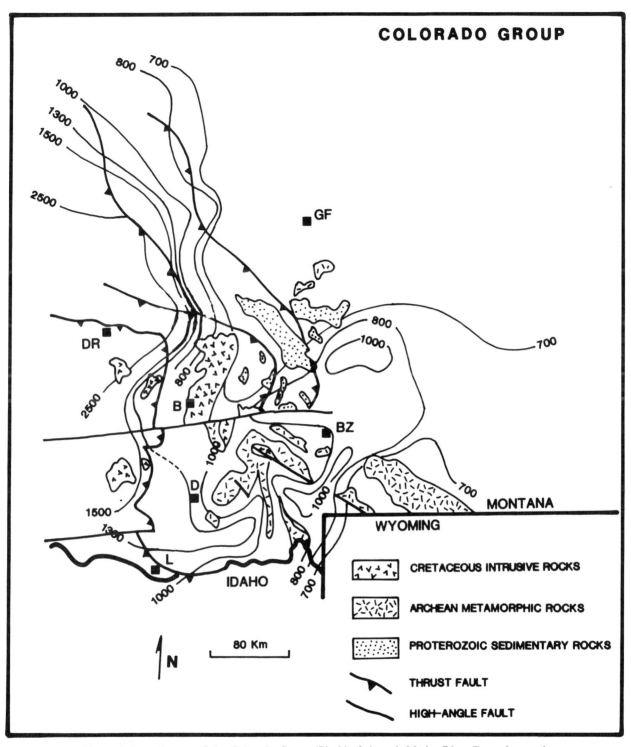

Figure 6. Isopach map of the Colorado Group (Blackleaf through Marias River Formations and equivalents) in western Montana. Major thrust plates have been palinspastically restored according to Peterson (1981). Isopach contours are in meters. Modified from Schwartz (1983) and Peterson (1981). See Figures 4 and 5 for city symbols.

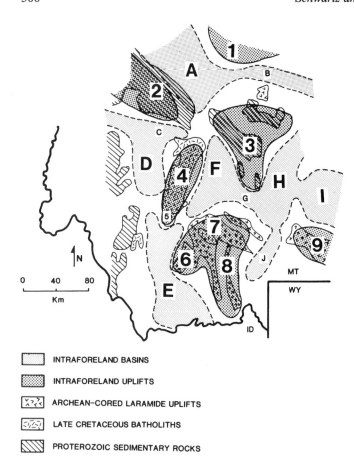

INTRAFORELAND BASINS

INTRAFORELAND UPLIFTS

ARCHEAN-CORED LARAMIDE UPLIFTS

LATE CRETACEOUS BATHOLITHS

PROTEROZOIC SEDIMENTARY ROCKS

Figure 7. Schematic map showing the distribution of postulated Cretaceous intraforeland uplifts and basins, metamorphic-cored Laramide (Late Cretaceous–Eocene) uplifts, outcrops of Proterozoic strata (Belt Supergroup), and Late Cretaceous batholiths. Numbered intraforeland uplifts are: 1, Sweetgrass Arch; 2, Lewis-and-Clark; 3, Belt; 4, Boulder; 5, Highland; 6, Blacktail-Snowcrest; 7, Tobacco Root–Ruby; 8, Madison-Gravelly; and 9, Beartooth. Lettered intraforeland basins are: (A) Sun River; (B) Belt; (C) Clark Fork; (D) Deerlodge; (E) Beaverhead; (F) Elkhorn; (G) Central Montana trough; (H) Maudlow; (I) Crazy Mountains; and (J) Gallatin.

Crazy Mountains trough; and (3) smaller scale basins, or structural "sags," oriented approximately transverse to the larger, elongated structural elements. The roughly north-south–trending intraforeland basins are referred to as the Maudlow, Gallatin, Elkhorn, Sun River, Deerlodge, and Beaverhead Basins (Fig. 7). Transverse sags occupied structural lows between or across positive elements and connected the larger second-order basins. The identifiable transverse sags include the Clark Fork sag (Gwinn, 1965), Belt basin (not to be confused with the Proterozoic Belt basin), a narrow zone between the Boulder-Highland and Tobacco Root–Ruby highs connecting the Elkhorn and Deerlodge basins, and a zone across the western Madison-Gravelly high (south of the Blacktail-Snowcrest high) that may have partially connected the Gallatin and Beaverhead Basins.

Lithofacies and paleocurrent patterns

Kootenai Formation—background. DeCelles (1986) subdivided the Kootenai in southwestern Montana into eight lithologically distinct members (Fig. 3). The coarse-grained members (Basal Conglomerate, First and Second Sandstones) are most useful in determining intraforeland configuration because of the occurrence of particular sandstone body types and their associated paleocurrent patterns. The calcareous members and fine-grained members are of more limited use in defining intraforeland basin geometry because of poor exposure and lack of paleocurrent indicators. However, limestone and fine-grained siliciclastic rocks (mostly mudstone) embody more than 50 percent of the Kootenai and thus represent significant intervals of sedimentation in the foreland basin of southwestern Montana. Various aspects of both the calcareous and fine-grained members are discussed in greater detail by Suttner (1969), Walker (1974), James (1977, 1980), Holm and others (1977), Suttner and others (1981), Schwartz (1983), DeCelles (1984, 1986), and Thompson (1984).

DeCelles (1986) discussed the nature of the Kootenai-Morrison contact and the distribution of basal Kootenai lithologies, which provide supporting evidence for active tectonism within the foreland prior to Kootenai sedimentation. The evidence includes local angular relationships between the Kootenai and Morrison Formations; laterally restricted occurrences of the Basal Conglomerate Member in inferred paleovalleys on the Morrison unconformity surface; pinching out of sandy fluvial lithofacies against paleovalley flanks; and a local occurrence of angular limestone (Ellis?) cobbles in the Gravelly Range, suggesting erosion of pre-Morrison strata.

Kootenai coarse-grained members. The Kootenai coarse-grained members (Basal Conglomerate, First and Second Sandstones) were deposited by three different types of fluvial systems (DeCelles, 1986). The Basal Conglomerate and First Sandstone are interpreted respectively as the deposits of gravel-dominant and sand-dominant braided stream systems. The Second Sandstone is interpreted as the deposits of a highly aggradational, transport-inefficient, probably anastomosed system (DeCelles, 1986). Detailed sedimentological, paleocurrent, and compositional data indicate that, at least during deposition of the First and Second Sandstones, the foreland basin was partitioned into several discrete intraforeland basins (DeCelles, 1984, 1986; Thompson, 1984). This complex of intraforeland basins received detritus from the Cordilleran fold-thrust belt, as well as uplifted intraforeland elements that occupied positions presently marked by Archean-cored Laramide uplifts.

At least four intraforeland uplifts were active during deposition of the First Sandstone, including the Boulder-Highland, Tobacco Root–Ruby, Madison-Gravelly, and Beartooth highs (Fig. 8; DeCelles, 1986). The same intraforeland uplifts were active and probably more pronounced during deposition of the Second Sandstone (Fig. 9). Sedimentological data suggest that the Blacktail-Snowcrest uplift also was initiated during deposition of

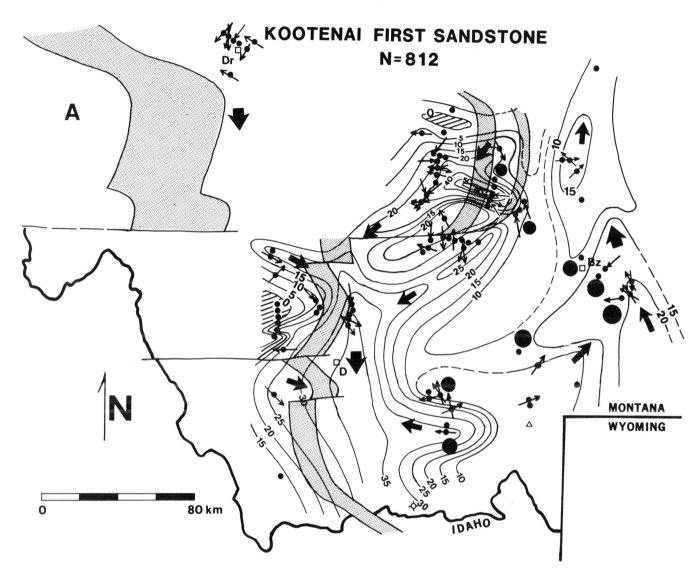

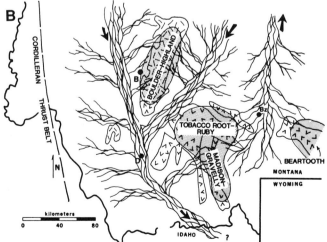

Figure 8. A, Map showing isopach contours (in meters) and paleocurrent data from the Kootenai First Sandstone. Small arrows indicate mean orientations of axes of large-scale trough cross-strata determined from 10 to 30 measurements of trough limbs per station (see DeCelles and others, 1983). All paleocurrent data are from major channel facies. Large arrows represent generalized, inferred paleodrainage directions. Large solid circles depict the relative maximum sizes (from 0.5 to 2 cm) of pebbles in conglomeratic lithofacies. Shaded areas represent gaps produced by palinspastic restoration of major thrust plates. Small solid circles indicate section locations. See Figure 4 for city symbols. Modified from DeCelles (1986). N = number of paleocurrent data. B, Map showing schematic representation of drainage patterns, stream morphologies, and intraforeland uplifts (shaded) during deposition of the Kootenai First Sandstone. The positions of Archean-cored Laramide uplifts and Late Cretaceous batholiths are also shown. Modified from DeCelles (1986).

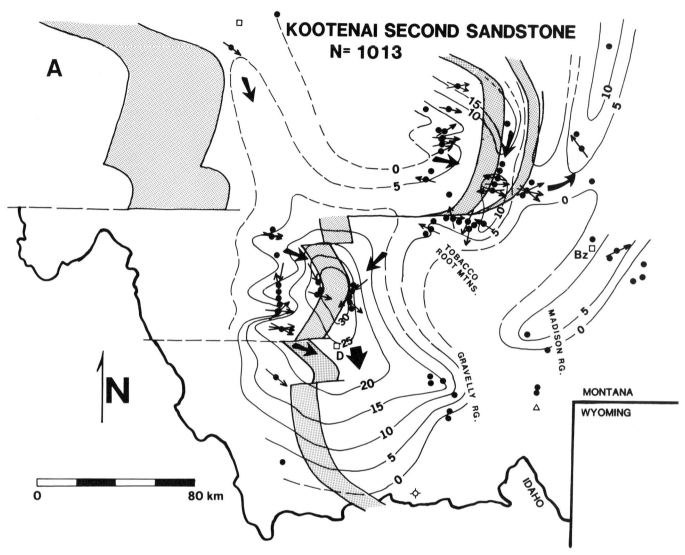

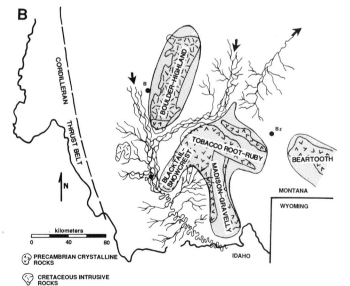

Figure 9. A, Map showing isopach contours (in meters) and paleocurrent patterns from the Kootenai Second Sandstone. See Figure 8 for explanation of arrows, shaded areas, and city symbols. From DeCelles (1986). N = number of paleocurrent data. B, Map showing schematic representation of drainage patterns, stream morphologies, and intraforeland uplifts (shaded areas) during deposition of the Kootenai Second Sandstone. Modified from DeCelles (1986).

the Second Sandstone. DeCelles (1986) suggested that the Second Sandstone fluvial system in the Beaverhead and Elkhorn Basins owed its highly aggradational character partly to elevation of base level upstream from the axis of the incipiently rising Blacktail-Snowcrest intraforeland uplift.

Major intraforeland fluvial-channel complexes of the First and Second Sandstones were confined to the axial realms of several intraforeland basins. The Beaverhead Basin was occupied by generally southward-flowing systems that were fed by drainage systems of the Deerlodge and Elkhorn Basins (Figs. 8, 9). Drainage in the Maudlow Basin was generally northward, being fed by systems that probably headed in the vicinities of the Madison-Gravelly and Beartooth highs (Figs. 8, 9).

Collective evidence for syndepositional tectonism and renewed differential subsidence during early Kootenai deposition includes: (1) initiation of a long-term cycle of first-order basin subsidence; (2) abrupt coarsening to conglomerate and sandstone above mudstone-dominated Morrison strata; (3) abrupt compositional change from quartzose Morrison sandstones to sedimentary and metamorphic lithic-rich Kootenai sandstones; (4) strong facies and paleodispersal control by intraforeland elements, including local base-level control; (5) local thickening of sandstone channel complexes adjacent to inferred paleo-uplifts that occupied sites of present fault-controlled structures such as the Madison-Gravelly uplift and the southwest Montana transverse zone; and (6) apparent temporal correlation with movement on thrust plates in the Idaho-Wyoming-Utah thrust belt and tectonic events in the westward-adjacent Salmon River suture zone of Lund and Snee (1988).

Kootenai calcareous members. The Kootenai Lower and Upper Calcareous Members were deposited in dominantly fluviolacustrine environments in southwestern Montana (James, 1977, 1980). The Upper Calcareous Member, also known informally as the gastropod limestone, is transitional with the overlying Blackleaf Formation and comprises lacustrine, fluviolacustrine, and tidal-channel facies (James, 1980; Schwartz, 1983).

The Lower and Upper Calcareous Members and the correlative Peterson and Draney Limestones of northern Utah and western Wyoming represent two phases of terrestrial carbonate deposition over a vast portion of the Cordilleran Foreland Basin. A combination of tectonic control on basin geometry, diminished terrigenous supply, exposure of carbonate source-terranes, and a possible association with sea-level rise resulted in development of the carbonate-lacustrine systems (Holm and others, 1977; Schwartz, 1983).

Earlier thrusting had resulted in the development of first-order foreland subsidence between Cordilleran uplands to the west and a structural hinge zone in the region of the present Boulder batholith. Intraforeland partitioning during deposition of the Upper Calcareous Member is again clearly indicated by regional isopach patterns (Fig. 10). Although first-order, eastward thinning is apparent (James, 1977), zones of significant thickening exist in the Deerlodge, Beaverhead, and Elkhorn Basins. Areas of thin, or missing, strata occur over the Boulder-Highland,

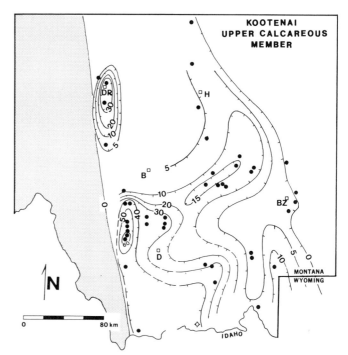

Figure 10. Map showing isopach contours (in meters) of the Kootenai Upper Calcareous Member (or "gastropod limestone"). Data are recontoured from James (1977). Shaded area on left represents zone where the Kootenai has been removed by erosion during uplift of the frontal fold-thrust belt.

Tobacco Root–Ruby, and Madison-Gravelly highs. These trends essentially mimic isopach patterns of the Kootenai First and Second Sandstone Members. Ponding of the internal drainage system led to widespread lake development, and the presence of intraforeland positive elements in southwestern Montana resulted in discontinuous carbonate depocenters (Schwartz, 1983; DeCelles, 1986).

Overlying fine-grained rocks of the lowermost Blackleaf Formation in the western portion of the study area were deposited in transitional marine settings during the early Albian transgression into southwestern Montana. Blackleaf rocks that overlie the Upper Calcareous Member in the eastern study area consist of lower shoreface to offshore siliciclastic facies that were deposited during the same transgression. Similarly, a quartzose burrowed unit of probable marine affinity is associated with the Lower Calcareous Member in the Great Falls area, suggesting a possible small-scale, middle-Kootenai transgression (Walker, 1974; S. Vuke, personal communication, 1986).

Kootenai fine-grained members. The Kootenai fine-grained members consist dominantly of variegated (red and green) claystone and siltstone with abundant limestone nodules mottling, massive bedding, and local zones of bioturbation. Most of these rocks consist of paleosols deposited in overbank settings (Thompson, 1984; DeCelles, 1986). Associated subenvironments included localized ephemeral ponds, lakes, swamps, and mud-dominant fluvial channels. In addition, small fluvial-channel bodies of sandstones and conglomerate are isolated within the Upper Fine-Grained Member of the western study area (Pioneer Mountains area).

The abundance of clay and silt, and the near-exclusion of sand and gravel in the fine-grained members, are significant with regard to depositional environment(s), source terranes, and tectonic implications. Although the most popular interpretation is that tectonic quiescence and subsequent erosion in the marginal thrust-belt resulted in a decrease in fluvial gradient and a diminished supply of coarse sediment (Suttner, 1969; Walker, 1974; Suttner and others, 1981), other potential factors must be considered. The lacustrine limestones reflect ponding of the internal drainage system, which in turn, may have exerted base-level control on adjacent fluvial systems. In addition, the abundance of mud may have been partially related to provenance. The abundance of illite in Kootenai mudstones (Suttner, 1968; DeCelles, 1984, 1986) and the presence of illite-rich, foliated, sand-sized clasts in associated channel sandstones suggest significant derivation from illite-rich argillites (James, 1977; DeCelles, 1986). Similar lithologies compose much of the Proterozoic Belt Supergroup. Belt source areas in the fold-thrust belt (Suttner, 1969) and the Belt Arch complex (James, 1977) have been proposed. However, an intermittent dominance of argillite-rich (Belt) source lithologies is not a fully adequate explanation for the alternation of sandstone and siliciclastic fine-grained intervals. The simultaneous exposure of upper Paleozoic chert and quartzose source lithologies during deposition of the fine-grained members is also indicated by compositions of sandstones within the fine-grained members and by bounding coarse-grained members of both the Kootenai and Blackleaf Formations. Thus, source lithologies of Proterozoic to Late Paleozoic age were contemporaneously exposed, and it is unlikely that a punctuated dominance of Belt lithologies in the source area produced cyclic influxes of clay and silt.

Schwartz (1983) postulated that the Kootenai limestones reflect periods of basin subsidence combined with decreased intraforeland uplift and decreased siliciclastic influx from all source areas. The difference between this and previous hypotheses is that periodic unroofing of carbonate-dominant source rocks would not be required. Instead, a more likely situation of widespread but low-relief exposure of multiple source lithologies (including abundant Paleozoic carbonates to supply solutes) allowed carbonate sedimentation to dominate in the clastic-starved foreland. Although not stated by Schwartz (1983), it was reasoned that thrust-load–induced (isostatic) subsidence continued in the foreland basin while tectonic uplift in the fold-thrust belt, and therefore the siliciclastic sediment supply, diminished. However, in addition to all of the above, the combination of mixed source lithologies (capable of simultaneously producing texturally and compositionally diverse sediment) and the presence of somewhat cyclic stratigraphic packages in both the Kootenai and Blackleaf Formations suggest even further controls on large-scale sediment differentiation and cyclic input to synorogenic basins (McLean and Jerzykiewicz, 1978).

Blackleaf Formation—background. The Blackleaf Formation consists of 150 to 640 m (490 to 2,100 ft) of sandstone, shale, mudstone, and volcaniclastic rocks (Fig. 3). These rocks also show vertical and lateral changes in composition and facies, which are related to paleotectonic control, and—more so than with the Kootenai—to sea-level control on sedimentation. Most lithofacies, and some compositional properties of sandstone and conglomerate, exhibit significant differences between the eastern and western halves of the study area. Regional comparisons have been facilitated by subdividing the formation into four informal lithostratigraphic intervals, two of which are relatively coarse-grained (intervals A and C), and two of which are mudstone-dominated (intervals B and D; Fig. 3). The nomenclature of stratigraphic equivalents to the intervals has been summarized by Schwartz (1972; 1983), and a more recent evaluation of Blackleaf stratigraphy in southwestern Montana is presented by Dyman and Nichols (1988). In contrast to recently published data from the Kootenai Formation (DeCelles, 1986), many pertinent aspects of Blackleaf sedimentology are not available in the literature. Sedimentologic details, corresponding interpretations, and comprehensive references are therefore presented in Appendix 2 (on microfiche, in pocket on back cover), which serves as a basis for the following summary discussion of Blackleaf sedimentation and tectonics in southwestern Montana.

The Kootenai-Blackleaf contact is essentially conformable in the fluvial-dominated western study area and locally unconformable in the marine-dominated eastern study area (Roberts, 1972; Schwartz, 1972, 1983; James, 1977; Vuke, 1982). The regional nature of the contact, however, reflects preservational bias for sediments deposited within intraforeland basins rather than atop intraforeland highs.

In the eastern study area, the Kootenai-Blackleaf contact is locally disconformable in the Livingston area, where the lower sandstone member of the Blackleaf equivalent commonly fills topographic depressions on an erosional surface (Roberts, 1972). A short distance to the west, in the Bozeman area, the contact appears to be gradational (Schwartz, 1972; James, 1977), indicating continuous sedimentation. North of the Bozeman area, on the Sweetgrass Arch, the Kootenai-Blackleaf contact is more extensively disconformable (Cobban and others, 1976), indicating the presence of a low-relief uplift of larger scale than the uplift in the Livingston area. In general, local unconformities in the eastern study area represent areas where the Kootenai surface was slightly elevated and subaerially eroded prior to the Albian transgression and/or areas where marked shoreface erosion occurred during transgression over the irregular Kootenai surface. In addition, later Cretaceous unconformities indicate positive regions in the Boulder batholith–Highland Mountains area and in the Madison-Gravelly area. In the western study area, most Kootenai and Blackleaf facies are exposed in intraforeland-basin settings where sedimentation was relatively continuous.

Evidence for shoreface erosion during Albian transgression is not apparent in the western study area. There, the Kootenai and Blackleaf are generally conformable owing to continuous subsidence and alluvial sedimentation within intraforeland basins, followed by low-energy marine inundation. Sedimentologic properties of individual Blackleaf intervals support patterns of suspected positive elements, as indicated by the Blackleaf-Kootenai unconformity patterns.

Blackleaf Formation: General basin architecture. The depositional systems associated with each Blackleaf interval varied across the foreland in a twofold manner. First, large-scale (first-order) regional differences between the western and eastern halves of the study area reflect relative proximity to the thrust-belt, with upland, nonmarine-dominated intraforeland-basin settings in the western part of the foreland, and lower lying, marine-dominated basinal settings in the more distal eastern region. Second, smaller scale (second-order) patterns of thickness, lithofacies, and paleocurrent directions within these first-order patterns demonstrate strong control of intraforeland uplifts on the lateral distribution and dynamics of both marine and nonmarine systems.

During Blackleaf deposition, the foreland became increasingly partitioned, and intraforeland uplifts effectively served as both source areas and barriers to cross-basin dispersal. As during Kootenai deposition, the Boulder-Highland, Tobacco Root–Ruby, Madison-Gravelly, Blacktail-Snowcrest, and Beartooth uplifts were active. Blackleaf data also indicate control on sedimentation by at least three other intraforeland uplifts, including the Lewis-and-Clark, Belt, and Sweetgrass–Milk River uplifts. Paleocurrent patterns reflect divergent fluvial transport away from subaerial intraforeland uplifts and longitudinal transport in trunk systems along basin axes (Figs. 11-13).

Blackleaf interval A. Interval A in the western study area represents a siliciclastic-dominated transition from Kootenai carbonate-lacustrine deposition to fluvial, estuarine, and locally marine settings. Lithofacies data (Appendix 2) indicate that this transition was associated with localized transgression of the Early Cretaceous sea into lower elevation, axial regions of the Beaverhead, Clark Fork, and Deerlodge intraforeland basins (Figs. 7, 11). In the eastern study area, widespread submergence is reflected by lower shoreface to shallow-offshore facies, including storm-controlled–ridge sandstone bodies (Stine, 1986). Although transgression of the Cretaceous sea occurred regionally (Kiowa–Skull Creek transgression of Kauffman, 1977), coarsening above the Kootenai Upper Calcareous Member in the western study area resulted from increased lithic-rich fluvial sand deposition. We interpret this nonmarine coarsening as a response to coeval tectonic rejuvenation.

Blackleaf interval B. Transgression reached a maximum (T5 of Kauffman, 1977) during deposition of the dark gray to black, shale-dominated interval B. In the western study area, much of interval B was deposited in brackish swamps, bays, and estuarine bodies of water. In most of the eastern study area, mud was deposited in marginal marine and offshore dysaerobic to anaerobic settings (Roberts, 1972; Schwartz, 1972; Vuke, 1982). Relative tectonic quiescence is suggested by a marked absence of coarse detritus in brackish settings that were situated proximal to

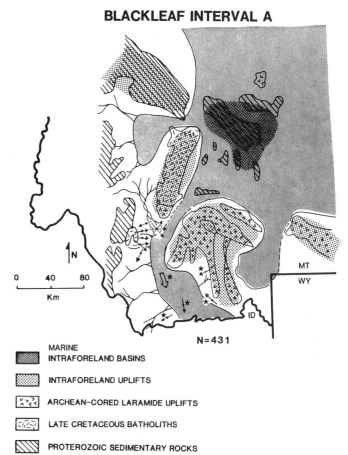

BLACKLEAF INTERVAL A

MARINE
INTRAFORELAND BASINS

INTRAFORELAND UPLIFTS

ARCHEAN–CORED LARAMIDE UPLIFTS

LATE CRETACEOUS BATHOLITHS

PROTEROZOIC SEDIMENTARY ROCKS

Figure 11. Map showing paleocurrent patterns and schematic representation of nonmarine paleodrainage systems, areas of marine inundation, and postulated intraforeland uplifts during deposition of Blackleaf interval A. See Figure 8A for explanation of paleocurrent symbols. Stars indicate data from Dyman (1985a). N = number of paleocurrent data.

intraforeland uplifts. The combined development of thick shale zones, general paucity of fauna, minor bioturbation within much of the shale, and the preservation of abundant organic matter probably resulted from sedimentation in more rapidly subsiding portions of the bathymetrically irregular, structurally partitioned foreland (Appendix 2; Hallam and Bradshaw, 1979; Hallam, 1981). The areas of relatively thick shale coincide with differentially subsiding intraforeland basins as independently established by data from all other Kootenai and Blackleaf intervals. This same relationship holds for interval D.

Blackleaf interval C. During deposition of interval C, fluvial-dominated, sandy deltas prograded into estuarine or restricted marine bodies of water along basin axes in the western study area (Clark Fork and Beaverhead Basins; Fig. 12). A sandy, braided fluvial system developed coevally along the western flank of the Beaverhead Basin. In the eastern study area, a fluvial-dominated delta prograded northeastward along the axis of the Gallatin intraforeland basin, reflecting primary drainage from the Madison-Gravelly high (Fig. 12). Large-scale submarine bars or

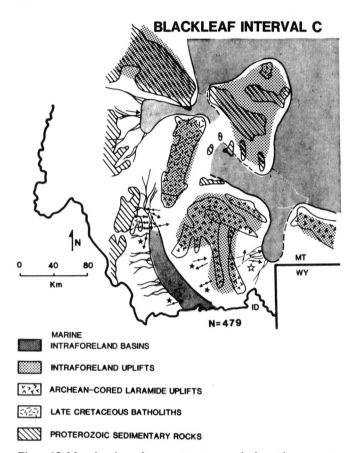

BLACKLEAF INTERVAL C

0   40   80
Km

N=479

MT
WY

ID

MARINE
INTRAFORELAND BASINS

INTRAFORELAND UPLIFTS

ARCHEAN-CORED LARAMIDE UPLIFTS

LATE CRETACEOUS BATHOLITHS

PROTEROZOIC SEDIMENTARY ROCKS

Figure 12. Map showing paleocurrent patterns and schematic representation of nonmarine paleodrainage systems, areas of marine inundation, and postulated intraforeland uplifts during deposition of Blackleaf interval C. See Figure 8A for explanation of paleocurrent symbols. Solid stars indicate data from Dyman (1985a); open stars indicate data from Vuke, 1982, 1984). N = number of paleocurrent data.

barrier-island sand bodies developed in shallow-marine settings, at least some of which were localized atop submarine positive elements (e.g., Sweetgrass Arch). This progradational coarsening episode was temporally associated with a middle Albian regression. Uplift of intraforeland source areas and progressive erosion is indicated by a significant increase in total lithic content and mineralogic variety within marine and nonmarine sandstone bodies. Widespread tectonism occurred during this time interval, as indicated by Weimer's (1978, 1983) evidence for movement of structural elements and tectonic control on sedimentation in the distal foreland of Wyoming and Colorado.

Blackleaf interval D. The vertical sequence of interval D lithologies in the eastern study area indicates increasingly deeper marine, mud-dominated deposition associated with a late–Early Cretaceous transgression prior to the late Albian–early Cenomanian maximum regression (R5 of Kauffman, 1977; Vuke, 1984). The early phase of the transgression witnessed the development of muddy delta-plain and coastal systems. With maximum transgression, locally restricted bodies of marine to brackish water

occupied intraforeland basins. Normal-marine sedimentation occurred in less confined basins and over subaqueous positive elements (e.g., Sweetgrass Arch). Alluvial-plain settings dominated in the western study area (Fig. 13). These systems were characterized by straight to sinuous, sand-choked channels with muddy, stable banks, sandy crevasse splays, and muddy overbank and lacustrine facies. Sediment influx to more western locales, both within the study area and regionally (Vuke, 1984), was sufficient to result in progradation and the development of nonmarine facies in spite of transgression. For the first time since lower Kootenai deposition, significant amounts of proximally derived, extraformational gravel were delivered to the foreland-basin complex. The combined occurrence of conglomerate and tuff, together with evidence for differential subsidence of intraforeland elements (Appendix 2), signals syndepositional tectonism. Source terranes included Precambrian sedimentary rocks and low-grade metamorphics exposed within intraforeland uplifts.

Frontier Formation—background. The lack of published information on the sedimentology of the Frontier Formation in western Montana is comparable to the paucity of available information about the Blackleaf. Thus we present sedimentological details of the Frontier in Appendix 3 and adopt the format of the foregoing section on the Blackleaf for the following discussion of Frontier Formation sedimentology and tectonics.

Schwartz (1972, 1983) initially placed conglomerates and thick sandstones that overlie volcaniclastic Blackleaf rocks into his interval D of the Blackleaf Formation in the northern Beaverhead Basin (Pioneer Mountains–McCartney Mountain area). These coarse-grained, volcaniclastic units of the Beaverhead Basin, and similar rocks in the Clark Fork Basin (Drummond area; Gwinn, 1960, 1965; Schwartz, 1972), formed the basis for Schwartz's (1983) proposal of a late Albian (Blackleaf) tectonic episode. However, recent work (Dyman, 1985a; Dyman and Nichols, 1988) documents a Cenomanian to Turonian age for the conglomerates and overlying finer grained lithologies in extreme southwestern Montana (southern Beaverhead Basin). These lithologies are more similar to the Frontier type section in southwestern Wyoming (Veatch, 1907; Cobban and Reeside, 1952) than the age-equivalent Marias River Shale of the Sweetgrass Arch (Cobban and others, 1976). In the Beaverhead Basin, the lower contact of the Frontier is placed at the base of the first thick conformable sandstone or conglomerate above the base of interval D, or at the unconformity in the Gravelly Range, Snowcrest Range, and Lima Peaks areas (Dyman, 1985a). An upper contact is presently being established in the southern Beaverhead Basin, along the paleobasin axis (Shine Hill area, 8 km south of Lima; T. S. Dyman, personal communication, 1986). Stratigraphic relations in the Drummond area are as yet unclear (Appendix 3). Stratigraphic relations in the eastern province are relatively simple and are summarized by Roberts (1972).

Basal, coarse-grained lithologies of Frontier age, usually including conglomerate, occur throughout much of the central Cordilleran Foreland Basin (Schmitt, 1985). These lithologies, and corresponding lithostratigraphic correlatives of undetermined

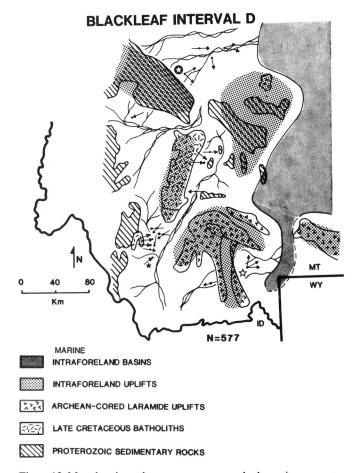

BLACKLEAF INTERVAL D

N=577

0 40 80
Km

MARINE
▓ INTRAFORELAND BASINS

▒ INTRAFORELAND UPLIFTS

⊠ ARCHEAN-CORED LARAMIDE UPLIFTS

⊠ LATE CRETACEOUS BATHOLITHS

⧅ PROTEROZOIC SEDIMENTARY ROCKS

Figure 13. Map showing paleocurrent patterns and schematic representation of nonmarine paleodrainage systems, areas of marine inundation, and postulated intraforeland uplifts during deposition of Blackleaf interval D. See Figure 8A for explanation of paleocurrent symbols. Solid star indicates data from Dyman (1985a); open star in southeastern study area indicates data from Vuke (1982, 1984); partially solid star in north-central study area indicates data from Mudge and Sheppard (1968). N = number of data, exclusive of those from Mudge and Sheppard (1968).

age within the study area, serve as a collective signal of tectonism. Cobban and Reeside (1952) described a correlative sequence in Wyoming where nonmarine lithofacies, including volcaniclastic sandstones, are overlain by finer grained, predominantly marine strata. A similar stratigraphic relationship occurs in the Livingston area, where a lenticular pebble-cobble conglomerate occurs within the coarser Boulder River Sandstone Member of the Frontier Formation (Roberts, 1972). Roberts (1972) suggested that sedimentation took place in shallow, brackish water of the regressive Late Cretaceous sea and that the sudden deposition of coarse detritus in much of Montana and western Wyoming resulted from regional uplift in western Montana or eastern Idaho. A more subtle, but similar, pattern occurs in shallow-marine rocks over the Sweetgrass Arch, where a coarse interval in the uppermost part of the Bootlegger Member (Blackleaf Formation; latest Albian to early Cenomanian age) overlies finer grained interval D lithofacies. The coarse interval is overlain by fine-

grained, offshore (deeper) marine strata of Cenomanian age (Cobban and others, 1976).

Thus, in the Frontier Formation and time-equivalent rocks, there exists a vertical sequence pattern consisting of (1) relatively abrupt coarsening above finer grained, late Albian-aged Blackleaf strata; and (2) subsequent deposition of finer grained strata associated with low-gradient fluvial or deeper marine settings during Cenomanian to Turonian time. With this pattern and age relationship in mind, it is possible to identify corresponding genetic sequences within nonmarine-dominated Frontier strata in the Beaverhead Basin and nonmarine-dominated strata presently assigned to the uppermost Blackleaf Formation in the Sun River Basin and in the Clark Fork Basin (Appendix 3, on microfiche in pocket inside back cover).

Frontier Formation—sedimentation in western study area. The lower Frontier sequence in the western study area coarsens abruptly above a laterally variable, conformable to unconformable contact. Gravel-dominant braided streams occupied higher elevation areas on the flanks of intraforeland basins, whereas isolated sand-dominant, sinuous channels developed in more distal, lower gradient intraforeland-basin settings (Fig. 14). In the western study area, the overlying Frontier sequence records deposition in muddy alluvial-plain to brackish and shallow-marine settings during a subsequent period of tectonic quiescence. Lithofacies, paleocurrent, and compositional data, although limited, are consistent with evidence from the Kootenai and Blackleaf Formations for structural partitioning in southwestern Montana. In particular, these data indicate divergent fluvial transport southwestward toward the Clark Fork Basin and eastward toward the Sun River Basin (Fig. 14), away from the intervening Lewis-and-Clark high, where different source-rock associations were exposed in the separate drainage systems (Appendix 3). In the Beaverhead Basin, gravel-dominant streams occupied higher elevation areas on the flanks of the basin, whereas isolated sand-dominant, sinuous channels developed in more distal, lower gradient settings. In addition, paleocurrent data indicate convergent sediment transport toward the axis of the Beaverhead Basin (Fig. 14). The combination of paleocurrent and unconformity data (Dyman, 1985a) indicates that the ancestral Blacktail-Snowcrest uplift increasingly partitioned the Beaverhead basin. A northward-directed paleocurrent component (Dyman, 1985a) reflects a major drainage reversal within the basin, analogous to the pattern of northward drainage in the modern Beaverhead intermontane basin.

Initial coarser grained, progradational Frontier sedimentation was concurrent with, or shortly followed, a maximum in Late Albian to Early Cenomanian eustatic regression (R5 of Kauffman, 1977). However, lithofacies development was also related to an episode of foreland tectonism. In southwestern Montana, a tectonic episode associated with initial Frontier deposition is indicated by: (1) abrupt coarsening (including conglomerate) above finer grained, volcaniclastic strata of Blackleaf interval D; (2) continued deposition of tuff and epiclastics; (3) erosion of igneous and middle- to high-rank metamorphic (Archean?) rocks located within the eastern study area; (4) major drainage reversal in the Beaverhead Basin; (5) temporal correlation with movement on thrust plates in southwesternmost Montana and the Idaho-Wyoming-Utah region (Fig. 2); and (6) temporal correlation with tectonic events in the westward adjacent Cordillera, including a major thermal event (101 to 99 Ma) along the Salmon River suture zone in western Idaho (Lund and Snee, 1988). This tectonic episode was followed by a period of tectonic quiescence and eustatic transgression (T6 of Kauffman, 1977), prior to a culminating Late Cretaceous (Campanian-Maastrichtian) tectonic event. This latter event is structurally and stratigraphically well-documented, and involved deposition of the Elkhorn Mountains Volcanics, Golden Spike Formation, Livingston Group, Sphinx Conglomerate, Lima and Beaverhead Conglomerates, and coarse-grained equivalents (e.g., Wilson, 1970; DeCelles and others, 1987).

INTRAFORELAND UPLIFT: FOREBULGE OR FORELAND REACTIVATION?

Virtually all models for load-driven flexure of the lithosphere predict the development of a linear forebulge (or outer bulge) along the cratonward periphery of the foreland basin (Walcott, 1970; Beaumont, 1981; Jordan,1981; Schedl and Wiltschko, 1984; Quinlan and Beaumont, 1984). Oft-cited examples of forebulges include the Nashville Dome–Cincinnati Arch–Findlay Arch–Algonquin Arch complex of the Appalachian foreland region and the Sweetgrass Arch of northwestern Montana (Beaumont, 1981; Lorenz, 1983). The possibility thus exists that the intraforeland uplifts of southwestern Montana were actually manifestations of migratory forebulge uplift (e.g., Quinlan and Beaumont, 1984). However, the predicted behavior of a forebulge does not match the apparent behavior of the intraforeland uplifts in two significant ways.

1. The intraforeland uplifts and basins of this study formed an irregular, nonlinear pattern throughout the first-order foreland basin. Although absolute dates are not available for the activation times of the intraforeland uplifts, regional lithostratigraphic correlations suggest that intraforeland uplifts occurred coevally throughout the foreland basin. If the intraforeland uplifts were activated by forebulge flexure and migration, they would be expected to occur along a linear zone parallel to the fold-thrust belt. Migration of the forebulge would have caused time-transgressive uplift across the basin, rather than synchronous uplift and subsidence at various locales throughout the basin.

2. The intraforeland uplifts seem to have occupied sites of long-term structural reactivation, dating back to Proterozoic time. Many of these structures were probably related to crustal and, presumably, lithospheric inhomogeneities produced during Proterozoic rifting along the western continental margin (Harrison and others, 1974; Sears, 1983; Winston and others, 1984).

We therefore conclude that the intraforeland elements were not primarily related to forebulge development and/or migration. The widespread reactivation of intraforeland structures was su-

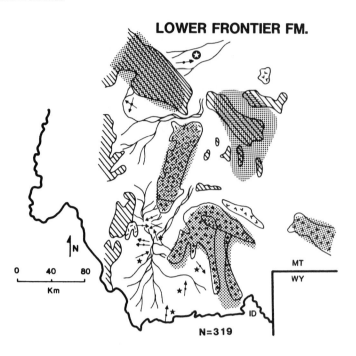

LOWER FRONTIER FM.

N=319

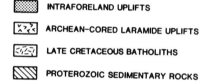

▦ INTRAFORELAND UPLIFTS

⬚ ARCHEAN-CORED LARAMIDE UPLIFTS

⬚ LATE CRETACEOUS BATHOLITHS

⧄ PROTEROZOIC SEDIMENTARY ROCKS

Figure 14. Map showing paleocurrent patterns and schematic representation of nonmarine paleodrainage systems and postulated intraforeland uplifts during deposition of the lower Frontier Formation. See Figure 8A for explanation of paleocurrent symbols. Solid stars indicate data from Dyman (1985a); circled solid star in north-central study area indicates data from Mudge and Sheppard (1968). N = number of paleocurrent data, exclusive of those from Mudge and Sheppard (1968).

perimposed upon a first-order, load-induced flexure of the lithosphere. We consider the Sweetgrass Arch to be a low-relief intraforeland uplift, probably associated with a buried structure beyond the northern end of the Laramide structural province.

SUMMARY AND CONCLUSIONS

Sedimentological data from the Cretaceous Kootenai, Blackleaf, and lower Frontier Formations, in conjunction with data from bounding stratigraphic intervals, have been used to determine the paleogeographic and structural development of the Cordilleran Foreland Basin in western Montana and to synthesize the relationships between sedimentation and tectonism. Evidence for structural partitioning is summarized in Table 1. Conclusions of a broader scope are presented below.

The Cordilleran Foreland Basin in southwestern Montana may be considered in terms of intersecting first- and second-order basin geometries. The larger scale (300 to 400 km wide), first-

TABLE 1. SUMMARY OF EVIDENCE FOR BASIN PARTITIONING IN FORELAND OF SOUTHWESTERN MONTANA

Criterion		Description	Example
Formation and Member Thickness		Multiple zones of thickening and thinning indicate discrete intraforeland uplifts and basins. Zones of thickening may correspond with intraforeland basin axes, which tend to parallel axes of intraforeland uplifts.	Kootenai First and Second Sandstones and Upper Calcareous Member; Blackleaf intervals A, C, and D.
Unconformities	Angular	Indicates major intraforeland uplift and erosion.	Morrison-Kootenai unconformity
	Disconformity	May result from transgression over topographically complex foreland. Should be characteristic of areas of intraforeland uplift, but may not be present in intraforeland basins.	Blackleaf-Frontier contact in Beaverhead basin and Blacktail-Snowcrest uplift.
Nonmarine Facies		Complex isopach and paleocurrent patterns indicate intraforeland partitioning. Trunk systems generally parallel axes of uplifts, but tributaries diverge from flanks of intraforeland uplifts. Decreased fluvial gradients and ponding indicate elevated base level, possibly owing to subsidence.	Kootenai First and Second Sandstones, Upper Calcareous Member, Blackleaf intervals C and D.
Marine Facies		Submarine intraforeland uplifts "anchor" shallow-marine sandstone bodies. Muddy facies thicken toward basin axes. Confinement of intraforeland basins between uplifts results in local estuarine and reducing conditions.	Blackleaf intervals B and D.
Compositional Effects		Gross framework mineralogy indicates a dominance of thrust-belt sources, but local concentrations of low-rank metasedimentary, volcanic, and feldspathic clasts and heavy minerals indicate intraforeland sources and dispersal barriers.	Kootenai and Blackleaf sandstones.
Textural Effects		In both nonmarine and marine systems, grain size decreases away from intraforeland uplifts. Relatively coarse- and fine-grained fluvial systems may contemporaneously occupy separate intraforeland basins.	Kootenai First Sandstone, Blackleaf interval C (Beaverhead basin), interval D (eastern province).

order basin had a relatively simple geometry characteristic of thrust-sheet–loaded forelands. Second-order elements consisted of smaller (e.g., 100 km long and 20 to 70 km wide), elongated intraforeland uplifts and basins that occurred within the developing first-order basin and the adjacent craton. Overall, the foreland basin experienced a long history of increasingly intense tectonic activity. The amount of structural and topographic relief of the intraforeland uplifts increased markedly through time and culminated in the Laramide orogeny.

The Cretaceous rocks of western Montana must be viewed within the broader context of the evolving Cordillera and its adjacent foreland basin. We suggest that signs of Cordilleran thrusting and intraforeland partitioning of the incipient foreland basin are evident in the Middle to Late Jurassic Ellis Group and Morrison Formation. Development of first-order foreland-basin subsidence in western Montana coincided with deposition of the Kootenai. In general, the stratigraphic sequence suggests eastward migration of the thrust belt and first-order basin into regions of widespread second-order structures that were episodically reactivated.

Source areas for the partitioned foreland consisted of the Cordilleran fold-thrust belt, intraforeland uplifts, and the craton. The effectiveness of each source area varied as tectonic controls and relative sea level changed. In addition, topography and bathymetry exerted major control both on the lateral distribution and dynamics of depositional systems. During nonmarine phases, sediment was transported by fluvial systems toward and along intraforeland-basin axes. Decreased terrigenous influx, associated with continued first-order basin subsidence, led to the widespread development of carbonate lacustrine systems. Marine inundation of the topographically complex foreland basin resulted in a highly embayed shoreline, and at least locally restricted bodies of water, which were flanked by shallow-marine and nonmarine facies.

The Kootenai–lower Frontier sequence represents an approximately 20-m.y. megacycle of episodic sedimentation related to nearly coeval thrust-belt and intraforeland tectonic episodes (five or six total). Episode maxima mark the boundaries of the megacycle and are characterized by coarse sand and gravel deposition, development of local unconformities, mixed thrust-belt and intraforeland provenance, fluvial gradient increase, and basin overfilling (i.e., Kootenai Basal Conglomerate and lowermost Frontier Formation). The medial portion of the megacycle (Kootenai Middle Fine–Grained Member through Blackleaf interval B) is characterized by textural fining, decreased fluvial gradients, and widespread nonmarine ponding or marine transgression, suggesting quiescence and continued basin subsidence (or basin underfilling). Radiometric dates from the Salmon River suture zone in Idaho (Lund and Snee, 1988) suggest close temporal correspondence between tectonic events in the adjacent Cordillera, intraforeland uplifts, and foreland sedimentary responses. Changes in eustatic sea level exerted an important but secondary control on foreland sedimentation.

In spite of the presence of intraforeland uplifts, the stratigraphic record in southwestern Montana generally supports the temporal aspects of first-order basin evolution and sedimentation predicted by the model for load-driven flexure and subsequent relaxation of a viscoelastic lithosphere (e.g., Quinlan and Beaumont, 1984). However, some other, yet unspecified, model is required to explain the second-order effects described herein. We

suggest that such a model must take into account the inherent compositional and structural inhomogeneities of the crust and tectonic reactivation (e.g., through crustal shortening or bending) in a foreland setting.

ACKNOWLEDGMENTS

We gratefully acknowledge T. S. Dyman for thoughtful and critical reviews of earlier versions of this paper. Additional reviews and suggestions by C. F. Vondra and an anonymous reviewer clarified and improved the content of the paper. We thank L. J. Suttner, D. E. Wuellner, W. Brewer, S. M. Vuke-Foster, J. H. Meyers, W. C. James, E. P. Kvale, C. Beaumont, T. E. Jordan, and M. Covey for helpful and informative conversations. Field work was supported in part by the U.S. Geological Survey (to R.K.S.), by Chevron U.S.A. (to P.G.D.), and by Allegheny College Faculty Development Grants (to R.K.S.). Finally, we thank C. J. Schmidt and W. J. Perry, Jr., for their patience and editorial skills.

REFERENCES CITED

Note: Some citations are located in Appendices 1 and 2, on microfiche inside back cover.

Aigner, T., 1985, Storm depositional systems; Lecture notes in earth sciences: New York, Springer-Verlag, v. 3, 174 p.

Allmendinger, R. W., and Jordan, T. E., 1981, Mesozoic evolution, hinterland of the Sevier orogenic belt: Geology, v. 9, p. 308–313.

—— , 1984, Mesozoic structure of the Newfoundland Mountains, Utah; Horizontal shortening and subsequent extension in the hinterland of the Sevier Belt: Geological Society of America Bulletin, v. 95, p. 1280–1292.

Allmendinger, R. W., Miller, D. M., and Jordan, T. E., 1984, Known and inferred Mesozoic deformation in the hinterland of the Sevier belt, northwest Utah: Utah Geological Association Publication 14, p. 21–34.

Armstrong, R. L., and Suppe, J., 1973, Potassium-argon geochronometry of Mesozoic igneous rocks in Nevada, Utah, and southern California: Geological Society of America Bulletin, v. 84, p. 1375–1392.

Armstrong, R. L., Taubeneck, W. H., and Hales, P. O., 1977, Rb-Sr and K-Ar geochronometry of Mesozoic granitic rocks and their Sr isotopic composition, Oregon, Washington, and Idaho: Geological Society of America Bulletin, v. 88, p. 397–411.

Baker, V. R., 1978, Adjustment of fluvial systems to climate and source terrain in tropical and subtropical environments, *in* Miall, A. D., ed., Fluvial sedimentology, Canadian Society of Petroleum Geologists Memoir 5, p. 211–230.

Beaumont, C., 1981, Foreland basins: Geophysical Journal of the Royal Astronomical Society, v. 65, p. 291–329.

Berkhouse, G. A., 1984, Sedimentology and diagenesis of the Lower Cretaceous Kootenai Formation in the Sun River Canyon area, northwestern Montana [M.A. thesis]: Bloomington, Indiana University, 151 p.

Bird, P., 1984, Laramide crustal thickening event in the Rocky Mountain foreland and Great Plains: Tectonics, v. 3, p. 741–758.

Burchfiel, B. C., and Davis, G. A., 1972, Structural framework and evolution of the southern part of the Cordilleran orogen, western United States: American Journal of Science, v. 272, p. 97–118.

Burden, E. T., 1984, Terrestrial palynomorph biostratigraphy of the lower part of the Mannville Group (Lower Cretaceous), Alberta and Montana, *in* Scott, D. F., and Glass, D. J., eds., The Mesozoic in middle North America: Canadian Society of Petroleum Geologists Memoir 9, p. 249–270.

Byers, C. W., 1977, Biofacies patterns in euxinic basins; A general model, *in*

Cooke, H. E., and Enos, P., eds., Deep-water carbonate environments: Society of Economic Mineralogists and Paleontologists Special Publication 25, p. 5–17.

Caldwell, W.G.E., 1984, Early Cretaceous transgressions and regressions in southern interior plains, *in* Scott, D. F., and Glass D. J., ed., The Mesozoic of middle North America: Canadian Society of Petroleum Geologists Memoir 9, p. 173–203.

Cannon, J. L., 1966, Outcrop examination and interpretation of paleocurrent patterns of the Blackleaf Formation near Great Falls, Montana: Billings Geological Society 17th Annual Field Conference Guidebook, p. 71–111.

Cant, D. J., 1985, Western Canada Foreland Basin; Controls on sedimentation; International Symposium on Foreland Basins, Freibourg, Switzerland: Freibourg, Switzerland, International Association of Sedimentologists, p. 40.

Chisholm, W. A., 1963, The petrology of Upper Jurassic and Lower Cretaceous strata of the Western Interior: Wyoming Geological Association and Billings Geological Society First Joint Field Conference Guidebook, p. 71–86.

Cobban, W. A., and Reeside, J. B., 1952, Correlation of the Cretaceous formations of the Western Interior of the United States: Geological Society of America Bulletin, v. 63, p. 1011–1044.

Cobban, W. A., Erdmann, C. E., Lemke, R. W., and Maughn, E. K., 1976, Type sections and stratigraphy of the members of the Blackleaf and Marias River Formations (Cretaceous) of the Sweetgrass Arch, Montana: U.S. Geological Survey Professional Paper 974, 66 p.

Collinson, J. W., and Hasenmuller, W. A., 1978, Early Triassic paleogeography and biostratigraphy of the Cordilleran miogeosyncline, *in* Howell, D. G., and McDougall, K. A., eds., Mesozoic paleogeography of the western United States: Pacific Section, Society of Economic Paleontologists and Mineralogists, Pacific Coast Paleogeography Symposium 2, p. 175–188.

Coney, P. J., 1972, Cordilleran tectonics and North American plate motion: American Journal of Science, v. 272, p. 603–628.

Coney, P. J., Jones, D. L., and Monger, J.W.H., 1980, Cordilleran suspect terranes: Nature, v. 288, p. 329–333.

Cross, T. A., and Pilger, R. H., 1978, Tectonic controls of Late Cretaceous sedimentation, Western Interior, U.S.A.: Nature, v. 274, p. 653–657.

Daugherty, F. W., and Vitaliano, C. J., 1969, Sand Creek sill complex, Madison and Gallatin Counties, Montana: Geological Society of America Abstracts with Programs, v. 5, p. 19–20.

Davis, G. A., Monger, J.W.H., and Burchfiel, B. C., 1978, Mesozoic construction of the Cordilleran "collage," central British Columbia to central California, *in* Howell, D. G., and MaDougall, K. A., eds., Mesozoic paleogeography of the western United States: Pacific Section, Society of Economic Paleontologists and Mineralogists, Pacific Coast Paleogeography Symposium 2, p. 1–32.

DeCelles, P. G., 1984, Sedimentation and diagenesis in a tectonically partitioned, nonmarine foreland basin; The Lower Cretaceous Kootenai Formation, southwestern Montana [Ph.D. thesis]: Bloomington, Indiana University, 423 p.

——— , 1986, Sedimentation in a tectonically partitioned nonmarine foreland basin; The Lower Cretaceous Kootenai Formation, southwestern Montana: Geological Society of America Bulletin, v. 97, p. 911–931.

DeCelles, P. G., Langford, R. P., and Schwartz, R. K., 1983, Two new methods of paleocurrent determination from trough cross-stratification: Journal of Sedimentary Petrology, v. 53, p. 629–642.

DeCelles, P. G., and 15 others, 1987, Laramide thrust-generated alluvial-fan sedimentation, Sphinx Conglomerate, southwestern Montana: American Association of Petroleum Geologists Bulletin, v. 71, p. 135–155.

Demaison, G. J., and Moore, G. T., 1980, Anoxic environments and oil source bed genesis: American Association of Petroleum Geologists Bulletin, v. 64, p. 1179–1209.

Deuser, W. G., 1974, Evolution of anoxic conditions in Black Sea during Holocene, *in* Degens, E. T., and Ross, D. A., eds., The Black Sea; Geology, chemistry, and biology: American Association of Petroleum Geologists Memoir 20, p. 133–136.

Dickinson, W. R., 1976, Sedimentary basins developed during evolution of Mesozoic–Cenozoic arc–trench system in western North America: Canadian Journal of Earth Sciences, v. 13, p. 1268–1287.

Dickinson, W. R., and Snyder, W. S., 1978, Plate tectonics of the Laramide orogeny: Geological Society of America Memoir 151, p. 355–366.

Dyman, T. S., 1985a, Stratigraphic and petrologic analysis of the Lower Cretaceous Blackleaf Formation and the Upper Cretaceous Frontier Formation (lower part), Beaverhead and Madison Counties, Montana [Ph.D. thesis]: Pullman, Washington State University, 216 p.

——— , 1985b, Petrographic data from the Lower Cretaceous Blackleaf Formation and lower Upper Cretaceous Frontier Formation in Beaverhead and Madison Counties, Montana: U.S. Geological Survey Open-File Report 85-592, 19 p.

Dyman, T. S., and Nichols, D. J., 1988, Stratigraphy of mid-Cretaceous Blackleaf and lower part of the Frontier Formations in parts of Beaverhead and Madison Counties, Montana: U.S. Geological Survey Bulletin 1773 (in press).

Engebretson, D. C., Cox, A., and Thompson, G. A., 1984, Correlation of plate motions with continental tectonics: Laramide to Basin-Range: Tectonics, v. 3, p. 115–119.

Ettensohn, F. R., 1985, Controls on development of Catskill Delta complex basin-facies, *in* Woodrow, D. L., and Savon, W. D., eds., The Catskill Delta: Geological Society of America Special Paper 201, p. 65–77.

Evernden, J. F., and Kistler, R. W., 1970, Chronology of emplacement of Mesozoic batholith complexes in California and western Nevada: U.S. Geological Survey Professional Paper 623, 42 p.

Fox, N. A., 1982, Facies relationships and provenance of the Swift Formation (Jurassic) southwestern Montana [Ph.D. thesis]: Bozeman, Montana State University, 104 p.

Graham, S. A., and 14 others, 1986, Provenance modelling as a technique for analyzing source terrane evolution and controls on foreland sedimentation, *in* Allen, P., and Homewood, P., eds., Foreland basins: International Association of Sedimentologists Special Publication 8, p. 425–436.

Greenwood, W. R., Wallace, C. A., and Selverstone, J. E., 1979, The structural environment and controls of Cretaceous volcanism and plutonism in the Boulder batholith region, Montana: Geological Society of America Abstracts

with Programs, v. 11, p. 435.

Gwinn, V. E., 1960, Cretaceous and Tertiary stratigraphy and structural geology of the Drummond area, west-central Montana [Ph.D. thesis]: Princeton, New Jersey, Princeton University, 165 p.

——— , 1965, Cretaceous rocks of the Clark Fork Valley, central-western Montana: Billings Geological Societh 16th Annual Field Conference Guidebook, p. 34–57.

Gwinn, V. E., and Mutch, T. A., 1965, Intertongued Upper Cretaceous volcanic and non-volcanic rocks, central-western Montana: Geological Society of America Bulletin, v. 76, p. 1125–1144.

Hall, W. B., 1961, Geology of part of the upper Gallatin valley of southwestern Montana [Ph.D. thesis]: Laramie, University of Wyoming, 238 p.

Hallam, A., 1981, Facies interpretation and the stratigraphic record: San Francisco, California, W. H. Freeman and Company, 192 p.

Hallam, A., and Bradshaw, M. J., 1979, Bituminous shales and oolitic ironstones as indicators of transgressions and regressions: Journal of the Geological Society of London, v. 136, p. 157–164.

Hamilton, W., 1978, Mesozoic tectonics of the western United States, *in* Howell, D. G., and McDougall, K. A., eds., Mesozoic paleogeography of the western United States: Pacific Section, Society of Economic Paleontologists and Mineralogists, Pacific Coast Paleogeography Symposium 2, p. 33–70.

Harper, G. D., and Wright, J. E., 1984, Middle to Late Jurassic tectonic evolution of the Klamath Mountains, California-Oregon: Tectonics, v. 3, p. 759–772.

Harrison, J. E., Griggs, A. D., and Wells, J. D., 1974, Tectonic features of the Precambrian Belt basin and their influence on post-Belt structures: U.S. Geological Survey Professional Paper 866, 15 p.

Hayes, B.J.R., 1984, Stratigraphy and petroleum potential of the Swift Formation (Upper Jurassic) southern Alberta and north-central Montana: Montana Geological Society Field Trip and Symposium volume, p. 143–157.

Heller, P. L., and 7 others, 1986, Timing of initiation of the Sevier orogeny, Idaho-Wyoming and Utah thrust belts: Geology, v. 14, p. 388–391.

Henderson, L. J., Gordon, R. G., and Engebretson, D. C., 1984, Mesozoic aseismic ridges on the Farallon plate and southward migration of shallow subduction during the Laramide orogeny: Tectonics, v. 3, p. 121–132.

Holm, M. R., James, W. C., and Suttner, L. J., 1977, Comparison of the Peterson and Draney limestones, Idaho and Wyoming, and the calcareous members of the Kootenai Formation, western Montana: Wyoming Geological Association Guidebook 29th Annual Conference, p. 259–270.

Howard, J. D., and Frey, R. W., 1973, Characteristic physical and biogenic sedimentary structures in Georgia estuaries: American Association of Petroleum Geologists Bulletin, v. 57, p. 1169–1184.

——— , 1975, Estuaries of the Georgia coast, U.S.A.; Sedimentology and biology: Frankfurt am Main, Senckenbergiana Maritima, v. 7, 307 p.

Ingersoll, R. V., and Schweickert, R. A., 1986, A plate-tectonic model for Late Jurassic ophiolite genesis, Nevadan orogeny and forearc initiation, northern California: Tectonics, v. 5, p. 901–912.

Irving, E., Monger, J.W.H., and Yole, R. W., 1980, New paleomagnetic evidence for displaced terranes in British Columbia: Geological Association of Canada Special Paper 20, p. 441–456.

James, W. C., 1977, Origin of marine-nonmarine transitional strata at the top of the Kootenai Formation, southwestern Montana [Ph.D. thesis]: Bloomington, Indiana University, 433 p.

——— , 1980, Limestone channel storm complex (Lower Cretaceous) Elkhorn Mountains, Montana: Journal of Sedimentary Petrology, v. 50, no. 2, p. 447–456.

Jordan, T. E., 1981, Thrust loads and foreland basin evolution, Cretaceous, western United States: American Association of Petroleum Geologists Bulletin, v. 65, p. 2506–2520.

Jordan, T. E., Flemings, P. B., and Beer, J. A., 1988, Dating thrust fault activity by use of foreland basin strata, *in* Paola, C., and Kleinspehn, K., eds., New perspectives in basin analysis: New York, Springer-Verlag, p. 307–330.

Kauffman, E. G., 1975, Dispersal and biostratigraphic potential of Cretaceous benthonic bivalvia in the Western Interior: Geological Association of Canada Special Paper 13, p. 162–194.

—— , 1977, Geological and biological overview; Western Interior Cretaceous basin: Mountain Geologist, v. 14, p. 75–99.

Klepper, M. R., Weeks, R. A., and Ruppel, E. T., 1975, Geology of the southern Elkhorn Mountains, Jefferson and Broadwater Counties, Montana: U.S. Geological Survey Professional Paper 292, 82 p.

Kvale, E. P., 1986, Paleoenvironments and tectonic significance of the Upper Jurassic Morrison/Lower Cretaceous Cloverly Formations, Bighorn Basin, Wyoming [Ph.D. thesis]: Ames, Iowa State University, 191 p.

Lageson, D. R., 1985, Tectonic evolution of the Bridger Range and adjacent regions, southwest Montana: Bozeman, Montana, Tobacco Root Geological Society Guidebook to 10th Annual Field Conference, p. 10.

Lawton, T. F., 1985, Style and timing of frontal structures, thrust belt, central Utah: American Association of Petroleum Geologists Bulletin, v. 69, p. 1145–1159.

Lorenz, J. C., 1983, Lithospheric flexure and the history of the Sweetgrass Arch northwestern Montana, *in* Powers, R. B., ed., Geologic studies of the Cordilleran thrust belt, 1982: Denver, Colorado, Rocky Mountain Association of Geologists, p. 77–89.

Lund, K., 1984, Tectonic history of a continent–island arc boundary, west-central Idaho [Ph.D. thesis]: University Park, Pennsylvania State University, 207 p.

Lund, K., and Snee, L. W., 1988, Metamorphism, structural development, and age of the continent–island arc juncture in west-central Idaho, *in* Ernst, G., ed., Metamorphism and crustal evolution in the western conterminous United States, Rubey Volume 7: Los Angeles, University of California (in press).

McGookey, D. P., 1972, Cretaceous system *in* Geologic atlas of the Rocky Mountain region, United States of America: Denver, Colorado, Rocky Mountain Association of Geologists, p. 190–228.

McLean, J. R., and Jerzykiewicz, T., 1978, Cyclicity, tectonics and coal, *in* the Brazeau-Paskapoo Formations, Coal Valley area, Alberta, Canada, *in* Miall, A. D., ed., Fluvial sedimentology, Canadian Society of Petroleum Geologists Memoir 5, p. 441–468.

Meyers, J. H., 1981, Carbonate sedimentation in the Ellis Group (Jurassic) on the southern flank of the Belt Island, southwestern Montana: Montana Geological Society Field Conference and Symposium Guidebook to southwest Montana, p. 83–91.

Miller, E. L., Gans, P. B., Wright, J. E., and Sutter, J. F., 1987, Metamorphic history of the east-central Basin and Range Province; Tectonic setting and relationship to magmatism, *in* Ernst, W. G., ed., Metamorphic and crustal evolution, western coterminous United States, Rubey Volume 7: Los Angeles, University of California (in press).

Monger, J.W.H., Price, R. A., and Tempelman-Kluit, D. J., 1982, Tectonic accretion and the origin of the two major metamorphic and plutonic welts in the Canadian Cordillera: Geology, v. 10, p. 70–75.

Mudge, M. R., 1972, Pre-Quaternary rocks of the Sun River area, northwestern Montana: U.S. Geological Survey Professional Paper 663-A, 138 p.

Mudge, M. R., and Sheppard, R. A., 1968, Provenance of igneous rocks in Cretaceous conglomerates in northwestern Montana, *in* Geological Survey Research 1968: U.S. Geological Survey Professional Paper 600-D, p. D137–D146.

Nichols, D. J., Perry, W. J., and Haley, J. C., 1985, Reinterpretation of the palynogy and age of Laramide syntectonic deposits, southwestern Montana, and revision of the Beaverhead Group: Geology, v. 13, p. 149–153.

Oldow, J. S., Avé Lallement, H. G., and Schmidt, W. J., 1984, Kinematics of plate convergence deduced from Mesozoic structures in the western Cordillera: Tectonics, v. 3, p. 201–227.

Perry, W. J., Jr., and Sando, W. J., 1983, Sequence of deformation of Cordilleran thrust belt in Lima, Montana region, *in* Powers, R. B., ed., Geologic studies of the Cordilleran thrust belt, 1982: Denver, Colorado, Rocky Mountain Association of Geologists, p. 137–144.

Peterson, J. A., 1972, Jurassic System, *in* Geological atlas of the Rocky Mountain region, United States of America: Denver, Colorado, Rocky Mountain Association of Geologists, p. 177–189.

—— , 1981, General stratigraphy and regional paleostructure of the western

Montana overthrust belt: Montana Geological Society 1981 Annual Field Conference Guidebook, p. 3–35.

Poole, F. G., and Wardlaw, B. R., 1978, Candelaria (Triassic) and Diablo (Permian) Formations in southern Toquima Range, central Nevada, *in* Howell, D. G., and McDougall, K. A., eds., Mesozoic paleogeography of the western United States: Pacific Section, Society of Economic Paleontologists and Mineralogists, Pacific Coast Paleogeography Symposium 2, p. 271–276.

Posamentier, H. W., and Vail, P. R., 1988, Eustatic controls on clastic deposition, *in* Wilgus, C. K., Van Wagner, J., Mitchum, R., and Posamentier, H. W., eds., Sea level research; An integrated approach: Society of Economic Paleontologists and Mineralogists Special Publication 41 (in press).

Price, R. A., 1973, Large-scale gravitational flow of supracrustal rocks, southern Canadian Rockies, *in* Delong, K. A., and Scholten, R., eds., Gravity and tectonics: New York, John Wiley and Sons, p. 491–502.

Quinlan, G. M., and Beaumont, C., 1984, Appalachian thrusting, lithospheric flexure, and the Paleozoic stratigraphy of the Eastern Interior of North America: Canadian Journal of Earth Sciences, v. 21, p. 973–996.

Roberts, A. E., 1972, Cretaceous and early Tertiary depositional history of the Livingston area, southwestern Montana: U.S. Geological Survey Professional Paper 526-C, 120 p.

Robinson, G. D., Klepper, M. R., and Obradovich, J., 1968, Overlapping plutonism, volcanism, and tectonism in the Bouler batholith region, western Montana: Geological Society of America Memoir 116, p. 557–576.

Royse, F., Jr., Warner, M. A., and Reese, D. L., 1975, Thrust belt structural geometry and related stratigraphic problems, Wyoming–Idaho–northern Utah: Denver, Colorado, Rocky Mountain Association of Geologists 1975 Guidebook, p. 41–54.

Ruppel, E. T., and Lopez, D. A., 1984, The thrust belt in southwest Montana and east-central Idaho: U.S. Geological Survey Professional Paper 1278, 41 p.

Ruppel, E. T., Wallace, C. A., Schmidt, R. G., and Lopez, D. A., 1981, Preliminary interpretation of the thrust belt in southwest and west-central Montana and east central Idaho: Montana Geological Society Field Conference and Symposium Guidebook to southwest Montana, p. 139–159.

Ryder, R. T., and Scholten, R., 1973, Syntectonic conglomerates in southwest Montana; Their nature, origin, and tectonic significance: Geological Society of America Bulletin, v. 84, p. 773–796.

Ryer, T. A., 1977, Patterns of Cretaceous shallow-marine sedimentation, Coalville and Rockport areas, Utah: Geological Society of America Bulletin, v. 88, p. 177–188.

Saleeby, J. B., 1983, Accretionary tectonics of the North American Cordillera: Annual Review of Earth and Planetary Science, v. 15, p. 45–73.

Schedl, A., and Wiltschko, D. W., 1984, Sedimentological effects of a moving terrain: Journal of Geology, v. 92, p. 273–287.

Scholten, R., 1957, Paleozoic evolution of the geosynclinal margin north of the Snake River Plain: Geological Society of America Bulletin, v. 68, p. 151–170.

Schmidt, C. J., and Garihan, J. M., 1983, Laramide tectonic development of the Rocky Mountain foreland of southwestern Montana, *in* Lowell, J. D., and Gries, R. B., eds., Rocky Mountain foreland basins and uplifts: Denver, Colorado, Rocky Mountain Association of Geologists, p. 193–218.

Schmidt, C. J., and Hendrix, T. E., 1981, Tectonic controls for thrust belt and Rocky Mountain foreland structures in the northern Tobacco Root Mountains–Jefferson Canyon area, southwestern Montana: Montana Geological Society Field Conference and Symposium Guidebook to southwest Montana, p. 167–180.

Schmidt, C. J., and O'Neill, J. M., 1983, Structural evolution of the southwest Montana transverse zone, *in* Powers, R. B., ed., Geologic studies of the Cordilleran thrust belt: Denver, Colorado, Rocky Mountain Association of Geologists, p. 193–218.

Schmitt, J. G., 1985, Synorogenic sedimentation of upper Cretaceous Frontier formation conglomerates and associated strata, Wyoming-Idaho-Utah thrust belt: The Mountain Geologist, v. 22, no. 1, p. 5–16.

Schwartz, R. K., 1972, Stratigraphic and petrographic analysis of the Lower Cretaceous Blackleaf Formation, southwestern Montana [Ph.D. thesis]:

Bloomington, Indiana University, 268 p.

—— , 1983, Broken Early Cretaceous foreland basin in southwestern Montana; Sedimentation related to tectonism, *in* Powers, R. B., ed., Geologic studies of the Cordilleran thrust belt, 1982; Denver, Colorado, Rocky Mountain Association of Geologists, p. 159–184.

Sears, J., 1983, A continental margin ramp in the Cordilleran thrust belt along the Montana lineament: Geological Society of America Abstracts with Programs, v. 15, p. 682.

Sears, J., and Schmitt, J. G., 1987, Terrane accretion and transform faulting; Controls on the evolution of the Sevier foreland basin in Montana: Geological Society of America Abstracts with Programs, v. 19, p. 837.

Skipp, B., and Hall, W. E., 1980, Upper Paleozoic paleotectonics and paleogeography of Idaho, *in* Fouch, T. D., and Magathan, E. R., eds., Paleozoic paleogeography of the west-central United States: Society of Economic Paleontologists and Mineralogists, Rocky Mountain Paleogeography Symposium 1, p. 387–422.

Speed, R. C., 1978, Paleographic and plate tectonic evolution of the early Mesozoic marine province of the western Great Basin, *in* Howell, D. G., and McDougall, K. A., eds., Mesozoic paleogeography of the western United States: Pacific Section, Society of Economic Paleontologists and Mineralogists, Pacific Coast Paleogeography Symposium 2, p. 253–270.

Stine, A. D., 1986, Sedimentology of the Early Cretaceous Lower Sandstone Member of the Thermopolis Shale, southwestern Montana [M.S. thesis]: Boseman, Montana State University, 62 p.

Suppe, J., 1985, Principles of structural geology: Englewood Cliffs, New Jersey, Prentice-Hall, Inc., 537 p.

Sutter, J. F., Snee, L. W., and Lund, K., 1984, Metamorphic, plutonic, and uplift history of a continent–island arc suture zone, west-central Idaho: Geological Society of America Abstracts with Programs, v. 16, p. 670–671.

Suttner, L. J., 1968, Clay minerals in the Upper Jurassic–Lower Cretaceous Morrison and Kootenai Formations, southwestern Montana: Wyoming Geological Association Bulletin, v. 1, p. 5–14.

—— , 1969, Stratigraphic and petrographic analysis of Upper Jurassic–Lower Cretaceous Morrison and Kootenai Formations, southwest Montana: American Association of Petroleum Geologists Bulletin, v. 43, p. 1391–1410.

Suttner, L. J., and Basu, A., 1985, The effect of grain size on detrital modes; A test of the Gazzi-Dickinson point-counting method; Discussion: Journal of Sedimentary Petrology, v. 55, p. 616–617.

Suttner, L. J., and Schwartz, R. K., 1969, Petrographic vertical profile study of a barrier island–marine shelf sandstone complex: Geological Society of America Abstracts with Programs, part 5, p. 80.

Suttner, L. J., Schwartz, R. K., and James, W. C., 1981, Late Mesozoic to Early Cenozoic foreland sedimentation in southwest Montana: Montana Geological Society Field Conference and Symposium Guidebook to Southwest Montana, p. 93–104.

Suttner, L. J., DeCelles, P. G., and Berkhouse, G. A., 1985, Tectonic controls on Early Cretaceous sedimentation in the foreland basin of western Montana, U.S.A.: Friebourg, Switzerland, International Symposium on Foreland Basins Abstracts with Programs, p. 120.

Swift, D.J.P., Hudelson, P. M., and Brenner, R. L., 1987, Shelf construction in a foreland basin; Storm beds, shelf sandbodies, and shelf-slope depositional sequences in the Upper Cretaceous Mesaverde Group, Book Cliffs, Utah: Sedimentology (in press).

Thompson, T. A., 1984, Limestone pebble conglomerates in the Early Cretaceous foreland basin in southwestern Montana; Origin and significance [M.S. thesis]: Bloomington, Indiana University, 73 p.

Tilling, R. I., Klepper, M. R., and Obradovich, J. D., 1968, K-Ar ages and time span of emplacement of the Boulder batholith, Montana: American Journal of Science, v. 266, p. 671–689.

Veatch, A. C., 1907, Geography and geology of a portion of southwestern Wyoming, with special reference to coal and oil: U.S. Geological Survey Professional Paper 56, 178 p.

Vuke, S. M., 1982, Depositional environments of the Cretaceous Thermopolis, Muddy, and Mowry Formations, southern Madison and Gallatin Ranges, Montana [M.S. thesis]: Missoula, University of Montana, 141 p.

—— , 1984, Depositional environments of the early Cretaceous western interior seaway in southwestern Montana and the northern United States: Canadian Society of Petroleum Geologists Memoir 9, p. 127–144.

Walcott, R. L., 1970, Flexural rigidity, thickness, and viscosity of the lithosphere: Journal of Geophysical Research, v. 75, p. 3941–3954.

Walker, T. F., 1974, Stratigraphy and depositional environments of the Morrison and Kootenai Formations in the Great Falls area, Montana [Ph.D. thesis]: Missoula, University of Montana, 195 p.

Weimer, R. J., 1978, Influence of Transcontinental arch on Cretaceous marine sedimentation; A preliminary report, *in* Pruit, J. D., and Coffin, P. E., eds., Symposium, Energy Resources of the Denver Basin: Denver, Colorado, Rocky Mountain Association of Geologists, p. 211–222.

—— , 1983, Relation of unconformities, tectonics, and sea level changes, Cretaceous of the Denver Basin and adjacent areas, *in* Howell, D. G., and McDougall, K. A., eds., Mesozoic paleogeography of the western United States: Pacific Section, Society of Economic Paleontologists and Mineralogists, Pacific Coast Paleogeography Symposium 2, p. 359–376.

Wilson, M. D., 1970, Upper Cretaceous–Paleocene synorogenic conglomerates of southwestern Montana: American Association of Petroleum Geologists Bulletin, v. 54, p. 1843–1867.

Wiltschko, D. V., and Dorr, J. A., 1983, Timing of deformation in overthrust belt and foreland of Idaho, Wyoming, and Utah: American Association of Petroleum Geologists Bulletin, v. 67, p. 1304–1322.

Winston, D., Woods, M., and Byer, G. B., 1984, The case for an intracratonic belt–Purcell basin; Tectonic, stratigraphic, and stable isotopic considerations: Montana Geological Society Field Conference and Symposium Volume, p. 103–118.

Wright, J. E., and Miller, E. L., 1986, An expanded view of Jurassic orogenesis for the western United States Cordillera: Geological Society of America Abstracts with Programs, v. 18, p. 201.

Young, S. W., 1985, Structural history of the Jordian Creek area, northern Madison Range, Madison County, Montana [M.S. thesis]: Austin, University of Texas, 125 p.

Zen, E-an, Marvin, R. F., and Mehnert, H. H., 1975, Preliminary petrographic, chemical, and age data on some intrusive and related contact metamorphic rocks, Pioneer Mountains, southwestern Montana: Geological Society of America Bulletin, v. 86, p. 367–370.

Manuscript Accepted by the Society June 13, 1988

Geological Society of America
Memoir 171
1988

Tectonic and sedimentary evolution of the northern Green River basin, western Wyoming

Mark W. Shuster* and James R. Steidtmann
Department of Geology and Geophysics, University of Wyoming, Laramie, Wyoming 82071

ABSTRACT

Studies of the provenances, facies, and subsidence histories of Upper Cretaceous and lower Tertiary strata in conjunction with flexural modeling document the tectonic origin and sedimentary evolution of the northern Green River basin in western Wyoming. The area evolved from being part of the Sevier foreland into a nonmarine intermontane basin with the uplift of the Wind River and Gros Ventre Ranges during late Cretaceous time, and by early Tertiary time, subsidence and sedimentation related to these uplifts dominated the northern Green River basin.

Sandstone compositions and paleocurrent data indicate an abrupt change in provenance at the beginning of Paleocene time, marking the progressive uplift and erosion of the Wind River and Gros Ventre highlands. Sandstones changed from dominantly sedimentary lithic compositions to dominantly feldspathic compositions when the crystalline core of the Wind River Range was breached. Similarly, paleocurrent trends changed from southeasterly flow directions southward and southwestward, as both the Gros Ventre and Wind River uplifts flooded the basin with detritus.

The alluvial sandstone architecture of Upper Cretaceous and lower Tertiary rocks was analyzed in order to document the interaction of allocyclic controls and depositional facies as related to the subsidence history of the basin. This approach proved to be successful only where complicating factors, such as climate and source lithology, could be adequately constrained. Analyses of facies within the lenticular sandstone and shale sequence (Campanian) and the Hoback Formation (Paleocene) suggest deposition during rapid subsidence. The alluvial architecture of Eocene strata (Pass Peak and Wasatch formations) of the Hoback area cannot be easily interpreted in terms of subsidence. Rapid subsidence is indicated for the LaBarge Member of the Wasatch Formation in the Big Piney–LaBarge area.

Subsidence analysis for the Hoback, Pinedale anticline, and LaBarge areas documents the patterns and timing of tectonically induced subsidence. A subsidence event occurring at approximately 120 to 115 Ma was probably related to thrusting in the Idaho-Wyoming thrust belt. Another subsidence event at approximately 90 Ma may indicate initial uplift of the Wind River block. The very rapid subsidence event in the Pinedale anticline area during Maastrichtian time is not evident in subsidence curves from the Hoback and LaBarge areas, and thus is probably a manifestation of loading by the Wind River thrust. Rapid subsidence during Paleocene time in the Hoback area is attributed to loading from the Darby thrust and Gros Ventre uplift.

Two-dimensional profiling of the northern Green River Basin shows that the basin can be effectively modeled as a flexural depression resulting from extrabasinal and intrabasinal loading on an elastic lithosphere. Two distinct models were used to confirm

---

*Present address: Shell Development Co., P.O. Box 481, Houston, TX 77001.

regional compensation and the flexural response to loading of the lithosphere. Modern basin geometry analysis tested for regional compensation by comparing modeled deflections with observed basin geometry for a given load configuration. Sediment thickness profiling was used to determine the maximum thickness of sedimentary rocks that could have accumulated in the tectonic depression resulting from Darby, Prospect, and Wind River thrusting (assuming instantaneous uplift and adequate sediment supply). Both models are consistent with the concept of basin-margin tectonic loading as the main cause of subsidence in the Green River basin.

INTRODUCTION

The tectonic and sedimentary evolution of the northern Green River basin was a response to both thrusting in the Idaho-Wyoming thrust belt and basement uplift in the Rocky Mountain foreland. Evidence of this genetic relationship is recorded in both the subsidence history and sedimentary fill of the basin. Because major thrusts in the Idaho-Wyoming thrust belt young toward the foreland, the chronologic and geometric relations between these two tectonic provinces, displayed in zones of impingement, relate mainly to the youngest thrusting events. In contrast, the tectogenic sedimentary record in basins along this transition reflects the long-term evolution of tectonic controls in both areas.

The tectonic controls on basin development are recorded in the lithology, facies patterns, and geometric distribution of its sedimentary fill. Intrabasinal tectonism, specifically subsidence, influences the types and geometries of sedimentary facies and the position of depocenters through time. Extrabasinal tectonism, specifically uplift, exerts control on the composition and texture of the basin fill and the character of facies proximal to uplifts. Our analysis of the sedimentary fill in the Northern Green River Basin yields information pertinent to understanding both intrabasinal and extrabasinal controls.

Geologic setting

The geologic setting of the northern Green River basin is shown in Figure 1. The basin is triangular in plan view, bounded by the Idaho-Wyoming thrust belt to the west, the Gros Ventre Range to the north and northeast, and the Wind River Range to the east. The basin opens southward into the greater Green River basin consisting of the Great Divide, Washakie, and Sand Wash basins (Sullivan, 1980).

The thrust belt consists of thrusted and concentrically folded Paleozoic and Mesozoic miogeoclinal sedimentary strata (Armstrong and Oriel, 1965; Royse and others, 1975). The major thrusts are eastward-vergent and are thought to be progressively younger to the east (Royse and others, 1975). Ramps in the major thrusts appear to have been reactivated by normal faulting during late Tertiary extension (Royse and others, 1975).

The core of the Wind River uplift consists of Archaean gneisses, metasedimentary rocks, metamorphosed granites, and metamorphosed mafic and ultramafic rocks (Love and Christiansen, 1985). The east side of the range consists of dip slopes of Paleozoic and Mesozoic strata. On the west side, the northeast-dipping Wind River thrust bounds the range but is buried by lower Tertiary sediment over its full extent. In the southern part of the range, in the Oregon Buttes area, the fault is expressed at the surface by Reds Cabin Monocline (Steidtmann and others, 1983). Associated faults in the core of the range are visible in the north (Love and Christiansen, 1985) and inferred for the southern part (Steidtmann and others, 1983; Shuster, 1986). Postcompressional collapse of the toe of the Wind River thrust is marked by the presence of the Continental normal fault (Love and Christiansen, 1985; Steidtmann and others, 1983). The corrected dip of the Wind River thrust, interpreted from the COCORP line, is about 40° (Zawislak and Smithson, 1981), but may be shallower elsewhere (Berg, 1962; Gries, 1983). About 15 km of horizontal shortening can be calculated for the 40° fault dip (Hagen and others, 1985).

The Gros Ventre uplift consists of Archean granitic rocks and Paleozoic and Mesozoic strata (Dorr and others, 1977), although the amount of exposed Precambrian basement is much less than that in the Wind River Range. The major bounding fault, the Cache thrust, is on the southwest margin of the range and dips to the northeast.

The Upper Cretaceous and lower Tertiary stratigraphy of the northern Green River basin sedimentary fill is shown in Figure 2. All of these rocks are nonmarine units of sandstone, shale, siltstone, and conglomerate including occasional coal and freshwater limestone. In the Hoback area the complete Upper Cretaceous–lower Tertiary section is exposed on the hanging wall of the Game Hill fault (Dorr and others, 1977). This stratigraphy is compiled from the four reference sections noted in Figure 1.

Previous work

The structural geology of the western basin margin (Idaho-Wyoming thrust belt) has been described by Armstrong and Oriel (1965), Royse and others (1975), Dorr and others (1977), Dixon (1982), and Lamerson (1983). As a whole, these workers have documented the "thin-skinned" nature of deformation and the eastward succession of major thrusts, both of which are important to understanding the tectonic origin of the basin (Jordan, 1981; Shuster and Steidtmann, 1983; Hagen and others, 1985; Shuster, 1986).

The structural geology of the foreland Gros Ventre and Wind River uplifts has been discussed by Berg (1961, 1962, 1963), Sales (1968), Smithson and others (1978), Dorr and oth-

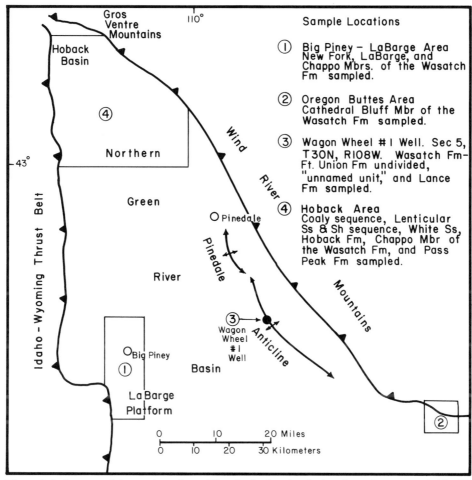

Figure 1. Index map of the northern Green River basin showing the locations of areas sampled in this study.

ers (1977), and Brewer and others (1980). These workers have shown that these uplifts formed as a result of basement-involved thrusting. The timing of basin-margin deformation pertinent to the evolution of the northern Green River basin is presented by Berg (1961), Dorr and others (1977), Steidtmann and others (1983), Wiltschko and Dorr (1983), and Shuster (1986). The general stratigraphy and sedimentology of Upper Cretaceous–lower Tertiary rocks is given by Oriel (1962, 1969), Steidtmann (1968), West (1969), Spearing (1969), Curry (1973), Guennel and others (1973), Dorr and others (1977), Sullivan (1980), and Law (1981, 1984).

New theories proposed for the tectonic origin of the northern Green River basin (Shuster and Steidtmann, 1983; Hagen and others, 1985) indicate that subsidence of the basin resulted from tectonic loading by basin-margin uplifts, notably the thrust belt and Wind River uplifts. Moreover, fission-track thermochronology of the Wind River Range (Shuster, 1986) has provided constraints on the timing and uplift rates of this foreland uplift, and Law (1984), Naeser (1984), Pollastro and Barker (1984), and Prensky (1984) have presented data pertinent to the stratigraphy and burial history of the basin.

Investigative approach

Sandstone composition and paleocurrent analyses of Upper Cretaceous and lower Tertiary nonmarine strata were used to determine source lithologies and timing of uplift. The Paleocurrent measurements of both trough axes and planar cross-beds from fluvial sequences were taken to delineate paleo-flow directions. The provenance of these sediments documents the evolving history of sedimentary fill in the basin. The subsidence history of the basin was investigated using alluvial-sandstone architecture analysis (Allen, 1978; Blakey and Gubitosa, 1984) in conjuction with subsidence curve (backstripping) analyses (Steckler and Watts, 1978). These procedures identify the interaction of sedimentation and subsidence within the basin, as well as the timing and nature of tectonically driven subsidence events.

Because there was a large component of tectonically driven subsidence during the Late Cretaceous–early Tertiary history of the basin, we propose a model that accounts for the tectonic downwarping of the basin by lithospheric flexure under tectonic and sedimentary supracrustal loads. This model does not include the effects of erosion and redistribution of load through time but investigates the maximum amount of sediment-fill that could be accommodated from the tectonic loading, assuming instantaneous uplift and adequate sediment supply.

PROVENANCE

Upper Cretaceous sandstones, Hoback Basin, Pinedale Anticline, and northeast Rock Springs Uplift

Sandstones of Campanian age in the Hoback basin (coaly sequence, lenticular sandstone and shale sequence, and the white sandstone) are litharenites (Folk, 1980). The major framework constituents, in decreasing order of abundance, are quartz (monocrystalline), detrital phosphatic chert, detrital lithic fragments, potassium feldspars, plagioclase, carbonate lithic fragments, muscovite, biotite, and assorted accessory heavy minerals, the most common of which are zircon, garnet, and magnetite (Fig. 3).

Core from the Wagon Wheel No. 1 borehole, Sec.5,T.30N., R.108W., was sampled to determine sandstone compositions in uppermost Cretaceous strata. The sandstones are litharenites (Folk, 1980) and are plotted on a Q:F:L: ternary diagram in Figure 3. Compositions of these sandstones are almost identical to those of other Cretaceous sandstones in the Pinedale anticline (Keighin, 1984). The major constituents, in decreasing order of abundance, are quartz, detrital chert, detrital lithic fragments, and carbonate lithic fragments, with minor amounts of micaceous minerals and accessory heavy minerals.

Sandstone bodies in the Lance Formation on the Rock Springs Uplift were sampled to further define compositions of Cretaceous strata. The normalized compositions for Q:F:L are shown in Figure 3. All samples are litharenites, according to Folk (1980). The major framework grains, in decreasing abundance, are monocrystalline quartz, detrital chert, and detrital lithic fragments. A small amount of plagioclase is also present and is relatively unaltered.

Lower Tertiary strata: Pinedale Anticline, and LaBarge–Big Piney area

Sandstone from the lower Tertiary units in the Pinedale Anticline (unnamed unit, Fort Union Formation, and Wasatch Formation; Law, 1985) range in composition from feldspathic

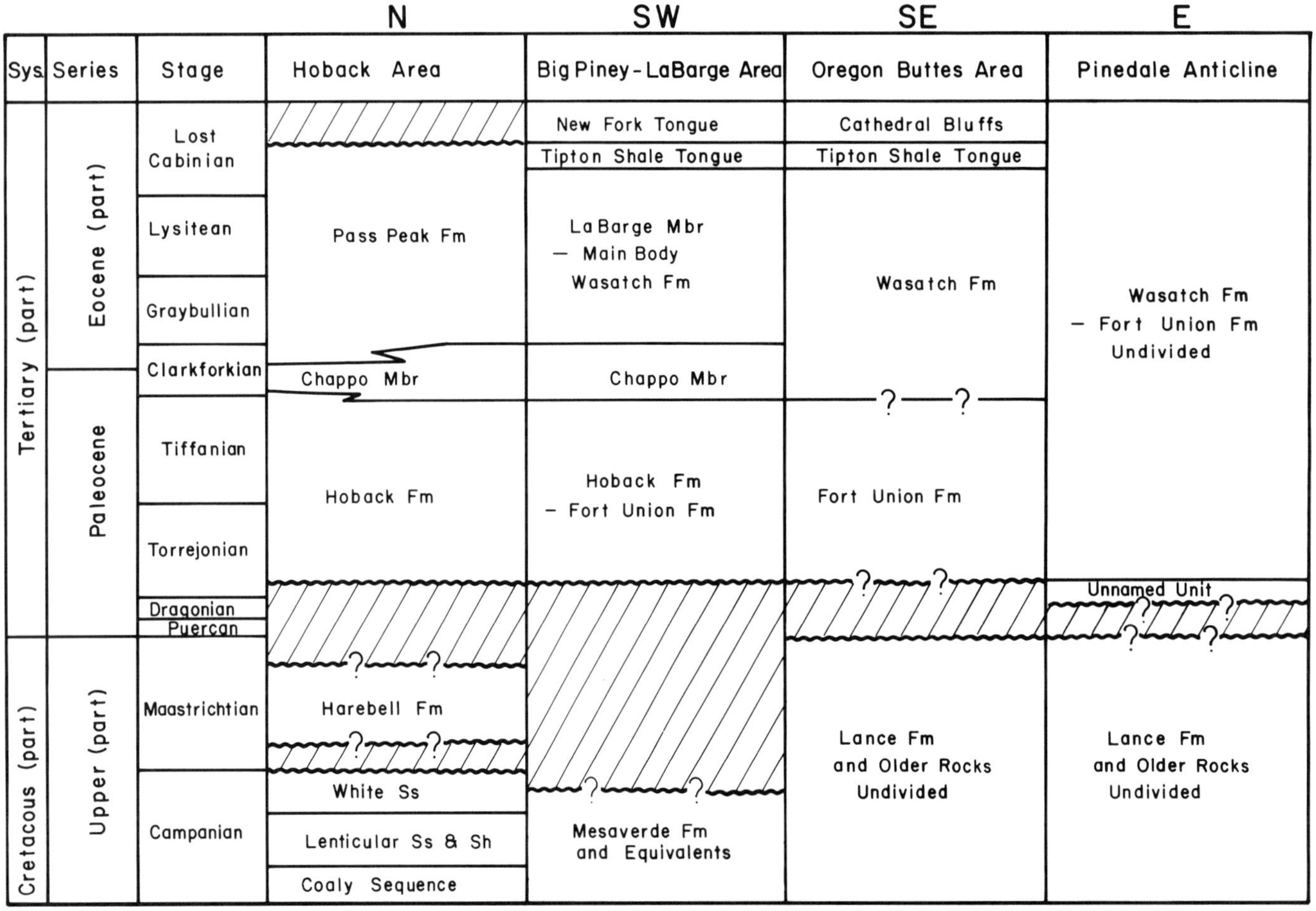

			N	SW	SE	E
Sys.	Series	Stage	Hoback Area	Big Piney–LaBarge Area	Oregon Buttes Area	Pinedale Anticline
Tertiary (part)	Eocene (part)	Lost Cabinian	Pass Peak Fm	New Fork Tongue	Cathedral Bluffs	Wasatch Fm – Fort Union Fm Undivided
				Tipton Shale Tongue	Tipton Shale Tongue	
		Lysitean		LaBarge Mbr – Main Body Wasatch Fm	Wasatch Fm	
		Graybullian				
		Clarkforkian	Chappo Mbr	Chappo Mbr	?—?	
	Paleocene	Tiffanian	Hoback Fm	Hoback Fm – Fort Union Fm	Fort Union Fm	
		Torrejonian			?—?	Unnamed Unit
		Dragonian Puercan				
Cretaceous (part)	Upper (part)	Maastrichtian	Harebell Fm		Lance Fm and Older Rocks Undivided	Lance Fm and Older Rocks Undivided
		Campanian	White Ss	Mesaverde Fm and Equivalents		
			Lenticular Ss & Sh			
			Coaly Sequence			

Figure 2. Upper Cretaceous and lower Tertiary stratigraphy of the northern Green River basin. Compiled from Oriel (1962, 1969), Steidtmann (1968), West (1969), Spearing (1969), Guennel and others (1973), Dorr and others (1977), Sullivan (1980), and Law (1981, 1984).

litharenite to arkoses. The major framework components of these sandstones are quartz, microcline, plagioclase and plutonic rock fragments, and detrital lithic fragments.

Lower Tertiary sandstones of the Hoback basin show a much greater range in composition (Fig. 4). More important, the change in composition reflects the general stratigraphic position of the samples. Paleocene-age samples (Hoback Formation) are litharenites, whereas Eocene-age samples (Chappo Member, Wasatch Formation, and Pass Peak Formation) range in composition from arkoses to feldspathic litharenites (Fig. 4; Steidtmann, 1968; Shuster, 1986). This general change in Q:F:L ratios in Paleocene and Eocene rocks is marked also by the appearance of metamorphic and plutonic lithic fragments, a relative decline of sedimentary lithic fragments, and the increase of biotite, muscovite, hornblende, and garnet accessory minerals.

The normalized compositions of eight samples from the La-Barge and New Fork members of the Wasatch Formation are shown in Figure 4. These sandstones range in composition from feldspathic litharenites to arkoses. The predominant framework grains are undulose and nonundulose quartz, microcline, detrital lithic fragments, plagioclase, and metamorphic rock fragments.

Discussion

Sandstone compositions and paleocurrent data (Figs. 3, 4) for the coaly sequence, lenticular sandstone and shale sequence, and the white sandstone indicate that they were eroded from sedimentary terranes to the northwest in the Idaho-Wyoming

salient of the thrust belt. The compositional data indicate that the source terrane supplied a large amount of phosphatic chert and detrital lithic fragments as well as quartz, indicating that the Phosphoria Formation supplied sediment to at least some of these Campanian strata.

Compositional and paleocurrent data from Paleocene strata to the north (Fig. 4) suggest that highlands located in the Idaho-Wyoming thrust belt to the west were the major source for these rocks, with some subsidiary contribution from Gros Ventre highlands to the north and northeast (Dorr and others, 1977). The easterly-southeasterly flow directions could not have been maintained for a great distance because of the buttressing effect of the Wind River Range, and flow was diverted toward the south. The lack of exposed Paleocene rocks in the basin center obscures the interpretation, but presumably a zone of compositional mixing exists where coeval drainage systems merged. This zone was documented, in part, by Spearing (1969) and Steidtmann (1968) for the upper Hoback Formation and Pass Peak Formation, respectively. The uppermost Paleocene Chappo Member of the Wasatch Formation (Oriel, 1969) also appears to be mainly lithic at its type locality west of LaBarge, Wyoming, although no modal analyses were done. Thus, it too was most likely derived from thrust-belt highlands.

The interpretation of paleocurrent and compositional information from the Wasatch Formation in the LaBarge area (Fig. 4) is not as straightforward. The feldspathic compositions indicate that a crystalline source within the Precambrian core of the Wind River Range is the most likely source terrane. The Precambrian

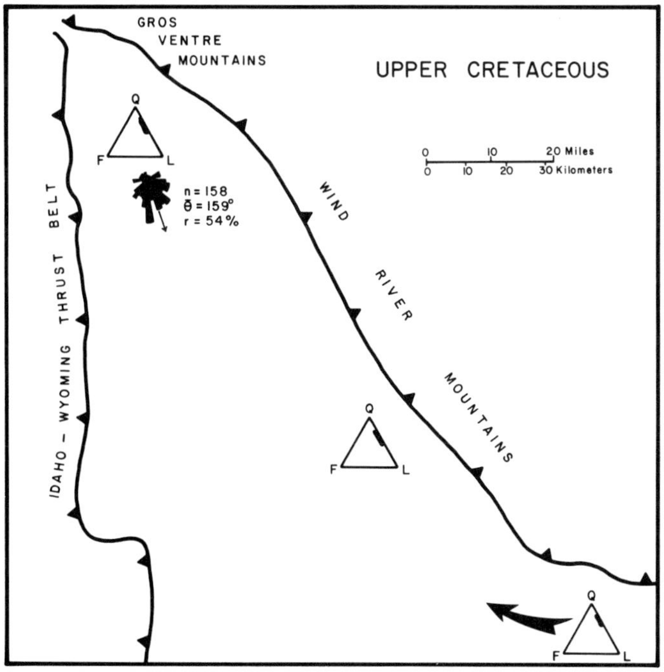

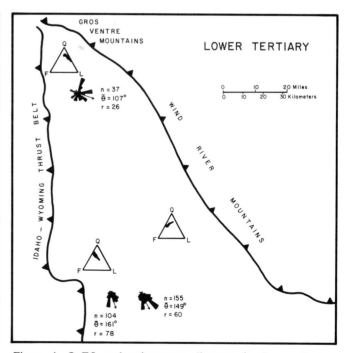

Figure 3. Qt:F:L and paleocurrent diagrams for Upper Cretaceous sandstones. Paleocurrent data includes both trough and planar cross-bedding measurements. n = No. of measurements, θ = vector mean azimuth, r = magnitude of resultant vector (percent).

Figure 4. Qt:F:L and paleocurrent diagrams for Lower Tertiary sandstones. Paleocurrent data includes both trough and planar cross-bedding measurements. n = No. of measurements, θ = vector mean azimuth, r = magnitude of resultant vector (percent).

rocks in the Gros Ventre Range to the north had not yet been breached (Dorr and others, 1977), and there were few, if any, crystalline rocks exposed in the thrust belt. However, paleocurrent data (Fig. 4) indicate transport from the north or northwest. The explanation of this apparent inconsistency may be that by this time (early Eocene) sediment provenance in the northern Green River basin was so dominated by uplift and erosion of the Wind River block that the drainage was pushed to the far western edge of the basin where it continued its southerly direction.

The Lance Formation and its equivalent to the north, the Harebell Formation, were derived from preexisting sedimentary terranes, although at this point it is impossible to determine the exact location of the sources. Lance Formation sandstones from both the Wagon Wheel No. 1 core (Law, 1984) and the northeast flank of the Rock Springs uplift are fine-grained litharenites. Work by Pryor (1961) and fission-track work (Shuster, 1986) suggest that uplift of the Wind River Range had begun by Campanian time. Thus, lithic material in the Lance Formation and equivalent could have been derived from erosion of the sedimentary cover of the Wind River highlands, but lacking good paleocurrent data, we cannot rule out a source in the uplifted Mesozoic and Paleozoic rocks of the Idaho-Wyoming thrust belt.

Paleocene strata, including the Hoback Formation, Fort Union Formation, Chappo Member of the Wasatch Formation, and the unnamed unit of Law and Nichols (1982) are the oldest units that can be documented to have been derived from the basement-involved Gros Ventre and Wind River uplifts. The "unnamed unit" cored in the Wagon Wheel No. 1 Well lies stratigraphically below the Torrejonian Hoback Formation (Guennel and others, 1973) and is presumed to be early Torrejonian or Dragonian in age. Clearly, the feldspathic content of these rocks indicates a crystalline source, and the stratigraphic position of the "unnamed unit" indicates that the Precambrian core of the Wind River Range was breached earlier than previously thought. Moreover, much of the Phanerozoic section on the Wind River block had already been removed by erosion, indicating significant uplift in late Cretaceous time. In summary, analyses of sandstone compositions and paleocurrent data for Campanian through early Eocene rocks in the northern Green River basin indicate that the main controls on sedimentation shifted from mainly western thrust belt sources in late Cretaceous times to basement-involved sources to the east by Paleocene time.

SUBSIDENCE ANALYSES

Introduction

The uppermost Cretaceous and Paleocene sedimentary record of the northern Green River basin consists wholly of nonmarine deposits (Law, 1984; Dorr and others, 1977; Love and others, 1963). These strata were deposited during intrabasinal (subsidence) and extrabasinal (uplift) tectonism as the basin was molded into its present form. The nonmarine depositional systems were influenced by the ongoing tectonism, and the sedimentary facies observed today reflect that tectonic influence.

The sandstone architecture of an alluvial sequence is a product of both autocyclic and allocyclic controls. More specifically, the spatial distribution of sandstone channels in overbank deposits is a function of the scale and mode of behavior of a river system, the rate of avulsion, and the subsidence rate of the alluvial plain (Allen, 1978). If all other factors are constant, the sandstone geometry is dependent on subsidence rate. The complexities of the fluvial system, in terms of its response to varied autocyclic and allocyclic controls obscure, and in some cases occlude, information pertinent to the specific tectonic setting. However, recent work by Blakey and Gubitosa (1984) and Shuster and Steidtmann (1987) suggest that qualitative information pertinent to the subsidence history can be gleaned from the sedimentary record through detailed facies analysis and careful consideration of climate and source lithology.

For the most part, tectonic subsidence of a basin is a nearly instantaneous response to load emplacement (Jordan, 1981). Therefore, the subsidence history of a basin can be used to delineate the timing of loading events. Heller and others (1986) applied this approach to determine the timing of initial thrusting in the Idaho-Wyoming thrust belt. In our study we have used the subsidence analysis technique (assuming an Airy-type isostatic model) of the northern Green River basin to determine the time of basin-margin loading by thrusts.

Stratigraphic data were compiled from the literature and from our observations of the basin's sedimentary record. Types of data include lithology, porosity, paleobathymetric estimates, and biostratigraphic age control. Porosity-depth corrections used in the "backstripping" procedure were modified after exponential functions presented by Rieke and Chilingarian (1974) and Sclater and Christie (1980). The time scale is from Palmer (1983). Water depths were estimated by faunal assemblages or interpretations of depositional environments as follows: fully marine facies = 60 to 300 m; shallow marine facies = 0 to 60 m, and nonmarine facies = 0 to 300 m above sea level. The data and procedures are described in detail by Shuster (1986).

Campanian strata, Hoback area

A complete discussion of the alluvial sandstone architecture of Campanian strata in the Hoback area is given by Shuster (1986) and Shuster and Steidtmann (1987). Approximately 1,000 m of Campanian nonmarine strata are exposed in the Hoback area. These strata consist of shale, sandstone, coal and fresh-water limestone. The coaly sequence and lenticular sandstone and shale sequence are the depositional products of low-sinuosity, low-gradient, fixed-channel fluvial systems (Shuster, 1986; Shuster and Steidtmann, 1987). The overlying white sandstone (30 m thick), consisting entirely of sandstone and chert pebble conglomerate, was deposited by low-sinuosity, high-gradient, meandering or braided fluvial systems (Shuster, 1986; Shuster and Steidtmann, 1987).

The alluvial sandstone architecture of the coaly sequence and lenticular sandstone and shale sequence was deposited on a

rapidly subsiding alluvial plain. Moreover, Shuster and Steidtmann (1987) suggested that the subsidence was induced by coeval tectonic loading in the thrust belt to the west and that the
overlying white sandstone represents post-thrusting progradation. Regardless of the specific interpretation, the predominantly fine-grained Campanian fluvial system contains lenticular
ribbon and multistory ribbon sandstone channels, poorly developed but ubiquitous paleosol horizons, and limestone, which,
together with relatively unchanging provenance, suggest rapid
subsidence in light of Allen's (1974, 1978) observations.

Hoback Formation

Detailed sedimentology of the Hoback Formation, as defined by Guennel and others (1973), was presented by Spearing
(1969) and summarized by Dorr and others (1977). The unit is
predominantly fine grained, and consists of shale, siltstone, sandstone, conglomerate, coal, and fresh-water micritic limestone.
The composition and facies of this formation are similar to those
of the lenticular sandstone and shale sequence, although the basal
Hoback Formation is notably conglomeratic. The total thickness
of the Hoback Formation is about 2,000 m, about 10 percent of
which is sandstone. Most of the sandstone bodies are splay deposits into paludal or lacustrine interfluve environments. They are
thin (<1 m) and contain small-scale cross-stratification. Rare
channel deposits are lenticular and isolated.

The sedimentary facies of the Hoback Formation are the
depositional products of low-gradient alluvial systems with associated marsh, paludal, and lacustrine environments. Spearing
(1969) suggested that facies characteristics and vertebrate remains
indicate that the climate during Hoback deposition was generally
warm and humid. We did not conduct detailed studies of paleosols, but reconnaissance examination suggests that they are not
particularly well developed, even though rooted horizons are
ubiquitous.

By analogy with the previous arguments made for the Campanian lenticular sandstone and shale sequence, sedimentary facies of the Hoback Formation also suggest deposition during
rapid basin subsidence. This interpretation is based on (1) the
isolated nature of alluvial channel sandstones (Allen, 1978), (2)
the ubiquitous lacustrine and paludal deposits indicative of a
poorly drained flood plain, and (3) numerous but poorly developed paleosol horizons (Allen, 1974).

Chappo Member, Wasatch Formation

The Chappo Member of the Wasatch Formation exposed in
the Hoback area is approximately 600 m thick and consists
mainly of shale, siltstone, and sandstone. This unit was interpreted by Dorr and others (1977) to represent alluvial flood-plain
deposition during a somewhat drier climate than was the case for
the Hoback Formation. In general, channels in the Chappo
Member are similar to the high-gradient low-sinuosity channels
of the Saskatchawan braided model (Miall, 1978). Apparently

the fine-grained lithologies in the Chappo were derived from
Triassic red beds in the source area. If that was the case, then the
overall facies patterns may be the result of provenance control
rather than active subsidence. Similar provenance controls on
bedding trends have been documented for foreland sedimentation
in southwestern Montana (Graham and others, 1986).

Pass Peak Formation

The Pass Peak Formation, described in detail by Steidtmann
(1968), is approximately 500 m thick. The unit consists predominantly of medium to coarse-grained sandstone, siltstone, conglomerate, and shale. Steidtmann (1968) interpreted these strata as
being deposited by braided streams in an alluvial fan setting
(coarse-grained depsoits) and by meandering and braided streams
in alluvial plain settings. Examination of the sandstone channels
suggests that stacked multilateral bodies (Allen, 1978) predominate. These sandstone bodies range in thickness from 3 to 25 m,
with most ranging between 12 and 20 m, and extend laterally
from 75 to 4,500 m (Steidtmann, 1968). They are surrounded by
shale and siltstone that are are laterally continuous. The presence
of these laterally continuous fine-grained strata indicate that winnowing of fine-grained material was not complete. Some nonmarine limestones are intercalated with the shaley deposits,
suggesting the presence of small lakes in interfluve areas.

Presumably, the increased aridity seen in the Chappo Member continued throughout Pass Peak deposition. Moreover,
source-rock controls on depositional facies were similar for the
Pass Peak deposition. Also, facies reconstructions of the Pass
Peak Formation indicate that these deposits were for the most
part proximal to their sources (Steidtmann, 1968). This setting
argues against application of Allen's (1978) model to interpretation of the subsidence history. If the architecture of the Pass Peak
Formation is compared with that of the Hoback Formation and
lenticular sandstone and shale sequence, an apparent slowing of
subsidence is indicated; however, this may actually relate to
source control rather than subsidence.

Wasatch Formation, LaBarge–Big Piney Area

The stratigraphy of the Wasatch Formation in the northwestern part of the Green River basin is summarized by Oriel
(1962, 1969). We examined three subunits in the LaBarge area:
the Chappo and LaBarge Members and the New Fork Tongue
(Fig. 2).

The Chappo Member consists of thin (<2 m), ripple-
stratified sandstones with rooted horizons at the top. The sandstones are enveloped in shale and siltstone, which together
represent alluvial plain and splay deposition. The presence of
multiple paleosol horizons indicates several periods of subaerial
exposure.

The LaBarge Member consists of isolated, thick (>5m),
medium- to fine-grained sandstone bodies, thin (<1m), fine-
grained sandstone bodies, siltstone, and mudstone. The thick sand-

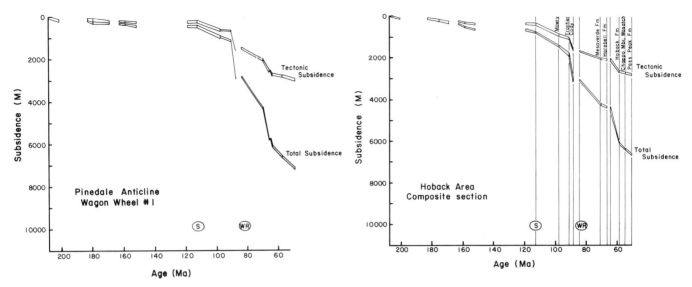

Figure 5. Subsidence curves for the Pinedale anticline area. The sedimentary column was backstripped and corrected for compaction following the procedures outlined by Steckler and Watts (1978). See text for further explanation. Stratigraphic data are presented in Shuster (1986). S and WR refer to the inferred initiation of Sevier and Wind River thrusting, respectively.

Figure 6. Subsidence curves for the Hoback area. The sedimentary column was backstripped and corrected for compaction following the procedures outlined by Steckler and Watts (1978). See text for further explanation. Stratigraphic data are presented in Shuster (1986). Modified from Heller and others, 1986. S and WR refer to the inferred initiation of Sevier and Wind River thrusting, respectively.

stone bodies show erosive bases, typically fine upward, and are predominantly trough cross-stratified. Some of the trough sets are extremely large (>1 m thick) and unusually long (as much as 5 m). The thin, fine-grained sandstones are ripple-stratified and laterally extensive (as much as 2 km in some cases). Occasionally, these thin sandstones show evidence of rooting at their tops. The large sandstone bodies are channel fills of large river systems. The facies associations and predominance of trough cross-stratification suggest that these rivers were mixed-load meandering systems (Jackson, 1976, 1978) with associated large splays. The overbank facies contain ubiquitous, laterally continuous paleosol horizons (E. H. Southwell, personal communication, 1985).

Because of climatic changes during the Eocene (MacGinitie, 1969), it is difficult to interpret the Chappo and LaBarge members in terms of tectonic control. However, these deposits were relatively distal and were fed, for the most part, from the Wind River highlands, so that local source influences were minimal. If climatic effects on these facies assemblages were also minimal, the isolated nature of the sandstone channels and the large proportion of fine-grained rocks to sandstone would indicate relatively rapid subsidence (Blakey and Gubitosa, 1984).

The alluvial sandstone architecture of the New Fork Tongue is notably different from that of the underlying LaBarge Member. The New Fork Tongue consists of multilateral sandstone bodies 10 to 20 m thick that are laterally continuous for more than 5 km without major changes in thickness. These sandstones appear to be coalesced meandering river deposits showing well-developed point bar assemblages with rooted zones at the top (Southwell and Shuster, 1985).

Alluvial sandstone architecture suggests that subsidence rates decreased during deposition of the New Fork Tongue. It is unlikely that provenance exerted significant control because of the distal nature of the deposit with its source in the Wind River Range. The drying climatic trend may have influenced the sandstone geometries to some degree (Southwell and Shuster, 1985), but we are unable to assess this effect.

Subsidence curves

Three subsidence curves for the northern Green River basin were produced using different stratigraphic sections (Figs. 5, 6, 7). Figure 5 shows the Jurassic–Cretaceous–early Tertiary subsidence history for the Pinedale anticline area. The upper Cretaceous–lower Tertiary stratigraphic data were assembled from the El Paso Natural Gas Company Wagon Wheel No. 1 well. The Rainbow Resources 1-34 Federal Pacific Creek borehole provided the data for the Jurassic and lower Cretaceous section. A subsidence history for the Hoback area, compiled from surface stratigraphy, is shown in Figure 6. The Late Cretaceous–Early Tertiary subsidence history for the LaBarge platform is shown in Figure 7. Data for the LaBarge area were taken from the No. 1 USA AMOCO A-E borehole (Sec. 7,T.27N.,R.111W.) (see Shuster, 1986, for data tables).

Examination of the subsidence curves shows that the greatest amount of net subsidence occurred in the Pinedale anticline area (3,000 m of isostatic subsidence). The Hoback area curves document a net total isostatic subsidence of about 2,900 m. Although the LaBarge results cannot be directly compared to the

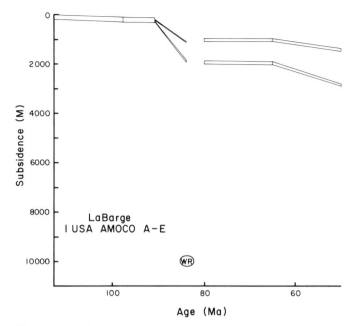

Figure 7. Subsidence curves for the LaBarge area. The sedimentary column was backstripped and corrected for compaction following the procedures outlined by Steckler and Watts (1978). See text for further explanation. Stratigraphic data are presented in Shuster (1986).

other curves because of the absence of Jurassic and Early Cretaceous data, the isostatically modeled subsidence for the Late Cretaceous–early Tertiary (~1,300 m) is significantly less than that of the other curves.

Discussion

The subsidence curves (Figs. 5, 6) show the timing of the initiation of the Sevier orogeny, as interpreted by Heller and others (1986), and the timing of the initial Wind River uplift. The interpretation by Heller and others of first Sevier thrusting coincides with the rapid subsidence event at 119 Ma. Apatite fission-track data suggest that Wind River uplift began between 80 and 90 Ma (Shuster, 1986) and may have increased the total subsidence in the Pinedale anticline area. The Maastrichtian subsidence in the Pinedale anticline area probably also reflects tectonic loading by the Wind River block, inasmuch as this event is not seen in curves from areas far away from this uplift. The Paleocene rapid subsidence event in the Hoback area (Fig. 6) may be due to contemporaneous tectonic loading by both Darby thrusting and the Gros Ventre uplift. Paleocene uplift of these areas is well-constrained by the sedimentological observations of Dorr and others (1977) and those presented earlier in this chapter.

Some of the results of facies analysis are consistent with these subsidence curves while others are inconclusive. The very rapid subsidence indicated by the facies patterns of the Hoback Formation is also identified by the backstripping procedure. Subsidence rates slowed during the Eocene, but both subsidence

curves from the Pinedale and Hoback areas and facies patterns in the LaBarge Member indicated that it was still relatively rapid. Facies patterns in the Eocene strata of the Hoback area could not be adequately interpreted because of the potential effects of provenance and climatic controls. Similarly, the apparent slow-down of subsidence rates during deposition of the New Fork Member cannot be adequately evaluated because the resolution of the subsidence curves (i.e., age control) is too coarse and because climatic effects are unknown.

FLEXURAL MODELING

Introduction

Several mechanisms and models have been proposed for basin development in oceanic or continental margin settings, but because the Laramide Green River basin evolved in an intermontane setting, mechanisms such as thermal contraction and crustal extension are not appropriate. Intuitively, an intermontane basin bounded by a thrust belt and a basement-involved thrust would be tectonically loaded, and for this reason a flexural model for the northern Green River Basin was tested.

Several workers have already proposed tectonically loaded flexural models for basin development. Jordan (1981) modeled the western interior foreland basin. Beaumont (1981) proposed a viscoelastic model for the Alberta foreland basin. Quinlan and Beaumont (1984) suggested that the Appalachian basin formed as a multistage foreland basin due to thrust loading. Lambeck (1983) suggested that the intracratonic basins of central Australia formed as a result of loading on a highly compressed lithosphere. Royden and Karner (1984) concluded that there were insufficient loads to form the Appenine and Carpathian basins. Schedl and Wiltschko (1984) examined the theoretical effects of loading and resultant flexure in foreland basin settings. Most recently, Hagen and others (1985) suggested that the Laramide intermontane basins of the Wyoming foreland province developed in response to loading. Taken as a whole, these studies reflect the importance of flexure in the development basins in compressive settings.

Although the uplift of the Wind River Range has been documented by apatite fission-track dating (Shuster, 1986), the paucity of age control and the lack of absolute age constraints on the timing of thrusting in the Sevier belt make time-dependent, step-wise modeling of the northern Green River basin difficult to constrain. Therefore, the models used in this study are designed to bypass time-dependency and look at the present-day state of the northern Green River basin in terms of lithospheric deflection and the maximum amount of sediment that could have accumulated in the flexural depression induced by tectonic loading.

Two methods were used to examine the role of flexure from extrabasinal loading in the evolution of the northern Green River basin. The first analyzes present-day geometry of the basin, while the second examines the stratigraphic thickness of lower Tertiary rocks that could have accumulated in the depression caused by loading.

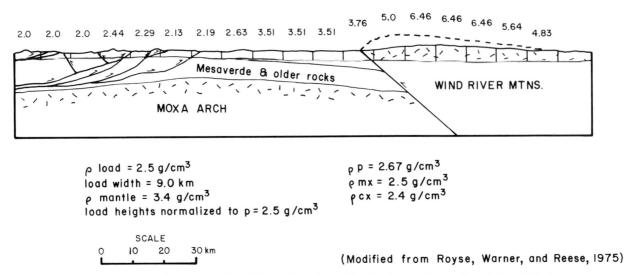

Figure 8. Generalized cross section of the northern Green River basin and adjacent thrust belt and Wind River uplift showing load profiles and densities used in the flexural model (modern basin geometry). No vertical exaggeration.

Modern basin geometry

Two-dimensional profiling was used to examine the present-day basin geometry in order to test for regional compensation and to constrain lithosphere rigidity. The profiling uses a BASIC computer program (Shuster, 1986) that models the lithosphere as an infinite elastic beam using flexural rigidities of 10^{21}, 10^{22}, and 10^{23} Nm. A generalized cross section from Royse and others (1975) was used as the basis for assembling the loads, with the top of the Mesaverde Formation as a datum line. The cross section was slightly altered utilizing a dip for the Wind River fault in accordance with the Zawislak and Smithson (1981) interpretation of COCORP seismic data across the southern Wind River Range. Upper crustal densities were approximated from the estimates of Smithson and others (1978). All load thicknesses were normalized for a load density of 2.5 g/cm^3 to ease computation. A mantle density of 3.4 g/cm^3 was used. The cross section with load profiles and densities is shown in Figure 8.

Sediment thickness profiling

Sediment thickness profiling is also a two-dimensional approach to modeling. However, this case tests whether the present sediment thickness (over a given time) is what would be expected from the extrabasinal loading and the intrabasinal load of the sediment. This technique is described in detail by Shuster (1986).

For the northern Green River basin, sediment thickness profiling was done for the early Tertiary under the premise that deposition of the lower Tertiary units (Fort Union–Wasatch and equivalents) was genetically related to loading by the Darby, Prospect, and Wind River faults. Maximum sediment thickness profiles were calculated for the Darby, Prospect, and Wind River

loads at flexural rigidities of 10^{21}, 10^{22}, and 10^{23} Nm. These profiles were then summed to give the predicted total sediment thickness profile. The maximum Darby and Prospect loads were assembled using the base of Paleocene and Eocene rocks, respectively, as data lines. The cross section of Royse and others (1975) provided geometric constraints for constructing these loads. Figures 9 and 10 show the load geometries of the Darby and Prospect thrusts respectively. The Darby load accommodates a remnant of the Absaroka thrust that was moved in piggy-back fashion on the Darby thrust. Palinspastic restoration of the Darby-Prospect system indicates that the toes of both faults (assuming instantaneous uplift and no erosion) would have had approximately the same eastward extent. This latter assumption is in in keeping with the model of Willemin (1984) for thrust toe movement and allows the fill for each thrust to be summed directly.

The Wind River thrust load was constructed from data of Royse and others (1975), Zawislak and Smithson (1981), and Smithson and others (1978). Flattening of the thrust near the surface and imbricate thrusts (Steidtmann and others, 1984) were not taken into account because their effects on loading were determined to be minimal. The load diagram for the Wind River thrust is shown in Figure 11.

Results

The results of modern-basin geometry profiling are shown in Figure 12. Predicted depth to top of Mesaverde Formation profiles for flexural rigidities of 10^{21}, 10^{22}, and 10^{23} Nm are plotted against the observed profile (Curry, 1973). The profiles for rigidity values of 10^{21} and 10^{22} Nm best fit the observed profile at basin margins; however, all of the curves underestimate the depth in the central portion of the basin. The maximum divergences for

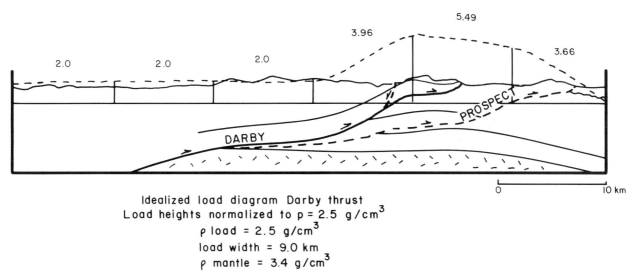

Figure 9. Load diagram for the Darby thrust as used in the sediment thickness profiling (see text). Reconstruction based on cross section X-X' (Royse and others, 1975). No vertical exaggeration.

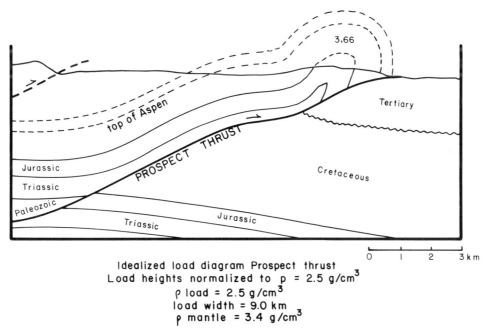

Figure 10. Load diagram for the Prospect thrust as used in the sediment thickness profiling (see text). Reconstruction based on cross section X-X' (Royse and others, 1975). No vertical exaggeration.

the three predicted profiles are 1,000 m (10^{21} Nm), 800 m (10^{22} Nm), and 1,300 m (10^{23} Nm), or in other words, the profiles explain 75, 80, and 67 percent of the observed depression, respectively. Because the 10^{22}-Nm profile is the closest approximation to the observed profile, both in divergence and shape, it is accepted as the best fitting curve.

The observed divergence may be related to: (1) intrabasinal perturbations, such as the Pinedale anticline; (2) viscoelastic rather than elastic lithospheric response; (3) other nearby loads, such as the Teton and Gros Ventre Ranges, which were neglected in the two-dimensional model; and (4) unidentified intra- or sub-crustal loads.

Figure 13 shows the total sediment thickness profiles modeled at flexural rigidities of 10^{21}, 10^{22}, and 10^{23} Nm compared to the observed depth to Mesaverde profile (the effective post-Mesaverde sediment thickness), and the Fort Union–Wasatch

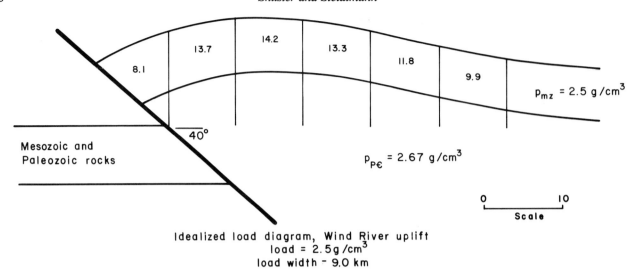

Figure 11. Load diagram for the Wind River thrust as used in the sediment thickness profiling (see text). Reconstruction based on data from Smithson and others (1978) and Zawislak and Smithson (1981). No vertical exaggeration.

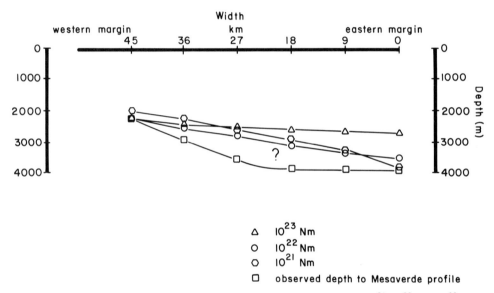

Figure 12. Results of modern basin geometry profiling for flexural rigidities of 10^{21}. 10^{22}, and 10^{23} Nm. See text for explanation.

isopach profiles. The 10^{21}-Nm profile is somewhat anomalous in that it shows significant thinning at the 18-km mark (Fig. 13). This feature can be explained by a significantly smaller half-wavelength for the flexural curves at 10^{21}-Nm rigidity and interference of the flexural curves produced by Wind River and Darby-Prospect loads.

The 10^{22} and 10^{23} profiles each overestimate and are subparallel to both the post-Mesaverde sediment thickness profile and the Fort Union–Wasatch isopach profiles, which, according to the rationale of sediment thickness profiling, suggests that the observed sedimentary thickness is consistent with the concept of subsidence by flexure. Although both curves diverge significantly from the observed thicknesses on the east and west margins, both predicted profiles are subparallel to those observed and reasonably fit the geometry of the sediment distribution. Furthermore, both curves predict a thicker accumulation near the Wind River front and less sediment toward the west as is observed.

Discussion

Some of the uncertainties in the modeling procedures have already been mentioned. Whether the lithosphere behaves elastically or viscoelastically is pertinent to our conclusions. Elastic behavior assumes that response of the lithosphere to a load is

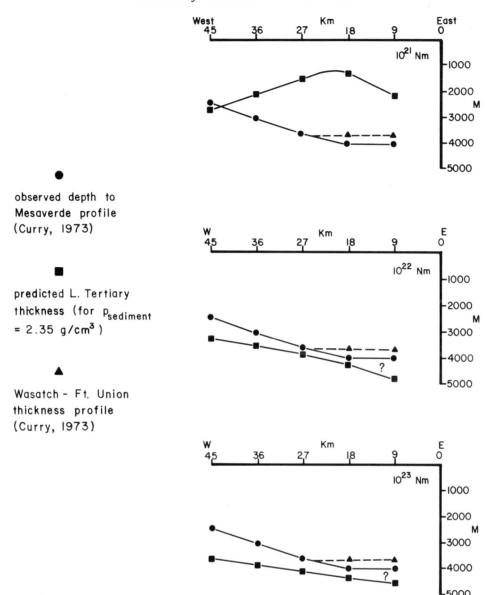

Figure 13. Results of sediment thickness profiling for flexural rigidities of 10^{21}, 10^{22}, and 10^{23} Nm. See text for explanation.

instantaneous. Viscoelastic behavior assumes that there is a viscous component to the lithosphere, which is manifested by relaxation under a load and which is time-dependent. This would result in continued subsidence after initial elastic flexure. More detailed discussions of lithosphere rheology are given by Walcott (1970), Beaumont (1978, 1981), and Karner and others (1983). In the case of the Green River basin, if the lithosphere was behaving viscoelastically, then the additional depression seen in the center of the observed present-day profile (Fig. 13) may be due to relaxation. The accuracy of mantle and upper crustal densities used is particularly critical to the validity of our modeling. Densities used are based on estimates from the literature, but even small changes—particularly in the mantle density—could significantly alter the predicted flexural response.

We also acknowledge that time-dependent sediment redistribution models yield less total flexural deflection than the model presented here. However, the results of these other models are dependent on rates and patterns of uplift, denudation, and deposition, as well as the paleo-uplift and basin topographies. In this study these variables are, at best, poorly known. Finally, in the method of sediment thickness profiling, we have assumed instantaneous uplift and adequate sediment supply without erosion of the tectonic loads. We fully realize that uplift was not instantaneous and that sediments were derived from the erosion of uplifting blocks. However, we have presented the results of this first approximation to show that flexure of the lithosphere due to tectonic and sedimentary loading was the major cause of subsidence in the northern Green River basin.

CONCLUSIONS

The results of our study of the sedimentary and tectonic evolution of the Green River basin suggest the following conclusions:

1. Provenance evidence indicates that during the Late Cretaceous, most sediment supplied to the Green River basin was from uplifts in the thrust belt to the northwest. By early Paleocene time, however, the Precambrian core of the Wind River Range was already shedding feldspathic sediments, indicating that uplift was initiated sometime earlier, when the Paleozoic and Mesozoic cover was stripped.

2. Analyses of alluvial sandstone architecture indicate that there was rapid subsidence in the Hoback area during the Campanian and Paleocene. Similar analyses in younger strata are inconclusive.

3. Subsidence analyses for the northern, western, and eastern parts of the basin indicate a rapid subsidence event, approximately 120 to 115 Ma, that was probably related to thrusting to the west. Another time of rapid subsidence occurred about 90 Ma and was probably related to initial uplift of the Wind River block.

4. Two-dimensional flexural modeling of the northern Green River basin indicates that basin geometry and the thickness of tectogenic sediments can be explained by sedimentary loading within the basin and tectonic loading of the basin margins by the thrust belt and Wind River block.

ACKNOWLEDGMENTS

This research was supported by the Arco Exploration Company, AMOCO Production Company, and Marathon Oil Company, and by National Science Foundation Grant EAR-8108938 (to J.R.S.).

REFERENCES CITED

Allen, J.R.L., 1974, Studies in fluviatile sedimentation: Implications of pedogenic carbonate units, Lower Old Red Sandstone, Anglo-Welsh outcrop: Geological Journal, v. 9, pt. 2, p. 181.
—— , 1978, Studies in fluviatile sedimentation; An exploratory quantitative model for the architecture of avulsion controlled alluvial suites: Sedimentary Geology, v. 21, p. 129–147.
Armstrong, F. C., and Oriel, S. S., 1965, Tectonic development of the Idaho-Wyoming thrust belt: American Association of Petroleum Geologists Bulletin, v. 49, p. 1847–1866.
Beaumont, C., 1978, The evolution of sedimentary basins on a viscoelastic lithosphere; Theory and examples: Geophysical Journal of the Royal Astronomical Society, v. 55, p. 471–497.
—— , 1981, Foreland basins: Geophysical Journal of the Royal Astronomical Society, v. 65, p. 291–329.
Berg, R. R., 1961, Laramide tectonics of the Wind River Mountains, *in* Symposium on Late Cretaceous rocks; Wyoming: Wyoming Geological Association 16th Annual Field Conference Guidebook, p. 70–80.
—— , 1962, Mountain flank thrusting in Rocky Mountain foreland, Wyoming and Colorado: American Association of Petroleum Geologists Bulletin, v. 46, p. 704–707.
—— , 1963, Laramide sediments along the Wind River thrust, Wyoming, *in* Childs, O. E., and Beebe, B. W., eds., Backbone of the Americas: American Association Petroleum Geologists Memoir 2, p. 2019–2032.
Blakey, G. C., and Gubitosa, R., 1984, Controls of sandstone body geometry and architecture in the Chinle Formation (Upper Triassic), Colorado Plateau: Sedimentary Geology, v. 38, p. 51–86.
Brewer, J. A., Smithson, S. B., Oliver, J. E., Kaufman, S., and Brown, L. D., 1980, The Laramide orogeny; Evidence from COCORP deep crustal seismic profiles in the Wind River Mountains, Wyoming: Tectonophysics, v. 62, p. 165–189.
Curry, W. H., III, 1973, Late Cretaceous and early Tertiary rocks, southwestern Wyoming: Wyoming Geological Association 25th Annual Field Conference Guidebook, p. 79–86.
Dixon, J. S., 1982, Regional structural synthesis, Wyoming salient of western overthrust belt: American Association of Petroleum Geologists Bulletin, v. 66, p. 1500–1531.
Dorr, J. A., Jr., Spearing, D. R., and Steidtmann, J. R., 1977, Deformation and deposition between a foreland uplift and an impinging thrust belt; Hoback Basin, Wyoming: Geological Society of America Special Paper 177, 82 p.
Folk, R. L., 1980, Petrology of sedimentary rocks: Austin, Texas, Hemphill, 182 p.
Graham, S. A., Tolson, R. B., DeCelles, P. G., and others, 1986, Provenance modeling as a technique for analyzing source terrane evolution and controls on foreland sedimentation, *in* Allen, P. A., and Homewood, P., eds., Foreland basins: International Association of Sedimentologists Special Publication No. 8, p. 425–436.
Gries, R., 1983, Oil and gas prospecting beneath the Precambrian of foreland thrust plates in the Rocky Mountains: American Association of Petroleum Geologists Bulletin, v. 67, p. 1–28.
Guennel, G. K., Spearing, D. R., and Dorr, J. A., Jr., 1973, Palynology of the Hoback Basin: Wyoming Geological Association 25th Annual Field Conference Guidebook, p. 173–185.
Hagen, E. S., Shuster, M. W., and Furlong, K. P., 1985, Tectonic loading and subsidence of intermontane basins; Wyoming foreland province: Geology, v. 13, p. 585–588.
Heller, P. L., Bowdler, S. S., Chambers, H. P., Coogan, J. C., Hagen, E. S., Shuster, M. W., and Winslow, N. S., 1986, Timing of initiation of the Sevier orogeny, Idaho-Wyoming and Utah thrust belts: Geology, v. 14, p. 388–391.
Jackson, R. G., II, 1976, Depositional model of point-bars in the lower Wabash River: Journal of Sedimentary Petrology, v. 46, p. 579–594.
—— , 1978, Preliminary evaluation of lithofacies models for meandering alluvial streams, *in* Miall, A. D., ed.: Fluvial sedimentology, Canadian Society Petroleum Geology Memoir 5, p. 413–430.
Jordan, T. E., 1981, Thrust loads and foreland basin evolution, Cretaceous, western United States: American Association of Petroleum Geologists Bulletin, v. 65, p. 2506–2520.
Karner, G. N., Steckler, M. S., and Thorne, J. A., 1983, Long-term thermomechanical properties of the continental lithosphere: Nature, v. 304, p. 250–253.
Keighin, C. W., 1984, Petrography and selected reservoir characteristics of some Tertiary and Cretaceous sandstones, Pinedale anticline, Sublette County, Wyoming, *in* Law, B. E., ed., Geological characteristics of low-permeability Upper Cretaceous and Lower Tertiary rocks in the Pinedale anticline area, Sublette County, Wyoming: U.S. Geological Survey Open-File Report 84–753, p. 16–22.
Lambeck, K., 1983, Structure and evolution of the intercratonic basins of central Australia: Geophysical Journal of the Royal Astronomical Society, v. 74, p. 843–886.
Lamerson, P. R., 1983, The Fossil basin and its relationship to the Absaroka thrust system, Wyoming and Utah, *in* Powers, R. B., ed., Geologic studies of the Cordilleran thrust belt, 1982: Denver, Colorado, Rocky Mountain Association Geologists, p. 279–340.

Law, B. E., 1981, Section C-C' subsurface correlations of some upper Cretaceous and Tertiary rocks, northern Green River Basin, Wyoming: U.S. Geological Survey Open-File Report 81-663, 1 sheet.
—— , 1984, Structure and stratigraphy of the Pinedale anticline, Wyoming, *in* Law, B. E., ed., Geological characteristics of low-permeability Upper Cretaceous and Lower Tertiary rocks in the Pinedale anticline area, Sublette County, Wyoming: U.S. Geological Survey Open-File Report 84-753, p. 6–16.
Law, B. E., and Nichols, D. J., 1982, Subsurface stratigraphic correlations of some Upper Cretaceous and Lower Tertiary rocks, northern Green River Basin, Wyoming [abs.], *in* Subsurface practices in geology and geophysics: University of Wyoming, Department of Geology and Geophysics, p. 17.
Love, J. D., and Christiansen, A. C., 1985, Geologic map of Wyoming: Wyoming Geological Survey, scale 1:500,000.
Love, J. D., McGrew, P. O., and Thomas, H. D., 1963, Relationship of latest Cretaceous and Tertiary deposition of deformation to oil and gas in Wyoming, *in* Childs, O. E., and Beebe, B. W., eds., Backbone of the Americas: American Association of Petroleum Geologists Memoir 2, p. 196–208.
MacGinitie, H. D., 1969, The Eocene Green River flora of northwestern Colorado and northeastern Utah: University of California Publications in Geological Sciences, v. 83, 140 p.
Miall, A. D., 1978, Lithofacies and vertical profile models in braided river deposits; A summary, *in* Miall, A. D., ed., Fluvial sedimentology: Canadian Society Petroleum Geologists Memoir 5, 597–604.
Naeser, N., 1984, Fission-track ages from the Wagon Wheel #1 well, northern Green River Basin, Wyoming; Evidence from recent cooling, *in* Law, B. E., ed., Geological characteristics of low-permeability Upper Cretaceous and Lower Tertiary rocks in the Pinedale anticline area, Sublette County, Wyoming: U.S. Geological Survey Open-File Report 84-753, p. 66–78.
Oriel, S. S., 1962, Main body of Wasatch Formation near LaBarge, Wyoming: American Association of Petroleum Geologists Bulletin, v. 46, p. 2161–2614.
—— , 1969, Geology of the Fort Hill Quadrangle, Lincoln County, Wyoming: U.S. Geological Survey Professional Paper 594-M, 40 p.
Palmer, A. R., 1983, The decade of North American Geology 1983 geologic time scale: Geology, v. 11, p. 503–504.
Pollastro, R. M., and Barker, C. E., 1984, Geothermometry from clay minerals, vitrinite reflectance, and fluid inclusions; Applications to the thermal and burial history of rocks cored from the Wagon Wheel #1 well, Green River Basin, Wyoming, *in* Law, B. E., ed., Geological characteristics of low-permeability Upper Cretaceous and Lower Tertiary rocks in the Pinedale anticline area, Sublette County, Wyoming: U.S. Geological Survey Open-File Report 84-753, p. 78–95.
Prensky, S. E., 1984, A gamma-ray anomaly associated with the Cretaceous-Tertiary boundary in the northern Green River Basin, Wyoming, *in* Law, B. E., ed., Geological characteristics of low-permeability Upper Cretaceous and Lower Tertiary rocks in the Pinedale anticline area, Sublette County, Wyoming: U.S. Geological Survey Open-File Report 84-753, p. 22–36.
Pryor, W. A., 1961, Petrology of Mesaverde sandstones in Wyoming: Wyoming Geological Association 16th Annual Field Conference Guidebook, p. 34–36.
Quinlan, G. M., and Beaumont, C., 1984, Appalachian thrusting, lithospheric flexure, and the Paleozoic stratigraphy of the eastern interior of North America: Canadian Journal of Earth Sciences, v. 21, p. 973–996.
Rieke, H. H., III, and Chilingarian, G. V., 1974, Compaction of argillaceous sediments: Developments in Sedimentology, v. 16, 424 p.
Royden, L., and Karner, G. D., 1984, Flexure of the continental lithosphere beneath Apennine and Carpathian foredeep basins: Nature, v. 309, p. 142–144.
Royse, F., Jr., Warner, M. A., and Reese, D. L., 1975, Thrust belt structural geometry and related stratigraphic problems, Wyoming-Idaho-northern Utah, *in* Bolyard, D. W., eds., Deep Drilling frontiers of the central Rocky Mountains: Denver, Colorado, Rocky Mountain Association of Geologists Symposium, p. 41–54.

Sales, J. K., 1968, Crustal mechanics of Cordilleran foreland deformation; A regional and scale model approach: American Association of Petroleum Geologists Bulletin, v. 52, p. 2016–2044.
Schedl, A., and Wiltschko, D. V., 1984, Sedimentological effects of a moving terrain: Journal of Geology, v. 92, p. 273–287.
Sclater, J. G., and Christie, P.A.F., 1980, Continental stretching; An explanation of the post-mid-Cretaceous subsidence of the central North Sea Basin: Journal Geophysical Research, v. 85, p. 3711–3739.
Shuster, M. W., 1986, The origin and sedimentary evolution of the northern Green River basin, western Wyoming [Ph.D. thesis]: Laramie, University of Wyoming, 323 p.
Shuster, M. W., and Steidtmann, J. R., 1983, The origin and development of the northern Green River Basin; A stratigraphic and flexural study [abs.]: American Association of Petroleum Geologists Bulletin, v. 67, p. 1356.
—— , 1987, Fluvial-sandstone architecture and thrust-induced subsidence, northern Green River Basin, Wyoming, *in* Ethridge, F. G., Flores, R. M., and Harvey, M. D., eds., Recent developments in fluvial sedimentology: Society of Economic Paleontologists and Mineralogists Special Publication No. 39, p. 279–286.
Smithson, S. B., Brewer, J., Kaufman, S., Oliver, J., and Hurich, C., 1978, Nature of the Wind River thrust, Wyoming, from COCORP deep-reflection data and from gravity data: Geology, v. 6, p. 648–652.
Southwell, E. S., and Shuster, M. W., 1985, Nonmarine biogenic structures in fluvial facies of the Lower Tertiary Greater Green River Basin, Wyoming: Society of Economic Paleontologists and Mineralogists Annual Midyear Meeting Abstracts, v. 2, p. 85.
Spearing, D. R., 1969, Stratigraphy, sedimentation, and tectonic history of the Paleocene-Eocene Hoback Formation of western Wyoming [Ph.D. thesis]: Ann Arbor, University of Michigan, 179 p.
Steckler, M. S., and Watts, A. B., 1978, Subsidence of the Atlantic-type continental margin off New York: Earth and Planetary Science Letters, v. 41, p. 1–13.
Steidtmann, J. R., 1968, Sedimentation, stratigraphy, and tectonic history of the Early Eocene Pass Peak Formation, central-western Wyoming [Ph.D. thesis]: Ann Arbor, University of Michigan, 145 p.
Steidtmann, J. R., McGee, L. C., and Middleton, L. T., 1983, Laramide sedimentation, folding, and faulting in the southern Wind River Range, Wyoming, *in* Lowell, J. D., and Gries, R., eds., Rocky Mountain foreland basins and uplifts: Denver, Colorado, Rocky Mountain Association Geologists, p. 161–168.
Steidtmann, J. R., Hurst, D. J., and Shuster, M. W., 1984, Structural evolution of part of the Wyoming thrust belt and foreland: A sedimentary tectonic approach: Geological Society of America Abstracts with Programs, v. 16, p. 667.
Sullivan, R., 1980, A stratigraphic evolution of the Eocene rocks of southwestern Wyoming: Geological Survey of Wyoming Report of Investigations no. 20, 50 p.
Walcott, R. I., 1970, Flexural rigidity, thickness, and viscosity of the lithosphere: Journal of Geophysical Research, v. 75, p. 3942–3951.
West, R. M., 1969, Geology and vertebrate paleontology of the north-eastern Green River Basin, Wyoming: Wyoming Geological Association 21st Annual Field Conference Guidebook, p. 77–93.
Willemin, J. H., 1984, Erosion and the mechanics of shallow foreland thrusts: Journal of Structural Geology, v. 6, p. 425–432.
Wiltschko, D. V., and Dorr, J. A., Jr., 1983, Timing of deformation in overthrust belt and foreland of Idaho, Wyoming, and Utah: American Association of Petroleum Geologists Bulletin, v. 67, p. 1304–1322.
Zawislak, R. L., and Smithson, S. B., 1981, Problems and interpretation of COCORP deep seismic reflection data, Wind River Range, Wyoming: Geophysics, v. 46, p. 1684–1701.

MANUSCRIPT ACCEPTED BY THE SOCIETY FEBRUARY 9, 1988

Printed in U.S.A.

Geological Society of America
Memoir 171
1988

Depositional response of Pigeon Creek Formation, Utah, to initial fold-thrust belt deformation in a differentially subsiding foreland basin

Peter Schwans
Department of Geology and Mineralogy, 107 Mendenhall Laboratory, The Ohio State University, 125 S. Oval Mall, Columbus, Ohio 43210-1398

ABSTRACT

Unconformity-bounded depositional sequences represent primary units of chrono-stratigraphic significance. Two regional unconformities are recognized and employed to stratigraphically subdivide an alluvial foreland basin fill sequence, documenting earliest Cordilleran foreland basin subsidence and sedimentation in Utah. First, stratigraphic nomenclature of syntectonic Lower Cretaceous strata is redefined on a sequence-stratigraphic basis using new paleontologic, sedimentologic, and lithostratigraphic data. A new stratotype and name, Pigeon Creek Formation, is introduced for rocks that had previously been assigned to the Lower Cretaceous Morrison(?) Formation and Indian-ola Group Undifferentiated of central Utah. Two members are recognized. Rocks of the lower Pigeon Creek member were deposited east of the thrust front during Neocomian to mid-Aptian time in an ephemeral braided stream system featuring a muddy flood basin with interspersed lacustrine depressions. Later, conglomerates and intercalated mudstones of the upper Pigeon Creek member were deposited in eastward-shedding, sheet flood–dominated fan systems during late Aptian to late Albian time. Together, the braided stream and overbank clastics of the Pigeon Creek Formation document initial thrust uplift and sedimentation in a laterally restricted foreland basin that is only subsiding near the thrust load.

Second, the Pigeon Creek Formation, together with correlative strata in eastern Utah and western Colorado, is placed into a regional sequence-stratigraphic framework. By defining the bounding unconformities, the extent of the hiatuses, and the age range of the sequence strata, the formation is shown to form a depositional sequence of regional extent bounded by globally recognized unconformities. Contrary to the work of others, this study interprets initial thrusting and basin subsidence to have occurred as early as late Neocomian time and to be evidenced by the substantive basinal preservation of the fines of the lower Pigeon Creek member adjacent to the thrust front. Initial uplift occurred above subsurface thrust ramps, resulting in source terranes dominated by fine-grained lower Mesozoic strata. Conversely, conglomerates of the upper Pigeon Creek member are postorogenic in nature and merely indicate hanging-wall emergence during the late Aptian and Albian. Clast distributions define an unroofing sequence following the erosive breaching of an emergent thrust terrane. Sedimentation in coeval, yet separate, depositional systems in central Utah, however, remained uninfluenced by initial basin subsidence. Larger scale foreland basin subsidence in Utah did not occur prior to late Albian time. Finally, three phases of tectonic deformation and differential Cordilleran foreland basin subsidence are identified on the basis of the sequence-stratigraphic analysis of alluvial foreland basin strata in Utah.

531

INTRODUCTION AND PURPOSE

The Late Jurassic to Early Cretaceous western margin of North America was dominated by subduction of oceanic lithosphere beneath the continent. Coeval to continental margin deformation, eastward-directed thrusting, and folding during the Early Cretaceous resulted in the formation of the Sevier overthrust belt (Royse and others, 1975; Burchfiel, 1980; Allmendinger and others, 1983; Wiltschko and Dorr, 1983) (Fig. 1). Initial foreland basin deformation to the impingent fold-thrust belt was marked in Montana and Wyoming (Armstrong, 1968; Jordan, 1981), for example, by a tectonic partitioning of the foreland basin by intraforeland structural elements and paleotopographic highs (Schwartz, 1983; Christopher, 1984; DeCelles, 1986). Little is known, however, about the character of initial uplift in the Utah segment of the Sevier belt and such factors as the type of sedimentation response in the incipient foreland basin, the time-dependent rate of change in the capability of the incipient foreland basin to store sediment, and the character of the earliest syntectonic clastic wedges.

Tectonics and sedimentation have been linked in the Montana–Idaho–Wyoming–northeastern Utah segment of the Sevier belt for the Late Cretaceous and Tertiary thrust systems and related synorogenic deposits (Royse and others, 1975; Allmendinger and Jordan, 1981; DeCelles, 1986). In Utah, eastward-directed thrust movement emplaced Precambrian, upper Paleozoic, and lower Mesozoic strata, in an imbricate fashion, over strata as young as Jurassic Navajo Sandstone (Christiansen, 1952; Hickcox, 1971; Burchfiel and Hickcox, 1972; Villien and Kligfield, 1986). Timing of earliest tectonism in central Utah, however, remains controversial with respect to onset and style of foreland basin deformation, and the identification and character of the synorogenic deposits.

Spieker (1946), Armstrong and Oriel (1965), and Armstrong (1968) suggested that deformation began during Early Cretaceous or possibly Late Jurassic. Burchfiel and Hickcox (1972) considered Lower Cretaceous strata to be the first clear synorogenic sediments. Fouch and others (1983) related the Cenomanian to Turonian Sanpete Formation of the Indianola Group to an early episode of thrust-fault activity in central Utah, whereas Lawton (1985), as well as Villien and Kligfield (1986), identified thrusting to have been continuous from Albian until late Campanian. Most recently, Heller and others (1986) suggested, based on subsidence analyses of sedimentary sequences, that initiation of thrust movement was recorded by basal Indianola Group conglomerates and was no older than Albian.

This chapter reevaluates the lithostratigraphic and sedimentologic characteristics of Lower Cretaceous clastic rocks in central Utah, and identifies and characterizes earliest foreland basin deposition in response to thrust initiation in the Utah segment of the Sevier belt. Lower Cretaceous strata, including rocks informally assigned by Spieker (1946, p. 125) to the Lower Cretaceous Morrison(?) Formation, are redefined by introducing a new stratotype and name, Pigeon Creek Formation. Pigeon Creek deposi-

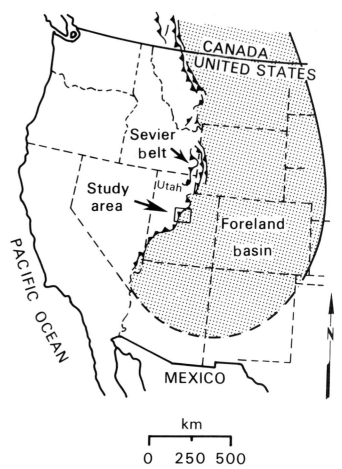

Figure 1. Map showing the Sevier fold-thrust belt and Late Cretaceous foreland basin area. Inset rectangle shows area covered by location map in Figure 2. Based on McGookey (1972).

tional architecture is analyzed, and the character of incipient Sevier belt deformation in central Utah is documented. Finally, the chapter introduces a tectonostratigraphic framework for Lower Cretaceous strata in central Utah in order to provide an understanding of fold-thrust belt and foreland basin interaction.

LOWER CRETACEOUS STRATIGRAPHY: PIGEON CREEK FORMATION

Problem and history

Age assignments for Lower Cretaceous rocks in central Utah have been ambiguous since Spieker (1946, 1949) first described the area (Fig. 2). A sequence of variegated shales, sandstones, conglomerates, and minor fresh-water limestones in the Wasatch Plateau, the Sanpete Valley area, and as far north as Thistle, was designated by Spieker (1946) as Morrison(?) Formation (Figs. 2, 3). Spieker (1946, p. 125) stated in his definition that ". . . above the marine Jurassic and beneath the marine Colorado in the Salina Canyon section and in the section east of Thistle, there is a succession of variegated shales, sandstones, and conglomerates [that is] here designated Morrison(?) formation." The name was introduced by Spieker (1946) based on stratigraphic position and lithologic similarities of the rocks with the Upper Jurassic Morrison Formation of Colorado.

According to Spieker (1946), the Morrison(?) Formation in the Salina district rests on Upper Jurassic Twist Gulch Formation of marine origin (Figs. 2, 3). Concerning the nature of the Morrison(?)/Arapien shale contact in Salina Canyon, Spieker (1946, p. 125) stated ". . .[it] is by no means clear-cut, but rather suggests intertonguing; above the first few feet of yellow sandstone, ochre shale, and conglomerate are thin-bedded red and gray shales just like those of the Arapien." Morrison(?) clastic rocks are overlain by rocks of the Upper Cretaceous Indianola Group (Spieker, 1946) (Fig. 3). Elaborating on the nature of the contact, Spieker (1946, p. 125) concluded that in ". . . the Salina Canyon section not only is the basal boundary of the Morrison(?) indefinite, but its upper limit is likewise difficult to determine." The Morrison(?)/Sanpete Formation contact in Salina Canyon was drawn by Spieker (1946, p. 125) at the ". . . line of greatest apparent change between colored rocks of Morrison aspect and the dominantly buff and gray rocks of the type common in the regional Upper Cretaceous." Spieker concluded, "but there is no clear-cut line of division." For the western Wasatch Plateau and areas to the west, Spieker (1946, p. 125) stated that ". . . no strata have ever been assigned to the Morrison formation, but it is possible that some of the conglomerates and red beds included in the Indianola Group (undifferentiated) are the same as the unit here designated Morrison(?)" (Fig. 3).

This inability to separate the Lower Cretaceous Morrison(?) Formation from the Upper Cretaceous Indianola Group has resulted in repeated misinterpretations of these strata and has greatly hindered correlation of Lower Cretaceous rocks in central Utah. In the western part of the Gunnison Plateau, for example, Spieker (1949, p. 105) identified red beds below the ". . . typical red conglomerate of Indianola" and he concluded that these beds ". . . may belong in Morrison(?) formation." Hunt (1950), however, mapped the same red beds as Jurassic Twist Gulch. Hardy and Zeller (1953) mapped similar red conglomerates and shales to the south in Little Salt Creek (Fig. 2) as Indianola Group (undifferentiated), noting, however, that ". . . the lower portions of the conglomerate may be Lower Cretaceous, or perhaps Upper Jurassic" (Hardy and Zeller, 1953, p. 1277). Stokes (1972) examined Morrison(?) outcrops in the type area and concluded that the rocks belonged mostly, if not entirely, in the Early Cretaceous.

More recently, Standlee (1983) suggested that all strata previously mapped as Morrison(?) in the Salina-Gunnison Plateau districts be assigned to the Lower Cretaceous Cedar Mountain Formation of east-central Utah. Lawton (1985), however, designated all Morrison(?) strata equivalent to the Jurassic Morrison Formation and included the upper parts of Standlee's Morrison(?) strata in the Upper Cretaceous Sanpete Formation of the lower Indianola Group. Witkind and others (1986) assigned an Early Cretaceous age to the Morrison(?) strata. Witkind and

Maley *in* Witkind and others (1986) correlated lower Morrison(?) strata with the Cedar Mountain Formation and tentatively assigned upper Morrison(?) conglomerates to Spieker's (1946) Indianola Group (undifferentiated) (Fig. 3). Standlee (*in* Witkind and others [1986]), however, assigned all Morrison(?) strata to the Cedar Mountain Formation (Fig. 3). In a recent correlation of these rocks, Weiss and Roche (1987, this volume) use the name Cedar Mountain for the beds formerly identified as part of the lower Morrison(?) and extended the base of the Upper Cretaceous Indianola Group to incorporate strata formerly recognized

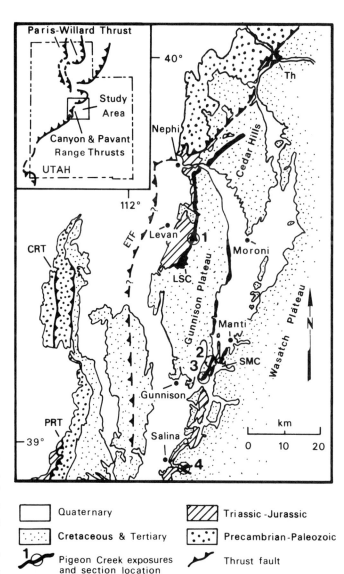

Figure 2. Generalized geologic map of western margin of foreland basin in study area in central Utah. Teeth on thrust faults are on upper plates. Pigeon Creek section locations: 1, Pigeon Creek Canyon, the type locality; 2 and 3, southeastern Gunnison Plateau; 4, Salina Canyon; CRT = Canyon Range thrust; ETF = Eastern thrust fault limit and surface trace of lower Pavant plate (after Villien and Kligfield, 1986); LSC = Little Salt Creek; PRT = Pavant Range thrust; SMC = Six Mile Canyon; Th = Thistle.

as part of the upper Morrison(?). Despite these varied attempts to correlate Lower Cretaceous strata of central Utah, the problem still remains whether Spieker's Morrison(?) beds above the Jurassic Twist Gulch Formation correlate with the Upper Jurassic Morrison (Lawton, 1985), the Lower Cretaceous Cedar Mountain (Standlee, 1982), undifferentiated Indianola Group (Witkind and others, 1986), and/or the even younger part of the Indianola Group (Weiss and Roche, this volume).

Definition and description

Name and stratotype. Detailed stratigraphic analyses of Spieker's Morrison(?) strata, and of conglomerates of the undifferentiated Indianola Group in the Salina-Gunnison Plateau district by Stuecheli (1984), Stuecheli and Collinson (1984), and Schwans (1985, 1986), combined with the interpretation of new palynomorph data and other age data, have allowed critical reevaluation of Lower Cretaceous rocks in central Utah. A new name, Pigeon Creek Formation, is introduced herewith to replace Spieker's Morrison(?) Formation (Fig. 3). Rocks similar to the Morrison(?) that were erroneously placed by Spieker and his students (Schoff, 1951; Hardy and Zeller, 1953) into the undifferentiated Indianola Group and/or the Twist Gulch Formation (Hunt, 1950), are also included in the Pigeon Creek Formation. This revision of the stratigraphic nomenclature of Lower Cretaceous rocks in central Utah intends to resolve the problem of poorly defined Lower Cretaceous stratotypes, as well as refrain from unwarranted expansion of stratigraphic units. The name Morrison(?) is abandoned, and the new unit, Pigeon Creek Formation, which incorporates Spieker's Morrison(?) strata and his ". . . typical red conglomerate of Indianola [character]" (Spieker, 1949, p. 105), is established (Fig. 3).

The Pigeon Creek Formation is named after Pigeon Creek Canyon (Levan 7½-minute Quadrangle, Sec.25,T.14S.,R.1E.) (Fig. 2, section location 1) where it forms a 975-m-thick, moderately eastward-dipping sequence of red mudstones, minor limestones, pebbly sandstones, and abundant conglomerates (Fig. 4). Two lithologically distinct members are recognized at the type locality: a lower member that is 185 m thick and consists predominantly of red mudstones, intercalated pebbly channel-form and sheet sandstones, sheet conglomerates, and minor fresh-water limestones; and an upper member that is 790 m thick and comprises a succession of sheet conglomerates and thin beds of intercalated red mudstones (Figs. 4, 5). The Pigeon Creek rocks in measured sections in the southeastern part of the Gunnison Plateau (Figs. 6, 7) and in the Salina area (Fig. 8), however, are much thinner, with thicknesses of the lower and upper members ranging from 100 to 200 m, and from 150 to 250 m, respectively.

The upper member of the Pigeon Creek Formation is, at its type locality and along the west side of the Gunnison Plateau, a prominent cliff-former (Fig. 4). At the type section, the upper member comprises parts of Spieker's undifferentiated Indianola Group (Spieker, 1946, p. 129), or what Spieker (1949, p. 105) called ". . . typical red conglomerate of Indianola [character]," as well as Hunt's (1950, p. 195–199) units 125 through 174. Similar units to the south, in Little Salt Creek, were mapped by Hardy and Zeller (1953) as Indianola Group (undifferentiated). The lower member is exposed at the type locality in slopes below the cliff-forming upper member (Fig. 4). The lower member consists partly of what Hunt (1950, p. 199–202) identified as upper Twist Gulch, or his units 85 through 125. Spieker (1949) referred to these units only informally in his road log and stated that the ". . . beds [below the typical red conglomerate of Indianola] may belong in [the] Morrison(?) formation" (Spieker, 1949, p. 105).

The contact between the upper and lower member of the Pigeon Creek Formation at the type locality is above the massive mudstone featuring a succession of a few thin, ledge-forming sheet conglomerate beds, and below the thick, cliff-forming conglomerate sequence with few thin mudstone interbeds (Figs. 4, 5). The contact between the upper and lower member is easily

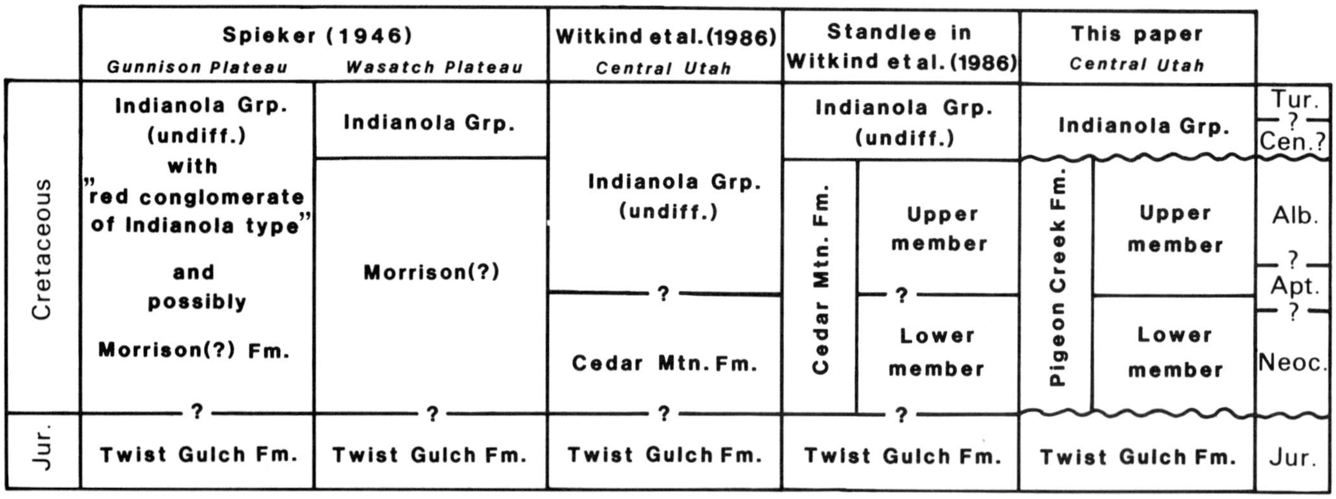

		Spieker (1946)		Witkind et al.(1986)	Standlee in Witkind et al. (1986)		This paper	
		Gunnison Plateau	*Wasatch Plateau*	*Central Utah*			*Central Utah*	
Cretaceous		Indianola Grp. (undiff.) with "red conglomerate of Indianola type" and possibly Morrison(?) Fm.	Indianola Grp.	Indianola Grp. (undiff.)	Indianola Grp. (undiff.)		Indianola Grp.	Tur. ? Cen.?
			Morrison(?)		Cedar Mtn. Fm.	Upper member	Pigeon Creek Fm. Upper member	Alb. ? Apt.
				———?		———?		———?
				Cedar Mtn. Fm.		Lower member	Lower member	Neoc.
		———?	———?	———?	———?			
Jur.		Twist Gulch Fm.	Twist Gulch Fm.	Twist Gulch Fm.	Twist Gulch Fm.		Twist Gulch Fm.	Jur.

Figure 3. Stratigraphic chart for central Utah showing previous correlations of Lower Cretaceous rocks by various authors and the revised stratigraphic correlation for Lower Cretaceous strata in west-central Utah as proposed by this study.

Figure 4. Type locality of Pigeon Creek Formation in Pigeon Creek Canyon, 6 km east of the town of Levan (section location 1 in Fig. 2). Lower member crops out in foreground below white line and upper member forms cliff faces in background above white line. View is to the east.

identified in all the sections measured in the study area (Figs. 6, and 7).

Composition, provenance. Conglomerates of the Pigeon Creek Formation are dominated to varying degrees by carbonate clasts and quartzite clasts (Fig. 5). Significant amounts of angular chert pebbles occur only in the lower member and in the lower part of the upper member (Figs. 5, 9). Chert pebbles are brown-green to light brown and were most likely derived from upper Paleozoic carbonates to the west that were of Permian age. Conodonts from various types of carbonate clasts identified by J. Geitgey (personal communication, 1987) indicate that late Paleozoic age (Devonian and Mississippian) carbonate clasts occur predominantly in the lower part of the upper member, whereas carbonate clasts of early Paleozoic age (Ordovician) are found throughout the formation (Fig. 5). The distribution of carbonate clasts is that of an inverse stratigraphy. Quartzite clasts reflect the entire range of Precambrian and Cambrian quartzites, such as the red to purple quartzite and conglomerate of Protero-zoic age, the pink to light gray Tintic Quartzite of Cambrian age, and the olive green quartzites belonging to the Cambrian Ophir Formation. The quartzite clasts, however, occur in varying amounts throughout the section (Figs. 5, 9).

Sandstones of the Pigeon Creek Formation were determined by Stuecheli (1984) to be composed of reworked sedimentary detritus, such as reworked overgrown quartz, abundant carbonate lithic detritus, minor feldspar and chert, and a few stable to ultrastable heavy minerals including tourmaline, zircon, and sphene. The mudstones that dominate the lower member are mostly of smectitic clay (Stuecheli, 1984).

Eastward-directed thrust movement in Utah along the Pa-vant thrusts emplaced Precambrian/Cambrian quartzites and Paleozoic carbonates over strata as young as the Jurassic Navajo Sandstone (Hickcox, 1971; Villien and Kligfield, 1986). The compositional character of Pigeon Creek rocks suggests deriva-tion of the clastics from a tectonically controlled western source during the Early Cretaceous. The presence of a large amount of fines in the lower member reflects a source dominated by Meso-zoic fine-grained siliciclastics, as well as chert-bearing upper Paleozoic carbonates (Fig. 9). The significant amounts of smectitic clay in the mudstones of the lower member also suggest influx of airborne ash from a volcanic source during mudstone deposition. Upper member conglomerate distribution reflects the partial and successive unroofing of an emergent thrust terrane domi-nated by lower Paleozoic carbonates and Precambrian/Cambrian quartzites.

Geographic distribution, dimensions. The Pigeon Creek strata crop out as far north as Thistle and as far south as Salina. Pigeon Creek rocks crop out continuously along the west side of the Gunnison Plateau as far south as Little Salt Creek. On the east side of the plateau, however, they occur only in a few isolated outcrops (Fig. 2). Measured stratigraphic thicknesses range from 150 m in Salina Canyon (Fig. 8) to a maximum of 975 m at the type locality in Pigeon Creek Canyon (Fig. 5). At Thistle, Spieker (1946) reported approximately 600 m of Morrison(?) mudstone, which is identified in this study as the lower member of the Pigeon Creek Formation. Jefferson (1982) measured 400 m of red Morrison(?) strata in the Cedar Hills area, which are shown here as Pigeon Creek strata (Fig. 2).

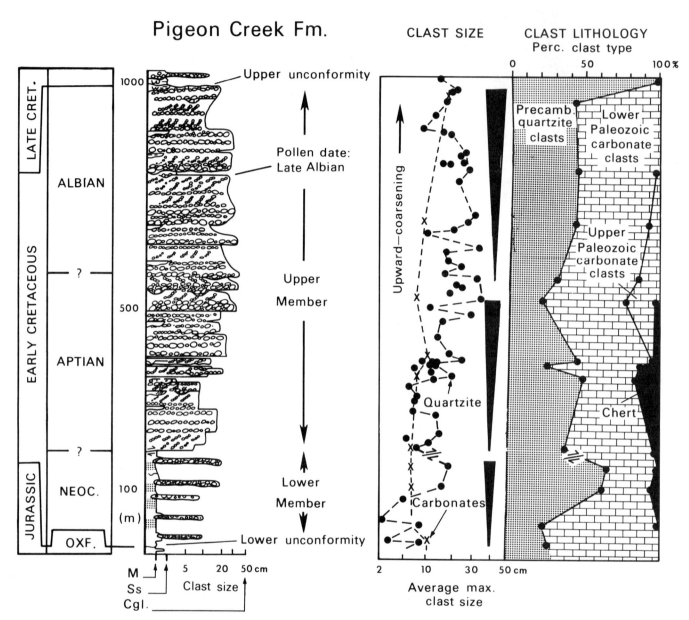

Figure 5. Measured Pigeon Creek stratotype in Pigeon Creek Canyon (Sec.25,T.14S.,R.1E.) (section location 1 in Fig. 2). Pigeon Creek Formation rests disconformably on Jurassic Twist Gulch and is disconformably overlain by strata of the Upper Cretaceous Indianola Group Undifferentiated. Measured section shows subdivision of formation and internal organization of type section. Note the upward-coarsening trend in the average maximum clast sizes, and the reverse stratigraphic order of the clast lithologies. Line connecting crosses (carbonate clast sizes) and full circles (quartzite clast sizes) shows clast size trend.

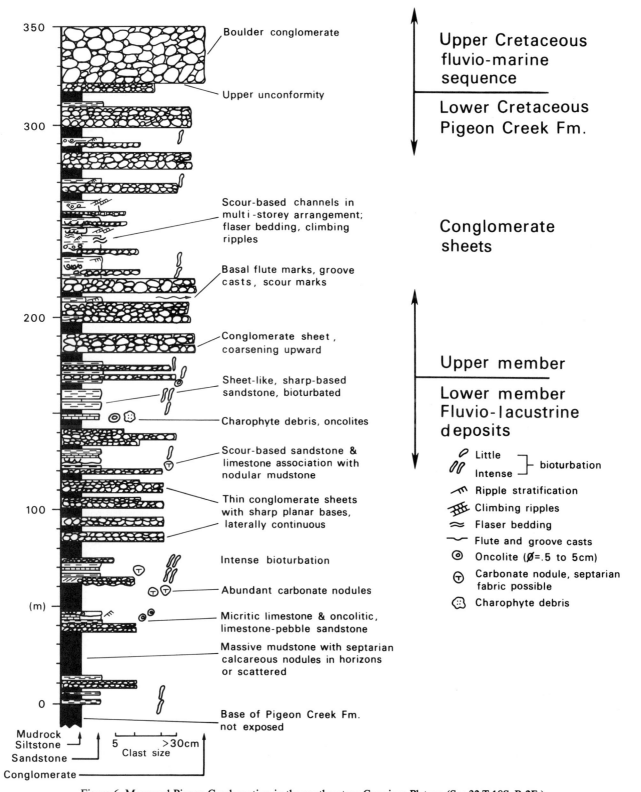

Figure 6. Measured Pigeon Creek section in the southeastern Gunnison Plateau (Sec.32,T.18S.,R.2E.) (section location 2 in Fig. 2), 10 km south of Manti. Section shows the fluvio-lacustrine deposits of the lower member and the sheet conglomerates of the upper member. Note the up-section coarsening and thickening trend of individual conglomerate sheets, as well as the clusters of channel-form sandstones. Boulder conglomerate at top is assigned to Upper Cretaceous Indianola Group and overlies Pigeon Creek strata disconformably.

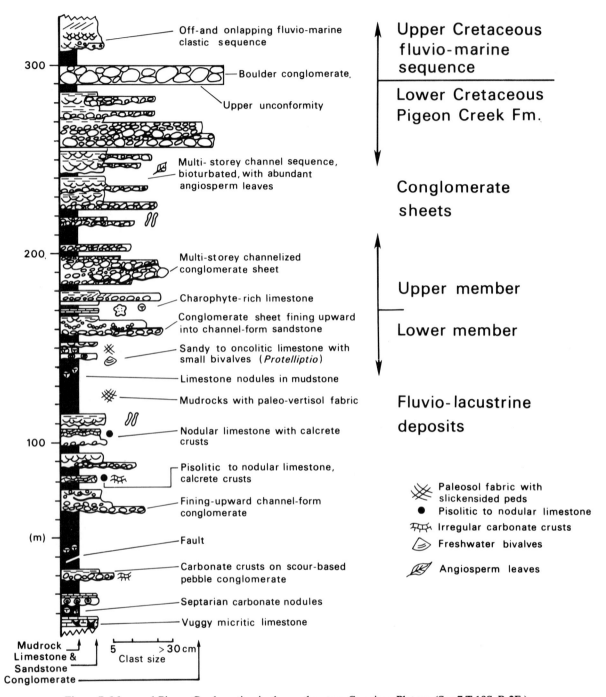

Figure 7. Measured Pigeon Creek section in the southeastern Gunnison Plateau (Sec.7,T.19S.,R.2E.) (section location 3 in Fig. 2), with Upper Cretaceous Indianola Group strata resting disconformably on strata of the Upper Pigeon Creek member. Note massive micritic limestone at base of section, and the presence of thin limestone units and calcrete crusts and of *Protelliptio* in the lower member. Angiosperm leaves are associated with multi-storey channel-form sandstone sequences in the upper member. Palynomorphs reported by Weiss and Roche (this volume) were recovered from the bivalve-bearing limestone.

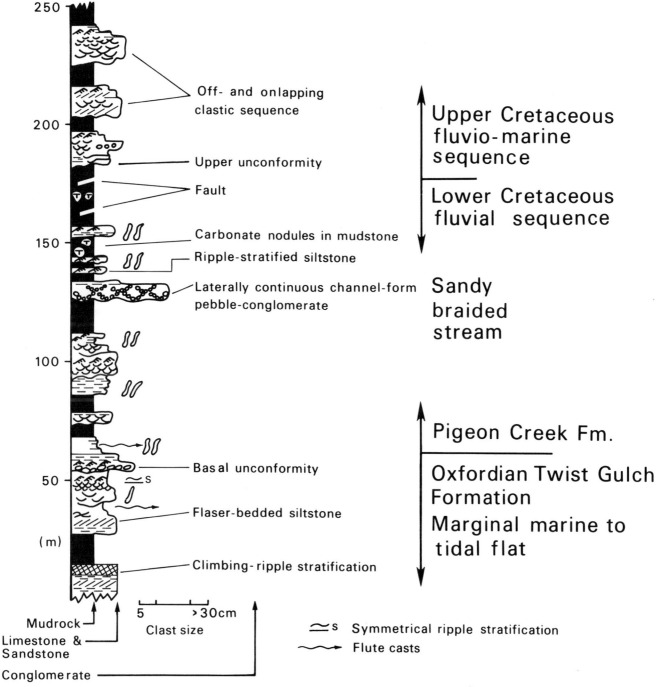

Figure 8. Measured Pigeon Creek section in Salina Canyon (Sec.33,T.21E.,R.1E.) (section location 4 in Fig. 2). Scour-base conglomerates, sheet sandstones, channel-form sandstones with wings of ripple-stratified sandstones are clustered in a multi-storey arrangement and intercalated in thick mudstones. Pigeon Creek channel-form sandstones overlie thinly laminated Jurassic Twist Gulch sandstones and siltstones along a scoured contact. Transitional alluvial to marine Sanpete sandstones rest on scour-base Pigeon Creek sandstones.

The depositional strike of the Pigeon Creek Formation parallels the structural strike of the fold-thrust belt. Pigeon Creek strata are thickest nearest the thrust front and thin rapidly to the east, to the north, and to the south of the type locality (Fig. 9). The conglomerates are coarsest at the stratotype in the west and fine rapidly to the southeast and east (Fig. 9). The large-scale depositional geometry of the clastic Pigeon Creek Formation is wedge-shaped down the depositional dip and lens-shaped along the depositional strike.

Boundaries and age

Boundaries. At the type section, the alluvial clastics of the Pigeon Creek Formation rest disconformably on marine clastics of the Upper Jurassic Twist Gulch Formation, and are disconformably overlain by rocks of the undifferentiated Upper Cretaceous Indianola Group (Fig. 5).

The base of the Pigeon Creek Formation is below the lowest exposed channel-form or sheet sandstone that is characteristic of the Pigeon Creek, and is above the uppermost exposed marine Twist Gulch strata (Hunt, 1950, his unit 85, p. 199). At the lower contact, Twist Gulch is separated from Pigeon Creek strata by the

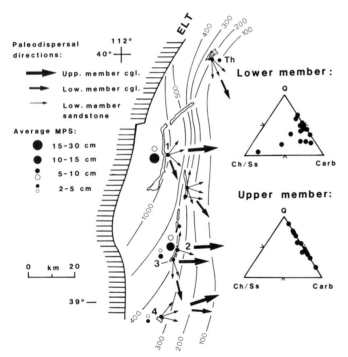

Figure 9. Map showing isopachs (in meters), triangular plots of clast lithologies (normalized to 100 percent chert/sandstone, carbonate, and quartzite), average maximum particle sizes (MPS), and paleodispersal directions for Pigeon Creek Formation. Filled circles indicate MPS of upper member clastics; open circles, MPS of lower member clastics. Small arrow indicates mean orientation of trough cross-strata in lower member sandstones determined from 5 to 15 measurements of trough limbs per station; medium-sized arrow (lower member) and large arrow (upper member) represent paleocurrent directions obtained from clast imbrication and orientation of gravel-furrows. Numbers indicate section locations shown in Figure 2; ELT = eastern limit of thrusting for Pavant Range thrust (after Villien and Kligfield, 1986).

following criteria: (1) red to ochre Pigeon Creek sandstones occur as channel-forms and sheets that are interbedded with massive red to gray mudstones, whereas the underlying beds of red and silty Twist Gulch mudstone are tabular and thin bedded, and exhibit abundant, thinly laminated to rippled sandstones and siltstones; (2) lower member Pigeon Creek sandstones are coarse grained to pebbly, and consist of reworked sedimentary detritus, such as chert and carbonate lithic detritus and, to a very minor extent, feldspar—in contrast, Twist Gulch sandstones are fine grained, contain traces of glauconite (Hardy, 1952; Standlee, 1983) but no chert pebbles, and are markedly feldspathic; and (3) the external geometry and the internal structure of Pigeon Creek beds indicate that deposition occurred under unidirectional flow conditions in an alluvial environment, whereas Twist Gulch strata were deposited under nonunidirectional flow conditions in a marine to tidal flat environment.

The above-described differences in lithologic character and depositional environment that occur at the Pigeon Creek/Twist Gulch contact are consistent throughout the study area. These differences indicate a significant depositional hiatus, which separates the Jurassic Twist Gulch from the Lower Cretaceous Pigeon Creek Formation (Figs. 3, 5, 10).

The top of the Pigeon Creek stratotype is above the uppermost exposed unit of Pigeon Creek conglomerate and intercalated red mudstones of sheet geometry; it is at the base of the lowest white to yellowish weathering channel-form sandstone and pebble-conglomerate that characterize strata of the Upper Cretaceous Indianola Group (undifferentiated). The Indianola Group exhibits quartzite-pebble to coarse-grained quartzose sandstones interbedded with thin-bedded pink clastic limestones. The conglomerates of the Pigeon Creek Formation, however, are much coarser, and channel-fills are scarce to absent. The most prominent clasts in the Pigeon Creek rocks are gray to dark gray carbonates, and red to purple and olive green to brown quartzites. The beds overlying the Pigeon Creek stratotype rocks are what Hunt (1950, p. 46) identified in the Gunnison Plateau as the "red zone" (i.e., all strata above Hunt's unit 174, p. 195), and their base is herein defined as the base of the Upper Cretaceous Indianola Group (undifferentiated) in the Gunnison Plateau area (Fig. 3).

The contact between the Indianola Group (undifferentiated) and the Pigeon Creek Formation in the study area is interpreted to represent a disconformity for the following reasons: (1) the abrupt disappearance of large and mineralogically unstable carbonate clasts at the contact coincides with the sudden appearance of mineralogically stable white to pink quartzite pebbles in the overlying Indianola Group strata; (2) the clast sizes of all clast types present change at the contact from cobble size below the contact to pebble- to granule- and sand-sized material above the contact (Fig. 5); and (3) the abrupt change in depositional character at the contact, from sheet conglomerate and intercalated mudstone to channel-form sandstone and detrital carbonate, reflects a significant change in the style of transport and deposition, as well as in the character of the sediment load.

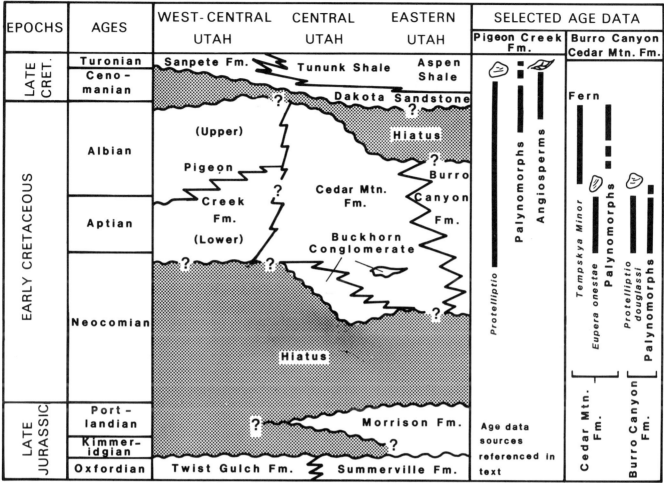

Figure 10. Revised sequence-stratigraphic chart for the Lower Cretaceous in Utah showing the unconformity-bounded Pigeon Creek–Cedar Mountain depositional sequence and selected age data. Note the varying stratigraphic range of the hiatuses. Compiled from McGookey (1972), Fouch and others, (1983), and Tschudy and others (1984).

The abrupt change in the distribution of clast lithologies and clast sizes at the top of the Pigeon Creek Formation are attributed to winnowing and weathering of Pigeon Creek strata during an extended period of nondeposition and erosion prior to Indianola deposition. The differences in the style of bedding, the energy conditions during deposition, together with the change in source of sediment across the contact, not only indicate a period during which a significant break in deposition occurred, but also reflect a distinct change in the character and the style of the depositional systems. The changes at the Indianola/Pigeon Creek contact occur throughout the study area and are evidence of the existence of a major depositional hiatus in the stratigraphic succession (Fig. 10).

In summary, Pigeon Creek strata in central Utah comprise an unconformity-bounded package of rocks (Figs. 3, 10) that incorporates Spieker's Morrison(?) Formation and the ". . . typical red conglomerate of Indianola [character]" (Spieker, 1946, p. 105). The unconformities bounding the Pigeon Creek clastic wedge show evidence of a significant depositional hiatus. Such basic unconformity-bounded units of regional extent have recently been described as a separate kind of stratigraphic unit and are called synthems (ISS Classification, 1987).

Age. Palynomorphs of late Albian age were recovered by Standlee (1983, p. 367) in Pigeon Creek Canyon (Fig. 2, section location 1) 600 m above the base of what was called undifferentiated Indianola Group (S. N. Nelson, personal communication, 1985) and what is here designated as the upper member of the Pigeon Creek Formation (Fig. 5). Pollen assemblages indicating various Late Cretaceous ages (Coniacian to Campanian) (S. N. Nelson, personal communication, 1986) were recovered during the present study from Indianola Group rocks at various localities in the northern Gunnison Plateau. Nondistinct nonmarine palynomorphs of Late Cretaceous age (D. J. Nichols, written communication, 1981) were recovered in the southeastern part of the Gunnison Plateau (Fig. 2, section locations 2 and 3) from Upper Cretaceous Indianola Group rocks that overlie conglomerates of the upper Pigeon Creek member (Figs. 6, 7). The Sanpete Formation (Fig. 10) at its type locality in Six Mile Canyon (Fig. 2) is of Cenomanian(?) to Turonian age (Cobban, 1976; J. H. Hanley, personal communication, 1982) and disconformably overlies lower member strata of the Pigeon Creek Formation.

Leaf impressions from sandstones of the upper Pigeon Creek member in the southeastern part of the Gunnison Plateau (Fig. 7) were identified, based on their veination patterns, as likely examples of primitive angiosperms of early Cenomanian to no older than late Albian age (S. L. Wing, written communication, 1984). Bivalves belonging to the fresh-water Genus *Protelliptio* were recovered by Stuecheli (1984) from a sandy to oncolitic limestone near the top of the lower member in the southern part of the Gunnison Plateau (Fig. 7). Genus *Protelliptio* has been reported in western North America from rocks ranging in age from late Neocomian (Barremian) to middle Cenomanian (J. H. Hanley, written communication, 1982). Palynomorphs found by Weiss and Roche (this volume) in the bivalve-bearing limestone have yielded an Albian to Cenomanian age range. Witkind and others (1986) recovered plant microfossils of Aptian to Albian age in the southeastern part of the Gunnison Plateau from mudstone lenses intercalated in conglomerate beds in a part of the section that is here called upper member of the Pigeon Creek Formation (Fig. 7).

Although some of the plant microfossils from both members are of longer range, evidence from the present study strongly suggests a late Neocomian to Aptian age range for the lower Pigeon Creek member and a late Aptian to predominantly Albian age range for the upper member of the Pigeon Creek Formation (Figs. 3, 6, 10). The Pigeon Creek Formation rests disconformably on Jurassic Twist Gulch strata and is separated from overlying Indianola Group by a major depositional hiatus that probably encompasses part of the latest Albian to early Cenomanian. Strata equivalent to the Sanpete Formation of predominantly Turonian age truncate the underlying Pigeon Creek Formation.

REGIONAL RELATIONSHIPS OF LOWER CRETACEOUS STRATA

Bounding unconformities

The disconformity at the base of the Pigeon Creek wedge is analogous to the Neocomian to early Aptian unconformity (Figs. 10, 11) that marks the base of the Cretaceous in the foreland basin (McGookey, 1972; Weimer, 1984). The formations overlying this regional unconformity include: (1) the Kootenai Formation in Montana (Suttner, 1969; DeCelles, 1986); (2) the Draney-Smoot-Smiths Formation interval, the Lakota and Wayan Formations, and the Gannett Group in Wyoming and Idaho (Eyer, 1969; Rubey, 1973; Schmidt and others, 1981; Sippel and others, 1981); and (3) the Cedar Mountain and Burro Canyon formations of eastern Utah and western Colorado, respectively (Hale and Van DeGraaf, 1964; Young, 1960, 1970; Stokes, 1972; Tschudy and others, 1984; Yingling, 1987) (Fig.

12). In the study area, the Neocomian to early Aptian unconformity is interpreted to have resulted from erosion during earliest foreland basin deformation. During this stratigraphic interval, however, depositional systems in east-central Utah remained largely unaffected by Sevier deformation and basin subsidence.

The disconformity truncating the top of the Pigeon Creek Formation in west-central Utah is correlative with the depositional hiatus that resulted from the southwestward-directed advance of the incipient seaway in Utah during the middle Albian to Cenomanian to early Turonian (Figs. 10, 11) (Lessard, 1973; Fouch and others, 1983; Vuke, 1984; Weimer, 1984; Schwans, 1986). Regional onlap against this surface is expressed, for example, by the Muddy Sandstone and the Dakota Sandstone that onlap the upper Cedar Mountain Formation along an erosional contact in central Utah (Young, 1960; Yingling, 1987), and by the marine Tununk Shale that is correlative to the Sanpete Formation in the study area (Figs. 11, 13). The transitional alluvial to marine strata overlying the Albian to Cenomanian unconformity reflect progressive marine deposition in response to widespread and unrestricted foreland basin subsidence during the Albian to Turonian. Widespread foreland basin subsidence occurred in response to thrust load emplacement in the Sevier belt of west-central Utah during the late Aptian to Albian.

Strata forming the depositional sequence

The depositional sequence of regional extent is composed of the Neocomian to late Albian Pigeon Creek Formation of west-central Utah and the Neocomian to Aptian and Albian Cedar Mountain Formation of east-central Utah. Together, these formations constitute a composite depositional wedge that records foreland basin deposition and deformation between the time of onset of earliest tectonic uplift in the Sevier belt and marine deposition during the middle Albian to early Turonian.

The similarity in stratigraphic position, chronostratigraphic range, and gross lithologic character between Pigeon Creek rocks and the Cedar Mountain Formation has led various workers to propose incorporating the strata here called Pigeon Creek Formation with the Cedar Mountain Formation (Fig. 3) (Standlee, 1982; Witkind and others, 1986; Weiss and Roche, this volume). The establishment of a composite Cedar Mountain/Pigeon Creek stratotype under the name Cedar Mountain Formation, however, would result in the formation of a stratigraphic unit incorporating rocks that are distributed over a large area and that display distinctly different lithologic, depositional, and stratigraphic characteristics. The grouping of these strata in the same formation would thus equate strata that are very different by exactly those characteristics that mark them as stratigraphic units of formational rank.

The following differences characterize the Cedar Mountain and Pigeon Creek Formations:

1. Stratotype subdivision: Pigeon Creek strata comprise a fine-grained lower member and a coarse-grained upper member, whereas the coarse Buckhorn Conglomerate member of the

Cedar Mountain Formation constitutes the base for the Cedar Mountain shales and sandstones (Fig. 10).

2. Dimensions, geometries: Pigeon Creek strata parallel the structural strike of the Sevier belt, are thickest nearest the thrust front, and thin to the east. They are completely absent east of the western base of the Wasatch Plateau and occur only within a restricted basinal area adjacent to the thrust front (Fig. 9). Conversely, Cedar Mountain rocks are of varying stratigraphic thickness and widely distributed throughout east-central Utah, and pinch out repeatedly against the intermittent topographic highs (Fig. 14).

3. Dispersal, provenance: The provenance and dispersal of Pigeon Creek clastics are directly related to thrust initiation in the Sevier belt and subsequent denudation of the allochthonous complexes during the Neocomian to late Albian (Fig. 9). Dispersal directions and modal clast pebble data, as well as the erosional relief at the Buckhorn Conglomerate/Morrison contact, however, indicate that Buckhorn Conglomerate (lower Cedar Mountain Formation) deposition occurred in various superposed, east- to northeastward-shedding incised drainage systems. Chert is the most abundant constituent in the Buckhorn Conglomerate (Fig. 14). Yingling (1987) suggested its derivation from Paleozoic sources to the southwest and south. Contrary to the conglomerate clast composition of the upper Pigeon Creek member, pebble composition data from sandstone channel bodies of the upper Cedar Mountain Formation reflect the significant influence of local source areas that were active during the Aptian-Albian within Utah and south of Utah (Fig. 14) (Young, 1960, 1970;

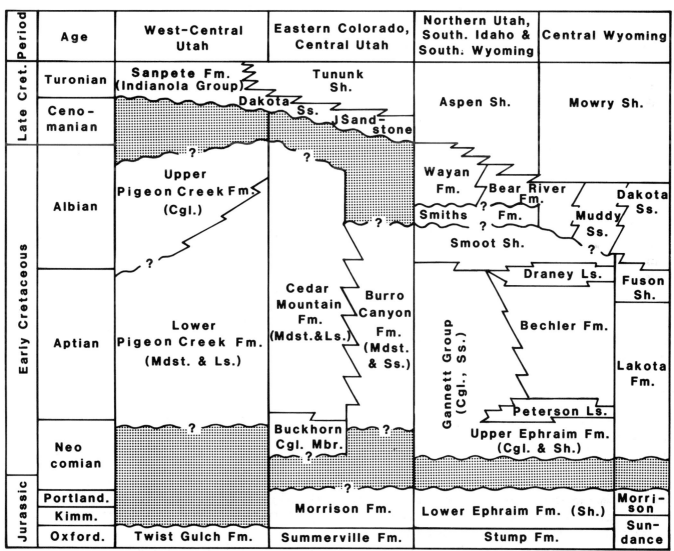

Figure 11. Revised sequence-stratigraphic chart for Lower Cretaceous strata in Utah and adjacent areas. Left side of diagram shows west to east relationships and right side of diagram north to south relationships of various formations. Note that the depositional hiatus above and below the Pigeon Creek–Cedar Mountain sequence in Utah is represented in areas to the north by other formations (see text for details). Compiled from McGookey (1972), Wiltschko and Dorr (1983), Fouch and others (1983).

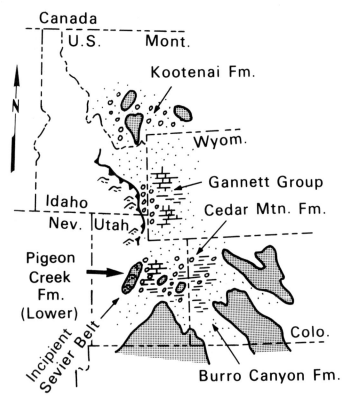

Figure 12. Neocomian to early Aptian paleogeography. Shaded areas depict paleotopographic highs in the incipient foreland basin situated in Montana, Colorado, and central Utah. Deposition of lower member Pigeon Creek strata occurred during this period in a restricted basinal area adjacent to the tectonic Sevier uplands (stippled), whereas the strata of the lower Cedar Mountain Formation (Buckhorn Conglomerate) in east-central Utah were deposited in a nonsubsiding foreland basin segmented by topographic highs. Adapted from Young (1960, 1970), McGookey (1972), Wiltschko and Dorr (1983), Weimer (1984), DeCelles (1986).

Peterson, 1986). Paleocurrent vectors from upper Cedar Mountain strata document an eastward to northeastward dispersal (Young, 1970; Yingling, 1987). At the same time, conglomerates of the upper Pigeon Creek member were shed eastward off the rising Sevier fold-thrust belt (Fig. 14).

4. Stratigraphic relationships: Lateral continuity between exposures of the Pigeon Creek and Cedar Mountain Formations has not been documented. The Cedar Mountain Formation features numerous, well-documented intraformational disconformities of varying chronostratigraphic range (Young, 1960; Tschudy and others, 1984), whereas the Pigeon Creek Formation comprises a 975-m-thick wedge of syntectonic clastics deposited adjacent to the thrust front. Consequently, the Cedar Mountain Formation already represents a composite stratotype where the total range of the unit has yet to be demonstrated. Pigeon Creek rocks, however, do not exhibit depositional breaks within their stratigraphic succession.

In summary, unconformity-bounded units of regional to interregional extent are useful for providing a framework for the stratigraphic analysis of sedimentary basins (ISS Classification, 1987). They are especially useful in situations where the stratigraphic breaks may have great significance in deciphering the complex geologic history of a basin area and where genetically unrelated units together record the history of basin deformation. Based on the formational differences presented above, the incorporation of Pigeon Creek strata into the Cedar Mountain Formation, as proposed by various workers (Fig. 3), does not seem warranted. The Pigeon Creek and Cedar Mountain Formations are genetically and lithostratigraphically unrelated unconformity-bounded units. Together, however, they record the deformation history of the evolving foreland basin during the Early Cretaceous. The Pigeon Creek and Cedar Mountain Formations can be regarded in that context as a synthem (ISS Classification, 1987).

PIGEON CREEK DEPOSITIONAL ARCHITECTURE

Lithofacies and facies assemblages

The lithofacies and the facies assemblages of the 975-m-thick, mudstone-rich, conglomeratic Pigeon Creek Formation document the changes in source area composition and structural style that occurred with the onset of Sevier fold-thrust belt formation. The Pigeon Creek Formation is subdivided into a lower fine-grained member and an upper conglomeratic member (Fig. 10). The lower member consists of, in order of decreasing abundance, mudstone, coarse-grained pebbly sandstone, and limestone. The upper member consists of a variety of conglomerate and associated sandstone. Strata of the upper member occur as 5- to 10-m-thick conglomerate sheets interbedded with mudstones, or as laterally adjacent and vertically superposed amalgamated conglomerate sheets with intercalated mudstone units (Figs. 5 through 8). Three major lithofacies are distinguished in the Pigeon Creek Formation: sheet conglomerate; scour-based conglomerate to sheet sandstone; and associated limestone, mudstone, and sandstone. Each lithofacies, and if present, each subfacies, will be discussed with respect to its environment of deposition, lateral relationship to other subenvironments, and its tectonic and/or climatic implications.

Sheet conglomerate facies. *Description.* Pigeon Creek conglomerates accumulated in sheet-like bodies that are a few hundreds of meters to a kilometer wide in cross section, and as much as 10 m thick. Each sheet consists of several 2- to 5-m-thick, upward-fining sequences with intercalated mudstones. Individual upward-fining sequences within the conglomerate sheets are interconnected and amalgamated laterally to form the large-scale sheet geometry. The conglomerate sheets either form a thick wedge consisting of vertically and laterally amalgamated sheets separated by 0.5- to 1-m-thick, laterally discontinuous mudstone and siltstone beds (Fig. 15), or they occur as sheet-like bodies interbedded with mudstones that are tens of meters thick (Fig. 16).

The discontinuous beds of mudstone and sandstone are 0.1 to 0.2 m thick and drape underlying conglomerates. The contacts

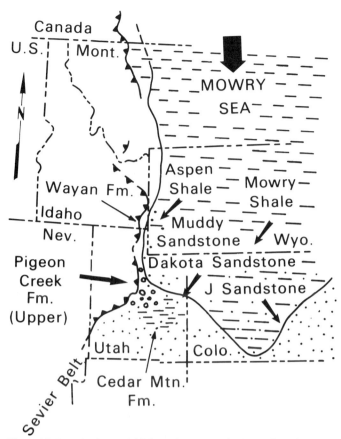

Figure 13. Late Aptian and Albian paleogeography. Incursion of seaway and resulting regional onlap of marine clastics against the upper boundary of the Pigeon Creek–Cedar Mountain synthem is represented by various formations. Upper member Pigeon Creek conglomerates were deposited during that time basinward of the emergent thrust terrane. Adapted from McGookey (1972), Wiltschko and Dorr (1983), Vuke (1984), and Weimer (1984).

between the sequences are sharp but rarely erosional. Well-defined conglomeratic channel fills within sheets are scarce. The sheets have planar to slightly undulatory bases developed directly on underlying mudstones (Fig. 17). Basal surfaces exhibit small-scale (10 to 50 cm deep) gravelly furrows, obstacle scours, and abundant flute, load, and drag marks (Fig. 18). Margins of individual large-scale sheets are dominated by sandstone featuring small channel fills. These channel fills commonly have extensive wings of siltstone that interfinger laterally with the mudstones surrounding the conglomerate sheet. Sheet-margin sandstones exhibit well-developed stratification and are extensively bioturbated. In sections more distal to the tectonic front, individual large-scale conglomerate sheets overlap laterally, and are offset vertically by thick mudstones.

The conglomerates commonly show crude normal grading, with clasts oriented subhorizontally to bedding. The conglomerates exhibit poor sorting, a polymodal grain-size distribution, an average maximum diameter of 5 to 50 cm, and are clast-supported. An upward-fining sequence ranges from unstratified

and disorganized at the base, to crudely horizontally stratified toward the top. This upward increase in the degree of internal organization is accompanied by an overall grain-size decrease from cobble/boulder sizes at the base to cobble/pebble sizes at the top. Fine-grained, horizontally laminated or rippled sandstones cap most of the conglomerate sheets.

Vector means of clasts with a(t) b(i) imbrication, and of elongation directions of gravelly furrows, yield a southeastward transport direction for lower member Pigeon Creek conglomerates, whereas vector means of upper member sheet conglomerates show eastward dispersal (Fig. 9). Furthermore, clast sizes in the conglomerates of the upper member decrease away from the stratotype, suggesting a dispersal direction similar to that obtained from associated imbrication data (Fig. 9).

Interpretation. The Pigeon Creek sheet conglomerate facies was deposited in a sheet flood–dominated alluvial fan system proximal to the thrust front. The paleoflow directions and the facies character reflect the transverse supply of conglomerate and

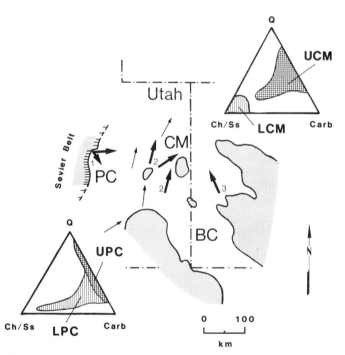

Figure 14. Schematic representation of Early Cretaceous paleodispersal patterns and modal pebble/clast lithologies of Pigeon Creek and Cedar Mountain strata. Shaded areas represent paleotopographic highs (McGookey, 1972; Peterson, 1986). Arrows at location 1 show paleodrainage directions for lower (smaller arrow) and upper Pigeon Creek member (larger arrow). Arrows at location 2 show paleoflow directions from Buckhorn Conglomerate exposures (Yingling, 1987). Arrow at location 3 represents regional paleodrainage direction for the Cedar Mountain–Burro Canyon interval (Young, 1960, 1970). Small arrows depict paleoflow direction from sandstone channel bodies of the upper Cedar Mountain Formation (Harris, 1980; Yingling, 1987). BC = Burro Canyon Formation; CM = Cedar Mountain Formation; LCM = Lower Cedar Mountain clast lithologies; LPC = Lower Pigeon Creek member clast lithologies; PC = Pigeon Creek Formation; UCM = Upper Cedar Mountain Formation clast lithologies; UPC = Upper Pigeon Creek member clast lithologies.

Figure 15. Sheet conglomerate facies in Little Salt Creek Canyon (for location, see Fig. 2) forming 2- to 5-m-thick, amalgamated sheets (between solid lines) separated by thin mudstones. Scour-based conglomerate channel fills occur toward the top of individual sheets (channel bases are dashed lines). View is to the south.

Figure 16. Overturned (to the right) Pigeon Creek depositional sequence exposed at location 2 (in Fig. 2). Lower member mudstones overlie Jurassic (J) along basal disconformity (solid line to left) and crop out in far background. Overlying conglomerate sheets and interbedded mudstones (right of dashed line) of the upper member are truncated by Tertiary (T) strata along angular unconformity (solid line to right). View is to the south.

Figure 17. Depositional base of upright-standing conglomerate sheet of the upper Pigeon Creek member in the southern Gunnison Plateau (between section locations 2 and 3 in Fig. 2). The exposure shows broad, channel-like scours and narrow, elongate obstacle-scours. View is to the south. Note arrow at right pointing to scale next to hammer (45 cm long).

minor sand from adjacent tectonic uplands onto a gravelly fan surface of low relief. Distally from the thrust front, conglomerate—intermixed to a greater degree with sand and mud—formed composite sheet flood deposits that interfingered with and terminated in a muddy flood plain. The association of conglomerate sheets encased in thick mudstones represents the interfingering of a sheet flood–dominated fan system with a basinal mud zone that lies downstream from, as well as transverse to, the gravelly fan bodies.

The depositional geometry, coarseness, poor sorting, and internal organization of the conglomerate sheets is interpreted to have resulted from rapid deposition in shallow water by high-discharge flows with relatively high sediment concentrations. The superposition of vastly different grain sizes within the conglomerates, and the vertical, as well as lateral, association of conglomerate beds and massive mudstones, suggests sedimentation under discontinuous flow conditions with variable flow competence and character of load. The absence of cross-stratification in the conglomerates indicates that significant bed surface topography was not developed to allow avalanching of gravel.

Transport and deposition of the clastics thus occurred under repeated flood stage conditions, in a shallow-braided braidplain featuring extremely variable and discontinuous discharge. Minor floods affected only areas within the braidplain and reworked the deposits at various times. Lateral continuity of conglomerate sheets results from the amalgamation and lateral overlap of individual upward-fining sequences caused by the migration of active

fan segments and/or by avulsion-controlled switching of the braidplain segments.

In his classification of alluvial systems, Friend (1983) described deposits of similar geometry and nature, as deposits of a coarse- to fine-grained alternating bedload- and suspension load–dominated sheetflood system. The lateral overlap, as well as the vertical offset of the large-scale sheets by thick successions of basinal fines, reflects the lateral sweeping of adjacent gravelly braidplains or low-relief fans in a continuously subsiding basin. Similar ancient, mixed coarse- to fine-grained sheet-flood sequences have been described by Stear (1983), Wells (1983, 1984), and Van Der Meulen (1986), as typical accumulates of an actively subsiding basin with close proximity to a tectonically active source. Stratification similar to the Pigeon Creek type has been described, for example, by Rust (1978) and Hein and Walker (1977) from modern proximal-braided outwash fans. Ferguson and Werrity (1983) related modern-day mixed conglomerate and sand sheets, similar to the Pigeon Creek type, to repeated flood-stage deposition with minor episodes of reworking.

Scour-base conglomerate and sheet sandstone facies.
Description. Pebbly to cobbly conglomerates and coarse to pebbly sandstones occur gradationally together and form sandy conglomeratic lenses, channel-form bodies, and sheet sandstones (Fig. 18). The conglomerate and sandstone facies form individual upward-fining sequences 2 to 5 m thick. The facies commonly constitute the top of the underlying sheet conglomerate facies or

Figure 18. Close-up of conglomerate sheet base shown in Figure 17. Shallow flute and load marks are visible to left of scale (15 cm long). An elongate drag or groove mark cuts across exposure from lower left to upper right. View is to the west.

Figure 19. Individual 2- to 4-m-thick, upward-fining conglomerate to mudstone sequence (between solid lines). Unit is overturned to the west (right). Sequence consists of a lower conglomerate sheet (CS) and an upper massive mudstone (F). Stratified conglomerate (Cs) at base (to right of solid line) is overlain by channel-form, trough cross-bedded, pebbly sandstones (Sp) and horizontally to ripple-stratified wings of sheet sandstone (Shr) (to right of dashed line). Massive mudstone (F) forms top of upward-fining package. Note scale = 1 m. Location is just north of section location 2 in Figure 2. View is to the south.

occur as clusters of pebbly channel-form sandstone bodies within the mudstone. Several subfacies are distinguished within the conglomerate and sandstone facies: scour-base conglomerates (50 percent), channel-form trough cross-bedded conglomerates to pebbly sandstones (30 percent), and sheet sandstones and siltstones (20 percent). The typical vertical succession of the facies features a conglomerate sheet overlain by channel-form conglomerates along a scoured contact, which in turn grades upward into trough cross-bedded sandstones capped by extensive sheet sandstones and siltstones (Fig. 19).

The scour-base conglomerate subfacies is trough cross-stratified, texturally mature, and fine-grained, with average clast sizes of 2 to 5 cm in diameter. The subfacies exhibits well-developed imbrication and a polymodal grain-size distribution. Individual beds are lenticular, with distinctly erosional, sharp, and convex-upward bases. The channel-form subfacies commonly rests on the sheet conglomerate facies (Fig. 15).

The trough cross-bedded pebbly sandstone subfacies exhibits internal scours and reactivation horizons with gravelly lags. Trough cross-stratification varies in scale, with large troughs found near the base and small-scale troughs and climbing-ripple stratification near the top of the facies units. The cross-bedded pebbly sandstones constitute small symmetrical scour-base channel-fills that are associated with the scour-base conglomerates.

The channel-form sandstones show prominent red-white mottling and bioturbation along their bases and in the lateral wings (Fig. 20). Individual burrows are typically several millimeters to a centimeter in diameter, cylindrical in form, vertical to oblique to bedding in orientation, and in some cases exhibit

Figure 20. Exposed base of channel-form sandstone featuring pedogenic mottling around burrows of *Skolithos* sp. and *Muensteria* sp. Exposure is at location 2 in Figure 2 with view to the west.

meniscus-shaped backfilling. The burrows can be identified as *Muensteria* sp., based on the lack of wall structure, the ornamentation, and the cylindrical morphology. A second type of burrow without wall lining, ornamentation, and branching, but with a structureless fill, is interpreted as *Skolithos* sp.

The white mottles are found at the bases of channel-forms and appear as white halos around large individual burrows, or, if irregularly shaped, incorporate numerous burrows (Fig. 20). The mottled areas are significantly depleted in iron, but not in silica. Underlying mudstones are characterized by high iron contents and feature calcite concretions scattered along the base of the channel-form sandstones. The channel-form sandstones contain abundant macerated plant material, with one horizon exhibiting a concentration of well-preserved impressions of primitive angiosperm leaves that were identified as late Albian to no older than Cenomanian (S. L. Wing, written communication, 1984).

Channel-form sandstones grade upward and laterally into finer grained sheet sandstones and siltstones that cap the sheet conglomerate facies. The sheet sandstones to siltstones drape the underlying conglomerates and are commonly overlain by mudstones. The sandstones and siltstones may also form extensive wings to the channel-form sandstones, when these occur as clusters of channel-form bodies within thick mudstone. The sandstone sheets are horizontally stratified at their bases and exhibit climbing-ripple stratification near their tops. Paleocurrent data from trough cross-strata in lower member sandstones show a wider spread of vector means as compared to the southeastward dispersal direction from imbrication data of associated conglomerates (Fig. 9).

Interpretation. The three subfacies are interpreted to represent the reworking of gravel and the deposition of sand and minor gravel in a predominantly sandy ephemeral bedload system along the lateral and downstream margins of the gravelly fan systems. The vertical superposition and lateral association of the three subfacies represent waning flow conditions and surficial reworking of the larger conglomerate sheets along sheet margins and on sheet tops. The infilling of active lateral and cross-over channels that formed with postflood bar emergence produced the conglomeratic to sandy scour-base channel fills on top of the larger conglomerate sheets. Sand and minor gravel deposition within these channels occurred in small transverse and lateral bars. Avulsion-controlled rapid migration of the predominantly sandy bedload channels caused minor surficial reworking of the tops of the conglomerate sheet and deposition of sand-sized to silt-sized material in nearby overbank areas. Sheet sandstones, deposited as wings to the shallow symmetrical bedload channels, drape the conglomerates or were deposited along the margins of the larger conglomerate sheets. Minor floods in the various segments of the shallow-braided braidplain and the lateral, as well as downflow, margins of the braidplain resulted in: (1) the infilling of channels on bar platforms by sandy bar-top washover (cross-bedded channel-form sandstones); (2) the deposition of horizontally stratified sands in overbank areas and on bar tops by sheet flow (sheet sandstones); and (3) the transport of sandy bedload into floodplain areas adjacent to the braidplain via small symmetrical sandy bed-load channels (channel-form clusters). The dispersion of the vector means of the three subfacies reflects the variations in flow directions with waning flood stage, braidplain margin deposition, and/or bar-top washover flow during minor flood events (Fig. 9).

The repeated modification of braided stream deposits by minor floods is common in modern braided streams (Williams and Rust, 1969; Costello and Walker, 1972). The transition from conglomeratic sheet flood deposition during flood conditions to conglomeratic-incised and sandy shallow-braided channels during later waning flow conditions is known from modern sheet flood systems from distal alluvial fans. Blair (1987) and Ferguson and Werrity (1983) documented a variety of sedimentary structures similar to those found in Pigeon Creek rocks for sediments deposited under unconfined flow regimes on modern alluvial fans. The transition sheet conglomerate to clusters of channel-form sandstones to mottled, flat sheets of sandstone and siltstone in a downflow direction, as well as in a lateral sense, as has been illustrated in the Pigeon Creek system (Figs. 6, 7, 8), is well documented from other ancient sheet flood–dominated braided stream environments (Larsen and Steel, 1978; Hubert and Hyde, 1982; Wells, 1984).

Limestone to mudstone to sandstone facies. *Description.* The lower member of the Pigeon Creek Formation consists of massive mudstones with carbonate nodules (50 percent), interbedded thin siltstone beds (10 percent), channel-form limestone-pebble to oncolitic sandstones (30 percent), thick micritic limestones (7 percent), and several thin sandy limestones (3 percent). The micritic limestones form 0.5- to 10-m-thick units that are laterally continuous for several hundred of meters to a kilometer. Several sandy and thin limestone units no thicker than 2 m are found at various stratigraphic levels in the lower member (Figs. 6, 7). The thin, sandy limestone units are laterally continuous over distances of 5 to 10 m and are commonly associated with the channel-form sandstone subfacies. The micritic limestones are massive or thick bedded to well laminated, and contain sparse, sandy layers or laminar concentrations of densely packed, ovoid to spheroidal grains of micrite and/or larger oncolites. Lamination is typically disrupted or destroyed by nodular and banded calcrete crusts. On a microscopic scale, limestones contain abundant micritic intraclasts, and small pisolitic and oncolitic grains coalesced in zones. These oolitically textured zones are laterally discontinuous and commonly capped by irregular calcrete laminae. Nuclei of the ooid grains consist of micritic fragments or, in some cases, pebbles and/or bivalves. The limestone subfacies grades laterally and vertically into ripple-stratified calcareous sandstones and channel-form sandstones.

Macrofossils in the limestones are preserved as molds of gastropods and bivalves, or as abundant charophyte debris. Bivalves belonging to Genus *Protelliptio* (J. H. Hanley, written communication, 1982) were found in one horizon in the upper part of the lower member of the Pigeon Creek Formation (Fig. 7).

Units of channel-form limestone-pebble to oncolitic sandstones form clusters of channel bodies (10 to 50 m wide and 1 to 5 m thick), which overlie limestones along convex-upward contacts, and occur along the depositional edges of the limestone beds. These calcarenites are dolomitic and commonly exhibit abundant internal scours and gravelly lags. Stratification consists of hierarchically arranged large- to small-scale trough cross-stratification. Thin-bedded, rippled siltstones and sandstones form the wings to the small channel fills and are intercalated in the massive mudstones.

The mudstones are 10 to 50 m thick and exhibit intercalated sandstone channel bodies or clusters of sandstone channel bodies. The mudstones exhibit repeated intercalations of red to mottled mudstone horizons, dark gray to gray to white mudstone horizons, and thin, cross-laminated sand and siltstone layers. The dark gray to gray mudstone horizons are characterized by a distinct pedogenic fabric featuring slickensided surfaces. The white mudstone horizons contain abundant burrowed zones, stacked zones or beds of coalesced calcrete nodules. The gray mudstone units and calcrete zones are commonly found in association with the channel-form sandstones and the siltstone wings. Individual calcrete nodules range from 1 to 5 cm in diameter (Fig. 21), whereas coalesced nodules are as much as 30 cm in diameter and show bands of laminated calcrete along their tops.

The pedogenic fabric in the dark gray mudstones consists of a blocky internal structure. Individual blocks are prismatic and are bounded by well-developed cleavage planes with slickensided surfaces that generally meet at steep angles and form wedge-shaped units (Fig. 21). Thin section studies of the prismatic mudstone blocks revealed a similar microfabric within the macroscopic peds; domains of finely layered, oriented clays bind prismatic fields of more randomly oriented clay. Smectite and mixed-layer clays are the dominant clay minerals (Stuecheli, 1984).

Interpretation. The limestones, mudstones, and sandstones making up the lower member of the Pigeon Creek Formation represent overbank deposition along the margins of the sheet-flood fan system and sandy to muddy flood-basin deposition in the basinal mud zone. The facies association constitutes the floodplain systems that formed the axial part of a basin oriented parallel to the tectonic uplands; this basin was periodically supplied with detritus by the ephemerally active fan systems.

The channel-form sandstone facies represent a mixed-load ephemeral braided stream environment, whereas the mudstone and limestone facies represent playa lake and flood-basin deposits that were repeatedly modified by fluvial processes during periods of inundation. Burrowing, plant growth, and postdepositional pedogenic processes reworked the mudstones and destroyed most sedimentary structures in the flood-basin deposits. Sandy stream sedimentation in flood-basin areas occurred with ephemeral inflow into overbank areas and the flood plain. Active stream deposition thus occurred in immediate proximity to flood-basin suspension deposition.

Mudstone microfabrics similar to those in the Pigeon Creek mudstones are produced by modern pedologic processes characterizing the vertisols (Brewer, 1976; Ahmad, 1983). According to Brewer (1976), modern vertisol structure is dominated by the behavior of clay minerals in seasonal wetting and drying cycles, which result in a sequence of ped disruption, development of

Figure 21. Calcareous blocky macrofabric of paleosol horizon in mudstones of lower Pigeon Creek member, just south of location 3 in Figure 2. Prismatic blocks show cleavage planes with slickensided surfaces (small arrows), forming wedge-shaped peds. Slickensided surfaces converge in a downward direction (large arrow) with respect to former paleosurface. View is to the northeast.

shear planes, clay orientation, and disintegration into prismatic fields. The shrinkage and expansion of the clay during repeated wetting and drying results in a system of cross-cutting cracks and planes.

The Pigeon Creek mudstone fabric and the near-surface to surface accumulation of pedogenic calcrete is interpreted to have resulted from the repeated wetting and drying of ephemerally inundated flood basins under a seasonal wet-dry climate. Soil formation probably occurred for extended periods of time, whereas other portions of the flood plain may have been subjected to relatively permanent saturation.

Synchronously to mudstone pedogenesis, carbonates accumulated in shallow and unstratified playa lakes. The shallow-water bodies shrank and expanded with ephemeral inflow into the flood basins. Repeated subaerial exposure of the carbonates resulted in brecciation, mud cracking, bioturbation, and calcrete formation. Shoreline oscillations caused the subaerial, as well as fluvial, modification of sediments along the playa lake margins. Channel bodies with limestone-pebble and oncolitic channel-fills, which truncate the lacustrine deposits and also occur along the depositional edges of the playa deposits, are interpreted to represent small bed-load channels discharging into the lacustrine depressions. The spatial distribution of the channel bodies suggests rapid lateral migration of channels by avulsion. Two distinct channel-margin environments are recognized: (1) laterally continuous, horizontally stratified sheet sandstones that were depos-

ited in crevasse splays extending into the surrounding flood plain; and (2) thin, rippled siltstones deposited immediately adjacent to the channel margin. Bed-load transport in channels occurred in close proximity to suspension deposition in the playa lakes.

The deposition of large amounts of fines in association with gravelly fan systems is poorly documented. Regardless of channel pattern, however, all rivers experience overbank deposition via crevasse channels and sheet floods. The supposition that all braided rivers are so laterally unstable that flood plains do not exist is probably an expression of modern studies of braided alluvial fan systems (Bridge, 1985). It is thus erroneous to assume that the association of large-scale gravelly sheets and large amounts of fines is incompatible with alluvial fan/braided stream and flood-basin deposition models.

Consequently, the large amounts of fines in the lower member of the Pigeon Creek Formation, together with the intercalated conglomerate sheets, are interpreted to represent a sheet flood system consisting of a wide braidplain terminating in a muddy flood plain. The Pigeon Creek sheet flood system lay fixed through time, forming a bajada and the thick basin-fill adjacent to the tectonic Sevier uplands. Ancient associations of large amounts of fines with gravelly fan systems similar to that of the Pigeon Creek, have been described by Ramos and Sopena (1983), Stear (1983), Wells (1983), and others. Van Der Meulen (1986) described a gravelly, sheet flood–dominated braidplain terminating in a muddy flood plain from the Buntsandstein of Spain. Graham

(1983) and Tunbridge (1984) described mixed massive clay and sandy sheet flood deposits in the distal areas of ephemeral Devonian braided streams.

FORELAND BASIN DEFORMATION AND DEPOSITIONAL RESPONSE

The model

Tectonism and climatic variance strongly influence the depositional style and lithologic composition of sediments of actively subsiding foreland basins (Miall, 1970; Heward, 1978a, b). Climate controls weathering and the variability of discharge, thereby affecting the relief and sediment flux within the basin (Garner,1959; Schumm, 1976, 1981). Tectonism and basin subsidence affect the broader features of the basin architecture, such as the vertical aggradation rates and channel densities of rivers (Allen, 1978; Smith and Smith, 1980), internal and external forms of sediment bodies (Leopold and Wolman, 1957; Friend, 1978, 1983), and the positions and orientations of rivers (Friend, 1983; Miall, 1983). The greatest thickness of foreland basin fill occurs adjacent to the thrust front as a result of increased subsidence rates nearest the thrust terranes with the flexural response of the lithosphere to the combined thrust and sediment load (Jordan, 1981). Rate of uplift and subsidence, as well as the changes in climate, determine the degree and type of siliciclastic influx into the basin and provide the necessary base-level control for the diversion of river patterns (Garner, 1979; Miall, 1983).

A key element of the foreland basin fill is its syntectonic character. The presence of conglomeratic alluvial sequences in basin fills has commonly been interpreted to represent major phases of basin alluviation related to pulses of uplift (Miall, 1970; Steel and others, 1977; Steel and Aasheim, 1978). Less obvious and less often discussed, however, is the significance of finer grained sediments in tracking the timing of thrusting recorded by associated clastic wedges in a foreland basin. Furthermore, the impact on foreland basin sedimentation of a lithologically diverse source terrain, whose structural behavior changes through time and space, remains, with few exceptions, largely unanswered (Graham and others, 1986; Lawton, 1986; Schwab, 1986).

Flood-plain and alluvial fan systems adjacent to the thrust front of an incipient foreland basin are thus important components in the spectrum of sedimentary environments that are modified by basin subsidence. The age of the clastics and their relationship to the various subenvironments of the alluvial fan and flood-plain system are a reflection of the time and the rate of uplift. An abrupt increase in the degree of basinal preservation of the fine-grained, as well as the coarse-grained, clastics indicates that increased rates of basinal subsidence coincide with pulses of uplift.

Application to the Pigeon Creek Formation

The lithologies of the Pigeon Creek Formation, their compositional changes, and the association of facies offer great inter-

pretive potential for modeling emergence and erosional stripping of thrust terrane and foreland basin subsidence in response to thrust load emplacement. Pigeon Creek strata were deposited adjacent to the incipient Cordilleran belt at the western edge of a broader Rocky Mountain foreland. Accumulation of Pigeon Creek strata was independent of clastic deposition in east-central Utah, where erosional and remnant topographies acted as interfluves to the Early Cretaceous drainages. Pigeon Creek provenance was directly related to the discrete tectonically controlled sources of the Sevier belt. Partial unroofing and dissection of the incipient Sevier uplifts caused successive erosional exposure of the Mesozoic and Paleozoic and Precambrian strata, resulting in an inverted stratigraphy in the Pigeon Creek clastics.

The thick mudstones of the lower Pigeon Creek member are related to source terranes dominated by fine-grained Mesozoic strata. Uplift of source areas may have been anticlinal above subsurface thrust ramps or along the leading edge of the emergent thrust. Erosive breaching of the anticlinal uplifts provided upper to lower Paleozoic detritus to the drainages. Initial basin subsidence during early anticlinal uplift in the Neocomian to early Aptian is recorded by the preservation of large amounts of fines in a distinctly basin-shaped area adjacent to the tectonic uplands. The degree of basin subsidence was restrained and restricted to areas proximal to the thrust front.

Lower member Pigeon Creek strata were deposited in ephemeral conglomeratic to sandy sheet flood fan systems that were transverse to and terminated in a mud-dominated flood basin featuring playa lakes (Fig. 22A). Lower member facies associations and dispersal directions indicate that deposystems were deflected to become longitudinal with respect to the axis of the basin and the incipient thrust front.

Subsequent hanging-wall emergence and thrust-nappe formation, as well as thrust loading, changed base-level in the basin more significantly during the late Aptian and Albian. The erosional breaching of thrust-nappe complexes most likely occurred along fracture zones and structural lows of the allochthon. Consequently, upper Paleozoic carbonates and Precambrian/Cambrian quartzites became increasingly available to the Pigeon Creek drainages. The conglomeratic clastics of the upper member were deposited in eastward-shedding, ephemeral, sheet flood–dominated fan systems that prograded eastward over the mudstone-dominated lower member (Fig. 22A). The preservation of a 600-m-thick wedge of conglomerate in basinal areas adjacent to the thrust front indicates that the basinal response was rapid, with subsidence now less restrained and less restricted to discrete areas proximal to the thrust front.

CONCLUSIONS

Based on the lithostratigraphic, chronostratigraphic, and depositional considerations presented, the incorporation of Pigeon Creek strata into the Cedar Mountain Formation, as proposed by various workers, does not seem warranted. The Pigeon Creek and Cedar Mountain Formations together, however, form

Pigeon Creek Fm. — Depositional Model

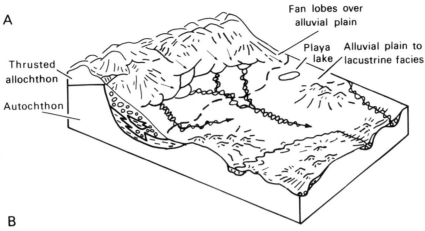

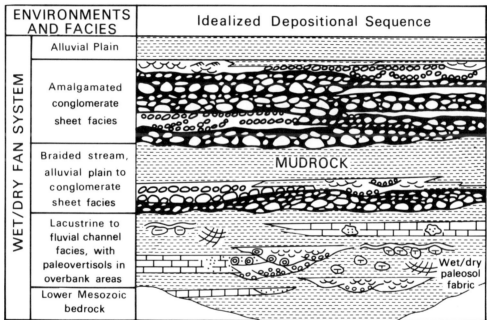

Figure 22. A, Depositional model for Pigeon Creek Formation featuring wet/dry alluvial fan, braided stream, and flood-basin environments. Sheet conglomerates are deposited in laterally overlapping fan bodies forming a low-relief bajada adjacent to the thrust front. Flood-plain environments are dominated by overbank fines and playa lakes. B, Idealized Pigeon Creek depositional sequence illustrating the lateral and vertical facies associations and related environments for the alluvial foreland basin fill.

an unconformity-bounded unit of regional to interregional extent. The apparent differences in the depositional and formational character of the two formations that compose the Pigeon Creek–Cedar Mountain synthem, are useful for developing an understanding of sedimentation response to earliest foreland basin evolution.

Earliest foreland basin deposition in Utah is marked by the thick sequences of syntectonic Pigeon Creek strata that were deposited proximal to the incipient thrust front in restricted areas of subsidence. Synchronous deposition of thin Cedar Mountain strata in the broader foreland, however, occurred throughout a vast and unrestricted area showing little or no subsidence. These

apparent differences in the dynamics of early foreland basin subsidence between areas proximal and distal to the thrust front are also documented by the existence of multiple superposed intraformational unconformities in the Cedar Mountain Formation, which are absent from the Pigeon Creek Formation.

Earliest foreland basin subsidence in Utah, as shown by this study, was initially restrained and restricted to areas most proximal to the thrust front. Contrary to other workers, the accumulation of thick flood basin and lacustrine fines in a narrow and elongate basin during the Neocomian to early Aptian is interpreted in this study to document the onset of Sevier deformation and basin subsidence. At the same time, the broader foreland to the east featured drainages undergoing repeated degradation, rather than aggradation. The formation of a discrete conglomeratic wedge during the late Aptian and Albian is interpreted to reflect hanging-wall emergence and thrust terrane erosion, which thus postdates the time of initial uplift and foreland basin subsidence. Subsequent to thrust loading in the Sevier belt, large-scale foreland basin deformation was initiated in areas to the east. Similar depositional responses to foreland basin deformation have been described by Schedl and Wiltschko (1984) in the Idaho-Wyoming sector, and by Schwartz (1983) and DeCelles (1986) in the southwestern Montana sector of the thrust-fold belt. More work is necessary, however, to further comprehend the complex patterns of foreland basin deformation during the early stages of subsidence.

The tectono-sedimentologic evolution of the Lower Cretaceous Pigeon Creek Formation in central Utah can be summarized in several phases that reflect the changes in the style of tectonic deformation and basin subsidence.

Phase 1. Thrust-related anticlinal uplift in the Utah segment of the Sevier belt may have developed as early as latest Neocomian and as late as early Aptian time. Erosion of predominantly Mesozoic strata resulted in a high influx of mainly fine-grained detritus into a narrow basin that formed parallel to the tectonic uplands. Uplift-related base-level changes caused basinal alluviation in areas proximal to the thrust front and formed, together with a seasonality in precipitation under a wet/dry climate, the distinct ephemeral braided stream, flood-basin, and playa facies association of the lower Pigeon Creek member (Fig. 22B). Such climatic changes may have resulted from the orographic effects of the incipient Sevier belt. Drainages synchronously active in east-central Utah, however, remained uninfluenced by Sevier belt activities. Buckhorn Conglomerate clastics were deposited in various superposed bed-load to mixed-load drainage systems that incised and later filled the erosional valleys and gullies in the Jurassic Morrison Formation.

Phase 2. Renewed tectonic activity as early as late Aptian and throughout Albian time, probably along the Pavant thrust, resulted in thrust emergence and thrust-nappe formation. The conglomeratic clastics of the upper Pigeon Creek member were shed eastward and prograded over the flood-basin fines of the lower member in laterally overlapping sheet flood–dominated fan systems (Fig. 22A and B). The gradual thickening of chronostratigraphically equivalent strata in the upper Cedar Mountain Formation toward the west is an indication that foreland basin subsidence had become less restricted and restrained, and had progressed farther to the east during Albian time.

Phase 3. Seaway advances into northern Utah and Colorado during the later part of widespread foreland basin subsidence in the late Albian and Cenomanian resulted in the onlap of the marine Dakota Sandstone against Cedar Mountain strata in east-central Utah. Equivalent Cenomanian(?) to Turonian sandstones of the Upper Cretaceous Indianola Group in the study area overlie the Lower Cretaceous Pigeon Creek wedge with apparent disconformity.

ACKNOWLEDGMENTS

I am very grateful to Mary Dylewski for her support, unsurpassed editorial skills, and patience throughout this project. I thank Philip J. Stuecheli for his contributions in field mapping and aspects of the sedimentology, and James W. Collinson for his comments and discussions. I am grateful to Chris Schmidt and other reviewers for their critical, but constructive, reviews. I thank Steve Jacobsen and Sheldon Nelson of Chevron U.S.A., Inc., for providing the palynological data, and Jim Geitgey of Atlantic Richfield Oil and Gas Company for identifying the conodonts. Karen Tyler did some of the drafting. This research is part of a Ph.D. dissertation and was supported by grants from the American Association of Petroleum Geologists Grant-In-Aid, Atlantic Richfield Oil and Gas Company, Chevron Field Studies Fund, Shell Western Exploration and Production Company, Sigma XI, The Research Society, and by Grant 3491-85 from the Geological Society of America.

REFERENCES CITED

Ahmad, N., 1983, Vertisols, *in* Wilding, L. P., Smeck, N. E., and Ball, G. F., eds., Pedogenesis and soil taxonomy; Part 2, Developments in soil sciences: New York, Elsevier Science Publishing Co., Inc., p. 91–123.

Allen, J.R.L., 1978, Studies in fluviatile sedimentation; An exploratory quantitive model for the architecture of avulsion-controlled alluvial suites: Sedimentary Geology, v. 21, p. 129–147.

Allmendinger, R. W., and Jordan, T. E., 1981, Mesozoic evolution, hinterland of the Sevier orogenic belt: Geology, v. 9, p. 308–313.

Allmendinger, R. W., Sharp, J. W., von Tish, D., Serpa, L., Brown, L., Kaufman, S., and Oliver, J., 1983, Cenozoic and Mesozoic structure of the eastern Basin and Range, Utah, from COCORP seismic-reflection data: Geology, v. 11, p. 532–536.

Armstrong, F. C., and Oriel, S. S., 1965, Tectonic development of Idaho-Wyoming thrust belt: American Association of Petroleum Geologists Bulletin, v. 50, p. 2614–2621.

Armstrong, R. L., 1968, Sevier orogenic belt in Nevada and Utah: Geological Society of America Bulletin, v. 79, p. 429–458.

Blair, T. C., 1987, Sedimentary processes, vertical stratification sequences, and geomorphology of the Roaring River alluvial fan, Rocky Mountain National Park, Colorado: Journal of Sedimentary Petrology, v. 57, p. 1–18.

Brewer, R., 1976, Fabric and mineral analysis of soils: Huntington, New York, Robert E. Krieger Publishing Co., 482 p.

Bridge, J. S., 1985, Paleochannel patterns inferred from alluvial deposits; A critical evaluation: Journal of Sedimentary Petrology, v. 55, p. 579–589.

Burchfiel, B. C., 1980, Plate tectonics and the continents; A review, *in* Continental tectonics: National Academy of Sciences Studies in Geophysics, p. 15–25.

Burchfiel, B. C., and Hickcox, C. W., 1972, Structural development of central Utah, *in* Baer, J. L., and Callaghan, E., eds., Plateau–Basin and Range transition zone, central Utah: Utah Geological Association Publication 2, p. 55–73.

Christiansen, F. W., 1952, Structure and stratigraphy of the Canyon Range, central Utah: Geological Society of America Bulletin, v. 63, p. 717–740.

Christopher, J. E., 1984, The Lower Cretaceous Mannville Group, northern Williston Basin region, Canada, *in* Stott, D. F., and Glass, D. J., eds., The Mesozoic of middle North America: Canadian Society of Petroleum Geologists Memoir 9, p. 109–126.

Cobban, W. A., 1976, Ammonite record from Mancos Shale of the Castle Valley–Price–Woodside area, east-central Utah: Brigham Young University Geology Studies, v. 22, p. 117–126.

Costello, W. R., and Walker, R. G., 1972, Pleistocene sedimentology, Credit River, southern Ontario; A new component of the braided river model: Journal of Sedimentary Petrology, v. 42, p. 389–400.

DeCelles, P. G., 1986, Sedimentation in a tectonically partitioned, nonmarine foreland basin; The Lower Cretaceous Kootenai Formation, southwestern Montana: Geological Society of America Bulletin, v. 97, p. 911–931.

Eyer, J. A., 1969, Gannett Group of western Wyoming and southeastern Idaho: American Association of Petroleum Geologists Bulletin, v. 53, p. 1368–1390.

Ferguson, R. I., and Werritty, A., 1983, Bar development and channel changes in the gravelly River Feshie, Scotland, *in* Collinson, J. D., and Lewin, J., eds., Modern and ancient fluvial systems: International Association of Sedimentologists Special Publication 6, p. 181–193.

Fouch, T. D., Lawton, T. F., Nichols, D. J., Cashion, W. B., and Cobban, W. A., 1983, Patterns and timing of synorogenic sedimentation in Upper Cretaceous rocks of central and northeast Utah, *in* Reynolds, M. W., and Dolly, E. D., eds., Mesozoic paleogeography of the west-central United States: Denver, Colorado, Rocky Mountain Section of the Society of Economic Paleontologists and Mineralogists Rocky Mountain Paleogeography Symposium 2, p. 305–336.

Friend, P. F., 1978, Distinctive features in some ancient river systems, *in* Miall, A. D., ed., Fluvial sedimentology: Canadian Society of Petroleum Geologists Memoir 5, p. 531–542.

—— , 1983, Towards the field classification of alluvial architecture or sequence, *in* Collinson, J. D., and Lewin, J., eds., Modern and ancient fluvial systems: International Association of Sedimentologists Special Publication 6, p. 345–353.

Garner, H. F., 1959, Stratigraphic-sedimentary significance of contemporary climate and relief in four regions of the Andes Mountains: Geological Society of America Bulletin, v. 70, p. 1327–1368.

—— , 1979, Coarsening-upward cycles in the alluvium of Hornelen basin (Devonian), Norway; Sedimentary response to tectonic events; Discussion and reply: Geological Society of America Bulletin, v. 90, p. 121–124.

Graham, J. R., 1983, Analysis of the Upper Devonian Munster Basin; An example of a fluvial distributary system, *in* Collinson, J. D., and Lewin, J., eds., Modern and ancient fluvial systems: International Association of Sedimentologists Special Publication 6, p. 473–483.

Graham, S. A., Tolson, R. B., DeCelles, P. G., Ingersoll, R. V., Bargar, E., Caldwell, M., Cvazza, W., Edwards, D. P., Follo, M. F., Handschy, J. F., Lemke, L., Moxon, I., Rice, R., Smith, G. A., and White, J., 1986, Provenance modelling as a technique for analyzing source terrane evolution and controls for foreland sedimentation, *in* Allen, P. A., and Homewood, P., eds., Foreland basins: International Association of Sedimentologists Special Publication 8, p. 425–436.

Hale, L. A., and Van DeGraaf, F. R., 1964, Cretaceous stratigraphy and facies patterns, northeastern Utah and adjacent areas, *in* The geology and mineral resources of the Uinta Basin; Utah's hydrocarbon storehouse: Intermountain Association of Petroleum Geologists 13th Annual Field Conference Guidebook, p. 115–138.

Hardy, C. T., 1952, Eastern Sevier Valley, Sevier and Sanpete Counties, Utah: Utah Geological and Mineral Survey Bulletin, v. 43, 98 p.

Hardy, C. T., and Zeller, H. D., 1953, Geology of the west-central part of the Gunnison Plateau: Geological Society of America Bulletin, v. 64, p. 1261–1278.

Harris, D. R., 1980, Exhumed paleochannels in the Lower Cretaceous Cedar Mountain Formation near Green River, Utah: Brigham Young University Geology Studies, v. 27, p. 51–66.

Hein, F. J., and Walker, R. G., 1977, Bar evolution and development of stratification of the gravelly, braided Kicking Horse River, British Columbia: Canadian Journal of Earth Sciences, v. 14, p. 562–570.

Heller, P. L., Bowdler, S. S., Chambers, H. P., Coogan, J. C., Hagen, E. S., Shuster, M. W., Winslow, N. S., and Lawton, T. F., 1986, Time of initial thrusting in the Sevier orogenic belt, Idaho-Wyoming, and Utah: Geology, v. 14, p. 288–291.

Heward, A. P., 1978a, Alluvial fan and lacustrine sediments from the Stephanian A and B (La Magdalena, Cinera-Mtallana, and Sabaro) coalfields, northern Spain: Sedimentology, v. 25, p. 451–488.

—— , 1978b, Alluvial fan sequences and megasequence models, with examples from the Westphalian D-Stephanian B coalfields, northern Spain, *in* Miall, A. D., ed., Fluvial sedimentology: Canadian Society of Petroleum Geologists Memoir 5, p. 669–702.

Hickcox, C. W., 1971, The geology of a portion of the Pavant Range allochthon, Millard County, Utah [Ph.D. thesis]: Ann Arbor, Michigan, University Microfilms International, 67 p.

Hubert, J. F., and Hyde, M. G., 1982, Sheet flow deposits of graded beds and mudstones on an alluvial sandflat-playa system; Upper Triassic Blomidan redbeds, St. Mary's Bay, Nova Scotia: Sedimentology, v. 29, p. 457–474.

Hunt, R. E., 1950, The geology of the northern part of the Gunnison Plateau, Utah [Ph.D. thesis]: Columbus, Ohio State University, 267 p.

ISS, International Subcommission on Stratigraphic Classification, Salvador, A., chairman, 1987, Unconformity-bounded stratigraphic units: Geological Society of America Bulletin, v. 98, p. 232–237.

Jefferson, W. S., 1982, Structural and stratigraphic relations of Upper Cretaceous to Lower Tertiary orogenic sediments in the Cedar Hills, Utah, *in* Nielson, D. L., ed., Overthrust belt of Utah: Utah Geological Association Publication 10, p. 65–80.

Jordan, T. E., 1981, Thrust loads and foreland basin evolution, Cretaceous, western United States: American Association of Petroleum Geologists Bulletin, v. 65, p. 2506–2520.

Larsen, V., and Steel, R. J., 1978, The sedimentary history of a debris-flow dominated, Devonian alluvial fan; A study of textural inversion: Sedimentology, v. 25, p. 37–59.

Lawton, T. F., 1985, Style and timing of frontal structures, thrust belt, central Utah: American Association of Petroleum Geologists Bulletin, v. 5, p. 1145–1159.

—— , 1986, Compositional trends within a clastic wedge adjacent to a thrust-fold belt, Indianola Group, central Utah, U.S.A., *in* Allen, P. A., and Homewood, P., eds., Foreland basins: International Association of Sedimentologists Special Publication 8, p. 411–423.

Leopold, L. B., and Wolman, M. G., 1957, River channel patterns; Braided, meandering, and straight: U.S. Geological Survey Professional Paper 282-B, p. 39–84.

Lessard, R. H., 1973, Micropaleontology and paleoecology of the Tununk Member of the Mancos Shale: Utah Geological and Mineral Survey Special Study 45, 28 p.

McGookey, D. P., 1972, Cretaceous System, *in* Mallory, W. W., ed., Geologic atlas of the Rocky Mountain region, U.S.A.: Denver, Colorado, Rocky Mountain Association of Geologists, p. 190–228.

Miall, A. D., 1970, Devonian alluvial fans, Prince of Wales Island, Arctic Canada: Journal of Sedimentary Petrology, v. 40, p. 556–571.

—— , 1983, Basin analysis of fluvial sediments, *in* Collinson, J. D., and Lewin, J., eds., Modern and ancient fluvial systems: International Association of Sedimentologists Special Publication 6, p. 279–285.

Peterson, F., 1986, Jurassic paleotectonics in the west-central part of the Colorado Plateau, Utah and Arizona, *in* Peterson, J. A., ed., Paleotectonics and sedimentation: American Association of Petroleum Geologists Memoir 41, p. 563–595.

Ramos, A., and Sopena, A., 1983, Gravel bars in low-sinuosity streams (Permian and Triassic, central Spain), *in* Collinson, J. D., and Lewin, J., eds., Modern and ancient fluvial systems: International Association of Sedimentologists Special Publication 6, p. 301–312.

Royse, F., Jr., Warner, M. A., and Reese, D. L., 1975, Thrust belt structural geometry and related stratigraphic problems, Wyoming-Idaho-northern Utah, *in* Bolygard, D. W., ed., Deep drilling frontiers of the central Rocky Mountains: Denver, Colorado, Rocky Mountain Association of Geologists, p. 41–55.

Rubey, W. W., 1973, New Cretaceous formations in the western Wyoming thrust belt: U.S. Geological Survey Bulletin 1372-I, 35 p.

Rust, B. R., 1978, Depositional models for braided alluvium, *in* Miall, A. D., ed., Fluvial sedimentology: Canadian Society of Petroleum Geologists Memoir 5, p. 605–625.

Schedl, A., and Wiltschko, D. V., 1984, Sedimentological effects of a moving terrain: Journal of Geology, v. 92, p. 273–287.

Schmidt, J. G., Sippel, K. N., and Wallen, B. B., 1981, Upper Jurassic through lowermost Cretaceous sedimentation in the Wyoming-Idaho-Utah thrust belt; I. Depositional environments and facies distribution [abs.], *in* Sedimentary tectonics; Principles and applications: Department of Geology, University of Wyoming, Wyoming Geological Survey, and Wyoming Geological Association Conference Notes May 3–5, p. 26–27.

Schoff, S. L., 1951, Geology of the Cedar Hills: Geological Society of America Bulletin, v. 62, p. 619–646.

Schumm, S. A., 1976, Episodic erosion; A modification of the geomorphic cycle, *in* Melhorn, W. N., and Flemal, R. C., eds., Theories of landform development; Proceedings 6th Geomorphology Symposium: State University of New York at Binghamton, p. 69–85.

—— , 1981, Evolution and response of the fluvial system; Sedimentological implications, *in* Ethridge, F. G., and Flores, R. M., eds., Recent and ancient nonmarine depositional environments; Models for exploration: Society of Economic Paleontologists and Mineralogists Special Publication 31, p. 19–29.

Schwab, F. L., 1986, Sedimentary "signatures" of foreland basin assemblages; Real or counterfeit? *in* Allen, P. A., and Homewood, P., eds., Foreland basins: International Association of Sedimentologists Special Publication 8, p. 395–410.

Schwans, P., 1985, Fanglomerate deposition in the foreland of the Sevier Overthrust Belt, control, facies, and timing of earliest syntectonic deposition in Utah, western U.S. [abs.]: Proceedings 3rd International Fluvial Sedimentology Conference, Fort Collins, Colorado, p. 34.

—— , 1986, Early Cretaceous depositional sequence evolution in the foreland of the Sevier overthrust belt in west-central Utah: Geological Society of America Abstracts with Programs, v. 18, p. 411.

Schwartz, R. K., 1983, Broken Early Cretaceous foreland basin in southwestern Montana: Sedimentation related totectonism, *in* Powers, R. B., ed., Geologic studies in the Cordilleran thrust belt, 1982: Denver, Colorado, Rocky Mountain Association of Geologists, v. 1, p. 159–184.

Sippel, K. N., Schmidt, J. A., Wallen, D. B., and Moran, M. E., 1981, Upper Jurassic through lowermost Cretaceous sedimentation in the Wyoming-Idaho-Utah thrust belt; II. Provenance and tectonic implications [abs.], *in* Sedimentary tectonics; Principles and applications: Department of Geology, University of Wyoming, Wyoming Geological Survey, and Wyoming Geological Association Conference Notes May 3–5, p. 28–29.

Smith, D. G., and Smith, N. D., 1980, Sedimentation in anastomosed river system; Modern and ancient examples in Alberta, Canada: Journal of Sedimentary Petrology, v. 50, p. 157–164.

Spieker, E. M., 1946, Late Mesozoic and early Cenozoic history of central Utah: U.S. Geological Survey Professional Paper 205-D, p. 117–161.

—— , 1949, The transition between the Colorado Plateaus and the Great Basin in central Utah: Utah Geological Society Guidebook to the Geology of Utah, v. 4, 106 p.

Standlee, L. A., 1983, Structure and stratigraphy of Jurassic rocks in central Utah; Their influence on tectonic development of the Cordilleran foreland thrust belt, *in* Powers, R. B., ed., Geologic studies of the Cordilleran thrust belt, 1982: Denver, Colorado, Rocky Mountain Association of Geologists, v. 1, p. 357–382.

Stear, W. M., 1983, Morphological characteristics of ephemeral stream channel and overbank splay sandstone bodies in the Permian Lower Beaufort Group, Karoo Basin, South Africa, *in* Collinson, J. D., and Lewin, J., eds., Modern and ancient fluvial systems: International Association of Sedimentologists Special Publication 6, p. 405–420.

Steel, R. J., and Aasheim, S. M., 1978, Alluvial sand deposition in a rapidly subsiding basin (Devonian, Norway), *in* Miall, A. D., ed., Fluvial sedimentology: Canadian Society of Petroleum Geologists Memoir 5, p. 385–412.

Steel, R. J., and others, 1977, Coarsening-upward cycles in the alluvium of Hornelen Basin (Devonian), Norway; Sedimentary response to tectonic events: Geological Society of America Bulletin, v. 88, p. 1124–1134.

Stokes, W. L., 1972, Stratigraphic problems of the Triassic and Jurassic sedimentary rocks of central Utah, *in* Baer, J. L., and Callaghan, E., eds., Plateau-Basin and Range transition zone, central Utah: Utah Geological Association Publication 2, p. 21–28.

Stuecheli, P. J., 1984, The sedimentology, depositional setting, and age of the Morrison(?) Formation in central Utah [M.S. thesis]: Columbus, Ohio State University, 104 p.

Stuecheli, P. J., and Collinson, J. S., 1984, Sedimentology of synorogenic conglomerates of the Lower Cretaceous Morrison(?) Formation, central Utah: Geological Society of America Abstracts with Programs, v. 16, p. 200.

Suttner, L. J., 1969, Stratigraphic and petrographic analysis of Upper Jurassic-Lower Cretaceous Morrison and Kootenai Formations, southwest Montana: American Association of Petroleum Geologists Bulletin, v. 53, p. 1391–1410.

Tschudy, R. H., Tschudy, B. D., and Craig, L. C., 1984, Palynological evaluation of Cedar Mountain and Burro Canyon Formations, Colorado Plateau: U.S. Geological Survey Professional Paper 1281, 21 p.

Tunbridge, I. P., 1984, Facies model for a sandy ephemeral stream and clay playa complex; The Middle Devonian Trentishoe Formation of North Devon, U.S.: Sedimentology, v. 31, p. 697–717.

Van Der Meulen, S., 1986, Sedimentary stratigraphy of Eocene sheetflood deposits, southern Pyrenees, Spain: Geological Magazine, v. 123, p. 167–183.

Villien, A., and Kligfield, R., 1986, Thrusting and synorogenic sedimentation in central Utah, *in* Peterson, J. A., ed., Paleotectonics and sedimentation: American Association of Petroleum Geologists Memoir 41, p. 281–307.

Vuke, S. M., 1984, Depositional environments of the Early Cretaceous western interior seaway in southwestern Montana and the northern United States, *in* Stott, D. F., and Glass, D. J., eds., The Mesozoic of middle North America: Canadian Society of Petroleum Geologists Memoir 9, p. 127–144.

Weimer, R. J., 1984, Relation of unconformities, tectonics, and sea-level changes, Cretaceous of Western Interior, U.S.A., *in* Schlee, J. S., ed., Interregional unconformities and hydrocarbon accumulation: American Association of Petroleum Geologists Memoir 36, p. 7–36.

Wells, N. A., 1983, Transient streams in sand-poor redbeds; Early Middle Eocene Kuldana Formation of northern Pakistan, *in* Collinson, J. D., and Lewin, J., eds., Modern and ancient fluvial systems: International Association of Sedimentologists Special Publication 6, p. 393–403.

—— , 1984, Sheet debris flow and sheetflood conglomerates in Cretaceous cool-maritime alluvial fans, South Orkney Islands, Antarctica, *in* Koster, E. H., and Steel, R. J., eds., Sedimentology of gravels and conglomerates: Canadian Society of Petroleum Geologists Memoir 10, p. 133–145.

Williams, P. F., and Rust, B. R., 1969, The sedimentology of a braided river: Journal of Sedimentary Petrology, v. 39, p. 649–679.

Wiltschko, D. V., and Dorr, J. A., 1983, Timing of deformation in overthrust belt and foreland of Idaho, Wyoming, and Utah: American Association of Petroleum Geologists Bulletin, v. 67, p. 1304–1322.

Witkind, I. J., Standlee, L. A., and Maley, K. F., 1986, Age and correlation of Cretaceous rocks previously assigned to the Morrison(?) Formation, Sanpete–Sevier Valley area, central Utah: U.S. Geological Survey Bulletin 1584, 9 p.

Yingling, V. L., 1987, Timing of initiation of the Sevier orogeny; Morrison and Cedar Mountain Formations and Dakota Sandstone, east-central Utah [M.S. thesis]: Laramie, University of Wyoming, 169 p.

Young, R. G., 1960, Dakota Group of Colorado Plateau: American Association of Petroleum Geologists Bulletin, v. 44, p. 156–194.

—— , 1970, Lower Cretaceous of Wyoming and the southern Rockies: Mountain Geologist, v. 7, p. 105–121.

MANUSCRIPT ACCEPTED BY THE SOCIETY FEBRUARY 9, 1988

Geological Society of America
Memoir 171
1988

The Cedar Mountain Formation (Lower Cretaceous) in the Gunnison Plateau, central Utah

Malcolm P. Weiss and Michael G. Roche*
Department of Geology, Northern Illinois University, DeKalb, Illinois 60115

ABSTRACT

Along the southeast flank of the Gunnison Plateau, southwest of Sterling, Utah, red and violet mudstones, some of which contain limy nodules and "gastroliths," and interbedded sandstones, conglomerates, and thin limestones, have long been considered a possible correlative of the Jurassic Morrison Formation, and are often mapped as "Morrison(?)." The lower 134-m interval is now known to conformably underlie strata containing fossils of Cretaceous age (Albian-Cenomanian); it contains limy nodules, oncolites, limestone beds, and bright red mudstones, and is assigned to the Cedar Mountain Formation of Early Cretaceous age. The upper part of the sequence underlies sandstone like the Sanpete Formation, and is assigned to an as-yet unnamed basal unit of the Indianola Group, of which the Sanpete was heretofore the lowest formation recognized. The names Morrison and Morrison(?) are abandoned for outcrops in central Utah.

The very limited areas of outcrop of these units in the deformed east front of the Gunnison Plateau are identified and described, in revision of earlier published work. Exposures of the Cedar Mountain Formation at the north end of the Gunnison Plateau and along its west flank are described for the first time; they show an irregular trend of southward thinning. Substitution of Cedar Mountain for the lower part of the Morrison(?) means that true Morrison strata (i.e., Jurassic) do not occur in central Utah and that there is a record of Lower Cretaceous terrestrial sedimentation in central Utah from near Thistle, 35 km (22 mi) northeast of the plateau, through the Gunnison Plateau, and down to Salina Canyon, 25 km (16 mi) south of the plateau. Under this new interpretation the earliest stages of the Sevier Orogeny are represented by the Cedar Mountain Formation (lower part of the former Morrison? Formation); this interval probably is Early Cretaceous in age rather than Jurassic.

INTRODUCTION

The Gunnison Plateau (or San Pitch Mountains) (Fig. 1) lies in the middle of the state of Utah and is the northwesternmost element of the Colorado Plateaus Province (Witkind and Weiss, 1985; Witkind and others, 1987). It is part of the High Plateaus Section of the Colorado Plateaus and has a mixture of geologic features from the Plateau Province and the Great Basin. The Mesozoic and Cenozoic strata are more similar to those of regions to the east, although some units occur in the Great Basin. The folded structures in Cretaceous and younger rocks are open like

those to the east, rather than thrust and overturned as they are in the eastern Great Basin. By contrast, the older rocks of the Gunnison Plateau are strongly deformed everywhere. The Jurassic-Tertiary beds are deformed on the east front, and the plateau is bounded by faults and cut through by many high-angle normal faults. All of these are features of the Basin and Range Province.

Most of the geologic mapping of the Gunnison Plateau has been done by students of the late E. M. Spieker, a pioneer student of central Utah geology. Most of that work was done more than 30 years ago, before topographic maps became available. Although largely unpublished, the work has been integrated into maps on a scale of 1:100,000 prepared by the U.S. Geological

---
*Present address: Testing Service Corporation, 457 East Gundersen Drive, Carol Stream, Illinois 60188.

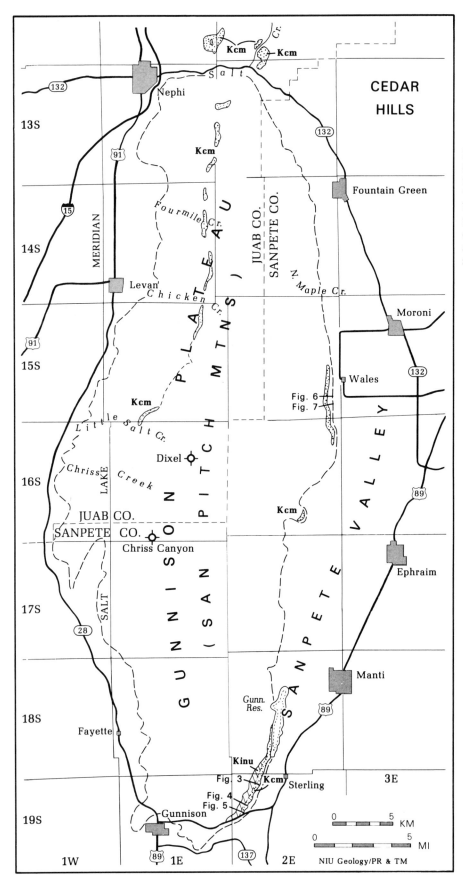

Figure 1. Index map of part of central Utah (modified from Weiss, 1982). Localities and sections described and illustrated (Figs. 3 through 7) are indicated by short labeled lines. The larger bands of Cedar Mountain (Kcm) are stippled; the new basal Indianola unit (Kinu) outcrop has diagonal lines. Dixel and Chriss Canyon wells are also shown (⬦). Line of long dashes represents edge of Gunnison Plateau.

Survey (Witkind and Weiss, 1985; Witkind and others, 1987). This newer work, as well as recent thesis work by students at Brigham Young, Northern Illinois, and Ohio State Universities, has carried forward that begun by Spieker and his students.

Two problems have long puzzled students of the Gunnison Plateau. The identity and historical significance of red beds at the southeastern corner of the plateau, mapped as Morrison(?) Formation by Spieker (1949), have never been clarified, even though Stokes (1972) believed the red beds probably belong to the Cedar Mountain Formation, whose type area is the San Rafael Swell. Also, the origin of the structures within and bordering the plateau is still a much-discussed matter; traditional interpretations of regional compression and uplift have been challenged recently by Witkind (1982, 1983), who has ascribed most of the folded and faulted features to salt diapirism occurring episodically from the Late Cretaceous to the present. Detailed subsurface data, however, show the structural history can be explained wholly in terms of thrust faults and subsequent motion reversal during extension (Standlee, 1983; Lawton, 1985). This chapter focuses on the first of these long-standing problems, the stratigraphy.

The stratigraphic columns used recently for central Utah (Fig. 2) imply a full record of Jurassic sediments and a hiatus of the entire Early Cretaceous, even though Armstrong (1968) theorized that Sevier deformation may have begun in either Late Jurassic or Early Cretaceous. The revised correlation (Stuecheli and Collinson, 1984; Roche, 1985; Witkind and others, 1986) makes the hiatus range from the Latest Jurassic to pre-Albian Cretaceous, which means the Sevier Orogeny began in the Early Cretaceous in central Utah. Heller and others (1986) have come to much the same conclusion for northern Utah and Wyoming.

The problem

A sequence of steeply dipping, mostly red, mudstones and conglomerates that are concordant with east-dipping, overturned beds of the Cretaceous Indianola Group crop out along the southeastern flank of the Gunnison Plateau (Fig. 1). Both are overstepped from the west by North Horn and Flagstaff beds that lie in angular unconformity on the older units. The red bed sequence is exposed along the west side of the Gunnison Reservoir, opposite Sterling, and southwestward for about 8 km (5 mi) to U.S. Highway 89 (Fig. 1). The best exposures with the greatest thicknesses are toward the highway, where a section was measured by A. J. Eardley in 1929 (E. M. Spieker, personal communication, 1957).* These red beds overlie marine mudstones of the Jurassic Twist Gulch Formation (Fig. 2) in the west part of the antiform† that occupies the south end of Sanpete Valley, between the Gunnison Plateau and Sixmile Canyon just east of Sterling.

---

*Eardley's notebook is in the Spieker archive of Orton Memorial Geological Library, Ohio State University.

†L. A. Standlee (personal communication, 1986) has pointed out that this may be an anticline as traditionally explained, or produced by a major thrust.

The red bed sequence was previously believed to be nonfossiliferous, but thin intervals containing microfossils and a few poorly preserved macrofossils have been found (Stuecheli, 1984; Roche, 1985; Witkind and others, 1986). Fouch and others (1983, p. 12) refer to a continuum in this locality of Morrison–Cedar Mountain?–Indianola.

A similar red bed sequence lies in a comparable position beneath the Indianola Group along Soldier Fork east of Thistle, 85 km (56 mi) to the northeast of Sterling (Fig. 1), and in Salina Canyon, 25 km (16 mi) to the south of Sterling (Spieker, 1946). Spieker and Reeside (1926) had earlier recognized the similarity of the sequence in Salina Canyon to the Morrison Formation farther east. Eardley identified the difficult and apparently nonfossiliferous section along Hwy. 89 as Morrison, and Spieker concurred (E. M. Spieker, personal communication, 1957).

Spieker later realized that some of the rock types in the so-called Morrison resemble some in the Indianola Group, and that he could find no unconformity between these units, and so he adopted the name Morrison(?) for these red beds (Spieker, 1946). The unit has heretofore not been mapped or recognized on the west side of the Gunnison Plateau (Hardy and Zeller, 1953; Hunt, 1950).

Work on the Morrison Formation of the San Rafael Swell by W. L. Stokes (1944, 1952) showed that some beds previously assigned to the Morrison are really Early Cretaceous, and he applied the name Cedar Mountain Formation (Stokes, 1944) to these younger beds. The concept raised the possibility that the Morrison(?) beds of central Utah are a part of or equivalent to the Cedar Mountain Formation and are younger than Jurassic, but little work was done on this possible correlation. Stokes, however, anticipated the recognition of the Cedar Mountain in Sanpete Valley (Stokes, 1972). Moreover, the virtual lack of macrofossils in the Morrison(?) beds in central Utah delayed certain recognition there of the Cedar Mountain. Further, Cretaceous microfossils have been collected from the unit at several times and places in recent years (Stuecheli, 1984; Roche, 1985; Witkind and others, 1986). The Morrison Formation may, of course, be diachronous, but the nomenclature has not developed along that line.

A different assignment of the former Morrison(?) beds along Hwy. 89 west of Sterling was published by Taylor (1980), who incorrectly mapped them as North Horn Formation. We first redefine units in the southeast corner of the Gunnison Plateau, then along the deformed east flank of the plateau, and then describe occurrences of the Cedar Mountain Formation on the west and north sides of the plateau.

CEDAR MOUNTAIN FORMATION IN THE TYPE AREA

Stokes (1944) described the Cedar Mountain Shale as variegated beds lying above the Buckhorn Conglomerate and beneath the locally pebbly yellow sandstones of the Dakota(?) near Cedar Mountain on the north end of the San Rafael Swell. He remarked

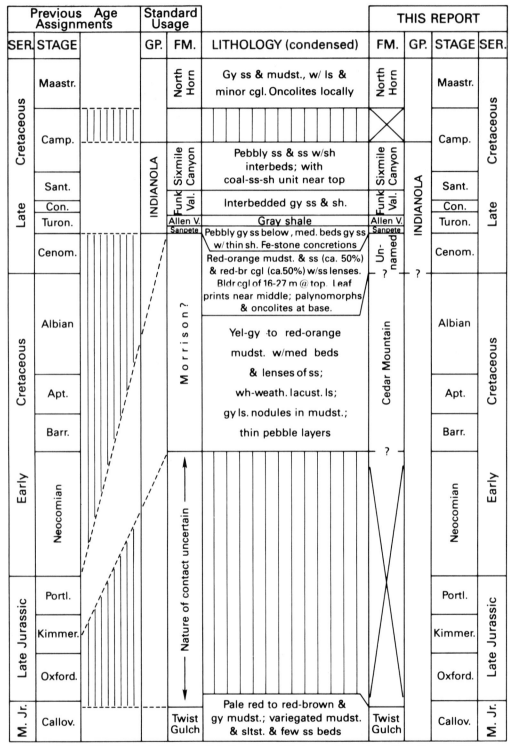

Figure 2. Simplified Geologic Column of late Jurassic and Cretaceous interval, southern Sanpete Valley. Allen Valley–Sixmile Canyon Formations are not exposed in the southeastern Gunnison Plateau. Villien (1984) has given the age of the Twist Gulch Formation as Aptian to Albian, based on palynomorphs from one sample, but there is no consensus yet on this drastic change of age assignment. Villien later placed the Twist Gulch in the Barremian and most of the Aptian (Villien and Kligfield, 1986, Fig. 3).

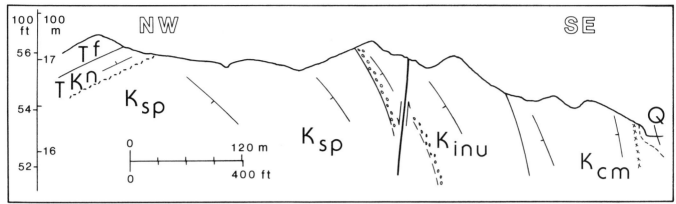

Figure 3. Stratigraphy and structure at the Radio Tower Valley section (modified from Roche's No. 13, 1985). Tf = Flagstaff, TKn = North Horn, Ksp = Sanpete, Kinu = Indianola, new basal unit, Kcm = Cedar Mountain, Q = valley fill. Line of xxx marks the limestone bed low in the Kcm. Line of circles represents the big boulder bed at top of new unit of the Indianola. Facing and dip of beds at the surface are shown by lines having short line on the tops of the strata. Throw on fault indeterminate.

on its similarity to the Brushy Basin Shale Member of the Morrison, but believed lithic differences were distinct and regionally persistent enough to justify a new formation. Fossil evidence subsequently showed that the Cedar Mountain is Early Cretaceous in age (Stokes, 1952), and he concluded that the sedimentary change from the upper member of the Morrison (Brushy Basin Shale) to the Buckhorn Conglomerate, which resembles lithic changes at the Jurassic-Cretaceous boundary elsewhere in the western interior, strongly suggests an Early Cretaceous age for the Buckhorn as well.

The Cedar Mountain Shale lies in sharp contact on the Buckhorn Conglomerate, has duller colors than the Brushy Basin Shale, lacks the many clearly bounded color bands of the older unit, and in the type area is light red to purple in the lower part, and gray to white in the upper part. Calcareous nodules and "gastroliths" are conspicuous by their abundance throughout the Cedar Mountain; Stokes (1944) noted that the "gastrolith" clasts are of rock types found in the underlying Buckhorn, and that the "gastroliths" themselves are nearly confined to the Cedar Mountain. It is now known that some of the calcareous nodules of the Cedar Mountain are oncolites, whereas others are structureless.

Stokes (1944) named both the Cedar Mountain Shale and the underlying Buckhorn Conglomerate, but later (1952) cited "Cedar Mountain formation" and "Buckhorn conglomerate member" as parts of the Cedar Mountain Formation. Hale and Van de Graaff (1964) applied Cedar Mountain to both units, made the Buckhorn a member of the Cedar Mountain Formation, and left the shale/mudstone unit as an unnamed member. As the Buckhorn is not present in central Utah, we prefer Stokes's original concept, named formation. The Cedar Mountain Formation in its type area is latest Aptian and Albian in age (Hintze, 1985). Zircons from the lower part of the Cedar Mountain Formation east of Capitol Reef National Monument show it is Late Albian (B. J. Kowallis, personal communication, 1987), which conforms to the paleontological conclusions of Tschudy and others (1984).

Bentonites in the Morrison at the same locality east of Capitol Reef have been dated by fission tracks in zircons (Kowallis and others, 1986; Kowallis and Heaton, 1987). The bulk of the Morrison there is Tithonian, but the upper one-quarter of its Brushy Basin Member is middle Albian.

SOUTHEAST GUNNISON PLATEAU

The outcrops of Morrison(?) beds along the flank of the Gunnison Plateau southward from the Gunnison Reservoir to U.S. Highway 89 are the most complete and best exposures of this equivocal unit (Figs. 1, 2). Witkind and others (1986) consider the age assignment of this unit and its correlation with beds elsewhere in the Colorado Plateau in detail. Stuecheli (1984) studied the sedimentation and environment of deposition as well as the age of the Morrison(?) beds. We do not duplicate their work, but wish merely to establish the identity of the beds at this locality as a reference for discussion of their correlatives elsewhere on the Gunnison Plateau. Roche (1985) studied equivocal rock units heretofore variously assigned to the Indianola or to the Morrison(?), along the east front of the Gunnison Plateau, from Hwy. 89 northward to Wales and beyond. Not far north of Wales (Fig. 1) the unit is truncated structurally, as the subjacent Twist Gulch Formation is reverse-faulted against the Indianola and Price River sandstones and conglomerates (Weiss, 1982).

Roche (1985) studied three sections (Tables 1, 2; Figs. 3, 4, 5) in the Morrison(?) beds between the Gunnison Reservoir and Hwy. 89, all in T.19S.,R.2E.,SLM. Stuecheli (1984) measured the section of Table 2 and several others in the vicinity. The Morrison(?) contains palynomorphs no older than Cenomanian (*Complexiopollis* cf. *patulus* and *Seductisporites* sp., S. M. Nelson, personal communication, 1984) (Roche, 1985) and limited mollusks and plants no older than early Cenomanian or late Albian (Stuecheli, 1984). The palynomorphs and some molluscs occur in a dark gray mudstone near the middle of Roche's Section 14E (Table 2); Stuecheli (1984) also found angiosperm leaf

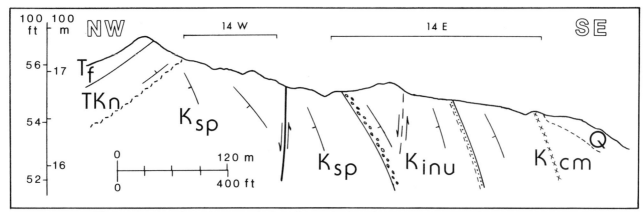

Figure 4. Stratigraphy and structure in the valley south of Radio Tower Valley (modified from Roche's No. 14, 1985); east and west parts described in Table 2. Formation and other symbols same as in Figure 3. Row of dots represents a limy sandstone with many oncolites in it; the dashed line stratigraphically above it represents a lag accumulation of chert pebbles. The fossiliferous dark gray mudstone lies directly on this unit. Throw on fault is indeterminate.

prints of late Albian to early Cenomanian age in sandstones above the dark mudstone. Thus, the younger part of the Morrison(?) is not Jurassic; we believe also that the older part can be shown to be the Early Cretaceous Cedar Mountain Formation because of close lithologic similarity to the type Cedar Mountain. The Buckhorn Conglomerate, or equivalent, does not occur in Central Utah.

A number of additional fossils, mostly nonmarine palynomorphs, are identified by Witkind and others (1986). They, too, separate the old Morrison(?) into the same two units, of which the lower contains only nondiagnostic Jurassic–Early Cretaceous species. The lower part of the upper unit, however, contains 12 species of Aptian–early Albian age (Witkind and others, 1986).

The upper unit is not like the Cedar Mountain and, as we show, does not correspond with the rocks of the lower part of the Indianola Group across Sanpete Valley; it does, however, underlie sandstones that do. Roche (1985) concluded that these possibly Upper Cretaceous beds must be a heretofore-unrecognized formation of the Indianola Group (Fig. 2). He called them, informally, the "Gunnison Formation," but if other workers support this view, a different name will be required. Dating of the basal Indianola Group as no older than late Albian is reinforced by Roche's discovery of an angiosperm leaf in a 1-m micrite bed a few meters above the base of the Indianola at North Maple Canyon (Fig. 1; see Fig. 14 in Weiss, 1982). The leaf was identified as a platanoid angiosperm (sycamore-like) by J. A. Wolfe of the U.S. Geological Survey. Similarly, late Albian palynomorphs have been discovered low in the Indianola conglomerates at Chicken Creek, on the west side of the Gunnison Plateau (Standlee, 1983; Lawton, 1985), not far above Cedar Mountain strata discussed later in this chapter.

The exposures along Hwy. 89 (Fig. 5) were not measured, but the units correspond along strike with those farther north (Tables 1, 2; Figs. 3, 4). The identity of the units shown in Figure 5 differ somewhat from those of Weiss (1982), but the changes

do not affect the parts of the old Morrison(?) Formation, namely the Cedar Mountain (Kcm) and the new basal unit of the Indianola Group (Kinu). One important aspect of the conglomerates in the Cedar Mountain and Indianola (new unit) in this vicinity, and not evident from the condensed sections, is that the proportion of limestone clasts decreases northward from about 76 percent to about 15 percent in the vicinity of Wales (Fig. 1), 32 km (20 mi) north (Roche, 1985).

Summary

We believe that the conditions set forth above justify the recognition of the Lower Cretaceous Cedar Mountain Formation in the Gunnison Plateau, and the recognition of a new unit of the Indianola Group—one that underlies the Sanpete Formation, traditionally regarded as the basal part of the group (Fig. 2). The first conclusion was foreseen by Stokes (1972) and demonstrated by Witkind and others (1986), but not the second. The new unit is Aptian to Cenomanian, on paleontological grounds, lithically distinct from the Cedar Mountain by the abundance of conglomerate and the absence of limy nodules, and differs from the Sanpete Formation by the abundance of conglomerate. We believe that a new name should not be put forward now, but that our interpretation of this very difficult sequence of rocks should be supported or revised by other workers before such a step is made. The Morrison is vacated in this area, with or without the query. The Cedar Mountain and the new lower unit of the Indianola make up the Morrison(?) Formation of Weiss (1982) here in the southeast corner of the plateau.

This interpretation has the youngest Jurassic marine beds (the Callovian Twist Gulch Formation) succeeded by marginal marine and terrestrial rocks of Early Cretaceous age—Albian or older. This sequence may require a disconformity and considerable hiatus between the youngest Jurassic and the oldest Cretaceous beds; the interval is not exposed on the east side of the Gunnison Plateau.

T. F. Lawton (personal communication, 1986) has objected to calling the lower part of the old Morrison(?) Cedar Mountain Formation, for the latter cannot be traced into central Utah, and we know the age only of the upper limit in central Utah. Even so, it seems reasonable to recognize the Cedar Mountain Formation in central Utah because of lithic similarity to beds in its type region. If future work proves this wrong, only the identification need be changed; no new formation will need to be suppressed. The absence of the Buckhorn Conglomerate or equivalent strata suggests that the whole unit may be Early Cretaceous in age. The several lithofacies are doubtless diachronous and only more dated samples will resolve the uncertainties.

The alluvial mudstones and sandstones and the few piedmont conglomerates of the Cedar Mountain Formation of this report record the initial effects of the Sevier Orogeny, and show that it began in Early Cretaceous time rather than the Late Jurassic. Stuecheli (1984) and Stuecheli and Collinson (1984) came to the same conclusion, and the former suggested the whole unit may be the Cedar Mountain Formation. This revised timing accords with that suggested by Heller and others (1986) for northern Utah and adjacent areas. Schwans (this volume) shows that these sediments resulted from initiation of thrusting in the Sevier orogenic belt.

Schwans (this volume) has studied the sedimentary tectonics of these rocks and made comparisons with other parts of the foreland basin to the south and north. He also concluded that these rocks are Early Cretaceous in age, and named the old Morrison(?) the Pigeon Creek Formation, from a locality on the west side of the Gunnison Plateau. Schwans divides the Pigeon Creek into lower and upper members, of which the lower is coextensive with the Cedar Mountain Formation of this paper. The upper is a thick wedge of conglomerate at its type section; Schwans infers that the conglomerate grades by facies change and intertonguing southeastward to the mixed conglomerate and mudstone unit identified in this report as the unnamed new basal unit of the Indianola Group.

EAST GUNNISON FRONT

Roche (1985) made comparisons between the Twist Gulch, Morrison(?) and Indianola (undiff.) Formations along the east flank of the Gunnison Plateau (Table 3; Figs. 6, 7), where they are poorly exposed, broken, and bent upward and westward against the main body of the plateau as a result of reverse faulting (Weiss, 1982). Because of the complex structure, small exposures, and uncertain identities, the Morrison(?) and Indianola were mapped as Cretaceous-Jurassic undifferentiated by Witkind and others (1987). The difficulty of distinguishing these two rock units there has troubled geologists for a long time. Roche made comparisons of the stratigraphy and petrology of known and equivocal beds at 12 localities between his section 13 (Fig. 3) and North Maple Canyon (Fig. 1), and with those at the southeast corner of the plateau, just described. The petrographic and stratigraphic features of the three units are given briefly below and

TABLE 1. CONDENSED STRATIGRAPHIC SECTION AT RADIO TOWER VALLEY*

North Horn Formation: 45 m of interbedded mudstone and sandstone dips 25 to 40° NW in angular unconformity over Sanpete sandstone, above and 0.4 km (0.25 mi) west of the measured section.

Indianola Group (Sanpete Formation): pinkish gray to yellowish brown sublitharenite (44 percent)—some fine to medium and some medium to coarse grained, some pebbly, some trough cross-beds in decimeter sets; and local ironstone concretions 1 to 4 cm in diameter. Covered and poorly exposed intervals of gray mudstone (55 percent). Conglomerate (1 percent). Beds strike N34°E, dip 38°SE, and are overturned. These rocks are similar to the basal beds of the Indianola exposed across Sanpete Valley—the Sanpete Formation. Only lower 45 m of 340 m total measured.

Indianola Group (new unit): mudstone (61 percent), conglomerate (38 percent), and sandstone (1 percent) that resemble those of enclosing units. The sandstone and mudstone are rather like those in the Cedar Mountain, except for the lack of limestone nodules. The sandstone displays parallel-, cross-, and graded bedding. The proportion of limestone clasts in the conglomerate increases slightly up-section, but the top of the unit is marked by a conspicuous quartzite-boulder bed 27 m thick, with clasts as much as 1 m in diameter. All beds strike N34°E, and are overturned; the dip decreases from about 60°SE near the base of the section to 38°E near the top of the section. The unit is 288 m thick. The degree to which the fault shown in Figure 3 distorts the section is not known.

Cedar Mountain Formation: varicolored mudstone (94 percent) with minor sublitharenite and lenses of conglomerate and limestone (6 percent); mudstone is reddish orange or reddish brown or light gray to yellowish gray—the gray beds contain many limestone nodules. The sandstone is moderate reddish orange, fine grained, and locally crossbedded. The pebble conglomerate is reddish, and the clasts are about 60 percent quartzite and 40 percent limestone. At the base of the unit is an unfossiliferous, gray-weathering, pale red, sandy intrasparite with oncolites. It changes facies to a white-weathering micrite. Only 93.5 m of the unit are exposed here. The strike is consistently N34°E, the dip decreases from 80°SE and overturned at base to about 60°SE at the top of the unit.

*See Figure 3 (from Section 13 of Roche, 1985). From center NW1/4 Sec. 5 to center NE1/4NE1/4 Sec. 6.

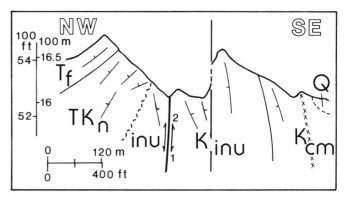

Figure 5. Stratigraphy and structure on the slope along Hwy. 89 (revised from Weiss, 1982, and Roche's section No. 15, 1985). Symbols as in Figures 3 and 4; vertical exaggeration ×2. Attitudes in the North Horn vary from top to bottom of the outcrop, and have suggested an unconformity within the unit (Weiss, 1982). We now believe (M. P. Weiss, unpublished data) that the fault surface, which has undergone two motions, is curved at the outcrop, and that the anomalous North Horn dips result from drag during the first movement on the fault (down to east). Because the outcrop face is oblique to the strike, the right half of the section is brought forward along strike 300 m at the match line.

TABLE 2. CONDENSED STRATIGRAPHIC SECTION IN VALLEY SOUTH OF RADIO TOWER VALLEY*

North Horn Formation: ca. 50 m of interbedded mudstone and sandstone dips about 30° WNW in angular unconformity over Sanpete sandstone and conglomerate.

Indianola Group (Sanpete Formation): gray to yellowish gray poorly exposed mudstone (65 percent), with interbedded medium to thick beds of yellowish gray to yellowish orange fine and medium-grained sandstone (17 percent), capped by 21.5 m of conglomerate (17 percent) of cobbles and boulders of quartzite and limestone (50:50). Much of the sandstone (sublitharenite) is trough cross-bedded in decimeter sets, and ironstone concretions of pebble and small cobble size are common. A thin silty micrite lies 4 m below the conglomerate. All 122 m of upper Sanpete is overturned and dips about 70°SE.

Quaternary fill in valley
Normal fault (Fig. 4)
Sanpete sandstone between the fault and base of the formation (Fig. 4) was not measured, but resembles the measured upper part. Total Sanpete exposed is about 220 m, but loss or gain in fault is not known.

Indianola Group (new unit): pale red to reddish orange conglomerate (42 percent) interbedded with reddish orange or yellowish gray fine-grained sublitharenite (17 percent) with sparse cross-bedding, and gray to reddish mudstone (41 percent) that is mostly poorly exposed. Conglomerate is mostly of pebbles and cobbles, and the 16.5 m unit of quartzite boulders (to 1 m diameter) at the top of the unit is continuous with that in Section 13. All beds are overturned and dip 62°E. Stuecheli (1984) collected late Albian - early Cenomanian leaf impressions from near the middle of this unit. A medium gray mudstone 1 m thick, and about 1.5 m above base of the unit, contains palynomorphs of Cenomanian—Coniacian age (S.N. Nelson, personal communication, 1984) and *Protelliptio* sp. (Stuecheli, 1984), which ranges from the Barremian to the Cenomanian. The basal bed beneath this mudstone is a highly calcareous pebbly friable sandstone that contains a lag deposit of oncolites and black and gray chert; it becomes mudstone along strike. This unit is 167 m thick, strikes N31°E, is overturned and dips 62°SE at the top.

Cedar Mountain Formation: yellowish gray, grayish red, reddish brown, and light red mudstone (81 percent), mostly medium-bedded grayish red to reddish brown fine to coarse-grained sublitharenite (10 percent), light gray to brownish gray micrite (6.6 percent), and one 3-m bed of reddish-orange-brown pebble and cobble conglomerate (2 percent). All are overturned and dip 35°E. Except for one micritic limestone below the middle, most of the limestone is a light brownish gray micrite at the base of the section that weathers brilliant white and is continuous along the outcrop from Section 13. The mudstone is very calcareous and two very thick beds, below the middle and near the top, contain abundant irregularly spheroidal limestone nodules. The 133.5 m exposed is not a complete thickness. The beds strike N35°E, are overturned, and dip 65°SE.

*See Figure 4 (from No. 14 of Roche, 1985). Part 14 W (see Fig. 4) from center E1/2 NE1/4 SW1/4 to SE1/4 SW1/4 NW1/4 Sec. 7; Part 14 E from NE1/4 SW1/4 NW1/4 to SE1/4 NW1/4 NW1/4 Sec. 7.

summarized in Table 3. His identifications at each locality, and comparisons to those of Weiss (1982) are detailed in Roche (1985). A major revision of Weiss's work in Deer Canyon and a section in North Coal Canyon are shown in Figures 6 and 7. The term Cedar Mountain is used hereafter in this chapter in place of Morrison(?).

Petrography

The three formations—Twist Gulch, Cedar Mountain, and unnamed lowest Indianola—have both similarities and important

differences (Table 3). Twenty-five modal analyses of sandstones show that many Cedar Mountain samples have larger percentages of monocrystalline quartz, polycrystalline quartz, chert, carbonate rock fragments, and sedimentary rock fragments, but the averages are not significantly higher than those of the other two units. Heavy mineral species and fractions are of no help. Distinctive features (Table 3) are feldspars (K-feldspars and plagioclase), the sums of kinds of lithic grains, color, and proportions of conglomerate.

Dusky brown spheroidal ironstone concretions are found only in beds otherwise identifiable as Indianola Group (undiff.). Calcite is the principal cement in all the units, and all are weakly cemented. Minor siliceous pore fillings are apparently confined to the Indianola Group. The Twist Gulch Formation is mostly mudstone and siltstone, and its sparse sandstone is less well sorted.

Except for the unfossiliferous micrite and intrasparite low in the Cedar Mountain, limestone is scarce in the three units. All the limestone is fresh water in origin, probably deposited in ponds and lakes; perhaps the oncolites were also from streams (Weiss, 1969, 1970). No limestone is known in the Twist Gulch Formation. Except for the leaf-bearing micrite bed in the basal Indianola at North Maple Canyon (discussed earlier), limestone is confined to the Cedar Mountain in the form of nodules in mudstone, oncolites in conglomerate, oncolitic micrites, and sparites, and micrites. There seems to be no gradation between true oncolites and the limy nodules. The oncolites are markedly layered and show the irregularity of structure and "mossy" layers typical of algal-sedimentary deposits; the nodules are homogeneous and structureless, irregular lumps.

Modal analyses of 14 conglomerates show those of the Cedar Mountain and Indianola (undiff.) are similar in many respects: clast type, average clast size, and matrix material. The clasts are mostly (95 percent) quartzite and limestone/dolomite, with minor amounts of sandstone and chert. The assignment of a conglomerate to a particular formation derives from the color of the associated mudstone, the oncoliths in some conglomerates, and the calcareous nodules in mudstones associated with those conglomerates. Samples from units otherwise considered to be either Cedar Mountain or Indianola do not separate on ternary diagrams of clast types (Roche, 1985); even so, Roche detected in both formations an increase in the carbonate-clast fraction from about 15 percent to 75 percent southward along the plateau front. This accords with a similar trend noted in the Indianola conglomerates on the west side of the plateau (the Price River of Hardy and Zeller, 1953). Such areal differences arose, no doubt, from differences in the provenance and axes of dispersal. Stuecheli (1984) found no differences in the vertical distribution of clast composition in the southeastern corner of the plateau, in either the Cedar Mountain or the Indianola.

The calcareous mudstones of all three units are composed of subequal amounts of silt and clay, with calcite, and typically have no fissility. X-ray diffraction analysis shows the prevalent mineral fines of all three units are, in decreasing order of abundance, quartz, montmorillonite, and illite, except that feldspar (mainly

TABLE 3. PETROGRAPHIC SUMMARY OF SELECTED ROCK UNITS

Formation	Mean percents in sandstone*		Colors		Conglomerate†
	Feldspar	Lithic Grains	Sandstone	Mudstone	
Indianola (Sanpete Fm.)			Yellow-gray and orange-gray	Light gray to yellow-gray	Rare
Indianola (new unit)	<1	7.6	Red-orange and yellow-gray	Gray-red	Abundant; many beds
Cedar Mountain	<1	18	Bright red-orange (10R6/6) and red-brown (10R4/6); some pale red and gray, some variegated	Bright red-orange, plus some gray, pale red, red-brown, and red-purple	Few, in upper part
Twist Gulch	5	10.8	Dull pale red (5R6/2), some variegated with gray	Light gray to pale red, variegated or mottled	None

*Applies equally to matrix of conglomerate.
†Clasts are all of similar composition.

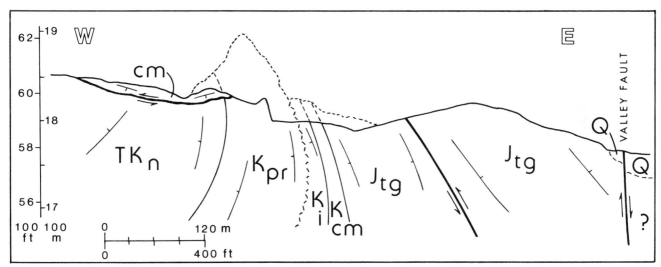

Figure 6. Stratigraphy and structure through stream gap in Deer Canyon, southwest of Wales (revised from Weiss, 1982, and Roche, 1985). Formation symbols as before, plus Jtg = Twist Gulch, Ki = Indianola undifferentiated (Sanpete?) and Kpr = Price River (= basal North Horn of Lawton, 1985). The dashed line is profile of ridge north of creek. Cedar Mountain Formation is much attenuated in tight fold, and may be bounded by faults. The Price River Formation may be reverse-faulted against the North Horn ("Termination Canyon" of Burma and Hardy, 1953).

microcline) is second most abundant in the Twist Gulch mudstone. All red beds have some hematite. The best distinguishing characteristics among the three is still the colors and conglomerate (Table 3). Although dull in its type area, the Cedar Mountain here is more brightly colored. In the Gunnison Plateau exposures, orange-red shades prevail, although medium to light gray, pale red, reddish brown, reddish purple, and mixtures of these hues also occur. Mudstone having these colors is likely to have limy nodules and some gastroliths, although fewer of the latter than the type area or the southeastern corner of the plateau. The few light gray to yellowish gray mudstones exposed are considered to belong to the Indianola Group.

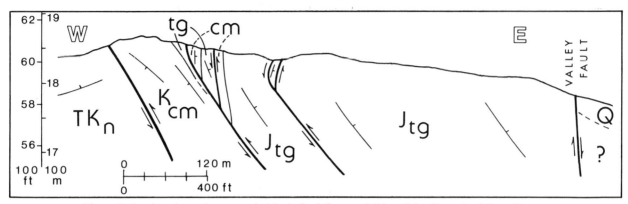

Figure 7. Stratigraphy and structure in North Coal Canyon 0.5 km (0.3 mi) south of Deer Canyon (Fig. 6) (modified from Roche, 1985). Formation symbols as in other figures.

Stratigraphy

Recognition and characterization of the Cedar Mountain Formation and the pre-Sanpete beds of the Indianola Group (lower and upper members, respectively, of the Pigeon Creek Formation of Schwans, this volume) along the southeastern corner of the Gunnison Plateau serve as a standard to identify the various discontinuous exposures of sub–Price River/North Horn beds (KJ$_u$ of Witkind and others, 1987) along the east front of the plateau. We are unable to recognize reliably the new unit of the Indianola north of the Gunnison Reservoir (Fig. 1), and therefore assign all non–Twist Gulch and non–Cedar Mountain beds to the Indianola (undiff.). This revision of units recognized along the east face of the Gunnison Plateau shows that the Indianola Group rests apparently conformably on the Cedar Mountain at the southeast. However, the basal Indianola beds (Sanpete?) lie with moderate angular discordance on the Jurassic Twist Gulch in the northeast part of the plateau (Fig. 1, North Maple Canyon; Weiss, 1982); this surface may be an unconformity or a reverse fault. Probably the Cedar Mountain–Indianola sequence infilled an irregular topography (see Schwans, this volume, for other examples).

The restudy suggests that the KJim of Weiss (1982, Fig. 8) may be the new lower unit of the Indianola, and shows that the Jm of Weiss (1982, Figs. 7, 10, 11, 12) is really the Cedar Mountain Formation; furthermore, the westernmost Jatg in Figure 7 (Weiss, 1982) is right side up.

WEST GUNNISON FRONT

While compiling the work of Hardy and Zeller (1953) and Hunt (1950) onto topographic maps for the Manti and Nephi 30- by 60-minute Quadrangles (Witkind and others, 1987; Witkind and Weiss, 1985), Weiss realized that the cliffs of Indianola conglomerate along the west front of the mountain are underlain by brightly colored mudstones rather like those reassigned here to the Cedar Mountain Formation. The unit is exposed only locally on the west side, for it slumps readily at the foot of the high scarp

of Indianola. Earlier it was mapped with the Twist Gulch Formation (Hunt, 1950; Witkind and Weiss, 1985). Workers familiar with the section in the San Rafael Swell recognize the Cedar Mountain Formation along the west toe of the Gunnison cliffs without any difficulty (e.g., H. Doelling, L. Hintze, G. Willis, I. Witkind). Further, Witkind mapped the Cedar Mountain Formation in the northwest part of the Cedar Hills, above the village of Indianola, and along Soldier Fork east of Thistle (Witkind and Weiss, 1985). Those localities form a trend consonant with a belt of Cedar Mountain down the west side of the Gunnison Plateau, and Standlee (1983) identified the Cedar Mountain in wells in the west-central part of the plateau (Fig. 1).

Detailed work on the west side of the plateau has since been done from Mt. Nebo to Chriss Creek and in the western salient of the Cedar Hills, a region veneered with volcaniclastics, that adjoins the Gunnison Plateau at the northeast corner (Auby, 1987; Banks, 1986; Biek, 1988; McDermott, 1988). The Cedar Mountain Formation is exposed intermittently from the south flank of Mt. Nebo in the Nephi quadrangle nearly to Little Salt Creek in the middle of the Chriss Canyon quadrangle, a distance of about 29 km (18 mi) (Fig. 1), and consists of abundant pastel mudstone, bright reddish-orange mudstone, and varicolored mudstone. Lavender mudstone is conspicuous in the northern part, and pale red, reddish brown, and reddish orange are more common in the middle of the outcrop belt. Mudstone dominates the section in the north (70 to 75 percent) where dolomitic limestone beds 1 to 2.5 m thick make up less than 5 percent of the lower 50 m of the unit (Biek, 1988). North of Hwy. 132 the unit coarsens up-section, grading into the Indianola; pebble conglomerate totalling at least 10 percent is restricted to the upper part of the unit (Biek, 1988). Sandstone and a few beds of grit complete the section. Abundance of conglomerate in the Cedar Mountain decreases rapidly southward over about 5 km, so that south of Hwy. 132 it composes only a small percentage of the formation (Biek, 1988); however, the sandstone and siltstone content increases, so that, with conglomerate, it makes up 40 percent of the unit in the area east of Levan (Auby, 1987). A contact between the lower mudstone part and the upper part with conglomerates is not readily mappable because of the facies changes and scarcity of undisturbed exposures (Biek, 1988). Southeast of Nephi, two 2-m oncolitic limestone lenses occur in the uppermost Cedar Mountain.

The limestone is light gray or light purplish gray, as are the limy nodules that are common locally in the mudstones. A few limestone beds are highly oncolitic (Biek, 1988). Limy nodules, angular fragments of clear and white layered chalcedony, and a few gastroliths weather out to the surfaces of the mudstone, as also do carbonate and quartzite pebbles and cobbles from the conglomerates. As for the cobbles, it is difficult to be sure whether they are truly from the Cedar Mountain or merely colluvial lag from the overlying Indianola because the clasts in both units are similar. The gastroliths are always most common in association with limy nodules, and neither occurs in the Indianola.

The Cedar Mountain is 208 m thick at Rees Flat northeast of Nephi, 185 m thick near Fourmile Creek southeast of Nephi, and 94 m thick on Chicken Creek east of Levan (Fig. 1) (Auby, 1987; Biek, 1988). From Chicken Creek (where the lower Indianola has yielded late Albian palynomorphs (Standlee, 1983; Lawton, 1985) southward, the Cedar Mountain strike belt lies in back valleys sheltered by high foothills to the west, so that it is well watered, heavily wooded, and poorly exposed. Just north of Little Salt Creek is a 120-m-thick covered interval between a thick red-brown sandstone typical of the upper Twist Gulch and the lowest massive conglomerate of the Indianola (McDermott, 1988). A mile north on strike, this interval is partly exposed and contains Cedar Mountain mudstone. Standlee (1983, Figs. 4, 5) recorded conglomerate (symbolized by error as oolitic limestone: personal communication, L. A. Standlee, 1986) and mudstone with limestone above the Twist Gulch in both the Dixel and Chevron USA No. 1 Chriss Canyon wells, 5 km (3 mi) southeast and 10 km (6 mi) south, respectively, of Little Salt Creek (Fig. 1), and identified that interval as Cedar Mountain, of "uncertain thickness." Thus, it must indeed underlie this part of the plateau, although it thins irregularly southward. The thinning may be structural, for the dip of the superjacent Indianola beds increases southward from about 20° near Nephi to about 40° on Little Salt Creek; the soft Cedar Mountain mudstone may have attenuated in the tighter folding.

Despite the slumping and wash of nodules, oncolites, and larger clasts downslope, the contact with the Twist Gulch is mappable, because no such particles occur in the Twist Gulch and it is always distinctly brownish red. Only two outcrops of the Twist Gulch/Cedar Mountain contact are known on the western belt; just east of Rees Flat, northeast of Nephi, the contact is not well exposed, but appears to be gradational (Biek, 1988). The basal Cedar Mountain is disconformable upon the Twist Gulch Formation, with channeling, on Chicken Creek, east of Levan (W. Auby, personal communication, 1986). The upper contact is gradational, as pebble and cobble conglomerate becomes more abundant and coarser upward in the Cedar Mountain. The mudstones interbedded with the sandstones and conglomerates of the basal Indianola are also colored rather like those of the Cedar Mountain. This gradation recalls the same condition of this contact in the southeastern corner of the plateau, already described. This succession, however, is not directly comparable to that on the southeastern flank of the Gunnison Plateau because the Sanpete Sandstone there cannot be correlated definitely with the Indianola conglomerates here. There the Cedar Mountain grades into the new basal Indianola member. Here on the west side, a 16- to 26-m-thick cobble and boulder conglomerate ledge (illustrated by Lawton, 1982, p. 204), thickening southward, marks the base of the mostly conglomeratic Indianola (Auby, 1987; Biek, 1988).

Pigeon Creek, the type section of the Pigeon Creek Formation of Schwans (this volume), lies just 2.5 km (1.5 mi) north of Chicken Creek (Fig. 1) on the northwest flank of the Gunnison Plateau. Schwans's lower Pigeon Creek member is the Cedar Mountain of this report. The upper member of the type Pigeon Creek is the lower 782 m (2,565 ft) of the Indianola Group.

CEDAR HILLS

An occurrence of the Cedar Mountain Formation in the western part of the Cedar Hills and at the north of the Gunnison Plateau (Fig. 1) is described to integrate the outcrops already described with those farther northeast in the Cedar Hills and in the northwest corner of the Wasatch Plateau (Witkind and Weiss, 1985). Jefferson (1982) was the first to suggest that the Cedar Mountain Formation might occur in the Cedar Hills; he identified 400 m of strata, previously included with the Indianola, as Morrison(?), and correlated the unit definitely with the "Morrison(?)" of the southeastern Gunnison Plateau and elsewhere. Although he did not take the step of naming the unit Cedar Mountain, he observed properties that clearly mark the unit as Cedar Mountain: " . . . highly polished red and brown chert pebbles not found in the Indianola Group," and fresh-water limestones with rip-up clasts, stromatolites, and oncolites. Jefferson also considered the unit to be Early Cretaceous(?) in age. The outcrop belt he mapped is north of Hop Creek Ridge, along the middle fork of Pole Creek (Witkind and Weiss, 1985). Although concerned directly with the Indianola Group, Lawton (1982, Fig. 2) recognized that part of the so-called Jurassic outcrop throughout the region may be Lower Cretaceous rocks. Witkind (Witkind and Weiss, 1985) mapped the Cedar Mountain at the locality described by Jefferson and also north of Indianola and east of Thistle.

Banks (1986) mapped newly recognized outcrops of Cedar Mountain astride Salt Creek just north of Utah Hwy. 132. The area is very severely deformed, because it is close to the Nebo thrust, and the thickness cannot be determined accurately; Banks has estimated it is between 305 and 455 m. The rocks are reddish orange mudstones (55 to 60 percent) with many beds of sandstone (10 percent), grit (5 percent), fresh-water limestone (10 percent), and conglomerate (15 to 20 percent). The mass is part of that mapped as T(Ja), or Arapien Shale intruded as a diapiric mass (Witkind and Weiss, 1985), and the Arapien does crop out along the axis of an antiform centered on Salt Creek (Fig. 1). The mixed gray and red Arapien mudstone of the region is not unlike the Cedar Mountain mudstone, but the presence of abundant oncolites and some white limy nodules and reddish brown highly polished chert pebbles ("gastroliths") identifies the outcrops as Cedar Mountain Formation.

The sandstone is grayish orange or grayish pink and medium gray, is 95 percent medium and coarse grains, is thin- to thick-bedded, and has some planar cross bedding. The grit is light brown, and consists of 80 percent fine grit with a sandy and silty matrix. The limestone is white to medium light gray, has many small oncolites, and is medium- to thick-bedded. The conglomerate is mostly in the pebble range, with 65 percent clasts and 35 percent matrix of high-quartz sandstone, and is medium- to thick-bedded. The pebbles consist, in decreasing order of abundance, of varieties of quartzite, limestone, and reddish brown chert. Limy nodules occur in the mudstones, but are not numerous; "gastroliths" of reddish brown chert or very fine-grained quartzite occur in the mudstone and in the conglomerate. The base of the Cedar Mountain is not exposed, for it is intruded by a salt diapir, mapped by Witkind (Witkind and Weiss, 1985); the Cedar Mountain is overlain by the Indianola—in possible disconformable contact, according to Banks (1986).

CONCLUSIONS

The Cedar Mountain Formation, of late Early Cretaceous age (probably late Albian), is known to underlie the Gunnison Plateau, where it is stratigraphically between the Jurassic (Callovian) Twist Gulch Formation and the Upper Cretaceous (Cenomanian to Campanian) Indianola Group. It also occurs in similar stratigraphic position in the Cedar Hills and the Wasatch Plateau. The formation is the lower part of the unit identified as Morrison Formation or Morrison(?) Formation in previous work. In the Cedar Hills and along the west flank of the Gunnison Plateau, it thins southward over 40 km (25 mi) from 400 to 455 m (Jefferson, 1982; Banks, 1986) to 100 to 120 m (McDermott, 1988). Along the southeast flank of the Gunnison Plateau, the Cedar Mountain Formation is overlain by a sequence of mudstones and conglomerates of Albian-Cenomanian age (Stuecheli, 1984; Roche, 1985; Witkind and others, 1986) that have in the past also been included in the Morrison or the Morrison(?). We believe that this unit should be recognized as a new, lowest interval of the Indianola Group. It lies beneath mostly sandstone and conglomerate beds that long have been identified as the Sanpete Formation of the Indianola Group. Until this interpretation is confirmed, however, we prefer not to establish a new stratigraphic name for the unit; Schwans (this volume) argues for an alternative view. The Cedar Mountain Formation, together with the new unit of the Indianola Group, records the Early Cretaceous beginning of the Sevier Orogeny.

ACKNOWLEDGMENTS

Many persons have been helpful in the field and in discussions of possible interpretations, including J. W. Collinson, C. E. Corbato, L. A. Standlee, P. J. Stuecheli, D. D. Wilson, and I. J. Witkind. Lehi Hintze, Hellmut Doelling and Grant Willis were of very great help to the four men (W. L. Auby, R. L. Banks, R. F. Biek, and J. G. McDermott) who mapped the north and west sides of the Gunnison Plateau in 1985, and who contributed to this chapter. Joanna Wood typed the report several times and with great skill. We were fortunate to have constructive suggestions about the manuscript from Corbato, T. F. Lawton, G. E. Moore, Standlee, L. J. Suttner, and Witkind.

REFERENCES CITED

Armstrong, R. L., 1968, Sevier orogenic belt in Nevada and Utah: Geological Society of America Bulletin, v. 79, p. 429–458.

Auby, W. L., 1987, Geology of the Levan 7½-minute Quadrangle, Juab County, Utah [M.S. thesis]: DeKalb, Northern Illinois University, 213 p.

Banks, R. L., 1986, Geology of the Fountain Green North 7½-minute Quadrangle, Juab and Sanpete Counties, Utah [M.S. thesis]: DeKalb, Northern Illinois University, 246 p.

Biek, R. F., 1988, Geology of the Nephi 7½-minute Quadrangle, Juab County, Utah [M.S. thesis]: DeKalb, Northern Illinois University, 576 p.

Burma, B. H., and Hardy, C. T., 1953, Pre-North Horn orogeny in Gunnison Plateau, Utah: American Association of Petroleum Geologists Bulletin, v. 37, p. 549–553.

Fouch, T. D., Lawton, T. F., Nichols, D. J., Cashion, W. B., and Cobban, W. A., 1983, Patterns and timing of synorogenic sedimentation in Upper Cretaceous rocks of central and northeast Utah, *in* Reynolds, M. W., and Dolly, E. D., eds., Mesozoic paleogeography of the west-central United States: Society of Economic Paleontologists and Mineralogists Rocky Mountain Paleogeography Symposium no. 2, p. 305–336.

Hale, L. A., and Van de Graaf, F. R., 1964, Cretaceous stratigraphy and facies patterns, northeastern Utah and adjacent areas, *in* Sabatka, E. F., ed., Geology and mineral resources of the Uinta Basin: Intermountain Association of Petroleum Geologists 13th Annual Field Conference Guidebook, p. 115–138.

Hardy, C. T., and Zeller, H., 1953, Geology of the west-central part of the Gunnison Plateau, Utah: Geological Society of America Bulletin, v. 64, p. 1261–1278.

Heller, P. L., Bowdler, S. S., Chambers, H. P., Coogan, J. C., Hagen, E. S., Shuster, M. W., Winslow, N. S., and Lawton, T. F., 1986, Time of initial thrusting in the Sevier Orogenic Belt, Idaho-Wyoming and Utah: Geology, v. 14, p. 388–391.

Hintze, L. F., 1985, Correlation of stratigraphic units of North America (COSUNA) project; Great Basin Region: American Association of Petroleum Geologists Correlation Chart Series.

Hunt, R. E., 1950, The geology of the northern part of the Gunnison Plateau, Utah [Ph.D. thesis]: Columbus, Ohio State University, 267 p.

Jefferson, W. S., 1982, Structural and stratigraphic relations of Upper Cretaceous to Lower Tertiary orogenic sediments in the Cedar Hills, Utah, *in* Nielson, D. L., ed., Overthrust belt of Utah: Utah Geological Association Publication 10, p. 65–80.

Kowallis, B. J., Heaton, J. S., and Bringhurst, K., 1986, Fission-track dating of volcanically derived sedimentary rocks: Geology, v. 14, p. 19–22.

Kowallis, B. J., and Heaton, J. S., 1987, Fission-track dating of bentonites and bentonitic mudstones from the Morrison Formation in central Utah: Geology, v. 15, p. 1138–1142.

Lawton, T. F., 1982, Lithofacies correlations within the Upper Cretaceous Indianola Group, central Utah, *in* Nielson, D. L., ed., Overthrust belt of Utah: Utah Geological Association Publication 10, p. 199–213.

——, 1985, Style and timing of frontal structures, thrust belt, central Utah: American Association of Petroleum Geologists Bulletin, v. 69, p. 1145–1159.

McDermott, J. G., 1988, Geology of the Chriss Canyon 7½-minute Quadrangle, Juab and Sanpete Counties, Utah [M.S. thesis]: DeKalb, Northern Illinois University.

Roche, M. G., 1985, Morrison(?) Formation of central Utah reassigned [M.S. thesis]: DeKalb, Northern Illinois University, 176 p.

Spieker, E. M., 1946, Late Mesozoic and Early Cenozoic history of central Utah: U.S. Geological Survey Professional Paper 205-D, p. 117–161.

——, 1949, The transition between the Colorado Plateaus and the Great Basin in central Utah: Utah Geological Society Guidebook to the Geology of Utah, no. 4, 106 p.

Spieker, E. M., and Reeside, J. B., Jr., 1926, Upper Cretaceous shoreline in Utah: Geological Society of America Bulletin, v. 37, p. 429–438.

Standlee, L. A., 1983, Structure and stratigraphy of Jurassic rocks in central Utah; Their influence on tectonic development of the Cordilleran Foreland Thrust Belt, *in* Powers, R. B., ed., Geologic studies of the Cordilleran thrust belt, 1982: Denver, Colorado, Rocky Mountain Association of Geologists, v. 1, p. 357–382.

Stokes, W. L., 1944, Morrison Formation and related deposits in and adjacent to the Colorado Plateau: Geological Society of America Bulletin, v. 55, p. 951–992.

——, 1952, Lower Cretaceous in Colorado Plateau: American Association of Petroleum Geologists Bulletin, v. 36, p. 1766–1776.

——, 1972, Stratigraphic problems of the Triassic and Jurassic sedimentary rocks of central Utah, *in* Baer, J. L., and Callaghan, E., eds., Plateau-Basin Range transition zone, central Utah: Utah Geological Association Publication 2, p. 21–28.

Stuecheli, P. J., 1984, The sedimentology, depositional setting, and age of the Morrison(?) Formation in central Utah [M.S. thesis]: Columbus, Ohio State University, 137 p.

Stuecheli, P. J. and Collinson, J. W., 1984, Sedimentology of synorogenic conglomerates of the Lower Cretaceous Morrison(?) Formation, central Utah: Geological Society of America Abstracts with Programs, v. 16, no. 3, p. 200.

Taylor, J. M., 1980, Geology of the Sterling Quadrangle, Sanpete County, Utah: Brigham Young University Geology Studies, v. 27, pt. 1, p. 117–135.

Tschudy, R. H., Tschudy, B. D. and Craig, L. C., 1984, Palynological evaluation of Cedar Mountain and Burro Canyon Formations, Colorado Plateau: U.S. Geological Survey Professional Paper 1281, 24 p.

Villien, A., 1984, Central Utah deformation belt [Ph.D. thesis]: Boulder, University of Colorado, 283 p.

Villien, A., and Kligfield, R. M., 1986, Thrusting and synorogenic sedimentation in central Utah, *in* Peterson, J. A., ed., Paleotectonics and sedimentation in the Rocky Mountain region, United States: American Association of Petroleum Geologists Memoir 41, p. 281–308.

Weiss, M. P., 1969, Oncolites, paleoecology, and Laramide tectonics, central Utah: American Association of Petroleum Geologists Bulletin, v. 53, p. 1105–1120.

——, 1970, Oncolites forming on snails (*Goniobasis*): Journal of Paleontology, v. 44, p. 765–769.

Weiss, M. P., 1982, Structural variety on east front of the Gunnison Plateau, central Utah, *in* Nielson, D. L., ed., Overthrust belt of Utah: Utah Geological Association Publication 10, p. 49–63.

Witkind, I. J., 1982, Salt diapirism in central Utah, *in* Nielson, D. L., ed., Overthrust belt of Utah: Utah Geological Association Publication 10, p. 13–30.

——, 1983, Overthrusts and salt diapirs, central Utah, *in* Miller, D. M., Todd, V. R., and Howard, K. A., eds., Tectonic and stratigraphic studies in the eastern Great Basin: Geological Society of America Memoir 157, p. 45–59.

Witkind, I. J., and Weiss, M. P., 1985, Preliminary geologic map of the Nephi 30 by 60-Minute Quadrangle, Carbon, Emery, Juab, Sanpete, Utah, and Wasatch counties, Utah: U.S. Geological Survey Open-File Report 85-446, scale 1:100,000.

Witkind, I. J., Weiss, M. P. and Brown, T. L., 1987, Geologic map of the Manti 30 by 60-minute Quadrangle, Carbon, Emery, Juab, Sanpete, and Sevier Counties, Utah: U.S. Geological Survey Miscellaneous Investigations Map I-1631, scale 1:100,000.

Witkind, I. J., Standlee, L. A., and Maley, K. F., 1986, Age and correlation of Cretaceous rocks previously assigned to the Morrison(?) Formation, Sanpete-Sevier Valley area, central Utah: U.S. Geological Survey Bulletin 1584, 9 p.

Manuscript Accepted by the Society February 9, 1988

Printed in U.S.A.

Index

[Italic page numbers indicate major references]

Typeset by WESType Publishers Services, Inc., Boulder, Colorado
Printed in U.S.A. by Malloy Lithographing, Inc., Ann Arbor, Michigan